HOLT Health

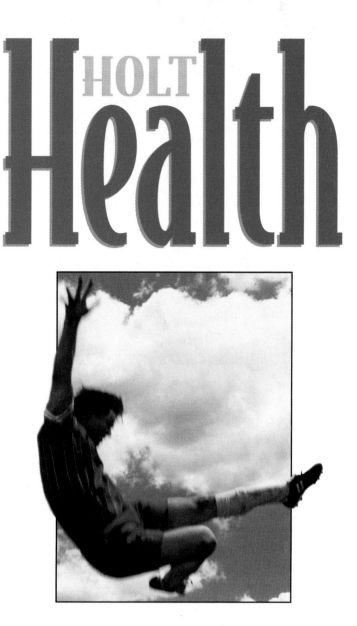

Annotated Teacher's Edition

Jerrold Greenberg, Ed.D.
University of Maryland
College Park, MD

Robert Gold, Ph.D.
University of Maryland
College Park, MD

HOLT, RINEHART AND WINSTON
Harcourt Brace & Company

Austin • New York • Orlando • Atlanta • San Francisco
Boston • Dallas • Toronto • London

ACKNOWLEDGMENTS

Contributing Authors

Clint Bruess, Ed.D.
University of Alabama at Birmingham
Birmingham, AL

George Dintiman, Ph.D.
Virginia Commonwealth University
Richmond, VA

Susan Laing
Southeast Regional Medical Education
 Center
Birmingham, AL

Staff Credits

Executive Editor
Ellen Standafer

Managing Editor
William Wahlgren

Project Editors
Jean Armstrong
Janis Gadsden
Christopher Hess
Meredith Phillips
Tracy Schagen

Copyediting
Steve Oelenberger, *Copyediting
 Supervisor*
Amy Daniewicz
Denise Haney

Editorial Permissions
Janet Harrington

Book Design
Christine Schueler, *Design Manager*
José Garza

Image Services
Greg Geisler, *Art Director*
Michelle Rumpf
Elaine Tate

Photo Research
Peggy Cooper, *Photo Research Manager*
Caroline Robbins

Photo Studio
Sam Dudgeon, *Senior Staff Photographer*
Victoria Smith

Media Design
Joe Melomo, *Design Manager*

Cover Design
Nantucket Design

Manufacturing
Michael Roche

Electronic Publishing
Carol Martin, *Electronic Publishing
 Manager*
Barbara Hudgens, *Electronic Publishing
 Supervisor*
Heather Jernt, *Project Coordinator*
JoAnn Brown
Mercedes Newman
Rina Ouellette
Michele Ruschaupt
Charlie Taliaferro
Ethan Thompson

Prepress
Beth Prevelige, *Senior Production
 Manager*
Simira Davis
Rose Mayo Degollado
Sergio Durante
Beth Sample

Media
Kim Anderson, *Production Manager*
Susan Mussey

Acknowledgments

Teacher Reviewers

Beth Barry, M.P.H., C.H.E.S.
Health Education Consultant
Richland County School District One
Columbia, SC

Alan D. Blakely
Newfound Regional High School
Bristol, NH

Janice E. Burke, M.A.
Reed High School
Sparks, NV

Cathleen Chavez
Chinle High School
Chinle, AZ

Burney Drake
Shelby High School
Shelby, NC

John A. Garcia
Castro Valley High School
Castro Valley, CA

Geri Grocki, M.S.
Weston Public Schools
Weston, CT

Debra C. Harris, Ph.D.
West Linn High School
West Linn, OR

**Virginia "Ginger" Lawless, M.E.,
   C.H.E.S.**
Fort Bend Independent School District
Sugar Land, TX

Marie Lesko, M.A., C.H.E.S.
Health Education Department Chair
Hopewell Area School District
Aliquippa, PA

Loretta McHan
Crockett High School
Austin, TX

Shirlee Nelson
Greenacres Elementary
Pocatello, ID

Michael J. Palazzo
West Torrance High School
West Torrance, CA

Becky Reeder
Jacksonville Middle School
Jacksonville, TX

Ann C. Slater, Ed.D., C.H.E.S.
Irmo Middle School, Columbia, SC;
Adjunct Assistant Professor
University of South Carolina
Columbia, SC

Denise Swan
Naugatuck High School
Naugatuck, CT

Linda S. Tucker
Silver Creek High School
Sellersburg, IN

Pamela Cates White
San Marcos High School
San Marcos, TX

Content Reviewers

Timothy Aldrich, Ph.D.
Director
Central Cancer Registry
Raleigh, NC

Linda A. Berne, Ed.D., C.H.E.S.
Professor
University of North Carolina
Charlotte, NC

Robert W. Boyce, Ph.D., F.A.C.S.M.
Owner
Robert Boyce Health Promotion
Charlotte, NC

Diane Brinkman, M.D.
Physician
Austin Regional Clinic
Austin, TX

Ileana Corbelle, LMSW-ACP
Clinical Director
Austin Rape Crisis Center
Austin, TX

Doris Dedmon, R.N.
Nurse
Shelby, NC

Deborah A. Fortune, Ph.D., C.H.E.S.
Director, HIV/AIDS Project
American Association for Health
   Education
Reston, VA

B. Don Franks, Ph.D.
Professor and Chair
Department of Kinesiology
Louisiana State University
Baton Rouge, LA

Bob Frye
Health Consultant
Raleigh, NC

Steve Furney, Ed.D., M.P.H., C.H.E.S.
Professor and Director, Health Education
   Division
Southwest Texas State University
San Marcos, TX

Judy Harris, R.N., C.H.E.S.
Director, Institute for Health Professionals
Portland Community College
Portland, OR

James Heffley, Ph.D.
Nutrition Counseling Service
Austin, TX

Carol Higy, Ed.D.
Title III Program Coordinator
University of North Carolina
Pembroke, NC

Donna J. Jones, M.Ed., A.T.C., L.A.T.
Athletic Trainer
Texas A&M University
College Station, TX

Gary Klukken, Ph.D.
Director, Student Counseling Services
   Center
University of Tennessee
Knoxville, TN

Nancy J. Lipinski, R.N.
Licensed School Nurse
Annandale District 876 Public Schools
Annandale, MN

**Arlene Marks Montgomery,
   LMSW-ACP**
Lecturer
University of Texas
Austin, TX

Emily Ousley, C.N.M.
Certified Nurse Midwife
Lawndale, NC

Barbara L. Potts, R.D., L.D.
Cooper Clinic
Dallas, TX

Robert Wandberg, Ph.D.
John F. Kennedy Senior High School
Bloomington, MN

Royal E. Wohl, Ph.D., C.H.E.S.
Lecturer
Washburn University
Topeka, KS

Kenneth A. Zeno, C.H.H.D.
Director
Center for Health & Human
   Development
West Peabody, MA

Table of Contents

PRESENTS THE DECISION-MAKING MODEL USED THROUGH-OUT THE TEXT.

U N I T   F O U R

Protecting Your Health in a Drug Society 242

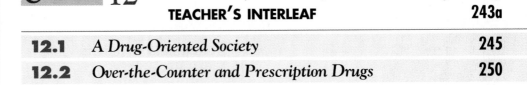

UNIT FIVE

Family Life, Sexuality, and Social Health 322

U N I T S I X

UP-TO-DATE
INFORMATION
ON THE NATURE OF
THE DISEASE, HOW
IT IS TRANSMITTED,
AND WHAT BEHAV-
IORS ARE SAFE AND
UNSAFE.

U N I T S E V E N

U N I T   E I G H T

AN EXPANDED BODY SYSTEMS HANDBOOK PROVIDES INFORMATION ON HUMAN ANATOMY AND PHYSIOLOGY AND HELPS STUDENTS UNDERSTAND HOW THEIR LIFESTYLE CAN AFFECT THEIR BODY.

$\mathscr{L}ife$ SKILLS:

What Would You Do ❓ Making Responsible Decisions

Cultural DIVERSITY

Check Up

HOLT Health

Philosophy and Objectives

THE HEALTH CURRICULUM AND TODAY'S TEENS

The changing focus of the high school health curriculum over the last 10 years has been dramatic. The role of the health teacher has become critically important in helping students adjust and adapt to the challenges of adolescence. No single age group is more subject to avoidable health risks, and a quality health course can help teens recognize and avoid these risks. Our goal is to provide the instructional support you need to present a health course that meets the needs of today's teens by focusing on health issues from an adolescent perspective.

From page one of *Holt Health*, you'll see it's different. Your students will want to read the text because it's relevant to them. They'll want to discuss what they've read because it's relevant to how they live today. As a result, the *Holt Health* classroom is highly interactive. Life Skills and Decision-Making Skills form the core of the program. Students apply these skills in making choices on health and lifestyle issues.

"I'm trying to make my own decisions now and not do things just because my friends are doing them."

Beatriz

Establishing Links to the Community
The *Holt Health* program recognizes that health education is not restricted to the school environment. Throughout *Holt Health*, students are expected to look at resources in the community related to particular health issues.

Section

7.4   *Seeking Help*

· · · · ·

Objectives

- Describe the signs of mental and emotional health problems.

- List community resources that help with mental and emotional problems.
  LIFE SKILLS: Using Community Resources

- Differentiate among types of treatment for mental and emotional problems.

Blood Alcohol Level's Effect on Death Risk	
BAL	**Chance of Dying**
.02–.04	1.5 times as likely
.05–.09	11 times as likely
.10–.14	48 times as likely
.15+	380 times as likely

(FIGURE 13-11) Drinking alcohol in any amount can put a person's life in danger.

Breaking the Law

People under 21 break a law every time they have any alcohol (except under special circumstances, such as religious purposes). Like all crimes, getting caught drinking alcohol under the age of 21 can lead to arrest, a fine, and even a criminal record. Many teenagers have decided that they'd rather not risk their futures by drinking alcohol now. In addition, driving while under the influence of alcohol is illegal for people of all ages. A person does not have to be in an accident in order to be caught driving drunk—the driver of any car exceeding the speed limit or noticeably weaving through traffic is subject to inspection and a possible blood alcohol level test.

Losing Control

One of the best reasons not to drink is that alcohol can make a person lose control. Drinking to the point of intoxication can remove inhibitions completely. As a result, drunk people may find themselves doing things they regret.

For example, Krystal and Claudio are the school's most popular couple. Wher-

ever they go is *the* place to be. Whatever they do, everyone wants to do too. It's a secret, but one thing they *haven't* done is have sexual intercourse.

Claudio lives with his grandmother, who happens to be out of town for the weekend. He takes advantage of this opportunity, and throws the year's wildest party. By the end of the night, everyone is very drunk, including Claudio and Krystal. The house is severely damaged: the stereo is broken beyond repair, and part of the carpet has been badly burned.

Claudio doesn't know any of this yet, because Krystal has suddenly decided she's ready to have sex with him. The two of them have stumbled to his bedroom.

Hours later, Claudio wakes up, horrified and ashamed. He hadn't wanted it to be like that. How could he have been so stupid? He knows they both made a mistake and that it's too late to go back now. What if Krystal gets pregnant? What about sexually transmitted diseases? Claudio knows that if they hadn't been drunk, they wouldn't have lost control.

Teenagers who drink are more likely to engage in activities that conflict with their

personal and parental values. These actions can result in conflicts with family and friends, feelings of guilt, unwanted pregnancies, sexually transmitted diseases, and damage to public or personal property.

Standards Set by Parents or Guardians

Many teenagers decide not to drink because they want to abide by the standards set by their parents or guardians. Chances are that a lot of students in your class have decided not to drink for this reason.

An Alcohol-Free Life

People who choose not to drink do so because they like being sober. They find that being drunk interferes with a lot of activities they enjoy—like taking part in sports, or going to the movies, or socializing with friends, or reading. Being sober allows them to get the most out of the things that make them happy.

270 CHAPTER 13 ALCOHOL: A DANGEROUS DRUG

What Would You Do ?

Making Responsible Decisions

Should You Let Him Drive You Home?

You're at a party, and it's getting late. Your friend Cliff, who drove you to the party, says he's ready to drive you home. He tells you he hasn't been drinking, but you're pretty sure he's had at least two or three beers. What would you do?

Remember to use the decision-making steps:

1. State the Problem.
2. List the Options.
3. Imagine the Benefits and Consequences.
4. Consider Your Values.
5. Weigh the Options and Decide.
6. Act.
7. Evaluate the Results.

(FIGURE 13-12) Life's healthiest and drinking alcohol.

ENGAGING NARRATIVE

The harsh realities confronting today's teens are presented through compelling and compassionate scenarios.

HOLT HEALTH: THE SELF-HELP BOOK FOR TEENS

Building Self-Esteem

People who feel good about themselves can more readily identify and avoid unhealthy risk-taking behaviors. Recognizing this fact, you will find a full chapter on self-esteem in the *Holt Health* program. This chapter helps students recognize their own self worth and the importance of acting responsibly toward others. Teens today are so heavily influenced by the media. They are consistently bombarded with images and models of how to look and act. *Holt Health* breaks through the stereotypes in helping students learn to appreciate themselves as individuals and appreciate the diversity among people.

Cultural Diversity

Holt Health reflects the diversity among people, not only in appearance, but in attitudes and beliefs. Throughout the text, students encounter the message to treat all others with dignity and respect. In special Cultural Diversity features, students examine the cultural norms related to health issues.

NATIONAL HEALTH EDUCATION STANDARDS

The National Health Education Standards, established in 1995, give direction for achieving excellence in health education. Since it is through education set into personal action, rather than through biomedical advances, that the nation's health will improve, these standards aim to increase an individual's capacity to use basic health information and services in ways that enhance health. They accomplish this by providing a framework of knowledge and skills broad enough and flexible enough to meet the needs of distinct students, families, schools, and communities. Each Unit Opener in *Holt Health* links components of the program to the national standards. Allying day-to-day instruction with national, state, and local concerns helps students become critical thinkers and problem solvers, responsible and productive citizens, self-directed learners, and effective communicators.

STANDARDS*

1. *Students will comprehend concepts related to health promotion and disease prevention.*

2. *Students will demonstrate the ability to access valid health information and health-promoting products and services.*

3. *Students will demonstrate the ability to practice health-enhancing behaviors and reduce health risks.*

4. *Students will analyze the influence of culture, media, technology, and other factors on health.*

5. *Students will demonstrate the ability to use interpersonal communication skills to enhance health.*

6. *Students will demonstrate the ability to use goal-setting and decision-making skills to enhance health.*

7. *Students will demonstrate the ability to advocate for personal, family, and community health.*

*"This represents the work of the Joint Committee on National Health Education Standards. Copies of *National Health Education Standards: Achieving Health Literacy* can be obtained through the American School Health Association, Association for the Advancement of Health Education or the American Cancer Society."

Holt Health

Building Skills for a Lifetime

LIFE SKILLS DEVELOPMENT

The purpose of any health course is to develop subject area content in a way that applies to daily life. *Holt Health* shows how one's quality of life, now and in the future, is intimately tied to avoiding health risks. Those risks can only be identified through health instruction. The development of Life Skills in *Holt Health* is an integral part of the total course. To emphasize the development of these skills, you will find them clearly labeled in the Life Skills feature pages throughout the text. The feature strand can be divided into the following categories that correspond to most curriculum objectives.

LIFE SKILLS CATEGORIES

Solving Problems	*Communicating Effectively*
Coping	*Being a Wise Consumer*
Setting Goals	*Making Responsible Decisions*
Resisting Pressure	*Practicing Self-Care*
Assessing Your Health	*Intervention Strategies*
Using Community Resources	

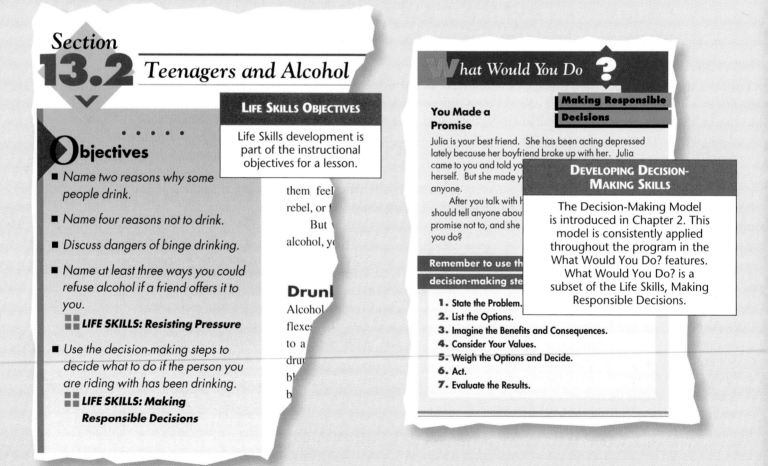

Section 13.2 Teenagers and Alcohol

LIFE SKILLS OBJECTIVES

Life Skills development is part of the instructional objectives for a lesson.

Objectives

■ *Name two reasons why some people drink.*

■ *Name four reasons not to drink.*

■ *Discuss dangers of binge drinking.*

■ *Name at least three ways you could refuse alcohol if a friend offers it to you.*
LIFE SKILLS: Resisting Pressure

■ *Use the decision-making steps to decide what to do if the person you are riding with has been drinking.*
LIFE SKILLS: Making Responsible Decisions

them feel
rebel, or
But
alcohol, y

Drunk

Alcohol
flexes
to a
dru
b
b

What Would You Do ?

Making Responsible Decisions

You Made a Promise

Julia is your best friend. She has been acting depressed lately because her boyfriend broke up with her. Julia came to you and told yo
herself. But she made y
anyone.

After you talk with h
should tell anyone abou
promise not to, and she
you do?

Remember to use th

decision-making ste

1. State the Problem.
2. List the Options.
3. Imagine the Benefits and Consequences.
4. Consider Your Values.
5. Weigh the Options and Decide.
6. Act.
7. Evaluate the Results.

DEVELOPING DECISION-MAKING SKILLS

The Decision-Making Model is introduced in Chapter 2. This model is consistently applied throughout the program in the What Would You Do? features. What Would You Do? is a subset of the Life Skills, Making Responsible Decisions.

LIFE SKILLS FEATURES

These features in the pupil's text include activities to develop the Life Skills in the program.

LifeSKILLS: Assessing Your Health

Self-Esteem Scale

On a separate sheet of paper, write the letter that most accurately describes how you feel:

1. I feel that I'm a person of worth, at least equal to others.
a. Strongly agree
b. Agree
c. Disagree
d. Strongly disagree

2. I feel that I have a number of good qualities.
a. Strongly agree
b. Agree
c. Disagree
d. Strongly disagree

3. All in all, I am inclined to feel that I am a failure.
a. Strongly agree
b. Agree
c. Disagree
d. Strongly disagree

4. I am able to do things as well as most other people.
a. Strongly agree
b. Agree
c. Disagree
d. Strongly disagree

5. I feel I do not have much to be proud of.
a. Strongly agree
b. Agree
c. Disagree
d. Strongly disagree

6. I take a positive attitude toward myself.
a. Strongly agree
b. Agree
c. Disagree
d. Strongly disagree

7. On the whole, I am satisfied with myself.
a. Strongly agree
b. Agree
c. Disagree
d. Strongly disagree

8. I wish I could have more respect for myself.
a. Strongly agree
b. Agree
c. Disagree
d. Strongly disagree

9. I feel useless at times.
a. Strongly agree
b. Agree
c. Disagree
d. Strongly disagree

10. At times I think I am no good at all.
a. Strongly agree
b. Agree
c. Disagree
d. Strongly disagree

Scoring. To score the scale and derive a measure of your self-esteem, follow these instructions.

The positive responses for the questions are as follows:

question 1: (a) or (b)
question 2: (a) or (b)
question 3: (c) or (d)
question 4: (a) or (b)
question 5: (c) or (d)
question 6: (a) or (b)
question 7: (a) or (b)
question 8: (c) or (d)
question 9: (c) or (d)
question 10: (c) or (d)

For each positive answer that you chose, give yourself one point. The range of scores on this self-esteem scale is 0–10. The higher the score, the better your self-esteem.

180 Chapter 8 Building Self-Esteem

8.1 The Importance of Self-Esteem 181

LifeSKILLS: Communicating Effectively

Showing Love Nonsexually

The teenage years are a time of strong sexual feelings. Even though you know that choosing abstinence is the best way to avoid STDs, you may want to show your affection for someone by becoming sexually intimate.

When you are in love and really care for someone, it's natural to want to show it. But sexual intercourse is not the only way to show affection. For example, one of the nicest things you can do for a person is to listen to what he or she has to say with genuine interest. This shows that you take the person seriously and that his or her thoughts and feelings are important to you.

On a separate sheet of paper, write down at least 10 other ways besides sex that you can show you love your girl-friend or boyfriend.

476 Chapter 22 Sexually Transmitted Diseases

As you already learned, delaying or abstaining from sexual intimacy is called sexual abstinence. If you decide to practice abstinence until you are older, that doesn't mean that you will not have sexual feelings for someone in the meantime. There are many safe ways to express sexual affection for someone. Talking, hugging, and holding hands, for example, are the safest possible expressions of feelings.

In spite of the messages you may be getting from music, movies, TV, or even your friends, the truth is that many teenagers are not sexually active. Teenagers... to delay sexual intimacy for a v... reasons. For some teens it is a ... avoiding sexually transmitted dis... for delaying intimacy involve... goals and values. People are ge... pier when they live up to their... accomplish their goals.

Remember, if two people... sexual activity until marria... faithful to each other, they w... from STDs.

LIFE SKILLS WORKSHEETS

These creative activities extend and reinforce the skill development in the pupil's text. They are part of the *Holt Health* Teaching Resource Supplements.

Chapter **14**

Tobacco: Hazardous and Addictive

LifeSKILLS

...ity A: Communicating Effectively

...municating With Smokers

...otect themselves from cigarette smoke, nonsmokers need to learn how ...mmunicate effectively with smokers about maintaining a smoke-free ...onment. How would you respond to each of the following situations?

...ara was walking down the hall at school when she caught a whiff of cigarette smoke. She followed ...e smell and saw a younger student snuffing out a cigarette inside her locker. What would you do if ...ou were Lara and why?

...an drove up to a self-service gas station and noticed that the woman at the pump next to him was ...moking as she pumped gas into her car. What would you do if you were Juan? Why?

3. Cheryl's aunt is in the hospital recovering from kidney surgery. While Cheryl is visiting, her aunt's hospital roommate lights up a cigarette. Cheryl doesn't think smoking is permitted in her aunt's hospital room, and she knows smoke makes her aunt uncomfortable. What would you do if you were Cheryl?

Life Skills 14A 35

LIFE SKILLS ASSESSMENT

To ensure that the skills are being mastered, every Chapter Review contains a series of questions in the Life Skills Check section. These questions measure students' abilities to apply what they've learned.

Life Skills Check

1. Using Community Resources
Your cousin confided that she often feels as if she is losing control with her children and that she is afraid she might hurt them. What could you advise her to do?

2. Making Responsible Decisions
Katie's parents seem to criticize everything she does. They are hardly ever at home, and when they are, Katie never hears one kind or encouraging word from them. The situation has gotten so bad that she is thinking about running away. What alternatives does Katie have?

3. Coping
You like Ray a lot and enjoy some degree of sexual intimacy, but you do not want to have intercourse with him. The last time you were on a date, he assumed that because you enjoyed kissing him, you didn't want him to stop—you had to be really firm. The two of you are supposed to go out tonight. What should you do?

INSTRUCTIONAL AIDS

Your Partner in Quality Health Instruction

The *Holt Health* program provides a number of unique features designed to meet the instructional challenges you face in teaching health to high school students. Its wellness approach to health requires that the course be introspective but remain sensitive to students' feelings and need for privacy. The features shown here will help you implement the program in a manner that fosters health-enhancing evaluation of behaviors and lifestyle. The reflections are private and are to be shared on a voluntary basis only.

SECTION 7.1

Personal Health Inventory

Have students complete the Personal Health Inventory for this chapter.

THE QUESTION BOX

One important goal of *Holt Health* is to deal with the questions students have about their own health by encouraging dialogue on these topics. This will help students understand how their actions and the environment they live in can have an impact on their health. To address this goal, the Question Box feature is found in every chapter opener. Students anonymously submit any questions they may have about the topics to be covered in the chapter. This allows you to build lesson plans that deal with the specific concerns of your students and to encourage dialogue in these areas.

Question Box

Have students write out any questions they have about health and wellness, as it pertains to teens and their families, and put them in the Question Box.

Sensitivity *ALERT*

The discussion of health or wellness may make some students uncomfortable. They may have a health problem or someone close to them who is ill. They may feel that everyone will think they are different or unacceptable because of these problems. Prepare the class to be respectful of privacy and sensitive to the feelings of others. Help them see that someone with a physical health problem may more than compensate in the other aspects of health.

PERSONAL HEALTH INVENTORY

These confidential worksheets come at the beginning of each chapter. Some worksheets allow students to examine their prior knowledge of the subject presented in the chapter. Others provide students with a means of evaluating their own behavior in regard to the health issues presented in the chapter. This allows each student to discover how the content of the chapter may be relevant to his or her life. The Personal Health Inventories are a part of the *Holt Health* Teaching Resource Supplements.

SENSITIVITY *ALERT*

Today's students come from very diverse backgrounds and as such they have had very diverse experiences. The likelihood of having a student who has had direct experience with abuse, violence, addiction, and even AIDS is very high. To assist you in covering potentially sensitive areas, each text chapter includes a Sensitivity ALERT with notes on covering potentially sensitive subjects in the chapter.

Section 8.2 Lesson Plan

MOTIVATE

✎ **Journal 8C**
Expectations of Yourself

This may be done as a warm-up activity. Most teenagers feel dissatisfied with themselves to some degree, often because of unreasonable expectations they place on themselves. Encourage students to write in their Journal,

completing this statement: "I would feel really good about myself if I ____ ." Then ask them to discuss whether their expectation is reasonable

TEACH

Reinforcement
Fighting Low Self-Es

Taking responsibility fo themselves may be ha with low self-esteem

182 BUILDING SELF-ESTEEM

THE JOURNAL

The Journal provides a vehicle for students to privately reflect and express their feelings and opinions on many health issues. Often the Journal is used to record answers to warm-up activities that begin lessons. Students then use these answers to contribute to the class discussion once the class begins. The Journal is referred to throughout the Annotated Teacher's Edition, and is part of the *Holt Health* Teaching Resource Supplements.

CHECK UP

The Check Up feature helps students assess various aspects of their knowledge and behavior as each relates to wellness. Collect students' anonymous answers, and use them as a spring board for class discussions.

SECTION 6.1

Check Up

Have students turn in their answers to the Check Up questions anonymously and then discuss the responses with the class. As these topics are quite personal in nature, there will probably be differences of opinion about what constitutes proper care.

Check Up

How Well Do You Take Care of Yourself?

Which of the following actions do you take to improve your appearance and health?

- Wash skin regularly with soap and water
- Use a sunscreen of at least 15 SPF when outdoors
- Watch any moles for changes in their appearance
- Wash hair regularly
- Limit the use of electric hair dryers and curlers
- Brush teeth at least twice a day
- Floss teeth once a day

PLAN FOR ACTION

A health program is effective if the education the student receives causes a positive change in lifestyle or behavior. Unless that change occurs, the instruction has been ineffective. The confidential Plan for Action helps you assess goals for behavioral change. Each Plan for Action in the Chapter Review requires students to develop a life plan that reflects their understanding of the ideas and concepts in the chapter.

Plan for Action . . . .

List one or two stressors in your life and devise a plan to lower your stress level using the suggestions in this chapter.

. . . . .
CHAPTER REVIEW **211**

Plan for Action . . . .

Plan a balanced weekly exercise program to fit your own personal needs.

Plan for Action . . . .

Friends and family can support a dying person and each other. List three things you can do in the future to help a dying friend.

HOLT Health

In-Text Handbooks

The Digestive System

The digestive system allows your body to take in and process food to nourish its cells. Digestion begins in the mouth and continues in the stomach and the small intestine. Other digestive organs, such as the pancreas, liver, and gallbladder, contribute to the process of digestion.

◆ MOUTH

Digestion begins in the mouth with three pairs of **salivary glands.** The smell, and even the thought, of food causes these glands to increase their production of saliva. **Saliva** contains enzymes that break down starches and other complex carbohydrates in food. As a person chews, food is broken into small pieces and mixed with the saliva, which moistens it, making it easier to swallow. Once the food is chewed sufficiently, swallowing forces it into the esophagus.

◆ ESOPHAGUS AND STOMACH

After food is swallowed, it passes through a muscular tube called the **esophagus** and enters the **stomach.** Glands in the stomach lining secrete a variety of enzymes and other chemical compounds. These secretions aid in digesting the food and are collectively called **gastric juices.** Most of the protein and carbohydrates in food are broken down in the stomach. The churning action of the

...like motion called
...sis pushes food
... the esophagus
... the stomach.

Mouth
Esophagus
Liver
Stomach
Gall-
bladder
Pancreas
Small
intestine
Large
intestine
(colon)
Rectum
Anus

◆ SMALL INTESTINE

Digestion is completed in the **small intestine.** Enzymes secreted by the liver and pancreas enter the portion of the small intestine close to the stomach. The digestion of carbohydrates and proteins continues, and the digestion of fats occurs. The remainder of the small intestine has the critical function of absorbing the digested food.

The walls of the small intestine are covered with tiny projections called **villi.** Each villus contains capillaries and lymph vessels and is covered with hairlike projections called **microvilli.** Nutrients move from the small intestine into the capillaries, where they are transported to the cells of the body. The presence of the villi and microvilli increases the total surface area available for nutrient absorption. In fact, for the average person, the total surface area available for nutrient absorption is larger than a tennis court! The middle section of the small intestine contains the greatest concentration of villi, and most absorption takes place there.

Villi
Microvilli
Capillaries

◆ PANCREAS, LIVER, AND GALLBLADDER

The small intestine produces only a few digestive enzymes. Others are supplied by the pancreas and the liver. These organs communicate with each other through hormonal messages that coordinate their enzyme secretions. The **pancreas** secretes enzymes that are active in the digestion of carbohydrates, proteins, and fats. The **liver** secretes a greenish fluid called **bile.** Bile enables large molecules of fat to be broken down. The **gallbladder,** a small, muscular, green sac attached to the liver, stores excess bile until it is needed. The pancreas and the liver have other functions as well. The liver is vital in regulating metabolism. Toxins, such as drugs and alcohol, are broken down by the liver. It also filters damaged red blood cells, debris, and pathogens from the bloodstream. The pancreas produces insulin, which is vital in regulating blood-sugar levels.

◆ LARGE INTESTINE

Undigested food moves into the **large intestine,** or colon, where water is absorbed from the waste and returned to the bloodstream. No food absorption takes place here. Peristalsis moves the solid waste, called feces, through the colon to the **rectum.** Here, it is stored briefly and then eliminated from the body through an opening called the **anus.**

675

Body Systems Handbook (side tab)

BODY SYSTEMS HANDBOOK

Holt Health is a wellness approach focused on everyday living. In keeping with that philosophy, you will find technical background on human body systems in an expanded Body Systems Handbook. This structure gives you the flexibility to integrate the coverage of a particular body system as needed with a core chapter. For example, when studying Chapter 4, Nutrition Principles, you could have students use the Handbook to review the parts and functions of the digestive system.

Emergency medical technicians, or EMTs, must react quickly to administer medical care in emergency situations.

2784N

◆ EMERGENCY MEDICAL TECHNICIAN

An **emergency medical technician** (EMT) provides quick medical attention in emergency situations, such as automobile accidents. EMTs are trained to assess the seriousness of an injury or illness and to provide care for victims of heart attacks, near drownings, motor-vehicle accidents, accidental poisoning, and serious wounds. EMTs treat victims at the scene of the accident and often transport them to hospitals for additional medical care.

An emergency medical technician must be at least 18 years old, hold a high-school diploma, and have a valid driver's license. After completing an extensive training program, those certified as EMTs find jobs at hospitals, police or fire departments, or with private companies. With advanced training, a person can earn an EMT paramedic rating, which enables him or her to perform more advanced medical procedures.

◆ NURSE

A **nurse** works to care for those in need of medical attention. Depending on their level of training and their specialty, nurses perform a variety of duties, such as performing physical exams, observing and assessing patient symptoms, administering medication and treatments, and helping patients with proper nutrition, personal hygiene, and general health care.

Registered nurses (RNs) are licensed to practice by a state board. States have different education requirements that may include a diploma, an associate degree, or a bachelor's degree from an accredited college or university. With additional specialized training, an RN may become a nurse practitioner (NP). Licensed practical nurses (LPNs) usually complete a two-year college program or a technical-school program. In addition to many hours of clinical experience during their schooling, nurses must pass a state-board examination before they can be hired.

This surgical nurse has received special training to allow her to assist physicians in performing surgery.

◆ DENTAL LABORATORY TECHNICIAN

A **dental laboratory technician** makes retainers, dentures, braces, bridges, and crowns according to a dentist's exact specifications. He or she must have excellent manual dexterity, because precision and accuracy are crucial to the perfect fit of dental devices.

Most dental laboratory technicians acquire their skills in commercial laboratories. On-the-job training also is provided by hospitals and federal agencies. Schooling without the actual hands-on training takes about two years. Training with no formal schooling can last as long as five years.

The procedures followed by a dental laboratory technician require manual dexterity and artistic ability.

A dentist treats patients for diseases of the teeth and gums and repairs mechanical damage to the teeth to improve their appearance or function.

◆ DENTIST

A **dentist** examines and treats patients for diseases and conditions of the teeth and gums. A general dentist checks teeth for abscesses, fills decayed teeth, determines whether orthodontic devices are needed, and instructs his or her patients on home dental care. He or she also does the preliminary work for fitting a patient with dentures, crowns, or bridges. As with physicians, there are many dental specialties as well.

After successfully completing college and four years of dental school, every aspiring dentist must pass many practical and written examinations as well as a state board exam. Specialists must complete two to three years of additional study and pass exams in their field of specialization.

686

687

Health Careers Handbook (side tab)

HEALTH CAREERS HANDBOOK

In keeping with *Holt Health*'s emphasis on establishing links to the larger community, the Health Careers Handbook presents a wide range of health-related career opportunities. Students become aware of the variety of careers associated with health care, what the positions entail, and what qualifications they will need to enter each field.

HOLT Health
Course Options

PACING THE COURSE:
FULL AND ALTERNATIVE COURSES OF STUDY

Holt Health is a comprehensive one-year course of 28 chapters divided into eight units. You may cover the units in any order you wish. Additionally, you can select units and chapters according to the time frame and content requirements of your local school district or the interests of your students. The following course outlines can be used as a guide for a full-year course and one-semester courses.

FULL COURSE

ONE-YEAR (36 WEEK) COURSE   28 CHAPTERS

Unit 1 Introduction to Health and Wellness
Chapters 1, 2...*3 weeks*

Unit 2 Health and Your Body
Chapters 3, 4, 5, 6..................................*5 weeks*

Unit 3 Health and Your Mind
Chapters 7, 8, 9, 10, 11..........................*5 weeks*

Unit 4 Protecting Your Health in a Drug Society
Chapters 12, 13, 14, 15..........................*6 weeks*

Unit 5 Family Life, Sexuality, and Social Health
Chapters 16, 17, 18, 19, 20....................*7 weeks*

Unit 6 Diseases and Disorders
Chapters 21, 22, 23, 24..........................*6 weeks*

Unit 7 Health and Society
Chapters 25 and 26................................*2 weeks*

Unit 8 Safety and Emergency Care
Chapters 27 and 28................................*2 weeks*

MENTAL-HEALTH COURSE

ONE-SEMESTER (18 WEEK) COURSE   15 CHAPTERS

Unit 1 Introduction to Health and Wellness
Chapters 1, 2...*2 weeks*

Unit 2 Health and Your Body
Chapter 5 ....*1 week*

Unit 3 Health and Your Mind
Chapters 7, 8, 9, 11................................*6 weeks*

Unit 4 Protecting Your Health in a Drug Society
Chapters 12, 13, 14, 15..........................*5 weeks*

Unit 5 Family Life, Sexuality, and Social Health
Chapters 17, 19, 20................................*3 weeks*

Unit 7 Health and Society
Chapter 25 ....*1 week*

PHYSICAL-HEALTH COURSE

ONE-SEMESTER (18 WEEK) COURSE   17 CHAPTERS

Unit 1 Introduction to Health and Wellness
Chapters 1, 2...*2 weeks*

Unit 2 Health and Your Body
Chapters 3, 4, 5, 6..................................*4 weeks*

Unit 4 Protecting Your Health in a Drug Society
Chapters 12, 13, 14, 15..........................*5 weeks*

Unit 5 Family Life, Sexuality, and Social Health
Chapter 16 ....*1 week*

Unit 6 Diseases and Disorders
Chapters 21, 22, 23, 24..........................*4 weeks*

Unit 7 Health and Society
Chapters 27 and 28................................*2 weeks*

HEALTH SURVEY

ONE-SEMESTER (18 WEEK) COURSE   15 CHAPTERS

Unit 1 Introduction to Health and Wellness
Chapters 1, 2...*2 weeks*

Unit 2 Health and Your Body
Chapters 3, 4...*3 weeks*

Unit 3 Health and Your Mind
Chapters 7, 8...*2 weeks*

Unit 4 Protecting Your Health in a Drug Society
Chapters 12, 13, 14, 15..........................*5 weeks*

Unit 5 Family Life, Sexuality, and Social Health
Chapters 16, 20..*2 weeks*

Unit 6 Diseases and Disorders
Chapters 21, 22, 23................................*4 weeks*

HOLT HEALTH ANNOTATED TEACHER'S EDITION

TEACHER'S INTERLEAF PAGES

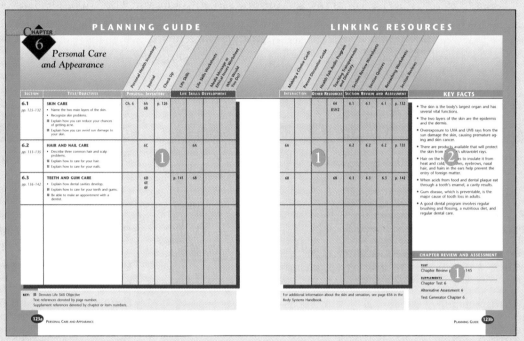

LINKING RESOURCES/PLANNING GUIDES

1 **The Planning Guide** and **Linking Resources** help you in selecting all of the appropriate materials for a text section. You can see at a glance all the resources you can select from when covering a particular chapter. The color-coded columns call out which resources are related to Personal Inventory, Life Skill Development, Interaction, or Section Review and Assessment.

2 **Key Facts** gives you a quick overview of the important ideas of the chapter.

UNIT OPENERS

3 **Chapter Overview** gives you a quick summary of the material presented in the chapter.

4 **Unit Preview** gives you a concise overview of the important concepts developed in the unit.

5 **National Health Education Standards** table shows which standards are supported by information and activities found in the unit chapters.

CHAPTER OPENERS

6 **Getting Started** uses the chapter photograph as a springboard to help you begin a discussion of the chapter theme.

7 **Myths and Misconceptions** helps you dispel faulty thinking students may have on the chapter's subject matter.

UNIT OPENER PAGES

TEACHER'S WRAP

Holt Health Instructional
Model The instructional
model for *Holt Health*
consists of three phases.

⑧ PHASE 1: MOTIVATE

*Self-Reflection and
Assessment of Prior
Knowledge*

You'll find specific features
in the Annotated Teacher's
Edition for beginning the
chapter and each lesson with
the student Journal or other
motivating activity.

⑨ PHASE 2: TEACH

Processing Information

This stage of instruction focuses
on the strategies you use to
cover the key concepts of the
chapter. The Annotated
Teacher's Edition gives you
a wide range of highly interactive strategies including class
discussion, cooperative learning
activities, role playing, games,
reinforcement strategies, and
journal writing activities.

⑩ PHASE 3: ASSESS

Evaluate Understanding

This stage of instruction focuses
on evaluating students' understanding of the subject matter.
Holt Health provides a number
of strategies including Section
Reviews, Chapter Reviews,
Closure Activities, and Alternative Assessment Strategies.
To learn more about the complete assessment plan for *Holt
Health* turn to pages 26T–27T.

HOLT Health
TEACHING RESOURCE SUPPLEMENTS (IN COPYMASTER FORM)

The *Holt Health* Teaching Resource Supplements include a wealth of reproducibles that provide everything you need to supplement your basic health program. The following individual booklets contain worksheets that support class discussion, group interaction, and individualized instruction for today's dynamic health classroom. The assessment booklets contain a complete evaluation program with options for alternative assessment and reteaching.

Lesson Plans

Personal Health Inventories and Journal (includes Personal Pledges)

Life Skills Worksheets with Answer Key (includes Evaluating Media Messages/Ethical Issues in Health)

Section Reviews with Answer Key

Section Quizzes with Answer Key

Reteaching Worksheets with Answer Key

Chapter Tests and Alternative Assessments with Answer Key

Parent Discussion Guide—English/Spanish

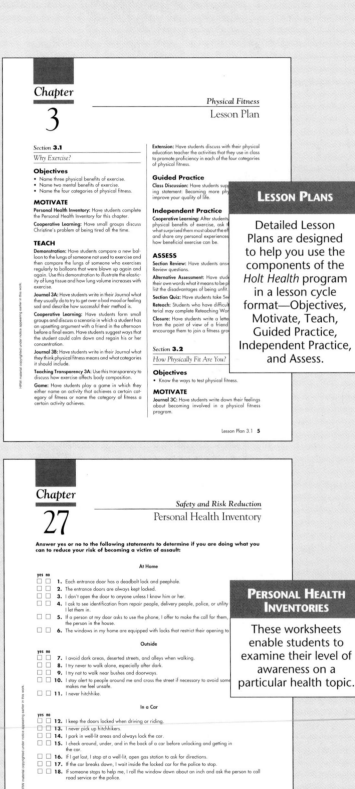

LESSON PLANS

Detailed Lesson Plans are designed to help you use the components of the *Holt Health* program in a lesson cycle format—Objectives, Motivate, Teach, Guided Practice, Independent Practice, and Assess.

JOURNAL ENTRIES

The confidential Journal Entries provide students with an opportunity to explore in writing their values, beliefs, feelings, and opinions on a variety of health-related topics.

PERSONAL HEALTH INVENTORIES

These worksheets enable students to examine their level of awareness on a particular health topic.

ALERT: All Journal Entry, Personal Health Inventory, and Personal Pledge worksheets are designed for the students' private reflections and are not intended to be collected.

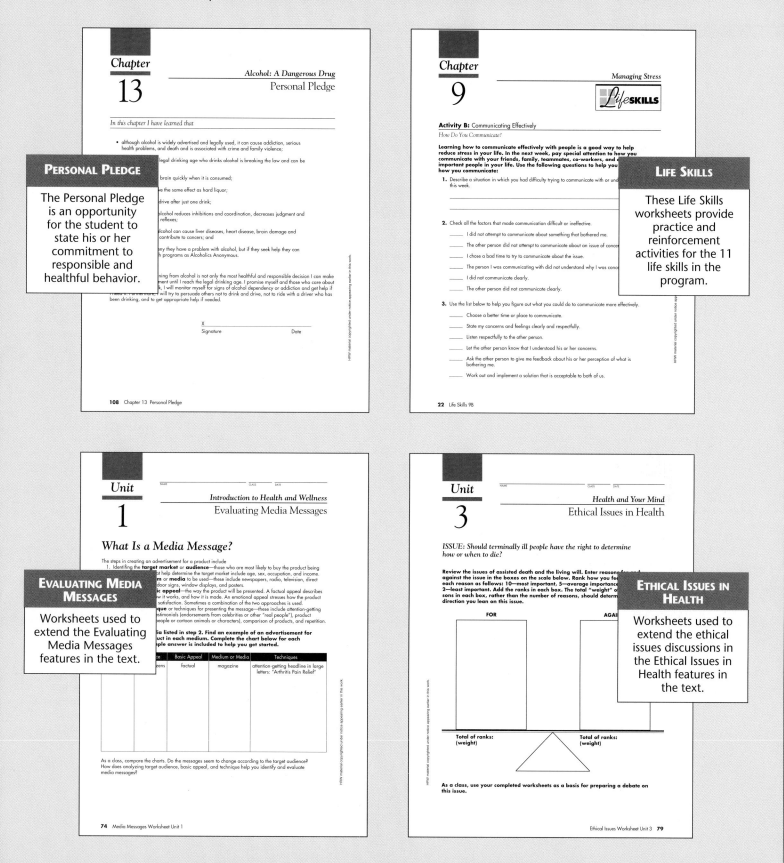

PERSONAL PLEDGE

The Personal Pledge is an opportunity for the student to state his or her commitment to responsible and healthful behavior.

LIFE SKILLS

These Life Skills worksheets provide practice and reinforcement activities for the 11 life skills in the program.

EVALUATING MEDIA MESSAGES

Worksheets used to extend the Evaluating Media Messages features in the text.

ETHICAL ISSUES IN HEALTH

Worksheets used to extend the ethical issues discussions in the Ethical Issues in Health features in the text.

TEACHING RESOURCE SUPPLEMENTS (IN COPYMASTER FORM)

Chapter 11

NAME ___ CLASS ___ DATE ___

Preventing Suicide
Section Review

Section **11.1** *Teenage Suicide: A Serious Problem*

Part I

There are many myths surrounding suicidal behavior, and if they are believed they can have serious consequences. Identify each of the following statements as a myth or fact by writing M or F in the blanks:

_____ **1.** All people who commit suicide are mentally ill.

_____ **2.** Most people who commit suicide have talked about it before.

_____ **3.** Suicide is a behavior that is not inherited.

_____ **4.** If you ask a person if he or she is considering suicide, you will encourage that person to commit suicide.

_____ **5.** If a person makes a suicidal threat while drunk or high on drugs, it isn't serious.

_____ **6.** People who talk about killing themselves rarely commit suicide.

_____ **7.** A suicide attempt is often a cry for help to live.

_____ **8.** Suicide usually occurs without warning.

_____ **9.** Many people consider suicide for only a brief period in their life.

_____ **10.** When a suicidal person suddenly seems calm and serene, there is no longer any danger of suicide.

46 Section Review 11.1

SECTION REVIEWS

Worksheets that focus on reading comprehension and concept review.

Section Review cont.

Part II

Find the path that includes *all* the things that might help reduce the risk of teen suicide and avoids *all* the things that could increase the risk.

START

Rising divorce rate

Moving from place to place

Strong family support

Alcohol and drug abuse

Pressure to succeed in school

Nearby friends and relatives

Physical, emotional, or sexual abuse

Glamorized images of suicide

Abstaining from drugs and alcohol

Loving, caring parents

Help from people who care

STAY ALIVE

Section Review 11.1 **47**

Chapter 10

NAME ___ CLASS ___ DATE ___

Coping With Loss
Section Quiz

Section **10.1** *Death and Dying*

Part I

Listed below are five stages terminally ill people generally pass through as they face death. In the spaces provided, describe what a person might feel, think, or do during that stage and how you might help someone in

---

SECTION QUIZZES

Quick assessment sheets to motivate students to keep up with their classwork.

---

5. Acceptance:

Part II

Answer the question in the space provided.

6. Do all people go through these stages in the same order? Explain.

Section Quiz 10.1 **29**

Chapter 12

NAME ___ CLASS ___ DATE ___

The Use, Misuse, and Abuse of Drugs
Reteaching

Section **12.2** *Over-the-Counter and Prescription Drugs*

Part I

Complete the network tree about OTC drugs by using terms from the list below. Then choose terms to complete statements about the negative effects of OTC drugs. Some terms can be used more than once, others may not be used at all.

acetaminophen   relieve pain   appetite suppressants
mild sleeping pills aspirin   ibuprofen
increase alertness   induce sleep   cold remedies
antihistamines   reduce appetite   cough syrup with alcohol

OTC drugs

common types

1. analgesics   **2.** sedatives   **3.** stimulants

positive effects	examples	*positive effects*	examples	*positive effects*	examp
relieve pain	a.	a.	b.	a.	b.
	b.		c.		c.
	c.				d.

Part II

Answer the questions in the spaces provided.

4. What analgesic can cause stomach irritation and bleeding and is associated with Reye's syndrom

5. What medicines can cause drowsiness and dizziness and should not be taken before driving a car?

6. What OTC preparations containing stimulants and caffeine can cause high blood pressure and increased heart rate?

34 Reteaching 12.2

RETEACHING

Worksheets to reinforce or represent the more difficult concepts in a section in a clear, straightforward manner.

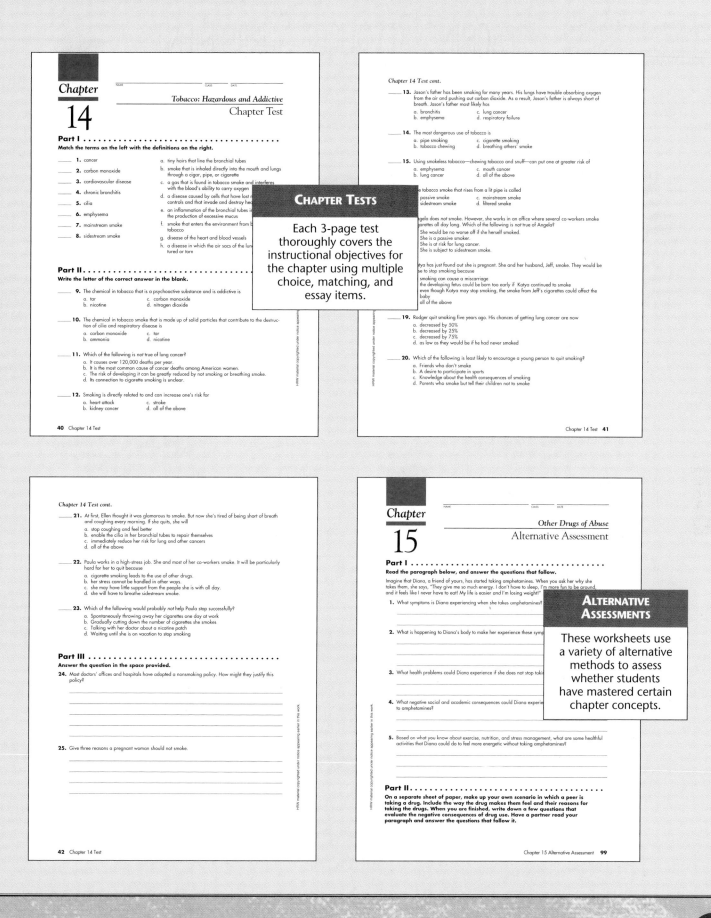

Chapter 14

NAME _____ CLASS _____ DATE _____

Tobacco: Hazardous and Addictive
Chapter Test

Part I . . . .
Match the terms on the left with the definitions on the right.

____ **1.** cancer
____ **2.** carbon monoxide
____ **3.** cardiovascular disease
____ **4.** chronic bronchitis
____ **5.** cilia
____ **6.** emphysema
____ **7.** mainstream smoke
____ **8.** sidestream smoke

a. tiny hairs that line the bronchial tubes
b. smoke that is inhaled directly into the mouth and lungs through a cigar, pipe, or cigarette
c. a gas that is found in tobacco smoke and interferes with the blood's ability to carry oxygen
d. a disease caused by cells that have lost [their] controls and that invade and destroy hea[lthy cells]
e. an inflammation of the bronchial tubes i[n] the production of excessive mucus
f. smoke that enters the environment from b[urning] tobacco
g. disease of the heart and blood vessels
h. a disease in which the air sacs of the lun[gs are rup-]tured or torn

Part II . . . .
Write the letter of the correct answer in the blank.

____ **9.** The chemical in tobacco that is a psychoactive substance and is addictive is
a. tar
b. nicotine
c. carbon monoxide
d. nitrogen dioxide

____ **10.** The chemical in tobacco smoke that is made up of solid particles that contribute to the destruction of cilia and respiratory disease is
a. carbon monoxide
b. ammonia
c. tar
d. nicotine

____ **11.** Which of the following is not true of lung cancer?
a. It causes over 120,000 deaths per year.
b. It is the most common cause of cancer deaths among American women.
c. The risk of developing it can be greatly reduced by not smoking or breathing smoke.
d. Its connection to cigarette smoking is unclear.

____ **12.** Smoking is directly related to and can increase one's risk for
a. heart attack
b. kidney cancer
c. stroke
d. all of the above

40   Chapter 14 Test

Chapter 14 Test cont.

____ **13.** Jason's father has been smoking for many years. His lungs have trouble absorbing oxygen from the air and pushing out carbon dioxide. As a result, Jason's father is always short of breath. Jason's father most likely has
a. bronchitis
b. emphysema
c. lung cancer
d. respiratory failure

____ **14.** The most dangerous use of tobacco is
a. pipe smoking
b. tobacco chewing
c. cigarette smoking
d. breathing others' smoke

____ **15.** Using smokeless tobacco—chewing tobacco and snuff—can put one at greater risk of
a. emphysema
b. lung cancer
c. mouth cancer
d. all of the above

____ **16.** [The] tobacco smoke that rises from a lit pipe is called
[a.] passive smoke
[b.] sidestream smoke
c. mainstream smoke
d. filtered smoke

____ **17.** [An]gela does *not* smoke. However, she works in an office where several co-workers smoke [ciga]rettes all day long. Which of the following is *not* true of Angela?
[a.] She would be no worse off if she herself smoked.
[b.] She is a passive smoker.
[c.] She is at risk for lung cancer.
[d.] She is subject to sidestream smoke.

____ **18.** [Kat]ya has just found out she is pregnant. She and her husband, Jeff, smoke. They would be [wi]se to stop smoking because
[a.] smoking can cause a miscarriage
[b.] the developing fetus could be born too early if Katya continued to smoke
[c.] even though Katya may stop smoking, the smoke from Jeff's cigarettes could affect the baby
[d.] all of the above

____ **19.** Rodger quit smoking five years ago. His chances of getting lung cancer are now
a. decreased by 50%
b. decreased by 25%
c. decreased by 75%
d. as low as they would be if he had never smoked

____ **20.** Which of the following is least likely to encourage a young person to quit smoking?
a. Friends who don't smoke
b. A desire to participate in sports
c. Knowledge about the health consequences of smoking
d. Parents who smoke but tell their children not to smoke

Chapter 14 Test   41

Chapter 14 Test cont.

____ **21.** At first, Ellen thought it was glamorous to smoke. But now she's tired of being short of breath and coughing every morning. If she quits, she will
a. stop coughing and feel better
b. enable the cilia in her bronchial tubes to repair themselves
c. immediately reduce her risk for lung and other cancers
d. all of the above

____ **22.** Paula works in a high-stress job. She and most of her co-workers smoke. It will be particularly hard for her to quit because
a. cigarette smoking leads to the use of other drugs.
b. her stress cannot be handled in other ways.
c. she may have little support from the people she is with all day.
d. she will have to breathe sidestream smoke.

____ **23.** Which of the following would probably *not* help Paula stop successfully?
a. Spontaneously throwing away her cigarettes one day at work
b. Gradually cutting down the number of cigarettes she smokes
c. Talking with her doctor about a nicotine patch
d. Waiting until she is on vacation to stop smoking

Part III . . . .
Answer the question in the space provided.

24. Most doctors' offices and hospitals have adopted a nonsmoking policy. How might they justify this policy?

_____
_____
_____
_____

25. Give three reasons a pregnant woman should not smoke.

_____
_____
_____
_____

42   Chapter 14 Test

Chapter 15

NAME _____ CLASS _____ DATE _____

Other Drugs of Abuse
Alternative Assessment

Part I . . . .
Read the paragraph below, and answer the questions that follow.

Imagine that Diana, a friend of yours, has started taking amphetamines. When you ask her why she takes them, she says, "They give me so much energy. I don't have to sleep, I'm more fun to be around, and it feels like I never have to eat! My life is easier *and* I'm losing weight!"

1. What symptoms is Diana experiencing when she takes amphetamines?

_____

2. What is happening to Diana's body to make her experience these symp[toms]?

_____
_____

3. What health problems could Diana experience if she does not stop takin[g the drug]?

_____
_____

4. What negative social and academic consequences could Diana experie[nce due] to amphetamines?

_____
_____

5. Based on what you know about exercise, nutrition, and stress management, what are some healthful activities that Diana could do to feel more energetic without taking amphetamines?

_____
_____
_____

Part II . . . .
On a separate sheet of paper, make up your own scenario in which a peer is taking a drug. Include the way the drug makes them feel and their reasons for taking the drugs. When you are finished, write down a few questions that evaluate the negative consequences of drug use. Have a partner read your paragraph and answer the questions that follow it.

Chapter 15 Alternative Assessment   99

CHAPTER TESTS

Each 3-page test thoroughly covers the instructional objectives for the chapter using multiple choice, matching, and essay items.

ALTERNATIVE ASSESSMENTS

These worksheets use a variety of alternative methods to assess whether students have mastered certain chapter concepts.

HOLT Health

TEACHING RESOURCE SUPPLEMENTS

HEALTH TALK AUDIO CD PROGRAM ENGLISH/SPANISH

The audio CD program addresses the needs of auditory learners or students with English language difficulties. For selected chapters, the audio program reviews key concepts in English or Spanish.

TEST GENERATOR

This teacher utility software can be used to construct customized chapter tests from a bank of over 1200 items. Available for Macintosh® and IBM® and compatible PCs.

TEACHING TRANSPARENCIES

The set of 64 transparencies includes teaching diagrams from the chapters and the Body Systems Handbook, plus some new diagrams to be used with specific teaching strategies in the Annotated Teacher's Edition.

HOLT HEALTH
Figure 28-2
28A
Rescue Breathing

1. Open the airway by tipping the head back and lifting the chin.
2. Check for breathing by placing your cheek next to the person's nose and then listening and feeling for breath.
3. If the victim is not breathing, pinch the nose closed with one hand while keeping the airway open by holding the chin up with the other hand.
4. Tightly seal your mouth over the victim's mouth and blow air into the victim's lungs, or hold the mouth closed and blow into the nose.
5. After two breaths, check for a pulse and signs of breathing.
6. Continue to give one slow breath every 5 seconds until medical help arrives, you are too exhausted to continue, or the victim begins to breath.

For young children and babies:
1. Blow into the mouth and nose at the same time.
2. Give one breath every 3 seconds.
3. Use smaller puffs of breaths, because the lungs are smaller.

HOLT HEALTH
Figure 16-12
16C
Fertilization

The egg continues to divide.
The egg divides into two cells.
Fallopian tube
Ovary
The egg implants itself in the uterine wall. It is now called an embryo.
The sperm fertilizes the egg.
cavity
Vagina
Cervical opening

HRW material copyrighted under notice appearing earlier in this work.

PARENTAL SURVEY

Complete the following survey together.

A decision-making model (Figure 2-4 in *Holt Health*) is a series of steps that can help a person make a better informed and more responsible decision. The model has seven steps. The steps that follow are out of order. Together, discuss the order in which you think they should be arranged. Place a number (1–7) on each line.

• Consider your values.

• Evaluate the results.

THE EXTRA MILE

Imagine that a good friend is pressuring you to start smoking cigarettes. Using a decision-making model as a guide, write down any information that might help you decide what to do.

State the Problem: _____

List the Options: _____

Imagine the Benefits and Consequences: _____

Consider Your Values: _____

Evaluate Options and Decide: _____

Making Responsible Decisions
Parent Letter

Chapter 2

Dear Parent/Guardian,

In the years to come, your teen will be making decisions that impact his or her physical, emotional, and spiritual health. The purpose of this Health Education class is to provide students with the knowledge and resources they need to make responsible and well-informed decisions about their health. As the course progresses, students will be asked to explore their values, opinions, and beliefs as they address these issues. It is important that students receive mature guidance in the classroom and at home as they address these issues.

In the next few weeks, your son or daughter's Health Education class will focus on the subject of making responsible decisions. The decisions your teen makes today will influence not only how long he or she lives, but also the quality of his or her life years from now. This chapter will introduce a seven-step decision-making model designed to help young adults arrive at healthful, logical, and rational decisions in a systematic way. Students will learn that responsible decision making is an essential part of a healthful lifestyle.

Other areas covered in this chapter include life expectancy, personal values, and how to improve one's quality of life. We will also discuss the top three causes of death both for young people 15 to 24 years old and people 55 to 64 years old in America today.

You can actively support your teen's progress in Health by communicating with him or her about the topics covered in this course. To aid this communication, I have included worksheets for you to complete with your teen. These worksheets include a Parental Survey, which introduces topics covered in the course, and a worksheet entitled The Extra Mile, which provides guidance for a more in-depth discussion. Your signature at the end of this material will verify that this home interaction has taken place.

Thank you in advance for your time, cooperation, and support.

Sincerely,

_____
Health Teacher

Chapter 2 Parent Discussion Guide 1

Chapter 2 Parent Discussion Guide 3

PARENT DISCUSSION GUIDE

This copymaster booklet contains parent letters and discussion guides for 16 key chapters in the text. This program is designed to encourage discussion of important health issues between teens and parents or guardians.

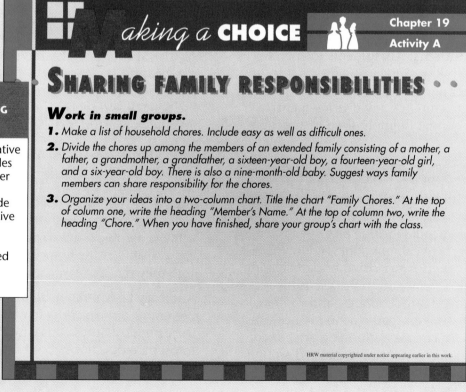

Making a CHOICE

Chapter 19

Activity A

SHARING FAMILY RESPONSIBILITIES

Work in small groups.

1. Make a list of household chores. Include easy as well as difficult ones.

2. Divide the chores up among the members of an extended family consisting of a mother, a father, a grandmother, a grandfather, a sixteen-year-old boy, a fourteen-year-old girl, and a six-year-old boy. There is also a nine-month-old baby. Suggest ways family members can share responsibility for the chores.

3. Organize your ideas into a two-column chart. Title the chart "Family Chores." At the top of column one, write the heading "Member's Name." At the top of column two, write the heading "Chore." When you have finished, share your group's chart with the class.

MAKING A CHOICE COOPERATIVE LEARNING STRATEGIES

This boxed set of cooperative learning activities includes two activities per chapter and 6 copies of each activity so you can divide the class into 6 cooperative groups. Spanish copymasters of each activity card are included in the accompanying *Teacher's Notes*.

FOR STUDENTS WITH SPECIAL NEEDS

Today's classroom is composed of students that have varying abilities and different learning styles. To accommodate the needs of these students, the *Holt Health* program includes optional activities and alternative instructional approaches for students with Limited English Proficiency (LEP), At-Risk students who have special needs in motivation, students who are Less-Advanced, and students with different learning styles—Visual, Auditory, and Kinesthetic.

In addition to the suggested chapter activities listed in this section of the Teacher's Guide, many of the Vocabulary and Extension activities found on the Highlights/Strategies page at the end of each chapter will accommodate the needs of one of these groups of students. Also, the English version of the Health Talk Audio CD program is an excellent aid for Auditory Learners, LEP students, and any other student for whom written English is a hindrance to learning. Use the Spanish version of the Health Talk Audio CD program for students who are more proficient in Spanish.

CHAPTER 1

LEP Students: Appoint a team of students who have a grasp on what total health means. Have them draw up a questionnaire that can be used to assess a student's health profile. (Questions might include: Do you enjoy doing things with other people? Are you comfortable with the way your body looks and feels? When you want to, can you tell people how you feel? Do you have enough energy for your daily activities? for sports?) When the questionnaire is ready, the team can use it on a one-on-one basis, posing the questions to LEP students and making sure they understand what total health comprises. Then have the LEP students switch roles and ask the questions to those who prepared the questionnaire.

Less-Advanced Students: Ask students to analyze the Life Skills Health Risks Survey and list each section of the survey under one of the five components of health. Discuss with students any disagreements about which component is emphasized in a section.

CHAPTER 2

Visual Learners: Students may benefit from a display of images that focus on lifestyle decisions. Such images might be paired and could include pictures of alcoholic beverages versus healthful drinks; young people watching television versus exercising or participating in sports; foods high in fat and sugar versus those high in fiber, complex carbohydrates, and vitamins; teens in gangs versus teens participating in positive activities, such as sports, the performing arts, or computer clubs. The display might be organized around a key phrase such as "Decisions for Life."

Auditory Learners: Have students form small groups. Provide each group with a cassette tape on which a young person's lifestyle decision is described. (Examples might include opting not to go to college, deciding to work 30 hours a week during high school, buying a motorcycle, taking up smoking, cutting out fatty foods.) Have each group discuss the likely short-term and long-term effects of the decision they heard on the tape. After ranking the most important effects, students can record their responses and a statement telling whether they think the decision was responsible. The class can listen to each group's tape and discuss their reactions.

CHAPTER 3

At-Risk Students: Have these students identify an exercise or sport the appeals to them or that they already participate in. Have them investigate the benefits of the activity and report their findings to the class. If feasible, have students include a demonstration.

Visual Learners: Use aerobic fitness videos to demonstrate the typical exercises that will help students become fit. Make the videos available before or after class—if this complies with school policy—to students who may wish to work with others to achieve aerobic fitness. Find out which fitness videos are available at the library. Preview them to make sure they meet safety standards for teenagers.

Auditory Learners: Invite members of a school team, preferably a male and a female athlete, to discuss their physical fitness tips with students. Ask students to prepare questions about fitness that they would like answered.

Kinesthetic Learners: Give students index cards with situations related to physical fitness that would lend themselves to role-playing or skits. Index cards might include a student who hates sports but knows that he or she needs physical exercise; a student who spends three hours a day watching television and gets no exercise; a friend who is discouraged because he diets but can't seem to lose weight.

CHAPTER 4

LEP Students: Provide students with magazine pictures of foods, from each food group, that clearly belong to their particular group. Have students construct a large food pyramid and place the pictures in the appropriate group. Then have students write out English labels for the foods and place them on the pictures so that the name does not show but can be viewed by flipping the label over. Students can quiz each other on the names of the foods. In addition, students could include foods from their own cultures that may be unknown to other students. You may want to extend this activity to common food products that belong to several food groups. Students may find it helpful to practice distinguishing between similar foods, for example, a sausage pizza verses a mushroom pizza or a ham-and-cheese sandwich verses a tuna on rye.

Kinesthetic Learners: Have students bring to class an assortment of food items and supplement them as necessary to represent the groups on the food pyramid. Ask small groups to select a variety of foods that would provide a balanced diet for one day. Rate students' selections for nutritional balance and adequacy.

Auditory Learners: Have students interview a nutritionist or prepare questions for a nutritionist guest speaker and take notes on the answers they receive. Suggest that each student focus on one area, such as nutrients, menu planning, or evaluating diets.

CHAPTER 5

Visual Learners: Show students a selection of books and advertisements dealing with diets and plans for losing weight. Students can make a bulletin-board display of such items and then a chart listing the points in a balanced plan for weight reduction.

At-Risk Students: Show students an exercise video and stress the popularity of such items in weight control plans. Allow students to critique the video. They may wish to learn some of the routines and put on a demonstration for the rest of the class.

CHAPTER 6

At-Risk Students: Provide students with a variety of empty containers of sunscreen and sun block products. (You could organize a class drive to collect containers.) Have students read the ingredient labels to determine which products block UVA and UVB rays and classify the containers accordingly. Then have students develop a presentation that explains the differences in the products, including the SPF.

Kinesthetic Learners: Invite a dental hygienist, dentist, or school nurse to demonstrate the correct teeth-cleaning technique. Allow students to handle the models and equipment used and to practice the techniques demonstrated.

CHAPTER 7

LEP and At-Risk Students: To help students connect the names of common defense mechanisms with the behaviors these mechanisms describe, have them draw and label cartoons illustrating defense mechanisms. You might wish to display the cartoons on a bulletin board.

CHAPTER 8

Auditory Learners: Students who learn best by listening and speaking can spend several days making notes on comments they hear that signal how people value themselves. They can then analyze these comments and the contexts in which they occurred. For each negative comment, ask that they recreate the context and act out the scene, replacing the negative with a positive "I" statement.

Kinesthetic Learners: The body image projected by an individual depends on posture, gesture, manner of moving, and so on. For kinesthetic learners, suggest a three-day period in which they observe others and themselves. Ask them to isolate and demonstrate five elements of body language that communicate low self-esteem, and then model replacement behaviors that project a positive self-image.

At-Risk Students: Assist students in creating personal profiles of their self-esteem. Formats can be individualized, and headings might include "Who I Am" (likes, dislikes, strengths, weaknesses), "Starring Me!" (things I do well), "A Change Artist" (negatives I can do something about and a plan for changing them), and "The Feel-Good Gang" (people in my support group, or who I want in my support group).

Chapter 9

LEP Students: LEP students often experience stress and frustration over their inability to express themselves well in English. Have LEP students create a list of communication situations that they have found stressful. Then have them discuss the situations and share any successful techniques they have for dealing with the situations described or the stress involved. Interested native English speakers could help by suggesting nonverbal cues that could help in communication.

Visual Learners: Have students collect newspaper and magazine photos of both stressed and happy faces. Ask them to write a description of how the stressed and happy faces differ.

Kinesthetic Learners: Students may find regular contact with a pet helpful in reducing stress. Have students report to the class on the stress-reducing effects of pets, using as references stress-management books and articles, which can be found through *Academic Abstracts* on CD or in *The Reader's Guide to Periodical Literature.* Some students may wish to report on their personal experience with pets and stress reduction.

Chapter 10

Visual Learners: Have students gather, photograph, and draw images that to them best illustrate the key concepts of stages in dying, death with dignity, hospice care, and mourning for the dead. Have them arrange these images, along with the key words or phrases, in original collages.

LEP Students: Students can develop pantomimes that communicate helpful responses to a terminally ill person by friends, family, and hospice workers. For each skit, the performers should write a simple explanation and read it to the audience after performing.

Chapter 11

Auditory Learners: Have students organize a mock radio panel presentation on teenage suicides. Topics that could be addressed include facts and myths about suicide, warning signs of suicide, and how to help suicidal people.

Kinesthetic and Visual Learners: Have groups of three students act out brief conversations between friends in which one friend says something that is a warning of possible suicidal thoughts. The other student should model one of the helping behaviors (active listening, empathetic response, or acknowledgment of the seriousness of the person's problem). The dialogue should then be repeated with the third student acting as a moderator who freezes the action at certain points to comment on what the warning is and how the listener is responding to it.

Chapter 12

Less-Advanced Students: Have students create a mobile, poster, or other visual display in which the chapter's vocabulary is highlighted. They could write each of the terms on one side of a card or a cutout shaped like a pill or bottle, and the definition on the other side.

LEP Students: Have students for whom English is a second language look to see if prescription and over-the-counter medications in their home have directions in their native language. If not, have students ask pharmacists near their home if directions in their native language are available for most drugs. Have them prepare a list of precautions they have learned about in class that may help their family.

Chapter 13

At-Risk Students: Using Figure 13-4 as a guide, have students develop a presentation that includes visuals on how alcohol is absorbed, distributed, and eliminated by the body. Have students relate this process to why a person who have a drink or two begins to become intoxicated. Students could work alone, with a partner, or with a small group, depending on which situation is most comfortable for them.

Less-Advanced Students: Have students bring to class newspaper and magazine articles about alcohol-related traffic accidents, or have them take notes on such accidents during newscasts. Ask them to highlight the blood alcohol level (BAL) when indicated, and place these articles on the classroom bulletin board.

CHAPTER 14

Visual Learners: Have students prepare a display of anti-smoking posters, available from organizations such as the American Cancer Society, and cigarette ads from magazines. Use the display as the basis for a class discussion of the feelings that tobacco companies try to evoke in people to get them to smoke a particular brand, such as the need to belong, the desire to be popular, and the desire to be successful.

At-Risk Students: Have students conduct a survey of adults or teenagers they know who have successfully quit smoking cigarettes. They should prepare a list of questions, which might cover reasons for smoking in the first place, reasons for quitting, and methods used to quit. Have them present their findings to the class in an oral report, skit, or set of graphs.

CHAPTER 15

Visual Learners: For students who learn best visually, you may wish to show the video series *Straight Talk About Drugs.* This series contains three videos: *Tranquilizers and Sedatives; Stimulants and Narcotics;* and *Psychedelics, PCP, and Dangerous Combinations.* The series provides information about the effects of drugs, addiction, the dangers of combining drugs, and rehabilitation programs. The videos may be available at your library or can be obtained at Guidance Associates, Communications Park, Box 3000, Mount Kisco, NY 10549. Call 1-800-431-1242.

At-Risk Students: Have students create a newspaper for circulation among younger students that carries an antidrug message. They could do this by collecting articles from newspapers and magazines or by writing their own feature stories, news stories, cartoons, and editorials.

CHAPTER 16

Visual Learners: Students will benefit from a display of images that trace the development of a human from conception through birth and the first 10 years of life. Have students locate pictures or make drawings that represent conception, pregnancy, childbirth, infancy, and the stages of childhood. These can be placed on a time line fixed to a bulletin board, wall, or chalkboard.

CHAPTER 17

LEP Students: Students might benefit from the active-listening technique in Section 17.2. Give students extra practice in this method by helping them prepare cards with the chapter's vocabulary words and definitions. Have them take turns reading aloud and actively listening to the words and definitions.

At-Risk Students: Emphasize to students the social, educational, and financial disadvantages of teen pregnancy. Then have students review the section "Risks of Teenage Sexual Intimacy." Students should then create a mock television news magazine segment on these risks. One student could be the host and other students could take the roles of reporters for each of the three subsections. After reviewing each group's final run-through, have the groups present their segments to the class.

CHAPTER 18

Visual Learners: Have students create a time line of their own showing the three stages of adulthood as they hope to experience them. Encourage students to illustrate important life events they may anticipate, such as career, marriage, family, new home, losses, etc. For example, students might draw pictures of themselves at different ages, and write articles or letters to show possible achievements or experiences.

At-Risk Students: Have students interview school counselors and any teenagers who are married and/or parents to learn about the special needs and problems of teen marriage and parenthood. They can present their findings in a panel, and take questions from the audience afterward.

CHAPTER 19

Less-Advanced Students: Create a bulletin board titled "Coping With Change in the Family." In the center of the display, pin a phrase describing a change that affects family dynamics (such as "Serious Illness," "Divorce and Remarriage," "New Baby," or "Unemployment"). Have students fill the board with illustrations and written suggestions for how family members support each other, communicate, and adapt responsibilities to cope with this change. Pin up new phrases and solicit new student contributions as chapter study progresses.

At-Risk Students: Have students write fantasy stories about living in their ideal families. With whom would they live? Where would they live? What kinds of activities would the family members share? What would be unique about their relationship with each member of the family? Then have them write a few sentences telling how they might make choices and plans to realize some of their ideals about family living.

CHAPTER 20

At-Risk Students: Have students find information and statistics on gangs in your area. Supply a list of possible sources for data (police department, family services agencies, and so on). Suggest that students gather information on crimes and deaths related to gangs, as well as what happens to gang members over time. They can communicate to the class what they learn from their research through an oral presentation or a visual display.

Visual/Auditory Learners: Have students write skits about and act out interpersonal conflicts that could lead to violence or abuse. Have them act out the scenes a second time, showing how communication skills and appropriate reaction could defuse the situation. You may want to suggest that students use the RESPECT method for resolving conflicts (described in Chapter 17). If possible, have students videotape and narrate the skits, using a student narration followed by a class viewing and discussion.

CHAPTER 21

Auditory Learners: Prepare cards containing the following information. Card 1: names of the five types of pathogens (for Section 21.1), Card 2: the five ways in which diseases are spread (21.1), Card 3: the body's six initial defenses (21.2), Card 4: the three immunity types (21.2), and Card 5: the nine diseases headlined in the text (21.3). Have pairs of students use the cards to query each other to define each term.

Visual Learners: Have students find appropriate pictures and ads to construct a scrapbook on infectious diseases. This might include photos of people from various nations.

CHAPTER 22

Visual Learners: For students who learn best visually, show a video about STDs, such as *Sexually Transmitted Diseases: Causes, Prevention and Cure,* video (Guidance Associates). Discuss the film afterwards to find out what topics students have questions about. Have them write any positive or negative thoughts they had about the film.

Auditory Learners: Give pairs or small groups of students several questions about the four most common STDs. Students should reach a consensus about the answers and record both the questions and answers. Students can then listen to a question, stop the tape, and answer the question orally. By listening to the taped answer, students can check their knowledge of the subject.

CHAPTER 23

LEP Students: Have students read the book *Straight Talk About Sexually Transmitted Diseases* (Facts on File, Incorporated, 1993), by Brodman, Michael, M.D., John Thacker, and Rachael Kranz. Have pairs of LEP students present their findings to the class. You may want to partner each pair with a native English speaker who have a strong grasp of the subject matter. That student could answer any questions the LEP student has about developing their presentation.

Visual Learners: Collect images that reinforce key points of the chapter. Display them on a bulletin board or on posters. Images might include young people enjoying each other's company in a nonsexual way, the action of a virus in a cell, people who are ill with AIDS, and young people with tattoos or pierced ears. Have students make collages showing positive ways of expressing affection nonsexually.

CHAPTER 24

Kinesthetic Learners: Develop a concept map for the material in section one and draw the map on a large piece of paper. Then cut the map apart into puzzle sections for the students to reassemble. Challenge students to make their own puzzles for sections two and three.

Kinesthetic Learners and Less-Advanced Students: Some students may have difficulty in remembering the different hereditary, congenital, autoimmune, and degenerative diseases. Write these titles each on a separate index card. Give students self-stick note sheets on which to write the names of the diseases discussed in the chapter. Have them stick each name under the proper category of disease.

CHAPTER 25

Visual Learners: Have students collect pictures from magazines and newspapers showing a variety of unspoiled ecosystems, the effects of pollution in different settings, and the causes of pollution. Use these pictures as you discuss ecosystems and pollution.

At-Risk Students: Organize a project to improve the environment in and around the school. Allow students to select tasks that they wish to participate in, and provide recognition for students' accomplishments.

LEP Students: Many terms from this chapter are drawn from the fields of science and medicine. Have pairs of students write these terms on a set of index cards and have them write the definitions on a second set of cards. Have these pairs of students work together, matching terms and definitions.

CHAPTER 26

LEP Students: Provide students with one index card for each vocabulary term for this chapter. Ask them

to write the term on one side of the card and the definition on the other and practice saying the terms and defining them.

Less-Advanced Students: To help students identify quackery, have them find examples of quack advertising in magazines, using Figure 26-7 for guidance. Alternatively, have students poll friends and relatives for any experiences they may have had with quack products. Students could then report these experiences to the class.

CHAPTER 27

Visual Learners: Have students draw, sketch, paint, or use other means to illustrate a scene in which an accident is bound to happen. Ask them to imagine dangerous circumstances around the home, at school, or in another familiar place. Display their pictures in the classroom.

At-Risk Students: Have students interview family members, neighbors, or fellow students to compile statistics on one category of accident each. They could choose recreational, home repair, automobile, and so on. They should ask for information about the victim, time of day, state of health, and so on. Then have students combine their data to make a complete set of statistics. What seem to be the most common causes among the accidents they covered? Are some people more accident-prone than others? Have them present their statistical conclusions to the class.

CHAPTER 28

Kinesthetic Learners: Students might be helped by practicing the first-aid skills learned in this chapter in role-playing situations.

At-Risk Students: During role-playing situations, assign these students roles that involve decision making and treatment. Such assignments will help build self-esteem.

LEP Students: Have students make a chart that lists the types of emergencies covered in this chapter. Then ask them to write in the chart any words concerning each emergency that they do not understand. Go over the charts with them to clarify definitions.

UNIT 1

INTRODUCTION TO HEALTH AND WELLNESS

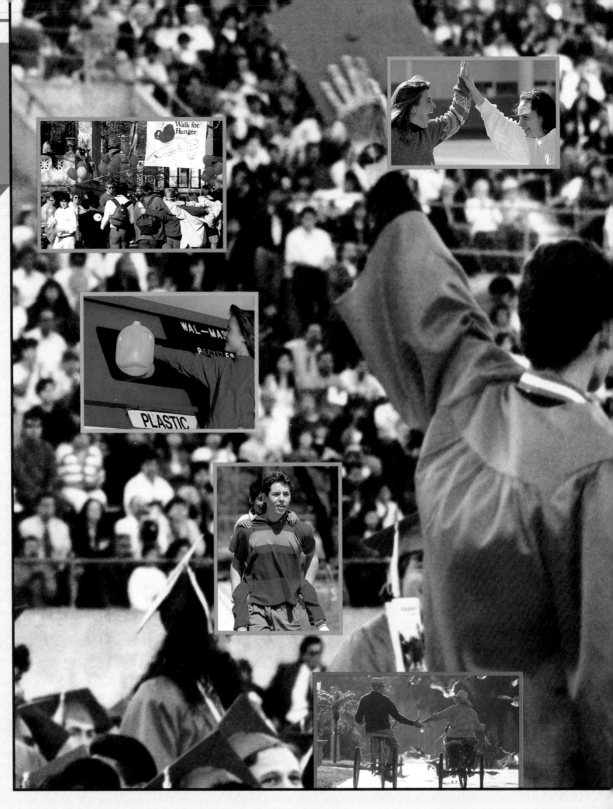

CHAPTER OVERVIEWS

CHAPTER 1

HEALTH AND WELLNESS: A QUALITY OF LIFE

This chapter introduces the concept of wellness and describes the five components of health—physical, social, mental, emotional, and spiritual. It provides a health-illness continuum on which students can plot their total health status. The chapter explains the relationships of health, self-esteem, social support, and physical fitness to wellness. In the second section, students are introduced to the idea of making healthy decisions by looking at teen health risks and completing a survey.

CHAPTER 2

MAKING RESPONSIBLE DECISIONS

Students learn how responsible decision making is related to health and wellness. The leading causes of death in young people and older people are discussed and related to the short-term and long-term consequences of health-related decisions. A decision-making model is presented. Students follow a fictional character through the process of decision making using the model. Then they are asked to apply the model to a real or invented situation of their own.

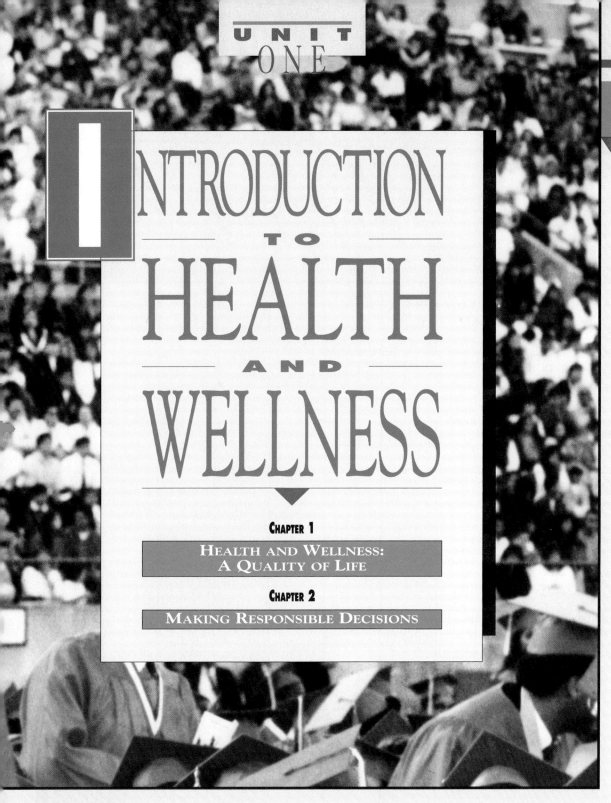

INTRODUCTION TO HEALTH AND WELLNESS

CHAPTER 1

HEALTH AND WELLNESS:
A QUALITY OF LIFE

CHAPTER 2

MAKING RESPONSIBLE DECISIONS

UNIT PREVIEW

This unit helps students understand what constitutes health and how it is related to total wellness. Through gaining this understanding, assessing their own health, and identifying their health risk factors, students begin thinking about managing their own health. The most important component of health management is responsible decision making. A decision-making model is provided to help students in this process. The chart below links the information and skills presented in this unit to the National Health Education Standards.

Unit 1	NATIONAL HEALTH EDUCATION STANDARDS*						
STANDARD	1	2	3	4	5	6	7
Chapter 1	•			•			
Chapter 2	•			•		•	

* For full text listing of each standard, see page 15T.

PLANNING GUIDE

Health and Wellness: A Quality of Life

SECTION	TITLE/OBJECTIVES	PERSONAL INVENTORY			LIFE SKILLS DEVELOPMENT			
		Personal Health Inventory	Journal	Check Up	Life Skills	Life Skills Worksheets	Media Message or Ethical Issues Worksheet	What Would You Do?
1.1 pp. 5–10	**HEALTH AND YOU** • Explain how the five components of health provide a picture of overall health. • Describe the difference between wellness and health. ▪ Plot your current state of health on the health-illness continuum. • Describe the ways in which self-esteem, social support, health, and wellness are related. • Describe the health benefits of physical fitness.	Ch. 1	1A					
1.2 pp. 11–16	**HEALTH CONCERNS IN THE UNITED STATES** • Compare the leading causes of death at the turn of the 20th century with the leading causes of death today. • Relate the lifestyle factors that contribute to disease to the leading causes of death in the United States. ▪ Identify your current lifestyle behaviors that reduce your health risks.		1B		p. 14	1A		

KEY: ▪ Denotes Life Skill Objective
Text references denoted by page number.
Supplement references denoted by chapter or item numbers.

HEALTH AND WELLNESS: A QUALITY OF LIFE

LINKING RESOURCES

	Making a Choice Cards	Parent Discussion Guide	Health Talk Audio Program	Teaching Transparencies and Directory	Section Review Worksheets	Section Quizzes	Reteaching Worksheets	Section Reviews
	INTERACTION		**OTHER RESOURCES**	**SECTION REVIEW AND ASSESSMENT**				
	1A			1A	1.1	1.1	1.1	p. 10
	1B			1B	1.2	1.2	1.2	p. 13

KEY FACTS

- The five major components of health—physical, social, mental, emotional, and spiritual—must be in balance for you to be truly healthy.

- Health is the state of well-being that comes from realizing your potential in each of the five components of health. Optimal health is known as wellness.

- Achieving wellness involves making the right choices and behaving in a way that maximizes your health.

- Self-esteem, or feeling good about yourself, is important to health and wellness.

- Social support helps you to manage stressors without becoming ill.

- Many teen health issues involve decisions that a teen can control.

- Unhealthful lifestyle choices are risk factors for both of today's leading causes of death—heart disease and cancer.

CHAPTER REVIEW AND ASSESSMENT

TEXT

Chapter Review pp. 18–19

SUPPLEMENTS

Chapter Test 1

Alternative Assessment 1

Test Generator Chapter 1

Using the Chapter Photograph

Ask students how the person in the picture presents an image of wellness. Discuss what they think it means to be healthy. Is health limited to physical well-being? What other things contribute to it?

 Question Box

Have students write out any questions they have about health and wellness, as it pertains to teens and their families, and put them in the Question Box.

Sensitivity *ALERT*

The discussion of health or wellness may make some students uncomfortable. They may have a health problem or someone close to them who is ill. They may feel that everyone will think they are different or unacceptable because of these problems. Prepare the class to be respectful of privacy and sensitive to the feelings of others. Help them see that someone with a physical health problem may more than compensate in the other aspects of health.

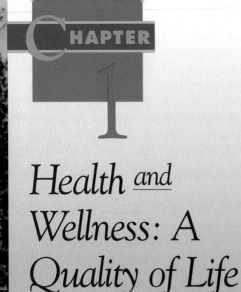

CHAPTER

1

Health *and* Wellness: A Quality of Life
◆ ◆ ◆ ◆

Section 1.1 Health and You

Section 1.2 Health Concerns in the United States

■ **Lifestyle plays an important role in managing your overall health. Forming satisfying relationships and engaging in physical activity help make you healthy.**

MYTHS & MISCONCEPTIONS

- **If you are physically fit, you are perfectly healthy.** Some people are physically fit but are not socially, mentally, emotionally, or spiritually healthy.

- **Heart disease and cancer just run in some families; there's nothing that can prevent it.** While the risks for developing some types of heart disease and cancer are highly influenced by genetic makeup, there are also lifestyle risk factors that influence them. Physicians emphasize that regular exercise, a proper diet, periodic medical exams, stress management, avoidance of tobacco and illegal drugs, and moderation in consumption of alcohol greatly reduce your chance of dying from either disease.

- **Because of advances in medicine, today's teens are much healthier than teens were in the early 20th century.** In some respects this is true. However, teens today face different health problems, and some new ones are life threatening.

Tara looked at her schedule. Fourth-period health was coming up next. Now that was the last class she felt like taking. Health class in grade school had been boring. Memorizing parts of the body and reading about diseases was not something she looked forward to doing again.

Right now all she could think about were the problems at home. Her mother's drinking was getting worse. Everything seemed to fall apart during the divorce. Her parents continued to argue all the time and Tara really felt caught in the middle. Her younger sister was talking about running away. Tara felt helpless in dealing with it all. Who could she turn to?

Section 1.1 — Health and You

Objectives

- Explain how the five components of health provide a picture of overall health.

- Describe the difference between wellness and health.

- Plot your current state of health on the health-illness continuum.
  - **LIFE SKILLS: Assessing Your Health**

- Describe the ways in which self-esteem, social support, health, and wellness are related.

- Describe the health benefits of physical fitness.

You are at one of the most exciting yet challenging times of your life. You are no longer a child who requires constant care and the closeness of family. Your adult identity is in the early stages of formation. Your body is changing as you make this transition from child to adult. Your relationships with your friends and family are changing too. You want to spend more time with your friends and less with your family. Your family may be adjusting well to your need for independence or you may feel that you are still being treated like a child. The teen years are a time of adjustment to many new freedoms and responsibilities. It can also be a time of tremendous conflict in your relationships with your family and friends. During this time, you will establish habits and views that you will carry with you throughout your life.

You are faced with many choices that can have a major effect on your future. You know it is unhealthy to smoke, or to use alcohol. In fact, if you are under 21 it is illegal to use alcohol. However, an occasion may arise where you are offered tobacco, alcohol, or other drugs. Virtually every Ameri-

Background
Choosing a Healthful Lifestyle
Most subjects taught in school increase a student's knowledge and experience. The study of health can impart more than knowledge and experience. It can set the course for a change of lifestyle that should lead to a fuller, more rounded life. When students make health-enhancing decisions about lifestyle issues, they improve the quality of their own life, cause a positive impact on the lives of those near them, and prolong the time they have to lead productive lives.

Personal Health Inventory
Have students complete the Personal Health Inventory for this chapter.

Section 1.1 Lesson Plan

MOTIVATE

Journal 1A
Concerns About Health

This may be done as a warm-up activity. Encourage students to record in their Journal some of their interests, concerns, or goals about their health. Also, have them discuss some ways they intend to address any of the issues they listed. In addition, ask students to write their reactions and feelings about Tara's situation. What advice would they give her?

Cooperative Learning
Tara's Problems

Have students form groups to discuss the problems Tara is facing and how this might affect her health. Ask them to tell how they might react to the same problems. Have them offer suggestions of what Tara can do to get help.

Background
Health as Adaptation

Health is the successful adaptation to each challenge—physical, mental, emotional, or spiritual—in the everyday environment. These adaptations may be in response to genetic makeup, microbes, carcinogens, pollutants, pressures, and problems. In order to reach optimal health, or wellness, people need to be aware of their needs in each of these areas. They also need to know how to meet these needs. The information and activities in this book can help teens understand how to assess their health and how to make lifestyle decisions that promote wellness.

can teen has to make decisions concerning these issues.

You may now be experiencing problems in your life that have a profound effect on your health both now and in the future. The story about Tara in the introduction to this chapter is an example. Tara's family is not functioning properly. Everyone is under a lot of stress. Tara's mother has an alcohol abuse problem. Tara and her family need help. One goal of this course is to give you the knowledge you need to work through problems like these, should you be going through them now or sometime in the future. Throughout the text, you will be encouraged to seek help when you can't re-

solve a problem on your own. You will find out where in your community you can get help for yourself or others close to you. This course will put you in an active role in managing your health.

Describing Health

How do you generally respond when someone asks ''How are you?'' If you respond that you are ''fine,'' take a moment to write down what you think it means to feel fine. If you respond in some other way, write down what your response really means. If you are not fine, are you sick? Now look at your description. How you feel is really part of describing your health.

Cultural DIVERSITY

Being Healthy— What Does It Mean?

Health means different things to different cultures. In the United States, slender people are viewed as healthy and attractive. But in some less prosperous cultures, thin people are viewed as unhealthy and less attractive. A fuller figure is a sign of having enough money to eat well and is considered desirable and healthy. These examples show how physical health can be defined by one's cultural beliefs.

Mental health can also be defined culturally. In the United States, a retired older relative who desires to meditate and prepare for death would probably be considered strange or even mentally ill, whereas in India, this decision would

be understood as the fulfillment of one of the stages of a religious Hindu's life. A bank clerk in Milwaukee makes an appointment with a mental health therapist when he starts hearing voices, but an Inuit shaman expects to hear voices because he relies on advice from the invisible world. Again, how behavior is viewed depends on the culture of the person viewing it.

Remedies for treating illnesses can also be linked to culture. In some Jewish households, chicken soup is a medicine for various illnesses. A vitamin pill might be chosen to boost an Arizona accountant's energy level, but ginseng root might be the remedy in China. A housewife in Virginia could choose either of these, but chooses the ginseng because her mother and grandmother prepared the roots using an old family recipe.

TEACH

Class Discussion
Components of Health

Write on the chalkboard, "Health is not just the absence of disease." Ask: **What does this mean?** *[People can be without physical problems and still not be healthy if, for example, they are mentally or emotionally ill.]* **When might you be without physical disease and still not have physical health?** *[If you do not*

have a disease but you lack physical fitness; you might not have energy to do homework, engage in outside activities, and socialize with friends. If so, you are not physically healthy.] **How would you describe people who are socially healthy?** *[People who are socially healthy have friends with whom they spend time and discuss problems. They interact well with people and have satisfying relationships.]* **How can you tell if someone is mentally healthy?** *[If someone has a sense of self-worth, is*

open to new ideas, and can cope with stressful situations, he or she has good mental health.] **What is meant by spiritual health?** *[People have spiritual health if they are working to find peace with themselves and those around them, either with the help of religion or by relying on their own individual life purpose.]*

Health was once thought to be the absence of disease. Health is now described in much broader terms, because we know so much more about what it takes to be healthy. There are five major components of health—physical health, social health, mental health, emotional health, and spiritual health. All five components must be in balance for you to be truly healthy.

Physical Health

Physical health covers those aspects of health related directly to the body. Your weight, strength, and the way your body functions are physical characteristics that are part of your physical health.

The absence of disease is part of physical health. Being physically healthy means you can get through your day at school and still have the energy to do your homework, engage in outside activities, and socialize with friends. Developing your physical fitness improves your physical health.

Audra is on the track and volleyball teams. She gets a lot of exercise and picks foods that keep her performance level high. Her boyfriend, Josh, has been smoking for two years. Because he smokes, Josh often skips meals and snacks throughout the day instead. He had five colds last winter alone. Audra is obviously doing a better job than Josh in attending to her physical health.

physical health:

your physical characteristics and the way your body functions.

Making a Choice 1A
Assign the Assessing Attitudes card. The card asks students to consider which statements reflect attitudes that are emotionally healthy.

One culture's practices may be slowly adopted by others. Once condemned as superstition, the ancient Chinese healing art of acupuncture is now being used in the West to relieve pain. Many western physicians and scientists believed acupuncture was nothing more than mind over matter until first-hand observation of the results changed their opinions. Now several kinds of treatment for pain relief apply the ideas of acupuncture for pain relief. This and other forms of traditional medicine from Eastern cultures are gaining a new degree of acceptance and scientific respect in the Western world.

There is one word, however, that is central to the definition of health in many cultures. That word is *balance,* or *harmony.* Good health is achieved by balancing mind, body, and spirit so that they work together in harmony. Harmony is the aim of the Navajo "Blessing Way" ceremony. Using chants and meditation, this ceremony brings an individual back into balance. Harmony is also the aim of holistic healing methods, in which all levels of an individual are treated and brought into balance. Once balanced, vitality flows through and connects all parts of an individual's life and thought.

Regardless of how your culture defines health and beauty, remaining open to new and different ideas not only will enrich your appreciation of culture diversity but also may expand your own view of health.

Role-Playing
Being Emotionally Healthy

Present a scenario that most teens would find emotionally challenging, for example, one person in a group project hasn't done his or her share on a project that is due soon. Brainstorm to make a list of statements that accept the challenge of finishing the project and a list of statements that place blame. Have students role-play each. Discuss which of the statements could help the project reach completion on time. Ask students which statements are unlikely to be helpful and why.

 ## Cooperative Learning
Benefits of Social Support

Have students work in groups of three or four to discuss which aspects of Josh's lifestyle might contribute to his frequent colds. What helpful, nonjudgmental support could Josh's friends provide to help him see how to improve his health? Each group should list several suggestions to share with the class. As a class, discuss the various suggestions, and decide which ones would be most likely to help Josh.

Cooperative Learning
Promoting Wellness

Have students form groups to develop a radio campaign focusing public attention on wellness. They should write 10-, 30-, and 60-second spots promoting their ideas of the concept of wellness. Have students perform their announcements for the class or record them to make a class tape.

Section Review Worksheet 1.1

To reinforce the concepts presented in this section, assign Section Review Worksheet 1.1.

Section Quiz 1.1

Have students take Section Quiz 1.1.

Reteaching Worksheet 1.1

Students who have difficulty with the material may complete Reteaching Worksheet 1.1.

---

social health:

interactions with people to build satisfying relationships.

spiritual health:

maintaining harmonious relationships with other living things and having spiritual direction and purpose.

health:

state of well-being that comes from a good balance of the five aspects of health.

wellness:

optimal health in each of the five aspects of health.

mental health:

the ability to recognize reality and cope with the demands of daily life.

emotional health:

expressing feelings in an appropriate way.

Social Health Your **social health** involves interacting with people and your environment. Having satisfying relationships is a major part of your social health. Your social health development started when you were an infant and began interacting with parents and others in your family. Your social skills will continue to develop more fully now that you are a teen interacting with your peers. Your social health is influenced by your social networks and the support that you get from the people that you care about and love. Your social connections actually help to determine your state of physical and emotional health. During times of crisis and ill health, your network of family and friends becomes an especially important source of support. Your family, close friends, and the formal and informal groups to which you belong form your social networks. Healthy connections with these groups give you a sense of belonging and help you feel good about yourself. Being considerate of others, sharing your true feelings, serving your community, and asking for help when you need it are part of being socially healthy.

Mental Health The state of mind that enables you to cope with the emotional demands of your everyday life is described as **mental health**. Being mentally healthy means you can accept new ideas and recognize the reality of a situation. You have a sense of self-worth and tolerate things that are different. You can cope with stressful situations because you know that stress is a part of life that you can manage. You work to develop your individual strengths and accept your weaknesses.

Emotional Health Your ability to express feelings in appropriate ways defines your **emotional health**. While everyone experiences unpleasant or negative feelings

at one time or another, emotionally healthy people can overcome the difficulties. An emotionally healthy person enjoys life and views hardships or difficulties as challenges. An emotionally healthy person can express anger without violence and sadness without serious depression.

Spiritual Health **Spiritual health** involves your relationship to other living things and the role of spiritual direction in your life. This description means different things to different people. For some people, spiritual health is defined by a religion. For others, it involves understanding your individual purpose in life. Being spiritually healthy means you are working to achieve your spiritual potential and to find harmony in living. You are at peace with yourself and those around you.

Health and Wellness

These five aspects of health contribute to your overall health. It should be obvious that if you are physically fit, but you cannot get along with your teachers and parents, then you are not completely healthy. If you are very active in your church, synagogue, and community, but feel depressed and anxious most of the time, you are not completely healthy. **Health** can now be formally defined as the state of well-being that comes from realizing your potential in each of the five aspects of health. Optimal health is described by the term **wellness**. A state of wellness is experienced by looking at your overall health as a range of possibilities.

Health-Illness Continuum Your overall health can be illustrated by a plot on the health-illness continuum shown in Figure 1-1. Plotting your health position on the continuum involves looking at your health status in each of the five aspects of health. The right side of the continuum represents optimum health or wellness, an ideal state.

● ● ● TEACH continued

Demonstration
Health-Illness Continuum

Make a health-illness continuum for the bulletin board. Pass out index cards. Ask students to write on the cards an activity that will help them move in the right direction along the continuum. Their activities may be expressed in the affirmative (eating right) or stated negatively (not using alcohol).

Have them tape their cards to appropriate places on the continuum. After students have attached their cards, discuss how engaging in any harmful activities would hinder their progress on the continuum to health.

 Teaching Transparency 1A
Five Dimensions of Health

Use this transparency as a focal point for a discussion on how practicing health-enhancing behaviors is related

to disease prevention and maintaining a satisfactory quality of life.

Extension
Promoting Health in the Community

Ask students to find community-sponsored events that promote physical, mental, emotional, social, or spiritual health. Have them collect posters or brochures that describe and illustrate the events. Next, have

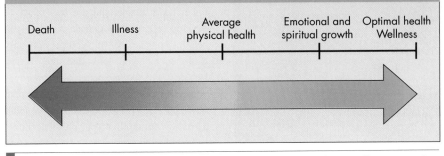

HEALTH-ILLNESS CONTINUUM

Death | Illness | Average physical health | Emotional and spiritual growth | Optimal health Wellness

(FIGURE 1-1) **Your health status on the continuum depends on how well you attend to each of the five areas that make up your total health picture.**

Achieving wellness involves making choices and behaving in ways that benefit your health. Making life-threatening choices like abusing alcohol or extreme dieting puts you on the left side of the continuum, which is the path to illness or an early death.

Self-Esteem and Wellness In order to achieve wellness, you have to feel good about yourself. Feeling good about yourself is called having positive **self-esteem**. You can be free of disease, you can get good grades in school, you can have nice friends, and be physically fit, but if you don't feel good about yourself you have not reached a state of wellness. In fact, when you get to Chapter 9, Managing Stress, you will discover that low self-esteem can actually make you physically ill. The stress you feel from not feeling good about yourself reduces your ability to fight off disease. So how you feel about yourself is related not only to your mental and emotional health, but is also related to your physical health.

Self-esteem is such an important component of health and wellness that it is a theme of this book. Chapter 8 focuses on self-esteem and what you can do to improve your self-esteem if you need to. Throughout this book you will see surveys that help

you learn more about yourself. Sometimes your strengths will show up. At other times, you'll see areas where you might want to change what you know, what you believe, what you say, or what you do. Everyone will find areas that can be improved. After all, no one is perfect.

Wellness Involves Social Support It is quite clear to people in the health profession that people need people. In fact, there is a name given to the benefits one gets from

self-esteem:

feeling good about yourself and your abilities.

(FIGURE 1-2) **Building relationships and receiving support from others is essential to your overall health and wellness.**

Review Answers

1. Answers may include the following information: if a person is not physically healthy, he or she may not be able to see or spend time with friends. This could affect social health and cause stress. If the person cannot control this stress, it may affect mental and emotional health. If the person has a serious illness, he or she may lose or question religious faith.

2. To be healthy, one must have a balance of good physical, social, mental, emotional, and spiritual health. To reach a state of wellness, one must feel good about oneself.

students decide which aspects of wellness each event promotes. For example, a Fourth of July picnic organized by a civic organization may promote social health, and free blood pressure exams by a local clinic may promote both physical and social health. Then have students display the information they collected on a bulletin board.

Answers to Questions 1 and 2 are on p. 9.

3. Being physically fit helps a person stay physically healthy and control weight and stress. Controlling stress helps improve a person's mental and emotional health. If the person gets exercise in activities that require group participation, such as team sports, he or she also improves social health. All of these factors help a person feel good about himself or herself and in this way improve self-esteem.

4. Answers may include people students trust, such as friends, family members, teachers, school counselors, and religious leaders.

5. Answers should reflect actions that will lead to greater physical, social, mental, emotional, or spiritual health.

(FIGURE 1-3) **Physical activity can improve your physical health as well as provide for your social health.**

social support:

deriving positive feelings from sharing life situations with others.

talking to others about joys, sorrows, problems, and stressors. It's called **social support**. It is now well known that a lot of stress in your life can make you physically sick. However, if you have social support, it is more likely you'll be able to manage stressors without becoming ill. Hasn't there been a time when you felt better about a bad situation after discussing it with a friend or relative? Throughout this course you will be encouraged to seek the help or advice of someone you can trust when you are having a problem. The purpose of this course is to give you a set of skills that will enable you to live a healthy lifestyle. Employing these skills when needed throughout your life keeps you on the path to wellness.

physical fitness:

a state in which your body can meet daily life demands.

Wellness and Physical Fitness **Physical fitness** is a state in which your body can meet the daily demands of living. It means you have a healthy heart, blood vessels, and lungs (cardiorespiratory endurance), and that you have sufficient muscular strength,

endurance, flexibility, agility, balance, and coordination. People who are fit have fewer heart attacks and are less likely to develop diseases like diabetes. When you become physically fit, you're not only healthier but you look and feel better. Looking and feeling better also improves your self-esteem, and you have already read how important that is. In Chapter 3 you will learn how to improve your physical fitness by developing a personal fitness program and then working to stick to it.

There is much you can do if you make up your mind to do it. Your potential is unlimited. Bob Weiland realized this when he decided to compete in the Marine Corps Marathon. It took him 79 hours and 57 minutes to complete the 26.2 miles. Despite having lost his legs in Vietnam and having to propel himself with his hands and no wheelchair, Bob finished the course.

Review

1. How might a physical health problem, such as a disease, affect the other components of your health?

2. Why is self-esteem so important to overall health?

3. How can being physically fit improve your self-esteem?

4. List the people you use for social support.

5. **Critical Thinking** List two things you could do to improve your position on the health-illness continuum.

ASSESS

Section Review

Have students answer the Section Review questions.

Alternative Assessment
Realizing Your Health Potential

Have students explain what is meant by realizing their potential in each of the five aspects of health. For each aspect, have students make a list of be-

haviors ranging from least healthful to most healthful. For instance, a list could include behaviors ranging from eating junk food for lunch every day to almost always taking the time to prepare a wholesome lunch. Another list could include behaviors ranging from expressing anger by hitting someone to talking the problem out.

Closure
Self-Esteem/Health Relationship

Have students write a letter to a friend expressing concern about a fictitious mutual friend who is showing signs of low self-esteem. The letter should also express concern about the mutual friend's numerous minor health problems. Students' letters should include information on how the two problems may be related, and students should make suggestions of what they could do to provide support for their friend.

Section 1.2

Health Concerns in the United States

Objectives

- *Compare the leading causes of death at the turn of the 20th century with the leading causes of death today.*

- *Relate lifestyle factors that contribute to disease and to the leading causes of death in the United States.*

- *Identify your current lifestyle behaviors that reduce your health risks.*

- **LIFE SKILLS: Assessing Your Health**

In the early 1900s, the major health issue facing teens was early death due to diseases caused by microorganisms that spread from person to person. Today the **communicable diseases** that caused deaths in the early 1900s have either been controlled or wiped out, but lifestyle factors have taken their place as the major threat to teen health. Your choices and your behaviors, including how, when, and where you socialize or resolve problems, are part of your lifestyle. Figure 1-4 shows how unhealthy lifestyle behaviors relate to overall causes of death.

Teen Health Issues

One in five teens in the United States has at least one serious health problem. Figure 1-5 gives some teen health statistics. Did you know that each year 3 million teens are infected with a sexually transmitted disease? This statistic is especially alarming when you realize that one of those diseases

is HIV infection, which leads to AIDS and ends in death.

Teens and Risk

Taking risks is a natural part of living. For teens, it's part of growing up. Everything you do has some risk involved. Each action you take has a consequence. Most of your daily actions pose little risk; the results of those actions don't seriously threaten your life or your health. Other actions carry great risk; their consequences may actually threaten your life. This course will help you recognize the risks that exist for you as a teen. If you are like most other teens, you think that no harm will come to you. Because of that belief, you may be willing to take risks that can have serious consequences. Assessing risks and considering the possible consequences of your actions is a part of moving through adolescence into

communicable disease:

a disease that is passed from person to person by an organism.

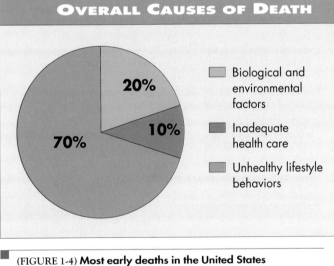

OVERALL CAUSES OF DEATH

20%

10%

70%

- Biological and environmental factors
- Inadequate health care
- Unhealthy lifestyle behaviors

(FIGURE 1-4) **Most early deaths in the United States are related to lifestyle factors.**

Background
Preventive Health Care

Most Americans have been oriented toward crisis health care. When they are sick, they concentrate on getting well. More recently, interest has turned to preventive health care. This approach has a much broader goal than overcoming a particular illness. Preventive health care focuses on removing the obstacles to good health before a person becomes ill, and on promoting wellness in all its aspects. Preventive care helps a person postpone or avoid many illnesses.

Life Skills Worksheet 1A

Assign the Determining Your Family Health History Life Skills Worksheet.

Section 1.2 Lesson Plan

MOTIVATE

Journal 1B
Teen Health Problems

This may be done as a warm-up activity. Encourage students to record in their Journal their opinions about some of the most pressing health issues facing teens today. Then have students choose one of these issues and discuss how it could affect them directly.

Class Discussion
What Is Lifestyle?

Discuss the concept of lifestyle. As a class, develop a list of conditions or behaviors that could be considered a part of lifestyle, for example, where people live, their typical diet, how they spend their free time, how physically active they are, how much they socialize, etc. Help students realize that all these factors determine what we refer to as an individual's lifestyle.

TEACH

Class Discussion
Overall Causes of Death

Have students look at Figure 1-4, which shows the Causes of Death in the United States. Ask them to speculate about why the percentage of deaths caused by lifestyle choices is so high. Ask: **What are some lifestyle choices that you think contribute to death or diminished quality of life?**

11

Making a Choice 1B

Assign the Looking at Causes of Death card. The card asks students to discuss strategies that could be used to reduce the number of deaths due to certain causes.

Section Review Worksheet 1.2

To reinforce the concepts presented in this section, assign Section Review Worksheet 1.2.

Section Quiz 1.2

Have students take Section Quiz 1.2

Reteaching Worksheet 1.2

Students who have difficulty with the material may complete Reteaching Worksheet 1.2.

---

adulthood. Taking responsibility for your actions is a sign of maturity and well-being.

National Health Risks

Pneumonia, tuberculosis, and influenza (flu) were the leading causes of death in the United States in the early part of this century. These three diseases fall into the category of communicable diseases, which means a person can get the disease from someone else. The government responded to this health problem by enacting laws on quarantine (isolation of disease victims), sewage disposal, and food and water sanitation. These actions caused a significant reduction in the number of people that got communicable diseases.

Figure 1-6 shows the 10 leading causes of death in the United States today and the factors that contribute to those causes. Contributing factors can actually be controlled by the choices made and the actions taken. In other words, most of the premature deaths and disabilities in the United States could be prevented. If people would exercise regularly, eat properly, have periodic medical exams, avoid the use of tobacco, and manage stress, more premature deaths could be avoided.

Developing Life Skills

Health professionals and medical professionals now stress prevention as their guiding principle to achieving wellness. Community health specialists have taken a more active role in educating the public concerning healthy living practices and disease prevention. Many hospitals and clinics now sponsor health education programs for the public that focus on diet, exercise, stress reduction, and emotional well being. It is believed that these programs will help reduce health care costs by getting people to accept more responsibility for their health.

In keeping with the prevention philosophy, Life Skills pages throughout this text help you apply what you learn in this class. The first Life Skills, on page 14, helps you identify your potential health risks.

Stopping to assess your behavior or feelings about a subject or issue may be a difficult task, but it is something that you will be frequently asked to do in this course. A journal will be a handy place to record this information. You may not want to admit that you are having trouble coping

Teen Health Statistics

38% of high school students reported they had been in a fight within the last year.

20% of high school students reported that they have carried a weapon.

24% of teens have considered suicide. Almost 9% of teens have attempted suicide.

34% of teens smoke cigarettes, and more than half of these teens buy their own cigarettes even though this is illegal for most teens.

Over 53% of high school students report having had intercourse.

More than 800,000 teens between the ages of 15-19 become pregnant each year.

Only 15% of teens regularly eat the recommended daily amount of fruits and vegetables.

38% of teens have ridden in a vehicle with a driver who had been drinking alcohol.

25% of teens report using marijuana; 51% used alcohol.

(FIGURE 1-5) **Teen health problems are widespread and varied. All these statistics involve health-related decisions that you can control in managing your own health.**

• • • TEACH continued

[Responses will vary but will probably include behaviors such as smoking, eating junk food, and not getting any exercise.] Make a list of students' responses, which can be saved and used when viewing Teaching Transparency 1B.

Writing
Teen Health Statistics

As a class, review Figure 1-5, Teen Health Statistics. Then ask students to write a brief essay giving their comments on one or two of the statistics. If some students have difficulty getting started, suggest one of the following topics: why they think the figures are so high for some statistics, whether they believe that the statistics could be modified by making health-enhancing

decisions, or if any of the statistics reflect something that is common in their school.

Teaching Transparency 1B
Underlying Causes of Death

Review the list of lifestyle choices that contribute to death or diminished quality of life that the class compiled when discussing Figure 1-4. Then use this transparency of the histogram in

12 HEALTH AND WELLNESS: A QUALITY OF LIFE

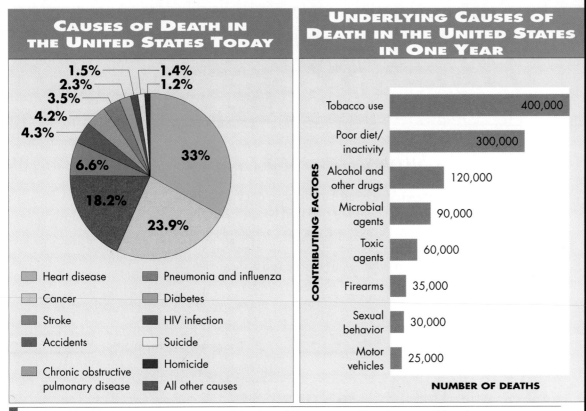

CAUSES OF DEATH IN THE UNITED STATES TODAY

- 1.5%
- 2.3%
- 3.5%
- 4.2%
- 4.3%
- 1.4%
- 1.2%
- 33%
- 6.6%
- 18.2%
- 23.9%

- ☐ Heart disease
- ☐ Cancer
- ☐ Stroke
- ☐ Accidents
- ☐ Chronic obstructive pulmonary disease
- ☐ Pneumonia and influenza
- ☐ Diabetes
- ☐ HIV infection
- ☐ Suicide
- ☐ Homicide
- ☐ All other causes

UNDERLYING CAUSES OF DEATH IN THE UNITED STATES IN ONE YEAR

CONTRIBUTING FACTORS

Tobacco use	400,000
Poor diet/ inactivity	300,000
Alcohol and other drugs	120,000
Microbial agents	90,000
Toxic agents	60,000
Firearms	35,000
Sexual behavior	30,000
Motor vehicles	25,000

NUMBER OF DEATHS

(FIGURE 1-6) **Today most leading causes of death could be prevented by changes in lifestyle.**

with a situation at home or that you are under too much pressure from friends or family. You may be much more comfortable expressing these feelings in the journal.

Keep a copy of your answers to this first Life Skills survey in your journal. Complete the survey again at the end of the course to find out if you have reduced your health risks. Other Life Skills pages will cover the following areas.

- Solving Problems
- Coping
- Setting Goals
- Resisting Pressure
- Assessing Your Health
- Using Community Resources Effectively
- Communicating Effectively
- Being A Wise Consumer

- Making Responsible Decisions
- Practicing Self-Care
- Intervention Strategies

*R*eview

1. List three health-related decisions that you might make in the next year.

2. In what ways do your health risks differ from those of your grandparents when they were teens?

3. How might the Life Skills listed on this page assist you in reducing your health risks?

SECTION 1.2

Review Answers
1. Answers will vary but may include not drinking, not driving with someone who has been drinking, not putting myself at risk of a sexually transmitted disease or pregnancy, talking to a trusted friend or family member about my concerns, not smoking, and not using drugs. Accept any answer that moves students toward optimal health.
2. In the early 1900s, people were at a much greater risk of dying from a communicable disease than they are today. Most of those communicable diseases are now controlled, but the risk of developing a lifestyle-related disease is very high.
3. Answers will vary but should reflect an understanding of the relationship between good health and the ability to identify and implement health-enhancing behaviors.

Figure 1-6 to compare the actual factors contributing to premature death and disability with the class's list.

Debate the Issue
Changing Lifestyle: Is It Worth It?

Divide the class into two teams to debate the question: If having good health means changing your lifestyle, is it worth the effort? Students on both sides of the argument should support their positions with information about how a change of lifestyle can affect the

health of teens. Encourage students to express their own opinions on the topic after the debate is over.

Class Discussion
What Are Life Skills?

Discuss whether the ability to manage diet, exercise, stress, and emotional well-being is a skill that can be learned. Review the Life Skills on page 13. Ask students what they think each category means. Emphasize that Solving Problems includes conflict resolution

and that Coping includes stress management. Assessing Your Health is a way of discovering what your health needs are, and Practicing Self-Care is a way of taking care of those needs once you have identified them.

Writing
Open Letter to Teens

Encourage students to write an open letter to teens, based on the information and statistics in this section. Have

LifeSKILLS: Assessing Your Health

Have students identify their behavior in each of the six sections in the Health Risks Survey by writing on a separate piece of paper the number that corresponds to their usual practice. Have students do this exercise independently, in order to benefit from the experience.

Health Risks Survey

The United States government developed the following questionnaire to help people assess their health behavior and their health risks. The questionnaire has six sections. Answer each item on a separate piece of paper by listing the number corresponding to the answer that describes your behavior. Then add the numbers you have circled to determine your score for that section.

Eating Habits

	Almost Always	Some-times	Almost Never
1. I eat a variety of foods each day, such as fruits and vegetables, whole grain breads and cereals, lean meats, dairy products, dry peas and beans, and nuts and seeds.	4	2	0
2. I limit the amount of fat, saturated fat, and cholesterol I eat (including fats in meats, eggs, butter, cream, shortenings, and organ meats such as liver).	2	1	0
3. I limit the amount of salt I eat by not adding salt at the table, avoiding salty snacks, and having my meals cooked with only small amounts of salt.	2	1	0
4. I avoid eating too much sugar (especially frequent snacks of sticky candy or soft drinks).	2	1	0

Your Eating Habits Score: _____

Exercise and Fitness

	Almost Always	Some-times	Almost Never
1. I maintain a comfortable weight, avoiding overweight and underweight.	3	2	0
2. I exercise vigorously for 15 to 30 minutes at least three times a week (examples include running, swimming, brisk walking).	3	2	0
3. I do exercises that enhance my muscle tone for 15 to 30 minutes at least three times a week (examples include yoga and calisthenics).	2	1	0
4. I use part of my leisure time to participate in individual, family, or team activities that increase my level of fitness (such as gardening, bowling, golf, or baseball).	2	1	0

Your Exercise and Fitness Score: _____

• • • TEACH continued

them include what impressed them most about the statistics. Let them share their letters in small groups or with the class.

Extension
Making a Choice

Have students notice which foods sold in the school cafeteria or restaurants are healthful and which are less healthful. Have them prepare humorous posters that encourage students to choose healthful foods.

Section Review

Have students answer the Section Review questions.

Alternative Assessment
Time of Regrets

Have students make up a skit featuring a person disabled by heart disease who recalls various scenes from his or her youth—smoking for the first time, getting no exercise, eating too many fatty foods. Have students discuss which lifestyle changes would have helped this person avoid heart disease and the diminished quality of life that it causes.

Stress Control

	Almost Always	Some-times	Almost Never
1. I enjoy school or other work I do.	2	1	0
2. I find it easy to relax and express my feelings freely.	2	1	0
3. I recognize early, and prepare for, events or situations likely to be stressful for me.	2	1	0
4. I have close friends, relatives, or others whom I can talk to about personal matters and call on for help when needed.	2	1	0
5. I participate in group activities (such as church/synagogue or community organizations) or hobbies that I enjoy.	2	1	0

Your Stress Control Score: _____

Safety

	Almost Always	Some-times	Almost Never
1. I wear a seat belt while riding in a car.	2	1	0
2. I avoid driving, or getting in a car with someone else who is driving, while under the influence of alcohol and other drugs.	2	1	0
3. I obey the traffic rules and observe the speed limit when driving or ask others to do so when driving in a car with them.	2	1	0
4. I am careful when using potentially harmful products or substances (such as household cleaners, poisons, and electrical devices).	2	1	0
5. I avoid smoking in bed.	2	1	0

Your Health Score: _____

Alcohol and Other Drug Use

	Almost Always	Some-times	Never
1. I avoid drinking alcoholic beverages.	4	2	0
2. I avoid using alcohol or other drugs (especially illegal drugs) as a way of handling stressful situations or the problems of my life.	3	1	0
3. I read and follow the label directions when using prescription and over-the-counter drugs.	3	1	0

Your Alcohol and Drugs Score: _____

Tobacco Use

	Almost Always	Some-times	Almost Never
1. I avoid smoking cigarettes.	4	1	0
2. I do not use chewing tobacco, smoke a pipe, or smoke cigars.	3	1	0
3. I avoid areas where others are smoking.	3	1	0

Your Tobacco Use Score: _____

Closure
Changing Lifestyle

Have students explain in their own words how changes in lifestyle could mean better health.

Your Health Score

Make sure you have figured your score for each of the six sections.
Use the scale that follows for assessing each section.

Tabacco Use	Alcohol and Drug Use	Eating Habits	Exercise and Fitness	Stress Control	Safety
10	10	10	10	10	10
9	9	9	9	9	9
8	8	8	8	8	8
7	7	7	7	7	7
6	6	6	6	6	6
5	5	5	5	5	5
4	4	4	4	4	4
3	3	3	3	3	3
2	2	2	2	2	2
1	1	1	1	1	1

Interpreting Your Scores

Scores of **9 or 10** are excellent! You are putting your knowledge to work for you by practicing good health habits.

Scores of **6 - 8** indicate your health practices in this area are good, but there is room for improvement. Look again at the items you answered with a "Sometimes" or an "Almost Never." What changes can you make to improve your score?

Scores of **3 - 5** mean you have behaviors that put your health at risk.

Scores of **0 - 2** mean you may be taking serious, unnecessary risks with your health. This course will make you aware of the risks and what to do about them.

Fill out this survey again at the end of your health course. Our goal is to give you the information you need to improve your scores.

Highlights

Summary

- Health is more than the absence of disease; it is the state of mental, physical, and social well-being.

- The concept of health requires a balance of five components: physical health, social health, mental health, emotional health, and spiritual health.

- A state of wellness is achieved by looking at your total health picture from a positive perspective.

- Making choices and behaving in a way that maximizes your health are the strongest positive influences on your level of wellness.

- To achieve wellness, you have to feel good about yourself.

- If you have social support, it is more likely you'll be able to manage stressors without becoming ill.

- Most of the health issues affecting teens are related to lifestyle.

- The major health dangers for teenagers today include accidents, suicide, homicide, unwanted pregnancy, and sexually transmitted diseases.

Vocabulary

physical health your physical characteristics and the way your body functions.

social health interactions with people to build satisfying relationships.

mental health the ability to recognize reality and cope with the demands of daily life.

emotional health expressing feelings in an appropriate way.

spiritual health maintaining harmonious relationships with other living things and having spiritual direction and purpose.

health state of well-being that comes from a good balance of the five aspects of health.

wellness optimal health in each of the five aspects of health.

self-esteem feeling good about yourself and what you can do.

social support deriving positive feelings from sharing life situations with others.

physical fitness a state whereby your body can meet daily life demands.

communicable disease a disease that is passed from person to person by an organism.

SUMMARY
Have students read the summary to reinforce the concepts they learned in Chapter 1.

VOCABULARY
Have students write a brief public service announcement (PSA) or jingle using as many of the vocabulary words as possible. The PSA or jingle should tell what is included in the study of health and should be appropriate for teens. Students can present their work in written form for display, or they can record their work on cassette tape.

EXTENSION
Have students make health and wellness posters to be displayed throughout the school and community. The posters should show some aspect of health related to teens and should include suggestions for solving teen health-related problems.

Chapter Review

CHAPTER REVIEW

Concept Review

1. health
2. physical health
3. social health
4. spiritual health
5. health-illness continuum
6. self-esteem
7. social support
8. health-related physical fitness
9. lifestyle diseases
10. choices

Expressing Your Views

Sample responses:

1. somewhere near "Average Health"

2. Today, more people are working out or walking regularly than in the past. People are more concerned about their diet. There are many more articles about health and fitness in newspapers and magazines.

3. abusing alcohol and other drugs, unprotected sexual intercourse

4. The biggest risk is being involved in an accident with another car or with a pedestrian. This accident could lead to injury or death. The risks of being involved in an accident and being injured can be reduced by wearing a seat belt, not driving while under the influence of alcohol or drugs or riding in a car with someone else driving under the influence of alcohol and other drugs,

Concept Review . . . .

1. The well-being of your body, your mind, and your relationships with other people is called _____.

2. _____ refers to the care of your body and the way your body functions.

3. The way people get along with one another and make and keep friends is called _____.

4. _____ means maintaining harmonious relationships with other living things and having spiritual direction and purpose.

5. A special scale that shows your total health has many levels is called a _____.

6. Feeling good about yourself is called having positive _____.

7. The benefit one gets from talking about joys, sorrows, problems, and stressors is called _____.

8. _____ is the foundation of wellness.

9. Communicable diseases have been replaced by _____ _____ as the leading causes of death in the United States.

10. The _____ you make about how you live have a direct impact on your overall health.

Expressing Your Views . . . .

1. Benton is 15 years old. He has started to exercise regularly, has lowered his fat intake, and doesn't drink alcohol. Where would you place him on the Wellness Continuum?

2. What are some of the indications that Americans are becoming more fitness oriented?

3. Most of the health issues facing teens today are determined by lifestyle. In your opinion, what are the two risk behaviors that will most influence a teen's health?

4. Demetra just received her driver's license. What are some of the risks involved in driving a car? What do you think Demetra could do to reduce the risks?

obeying traffic rules, and observing the speed limit when driving, as well as asking others to do these things when you are riding in a car with them.

Life Skills Check

Sample responses:

1. Eat a healthy diet that is low in fat, salt, and sugar; maintain a comfortable weight and exercise regularly; learn to control stress; avoid smoking cigarettes; avoid

drinking alcoholic beverages; avoid using drugs, especially illegal drugs; and practice safety behaviors, such as wearing a seat belt when riding in a car.

2. someone from my support group, such as parents, a teacher, a counselor, a coach, or a religious leader

3. Lists and explanations will vary for each student.

Life Skills Check . . . .

1. Assessing Your Health

You are content with your current state of wellness, but you would like to make sure you are healthy in the years to come. What are some things you could do now to ensure your future well-being?

2. Assessing Your Health

Lately you have not been getting along with your friends or family. The stress in your life is sometimes almost overwhelming. Often you just want to be alone. Who could you talk to? Explain your choice.

3. Assessing Your Health

Keep a list of all the choices you make for one day. How many of them are related to health? Explain how they are related.

Projects . . . .

1. Interview a person over age 50 and a person over age 70 to find out what health problems were most common during their teenage years. Prepare a brief report to the class comparing what you learned in the two interviews with what you learned in this chapter about health problems facing teens today.

2. Collect newspaper or magazine pictures that depict healthful behaviors and harmful behaviors. Glue these pictures on a poster board. Show your poster to the class and discuss how advertisements can influence your health choices both positively and negatively.

Plan for Action . . . .

Identify one healthful behavior from the Health Risks Survey that isn't now included in your daily life and that could positively affect your health. Make a month-long plan to adopt that behavior, and do weekly check-ups to track your progress.

Projects

Have students plan and carry out the projects for health and wellness within the school and community.

Plan for Action

Have students make a calendar for their monthlong plan. The space for each date should be big enough to write in. Every day, have students indicate whether they included the target behavior in their daily routine. At the end of each week, students can do a self-check to see how their plan is progressing. Suggest that students who are unable to include their target behavior reevaluate their plan. They may need to choose a different target behavior to work toward.

ASSESSMENT OPTIONS

Chapter Test
Have students take the Chapter 1 Test.

Alternative Assessment
Have students do the Alternative Assessment activity for Chapter 1.

Test Generator
The Test Generator contains additional assessment items for this chapter.

PLANNING GUIDE

2

Making Responsible Decisions

SECTION	TITLE/OBJECTIVES	Personal Health Inventory	Journal	Check Up	Life Skills	Life Skills Worksheets	Media Message or Ethical Issues Worksheet	What Would You Do?
		PERSONAL INVENTORY			**LIFE SKILLS DEVELOPMENT**			
2.1 *pp. 21–23*	**WHY DOES HEALTH INVOLVE SO MANY DECISIONS?** • Name the top three causes of death of people ages 15–24. • Explain how decisions made today can affect how long you live. • Name the top three causes of death of people ages 55–64. • Explain how decisions made today can affect your quality of life when you are older.	Ch. 2	2A					
2.2 *pp. 24–30*	**HOW TO MAKE A RESPONSIBLE DECISION** • Name the steps of the decision-making model presented in this chapter. • Discuss the importance of values to responsible decision making. ▪▪ Demonstrate the ability to use a decision-making model to make a responsible decision.		2B 2C			2A	Unit 1	p. 29

KEY: ▪▪ Denotes Life Skill Objective

Text references denoted by page number.

Supplement references denoted by chapter or item numbers.

LINKING RESOURCES

	Making a Choice Cards	Parent Discussion Guide	Health Talk Audio Program	Teaching Transparencies and Directory	Section Review Worksheets	Section Quizzes	Reteaching Worksheets	Section Reviews
	INTERACTION		**OTHER RESOURCES**	**SECTION REVIEW AND ASSESSMENT**				
		Ch. 2	Ch. 2	2A 2B 2C	2.1	2.1	2.1	p. 23
	2A 2B			2D	2.2	2.2	2.2	p. 30

KEY FACTS

- Responsible decision making provides a measure of control over personal health.

- Lifestyle choices contribute directly to quality and length of life.

- A person born in the United States today has a life expectancy of 76 years.

- The leading causes of death among people 15 to 24 are unintentional injuries, homicide, and suicide. The use of alcohol or other drugs greatly increases the odds of being hurt or killed in one of these ways.

- The leading causes of death among people 55 to 64 are cancer, heart disease, and chronic obstructive pulmonary disease.

- Responsible decisions may be made by using a decision-making model.

- Honesty, trustworthiness, personal responsibility, self-control, and social justice are values most people in our society consider important.

- When under pressure to make a quick decision, consider your values first.

CHAPTER REVIEW AND ASSESSMENT

TEXT
Chapter Review pp. 32–33

SUPPLEMENTS
Chapter Test 2

Alternative Assessment 2

Test Generator Chapter 2

GETTING STARTED

Using the Chapter Photograph

Ask students to list some decisions the people in the photograph might have made before coming to the party or may have to make before it ends. Then ask students to pick out those decisions that might have serious consequences and to explain why. Have them name and discuss several other key decisions young people must make.

 Question Box

Have students write out any questions they have about how to make good decisions and put them in the Question Box.

Sensitivity *ALERT*

Discussion of important lifestyle decisions may make some students uncomfortable. Those who are coping with alcoholism or addiction, or who have family members who are coping with either, may withdraw or respond angrily. They may also feel that revealing any personal information would show disloyalty to family.

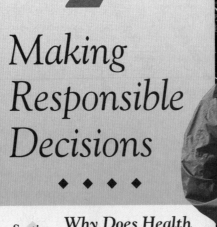

CHAPTER 2

Making Responsible Decisions

◆ ◆ ◆ ◆

Section 2.1 Why Does Health Involve So Many Decisions?

Section 2.2 How to Make a Responsible Decision

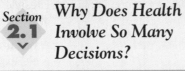

When you are a teenager, making responsible decisions is often difficult. But if you learn a method of making choices that takes into account your values, you will be able to live with your decisions.

MYTHS & MISCONCEPTIONS

- **No one can help you make decisions; you must make them for yourself.** Actually, discussing choices with a trusted friend or with an adult whose judgment you respect may help you see a situation more objectively, may provide further insight, and may help you discover options you wouldn't have though of on your own.

- **If the outcome of a decision isn't what I expected, then I made the wrong decision.** Events beyond a person's control may prevent the desired outcome.

- **The best decision is the one with an immediate, positive outcome.** An action that has a pleasant, immediate outcome may have disastrous long-term results. On the other hand, some decisions result in unpleasant, short-term consequences but positive future results.

Richard can't decide what to do. His friend Nicole asked him if he wants to go to a party with her and her friend Selena this Saturday night. Richard has always wanted to ask Selena out but has been afraid she would turn him down. Going to this party would be the perfect way to get to know her without putting his pride on the line. But Richard has a big problem. He figures that a few people may be drinking alcohol at this party, and he decided last year that he didn't want to drink. First of all, he knows it's illegal for teenagers to drink alcohol. In addition, his brother was arrested twice for drunken driving and finally went into an alcoholism treatment program. Even though his brother is doing better now, Richard doesn't want to go through what his brother did. So far he's been able to stick to his decision. He's worried, though, that at this party someone may offer him a drink, and that he'll feel pressured to take it. What should he do? What would you do?

Section 2.1
Why Does Health Involve So Many Decisions?

Objectives

- *Name the top three causes of death of people ages 15–24.*
- *Explain how decisions made today can affect how long you live.*
- *Name the top three causes of death of people ages 55–64.*
- *Explain how decisions made today can affect your quality of life when you are older.*

This is not the first time that Richard has had to make a difficult choice. Each day *everyone* faces decisions. Some choices are pretty easy to make—like deciding which shoes to wear, or which shoe to put on first. But other decisions have important consequences for your health, and these are often the difficult ones to make. In this chapter you'll learn a method for making responsible decisions that you can use for the rest of your life.

Responsible decision making is an important part of health; the choices you make give you a great deal of control over your own health.

The decisions you make could be more important to your health than any other factor. Your lifestyle—your way of living—could affect your health more than the traits you inherited from your parents, more than your environment, and more than the kind of health care you get.

Sometimes the choices you make affect your health immediately. Other times, the consequences are not seen until many

 Personal Health Inventory

Have students complete the Personal Health Inventory for this chapter.

 English/Spanish CD Audio Program

Use the English/Spanish Health Talk audio program for students who need audio reinforcement of the concepts presented.

Parent Discussion Guide

Send home the Parent Letter for Chapter 2. As you progress through the chapter, send home the Parental Survey and The Extra Mile.

Section 2.1 Lesson Plan

MOTIVATE

Journal 2A
Richard's Dilemma

This may be done as a warm-up activity. Have students write down in their Journal their reactions to Richard's dilemma. Ask them to tell what they would decide and to explain why.

TEACH

 Teaching Transparency 2A
Leading Causes of Death

Show the transparency of the histogram in Figure 2-1, which shows the leading causes of death for people 15 to 24 years old. Have students discuss how choices young people make might lead to death from one of the causes shown. Ask students why they think that unintentional injuries

(accidents) account for the most deaths. Discuss possible contributing factors, such as a greater willingness to participate in risky behaviors, curiosity that leads to dangerous experimentation, inexperience that results in carelessness, and impulsiveness.

Section Review Worksheet 2.1

To reinforce the concepts presented in this section, assign Section Review Worksheet 2-1.

Section Quiz 2.1

Have students take Section Quiz 2.1.

Reteaching Worksheet 2.1

Students who have difficulty with the material may complete Reteaching Worksheet 2.1.

---

years later. The choice that Richard has to make about the party is one that can have both short-term and long-term consequences for his health.

Short-Term Consequences of Health Decisions

Many decisions will affect your life today and in the coming weeks. Getting enough sleep, eating properly, managing your time, and staying active may help you fight off viruses and bacteria that could cause a cold, the flu, or a sore throat. In a similar way, your skin is affected by your activity habits, your diet, your use of alcohol and other drugs, and sun exposure. Think of other ways in which your decisions affect your appearance or your physical health.

Your emotions can also be affected by decisions you made last night or on the weekend. When you're tired, you may be-

unintentional injuries:

injuries that are not the result of purposeful acts.

come emotional and upset at things that wouldn't usually bother you. When you're rested, you can better handle new situations or stressful events. In what other ways might your decisions and health habits affect your emotions today or later this week? How might these emotions affect your health?

While you're young, you believe your whole life is ahead of you; however, the consequences of some health decisions can be dramatic, immediate, and anything but short-term. Figure 2-1 shows the top six causes of death among young people 15 to 24 years old. These causes of death are often directly related to the choices a person makes. **Unintentional injuries** are the leading cause of death for teens. These injuries are not the result of purposeful acts. They include deaths involving motor vehicles. Unintentional injuries are no longer considered accidents, because at least 85% of them could have been prevented.

 (FIGURE 2-1) These charts show the leading causes of death for young people (left) and for older people (right). The decisions you make now can affect your health immediately *and* later in your life. (Source: United States Department of Health and Human Services.)

● ● ● TEACH continued

Reinforcement
Prevention of Accidents

Some students may be shocked by the statistics in Figure 2-1. Tell students that the total number of teen deaths each year is low compared to the number of deaths in other age groups. Many accidental deaths among teens are tragic because they are preventable. Ask

them to speculate about ways that accidents can be prevented.

 Teaching Transparency 2B
Teen Health Priorities

Use this transparency as a focal point for a discussion of the types of health problems that teens face today. Have the class evaluate the list. Where on the list do their health concerns fit? If necessary, add categories to the list.

Teaching Transparency 2C
Causes of Cancer

Use this transparency to discuss the causes of cancer. Ask students to identify what percentage of cancers are a result of personal behavior and are therefore preventable.

Extension
Health and Lifestyle

Invite a health counselor or other health professional to speak to the class about the impact that poor

(FIGURE 2-2) **Health decisions can have immediate consequences. A decision to wear a helmet while bicycling can save your life.**

Long-Term Consequences of Health Decisions

Some decisions might not have immediate consequences for your health, but they can determine what your life will be like when you are older. Look again at Figure 2-1. The top three causes of death among people between the ages of 55 and 64 are:

1. cancer
2. heart disease
3. chronic obstructive pulmonary disease

Each of these causes of death is often the result of choices made early in life. People who choose to smoke, for instance, are much more likely to get lung cancer than those who don't. Smoking begun in the teenage years and continued over long periods of time is the cause of most deaths due to lung cancer.

Suppose a man succeeded in living all the years of his life expectancy. But during the last 20 of those years he was always sick and in pain. He had emphysema, a lung disease, as a result of smoking cigarettes since the age of 16. Even though he lived a *long* life, his **quality of life** was poor. Quality of life is the degree to which a person lives life to its fullest capacity with enjoyment and reward.

If Richard's brother hadn't taken steps to recover from his alcoholism, he could have developed any number of ailments that would have severely damaged his quality of life. You are not likely to have a good quality of life if you smoke for 40 years and get emphysema. Similarly, you probably won't have a good quality of life if you develop heart disease as a result of poor diet and inadequate exercise.

You may not be able to do all the things you would like to do in your later years unless you make healthy choices now. The decisions you make today will influence not only how long you live, but also how you *feel* years from now.

quality of life:
the degree to which a person lives life to its fullest capacity with enjoyment and reward.

Review

1. Name the top three causes of death of people ages 15–24.

2. Explain how decisions made today can affect how long you live.

3. Name the top three causes of death of people ages 55–64.

4. Explain how decisions made today can affect your quality of life when you are older.

5. **Critical Thinking** If Richard's brother hadn't decided to quit drinking, how do you think his quality of life would be affected if he lived into his fifties?

SECTION 2.1

Review Answers

1. unintentional injury, homicide, suicide

2. Answers will vary. Sample response: Decisions concerning safety, such as wearing a helmet when riding a bicycle or wearing a seat belt when riding in a car, can protect a person from serious injury and even death. Also, decisions to not drink and not use drugs can greatly reduce a person's risk of being involved in an accident or developing health problems.

3. cancer, heart disease, chronic obstructive pulmonary diseases

4. Decisions that affect one's health—such as smoking, drinking alcohol, using drugs, getting little or no exercise, and eating a poor diet—can decrease the quality of life as a person gets older.

5. Answers will vary. Sample response: Richard's brother might have developed ailments that would be damaging to his overall health and quality of life. For example, his ailments might have prevented him from keeping a steady job or participating in activities he enjoys.

lifestyle decisions have on health. Such a resource can provide firsthand observations about anonymous case histories as well as an objective perspective about health choices that have dramatic short-term and long-term effects.

ASSESS

Section Review

Have students answer the Section Review questions.

Alternative Assessment

Have students write a paragraph analyzing a decision that could lead to poor quality of life decades from now. They should describe the decision, list specific health outcomes, and explain the short-term or long-term effects of the decision.

Closure
Wellness Contract

Introduce the concept of a wellness contract aimed at reaching a specific health goal. The contract should include a long-term goal and an action that would help the student reach that goal. For example, walking home once a week would be a first step toward the goal of increased physical fitness. Have each student draw up a contract that includes: a health goal, a realistic action that will help reach that goal, a specific time period for the action, a system for keeping track of and evaluating the effort, date, and student's signature.

Background

Cognitive Dissonance

Psychologists use a theory called cognitive dissonance to explain people's tendency to avoid inconsistency in their beliefs. When a person experiences a discrepancy between two thoughts (cognition), tension results. To reduce this tension, the person modifies one of the thoughts. The modification, however, is not always realistic. This can affect the evaluation of a decision. If a person is pleased with an outcome, he or she may credit the decision even though it had little or nothing to do with the result. If a person is displeased with an outcome, he or she may irrationally blame outside forces even though the results stem from the decision. When a person does not evaluate a decision realistically, he or she can make false or even destructive conclusions.

Section 2.2

How to Make a Responsible Decision

Objectives

- Name the steps of the decision-making model presented in this chapter.

- Discuss the importance of values to responsible decision making.

- Demonstrate the ability to use a decision-making model to make a responsible decision.
  LIFE SKILLS: Making Responsible Decisions

decision-making model:

a series of steps that helps a person make a responsible decision.

Why is it necessary to teach people how to make decisions? Don't people just naturally learn how? No, it doesn't always work that way. Many people—perhaps most of us— have great difficulty making decisions, and then worry about it long after the choice has been made. "Did I do the right thing?" they wonder. "What if I had made the other decision?" A lot of people need specific instructions before they know how to make responsible decisions.

A Decision-Making Model

In this section you'll see how Richard uses a **decision-making model** to make his choice. A decision-making model is a series of steps that helps a person make a responsible decision.

The decision-making model used in this textbook is shown in Figure 2-4. Follow along as you see Richard go through the steps to make his decision.

(FIGURE 2-3) **When making a difficult decision, it often helps to talk with someone you trust, such as a parent, teacher, counselor, or friend.**

Section 2.2 Lesson Plan

MOTIVATE

Journal 2B
Difficult Decisions

Have students write in their Journal about a decision they had difficulty making and then worried about afterward.

Role-Playing
Making the Right Decision

Have students select one or more of the following scenarios to role-play:

- A friend offers a ride to two teens. The car already has six passengers. Without a ride, the two teens will have a 2-mile walk to the beach.

- Your best friend went to a game instead of doing homework and asks to borrow your homework before class.

- Richard goes to the party, where someone offers him a beer.

Encourage participants to resolve each scenario. Discuss what might happen next as a result of their decisions.

Step 1.	• State the Problem
Step 2.	• List the Options
Step 3.	• Imagine the Benefits and Consequences
Step 4.	• Consider Your Values
Step 5.	• Weigh the Options and Decide
Step 6.	• Act
Step 7.	• Evaluate the Results

(FIGURE 2-4) **A decision-making model is a series of steps that helps a person make a responsible decision. Richard used the steps shown above to make his decision about the party.**

Step 1. State the Problem The first step in making a decision is to state the problem clearly. This is how Richard states his problem: ''Should I go to the party even though I don't want to drink?''

Step 2. List the Options Before deciding what to do, Richard needs to list all the options. As he sees it, these are his options:

1. Go to the party and refuse a drink if it is offered.
2. Stay home and watch reruns of ''Who's the Boss?''

Not very appealing options. Surely there are other alternatives. Well, Richard thinks, he could tell Nicole and Selena ahead of time that he isn't going to drink.

That way they might not try to pressure him into drinking. So now he has a third option:

3. Go to the party, and tell Nicole and Selena ahead of time that he is not going to drink.

Richard can't think of any more options. It seems that he will have to choose among these three. But that's not necessarily true. A person in the middle of trying to solve a problem may not be able to *recognize* all the options.

If Richard discusses his problem with other people, however, they may be able to think of other options or at least provide additional information. In this case, Richard talks to his good friend Carlos about his dilemma. Carlos tells him he has heard that

 Making a Choice 2A

Assign the When Others Are Drinking card. The card asks students to role-play a situation in which a couple decide what to do at a party where drinking is occurring.

Evaluating Media Messages

Have students read this Unit 1 feature on pages 34–35. Then have them complete its companion worksheet.

TEACH

 Teaching Transparency 2D
Decision-Making Model

Use this transparency of Figure 2-4 to discuss the steps in the decision-making model. Ask: **Which steps do you think are most important? Which do you think could be left out? Why? When do you think using this model would be most helpful?**

Class Discussion
Consulting Others

Ask students how they would decide whom to talk to when trying to make an important decision. You might place the following factors on the board and encourage students to think of others:

• knows me well
• is trustworthy
• is an expert on the subject
• has common sense and good judgment
• knows the situation or has made a similar decision

Have students discuss the relevance of each factor to decision making.

Making a Choice 2B

Assign the Values card. The card asks students to consider how individual values may differ among students and to discuss the effects of making decisions that are inconsistent with one's values.

values:

a person's strong beliefs and ideals.

Selena doesn't drink either. Richard hadn't even considered that possibility. "What about going to a movie?" Carlos suggests. "That way you can see Selena but not have to worry about drinking." So now he has a fourth option:

4. Persuade Nicole and Selena to go to a movie instead of the party.

If Selena doesn't drink, Richard thinks, he might have a pretty good chance of getting the girls to change their plans.

Having someone to talk to whose opinions you trust is a valuable asset. It's important to remember, though, that you don't want to be persuaded to do something that isn't good for you.

Step 3. Imagine the Benefits and Consequences of Each Option

Many people have the hardest time with this step because they don't want to think about all the painful things that could happen as a result of choosing some of their options. But that's why this step is so important. In the long run, it's less painful to just imagine the consequences of a bad decision than to actually *experience* the consequences.

Take some time and carefully think through the benefits and negative consequences of each of your options. Make separate lists of the short-term consequences and the long-term consequences. A solution that solves the immediate problem might have terrible consequences later. And a solution that has uncomfortable consequences at first can be the best one in the long run.

Figure 2-5 shows the possible benefits and negative consequences that Richard imagined during his decision-making process. Remember that this is how *Richard* saw his situation. If you had Richard's problem, your lists of benefits and consequences might be entirely different.

Step 4. Consider Your Values

The next step in making a responsible decision is to think about how each option fits with your **values.** There are many definitions of the word "values," but when you see the word in this book it means a person's strong beliefs and ideals.

Your values allow you to choose between good and bad, and between right and wrong. Your values show the kind of person you are and what you care most about.

A person's values develop over time and are influenced by the teachings of family, culture, and religious and spiritual leaders. It's important to realize that not everyone will share your values. Each person develops his or her own value system, based on individual life experiences. However, there are some values that seem to be important to people from many backgrounds and cultures. These values, which are sometimes called "universal values," are:

- honesty
- trustworthiness
- responsibility to oneself and others
- self-control
- social justice

Richard feels that the value most relevant to his problem is responsibility to himself and others. It is very important to Richard to protect himself from harm. It is also important to him to avoid needlessly hurting his family. If he developed a drinking problem like his brother's, it would cause his family a lot of pain.

He also recognizes that his problem involves self-control. He had vowed to himself that he would not drink, and he doesn't want to break his promise to himself by losing control.

When Richard looks over his list of options, he sees that Option 2 and Option 4 fit his values. If he chooses either of these options, he will be certain not to drink.

• • • TEACH continued

Class Discussion
Ranking Values

Have students study the bulleted list of "universal values" and rank them from most important to least important. If a value that is important to them is not listed, ask them to add it. Tally the results on the chalkboard. Stress that people's values differ, just as students' opinions about the relative importance of specific values differ.

Demonstration
Values and Behavior

Ask students to draw a visual map to represent the relationship between personal values and behavior. You might copy the clearest visual map on the chalkboard or on an overhead transparency. Then trace the path on the visual as students name a value and suggest a behavior that proceeds from it. For example, value—respect for other people; behaviors—listening

when others talk, respecting opposing points of view.

Reinforcement
Deciding on a Plan

For the following situation, ask students to suggest a plan Maria could follow to help her carry out her decision:

Maria decides that she is going to exercise regularly to lose weight and get in shape. She feels good about her decision. A month later, however, she still has not begun to exercise.

Richard's Options

(FIGURE 2-5)

Options	Possible Benefits	Possible Short-Term Negative Consequences	Possible Long-Term Negative Consequences
1. Go to the party and hope that I am not tempted to drink.	I will be sure to spend the evening with the girls.	I may drink and feel guilty about it. I may drink and lose the chance to go out with Selena, since she doesn't drink. I may drink and end up in a dangerous situation, such as driving while drunk.	If I drink after I've decided not to drink, I could become a problem drinker like my brother. The negative consequences of being a problem drinker would take all day to list. Some of them are increased risk of injuries, physical illness, emotional depression, and damaged relationships with people I care about.
2. Stay at home and watch reruns.	I will not have to deal with the pressures to drink alcohol. I will keep my promise to myself about not drinking.	I will not get to spend the evening with the girls.	The girls might think I'm no fun.
3. Go to the party but tell Nicole and Selena ahead of time that I am not going to drink.	I will have a better chance of keeping my promise to myself about not drinking than if I choose Option 1.	I might drink anyway and have the same possible short-term consequences of Option 1.	If I drink, I have the same possible long-term consequences of Option 1. In addition, I might lose the respect of Nicole and Selena if I drink after I said I would not.
4. Persuade Nicole and Selena to go to a movie instead of the party.	I will get to spend the evening with the girls. I will know that Nicole and Selena would rather spend time with me than go to the party. I will keep my promise to myself about not drinking. I may improve my chances with Selena, since she doesn't drink.	Nicole and Selena might insist on going to the party, with or without me. If I do convince them to go to the movie instead, they may still feel a little upset about not going to the party.	If they don't want to go to the movie, the girls might think I'm no fun.

(Students may suggest some of the following: Decide on specific exercises she enjoys and can realistically do. Plan an exercise schedule that fits into her daily schedule. Ask a friend to exercise with her regularly. Make a chart to show improvements. Allow herself a small reward for each goal reached.)

Debate the Issue
Decisions Under Pressure

Have the class divide into two teams to debate the following question: When you have to make a decision quickly, under pressure, should you always go with your first, instinctive response? Students on both sides should support their arguments with information they have learned about decision making and values. Have students suggest guidelines they think are important in making quick decisions under pressure.

Extension
Observing Decision Making

Many cities broadcast city council meetings on television. Record a session and show it to the class. Determine what, if any, decisions were made at the meeting. Analyze how they were made. Evaluate the decision-making process used. Identify any obstacles. If

HOW TO MAKE A RESPONSIBLE DECISION **27**

Section Review Worksheet 2.2

To reinforce the concepts presented in this section, assign Section Review Worksheet 2-2.

Section Quiz 2.2

Have students take Section Quiz 2.2

Reteaching Worksheet 2.2

Students who have difficulty with the material may complete Reteaching Worksheet 2.2.

Step 5. Weigh the Options and Decide

The next step is to weigh your options and make the decision. Carefully examine the possible benefits and negative consequences of each option. Which option has the most benefits and the fewest negative consequences? Pay special attention to the long-term consequences of the options.

Most important, remember what you learned in Step 4—how the options fit your values. If you have trouble deciding between two options that seem equally desirable, choose the one that better reflects your strong beliefs and ideals. There is a very practical reason to act in accordance with one's values: When people go against their values, they are likely to feel bad about themselves. Always ask yourself, ''How will I feel about myself later if I choose this option?''

Richard knows that Options 1 and 3 are not compatible with his values because they might lead to drinking. Option 2, to stay home, *is* compatible with his values. But it doesn't have as many benefits as Option 4, to persuade the girls to go to a movie instead of the party.

Option 4 has more benefits than any of the other options, does not have many negative consequences, and is consistent with his values. It has now become clear to Richard that Option 4 is the best option for him.

He has made a responsible decision.

Step 6. Act

It may seem that things should be smooth sailing after you finally make a decision. You just *do* it, right? In reality, it takes some thought and planning

> **❝***I don't want to drink, but it's hard when some people at a party may be drinking.***❞**
>
> Richard

• • • TEACH continued

you are unable to obtain such a video, ask a member of another organization, such as the chamber of commerce, to visit the class. Have him or her talk about the decision-making process the organization uses.

to ensure that you will act on your decision. Richard made the following list of actions he would take to implement his decision:

1. I will find out ahead of time which movies will be showing the night of the party and make a note of several that sound good.
2. I will make sure I can get the car that night so I can drive everyone to the theater.
3. I will tell Nicole and Selena about all the good movies showing in town and ask them if they would like to go to one of them instead of going to the party.
4. I will be prepared to tell them the truth if they ask me why I don't want to go to the party.

Step 7. Evaluate the Results   Once the decision is made and you have acted on the decision, you should evaluate the results.

Ask yourself the following questions. How well did the decision work out? How well did you identify the potential benefits and negative consequences of the option you chose? How can you improve the way you make decisions in the future?

As it turned out, Nicole and Selena went along with his idea to go to the movie. Nicole was a little reluctant because she had been looking forward to the party, but Selena was happy to avoid the pressure to drink. No one quizzed Richard about why he didn't want to go to the party. All three had a good time at the movie, and Richard got to know Selena better. When Richard evaluated the results, he felt he had made the best decision possible.

But what if the situation had turned out differently? What if the girls had refused to go with him and had made fun of him? It wouldn't mean that he had made the wrong decision. It would mean that no matter how good his decision was, he couldn't control other people's behavior. All Richard could

control was his *own* behavior. A good decision is not necessarily one that works out well, but one that is made responsibly.

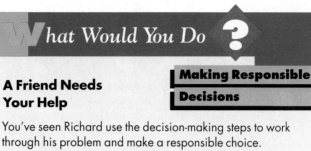

A Friend Needs Your Help

Making Responsible Decisions

You've seen Richard use the decision-making steps to work through his problem and make a responsible choice. Now practice using those same steps by making a decision about what you would do if faced with the following dilemma.

You know your friend Juliette has been depressed lately, but every time you ask her what's wrong, she changes the subject. Then one day you notice a bruise on her face that she's tried to cover with makeup. At first she tells you that she got hit in the face with a softball, but then, leaning against her locker and crying, she admits that her stepfather beat her up. "He knocks me around every time he has a bad day at work," Juliette says. "Mom doesn't even know about it because she gets home from work after he does."

"Why don't you tell your mother about it?" you ask. But Juliette shakes her head. "I don't want to break up Mom's marriage. She's happier now than she's been in a long time."

That night you keep thinking about Juliette. You want to help your friend, but you don't want to make her situation worse. What would you do?

Remember to use the decision-making steps:

1. State the Problem
2. List the Options
3. Imagine the Benefits and Consequences
4. Consider Your Values
5. Weigh the Options and Decide
6. Act
7. Evaluate the Results

 What Would You Do ?

Answers will vary. Accept any answers that demonstrate students' abilities to comprehend and apply the decision-making model to a chosen dilemma.

Life Skills Worksheet 2A
Assign the Making Immediate Decisions Life Skills Worksheet.

Review Answers

1. (1) state the problem, (2) list the options, (3) imagine the benefits and consequences of each option, (4) consider your values, (5) weigh the options and decide, (6) act, (7) evaluate the results

2. Values are important when making a decision because values enable people to choose between what they think is right and what they think is wrong. Also, if people go against their values when making a decision, they are likely to feel bad about themselves, which will lower their self-esteem.

3. Accept any response that shows an understanding of the decision-making model.

4. Answers will vary. Accept any reasonable response. Answers may include honesty, trustworthiness, responsibility to oneself and others, self-control, and social justice.

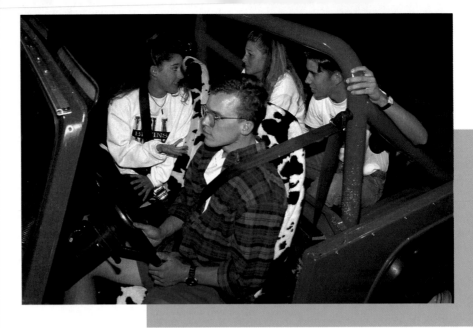

(FIGURE 2-6) **What if you're riding around in a car with friends and you have to make a quick decision about whether to go to a party? When under this kind of pressure, consider your values first.**

What Happens When You Have to Make a Quick Decision? Because Richard had plenty of time before the night of the party, he was able to systematically follow the decision-making steps. He was lucky that time. But let's say Richard was riding around in a car with some friends who wanted to go to a beer party right then. He wouldn't be able to whip out his notebook and pencil and make lists of the options, benefits, and consequences. He would have to respond immediately.

When under pressure, it is best to consider your values first. It also helps if you have practiced the decision-making steps many times before. Then the process would come almost naturally. The ''What Would You Do?'' activity on the previous page will give you an opportunity to sharpen your decision-making skills in preparation for the times when you have to make quick decisions.

Review

1. Name the steps of the decision-making model presented in this chapter.

2. Why are values important in making responsible decisions?

3. ▪▪ **LIFE SKILLS: Making Responsible Decisions** Here is your dilemma: You are very attracted to someone in your school named Kris, but a friend recently told you that Kris smokes. Decide whether you should pursue your interest in Kris, using the steps of the decision-making model.

4. **Critical Thinking** Name three values that are very important to you.

ASSESS

Section Review

Have students answer the Section Review questions.

Alternative Assessment
Evaluating a Decision

Have students use the decision-making model to write an evaluation for a decision that they may have personally made or that they studied in this sec-tion. The evaluation should state the problem, describe the action taken and the consequences of the action, and explain whether or not the results were satisfactory.

 Closure—Journal 2C
Taking Responsibility

In their Journal, have students make a list of things people do or say to deny responsibility for poor decisions or negative actions. (Starter examples might include statements such as the following: "_____ made me do it." "Everybody does that." "It wasn't my fault.") Then have students tell how these excuses could cause problems.

Highlights

CHAPTER **2**
HIGHLIGHTS
STRATEGIES

Summary

- People who are able to make responsible decisions have a great deal of control over their own lives.

- The top three causes of death among Americans between the ages of 15 and 24 are accidental injury, homicide, and suicide. Each of these can directly result from the choices a person makes.

- The top three causes of death for Americans between the ages of 55 and 64 are cancer, heart disease, and chronic obstructive pulmonary disease. Each of these can result from choices made early in life, such as smoking.

- A person who has a high quality of life leads a life that is full of enrichment and reward.

- There is a series of steps you can learn that will help you make responsible decisions.

- Talking to someone whose opinions you trust can help you make a decision. Be sure, though, that you are not persuaded to make a decision to do something that is bad for you.

- A person's values, or strong beliefs and ideals, can be influenced by family, culture, and religious and spiritual leaders.

- Whenever you are under pressure to make a quick decision, make sure you consider your own values first.

- The most important values include honesty, trustworthiness, responsibility to oneself and others, self-control, and social justice.

Vocabulary

unintentional injuries injuries that are not the result of purposeful acts.

quality of life the degree to which a person lives life to its fullest capacity with enjoyment and reward.

decision-making model a series of steps that helps a person make a responsible decision.

values a person's strong beliefs and ideals.

CHAPTER

2

Chapter Review

CHAPTER REVIEW

Concept Review

1. unintentional injury, homicide, suicide
2. cancer, heart disease, chronic obstructive pulmonary diseases
3. alcohol, drugs
4. quality of life
5. emphysema
6. quality of life
7. state the problem
8. values
9. beliefs, ideals
10. evaluate the results

Expressing Your Views

1. eating nutritious snacks and a well-balanced diet, exercising, not smoking, not using illegal drugs, not drinking alcohol, wearing protective items or devices when necessary
2. Answers will vary. Accept any response that indicates serious reflection on the issue and an understanding of the consequences of questionable decisions.
3. Answers will vary. Sample response: We might not be able to remain friends. If she continues to drink, she could be hurt or killed in a car accident. Also, she could become an alcoholic.

Concept Review . . . .

1. The top three causes of death of people ages 15–24 are _____ , _____ , and _____ .

2. The top three causes of death of people ages 55–64 are _____ , _____ , and _____ .

3. It has been shown that the use of _____ and other _____ greatly increases the chances that a person will experience serious injury, be involved in violence, or commit suicide.

4. Health decisions you make today will have a profound effect on your future _____ .

5. If you choose to smoke, you are more likely to get lung cancer or _____ , a lung disease.

6. The degree to which a person lives life to its fullest capacity with enjoyment and reward is known as _____ .

7. The first step in making a decision is to _____ .

8. Your _____ allow you to choose between right and wrong and show the kind of person you are.

9. If you have trouble deciding between two options that seem equally desirable, choose the one that better reflects your strong _____ and _____ .

10. Once a decision is made and you have acted on the decision, the next step in the decision-making process is to _____ .

Expressing Your Views . . . .

1. What are some changes you could make in your lifestyle to improve your quality of life in later years?

2. You have a friend who smokes cigarettes and is reluctant to quit. He says smoking has never made him feel sick, and that it's not going to harm him.
    What would you tell him?

3. Your best friend was drinking at the party Saturday. You think she may be drinking often, but you're not sure whether you should say something to her about it. What do you think you should do? What are some long- and short-term consequences for her health?

Life Skills Check

1. Answers should include using the steps of the decision-making model to decide what to do in this situation.
2. Answers should include using the decision-making model to decide what to do in this situation.

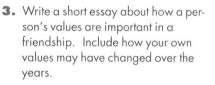

Life Skills Check . . . .

1. Making Responsible Decisions

Terry is someone you've always wanted to be friends with, so you're pretty happy the two of you have started to do stuff together. Unfortunately, one thing Terry really likes to do most is skip class and go to the park. You haven't done it yet, but Terry wants the two of you to cut math class Friday. You don't want to miss the class; you have a quiz the next week, and you'd feel really funny about cutting a class anyway. But you also don't want to lose Terry's friendship. What would you do?

2. Making Responsible Decisions

Some close friends of yours have started using alcohol and other drugs on a regular basis. Using the steps of the decision-making model, decide whether you want to continue associating with this group of friends.

Projects . . . .

1. Design a bulletin board that displays the leading causes of death for Americans between the ages of 15 and 24, and for those between the ages of 55 and 64. Suggest ways to reduce the number of deaths from these causes.

2. Work with a group of students to come up with a list of problems for which the decision-making model might be useful. What issues would not be suitable for the model?

3. Write a short essay about how a person's values are important in a friendship. Include how your own values may have changed over the years.

4. Work with a partner to find magazine pictures that show people attempting to improve their quality of life. Create a collage on a poster board using the pictures you have found. Next to the collage, list the ways the people in the pictures are striving for a more satisfying life.

Plan for Action . . . .

Make a list of four situations that require a spur of the moment decision that could negatively affect your health. Select one situation and use the decision-making model to make a decision about what to do.

Projects

Have students plan and carry out the projects for responsible decision making.

Plan for Action

Discuss with the students the nature of quick decisions. Brainstorm to make a list of situations that might require a quick decision. Discuss how the model shown in the text could be applied to one of the situations listed. Then have students make their own list and complete the activity.

ASSESSMENT OPTIONS

Chapter Test
Have students take the Chapter 2 Test.

Alternative Assessment
Have students do the Alternative Assessment activity for Chapter 2.

Test Generator
The Test Generator contains additional assessment items for this chapter.

Evaluating Media Messages

Issues in Health

EVALUATING MEDIA MESSAGES

What Is a Media Message?

Have students read the Evaluating Media Messages feature. Discuss with students their responses to the situation described: Have they ever felt they wanted something because of the image presented in an advertisement? Have they bought something based on media persuasion? Were they pleased with the decision? Or, have there been times when their best interests were not the same as those of the seller? If so, how could they be better prepared the next time they have such a decision to make?

What Is a Media Message?

Mike needs some new athletic shoes. Like many of his friends, Mike wants a popular name brand endorsed by famous athletes. He loves to think that wearing those particular shoes will impress his friends and make him more popular at school. Unfortunately, the shoes cost three times as much money as Mike has to spend. When Mike asks his father if he will help with the purchase, his father says no.

"Come on, Dad," Mike says. "All the NBA stars are wearing these shoes. They're the best!"

"That may be, Mike," his father replies, "but they are not the best choice for you. They're just too expensive. Before you make a decision based only on the influence of a media message, why don't you do a little research on several kinds of shoes."

"Okay, Dad," Mike agrees. "But what's a media message, anyway?"

Most advertisers take advantage of our tendency to make decisions based on emotion rather than reason.

As Mike's father explained, media messages are the information conveyed by television, radio, magazines, newspapers, and other types of mass media (forms of communication that reach large numbers of people). They are found primarily in advertisements, television programs, and movies, but are also found in news stories, art, literature, and even rock music lyrics.

Media messages not only contain information but also express social values and persuade people to make judgments and to take certain actions. Because such messages reach so many people, they greatly affect people's opinions of what is normal, attractive, successful, and even healthy. Often, the forms of persuasion used in media messages encourage people to make decisions based on emotion rather than reason. Consequently, the purpose, source, and nature of any media message should be carefully evaluated before making a decision based on the message.

The ads that make Mike feel he must have a certain type of athletic shoes are examples of media messages designed to persuade. Some of the ads mention comfort, foot support, durability, and endorsements by medical experts, which are all logical reasons for buying a particular shoe. But many ads rely on visual images of athletes wearing that brand of athletic shoes. The athletes project an image of attractiveness and success that is emotionally appealing. By association, whatever the athlete is wearing, eating, or doing may be perceived as contributing to the athlete's attractiveness and success. This is why Mike feels that if he wears the same athletic shoes, he too will be attractive and successful.

All of us have a tendency to make decisions based on emotion rather than reason. Most advertisers take advantage of this tendency. When evaluating media messages like athletic-shoe ads, it is important to remember the purpose of the ads—to sell shoes and make money for the shoe companies. The athletes also make money by doing the ads. Such interests may conflict with the best interests of buyers.

Once Mike understood how and why he came to desire the expensive athletic shoes, he realized that he would rather base his decision on his own best interests. After making a list of several types of athletic shoes and their features, Mike talked to some of the coaches at school about how the different brands compare in terms of performance and durability. By applying the decision-making model he learned in health class, Mike finally chose a style that is more comfortable, lasts longer, and costs a lot less money than the brand he wanted originally.

It also provides good foot support and looks great. Even though Mike's choice still costs more money than he has, it is clearly his best choice overall. And his father agreed to help with the purchase after all.

ritical Thinking

1. Find several ads for a common item such as a type of clothing, a toy, a kids' cereal, a type of sporting equipment, or an automobile. Analyze the ads for the media messages they convey.

   • What information is given upfront?
   • What information is unspoken or in the background?
   • What type of media—print, radio, or television—does each ad use? Which do you think is the most effective?
   • Does the ad appeal to your emotions or your sense of reason?
   • Choose what you think is the best ad upon which to base a decision to buy.

2. For each ad you analyzed for item 1, ask yourself the following questions.

   • How will I benefit if I buy what the ad is trying to sell?
   • How will the advertiser benefit if I buy what the ad is trying to sell?

CHAPTER OVERVIEWS

CHAPTER 3

PHYSICAL FITNESS

This chapter explains the mental and physical benefits of exercise and describes the four categories of physical fitness. It explores ways to improve fitness and provides tests for judging it. The differences between aerobic and anaerobic exercise are explained, and examples are given. Students learn about the dangers of steroid abuse, how to avoid injury while exercising, and how to determine target heart rate. The chapter helps students set exercise goals and design an exercise schedule. It emphasizes the importance of sleep in maintaining fitness, explains the stages of sleep, and provides suggestions for coping with insomnia.

CHAPTER 4

NUTRITION PRINCIPLES

The chapter opens with a discussion of how hunger, appetite, and environment affect food choices. This is followed by a presentation of the functions of the essential nutrients and the problems that nutrient deficiencies can cause. Students learn to define their nutritional needs, classify foods into appropriate groups, and interpret food labels. This prepares them to apply guidelines in order to make healthful food choices and to understand the special nutritional needs of selected populations. They also learn

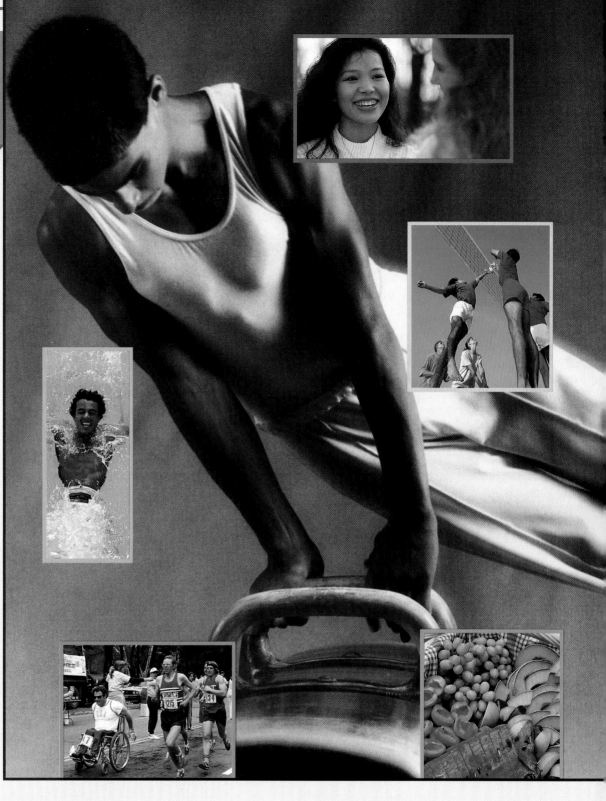

to recognize the symptoms of food-borne illnesses and how to prevent the bacterial contamination of food.

the digestive system, ways to treat them, and the differences between food allergies and food intolerances.

CHAPTER 5

WEIGHT MANAGEMENT AND EATING DISORDERS

Basic information about maintaining an ideal weight is presented in this chapter. Students learn how the body uses energy, how to determine ideal weight, and how to lose or gain weight sensibly. Then they learn how to recognize eating disorders and avoid developing them. Next, students learn about disorders that affect

CHAPTER 6

PERSONAL CARE AND APPEARANCE

Personal hygiene is important to self-esteem *and* to health. In this chapter, students learn to care for their skin, hair, nails, teeth, and gums. They also learn about the structure of the skin, hair, and teeth, and how to recognize and deal with skin, hair, and dental problems. In addition, students learn how to choose a dentist and make a dental appointment.

HEALTH AND YOUR BODY

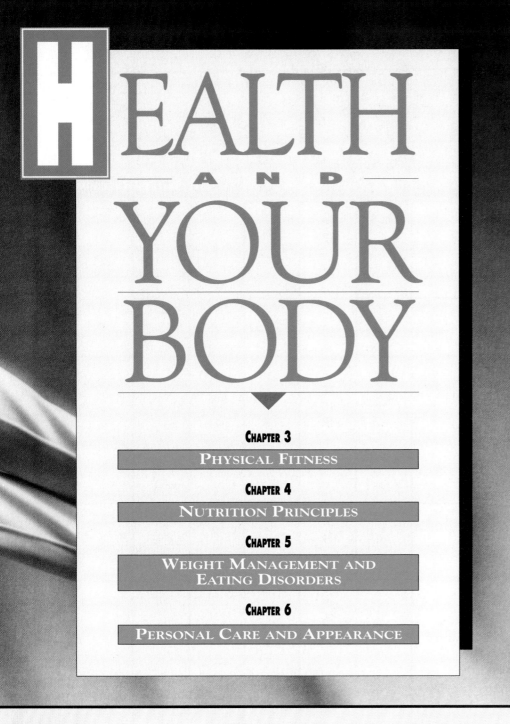

CHAPTER 3
PHYSICAL FITNESS

CHAPTER 4
NUTRITION PRINCIPLES

CHAPTER 5
WEIGHT MANAGEMENT AND
EATING DISORDERS

CHAPTER 6
PERSONAL CARE AND APPEARANCE

UNIT PREVIEW

The information presented in this unit will help students make good choices in exercise, eating, and personal care. They learn the components of physical fitness, the elements of a nutritious diet, how to determine an ideal weight, and how to care for their skin, hair, nails, teeth, and gums. Students also learn how to identify problems in the areas and are given suggestions for dealing with them. The chart below links the information and skills presented in this unit to the National Health Education Standards.

Unit 2	NATIONAL HEALTH EDUCATION STANDARDS*						
STANDARD	1	2	3	4	5	6	7
Chapter 3	•		•			•	•
Chapter 4	•	•	•			•	•
Chapter 5	•		•	•	•	•	
Chapter 6	•	•	•	•	•	•	

* For full text listing of each standard, see page 15T.

CHAPTER 3

Physical Fitness

SECTION	TITLE/OBJECTIVES	PERSONAL INVENTORY			LIFE SKILLS DEVELOPMENT				
		Personal Health Inventory	Journal	Check Up	Life Skills	Life Skills Worksheets	Media Message or Ethical Issues Worksheet	What Would You Do?	
3.1 *pp. 39–43*	**WHY EXERCISE?** • Name three physical benefits of exercise. • Name two mental benefits of exercise. • Name the four categories of physical fitness.	Ch. 3	3A 3B						
3.2 *pp. 44–45*	**HOW PHYSICALLY FIT ARE YOU?** ▪▪ Know the ways to test physical fitness.		3C 3D						
3.3 *pp. 46–53*	**ABOUT EXERCISE** • Know the difference between aerobic and anaerobic exercise. • Name three examples of aerobic exercise. • Name three effects of steroid abuse. • Know what to do to avoid basic injuries. ▪▪ Know the range of your target heart rate.		3E 3F 3G 3H		p. 49				
3.4 *pp. 54–59*	**GETTING STARTED** • Set your exercise goals. • Design your own exercise schedule.		3I 3J			3A			
3.5 *pp. 60–62*	**SLEEP** • Know the two different categories of sleep. • Describe what happens during each phase of the sleep cycle. • Name two ways to cope with insomnia. ▪▪ Know how much sleep you need each night.		3K 3L			3B			

KEY: ▪▪ Denotes Life Skill Objective

Text references denoted by page number.

Supplement references denoted by chapter or item numbers.

LINKING RESOURCES

INTERACTION		OTHER RESOURCES		SECTION REVIEW AND ASSESSMENT			
	Ch. 3	Ch. 3	3A BSH4	3.1	3.1	3.1	p. 43
			BSH5	3.2	3.2	3.2	p. 45
3A 3B			BSH6 BSH7	3.3	3.3	3.3	p. 53
			3B 3C	3.4	3.4	3.4	p. 59
				3.5	3.5	3.5	p. 62

For information about the skeletal, muscular, and circulatory systems, see pages 662–664, 665–667, and 668–670 in the Body Systems Handbook.

KEY FACTS

- Exercise benefits the body by increasing energy levels, strengthening bones, decreasing cholesterol levels, lowering blood pressure, and reducing body fat.

- Exercise benefits the mind by reducing anxiety and depression. It causes an increase in endorphins, which affect an individual's mood.

- Aerobic exercise helps improve the respiratory and circulatory systems.

- Rules to remember when exercising: F, frequency—3 or 4 times a week; I, intensity—at or just above target heart rate; T, time—at least 30 minutes of exercise, including a warm up and a cool down.

- To treat basic injuries, remember PRICE: physician, rest, ice, compression, elevation.

- Anabolic steroids are illegal, dangerous drugs which cause physical and behavioral problems.

- Exercise increases the time spent in stage III and IV NREM sleep, in which most body rest and restoration takes place.

CHAPTER REVIEW AND ASSESSMENT

TEXT

Chapter Review pp. 64–65

SUPPLEMENTS

Chapter Test 3

Alternative Assessment 3

Test Generator Chapter 3

GETTING STARTED

Using the Chapter Photograph

Ask students if they think the basketball players in the photograph are physically fit. Have the students name the traits they think a physically fit person has. Ask students if they think a person has to be an athlete to be physically fit.

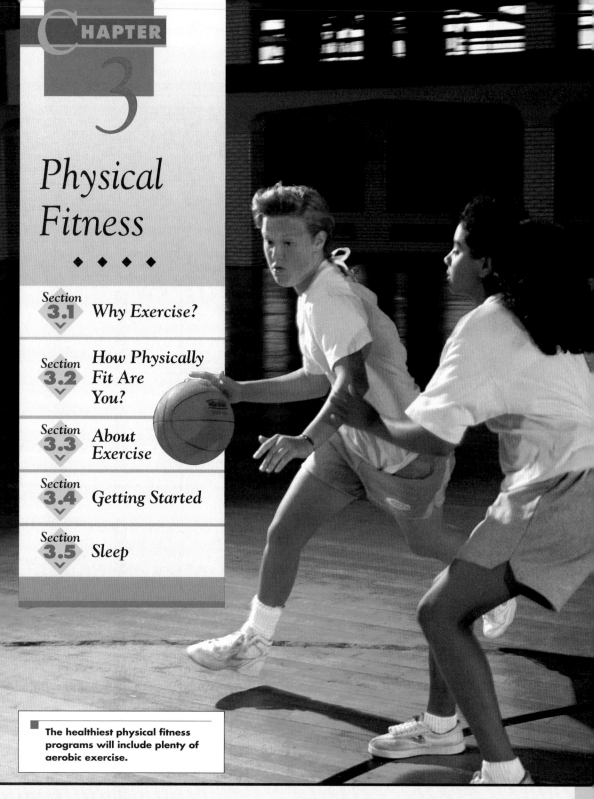

Question Box

Have students write out any questions they have about being physically fit and put them in the Question Box.

Sensitivity **ALERT**

Be aware of the feelings of students who are overweight or who, for whatever reason, are not physically fit. Students who are physically impaired may find a chapter on physical fitness disturbing. Some students may not have the economic resources to meet the equipment requirements of some physical activities. Make it a point to discuss the value of activities that are within everyone's means.

CHAPTER

3

Physical Fitness

◆ ◆ ◆ ◆

Section **3.1**	Why Exercise?
Section **3.2**	How Physically Fit Are You?
Section **3.3**	About Exercise
Section **3.4**	Getting Started
Section **3.5**	Sleep

The healthiest physical fitness programs will include plenty of aerobic exercise.

MYTHS & MISCONCEPTIONS

- **There is no such thing as exercising too much.** Some people become so addicted to exercise that it dominates their life.

- **If there is no pain while exercising, there is no gain in fitness.** Jogging, brisk walking, and cycling improve fitness without causing pain.

- **Just 10 minutes of aerobic exercise daily can help you become more fit.** You must spend 20 to 30 minutes doing an aerobic exercise for it to be beneficial.

- **Muscles turn to fat when a person stops working out.** Muscles can lose their tone and look flabby, but they cannot turn into fat, which is a different tissue.

- **Drinking water before exercising can cause stomach cramps.** Drinking water will prevent cramps, which are caused by dehydration.

Christine can't seem to stay awake anymore. She has to drag herself out of bed every morning, and at school she sits bleary-eyed in class, counting seconds until the bell rings. After staring into space at her after-school job, she barely begins her homework before nodding off, at around 8 P.M. Her friends, family, and teachers have noticed that she's been acting strange lately, and Christine herself is concerned about her lack of energy.

She's also worried about the layer of fat that she has recently noticed on her waist and the back of her arms. Christine knows that having some body fat is perfectly normal, but she also realizes that she has been eating too many sweets between meals. She wonders whether her busy, stressful life has something to do with her constant exhaustion and huge appetite. Then one day it dawns on her that she can't remember the last time she got any exercise.

Personal Health Inventory

Have students complete the Personal Health Inventory for this chapter.

English/Spanish CD Audio Program

Use the English/Spanish Health Talk audio program for students who need audio reinforcement of the concepts presented.

Parent Discussion Guide

Send home the Parent Letter for Chapter 3. As you progress through the chapter, send home the Parental Survey and The Extra Mile.

Section 3.1

Why Exercise?

Objectives

- *Name three physical benefits of exercise.*
- *Name two mental benefits of exercise.*
- *Name the four categories of physical fitness.*

You've probably heard all about how good exercise is for you. You know that it can help you develop muscles and lose weight. What you may not realize is that regular exercise helps you cope better with the stress and anxiety you probably face every day, and that it greatly increases your energy level. It can even help you avoid some serious diseases later on in life.

Some people like to exercise more than others. If you're the wide receiver on your school football team, you will have an easier time figuring out how to be physically active than if you hate the thought of lacing up a pair of sneakers. But exercising regularly does not have to mean competing against the best athletes in your class or taking a swimming lesson when it's freezing outside. Walking for half an hour before supper, or biking to school instead of taking the bus, is often enough to give your body the **exercise** it needs.

exercise:

physical activity that consists of a regular series of activities to train and strengthen the body.

Section 3.1 Lesson Plan

MOTIVATE

Cooperative Learning
Feeling Tired

Have students form small groups to discuss Christine's problem of being tired all the time. Ask them to discuss the following questions: How would you categorize Christine's condition? Have you ever felt as she does? What do you think was the basic cause of Christine's problem? What might happen if she continues in this way for a long period of time? What could she do to improve her condition? What experiences have you had that prove that exercise can help you feel less tired?

39

WHY EXERCISE?

Background
The Medical Benefits of Exercise

Research teams now credit exercise for a wide array of physical benefits, including the prevention, and even cure, of certain diseases. Osteoporosis, a disease caused by a loss of minerals in the bones, results in brittle bones that break easily. Weight-bearing and strength exercises can increase bone density and can reverse the process of loss of bone density. Recent findings also suggest that regular, moderate aerobic exercise may decrease the incidence of coronary heart disease by up to 50 percent. Other studies show an inverse relationship between exercise and certain cancers, particularly colon cancer. An intense exercise program is not necessary to receive these benefits. Small increases in daily activity can help people reduce their risk of disease and increase their feeling of well-being.

body composition:

the division of total body weight into fat weight and fat-free weight which includes bone and muscle.

For more information on where to seek help for anxiety and depression, see Chapter 7.

The Benefits of Exercise

Christine bought an exercise tape and started working out four times a week. It surprised her how quickly she started feeling better. Her energy level bounced back to normal, and she found it hard to believe that at one time she could barely stay conscious until early evening. By combining physical workouts with a new diet of nutritious, low-fat foods, she began to lose the extra weight.

In addition, Christine forgot that her days were once filled with depression and anxiety. Her dark moods lifted, and she no longer woke up in the morning with a sense of dread in the pit of her stomach. Her exercise routine became a part of her day-to-day life, so she no longer had to force herself to do the activities that improved her physical and mental well-being so dramatically.

Not everyone will get the same benefits from exercise as Christine. It could be that your body will not respond as easily or as quickly to physical activity. In addition, many teenagers are depressed or anxious—not because they haven't exercised, but because something is happening at school or at home that may be troubling them. If you are feeling sad or stressed out, and you don't think it has anything to do with the amount of exercise you've been getting, you may want to talk to someone, like a teacher, a coach, or a counselor. See Chapter 7, Mental and Emotional Health, for more information on this.

Physical Benefits All body systems benefit from regular physical activity, including exercise. When you perform a regular series of activities to train and strengthen your body, you are exercising. But there are occasions when you just need to walk to the store, climb a flight of stairs, mow the lawn, or wash the car. Although that's not formally exercise, it is physical activity, and it, too, benefits your physical health.

Many teens are concerned about weight gain. Christine herself was worried about the fat on her body. Exercise can help her achieve a **body composition** with the appropriate fat percentage to be healthy. Christine's exercise tape keeps her moving continuously for about 20 minutes. In doing so, she uses energy. At some point in time and with changes in her diet, Christine can reach a healthy weight. A healthy weight is one that is suited to her body build and the size of her bones. She'll be able to maintain her weight if she continues her physical activity, because physical activity is the key to long-term weight maintenance.

When Christine saw people exercising who looked trim, she wondered why they even needed to exercise. Exercise is not just for people who have fat to lose. Thin people have as much reason to exercise as not-so-thin people. While exercising, Christine is keeping her heart rate and breathing rate up which strengthens her heart, the muscles of her lungs, and her blood vessels. Not only do these tissues get stronger, but they also remain elastic, relaxing and contracting steadily as needed. This, in turn, reduces her risk for heart attack, stroke, and high blood pressure, which is often a result of the build-up of plaque in the blood vessels. Plaque forms within arteries in the heart, the brain, and throughout the body. These deposits can clog arteries in the heart and lead to a heart attack, or they can clog arteries in the brain and lead to a stroke. Plaque formation can begin in infancy, but regular exercise can slow down the build-up by raising the levels of chemicals in the blood that help to remove the fatty deposits.

Christine's tape also has an exercise segment to strengthen abdominal muscles. Stronger muscles in her abdomen help support her lower back. Given that back problems are often caused by weak muscles,

---

TEACH

Class Discussion
Benefits of Physical Fitness

Write on the chalkboard: Becoming more physically fit can improve your quality of life. Ask: **What are some examples that support this statement?** *[When a person is alert and feeling energetic, he or she can think better and respond better to other people. An energetic person can learn with less effort in school and can be more cooperative at home and at work.]* Record student contributions on the chalkboard. Ask students to suggest activities they enjoy that give them a beneficial physical workout. Discuss the effects of exercise on Christine—how she felt after she began using the exercise tape. Point out that while exercise cannot cure psychological problems, it can help relieve stress and moderate mood swings.

 Cooperative Learning
Were You Surprised?

After students read about the physical benefits of exercise, ask them to discuss what surprised them most about the effects of exercise. Have them share any personal experiences that document how beneficial exercise can be.

Christine is working to prevent lower back problems. Each time these and other strengthening exercises place a strain on her bones, her bones get stronger and more dense. Increased bone density will help Christine later in life when osteoporosis could otherwise result in brittle and easily broken bones. And because she is active, Christine is reducing her chances of getting diabetes as she moves into her forties.

In the short term, the moderate pace of her exercise tape will boost Christine's immune system. A strong immune system is necessary to prevent disease. Christine might find that she has fewer colds and sore throats during the coming winter. Other systems like her digestive and excretory systems are strengthened by regular exercise and adopting a more nutritious diet. Because she is now sweating regularly, Christine's skin is working more efficiently to remove wastes from her body. Research suggests she may also be reducing her risk of cancer with exercise.

Section Review Worksheet 3.1

To reinforce the concepts presented in this section, assign Section Review Worksheet 3.1.

Section Quiz 3.1

Have students take Section Quiz 3.1.

Reteaching Worksheet 3.1

Students who have difficulty with the material may complete Reteaching Worksheet 3.1.

Myths and Facts About Exercise

MYTH	FACT
No pain, no gain.	Exercise does not have to hurt in order to be effective. Jogging, walking, or cycling at a pace that allows you to carry on a normal conversation, for example, will improve your aerobic fitness without pain.
Drinking water right before exercising can cause stomach cramps.	Drinking water does not cause stomach cramps; dehydration does and drinking water before and during exercise prevents dehydration.
When you stop working out, your muscle will turn to fat.	It is impossible for muscle to turn into fat because muscle and fat are two different kinds of tissue.
There is no such thing as exercising too much.	Too much exercise can be unhealthy. Make sure that exercise is part of your life, but don't let it dominate every thought. Believe it or not, people have become addicted to exercise.
You can't be too thin.	Being underweight is possible, and can be very dangerous. If you do think you need to lose weight, set limits for yourself. Remember that you're dieting and exercising for your health. Overdoing either one can defeat this purpose.

(FIGURE 3-1)
Not everything you hear about exercise is true. Here are some examples of some popular but untrue statements.

Demonstration
Exercise and Your Lungs

Give students a new balloon to blow up. Most will find that at first the balloon resists being blown up. After several attempts, blowing up the balloon becomes very easy. Ask students to compare a new balloon with the lungs of someone who seldom exercises. Have them compare the lungs of someone who exercises regularly with the balloons that were blown up again

and again. (Both are more elastic.) Lung volume increases with exercise, and oxygen is transferred into the body more efficiently.

 Journal 3A
Coping With the Blues

Have students write in their Journal what they usually do to try to get over a bad mood or feeling sad. Ask them to describe how successful their method is and how long it usually takes to work.

 Cooperative Learning
Dealing With Stress

Present the following scenario to the class: On the afternoon before a final exam, a student has a big argument with a close friend. The student is so upset by the disagreement that he or she can't concentrate on studying. Divide the class into small groups. Have group members discuss how the upset person could calm down and regain

Background

Endorphins and Exercise

Endorphins are neuropeptides that seem to regulate emotional responses. They have pain-killing properties similar to morphine. Intense exercise induces the brain to increase its release of endorphins into the bloodstream. When an activity uses 60 percent of the maximum possible intake of oxygen, it causes a significant elevation of endorphin levels. Researchers think that this release of endorphins may explain why people feel better when they exercise.

Review Answers

1. Answers will vary but may include any of the following: Physical benefits include long-term weight maintenance; increased strength and elasticity in the heart and the muscles of the lungs and blood vessels; reduced risk of heart attack, stroke, and high blood pressure; decreased likelihood of back problems; increased

endorphin:

a substance produced inside the brain that has pain-killing effects.

physical fitness:

the ability to perform daily tasks vigorously and to perform physical activities while avoiding diseases related to a lack of activity.

Mental Benefits Studies have shown that aerobic exercise helps people with emotional problems control their mood swings. So it makes some sense that doing physical activity can help everyone cope with everyday anxiety and occasional, mild forms of depression. Exercise is good for your mental well-being for several reasons. First of all, knowing that you are doing something healthy for your body is very satisfying. Second, studies show that exercise improves your mood. According to research, certain types of physical activity may cause your brain to manufacture hormones called **endorphins**, which are natural substances that make you feel good. Vigorous physical activity helps your body produce greater amounts of endorphins, which may be part of the reason why people who get exercise on a regular basis are often more emotionally stable and more confident than those who don't.

People who are physically fit also tend to be less nervous and less stressed. Exercise relaxes your muscles and eases anxiety, which not only helps you cope with tensions during the day but also lets you put them aside at night, when you're trying to sleep. This is one reason why people who exercise regularly sleep better than those who don't. Another is that they are more tired. Physical activity may give you more energy during the day, but it makes you more tired at the right time—at night. You'll learn more about sleep later on in this chapter.

What's Physical Fitness?

Ask a few experts what **"physical fitness"** means, and you may very well get a few different answers. Most experts do agree that people who are physically fit (1) perform their day-to-day tasks with energy and vigor and (2) can participate in a variety of physical activities. They can do these while staying relatively clear of diseases related to a lack of exercise. Physical fitness can be divided into four categories:

- aerobic fitness
- muscular strength and endurance
- flexibility
- body composition

Aerobic Fitness Aerobic fitness refers to your body's ability to endure 10 minutes or more of continuous exercise. These activities increase the heart rate and use large muscles in a steady and continuous motion. They range from activities such as swimming, walking, or jogging to team sports such as basketball and soccer.

Muscular Strength and Endurance Muscular strength refers to the amount of force you generate using your muscles. Muscular endurance is the amount of force you can generate repeatedly using your muscles for an extended period. Attempting to lift a 300-pound sofa alone requires tremendous muscular strength. Unloading one hundred, 50-pound bags of potatoes takes a great deal of muscular endurance. To develop muscular strength and endurance you need to do exercises that force the muscles to move against a force heavier than normal.

Flexibility Flexibility refers to your body's ability to use its major joints fully. Peak flexibility is achieved in the teen years, but as one ages, joints become stiff and lose their range of motion if they are not stretched regularly. Flexibility can improve performance, reduce the risk of injury, and make your daily activities easier and more enjoyable.

Body Composition Body composition refers to the proportion of fat and fat-free tissue, such as muscle and bone, in your body. This proportion changes as your eating and activity habits change. Aerobic activity can reduce body fat. Resistance training increases muscle mass and bone density.

• • • TEACH continued

his or her concentration. Students should emphasize what they have learned about the mental benefits of exercise. Have each small group pick one of their suggestions to role-play for the entire class.

Journal 3B
What Is Physical Fitness?

Ask students to write in their Journal what they think physical fitness means. Have them list any categories that they think physical fitness would include.

 Teaching Transparency 3A
Ideal Body Composition for Adolescents

Use this transparency to discuss how exercise affects body composition. Ask: **If a teenager's percentage of body fat were above the ideal, how would regular participation in an aerobic activity change it?** [It would reduce the percentage of body fat.]

Game
Name the Category

Try this game after students have read about the four categories of physical fitness. Divide the class into groups and provide each group with a stack of cards. On each card list one of the four categories of physical fitness or an activity that helps a person achieve a particular category of physical fitness. Each team member selects a card. If the card has the name of a category, the player must name an activity that achieves that category of fitness. If the

Another way to think of physical fitness is to consider it in terms of your own needs and goals. If you are in good physical condition, you should be able to perform your everyday tasks without getting too tired to function. If you find that, like Christine, you're yawning at your desk a lot, you have trouble relaxing, and even low levels of exertion exhaust you, your physical fitness level may be lower than it should be. What about mood swings? Do you get depressed or anxious easily? These may also be symptoms of a lack of physical fitness, and they can disappear quickly if treated with a program of regular exercise.

Physical Fitness and Physical Disabilities

Have you ever tried pushing yourself in a wheelchair for 26 miles? Or sprinting for 100 meters with one real leg? How about pitching to major-league hitters when you have only one hand? Chances are you haven't. But think for a moment of how difficult these activities are, and then ask yourself: Can having a physical disability prevent a person from being physically fit?

Sharon Hedrick, Dennis Oehler, and Jim Abbott know the answer to that question. Hedrick, a paraplegic, used tremendous arm and shoulder strength to push her wheelchair to victory in an exhibition marathon race at the 1988 Olympics in Seoul, South Korea. Oehler, who lost his right leg in an automobile accident, wears a prosthesis, or an artificial leg. His time of 12.01 seconds in the 100-meter dash is a world record for athletes with disabilities, and is only 2 seconds slower than that of two-time Olympic champion Carl Lewis, who has two legs. Being born without a right hand did not stop Abbott, who is able both to throw and catch with his left hand, from winning 18 games for the California Angels in 1991.

(FIGURE 3-2) **Jim Abbott (left), who is missing a right hand, is a major-league pitcher. Paraplegic Sharon Hedrick (right) is a champion wheelchair marathoner.**

Of course, you don't have to perform athletic miracles in order to be in good physical condition. Most people who are physically fit could not win 18 games in the Major Leagues, but they do know how to keep themselves healthy. And just as physical disabilities do not stop world-class athletes from achieving greatness, they do not block people who want to be in good physical condition from doing so. Most important, the state of wellness—of being physically, emotionally, and spiritually healthy—is a realistic, reachable goal every person is capable of achieving. People with physical disabilities have as much chance as anyone does of leading long, full, healthy, and happy lives.

Review

1. Name two physical benefits and two mental benefits of exercise.

2. What are the four categories of physical fitness?

3. **Critical Thinking** Why is it important to be physically fit?

Answer to Question 1 begins on p. 42.

bone density and reduced risk of osteoporosis; increased strength of the immune system; increased strength of the digestion and excretory systems; increased endurance and flexibility; reduction of body fat; increased energy; and possible reduction of the risk of cancer. Mental benefits include the ability to cope better with stress and anxiety; better control over mood swings; improvement of overall mood; increased level of emotional stability; increased confidence; and more restful sleep.

2. aerobic fitness, muscular strength and endurance, flexibility, body composition

3. Answers will vary. Accept any answer that shows an understanding of the benefits of being physically fit. Answers may include that being physically fit improves overall physical health, helps control weight, improves mental health and well-being, helps control stress and anxieties, increases energy levels during the day, and enables one to sleep better at night.

---

card has the name of an activity, the player must name the category of physical fitness the activity will foster.

Extension
Promoting Physical Fitness in Gym

Encourage students to discuss with their physical education teacher what activities he or she uses in class to promote proficiency in each of the four categories of physical fitness.

ASSESS

Section Review

Have students answer the Section Review questions.

Alternative Assessment
Why Be Fit?

Ask students to explain in their own words what it means to be physically fit. Have them list the disadvantages of being unfit.

Closure
Giving Yourself Good Advice

Have students write letters to themselves from the point of view of a friend who wants to encourage them to join a fitness group. Tell them the letters should include advice on how they could become more physically fit.

Section Review Worksheet 3.2

To reinforce the concepts presented in this section, assign Section Review Worksheet 3.2.

 Section Quiz 3.2

Have students take Section Quiz 3.2.

Reteaching Worksheet 3.2

Students who have difficulty with the material may complete Reteaching Worksheet 3.2.

aerobic fitness:

the ability to endure at least 10 minutes of moderate activity.

Section 3.2 — How Physically Fit Are You?

Objectives

■ *Know the ways to test physical fitness.*

■ **LIFE SKILLS: Assessing Your Health**

Before you plan an exercise program or a program to increase your physical activity, assess your current fitness level. The following are some simple tests you can do to determine your current level of fitness.

Aerobic Fitness Level

Before you begin you will need to know how to take your pulse. Place the middle and index fingers of your right hand on your left wrist, just below the base of your thumb.

Can you feel your pulse? Using a second hand on a watch, count the beats for 10 seconds. Now you are ready to begin the test. Time yourself running or walking a mile as quickly as you can. As soon as you finish the mile, check your pulse for 10 seconds. Now multiply that number by six to determine your beats per minute. A rate between 100 and 140 means you are reasonably fit. Then check your time against Figure 3-3 to see where it falls.

Muscular Strength and Endurance Level

Lie on your back with your knees bent and your feet flat on the floor as shown in Figure 3-5. Cross your arms over your chest and rest your hands on your shoulders. Exhale as you tuck your chin toward your chest, curling your torso until your shoulder blades leave the floor. Inhale as you return

	Aerobic Fitness Standards: One-Mile Walk or Run	
The times below define a low level of fitness. If your time is slower for the mile, use the time shown as your first goal when you begin your program.		
Age	**Minimum Standards for Boys**	**Minimum Standards for Girls**
12	10 minutes	11 minutes, 35 seconds
13	8 minutes, 35 seconds	11 minutes
14–16	8 minutes, 10 seconds	12 minutes
17–19	8 minutes, 30 seconds	11 minutes, 30 seconds

(FIGURE 3-3) **If your times are faster than the ones shown in the table by a minute or more, your fitness level is moderate to high.**

Section 3.2 Lesson Plan

MOTIVATE

Journal 3C
Getting Started

Encourage students to write in their Journal their feelings about becoming involved in a physical-fitness program. If they have reservations about starting one, have them think of some ways to get past those feelings.

 44 PHYSICAL FITNESS

TEACH

Demonstration
Taking Your Pulse

Explain that the pulse is a throbbing of the arteries caused by the contractions of the heart. Have students sit still and find their pulse by placing three fingers on their wrist. Have students record the number of beats that they counted in 30 seconds. They should multiply the result by two to find their heart rate per minute. Then have

students jog in place for two minutes and take their pulse again while still standing. (Students should walk slowly around the room for a minute before sitting down.) Compare the two pulse rates. Ask students why they think that their heart rate changed as their exercise level changed. *(When the students increased their body activity, their cells needed more oxygen. The heart began to pump blood faster so that more oxygen could be delivered to the body's cells.)*

(FIGURE 3-4) **In order to test your muscular strength and endurance, see how many curl-ups you can complete in one minute.**

your shoulder blades to the floor, completing one curl-up in about 3 seconds. To be fit, girls should complete 33 to 35 curl-ups, boys between 40 and 44, in one minute.

To test your upper body, perform a pull-up test, using a horizontal bar that is high enough so that your feet don't touch the floor once you're up. Keep your arms and legs straight, and grasp the bar, palms facing away from you. Using your arms, raise your body until your chin is above the bar. Girls should be able to do one pull-up, and boys three to five, without stopping.

Flexibility Level

To test lower back and hamstring **flexibility,** sit on the floor as shown in Figure 3-5. Bend forward from your hips, and reach your arms forward without straining. Do this slowly several times, until you feel stretched. Repeat the reach and measure your distance. If you're flexible, you'll be able to reach between 1 and 4 inches past your feet.

Body Composition

Grasp a fold of skin from your abdomen with your thumb and forefinger. Now grasp the flesh on the back of your upper

(FIGURE 3-5) **The more flexible you are, the farther you can reach your arms beyond your feet in this ''box test.''**

arm, your thigh, and the back of your lower leg. If you can pinch more than an inch in any of these areas, consider changing your diet and increasing your physical activity.

Review • • • • •

1. ▦ *LIFE SKILLS: Assessing Your Health* What are four ways to test physical fitness?

2. *What areas of fitness do you need to improve?*

3. *Critical Thinking* Why is it a good idea to test your level of physical fitness before you begin an exercise program?

flexibility:

the ability to move muscles and joints through their full range of motion.

Review Answers

1. Aerobic—check the time it takes you to run or walk one mile; muscular strength and endurance— see how many curl-ups you can complete in one minute and how many pull-ups you can do without stopping; flexibility— see how far you can reach your arms beyond your feet in the box test; body composition— check to see if you can pinch more than an inch in the pinch-an-inch test.

2. Answers will vary according to each individual student's level of fitness.

3. Answers will vary. Accept any reasonable answer. Answers may include that by knowing your level of fitness you will know at what level to start and how to better structure an exercise program to improve the areas of weakness.

👥 Cooperative Learning
Test Yourself

Test for muscular endurance: Have volunteers demonstrate the proper method for doing the bent-knee curl-up. Let students work in pairs to test themselves on their muscular endurance. Have them record their number of curl-ups in their Journal.

Test for flexibility: Have volunteers demonstrate the test, and then allow students to work in pairs. Have them record in their Journal the number of inches they can reach.

Test for body composition: Have students do this test on themselves.

Extension
Your Mental Outlook

Invite a fitness instructor to speak about exercise and its relationship to one's appearance and mental outlook.

ASSESS

Section Review

Have students answer the Section Review questions.

Alternative Assessment
What's Wrong With Sitting Still?

Ask students to write an article titled "Inactivity Is Hazardous to Your Health" for the school newspaper.

✎ Closure–Journal 3D
Setting Goals

Ask students to write in their Journal their feelings about their own physical fitness and how they think they can improve their fitness level.

Section
3.3
About Exercise

Background

Health Effects of Aerobic Exercises

Over the last 25 years, health professionals have learned a lot about the positive health effects of regular aerobic exercise. It serves both as a preventative measure and as a treatment for many diseases and disorders. Most important, it can lower serum cholesterol levels, lower blood pressure, help keep arterial walls limber, and perhaps even help the body use insulin more effectively. Regular aerobic exercise can change body composition by reducing fat, especially in the abdominal region. It is this fat that seems to be the most closely linked to an increased risk of heart disease and diabetes.

While not everyone has the same aerobic potential, everyone can benefit from aerobic exercise and work toward meeting his or her potential. Emphasize that students should choose an exercise that they enjoy and that challenges the heart and lungs moderately.

Objectives

- *Know the difference between aerobic and anaerobic exercise.*
- *Name three examples of aerobic exercise.*
- *Name three effects of steroid abuse.*
- *Know what to do to avoid basic injuries.*
- *Know the range of your target heart rate.*

■ **LIFE SKILLS: Assessing Your Health**

aerobic exercise:

physical activity that increases the supply of oxygen to the muscles, and that can be continued for a period of time without resting.

You have just found out that physical fitness is divided into four categories. You should also know that exercise has different subsets as well:

- aerobic exercises are physical activities that continue for more than 10 minutes.
- anaerobic exercises are intense, all-out actions that last from a few seconds to a few minutes.

Aerobic Exercises

Aerobic exercises are the most important, most healthy things you can do for your body. Every time you run, walk, bike, or do any kind of aerobic activity for an extended amount of time, you breathe rapidly and your heartbeat temporarily increases. When this happens your lungs transfer more oxygen to your bloodstream. But most important, aerobic activity lowers your heart rate and helps your respiratory and cir-

culatory systems stay healthy. For these reasons, you should make sure you include at least one of the following aerobic exercises in your exercise schedule, no matter what your ultimate physical fitness goal is.

Walking Walking can be aerobic when it is brisk and raises your heart rate into your training zone. Slower-paced walking can also be aerobic if you carry three- or four-pound hand weights or a five-pound pack, or if you walk hills or stairs. Aerobic walking causes you to breathe harder and sweat, and it can stimulate endorphins and raise

■ (FIGURE 3-6) **Walking for an hour or so is a good way to exercise your muscles and relax your mind.**

Section 3.3 Lesson Plan

MOTIVATE

Class Discussion
Benefits of Aerobic Exercise

Write on the chalkboard, "Aerobic exercise is one of the most healthful things you can do for your body." Make a fish-bone map to record the reasons students offer to explain why this statement is true.

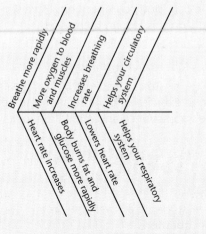

TEACH

Role-Playing
Convincing a Friend

Have students role-play a situation in which one student hates to do aerobic exercise. A friend tries to convince the reluctant student of the need to do aerobic exercise, perhaps linking some of the student's problems in school or at home to a lack of exercise. The friend should think of ways to coax the student to change his or her attitude toward exercise.

SECTION 3.3

your mood. Because its impact on the bones and joints is low, walking is a great way to begin a fitness program if you are trying to lose weight. Walking alone or with a friend can also give you a chance to catch up on your day, unwind, and relax.

Running Running is harder to do than walking, but you may find that the things it can do for you make the extra effort worthwhile. Studies show that running causes your brain to produce endorphins, and it burns calories at a faster pace than walking does. In addition, running causes you to breathe more rapidly, which, as you learned earlier, allows more oxygen into your system. This extra effort eventually increases your lung capacity. If you find that you're breathing very heavily after you've run a mile today, try running the same distance three times a week for a month. At that point you may very well laugh when you think about how tired and breathless it once made you.

Swimming and Biking Swimming and biking can give you the same benefits as running, but they may not be as convenient, because they require equipment that can be expensive. If you have a bike, you may find that you prefer cycling to running, or that it provides a good change of pace. Swimming is an excellent aerobic activity because it exercises not only your legs but also your arms and torso. If your school doesn't have a pool, try calling your neighborhood YMCA. These organizations often have good pools (as well as other exercise programs at a fair price).

Aerobic Exercise to Music Aerobic exercise to music can be an enjoyable way to increase your physical activity. In an aerobic class you use your entire body, which provides the same aerobic benefits as swimming or basketball. There are some important questions to consider before join-

(FIGURE 3-7) **Aerobic exercise to music is a great workout for just about every muscle in the body. If you want to do this type of exercise, make sure you find a class that is on the right level for you.**

ing a class. What kind of class is best suited to my fitness level? Should I select a class that is high, mixed, or low impact? What are the qualifications of the instructor? Is it someone who is well educated about aerobic exercise? Is the facility set up to accommodate aerobics classes? Answers to these questions can help you select the aerobics class that is best for you.

You can also get a good aerobics workout to music using a videotape at home. If you decide to purchase an aerobics exercise tape, be sure to do some research on the tapes available. Tapes made by celebrities may not provide the best kind of instruction or workout. Fitness magazines will often provide ratings of aerobics tapes that you can use to select the tape that is best for you.

Team Sports Team sports such as basketball, hockey, and soccer can give you many of the same benefits as other aerobic exercise, and they can become great social events, because they are activities you can do with friends. If you like playing team sports more than any of your friends do, find out if your neighborhood has pickup games

Journal 3E
Choosing an Exercise

Have students write in their Journal the aerobic exercises covered in the text that they would select for their exercise program. Tell them to explain why they think these exercises would work best for them. Have them include what they dislike about exercise.

Cooperative Learning
Favorite Forms of Exercise

Have students work in groups to survey the types of aerobic exercise enjoyed by members of the group. Along with stating the exercise of their choice, students should also explain why they find the exercise worthwhile. Each group should record its findings. Then have the groups share their data with the rest of the class by means of a class exercise preference chart. Ask

students to discuss whether knowing the preferences of their peers will influence their selection of one form of exercise over another.

ABOUT EXERCISE 47

Making a Choice 3A

Assign the Reasons for Exercising card. The card asks students to work in groups to brainstorm for excuses they have heard for not exercising and then to come up with ways to overcome obstacles to exercise.

Making a Choice 3B

Assign the Sports Safety card. The card asks the students to list safety rules to follow when participating in various sports and to recognize high-injury sports.

(FIGURE 3-8) **Anaerobic exercises develop speed and muscular strength.**

any activity enjoyable if you know some basic rules of fitness training.

Make Sure You Exercise Often Enough, Long Enough, and at the Right Intensity When you start a fitness program, you'll want to start slowly. Avoid doing too much, too soon. Once you're on your way, you'll need to progress gradually, doing more only as you become stronger and more fit.

Aerobic fitness requires intense activity at least three times per week. **Intensity** is the term used to describe how hard you're working. What is the intensity that is suited to you? The Life Skills feature on page 49 will help you answer that question as it relates to your aerobic training. You can monitor your heart rate as an estimate of intensity. When your heart rate falls within your target heart rate range, you are exercising at the proper intensity. If your heart rate is too low, you'll need to change something about your workout. Taking bigger steps, adding jumps, lifting your knees higher, moving your arms more, or increasing your speed will raise your heart rate. If your heart rate is too high, you'll need to lower the intensity. Shorten your stride, stop using your arms, slow down—all will lower intensity. When the intensity of your program is correct, you'll be perspiring slightly but you'll also be able to carry on a conversation. If you cannot pass this "can you talk" guideline, your intensity is too high. Likewise, if you're tired for more than an hour after your workout, your activity was too intense.

How long is long enough? A minimum of 20–30 minutes per day is recommended. You can do all of your aerobic work at once or split it into segments that are each 10 minutes or longer.

you can join. You may also want to call the YMCA in your neighborhood, which may be able to set you up with a team that matches your skills and ability.

anaerobic exercise:

physical activity that increases speed and muscular strength, and that cannot be continued for a few minutes without stopping.

Anaerobic Exercises

Because **anaerobic exercises** take so much immediate energy and effort, they make you breathe even more rapidly than aerobic activities. This type of exercise does not necessarily help the body's respiratory and circulatory systems, and it does not burn calories as effectively as aerobic exercises do. Anaerobic exercise will improve your speed and muscular strength. Sprinting, weight lifting, and gymnastics are three examples of anaerobic activities.

Some Basic Rules

When you like an activity, it is automatically enjoyable. But you can make almost

---

• • • TEACH continued

Class Discussion
Benefits of a Brisk Walk

Ask: **What are the physical benefits of aerobic exercise?** *[Helps control weight, helps your respiratory and circulatory systems stay healthy, lowers blood pressure and heart rate]* Have students discuss the mental and social benefits of aerobic exercise. Tell them to recall the effect of a long, brisk walk, alone or with a friend.

Journal 3F
Feelings About Sports

Have students use their Journal to describe their feelings about playing sports. Ask them to write both their positive and negative feelings.

Writing
Someone to Admire

Have students write a paragraph describing someone who is their ideal in the area of physical fitness. Tell them

the person does not have to be a sports figure or a well-known person. The person may be someone their own age who is concerned about physical fitness, or it may be a friend or family member.

Determining Your Target Heart Rate Range . . . . .

In order to find out your target heart rate range, you must know your maximum heart rate (MHR), which is the fastest your heart can possibly beat. If you happened to take your pulse the last time physical activity left you so worn-out that your heart pounded and you were completely breathless, you may know what your MHR is. If you didn't, you can find out your MHR by subtracting your age from 220.

Your target heart rate, or the pace you want your heart to beat when you exercise, should be between 60 percent and 80 percent of your maximum heart rate. In order to find your target heart rate range, multiply your MHR first by .6 to determine the lower end of the range, and then by .8 to determine the upper end of the range.

You can find your MHR and your target heart rate range by checking this chart:

Age	Maximum Heart Rate	Target Heart Rate Range
13	207	124-166
14	206	123-165
15	205	123-164
16	204	122-163
17	203	122-162
18	202	121-162

Life SKILLS

Have students practice finding their maximum heart rate and their target heart rate range. Tell them to follow the steps and perform the calculations in order to figure out these rates even when they do not have a chart available. Give each student an index card on which to record the information they need. Tell them to exercise and check their heart rate following the exercise, some time before the next class period.

Class Discussion
Aerobic vs. Anaerobic Exercise

Ask students to explain the difference between aerobic and anaerobic exercises. Ask for examples of both kinds of exercise. Encourage students to suggest characteristics or effects of each type of exercise through a series of questions such as the following: What effect does aerobic exercise have on the circulatory and respiratory systems? What effect does anaerobic exercise have on these systems?

Remind students that the value of aerobic exercise is that it can be continued for longer periods of time, providing the exerciser with enhanced respiratory and cardiovascular activity.

Journal 3G
Measuring Your Heart Rate

Have students write in their Journal how their exercising heart rate compares with the range in the Life Skills feature. Tell them to compare rates again after they have been exercising for some time.

Class Discussion
Frequency, Intensity, and Time

Write the letters F, I, and T on the chalkboard. Ask students what the initials stand for. Remind them that frequency, intensity, and time are important parts of their exercise program. Ask why warming up and cooling down are important in any exercise program.

Background
Reasons for Warming Up and Cooling Down

Warm-up involves a general body warming plus a specific warming related to the skills to be performed in a particular exercise. Studies show that proper warm-up lessens the possibility of injury because the process stretches and lengthens the muscles, putting less tension on any one part of the muscle. No more than 15 minutes should elapse between warm-up and the aerobic exercise. Cooling down properly decreases lactic acid levels in the blood and muscles. Lactic acid is a product of metabolism and results from the incomplete breakdown of sugar in the muscle cells. A buildup of lactic acid causes the muscles to feel tired and sore.

A good way to remember all this information is to think of the word FIT:

- F stands for frequency, which should be three to four times per week.
- I stands for intensity, which should be at or slightly above your target heart rate.
- T stands for time, which should be at least 30 minutes of continuous exercise.

Warm Up and Cool Down Every athlete talks about how important it is to warm up before doing any strenuous physical activity. It is a good rule of thumb to spend a few minutes walking or jogging, and then do some mild stretching to warm up your muscles and raise your body temperature before you begin exercising.

It's also important to cool down *after* you finish exercising. If you don't, you may get dizzy or feel nauseated, and your muscles can become sore and cramped. Don't stop moving immediately after a strenuous exercise. Slow down, but continue walking or moving for another five minutes or so, to cool down your muscles in the same way that you warmed them up.

Start Slowly No matter how impatient you are to get your body into top physical shape, don't begin your exercise program by doing too much too soon. If your goal is to run 5 miles without stopping, but you haven't run in a while, pushing yourself beyond your current limitations can hurt you both physically and mentally. You may find yourself nursing cramped muscles, struggling for breath, and figuring that you would rather do just about anything rather than set foot on a track again.

Here's another example. Let's say you're in a weight-training program, and your goal is to lift a certain amount of weight that seems impossibly heavy right now. The best way to reach your goal is to choose a program that forces you to lift

slightly more weight each workout. This is called using the progressive resistance principle, and it can and should be used in any type of exercise program you choose.

Vary Your Workout Just as you can get sick of hearing your favorite song too often, doing one exercise all the time can become boring. It can also injure your muscular and skeletal systems. Try to include a variety of aerobic exercises—called cross training—in your schedule. If you run one day, cycle another, and play tennis a third, you can both cut down on your chances of injury and keep yourself interested in each activity. This will help you receive the full benefit from each workout.

In addition, place some limits on the amount of exercise you do each week. Don't exercise intensely more than three or four times a week, and try to arrange your schedule so that you have a day to rest between each workout.

Avoiding Injuries

Even if you follow every exercise rule perfectly, you still run a small risk of injury when you exercise. The more physically fit you are, the lower this risk will be. But to be on the safe side, even if you are in terrific physical condition (and especially if you're not), read the following suggestions carefully and follow basic safety rules so you can keep your chances of getting hurt at a minimum.

Listen to Your Body Signals Make sure you pay close attention to the way your body is feeling. Minor aches and breathlessness are a normal part of exercise, but anything more serious than that—a sharp pain, for instance—probably means something is wrong and should not be ignored.

Even when everything seems fine, take time after each workout to let your body analyze things for you. Are you sweating?

• • • TEACH continued

Journal 3H
Changing Ideas

Have students write in their Journal whether their ideas about exercising have changed while reading this chapter. If they have changed, tell them to explain why this happened. If their ideas about exercising have not changed, ask them to explain why.

• • • TEACH continues on p. 52

If you're not, the workout was probably too light. If you're out of breath, are you still that way after 10 minutes of rest? If so, you may have exercised too hard. Of course it's normal to feel tired after exercising, but exhaustion that lasts for more than 24 hours is definitely a signal of some sort. Do you feel nauseated or dizzy? Next time you exercise, wait two minutes after the end of your workout, and then check your heart rate. If your pulse is more than five beats quicker than the upper limit of your target heartbeat range—and especially if you are experiencing these other symptoms as well—you must lighten your workouts.

When you're feeling ill, don't make things worse by exercising. It won't make you feel any less sick, and you'll be much better off if you rest instead. When you're completely well again, work out lightly for a few days before returning to your full exercise schedule, just to be on the safe side.

Dress for the Weather Don't let the fact that exercise increases your body temperature fool you into thinking that it's perfectly fine to exercise outdoors on extremely cold days without dressing properly. The best thing you can do when it's freezing outside is to exercise indoors. If you do insist on being outside, make sure you're dressed for it. Put on two or three layers of clothing instead of one heavy outfit. Wear a hat to keep your head warm, and make sure your ears, fingers, nose, and toes are covered properly. Keep your clothing as dry as possible, and take extra time warming up before you begin your workout.

Be even more careful on hot, humid days. Again, you're best off staying in a cool gymnasium when the weather's hitting 90 degrees, but if you do go out, wear light-colored, lightweight clothing. Never wear rubberized suits or try to lose weight by sweating. This could seriously overheat your body. Most important, drink lots of water before, during, and after your workouts. The water will keep you from becoming dehydrated, and it will help you sweat so you can stay cooler.

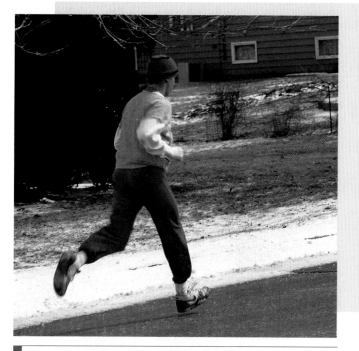

(FIGURE 3-9) **When you exercise in the cold, layer your garments. For the first layer, use a garment that draws (wicks) moisture from your skin. For the second layer, use a garment that absorbs the moisture. Add other layers as needed.**

Don't Be Just a Weekend Exerciser
It's always easier to find time to exercise on a Saturday or Sunday than it is during the week, especially during the school year. Unfortunately, exercising only on the weekends can be risky. People who rely on weekend activity to improve their aerobic fitness can overdo it, and they often find themselves nursing sprained ankles and sore knees after they have burned up the tennis court or running track. In addition, exercising only once a week will do little for your overall fitness level.

Background
Treating Injuries
Continuous application of a cold pack on an injured part of the body can cause tissue damage. To avoid this, an ice pack should be applied for 20 minutes every hour for a period of 1 to 72 hours, depending on the extent of the injury. Compression on an injured part decreases swelling and avoids hemorrhage.

Section Review Worksheet 3.3

To reinforce the concepts presented in this section, assign Section Review Worksheet 3.3.

Section Quiz 3.3

Have students take Section Quiz 3.3.

Reteaching Worksheet 3.3

Students who have difficulty with the material may complete Reteaching Worksheet 3.3.

If you can exercise only on weekends, make sure that you warm up thoroughly before each activity and that you take frequent breaks. If at all possible, try to find time for a short workout at least once during the week. By following these suggestions, you will make your weekend sports routine less hazardous to your health.

anabolic steroid:

an artificially made, complex substance that can temporarily increase muscle size.

How to Treat Basic Injuries

No matter how careful you are, accidents and injuries can happen. In case one happens to you, keep in mind the five simple actions—known as PRICE—involved in the emergency treatment of injuries:

(FIGURE 3-10) **If you think you've seriously injured yourself exercising, seek medical attention immediately.**

- P (physician): decide whether you need to see a doctor immediately, or whether it's safe to wait a few days.
- R (rest): stop exercising immediately, and stay off the body part you've injured. If you've hurt a leg, ankle, or foot, use crutches if you have them.
- I (ice): to keep swelling to a minimum, put ice on your injury as soon as possible.
- C (compression): wrapping a towel or bandage firmly around the ice also helps limit swelling.
- E (elevation): keep your injured limb raised above your heart level. This will drain extra fluid from the injury.

If you decide that you're not hurt badly enough to see a doctor—and make this decision very carefully—begin treating your injury as soon as you can. Apply ice, in periods of 15 to 20 minutes, until the swelling goes down. At that point, remove the ice and use moist-heat compresses instead. Once swelling has disappeared, pain is gone, and your range of motion is restored, you can usually start exercising again in four or five days. Be very careful when you do this—take extra care to follow the basic safety rules. You don't want to reinjure yourself and start the treatment process all over again.

Anabolic Steroids

Even if you're not a big sports fan, you may remember Canadian runner Ben Johnson, who was stripped of his gold medal after breaking the Olympic and World records in the 100-meter dash at the 1988 Olympics. Johnson, it turned out, had taken **anabolic steroids**, an illegal drug some athletes use to make them stronger and faster.

Steroids, which are made from a hormone called testosterone, do have some medical value. Doctors prescribe them to treat people with a blood condition called anemia, to help patients recovering from

---

Cooperative Learning
Getting the Word Out

Have students form small groups to advertise one of the basic rules of exercising. The groups may advertise by means of a poster, a slogan, a rap song, or any other method that would convey their message. Encourage students to be creative and to include reasons for the rule in their advertise-

ments. Let them share their advertisements in class.

Debate the Issue
Testing for Steroids

Let students debate the topic: Should student athletes be tested for steroids? Tell students to research the dangers of steroids and the violations that have been uncovered in the past. The teams should prepare arguments for their side of the debate. Remind them that for the sake of debate they can defend a position in which they do not be-

lieve. After presentations and rebuttals, the audience can question the debaters.

Extension
Interview

Suggest that students research one type of aerobic exercise—such as swimming, cycling, running, walking, or aerobic dancing—to determine how the time or distance covered in each exercise session should be increased over a period of several weeks. Students may wish to interview a coach to see how he or she increases player workouts.

surgery, and also to replace a missing hormone in people who have not grown properly. But steroids have also become very popular illegal drugs, because they can increase muscle size and body weight. Famous athletes are not the only ones known to use steroids—thousands of high school students have taken them as well.

Not only are steroids illegal, but they're also very dangerous. They can cause high blood pressure, liver damage, cancer, damage to the reproductive system, and facial deformities, as well as violent behavior and other psychiatric problems.

It's not always easy to know if someone is taking steroids, but some common symptoms of this type of drug abuse include the following:

- noticeable change in muscle mass
- dramatic increase in ability to lift heavy weights
- aggressive behavior
- dramatic amounts of acne

It may seem as though steroids have their advantages. After all, they can make you stronger and faster without your having to work too hard. Even so, they're not worth the risk. A lot of the damage they cause may be permanent. Why ruin your life over some extra muscle? And anyway, depending on steroids to make you look good robs you of the pleasure of achievement. It doesn't count for much if you're strong just because you took a drug. Finally, you don't need steroids to make you stronger and faster. By combining weight training with a healthy diet and a program of regular aerobic exercise, you can help your body produce natural hormones to make your muscles grow. For additional information on gaining body weight, read the Gaining Weight Safely section in Chapter 5. For more information on steroid abuse, see Chapter 15.

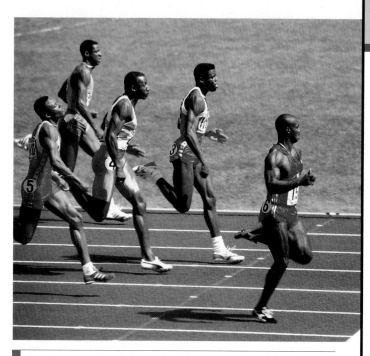

(FIGURE 3-11) **Ben Johnson (right) was stripped of his gold medal at the 1988 Olympic games when traces of anabolic steroids were found in his blood.**

eview

1. *Describe the difference between aerobic and anaerobic exercise.*

2. *Name two examples of aerobic exercises, and two examples of anaerobic exercise.*

3. **LIFE SKILLS: Assessing Your Health** *Your workouts are making you tired, and you wonder whether they may be too intense for you. What's a good way to find this out?*

4. *Critical Thinking Which is more important to overall physical fitness: aerobic exercise, or anaerobic exercise? Why?*

For more information on how to gain weight safely, see Chapter 5.

Anabolic Steroids are also discussed in Chapter 15.

SECTION 3.3

Review Answers

1. Aerobic exercises are physical activities that continue for more than 10 minutes. Anaerobic exercises are intensive actions that last no more than a few minutes.

2. Accept any correct answer. Examples of aerobic exercises include walking, running, cycling, swimming, and team sports. Examples of anaerobic exercises include sprinting, weight lifting, and gymnastics.

3. You could check your target heart rate.

4. Aerobic exercise is more important. Done often enough, long enough, and at the right intensity, it helps improve circulation, burns calories, produces energy, lowers blood pressure and heart rate, and increases your breathing rate. Aerobic exercise helps a person lose or control weight and helps a person's respiratory and circulatory systems stay healthy.

ASSESS

Section Review

Have students answer the Section Review questions.

Alternative Assessment
Defending Physical Education

Have students plan a mock school board meeting where the budget is being considered. Some board members are suggesting that the only way to balance the budget is to limit physical education classes. The physical education teacher has asked students and their parents to express their opinions before the school board. Have students meet in cooperative groups to plan their appeal to the school board. Let each group share their response with the class.

Closure
It Pays to Follow the Rules

Ask students why exercisers must follow the basic rules of exercise. *(To get the most out of exercising and to prevent injuries.)*

Background
The Need to Stay Active

The human body was made for physical activity and suffers when deprived of it. Just a few weeks of being confined to bed or to a wheelchair produces muscle atrophy, bone demineralization, and decreased aerobic capacity. People recovering from accidents or injuries, with the approval of their physicians, can participate in a limited exercise program. The same is true for people recovering from surgery. In the past, recovering patients were told to stay in bed. Now physicians know that recovery is faster when the body is somewhat active, and most people are encouraged to get up the day after their surgery. Because modern life is so sedentary, efforts must be made to meet the body's need for activity. Today more and more people are making time for regular exercise. Once they start an exercise program, many people wonder how they ever got along without one.

Section
3.4 Getting Started

Objectives

- Set your exercise goals.
- Design your own exercise schedule.

Now that you've read through all the rules and regulations of physical activity, not to mention the benefits of being physically fit, it's time to sit down and figure out what your exercise goals are. Then you can design a program that can help you meet them. Remember that your main ambition does not have to be to play basketball like Michael Jordan or tennis like Jennifer Capriati. It could be that you're looking to lose weight, or that you want to have more energy, or that you just want to stay healthy.

Your exercise schedule should reflect your personal goals, and may for that reason be very different from those of your close friends. That's why it's so important that you take plenty of time to design your own program.

Your Goals and How to Achieve Them

By now you most likely have some idea of what you want from your exercise program. In case you don't, here's a list and brief description of goals you may want to strive for. When you've decided what's best for you, look at Figure 3-13 to find out what type of exercises you should do.

Aerobic Fitness Earlier in this chapter you learned that when you are aerobically

(FIGURE 3-12) **Good exercise schedules leave time for some sort of physical activity every day of the week.**

Your Exercise Goals and How to Achieve Them

Goal	Type of Exercise	What to Do
Weight Loss	Aerobics	Four or more times a week, within your zone, 45–60 minutes
Better Health	Aerobics	Every other day, at 70–85% of your heart rate maximum, 30 minutes
Muscular Endurance and Good Body Composition	Resistance Training	Two or more times a week, 70–85% of the heaviest weight you can lift, 30 minutes maximum
Muscular Strength	Resistance Training	Three or more times a week, at 90% of the heaviest weight you can lift, enough to do 10 exercises and multiple sets eventually
Flexibility	Stretching	Each time you workout, 10 exercises, 3 reps each, hold each position 20 seconds or longer

(FIGURE 3-13) **Remember when you design your exercise program to keep your goals simple. Too much exercise too soon can do more harm than good.**

fit, not only is your body able to undergo 10 minutes or more of continuous exercise, but your circulatory system and respiratory system are working more efficiently. These health benefits are the most important part of physical fitness. Aerobic exercise is an important part of a total fitness program. Remember that if you start taking care of your circulatory and respiratory systems now, you can reduce your risk for disease.

Strength and Muscle Development
Muscles grow stronger and may increase in size through resistance training. Resistance training involves overcoming the resistance caused by the weight of another object or a force. Resistance can come from free weights, weight or hydraulic machines, rubberized resistance, or your body weight.

Your muscles will adapt to working with greater and greater resistance over time if you vary the following in your workout.

- load—the weight or force being overcome or moved
- repetitions—the number of times you repeatedly overcome the resistance without resting
- sets—groups of repetitions, separated by a rest period of 30 seconds to 3 minutes

Schedule" activity and indicate which goal or goals each type of exercise is appropriate for. Remind them that any exercise, even if it doesn't actually help them achieve a particular long-term goal, will contribute to their health and well-being.

Writing
Charting Exercise Goals

Encourage students to list their specific goals in one column and the type of exercise they will do to achieve their goals in a second column. Students should list how, and how often, they will do these exercises in a third column. They can base their table on the one in Figure 3-13.

• • • TEACH continues on p. 56

Background
Muscular Endurance

Muscular endurance involves the ability to contract the muscles repeatedly. After many repetitions, the muscle becomes tired and will not contract when a person wishes it to. An exercise program helps increase the possible number of contractions a muscle can make. The amount of force exerted in a single contraction indicates the strength of a muscle. Any muscle in the body becomes stronger with use.

Various Aerobic Activities and the Calories They Burn

Activity	Approximate Calories Burned (per minute)
Walking (3.75 miles per hour)	5
Badminton	6.6
Cycling (9.4 miles per hour)	6.8
Tennis (singles)	7.5
Swimming	8.3
Field Hockey	9.1
Basketball	9.4
Skiing	13
Handball	14.4
Ice Hockey	15.5
Walking Up Stairs	18
Running: 5.8 miles per hour	9.5
8.0 miles per hour	12.5
10.0 miles per hour	15
11.4 miles per hour	21.5
13.2 miles per hour	39

(FIGURE 3-14) **You have a wide range of choices in selecting aerobic activities that match your preferences and your schedule.**

Resistance training can increase strength, endurance, or both depending on how you change the three variables. Building strength requires that you use heavier loads (90% or more of your maximum) with fewer repetitions (1–5). Building endurance requires lighter loads (70–85% of your maximum) and higher repetitions (12–15). Building both strength and endurance requires 10–15 repetitions. A personal trainer or a physical educator can work with you to develop a program that will help you achieve your personal goals.

One set of muscles that deserves special attention is your abdominal muscles. (Actually there are four sets of abdominal muscles.) Strong abdominal muscles will protect your lower back from injury and support your internal organs. Figure 3-15 shows several beginning exercises for building abdominal strength and endurance.

Weight Control Exercise is a vital part of every weight-loss program. Consider the following facts.

- Exercise can decrease your appetite.
- Exercise burns calories.
- Exercise helps you lose fat without losing muscle.

You learned earlier that physical activity is the key to long-term weight management. Aerobic activities burn fat. Resistance exercises, which build stronger muscle and greater muscle mass, also play a part in weight control. When you increase your muscle mass with resistance exercises, you burn more calories during your workouts, and you'll also burn more calories when you're not active. As you lose fat, you can tighten and tone your muscles by regular, moderate resistance training. Just remember, though, that more is not always better. While exercise is healthful and a crucial part of reaching and maintaining a healthy weight, over-exercising can be dangerous.

• • • TEACH continued

Teaching Transparency 3C
Calories Burned

Have students review this transparency of the table found in Figure 3-14. Ask students which activities burn the fewest number of calories and which activities burn the greatest number of calories. Discuss which activities would be most helpful for someone interested in weight loss and a change in body composition.

Demonstration
Abdominal Exercises

Ask for student volunteers to demonstrate the exercises in Figure 3-15. Have students point out what a person has to bear in mind while doing the exercise in order to achieve the goal of that exercise. Ask: **Why is it important to develop the abdominal muscles?** *[Strong abdominal muscles will help protect the lower back from injury. They will*

also help support the internal organs, giving that "flat stomach" appearance.] **What can be achieved by exercising for weight control?** *[Exercise can decrease appetite, burn calories, and help you lose fat without losing muscle.]*

Journal 3J
Refining an Exercise Plan

Encourage students to write in their Journal the activities that they could realistically engage in on a regular basis and the number of calories burned by those activities in an hour.

• • • TEACH continues on p. 58

Life Skills
Worksheet 3A
Assign the Improving
Your Fitness Life Skills
Worksheet.

Reverse Curls

Lie on the floor with your arms by your sides. Knees are bent. Contract your lower abs to curl hips off the ground about 3 to 5 inches bringing knees towards chest. Slowly return to the floor. Do not ''whip'' your legs. Let the abs do the work. Remember to press your lower back into floor throughout the exercise.

Lower abdominal kips

Lie on the floor with your legs extended straight up toward the ceiling. Place your arms on the floor by your sides or extend them overhead. Inhale. Exhale as you push your heels toward the ceiling, tilting your pelvis upward while keeping your buttocks relaxed. Inhale as you lower your legs.

Bent knee curl-ups

Lie on the floor with your knees bent and your feet flat on the floor about one foot from your hips. Fold your arms across your chest or leave them by your sides. Exhale as you tuck the chin and curl the shoulder blades lifting them from the floor, toward your thighs. Inhale as you return to the floor.

Lying side bends

Lie on your side with your knees flexed and your thighs slightly forward. Fold the arm resting on the floor, across your chest. Extend your other arm along your side. Inhale. Exhale as you raise your shoulders off the floor and reach your extended arm toward your feet. Inhale as you return to the floor.

Feet high oblique curl

Lie on the floor with your legs supported on the seat of a chair or a high aerobic bench. Keep your thighs perpendicular to the floor. Place your hands so that your head rests on your fingertips. Inhale. Exhale, as you lift your right shoulder toward your left knee, while leaving the other shoulder on the floor. Inhale as you return to the floor and repeat the movement on the opposite side.

Feet high curl-ups

Lie on the floor with your legs supported on the seat of a chair or a high aerobic bench. Keep your thighs perpendicular to the floor. Fold your arms across your chest and inhale to begin. Exhale as you tuck the chin and curl the shoulder blades lifting them off the floor, toward the thighs. Inhale as you return to the floor.

(FIGURE 3-15) **These exercises can strengthen your abdominal muscles, but they can also cause injury if they are not done correctly. Check with your health or physical education teachers to be sure you are doing them correctly.**

Section Review Worksheet 3.4

To reinforce the concepts presented in this section, assign Section Review Worksheet 3.4.

Section Quiz 3.4

Have students take Section Quiz 3.4.

Reteaching Worksheet 3.4

Students who have difficulty with the material may complete Reteaching Worksheet 3.4.

Shoulder stretch
Hold onto an object about shoulder height. With hands on the support, relax and keep arms straight and chest moving downward, feet under hips, and knees slightly bent.

Hamstring (a)
While sitting down with knees slighty bent, reach foward from the hips until you feel a stretch in the back of your legs.

Hamstrings (b)
Keep only a slight bend in the front leg, with the other foot next to the inside of the leg. Bend forward at the hips until you feel slight pressure.

Hip
Lying on your back, relax and straighten both legs. Pull the left foot toward the chest. Repeat using the right foot.

Calf
Stand slightly away from a wall and lean forward with the lead leg bent and the rear leg extended. Move the hips forward with the heel of the straight leg on the ground until you feel a stretch in the calf.

Quadriceps
Stand on your left leg. Now bend your right leg at the knee, hold your ankle behind you, and pull upward slowly and gently until you feel a slight stretch in your thigh. Switch legs and repeat.

Archillies tendon and soleus
Bend the back knee slightly with the heel flat. Lean forward as in the calf stretch.

Groin (a)
With soles of the feet together, place hands around the feet and pull yourself forward.

Groin (b)
Move one leg forward until the knee is directly over the ankle. The back knee rests on the floor. Lean forward and hold.

(FIGURE 3-16) **Stretching exercises not only increase flexibility, but also decrease your chances of injury. Take time to stretch before doing any vigorous physical activity.**

• • • TEACH continued

Class Discussion
Stretching Exercises

Have students study the stretching exercises shown in Figure 3-16. You may want to have student volunteers demonstrate the exercises. Ask students to state the purpose of stretching exercises. Have them explain why these exercises prevent sports injuries.

Case Study
Physical Fitness and the Physically Impaired

Discuss the achievements of Sharon Hedrick, Dennis Oehler, and Jim Abbott, who were mentioned in Section 3.1. Call attention to the fact that these young athletes have won the respect of athletes and spectators alike. Discuss why physical fitness is important and possible for almost everyone.

Extension
Finding Resources

Suggest that students visit the library to select books or videos on physical fitness. Students who find interesting or helpful sources could share their findings by presenting a book talk or video talk to the class. The talk should include the item's full title and author, a brief overview of its contents, and a few statements about why the student found it helpful. Some students may prefer to tape their talks. If so, have those tapes available for free-time listening.

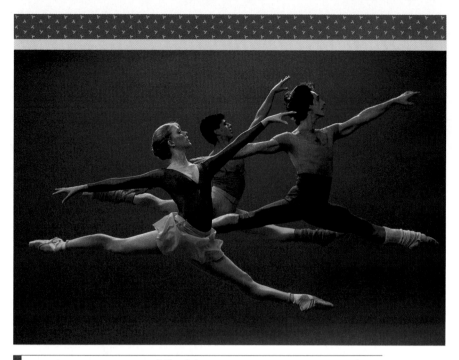

■ **(FIGURE 3-17) Having good flexibility is an important requirement for dancers and gymnasts.**

Increasing Flexibility Even if you are not a gymnast or a dancer, flexibility can still be a goal for you. Doing stretching exercises results in the kind of flexibility shown in Figure 3-17. Warming up and cooling down should be part of your regular exercise routine. Keep in mind that good flexibility helps prevent injuries. A good time to stretch the muscles you will be working is after your cardiovascular warm-up. Again after your aerobic segment, while your muscles are very warm and full of blood, stretch each in turn for 10–20 seconds.

Changing Body Composition

The most effective program for achieving healthy body composition includes adequate aerobic exercise and resistance training coupled with a balanced diet. Starving yourself or using steroids may give results in the short-term, but the long-term consequences are not worth the risks to your health. Regular physical activity and sensible eating habits make a long term plan for enhancing your health.

Review

1. *What are your exercise goals?*

2. *Write out a realistic exercise plan to achieve your goals.*

3. ***Critical Thinking*** *You and your friend want to work out together, but you have different exercise goals. How might this difference affect your plan and results?*

SECTION 3.4

Review Answers
1. Answers will vary but may include aerobic fitness, weight control, strength and muscle development, flexibility, and body composition.
2. Answers will vary. Accept any exercise schedule that shows an understanding of the relationship among exercise goals, type of exercise, and how often the exercise is performed.
3. Answers will vary. Accept responses that indicate that the friends can still do a portion of their workout together. This would include warm-ups, stretching, and probably some aerobic exercises.

ASSESS

Section Review
Have students answer the Section Review questions.

Alternative Assessment
Expectations for Exercise
Have students write a letter to a friend describing their physical exercise program and what they expect it will do for them. Perhaps they could encourage their friend to join them in becoming more physically fit.

Closure
Results of Planning
Have students sum up in a brief paragraph how they think planning a personal exercise program has changed their outlook about exercise.

Background
Sleep Deprivation

Recent research indicates that many Americans, particularly teenagers, suffer from chronic sleep deprivation. It is increasingly clear that lack of sufficient sleep is a common health risk. Some types of immune cells are less active when the body is sleep-deprived. Inadequate sleep is associated with an increased accident rate. In addition to these physical risks, sleep deprivation is associated with decreased job or school performance, moodiness, and a lessened ability to think creatively.

The number of hours of sleep a person needs varies from individual to individual; some people do fine with five hours a night, while others need eight to ten. It is known that teenagers and young adults need more sleep than preteens. How can someone tell if he or she suffers from mild sleep deprivation? Look for these signs: always needing an alarm to awaken; being sleepy even after a full night's sleep; and dosing off during class, at work, or when relaxed.

brain waves:

electrical patterns produced by the brain that fluctuate greatly during the sleep cycle.

Section 3.5
Sleep

Objectives

- *Know the two different categories of sleep.*
- *Describe what happens during each phase of the sleep cycle.*
- *Name two ways to cope with insomnia.*
- *Know how much sleep you need each night.*
  - **LIFE SKILLS: Solving Problems**

There is another aspect to physical fitness. No matter how strong, flexible, lean, and aerobically healthy you are, you're not going to feel or function well if you don't get enough sleep. Most high school students need about eight or nine hours of sleep, but you may find that you do fine with seven, or that you can't stay alert unless you've gotten ten. Whatever your personal requirements are, try to stick to them, because it is while you are asleep that your body recovers from the activities of the day that has just ended, and prepares itself for the new day ahead.

What Happens When You Sleep?

It may seem as though your body shuts off completely while you're asleep. This is not totally off the track, because your breathing and heart rate do slow down, and your blood pressure and body temperature drop slightly. But at the same time, your brain continues to recognize outside information,

so it remains about as active, in a different way, as it is when you're awake. It exhibits this activity in the form of **brain waves**, or electrical changes that take place in the brain. By studying these brain waves, scientists have been able to recognize the different stages of sleep, and what goes on in the brain during each phase.

The Sleep Cycle

Sleep can be divided into two categories. The first of these, called nonrapid eye movement sleep, or **NREM**, has four stages of its own. If you're like most teenagers, you spend only a short amount of time in stage I, which ends as soon as you have fallen asleep. When this happens, you enter stage II, in which your brain waves slow down. Those brain waves are at their slowest in stages III and IV, the phases of deepest sleep. Evidence indicates that the more you exercise, the more time you spend in stages

(FIGURE 3-18) **Your brain remains active and continues to process information when you are asleep.**

Section 3.5 Lesson Plan

MOTIVATE

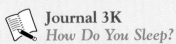
Journal 3K
How Do You Sleep?

This may be done as a warm-up activity. Have students use their Journal to write down the answers to these questions. How many hours of sleep do you generally get? How often do you have trouble sleeping at night?

TEACH

Cooperative Learning
How Much Sleep?

Divide the class into small groups, and have one member of each group be the reporter. Groups should record the number of hours of sleep their members usually get each day. Then have students discuss why they sometimes do not get enough sleep. Bring the class together, and use the sleep-per-

night figures to make a class histogram. Have reporters list common reasons for not getting enough sleep. See if groups have similar reasons. Have students draw conclusions from their findings.

Class Discussion
Sleep Stages

Review Figure 3-19, which shows the "Stages of Sleep." Point out that the sleeper goes from Stage I to Stage IV and back again before entering REM

III and IV. These stages are believed to be the phases at which the body does most of its resting and restoring. Even so, most people enter these stages only during the first half of the night.

As brain wave activity increases again, you pass back through the sleep stages. When you return to Stage I, you enter the second category of sleep—rapid eye movement, or **REM.** Your brain waves become similar to those of the waking state, and your eyes move back and forth rapidly. Most dreams occur during this time. Although you might not remember your dreams, researchers think that everyone dreams during REM sleep. During the course of your night's sleep, you will experience four or five sleep cycles. About a fourth of your total sleeping time will be REM sleep.

The function of sleep is poorly understood. What is known is that adequate sleep is essential to good health. Also, people who suffer from chronic lack of sleep are more prone to accidents.

Insomnia

Everyone has **insomnia,** or trouble sleeping, from time to time. You may find it hard to get to sleep when you've got a big exam the next day, for instance, or when you've eaten too much at dinner. Maybe it's hot outside, and you find your room stuffy even with the windows open. In general, these are temporary situations. When they disappear, your insomnia should too. But if you have had trouble sleeping over the course of a few months, it could be more serious.

Long-term insomnia can cause moodiness and concentration lapses. It can also wear down your immune system, making you more vulnerable to illness. If you have had trouble sleeping for a long period of time, it could be that you're not getting enough exercise. You know now that exer-

cise helps the sleeping process because it makes you more tired at the right time. If you are exercising regularly and still have trouble sleeping, you may want to see a doctor.

(FIGURE 3-19) **During a typical night you may pass through each stage of sleep four or five times.**

Tips for Sound Sleeping

If not everyone needs the same amount of sleep, how can you tell whether you're getting enough? You're the only one who can answer that question, so be honest about it. Recognize that you may need more sleep if you're feeling irritable, having trouble concentrating, or if you're just plain tired. It doesn't prove anything to stay up until 11:30 when you secretly felt like going to sleep at 10:00.

If you decide that you do need to get more sleep, or if you're suffering from insomnia, here are some ways to get back on track:

1. Keep a regular sleep schedule. Try to set a regular bedtime, so that you're "programmed" to get tired when it's time to turn in.
2. Go to bed when you're tired. It's pointless to stay up when you can't. If it's a little earlier than usual, enjoy the extra sleep you'll be getting.

REM:

(rapid eye movement) the dreaming part of the sleep cycle, in which the eyes move back and forth rapidly under the eyelids.

insomnia:

temporary or continuing loss of sleep.

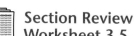

SECTION 3.5

Life Skills Worksheet 3B
Assign the Keeping a Sleep Journal Life Skills Worksheet.

Section Review Worksheet 3.5
To reinforce the concepts presented in this section, assign Section Review Worksheet 3.5.

Section Quiz 3.5
Have students take Section Quiz 3.5.

Reteaching Worksheet 3.5
Students who have difficulty with the material may complete Reteaching Worksheet 3.5.

sleep. Notice that in each successive cycle, the sleep phase is less deep and the REM phase is somewhat longer.

Journal 3L
Sleep Habits

Have students write in their Journal how they view their sleeping habits. How could they improve their sleeping habits? How would better sleep improve the quality of their lives?

Extension
Sleep Deprivation

Have students do research on sleep deprivation. Sometimes individuals are deprived of sleep for research. Sleep deprivation has also been used in brainwashing techniques. Have students find out why sleep deprivation can effectively be used in brainwashing.

Review Answers

1. NREM (nonrapid eye movement) and REM (rapid eye movement)

2. NREM: Stage I—ends when you have fallen asleep; Stage II—brain waves slow down; Stages III and IV—brain waves are at their slowest; this is the phase of deepest sleep when the body does most of its resting and restoring.
REM: brain waves similar to waking state; eyes move back and forth; dreams occur.

3. Answers will vary but may include: keep a regular sleep schedule, go to bed when you are tired, finish your exercise program at least three hours before bedtime, keep your room dark and quiet, don't lie in bed if you can't sleep, don't drink caffeine after about six at night, don't eat too late, don't rely on over-the-counter sleep medication.

4. Sample responses: I would go to sleep and set my alarm to get up an hour earlier in order to finish studying for the test.

5. Scientists have been able to recognize the different stages of sleep and what goes on in the brain during each stage.

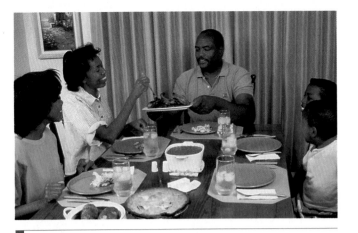

(FIGURE 3-20) **If at all possible, eat dinner early in the evening. A too-full stomach can keep you awake at night.**

3. Finish your exercise program at least three hours before bedtime. It's not a great idea to do anything too physically trying right before going to sleep. Instead, do some reading, listen to music, or watch a little television, to get your mind off your day.

4. Keep your room dark and quiet. You may love to listen to the radio, but if you're having trouble getting to sleep, it may be keeping you up. Try doing without it.

5. Don't lie in bed if you can't sleep. In general, tossing and turning won't help you fall asleep. Get out of bed and try reading. A warm bath or shower sometimes helps too.

6. Don't use alcohol or tobacco. Alcohol may cause drowsiness, but it does not help insomnia. Besides being addictive and dangerous, tobacco contains ingredients that stimulate your mind and body, and is therefore the worst thing to take late at night.

7. Don't drink caffeine, which is also a stimulant, after about 6 P.M. If you do drink soda at night, be sure that it's decaffeinated.

8. Don't eat too late. Indigestion or a too-full stomach can cost you precious hours of sleep. If at all possible, eat dinner before 6 P.M., and avoid snacking right before going to bed.

9. Don't rely on over-the-counter sleep medications. They may help you sleep for a night, but they often leave you groggy in the morning. And if they do work once, you may start to depend on them to get to sleep.

If you find that none of these help you get the sleep you need, see a doctor. Long-term insomnia can be caused by a number of things, from mental depression to poor eating habits. A health professional can determine what the problem is, and can often help you sleep well again in no time. Getting the sleep you need is probably the easiest part of any physical fitness program, and is well worth the time you put into it.

Review

1. Name the two categories of sleep.

2. Describe what happens during each phase of the sleep cycle.

3. Name two things you can do to help yourself sleep better.

4. **LIFE SKILLS: Solving Problems** You have a big test in the morning, and you know you haven't finished studying for it. But it's late, and you're getting really tired. What should you do?

5. **Critical Thinking** How does studying brain waves help scientists figure out what happens while we sleep?

ASSESS

Section Review

Have students answer the Section Review questions.

Alternative Assessment
Why Do We Need Sleep?

Ask students to write one or two paragraphs about why they think all mammals need sleep.

Closure
A Good Night's Sleep

Have students create a Tips List that gives advice on how to get a good night's sleep. Post the list somewhere in the classroom. Copies could be made available for students in other classes.

CHAPTER
3

Highlights

CHAPTER 3
HIGHLIGHTS
STRATEGIES

Summary

- Exercise offers benefits in four broad areas: aerobic fitness, muscle strength and endurance, body composition, and flexibility.

- Aerobic exercises such as walking, running, biking, and swimming can help your circulatory and respiratory systems stay healthy.

- Anaerobic exercises such as sprinting and weight lifting increase your muscle strength and muscle endurance.

- You can avoid many exercise injuries if you warm up correctly before your workout, and if you exercise regularly without pushing yourself.

- The sleep cycle consists of four stages of NREM sleep and a period of REM sleep.

Vocabulary

exercise physical activity that consists of a regular series of activities to train and strengthen the body.

endorphin a substance produced inside the brain that has pain-relieving properties.

flexibility the ability to move muscles and joints through their full range of motion.

body composition the division of total body weight into fat weight, and fat-free weight which includes muscle and bone.

aerobic exercise physical activity that increases the heart rate and supplies enough oxygen to the muscles so that the activity can be continued for a long period of time without resting.

anaerobic exercise physical activity that requires continuous effort over a short period of time, and that cannot be continued without resting.

anabolic steroid a drug that can temporarily increase muscle size.

brain waves electrical patterns produced by the brain that fluctuate greatly during the sleep cycle.

REM (rapid eye movement) the dreaming part of the sleep cycle, in which the eyes move back and forth rapidly under the eyelids.

insomnia temporary or continuing loss of sleep.

SUMMARY
Have students read the summary to reinforce the concepts they have learned in Chapter 3.

VOCABULARY
Have students write the vocabulary words and the definitions on index cards. The cards can be used to play "Concentration" as a way to review the vocabulary words. (In the game Concentration, all cards are placed face down. Players take turns turning over two cards. If the cards match, they are removed and that player receives a point. If the cards do not match, they are turned face down again.) Students may want to make up other games that use the vocabulary cards.

EXTENSION
Ask students to create a magazine page that touts the benefits of being physically fit. It could include slogans to stimulate interest and convey the benefits of physical fitness.

63

HIGHLIGHTS STRATEGIES

CHAPTER 3 ASSESSMENT

CHAPTER REVIEW

Concept Review

1. Exercise helps internal body tissues remain elastic. It can also lower blood pressure and lower your chances of having osteoporosis.

2. They produce a sense of pleasure and make you feel good.

3. Aerobic activity causes you to breathe rapidly for a longer period of time than anaerobic exercise does. Aerobic activity increases your heartbeat temporarily. As your heart beats more rapidly, more oxygen is transferred to your bloodstream. Anaerobic exercise makes you breathe even more rapidly, but for a shorter period of time. It does not benefit the respiratory and circulatory systems.

4. Exercise frequently, three to four times a week; exercise at an intensity at or slightly above your target heart rate; and exercise for 20–30 consecutive minutes.

5. Listen to your body signals, stop if you feel something is wrong, don't exercise if you are feeling ill, dress for the weather, don't be just a weekend athlete, warm up and cool down when exercising.

6. Remember PRICE. Decide whether you need to see a physician immediately, stay off of (and rest) the body part you have injured, put ice on your

CHAPTER 3

Chapter Review

Concept Review . . . .

1. What are some physical changes resulting from regular, moderate exercise that you can't see?

2. What effect do endorphins have on your body?

3. How does rapid breathing during aerobic activity differ from that which results from anaerobic activity?

4. What are the three basic rules to know before you begin an exercise program?

5. What are three ways to avoid injuries when exercising?

6. If an accident or injury happens, what are the five simple actions involved in emergency treatment?

7. Name three effects of steroid abuse.

8. Describe what happens to your body while you sleep.

9. How do you know if you are getting enough sleep?

Expressing Your Views . . . . . .

1. Do you think Americans are more physically fit today than a century ago? Why or why not?

2. You've noticed that the football team begins every practice session with stretching exercises and ends every session jogging around the track. Why do you think the coach has the players do this?

3. Tim is 15 years old and wants big muscles. What type of exercise would be helpful for him? Sophia is 14 years old and wants to help her heart and lungs stay healthy. She doesn't enjoy exercising alone. What type of exercise would be suitable for her?

4. Why is it important to set goals when you start an exercise program? How can knowing your current fitness level help you to set goals?

---

injury, compress the injury by wrapping a bandage around it and the ice, and elevate an injured limb above heart level.

7. Answers may include high blood pressure, liver damage, cancer, damage to the reproductive system, facial deformities, violent behavior, and psychiatric problems.

8. Your breathing and heart rate slow down, and your blood pressure and body temperature drop slightly.

9. You may need more sleep if you feel irritable, are having trouble concentrating, or if you feel tired.

Expressing Your Views
Sample responses:

1. No. Most Americans have sedentary jobs and they also commute to work by car, train, or bus instead of walking or riding a bicycle. Many American children watch television instead of exercising.

2. To warm and stretch the muscles before vigorous exercise in order to avoid injury; to cool down the muscles and to prevent them from becoming sore and cramped, as well as to prevent dizziness or nausea.

64 PHYSICAL FITNESS

Life Skills Check . . . . . .

1. Testing Physical Fitness
You would like to start an exercise program but you are not sure at what level you need to begin. What can you do to test your physical fitness?

2. Sleeping Well
Your friend has been having trouble sleeping at night. Often he is late to school or cancels weekend plans in order to catch up on sleep. What advice could you give your friend?

3. Determining Your Heart Rate
Work with a partner to identify each other's target pulse rates. One at a time, run in place for two or three minutes and take your pulse to find your MHR. Then determine your target pulse rate by using the directions on p. 47. What is your target pulse rate? Do you think this rate changes according to how fit you are?

Projects . . . .

1. Work with a group of students to find out what exercise, health, or sports facilities are available in or near your community. Are there swimming pools, tennis courts, jogging or biking trails, aerobics classes, basketball courts, or volleyball sand pits? If you live in a large city, each group might investigate one recreational area.

2. Design a survey to find out why people exercise. Think of four questions to ask, then work in a small group to collect and combine responses. Analyze the results to determine whether physical or psychological benefits were more motivating.

3. Write to the President's Council on Physical Fitness and request suitable programs or fitness norms for your age group. The address is
202 Pennsylvania Avenue NW
Suite 250
Washington DC 20004

Plan for Action . . . .

Plan a balanced weekly exercise program to fit your own personal needs.

3. anaerobic, such as weight lifting; any team sport that requires aerobic exercise

4. It is important to set a goal so that you can choose exercises that will help you meet that goal. If you know what your starting point is, you will be able to track your progress and exercise at the proper intensity, thereby avoiding injury and exhaustion.

Life Skills Check

1. You can do some simple tests to determine at what level you need to begin: aerobic, muscular strength and endurance, flexibility, and body composition.

2. Students should name three of the Tips for Sound Sleeping listed in Section 3.5.

3. Target heart rates will vary. No, the rate doesn't change, but how quickly you reach that rate will change.

Projects
Have the students plan and carry out projects for physical fitness education.

Plan for Action
Have students describe plans for their own physical exercise program. Ask students how their personal plans fulfill their exercise goals and have them respond to the plans of other students.

CHAPTER 4

Nutrition Principles

SECTION	TITLE/OBJECTIVES	PERSONAL INVENTORY			LIFE SKILLS DEVELOPMENT			
		Personal Health Inventory	Journal	Check Up	Life Skills	Life Skills Worksheets	Media Message or Ethical Issues Worksheet	What Would You Do?
4.1 pp. 67–69	**INFLUENCES ON FOOD CHOICES** • Describe the difference between hunger and appetite. ▪▪ Describe how different factors affect your food choices. • List the short-term consequences of making poor nutritional choices.	Ch. 4	4A 4B	p. 68				
4.2 pp. 70–81	**NUTRITIONAL COMPONENTS OF FOOD** • Describe the roles and functions of the six classes of dietary nutrients. • Identify problems that can occur from inadequate amounts of certain nutrients. • List recommended dietary levels for various nutrients. • Describe the differences among the various types of fats.		4C					
4.3 pp. 82–97	**ANALYZING YOUR NUTRITIONAL NEEDS** • Define the nutritional requirements for healthy teens. • Classify foods into the appropriate food groups. • Interpret food labeling to analyze nutritional breakdown. ▪▪ Make food selections that satisfy nutritional requirements using the Food Pyramid and Dietary Guidelines. • Identify special nutritional needs of selected populations.		4D	p. 84	p. 94	4A 4B 4C 4D		
4.4 pp. 98–100	**FOOD SAFETY** • Describe the symptoms common to food-borne illness. ▪▪ Discuss ways to prevent bacterial contamination of foods. • Locate the "use by" or "sell by" dates on common food items.							

KEY: ▪▪ Denotes Life Skill Objective

Text references denoted by page number.

Supplement references denoted by chapter or item numbers.

LINKING RESOURCES

INTERACTION		OTHER RESOURCES		SECTION REVIEW AND ASSESSMENT			
Making a Choice Cards	Parent Discussion Guide	Health Talk Audio Program	Teaching Transparencies and Directory	Section Review Worksheets	Section Quizzes	Reteaching Worksheets	Section Reviews
	Ch. 4	Ch. 4		4.1	4.1	4.1	p. 69
4A		BSH12		4.2	4.2	4.2	p. 81
4B			4A 4B	4.3	4.3	4.3	p. 97
				4.4	4.4	4.4	p. 100

For information about the excretion of water from the body, see pages 682–683 in the Body Systems Handbook.

KEY FACTS

- Hunger is the physical need for food; appetite is the desire for food. Healthful eating habits satisfy both and are culturally influenced.

- Adequate nutrition requires adequate intake of six essential nutrients: carbohydrates, fats, and proteins—which provide energy—plus vitamins, minerals, and water—which enable the body to utilize other nutrients.

- Many health problems and premature deaths are related to a poor diet.

- An excessive intake of fats and cholesterol by many Americans has increased the incidence of cardiovascular disease and cancer.

- Lack of fiber in the American diet contributes to certain diseases, such as colon cancer.

- The Food Pyramid is a guide that shows the number of servings that should be consumed daily of different kinds of foods.

- The Nutrition Facts label found on processed foods provides nutritional information about the food based on a 2,000-calorie diet. It is important to learn how to interpret the information on the label.

- Food poisoning is caused by foods that are cooked or stored improperly, that have passed their "sell by" date, or that are prepared using unsanitary utensils.

CHAPTER REVIEW AND ASSESSMENT

TEXT

Chapter Review pp. 102–103

SUPPLEMENTS

Chapter Test 4

Alternative Assessment 4

Test Generator Chapter 4

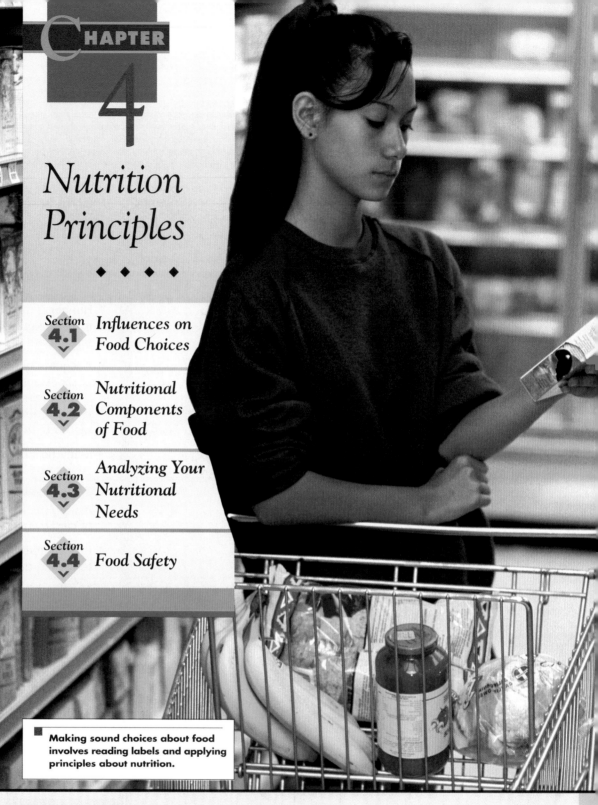

CHAPTER

4

Nutrition Principles

◆ ◆ ◆ ◆

Section **4.1** Influences on Food Choices

Section **4.2** Nutritional Components of Food

Section **4.3** Analyzing Your Nutritional Needs

Section **4.4** Food Safety

■ Making sound choices about food involves reading labels and applying principles about nutrition.

GETTING STARTED
• • • • • • • • • •

Using the Chapter Photograph

Ask students to describe the chapter photograph and compare it with that of Mary Ann at the snack machine. Discuss the food choices shown in the photos. Ask students how reading food labels can help people make healthful choices about their diets.

 Question Box

Have students write any questions they have about nutrition or diet and put them in the Question Box.

Sensitivity *ALERT*

Students who are seriously overweight or underweight may be reluctant to discuss eating habits. Some students may be reluctant to discuss diet because of religious or cultural food customs practiced at home. The privacy of such students should be respected; allow them to volunteer information.

MYTHS & MISCONCEPTIONS

• **Drinking 10 cups of any fluid fulfills the daily water requirement.** While most fluids contain a lot of water, they are not 100 percent water. Fluids that contain caffeine and alcohol act as diuretics, causing the body to eliminate more water than normal. They actually increase the body's need for fluids.

• **Athletes need extra protein, so they should consume a lot of meat and protein supplements.** Most athletes only need to replace the calories they expend. The percentages of nutrients in their diet should not change.

• **Eating right means cutting out snacks.** Many nutritionists recommend eating small snacks. What is important is to pick healthful snacks most of the time and to use moderation when eating ones that are high in fat and calories.

Mary Anne is really hungry and tired. She's got two more classes and then band practice. A snack would be great right about now. Standing in front of the vending machine, she wonders what to pick—chips, candy, gum, pretzels, or cookies. The candy bar looks really good, especially since Mary Anne feels she needs energy to stay awake through her next two classes and get through the band workout. A half-hour after eating the candy bar, she feels terrible. Could Mary Anne have made a better snack choice from the machine to satisfy her hunger and give her a boost of energy?

Section 4.1 — *Influences on Food Choices*

Objectives

- *Describe the difference between hunger and appetite.*
- *Describe how different factors affect your food choices.*
  - **LIFE SKILLS: Assessing Your Health**
- *List the short-term consequences of making poor nutritional choices.*

Picture yourself in this scene. Your best friend says she is hungry and wants a snack. You are not really hungry, but you decide to join her and eat anyway.

Hunger Selecting snacks and eating when you are not hungry are two situations that may be common in making choices about what and when you eat. To understand some important issues regarding food, you need to think about why you eat. There are two important terms that are related to

eating: hunger and appetite. **Hunger** is the body's physical response to the need for fuel. Your body uses food as the fuel to power the many chemical reactions that keep you alive and functioning. Hunger is a feeling you are born with. Symptoms of hunger include hunger pangs, weakness, dizziness, nausea, and a loss of concentration. Symptoms of hunger are relieved by eating. So how much should you eat? That is a question you will explore in detail in this chapter and the next one. For now, it is enough to say that you should eat until you feel full. The feeling of fullness you feel after eating is called *satiety*.

Appetite Hunger differs from appetite. **Appetite** describes your desire to eat based on the pleasure you get from eating certain foods. When you are dealing with appetite, you might ask, What do I want to eat? There are a number of factors that influence your appetite, such as the taste, texture, or aroma of certain foods. Your physical health can affect your appetite. If you are

hunger:
the body's physical response to the need for food.

appetite:
the desire to eat based on the pleasure derived from eating.

Section 4.1 Lesson Plan

MOTIVATE

 Journal 4A
Favorite Foods

This may be done as a warm-up activity. Ask students to think of a food that has always been a favorite of theirs, and ask why it is a favorite. Have them write in their Journal some of their memories associated with this food.

Class Discussion
Snack Choices

Ask students to name factors they think influenced Mary Anne's snack choice. *(preference, belief that it was the best source of energy, advertising, possible sugar or chocolate addiction)* Have volunteers suggest why the candy bar was a poor choice. *(Sugar and chocolate supply a spurt of energy and stimulation, but low energy and a depressant effect follow immediately.)*

TEACH

 Journal 4B
Motivations for Eating

Have students silently recall times when they have eaten when they were not hungry or continued to eat after they were full. Have them record in their Journal factors that affect their decisions about eating.

Up

Have students hand in their Check Up answers anonymously and tally results on the chalkboard. Encourage students to note trends and decide which factors seem most influential for them.

 Section Review Worksheet 4.1

To reinforce the concepts presented in this section, assign Section Review Worksheet 4.1.

 Section Quiz 4.1

Have students take Section Quiz 4.1.

 Reteaching Worksheet 4.1

Students who have difficulty with the material may complete Reteaching Worksheet 4.1.

Check Up

Charting Your Appetite

Answer the following questions related to hunger and appetite on a separate sheet of paper.

1. When is your desire to eat strongest?

2. When is your desire to eat weakest?

3. What moods cause an increase in your appetite?

4. What moods reduce your appetite?

5. What people affect your appetite?

6. What places cause an increase in your appetite?

7. What times of day do you notice an increase in your appetite?

8. At what times of day or in what situations do you eat, even if you aren't hungry? Why?

Now look at your responses. Do you have food habits that can lead to overeating? What changes can you make to have better control over your appetite?

(FIGURE 4-1) **Eating can be a highly social activity, causing you to eat even when you are not hungry.**

sick, you generally don't feel like eating. If you become very active, your appetite can change. The weather can affect your appetite. Some people lose their appetites when it is very hot outside, or they will only eat cold foods. Your culture and religion can have a major effect on your appetite. You may derive a lot of pleasure from eating certain foods that you grew up eating. You may also lose your appetite when presented with foods from another culture that appear unappealing to you.

Appetite refers to a desire for food. Hunger is your body telling you to eat. When hunger and appetite work together, you have a nice balance. But if you let appetite drive your eating behavior, you eat even when you are not hungry. When some people are depressed, they eat because they think they will feel better. Other people refuse to eat when they are depressed. Some people eat out of habit. They eat dinner at 5 P.M. whether they are hungry or not. All these reasons for eating help explain why so many people have trouble managing their weight. To strike the right balance between hunger and appetite, you need to understand when and why you eat.

What you should learn from this chapter is to make your food selections based on sound nutritional practices. Selecting foods in this way will help maintain your physical and emotional well-being. Figure 4-2 lists major health problems related to poor nutrition. For young people, there is another special issue related to diet. Young people who are overweight are more likely to become obese adults.

Environmental Factors There are several factors that influence your choice of foods and how much of them you eat. Perhaps most important among these factors are the social influences. The kinds of food you select are often determined by such

---

• • • TEACH continued

Class Discussion
Eating Habits and Health

Have students name all the factors they can think of that affect where, when, and how often a person eats. Write the list on the chalkboard and have volunteers identify factors that they think contribute to poor nutrition in America.

Role-Playing
Broadening Tastes in Food

If you have several students who are knowledgeable about the food of another region or country, pair them with students who are not familiar with the foods of those places. Then have them role-play ordering a meal in a restaurant in that country or region. The waiter can describe several dishes, and the customer can make a selection.

Extension
Ethnic Foods in Your Area

Encourage students to contact the local chamber of commerce and learn about ethnic restaurants in the area. Some students may prepare a graph showing how many different cultures are represented. Others may contact selected restaurants to learn about foods they serve.

• • • TEACH continued

Class Discussion
Eating Habits and Health

Have students name all the factors they can think of that affect where, when, and how often a person eats. Write the list on the chalkboard and have volunteers identify factors that they think contribute to poor nutrition in America.

Role-Playing
Broadening Tastes in Food

If you have several students who are knowledgeable about the food of another region or country, pair them with students who are not familiar with the foods of those places. Then have them role-play ordering a meal in a restaurant in that country or region. The waiter can describe several dishes, and the customer can make a selection.

Extension
Ethnic Foods in Your Area

Encourage students to contact the local chamber of commerce and learn about ethnic restaurants in the area. Some students may prepare a graph showing how many different cultures are represented. Others may contact selected restaurants to learn about foods they serve.

Some Health Problems Related to Diet

Short Term Conditions

Fatigue
Bad moods
Depression

Long Term Conditions

Obesity
Heart disease
Stroke
Adult-onset diabetes
High blood pressure
Cirrhosis of the liver
Tooth decay
Cancer (some types)
Birth of low birth weight babies
    with poor mental and physical
    development
Dietary deficiency diseases
    (such as scurvy)

(FIGURE 4-2)

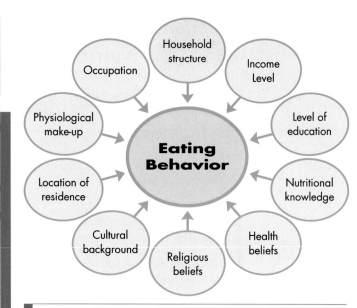

(FIGURE 4-3) **What you eat and when you eat is influenced by many factors. Describe how each of these factors affects your own food selections.**

things as your own family experiences, cultural heritage, cost, and other factors shown in Figure 4-3. For example, if you have grown up in the southwestern United States, you probably have eaten a lot of Mexican food even if it was not part of your ethnic background. Growing up on the East Coast, you might have eaten more seafood than someone who grew up in the Midwest Farm Belt. Your personality can also influence your food selections. Some people are very adventuresome about food and like to try new things. Other people feel very uncomfortable when faced with the thought of trying something new.

Review

1. How does hunger differ from appetite? Should you eat to satisfy hunger or to satisfy your appetite?

2. **LIFE SKILLS: Assessing Your Health** List two ways in which your ethnic background may affect the types of food you eat.

3. Describe two consequences of poor nutrition that could affect you as an adult.

4. *Critical Thinking* How do you know when you are hungry? How do you know when your appetite is at work?

Review Answers

1. Hunger is your body telling you to eat; appetite is your desire to have food. You should eat to satisfy your hunger.

2. Students may answer that some foods may be more appealing than others because of familiar ethnic dishes or spices. Ethnic holidays may influence the types of foods eaten and how they are prepared.

3. Answers may include fatigue, bad moods, depression, obesity, heart disease, diabetes, high blood pressure, tooth decay, cancer, and dietary deficiency diseases.

4. Signs of hunger include hunger pangs, weakness, dizziness, nausea, and a loss of concentration. Your appetite is at work when you are eating for reasons other than being hungry.

ASSESS

Section Review

Have students answer the Section Review questions.

Alternative Assessment
Psychology of Eating

Have students explain in their own words why many decisions to eat are based on psychological or emotional reasons rather than physical reasons.

Closure
Persuading People to Follow a Healthful Diet

Have students write a brief paragraph that attempts to persuade readers to follow a healthful diet in order to avoid health problems.

...and Disease

In adolescents, nutrition directly affects growth and development, dental health, and body composition. Poor diet contributes to the development of many chronic diseases that afflict American adults. For adults, coronary heart disease, some forms of cancer, stroke, non-insulin-dependent diabetes, and arteriosclerosis have been linked to a poor diet. While food is no longer scarce in the United States, undernutrition remains a problem for the isolated and some of the poor. In addition, there is a new problem— a pattern of overeating and dietary imbalance that leads to malnutrition. Americans whose diets follow this pattern place themselves needlessly at risk for many diseases.

essential nutrients:

six categories of substances from food that nourish the body: carbohydrates, fats, proteins, vitamins, minerals, water.

calorie:

a unit of measurement for energy. 1 nutrition calorie = 1 kilocalorie.

carbohydrates:

a class of nutrients containing starches, simple sugars, glycogen, and dietary fiber.

Section 4.2 — Nutritional Components of Food

Objectives

■ *Describe the roles and functions of the six classes of dietary nutrients.*

■ *Identify problems that can occur from inadequate amounts of certain nutrients.*

■ *List recommended dietary levels for various nutrients.*

■ *Describe the differences among the various types of fats.*

Nutrition refers to the study of the way in which the substances in food affect our health. Over the last 100 years, the American diet has changed drastically. It was not uncommon for a person's diet 100 years ago to reflect a heavy dependence on grains, fruits, and vegetables. While there is far more attention paid today to health and nutrition, the typical American diet is not as nutritionally balanced as that of our grandparents. Analyzing your eating patterns is very important because diet is related to six of the ten leading causes of death in the United States. Diet also plays a role in infant death, tooth decay, and being overweight, as shown in Figure 4-3.

In a national survey of 10th-graders, most students knew that too much fat, sugar, or salt is unhealthy. They knew these substances increase the risk of getting diseases such as heart disease and cancer. However, most students didn't know which foods are high in fat, sugar, salt, and fiber. It is clear that their eating patterns frequently included fried foods, nutrient-poor snack foods, and beverages high in sugar.

Basic Principles of Nutrition

Foods contain substances needed for growth and development. The substances are classified into six groups called **essential nutrients,** which are necessary for the maintenance of health. There are six categories of essential nutrients: *carbohydrates, fats, proteins, vitamins, minerals, and water.* Of these six groups, carbohydrates, fats, and protein provide energy for the body in the form of **calories** *. The remaining three nutrients—vitamins, minerals, and water—are essential for the body to use these other nutrients properly.

Carbohydrates The term *carbohydrate* comes from the names of the three chemical elements in carbohydrates: carbon, oxygen, and hydrogen. In fact, the oxygen and hydrogen in carbohydrates are in the same proportions as found in water. Therefore, we get the name carbo (carbon) and hydrate (water).

Carbohydrates are our main source of food energy. One gram of carbohydrate provides 4 calories of available energy.

Carbohydrates can be divided into three classes based on their size: simple sugars, short-chain sugars, and long-chain sugars. Simple sugars are also called monosaccharides. The most important simple sugar is glucose because it is the major energy source for cells in your body. Carbohy-

The nutrition calorie is actually a kilocalorie of energy (abbreviated kcal). There are 1000 calories in a nutrition calorie (sometimes spelled with a capital C).

Section 4.2 Lesson Plan

MOTIVATE

Cooperative Learning
Nutrition-Knowledge Challenge

Divide the class into small groups. List the six essential nutrients on the board as column headings. Have each group brainstorm to develop a list of facts about each nutrient—where it is found, what it does for the body, etc. Groups then share their information by writing their facts in the columns. Other groups can challenge information they believe is incorrect or improperly placed. Tell students that in this section they will learn about the different types of nutrients.

TEACH

Class Discussion
Sugar Sources

Bring in, or have students bring in, a variety of cans or labels from products that contain sugars. Read the ingredient labels to identify the sources of the sugar. Notice that some products will contain sugars from more than one source. Make a list of all the products that contain more than 10 percent of the daily recommended value of sugar

(FIGURE 4-4) **Complex carbohydrates have the added value of providing dietary fiber.**

Background
America's Sweet Tooth
Americans consume enormous quantities of sugar. Much of this sugar is hidden in prepared foods so the product will appeal to our sweet tooth. Even products such as canned soup may contain added sugar. The United States Department of Agriculture reports that over the last 20 years there has been a 16 percent increase in annual consumption of sugar per person. Sugars now account for approximately 21 percent of the calories in a typical American diet.

drates must be converted to glucose before they can be used as energy.

The carbohydrates in food except milk sugar (lactose) and glycogen are formed in plants. Simple sugars naturally occur in fruits, vegetables, honey, and molasses. The sugar you get from the sugar bowl is sucrose, a short-chain sugar. Sucrose is a disaccharide meaning that it is made from two monosaccharides.

Common long-chain sugars are starch, glycogen, and dietary fiber. These consist of long chains of simple sugars. Starches and fiber come from vegetables, potatoes, grains (such as rice, corn, wheat, and oats), and beans. Breads, cereals, and pasta are also made from grains. Almost all these sources of **complex carbohydrates** are low in fat and rich in vitamins, minerals, and fiber. Glycogen is "animal starch," a form of stored carbohydrate in the liver and muscles of animals.

Dietary fiber is a complex carbohydrate, but it does not provide energy (calories). Dietary fiber that does not dissolve in water is commonly called roughage because it provides bulk in the large intestine. Roughage helps to move undigested food through the digestive tract, preventing constipation and reducing the risk of certain diseases, such as colon cancer. Whole-grain wheat bran, corn, rice, corn bran, and rice bran are good sources of roughage. Some dietary fiber dissolves in water. This kind of fiber, found in oats and beans, helps to lower blood cholesterol and thus reduce the risk of cardiovascular disease. Fruits and vegetables contain both kinds of fiber.

Carbohydrates should make up 60 percent of your daily calories. Fewer than 10 percent of your day's calories should come from sugars. It is recommended that you consume between 20 and 35 grams of dietary fiber a day.

dietary fiber:

a subclass of complex carbohydrates with a high ratio of plant material that is not absorbed by the body.

complex carbohydrates:

a subclass of carbohydrates that includes starches, dietary fiber, and glycogen.

Sugars add calories to foods without adding nutritional value; thus the term *empty calories*. To reduce the amount of sugar (and calories) in their diets, teens need to become label readers and to take note of the types and amounts of sugars in foods before consuming them. The label may not say sugar (sucrose). Look for terms such as high-fructose corn syrup, fructose, lactose, dextrose, maltose, honey, syrup, corn syrup, molasses, fruit juice concentrate, or sorbitol. All of these terms are used to indicate added sugars.

in one serving. Remind students that most people consume several food items a day that contain some form of sugar. Just because a label shows less than 10 percent of the daily allowance of sugar, it doesn't mean that it's OK to eat it—you have to consider your total daily food intake first.

Class Discussion
Fiber Rich, Calorie Poor

Ask: **Why should you eat fiber-rich foods, since fiber isn't digested and provides no energy?** *[Fiber is essential for the proper functioning of the digestive tract. Fiber helps move undigested food through the digestive tract, preventing constipation and decreasing the risk of developing colon cancer. Fiber also helps*

lower blood cholesterol, thus reducing the risk of cardiovascular disease.]

Cooperative Learning
An Apple a Day

Have students work in small groups to list as many reasons as possible why an apple is a better snack than a candy bar. Suggest that they include both the positives of the fruit and the negatives of the candy.

Making a Choice 4A

Assign the Party Refreshments card. The card asks students to plan healthful refreshments for a party.

fats:

a class of nutrients that supply more energy per gram than carbohydrates or proteins.

saturated fats:

fats that contain single bonds between carbon atoms and the maximum number of hydrogen atoms bonded to carbon.

unsaturated fats:

fats that contain one or more double bonds between carbon atoms and have less than the maximum number of hydrogen atoms bonded to carbon.

Fat Fat is the most concentrated form of energy in food. Along with carbohydrates, fat is an important fuel for the body, yielding 9 calories per gram, or 252 calories per ounce. One tablespoon of fat contains about 13.5 grams of fat, or 120 calories. Like carbohydrates, fat consists of carbon, hydrogen, and oxygen, but these elements are arranged differently. And like glycogen, fat is stored in your body. Fat storage sites are called adipose, or fatty, tissue.

Fat in the diet belongs to a class of compounds called lipids. Lipids are essential for good health. Many hormones, including the sex hormones, are made from lipids. Several vitamins will dissolve only in fat. Fat takes a longer time to digest than either carbohydrates or protein, and it contributes to that sense of fullness that lasts for several hours after a meal.

Just as there are different kinds of dietary carbohydrates, there are also different kinds of dietary fat. They differ in their chemical structure which affects their physical state at room temperature and their fate in the body.

The long chains of carbon atoms in **saturated fats** have all bond sites filled with hydrogen atoms. Saturated fats are often solid at room temperature, because the carbon chains are straight and can be layered. Animal fats, like butter and lard, are essentially saturated fat. Saturated fats predominate in only two vegetable oils—palm oil and coconut oil. But other vegetable oils can become saturated, either completely or partially, through a process called hydrogenation.

Unsaturated fats are also made of long carbon chains. However these chains consist of multiple bonds between carbon atoms leaving fewer bonds sites available for hydrogen atoms. Therefore, all the carbon atoms are not saturated with hydrogen atoms. Vegetable oils and fish oils are unsaturated by nature. Monounsaturated fats

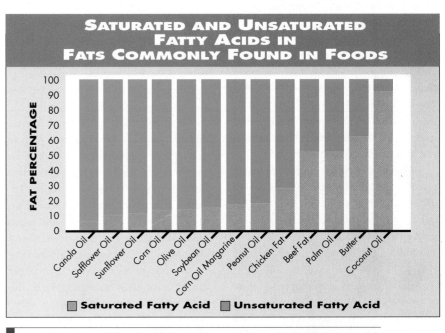

(FIGURE 4-5) **Avoid foods with ingredients that have high percentages of saturated fats.**

• • • TEACH continued

Demonstration

Fat in Snack Foods

Display a number of popular snack foods. For each, provide a craft stick marked off in tenths. Ask students to guess the percent of total calories that are fat. Then color in the portion of the stick that indicates the actual percentage of fat content. (Use product labels and the following equation to calculate: 1 gram fat = 9 calories.)

Reinforcement

There's Fat and There's FAT

Stress to students the importance of distinguishing between saturated fat and unsaturated fat. Have them study Figure 4-5 and name the types of oil or fat that contain more saturated fat than is healthful. (*chicken fat, beef fat, butter, palm oil, and coconut oil*)

Provide several snack food labels and ask students to determine (1) the grams of fat per serving and (2) the

ratio of saturated fat to unsaturated fat. Students can then rate each food according to a "health rating scale" they invent. Include snack foods such as chips, crackers, pretzels, cookies, and doughnuts.

Class Discussion

Favorite Foods and Fat

Refer students to Figure 4-7 on page 74 to discover other foods that are high in fat. Ask students which foods they eat too much of.

are liquid at room temperature, but they harden when refrigerated. Monounsaturated means that the bond between two carbon atoms is not saturated. Polyunsaturated fats have two or more carbon atoms that are not saturated.

Fats can play different roles in the development of disease. Saturated fats are linked to the development of cardiovascular disease and some forms of cancer. Monounsaturated and polyunsaturated oils appear to provide protection against the development of some of these diseases. But vegetable oils that have been hydrogenated are different. During hydrogenation, the bonding between carbon atoms in vegetable oils changes, producing fats called *trans* fats. Trans fats don't spoil rapidly and can be reused longer. However, trans fats behave like any other saturated fat in the body.

To reduce your risk of cardiovascular disease, cancer, and diabetes, limit the total amount of fat in your diet to no more than 30 percent of your day's total calories. Figure 4-7 shows the percentages of calories from fat in various foods. Compare the foods shown with what you normally eat.

Cholesterol **Cholesterol** is a fatlike substance found in some foods of animal origin. It is also produced by the liver. Cholesterol is part of the membrane around a cell, and it provides some protective cover-

ing to nerve fibers in the body. It is essential for the production of vitamin D and bile salts, which are used in the digestion of lipids. Cholesterol is also needed for the production of certain sex hormones. The body makes all the cholesterol it needs.

You may have heard two different terms associated with cholesterol, **high-density lipoproteins (HDL)** and **low-density lipoproteins (LDL)**. HDL is sometimes referred to as good cholesterol because it is thought to provide some protection against heart disease. LDL carries cholesterol and other fats from the digestive system through the blood to the body's cells. The amount of LDL in the blood is regulated by LDL receptors on cells. If there is too much cholesterol in the blood, it can build up on the walls of blood vessels. Eventually, these deposits can clog arteries and restrict the supply of oxygenated blood to the heart, resulting in a heart attack. It is now generally agreed that cholesterol levels in the blood should be below 200 milligrams per deciliter (mg/dL).

Diets that are high in fat increase blood cholesterol levels. Saturated fat is thought to cause the increase in cholesterol level by affecting the LDL cholesterol absorbed by the liver. Therefore dietary guidelines suggest reducing the intake of foods that are high in saturated fat to help lower cholesterol levels.

HDL:

(high-density lipoproteins) compounds that remove cholesterol from the blood and transport it back to the liver.

LDL:

(low-density lipoproteins) compounds that carry cholesterol to cells for cell processes.

cholesterol:

a fatlike substance that is part of all animal cells and is needed for the production of some hormones and fat digestion.

(FIGURE 4-6) **Heart disease resulting from clogged arteries can be the long-term effect of a diet that is high in cholesterol. The artery on the right is completely blocked with plaque. Start now to monitor cholesterol levels throughout your life.**

Reinforcement
Cholesterol Confusion
Write on the chalkboard:
CHOLESTEROL ≠ FAT
Explain that foods with no cholesterol are not necessarily low in fat. Have students refer again to snack food labels and compare cholesterol with fat content. Also write on the board:
CHOLESTEROL INTAKE ≠ CHOLESTEROL IN BLOOD
Stress the fact that eating foods that

contain no cholesterol is not a guarantee that you will have a low cholesterol blood serum level. Many factors influence the level and types of cholesterol circulating in the blood. However, eating foods high in saturated fats can increase your cholesterol level. When saturated fats are digested, they circulate in the bloodstream as forerunners of the components of LDL ("bad cholesterol"). The body can then use these components to build LDL.

Class Discussion
Limiting Cholesterol
Ask: **If cholesterol is essential, why should you worry about how much you eat?** *[The body makes cholesterol to fill its needs. Ingesting great amounts of cholesterol and saturated fats can lead to a buildup of the fatlike substance in the artery walls, which ultimately can lead to heart disease. In addition, high cholesterol is linked to some kinds of cancer.]*

Background
Cholesterol

Physicians now think that the best way to evaluate a person's cholesterol level is to look at the ratio of the total cholesterol level to the HDL level. To find this ratio, divide the total cholesterol level by the HDL level. Although a ratio between 5 and 9 is considered normal, a ratio of four or less is associated with a decreased risk of heart disease. One study showed that men whose ratio was less than 3 have a 60 percent lower risk for developing heart disease than those in the normal range.

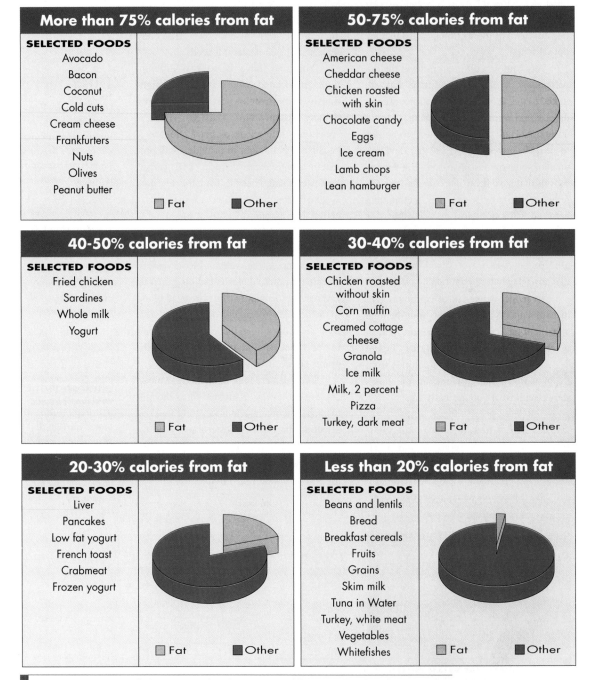

PERCENTAGE OF CALORIES FROM FATS

More than 75% calories from fat

SELECTED FOODS
Avocado
Bacon
Coconut
Cold cuts
Cream cheese
Frankfurters
Nuts
Olives
Peanut butter

☐ Fat ☐ Other

50-75% calories from fat

SELECTED FOODS
American cheese
Cheddar cheese
Chicken roasted with skin
Chocolate candy
Eggs
Ice cream
Lamb chops
Lean hamburger

☐ Fat ☐ Other

40-50% calories from fat

SELECTED FOODS
Fried chicken
Sardines
Whole milk
Yogurt

☐ Fat ☐ Other

30-40% calories from fat

SELECTED FOODS
Chicken roasted without skin
Corn muffin
Creamed cottage cheese
Granola
Ice milk
Milk, 2 percent
Pizza
Turkey, dark meat

☐ Fat ☐ Other

20-30% calories from fat

SELECTED FOODS
Liver
Pancakes
Low fat yogurt
French toast
Crabmeat
Frozen yogurt

☐ Fat ☐ Other

Less than 20% calories from fat

SELECTED FOODS
Beans and lentils
Bread
Breakfast cereals
Fruits
Grains
Skim milk
Tuna in Water
Turkey, white meat
Vegetables
Whitefishes

☐ Fat ☐ Other

(FIGURE 4-7) **You might be surprised at the amount of fat some foods contain. Learn how to determine these percentages later in this chapter.**

• • • TEACH continued

Demonstration
Clinical Bloodwork to Show Serum Cholesterol Levels

To help students differentiate HDL from LDL, ask a medical lab or a doctor's office for a facsimile of a lab form for bloodwork, showing hypothetical results for a patient's levels of cholesterol in general and broken down into HDL and LDL levels. Or, you may prefer to use the following example.

TEST NAME	RESULT	UNITS	NORMAL RANGE
Cholesterol	190	mg/dL	120 – 200
LDL	170*	mg/dL	130 – 160
HDL	20**	mg/dL	30 – 90

*High level may mean higher risk; desirable LDL = 130 mg/dL or less; 130–159 mg/dL = borderline level.
**Low level may mean higher risk; HDL should be above 35 mg/dL.

Copy the form for viewing on the overhead projector or chalkboard and help students read and interpret the data. The example included here shows that a normal range cholesterol level may, when further broken down to show HDL and LDL, reveal a high level of LDL, or "bad cholesterol."

Class Discussion
Complete Versus Incomplete

Help students see that proteins supplied by plants are not inferior because they are incomplete. Ask: **How is it**

Creating Complete Proteins

To create a complete protein, combine foods from at least two of the following groups at a single meal:

Legumes   dry beans and peas (navy, lima, pinto, black, soybeans), soybean curd (tofu), soy flour, peanuts, peanut butter

Grains   whole grains (barley, oats, rice, rye, wheat), corn, pasta

Nuts, seeds   almonds, pecans, walnuts, sunflower seeds, pumpkin seeds, sesame seeds

(FIGURE 4-8) **When selecting nuts and seeds to create complete proteins, limit the amount you eat because they are high in fat.**

Proteins Like carbohydrates and fats, **proteins** are made of carbon, hydrogen, and oxygen, but they also contain nitrogen. Proteins play a unique role in the growth and repair of body tissues. All cells contain some protein. It is also found in antibodies and some hormones. Enzymes that speed up the rate of chemical reactions in the body are proteins.

All proteins are made of amino acids. There are 20 amino acids; 11 of them can be made in the body and 9 others must be supplied by food. The 9 amino acids that cannot be produced in the body are called **essential amino acids.**

Because proteins perform so many necessary functions, you can see that the foods you select should include good sources of protein. However, the proteins found in the human body are not supplied directly from food. During digestion, proteins in food are broken down to their amino acids. These amino acids are the building blocks of new proteins for growth and tissue repair.

The proteins in food are sometimes classified as complete or incomplete proteins. A **complete protein** is one that contains all nine essential amino acids; an **incomplete protein** contains only some of these nine amino acids. Generally, foods that come from animal products (meat, poultry, fish, and milk products) contain complete proteins. Most proteins that come from plant sources are incomplete. It is possible, however, to get the proper amount of complete proteins from plant sources by selecting various protein sources so that all essential amino acids are supplied. Figure 4-8 contains a recommendation on how to select from a mix of plant foods to achieve a diet that has complete proteins. Proteins should make up about 10 percent of your daily caloric intake for adequate nutrition.

proteins:

class of nutrients consisting of long chains of amino acids, which are the basic components of body tissue and provide energy.

complete protein:

a protein that contains all nine essential amino acids.

incomplete protein:

a protein that lacks one or more of the essential amino acids.

essential amino acids:

a group of nine amino acids that cannot be manufactured by the body and must be supplied by food.

Background
A Teen's Eye View of Nutrition
Young people are likely to regard advice to eat a healthy diet to prevent chronic disease and health problems as something that applies to middle-aged and elderly people—not to them. However, poor eating habits and poor nutrition harm them now, even in terms of their long-term health. The heart disease, cancer, and diabetes that afflict many elderly people in American society began much earlier in their lives; prevention requires changing habits at a younger age. In addition, autopsies of young accident victims have shown early signs of plaque buildup in arteries. The best time for teens to start a healthful diet for life is now.

---

possible to provide your body with all essential amino acids if you eat incomplete proteins in plant food? *[Eating certain combinations of plant proteins provides all the essential amino acids.]* What would be an advantage of getting most of your protein from plant sources? *[If you provided enough of the right kinds of amino acids, you would at the same time boost your intake of vitamins, minerals, fiber, and complex carbohydrates, which are all more likely to be lacking than protein in the American diet.]*

Cooperative Learning
Picturing Plenty of Protein
Have small groups of students locate and clip pictures of foods that are good sources of protein. They should divide the pictures into foods that provide complete or incomplete proteins. Then have students arrange incomplete proteins into combinations that form complete proteins.

• • • TEACH continues on p. 76

Fat Soluble Vitamins

Vitamin	Function	Sources	Deficiency
A	Maintains healthy eyes, skin, bones, teeth, keeps lining of digestive tract resistant to infection	Milk products, liver, yellow fruits and vegetables, dark-green leafy vegetables	Night blindness, impaired growth
D	Promotes normal growth, works with calcium and phosphorus in building bones and teeth	Fish-liver oils, fortified milk, liver, egg yolk, salmon, tuna	Rickets (inadequate growth of bones and teeth)
E	Prevents destruction of red blood cells; needed for certain enzymes to function	Wheat germ, vegetable oils, legumes, nuts, dark green vegetables	Red blood cell rupture causing anemia
K	Assists with blood clotting, bone growth	Green, leafy vegetables and vegetable oils, tomatoes, potatoes	Slow clotting of blood, hemorrhage

(FIGURE 4-9) **Fat-soluble vitamins can be stored in the body, while water-soluble vitamins (shown on the next page) cannot. It is best to obtain vitamins from food sources rather than from vitamin supplements.**

vitamins:

organic substances that assist in the chemical reactions that occur in the body.

Vitamins **Vitamins** are compounds that help regulate certain chemical reactions in the body. Though vitamins do not supply energy, they are essential for good health. The only vitamins the body can make are vitamins D and K.

Vitamins are grouped into two different categories: those that are fat soluble and those that are water soluble. *Fat soluble* means that the substance dissolves in fat. Fat-soluble vitamins include vitamins A, D, E, and K. Because they dissolve in fat, these vitamins can be stored in body fat. A balanced diet, which you will learn about in the next section, provides the right levels of fat-soluble vitamins and the fats needed to store these vitamins. If a person takes in high levels of fat-soluble vitamins either from food or from vitamin supplements, the excess is stored in the liver or skin and may be harmful. Figure 4-9 lists the fat-soluble vitamins, their sources, and their importance to health.

Water-soluble vitamins like the B group and vitamin C are not stored in the body. Because water-soluble vitamins dissolve in water, any excess is excreted in urine. Therefore, you must have consistent sources of water-soluble vitamins to prevent deficiency diseases. Figure 4-9 also lists the water-soluble vitamins, their sources, and their importance to health. A well-

---

• • • TEACH continued

Game
Vitamin Spin

Make a wheel with the 13 vitamins listed on it, and a spinner. A student team spins the wheel and must describe a function, one source, and a deficiency related to the vitamin landed on. The majority of team members must agree with the answers provided by the spokesperson. For each correct answer, the team wins 5 points. If all three answers are correct, the team spins again. A vitamin may be used more than once, but answers should not be duplicated.

Class Discussion
Some Things Bear Repeating

Have students explain why it's a good idea to eat foods rich in vitamins C and B every day. Ask them to respond to the following scenario:

Suppose a healthy person who has had an adequate diet is shipwrecked on an island. There is water on the island but no food. The person is rescued one month later.
Ask: **Which vitamins will the person need most?** *[B and C]* **Why?** *[The body cannot store them; they must be replenished daily.]*

Debate the Issue
Vitamin Pills

Have two teams of students debate the question: Should teens take vitamin pills? Each team will need time to collect

Water Soluble Vitamins

Vitamin	Function	Sources	Deficiency
B$_1$ Thiamine	Assists with conversion of carbohydrates to energy, normal appetite and digestion, nervous system function	Pork products, liver, legumes, enriched and whole grain breads, cereals, nuts	Beriberi (inflamed nerves, muscle weakness, heart problems)
B$_2$ Riboflavin	Assists with nerve cell function, healthy appetite and release of energy from carbohydrates, protein, and fats	Milk, eggs, whole grain products, green leafy vegetables, dried beans, enriched breads, cereals, and pasta	Cheilosis (skin sores on nose and lips, sensitive eyes)
B$_3$ Niacin	Maintenance of normal metabolism, digestion, nerve function, energy release	Red meats, organ meats, fish, enriched breads and cereals	Pellagra (soreness on mouth, diarrhea, irritability, depression)
B$_6$ Pyridoxine	Necessary for normal carbohydrate, protein and fat metabolism	Whole grain products, fish, bananas, green leafy vegetables	Anemia, dermatitis
B$_{12}$	Necessary for formation of red blood cells; normal cell function	Lean meats, liver, egg products, milk, cheese	Pernicious anemia, stunted growth
Folacin	Necessary for formation of hemoglobin in red blood cells; necessary for production of genetic material	Green vegetables, liver, whole grain products, legumes	Anemia, diarrhea
Pantothenic Acid	Assists with energy release from carbohydrates, protein, and fats; used to produce some hormones	Whole grain cereals, liver, green vegetables, eggs, nuts	Reduced resistance to stress
Biotin	Necessary for normal metabolism of carbohydrates and some other B vitamins	Organ meats, egg yolks, green vegetables	Skin disorders, hair loss
C Ascorbic Acid	Needed for normal development of connective tissue, including those holding teeth; wound healing; use of iron	Citrus fruits, melons, green vegetables, peppers	Scurvy (slow healing of wounds, bleeding gums and loose teeth)

information and organize presentations. After both sides of the issue have been presented and rebuttals given, have the rest of the class tell which arguments were most convincing, and why.

Class Discussion
Vitamin Megadoses

Students should be aware of the negative effects of large doses of vitamin supplements. Ask: **What might happen if you take megadoses of vitamin A or E?** *[The body would use what it needs. Then it would store these fat-soluble vitamins, even to a toxic level.]* **What are the effects of megadoses of vitamin C?** *[The body will excrete the excess, wasting the vitamins.]*

• • • TEACH continues on p. 78

Background

Getting Enough Calcium

Research shows that many women and teenagers do not get enough calcium. Experts in the field of nutrition say that teenagers need between 1200 and 1400 mg of calcium daily to build strong bones. For girls especially, failure to consume adequate calcium will greatly increase the risk for developing osteoporosis later in life. A sufficient and varied diet is the preferred method of obtaining calcium. Good dietary sources include milk and other dairy products; figs; broccoli; dark, leafy green vegetables; beans, especially soybeans; canned salmon consumed with the bones; and seeds and nuts, especially almonds. Many products that are high in calcium are also high in fat. However, it is important not to sacrifice calcium to achieve a low-fat diet. A recent study of 900 ten-year-olds revealed that those who obtained less than 30 percent of their calories from fat had diets that were deficient in vitamins and

• • • BACKGROUND continues on p. 79

minerals:

inorganic substances that are generally absorbed to form structural components of the body.

Minerals Minerals are naturally occurring substances that contribute to the normal functioning of the body. Unlike vitamins, which are produced and found in living materials, minerals are not produced by living organisms. More than 20 minerals are necessary for healthy functioning. Figure 4-10 contains a summary of some essential minerals.

Minerals are divided into two categories: macrominerals, which include calcium, chlorine, magnesium, phosphorus, potassium, sodium, and sulfur; and trace minerals, which include chromium, fluorine, copper, iodine, iron, manganese, selenium, and zinc. Macrominerals are needed in larger amounts by the body, and trace minerals are needed in smaller quantities. All minerals are found in nature in combination with other minerals. Their combinations are known as *salts*. When salts are in solution, they dissolve to form charged particles that are capable of conducting an electric current. These dissolved salts are called *electrolytes*.

Proper electrolyte balance is needed to keep the body's internal environment stable. Sodium and chlorine are two minerals that have received a lot of attention because of their role in regulating fluid balance. An excess of sodium has been linked to high blood pressure.

Ordinary table salt is a combination of sodium and chlorine, and it is a major source of *sodium* in the diet. One teaspoon of table salt provides about 2,000 mg of sodium. The amount of sodium inside and outside of your body cells must be kept in a delicate balance, and a diet high in salt may upset this balance. Health problems linked

balanced diet provides enough of each of the necessary vitamins; no vitamin supplements should be necessary.

to high salt intake include high blood pressure, abnormal heart rhythms, fluid around the heart, and overburdened kidneys. For this reason, it is recommended that your daily sodium intake be less than 3,000 mg. Because the link between salt and heart problems has been so publicized, most people watch the amount of salt they use to season food. The bulk of excess salt in the diet comes from packaged foods and fast, convenient foods.

The role of *calcium* and *magnesium* in bone growth and development makes them minerals of major importance. As a teen, you might not worry about your bones thinking that diseases such as osteoporosis only affect older people. But you are building bone now, and the amount of bone that you build before age 35 will influence whether you develop weakened and brittle bones as you age. Calcium and magnesium are two minerals that help build dense, strong bones. Dark green, leafy vegetables are high in magnesium and calcium, and dairy products are high in calcium. These two minerals are also responsible for efficient muscular contraction and relaxation. When you eat a varied diet balanced in both minerals, you will also be consuming other needed minerals.

Growth that occurs during adolescence requires a tremendous amount of energy— to run normal body systems. Iron deficiency anemia, which is due to a lack of iron in the diet and is common in both males and females, can result in fatigue. If you do not eat a lot of foods that are rich in iron, you can improve the absorption of iron by including more vitamin C in your diet. Vitamin C makes the iron in plant foods more available to your body.

Water Water is an essential compound in your diet. About two-thirds of your body

---

• • • TEACH continued

Class Discussion

Minerals Stand Alone

Ask: **How do minerals differ from other nutrients?** *[They are not produced by organisms.]* **Do you need macrominerals more than you need trace minerals?** *[No. You need macrominerals in larger doses than trace minerals, but both types are essential.]*

Class Discussion

Minerals Up Close and Personal

Have students refer to Figure 4-10 and identify the macrominerals and the trace minerals. Ask them to assess their diets and note any deficiencies they may have. Encourage students to discuss reasons why calcium and sodium intake should be kept at recommended doses. *(Calcium deficiency leads to bone weakness and osteoporosis; excess sodium intake is thought to be*

related to heart disease and high blood pressure.)

Class Discussion

Salt Without Shakers

Ask: **How can a person who uses no table salt be getting adequate sodium in his or her diet?** *[Many foods contain some naturally-occurring sodium, and most processed foods contain high levels of added sodium. In addition, sodium intake comes in forms other than sodium chloride, for example, MSG and sodium nitrate.]*

Listing of Important Minerals and Their Function

Mineral	Function	Sources
Calcium	Necessary for normal growth of bones and teeth, transmission of nerve cell impulses, muscle contraction	Milk and dairy products, dark leafy green vegetables
Chromium	Necessary for proper blood sugar regulation and insulin activity	Cheese, plums, apple juice, prunes, peanuts and peanut butter, corn and corn oil, mushrooms
Copper	Needed for normal production of hemoglobin, bone, and melanin (involved in skin color)	Liver, shellfish, legumes, nuts, whole-grain products
Iodine	Essential for production of thyroid hormone	Iodized salt, seafood
Iron	Found in hemoglobin; needed for some enzymes	Organ meats, red meat, whole grains, dark green vegetables, legumes
Magnesium	Needed for chemical reactions during metabolism	Milk, dairy products, green leafy vegetables
Manganese	Used in enzymes for synthesis of cholesterol, formation of urea, normal function of nervous tissue	Whole grain products, leafy green vegetables, fruits, legumes, nuts
Potassium	Helps maintain normal metabolism, nerve and muscle function	Meats, poultry, fish, fruits, vegetables
Selenium	Needed for healthy heart function, protects against heavy metal toxicity	Tuna and other seafood, whole grains, organ meats, molasses, Brazil nuts
Sodium	Essential for proper water balance in cells and tissues; nerve cell conduction	Table salt, high salt meats (ham), cheeses, crackers
Sulfur	Found in several amino acids	Meats, milk, eggs, legumes, nuts
Zinc	Needed for several digestive enzymes; plays a role in respiration, bone and liver metabolism, and healing of wounds	Seafood, meats, milk, poultry

(FIGURE 4-10) **The amount of minerals you need to consume each day measures out to about a tablespoon. You need greater amounts of minerals than vitamins.**

minerals, including calcium. A low-fat diet should include low-fat or nonfat dairy foods plus vegetables high in calcium. Note that a number of factors influence calcium absorption. Vitamin D enhances it. High levels of sodium and animal protein, excessive caffeine consumption, and the use of steroids may reduce absorption. Also, the aluminum in antacids may increase calcium excretion and therefore should not be used on a regular basis without medical supervision.

Cooperative Learning
Bone Builders

Have students bring to class labels from calcium-rich foods and work in groups to determine several ways to supply the 1,200 mg of calcium they need every day. Suggest they use a form like the one at right to record their data.

Food	Serving size	mg calcium/serving	No. of servings needed

Journal 4C
Water Intake

Have students note in their Journal how much water they drink in a day. Suggest that they list times during the day when it would be convenient to have a drink of water.

Class Discussion
Importance of Water

Ask: **Why might water be considered the most important of the six nutrients?** [It makes up the greatest part of the body; it provides a medium for essential body reactions and keeps levels of other nutrients in balance; water regulates temperature and allows passage of gases, nutrients, and wastes.]

Section Review Worksheet 4.2

To reinforce the concepts presented in this section, assign Section Review Worksheet 4.2.

Section Quiz 4.2

Have students take Section Quiz 4.2

Reteaching Worksheet 4.2

Students who have difficulty with the material may complete Reteaching Worksheet 4.2.

Review Answers

1. Complex carbohydrates supply the body with energy as well as vitamins, minerals, proteins, and fiber.

2. fat

3. If calcium levels are low during the developmental years, the body will not be able to build strong bones. As a result, the bones will weaken and become brittle with age. Adequate calcium intake is also important for building strong teeth.

---

weight is water (65 to 70 percent in males, 55 to 65 percent in females). The percentage of water in the body depends on the amount of body fat a person has. People with high percentages of body fat have lower percentages of body water than normal. Much of this water is found inside your cells. The remaining water is found in the spaces surrounding cells, and in your bloodstream. Most body fluids, such as blood and digestive juices, are 80 percent water. If a 16-year-old male weighs 150 pounds, as much as 105 pounds of that weight is water. Similarly for a 16-year-old female weighing 120 pounds, as much as 78 pounds of that weight is water. The impor-

tance of water in the diet becomes obvious when you look at all the ways the body uses water to maintain its stability.

Functions of Water in the Body

1. All body functions are the result of chemical reactions. Most chemical reactions in the body can occur only in a water medium because substances dissolve in water.

2. The speed at which some of these chemical reactions occur is affected by how acidic body fluids are. Water helps maintain acidity at the proper levels.

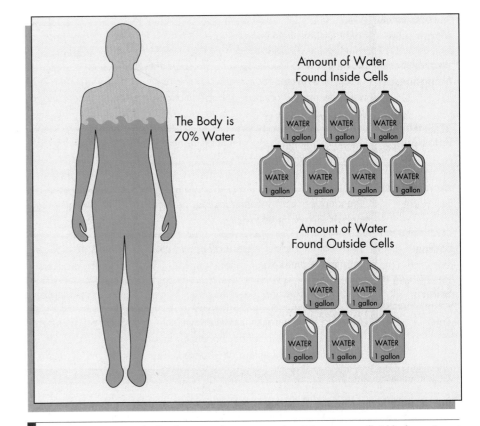

(FIGURE 4-11) **Since the body is mostly water, maintaining proper fluid balance is critical for good health.**

••• TEACH continued

Demonstration
Thirsty Cells

You can model the process that stimulates thirst: excess sodium in the blood causes water to move out of cells and into the blood. In other words, water diffuses across cell membranes to equalize the concentration of solutions. This can be illustrated with a small clear cup containing colored

water (representing the cell) and a clear glass container of salt water (representing the fluid around the cell). Cover the cup of colored water with a piece of fine cheesecloth or an old nylon stocking, and secure it with a rubber band. Lower it carefully into the container of salt water. Over time, colored water should diffuse through the fabric "cell membrane" into the surrounding salt water. Explain that water leaves the cells to try to correct the imbalance of sodium concentration in the

blood. This triggers a signal to the brain, resulting in a feeling of thirst.

Reinforcement
Who Needs Water?

Most Americans fail to drink enough water. Remind students of the following.

1. Body processes and cell maintenance cannot proceed normally without adequate water intake. Dehydration doesn't just make you feel bad; it is actually bad for your body!

3. Water is a product of the chemical reactions that supply energy to drive your body processes.
4. Water in body fluids provides a medium to transport gases, nutrients, and waste products throughout the body.
5. Water helps regulate body temperature. Water loss through perspiration helps cool the body.

Dehydration Water is so vital that it is rare to live for more than 10 days without water, even though you could live several weeks without food. When the amount of water you excrete exceeds the amount of water you take in, you are in a state of **dehydration.** Dehydration can occur as a result of heavy physical activity or an illness that includes vomiting, diarrhea, or fever. Situations that cause you to sweat profusely can also cause dehydration if you are not drinking enough water. Drinking too much alcohol or eating a high-protein diet can also cause dehydration. A prolonged state of dehydration can lead to kidney failure and death.

We take in water by drinking fluids and eating. Many foods contain large amounts of water. You need to consume at least one-half ounce of water daily for every pound of body weight, which totals at least two quarts. If you are very active or live in a very hot climate, extreme water loss through sweating could interfere with your body's functions.

A simple way to find out if you're adequately hydrated is to check the color of your urine throughout the day. If it is clear and uncolored, your water intake is adequate. If it is colored to any degree, you need to drink more water. If it is highly colored, you definitely need to increase your intake. It is especially important to drink enough water if you are trying to lose weight.

(FIGURE 4-12) **Drinking water after heavy activity replaces fluids lost from sweating.**

Review

1. Describe the importance of complex carbohydrates in the diet.

2. Which nutrient supplies the most calories per ounce?

3. How does a low calcium intake affect the body?

4. Why should you limit the amount of sodium in your diet?

5. Why are saturated fats to be avoided in making food selections?

6. How much of your daily caloric intake should come from carbohydrates, fats, and proteins?

7. Why do you need to have some fat in your diet?

8. *Critical Thinking* Why is it misleading to label peanut butter as having "no cholesterol"?

dehydration:
a state in which the body has lost more water than has been taken in.

Answers to Questions 1–3 are on p. 80.

SECTION 4.2

4. High levels of sodium have been linked to high blood pressure, abnormal heart rhythms, fluid around the heart, and overburdened kidneys.

5. Saturated fats contain large amounts of LDLs, which have been associated with cardiovascular disease. High fat intake has also been associated with diabetes and certain cancers.

6. 60 percent carbohydrates; no more than 30 percent fats; about 10 percent proteins

7. Fat is a concentrated source of energy and is an important body fuel. Fats are an important ingredient in many hormones, and some vitamins are soluble only in fat.

8. Many people think that "no cholesterol" also means no fat or low fat. Because cholesterol is found only in animal products, peanut butter cannot contain cholesterol. However, more than 75 percent of the calories in peanut butter come from fat, and more than 10 percent of that fat is saturated fat, which is linked to increased risk of heart disease.

2. Some things people think they can substitute for water actually cause their bodies to lose water. For example, alcohol and drinks containing caffeine (like many soft drinks) act as diuretics; that is, they cause water to be pumped out of the body.

Extension
Salt Watch

Have students interview adults who are monitoring their sodium intake, to learn what methods they use to reduce their salt consumption.

ASSESS

Section Review

Have students answer the Section Review questions.

Alternative Assessment
Good Food Salesmanship

Have students bring in fresh foods or pictures of them to "sell" to the class. Each must persuade other students of the food's value in promoting good health by explaining its nutrients.

Closure
Importance of Fats

Have students explain the pros and cons of fats—why we need fats in the diet—but not too many.

Section 4.3
Analyzing Your Nutritional Needs

Objectives

- *Define the nutritional requirements for healthy teens.*

- *Classify foods into the appropriate food groups.*

- *Interpret food labeling to analyze nutritional breakdown.*

- *Make food selections that satisfy nutritional requirements using the Food Pyramid and Dietary Guidelines.*
  - **LIFE SKILLS: Making Responsible Decisions**

- *Identify special nutritional needs of selected populations.*

Knowing about the principles of nutrition is just the first step in improving your health. Putting those principles into action is the next and most important step.

The Dietary Guidelines for Americans were developed to reflect what is currently known about the effect that diet has on health. The guidelines listed in Figure 4-13 provide a profile of a healthful diet and focus on seven eating practices.

Balance of Energy From Nutrients

Recall that three nutrients provide calories—carbohydrates, proteins, and fats. Balancing the calories from these three nutrient groups is the key to improving your diet. When you balance the calories provided by these larger nutrients, many of the nutrients needed in smaller quantities fall into place.

The Daily Reference Values listed in Figure 4-14 describe the percentage of your daily calories that should come from carbohydrates, protein, and fat. These values were designed to help you follow the recommendations of the general guidelines in Figure 4-13. Notice that most of these values can be found in the Nutrition Facts portion of a food label. If you can improve

(FIGURE 4-13) **These recommendations were released in 1990 from the U.S. Department of Agriculture (USDA) and the U.S. Department of Health and Human Services (USDHHS).**

Dietary Guidelines for Americans

Eat a variety of foods.

Maintain a healthful weight.

Choose a diet that is low in fat, saturated fat, and cholesterol.

Choose a diet with plenty of fruits, vegetables, and grain products.

Use sugars only in moderation.

Use salt and other forms of sodium only in moderation.

For adults who drink alcohol, do so only in moderation.

Daily Reference Values (DRVs)

Food component	Daily Reference Value
Total fat	65 g, 30% of total energy requirement
Saturated fat	20 g, 10% of total energy requirement
Cholesterol	300 mg
Total carbohydrate	300 g, 60% of total energy requirement
Dietary fiber	25 g
Protein	50 g, 10% of total energy requirement
Potassium	3500 mg
Sodium	2400 mg

(FIGURE 4-14) **Daily Reference Values are used as the standard for food labels which show the percentages of nutrients suggested for a 2,000 calorie diet.**

(FIGURE 4-15) **Reference Daily Intakes (RDIs) have replaced the U.S. Recommended Dietary Allowances (RDAs), which were once the accepted nutrition standard.**

your diet on a daily basis, then in the long run you'll be making choices about foods that match the dietary guidelines. There may be some days when you find it more difficult to follow the guidelines. One or two-less-than perfect days out of a week don't hurt your efforts to improve your nutrition.

Getting the nutrition you need during your teen years doesn't mean you have to completely give up your favorite foods. But if your favorite foods are high in sugar, calories, and fat, or if your favorite foods are low in fiber or other essential nutrients, you may need to make some changes to your diet to increase its nutritional value and follow the dietary guidelines. As a teen, you have an even greater need for some nutrients because your body is changing.

In some situations, the nutritional needs of a teen differ from those shown in Figure 4-15. For instance, vegetarians, athletes, and teen mothers have additional nutritional requirements that must be met to maintain health.

Some Vitamin and Mineral Reference Daily Intakes (RDIs)

(for adults and children 4 or more years of age)

Mineral/Vitamin	Quantity
Calcium	1 g (gram)
Iron	18 mg (milligrams)
Magnesium	400 mg
Copper	20 mg
Vitamin A	5,000 IUs (international units)
Vitamin C	60 mg
Vitamin D	400 IUs
Vitamin E	30 IUs

TEACH

Class Discussion
Dietary Guidelines

Discuss the Dietary Guidelines shown in Figure 4-13. Ask: **What are the purposes of these guidelines?** *[to provide a profile of a healthful diet, to focus on seven eating practices, and to provide information about the effect of diet on health]* Discuss the meaning of terms such as *healthful, low, plenty,* and *moderation.* Ask: **Why do you think these terms are used rather than specific recommendations?** *[Answers should stress that because individuals are so different, it is not possible to make specific recommendations that are valid for everyone. In order to know what is "low" or "high," individuals need to use the information in this chapter to determine what is ideal (the most healthful) for them.]*

Cooperative Learning
Daily Reference Values

In small groups or pairs, have students design and make their own daily reference charts using Figures 4-14 and 4-15 as information sources. Although students can organize the information as they wish, suggest that a pie chart is an effective way to present the data given in percentages. Students can use these charts later when they evaluate their own diet or plan a new one.

Class Discussion
The Shape of Balanced Nutrition

Ask: **Why is the pyramid a good shape to illustrate the needs for**

Check Up

Have students turn in their choices for the two items and tally the answers on the board. Discuss the answers to items many students got wrong.

Check Up

How Much Do You Know About Food Selection?

From the statements listed below, choose the best answer. Then check the correct answers below.

1. Cooking practice that increases fat in foods
   baking   broiling   frying   don't know

2. Boiling vegetables reduces vitamins
   yes   no   don't know

3. Salt in peanut butter-and-jelly sandwich compared with a hot dog
   less salt   more   same   don't know

4. Salt in canned vegetables compared with frozen
   less salt   more   same   don't know

5. Fat in frozen yogurt compared with ice cream
   less fat   more   same   don't know

6. Fiber in corn flakes compared with bran cereal
   less fiber   more   same   don't know

7. Fiber in baked beans compared with baked potato
   less fiber   more   same   don't know

8. Eating fatty foods may cause
   cavities   stomach cancer
   heart disease   don't know

9. Eating too little fiber may cause
   colon cancer   high blood pressure
   heart disease   don't know

10. Eating sugar may cause
    heart disease   low blood pressure
    cavities   don't know

11. Amount of iron needed by females compared with males
    less iron   more   same   don't know

12. Amount of calcium needed by teenagers compared to middle-aged women
    less calcium   more   same   don't know

1) frying; 2) yes; 3) less salt; 4) more salt; 5) less fat; 6) less fiber; 7) more fiber; 8) heart disease; 9) colon cancer; 10) cavities; 11) more iron; 12) more calcium

Categorizing Foods— The Food Pyramid

You should know by now that the best nutritional strategies include eating a variety of foods. When you choose a variety of foods, your diet can supply all your daily requirements. One way to select from a variety of foods is by grouping them. The idea of four basic food groups was once used to group foods for nutritional purposes. In May 1992, the U.S. Department of Agriculture provided a new way of categorizing foods called the Food Pyramid, shown in Figure 4-16 on the next page.

Let's look at how the Food Pyramid should be used in planning your diet. The pyramid organizes foods into groups based on the Dietary Guidelines. Notice that the bread, cereal, rice, and pasta group is on the bottom. This placement indicates that foods from this group should be the largest part of your diet. Each day, you should have 6 to 11 servings from this group for good health. Figure 4-17 shows some foods that are part of this group.

As you move up the pyramid, you see that you need fewer servings from the remaining groups to be healthy. For example, you need 3 to 5 servings daily from the vegetable group and 2 to 4 servings from the fruit group. You need only 2 to 3 servings from the milk, yogurt, and cheese group, and the same number of servings from the meat, poultry, fish, dry beans, eggs, and nuts group. Finally, at the top of the pyramid you find fats, oils, and sweets. Foods in this category are not part of a food group. These foods should be selected sparingly as part of your diet.

Bread, Cereal, Rice, and Pasta Group

Foods from this group are made from whole grains and grain products. The term "cereal" is used to describe the food crops— rice, wheat, and corn. These grains supply more than half of the energy humans use

---

• • • TEACH continued

various food groups? [We need a broad base of breads, cereals, rice, and pasta, which fits the broad base of the pyramid. Lesser, but still substantial, requirements for vegetables and fruits fit on the next layer of the pyramid. Still fewer servings of milk and meat groups fit on the next layer. The small triangle on the top represents the few fats and sweets needed.]

Class Discussion
Diets: What Should You Cut?

Ask: **Why are limitations placed on foods in the top three groups of the pyramid rather than on the bottom three?** [The first three groups are relatively high in fat, protein, or sugar and are related to the most pressing health problems in our society. They are also the highest in calories. The bottom three groups are generally low in fat and high in fiber, minerals, vitamins, and water. Complex carbohydrates are linked with a low incidence of cancer and heart disease. They also are low in calories.]

Reinforcement
America's Upside-Down Food Triangle

Emphasize to students the relative area given to each food group. Far too often, young people's eating habits reverse these proportions. Many people still believe that the base group is fattening, and curtail their intake of complex carbohydrates when dieting. As a result, their intake is insufficient.

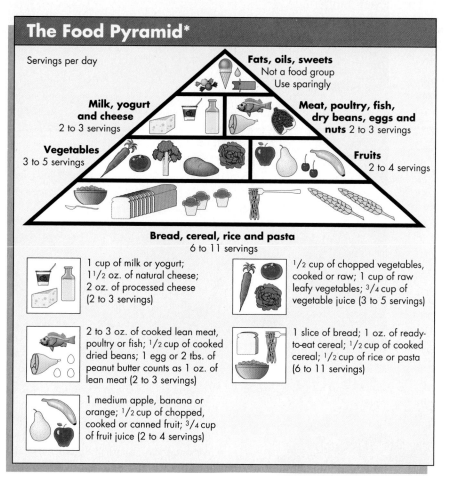

The Food Pyramid*

Servings per day

Fats, oils, sweets
Not a food group
Use sparingly

Milk, yogurt and cheese
2 to 3 servings

Meat, poultry, fish, dry beans, eggs and nuts 2 to 3 servings

Vegetables
3 to 5 servings

Fruits
2 to 4 servings

Bread, cereal, rice and pasta
6 to 11 servings

1 cup of milk or yogurt; 1¹/₂ oz. of natural cheese; 2 oz. of processed cheese (2 to 3 servings)

¹/₂ cup of chopped vegetables, cooked or raw; 1 cup of raw leafy vegetables; ³/₄ cup of vegetable juice (3 to 5 servings)

2 to 3 oz. of cooked lean meat, poultry or fish; ¹/₂ cup of cooked dried beans; 1 egg or 2 tbs. of peanut butter counts as 1 oz. of lean meat (2 to 3 servings)

1 slice of bread; 1 oz. of ready-to-eat cereal; ¹/₂ cup of cooked cereal; ¹/₂ cup of rice or pasta (6 to 11 servings)

1 medium apple, banana or orange; ¹/₂ cup of chopped, cooked or canned fruit; ³/₄ cup of fruit juice (2 to 4 servings)

*Source: U.S. Department of Agriculture and Department of Health and Human Services

■ (FIGURE 4-16) **The Food Pyramid replaces the four food groups concept.**

daily. Foods derived from these cereal crops are good sources of complex carbohydrates and dietary fiber. They are generally low in fat and high in B vitamins. "Generally low in fat" means you should look at labels to determine if the food selection from this group is low in fat. Recommended serving sizes from this group include one slice of bread, one-half cup of cereal, or one-half cup of pasta.

Foods to Limit: Foods containing a lot of butter or eggs should be limited. For example, the following could be very high in fat, cholesterol, and calories: butter rolls, croissants, cheese breads, egg breads, store-bought donuts, muffins, sweet rolls, and biscuits. Buttered popcorn (including microwave products), foods made with coconut or palm oil, soups made with cream, and high-fat meats should also be limited.

Background
More Guidelines on Healthful Dieting

Dieting can have unexpected bad side effects if calories are reduced too drastically. In general, a diet that includes less than 1,000–1,200 calories a day (1,500 for a large person) stresses the body. The restricted intake has long-term implications. It triggers a survival mechanism, causing the dieter to lose muscle mass, the metabolism to slow down, and the percent of body fat to increase. The body converts mass to fat because it requires fewer calories to be maintained. Result: the body needs fewer calories than before the diet. After the diet, a return to normal food intake causes weight gain because the body has changed its method of handling energy supplies.

Sweets and fats, which should be eaten sparingly, are actively promoted by advertisers.

Class Discussion
Don't Butter Me Up

Ask: **How can some bread, cereal, rice, and pasta products be undesirable if everyone needs a high percentage of complex carbohydrates?** *[When made with butter, lard, vegetable shortening, or eggs, breads and other* *baked goods can be high in cholesterol and saturated fat. Rice or pasta served with a fatty sauce or butter presents the same problem.]* **What is the disadvantage of purchasing fresh bread or other baked goods?** *[Unlike packaged baked goods, fresh ones seldom have Nutrition Facts labels, and often contain high amounts of fat and sugar.]* **What is an advantage?** *[They usually do not contain additives or preservatives.]*

• • • TEACH continues on p. 86

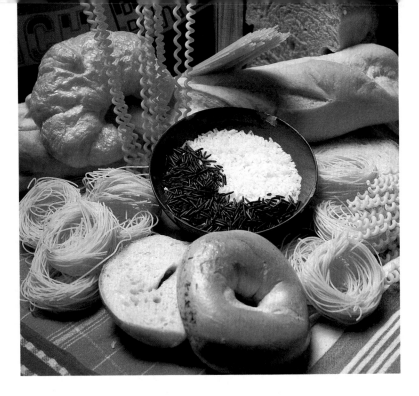

(FIGURE 4-17) **You should have 6 to 11 servings daily from foods in the bread, cereal, rice, and pasta group. Limit sweet bakery in favor of low-sugar, complex carbohydrates.**

(FIGURE 4-18) **Signs in most produce markets remind you to "Eat Five a Day," which means you should eat at least five servings of fruits and vegetables daily.**

Vegetable Group Foods from this group are high in vitamins, minerals, and carbohydrates and very low in fat. All vegetables are part of this group and are generally good sources of dietary fiber. These foods generally supply the best nutrition for the fewest calories.

The size of a serving is a half-cup of cooked or raw vegetables, a cup of raw leafy vegetables, or three-fourths cup of vegetable juice. Select a vegetable or fruit that is high in vitamin C at least once a day. Select vegetables and fruits that are high in vitamin A several times a week.

Vitamin C-rich vegetables: asparagus, broccoli, brussel sprouts, cabbage, greens (mustard, kale, collard, beet), green pepper, potatoes, spinach, and tomatoes.

Vitamin A-rich vegetables: broccoli, carrots, greens, pumpkin, romaine lettuce, spinach, sweet potatoes, tomatoes, and winter squash.

••• TEACH continued

Demonstration
Your Fruit and Veggie IQ

Challenge students to bring in fruits and vegetables they think other students may not have tried. (Some possibilities include kale, artichoke, mango, plantain, papaya, kiwi, kohlrabi, winter squash, and ugli fruit.) If possible, students should include nutritional information about the item they bring in.

They may want to include a recipe for its preparation. Place each item at a separate station, and have students rotate through the stations to examine the foods. Include a question-and-answer session in which students can ask any questions they have about the fruits and vegetables.

Demonstration
The Meaning of Lean

The differences in fat content of various grades of ground beef can be dra-

matically illustrated. In separate skillets, cook one-fourth of a pound of ground beef with various fat levels, such as 90 percent, 80 percent, etc. Pour off the fat from each cooked portion, and measure it. Have students view the different quantities of fat, and comment on the difference between eating a hamburger made of regular meat versus eating one made of reduced-fat meat. To dramatize that animal fat is saturated, allow the samples to congeal before discarding.

Foods to Limit: Though most fruits and vegetables are low in fat, avocados and olives should be limited, as they are high in fat and therefore high in calories.

Fruit Group Foods from this group are also high in vitamins and minerals while being low in fat. Like vegetables, fruits are also good sources of dietary fiber. The fiber content of raw fruit or dried fruit is much higher than that of fruit juices. If you prefer fruit juice, drink 100 percent juice. Fruit drinks do not have the same nutritional value as juices. If you eat canned or frozen fruits, select those packed in light syrups or natural juices.

The size of a serving is one medium-sized piece of fresh fruit, such as an apple, banana, or orange; one-half cup of chopped, cooked, or canned fruit; or three-fourths cup of fruit juice. In making selections in this group, you should also look for good sources of vitamins A and C.

Vitamin C-rich fruits: tomatoes, cantaloupe, grapefruit, oranges, and tangerines.

Vitamin A-rich fruits: tomatoes, apricots, cantaloupe, mango, papaya, and peaches.

Milk, Yogurt, and Cheese Group All dairy products are found in this group. This group provides the best sources of calcium, good sources of protein, vitamins A and D, and some minerals. Teens and young adults are still building their bones and need the calcium supplied by five servings a day from this group. One cup of milk or yogurt, one and one-half ounces of cheese, or two ounces of processed cheese are recommended serving sizes.

Foods to Limit: Milk products with more than 1 percent fat should be limited. This includes buttermilk and yogurt made from whole milk; condensed milk, evaporated milk, all types of cream, nondairy cream substitutes, and any sour cream sub-

(FIGURE 4-19) **You should have two to three servings daily from foods in the milk, yogurt, and cheese group. Limit cheese and milk products with high fat content. Those items shown are good low-fat selections.**

stitutes with palm oil. Also limit cheeses with more than 2 grams of fat per ounce of cheese, such as cream cheese, creamed cottage cheese, and most processed cheeses.

Meat, Poultry, Fish, Dry Beans, Eggs, and Nuts Group These foods are high in protein and B vitamins, and are also good sources of certain minerals. Foods from this group can be very high in fat and cholesterol. Good choices are the leanest possible cuts of any meat. Skinless poultry and fish are preferred selections over red meat. The new turkey-based products, such as turkey hot dogs, cold cuts, and sausages are the food industry's way of providing foods with less fat than the pork or beef versions. The serving size for this group would be 2 to 3 ounces of cooked lean meat, poultry, or fish. One egg or 2 tablespoons of peanut butter count as 1 ounce of lean meat.

Foods to Limit: Select low-fat meats with no more than 2 grams of fat per ounce

Role-Playing
Breaking the Burger Habit

Ask for volunteers to role-play a group of friends ordering dinner at a fast-food restaurant. One student should try to convince the others to change the standard order—burger, fries, and a soda. Other students should demonstrate peer pressure not to change. Have student observers comment on the realism of the dialogue and suggest additional arguments in favor of ordering more healthful food.

Game
Calorie Countdown

Create a number of food cards to represent typical breakfast, lunch, and dinner foods. Glue food pictures to one side of a 4 x 6 in. card. On the opposite side, write the number of calories and grams of fat per serving. Divide the class into teams, and tell them that the goal is to create a daily meal plan with 1600 calories and 53 or fewer grams of fat. One team should select foods without looking at

the back of the cards, then count the total calories and fat in the day's meals. Have other teams take their turns, and then compare the results. The team or teams that come closest to the goal are the winners.

 Teaching Transparency 4A
Nutrients in Food

Use this transparency to relate the information in the food pyramid to the foods discussed here and the nutrients discussed in Section 4-2.

Background

What's for Dessert?—Sugar and Fat

Western societies consume a diet very high in sugar and fat. Sweet desserts combine these two nutrients in great amounts; for example, in chocolate products, sugar and fat typically account for 80 to 90 percent of total calories. The combination of sugar and fat make them uniquely tasty, but studies show that this combination is also uniquely fattening. Data from nutritional studies indicate that eating sugar/fat mixtures leads to the deposit of more body fat than does eating an equal amount of sugar and fat at different times of the day.

(FIGURE 4-20) **You should select two to three servings daily from foods in this group. Select low-fat ways to prepare meats, fish, eggs, and poultry. Note that nuts and beans are also part of this group.**

of meat. Limit bacon, sausage, corned beef, pastrami, ribs, regular ground meat, goose, duck, and organ meats. Though liver is high in cholesterol, it is very rich in iron and vitamins. Liver provides important nutrients and should be eaten in moderation. Peanut butter and most nuts are high in fat and should be eaten sparingly.

Fats-Sweets The top of the pyramid contains foods that are high in calories, sugars, and fats but are low in nutrients. This section of the pyramid also contains beverages, that are high in sugar, and other drinks, such as coffee, tea, and alcohol, that provide little or no nutrition. Refined sugars and natural sweetners like honey, molasses, and maple syrup and refined sugars are part of this section along with foods high in sugars, such as candy bars, cakes, and pies. Foods high in fat also belong in this section. High-fat diets have been linked to increased risk of heart disease and certain kinds of cancer. In

addition, foods from this group contribute to obesity. Therefore, all the foods that fall in this category should be used sparingly. In fact, it is better to go several days without eating foods from this group.

Nutritional Labeling

The food pyramid is a giant step forward in "seeing" what makes a healthful diet. When the food pyramid was introduced, many changes were taking place in the ways government agencies were educating the public about food selection. Unlike other countries where deficiencies of protein and calories still exist, the United States has an abundance of food. The dietary deficiency diseases are rarely seen anymore in our country. But the United States has two primary nutritional problems affecting the health of its children, teens, and adults: consuming too many calories and not getting enough exercise.

One of the most significant changes aimed at educating the public has been the new food label. Figure 4-21 shows you an example of how the label's information can help you make smart food choices and follow the dietary guidelines.

Reading Labels

The new label gives information about the nutrients that make it easier to determine which foods fall within your guidelines for kinds of fat, complex carbohydrates, fiber, and sugar. Few foods are exempt from the labeling requirements. The labeling standards prevent misleading claims about foods advertised as "low fat," "low cholesterol," "reduced sugar," or "fat free."

Serving Size—The Basis of Comparison If you eat more or less than the serving size, you'll need to adjust the amount of each nutrient to reflect your serving.

• • • TEACH continued

Class Discussion

What's on a Food Label?

Have students use Figure 4-21 as a reference, and ask: **What is the serving size?** *[about 3/4 cup, or 30 g]* **Assuming the person eating the cereal uses no milk, how many calories are in one serving?** *[120]* **How many of those calories are from fat?** *[15]* **What is the total fat content, and how much of that fat is saturated?**

[2 g, none] **What does the 3% Daily Value for fat mean?** *[One serving provides 3 percent of a person's fat requirement for one day, based on a 2,000 calorie diet.]* **Does this cereal contain any cholesterol?** *[no]* **How much of the carbohydrate content is fiber?** *[3 g out of 25 g]* **What percent of the Daily Value of iron does the cereal provide?** *[25 percent]* **How does eating the cereal with one-half cup skim milk change the nutritional value?** *[It increases the total calories and calories from fat; it adds additional*

cholesterol, sodium, potassium, carbohydrates, thiamin, riboflavin, phosphorus, zinc, and vitamins A, C, and D.]

Class Discussion

Rounding Out Breakfast

After students have analyzed the nutrition of the cereal shown in Figure 4-21, have them suggest other foods that could be added to make a well-rounded breakfast. *(Suggestions may include skim milk, sliced fruit or fruit juice, and whole-wheat toast with margarine.)*

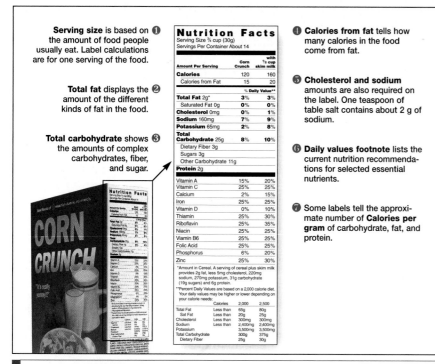

Serving size is based on ❶ the amount of food people usually eat. Label calculations are for one serving of the food.

Total fat displays the ❷ amount of the different kinds of fat in the food.

Total carbohydrate shows ❸ the amounts of complex carbohydrates, fiber, and sugar.

❹ Calories from fat tells how many calories in the food come from fat.

❺ Cholesterol and sodium amounts are also required on the label. One teaspoon of table salt contains about 2 g of sodium.

❻ Daily values footnote lists the current nutrition recommendations for selected essential nutrients.

❼ Some labels tell the approximate number of Calories per gram of carbohydrate, fat, and protein.

(FIGURE 4-21) **The listing of Nutrition Facts on food labels is now required by law. You can use these data to make informed choices about foods so that your diet fits the Dietary Guidelines for Americans.**

Life Skills Worksheet 4A
Assign the Examining Food Labels Life Skills Worksheet.

Labeling about Calories
Excess calories is one reason for weight gain.

Terms You Should Know

Calorie-free: fewer than 5 calories per serving

Low calorie: 40 calories or less per serving

Reduced or fewer calories: at least 25 percent fewer calories per serving than the reference food

Labeling about Sugar
Sugar values on the label include naturally occurring sugars, such as milk sugar, and refined sugars added during processing. However, the nutrition label does not account for longer-chain sugars in the food. To keep your sugar intake at or below 10 percent of your day's calories, you'll need to read the ingredient list. Ingredients such as *sugar* (sucrose), *fructose*, *maltose, lactose, honey, syrup, corn syrup, high-fructose corn syrup, molasses,* and *fruit juice concentrate* indicate added sweeteners. If any of these ingredients appears first or second or if several of them appear in the list, the food is probably high in sugar.

Terms You Should Know

Sugar free: there is either no sugar in the food or less than 0.5 gram per serving

No sugar added, Without added sugar: no sugars or ingredients that contain sugars have been added and processing does not increase the sugar content above the amount that is naturally found in the ingredients

Reduced sugar: contains at least 25 percent less sugar per serving than the reference food

Cooperative Learning
Reading Food Labels

Provide small groups of students with identical copies of a label from a food product. Assign each group one of the following areas to evaluate: calories, sugar, fat, fiber, or carbohydrates. Using the information on pages 88–90 as a guide, each group should comment on their topic. For example, if the product contains 3 g of fiber, that group might say, "This product contains 3 g of fiber per serving, which classifies it as a good source." Groups should make their report to the entire class and can be challenged if another group disagrees with their assessment.

• • • TEACH continues on p. 90

Life Skills Worksheet 4B

Assign the Planning a Menu Life Skills Worksheet.

NUTRITIONAL ANALYSIS OF FAST FOOD LUNCH

933 Total Calories

Protein..............13%
Total Fats 42%
Complex Carbohydrates ..28%
Sugar...............16%

■ Protein ☐ Complex Carb
■ Total Fat ☐ Other

■ (FIGURE 4-22) The fast-food diet is high in calories and fat. Compare these values to the guidelines in Figure 4-14.

Labeling About Fat The label makes total fat and saturated fat values very visible, but reading the ingredients list will give you a more complete picture. The values listed on the label include all naturally saturated fats unless there is less than 0.5 g. If you want to limit your intake of saturated fat from both animal and vegetable sources, read the label and look for the words *hydrogenated* or *partially hydrogenated* used to describe a vegetable oil. Even though these vegetable oils are naturally unsaturated before hydrogenation, they will not be included as unsaturated fat.

Know Your Fat Limit

	Daily calorie level			
	1600	**2000**	**2500**	**2800**
Total fat (grams)	52	65	81	91
Saturated fat (grams)	18	20	25	31

Labeling About Fiber If the labeling claims that the product is high in fiber, either the food must be low in fat or the level of total fat must appear next to the high-fiber claim.

Terms You Should Know

High fiber: 5 grams or more per serving
Good source of fiber: between 2.5 and 5 grams per serving
More or added fiber: at least 0.5 grams more per serving than the reference food

Labeling about Carbohydrates The label will provide values for the amount of dietary fiber, but it will make no distinction between fiber in the food that dissolves or does not dissolve. If you are trying to calculate the number of calories from carbohydrates, don't include the grams of fiber in the calculation. Fiber does not provide calories.

General Labels Food manufacturers sometimes alter food in order to make it more appealing to the consumer, who may be concerned about the number of calories, the sodium level, or the fat content. Two terms, *light* and *lite* are commonly used to

Teaching Transparency 4B
Dietary Guidelines for Americans

Use this transparency of Figure 4-13 to review the dietary guidelines, and discuss how the Guidelines for Improving Your Food Selections relate to them.

Class Discussion
Strategies for Lower Sugar and Fat Intake

After students have read the guidelines for improving food selections, ask them to suggest realistic substitutes for soft drinks or sodas that are lower in sugar (club soda, fruit juice and fruit juice blends, milk, herbal tea, plain water or specialty waters). Then have them review the guidelines for reducing dietary fat. Ask the class to vote on

their "top five"—the five guidelines for reducing fat intake that can be most realistically implemented.

Debate the Issue
How Much Fast Food?

Have students debate this issue: Teenagers should limit their fast-food meals to no more than three a week. Allow time for students to gather information about fast-food meals. Be certain that students consider factors such as the nutritional content of fast-compare these altered foods with their reference foods and may mean one of two things:

- the altered product contains one-third fewer calories or half the fat of the reference food, or
- the sodium content of a low-calorie, low-fat food has been reduced to half of its original sodium content.

The American Diet

How does the American diet compare with recommended dietary guidelines? A meal that is fairly standard for teenagers consists of a hamburger, a large order of french-fried potatoes, and a cola drink. According to the Daily Reference Values for a 2000 calorie diet, 200 calories (10 percent) should come from protein. For a 2500 calorie diet, 250 calories (10 percent) should come from protein. In a day, no more than 30 percent of your total calories should come from fats, 10 percent from proteins, and 60 percent from carbohydrates. Figure 4-22 is a summary of the nutritional content of this fast food.

As you can see, this one meal provides more than 46 percent of the caloric intake of a 2000 calorie diet and more than 37 percent of a 2500 calorie diet. This meal contains an appropriate amount of protein, but far too much fat and far too few complex carbohydrates.

Guidelines for Improving Your Food Selections

Now that you have read about basic nutrition principles, you can use the following points to guide you in making nutritious food selections.

1. **Sugars**
   To reduce the amount of refined sugars in your diet you can

a. reduce the number of soft drinks you have each day.
b. eat fresh fruit for dessert instead of baked goods.
c. read food labels and reduce your intake of foods high in sugar.
d. reduce the amount of sugar you add to foods.

2. **Complex Carbohydrates**
   To increase the percentage of complex carbohydrates in your diet you can
a. eat more fruits, vegetables, cereals, breads, and legumes at each meal.
b. eat fresh fruits as snacks.
c. increase the number of whole-grain products you eat (such as whole-wheat bread rather than white bread).
d. eat more pasta, noodles, and rice.

3. **Fats**
   To reduce the amount of fat in your diet you can
a. substitute complex carbohydrates for foods high in fat.
b. reduce the amount of high-fat meats you eat (for example, regular hamburger, ribs, sausages, and hot dogs).
c. eat lean meats (for example, white chicken meat roasted without the skin).
d. increase the amount of fish in your diet as a substitute for meats.
e. reduce the amount of nuts, peanuts, and peanut butter in your diet.
f. trim fat from meat before cooking.
g. limit fried foods.
h. bake, broil, or cook meats so that fat will drain away from food as it is cooked.
i. substitute skim or low-fat milk for whole milk.
j. use low-fat salad dressings.
k. reduce the amount of butter or margarine you use.
l. reduce your use of eggs.

Life Skills Worksheet 4C
Assign the More for Your Money Life Skills Worksheet.

food meals, the broadening of fast-food menus to include more healthful choices, the needs of today's families, teen food preferences, and peer pressure.

Role-Playing
Making a Shopping List

Have pairs of students take turns role-playing friends making a shopping list for one day's menu. One student can criticize the other's choice of breakfast, snack, or other food. The other must

defend the choice by providing facts about the item's nutritional value. Have the class comment about how convincing the actors are and whether their choices are healthful.

Reinforcement
More Than the Price Is Wrong

Processed foods not only are generally more expensive ounce-per-ounce than fresh foods, but also are likely to contain more saturated fats, sodium, and sugar. These ingredients are added to

increase a product's shelf life and enhance its taste. Encourage students to read labels on processed foods to become aware of the "hidden" calories from fats and sugars and the high sodium levels found in some of them.

Background

The Chinese Diet

Studies suggest that the traditional Chinese diet is much better for your health than the American standard. The Chinese consume a third of the fat Americans do and twice as much starch, and their plant-rich diet includes three times as much dietary fiber. Only 7 percent of protein in the Chinese diet comes from animal sources, whereas 70 percent of Americans' protein comes from animals. Unfortunately, most Chinese restaurants in the United States prepare their dishes to suit American tastes. As a result, the food often contains unacceptably high levels of sodium and fat. When ordering Chinese food, it's best to choose steamed dishes or ones that have been stir-fried in a small amount of oil.

Cultural DIVERSITY

Dietary Patterns and Food Selection Tips

Although most Americans eat many of the same kinds of foods, people have some distinct dietary patterns based on their cultural backgrounds.

Jewish Foods Jewish dietary laws originated as the "Rules of Kashruth," and all foods prepared according to these rules were called "kosher." Most of these laws today apply to the methods of slaughter, preparation, and serving of meat products, and to restrictions on the combination of meat, fish, and egg products. There are also special foods to commemorate or celebrate special occasions, such as challah (white bread), gefilte fish (chopped fish), matzoh

(unleavened bread), and potato latkes (fried grated potatoes).

African-American Foods The African-American diet includes nutritious items, such as collard greens, sweet potatoes, corn bread, rice, black-eyed peas, lima beans, kidney beans, navy beans, and pinto beans. This selection of foods provides good sources of vitamins A and C, protein, and complex carbohydrates. Fish and chicken are commonly used instead of red meat. Salt, butter, fatback, and salt pork are used in flavoring foods. Limiting items high in salt and fat provides an African-American diet with the nutrients for good health.

Mexican Foods Today's Mexican food customs represent a blend of the food habits of early Spanish settlers in this country and Native-American tribes from the southwest. With this mixing of customs, three foods emerged as important: dried beans, chiles (chili peppers), and corn. Corn is the basic grain for breads and cereals. Masa is a dough made from dried corn that is soaked in water and lime, boiled, then ground into a paste-like dough. This dough is made into tortillas.

Puerto Rican Foods Although Puerto Rico shares a common heritage with Mexico, Puerto Rican foods include many fruits and vegetables not available in Mexico, such as viandas (starchy fruits and vegetables: yams, sweet potatoes, green bananas, and cassava). A typical day's menu might include coffee for breakfast, viandas and codfish for lunch, and rice, beans, and viandas for dinner.

• • • TEACH continued

Writing

Adventures in International Cuisine

Ask students to select a distinctive cultural cuisine they think they would like to try. Have them write about several opportunities they might create to try these foods: purchase the items from a specialty grocery store or the ethnic foods aisle of supermarket; borrow a cookbook from library; ask a friend, relative, or neighbor who is an expert; or go to an ethnic restaurant. After they have tried the food, students can write a description of the experience.

Writing

A Menu With Cosmopolitan Flair

Students who are familiar with the foods of another culture can imagine they are opening a restaurant specializing in the foods of that culture. Have them write food descriptions for their menus. Their object is to entice the restaurant customer to try a variety of healthy foods from that culture.

 ## Cooperative Learning

Cooking Up Good Health— International Style

Assemble a collection of cookbooks of other countries—library offerings may

Life Skills Worksheet 4D
Assign the Evaluating Your Diet Life Skills Worksheet.

Chinese Foods Chinese cooking is based on enhancing the natural flavor of foods and preserving their color and texture. Chinese prefer to cook fresh foods quickly, stir-frying them. Vegetables are cooked slightly to retain crispness, flavor, and vitamins.

Japanese Foods The Japanese diet contains far more seafood, particularly raw fish, than does the Chinese diet. A traditional Japanese meal might begin with unsweetened tea, followed by tofu or soybean cake served with raw fish (sashimi) or radish (komono), followed by broiled fish, vegetables, steamed rice, fruits, soup, and more tea.

Selecting Foods from Other Cultures

Italian Pasta is a good choice for carbohydrates. Select vegetable sauces without cream, and dishes without a lot of high-fat cheese and meat. Italian ices are good, low-calorie choices for desserts.

Oriental Choose steamed, broiled, or stir-fried dishes rather than deep-fried. Limit your use of soy sauce, which is high in sodium. Select noodle dishes with soft noodles rather than hard noodles, which are fried. Dishes with tofu are high in protein and low in calories.

French Avoid foods with rich sauces like hollandaise and bechamel that are very high in fat and cholesterol. Select foods prepared in wine sauces and ask how the sauce is prepared, to assure that it is low in fat and calories. Foods from southern France are generally prepared with olive oil and with lots of vegetables, which would provide more nutrition with fewer calories.

Greek Select Greek salads, but use the cheese, anchovies, and olives sparingly, as they are high in fat and sodium. Select fish dishes or broiled shish kebab. Avoid dishes with phyllo dough because they are generally made with lots of butter.

Eastern Indian Foods from this culture are generally low in saturated fat and cholesterol. Look for seekh kabob, marinated lamb or chicken, and fish cooked in clay pots. Avoid foods cooked in coconut milk or cream, as they are high in saturated fat.

Mexican Limit tortillas that are fried with lard. Select shrimp or chicken tostadas made with corn tortillas that are baked. Look for dishes without cheese or ask for the cheese on the side. Rice and beans are good choices because they are low in fat and provide complete protein. Limit refried beans as they are often cooked in lard.

Middle Eastern Select dishes made with vegetables, grains, and spices, like couscous or steamed bulgur, topped with vegetables or chicken. Shish kebab is also a good choice as long as it is not basted in butter. Fresh fruits such as melons, figs, and grapes are excellent choices for dessert.

Southeast Asian Limit deep-fried foods and cream soups. Select stir-fried dishes with fresh vegetables and small portions of meat or fish. Grilled meat dishes and hot-and-sour soup are also good low-fat choices.

be supplemented by books brought from home. Set up a small group to represent each cuisine. Within each group, allow students time to explore the ingredients and preparation methods for typical foods of the culture. Their goal is to prepare a 3 to 5 minute presentation describing the healthfulness and balance of ingredients of several recipes.

• • • TEACH continues on p. 94

Life SKILLS

Review the directions for logging in foods and beverages. Be certain that students understand what constitutes a serving. Students can copy the log form or use Life Skills Worksheet 4A to record their eating habits.

Background
Common Vegetables and Amino Acids

Researchers have found that 11 different vegetable juices contain the types of free amino acids necessary for protein building. Careful blending of the juices from various fruits, vegetables, and seeds can produce a drink that contains all 20 of the essential amino acids. There is no such juice on the market right now, but with additional research, it could become one of the foods of the twenty-first century.

LifeSKILLS: Being a Wise Consumer

Checking Your Diet Against the Food Pyramid

The first step toward developing healthful eating habits is to identify how you're currently eating. Keep a food and beverage diary for three days. Stick to these guidelines when making entries in your diary. For each day . . .

1. Write down everything you eat and drink at each meal, record all snacks. write down the time you eat as well.

2. Be specific when you identify the food at each meal and snack. Is it whole wheat bread or white bread? Is it lowfat yogurt or fat-free yogurt? Instead of writing "hamburger," specify 1 burger bun, 3 ounces of meat, 1 slice of tomato, 1 tablespoon of mayonnaise.

3. Be precise when you record the amounts of food. For instance, write 1 cup of cereal instead of a bowl. You may need to measure to be sure of the exact amount you are eating.

4. Record how the food was prepared. Was it baked, broiled, fried, fresh, or frozen?

Next, make a list of how many servings you should be eating daily from each group in the food pyramid, and compare each day of your log to the list.

How did you do?
Is there one group that is especially high or low?
How could you improve that one group?

Food group	Recommended number of servings	My servings for the day	Number over or under (+ or −)
Bread and cereal group	_____	_____	_____
Vegetable group	_____	_____	_____
Fruit group	_____	_____	_____
Dairy products group	_____	_____	_____
Protein foods group	_____	_____	_____
Fat and sugar group	_____	_____	_____

• • • TEACH continued

Cooperative Learning
Ranking Advertised Products

Ask students to bring in the packaging from a food product they see advertised. Divide the class into small groups to study the ingredients list on one or two of the labels, and classify the ingredients in them according to the food pyramid groupings. Most products will contain nutrients from more than one group. As a class, rank the products according to their nutritional values and decide which are healthful choices and which should be eaten in moderation.

Class Discussion
What's the Motivation?

Ask: **What do you think it would take to convince teens to switch from unhealthful snack foods to healthful snack foods?** *[Responses may include education about food choices, a desire to be healthier, a conviction that some snack items really do harm their health, better advertising of health-enhancing snacks, and better availability of such snacks.]*

Journal 4D
Plan for Improving Your Diet

Have students write in their Journal a plan for improving their food selections. Students should choose several

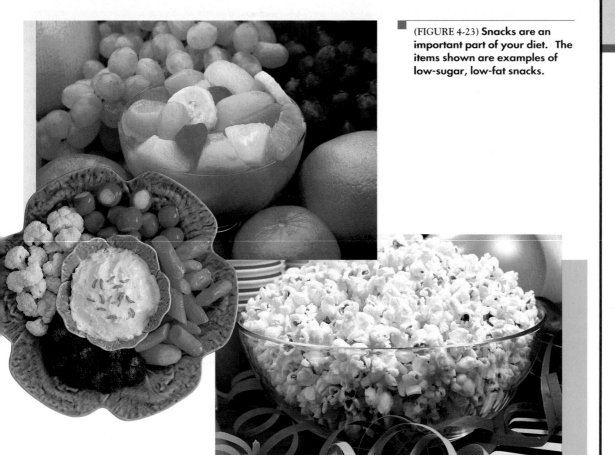

(FIGURE 4-23) **Snacks are an important part of your diet. The items shown are examples of low-sugar, low-fat snacks.**

Background
Vegetarian Diets and Health

Recent studies of people on vegetarian diets have documented some clear-cut benefits of vegetarianism, including the following:

• a 40 percent lower death rate from cardio-vascular disease than the average American

• 41 percent fewer deaths from cancer

• a reduced risk of adult-onset diabetes

Doctors still recommend caution. Other factors, such as exercise and abstaining from smoking, could be partly responsible for the observed benefits. Some health experts say that it may not be necessary to eliminate meat completely. Diets that include small portions of lean meat or fish may be just as healthful. In addition, there is probably little or no benefit from a meatless diet that includes large portions of high-fat dairy products and fried foods.

Snacks

Snacking is a large part of the American diet. Snacking, in and of itself, is not a bad habit. Some nutritionists actually recommend small meals and snacks rather than three large meals per day. Most weight loss programs include snacks as part of the meal plan. What are nutritious snacks? Where do they fit into your overall diet?

Fruits Fresh fruits, dried fruits, or canned fruits without added sugar provide vitamins and are a quick energy source. Fruit ices and sorbets make good low-calorie substitutes for ice cream.

Vegetables Fresh vegetables are low in fat and low in calories.

Grains Baked tortilla chips, low-fat snack chips (read the labels), pretzels, unbuttered popcorn, whole-grain homemade baked goods (using low-fat ingredients), ginger-snaps, newtons, and angel food cake can be low in fat and calories.

Milk products Low-fat or nonfat yogurts and cheeses make excellent snacks.

Foods to Limit: The following are high in sugar or fat and provide little nutrition: all types of candy, store-bought cookies, pies, cakes, coconut, deep-fried chips, desserts with cream or cream cheese, specialty ice creams, and milk shakes made with whole milk and ice cream.

suggestions from the Dietary Guidelines for Americans or the Guidelines for Improving Your Food Selections and explain how they will implement the suggestions in their own diet. Suggest that students review their progress on each suggestion during the next few weeks.

• • • TEACH continues on p. 96

Making a Choice 4B

Assign the Eating Away From Home card. The card asks students to plan a healthful diet for people who are away from home and assess the availability of healthful food options in the community.

Section Review Worksheet 4.3

To reinforce the concepts presented in this section, assign Section Review Worksheet 4.3.

Section Quiz 4.3

Have students take Section Quiz 4.3.

Reteaching Worksheet 4.3

Students who have difficulty with the material may complete Reteaching Worksheet 4.3.

Selecting Foods When Eating Out

There are healthful choices in almost any restaurant, if you take the time to look and give some thought to your choices. Remember the nutritional principles that guide your choices in other settings. Order your meal by selecting a variety of foods from several food groups in the pyramid, and try not to overeat. If you watch what you eat for most of the week, one meal—even one that is high in calories, fat, and sodium—will not cause a problem if you are a healthy person. Rather than avoiding certain things when you eat out, take positive steps.

- If you want salad dressings, toppings, gravies, or other high-fat additions to food, ask for them to be brought "on the side," and use only small amounts.
- When possible, choose low-fat alternatives, such as fish, pasta with vegetables, chicken with its skin removed, low-fat milk or cheese, and baked potatoes instead of fried potatoes.
- Even most fast-food restaurants now offer alternative menus. When possible, choose broiled or baked foods rather than fried foods.
- Choose whole-grain breads or bagels rather than biscuits.

Teenage Nutritional Needs

The onset of puberty brings many bodily changes. During the teenage years maturation speeds up, creating greater demands on body processes. The hormonal changes that control the development of sex characteristics have an important influence on growth and development.

Both boys and girls experience increased demands for energy, protein, vitamins, and minerals to deal with developmental changes. When you snack to get energy, select snacks with nutritional value rather than candy bars or high-fat desserts. You really need protein for muscle growth, along with calcium and iron for other developmental changes. Teens tend to stop drinking milk as they get older. Carbonated beverages do not provide the calcium you need to increase your bone density. Girls must take care to select foods high in iron, since they begin to lose iron when menstruation begins. This iron loss results in fatigue and iron-deficiency anemia. Select foods high in vitamins and minerals.

To summarize, the most common dietary deficiencies seen among teenagers involve a lack of vitamins and minerals such as B, C, A, iron, and calcium.

Nutritional Needs of Pregnant Women As with the teenage years, pregnancy carries with it increased demands for nutrients. The development of the fetus is a period of rapid physical growth from the fertilized egg to a full-term baby. Good nutrition during this time is a major factor in determining the baby's overall health. Pregnant women need to increase the number of calories they consume to meet energy demands and to increase the amount of protein to make tissues. For example, protein is necessary for growth of the placenta, growth of breast and uterine tissue, formation of amniotic fluids, and increased blood volume, all of which provide the right environment for the growing fetus.

Getting adequate nutrition without excessive weight gain is a challenge for the pregnant mother. Eating from all but the top group in the food pyramid will help both the mother and the developing infant.

Vegetarian Diets

Vegetarians choose not to eat meat and meat products. Some also avoid dairy products. The number of vegetarians in this country

---

Class Discussion
Special Nutritional Needs and Risks

Stress the risks teens take when they fail to eat a balanced diet, especially pregnant teens. A diagram such as the one shown on the right might be placed on the chalkboard as students provide causes of poor teen nutrition and list possible results.

Effects
Deficiency diseases
Anemia
Obesity
Stress

Poor food choices
Inadequate nutrition

Peer pressure
Anxiety
Fad diets
Junk food preference
Ignorance

Causes

Class Discussion
Going Meatless

Discuss why a person might decide to become a vegetarian. Ask students what measures vegetarians need to take to be certain their diets contain sufficient nutrients. *(They need to be certain that their diets contain the amino acids needed for protein synthesis. If no dairy products or eggs are included, a vitamin B_{12} supplement is necessary.)*

appears to be increasing each year, and contrary to what many believe, a vegetarian diet can be healthful. However, because plant products do not contain complete proteins, it is important for vegetarians to be aware of protein requirements. Vegetarians must eat a variety of foods to get a mix of proteins that will supply all of the essential amino acids. Since vitamin B_{12} is found only in animals, vegetarians must take a B_{12} supplement if no dairy or meat products are eaten. There are some distinct health benefits of a vegetarian diet, but to be nutritionally successful, it does take some planning within the food pyramid, especially for proteins. It may be wise to work with a licensed dietitian or nutritionist if you are a vegetarian or want to become one.

Nutrition and Athletes

Teens who are athletes need a slightly greater amount of protein than teens who are not athletes. Under ordinary conditions, proteins are not used for fuel like carbohydrates and fats are, but in endurance events some amino acids are actually used for fuel. To use fuel rapidly, an increase in protective nutrients called antioxidants is needed. Leafy vegetables are a good source of antioxidants and should be included in every athlete's diet.

Athletes must be well hydrated if they are to perform their best. For activities lasting under two hours, water can adequately replace any fluid that has been lost. In events lasting longer than two hours, however, both water and electrolytes must be replaced. Sports drinks that are low in sugar are recommended for use during prolonged endurance events. Some newer drinks now include dextrins, carbohydrates that are readily digested and available to the body for immediate use.

Nutrition plays a vital role in successful athletic performance. An athlete can plan what foods to eat in order to store the proper kind of fuel needed for a future event. Short, intense events require plenty of stored carbohydrates, made readily available through the right kind of training. Endurance events require stored fats, stored carbohydrates, and some selected amino acids. Attention to good nutrition year round can help athletes achieve their goals.

Review

1. Describe what is meant by each of the Dietary Guidelines for Americans.

2. To which group on the food pyramid, do you think each of the following foods belongs?
   a. tortilla   e. peanut butter
   b. rice   f. salmon
   c. bean sprouts   g. salsa
   d. olives   h. bran muffin

3. Look at Figures 4-14 and 4-15.
   a. How much vitamin C do you need per day?
   b. What percentage of your daily calories should come from saturated fat?

4. **Critical Thinking** A beef burrito weighs 206 grams. The burrito supplies 430 calories and has 21 grams of fat. What percentage of the burrito's total calories comes from fat? How does your answer compare with the dietary guidelines?

SECTION 4.3

Review Answers

1. Answers will vary, but students should explain something they have learned about each of the seven guidelines.
2. a. Bread, cereal, rice and pasta group
b. Bread, cereal, rice and pasta group
c. Vegetable group
d. Fats, oils, sweets group
e. Fats, oils, sweets group
f. Meat, poultry, fish, dry beans, eggs and nuts group
g. Vegetable group
h. Bread, cereal, rice and pasta; depending on the recipe, it may contain something from the fats, oils, sweets group
3. a. 60 mg
b. 10 percent
4. 21 g of fat at 9 calories per gram equals 189 calories from fat. Divide this by 430 total calories, and it equals approximately 0.44. Multiply this by 100, and it equals 44 percent fat. Because the total percentage calories from fat should not exceed 30 percent, this is far too much fat from one source. (Dividing the burrito's total weight, 206 g, by 21 g of fat tells what percent of the total weight is fat. It does not address the calorie issue.)

Extension
Food and Advertising

Have students keep a log of television commercials about food for one weekend. They should analyze the types of food promoted and make a graph to show where these foods fit on the food pyramid. Students should then write a critique of the ads from a nutritionist's point of view.

ASSESS

Section Review

Have students answer the Section Review questions.

Alternative Assessment
Using the Food Pyramid

Have students draw a food pyramid with the food groups represented and write a healthful day's menu around it, drawing arrows from each item to its

food group and totalling the numbers of servings for each group for the day.

Closure
Evaluating Food Labels

Provide each student with a food label to study. Ask that students write a paragraph evaluating the food's fat, sugar, and sodium contents, calories per serving, and percentages of the Daily Reference Values.

Background
Food Poisoning—Costs and Causes
Each year in the United States, food poisoning kills an estimated 9,000 people and sickens millions of others. The most vulnerable are young children, old people, and people with weakened immune systems. Home-contracted cases of food poisoning far outnumber the cases you hear about in the media. Researchers say that damp sponges provide an ideal breeding ground for germs. In fact, kitchen sponges, dish cloths, counter tops, sinks, drains, and utensils harbor far more pathogens than almost any bathroom. In one study, 20 percent of the sponges and dish cloths contained *Staphylococcus aureus*, and 14 percent harbored *Salmonella*—both culprits in food poisoning. However, these kitchen germs can be removed fairly easily by cleaning. A brief scrub with detergent or kitchen cleaner followed by a good rinse will get rid of most germs. Also, keeping counters and sponges dry is a good way to reduce bacterial growth.

Section 4.4 Food Safety

Objectives
- Describe symptoms common to food-borne illnesses.
- Discuss ways to prevent bacterial contamination of foods.
  - **Life Skills: Being a Wise Consumer**
- Locate the "use by" or "sell by" dates on common food items.

Each year in the United states, millions of cases of food-borne illnesses occur. In most instances, food has been contaminated by bacteria, and the result is an illness that can cause a variety of unpleasant symptoms or—for those who are less healthy—death.

Symptoms of Food-Borne Illnesses
Food-borne illnesses usually affect the stomach and intestines. Common symptoms include diarrhea, cramping, fever, headache, vomiting, and exhaustion. Symptoms may appear as quickly as half an hour after eating, or they may not develop for several days or weeks. They usually last a couple of days or less, but they can last as long as 7–10 days. For most healthy people, food-borne illnesses are not serious, but for very young children, older people, and people who are already ill, food-borne illnesses may be life-threatening. When symptoms are severe, a medical doctor should be seen. For milder symptoms, lost fluids should be replaced and easily-digested meals can be eaten. Some ill-

nesses, like botulism, cause nerve problems, and emergency care is essential.

Bacteria and Food-Borne Illnesses
Contamination by bacteria can occur at any point in the food production process, but about 30 percent of all food-borne illnesses result from unsafe food handling at home. A wide range of foods can be affected, including meats, dairy products, unpasteurized fruit juice, fresh pasta, spices, chocolate, seafood, and even water. Other products that can be tainted by bacteria include egg products; tuna, potato, and macaroni salads; and cream-filled pastries. Poultry (usually chicken) is the food most often contaminated by disease-causing organisms.

Safe Food Buying Preventing food-borne illnesses actually begins during the trip to the supermarket. If any of the items on your shopping list are those that can be affected by bacterial contamination, pick up these foods and frozen foods last. Get them home quickly. Refrigerate or freeze foods right away if they are perishable. Figure 4-24 lists storage guidelines for foods that are commonly served in American homes.

Don't buy bulging cans or jars that are not tightly sealed. Look for "use by" or "sell by" dates, and buy small enough quantities that you can use all of the product before the expiration date. Dairy products and eggs are dated, as are other pasteurized foods, like juices. Place foods that perish quickly in their own bag with like items so their drippings don't contaminate other foods. When buying fish, buy from markets that get their supplies from state-

---

Section 4.4 Lesson Plan

MOTIVATE

Class Discussion
Was It Something I Ate?
Ask if any students have ever had food poisoning or any other food-borne illness. If students know the source of their food poisoning, write it on the board. Point out that doctors say that many cases of "24-hour stomach flu"

are actually mild cases of food poisoning. Tell students that in this section they will learn how to protect themselves against food-borne illnesses.

TEACH

Cooperative Learning
How Long Has This Been Here?
Review the food items in Figure 4-24, and then divide the class into small

groups. Have each group come up with a list of other food items that are stored in the refrigerator. Ask students to identify which foods on their lists could pose health risks. (*Risky foods include leftover prepared salads; hot dogs that have been open for too long; opened orange juice and other juices; opened milk and milk products; foods containing eggs; soups, especially cream soups; prepared frozen foods that were*

Cold Storage Periods for Common American Foods

Product	STORAGE PERIOD	
	Maximum Time In Refrigerator	Maximum Time In Freezer
Fresh ground meat	1–2 days	3–4 months
Fresh steaks and roasts	3–5 days	6–12 months
Fresh pork chops	3–5 days	3–4 months
Fresh ground pork	1–2 days	1–2 months
Fresh pork roast	3–5 days	4–8 months
Cured lunch meat	3–5 days	1–2 months
Cured sausage	1–2 days	1–2 months
Gravy	1–2 days	3 months
Lean fish (cod, etc.)	1–2 days	up to 6 months
Fatty fish (perch, salmon, etc.)	1–2 days	2–3 months
Whole chicken	1–2 days	12 months
Chicken parts	1–2 days	9 months
Chicken giblets	1–2 days	3–4 months
Cheese	3–4 weeks	*
Milk	5 days	1 month
Eggs, fresh in shell	3–5 days	do not freeze
Eggs, hard-boiled	1 week	do not freeze

*If cheese is frozen, the texture and taste will be affected.

(FIGURE 4-24) Labeling foods with a date of purchase can help you better determine when they are no longer safe to eat.

Section Review Worksheet 4.4

To reinforce the concepts presented in this section, assign Section Review Worksheet 4.4.

Section Quiz 4.4

Have students take Section Quiz 4.4.

Reteaching Worksheet 4.4

Students who have difficulty with the material may complete Reteaching Worksheet 4.4.

thawed but never cooked; and casserole dishes that have been stored for a week or more. Products safe for long-term storage include most pickles and relishes, salsas and salad dressings that did not require refrigeration before opening, mustards, ketchup, and bread products, except for foods such as dressing for poultry.) As a class, review each list, and ask students to discuss their experiences with risky products.

Extension
Expiration Dates

Have interested students bring in a variety of food packages that show "use by" or "sell by" dates and one or two packages that show "best if used by" dates. Caution students that the "use by" or "sell by" date does not apply to a product once it is opened. For example, an opened carton of milk may become slightly sour before its expiration date. Point out that "best if used by" dates refer to freshness, not spoilage, and indicate a date after which the flavor and texture may not be as good. Have students design an informative display of the collected packages.

Review Answers

1. diarrhea, cramping, fever, headache, vomiting, exhaustion

2. Answers will vary but should include some of the following information: look for "use by" dates, pick up perishables last and bag them separately, and purchase fish from state approved sources; refrigerate or freeze perishables immediately, follow product storage guidelines, store leftovers in tightly sealed containers, and avoid overcrowding the refrigerator; cook foods to the appropriate temperature and for a sufficient period of time; do not let unclean utensils or the raw juices from meat, fish, or poultry contaminate other foods; wash fruits and vegetables well; and thaw meats in the refrigerator or microwave. Accept any other precaution given on pp. 98–100.

3. Answers will vary. Lists may include cold cuts, milk, butter, yogurt, cottage cheese, eggs, orange juice and other juices, canned biscuits, packaged fresh meats, and packaged fresh poultry.

---

approved sources rather than at roadside stands or trucks. Check the meat and fish counters and salad bars for cleanliness, and be sure that different foods are kept apart.

Safe Food Handling The following guidelines can help ensure the careful handling of food to prevent the growth of disease-causing bacteria.

1. Keep foods in the refrigerator no longer than the period shown in Figure 4-24. Hot or cold foods left standing too long at room temperature may provide the climate bacteria need to grow.
2. Cooking foods at too low a temperature or for too short a time may not kill bacteria. Cook eggs well because even though they have a shell they can be infected by bacteria.
3. Knives and cutting surfaces that come into contact with a contaminated food can be a source of contamination to another food if they are not cleaned with hot soapy water. Use a clean platter for cooked meat rather then the one that held it when it was raw.
4. Wash fruits and vegetables well.
5. Always thaw frozen meats in the refrigerator or in the microwave, and then cook them right away.
6. Leftovers should be stored in tightly sealed containers in the refrigerator. Eggs should be stored in their own carton on a shelf in the refrigerator, which is colder than a tray in the door. Avoid overcrowding the refrigerator to allow air to circulate freely.
7. Eat leftovers quickly or discard them.
8. Make it a regular practice to review the "use by" dates for packaged products. Discard any foods that are no longer safe to eat. Look for "refrigerate after opening" directions on labels. Store products accordingly.
9. Mayonnaise and ketchup are best kept in the refrigerator, as their labels direct.
10. When storing canned or dry goods, move older items to the front of the shelf and use them first.

Eating Out Safely In one of the worst food-poisoning outbreaks ever in this country, contaminated hamburgers made 450 people sick and killed one toddler in 1992. The contamination was caused by a rare strain of *E. coli* bacteria that is normally found in animals. Had the meat been cooked well, the bacteria would have been killed. The Food and Drug Administration now requires that ground meat be cooked to 155°F, well above the pink stage. Ground meats are especially dangerous because the grinding equipment may be contaminated and ground meat has a larger surface area on which bacteria can multiply. It is best not to order a rare hamburger when eating out. In addition, other raw meat dishes and milk can also carry *E. coli.*

Review

1. What are the general symptoms of a food-borne illness?

2. What precautions should you always take when preparing or handling food?

3. **Life Skills: Being a Wise Consumer** Check your refrigerator and other food storage areas in your home. Make a list of at least 10 foods that have been marked with expiration dates.

ASSESS

Section Review
Have students answer the Section Review questions.

Alternative Assessment
Food Safety

Have students make a food safety chart that gives tips on how to avoid eating spoiled foods. As an alternative, they could write a series of public

safety announcements that offer tips to shoppers about expiration dates and food storage.

Closure
What Do You Think?

Divide the class into small groups. Provide each group with a list of foods, and ask them to state if the foods are OK to eat, risky, or dangerous. Have them explain their answers. Include a variety of foods, such as uncooked fish that has been in the refrigerator for

three days, cottage cheese that is unopened but past its expiration date, chips that have passed their "use by" date, etc. Compare the groups' responses.

Highlights

Summary

- Appetite refers to a desire to eat food. Hunger is your body telling you to eat. To get a good balance, appetite and hunger should work together.

- Diet is related to six of the ten leading causes of death in the U.S.

- The six categories of essential nutrients are carbohydrates, fats, proteins, vitamins, minerals, and water.

- The body's primary sources of energy are carbohydrates and fats.

- Cholesterol in the body is measured in two forms: high-density lipoproteins (HDL) and low-density lipoproteins (LDL).

- Water is needed for all body processes, for carrying nutrients to cells and waste to the kidneys, and for temperature regulation.

- The Food Pyramid organizes foods into five categories based on daily nutritional needs.

- The Food Pyramid and the U.S. Dietary Guidelines are guides for a healthful, well-balanced diet.

- Proper food handling practices can protect you from food-borne illnesses.

Vocabulary

carbohydrates a class of nutrients containing simple sugars, starches, glycogen, and dietary fiber.

saturated fats fats that contain single bonds between carbon atoms and the maximum number of hydrogen atoms bonded to carbon.

unsaturated fats fats that contain one or more double bonds between carbon atoms and have less than the maximum number of hydrogen atoms bonded to carbon.

cholesterol a fatlike substance that is part of all animal cells and is necessary for the production of some hormones and fat digestion.

proteins class of nutrients consisting of long chains of amino acids, which are the basic components of body tissue and can provide energy.

vitamins organic substances that assist in the chemical reactions that occur in the body.

minerals inorganic substances that are generally absorbed to form structural components of the body.

SUMMARY
Have students read the summary to reinforce the concepts they learned in Chapter 4.

VOCABULARY
Have students write a letter to the editor of a newspaper persuading teens to change their diet habits. They should use at least 10 of the vocabulary words.

EXTENSION
Have small groups of students work together to compile a Survivor's Handbook for Fast-Food Nutrition. The pamphlet could list specific menu items from different fast-food restaurants and tell why some are more nutritionally sound than others.

CHAPTER REVIEW
Concept Review

1. family experiences, cultural heritage, your personality, cost
2. Carbohydrates are the main source of energy; pasta. Fats store energy; butter. Proteins play a role in growth and repair of body tissues; meat. Vitamins and minerals are essential for good health; fruits. Water is needed for the body to function and to maintain its stability.
3. Simple carbohydrates are simple sugars and short-chain sugars that

are rapidly broken down into glucose and that provide a quick energy source. Complex carbohydrates are long-chain sugars, such as starch, glycogen, and dietary fiber. Except for dietary fiber, most complex carbohydrates are rich in vitamins and minerals.
4. Saturated fats generally come from animals and are often solid at room temperature because their carbon chains are straight and can be layered. Unsaturated fats come from plant sources and from fish.

They are usually liquid at room temperature. Their carbon chains have fewer bond sights available for hydrogen atoms. Therefore, their carbon atoms are not saturated with hydrogen atoms.
5. Cholesterol is a fatlike substance that is found in some foods that come from animals. It is also produced by the liver. Too much LDL cholesterol is a factor in the development of cardiovascular disease.

Concept Review

1. List four factors that influence the foods you choose.

2. List the six nutrients, then describe what each one does for the body. Name a food source for each nutrient.

3. What is the difference between simple carbohydrates and complex carbohydrates?

4. What is the difference between saturated fats and unsaturated fats?

5. What is cholesterol and how can it affect your health?

6. What can happen to your body if your diet is deficient in vitamins and minerals?

7. Why is water important to your diet?

8. Identify the five food categories on the food pyramid and list two foods from each group.

9. Explain the organization of the food pyramid.

10. Name four ways to reduce the amount of fat in your diet.

11. What can you do to help prevent osteoporosis?

12. Why do protein requirements increase during pregnancy?

13. List the daily dietary guidelines for fats, cholesterol, carbohydrates, and sodium.

14. In what ways can bacteria contaminate food?

Expressing Your Views

1. Studies have shown that many teenagers in the United States do not make nutritious food choices. Why do you think this is so?

2. Your younger brother loves sweets. He will often eat only a dessert at meal time and you have noticed that he eats sweet snacks all day. He says not to worry because he eats plenty of carbohydrates and they are a source of energy. However, you are concerned that his diet is not adequate. What advice could you give him?

3. Why is making food selections based on calories alone not a good method for planning your diet?

4. Why is it so important to drink at least 8 glasses of water each day?

Answers to Questions 1–5 are on p. 101.

6. You could develop a deficiency disease or an electrolyte imbalance.

7. Most chemical reactions in the body can occur only in a water medium; water helps maintain acidity at proper levels; water in body fluids provides a medium to transport gases, nutrients, and waste; and water helps to regulate body temperature.

8. Students should list the food categories shown in Figure 4-16 on page 85. Foods listed will vary; accept any correct answer.

9. The foods at the bottom should be the largest part of your diet. As you move up the pyramid, the food groups should make up a smaller part of your diet. Fats, oils, and sweets should be used only in small amounts.

10. Limit all milk products containing more than 1 percent fat; choose skinless poultry and fish over red meat; choose turkey-based hot dogs, cold cuts, and sausages; and eat peanut butter and other nut butters sparingly.

11. Increase the amount of calcium-rich foods in your diet, and get plenty of exercise.

12. to meet the demands of growth of the placenta, breast, and uterine tissue; formation of amniotic fluids; increased blood volume

13. Students should list the quantities shown in Figure 4-14, Daily Reference Value: fats, 65 g; cholesterol, 300 mg; carbohydrates, 300 g; and sodium, 2400 mg. These figures are based on a 2,000-calorie diet.

14. Foods can become contaminated if they are stored at improper temperatures, stored for too long a period of time, or if they come into contact with unclean utensils or with other products that are contaminated.

Expressing Your Views

1. Food choices are often influenced by peers; social pressure to be thin can cause teens to make inappropriate choices.

2. Sample response: I would tell him that although he is eating foods high in carbohydrates, they are simple carbohydrates that contain few vitamins and minerals. I would suggest that he eat more balanced meals and save the sweets for last.

Life Skills Check . . . . . .

1. Practicing Self-Care
You enjoy eating food from other cultures. You want to make healthful choices when selecting food at restaurants specializing in these dishes. Make a list of foods to avoid when you eat at each of the following restaurants: Italian, Oriental, French, Greek, Mexican, Eastern Indian, and Southeast Asian.

2. Practicing Self-Care
Calculate the percentage of calories from fat for 1 tablespoon of blue cheese salad dressing (about 14 grams). The tablespoon of salad dressing is 77 calories with 8 grams of fat.

Projects . . . .

1. Use your detailed food diary from the Life Skills feature to further analyze your diet. Using either a computer software package or a table of food values, analyze your diet for amounts of energy nutrients, fiber, cholesterol, sodium, iron, calcium, and vitamins A and C. What changes do you need to make in your diet?

2. Work with a group to obtain nutritional information from various fast-food restaurants (perhaps by asking for a menu). Analyze this informa-

tion and decide which foods are the healthiest and most nutritious in each type of restaurant. Write a consumer article for your school newspaper.

3. Bring to class a recipe for a cake, a pie, cookies, or some other dessert. Discuss ways to make substitutions in the recipes to reduce the fat, sugar, and salt. After making these substitutions, develop a "healthy dessert" recipe file with the class. Compile all of your recipes into a pamphlet and distribute the pamphlets throughout the school.

Plan for Action . . . .

The foods you eat every day have an effect on your overall health. Do you choose healthful foods every day? List five changes you will make in your food selections in order to achieve a more healthful diet.

---

3. Some foods contain calories that provide no nutrients.

4. Your body needs water to maintain its stability and to avoid dehydration.

Life Skills Check
1. Italian: cream sauces and high-fat cheeses and meats; Oriental: deep-fried food and soy sauce; French: rich sauces; Greek: dishes with high-fat cheese, anchovies, and olives, as well as those made with phyllo dough; Mexican: cheeses, deep-fried foods, and refried beans; Eastern Indian: foods cooked in coconut milk or cream; and Southeast Asian: deep-fried foods and cream soups.

2. 8 g of fat x 9 calories per g equals 72 calories from fat. Divide this number by 77 total calories, and it equals approximately 0.935. Multiply this by 100, and it equals 93.5 percent calories from fat.

Projects
Have students plan and carry out the projects on nutrition.

Plan for Action
Have students write down the five dietary changes they chose and post it where they will see the list each day. Suggest that they review the list before they start the day and make a mental plan of how they can implement at least three of the changes that day.

ASSESSMENT OPTIONS

Chapter Test
Have students take the Chapter 4 Test.

Alternative Assessment
Have students do the Alternative Assessment activity for Chapter 4.

Test Generator
The Test Generator contains additional assessment items for this chapter.

CHAPTER 5

Weight Management and Eating Disorders

SECTION	TITLE/OBJECTIVES	PERSONAL INVENTORY			LIFE SKILLS DEVELOPMENT			
		Personal Health Inventory	Journal	Check Up	Life Skills	Life Skills Worksheets	Media Message or Ethical Issues Worksheet	What Would You Do?
5.1 pp. 105–112	**METABOLISM AND IDEAL WEIGHT** ■ Describe how to determine your daily calorie expenditure. • List the factors that should be used to determine your ideal weight. • Identify the characteristics of fad diets. • Identify the characteristics of healthy weight-loss and weight-gain plans.	Ch. 5	5A 5B 5C		p. 109	5A		
5.2 pp. 113–117	**EATING DISORDERS** • List the health hazards of anorexia, bulimia, and pica. • Describe the characteristics of individuals most at risk for anorexia or bulimia. • Explain how eating disorders can be avoided.		5D 5E 5F	p. 114			Unit 2	p. 116
5.3 pp. 118–120	**DISORDERS AFFECTING THE DIGESTIVE SYSTEM** • List the most common digestive disorders. • Describe ways to treat constipation and diarrhea. • Describe the differences between food allergies and food intolerances.		5G 5H					

KEY: ■ Denotes Life Skill Objective

Text references denoted by page number.

Supplement references denoted by chapter or item numbers.

LINKING RESOURCES

			Making a Choice Cards	Parent Discussion Guide	Health Talk Audio Program	Teaching Transparencies and Directory	Section Review Worksheets	Section Quizzes	Reteaching Worksheets	Section Reviews
INTERACTION		**OTHER RESOURCES**		**SECTION REVIEW AND ASSESSMENT**						
5A	Ch. 5	Ch. 5					5.1	5.1	5.1	p. 112
							5.2	5.2	5.2	p. 117
5B		BSH9					5.3	5.3	5.3	p. 120

For additional information about digestion and disorders of the digestive system, see pages 674–676 in the Body Systems Handbook.

KEY FACTS

- Weight management involves balancing the body's energy needs against the number of calories consumed.
- The basal metabolism rate is the energy required to keep the body functioning when at rest.
- Body composition, determined by the ratio or fat to lean mass, is a key factor in determining ideal weight.
- Anorexia nervosa and bulimia are eating disorders that require both medical and psychological treatment.
- Constipation and diarrhea are sometimes caused by diet.
- Severe allergic reactions to food can be life threatening.
- Food intolerances usually can be managed by modifying the diet.

CHAPTER REVIEW AND ASSESSMENT

TEXT

Chapter Review pp. 122–123

SUPPLEMENTS

Chapter Test 5

Alternative Assessment 5

Test Generator Chapter 5

GETTING STARTED

Using the Chapter Photograph

Have students describe the girl in the photograph. What is she doing? Does she appear to have unusual or dangerous eating patterns? What, if anything, can you tell from the way she looks? Discuss the importance placed on weight and personal appearance in our society and the effects this may have on an individual's behavior.

 Question Box

Have students write out any questions they have about ideal weight, weight control, and eating disorders and put them in the Question Box.

Sensitivity *ALERT*

Discussions about weight and how to control it may cause embarrassment for some students. Those who are overweight or underweight are likely to be sensitive about these topics. Students may have relatives or friends who have eating disorders, or they may have such disorders. Encouraging students to reveal personal difficulties is not recommended.

CHAPTER
5

Weight Management and Eating Disorders

◆ ◆ ◆ ◆

Section 5.1 *Metabolism and Ideal Weight*

Section 5.2 *Eating Disorders*

Section 5.3 *Disorders Affecting the Digestive System*

■ **The focus on being thin has resulted in a major increase in eating disorders like bulimia.**

MYTHS & MISCONCEPTIONS

- **A person can't be too thin.** Being underweight can be detrimental to your heath. When carried to an extreme, as in anorexia, it is life threatening.

- **If my weight is normal, I don't need to worry about body fat.** Even if your weight falls within a range indicated on a weight table, you can have too much body fat. It is the ratio of lean mass to fat that is important.

- **A person with anorexia just doesn't want to listen to those offering help.** Anorexics are incapable of recognizing the danger of their condition. Medical intervention is imperative.

- **Diarrhea is unpleasant but not harmful.** Diarrhea can be a serious disorder, especially in infants. Severe diarrhea that lasts more than a day or chronic mild diarrhea can cause dehydration and require medical attention.

M argaret and her best friend, Dale, are 15 years old. Yesterday, Dale was rushed to the local hospital and almost died. When she was admitted to the hospital Dale weighed only 80 pounds. Margaret knew Dale had been dieting for a long time to "get thin." She tried to convince Dale that she was already thin and that she was "starving herself to death." But Dale would not listen. Every time Dale looked in the mirror, she complained about being fat. No one else saw her that way. Dale and her mother argued constantly about eating. It seemed that as Dale got thinner, she ate even less. She exercised all the time. Margaret didn't know how Dale found the strength. What was happening to Dale? Margaret wondered what was causing Dale to feel she had to be so thin, even when she was beginning to lose her health? Why couldn't Dale see that she was already thin? Why was she being so stubborn about eating? What could Margaret have done differently to help Dale? What can Margaret do now to help Dale recover? What can Dale's mother do?

Section 5.1

Metabolism and Ideal Weight

Objectives

- Describe how to determine your daily calorie expenditure.
  - **LIFE SKILLS: Assessing Your Health**

- List the factors that should be used to determine your ideal weight.

- Identify the characteristics of fad diets.

- Identify the characteristics of healthy weight-loss and weight-gain plans.

Weight Management Concepts

There isn't a day that goes by that you don't hear something about weight control or dieting. The TV is filled with weight-loss ads. The stores are filled with diet products. Yet many Americans are dangerously overweight. The chances of being overweight at some point during your life are high. Therefore, in this chapter you will study basic information about how your body uses calories and what you can do to maintain a weight that's good for your health. You can control your weight by knowing when and why you eat, and some-

Personal Health Inventory
Have students complete the Personal Health Inventory for this chapter.

English/Spanish CD Audio Program
Use the English/Spanish Health Talk audio program for students who need audio reinforcement of the concepts presented.

Parent Discussion Guide
Send home the Parent Letter for Chapter 5. As you progress through the chapter, send home the Parental Survey and The Extra Mile.

Section 5.1 Lesson Plan

MOTIVATE

Journal 5A
Concerns About Weight

This may be done as a warm-up activity. Encourage students to describe any concerns they may have about their weight in their Journal.

Role-Playing
The Diet Message

Have four or five students act as ad writers planning a commercial for a new diet pill. Have them suggest reasons why consumers should use the pill. Then have students compare the message with actual advertisements they have heard for diet pills. Ask students to discuss whether or not the reasons listed are the most important reasons for trying to lose weight.

Background

Weight Tables

Weight tables are usually based on life-expectancy data gathered by insurance companies. Most of them show desirable weights for adults, not teenagers. They are based on height and sometimes on body frame. The newer tables, however, take age into account and give a range for desirable weight. Although this is an improvement, a better way to calculate optimum weight is to measure body composition (the ratio of fat to lean mass). For this reason, most health educators recommend using a scale similar to the one shown in Figure 5-1.

basal metabolic rate:

energy needed to fuel the body's ongoing processes while the body is at complete rest.

energy-balance equation:

eating the same number of calories that you burn each day.

thing about your body's composition. Look back at the Check Up you answered on page 68. Do you often eat or overeat when you are not hungry?

How Your Body Uses Food Energy

Metabolism describes all the chemical reactions that occur in the body to break down food and build new materials. The body breaks down food so it can be used for energy and other purposes. But how much food do you need? The amount of calories you should consume is determined by two factors: basal metabolism rate and your level of activity. In Chapter 3 you learned how physical activity affects the amount of energy you expend each day. **Basal metabolic rate** (**BMR**) refers to the amount of energy it takes to keep your body functioning normally when you are at rest. These functions include breathing, circulating blood throughout the body, and providing energy to maintain cell function. BMR does not include the energy needed to digest food. BMR changes as you age, differs between men and women, and differs depending on your body type. A fit, lean individual will have a higher BMR than someone who weighs the same but has less muscle mass.

If you add your BMR to the energy required for all your activities during a 24-hour period, and to the energy needed to digest the food you have eaten, you end up with the energy your body needs. For example, if your BMR was 1000 calories, and your activity level required another 800 calories per day, your body would need approximately 180 calories to digest food. Your total energy requirement per day to maintain your current body weight is 1980 calories. This concept is called the **energy-balance equation** and is covered in the Life Skills on page 109. You can maintain your current body weight if you balance the number of calories you eat with the number of calories you burn.

Body Composition

The body is made of several kinds of tissue, including fat and **lean mass.** You learned in the last chapter that your diet must include some fat to maintain important body functions. For example, some vitamins can only be used by the body if they are dissolved in fat. The amount of fat that you need for normal functioning is called **essential fat.** Fat intake beyond essential fat is considered excess **storage fat.** Ordinarily, essential fat makes up no more than 3 percent of total

BODY FAT SCALE FOR TEENS

Approx. fat %	Males	Skinfold Caliper Measurement (millimeters)	Females	Approx. fat %
6	Very low	5	Very low	
10	Low	10		11.5
	Optimal	15	Low	15
		20	Optimal	
20		25		
	Moderately high	30	Moderately high	25
25		35		29.5
	High	40	High	
31		45		36
	Very high	50		
		55	Very high	
		60		

(FIGURE 5-1) **If your body fat measurements are outside the acceptable ranges, change your eating habits and level of physical activity.**

TEACH

Class Discussion
BMR

To help students grasp the concept of basal metabolic rate, compare it to energy use by a car that is in neutral with the motor running. Point out that even though the car is not moving, it is using energy—and that this is the minimal amount of energy required when the motor is running. Ask: **How would the minimal amount of energy differ in a car with a larger motor?** *[It is likely that more energy would be used.]* Point out that, like cars, people differ in their minimum energy requirements, or BMR. Have students discuss how the car in motion is similar to a person engaged in physical activity.

Class Discussion
Body Fat Scale for Teens

Have students look at the scale in Figure 5-1. Ask: **How is body fat measured?** *[The width of a skin fold is measured in millimeters.]* **Is a specific amount of body fat identified as "correct"?** *[No, ranges, ranked on a scale from very low to very high, are given.]* **How do the percentages of body fat differ from males to females?** *[Females have a slightly higher-fat-to-lean ratio than males.]*

(FIGURE 5-2) **The only way to determine your ideal weight is to start by having your body fat measured. Body fat can be measured using skin-fold calipers or by submersion in a tank of water.**

Life Skills Worksheet 5A
Assign the Comparing Weight-Loss Programs Life Skills Worksheet.

lean mass:
total body weight minus the weight due to fat.

essential fat:
the amount of fat needed for certain metabolic processes to occur.

storage fat:
excess fat stored in the body.

overweight:
weighing 10 percent more than one's recommended weight.

obesity:
a condition in which one weighs 20 percent more than the recommended weight.

body weight for men, and 10–12 percent for women. Desirable total body fat levels for teens range between 10 and 20 percent for males and between 15 and 25 percent for females. The higher fat composition for females is related to different hormonal needs for the reproductive system. A large percentage of your body weight is made of lean muscle, bone and body fluids.

Figure 5-1 shows the optimal body fat range for teen males and females. There is no fixed ideal body weight for each person. Ideal body weight is based on your age, your sex, and your frame size and bone structure. Height and weight charts are only guidelines. Rather than using height and weight charts, you should have your body fat measured to determine the relationship between fat and lean mass. This is a

better indicator for determining your ideal, healthy weight.

You store a pound of body fat when you eat 3500 calories more than you need. If you weigh 10 percent more than your ideal recommended weight, then you are considered **overweight**. The term **obesity** is used to describe a condition in which one weighs more than 20 percent over an ideal body weight. Being overweight is unhealthy, but being obese is a substantial risk to health and life.

Nathan is 18 years old, 5 feet 8 inches tall and weighs 170 pounds. His close friend Rico is also 18 and the same height, but Rico weighs 180 pounds. A height and weight chart suggests that both Nathan and Rico should weigh about 155 pounds. Nathan and Rico agree to be weighed in an

---

Reinforcement
Body Fat and Weight

Use the discussion that compares Nathan and Rico in terms of weight to stress the limited value of weight tables in determining what the healthy weight for a particular individual is. Point out that the amount of body fat is a significant factor in health—regardless of what the person's weight is.

Demonstration
Snacks and Calories

Have students list the kinds of snacks they favor. Then have them find out how many calories are in each of these snacks. (Students can check labels or they may have to look up calorie tables if the foods are unpackaged.) Students can calculate how many snack calories they consume on an average day.

 ## Cooperative Learning
Designing a Diet

Form small groups. Have students review the advice on losing weight safely, then prepare a sample day's diet and exercise program. They should suggest reasonable foods for breakfast, lunch, dinner, and snacks; recommend activities that keep the person active and away from food; and suggest exercises. Each group can post its plan for others to review.

Making a Choice 5A

Assign the Weight Control Practices card. The card asks students to review what they know about maintaining a healthy weight, to discuss how people could avoid poor eating habits, and to make a poster illustrating alternatives to negative eating habits.

underwater tank to determine their percentage of body fat. Nathan finds that 19 percent of his body weight is fat, while Rico measures 12 percent body fat. What do these measurements mean? To find out, you need to do some math to find Nathan's and Rico's actual body fat. Nineteen percent of 170 pounds is 32.3 pounds for Nathan, and 12 percent of 180 pounds is 21.6 pounds for Rico. Nathan has much more body fat than Rico, even though he weighs 10 pounds less. Now you see why height/weight charts may not be very useful. A person can have too much fat from overeating and lack of exercise, and still not be overweight according to a weight chart.

(FIGURE 5-3) **While there is a wealth of information available on losing weight, the guidelines are actually very simple. Avoid programs that promise unrealistic results.**

Body composition is a better predictor of health than height/weight ratios. Rather than losing weight, Nathan could lose fat by improving his nutritional choices and becoming active through exercise. He might actually gain muscle mass while reducing his percentage of body fat. Nathan could be healthier even though he would weigh more.

Weight Gain Can Occur Slowly

There are many ways you can put on weight without realizing it. Suppose your total energy expenditure is 1800 calories per day. Eating that level of calories you would maintain your present weight. Now imagine that you develop a habit of buying a package of pretzels after school and eating them on your way home. The label on the package tells you that this is a relatively low-fat snack with about 100 calories. Eating the pretzels adds 100 calories more each day than you need. Not much? Well, if you do not increase your exercise to compensate for these pretzels each day, by the end of the first week you will have eaten 500 calories more than you needed. In seven weeks this becomes 3500 calories and you gain a pound. By the end of the school year you have eaten enough (just one bag of pretzels a day) to add seven to eight pounds of body fat. Gaining weight over long periods of time does not always mean eating lots of food all at once. Being overweight or obese increases your risks of high blood pressure, diabetes, and elevated cholesterol. When someone is obese, the risk of death from coronary heart disease, cancer, diabetes, and stroke is substantial.

• • • TEACH continued

Class Discussion
Family Meals and Being Overweight

Have students discuss whether the foods selected and served in a family are a significant factor in whether a person is overweight. Do cultural factors play a role?

Debate the Issue
Discrimination Based on Weight

Have students debate the topic: Should individuals who are overweight or underweight be protected from discrimination in the workplace? Encourage students to view discrimination in a broad sense—not just from a legal perspective.

Journal 5B
Calculating Caloric Needs

Have students copy the calculation of their own caloric needs into their Journal. They can use the data to help determine what adjustments, if any, they need to make in their eating and activity habits to help them acheive or maintain a healthful weight.

• • • TEACH continues on p. 110

LifeSKILLS: Assessing Your Health

Calculating Your Caloric Needs . . . .

Your total caloric needs for the day depend on your BMR, your activity level, and the number of calories you need to digest food. The actual measurement of a BMR is very expensive. The formulas given here will give you rough estimates.

1. Calculating BMR Calories

Females
body weight (pounds) × 10 = BMR Calories

Males
body weight (pounds) × 11 = BMR Calories

2. Calculating Activity Levels

Activity Level	% BMR Calories	Multiply by
inactive	30	0.30
average activity	50	0.50
very active (some strenuous activity)	75	0.75

3. Calculating Calories Needed to Digest Food

(BMR Calories + Activity Calories) (0.1) = Digestion Calories

4. Total Calories needed = Step 1 + 2 + 3

Example
Marianne weighs 130 lb. Her activity level is average. Marianne needs 2145 calories to maintain her weight.

$$130 \text{ lb} \times 10 = 1300 \text{ BMR Calories}$$
$$0.50 \times 1300 = 650 \text{ Activity Calories}$$
$$\underline{1950 \times 0.1 = 195 \text{ Digestion Calories}}$$
$$2145 \text{ Total Calories}$$

Life SKILLS

Have students do the Life Skills activity in the text to determine their daily caloric needs and record their results as Journal entry 5B indicates below. Point out that their calculation is an approximation because they used an estimated BMR rather than their own BMR.

Background

Diet Centers and Diet Pills

Weight-loss products and plans are extremely popular, but it is good to keep in mind that they are often very profit-driven. Few people find any long-term weight loss from these methods. Two popular approaches to losing weight are taking over-the-counter diet pills and joining weight control programs. Diet pills may contain mild stimulants that tend to increase metabolic activity. In some cases, the pills contain an appetite suppressant. Weight loss achieved through pills is frequently temporary, since the pills are not supposed to be taken over a long period of time and they don't teach new eating habits.

Weight control programs often involve dietary restrictions coupled with group meetings that can include exercises. Many people find it impossible to stay with this type of program over a long period of time.

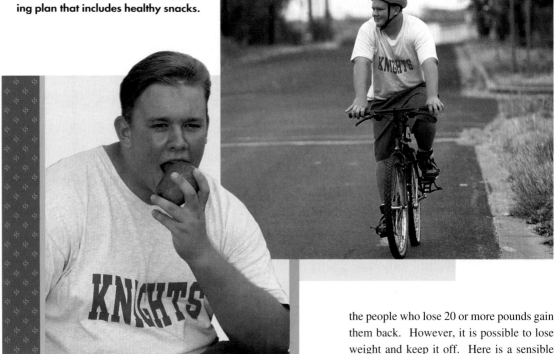

(FIGURE 5-4) Long-term weight loss involves exercise and a nutritious eating plan that includes healthy snacks.

Losing Weight Sensibly

If you determine that you need to lose weight, you should visit your doctor to help you develop a sensible weight loss plan. Your doctor will probably suggest you lose weight by reducing the number of calories you eat and increasing the number of calories that you burn. Your doctor may also tell you that it is possible to lose weight *too* rapidly and may refer you to a registered dietitian. Losing more than one or two pounds per week can be dangerous to your health. That is because during weight loss, stored fats are used for energy. As these fats are transported through the bloodstream to be metabolized, they can clog arteries.

Each year a large number of people try to lose weight. Those who go on diets are rarely successful. As many as 90 percent of

the people who lose 20 or more pounds gain them back. However, it is possible to lose weight and keep it off. Here is a sensible plan to lose fat and keep it off.

1. Establish a weight goal based on your excess body fat rather than body weight.
2. Teens are expected to gain weight each year as they are growing, so weight loss should not be extreme and calories shouldn't be cut back excessively. Active teens can safely consume 2000 calories, less active teens should consume no less than 1500 calories daily.
3. A combined program of diet and exercise is the most effective way to lose fat. Begin or maintain a moderate intensity (40–70% of your maximum heart rate) aerobic exercise program five to seven days a week. After 20 minutes of walking, your body uses more fats than carbohydrates for energy. The longer you walk, the more fat you burn.

• • • TEACH continued

Class Discussion

Gaining or Losing Weight

Have students compare the recommendations for losing weight with those for gaining weight. Ask: **What are the similarities between the two sets of advice?** [*Both involve an analysis of one's eating and exercise habits.*]

 Journal 5C
Diet Plans

Ask students to recall a diet plan that they have used or one that they have heard about. Have them write in their Journal the nature of the diet and their opinion on whether the diet promotes health.

Reinforcement

Safe Dieting

Whether attempting to gain or lose weight, a person must keep some important factors in mind.

1. Dieting is best done under a doctor's supervision.
2. Regular exercise is an important part of any diet.

4. Plan to lose no more than four pounds a month.

5. Use the Life Skills on page 109 to determine the calories you need daily to maintain your current weight.

6. To lose three pounds a month, create a deficit of 300 calories a day. Reduce your caloric intake (eat 150 calories less) and increase your calorie expenditure (burn 150 calories more).

7. Drink enough water daily using the guideline in Chapter 4.

8. Develop eating habits for a lifetime, rather than dieting habits for a short time.

9. Never skip meals. Eat several small meals a day, carefully selecting foods that meet the Dietary Guidelines.

10. Remember that the key to lifelong weight management is regular physical activity balanced against nutritious eating habits that provide adequate calories for health.

Gaining Weight Safely

Many teenagers are unhappy with the way they look. Very thin teenagers may find that being too thin can be stressful. Being too thin and wanting to gain weight can be just as frustrating as being too heavy and wanting to lose weight. The best strategies for overly thin teenagers are much the same as those for obese individuals. Check with a doctor or registered dietitian for safe weight-gain strategies and refer to the points listed for weight control. Modify them slightly to get a reasonable plan for weight gain. Add the following points.

1. Examine your eating patterns. Avoid skipping meals. If you have trouble eating three large meals a day, try eating six smaller meals. Be willing to try new foods. A well-balanced diet is easier to achieve when you eat a variety of foods.

2. Examine your snacking patterns. Do you snack close to mealtime? Snacking increases blood sugar levels, which reduces hunger and appetite. If you snack, do so at least two hours before a meal.

3. If you are sedentary, start to exercise. If you are exercising, increase your activity level. Exercise can increase your metabolism and you will feel less tired.

4. Eat a variety of foods. Look for nutritious foods (such as nuts and dried fruits) that are high in calories.

Remember that it takes an extra 3500 calories to gain one pound. If you can increase your caloric intake by 500 calories above what you burn each day, you should be able to gain about one pound a week.

Fad Diets

Because losing weight takes time and careful planning, many people turn to fad diets for the promise of quick and easy results. A **fad diet** is one that promises quick and unrealistic results. Because being thin seems to be so unrealistically valued in our society, people think being thin is the way to become popular. Obese people are often the subject of jokes and other kinds of discrimination. These are some of the reasons why fad diets are so popular. Fad diets take advantage of people's emotions and give them false hopes. These diets promise a quick fix for obesity and lead you to believe that weight loss takes little effort. Advertisements for fad diets are everywhere—on television, in magazines and newspapers, and on the radio. These ads may appear to be very sound approaches to weight loss. Some will deliver the desired weight loss.

There are two major problems with fad diets. They can be dangerous to your health and the weight that is lost, while using them,

fad diet:

a weight-loss plan that promises unrealistic results.

SECTION 5.1

 Section Review Worksheet 5.1
To reinforce the concepts presented in this section, assign Section Review Worksheet 5.1.

 Section Quiz 5.1
Have students take Section Quiz 5.1.

Reteaching Worksheet 5.1
Students who have difficulty with the material may complete Reteaching Worksheet 5.1.

3. Well-balanced meals are important, no matter what the weight goal.

4. Restricting the amount of fat in the diet is essential for weight loss. The reverse is true for weight gain.

Extension
Fads in Dieting

Have students, or groups of students, investigate the kinds of fad diets that are currently advertised and popular.

Ask them to gather information on the requirements of the diet, the weight loss (or gain) that is promised, and who, in particular, seems to be targeted by the advertisements (teenagers, women). You might also ask students to gather information on how the diets are advertised and what about them, if anything, is potentially dangerous.

Review Answers

1. Answers will vary depending on students' BMR and level of activity. Students should follow the steps in the Life Skills feature.

2. The primary factor is body composition (ratio of fat mass to lean). The goal should not be a particular weight, but rather a certain body-fat percentage as measured on a skin-fold test.

3. Fad diets can be dangerous. They often do not provide adequate nutrition and can sometimes lead to serious health problems. Also, it is difficult to maintain weight loss with a fad diet.

4. Lose weight gradually; change your diet to reduce the number of calories and the percentage of fats, proteins, and carbohydrates; increase exercise; eat only when hungry; and choose snacks that are low in fat and also nutritious, such as fruits and vegetables.

(FIGURE 5-5) **Fad diets can appear to be sound programs for weight loss. Don't be fooled. People have died from lack of nutrition from some fad diets. Follow a doctor's or dietitian's instructions for a weight-loss plan.**

generally returns when you go back to your old eating habits. Fad diets usually include eating plans that do not provide adequate nutrition. There have been numerous deaths related to fad diets, even medically supervised ones, which do not provide adequate calories and nutrients for healthy body function.

Very low calorie levels also cause a change in the body's metabolic rate. If calories are cut sharply, the body slows its rate of metabolism to function on fewer calories. When the dieting phase ends and the person resumes normal eating habits, more calories are provided so the body stores more fat to prepare for the next state of "starvation."

If you must lose weight because you have a higher than normal percentage of body fat, then ask yourself these questions before you invest the time and energy in a weight loss program: Does the program . . .

- involve qualified nutrition professionals?
- include a safe, personalized physical activity program?

- encourage slow, gradual weight loss?
- include all of the five major food groups in the Food Pyramid?
- fit your lifestyle?
- help you make positive changes in your eating behavior for a lifetime?
- have a weight maintenance program?

A "Yes" to all of these questions indicates a sound program.

Review

1. Calculate your daily caloric need.

2. What factors should be considered in assessing your ideal weight?

3. What are the drawbacks of fad diets?

4. What are the characteristics of a healthy weight-loss plan?

ASSESS

Section Review

Have students answer the Section Review questions.

Alternative Assessment
Weighty Advice

Have students write a paragraph describing the advice they would give to a friend who wanted to lose weight in order to become more popular.

Closure
Reaching a Healthful Fat-to-Lean Ratio

Have students write a newspaper or magazine article describing how a person can determine if he or she is overfat. The article should include tips for developing a program to lose or gain body fat as well as the dangers of fad dieting. Suggest that the articles include visuals. Students might want

to compile their articles into a newsletter and distribute it to other classes.

Section 5.2 Eating Disorders

Objectives

- List the health hazards of anorexia, bulimia, and pica.
- Describe the characteristics of individuals most at risk for anorexia or bulimia.
- Explain how eating disorders can be avoided.

Dale has carried weight control and dieting too far. She's become attached to a body image that is unreasonable. The only way to achieve that image involves endangering her health.

Think about the body image you would like to have. Does it suit you or is it the image of someone else? Your mind can be flooded with images of young, thin beautiful models as the ideal. As a result, you may feel you are too heavy or unattractive even when you are not.

It is far more important to visualize yourself as a fit, healthy person. Being fit and engaging in healthful behaviors should provide a body image that is right for you. The heavy emphasis on body image in today's society has produced a dramatic increase in the number of people suffering from eating disorders. In this section we want you to explore the emotional and physical effects of these disorders. Let's start by looking at how they come about in the first place. While eating disorders are not new diseases (there is evidence that they date back to the Middle Ages), it appears that the percentage of people affected by these disorders is increasing. An estimated one million teenagers are affected by eating disorders. As many as 85 percent of all people with these disorders are female.

There are many reasons why females are more likely to have these disorders. One of the major reasons is that thinness appears to be associated with femininity and sensuality in females. Another reason is that women often think thinness is a factor in being popular.

(FIGURE 5-6) **It is better to see yourself as a fit, healthy person than to try to look like a fashion model.**

Background
Diet Survey
In a recent national survey of high school students, slightly more than one-third of the girls identified themselves as overweight, while less than 15 percent of the boys did. Almost half the girls in the survey indicated that they were on a diet even though almost one-quarter of the same girls did not think they were overweight. Skipping meals, using diet pills, and forced vomiting after eating were the most frequently reported dieting practices.

Evaluating Media Messages
Have students read this Unit 2 feature on pages 146–147. Then have them complete its companion worksheet.

Section 5.2 Lesson Plan

MOTIVATE

Journal 5D
Concerns About Eating Disorders

This may be done as a warm-up activity. Encourage students who have concerns about eating disorders to record their concerns in their Journal. Students could also record their feelings concerning Dale and her troubles.

Cooperative Learning
Dale's Dieting Problem

Have students form small groups to discuss the kinds of pressure, including peer pressure, that might be contributing to Dale's disorder. Students should also consider ways in which an individual can be helped to resist such pressure.

TEACH

Class Discussion
Body Image Versus Self-Esteem

Elicit from students what they think society views as the ideal male and female body image. Then have them suggest definitions of the term *self-esteem*. Discuss the relationship between having low self-esteem and wanting to have an ideal body image.

Check Up

Check Up

Have students turn in anonymously their answers to the Check Up. Tally the results and discuss them. Encourage students to identify risky eating behaviors. Challenge them to find patterns in the way their classmates eat.

Background

Anorexia Nervosa

Studies indicate that anorexia nervosa occurs in as many as 1 in 100 females aged 12 to 18. The condition does occur in males, but at a much lower frequency. Its causes are still unclear, but research points to low self-esteem as a major underlying factor. Some research suggests that a student may hear about eating disorders in a health class and decide to use one as a temporary method of losing weight. This practice is risky because many teens find it difficult to resume normal eating habits.

It would be hard to overemphasize the dangers of anorexia. As an anorexic grows increasingly thin, normal gastrointestinal function is

• • • Background continues on p. 115

Are You at Risk for an Eating Disorder?

People with eating disorders will respond with a "yes" to most of the following questions.

1. Do you prefer to eat alone?
2. Are you terrified of being overweight?
3. Do you constantly think about food?
4. Do you "binge" (overeat drastically) occasionally?
5. Are you highly knowledgeable about the calorie content of all the foods you eat?
6. Do you always feel "stuffed" after meals?
7. Are you constantly weighing yourself?
8. Do you eat a lot of "diet" foods?
9. Do you over-exercise to burn all the calories you eat?
10. Do you take a long time to eat meals?
11. Are you frequently constipated?
12. Do you feel guilty when you eat sweet or fattening foods?
13. Do you feel the urge to throw up after eating?
14. Do you feel your life is controlled by food and eating?

If your responses suggest that you may be at risk for an eating disorder, it is suggested that you discuss your situation with an adult or doctor.

(FIGURE 5-7) **One sign of anorexia is excessive exercise.**

Anorexia Nervosa

anorexia nervosa:
an eating disorder in which the person refuses to eat because of a fear of weight gain.

Anorexia nervosa is a condition in which a person is constantly dieting and carrying this dieting to an extreme. The anorexic, like Dale in the story, is in a state of starvation. Someone who diets to lose much more weight than is necessary may be anorexic. Dale feels she is overweight. She cannot be convinced to stop dieting because she sees herself as fat. The anorexic is obsessed with becoming thin and doesn't recognize when she becomes dangerously thin. She may exercise excessively and will appear to have no appetite. Signs of hunger and appetite are there, but the anorexic does not respond to them.

In dealing with the anorexic, parents and friends may attempt to force the victim to eat. These attempts will generally make the problem worse. The anorexic becomes more determined not to eat. However, on occasion, the anorexic will eat to avoid the hassles of dealing with family or friends. Unfortunately, it is likely that the anorexic will then go to a private place and throw up to get rid of the food.

Anorexia often occurs as a result of emotional problems. The anorexic is generally described as the "perfect" child. These individuals are generally popular. They are characterized as obedient, respectful, and are often good students. Parents or guardians of anorexics may unknowingly be

---

• • • TEACH continued

Case Study
Christy Henrich

Christy Henrich was a promising gymnast who aspired to be on the 1988 U.S. Olympic team. Although she was only four feet eleven inches tall and weighed 95 pounds, a competition judge told her she was too fat to make the team. When Christy went on a severe diet, she probably didn't realize the danger she was in. By July 1994, Christy weighed less than 60 pounds. At that weight, her body could no longer perform the functions needed for life, and she died of multiple organ failure. Use this case study to discuss the problem of body image and self-esteem. Emphasize that anorexia is both an emotional and a physical disease. Once the starvation process reaches a certain point, the results cannot be reversed, even if a person wants to start eating again.

Role-Playing
I Need to Diet

Select two students; one will play the role of someone engaged in a dangerous dieting practice, and the other will play the role of a sympathetic but worried friend. The first player should disagree with the fact that dieting can be dangerous. The second player should express his or her concerns and tell the first player that dieting can lead to a serious eating disorder. As a class, discuss why a person with an eating disorder very domineering, or have unreasonable expectations of their child. Control over eating may be the only area where the anorexic feels he or she has firm control in this kind of an environment. Part of the recovery process often involves helping the anorexic gain independence.

Effects of Anorexia Nervosa The anorexic experiences other physical effects related to the excessive weight loss. Heart rate, BMR, and body temperature all drop to low levels. Because the fat stored in the body is used up, the body begins breaking down muscle tissue for energy. Loss of muscle tissue can cause permanent heart damage. When this disorder occurs during puberty, sexual maturity and growth will stop. Sometimes a girl feels threatened by sexual maturity and will use dieting and weight loss to avoid changes that come with growing up.

The anorexic has low self-esteem, which is generally the cause of the disorder. The state of starvation results in frequent depression. Relationships among family and friends can be strained as the anorexic becomes more and more obsessed with not eating.

Treatment As many as 10 percent of anorexics die of starvation without treatment. Treatment requires a team of professionals—physicians, nurses, psychiatrists, family psychologists, and dietitians—working together. Mental health counseling is required to successfully treat the disorder. A treatment plan is developed that deals with the physical effects of the disorder and the emotional reasons for its occurrence. Early treatment is essential to prevent permanent damage to one's health. Treatment may sometimes involve forced feeding on a temporary basis. The first priority of treatment is aimed at meeting nutritional deficiencies to prevent long-term medical problems.

Bulimia

Bulimia is a disorder in which a person binges on food. A binge involves eating large amounts of food over a very short period of time. This *bingeing* is then followed by *purging* (either throwing up or using laxatives). Bulimia generally appears from the teen years through adulthood. It is far more common in teenage girls than is anorexia. Bulimics are threatened by being overweight, but derive a lot of pleasure from going on a binge. However, feelings of guilt and fear of weight gain set in and purging occurs.

Effects of Bulimia A bulimic may throw up daily to purge. Throwing up causes the enamel on the teeth to dissolve from exposure to acid from the stomach. The teeth are more prone to decay. The salivary glands become large from overproducing saliva to prevent dehydration. Frequent throwing up

bulimia:

an eating disorder based on a cycle of bingeing and purging food.

Warning Signs of Bulimia

Recurring episodes of binge eating.

Feeling of a lack of control over eating behavior during the eating binges.

Regular practice of self-induced vomiting, using laxatives, or using diuretics.

Strict dieting, fasting, or engaging in vigorous exercise to prevent weight gain.

An average of two or more binge eating episodes a week for at least three months.

Persistent over-concern with body shape and weight.

(FIGURE 5-8) **Bulimia is diagnosed after careful evaluation of the patient. The signs above are used to make the diagnosis.**

altered. The stomach empties slowly, and the small intestine becomes unable to absorb the nutrients in food. Liver and kidney functions are impaired, and permanent damage to these organs may occur. Body chemicals become so imbalanced that heart failure often occurs. Early diagnosis and treatment are vital. Body weight must be restored as quickly as possible; this is the first goal of treatment. Hospitalization is usually required, and the therapeutic process generally lasts for a year or more.

Background
Understanding Bulimia
Bulimia and anorexia nervosa are related disorders. The same set of factors—personality type, family structure, socioeconomic class—are common to both. Unlike an anorexic, a person with bulimia may appear healthy. However, there are some warning signs. These include depression, inability to sleep well, talking about suicide, fear of appearing fat, and purchasing large quantities of food. Bulimia can lead to malnutrition and other health problems.

---

needs more help than a friend can provide and what teens can do if they have serious concerns about a friend.

Reinforcement
Anorexia Is Life Threatening
Emphasize that people with anorexia must have professional treatment. On the board, list this summary of the physical effects of anorexia: decreased thyroid activity; reduced blood pressure; lowered body temperature; mental disorders, especially depression; decreased bone density; altered organ function; utilization of muscle tissue as an energy source; severe imbalance in body chemistry; heart failure; and, in females, a disruption of the menstrual cycle.

 Journal 5E
An Anorexic Friend
Have students record in their Journal how they might feel toward, and react to, a friend who has anorexia nervosa.

 Cooperative Learning
Bulimia: A Serious Disorder
Have students work in small groups to think of ways they could be of help to a friend or classmate being treated for bulimia. (*Suggestions might include treating the condition like any other illness rather than something to be ashamed of, writing to them if they are in residential treatment, and being sensitive to food issues on social occasions.*)

What Would You Do?

Have students read about Pam's situation and think about how they would try to help her as a friend. Remind them to use the seven decision-making steps to help them come to a conclusion about the best course of action.

Section Review Worksheet 5.2

To reinforce the concepts presented in this section, assign Section Review Worksheet 5.2.

Section Quiz 5.2

Have students take Section Quiz 5.2.

Reteaching Worksheet 5.2

Students who have difficulty with the material may complete Reteaching Worksheet 5.2.

What Would You Do?

Making Responsible Decisions

Pam Is in Trouble

Imagine that your best friend, Pam, has been starving herself on a diet for a long time and you think she has gone too far. Every time you say something to her, she tells you that she is too fat. She says everyone makes fun of her because she is too fat and that if you were a real friend you would be supportive of what she is doing.

You have a feeling there is a problem. You have heard about anorexia nervosa. You think Pam is becoming anorexic. Pam gets very angry when you try to talk to her about her weight. It's obvious that your friendship is in trouble. What do you do?

Remember to use the decision-making steps:

1. State the Problem.
2. List the Options.
3. Imagine the Benefits and Consequences.
4. Consider Your Values.
5. Weigh the Options and Decide.
6. Act.
7. Evaluate the Results.

---

can disturb the electrolyte balance in the body and can result in abnormal heart rhythms and kidney damage. Bulimics may also use laxatives. Weight loss caused by using laxatives results from water loss. Excessive use of laxatives disturbs the normal bowel function. The bulimic may then need to continue taking laxatives for the bowels to function at all. The use of diuretics can also alter the electrolyte balance of the body. Excessive use of diuretics can also cause high blood pressure and dehydration.

The binge-purge cycle begins to dominate the bulimic's life. Depression is very common. The enormous food habit can be very expensive. A bulimic may have to go to great lengths in order to obtain the money to support a food habit.

Treatment Bulimia can be hard to diagnose because its victims appear to be of normal weight. The disorder becomes apparent only after the person has had the disorder for a long time.

Because the binge-purge cycle dominates the bulimic's eating patterns, some people with bulimia can no longer recognize when they feel full. The chemical signals the body produces to signal fullness may be at very low levels in people who have bulimia. Like anorexia, the emotional basis of this disorder lies in the individual's low self-esteem. Therapy includes training in appropriate nutritional eating habits. Patients are encouraged to engage in activities that develop confidence and build self-esteem.

Anorexia and Bulimia in Combination

About 30 to 50 percent of anorexics also go through binge-purge cycles. Throwing up is one way anorexics maintain their low calorie consumption and keep weight low. Having both disorders just increases the health risks you've read about for each disorder. Professional counseling would almost always be required to successfully treat someone with both disorders.

What Should You Do?

Recognize that eating disorders result from placing too much emphasis on body shape and weight. Because thinness is highly valued in the United States culture, these disorders occur more frequently here than in

---

• • • TEACH continued

Class Discussion
Anorexia and Bulimia

Have students discuss the similarities and differences between the disorders anorexia nervosa and bulimia. Elicit from students that both are emotional disorders in which low self-esteem is a factor. Both involve body image perceptions. Have students distinguish the constant dieting of the anorexic from the binge-purge cycle of the bulimic.

Journal 5F
Am I at Risk?

Have students record in their Journal whether or not they think that they are at risk for anorexia or bulimia. Encourage students to use the Check Up list on page 114 in determining their risk. If they think they are at risk, encourage them to identify the risk factors and to consider talking to someone who can help.

Cooperative Learning
A Plan for Fitness

Have students meet in groups to formulate a nutrition and exercise plan that they feel would have a positive effect on an individual's overall health and self-esteem. Have several groups of students present their plans to the class.

other parts of the world. The focus on thinness, an obsession with food, and a domineering family situation are prime factors in the cause of these disorders.

Being fit and eating nutritiously will help make you feel good about yourself. When you feel good about yourself, you are less likely to do things that could damage your health. Learn to be comfortable with your body and realize that there is only so much you can do to change it. In trying to be popular, remember that it is your personality that makes you the attractive person that you are.

If you have, or are at high risk for, an eating disorder, seek help now. Talk to an adult you trust. Figure 11-8 on page 235 gives a list of some of the people in your life with whom you could discuss your problem. A visit to the doctor and a complete physical would help you know where to start, if treatment is needed. There are now numerous eating disorder clinics throughout the country. Check the *Hospital* listing in your phone book for places you can call for help.

Treating these disorders is generally a long, slow process. These risky behaviors do not go away overnight and require professional treatment.

Pica

Pica is a little-known eating disorder that involves eating substances not normally considered as food. People experiencing pica have cravings for such things as clay, soil, or laundry starch. This disorder generally occurs among pregnant women. Most pica is reported among pregnant African-American women living in rural areas of the southern United States. The disorder is also found in certain groups living in Australia and Africa. There is some evidence to suggest that pica results from cultural beliefs

(FIGURE 5-9) **Setting a goal to be fit will help boost your self-esteem. When you feel good about yourself, you are less likely to do things that damage your health.**

related to pregnancy, along with changes in food preferences among pregnant women.

The health dangers of pica result from eating harmful bacteria that could be present in clay, soil, or laundry starch. Eating these substances can change the way minerals are absorbed by the body, and mineral deficiencies can result. Eating large quantities of clay can also block the intestines.

Review

1. What are the health risks of bulimia?

2. You think your best friend is bulimic. What signs do you look for to know for sure?

3. How is self-esteem related to some eating disorders?

pica:
an eating disorder in which the person eats nonfood substances like starch, clay, or soil.

Review Answers
1. tooth decay, enlarged salivary glands, disruption of the body's electrolyte balance, mineral deficiencies, dehydration and disruption of normal bowel functions, high blood pressure, behaviors similar to drug addicts
2. Answers may include eating binges, purging, concern about being overweight, and low self-esteem.
3. People with low self-esteem often judge themselves by unrealistic standards. This is particularly true in terms of physical appearance. They may think that if their bodies were different, they would be happier. This idea, coupled with a distorted perception of their appearance, can lead to eating disorders.

Extension
Karen Carpenter

Tell students about or have them research the life of Karen Carpenter, a recording star with The Carpenters. Talent, popularity, and success were not enough to shield her from anorexia nervosa. Although the disorder was recognized, she died from her illness. Have students try to determine what pressures could have led to her development of anorexia.

ASSESS

Section Review
Have students answer the Section Review questions.

Alternative Assessment
The Nature of Anorexia Nervosa

Ask students to imagine that they are going to give a presentation on eating disorders. Have them write or record a

lecture that includes the common characteristics of people with eating disorders, common symptoms, associated health risks, and treatments.

Closure
Eating Disorders

Have a speaker who specializes in eating disorders speak to the class about these disorders.

Section 5.3 Disorders Affecting the Digestive System

Background
Digestive Disorders

Personal habits often contribute to constipation. When the body's natural urge to eliminate waste products comes at an inconvenient time, people may postpone elimination. Neglecting the body's signals disrupts its rhythm and can cause constipation.

Mild diarrhea is seldom a problem, but acute or prolonged cases are a health concern, especially for young children. The resulting dehydration and loss of electrolytes can cause death. In such cases, medical treatment, which includes hospitalization and the use of rehydration fluids, can be necessary.

Because dairy products provide about 75 percent of the calcium in the American diet, teens should not self-diagnose lactose intolerance. Physicians use either a breath hydrogen test or a lactose tolerance test to diagnose the condition. A person, especially a female, who is lactose intolerant must manage his or her diet carefully so that it includes enough calcium.

Objectives

- List the most common digestive disorders.
- Describe ways to treat constipation and diarrhea.
- Describe the differences between food allergies and food intolerances.

diarrhea:

loose bowel movements that occur when food moves too quickly through the digestive system.

constipation:

a condition in which bowel movements are infrequent or difficult.

As with many other health-related issues, disorders of the digestive system are frequently related to personal choices, like eating behaviors. Overeating and eating foods that the body has difficulty digesting most frequently cause digestive problems. But digestive problems can also be the result of a specific disease. The most common signs and symptoms of digestive disorders include such things as pain in the chest and abdomen, nausea and vomiting, and constipation and diarrhea.

Constipation

Constipation refers to a condition in which a person has difficult or infrequent bowel movements. It usually results when too much water is removed from waste products in the large intestine. This loss causes difficulty in moving waste material through to the rectum. There are many reasons why constipation may occur, including such things as a low-fiber diet, not drinking enough fluids, lack of exercise, stress, or

some disease process. To prevent constipation, your diet should include plenty of fluids, foods high in fiber, and regular exercise. You should try to limit the number of high-fat foods you eat. These foods take longer to travel through your digestive system. If you have a problem with frequent constipation, you should see a physician to rule out the possibility of serious illness.

Diarrhea

Diarrhea occurs when food moves through the digestive system too quickly and there is not enough time for water to be removed. When this happens, the stools are loose and watery, and bowel movements may occur quite often. Usually diarrhea lasts for only a short period of time and stops without treatment. Even though the stools are watery, a person with diarrhea should drink plenty of liquids. The water that is normally removed from digested food in the large intestine is an important source of nutrients for the body. During diarrhea there is a loss of nutrients, and dehydration can occur. When a person has diarrhea for an extended period of time, the large loss of water can be very dangerous to health, or even fatal.

The electrolytes sodium, potassium, and chloride can also be lost during bouts of extended diarrhea—or through any large fluid loss (like heavy perspiration). The proper balance of electrolytes prevents problems resulting from dehydration, such as cramping, heat exhaustion, and heat stroke. Therefore, if diarrhea lasts for more than two days, a physician should always be consulted.

Section 5.3 Lesson Plan

MOTIVATE

Journal 5G
Food Preferences

This can be done as a warm-up activity. Suggest to students that they record in their Journal foods that they like very much and foods that they dislike. Then tell them to review their

lists and identify any foods that seem to cause digestive upset or allergic reactions.

TEACH

Class Discussion
Digestive Disorders

Most members of the class, if not all, will have experienced the common digestive disorders discussed here—con-

stipation and diarrhea. Stress that these disorders sometimes indicate the presence of a serious condition. Point out that chronic constipation can lead to laxative dependence. Students should also be made aware that diarrhea can be a very serious condition, particularly in infants, because they dehydrate very rapidly.

Food Allergies

Allergies brought about by food can cause reactions such as diarrhea, rashes, congestion, sneezing, and itchy, watery eyes. Food allergies are the result of the body's immune system responding to the food as if it were a disease-causing organism. The most common food allergies involve cow's milk, eggs, peanuts, wheat products, shellfish, and fish. The allergic responses are the result of the body's reaction to the foreign proteins in these foods. The most severe food allergy reaction is called anaphylactic shock. The victim of anaphylactic shock experiences severe itching, hives, sweating, tightness in the throat, and difficulty in breathing, followed by low blood pressure, unconsciousness, and eventually death. If you are diagnosed as having a specific food allergy (diagnosis should come from an allergist), you must avoid the food that produces the reaction. This means looking carefully at labels to determine if combination foods are made with substances you are allergic to.

Many allergies begin in infancy and are thought to result from introducing solid foods too early in the infant's diet. It is recommended that cow's milk not be given to infants until they are at least six months of age. Foods that commonly cause allergies should not be given to infants until they are past their first birthday. Certain chemical additives in foods (such as dyes) can also cause allergic reactions.

Food Intolerances

Negative reactions to specific foods that do not involve the body's immune system are called **food intolerances.** Lactose intolerance is one of the most common of these reactions. People with lactose intolerance cannot tolerate milk and milk products. Their bodies do not produce lactase, the

(FIGURE 5-10) **Consuming dairy products containing lactose such as those shown in the top photograph can cause extreme discomfort for individuals with lactose intolerance. The products shown above can be taken by lactose-intolerant individuals to breakdown lactose.**

enzyme that breaks down lactose in milk. Lactose intolerance is high among Asians, Africans, Native Americans, and African-Americans. Drinking milk if you don't produce lactase will cause you to experience bloating, diarrhea, gas, and severe cramps. Fortunately, people who have lactose intolerance can purchase milk already treated with lactase, or add special lactase drops to milk. Lactase tablets can also be used with meals that include milk products. If you have lactose intolerance, you need to be sure you still get an adequate supply of calcium in your diet.

food intolerance:

a negative reaction to food which is not brought about by the immune system.

SECTION 5.3

Background
Food Additives

Although there are many reasons why additives are put into food, most often they are used for one of four purposes—to add flavor, color, or texture to food, or to preserve food. Spices, natural flavors, and artificial flavors are added to enhance the taste of food. Coloring agents are used to make food look more appealing. Texturing additives are used to thicken food or to stabilize it, that is, to keep it from separating. Preservatives are added to prevent food from spoiling.

Other reasons for using food additives are to increase a food's nutritional quality, to help certain foods remain moist, and to prevent foods from becoming acidic or alkaline.

 Making a Choice 5B

Assign the Lactose-Free Foods card. The card asks students to consider ways of using lactose-free foods as substitutes for dairy products.

Journal 5H
Anxiety and Digestive Disorders

Have students record in their Journal any digestive problem they have experienced that may have been caused by anxiety, and have them describe how they handled it. Students who have not had such problems can give suggestions on how to handle anxiety-related digestive problems.

Case Study
Lactose Intolerance

Ask for a volunteer who knows that he or she has a lactose intolerance to describe how he or she handles the condition with respect to diet. Ask them to name some foods that contain "hidden" milk.

Debate the Issue
Eliminate Food Additives

Have teams debate the topic: Should food additives be banned because they cause serious health problems for some individuals? Have students propose measures to deal with the health problems created by food additives.

Section Review Worksheet 5.3

To reinforce the concepts presented in this section, assign Section Review Worksheet 5.3.

Section Quiz 5.3

Have students take Section Quiz 5.3.

Reteaching Worksheet 5.3

Students who have difficulty with the material may complete Reteaching Worksheet 5.3.

Review Answers

1. Answers may include chest and abdomen pain, cramping, nausea, vomiting, constipation, diarrhea, gas, and bloating.

2. Liquids prevent dehydration that occurs during diarrhea.

3. Food allergies, unlike food intolerances, involve the body's immune system. The immune system responds to the food as if it were an invading organism or germ.

Common Food Additives and Environmental Contaminants

Additive	Source	Side Effects
MSG	Oriental foods, processed meats	Chest pain, headache, sweating, burning feeling
Coloring agents	Beverages	Allergic reactions: rash, digestive problems
Sodium nitrite	Smoked meats: ham, bacon, sausage, cold cuts	Possible link to cancer
Sulfites (sulfur dioxide)	Potatoes, packaged foods, wine	Allergic reactions including anaphylactic shock
Estrogen	Meats	Possible link to cancer
Lead	Lead-containing paints and glazes	Lead poisoning
Mercury	Contaminated fish	Mercury poisoning

(FIGURE 5-11)

Other common intolerances include the inability to adequately digest substances such as prunes, blueberries, corn, and MSG (monosodium glutamate). MSG can produce a reaction often called "Chinese-restaurant syndrome" (MSG is commonly used in Chinese foods). MSG is an additive in many foods. Reactions to MSG include chest pain, headache, sweating, and a burning feeling.

Figure 5-11 shows some other additives commonly used in foods that can cause the body to react negatively. If you have a food intolerance you will need to check food labels carefully. When eating out, be sure to ask questions about the ingredients used in preparing the food.

Review

1. List the symptoms of a digestive disorder.

2. Why are liquids so important in treating diarrhea?

3. How does a food allergy differ from a food intolerance?

. . . TEACH continued

Extension
What's in Food?

Have students use library sources to investigate the kinds of foods in which additives are used. Have them read food labels to identify some foods that contain one or more additives. Have them catalog the possible side effects from eating each type of food.

ASSESS

Section Review

Have students answer the Section Review questions.

Alternative Assessment
Digestive Disorders

On the chalkboard create a reference table on digestive disorders while students provide the information. The table should contain four columns: Disorder, Causes, Symptoms, Treatment/Prevention.

Closure
Treating Digestive Problems

Ask students to explain how constipation can be prevented, and then to explain why diarrhea can be dangerous.

Summary

- The number of calories you should consume is determined by basal metabolism rate and your level of activity.

- The body is made of several kinds of tissue, including fat and lean mass. Females have a higher fat content than males.

- A person's ideal weight should be determined by the ratio of fat to lean mass.

- Obesity has serious health risks, including heart disease, cancer, diabetes, and stroke.

- Fad diets are rarely effective and can be dangerous to your health. Regular physical activity is the key to lifetime weight management.

- Anorexia nervosa is a starvation eating disorder that can result in depression, permanent heart damage, and even death.

- Bulimia can cause harmful changes in body organs.

- Some common digestive disorders are constipation, diarrhea, food allergies, and food intolerances.

Vocabulary

basal metabolic rate energy needed to fuel the body's on-going processes while the body is at complete rest.

energy-balance equation eating the same number of calories that you burn each day.

lean mass also known as the lean muscle mass portion of your body. It is your total body weight minus the weight due to fat.

essential fat the amount of fat needed for certain metabolic processes to occur.

storage fat excess fat stored in the body.

obesity weighing 20 percent more than one's recommended weight.

anorexia nervosa an eating disorder in which the person refuses to eat because of a fear of weight gain.

bulimia an eating disorder based on a cycle of bingeing and purging food.

pica an eating disorder in which the person eats nonfood substances like starch, clay, or soil.

constipation a condition in which bowel movements are infrequent or difficult.

diarrhea loose bowel movements that occur when food moves too quickly through the digestive system.

food intolerance a condition in which a reaction occurs to food that is not brought about by the immune system.

SUMMARY
Have students read the summary to reinforce the concepts they learned in Chapter 5.

VOCABULARY
Have students write a paragraph for a student newspaper using as many of the vocabulary terms as they can.

EXTENSION
Have students visit a grocery store or supermarket, paying attention to the locations on shelves, locations in the store, and size of displays devoted to foods that are high in fat.

CHAPTER REVIEW

Concept Review

1. basal metabolic rate (BMR)
2. body composition
3. diabetes, blood pressure, cholesterol
4. eat, burn
5. nutrition
6. bulimia
7. anorexia nervosa
8. fluids, fiber, exercise
9. diarrhea
10. lactose intolerance

Expressing Your Views

Sample responses:

1. I would tell Patricia that diets promising fast weight loss are not healthy, as they do not provide adequate nutrition. I would also tell her that height and weight charts are only a guide, not a specific target for body weight. There is no fixed ideal body weight for each person. I would also tell Patricia that she should have her body fat measured.

2. Thinness appears to be associated with femininity and sensuality in women, and most women think that thinness is a factor in being popular.

3. Daniel can drink milk in which the lactose has already been broken down by lactase. This type of milk is available for purchase or Daniel can add special lactase drops to regular milk. Daniel can

Concept Review

1. Your _____ refers to how fast your body burns calories.

2. Rather than using height and weight charts, you should examine your _____ as a better method of determining your ideal weight.

3. Being overweight or obese increases your health risks of _____, high _____, and elevated _____ .

4. A simple rule for healthy weight control is to _____ fewer calories than you _____ .

5. Fad diets can be dangerous to your health because they require food selections that do not provide adequate _____ .

6. A condition called _____ can lead to tooth decay and mineral deficiencies from repeated vomiting.

7. _____ is a condition in which a person is obsessed with becoming thin.

8. To prevent constipation, your diet should include plenty of _____ , foods high in _____ , and plenty of _____ .

9. When a person has _____ for an extended period of time, the large loss of water can be very dangerous to his or her health.

10. A common negative reaction to milk and milk products is called _____ .

Expressing Your Views

1. Patricia is 5'5" and weighs 140 pounds. She was surprised when she saw a height/weight chart at the doctor's office that gave her ideal weight as no more than 135 pounds. She is now looking for a diet that promises fast results. What would you advise her? What could you tell her about height/weight charts?

2. Anorexia nervosa and bulimia appear more often in girls than in boys. Why do you think this is true?

3. Daniel has lactose intolerance. How can he be sure his body gets enough calcium?

also use lactase tablets with meals that include milk products containing lactose. Daniel can be sure to get an adequate supply of calcium in his diet by eating calcium-rich foods that do not contain lactose, such as sardines.

Life Skills Check . . . . . .

1. Assessing Your Health
You will be traveling next summer on a long road trip. Most of your day will be spent riding in the car. Calculate your total calorie needs for the day. You'll be visiting relatives and you know that their eating habits differ from yours. What can you do to keep your caloric intake and calories burned in balance?

2. Making Responsible Decisions
You have just learned that you are allergic to milk. What kind of changes to your diet will you need to make in order to get the calcium that you need?

Projects . . . .

1. Your genetic makeup plays a role in determining your body composition. Recent evidence indicates that genes may also influence fat storage. In a small group, research what is currently known about the effect of genes on body size, fat storage sites, and weight. Develop a class or school exhibit that shows key facts about the influence of genes on body composition.

2. Locate weight loss programs in your community that advertise for teens. Gather information about each program so that you compare the distinct programs to the characteristics on page 112. Report your findings to the class.

Plan for Action . . . .

Eating patterns and food selection directly affect weight control. List four strategies you will use to help you gain, lose, or maintain your present weight depending on your individual needs.

Life Skills Check
Sample responses:
1. I know I need to watch the number of calories I take in and the number of calories I burn or I'll gain weight. On the trip I would eat more fruits and vegetables and avoid high-calorie snacks like chips and sodas. I will try to walk or do some simple exercises when we take breaks or in the evening. I will exercise every day while I'm there—I could go biking with my cousins—and not just sit around watching T.V. I'll try to eat only small portions of foods that I know are high in fat or calories.
2. I know I can't just eliminate milk products from my diet, so I'll use lactose-free or lactose-reduced dairy products. I will read labels to find "hidden" milk and add lactase drops to those foods when I eat them. I'll do some research to find out which non-dairy foods are high in calcium and include plenty of these foods in my diet.

Projects
Have students complete the projects on genetic makeup and body composition and on weight-loss programs.

Plan for Action
Ask students to discuss the role that weight control can play in a person's life and what role they would like it to play in their life. Then have them develop a personal strategy for weight gain, loss, or maintenance.

ASSESSMENT OPTIONS

Chapter Test
Have students take the Chapter 5 Test.

Alternate Assessment
Have students do the Alternative Assessment activity for Chapter 5.

Test Generator
The Test Generator contains additional assessment items for this chapter.

Personal Care and Appearance

SECTION	TITLE/OBJECTIVES	PERSONAL INVENTORY			LIFE SKILLS DEVELOPMENT			
		Personal Health Inventory	Journal	Check Up	Life Skills	Life Skills Worksheets	Media Message or Ethical Issues Worksheet	What Would You Do?
6.1 pp. 125–132	**SKIN CARE** • Name the two main layers of the skin. • Recognize skin problems. ▪▪ Explain how you can reduce your chances of getting acne. ▪▪ Explain how you can avoid sun damage to your skin.	Ch. 6	6A 6B	p. 126				
6.2 pp. 133–135	**HAIR AND NAIL CARE** • Describe three common hair and scalp problems. ▪▪ Explain how to care for your hair. ▪▪ Explain how to care for your nails.		6C			6A		
6.3 pp. 136–142	**TEETH AND GUM CARE** • Explain how dental cavities develop. ▪▪ Explain how to care for your teeth and gums. ▪▪ Be able to make an appointment with a dentist.		6D 6E 6F		p. 141	6B		

KEY: ▪▪ Denotes Life Skill Objective

Text references denoted by page number.

Supplement references denoted by chapter or item numbers.

LINKING RESOURCES

	Making a Choice Cards	Parent Discussion Guide	Health Talk Audio Program	Teaching Transparencies and Directory	Section Review Worksheets	Section Quizzes	Reteaching Worksheets	Section Reviews
	INTERACTION		**OTHER RESOURCES**		**SECTION REVIEW AND ASSESSMENT**			
				6A BSH2	6.1	6.1	6.1	p. 132
	6A				6.2	6.2	6.2	p. 135
	6B			6B	6.3	6.3	6.3	p. 142

For additional information about the skin and sensation, see page 656 in the Body Systems Handbook.

KEY FACTS

- The skin is the body's largest organ and has several vital functions.
- The two layers of the skin are the epidermis and the dermis.
- Overexposure to UVA and UVB rays from the sun damage the skin, causing premature aging and skin cancer.
- There are products available that will protect the skin from the sun's ultraviolet rays.
- Hair on the head serves to insulate it from heat and cold; eyelashes, eyebrows, nasal hair, and hairs in the ears help prevent the entry of foreign matter.
- When acids from food and dental plaque eat through a tooth's enamel, a cavity results.
- Gum disease, which is preventable, is the major cause of tooth loss in adults.
- A good dental program involves regular brushing and flossing, a nutritious diet, and regular dental care.

CHAPTER REVIEW AND ASSESSMENT

TEXT
Chapter Review pp. 144–145

SUPPLEMENTS
Chapter Test 6

Alternative Assessment 6

Test Generator Chapter 6

CHAPTER

6

Personal Care *and* Appearance

◆ ◆ ◆ ◆

Section 6.1	Skin Care
Section 6.2	Hair and Nail Care
Section 6.3	Teeth and Gum Care

Personal care involves more than just how you look. Taking care of yourself makes you feel better too.

MYTHS & MISCONCEPTIONS

- **Beach umbrellas provide adequate protection against sunburn.** Beach umbrellas provide little protection against sunburn because ultraviolet rays reflected from water and sand can be reflected into the area shaded by the umbrella.

- **Sunburn cannot occur on foggy, hazy, or overcast days.** Under these atmospheric conditions, the sun's ultraviolet rays are scattered but still cause sunburn.

- **Cocoa butter, baby oil, and mineral oil are effective sunscreens.** These products moisturize and minimize the sun's drying effects, but they do not prevent sunburn.

- **Shaving makes hair grow faster.** Hair roots, where hair growth begins, are located in the dermis. They are not affected by shaving at the skin level.

The day at the beach was perfect. David and Elena had a great time, swimming and listening to music and watching the waves. When they got home, though, David was red and sunburned all over. Elena told him he looked like a giant tomato. She was teasing, but it wasn't funny. When Elena touched his arm, it felt like a lit match on his skin.

◆
◆
◆
◆

David couldn't understand why he got sunburned and Elena didn't. They both used the same suntan lotion. They put it on at the same time. They were in the sun exactly the same amount of time—from 10:00 A.M. till 4:00 P.M. They both swam for the same length of time. Why did they have such different reactions to the sun?

Personal Health Inventory
Have students complete the Personal Health Inventory for this chapter.

Section
6.1 *Skin Care*

Objectives

- *Name the two main layers of the skin.*

- *Recognize skin problems.*

- *Explain how you can reduce your chances of getting acne.*
  LIFE SKILLS: Practicing Self-Care

- *Explain how you can avoid sun damage to your skin.*
  LIFE SKILLS: Practicing Self-Care

David discovered the reason for their different reactions to the sun when he talked with a pharmacist. The pharmacist explained that differences in tanning are due to a substance called melanin in the skin. The more melanin people have in their skin, the darker their skin is and the less likely they are to get sunburned. David is blond, blue-eyed, and fair complexioned, so he sunburned easily. Elena has dark eyes, black hair, and brown skin, so she tanned instead.

In this chapter, you'll learn to protect your skin from the sun and other hazards. You'll also learn how to take good care of your hair, nails, and teeth. And you'll learn that good grooming helps you stay healthy and improves your personal appearance.

Skin Care and How You Look

Care of the skin is an important part of your appearance. This is particularly true during the teen years. Your body has more chemicals called hormones now than when you were a child. Hormones affect your skin and how it looks. Why is it that one day you

Section 6.1 Lesson Plan

MOTIVATE

Journal 6A
Skin Care

This may be done as a warm-up activity. In their Journal, have students describe their present skin-care routine. Explain that this may be showering once a day or it may include something more elaborate.

Class Discussion
An Age-Old Concern

Tell students that archaeologists have learned that people have always been concerned with their appearance. As early as 4,000 B.C., the ancient Egyptians, both male and female, used cosmetics and perfumed oils. Grooming tools such as combs, mirrors, and razors have been found during archaeological excavations. (If possible, bring to class photographs or pictures that pertain to the history of cosmetics and self-adornment.) Ask students to suggest reasons why personal appearance is so important to humans.

Check Up

Have students turn in their answers to the Check Up questions anonymously and then discuss the responses with the class. As these topics are quite personal in nature, there will probably be differences of opinion about what constitutes proper care.

Check Up

How Well Do You Take Care of Yourself?

Which of the following actions do you take to improve your appearance and health?

- Wash skin regularly with soap and water
- Use a sunscreen of at least 15 SPF when outdoors
- Watch any moles for changes in their appearance
- Wash hair regularly
- Limit the use of electric hair dryers and curlers
- Brush teeth at least twice a day
- Floss teeth once a day

(FIGURE 6-1) **Having healthy skin helps you look and feel good.**

have a clear complexion and the next day it's full of pimples? It's because of hormones. You can't do anything to change the hormones in your body, but you *can* improve the look of your skin.

Functions of the Skin

The skin is the largest organ in the body. It is far larger than your lungs or your heart. While you may not think of your skin as an important organ, it actually has some very important functions.

1. to protect the body from germs and injury
2. to regulate body temperature
3. to transmit sensations such as pain or cold
4. to act as a weatherproof cover which can prevent dehydration
5. to excrete wastes
6. to synthesize vitamin D

TEACH

Class Discussion
Sunburn

Have students look at the photographs of David and Elena and speculate which one of the pair will sunburn more easily. Ask them to explain their thinking. Have them discuss their own experiences with sunburn. Find out whether any students have ever sunburned on

foggy, hazy, or overcast days, or on a sunny day while sitting beneath a beach umbrella. Ask students to name some remedies they have used to lessen the discomfort from sunburn. Point out that a serious sunburn needs to be treated by a physician.

Demonstration
The Weight and Size of Skin

To demonstrate the possible weight and size of the skin of an adult, provide students with a gallon of milk or a 7-pound weight to lift, and have them

use a yardstick to determine the amount of space covered by a 20-square-foot area.

 Teaching Transparency 6A
Structure of the Skin

Use this transparency of Figure 6-2 to point out the various parts that make up the skin's structure—such as a sweat gland, an oil gland, and a hair root. Ask students to identify each structure. Ask a volunteer to locate the epidermis and dermis layers.

Structure of the Skin

As you can see in Figure 6-2, the skin has two main layers—the **epidermis** and the **dermis**. Under these two layers is a layer of fatty tissue called the subcutaneous layer. The subcutaneous layer insulates the body from temperature changes and connects the skin to the body.

The Epidermis   The epidermis is the top layer of the skin. This is the part of the skin that you see. It is made up of cells that are replaced once a month, which means that none of the skin you see is over a month old.

The epidermis has small openings called pores. Pores are tunnels that lead to the skin surface from below the epidermis. Skin oil and sweat are carried in the pores up to the skin surface.

Melanin, the substance that gives skin its color, is found in the epidermis. Melanin protects the skin from the sun's rays and is produced whenever the skin is exposed to the sun. Melanin does not provide complete protection from the sun, and anyone can be sunburned. Melanin is also the substance that produces freckles.

The Dermis   The dermis is the skin layer just below the epidermis. It contains a network of blood vessels that carry heat and nutrients to the surface of the skin. The dermis has thousands of tiny hairs. The root of each hair is surrounded by oil glands. Oil from these glands travels along the hair to the surface of the skin. The oil keeps the skin moist, soft, and waterproof. Overproduction of oil can make the skin feel oily.

The dermis also has thousands of sweat glands that produce sweat to rid the body of excess water, salts, and wastes. When sweat evaporates, it cools the skin. About 1 quart of water is excreted in sweat every day, but most of the time it goes unnoticed. Physical activity causes increased sweating that is, of course, easy to see. Some sweat

(FIGURE 6-2) **The two main layers of the skin are the epidermis and the dermis. The epidermis is the layer you can see from the outside. The dermis is beneath the epidermis and contains the oil glands.**

glands release their moisture directly to the skin's surface. Other sweat glands release their moisture into a hair follicle in regions such as the armpits and groin. This secretion, rich in proteins and fatty acids, is decomposed by bacteria on the skin's surface, causing a distinct odor. These glands begin to function at puberty. Emotional stress and sexual changes promote secretion from these glands.

Nerves are also found in the dermis, allowing us to sense touch, pain, heat, and other sensations.

Skin Problems

One of the first things people see when they look at you is your skin, so it is especially frustrating when you have skin problems. Some skin problems, like acne, are common during the teen years. Other problems may occur at any time. The following are some of the most common problems.

Skin Blemishes   **Acne** is a term that is commonly used to label the skin eruptions

epidermis:

the very thin outer layer of the skin.

dermis:

the second layer of skin; the dermis contains the most important structures of the skin.

acne:

a condition in which the pores of the skin become clogged with oil; acne can take the form of blackheads, whiteheads, or pimples.

Background
Retin-A and Accutane
Retin-A and Accutane are drugs that are effective in treating acne. Both are vitamin A derivatives. Retin-A is applied topically and works to loosen the plugs of oil that stop up the pores of the skin. It may make the skin dry, and it increases the skin's vulnerability to damage by the sun's rays. While some advertisements tout its effectiveness as an anti-aging cream, Retin-A has only one FDA approved use—treatment of acne.

The drug Accutane is highly effective in treating severe acne that does not respond to other drug treatments; however, it has some undesirable and even dangerous side effects. It may cause peeling of the skin, headaches, nausea, and nosebleeds. In pregnant women, it can cause miscarriages and serious birth defects. Accutane <u>should not be used</u> by pregnant women or women who might become pregnant. For this reason, doctors prescribing Accutane and women using it need to go through a product education program.

Reinforcement
Functions of Skin

Review the functions of the skin. Stress that it is because these functions are so vital that severe burns can be life threatening.

Demonstration
Nerve Endings in Skin

Have students determine whether all areas of the skin contain the same number of nerve endings. Have a student hold two broomstraws together and gently press the arm of a blindfolded volunteer until the volunteer feels the pressure and identifies how many broomstraws he or she feels. Have the first student move the broomstraws slightly apart and repeat the procedure. Continue moving the broomstraws apart until the volunteer feels the touch of two broomstraws. Measure and record the distance between the broomstraws. Test other parts of the body, such as the cheek, shin, and fingertip. Students should find that the nerve endings are closest in the fingertips.

(FIGURE 6-3) **A pimple develops when bacteria infect a pore that is already clogged with oil.**

Background
Athlete's Foot

Athlete's foot can be caused by several different kinds of fungus and can vary in appearance. Warm, moist skin provides ideal growing conditions for fungus. For that reason, prevention of athlete's foot includes complete drying of the feet after bathing or swimming, especially between the toes, and paying attention to foot gear. Socks should be changed often and should be made of 100 percent cotton, and shoes should be made of leather or canvas. Because athlete's foot is slightly contagious, it is not a good idea to share towels or bathmats with a person who has athlete's foot.

associated with adolescence, but not all skin eruptions are diagnosed as acne, which is a medical condition. Acne is particularly common during the teen years when the skin can produce a lot of oil. There are three other types of skin blemishes: blackheads, whiteheads, and pimples. Blackheads occur when a pore becomes clogged with excess oil and dead skin cells. The combination of oil and dead cells turns black when it is exposed to the air. Whiteheads result from a clogged pore that is not exposed to the air, because the pore is covered by the epidermis. Pimples occur when a clogged pore becomes infected with bacteria. Daily cleansing can reduce the conditions that lead to bacterial infections.

What If You Have Skin Blemishes

Wash your face several times a day with a gentle cleanser to reduce the amount of oil and bacteria on your face.

If you use makeup on your skin, use products that are labeled "water-based." Oily cosmetics can clog the pores.

Do not squeeze or pick at pimples. Squeezing and picking can cause infection and scarring.

Try using an over-the-counter blemish medication containing benzoyl peroxide.

If you have a severe case of blemishes, see a dermatologist — a doctor who specializes in skin disorders. The dermatologist can prescribe medications and offer advice on ways to improve the condition of your skin.

(FIGURE 6-4)

(FIGURE 6-5) **If you have acne, but want to wear makeup on your skin, be sure to buy products that are labeled "water-based." Oil-based products can make acne worse.**

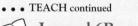

• • • TEACH continued

Journal 6B
Skin and Self-Confidence

In their Journal, have students write how they think the health of a person's skin affects his or her self-confidence and social acceptance.

Class Discussion
Causes of Acne

As a class, review the basic causes of teenage acne. *(Teenager's skin tends to be oily. The oil may block pores causing whiteheads, blackheads, or pimples.)*
Ask: **Where on the body does acne commonly occur?** *[The face and neck are the most usual sites, but acne also occurs on the back, shoulders, and chest.]* Point out that acne is most common in teenagers but it also occurs in adults. Explain that the cause of acne is not known. Some doctors

believe that heredity may be a major factor in the development of acne and in how severe the case will be. Many doctors believe that cosmetics are the leading cause of acne in adult women because oily moisturizers and foundations can clog pores.

Cooperative Learning
Controlling Body Odor

Divide the class into small groups and ask them to provide tips for controlling body odor. These tips may come from their own experience, from other people,

(FIGURE 6-6) **If you notice any changes in a mole, report it immediately to a doctor. A mole can become a malignant melanoma (shown above), a very serious cancer.**

Body Odor When bacteria on the skin attack sweaty secretions, they produce waste with an unpleasant odor. A diet high in animal proteins and animal fats may make this odor even stronger. Daily bathing or showering helps to remove the waste products. In addition, deodorants or antiperspirants may be used. Deodorants kill the bacteria and conceal body odor. Antiperspirants reduce the amount of perspiration and keep the bacteria from growing.

Foot Odor Foot odor can become offensive when the feet perspire heavily. To combat foot odor, be sure to wash your feet thoroughly every day. Wearing cotton socks and open-weave shoes will help reduce foot perspiration, and dusting the feet with plain talc will help absorb moisture. It is also a good idea to alternate pairs of shoes so they can dry out between wearings.

Moles A mole is a small round dark area on the skin. Most moles are not harmful; in fact, they are sometimes called "beauty marks." But just to be safe, report any changes in the size, color, or condition of the mole to a doctor, because these changes may indicate skin cancer.

Warts A wart is a small growth caused by a virus. Although there is no cure for warts, they are usually harmless. Often several warts will appear in the same area. The best treatment for warts is to have them removed by a doctor. If you use an over-the-counter product for wart removal, be very careful. Wart-removal products contain acid that may harm the surrounding skin if they are not applied carefully.

(FIGURE 6-7) **Athlete's foot is caused by a fungus. The symptoms are redness and itching.**

Athlete's Foot and Jock Itch Athlete's foot and other forms of a skin condition called ringworm are caused by microscopic fungi. Athlete's foot gets its name from locker room shower stalls where the fungus may grow and spread to bare feet.

Jock itch occurs in males around the genitals. Symptoms of both athlete's foot and jock itch are redness and itching. Personal cleanliness, using shower shoes, and keeping feet dry will help prevent the spread of the fungus.

SECTION 6.1

Background
Moles
At birth, most moles are present under the skin. When exposed to sunlight, they grow larger, become darker, and raise up above the normal surrounding skin. Moles are also found in areas covered by clothing but they are usually not as dark. Most moles are harmless, but changes in a mole should be reported to a physician, especially if it spreads, changes color, develops a black edge, bleeds, or becomes itchy. These may be symptoms of malignant melanoma, the most serious type of skin cancer. A mole that develops after adolescence may also be a symptom of malignant melanoma.

Background
Warts
Warts are caused by viral infections of the epidermis. The virus invades skin cells and makes them reproduce rapidly. They can spread to other body parts if they are picked, scratched, or touched, because viral infections are contagious. A wart usually disappears within 2 years.

---

or from the media. After the groups have generated their lists, have them create a master list and copy it on the chalkboard. Their tips may include

1. bathing frequently
2. changing clothes daily and laundering them frequently
3. using an underarm deodorant or antiperspirant to control odor
4. wearing fabrics such as cotton that allow moisture to escape
5. using underarm shields to protect clothing from perspiration

Reinforcement
Signs of Skin Cancer
Stress the importance of reporting to physicians any changes in moles, as the changes may be symptoms of malignant melanoma, the most serious type of skin cancer.

Reinforcement
Warts
Point out that warts are contagious—they can be spread from one part of the body to another, or from one person to another. Warts that grow in the mucous membranes of the penis or vagina are much like other warts but are considered to be a venereal disease (even if they were spread from a person's own fingers) because they can be spread by sexual contact. They should be treated by a physician.

Section Review Worksheet 6.1

To reinforce the concepts presented in this section, assign Section Review Worksheet 6.1.

 Section Quiz 6.1

Have students take Section Quiz 6.1.

Reteaching Worksheet 6.1

Students who have difficulty with the material may complete Reteaching Worksheet 6.1.

(FIGURE 6-8) **Impetigo is a bacterial infection that causes sores with crusts.**

Impetigo Impetigo is a common infection caused by bacteria, which causes sores with crusts on the skin. It begins in moist areas of the body, in areas where there is friction, and in cuts. Impetigo is most common in children, but may also occur in teenagers and adults. A photograph of impetigo is shown in Figure 6-8. If you think you have impetigo, it is best to seek medical attention.

Poison Ivy, Poison Oak, and Poison Sumac Many people have an allergic reaction to poison ivy, poison oak, or poison sumac. Touching these plants can cause redness, blisters, and severe itching. Each type of plant is shown in Figure 6-9. Memorize how they look so you can be sure to avoid them. Take the following precautions if you touch any of the three plants:

- Immediately wash the skin that came into contact with the plant.

Poison ivy   Poison oak   Poison sumac

(FIGURE 6-9) **Touching these plants can cause a painful allergic rash.**

• • • TEACH continued

Reinforcement
Poison Ivy Exposure

The following are some suggestions for dealing with poison ivy:

1. If exposed, change clothes as soon as possible.
2. After washing the exposed area with soap and water, apply rubbing alcohol.
3. Wash any clothes that came in contact with it.

4. If your dog or cat rubs against poison ivy, avoid skin contact with its fur and wash it using rubber gloves.
5. Be certain you can identify it.

Class Discussion
Sunburn and Time of Day

Ask: **At what time of day are you most likely to get a sunburn? Why?** *[The sun is strongest at midday because sunlight travels its shortest and most vertical route through the atmosphere.]*

Reinforcement
Slip, Slap, Slop

Tell students about the Australian expression "Slip, slap, slop." Slip into a long-sleeved shirt, slap on a hat, and slop on some sunscreen whenever you are going to be exposed to the sun for more than just a few minutes. Also, follow these precautions:

1. Avoid the midday sun.
2. Before purchasing a sunscreen, read its SPF, ingredient list, and directions carefully.

- If you have a mild allergic reaction, obtain a cream for it from a pharmacy.
- If you have a severe allergic reaction, see a doctor immediately.

Psoriasis Psoriasis is a condition in which red, raised patches appear on the skin. Later the skin becomes dry and flakes off. Areas most commonly affected are the elbows, knees, and scalp. See a doctor for treatment if you have this condition.

Skin and the Sun

Exposure to the sun can be very dangerous by causing damage to your skin now and in the future. Some of the dangers of exposure to the sun include sunburn, wrinkles, and skin cancer.

Sunburn Ultraviolet rays from the sun cause sunburn. Ultraviolet rays that damage skin come in two wavelengths and are known as either ultraviolet A (UVA) or ultraviolet B (UVB) rays. UVB rays burn the skin, so it is easy to see when you have been overexposed to this form of radiation. UVA rays affect the deeper layers of the skin. There is no warning when you have been overexposed. Both kinds of ultraviolet rays are strongest around midday.

(FIGURE 6-10) **Ultraviolet rays are at their most intense around midday. This is when you are most likely to get sunburned.**

It usually takes about four to six hours before you can feel the full effects of a sunburn. So even if you feel fine while you are out in the sun, remember that a sunburn won't show up until hours later.

People often have confused ideas about sunburn. Some people think you can get sunburned only on clear days. They don't realize that ultraviolet rays are also present on foggy and cloudy days. In addition, many people think that sunburning is limited to people with light skin. In fact, African-Americans and others with dark skin can also get sunburned.

Wrinkles The skin of people who spend a lot of time in the sun tends to age faster than others. They get wrinkles earlier, and they get more wrinkles as time goes on.

Skin Cancer People who spend a lot of time in the sun without protection or who had severe sunburns during youth are at a higher risk for getting skin cancer. Most skin cancers are easily treatable, but one type called malignant melanoma is very serious. Malignant melanomas are cancers of the cells that produce melanin. If you notice any change in a mole, you should see a physician immediately to make sure you don't have a melanoma.

More information about skin cancer can be found in Chapter 24.

Sun Protection **Sunscreens** and sunblocks are products that provide some protection from ultraviolet light. A product's ability to block the sun's rays is described by an SPF rating. SPF stands for *sun protection factor*. Figure 6-11 illustrates what different SPF values mean.

Sunscreens partially block UVB rays which burn the skin. Sunblocks partially filter the UVA rays which cause deeper skin damage. Reading the list of ingredients on

Skin cancer is also discussed in Chapter 24.

sunscreen:

a substance that blocks the harmful ultraviolet rays of the sun.

Background

Photosensitivity

Certain foods, cosmetics, and medications contain substances that cause photosensitivity in people, making them susceptible to severe sunburn with relatively short exposure to the sun. Common photosynthesizers include celery, figs, parsnips, many blue dyes, iodine, Tetracycline, and some antihistamines and perfumes. The dyes in tattoos can cause extreme photosensitivity in skin adjacent to the tattoo.

Background

UV Index

Many local weather reports now include a UV index. This index is a prediction of the amount of ultraviolet (UV) radiation that will reach Earth's surface during peak hours on a given day. A value ranging from 0 to 15 is assigned to the sunlight's intensity. This value is used to determine how long a person can safely stay out in the sun without burning. Knowing the UV index can help a person determine if he or she needs to apply sunscreen before going out.

---

3. If you decide to sunbathe, use adequate sunscreen. Stay out only 15 minutes the first time you sunbathe and increase this time by only 15 minutes on subsequent days. This will decrease your chance of getting a sunburn. **Note:** If you have a problem with acne, use an oil-free sunscreen.

Class Discussion
SPF Rating

Have students look at Figure 6-11 on page 132. Tell them that this chart is for someone who starts to burn after ten minutes in the sun. The SPF number is multiplied by 10 to determine how long this person can stay in the sun without burning. Ask: **If the SPF is 15, how long can this person stay in the sun?** *[up to 150 minutes]* **Why do you think the chart says "up to"?** *[the product could come off in water, to allow for individual differences, etc.]*

Extension
Don't Forget the Sunscreen

Have students work together to write a short fact sheet about the importance of protecting the skin against UVA and UVB rays, and make photocopies of it. Then have students poll the student body as to whether they use sunscreen or sunblock on a regular basis. Have students give a copy of the fact sheet to everyone who answers no.

Review Answers

1. epidermis and dermis

2. See a doctor and describe to him or her any changes in the size, color, and condition of the mole.

3. Keeping the face clean helps reduce the amount of oil and bacteria on the skin's surface.

4. by avoiding being out in the sun during midday because this is when the sun's rays are the most intense and by applying and reapplying a sunscreen of SPF 15 or higher to all areas exposed to the sun

5. Both are caused by fungi that thrive in warm, moist areas.

(FIGURE 6-11) **If you usually burn after 10 minutes in the sun, you can stay in the sun for up to 40 minutes (up to four times longer) by using a sunblock with an SPF of 4.**

SPF RATING AND TIME IN THE SUN

40   80   120   160   200   240   280   320

SPF 15...Up to 15 times longer

SPF 30...Up to 30 times longer

SPF 4...Up to 4 times longer

Unprotected

a product's label will tell you whether the product blocks UVA rays as well. Look for titanium or zinc in the ingredients list. If you go swimming, or sweat a lot while in the sun, you may need to reapply the product to be protected.

Wearing protective clothing, such as a hat or long sleeves and pants, also reduces your skin's exposure to the sun.

If you do get a sunburn, you can relieve the pain by applying wet, cool cloths to your burned skin and taking aspirin or acetaminophen. If the sunburn causes blisters or problems with your vision, you should get medical attention.

Review

1. Name the two main layers of the skin.

2. If you had a mole that changed color, what would you do?

3. ▨ **LIFE SKILLS: Practicing Self-Care** Why does washing the face with soap several times a day reduce a person's chances of getting acne?

4. ▨ **LIFE SKILLS: Practicing Self-Care** Explain how you can avoid sun damage to your skin.

5. **Critical Thinking** What causes the similarity in symptoms between athlete's foot and jock itch?

ASSESS

Section Review

Have students answer the Section Review questions.

Alternative Assessment
Maintaining Healthy Skin

Ask students to describe ways to keep their skin healthy.

Closure
Time in the Sun

Ask students what they would think of someone who sunbathes often and maintains a deep tan during the warm months. Would they try to change the person's mind? If this person asked them to join in marathon sunbathing sessions, would they?

Section 6.2

Hair and Nail Care

Objectives

- *Describe three common hair and scalp problems.*
- *Explain how to care for your hair.*
  ▪▪ **LIFE SKILLS: Practicing Self-Care**
- *Explain how to care for your nails.*
  ▪▪ **LIFE SKILLS: Practicing Self-Care**

Hair is important to not only our appearance but also our health. In the winter, we depend on hair to keep our heads warm. Throughout the year, we rely on the hair in our noses and ears to keep dust out of the body. And every time we blink, our eyelashes, which are specialized hair, protect the eyes.

Structure of Hair

The roots of the hair are in the dermis, where the hair starts growing. But hair cells die when they leave the dermis. That's why it doesn't hurt to have your hair cut—the hair is already dead.

Hair on the head grows for two to six years, then rests for several months. Lots of hair falls out after the rest period, but this is normal and should not cause any concern. It is typical to lose up to a hundred hairs a day, which isn't very many when you consider that most people have 100,000 to 200,000 hairs on their heads.

The part of the hair that we can see is called the hair shaft. The shape of the hair shaft determines whether hair will be straight, curly, or wavy.

Hair color is inherited. It is determined by the kind and amount of melanin in your hair. The melanin in hair decreases as people get older, causing their hair to turn gray and then white. The age at which hair turns gray is determined by heredity.

Thinning of the hair or baldness is an inherited condition affecting mainly men. It occurs with age, but can also result from illness. When hair loss is a result of illness, it is usually only a temporary loss.

Flat hair shafts = curly hair   Oval hair shafts = wavy hair   Round hair shafts = straight hair

▪ (FIGURE 6-12) **The shape of the hair shaft determines whether hair will be curly, wavy, or straight.**

Background
Head Lice

Head lice are tiny wingless insects that do not jump or fly. They live on the scalp and can usually be found behind the ears and at the back of the head of an infected person. Using six pairs of hooks in their mouths, they attach themselves to hair shafts. Head lice are difficult to see, but one sign of them is a persistent itching of the scalp. Close inspection of the hair will disclose nits—small silvery eggs attached to individual strands of hair. Personal cleanliness is not a total safeguard against head lice. They are transmitted from one infected person to another through the use of items such as combs, brushes, hats, hair decorations, towels, bedding, coats, even the headrests of airline, bus, and train seats.

Section 6.2 Lesson Plan

MOTIVATE

Journal 6C
On Hair

This may be done as a warm-up activity. Encourage students to write in their Journal what is important and what is not important to them about hair and nail care.

TEACH

Demonstration
Close Look at a Hair

Provide students with microscopes or powerful magnifying glasses. Ask them to pluck a hair from their head and examine it. Record student observations on the board.

Class Discussion
Healthy Hair

Ask students to describe the effects on hair of excessive blow-drying, bleaching, perming, and exposure to sun. Ask: **What role does heredity play in relation to hair?** *[It determines color, curliness, thinning or baldness, and the age at which it turns gray.]*

Debate the Issue
Rules About Hair

Tell students that many schools, organizations, and businesses dictate the standards for hair length and style for students and employees. Ask them to

Making a Choice 6A

Assign the Evaluating Personal Products card. The card asks students to identify and do research on products used on the hair and skin. Also, students must calculate the cost of a year's supply of a product and decide if the product's benefits justify its expense.

Life Skills Worksheet 6A

Assign the Practicing Personal Care Life Skills Worksheet.

Section Review Worksheet 6.2

To reinforce the concepts presented in this section, assign Section Review Worksheet 6.2.

Section Quiz 6.2

Have students take Section Quiz 6.2.

Reteaching Worksheet 6.2

Students who have difficulty with the material may complete Reteaching Worksheet 6.2.

Hair Care Tips

Get a good haircut that fits your lifestyle. Swimmers, for example, may want a short cut that doesn't require much styling.

Brush your hair to get the oil to the ends of the hair. Brushing also stimulates the scalp. It is best to brush with a natural bristle brush and to brush gently. If your hair gets tangled, don't yank at it. Instead, untangle it slowly.

Wash your hair regularly. Washing is good for both the hair and the scalp.

Rather than using a blow-dryer, let your hair dry naturally. Repeated use of blow-dryers can dry out hair. Electric curlers can also dry out hair.

Limit the number of perms you get, since they can damage the hair and scalp. Hair dyes and bleaches can also damage your hair.

(FIGURE 6-13)

Hair Care and Appearance

Taking care of your hair will keep it healthy and looking good. Some tips for keeping your hair in good condition are shown in Figure 6-13.

Keep in mind that you don't need to spend lots of money to have clean hair. Tests of a variety of shampoos have shown that inexpensive shampoos work just as well as the more expensive ones.

Hair and Scalp Problems

The most common problems that affect the hair and scalp can be prevented by good grooming practices. It is most important to shampoo regularly and to avoid sharing combs or brushes.

Dandruff Dandruff is dead skin that flakes off the scalp. People with oily scalps suffer most from dandruff. Washing hair more frequently is the most effective way to control the flaking. Dandruff shampoos with the following ingredients have been shown to be safe and effective for treating dandruff. These include salicylic acid, pyrithione zinc, sulfur, selenium sulfide, and coal tar. It is best to see a doctor for severe dandruff. Seborrhea and psoriasis look like dandruff but they may require prescription medication.

Head Lice Head lice, which are parasites that live in the scalp and hair, are shown in Figure 6-14. They cause almost unbearable itching. Head lice are often spread by the comb or brush of someone who is infected. If you have head lice, ask your doctor or pharmacist about medications that remove the lice. Thoroughly wash or discard clothing and bedding that has come into contact with your head. Do not share combs, brushes, or clothing with others, because this practice spreads the lice.

(FIGURE 6-14) **Head lice are easy to control with the right medication.**

• • • TEACH continued

debate whether these standards violate individual freedom of expression.

Reinforcement
Dandruff

Review the causes and remedies of dandruff. Point out that sometimes shampoo left over in the hair forms a scaly, dandruff-like residue. Rinsing shampoo completely out of the hair will eliminate the problem.

Reinforcement
Shaving Tips

The following shaving tips might be helpful for males who have acne:

1. Shave as infrequently as possible.
2. Use an electric razor. If you prefer to use a blade razor, use a new blade each time. Wash your face with soap and hot water to soften the beard. Lather shaving cream on your beard and leave it there for at least a minute before shaving.
3. When finished, rinse first with hot water, then with cold. An astringent can be used to remove excess oil and tighten the skin.
4. If shaving is intolerable, grow a beard.

Extension
Check It Out

Styles for hair, beards, and mustaches have changed throughout history. Some of the styles of the past seem quite comical to us today, while others seem perfectly normal. Have students research hairstyles that were popular during different historical periods, such

Ringworm Ringworm is caused by a fungus that forms a whitish ring on the skin. It is usually found on the scalp but can also appear on other parts of the body. Ringworm is easily spread to other people by the towels, combs, and brushes of a person who has it. A picture of a ringworm infection is shown in Figure 6-15. If you think you might have ringworm, see a doctor.

(FIGURE 6-15) **Ringworm is spread by sharing towels, combs, and brushes.**

Removing Unwanted Hair

The most common way to remove unwanted hair is to shave it off with a razor. The skin must first be moistened with water and soap or shaving cream. Otherwise the skin can dry out and is also more vulnerable to cuts and sores. Waxing is another hair-removal method, in which a wax is heated and applied to the skin. When the wax has cooled and hardened, it is stripped off, along with the hair. The effects are longer lasting than those of shaving, but waxing can be a bit painful. The only permanent method of hair removal is electrolysis. During elec-

trolysis, an electrical current is sent into each hair follicle. Like waxing, electrolysis can be painful, and it is also expensive.

Nails

Fingernail and manicure services in this country have grown to an estimated $5 billion industry. To improve the appearance of your natural nails, they should be trimmed regularly. The cuticle around the back of a nail can be pushed away and clipped if necessary. And the skin around nails can be moisturized periodically. Toenails can be clipped straight across to prevent ingrown nails. These practices plus a balanced diet can result in attractive nails without the expense of artificial nails. Artificial nails can pose some health risks. Some products used for gluing artificial nails or for removing the glue contain poisonous substances. Common nail problems resulting from the use of artificial nails include infections caused by bacteria, fungi, and the skin viruses that cause warts. Infections usually occur when the nails are left in place too long. If the tools used in a salon are not properly cleaned, they can also spread infections.

Review

1. Describe three common hair and scalp problems.

2. ▪▪ *LIFE SKILLS: Practicing Self-Care* Explain how to care for your hair.

3. ▪▪ *LIFE SKILLS: Practicing Self-Care* Explain how to care for your nails.

4. *Critical Thinking* Can a person live in the same house with someone who has ringworm and not get this condition? Explain your answer.

Review Answers

1. Dandruff is dead skin that flakes off the scalp. Head lice are parasites that live on the scalp and hair. Ringworm is a fungus and is characterized by whitish rings on the scalp and skin.

2. Get a haircut that fits your lifestyle; brush the hair to get oil to the ends of the hair; wash the hair regularly; don't overuse blow dryers and electric curlers; and limit the number of times the hair is permed or dyed.

3. Trim nails regularly; clip toenails straight across to prevent ingrown toenails; push back cuticles and clip loose pieces if necessary; moisturize skin around nails periodically; maintain a balanced diet; and, if you use artificial nails, go to a salon that sterilizes its tools, and don't keep the nails on for a long period of time.

4. Answers will vary. Sample response: It is possible, but ringworm is highly contagious so strict measures must be followed; the condition must be treated, and do not share towels, combs, brushes, or other personal items with the infected person.

---

as the Roman Empire, the American Colonial period, the 1930s, and the 1960s. Have students find out if any problems were associated with any of the hairstyles.

ASSESS

Section Review

Have students answer the Section Review questions.

Alternative Assessment
Hair Analysis

Do we make assumptions about people based on their hair? Collect examples of these assumptions from students and list them on the chalkboard under the headings BEARD, MUSTACHE, HAIR COLOR, LENGTH, and STYLE. Have students write a paragraph about the accuracy of the assumptions.

Closure
Hair and Scalp Problems

Have students identify common hair and scalp problems and their remedies.

Teeth and Gum Care

Background
Malocclusion and Orthodontia

Ideally, teeth should be straight and spaced regularly with no overlap or gaps, and they should be the right size for the jaw. However, few people have perfect teeth. *Malocclusion* is the term used to describe a condition in which the teeth of the upper and lower jaws fail to fit together properly. There are three main types of malocclusion: crowding, overbite, and underbite. Although there are several causes for malocclusion, the primary cause is heredity. Often people inherit a tooth pattern and jaw pattern that don't match well. Most occlusion problems can be solved by the use of dental braces or some other orthodontic appliance (orthodontia). However, some teeth may need to be extracted if the jaw is too crowded.

Objectives

- *Explain how dental cavities develop.*
- *Explain how to care for your teeth and gums.*
  ▪▪ **LIFE SKILLS: Practicing Self-Care**
- *Be able to make an appointment with a dentist.*
  ▪▪ **LIFE SKILLS: Being a Wise Consumer**

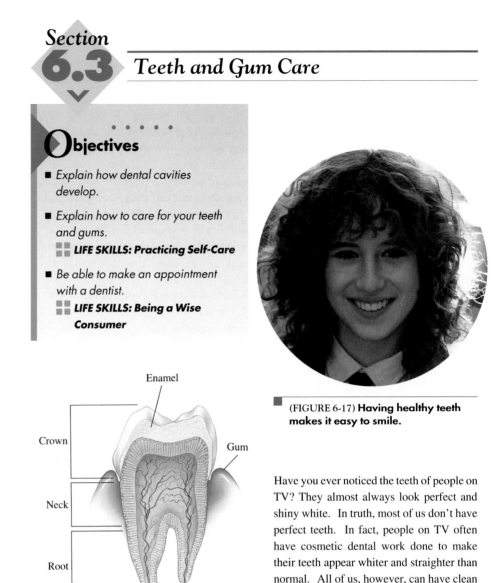

(FIGURE 6-17) **Having healthy teeth makes it easy to smile.**

Enamel

Crown

Gum

Neck

Root

Blood vessels

Nerve

(FIGURE 6-16) **The three main parts of the tooth are the crown, the neck, and the root. The crown is the part that is visible above the gums. Covering the crown is a substance called enamel, the hardest substance in the body.**

Have you ever noticed the teeth of people on TV? They almost always look perfect and shiny white. In truth, most of us don't have perfect teeth. In fact, people on TV often have cosmetic dental work done to make their teeth appear whiter and straighter than normal. All of us, however, can have clean teeth that are well cared for. It is simply a matter of good dental care.

Structure of a Tooth

The tooth is divided into three parts, which are shown in Figure 6-16. The crown is the visible part of the tooth above the gum. The neck is just below the gum line where the crown and root come together. The root is the part of the tooth below the gum line.

Section 6.3 Lesson Plan

MOTIVATE

Journal 6D
Feelings About Teeth

This may be done as a warm-up activity. Ask students to write in their Journal how they care for their teeth. Is there something else they think they could include?

TEACH

Reinforcement
Anatomy of a Tooth

Ask a student to draw on the chalkboard the parts of a tooth and label them. Point out that enamel, unlike other body tissues, cannot repair itself once it is damaged or worn down.

Journal 6E
Losing Primary Teeth

Ask students to record in their Journal their memories of losing their primary teeth. Do they remember how they felt when their first tooth fell out? Do they remember the feeling of having a loose tooth? Do they remember what it was like to eat with their front teeth missing?

The part of the tooth that we can see is covered by **enamel**, which is the hardest substance in the body. The only naturally occurring substance harder than enamel is a diamond. Even though it is extremely hard, enamel can still be eroded by decay. Beneath the enamel is soft tissue that contains blood vessels and nerve endings.

Types of Teeth

People have two sets of teeth during their life. First, they have 20 primary teeth—also called baby teeth—that are usually in by age three. These fall out, and permanent teeth start developing around the age of six. By the time people are grown, they have 32 permanent teeth. The four types of permanent teeth and their functions are shown in Figure 6-18.

Dental Problems

Common tooth problems include tooth decay and gum disease. Tooth decay is usually more common in children. Gum dis-

Incisors — Cut and tear food
Cuspids — Tear food into small pieces
Bicuspids — Tear and crush food
Molars — Grind up food

■ (FIGURE 6-18) **Each of the four types of permanent teeth has a different function in breaking up food before it is swallowed.**

ease is usually more common in adulthood. Taking a good care of your teeth can prevent cavities and gum diseases from developing.

Dental Cavity Figure 6-19 shows how a dental cavity develops. A dental cavity results from tooth decay. The decay begins when food is eaten and tiny food particles remain in the mouth. The food particles combine with bacteria and saliva to form

enamel:

the substance covering the crown of the tooth; hardest substance in the body.

SECTION 6.3

Making a Choice 6B

Assign the Teaching About Tooth Care card. The card asks students to review the guidelines for proper tooth and gum care and to develop a lesson plan for teaching younger children about tooth care.

Life Skills Worksheet 6B

Assign the Toothbrush Choices Life Skills Worksheet.

Decay

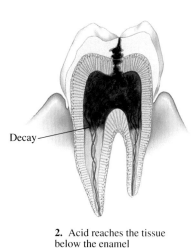

Decay

1. Acid eats through the enamel of a tooth.

2. Acid reaches the tissue below the enamel and causes infection.

■ (FIGURE 6-19) **Bacteria produce acids that eat away tooth enamel, eventually causing dental cavities.**

Reinforcement
Sequence of Cavity Formation

Copy the sequence below for cavity formation and ask students to put the steps in the proper order.

Acid attacks tooth enamel. (5)
Infection spreads to bone socket and tooth becomes abscessed. (7)
When saliva and food particles combine, plaque forms and coats the teeth. (3)
Tiny food particles remain between the teeth. (2)

Bacteria in plaque produce acid. (4)
Food is eaten. (1)
Acid eats through enamel and forms a cavity. (6)

Class Discussion
Braces

Students who are now wearing braces or who have had braces may wish to share their experiences with the class. They may want to bring a "before" photograph to class.

Demonstration
Brushing and Flossing

Ask a dentist or dental hygienist to bring dental models to class and demonstrate proper brushing and flossing techniques. If this is not feasible, perhaps your school nurse could demonstrate these techniques.

Background
Gum Disease

Gum disease is the major cause of tooth loss for adults over 40, but it can occur in children, too. Gum disease is caused by the buildup of plaque and calculus on the teeth. It can result in severe inflammation. The first stage of gum disease, called gingivitis, is typified by bleeding gums. If left untreated, gum disease can cause the destruction of the supporting tissues around the teeth. Pyorrhea or periodontitis is advanced gum disease. The gums begin to separate from the teeth and the space between them fills up with tartar, bacteria, and plaque. The teeth loosen and can fall out. Eventually, gum disease attacks and destroys the bone in which the teeth are anchored. Fortunately, gum disease will not cause permanent damage if treated early.

calculus:

hardened plaque.

plaque:

a film of food particles, saliva, and bacteria on teeth.

(FIGURE 6-20) **Gum disease is often caused by a buildup of calculus (tartar) on the teeth. If not treated by a dentist, gum disease can cause teeth to fall out.**

plaque, which coats the teeth with a very thin film. The bacteria which grows in the plaque produces an acid that eats through the enamel of the teeth. If the teeth are not cleaned, the enamel is eaten away until a cavity forms in the tooth. Cavities that are very small are not always easy to detect without an X ray, because they are not painful. A toothache may be a sign of decay that has reached the base of the tooth. If the infection spreads to the bone socket, the tooth can become abscessed. Other signs of decay include sensitivity to heat, to cold, and to pressure. If you have any of these sensations, see a dentist immediately. Your tooth will only get worse without treatment.

Bad Breath Most bad breath is the result of plaque, decayed teeth, and gum and throat infections. Mouthwashes may provide fresh breath for a little while, but it will not be lasting. In addition, mouthwashes usually contain alcohol, which can worsen a throat or tooth infection. Sometimes bad

breath results from eating strong-smelling foods—garlic, for example. A coated tongue may also cause bad breath. Most dentists recommend cleaning the tongue by brushing it with a toothbrush.

Gum Disease Gum disease is the leading cause of tooth loss in adults. It begins when a material called **calculus** builds up near the gums. Calculus, which is also known as tartar, is simply plaque that has hardened. Removing plaque at least once every 24 hours prevents it from becoming hard. Calculus must be removed at a dentist's office.

The first sign of gum disease is bleeding when the teeth are brushed. Later, the gums pull back from the teeth and form pockets that may fill with pus. The teeth may then loosen and fall out. Although more common in adults, gum disease can also occur during the teenage years. If treated early, it usually will not cause permanent damage or tooth loss. See a dentist if you think you might have gum disease.

Poor Alignment Usually the top teeth fit exactly over the bottom teeth. When they don't fit correctly, there is an alignment problem. Poor alignment may make it difficult to eat or speak or clean the teeth adequately. Sometimes poor tooth alignment is related to genetics. The bone structure of the jaw may be too small or too large for the teeth. Thumb-sucking may also play a role in poor alignment. Braces and other orthodontic devices are generally used to treat poor alignment, but sometimes tooth extraction and surgery may be required to correct the problem.

Dental Care

Good dental care involves more than just brushing your teeth. The behaviors that are most important to good dental care are: eating nutritious foods, brushing teeth, flossing teeth, and having regular dental checkups.

• • • TEACH continued

Reinforcement
Dental Care

Share the following suggestions for good dental care with students:

1. If you must have sweets, eat them during meals. Finishing a meal with cheese is a good idea, as cheese is effective in neutralizing acid formation.

2. Use disclosing tablets. They contain a dye that stains plaque and makes it

visible. Brushing and flossing removes the plaque and the stain.

3. Use floss to remove plaque, never toothpicks. Toothpicks can damage your gums.

4. Use a toothpaste with fluoride. Fluoride hardens the surface of the tooth and makes it more bacteria-resistant.

5. Tobacco use stains teeth and fouls breath.

 Journal 6F
My Own Dental Care

Ask students to record in their Journal how frequently they go for dental checkups. If they have had their teeth cleaned by a dentist or dental hygienist, have them describe it.

 Teaching Transparency 6B
Personal Care and Appearance

Use this transparency to review the problems, precautions, and treatments

Eating Nutritious Foods Foods high in sugar and acids can contribute to tooth decay. Eat a balanced diet rich in protein and minerals, along with raw fruits and vegetables. Avoid foods that stick to your teeth as they may promote tooth decay.

Flossing and Brushing Teeth Flossing before you brush loosens food particles so they can be brushed away. Dentists have discovered that harshly scrubbing the teeth may tear the gums and remove tooth enamel. The recommended way to brush is shown in Figure 6-21. You should brush your teeth twice a day. Always brush your teeth after you floss to remove dislodged particles.

Background
Root Canals
When decay reaches the inner portion of a tooth, or pulp, an infection that kills the nerve of the tooth can occur. If this happens, the pulp, including the nerve and its roots, must be removed. This process, called a root canal, should be performed only by a dentist trained in the procedure. The patient receives a local anesthesia, and the dentist drills a hole through the crown of the tooth. Using small files, the dentist then removes the pulp. It is extremely important that every bit of pulp, from crown to root tip, be removed, or the infection will reoccur. This process may require two or three office visits. The empty space within the tooth is then filled with a rubbery substance called gutta-percha, and the tooth is fitted with an artificial crown.

1. Hold the toothbrush at a 45-degree angle to the gums.

2. Move the brush gently in a circular motion on two teeth at a time. Don't brush hard! Gentle brushing will remove plaque without hurting your teeth.

3. Brush all the surfaces of your teeth, including the backs of teeth.

4. Continue until you have brushed all your teeth.

(FIGURE 6-21) **Brush your teeth at least twice a day, immediately after you eat if possible. Use a soft, flat brush that can reach all your teeth.**

relating to personal care and appearance described in the text.

Extension
Topics of Interest
Have individual students find information on one of the following topics and present brief reports on them to the class: use of the laser beam in dentistry, danger of mercury-type fillings, dentistry in the barbershop, and the technique of dental implants.

Community Dentistry
Dental examinations and work are expensive, and many insurance policies cover little, if any, of the cost. Have students investigate the availability of free or low-cost dental services in the communities where they live. Before starting the investigation, have students compile a list of questions such as: What services are available? How does a person qualify? What is the cost? What qualifications do the dentists and dental hygienists have? etc. Results can be compiled into a brochure or poster and posted where other classes can read it.

dental floss:

a special string that removes plaque from the teeth.

Flossing Teeth **Dental floss** is a special string sold at most supermarkets and drugstores. Flossing once a day will remove most plaque. Flossing is shown in Figure 6-22.

1. Cut off a piece of dental floss about 18 inches long.

2. Wrap the ends of the floss around your middle fingers.

3. Very gently push the floss between two teeth.

4. Pull the floss around one of the teeth to make a horseshoe shape with the floss. Gently move the floss up and down to clean the sides of that tooth.

(FIGURE 6-22)
Flossing removes the plaque between the teeth. You should floss your teeth every day.

5. Continue until you have flossed all your teeth. Use a clean section of floss on each tooth.

6. Rinse your mouth with water.

*Life*SKILLS: Being a Wise Consumer

Making a Dental Appointment . . . .

Making a dental appointment is something most teenagers haven't had any practice doing. It's actually quite easy to compare dentists and choose the one who suits your needs. You may already have a dentist or know of one you want to see. If not, follow these steps to choose a dentist and make an appointment.

1. Look in the yellow pages of the phone book under "Dentists" and find three dentists who are close to where you live or go to school.

2. Write down their phone numbers and call them.

3. Tell the receptionist who answers that you are just trying to get some information right now—you're not making an appointment. Ask how much an initial visit would cost to examine your teeth and clean them. This price will probably include X-rays of your teeth.

4. Ask when the office would be able to see you. Some dentists have a long waiting period, while others can see people quickly.

5. After calling all three offices, compare the costs of the dentists. Also compare the length of time you would need to wait before seeing each dentist.

6. Now you're ready to make an appointment with the dentist that you have chosen.

*Life*SKILLS

Have students do the Life Skills activity in the text, writing notes on paper as they complete the steps.

Section Review Worksheet 6.3
To reinforce the concepts presented in this section, assign Section Review Worksheet 6.3.

Section Quiz 6.3
Have students take Section Quiz 6.3.

Reteaching Worksheet 6.3
Students who have difficulty with the material may complete Reteaching Worksheet 6.3.

Review Answers

1. Bacteria in plaque produce an acid. This acid eats through the enamel of teeth. When the enamel gets eaten away, a cavity has formed. Left untreated, the cavity will reach the tissue below the enamel. Infection follows.

2. Brush twice daily; floss once a day; eat a balanced diet and avoid foods that promote tooth decay; and see a dentist for regular checkups.

3. Students should state the description given in Figure 6-22.

4. In the Yellow Pages, find the names of three dentists near where you live. Write down their names and phone numbers. Call their office to find out their fees and how soon the dentist could see you. Compare the information gathered and then choose a dentist. Call that dentist back to make an appointment.

5. Answers will vary. Sample response: Enamel protects the soft living tissue of the tooth against decay. Enamel is hard so that it does not wear away over the years as people use their teeth to chew food.

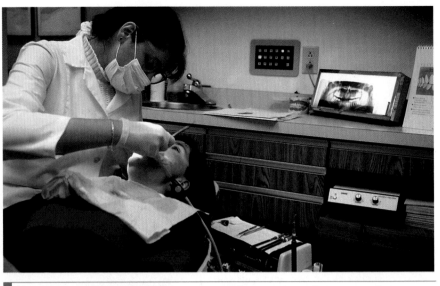

(FIGURE 6-23) **Dentists should always wear gloves and usually wear masks to protect themselves and their patients from infection.**

Dental Checkups How often do you think a person should see a dentist for a checkup?

- Every three months?
- Every six months?
- Every year?
- Every two years?

The answer depends on the person. Some people don't develop cavities or gum disease easily and may not need a checkup more often than every six months. Other people develop calculus even if they floss daily and brush their teeth regularly. They may need to have their teeth cleaned every three months. Most people do not need checkups more often than every six months.

Dentists and dental hygienists clean teeth with tools that look a little like pencils with scrapers on the end. They use these to scrape the calculus off the teeth and polish them. Most people experience very little discomfort with this process and are pleased with the result—nice, clean, polished teeth.

When teeth are flossed and brushed regularly, they usually stay nice-looking during the period between cleanings.

Review

1. Explain how dental cavities develop.

2. What are four things you can do to have healthy teeth?

3. **LIFE SKILLS: Practicing Self-Care** Describe how to floss the teeth.

4. **LIFE SKILLS: Being a Wise Consumer** Describe one method of choosing a dentist.

5. **Critical Thinking** What purpose do you think the enamel of teeth serves?

ASSESS

Section Review

Have students answer the Section Review questions.

Alternative Assessment
Healthy Teeth and Gums

Ask students to write a paragraph describing how to keep their teeth and gums healthy.

Closure
Overcoming Fear in the Dentist's Chair

Discuss the fears many people have of dentists. Ask students to suggest ways that people could get over their fears.

CHAPTER 6

Highlights

Summary

- The skin functions to protect the body from germs, to regulate body temperature, to transmit sensations such as pain, and as a waterproof cover that holds the body together.

- The epidermis and the dermis are the two main layers of the skin. The dermis contains oil and sweat glands as well as nerves.

- Blemishes, a common skin problem for teens, result when pores in the skin become clogged with oil. They usually can be controlled by washing frequently with soap and water.

- Other skin problems include moles, warts, athlete's foot and jock itch, impetigo, poison ivy, poison oak, poison sumac, and psoriasis.

- Changes in the size, color, or condition of a mole should be reported to a doctor because the changes may indicate skin cancer.

- Exposure to the sun can cause sunburn, wrinkles, and skin cancer. Use of a sunscreen is the most important action you can take to protect your skin from the sun.

- Hair insulates the head from heat and cold. Eyelashes and eyebrows protect the eyes from foreign matter. Hair in the nose and ears keeps foreign matter out of the nose and ears.

- A tooth is made up of a crown, a neck, and a root. The part of the tooth we see is covered by enamel.

- The bacteria in plaque produce acid, which eats through the enamel of teeth and causes decay.

- Good dental care includes brushing and flossing teeth, eating nutritious foods, and having regular checkups.

Vocabulary

epidermis the very thin outer layer of the skin.

dermis the second layer of skin; contains the most important skin structures.

acne a condition in which the pores of the skin become clogged with oil; acne can take the form of blackheads, whiteheads, or pimples.

enamel the substance covering the crown of the tooth.

plaque a film of food particles, saliva, and bacteria on teeth.

dental floss a special string that removes plaque from the teeth.

CHAPTER 6 HIGHLIGHTS STRATEGIES

SUMMARY
Have students read the summary to reinforce the concepts they have learned in Chapter 6.

VOCABULARY
Ask students to use each of the vocabulary words in a sentence having to do with personal care.

EXTENSION
Homeless people face practical problems in practicing personal care and hygiene. They may not have the financial resources to purchase the items they need, or there may not be a place where they can shower and shampoo regularly. Are there places in your community that supply toothpaste, toothbrushes, soap, shampoo, and other items for people in need of them? Are these places ever short of the supplies they need? Have students investigate the situation in their community. Students could then compile a list of what types and sizes of supplies are most needed and organize a drive to collect these items.

CHAPTER REVIEW

Concept Review

1. Answers can include: protects the body from germs and injury, regulates body temperature, transmits sensations such as pain or cold, acts as a weatherproof cover and prevents dehydration, excretes wastes, or synthesizes vitamin D.

2. epidermis: pores and melanin; dermis: blood vessels, hair follicles, oil glands, sweat glands, and nerves

3. fungus—athlete's foot, jock itch; bacteria—impetigo; virus—wart

4. when there is a change in size, color, or condition because these changes could indicate skin cancer

5. Sunscreens protect the skin from ultraviolet rays, which can cause sunburn, skin cancer, and wrinkles. The higher the SPF number, the more protection the sunscreen provides.

6. Hair insulates the head from heat and cold. Eyelashes and eyebrows protect the eyes from foreign matter. Hair in the nose and ears keeps dust out.

7. Dandruff appears when dead skin flakes off the scalp. Shampooing frequently can help control dandruff. Shampoos containing the following have proved safe and effective: salicylic acid, pyrithione zinc, sulfur, selenium sulfide, and coal tar.

Concept Review

1. What are three important functions of the skin?

2. Name two things found in each of the two layers of the skin.

3. Name a skin condition caused by fungus; by bacteria; by a virus.

4. When should a mole be checked by a doctor? Why?

5. Why is it important to use a sunscreen? What do the SPF numbers mean on suntan products?

6. How is hair important to our health?

7. Why does dandruff appear? What can you do to control it?

8. Head lice live in the scalp and hair. What are they and what should you do if you become infected with them?

9. Why is it important to take good care of your nails?

10. Name the three parts of a tooth. Which part(s) is above the gum line?

11. What is plaque? How can plaque removal help prevent cavities?

12. What are three things that can cause bad breath?

13. Who usually suffers from gum disease? What causes it and how can it be controlled?

Expressing Your Views

1. Julie has a mild case of acne. You notice that she wears heavy makeup to cover the pimples, and you often see her picking at her face. How will her behavior damage her skin? How would you advise her?

2. You are embarrassed to remove your shoes in public because when you do you have a very offensive foot odor. What could you do to relieve this problem?

3. You brush your teeth twice a day but lately you have noticed some sensitive areas on your teeth. What might this sensitivity mean? What can you do?

4. Your friend is bothered by unwanted hair on her face. She doesn't want to shave it off because it might make her skin rough and unattractive. What else can she do to get rid of the hair?

8. Head lice are parasites. Ask your doctor or pharmacist to recommend a medication to remove them. Also wash or discard clothing and bedding that have come in contact with your head. Do not share combs, brushes, or clothing.

9. Well-cared-for nails make a good impression and add to your self-confidence.

10. crown, neck, root; crown

11. Plaque is a film of food particles, saliva, and bacteria on teeth. Removing plaque removes the bacteria that produce the destructive acid that causes tooth decay.

12. Answers can include plaque, decayed teeth, gum and throat infections, strong smelling foods, or a coated tongue.

13. Adults. Gum disease is caused by a buildup of hardened plaque, or calculus, and can be controlled through regular brushing, flossing, and cleaning at the dentist's office.

Life Skills Check . . . . . .

1. Practicing Self-Care
You took a summer job as a lifeguard at a nearby pool. You have fair skin and you know you will be spending six hours a day in the sun. Should you take extra care to protect your skin from the sun? Why?

2. Being a Wise Consumer
Lamar has just moved to your community and needs to visit a dentist. He doesn't know any of the dentists in town, and he is not familiar with the streets. Explain how you would help him choose a dentist and make an appointment.

3. Practicing Self-Care
Your friend just made the diving team and is concerned about caring for her hair, since she will spend a lot of time in the water. Her shoulder-length hair appears dry and damaged. What advice can you give her?

Projects . . . .

1. Work with a group to learn what bacteria cause impetigo. How is this disease spread? How can this disease be stopped and controlled? Find out how your school system handles cases of impetigo. Make a report to your class.

2. Borrow two or three microscopes from the science department to examine the different shapes of hair shafts from you and your classmates.

Take turns viewing the different hair structures, then draw and label what you see.

3. Interview a dermatologist or dentist to find out the most common problems he or she encounters with teens. You might ask them what the main causes of the problems are and how they might be prevented. Summarize the information and present it to the class.

Plan for Action . . . .

A person's physical appearance reflects a person's health. List five improvements you can make regarding your grooming habits.

Expressing Your Views
Sample responses:
1. Her behavior can cause infection and scarring. I would tell Julie to wash her face several times a day with a gentle soap, to wear only water-base make-up, and not to pick at pimples. She may try over-the-counter medications containing benzoyl peroxide.
2. Wash my feet every day, wear cotton socks, dust my feet with talc, and alternate pairs of shoes.
3. decay; see my dentist as soon as possible
4. Use waxing or electrolysis.

Life Skills Check
1. yes, to protect your skin from wrinkles and skin cancer
2. Answers should reflect the steps given on page 141.
3. Cut her hair shorter, wear a swim cap, wash her hair after swimming, let her hair air dry, and don't use electric curlers or a curling iron.

Projects
Have students plan and carry out the projects on hair, skin, and dental care.

Plan for Action
Divide the chalkboard into these sections: Early Morning, Morning, Noontime, Afternoon, Evening, and Bedtime. Invite students to fill in personal-care activities that they might routinely do in one time slot. Have the class discuss the resulting schedule. Students can then develop their own schedule.

ASSESSMENT OPTIONS

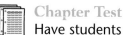
Chapter Test
Have students take the Chapter 6 Test.

Alternative Assessment
Have students do the Alternative Assessment activity for Chapter 6.

Test Generator
The Test Generator contains additional assessment items for this chapter.

Issues in Health

How In Is Thin?

EVALUATING MEDIA MESSAGES

How In Is Thin?
Have students read the Evaluating Media Messages feature. Then ask them to think of a person they know and like who does not fit the ideal body type as conveyed in the media. Have them suggest aloud, or list for themselves, attractive personality characteristics of that person. Then ask: In what way are the physical characteristics of the person important to you? Do they limit your relationship with the person? *[Encourage honest responses, which may include an admission that physical features are very important.]* **Do the other attractive features of the person seem as important, more important, or less important than the physical features? Have you ever found that a person you didn't think of as particularly attractive became attractive once you got to know the person?**

When Cara told Jennifer, "I love this dress, but it makes me look so fat!" Jennifer just stared at her friend. She wanted to say, "Cara, I hate it when you complain about being fat. You know I'm a lot bigger than you, and when you talk like that, it makes me feel huge!" Jennifer also wanted to tell her friend that she had started to worry about how thin Cara was getting and about what Cara was doing to get even thinner.

Does this sound familiar? Recent studies have shown that very few teenage girls are happy with their appearance, especially their weight. An alarming percentage of these girls report being overweight, even when their weight is healthy by medical standards. One source of such attitudes is the media messages about what is attractive that are found in advertisements, television programs, and movies.

The message to be thin can be both good and bad. Healthy people come in all shapes and sizes.

One of the strongest media messages in our culture is that thin is in and fat is out. Because marketing studies have shown that women's clothes sell better when pictured on thin models, girls get the strongest message to be thin. However, boys are also affected by media stereotypes. For males, attractiveness is usually associated with a muscular, athletic build. While this is a healthy model, a boy can also be healthy and fit without being muscular or athletic. Remember that the primary objective of most media messages is to sell something and that you do not have to look like a media stereotype to be healthy and happy.

When questioned about what they consider attractive, many teenagers automatically agree with the media stereotypes—the ultrathin girl and superjock boy—but only at first. As they continue to express their true attitudes and feelings, they tend to emphasize other, more important qualities:

"What I like most about Chad is that he's never boring. He has a great sense of humor and relates to people really well."

"What I love about Mai is that she knows what she wants out of life and really goes for it."

Issues in Health

''Jerry is really sensitive and sweet. He plans to have his own band someday. Because he is also a good student, he should have many options for the future.''

When you evaluate your attitudes toward personal appearance, be aware of how media messages influence you. Think about what the messages actually say and why they say what they do. Are they eroding your self-esteem? Are they causing you to engage in potentially harmful behavior? Also be aware of mixed messages. An example of a mixed message is a magazine article about proper nutrition and health that is surrounded by ads featuring extremely thin models. Ask yourself which of these messages is encouraging you to make realistic decisions that are truly in your best interest.

The message to be thin or athletic can be good or bad from a health standpoint. Naturally thin or athletic-looking people can be very healthy. However, these body types are not in the majority. Furthermore, healthy people come in all shapes and sizes. Too often, naturally full-figured people try to achieve the unrealistic goal of a fashion model's thin figure or athletic build by resorting to unhealthy behaviors.

Recently, many well-known personalities, including actors, fashion models, and athletes, have admitted that they engaged in unhealthy eating habits and took dangerous medications to maintain their weight and build. Several of these individuals now promote healthier lifestyles. One very moving appeal for a healthier lifestyle came from Lyle Alzado, a former NFL football player who died of cancer in 1992. Before he died, Mr. Alzado used the media to campaign against the use of steroids by athletes who want to increase their size

and weight. He believed that the steroids he took were the cause of his cancer.

Persuasive messages are a fact of life in our society. We can't eliminate them, but we can guard against being manipulated by them. With a clear understanding of your values and a strong sense of self-esteem, you can evaluate media messages and use them to your best advantage by using effective decision-making skills.

Critical Thinking

1. Find a picture of someone you think is really attractive, or describe a favorite actor or actress. Ask yourself:

- Do I really want to look like this person? Why?
- Does someone have to look like this person for me to be able to be friends with him or her?
- Why do I feel like this? Does this really match my values?
- If someone I cared for gained a lot of weight, would that change my feelings for that person? If I gained a lot of weight, would I understand if a friend tried to break off our friendship?
- Are my personal appearance and fitness goals realistic and healthy?
- What will I gain by attaining this goal? (Will I get a boyfriend/girlfriend if I lose five pounds?)
- What do I have to do to attain this goal? Is the effort worth it?

2. See if you can find an example of a mixed message in an advertisement, television program, or movie.

3. Name a movie or television program that contains characters who are attractive without fitting the stereotypical models of ''attractiveness.''

Or have you ever found that a person you initially thought of as very attractive didn't have much personality or wasn't very nice?

Students may also be interested to know that research shows that only 1 in 40,000 women have inherited the physical attributes required to be a model. Unfortunately, many young women's goal is to look like a model. They fail to see that other attributes are far more important than having a "perfect" body. Discuss how media messages can cause people to evaluate themselves in ways that are not healthful.

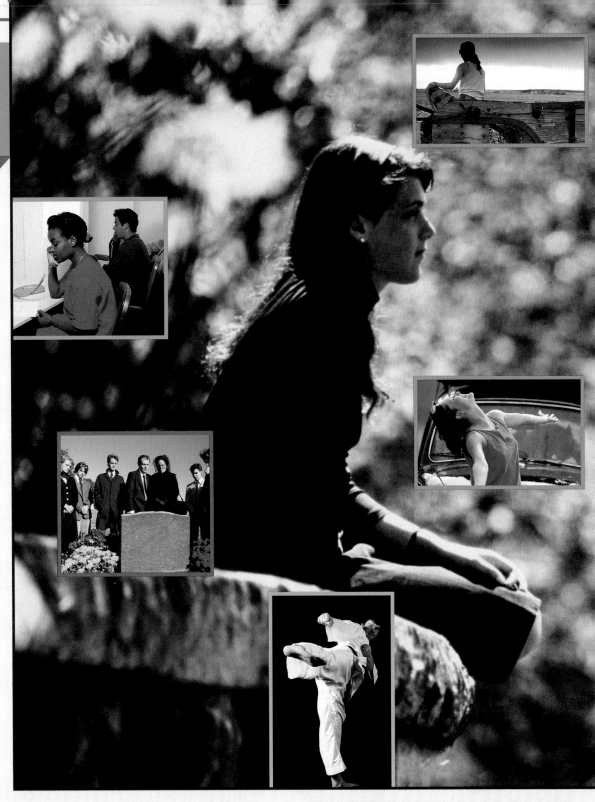

UNIT 3

HEALTH AND YOUR MIND

CHAPTER OVERVIEWS

CHAPTER 7

MENTAL AND EMOTIONAL HEALTH

This chapter describes the characteristics of a mentally healthy person. It defines emotions and explains their role in mental health. It offers suggestions for managing negative emotions and describes and evaluates defense mechanisms. Students are shown how to develop definitions of their self-concept and of their self-ideal. The chapter then describes categories of mental and emotional disorders. Students learn to recognize the signs of mental and emotional problems and the kinds of therapy that are available to help people deal with them.

CHAPTER 8

BUILDING SELF-ESTEEM

A definition of self-esteem opens the chapter. Then students learn how self-esteem develops and how to assess their own self-esteem. Students also learn how media messages can affect one's self-esteem. The chapter ends by offering students suggestions for raising self-esteem.

CHAPTER 9

MANAGING STRESS

Students learn that stress results from a combination of a stressor and a stress response, and that it may cause physical or mental disorders. A stress model is presented and ways to manage stressors on a daily basis are suggested. Strategies for managing stress over a lifetime complete the chapter.

CHAPTER 10

COPING WITH LOSS

This chapter offers information to help students cope with death and help a person who is dying. The five stages of adjustment to dying are described. The chapter also helps students deal with their grief and that of others.

CHAPTER 11

PREVENTING SUICIDE

Factors that may be responsible for the increase in teen suicides are presented. Students learn to distinguish between myth and fact regarding suicide and to recognize the warning signs. Intervention strategies for dealing with someone who is suicidal are suggested. Finally, students learn what to do if they feel suicidal.

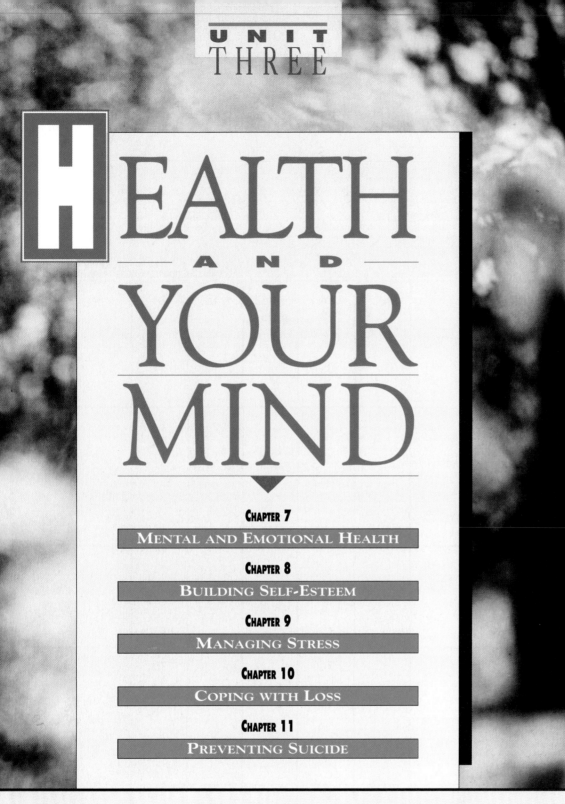

HEALTH AND YOUR MIND

CHAPTER 7
MENTAL AND EMOTIONAL HEALTH

CHAPTER 8
BUILDING SELF-ESTEEM

CHAPTER 9
MANAGING STRESS

CHAPTER 10
COPING WITH LOSS

CHAPTER 11
PREVENTING SUICIDE

UNIT PREVIEW

This unit deals with the role that emotions play in determining wellness. It helps students understand mental health and offers strategies for coping with emotional problems. Students learn that improving self-esteem is an important way to avoid self-destructive behaviors; they learn ways by which they might raise their own self-esteem. Students also receive suggestions for dealing with stress and for coping with death and grief. Finally, students learn to recognize the warning signs of suicide in others and how to cope with any suicidal feelings they may have. The chart below links the information and skills presented in this unit to the National Health Education Standards.

Unit 3	NATIONAL HEALTH EDUCATION STANDARDS*						
STANDARD	1	2	3	4	5	6	7
Chapter 7	•	•	•		•		•
Chapter 8			•	•	•	•	•
Chapter 9	•	•	•	•		•	
Chapter 10					•		•
Chapter 11	•		•	•	•	•	•

* For full text listing of each standard, see page 15T.

CHAPTER 7

Mental and Emotional Health

SECTION	TITLE/OBJECTIVES	PERSONAL INVENTORY			LIFE SKILLS DEVELOPMENT			
		Personal Health Inventory	Journal	Check Up	Life Skills	Life Skills Worksheets	Media Message or Ethical Issues Worksheet	What Would You Do?
7.1 *pp. 151–158*	**UNDERSTANDING MENTAL HEALTH AND EMOTIONS** • List the characteristics of a mentally healthy person. ▪▪ List qualities that can lead to happiness. ▪▪ List ways to manage negative emotions.	Ch. 7	7A 7B	p. 153 p. 157	p. 155	7A		
7.2 *pp. 159–162*	**DEFENSE MECHANISMS AND POSITIVE STRATEGIES** • Describe the purpose of defense mechanisms and how they can be helpful. ▪▪ Define your self-concept and self-ideal. • Relate Maslow's hierarchy of needs to self-esteem and self-ideal.					7B 7C		
7.3 *pp. 163–167*	**TYPES OF MENTAL AND EMOTIONAL DISORDERS** • Describe the differences among eating, organic, personality, somatoform, mood, and dissociative disorders.							
7.4 *pp. 168–172*	**SEEKING HELP** • Describe the signs of mental and emotional health problems. ▪▪ List community resources that help with mental and emotional problems. • Differentiate among types of treatment for mental and emotional problems.		7C		p. 170	7D		

KEY: ▪▪ Denotes Life Skill Objective
Text references denoted by page number.
Supplement references denoted by chapter or item numbers.

LINKING RESOURCES

Making a Choice Cards	Parent Discussion Guide	Health Talk Audio Program	Teaching Transparencies and Directory	Section Review Worksheets	Section Quizzes	Reteaching Worksheets	Section Reviews
INTERACTION	**OTHER RESOURCES**			**SECTION REVIEW AND ASSESSMENT**			
				7.1	7.1	7.1	p. 158
				7.2	7.2	7.2	p. 162
				7.3	7.3	7.3	p. 167
7A 7B			7A	7.4	7.4	7.4	p. 172

KEY FACTS

- A mentally healthy person feels good about himself or herself, relates well to others, and is able to work through normal life problems.

- Everyone experiences both pleasant and unpleasant emotions; it is important to learn how to express these emotions in a positive way.

- A healthful lifestyle, a feeling of some control over your life, meaningful relationships and work, and adaptability are important elements of a happy and fulfilling life.

- It is important to acknowledge negative emotions so that they can be addressed and managed in a positive way.

- Defense mechanisms are a means of coping and avoiding hurt; however, if overused, they allow people to put off facing an issue.

- Mental and emotional disorders may be categorized as organic (stemming from physical causes) or functional (due to internal struggles or related to surroundings).

- Intense fears, chronic sleeplessness, prolonged depression, and self-destructive behaviors can be signs of emotional or mental disorders.

- Professional help is available for those seeking help with emotional or mental problems.

CHAPTER REVIEW AND ASSESSMENT

TEXT

Chapter Review pp. 174–175

SUPPLEMENTS

Chapter Test 7

Alternative Assessment 7

Test Generator Chapter 7

GETTING STARTED

Using the Chapter Photograph

Ask students to describe the feelings expressed in the photographs. Are they pleasant or unpleasant emotions? Are they expressed appropriately? Discuss ways in which unpleasant feelings can be handled well and how pleasant feelings enhance a sense of well-being.

 Question Box

Have students write out any questions they have about mental illness or emotional health and put them in the Question Box.

Sensitivity *ALERT*

Most teens are experiencing an emotional roller coaster because of rapid physical and hormonal changes. They may need reassurance that their range and intensity of emotions are normal and that most mental disorders are rare. You may have a student who has a mental disorder or who has a family member with a mental disorder. These students may react to discussions of mental illness by withdrawing or becoming angry or defensive. Be sensitive to these students' feelings.

CHAPTER 7

Mental and Emotional Health

◆ ◆ ◆ ◆

Section **7.1**	Understanding Mental Health and Emotions
Section **7.2**	Defense Mechanisms and Positive Strategies
Section **7.3**	Types of Mental and Emotional Disorders
Section **7.4**	Seeking Help

■ **Emotionally healthy people feel a range of emotions and know how to express them in the right way.**

MYTHS & MISCONCEPTIONS

- **Mentally ill people are dangerous.** Most people who suffer from mental illness are not dangerous. In fact, many are so afraid of the world that they are more likely to withdraw from the world than to accost other people.

- **Mentally ill people always act crazy and will remain ill for life.** Only a small percentage of people who suffer from mental illness are always out of touch with reality. Most people with mental illness respond well to treatment; up to 80 percent of those who get appropriate treatment are able to lead normal, productive lives.

- **People should keep their emotional problems private and handle the problems by themselves.** Americans have traditionally hidden their mental and emotional problems, feeling that these problems are a sign of weakness. It is important to change this belief. Mental illness is highly treatable, and treatment can allow a person with a mental illness to have a normal, productive life.

Personal Health Inventory

Have students complete the Personal Health Inventory for this chapter.

Gena was really scared this time. Kevin had been so angry she was really afraid he would hurt her. Why was this happening? Why was he so mad? She thought about when they first met and started going together. He had been so nice. Lately though, Kevin was really possessive. He didn't like it when Gena talked to any other guys, and now he was beginning to be resentful of her girlfriends.

This last argument seemed so stupid. Gena was talking to Mr. Estrada, her history teacher, when Kevin walked up. That afternoon he told her he didn't want to see her talking to Mr. Estrada again. Gena couldn't believe it. When she tried to explain, he flew into a rage and pushed her against the wall. What was she going to do?

Section 7.1 *Understanding Mental Health and Emotions*

Objectives

- List the characteristics of a mentally healthy person.

- List qualities that can lead to happiness.
  ■ **LIFE SKILLS: Setting Goals**

- List ways to manage negative emotions.
  ■ **LIFE SKILLS: Coping**

People once thought of *mental health* as the absence of mental illness. Now it is defined in much more positive terms. Mental health refers to how you use the various aspects of health to achieve positive feelings about yourself and improve your ability to deal with problems. Do you feel good about yourself and the things you do? Can you cope with problems effectively? Do you have close friendships? Can you work through problems with your friends? If you can answer yes most of the time, you are probably mentally healthy.

It is important to recognize that there will be times when you will not feel good about yourself and times when you will have difficulty resolving problems. While having problems is normal, you can develop skills that will enable you to be more effective in dealing with problems.

The National Association for Mental Health describes someone with good mental health as having the following characteristics:

- feels comfortable with himself or herself
- has good relationships with others
- meets the demands of life

Section 7.1 Lesson Plan

MOTIVATE

Class Discussion
Gena's Choices

Discuss with students what Gena should do about Kevin's intense behavior. Why is she fearful? What are her options? What might be the result of each action?

 Journal 7A
Concerns About Emotions

After students have read and discussed the chapter opener, have them write in their Journal their concerns about negative emotions, such as anger, and tell what they think could be causing Kevin's anger.

TEACH

 Journal 7B
Defining Mental Health and Mental Illness

Have students complete the statements in their Journal about mental health and mental illness.

Life Skills
Worksheet 7A

Assign the Making Friends
Life Skills Worksheet.

Emotions Are Normal

Emotions are feelings in response to an activity or an experience. Understanding emotions and expressing them effectively are important parts of being mentally healthy.

Everyone has emotions, and they make you feel good or bad. Emotions themselves aren't good or bad, but the way you express emotions can be positive or negative. For example, feeling angry is okay, but expressing your anger by hitting someone is not.

You may feel happy one minute and sad the next. This change in feelings is actually very natural. Your body is changing rapidly, and your hormones can cause mood swings and dramatic changes in your emotions. Drugs and other substances can also have a profound effect on moods. For example, some people become very irritable if they consume too much caffeine. Scientists are studying the relationship between diet and mood.

(FIGURE 7-1) **Laughter makes you feel good. Keeping a sense of humor helps you deal with stress effectively.**

Expressing Emotions

You learn to express emotions based on past experiences. These experiences include what you learn from your interactions and from seeing how others react. You *model* your reactions on the reactions of someone else. It is important to recognize how to express your emotions in a positive way. Learning how to do this is a continual process. Instead of hitting someone when you're angry, you learn it is better to hit a pillow, or do some strenuous exercise, or tell someone you're angry. One valuable skill in expressing emotions positively is to think of a particular emotion and rehearse what you will do when it occurs.

Kinds of Emotions

We have the ability to feel a wide variety of emotions, from extreme happiness and joy to sadness and misery.

Love Love is the feeling of strong affection or caring for another person. Love can be a very strong emotion that grows deeper and stronger with time. We all have the need to love, and the need to be loved by others.

There are different types of love. You may feel love for the members of your family. You may also feel love for another person. That might be in the form of caring and loyalty to a friend, or in the form of romantic love. Romantic love is different from other forms of love because of the way you feel. Your heart beats faster when you think of the person you love, and you can't stand to be apart. Yet, sometimes it is hard to tell the difference between attraction and love.

Happiness Happiness is a feeling of joy and well-being or contentment. While happiness is an emotion, it is also a goal that drives people. Bookstores are filled with

● ● ● TEACH continued

Class Discussion
Feeling Emotional

Have students think of times that they felt more emotional than usual, and ask them what kinds of emotions they experienced. Then ask students to suggest different ways that people express the emotions discussed. (For example, people express worry in different ways. Some people withdraw and do not communicate, others become grouchy and do not communicate, and others talk constantly about how worried they are.) As a class, discuss the different ways a person might express an emotion and determine if the expression of the emotion is helpful or harmful.

Writing
Expressing Love

Have students write on the chalkboard a list of different kinds of love. Then have them write a second list of the feelings and actions that show love, or caring, for someone. Ask each student to focus on one type of love and write a poem, letter, or brief essay about how that love is expressed.

Reinforcement
Laughter Is Good Medicine

The act of laughing, even forcing laughter, has a positive impact on attitude and sense of well-being. Try having students monitor their state of mind and how they feel, then have books on how to achieve happiness—how to feel happy. The first step toward achieving this state is to recognize that you have some control over your life. Your attitude about life and how you react to situations are decisions only you make. Adopting a healthy lifestyle by following the guidelines you'll read about throughout this book will put you on the road to happiness. Here are some other things you can do to be happy.

- Establish close relationships with others.
- Work hard at tasks you find meaningful.
- Have a positive attitude.
- Think about what makes you happy and make time for those activities.
- Take good care of your body.
- Be organized, but flexible, so you can adapt to changes as they occur in your life.

Optimism Feeling optimistic means feeling that life experiences will be positive. It means realistically balancing the ups and downs of life and attempting to keep a positive attitude. Optimism is a healthy emotion that in turn affects your physical well-being. Is optimism part of your range of emotions? Do the following to find out.

Write down all the positive things you expect will happen to you in the future. Then list any of the bad things that you think could happen in the future as well. Now look at your lists. Have you described more positive things or more negative things? How could you revise your lists to look at each negative event with optimism?

Humor Humor provides a way of expressing some negative emotions in a more positive way. Laughing and finding humor in a stressful situation is a very healthy way of coping. Medical research has found that laughter can increase the effectiveness of your immune system in fighting disease.

Check Up

Assessing Your Mental Health

Answer the following questions and count the characteristics of good mental health that you possess.

1. Are you willing to assume responsibilities appropriate for your age?

2. Do you participate in activities appropriate to your stage of life?

3. Do you accept your responsibilities?

4. Do you solve problems rather than avoid them?

5. Do you make decisions with a minimum of worry?

6. Do you stick with a choice you make until new factors surface?

7. Are you satisfied with your accomplishments?

8. Do you recognize that thinking about a problem is the first step toward taking action?

9. Do you learn from failures or defeats?

10. Do you keep successes in perspective?

11. Do you enjoy working and enjoy playing?

12. Do you say no to negative situations even though they may provide temporary pleasure?

13. Do you say yes to situations that will be positive even though there may be some momentary displeasure?

14. Can you tell others when you are angry?

15. Can you show affection?

16. Can you endure frustration when the source cannot be changed or eliminated?

17. Can you make compromises in dealing with difficulties?

18. Can you concentrate and work at a single goal?

19. Do you recognize the challenges of life?

20. Can you develop and maintain family and intimate relationships?

Check Up

Discuss the questions with students before they answer them, having students provide suitable examples. You may want to collect students' anonymous answers and tally results for an overall perspective of the group's self-concepts.

---

them laugh for a full minute and note any changes. Experiment by beginning each class with this exercise. After a week, ask students to evaluate the value of laughter.

Class Discussion
Fear: Enemy or Friend?

Illustrate the usefulness of fear by asking students to describe incidents when being afraid helped them. Ask: **Why is it necessary for people to feel fear?** [*Fear heightens physical ability* *and quickens response time and can save your life.*] **When is fear harmful?** [*when it prevents you from living a normal life*] Have students list fears that are not helpful or reasonable.

• • • TEACH continues on p. 156

Background

Fight-or-Flight Response and Evolution

Fear and its physiological effects were great survival tools of the earliest humans. Dangers were everywhere and constant. To live, a human had to be able to respond quickly by fighting or running away. Because fear increases adrenalin production and provides energy to the major muscle groups, making an individual temporarily stronger, faster, and fiercer, it is not hard to see why natural selection favored this genetic trait. As humans evolved, this valuable characteristic was retained. Today, we don't face the same hazards as early humans, but we still possess this fight-or-flight response. The fear you feel, for example, as you wait to present a speech is the body gearing up for a situation it perceives as dangerous. (For more information about the fight-or-flight response, see the Body Systems Handbook, p. 678.)

(FIGURE 7-2) **It is normal to feel anger over an irritating situation. Exercise can provide a good outlet to relieve anger or it can just help you manage anger better.**

Fear Fear is the feeling of danger. When you are afraid, your heart beats faster to supply more blood to muscles. Your muscles become tense and your senses become more alert. All these reactions prepare your body to deal with danger. Your body returns to normal once you have dealt with the situation that caused the fear. It is important to work through fears so that the body doesn't stay in this state of alarm for an extended time.

Fears are often learned from experiences that you had when you were young. If you fell off a horse when you were nine years old, you might now be afraid to go riding. Fears also may be learned from other people, particularly your family. If your mother was robbed, you might be afraid to be alone at night. Some of these fears may be valid, while others may not be. For example, your parents probably told you never to accept rides from strangers when you were young. As a result, you may have developed a fear of strangers as a child that is still useful as you get older. However, as a child you may have been told not to go outside after dark. If you developed a fear of the dark as a consequence, that is not useful. Some fears, such as a fear of strangers, are useful because they are related to things that can cause you harm. But if a feeling of danger is not realistic, it is important to be able to manage that fear.

Managing Fear Two effective ways to manage fear are self-talk and environmental planning. *Self-talk* is saying things to yourself in order to view a fear more realistically. For example, if you are afraid of the dark, you might make the following self-talk statements:

1. I've never been hurt in the dark before. I probably won't be hurt in the dark now.
2. I sleep in a dark room every night and nothing bad ever happens to me.

3. It doesn't matter whether it's dark or light. It's whether the place or people are dangerous, and since they aren't in this place, there is nothing to fear.

Environmental planning involves re-arranging the environment to reduce your fear. For example, if you are afraid to fly on an airplane you could employ the following environmental planning strategies:

1. Travel with a friend or relative who can comfort you.
2. Bring something to read on the plane to take your mind off the fear.
3. Meditate or engage in some other form of relaxation exercise while flying.

Anger Anger is a strong feeling of irritation. Everyone feels angry at some time. The important thing is how you deal with the anger.

Life SKILLS

Review Americans' Top Ten Fears before students complete the exercise. Students should write suggestions independently, but they should share responses. You might break the class into groups that address the same or similar fears to make the sharing easier.

Life SKILLS: Coping

Managing Fears . . . .

Think about something that makes you afraid. With that situation in mind, answer the following questions.

1. What can you say to yourself to be less fearful in that situation?
   a. _____
   b. _____
   c. _____
   d. _____
   e. _____

2. How can you adjust your environment to be less fearful in that situation?
   a. _____
   b. _____
   c. _____
   d. _____
   e. _____

If you actually use this plan, it might help you to be less afraid.

Americans' Top Ten Fears

1. Snakes	39%
2. Heights	19%
3. Mice	15%
4. Flying	12%
5. Being closed in a small place	10%
6. Spiders/insects	9%
7. Thunder and lightning	9%
8. Being alone in a house at night	6%
9. Dogs	5%
10. Driving	3%

Background
Anger as a Coverup of Fear

Fear is often an underlying cause of anger, which in turn masks the fear. Because many people find it difficult to express vulnerability, they consciously or unconsciously express that fear as anger. For example, a parent may lash out angrily at a teen for coming home late, when the primary emotion was fear that the teen had been hurt in an accident. In the story, Kevin's fear that he will lose Gena is expressed as anger. Many people are not aware that they are expressing fear as anger.

Section Review Worksheet 7.1

To reinforce the concepts presented in this section, assign Section Review Worksheet 7.1.

Depression in relation to suicide is discussed in Chapter 11.

Anger is not experienced only in your mind. A physical reaction accompanies anger. This reaction varies but may include an increased heart rate and higher blood pressure, headaches, and nausea. It is important to find a positive release for these reactions. That is why exercise is recommended as a way to alleviate angry feelings.

Anger is negative if it is expressed in a violent form. Unfortunately, anger sometimes results in child abuse or spouse abuse. Too often, it also is expressed through aggressive behavior, such as fighting. In the introductory story, Kevin used violence to express his anger at Gena. If such behavior continues unchecked, Kevin will need professional help.

Managing Anger It is important to channel emotions appropriately so that anger can be expressed in a positive way. It is helpful to recognize your feelings and the source of the anger. Once you do this, you may wish to talk to the person with whom you are angry. You are likely to have the most positive results from the talk if you do not blame the other person. Keep in mind that other people, even if they make you angry, do not make you *express* your anger in a certain way. Recognizing this simple fact enables you to choose how, when, and to whom you express your anger.

If you are not able to talk with the person to resolve the problem, do something physical to release your anger and relieve some of the physical symptoms. Remember that it is not helpful to keep your feelings penned up inside.

Guilt Guilt is the feeling that you have done something wrong or are responsible for something bad happening. You may feel guilty after you have had an argument with someone you love. Or you may feel guilty if you have done something unintentionally that caused something bad to happen.

Guilt can be your cue to resolve a problem. Guilt may also drive you to do the right thing in a situation. You may be nice to someone you really don't like because you feel guilty if you're mean.

Managing Guilt If you feel guilty about something you've done, think about the source of your guilt. Have you done something wrong, or are you responding to how others see the situation? For example, if you have stood up to others during a conflict, have you allowed a parent or guardian to make you feel guilty for being assertive? Try not to be critical of yourself. If you've made a mistake, correct it and then move on. If you find guilt over an issue or problem to be overwhelming, seek professional help so you can work through the problem.

Depression Depression is a feeling of anxiety, loneliness, and despair. It can interfere with the ability to carry out daily activities. Symptoms of teenage depression may include the following:

- sleeping too much or too little
- feeling tired throughout the day
- lack of interest or lack of ability to concentrate
- loss of appetite
- loss of energy
- withdrawal from a group

Everyone feels sad or depressed occasionally, but extended depression may indicate a need for professional help. Serious depression can lead to suicide.

Several factors are linked to the development of depression.

- *Family History* The tendency for depression appears to be hereditary.

• • • TEACH continued
Role-Playing
Acting on Emotions

Divide the class into six groups and have each group create a role-playing situation illustrating anger, guilt, depression, jealousy, loneliness, or shyness. The scene should show what caused the emotion as well as how it was expressed. After each presentation, the class can evaluate the healthfulness of the expression of emotion or suggest other ways it might have been expressed.

Reinforcement
Chapter Cross-Reference

Depression, as a mood, generally refers to normal feelings of discouragement and sadness. It becomes a symptom of physical or mental illness when it is so severe as to hinder or halt normal functioning. Depression as a mental disorder is discussed later in this chapter, and is discussed as a contributing factor to suicide in Chapter 11.

Class Discussion
Building Confidence

Have students rate the self-help tips for overcoming shyness from most helpful to least helpful, explaining why they think as they do. Ask: **How might each tip help build self-esteem? Why might forcing yourself to be with people and to try new things help build confidence?** *[Students may say these actions will allay fears and make the shy person confident, if the strategies succeed.]*

156 MENTAL AND EMOTIONAL HEALTH

- *Major Life Stresses* Personal traumas such as neglect, abuse, or separation often precede depression.
- *Physical Illness* People who are physically ill are more likely to be depressed.
- *Substance Abuse* Alcoholics and abusers of other drugs have higher rates of depression.
- *Gender* Depression is more likely to occur in women.

Managing Depression When you feel depressed, try to identify why you feel the way you do. Once you do that, you'll be able to put things in perspective, and you may see that they really aren't that bad. Focus on the positive things in your life to keep you from dwelling on the things that aren't going so well. Talk to a trusted friend to help you with your perspective.

Get some exercise. When you get a workout your body produces chemicals that make you feel good. Exercise is a natural way to improve your outlook.

Jealousy Jealousy is the feeling of wanting something that someone else has or the fear of losing something that you have. For example, Mary's parents don't have much money. Mary works after school, but most of her money goes to help pay the family's expenses. Mary sees girls who don't have to work but have lots of nice clothes. Mary is jealous because they have things she would like but can't have.

The situation with Kevin in the introductory story shows an example of jealousy that results from the possibility of losing something. Kevin and Gena have been dating for six months. Gena has started tutoring Jordan after school. Kevin is jealous of Jordan because he has Gena's time and attention. He feels that his relationship with Gena is threatened by Jordan.

Check Up

Are You at Risk for Depression?

Depression occurs in people of all ages. By some estimates, 33 percent of teens are affected by depression. If feelings of depression last more than two weeks, help should be sought. To determine whether you (or a friend) are depressed, answer the following questions.

1. Do you have problems concentrating or making decisions?

2. Are you almost always tired, or do you have problems sitting still because you are so upset?

3. Do you sleep well? Are you sleeping much more or much less than usual?

4. Have you gained or lost a significant amount of weight?

5. Do you find that you no longer enjoy things that used to make you happy?

6. Do you feel worthless most of the time?

7. Do you have thoughts of death?

If you (or your friend) answered YES to five or more of these questions, speak with a mental health specialist.

Managing Jealousy If you are jealous of someone, you should discuss these feelings with the other person involved. Remember that people don't own other people, so they can't "lose" them. Jealousy is an emotion that can be very destructive if it is not controlled. In the introductory story, Kevin's jealousy was driving him to anger. That anger was expressed in a violent way. The jealousy is Kevin's problem, not Gena's. Gena's best course of action would be to stop seeing Kevin until he can get his emotions under control.

SECTION 7.1

Check Up

You may want to discuss some questions to be sure students put them in the appropriate context. For example, a change in diet or exercise patterns could be an alternative explanation for weight loss in some teens. Sleep pattern disturbances due to a busy schedule of practices, rehearsals, or work are not necessarily serious.

Students should complete the activity independently, but should be urged to talk to a trusted adult if they feel they are at risk. Students who acknowledge frequent thoughts of death or suicide are especially at risk.

 Section Quiz 7.1
Have students take Section Quiz 7.1.

Reteaching Worksheet 7.1
Students who have difficulty with the material may complete Reteaching Worksheet 7.1.

Cooperative Learning
The Shy and the Lonely

Shyness, loneliness, depression, and lack of confidence often go together. Discuss reasons why a person might feel all these emotions. Then have students work in groups to create a diagram showing how they are related. They could make one poster of their diagram and another showing or listing actions that can help a person overcome these negatives.

Extension
Helping Yourself to Happiness

Encourage students to search libraries, bookstores, and their own homes for self-help books on becoming happier, becoming more positive in outlook, or overcoming destructive emotions. Display the books, and ask volunteers to read and review several for the class.

Review Answers

1. Answers will vary but may include the following statements: I feel good about myself; I feel good about the things I do; I can deal with problems effectively; I have close friends; and I have good relationships with friends and members of my family.

2. Answers will vary but may include the following goals: find close relationships with others; work hard at tasks I find meaningful; have a positive attitude; think about what makes me happy, and make time for those activities; take good care of myself; and be organized and flexible.

3. Answers may include the following strategies: talk with the person with whom you are angry; do something physical, such as exercise, to relieve some of the physical symptoms of anger; and do not keep angry feelings pent up inside.

4. Answers will vary but may include these actions: call friends, join groups, and get involved in volunteer work.

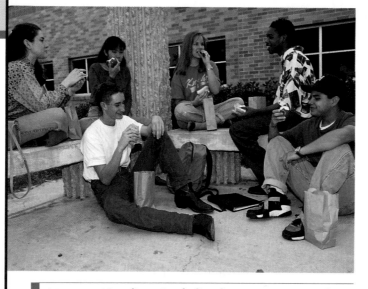

(FIGURE 7-3) **Loneliness is a feeling that you can manage by taking some action. Look for ways to interact with people.**

Loneliness Loneliness is a feeling of isolation or alienation. It is not the same as being alone. Being able to enjoy time by yourself is a part of good mental health. Loneliness can be a particular problem for teens, because in trying to become independent, teens sometimes alienate one another.

Managing Loneliness Engage in activities that will make you part of a group. Don't wait to be asked to join in. Take charge of your loneliness. Make the effort to contact your old friends. Get involved in volunteer work as an interest and way of meeting new people. There are times in life when you will be alone. Therefore it is a good idea to start now in being comfortable by yourself.

Shyness Shyness is the feeling of being timid or bashful. Shy people can appear to be less friendly or open. What often happens is that shy people are thought to be snobs or stuck up. Working to improve self-esteem will help in making shyness less of a problem. People who are confident are less controlled by feelings of shyness. Shyness is something that everyone feels at times.

Managing Shyness/Improving Self-Esteem If you are shy, you might try the following.

1. Make a list of your strengths and positive traits.
2. Never say things about yourself such as ''What a dummy,'' or ''Boy, am I stupid.'' These things make you feel inferior.
3. Purposely put yourself in situations with supportive people. As you do, you'll become more confident.
4. Do not spend time with people who make you feel badly about yourself. People who are always putting you down should be avoided. If the person putting you down is a family member and can't really be avoided, keep remembering your strengths and positive traits.
5. Don't be afraid to try new things or be afraid to fail. Failure teaches you lessons that help you grow as a person, and may lead to other opportunities that are successful.

Review

1. How would you know if you are mentally healthy?
2. List four goals you can set for yourself to achieve happiness.
3. Describe some positive strategies for managing anger.
4. **Critical Thinking** List three things you can do to keep from feeling lonely.

ASSESS

Section Review
Have students answer the Section Review questions.

Alternative Assessment
Good Humor Prescription

Ask students to write a paragraph describing a situation in which they could use humor to relieve an emotionally stressful incident. They should identify the emotion that needs management and explain how laughter would prevent the destructive expression of emotion and promote a healthier atmosphere.

Closure
Picture Your Emotions

Have each student select an emotion that is potentially harmful to mental health and draw a picture illustrating the expression of that emotion. Beneath the illustration, have students write two or three sentences explaining how the emotion can be healthfully channeled or managed.

Defense Mechanisms and Positive Strategies

Objectives

- Describe the purpose of defense mechanisms and how they can be helpful.
- Define your self-concept and self-ideal.
  - **LIFE SKILLS: Assessing Your Health**
- Relate Maslow's hierarchy of needs to self-esteem and self-ideal.

Background
Defense Mechanisms—Coping or Compounding Trouble?
Many teens are unaware that they use defense mechanisms. They may rely on them in part because they have not yet had the time and experience to integrate their emotions with their thought processes and reactions. In mature responses, a feeling is consciously understood and acted upon. For example, you may understand that you are frustrated by a situation and realize that you should talk it over and find some way to resolve the feeling. A teen may instead daydream to escape the feeling of frustration—a temporary relief that changes nothing. Simply by learning about defense mechanisms, students may begin to be aware of behaviors they carried out unconsciously.

Defense mechanisms are techniques you use to protect yourself from being hurt emotionally. They provide a way to deal with problems and maintain self-esteem. However, too much reliance on defense mechanisms is not healthy if they are used consistently to avoid facing an issue. Figure 7-4 is a listing of common defense mechanisms. Look through the list and think of one way to use each mechanism that would be helpful and one way that would be harmful.

Promoting Positive Mental and Emotional Health

Each day you are faced with problems or situations that affect your mental health. While it is easy to let your problems get you down, there are things you can do to stay mentally healthy. The road to good mental health starts with feeling positive about yourself, which means getting to know yourself thoroughly.

Self-Esteem Having high self-esteem is very important in developing and maintaining good mental health. Self-esteem is feeling good about yourself and the things you do. These feelings give you a sense of confidence. Take a moment to consider the positive things about yourself and the things you do well. Make a list of these. Pay particular attention to these positive aspects when you are feeling down. Chapter 8 will give you a number of strategies for building your self-esteem.

Sense of Control Another important factor for staying mentally healthy is acquiring a sense of control. High self-esteem gives you a sense of control. People with low self-esteem feel that events affecting their lives are beyond their control. These people have an *external locus of control.* Others believe they can control at least some aspects of their lives. These people have an *internal locus of control.* If you believe you are in control of a situation, you will do what you need to do to stay in control. If you think what you do influences your grades, you'll find out from your teacher how to do better. If you think you have no control over your grades, you won't bother. The reality is that you always have some control over your life. You need to work out the ways you can influence your future. You cannot solve problems by blaming others and bad luck for your situation.

As a teen, there are certain limits to the control you have. If you want to go to college and you don't have the money, that is a limitation. However, you can set college as a goal and begin to explore possible options

Section 7.2 Lesson Plan

MOTIVATE

Class Discussion
Putting Off Dealing With Emotions

Have students think of a time when they did not express how they felt about a situation. Ask: **Why did you put off expressing the feelings?** [They may suggest wanting to think over a response, to sort out the feelings, fear of rejection or violence, or feeling the emotion was unacceptable.] Ask students whether it is healthy or unhealthy to avoid expressing emotions.

TEACH

Role-Playing
Defense Mechanisms

Have students work in pairs or individually to role-play typical defense mechanisms. Have the rest of the class identify the mechanism being portrayed. Examples include lying to a friend about your feelings because you think the friend can't handle the truth (rationalization), blaming your best friend for keeping you out too late last night (projection), being rude to someone you are attracted to because you think they would never like you (reaction formation), whining when the library closes before you've finished your work (regression), and eating a giant ice cream sundae when you're feeling sad about a lost opportunity (substitution).

Life Skills
Worksheet 7B
Assign the Defense
Mechanisms Life Skills
Worksheet.

Life Skills
Worksheet 7C
Assign the Using
Maslow's Hierarchy
of Needs Life Skills
Worksheet.

Section Review
Worksheet 7.2
To reinforce the concepts
presented in this section,
assign Section Review
Worksheet 7.2.

Common Defense Mechanisms

Mechanism	Description	Examples
Compensation	covering a weakness by over-achieving in another area	focusing all your attention on sports because you think you are a better athlete than student
Daydreaming	escaping from an unpleasant situation by using your imagination	in the dentist's chair you focus on the fun you'll have over the weekend with friends because you hate being at the dentist
Denial	failure to accept reality	refusing to accept the death of a close friend or relative; refusing to accept that your relationship with a romantic friend is over
Displacement	the transfer of negative feelings about someone to someone else	you are very angry with your mother and you take out that anger in dealing with your sister or best friend
Projection	putting (projecting) negative feelings on someone else	blaming your teacher for failing a test when you did not study
Rationalization	justifying irrational behavior	not doing your homework one evening because you feel you've spent too much of your time on schoolwork
Reaction formation	expressing emotions that are the exact opposite of what you feel	acting like a clown in a group to hide your shyness
Regression	using childlike ways of expressing emotions like anger or disappointment	throwing a tantrum when you don't get to watch your favorite TV program
Repression	blocking out unpleasant memories	forgetting when you were in the hospital
Sublimation	redirecting bad or unacceptable behavior into positive behavior	channeling your aggression into an athletic sport where aggressive behavior is accepted
Somatization	converting emotions into bodily symptoms	getting stomach cramps every time final exams are scheduled

(FIGURE 7-4)

• • • TEACH continued

Class Discussion
Defining Locus of Control

Ask students to make a list of aspects of their lives over which they have some control and a second list of aspects over which they have no control. On the chalkboard, write the headings SOME CONTROL and NO CONTROL. Have students volunteer aspects of life from their lists, and write them under the appropriate heading. Review the two lists. Ask if anyone disagrees with the placement of an aspect. Are there any aspects that do not fit clearly into one of the two categories? Point out that often one's perception of control is a matter of one's perception of oneself. A self-confident person more actively looks for ways to positively affect his or her future.

Cooperative Learning
Self-Ideal

Have students work in small groups to distinguish cultural and individual factors that go into self-ideals. Each group should come up with a description of the ideal man and ideal woman, as defined in their social community. Then they should discuss how they see their own self-ideals as differing from the culturally defined one. Discuss whether the cultural ideal *actually* fits anyone.

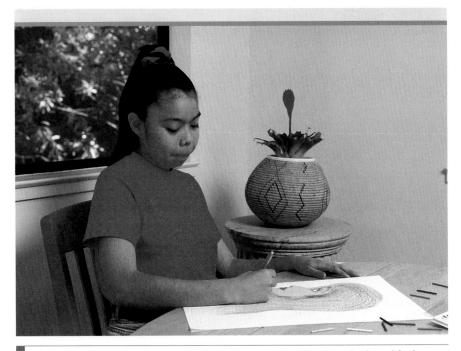

(FIGURE 7-5) **How closely does your self-concept match how you look and feel? What could you do to improve how you see yourself?**

for getting there. You may be able to seek financial aid or apply for scholarships. To look for ways to take charge of and solve a problem is to be mentally healthy. To give up and run away from your problems is to be unhealthy. If you focus on the negative, you'll be unhappy. If you focus on the positive, you'll be happier. Having a positive outlook will help improve and maintain your mental health.

Self-Concept Rating your level of self-esteem requires a thorough analysis of your **self-concept**, or self-image as it is sometimes called. It means looking realistically at how you see yourself.

Take out a piece of paper and draw a picture of yourself. Now look at the picture. Are you satisfied with the picture you've drawn? What kinds of things can you learn about how you feel about yourself by looking at the picture you've drawn? Do you see yourself as big or small? Did you draw yourself as happy or sad? Does your picture fill up the whole paper or is it off in a corner? Does your picture reflect a positive view of yourself?

Now think about what you would like your picture to look like. This image represents your **self-ideal**. Your self-ideal can be an image to strive for, as long as it is realistic. For example, if you are short you can't expect to achieve a goal of being tall. If you are sad, you can work at being happy. Your self-ideal should represent your feelings about yourself. Your self-ideal should be based on what you think, not on what your parents think, your friends think, or your teachers think.

Once you have a realistic self-ideal you can set reasonable goals for moving your self-concept closer to your self-ideal.

self-ideal:
your mental image of what you would like to be.

self-concept:
the current mental image you have of yourself.

Background
Abraham Maslow (1908–1970)
Abraham Maslow, best known for his theory of self-actualization, distinguished himself from psychologists in other schools of thought by focusing on well-adjusted people rather than on troubled patients. Whereas behaviorists saw people as controlled by instincts and environment, and psychoanalysts saw them as controlled by unconscious drives, Maslow and other humanistic psychologists saw people as motivated by a hierarchy of needs and controlled by their own values and choices. He saw integration of the self as the primary goal of psychotherapy.

 Section Quiz 7.2
Have students take Section Quiz 7.2.

Reteaching Worksheet 7.2
Students who have difficulty with the material may complete Reteaching Worksheet 7.2.

Class Discussion
Sliding Up and Down Maslow's Hierarchy

Have a volunteer define *hierarchy*. (*a system of things arranged in order of rank*) Refer students to Maslow's hierarchy, shown in Figure 7-6 on the following page. Stress that the hierarchy builds upward as more basic needs are met. Discuss the following questions: Which needs relate directly to survival? Which needs relate to emotional survival? How are these needs met for a small child? for a teen? for an adult? Point out that a person may progress up the pyramid and slide back down it numerous times. Also, few people achieve true self-actualization. Maslow himself felt that only one person in a hundred achieves self-actualization, or true fulfillment of potential.

Extension
Comic Strip Defense Mechanisms

Have students clip comic strips from the newspaper (or draw their own) to illustrate various defense mechanisms in action. Encourage them to create headings or sayings to label their comics, and display them on a bulletin board.

Review Answers

1. Defense mechanisms are used to protect a person from being emotionally hurt and to provide a way for the person to deal with problems and maintain self-esteem. Defense mechanisms can be misused when they are consistently used to avoid facing an issue.

2. Maslow's hierarchy includes, from the basic to the ultimate: physiological needs, safety-security needs, needs for love and affection, self-esteem, and self-actualization. You must develop a healthy self-esteem before you can meet your self-ideal. Self-esteem allows people to make decisions and set goals that will move them toward their self-ideal.

3. Answers will vary but may include the following: learn how you use defense mechanisms, work on improving your self-esteem by emphasizing the positive, acquire a sense of control over your life by taking action, identify your defense mechanisms and try not to rely on them too heavily, and do an analysis of your self-concept.

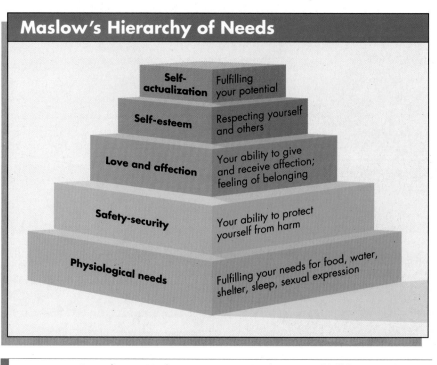

Maslow's Hierarchy of Needs

- **Self-actualization** — Fulfilling your potential
- **Self-esteem** — Respecting yourself and others
- **Love and affection** — Your ability to give and receive affection; feeling of belonging
- **Safety-security** — Your ability to protect yourself from harm
- **Physiological needs** — Fulfilling your needs for food, water, shelter, sleep, sexual expression

(FIGURE 7-6) **According to Maslow, you cannot reach a state of fulfillment without satisfying your basic physiological needs first. Each step in the pyramid requires that the needs in the section below have been met.**

Maslow's Hierarchy of Needs

Focusing on the positive aspects of human behavior was the subject of Abraham Maslow's work on emotional development. Maslow organized human needs by priority in achieving a state of wellness. Maslow's Hierarchy is shown in Figure 7-6. People grow emotionally when they can satisfy their needs from bottom to top of the hierarchy. Reaching the top of the scale represents the fulfillment of one's potential. This stage represents a state of wellness. Self-actualization and fulfillment may be your self-ideal. However, to reach this goal your self-esteem needs must be satisfied. You cannot grow emotionally without self-esteem.

Review

1. *Why do people use defense mechanisms? When are defense mechanisms misused?*

2. *List the phases in Maslow's hierarchy. How is your self-esteem related to self-ideal?*

3. ***Critical Thinking*** *List four things you can do to bring your self-concept closer to your self-ideal.*

ASSESS

Section Review

Have students answer the Section Review questions.

Alternative Assessment
Problem-Solving and Feeling in Control

Ask students to explain how a person's defense mechanisms and problem-solving strategies relate to his or her feeling of being in control. They should point out that defense mechanisms delay problem solving; the ability to resolve emotional issues strengthens an internal locus of control, and vice versa.

Closure
The Real "Me"

Have students describe in writing or with a drawing the differences they perceive in their own private, public, and ideal selves. Suggest that they keep their writing or drawing someplace where they can review it every month or two, using it as a reminder to work toward their self-ideal.

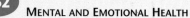

Types of Mental and Emotional Disorders

Objectives

- *Describe the differences among eating, organic, personality, somatoform, mood, and dissociative disorders.*

Everyone faces a variety of challenges. It may be the challenge of moving to a new town and making friends. Or it may be the challenge of rejection when you learn that the person you have a crush on doesn't feel the same about you. Most of the time, we are able to face challenges, learn from them, and move forward. Sometimes we are bogged down by them for a time. In these cases, our capacity to cope is exceeded, and the challenge interferes with our ability to function day to day. The inability to function for an extended period of time may be indicative of a mental or emotional disorder. The American Psychiatric Association has categorized mental and emotional disorders according to specific behaviors that people demonstrate. These mental and emotional disorder categories include the information in Figure 7-7. The diagnosis of a mental or emotional disorder should be made by a qualified doctor. People should never attempt to diagnose themselves or others just by reading a short description of a disorder in a textbook. If you are having difficulty, talk to a trusted adult. Counseling may help you deal with your problems. There is nothing wrong with seeking counseling. Seeking help for emotional problems is no different than seeking help for physical problems.

Organic Disorders

Mental and emotional disorders resulting from a *physical* cause are called **organic disorders**. There is evidence that some organic disorders are genetic. Other evidence indicates that these disorders develop as a response to various life experiences. Organic disorders may be caused by a physical illness, injury, or chemical imbalance. Because they involve the body as well as the mind, organic disorders are usually more serious than other types of mental and emotional problems.

An example of a physical illness causing an organic disorder is a brain tumor. A brain tumor can affect mood, speech, and comprehension. These won't improve until the tumor is removed. An example of an injury causing an organic disorder is a severe blow to the head. Brain cells may be destroyed during the injury and the functioning of the brain can be affected.

A chemical imbalance can also cause an organic disorder. For example, drinking alcohol or using other drugs may destroy brain cells, which in turn causes a chemical imbalance. The result can be an organic disorder. Brain cells may also be destroyed by lack of oxygen, such as when someone almost drowns. Chemicals help your brain send messages to your body. An imbalance in chemicals can affect the way you feel and act.

Eating Disorders

In Chapter 5, you learned about the characteristics of the two major eating disorders—anorexia and bulimia. The refusal to eat,

organic disorders:

mental and emotional disorders resulting from a physical cause.

Background
Chemical Imbalances in the Brain

Brain researchers are finding that many disorders once thought to be psychological in origin are the result of an imbalance of specific chemicals in the brain. Among the disorders are obsessive-compulsive disorder, panic disorder, and post-traumatic stress disorder. To treat these disorders, researchers are developing drugs aimed at specific receptors in the brain. These drugs treat the disorders but do not cure them. However, relieving the symptoms is a giant step. For example, one medication allows people with panic disorder to live without fear of recurring panic attacks.

Section 7.3 Lesson Plan

MOTIVATE

Class Discussion
Mental Disorders in the Media

Ask students to recall movies or programs that included a mentally ill character. (Films include *The Fisher King, Three Faces of Eve, One Flew Over the Cuckoo's Nest, I Never Promised You a Rose Garden, Ordinary People, Sybil, Prince of Tides,* and *What About Bob?.*)

What caused the character's crisis? What behaviors show that the person has lost the ability to function normally in society? What impression of mental illness is given in each film?

TEACH

Class Discussion
Organic Disorders

Ask: **What are three possible causes of organic disorders?** [*physical illness,*

injury, chemical imbalance] **Can a person's behavior bring about an organic disorder?** [*Yes, drug and alcohol use can impair brain cells, causing a chemical imbalance.*]

that is characteristic of anorexia, or the binge eating that is characteristic of bulimia are not the actual disorders. Anorexia and bulimia describe behaviors that are the result of deep emotional problems related to self-image and self-esteem.

Eating disorders are included again in this chapter because of their increasing frequency among teens. They are also included here because the cure for these disorders requires psychiatric treatment. The goal of therapy is to find the underlying cause of one's obsession with body image and weight. In some cases, family therapy is needed to provide insights into why the patient has an unrealistic and often negative image of himself or herself. Severe depression and some forms of sexual abuse are often associated with eating disorders.

Anxiety Disorders

You learned in Section 7.1 that fear is a protective emotion that helps you recognize and prepare for danger. It can be beneficial to you on occasions when you should feel afraid. For example, if you are contemplating doing something that is illegal, the fear of getting caught might prevent you from doing the wrong thing. In this case, the fear is helpful.

However, to be constantly afraid of things you should not fear is not normal.

Cultural DIVERSITY

Social Support and African-American Churches

You read at the beginning of this chapter that having good relationships with others—having social support—is an important part of being mentally healthy. Different people find this support in different ways. For many African-Americans, churches serve as an important base of social support.

In fact, African-American churches have a long history of providing support and a sense of community to their members. Almost from the beginning, the churches served as community centers where African-Americans could gather to socialize. In the segregated past, their churches were often the *only* public buildings where they could have large gatherings.

People still come together at churches for services, weddings, baptisms, concerts, suppers, socials, plays, parties, meetings, discussion groups, educational programs, and sports like basketball and softball. Most African-American churches are open at least four nights a week to accommodate all these events.

At times, the support African-American churches give is more than social; families in financial trouble often go to their churches for housing, clothing, and money. Recently, some churches have even begun addressing their members' health-care needs.

• • • TEACH continued

Class Discussion
When Fears Are Out of Control

Ask: **What are some biological purposes of fear?** *[In the evolution of humans, it served the useful purpose of preparing a person to fight or flee from danger; it heightens alertness and enhances physical prowess.]* **How do anxiety disorders differ from healthy fears?** *[They do not help you avoid danger but prevent you from living normally*

or enjoying life; they interfere with day-to-day function.]* Have volunteers point out ways in which each anxiety disorder expresses abnormal fear.

Reinforcement
Dissociative Disorders in Film and Fiction

Most students have read stories or seen movies about people suffering from amnesia or multiple personality disorder. Stress that these disorders are rare and are not usually as intense or dramatic as portrayed.

Case Study
Patty Duke Astin—Breaking the Manic-Depressive Cycle

In 1992, Patty Duke Astin went public with her story of two decades of suffering with manic-depressive disorder. Like most manic-depressives, she spent long periods in bed, battling severe depression that led to frequent suicide attempts. Finally diagnosed correctly, she received medical treatment and therapy that turned her life around. By telling her experience, Astin hopes to

Constant fear prevents you from participating in many aspects of a normal life. It can also damage you physically, because your body experiences a number of changes when you are afraid. Your heart rate speeds up, you perspire, and your blood pressure rises. If these changes occur most every day, they can be harmful and become the symptoms of an **anxiety disorder**. Phobias are the most well-known anxiety disorders. A fear of flying in a plane, of riding in an elevator, or of even leaving the house is a very real fear to someone with an anxiety disorder.

Anxiety disorders are the most common mental and emotional disorders. For some reason, anxiety disorders affect a greater percentage of women than men. Anxiety disorders either cause or are a contributing factor in many medical conditions for which Americans seek care.

Dissociative Disorders

A condition in which someone's personality changes dramatically is called a **dissociative disorder**. A person afflicted with a dissociative disorder believes that sometimes he or she is really someone else. People with dissociative disorders separate themselves from their real personality.

anxiety disorder:

a condition in which fear or anxiety prevents one from enjoying life and completing everyday tasks.

dissociative disorder:

a condition in which someone's personality changes to the point that the person believes that sometimes he or she is someone else.

In addition, churches have played a crucial role in the ongoing battle against racial discrimination. In the 1800s, African-American churches were active in the movement to abolish slavery. They were also part of the "underground railroad" that helped escaped slaves find their way to freedom.

Later, black religious institutions furnished much of the leadership for the civil rights movement. Two of the most important leaders of that time, Martin Luther King, Jr., and Malcolm X, began their civil rights work as religious leaders. King was a Baptist minister and Malcolm X was a speaker for the Nation of Islam. Today, African-American churches continue to work for social justice.

promote public awareness and understanding of the disorder, which is treatable in 90 percent of all cases.

Extension
Understanding Mental Disorders

Have students explore the library and community mental health clinics for books, articles, and pamphlets on specific mental disorders that interest them. They may work alone or in pairs to prepare a report, poster, or display that will educate the public about a mental disorder.

Background

"Split Personality"

In the past, schizophrenia was commonly called "split personality," but it should not be confused with the rare condition known as multiple personality disorder. Schizophrenics' logical thought processes are "split" off from fantasies that include hallucinations, delusions, and distortions of reality. Bizarre and sometimes dangerous behaviors result from these fantasies.

In the early 1960s, with the advent of antipsychotic drugs to treat serious mental conditions, almost all people with serious mental illnesses were "deinstitutionalized" (released from mental institutions). Most mental health officials today recognize that this policy has been a failure. There are thousands of mentally ill people, primarily schizophrenics, who do not receive adequate medication. It is estimated that about 30 percent of the nation's homeless—around 150,000 people—are seriously mentally ill.

Some Mental and Emotional Disorders

Type of Disorder		Characteristics
Eating Disorders	Anorexia	excessive dieting resulting in a state of self-starvation
	Bulimia	bingeing on food then purging to avoid weight gain
Anxiety Disorders	General Anxiety Disorder	constant feeling of anxiety and fear with physical symptoms like increased heart rate, shortness of breath, perspiration, shaking, and diarrhea
	Obsessive-Compulsive Disorder	persistent recurring thoughts accompanied with the need to repeatedly perform some action, such as repeatedly washing one's hands
	Panic Disorder	intense feelings of terror that occur suddenly without cause
	Phobia	persistent fear of something: Hydrophobia-fear of water; claustrophobia-fear of small, enclosed spaces; agoraphobia—fear of public places
Dissociative Disorders	Multiple Personality Disorder	having two or more distinct personalities which can show different physical conditions and are often the exact opposite of each other
	Amnesia	loss of memory
Mood Disorders	Depression	experiencing feelings of sadness, loneliness, and hopelessness for an extended period of time
	Bipolar Disorder (Manic-Depression)	experiencing exaggerated feelings of euphoria, irritability, depression; exaggerated mood swings; reckless behavior
Personality Disorders	Antisocial Personality Disorder	showing a preference to remain distant from others
	Paranoia	consistent mistrust of others for no reason
	Aggression	behavior that displays an inner conflict between being dependent and being assertive which results in erratic moods
Somatoform Disorders	Hypochondriasis	believing and showing signs of serious illness without any physical cause
Schizophrenia	Schizophrenia	impaired perceptions, thinking processes, emotional health, and physical activity

(FIGURE 7-7)

(FIGURE 7-8) **These two pictures of cats, drawn by an artist diagnosed with schizophrenia, show how the disorder can impair perception.**

Dissociative disorders occur infrequently. They are usually the result of a traumatic experience. For example, they may result from severe sexual, physical, or emotional abuse in childhood. These disorders may be the mind's way of avoiding the pain associated with a very unpleasant experience. Amnesia and multiple personality disorder are examples of dissociative disorders.

Mood Disorders

A **mood disorder** occurs when one mood, which is often an unhappy mood, is experienced almost to the exclusion of other feelings.

A mood disorder usually lasts a long time and interrupts a person's ability to complete daily activities. The most common mood disorder is depression. In any given year, severe depression affects 15 million Americans.

Personality Disorders

Traits that negatively affect a person's ability to get along with others are called **personality disorders.** These traits may affect a person's work, relationships, and sense of satisfaction with life. Most personality disorders are very difficult to treat because one's personality is difficult to change.

Somatoform Disorders

People with physical symptoms caused by emotional problems are said to have **somatoform disorders.** However, a person with a somatoform disorder has no actual physical illness. Hypochondriasis is an example of a somatoform disorder—hypochondriacs believe they are ill even though their physical symptoms are caused by psychological factors.

Review

1. How do eating disorders differ from personality disorders?

2. What disorders are related primarily to fears?

somatoform disorder:

an emotional condition in which there are physical symptoms but no identifiable disease or injury. The physical symptoms are caused by psychological factors.

mood disorder:

a condition in which one mood is experienced almost to the exclusion of other feelings.

personality disorder:

an emotional condition in which a person's patterns of behavior negatively affect that person's ability to get along with others.

SECTION 7.3

 Section Review Worksheet 7.3

To reinforce the concepts presented in this section, assign Section Review Worksheet 7.3.

 Section Quiz 7.3

Have students take Section Quiz 7.3.

 Reteaching Worksheet 7.3

Students who have difficulty with the material may complete Reteaching Worksheet 7.3.

Review Answers

1. Eating disorders are the result of deep emotional problems related to self-image and self-esteem. A personality disorder is an emotional condition in which a person's pattern of behavior negatively affects the person's ability to get along with others.
2. anxiety disorders

ASSESS

Section Review
Have students answer the Section Review questions.

Alternative Assessment
Dissociative and Personality Disorders

Have students write a paragraph explaining differences between dissociative and personality disorders, citing specific behaviors.

Closure
Anxiety and Mood Disorders

Have students take turns describing specific behaviors for others to classify as representative of mood disorders or anxiety disorders.

Background

Dorothea Lynde Dix (1802–1887)

Before the mid-1800s, mentally ill people were brutally treated. Often they were housed with criminals and denied basic human needs, such as proper food, clothing, and blankets. Dorothea Lynde Dix became aware of the dismal conditions of the prisons and almshouses in which the mentally ill were housed in the 1840s. She fought for legislation to improve these institutions. Her activities resulted in the construction or improvement of over 30 mental hospitals in the United States and Canada. She was also responsible for the reform of some of the deplorable conditions in these institutions.

Section 7.4 Seeking Help

Objectives

- Describe the signs of mental and emotional health problems.
- List community resources that help with mental and emotional problems.
  LIFE SKILLS: Using Community Resources
- Differentiate among types of treatment for mental and emotional problems.

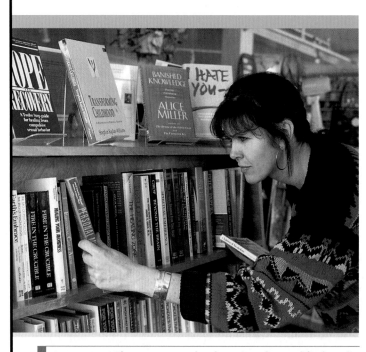

(FIGURE 7-9) **There are many books written by qualified medical and health professionals that can be of help in trying to deal with an emotional problem.**

Usually you can work through difficult times without outside help. Sometimes, though, you may need to ask for help from friends, parents, or relatives. There may be other times when your problems are so disturbing that it is important to seek professional help. That is when you need the assistance of a mental health specialist.

When to Seek Help for Mental and Emotional Health Problems

You may need to obtain professional help with your problems if you experience any of the following characteristics.

- a prolonged feeling of depression and hopelessness
- a feeling that life is out of control
- the inability to concentrate and make decisions
- difficulty getting along with family and friends
- intense fears
- persistent difficulty sleeping
- emotional problems coping with a physical illness
- inability to stop destructive behaviors like drinking, overeating, and abusing drugs

Mental and Emotional Health Services

If you need help or if someone you know needs help, contact a person you trust. That may be a parent, a teacher, a school counselor, a doctor, or a member of the clergy. Don't wait, thinking that the problems will clear up. Deep problems can only clear up if *you* take some action.

Section 7.4 Lesson Plan

MOTIVATE

Journal 7C
Mental and Emotional Health

As a warm-up activity, have students recall what they learned in Chapter 1 about mental and emotional health. In their Journal, have them describe in their own words the difference between emotional problems and mental illness.

Most communities provide mental and emotional health services. These services may be offered through community mental health centers, local hospitals, and numerous other agencies. Agencies like these in your community are listed in your local telephone book. Look in the phone book under *hospitals, social workers, psychologists, psychotherapists, mental health information,* and *treatment centers.*

In addition, hotline phone services are available in many communities. Where these exist, information and counseling are provided over the phone.

Mental and Emotional Health Therapies

Mental health specialists help people with mental and emotional health problems. For a description of the various types of mental health specialists, see the Career Appendix. The goal of therapy is to help a person work

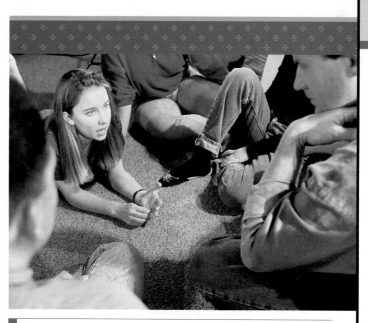

(FIGURE 7-10) **Support groups such as Al-Anon, Alateen, Alcoholics Anonymous, and many others can provide the support needed to work through specific emotional problems. The Yellow Pages of your phone book can provide information for contacting various support groups in your community.**

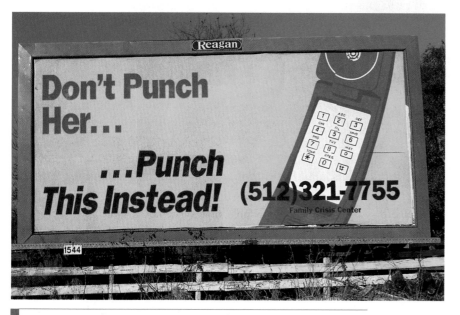

(FIGURE 7-11) **There are many sources of help in your community for emotional problems.**

SECTION 7.4

Life Skills Worksheet 7D

Assign the Help in Your Community Life Skills Worksheet.

Making a Choice 7A

Assign the Coping With Mental and Emotional Disorders card. The card asks students to discuss coping strategies for living with a family member who is mentally ill.

TEACH

Class Discussion
Mental Illness—Helping Yourself and Others

Ask students to name actions they could take if they believed a friend or relative were mentally ill. Allow students to argue the pros and cons of actions described and list the most valuable of these on the chalkboard. (*Some possible actions might include notifying a responsible adult, not leaving the person alone, and remaining calm and nonjudgmental.*) Stress that it takes a trained mental health professional to diagnose and treat mental illness. However, students should be aware of behaviors that indicate mental illness and should have thought of positive actions they can take.

Debate the Issue
Mental Health Treatment

Many insurance companies, especially HMOs, limit coverage for mental health services. For example, HMOs often will cover an older drug that is available in a generic form and is therefore inexpensive but will not cover a newer one that is more effective and has fewer side effects. Or a company will place a limit on the number of visits to a mental health professional it will cover. Have students debate this issue: Should insurance companies be able to deny coverage for mental health services? If so, how should these services be paid for?

Life SKILLS

Discuss the guidelines with students. If possible, ask a therapist to visit the class and discuss these issues of choice and treatment.

 Making a Choice 7B

Assign the Assessing Attitudes card. The card asks students to examine prevailing attitudes about counseling.

Section Review Worksheet 7.4

To reinforce the concepts presented in this section, assign Section Review Worksheet 7.4.

Section Quiz 7.4

Have students take Section Quiz 7.4.

Choosing a Therapist . . . .

At some time during your life, you or someone close to you will feel the need to seek professional counseling. In choosing a therapist, consider the following guidelines.

1. Check the background certification, experience, and credentials of the therapist. Does the therapist have a state license?

2. Find out how often you would see the therapist. Do you feel it is frequent enough to meet your needs?

3. Find out if the therapist has experience dealing with problems similar to yours.

4. Use an introductory session to determine whether you feel comfortable with the setting and how the therapist plans to work with you.

5. Look for signs that you are being treated with respect. Do you feel the therapist is concerned about your situation? Do you feel the therapist can be trusted with very personal information about your life? If you are not being treated in an appropriate manner, find another therapist. Do not ever feel you must continue with someone who makes you continually uncomfortable.

6. If during treatment you start to feel very uncomfortable, or if you do not feel you are making any progress, discuss the situation with your therapist. If you cannot resolve the issues, you should feel no obligation to continue with this therapist.

• • • TEACH continued

 Cooperative Learning
Community Mental Health Resources

Divide the class into small groups to gather information about mental health services. Supply a phone book to each group for locating local telephone numbers and addresses. You may also suggest that groups contact a national or state organization, such as the following, for free materials.

• National Mental Health Association, 1021 Prince St., Alexandria, VA 22314-2971 (703) 684-7722
• National Institute of Mental Health, 5600 Fishers Ln. 15C-105, Rockville, MD 20857 (301) 443-3673

Have groups compare lists to avoid duplication. Students within a group can divide their lists and call or write to various services and agencies to find out details of their operation—what is their principal role, what sorts of problems do they treat, what sorts of therapy do they offer, who is eligible, how expensive is therapy, what community outreach is available, how do they educate the public?

Class Discussion
Benefits of Group Therapy

Ask: **How might group therapy be beneficial to a person dealing with a specific crisis?** [It dispels the myth that one is alone with his or her problem; promotes social and communication skills; and provides sounding boards and support for trying out new behaviors.]

through difficulties so that he or she can return to normal activities and be more capable of dealing with challenges. Different therapies may be used.

Psychoanalysis Psychoanalysis is a form of therapy used to examine unresolved conflicts from the past. For example, Clancy earns extra money by doing odd jobs for people. But he tries to avoid anything that involves climbing over 5 ft. high on a ladder. He could make lots more money if he were not afraid of heights so he decided to undergo psychoanalysis. Clancy discovered during treatment that he had been stranded in a treehouse as a child when the ladder to the treehouse fell down. Although he had forgotten the incident, the fear he experienced made him terrified of heights. The psychoanalyst helped him discover the source of his fear, which may in turn help Clancy overcome his fear of heights.

The process of psychoanalysis was developed by Sigmund Freud. He believed that unresolved conflicts surface as problems later in life. The person examines experiences to improve awareness. The intent is that awareness helps the person understand and resolve the problems.

Behavioral Therapy Behavioral therapy focuses on the patient's behavior rather than on the underlying causes. The therapist helps the patient discover rewards for

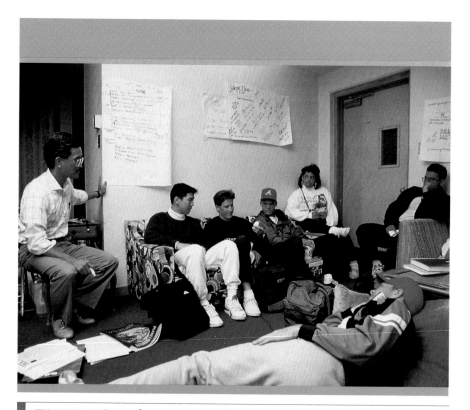

(FIGURE 7-12) **Group therapy can provide a supportive environment and a broader view for dealing with problems.**

SECTION 7.4

Reteaching Worksheet 7.4
Students who have difficulty with the material may complete Reteaching Worksheet 7.4.

Review Answers
1. Answers will vary but may include the following: the person might be depressed, feel that his or her life is out of control, be unable to concentrate and make decisions, have difficulty getting along with others, have intense fears, be unable to sleep, have emotional problems coping with illness, or be unable to stop destructive behaviors.
2. Answers will vary but should demonstrate a knowledge of what services are available in a community.

Teaching Transparency 7A
Mental and Emotional Health
Use this transparency to summarize the information in this chapter.

Extension
History of Treatment of Mentally Ill Patients

Until fairly recently in history, the mentally ill were treated as less than human. Have students research and report on ways different societies in different ages have treated the mentally ill. Some students may prefer to learn about the work of people who pioneered in mental health reform, such as Phillipe Pinel, Dorothea Lynde Dix, and Clifford Whittingham Beers.

Answers to Questions 1 and 2 are on p. 171.

3. Answers will vary but may include the following: What type of certification do you have? Do you have experience dealing with my type of problem? What degree do you hold? Do you have a state license? What are your fees? What are your hours? How often would I need to see you?

4. Behavior modification deals with an individual. It uses techniques that reward desirable behavior and ignore or punish undesirable behavior. Group therapy involves meeting with several people who have the same problem. The therapist and group members will often suggest solutions for other members' problems, as well as provide support.

5. Students might respond that they would seek the advice of a parent, teacher, coach, school counselor, school nurse, school social worker, or member of the clergy. Students may even call a hotline number for mental and emotional problems.

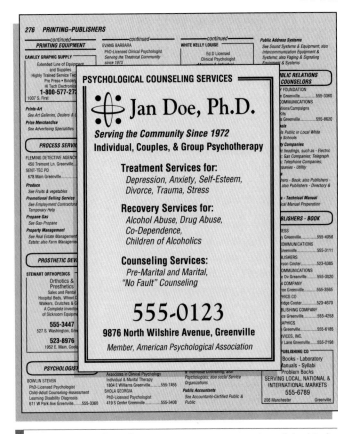

(FIGURE 7-13) **This advertisement is representative of the kind of mental health services provided by counselors.**

desirable behaviors and punishments for undesirable behaviors. This process is called behavior modification. Behavior modification programs help patients learn new ways to respond to situations, ways more effective than the ones they were using.

Group Therapy In group therapy, people with similar problems meet with a therapist to discuss their problems. Both the therapist and the group members suggest solutions, the idea being that the exchange of ideas and input from group members is more helpful than hearing only one perspective from a therapist.

Chemical Therapy Chemical therapy is the use of drugs to treat mental and emotional disorders. Drugs are prescribed to help control some symptoms of a disorder, such as aggressiveness, or to correct an imbalance of chemicals in the brain that can cause disorders like depression. It is important to note, though, that some drugs can have serious side effects. For example, an antidepressant may work very well in controlling depression in one patient while causing violent or suicidal behavior in someone else. This often is caused by a misdiagnosis or inappropriate use of a drug. As with any prescription medication, the use of chemical-therapy drugs should be closely monitored for serious side effects.

Review

1. How would you know if your best friend or someone in your family needed counseling?

2. List the places in your community where you could go if you were having an emotional problem. List one place you could go if you had an eating disorder. List two places you could go if there was a problem in your family that required counseling.

3. Make a list of four questions you would ask if you were choosing a therapist.

4. How does group therapy differ from behavior modification?

5. **Critical Thinking** If you were suffering from a mental or emotional problem, who would you go to for advice?

ASSESS

Section Review

Have students answer the Section Review questions.

Alternative Assessment
Giving Advice

Ask students to imagine they are advice columnists who have received a letter from a young girl. She is frightened by the way her mother has been acting lately and describes symptoms and behaviors indicative of manic-depressive disorder. Have each student write the girl's letter and a reply to it.

Closure
Qualifications of a Mental Health Specialist

With the class, compile a list of skills and personal qualities students think are important in a mental health professional. Write the ideas on the chalkboard. Students should be ready to explain why each characteristic they suggested is important.

Highlights

Summary

- According to the National Association for Mental Health, someone with good mental health feels comfortable with himself or herself, has good relationships with others, and meets the demands of life.

- It is important to express emotions in a positive way.

- Defense mechanisms provide a way to deal with problems and maintain self-esteem. Overuse of these mechanisms is not healthy.

- Maslow believed that all individuals can achieve self-actualization or a state of fulfillment if their basic physio-logical and psychological needs are met first.

- It is just as important to seek help for emotional problems as it is to seek help for physical problems.

- Most difficult times can be worked through without outside help. Sometimes, however, you may need to ask for help from friends, parents, or mental health specialists.

- Some therapies that certain specialists practice are psychoanalysis, behavioral therapy, group therapy, and chemical therapy.

Vocabulary

self-concept the current mental image you have of yourself.

self-ideal your mental image of what you would like to be.

organic disorders mental and emotional disorders resulting from a physical cause.

eating disorders compulsive eating behaviors caused by emotional problems and an obsession with body weight.

anxiety disorder a condition in which fear or anxiety prevents one from enjoying life and completing everyday tasks.

dissociative disorder a condition in which someone's personality changes to the point that the person believes that sometimes he or she is someone else.

mood disorder a condition in which one mood is experienced almost to the exclusion of other feelings.

personality disorder an emotional condition in which a person's patterns of behavior negatively affect that person's ability to get along with others.

somatoform disorder an emotional condition in which there are physical symptoms but no identifiable disease or injury. The physical symptoms are caused by psychological factors.

SUMMARY
Have students read the summary to reinforce the concepts they learned in Chapter 7.

VOCABULARY
Have students write a paragraph about mental and emotional health that uses a minimum of six of the chapter's vocabulary words correctly.

EXTENSION
Have students write true-false or multiple choice items for a mental illness awareness quiz. Go over these in class and have students select 10 items that they think would best educate the general public about mental illness. Suggest that students make posters that convey some of the items selected. Display the posters in the school or, if possible, in a public place such as the local library or community center.

CHAPTER REVIEW

Concept Review

1. has good relationships, meets the demands of life; Sample response: feels comfortable with himself or herself

2. Answers should include any four of the following: love—a strong feeling of affection for someone; happiness—feeling of joy or contentment; optimism—feeling that life experiences will be positive; humor—finding something funny in a situation; fear—feeling of danger; anger—strong feeling of irritation; guilt—feeling that you have done something wrong or are responsible for some mishap; depression—feelings of sadness and despair; jealousy—feeling of wanting something someone else has or of losing something you have; loneliness—feeling of isolation or alienation; or shyness—feeling of being timid or bashful.

3. As teens try to become independent they can sometimes alienate one another and feel lonely.

4. Feeling guilty can be a clue that you need to resolve a problem. Guilt may also drive you to do the right thing.

5. Defense mechanisms are often used to avoid facing an issue. If the issue is never resolved, it may become a bigger problem.

Concept Review . . . .

1. Which of the following characteristics define good mental health?
- fears new experiences
- has good relationships with others
- avoids responsibility
- has a negative attitude
- meets the demands of life

Add one characteristic of your own.

2. Identify and describe four emotions most people experience.

3. Why is loneliness a particular problem for teens?

4. In what way can guilt be a positive emotion?

5. Why should you avoid using defense mechanisms too frequently?

6. According to Maslow, when do people grow emotionally? What does reaching the top of the scale represent?

7. Name three possible causes of organic disorders. Are organic disorders more or less serious than other types of mental and emotional problems? Why?

8. Panic attacks and phobias are examples of what kind of disorder?

9. List three factors that are linked to developing depression.

10. Describe four treatments for mental disorders.

11. Why is behavior modification used in treating mental health disorders?

Expressing Your Views . . . .

1. Your text states that eating disorders are most often caused by pressure from peers or parents. Do you agree? Why or why not?

2. Martin decided to seek therapy for depression after his grandmother died. His friends have been very critical and told him that anyone who seeks counseling is weak. How should Martin respond to these people?

3. Every time Ruth fails at something she rationalizes her failure. Why do you think she does this? How could this behavior be harmful?

6. when they can satisfy their needs from the bottom to the top of the hierarchy; reaching one's potential

7. Genetic; response to life experiences; physical illness, injury, or chemical imbalance. Usually they are more serious because they involve the body as well as the mind.

8. anxiety disorders

9. Answers can include any three of the following: family history, major life stresses, physical illness, substance abuse, and gender.

10. Psychoanalysis is a form of therapy used to examine unresolved conflicts from the past. Behavioral therapy focuses on the patient's behavior rather than on the underlying causes of problems. Group therapy involves meetings of people with similar problems. Chemical therapy is the use of drugs to treat mental and emotional disorders.

11. Behavioral modification can help patients learn new, more effective ways to respond to situations.

Life Skills Check

1. Coping
You are angry because one of your friends borrowed your car and burned a hole in the seat. Now your friend refuses to help pay for the damage. How could you handle your anger in a positive way?

2. Using Community Resources
Your sister has been acting strangely for the past few months. You are worried about her and think she probably needs help. What advice would you give her? Where could she go for help?

3. Using Community Resources
Find out what 12-step programs are and make a list of those in your area. Include information on how these programs are connected to spiritual health.

Projects

1. Maslow thought Abraham Lincoln, Eleanor Roosevelt, and Thomas Jefferson were self-actualized people. Name someone you would add to Maslow's list and write a one-page essay describing your reasons for choosing this person.

2. Read *One Flew Over the Cuckoo's Nest* by Ken Kesey and note the mental disorders of the characters.

3. Work with a group to compile a list of activities in your school or community that promote good mental health. Suggest other activities that could be offered.

4. Why do you think some music is called the blues? Visit the library to find out the history of the blues. Prepare a brief report and presentation that includes some examples of blues music.

Plan for Action

The things people say about themselves often indicate how they feel about themselves. Write 10 statements about yourself in order to evaluate your self-concept, and devise a plan for improvement.

Expressing Your Views
Sample responses:
1. Yes. Functional disorders are not caused by any physical problems; therefore, they must be caused by the environment.
2. Martin should keep in mind that he is a stronger person for seeking help when he finds that he cannot cope with these feelings on his own.
3. Ruth is using rationalization to avoid facing an issue. This can be harmful because Ruth is not taking responsibility for her failure.

Life Skills Check
Sample responses:
1. I could do something physical to release my anger, such as exercise.
2. I would advise that she talk with a person she could trust, such as a teacher, a school counselor, our parents, or a religious leader.
3. Answers will vary, but lists should include the necessary information.

Projects
Have students complete the projects on mental health.

Plan for Action
After students write their statements, discuss what statements like these reveal about a person's self-concept. Remind the class that understanding one's self-concept can be a first step toward forming one's self-ideal. Reinforce the role of self-esteem in reaching this ideal.

ASSESSMENT OPTIONS

 Chapter Test
Have students take the Chapter 7 Test.

 Alternative Assessment
Have students do the Alternative Assessment activity for Chapter 7.

 Test Generator
The Test Generator contains additional assessment items for this chapter.

CHAPTER

8

Building Self-Esteem

SECTION	TITLE/OBJECTIVES	Personal Health Inventory	Journal	Check Up	Life Skills	Life Skills Worksheets	Media Message or Ethical Issues Worksheet	What Would You Do?
		PERSONAL INVENTORY			**LIFE SKILLS DEVELOPMENT**			
8.1 *pp. 177–181*	**THE IMPORTANCE OF SELF-ESTEEM** • Define self-esteem. • Describe how self-esteem develops. • Explain how media messages can affect one's self-esteem. ▪▪ Assess your own self-esteem.	Ch. 8	8A 8B		p. 180			
8.2 *pp. 182–186*	**HOW TO BUILD YOUR SELF-ESTEEM** • Name the best way to raise your self-esteem. • Name at least three other ways of raising your self-esteem. ▪▪ Make a plan to raise your own self-esteem.		8C 8D			8A 8B 8C 8D		

KEY: ▪▪ Denotes Life Skill Objective

Text references denoted by page number.

Supplement references denoted by chapter or item numbers.

LINKING RESOURCES

Making a Choice Cards	Parent Discussion Guide	Health Talk Audio Program	Teaching Transparencies and Directory	Section Review Worksheets	Section Quizzes	Reteaching Worksheets	Section Reviews
INTERACTION		**OTHER RESOURCES**		**SECTION REVIEW AND ASSESSMENT**			
8A	Ch. 8	Ch. 8		8.1	8.1	8.1	p. 179
8B			8A	8.2	8.2	8.2	p. 186

KEY FACTS

- Self-esteem is one's feeling of personal worth and acceptance. It impacts one's ability to sustain relationships and cope with life.

- Parents play a vital role in developing self-esteem in their children.

- The unrealistic standards the media presents can be a powerful negative influence on a person's self-esteem.

- It is possible, but not easy, for a person to increase his or her level of self-esteem.

- The most important part of raising self-esteem is accepting oneself.

- An important element of high self-esteem is appreciation of the worth of others and the ability to treat them with respect and compassion.

CHAPTER REVIEW AND ASSESSMENT

TEXT

Chapter Review pp. 188–189

SUPPLEMENTS

Chapter Test 8

Alternative Assessment 8

Test Generator Chapter 8

Using the Chapter Photograph

Ask students what they think the kids are doing and why they are doing it. Have students brainstorm for skills and qualities that they themselves have or would like to have. Encourage a wide variety of responses. Write the responses on the chalkboard. Discuss why people need to feel that they do something well or that they have admirable qualities.

Question Box

Have students write out any questions they have about self-esteem and how to acquire it and put them in the Question Box.

Sensitivity *ALERT*

The teenage years are a uniquely difficult time for building and maintaining self-esteem. Teens fear rejection by their peers because this is the group whose opinions matter most to them. The fear of rejection is even stronger in students with low self-esteem, who may not have close relationships with peers. Watch for feedback that may alert you to students who are more sensitive than most to rejection.

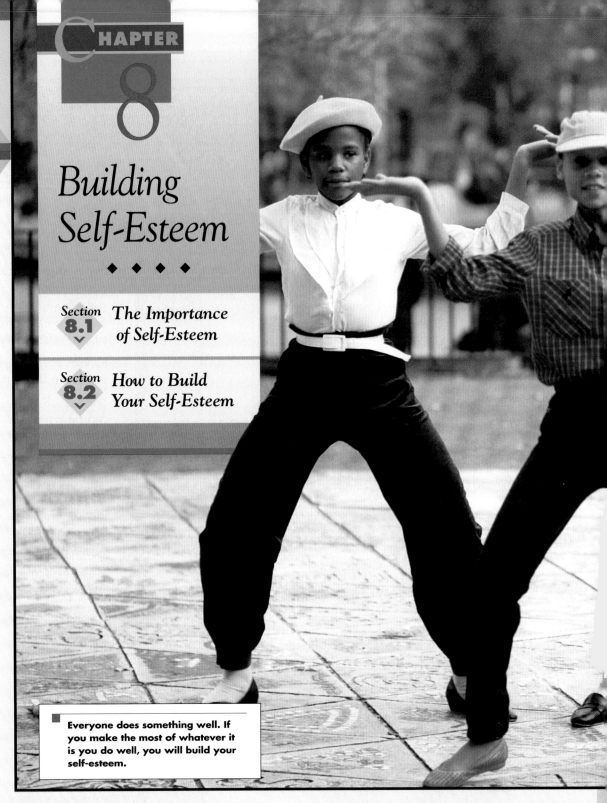

CHAPTER

8
Building Self-Esteem
◆ ◆ ◆ ◆

| Section 8.1 | The Importance of Self-Esteem |
| Section 8.2 | How to Build Your Self-Esteem |

Everyone does something well. If you make the most of whatever it is you do well, you will build your self-esteem.

MYTHS & MISCONCEPTIONS

- **Nobody likes to be around people who say good things about themselves.** People react most positively to individuals who recognize their own good qualities and show self-confidence without being egotistical.

- **Copying the mannerisms of someone in the "in crowd" causes you to lose your own personality.** The teenage years are an important time for both conformity and experimenting with self-expression.

Experimenting by copying the actions of someone you admire is normal. However, if you find it leads you to do things that go against your basic values, you need to reevaluate your behavior.

- **People who are good-looking always have a good self-image and high self-esteem.** People who don't feel good about their inner self tend to evaluate themselves unrealistically. An attractive person can be plagued by self-doubt and have an unrealistic, critical body image.

Lindsey feels ugly and unlikable. She compares herself with the models in the fashion magazines and wishes she could be as thin. When she looks in the mirror, she sees a chubby girl. Yet Lindsey is 5'3" tall and weighs only 105 lbs. She isn't really chubby at all. She constantly fantasizes about being popular, but feels that she doesn't have a chance. She is very shy and doesn't often talk to other students because she is afraid they won't like her.

Lindsey realizes that many people her age feel the way she does. However, she has made a silent promise to herself to find ways to feel better about herself and her life.

Section 8.1
The Importance of Self-Esteem

Objectives

- *Define self-esteem.*
- *Describe how self-esteem develops.*
- *Explain how media messages can affect one's self-esteem.*
- *Assess your own self-esteem.*
  - **LIFE SKILLS: Assessing Your Health**

Self-esteem is your pride in and acceptance of yourself. It is your sense of personal worth. When you feel worthwhile, you are able to make good decisions, experience acceptance from others, and give and receive love.

Lindsey has decided to improve her self-esteem. To do so, she must learn to respect herself, consider herself worthy, and avoid comparing herself with others.

Your self-esteem influences your relationships with your family, friends, teachers, and bosses. It affects how you do in school and at work. Low self-esteem can be very damaging, and has been linked to serious problems such as alcohol and drug abuse, eating disorders, suicide, and other self-destructive behaviors.

How Self-Esteem Develops

The development of self-esteem begins at birth. Early on, our feelings about ourselves tend to be a reflection of how we are treated by the people most important in our lives—usually our parents or guardians. We learn to see ourselves as we think they see us.

Most parents love their children and wouldn't knowingly do anything to damage their child's self-esteem. But parents are only human. Sometimes they don't say exactly what they mean. For example, a

self-esteem:

pride in and acceptance of yourself; sense of personal worth.

SECTION 8.1

 Personal Health Inventory
Have students complete the Personal Health Inventory for this chapter.

 English/Spanish CD Audio Program
Use the English/Spanish Health Talk audio program for students who need audio reinforcement of the concepts presented.

Parent Discussion Guide
Send home the Parent Letter for Chapter 8. As you progress through the chapter, send home the Parental Survey and The Extra Mile.

 Making a Choice 8A
Assign the Body Image card. The card asks students to examine changing cultural values with respect to body image.

Section 8.1 Lesson Plan

MOTIVATE

 Journal 8A
Lindsey's Decision

This may be done as a warm-up activity. Ask students to read about Lindsey's problem. Encourage them to write in their Journal their reactions to her feelings about herself.

Class Discussion
A Teenager's Self-Image

To start students thinking about how teenagers form perceptions of themselves, ask: **Why do you think Lindsey believes she is overweight? What might be some reasons she feels unlikable? Do you think her fears and concerns are grounded in a realistic view of herself? Why or why not?** [Student responses will vary. Try to elicit a wide variety of responses to explore.]

TEACH

Class Discussion
Feeling Good About Yourself

Have students personalize a definition of self-esteem by brainstorming for words that describe feelings associated with high self-esteem. (Students might suggest the following adjectives: confident, likable, valuable, content, capable, lovable, self-accepting, secure.) Next, have them do the same for

Background

Shaping Young Lives

Teacher expectations play a vital role in young students' success. One study of grade-school students and teachers involved an intelligence test. Teachers were told, following the test, which students ranked in the top 20 percent of the class. (Actually, the tests were not scored, and the names were picked at random.) Most of the students said to be at the top of the class had previously been considered average by the teachers. Nonetheless, teachers' attitudes toward these students now changed: they became more respectful and confident of the students' success; and their body language toward the students was more positive (smiling, eye contact, leaning toward student, nodding). In a follow-up, this 20 percent of the students tested significantly higher than other classmates on the IQ test. The superior performance was attributed solely to change in teacher attitude.

body image:
a person's perception of his or her appearance, level of fitness, and health.

parent might say, "I don't like you kids much when you're acting like this." The child may think the parent means, "I don't like you." It would be better if the parent said, "I get scared and nervous when you and your brother fight." That way, the parent makes it very clear that it is the behavior that is being criticized, not the worth of the child.

But most parents aren't psychologists. They may not even be aware that their words are so harsh. Most parents honestly want to support and encourage their children and help them feel loved, but they may not always succeed in communicating their support and love.

A more serious situation exists when parents neglect or abuse their children. Jonathan, for example, grew up without the care and attention he needed. He was a neglected child. His mom suffered from depression, and Jonathan remembers many

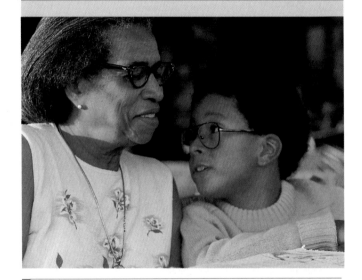

(FIGURE 8-1) **We make a decision about our own worth early in life based on how we think other people view us.**

days when she spent the entire day in bed. Jonathan's dad worked long hours, so he wasn't around much. It seemed that the only time his parents paid any attention to him was when he did something wrong. By the time he reached high school, Jonathan had very low self-esteem.

At some point during the first years of life, we make a decision about our own worth based on how we think others see us. The decision may not be a conscious one, but it is a decision nevertheless. After a while, it seems to be reality. We begin to look at our feelings and behaviors and think that's just the way we are.

Because self-esteem is based on a decision, it can be changed by making a new decision later in life. You, like Lindsey, can decide to raise your self-esteem.

Body Image, Media Messages, and Self-Esteem

Your **body image** is your perception of your appearance, level of fitness, and health. Sometimes it is difficult for teens to maintain a positive body image because so many natural physical changes are taking place during the teen years.

The fact that we are constantly exposed to media images that show "perfect" faces and bodies often negatively influences the way we see ourselves. This can lower self-esteem.

Teenage girls have an especially hard time because they sometimes feel that they must look unrealistically thin in order to be attractive. Lindsey looks at advertisements showing extremely thin women, and without realizing it, she accepts these women as a standard against which she must judge herself and her body. This gives her a negative body image.

••• TEACH continued
words associated with low self-esteem. *(Students might name the following descriptives: unwanted, dissatisfied, unassertive, weak, useless, inferior, withdrawn, frustrated.)*

Cooperative Learning
Guiding Children Without Criticism

Have students work in small groups to invent two or three situations in which

a parent must react to correct a child or keep the child safe from harm. For each situation, have the group write a command or comment that seems critical of the child and that might damage self-esteem. They should then write a second command that will correct the problem without undermining the child's feelings of worth.

Class Discussion
Society's Body Image

Have several magazines in which students can search for advertisements

projecting "desirable" body images. Allow students to react to them and to discuss their feelings about the standards society seems to set. Discuss issues such as what is meant by a perfect body, who decides what is perfect, and why anyone would want or need to be perfect.

Point out to students that many of the photographs they see in advertisements are computer-enhanced. Blemishes and shadows have been removed, color is added or changed, and body proportions are altered. If

(FIGURE 8-2) Standards of beauty change. In the 1950s, women with curves were considered attractive. A decade later, extremely thin women were fashionable. There is nothing wrong with any body type, but there *is* something wrong with media messages that encourage people to feel bad about their bodies.

The funny thing about advertising is that the ''perfect'' face and body change over time. Thin bodies for women are fashionable during one decade, and curvaceous bodies are stylish during another one. If you look at old advertisements, you see how ideals of beauty keep changing.

An important thing for Lindsey to remember is that there is nothing wrong with her body type. There *is* something wrong with an advertisement that makes her feel bad about herself. People of all body types can be attractive and accomplished—beauty and success often have more to do with confidence than with actual physical appearance.

Success comes in all kinds of ''packages.'' It comes to people of both sexes, of all ethnicities, and of all body types. Plain people, good-looking people, tall people, short people, and people with physical disabilities can all be successful. Lindsey could think of a well-known person in each of

these categories who has developed unique gifts and has become a star in his or her world.

Review

1. *Define self-esteem.*

2. *Describe how a person's self-esteem develops.*

3. *Explain how media messages can affect a person's self-esteem.*

4. **LIFE SKILLS: Assessing Your Health** *Describe what you have learned about your own self-esteem.*

5. *Critical Thinking* *How do you think poverty could contribute to low self-esteem?*

1. pride in, and acceptance of, oneself; a sense of personal worth

2. Self-esteem begins to develop at birth. People develop feelings about themselves based on how they are treated by important people in their lives, such as parents or guardians and other family members. Later, peers and teachers are important influences. Self-esteem is learned, and people come to see themselves as they *think* others see them.

3. By constantly showing "perfect" faces and bodies, the media presents an unrealistic standard against which many people judge themselves. This can lead to a negative body image and is damaging to a person's self-esteem.

4. Answers will vary depending on the students' individual evaluations of self-esteem.

5. Answers will vary. The students may answer that the inability to buy clothes and other material items that the media or peers deem necessary could lower a person's self-esteem.

students wonder how anyone could have such long, thin, well-shaped legs, the answer is probably that they don't without the computer's help.

Have students look at Figure 8-2, and ask: **What contradiction do you see in these two images of "beauty"?** [They represent different physical types, yet at different times each was considered beautiful.] **What danger do you see in letting media images dictate the kind of physical traits that are desirable?** [dissatisfaction with self because of an arbitrary, unreal standard; seeking to conform to

image by unhealthy dieting or even surgery; inability to accept self]

Cooperative Learning
Comparing Your Positives and Negatives

Suggest that students try this activity with family members who have read the Parent Letter on Building Self-Esteem or with a group of close friends. First, a student lists on a piece of paper what he or she sees as their best and worst physical features. Next, the group members write a positive comment about the student's physical

appearance. The student then compares his or her list with the comments. This comparison often reveals a positive feature the individual has but has never noticed.

Demonstration
Communicating Self-Image Through Body Language

Demonstrate for the class various postures, gestures, poses, and styles of movement that communicate positive

Section Review Worksheet 8.1

To reinforce the concepts presented in this section, assign Section Review Worksheet 8.1.

Section Quiz 8.1

Have students take Section Quiz 8.1.

Reteaching Worksheet 8.1

Students who have difficulty with the material may complete Reteaching Worksheet 8.1.

LifeSKILLS: Assessing Your Health

Self-Esteem Scale

On a separate sheet of paper, write the letter that most accurately describes how you feel:

1. I feel that I'm a person of worth, at least equal to others.
a. Strongly agree
b. Agree
c. Disagree
d. Strongly disagree

2. I feel that I have a number of good qualities.
a. Strongly agree
b. Agree
c. Disagree
d. Strongly disagree

3. All in all, I am inclined to feel that I am a failure.
a. Strongly agree
b. Agree
c. Disagree
d. Strongly disagree

4. I am able to do things as well as most other people.
a. Strongly agree
b. Agree
c. Disagree
d. Strongly disagree

5. I feel I do not have much to be proud of.
a. Strongly agree
b. Agree
c. Disagree
d. Strongly disagree

6. I take a positive attitude toward myself.
a. Strongly agree
b. Agree
c. Disagree
d. Strongly disagree

• • • TEACH continued

self-image and acceptance of others (erect but relaxed posture, energetic walk, firm handshake, sitting forward with hands open and maintaining eye contact, and so on). Contrast these with body language that communicates lack of confidence and rejection of others (slouching, scuffing floor with each step, averting eyes, stiffness, sitting back with arms and legs crossed, and so on).

Case History
Body Image and Self-Esteem

Have students revisit the stories of Jim Abbott, Sharon Hedrick, and Dennis Oehler on page 43. Suggest that these athletes are subject to the same bombardment of media messages that we all receive. How do students suppose the athletes avoided being discouraged by their situations? Interested students could locate articles about the experiences of one of the athletes and prepare a brief report for the class.

Journal 8B
Self-Esteem Scale

Have students write in their Journal their reaction to the self-esteem score they tallied.

Extension
Beauty of the Past

Have students locate and prepare copies of ideals of physical attractiveness for both men and women in an earlier time, such as the 1920s or the 1800s. Then have students work

7. On the whole, I am satisfied with myself.

a. Strongly agree

b. Agree

c. Disagree

d. Strongly disagree

8. I wish I could have more respect for myself.

a. Strongly agree

b. Agree

c. Disagree

d. Strongly disagree

9. I feel useless at times.

a. Strongly agree

b. Agree

c. Disagree

d. Strongly disagree

10. At times I think I am no good at all.

a. Strongly agree

b. Agree

c. Disagree

d. Strongly disagree

Scoring. To score the scale and derive a measure of your self-esteem, follow these instructions.

The positive responses for the questions are as follows:

question 1: (a) or (b)

question 2: (a) or (b)

question 3: (c) or (d)

question 4: (a) or (b)

question 5: (c) or (d)

question 6: (a) or (b)

question 7: (a) or (b)

question 8: (c) or (d)

question 9: (c) or (d)

question 10: (c) or (d)

For each positive answer that you chose, give yourself one point. The range of scores on this self-esteem scale is 0–10. The higher the score, the better your self-esteem.

together to prepare a time-line display showing how viewpoints have changed through the years.

ASSESS

Section Review

Have students answer the Section Review questions.

Alternative Assessment
Self-Esteem Indicators

Have students make sketches of two people, one with high self-esteem and one with low self-esteem. The sketches should show expression, posture, and other self-esteem indicators.

Closure
Letter to Yourself

Have students write a letter to themselves explaining why the teenage years are the most difficult in which to maintain high self-esteem and making suggestions for ways to avoid feeling unlovable or worthless.

Section
8.2 *How to Build Your Self-Esteem*

Background
Tips for Building Self-Esteem

Here are some ways of nurturing self-esteem in youth.

1. Give plenty of praise.
2. Praise effort, not just accomplishment.
3. Help the young person set realistic goals.
4. Avoid comparing the young person's efforts with others'.
5. Take responsibility for your own negative feelings. (Use "I" messages rather than blaming.)
6. Give real responsibility.
7. Show you care.

Objectives

- *Name the best way to raise your self-esteem.*
- *Name at least three other ways of raising your self-esteem.*
- *Make a plan to improve your own self-esteem.*

■■ **LIFE SKILLS: Building Self-Esteem**

As you read earlier, self-esteem is a decision we make about our worth as individuals. During childhood, our level of self-esteem is established based on how we see ourselves in relation to the adults around us and on the way we feel about ourselves as a result.

If you have low self-esteem, you can make a new, more accurate, and more positive decision about yourself. You can acknowledge the influence of your past, but resolve to move on. Your self-esteem is now your responsibility. It isn't easy to raise low self-esteem, but it can be done. By deciding to take responsibility for yourself and your own self-esteem, you can make big changes in the way you see yourself. You will be delighted when you discover how much more fun and rewarding your life can be when you feel good about yourself.

Accept Yourself

Learning to accept yourself is the best way to raise your self-esteem. This means learning to appreciate yourself and believing in your worth as a unique and special person.

How can you learn to accept yourself? First, realistically assess your strengths and weaknesses. Don't be modest. No one needs to know what you think your strengths are except you.

Second, try not to judge yourself by unrealistic standards. Don't, for example, compare your looks to those of the actors or actresses you see on television shows and in the movies. When you catch yourself thinking this way, stop and remind yourself of your uniqueness and special talents.

■ (FIGURE 8-3) **Accepting yourself just as you are is the most important part of raising your self-esteem. Although you aren't perfect, you are a unique and valuable person.**

Section 8.2 Lesson Plan

MOTIVATE

 Journal 8C
Expectations of Yourself

This may be done as a warm-up activity. Most teenagers feel dissatisfied with themselves to some degree, often because of unreasonable expectations they place on themselves. Encourage students to write in their Journal,

completing this statement: "I would feel really good about myself if I ____ ." Then ask them to discuss whether their expectation is reasonable.

TEACH

Reinforcement
Fighting Low Self-Esteem

Taking responsibility for how they view themselves may be hard for students with low self-esteem and intense feel-

ings of helplessness and hopelessness. Stress that the effects of past events in their lives need to be acknowledged but that these events do not have to control the future. Discussion of elements over which people do have control may be helpful to such students.

Class Discussion
Learning to Accept Yourself

Have students discuss which of the steps in learning to accept oneself would be most difficult for them. Then ask: **What phrases or statements can**

Third, decide that you are okay as you are, even though there are probably things about yourself you would like to change. Remember that even though you aren't perfect, you are a unique and valuable person. No one else has exactly the same gifts to offer the world. There isn't a single person anywhere who is perfect, and it certainly isn't necessary for *you* to be perfect.

Finally, only expend energy on changing things you have control over. You can't change your height or your body type, for instance, so don't spend time worrying about it. But you can work on developing new skills or interests, which would probably increase your self-esteem.

The more you accept and like yourself, the more others will accept and like you. If you project to others that you like yourself, they will be less likely to judge you or to pressure you to conform to their ideals. And even if they do, you will be less likely to cave in to their pressure.

Use Positive Self-Talk

We are constantly talking to ourselves—not necessarily out loud, but internally. Often this talk is negative. ''I'm such an idiot,'' you might say to yourself. ''Why did I do such a stupid thing?'' Talking negatively like this can damage your self-esteem over time.

When you use **positive self-talk**, on the other hand, you can raise your self-esteem. Positive self-talk is talking to yourself in a positive way about your characteristics and abilities. An example of positive self-talk might be: ''I did a great job on this project. I'm really good at this.''

When Lindsey feels nervous and uncomfortable around other students, she usually thinks, ''They think I'm no fun,'' or ''Why can't I ever think of anything interesting to say?'' Because she feels this way

and talks to herself this way, Lindsey often appears to be awkward and shy.

Suppose that Lindsey decided to use positive self-talk instead. She might say to herself, ''Sometimes I'm shy, but I can also be pretty funny, and people usually enjoy my company.'' If she continues to talk to herself this way and begins to believe what she says, Lindsey will be more likely to converse with other students. As she sees others respond to her more positively, Lindsey's confidence will grow. She will become more comfortable with other people, and her self-esteem will improve.

Be Good at Something

Everyone has something he or she does well. Make the most of whatever it is *you* do well. It might be playing guitar, making up dance steps, working with computers, playing basketball, telling stories, writing essays, making people laugh, being a good friend—the possibilities are endless. Even if it's something as seemingly trivial as being good at bicycle stunts, you'll develop more confidence in yourself if you cultivate your natural ability. Being very good at one thing will also make it easier for you to try new things. If you *know* that you're good at bicycle stunts, you probably won't feel as bad if you find out that you aren't very good at playing basketball.

Use ''I'' Statements

If you take responsibility for your feelings and words by using ''I'' statements, you will build self-esteem. People with low self-esteem are often afraid to do this because they fear criticism.

For instance, when Lindsey says, ''It is really hard to make friends,'' she is making a generalization that may not be true for other people. By beginning her statement with the impersonal pronoun ''it,'' she is

SECTION 8.2

Background
Cognitive Therapists
Cognitive therapists are trained to help people learn the skill of positive self-talk. They teach clients to talk to themselves in order to change the way they think about things and to affirm that their feelings are okay. They also help clients break problems down into manageable parts and work on one aspect at a time to avoid seeing the problem as a catastrophe and as something that cannot be overcome.

 Life Skills Worksheet 8A
Assign the Wise Self-Disclosure Life Skills Worksheet.

Life Skills Worksheet 8B
Assign the Finding Support Groups Life Skills Worksheet.

Life Skills Worksheet 8C
Assign the Choosing Supportive Relationships Life Skills Worksheet.

positive self-talk:

talking to yourself in a positive way about your characteristics and abilities.

you think of that might help you carry out these positive steps? [*Possibilities include: "I'm good at ____," "Nobody's perfect," "You can't believe everything on TV," "I'm as good as anybody else," and "I'm trying to change the things I can about myself. The things I can't change, I accept."*] Suggest that students write several such statements on 3×5 in. cards and post them in their rooms or lockers, where they will see them often.

Role Playing
Practicing Positive Self-Talk

Positive self-talk is a habit that can be learned. Assign pairs of students to role-play the positive, optimistic side of a hypothetical personality and the negative, pessimistic side. Have each actor pretend to be one of the sides and respond to various situations with suitable statements. Be sure students switch roles so that both experience positive self-talk.

A possible example follows.
Situation: *Joining a group at lunch*
Negative: What am I doing? They don't want me with them! I'll probably say something stupid and they won't like me.

Positive: They look friendly, and there's space at their table. This is a great opportunity to find out about their interests. I'll bet we have a lot of things in common.

**Life Skills
Worksheet 8D**

Assign the Evaluating
Behaviors Life Skills
Worksheet.

**Making a
Choice 8B**

Assign the Self-Image
Crutches card. The card
asks students to examine
the use of material items,
such as a car, as crutches
for self-esteem.

15 Ways to Boost Your Self-Esteem FIGURE 8-4

1. *Make a list of your good qualities and keep it with you at all times. Place extra copies on your mirror, in your school desk, or other places you will see it. Read over the list on a regular basis and at any time when you experience negative thoughts.*

2. *Avoid wasting time thinking about your negatives.*

3. *Seek new challenges in your life. Don't be afraid to try new things. Mastering a new task or ability can build self-esteem.*

4. *Avoid putting yourself down to others or to yourself. Accept compliments with a "thank you" and a smile.*

5. *Find something that you do very well and work to improve that skill.*

6. *Reward yourself when you accomplish a task or finish a project.*

7. *Accept the fact that neither you nor anyone else is perfect. Avoid dwelling on mistakes; laugh them off and continue with the positive.*

8. *Take a moment to look at yourself in the mirror each day and give yourself a verbal compliment.*

9. *Keep yourself well groomed, maintain a positive attitude, and develop a sense of humor to handle the difficult situations.*

10. *Join at least one activity that involves other people. Volunteer for service with an organization or group in your school or community.*

11. *Associate with other positive thinkers in your school and community. Create your own support group of friends who are a positive influence on you and your self-esteem.*

12. *Don't fight a fact; deal with it. Try to avoid thinking that people and things in your life that are out of your control should be different. They aren't, and that is the reality.*

13. *Accept that life does not have to be perfect for you to be happy. Happiness is a way of thinking; a content feeling, not constant euphoria.*

14. *Remember that sometimes bad things happen that are not within your control. Expect this and try not to let it set you back too much. Do the best you can to change what you can, and avoid dwelling on what you cannot change.*

15. *Remind yourself that each of us is important and valuable. Try to be the best "you" you can be. Remember, you're the best one for the job.*

• • • TEACH continued

Reinforcement
Mirror Talking

Suggest the following exercise for students to try at home in front of a mirror. Tell them the exercise may sound silly and may be hard to do at first, but that it really is effective if continued long enough. It amounts to reprogramming the way one looks at oneself. The exercise consists of looking at yourself in the mirror and saying aloud, "I really am a great person."

When this routine becomes comfortable, students should add a positive statement about themselves, such as, "I like the way I look today" or "I did a great job on my English project." Then suggest choosing a statement that calls attention to an attribute they have trouble accepting.

Teaching Transparency 8A
*15 Ways to Boost Your
Self-Esteem*

Use this transparency of Figure 8-4 to discuss with students the various ways they can help build their self-esteem.

(FIGURE 8-5) **A support group is a group of people who trust each other and can talk openly with each other. Having a support group can help you build your self-esteem.**

Section Review Worksheet 8.2

To reinforce the concepts presented in this section assign Section Review Worksheet 8.2.

Section Quiz 8.2

Have students take Section Quiz 8.2.

Reteaching Worksheet 8.2

Students who have difficulty with the material may complete Reteaching Worksheet 8.2.

not taking responsibility for her feelings. She could use an "I" statement instead: "I sometimes have trouble making friends." She is then talking about *her* feelings only.

When Lindsey said to her brother Scott, "You made me feel terrible when you told me that Sonya is smarter that I am," she was transferring responsibility for her own feelings to Scott. This is not an "I" statement—she is saying that *Scott* is responsible for *her* feelings. To take responsibility for her own feelings, Lindsey could say, "I felt hurt when you said that Sonya is smarter than I am."

Although it is easier to speak in generalities, it is important to clearly state how you feel.

Develop a Support Group

Few things can be as helpful in maintaining or enhancing your level of self-esteem as knowing people with whom you can share your joys and sorrows—a **support group.** A support group is composed of people in your life whom you trust and with whom you are able to talk openly.

Your support group can consist of friends you trust or family members who care for you. Members of your support group will not exert pressure on you. Instead, they help you to feel good about yourself.

Take a moment to write down the names of five people whom you would like in your support group. In the future, make an effort to spend more time with these people.

Self-disclosure—telling another person meaningful information about yourself—plays a central role in the development of positive self-esteem. When you share your true thoughts and feelings about yourself, you will learn how you are perceived by others through their responses. This process helps you see yourself more accurately. It can help a lot to learn that others often have the same doubts and fears that you do. You can also learn to better appreciate similarities and differences—the diversity among people—by sharing your feelings.

Self-disclosure is usually a gradual process between people. It's important to establish a relationship based on trust and mutual respect before you disclose personal details of your life.

self-disclosure:

telling another person meaningful information about yourself.

support group:

people in your life whom you trust and with whom you are able to talk openly.

Journal 8D
Personal Skills

Have students write in their Journal about one or more things they do well. Encourage them to explain how they acquired this skill (natural ability, practice, competition) and how it makes them feel about themselves.

Cooperative Learning
How You Can Boost Your Self-Esteem

Have students work in small groups to decide which five suggestions in Figure 8-4 seem most useful and then rank them. Have groups compare their rankings and explain their choices.

Demonstration
Taking Responsibility

Invite the school guidance counselor to give examples of general complaints that avoid responsibility or misplace blame. He or she can show how such comments can be recast as "I" statements that put the speaker in a position of responsibility.

Class Discussion
Identifying Support Groups

Ask students to name groups of people that they or someone their age might associate with. Write the group names on the chalkboard. Ask: **Among these groups, which ones are the most important? Which groups give people a sense of belonging? Which groups make a person feel good about himself or herself? Which groups can you trust?**

Review Answers

Resist Peer Pressure

Individuals who have low self-esteem usually do not have much confidence in their opinions or their decisions. Consequently, they are overly influenced by peers and by peer pressure.

Learning to trust yourself and your values builds confidence. The more you make your own decisions based on what you—not others—believe, the more confidence you will gain. This does not mean that you should ignore the advice or ideas of parents, friends, teachers, or others. It means that you should listen to your inner voice and make decisions based on what it is telling you.

When you make your own decisions, you and you alone are responsible for the outcome of those decisions. Have you ever seen people labor over a decision because their "gut feelings" were different from the advice they received from others?

> **❝**I'm trying to make my own decisions now and not do things just because my friends are doing them.**❞**
>
> Beatriz

You will notice that they tend to feel miserable afterward if they followed others' advice, only to find that their own path would have been the better one to take.

Act With Integrity

Once you appreciate your own worth, you can better appreciate the worth of other people. People with high self-esteem do not act as if they are only looking out for themselves. On the contrary, they treat others with respect and compassion. They act in ways that will help other people maintain high self-esteem.

It's easy to take advantage of those with low self-esteem by manipulating them or bullying them into doing what you want. But as a person of integrity, it is your responsibility to refrain from doing so.

When you act with integrity and responsibility toward others, you will feel good about yourself, and that will improve your self-esteem even more.

R eview

1. Describe the best way to raise your self-esteem.

2. Name at least three other ways to build your self-esteem.

3. ▓▓ **LIFE SKILLS: Building Self-Esteem** What steps will you take to improve your own self-esteem?

4. **Critical Thinking** Explain why people with high self-esteem do not have to put down other people in order to feel good about themselves.

Highlights

Summary

- Self-esteem is the confidence and satisfaction you have in yourself. It is influenced by the people and events of your early years.

- During childhood, we make decisions about our own worth based on how we think others see us. As we grow older, we become better equipped to make these decisions ourselves.

- Media messages can lower one's self-esteem by presenting unrealistic standards by which we judge ourselves. This can negatively influence our self-esteem because we look or act differently from actors or models.

- Learning to accept yourself is the best way to raise your self-esteem.

- By developing your natural abilities, you will develop more confidence in yourself. Being good at one thing will make it easier for you to take positive risks and develop new skills.

- You can build self-esteem if you take responsibility for your feelings by using "I" statements. It is important to state clearly what you mean rather than to speak in generalities.

- Trusting and sharing with a support group can help a person enhance or maintain self-esteem.

- You can improve your self-esteem by trying not to judge yourself by unrealistic standards, by deciding that you are okay as you are, and by trying to change only the things about yourself that are within your control.

- Talking in a positive way to yourself about yourself, and believing it, can improve your confidence and self-esteem.

Vocabulary

self-esteem pride in and acceptance of yourself; sense of personal worth.

body image a person's perception of his or her appearance, level of fitness, and health.

positive self-talk talking to yourself in a positive way about your characteristics and abilities.

support group a group of people in your life whom you trust and with whom you are able to talk openly.

self-disclosure telling another person meaningful information about yourself.

SUMMARY
Have students read the summary to reinforce the concepts learned in Chapter 8.

VOCABULARY
Divide the class into small groups and give each group one of the vocabulary words. Have the groups develop definitions for their terms and create dramatic ways to illustrate the concepts.

EXTENSION
Encourage students to make a "Who Am I?" file or book. In it they can keep a history of achievements, with photographs, summaries, etc. They may also devote a section to defining their positive qualities and things they enjoy doing. This can be expanded as they gain self-knowledge. Suggest that students complete their file or book with a list of positive changes they are making to nourish their feeling of self-worth.

CHAPTER REVIEW

Concept Review

1. self-esteem
2. body image
3. media
4. responsibility
5. strengths, weaknesses
6. positive self-talk
7. responsibility
8. support group
9. self-disclosure
10. peer pressure
11. integrity

Expressing Your Views

Sample responses:

1. If you do not have high self-esteem, you won't be able to have confidence in yourself, feel worthwhile, make good decisions, experience acceptance, or give and receive love. All of these factors negatively affect your relationships with family and friends and how you do in school and at work. Low self-esteem has been linked to self-destructive behaviors, such as alcohol and other drug abuse, eating disorders, and suicide.

2. Sylvia needs to accept herself. She needs to use her energy to change the things she can and accept those things she cannot change. She needs to talk to herself in a positive way and take responsibility for her feelings by using "I" statements.

3. Jeremy needs to trust himself and his values. He needs to listen to his

Concept Review . . . .

1. The degree to which a person likes or feels good about himself or herself is _____ .

2. Your _____ is your perception of your appearance, level of fitness, and health.

3. Messages from the _____ often cause us to have a low self-esteem by telling us we must look a certain way to be attractive.

4. By deciding to take _____ for yourself and your own self-esteem, you can make changes in the way you view yourself.

5. You can learn to feel good about yourself by accepting your _____ and _____ .

6. _____ is talking in a positive way to yourself about yourself.

7. Communication improves when you take _____ for your feelings and words by being specific and using "I" statements.

8. Friends or family members with whom you can speak openly are a _____ .

9. You can learn how you are perceived by others by how they respond to you, and you can see yourself more accurately, through _____ .

10. People with low self-esteem want to follow the crowd and often allow themselves to be influenced by _____ .

11. When you act with _____ and treat other people with respect and compassion, you will feel good about yourself.

Expressing Your Views . . . .

1. Some psychologists think that an individual's self-esteem is the most important influence on mental well-being. Why do you think self-esteem is so important?

2. Sylvia hates school because she feels as though she has no friends. She feels shy around other students because she thinks they're all more attractive than she is. What can Sylvia do to boost her self-esteem?

3. Sunday night, Jeremy sneaked out of the house after midnight to ride around and drink beer with his friends. Jeremy didn't really want to go, but he was afraid his friends would think he wasn't "cool." After he got home, Jeremy realized he had been doing a lot of things lately that he didn't really want to do. He decided that from now on he would resist this kind of peer pressure. What could Jeremy do to change?

inner voice and make decisions based on what it is telling him.

Life Skills Check

1. Answers will vary according to individual strengths and weaknesses.

2. Answers will vary but should indicate that Lee's behavior suggests that he does not feel good about himself and that he needs to take steps to improve his self-esteem, for only then will he be able to form satisfying friendships.

Life Skills Check . . . . . .

1. Assessing Your Health

You want to be able to accept yourself for what you are, but first you need to evaluate your self-esteem. As realistically as possible, make a personal inventory by listing as many strengths and weaknesses as you can about yourself. If your list of weaknesses is longer than your list of strengths, judge each weakness and decide whether you could view it in a more positive way. List ways you could improve your weaknesses and build on your strengths.

2. Building Self-Esteem

Lee appears to care only for his own feelings and becomes very defensive and upset if anyone criticizes his actions. You don't really consider yourself a close friend of his, but today he told you that he doesn't think anyone likes him much, and that he feels as if he doesn't have one true friend. How would you respond to this statement?

Projects . . . .

1. An essential part of building self-esteem is trying new things. When you volunteer in your community, it gives you a chance to develop your skills while helping other people, and this combination can be very gratifying. Call a local soup kitchen, nursing home, or homeless shelter to find out about ways that you can get involved. You will probably be regarded as a very important addition to the organization.

2. Work with a group to create and produce a skit involving characters with healthy self-esteem and with poor self-esteem. Show how both personalities deal with problems. Then have the audience decide which qualities of healthy self-esteem are missing or are present.

Plan for Action . . . .

An individual's self-esteem has a great impact on his or her mental health. Create a plan to raise your own self-esteem.

Projects

Have students plan and carry out the projects for building self-esteem.

Plan for Action

One way students could approach their plan is by identifying a few situations or activities that made them feel good or bad about themselves. Have students list one action they could take each week that would place them in an affirming situation, and one thing they will try to avoid. They also may find it helpful to partner their actions with a friend who has similar goals.

ASSESSMENT OPTIONS

Chapter Test
Have students take the Chapter 8 Test.

Alternative Assessment
Have students do the Alternative Assessment activity for Chapter 8.

Test Generator
The Test Generator contains additional assessment items for this chapter.

CHAPTER 9

Managing Stress

Section	Title/Objectives	Personal Inventory		Life Skills Development				
		Personal Health Inventory	Journal	Check Up	Life Skills	Life Skills Worksheets	Media Message or Ethical Issues Worksheet	What Would You Do?
9.1 *pp. 191–196*	**WHAT IS STRESS?** • Define stress. • Describe the stress response. • Name at least four stress-related disorders.	Ch. 9	9A 9B					
9.2 *pp. 197–205*	**HOW TO MANAGE STRESS** • Define stress intervention. • Explain why physical exercise is a good way to handle stress. ▦ Use selective awareness to change your interpretation of a stressor. ▦ Practice a relaxation technique that helps you to deal with stress.		9C 9D	p. 204	p. 201	9A 9B		
9.3 *pp. 206–208*	**MANAGING STRESS IS A LIFELONG PROCESS** • Explain how a support group helps a person deal with stress. ▦ Manage your time by setting goals and prioritizing. ▦ Know how to seek help if you or someone you know is overwhelmed by stress.		9E 9F		p. 207	9C 9D		

KEY: ▦ Denotes Life Skill Objective
Text references denoted by page number.
Supplement references denoted by chapter or item numbers.

LINKING RESOURCES

	INTERACTION	OTHER RESOURCES			SECTION REVIEW AND ASSESSMENT			
	Making a Choice Cards	Parent Discussion Guide	Health Talk Audio Program	Teaching Transparencies and Directory	Section Review Worksheets	Section Quizzes	Reteaching Worksheets	Section Reviews
	9A	Ch. 9	Ch. 9		9.1	9.1	9.1	p. 195
	9B			9A	9.2	9.2	9.2	p. 205
					9.3	9.3	9.3	p. 208

For additional information about the stress response, see page 678 in the Body Systems Handbook.

KEY FACTS

- Stress is a natural response that is experienced by everyone.
- Stress occurs when a situation (stressor) causes a stress response.
- Stressors can be positive or negative.
- The stress response is the body's physical reaction to a stressor.
- Prolonged stress can cause illness.
- Stress intervention techniques can be used to successfully manage stress.
- Everyone needs a support system of friends, family, teachers, or clergy to talk to if they feel troubled.
- Some stressors, especially those related to abuse, cannot be managed alone. If a person feels overwhelmed by such stressors, professional help is available.

CHAPTER REVIEW AND ASSESSMENT

TEXT
Chapter Review pp. 210–211

SUPPLEMENTS
Chapter Test 9

Alternative Assessment 9

Test Generator Chapter 9

GETTING STARTED

Using the Chapter Photograph

Ask students if taking exams is stressful for them. Does feeling stressed-out affect how well they do on tests? What could they do before the exam to help relieve the stress? Tell students that this chapter suggests some ways to recognize stress and to deal with it.

 Question Box

Have students write out any questions they have about stress and put them in the Question Box.

Sensitivity *ALERT*

Some of your students may have experienced— or may now be enduring—major stressors, such as a recent death in the family, divorce of parents, serious illness or accident, abuse, pregnancy, or suicidal thoughts. The practical advice in this chapter can especially benefit them. Always be alert to discomfort levels in students and provide opportunities for them to ask anonymous questions.

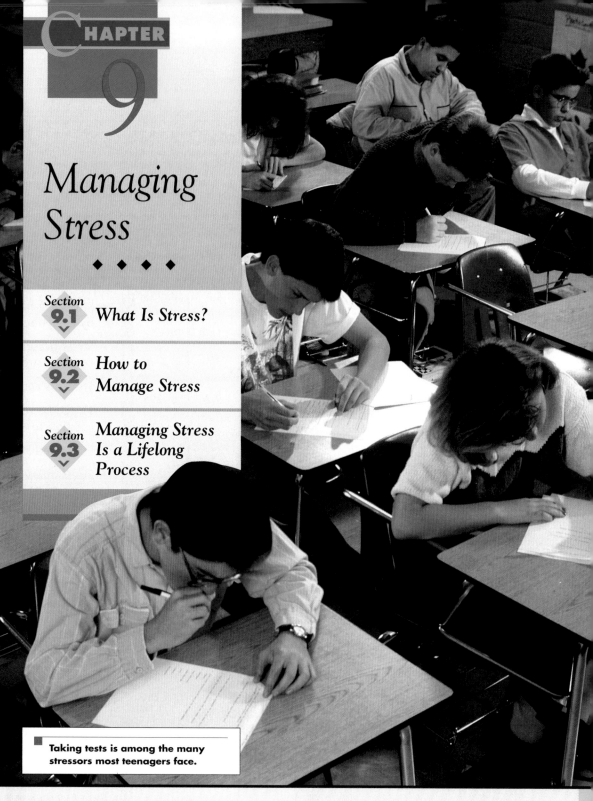

CHAPTER 9

Managing Stress

◆ ◆ ◆ ◆

Section 9.1 What Is Stress?

Section 9.2 How to Manage Stress

Section 9.3 Managing Stress Is a Lifelong Process

Taking tests is among the many stressors most teenagers face.

MYTHS & MISCONCEPTIONS

- **All stress is bad.** A reasonable amount of stress actually helps people to be more alert, perform better, and accomplish more. A completely stress-free life would probably be boring.

- **Needing help with stress management indicates a personal weakness.** Anyone, even the strongest of individuals, can become overwhelmed when under extreme stress. Seeking help is a positive action that indicates an understanding of one's own personal needs.

- **Other people don't feel as stressed and worried about making mistakes as I do.** Self-doubt and fear affect everyone at some time in their life. Many athletes and performers experience these feelings on a regular basis, but they have learned how to manage them.

Raquel had no idea how she was going to do it—the idea of getting up in front of her English class and giving a speech terrified her. What if she went totally blank and forgot everything she was going to say? Or what if she said something really stupid? What if everyone started laughing at her? What if . . . ? Just thinking about all the "what if's" made Raquel's heart start to pound and her hands start to sweat.

She could pretend to be sick and stay home the day she was supposed to give her speech, but she knew she would have to give it anyway when she went back to school. There wasn't any way out of it, and it was making Raquel a nervous wreck. In fact, she was so stressed-out about it that she couldn't even concentrate on *writing* the speech.

Section
9.1

What Is Stress?

Objectives

- *Define stress.*
- *Describe the stress response.*
- *Name at least four stress-related disorders.*

If you, like Raquel, have had physical reactions to a change in your life situation, you have experienced stress. It is perfectly natural to experience stress. All of us do. The key is learning how to manage stress so that it doesn't make you miserable or sick. In this chapter you'll find out about some techniques that can help you cope with the stress in your life.

Before you can cope with stress, you have to know how it develops. First, a situation arises that is new or potentially unpleasant. This situation is called a **stressor**.

In Raquel's case, the stressor was the speech that she had to give in her English class. Raquel felt anxious, her heart raced, and her hands started sweating when she thought about the speech. What she was experiencing was a **stress response**, the body's reaction to a stressor.

It is important to remember that stressors only have the *potential* to cause a stress response. For some people, giving a speech would not cause a stress response. It's only when a stressor does cause a stress response that stress results. Therefore, **stress** is the combination of the presence of a stressor and the occurrence of a stress response.

Stressors

Stressors can occur in almost every area of life. You may feel stress at home if your parents or guardians are not getting along with each other or if they are getting a divorce. It can also be stressful if one of your

stress response:

the body's reaction to a stressor.

stress:

the combination of a stressor and a stress response.

stressor:

any new or potentially unpleasant situation.

SECTION 9.1

Personal Health Inventory

Have students complete the Personal Health Inventory for this chapter.

English/Spanish CD Audio Program

Use the English/Spanish Health Talk audio program for students who need audio reinforcement of the concepts presented.

Parent Discussion Guide

Send home the Parent Letter for Chapter 9. As you progress through the chapter, send home the Parental Survey and The Extra Mile.

Section 9.1 Lesson Plan

MOTIVATE

Journal 9A
A Past Stressful Situation

This may be done as a warm-up activity. In their Journal, have students write down at least one stressful situation they have experienced. Have them note the stress response they felt and what they did to relieve it.

Cooperative Learning
Raquel's Situation

Have students form groups to discuss Raquel's situation. Ask: **What could Raquel do to relieve the stress?** *[Ask someone to help her prepare and practice the speech, breathe slowly and deeply, sit or lie down, and consciously relax.]* Students should also discuss how they have handled similar stressful situations.

Background

Five Stressor Categories

Psychologists identify five general stressor categories: biological (illness and problems one is born with); environmental (crowding, noise, poverty, disasters); thinking activities (exams, mental challenges); personal behavior (smoking, drinking alcohol, taking drugs, poor nutrition, poor sleep, little exercise); and life situations (death, relationships, personal events).

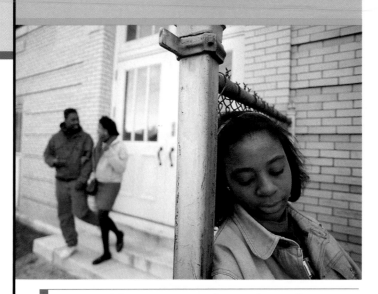

(FIGURE 9-1) **Stressors can come in many forms. If you are having trouble becoming part of a social group, you may experience stress as a result.**

parents remarries and you must move in with your new stepmother or stepfather. If you argue with your brother or sister, you might feel stress as a result.

At school, you may experience stress when you try out for a sport or the school play or if you have trouble becoming part of a certain social group. You may feel stress if you don't have the money to buy the clothes you want for a school dance or if other students pick on you.

Many stressors are connected to our self-concept, which is how we think of ourselves. We fear that we will look foolish in front of other people whose opinions we care about. That is why Raquel experienced stress when she had to give a speech. She was worried about other people's opinions, which could affect her opinion of herself. If you have these kinds of self-doubts and fears, be comforted in knowing that you are not alone. People of all ages and all occupations want others to think well of them, and this is just as stressful for them as it is for you.

A stressor can be something as simple as trying to get paper clips untangled, getting stuck at a red light when you're in a hurry, or getting a busy signal when you really need to talk with someone. If you let them, these kinds of "daily hassles" can add up and cause a tremendous amount of stress.

Even *positive* situations can be stressors. Getting married is a perfect example. It is a happy occasion, but because it involves a change in one's life situation, it can be just as stressful as a negative event. Making the all-star basketball team is another example of a positive life-changing event that can cause stress.

Having some stressors is perfectly normal and healthy. They motivate us to confront challenges and accomplish things. The ideal balance is to be able to deal with stressors effectively so we don't become ill from too much stress.

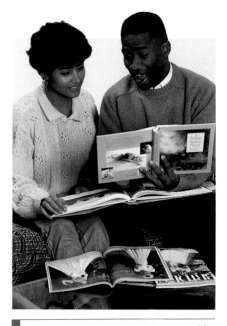

(FIGURE 9-2) **Even a positive event like getting married can be stressful because it involves a change in one's life situation.**

TEACH

Class Discussion
Life Science Analogy

Stress affects all living things. Ask students to consider these analogies: **If you moved a fern from shady, damp woods into a sunny, dry yard, how would the move stress the plant?** *[Moving the plant changes its environment, including temperature and wet-* ness. The plant will experience stress. It will not grow as it did in the woods, and it might die.] **How is this like a family moving from one place to another?** *[Moving changes a family's environment, creating stress due to the change of social contacts, work, schools, climate, and so on.]* **If a pet is often hit or yelled at, what might its stress responses be?** *[It might become depressed, lose its appetite, hide, try to run away, or become aggressive and* bite.] **How is this like a person's response to similar stress?** *[Essentially it is the same.]*

 Journal 9B
Life Changes

Have students read the caption for Figure 9-3. Then, in their Journal, ask them to write about any situations listed in the figure that they have experienced in the past 12 months and total their life-change units.

Life Changes of Teenagers

Life Event	Life-Change Units	Life Event	Life-Change Units
Getting married	101	Beginning to date	51
Being pregnant and unmarried	92	Being suspended from school	50
Experiencing the death of a parent	87	Having a newborn brother or sister	50
Acquiring a visible deformity	81	Having more arguments with parents	47
Going through a parent's divorce	77	Having an outstanding personal achievement	46
Becoming an unmarried father	77	Seeing an increase in the number of arguments between parents	46
Becoming involved with drugs or alcohol	76	Having a parent lose his or her job	46
Having a parent go to jail for a year or more	75	Experiencing a change in parents' financial status	45
Going through parents' separation	69	Being accepted at the college of your choice	43
Experiencing the death of a brother or sister	68	Being a senior in high school	47
Experiencing a change in acceptance by peers	67	Experiencing the serious illness of a brother or sister	41
Having an unmarried pregnant teenage sister	64	Experiencing increased absence from home of mother or father owing to change in occupation	38
Discovering you are an adopted child	64	Experiencing the departure from home of a brother or sister	37
Having a parent remarry	63	Experiencing the death of a grandparent	36
Experiencing the death of a close friend	62	Having a third adult added to the family	34
Having a visible congenital deformity	62	Becoming a full-fledged member of a religion	31
Having a serious illness requiring hospitalization	58	Seeing a decrease in the number of arguments between parents	27
Moving to a new school district	56	Having fewer arguments with parents	26
Failing a grade in school	56	Having a mother who begins to work outside the home	26
Not making an extracurricular activity	55		
Experiencing the serious illness of a parent	55		
Breaking up with a boyfriend or girlfriend	53		
Having a parent go to jail for 30 or fewer days	53		

(FIGURE 9-3) **Major changes in our lives can cause stress, even if they are positive events. To get an idea of how much your life has changed in the past year, add up the life-change units for the changes you experienced during the last 12 months. If your total score is less than 150, your life has changed little. If it is between 150 and 300, you have experienced moderate change. And if your score is over 300, your life has changed significantly.**

Role-Playing
That Stressful Feeling

Elicit from the class some common stressful situations, and write each one on the board. As a class, pick one or two of the situations to role-play. Develop a cast list and assign students to each role. Role-play the scenario two or three times using different casts. Afterward, have students discuss the stressors and the stress responses they experienced, including those that resulted from acting in the scene.

• • • TEACH continues on p. 194

Background
Stress and the Immune System

The connection between stress and illness is widely recognized. Dr. Hans Selye calls stress the "rate of wear and tear within the body." One study revealed that highly stressed air-traffic controllers had about five times the incidence of high blood pressure found in the general population. Allergists report that stress both initiates and worsens allergic attacks. (For more information about stress and the immune system, see the Body Systems Handbook, p. 681.)

Making a Choice 9A

Assign the Stress in Your Life card. The card asks students to discuss things they find stressful in their life and to draw a cartoon showing the humorous side of a stressful situation.

WHAT IS STRESS? **193**

Background

Other Responses to Stress

Other responses related to stress include nervous behavior (nail-biting, finger-drumming), smoking, increased use of alcohol and medications, eating too little or too much, sleeping too little or too much, careless driving and being accident-prone, and being absent-minded.

Section Review Worksheet 9.1

To reinforce the concepts presented in this section, assign Section Review Worksheet 9.1.

Section Quiz 9.1

Have students take Section Quiz 9.1.

The Stress Response

The stress response occurs because of the relationship between your brain and the rest of your body. Your brain recognizes a stressor and evaluates it. If your brain decides that the stressor isn't anything to worry about, nothing happens to your body. But if the stressor is seen as a threat, your brain tells your body to produce certain chemicals that contribute to the stress response. During a stress response, the physical changes shown in Figure 9-4 occur.

Why does the brain tell the rest of the body to respond this way? It doesn't seem as though the stress response would help us at all. It certainly didn't help Raquel prepare for her speech. When could the stress response possibly be helpful to us?

Well, imagine that you are walking down the street and a huge dog suddenly leaps at you from behind a garbage truck, snarling, teeth bared, and ready to bite you. What do you do? Do you try to defend yourself against the dog, or do you run away as fast as you can? Whichever you do—fight the dog or run away—will require you to act immediately and with great physical effort.

The stress response makes it possible for you to protect yourself. Your body produces the hormone called adrenaline, which gives you the rush of extra energy you need. Your breathing speeds up, which helps get more oxygen throughout your body. Your heart beats faster, which increases the flow of blood to your muscles. And your muscles tense up, which prepares you to move quickly.

At the same time these changes are occurring, other changes are also taking place throughout your body. Because all

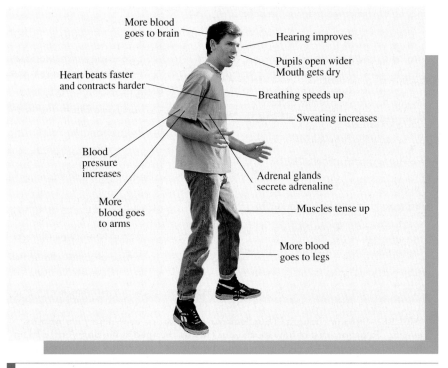

(FIGURE 9-4) **The physical changes of the stress response prepare the body to run away or stay and fight.**

• • • TEACH continued

Reinforcement

Physical and Nonphysical Threats

Students may wonder why our bodies respond identically to physical and nonphysical threats. Explain that humans evolved in a harsh environment, in constant physical threat from the natural elements and from animals and other humans. As a result, our stress response evolved as a survival mechanism. In today's environment, the old physical dangers to which our bodies are adapted are rare. Instead, our society provides nonphysical, emotional threats. Unfortunately, our environment has changed too fast for us to evolve new responses to nonphysical threats. Thus, when we feel threatened, our minds and bodies respond in the only way they know how—the physical stress response.

Class Discussion

Stress-Related Disorders

Invite students to talk about their own experiences with stress-related disorders and their observations of other people who have them. Ask if anyone in class has experienced getting a cold, tension headaches, or other disorders at a stressful time.

(FIGURE 9-5) **Giving a speech can cause the same stress response as being attacked by an animal.**

Reteaching Worksheet 9.1
Students who have difficulty with the material may complete Reteaching Worksheet 9.1.

Review Answers

1. Stress is a combination of the presence of a stressor and the occurrence of a stress response.

2. Answers will vary. Sample response: In addition to a general feeling of anxiety, the following physical changes occur: breathing speeds up, increasing the amount of oxygen throughout the body; the heart beats faster, increasing the blood flow to the muscles; and muscles tense up, preparing for quick movement. Also, sweating increases, hearing is improved, and the pupils open wider. Some functions slow down or stop. For example, less saliva is produced, so the mouth becomes dry, and digestion is altered, causing diarrhea or constipation.

your physical resources are mobilized to help you respond to danger, other body functions may take a back seat. The digestive system, for example, may begin to function strangely, causing diarrhea or constipation. Less saliva is produced, because it is a low priority to your body during times of physical danger. As a result, your mouth becomes dry.

The stress response is sometimes called the ''fight-or-flight'' response because it prepares you to either ''fight'' or ''take flight.'' It prepares you to do something *physical*. So when you are physically threatened and need to respond physically, the stress response is helpful to you.

However, your body also responds the same way to a *nonphysical* threat. For example, giving a speech can cause the same stress response as being attacked by an animal. But giving a speech, unlike defending yourself against an animal attack, does not require you to release stress in any physical way. The stress that is not released can make you physically ill.

Stress Can Make You Sick

It is estimated that from 60 to 80 percent of all physical and mental disorders are related to stress. Not all of these disorders, however, are *caused* by stress. Many of them are simply made worse by stress.

Asthma is a good example of a disorder than can be aggravated by stress. Let's say that you wheeze and you can't catch your breath when you are around cats. In this case, having trouble breathing is a completely physical reaction. It has nothing to do with stress.

Now imagine that you are under a lot of stress. Studies have shown that when you are under stress, especially long-term stress, your immune system suffers. Your asthmatic reaction to a cat may be much worse than it would normally be.

Some of the other diseases and disorders that are suspected of being related to stress include the following:

Extension
Clinic Visit

Suggest that students visit a mental health clinic to obtain pamphlets on dealing with stress. Display these in the classroom.

Answers to Questions 1 and 2 are on p. 195.

3. Answers may include colds and flu, tension headaches, backache, coronary heart disease, high blood pressure, chronic fatigue, mental illness, and possibly cancer.

4. Sample response: A stress-management program can help employees learn how to deal with and manage stress. As employees learn how to manage stress, they will experience less illness and therefore will be able to spend more days on the job and take fewer sick days.

- **Colds and Flu** Stress can weaken your immune system, the system of your body that defends against infection. As a result, a person under prolonged stress is more likely to become infected with cold and flu viruses. That person may also require more time than others to recover from these illnesses.

> **❝**I used to get a lot of headaches. Now that I'm doing relaxation exercises every day, they don't bother me as much.**❞**
>
> —— Sam

- **Tension Headaches** Stress causes the muscles in your neck and head to tense up, which can cause headaches.
- **Backache** Frequent tension in the muscles of the back can lead to backaches.
- **TMJ Syndrome** The joint that connects your upper jaw to your lower jaw is called the temporomandibular joint (TMJ). If stress causes a person to clench or grind the teeth, then pain in the joint, headaches, and dental problems can result.
- **Coronary Heart Disease** Some studies show that prolonged stress may cause changes in your body that may lead to a heart attack. One of these changes is an increased amount of cholesterol in the bloodstream.

  Cholesterol is a fatlike substance that can clog the arteries that supply blood to the heart. If a blockage of blood to the heart occurs, a heart attack may result.

- **High Blood Pressure** Part of the stress response is an increase in blood pressure. High blood pressure results when blood pushes harder than necessary against the inside of the blood vessels. It can eventually lead to the rupture of a blood vessel in the brain. This is called a stroke. A stroke can result in loss of speech and bodily movement, and even in death.
- **Chronic Fatigue** Prolonged stress can cause a person to feel tired all the time. This type of fatigue is different from the feeling one gets after strenuous physical exercise. Chronic fatigue is a *long-term* loss of energy.
- **Depression** Prolonged stress can wear a person down to the point of "burnout" or exhaustion. Depression can occur as a result of an advanced stage of burnout.

  There is even some evidence that people under prolonged stress may be more likely than others to develop cancer.

  Stress can also lead to injuries. When you are under stress, you aren't able to concentrate very well, which could increase your chances of having an accident.

Review

1. Define stress.

2. Describe the stress response.

3. Name at least four disorders that are caused by stress or made worse by stress.

4. **Critical Thinking** Many businesses offer stress-management programs to their employees. How could a stress-management program increase a company's profits?

ASSESS

Section Review

Have students answer the Section Review questions.

Alternative Assessment
Present Level of Stress

Have students write a paragraph describing their current level of stress. Do they have any of the signs of a stress response; if so, can they say why? If they are feeling no stress, is this a typical condition for them, or do they expect it to change soon? Are they taking any specific steps to keep their stress level low?

Closure
Upcoming Stressful Situations

Ask students to list and describe one or more stressful situations they expect to face during the next 12 months. Stressful situations might include a prom, a playoff game, a driving test, moving, breaking up with a girlfriend or boyfriend, or a serious illness in the family. Have students save their list for the next Closure.

Section 9.2

How to Manage Stress

Objectives

- Define stress intervention.
- Explain why physical exercise is a good way to handle stress.
- Use selective awareness to change your interpretation of a stressor.
  ■■ LIFE SKILLS: Coping
- Practice a relaxation technique that helps you to deal with stress.
  ■■ LIFE SKILLS: Coping

In this section you'll learn how to manage stressors as they come up on a daily basis by using the stress model shown below. Notice that the stress model consists of a series of steps, each step leading to the next. It is possible for you to take action to *stop* yourself from progressing from one step to the next.

The Stress Model

Step 1: A New or Potentially Unpleasant Situation (The Stressor) A situation which may trigger stress occurs.

Step 2: You Interpret the Situation as Threatening You interpret the situation as threatening, which leads to Step 3.

Step 3: Your Emotional Response You feel anxious, nervous, or insecure, which leads to the physical response in Step 4.

Step 4: Your Physical Response You experience the physical response, which leads to the negative consequences of Step 5.

Step 5: The Negative Consequences If nothing is done to relieve the stress, any number of consequences can result. Schoolwork may suffer, for example, as can a person's relationships with family and friends. A serious illness can also result from untreated long-term stress.

Signs of Stress

Physical Signs	Emotional and Mental Signs
Headaches	Anxiety
Dry mouth	Frustration
Teeth grinding	Mood swings
Shortness of breath	Depression
Pounding heart	Irritability
Indigestion	Nightmares
Diarrhea	Nervous laugh
Constipation	Worrying
Muscle aches	Confusion
Weight change	Forgetfulness
Fatigue	Poor concentration
Insomnia	Loneliness

(FIGURE 9-6) **This table shows some of the signs of stress. How many of these signs do you recognize in yourself? If you have more than a few, be sure to practice the stress interventions discussed in this chapter.**

Making a Choice 9B

Assign the Stress Intervention Role-Play card. The card asks students to describe a stressful situation, apply the stress model to the situation, identify stress interventions for the situation, and role-play the situation with and without the stress intervention. The class will discuss whether or not the stress interventions seemed successful.

Section 9.2 Lesson Plan

MOTIVATE

Journal 9C
Signs of Stress

This may be done as a warm-up activity. Ask students to study the signs of stress in Figure 9-6. In their Journal, have them write any of the signs that they experience when stressed. Tell them to annotate their list to show how often they experience each stress sign: D = daily, W = weekly, O = occasionally.

Class Discussion
A Personal Touch

Tell the students that studies rank your job as a teacher as very stressful. Then volunteer some examples of tasks or situations that a teacher deals with that are stressful. Indicate what the stressors are, such as overscheduling, difficult students, teaching concerns, and so on.

Life Skills
Worksheet 9A

Assign the Creating a Relaxation Corner Life Skills Worksheet.

The following examples will help you understand how the stress model works in a real-life situation.

Stress Sequence	Examples
Step 1. A New or Potentially Unpleasant Situation (The Stressor)	*Someone you are attracted to asks you to go to a movie with him or her.*
Step 2. You Interpret the Situation as Threatening	*You interpret this situation as threatening because you want to make a good impression and be able to go out with this person again. What if you say something dumb? What if this person doesn't think you are any fun?*
Step 3. Your Emotional Response	*During the movie, you start feeling nervous, doubtful, worried, and anxious.*
Step 4. Your Physical Response	*By the time the movie is over, you are sweating like crazy and your heart is racing in your chest.*
Step 5. The Negative Consequences	*You seem very nervous and you can't even talk about the movie later because you were too upset to pay much attention to it. The other person senses your unease and doesn't want to go out with you again.*

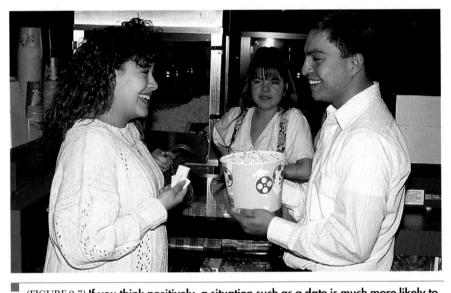

(FIGURE 9-7) **If you think positively, a situation such as a date is much more likely to turn out well. You can prevent a lot of stress by changing your interpretation of events and having realistic expectations.**

TEACH

Teaching Transparency 9A
The Stress Road

Use this transparency of Figure 9-8 to introduce the stress model. The model presents the five stages of stress as towns along a highway. Keep the transparency displayed throughout this section for reference in teaching and for use by students.

Game
The Stress Model

Have students form groups and play the Stress Model game to help them learn the five steps. Make sure the teaching transparency for the stress model is displayed for students' reference. Randomly choose students to name a step of the stress model and to give an example of the step. The examples of physical signs of stress do not have to be the same as those shown in Figure 9-6. A sample game involving five students is as follows: Step 1, a new

or potentially unpleasant situation occurs, for example, a student fails an exam; Step 2, you interpret the situation as threatening or nonthreatening, for example, threatening; Step 3, your emotional response, for example, fear and anxiety; Step 4, your physical response, for example, stomachache; and Step 5, the negative consequences, for example; parents are angry and the student is grounded until his or her grade in the subject improves. Repeat the cycle until every student has had at least two turns.

This scenario can be much different. Imagine that you have the same life situation (being asked out), but this time you decide that you're going to *interpret* the situation positively. "I must be a really fun person," you think. "I must be desirable." Because you think of the situation this way, you won't feel nearly as nervous or insecure, and none of the negative things that happened in the first scenario will occur. You have stopped yourself from progressing from one step to the next.

Think of the stress model as a map of a road that goes through the towns of "A New

or Potentially Unpleasant Situation," "You Interpret the Situation as Threatening," "Your Emotional Response," "Your Physical Response," and "The Negative Consequences." As with all roads, you can set up a roadblock anywhere along the way. Stress management is setting up roadblocks that prevent you from traveling to the next "town." The roadblocks you set up are stress interventions. A **stress intervention** is any action that prevents a stressor from resulting in negative consequences.

The following stress interventions, or roadblocks, are helpful in managing stress.

stress intervention:

any action that prevents a stressor from resulting in negative consequences.

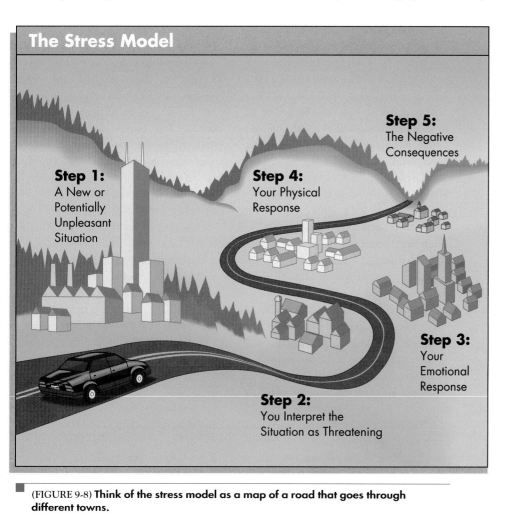

The Stress Model

Step 1: A New or Potentially Unpleasant Situation

Step 2: You Interpret the Situation as Threatening

Step 3: Your Emotional Response

Step 4: Your Physical Response

Step 5: The Negative Consequences

(FIGURE 9-8) **Think of the stress model as a map of a road that goes through different towns.**

Cooperative Learning
Stress Situations

Have students work in groups of four to write a stress situation, using the stress model. Tell them to write the five stress model steps down the left side of a sheet, and write what happens in each step on the right side. Have each group work with another group to critique and improve each other's situations.

Journal 9D
Dealing With Stressors

Ask students to create a three-column chart in their Journal. Explain that they are to list in the first column everyday situations that cause them stress. After they have read Eliminating Some Stressors on page 200, they should use the second column to explain in a phrase or two how they can eliminate the stress. After reading Changing Your

Interpretation of a Stressor, have students write in the third column what positive aspect they can focus on through selective awareness.

Class Discussion
Choosing an Intervention

Ask students to select some stressors from the chart they created in their Journal and write the stressors on plain paper. Collect the papers and place

Life Skills Worksheet 9B

Assign the How Do You Communicate? Life Skills Worksheet.

selective awareness:

focusing on the aspects of a situation that help a person feel better ("thinking positively").

Eliminating Some Stressors

If you were to list the situations that cause you stress, you would probably realize that you have a lot of stressors that occur regularly. If you are able to anticipate a common stressor, you may be able to find a way to remove it from your life. By getting rid of some of your stressors, you are setting up a stress intervention in front of Step 1 of the stress model.

For instance, if it is very difficult for you to wake up in the morning and this causes you to be late to school or work, you could go to sleep earlier at night. Or you could have someone you live with make sure you wake up on time. Either way, you would stop the progress of stress by eliminating one of your stressors.

If someone at your school is rude to you, you could eliminate or reduce that stressor by avoiding that person. If it isn't possible to avoid that person altogether, you could make sure that you are with a friend whenever you have to associate with that person.

The point to remember is that you have some control over the number of stressors in your life. One of the best ways to manage stress is to reduce the number of stressors in the first place. Which of _your_ stressors can you eliminate?

Changing Your Interpretation of a Stressor

The way you interpret events in your life is often more important than what the events actually are. Some people let themselves be distressed and bothered about insignificant things. Others seem never to be disturbed. Two people can have the same stressor, and one will experience a stress response while the other will not. To a great extent, each person determines how he or she reacts to situations and people. It's impossible to get rid of all the stressors in your life—getting the flu right before the school ski trip isn't something that you can control.

But you can try to look at your unfortunate situation in a positive light—in other words, you can change the way you interpret a stressor. When you change your interpretation of a stressor, you are setting up a roadblock in front of Step 2 of the stress model. To do this, you can use what is called **selective awareness,** or choosing to focus on the aspects of a situation that help you feel better. Selective awareness can be thought of as thinking positively.

If you can't go on the ski trip, you can at least try to find something positive in your situation. If might mean that you will get to spend time with your brother who will be on break from college during the week of

• • • TEACH continued

them in a box. Then draw the papers randomly from the box, and read the stressor. Have the class suggest and discuss the best intervention for that stressor: elimination, selective awareness, relaxation, or exercise.

• • • TEACH continues on p. 202

the trip. You hardly ever get to see him anymore, and this will be a good chance for the two of you to catch up.

A college student named Tatyana gave her father a good lesson in selective awareness. She wrote him from college that she had fallen out of her dormitory window, cracked her skull, and had been taken to the hospital. She wrote that while she was in the hospital, she fell in love with a man who was on parole from prison for physically abusing his first wife. Tatyana told her father that she and this man were planning to run away to get married.

At the end of the letter, however, she told him that she really hadn't fallen out of a window, hadn't been in the hospital, and hadn't met anyone with whom she had fallen in love. "But," she wrote, "I *did* fail chemistry, and I wanted you to put that in its proper perspective." Tatyana's father was not very upset about her failing chemistry

Life SKILLS

Ask volunteers to list five stressors and write a positive aspect of each.

Life SKILLS: Coping

Using Selective Awareness . . . .

Though you can eliminate some stressors from your life, you cannot get rid of all of them. You can, however, use selective awareness to make your stressors less disturbing. Selective awareness is choosing to focus on the aspects of a situation that make you feel better. For example, if your stressor is having to make a speech in one of your classes, you could choose to focus on the positive aspect of the situation—having a chance to present your ideas to others.

Make a list of five stressors in your life and then write the positive aspects of each one. It may also be helpful to take time just before you go to sleep each night to recall all the *good* things about the day. Pat yourself on the back for what you accomplished and the problems you handled successfully.

Background
Relaxation Techniques

Relaxation techniques work best when done regularly. The key is to set aside the same time daily, in a comfortable and quiet place—no radio, TV, talking, or disturbing noises. It's also important to have the cooperation of those around you, to assure encouragement and uninterrupted time.

because he focused on the fact that something much worse could have happened. Now *that* is using selective awareness!

The Life Skills activity on page 201 should help you to focus on the positive aspects of your stressors rather than on the negative aspects.

Using Relaxation Techniques

What if you're past the point of changing your interpretation of a situation? What if you are well on your way to becoming upset? One way to relieve your distress is to engage in some method of relaxation. When you do this, you are setting up a stress intervention in front of Step 3.

Different people relax in different ways. Some people like to listen to music. Others find that reading a book, watching television, or playing computer games helps them to relax. These activities have one thing in common: they take a person's mind off problems and hassles by focusing attention on another activity. Anything you do that changes the focus of your mind for a while can be relaxing.

Here are some other relaxation techniques that have been shown to be effective in helping people relax.

Meditation Meditation involves focusing on something that is repetitive or unchang-

ing. You can meditate by doing this simple, yet effective, exercise.
1. Sit down and close your eyes.
2. In your mind, repeat a word you find relaxing—maybe "calm," or "serene," or "one"—every time you breathe out.

After doing this meditation exercise for about 20 minutes, you will probably feel relaxed and energetic.

Progressive Relaxation Some people prefer to be more active while relaxing. Progressive relaxation can meet this need. Here is how you do progressive relaxation.
1. First, tense the muscles in one part of your body. You might tense the muscles in your shoulders, for example. Notice how it feels to have those muscles *tensed*.
2. Then relax the same part of your body that you just tensed. Notice how it feels to have those muscles *relaxed*.
3. Now go from one muscle group to another throughout your body, tensing and relaxing. Many people find that this technique works best when you start at the top of the body and work down to your feet.

This is called progressive relaxation because you "progress" from one part of your body to another. Progressive relaxation is a good technique to use any time you feel tense. It is also a good technique to practice daily, so that when you find yourself in a stressful situation, you can quickly relax the muscles in your body.

Body Scanning Even when you feel tense, there is always some part of your body that feels relaxed. Your shoulders may ache, for example, but your thighs may feel warm and relaxed. When you do body scanning, you search throughout your body for that one relaxed part, and when you find it, imagine the warm, relaxed feeling being transferred to the rest of your body.

• • • TEACH continued

Demonstration
Practicing Relaxation Techniques

Have students form small groups to practice some of the relaxation methods described in the text—meditation, progressive relaxation, body scanning, and imagery.

Class Discussion
Laughter Relieves Stress

Tell a joke in class or show cartoons from a book. Then discuss laughter as a method for reducing stress.

Extension
Stressful Occupations

Have students choose a profession or job they find interesting. Ask them to speculate about three stressors a

person in this profession might experience daily. Then have them suggest a stress-intervention strategy the person could use on the job.

Autogenic Training You can relax by imagining that your arms and legs feel heavy, warm, and tingly. When they feel this way, it means that you have let go of muscle tension and dilated the blood vessels in your arms and legs. Once your body is relaxed, think of peaceful images—perhaps a relaxing day at the beach or walking under the stars. Sitting quietly and thinking of certain images can help both your mind and body relax. Although you need to determine for yourself what images are relaxing to you, many people find the following images to be restful:

- the beach
- a park
- green pastures
- blue skies
- a starry night
- a meadow of flowers
- sunshine on your body
- a warm bath
- floating on water

SECTION 9.2

Section Review Worksheet 9.2
To reinforce the concepts presented in this section, assign Section Review Worksheet 9.2.

Section Quiz 9.2
Have students take Section Quiz 9.2.

Reteaching Worksheet 9.2
Students who have difficulty with the material may complete Reteaching Worksheet 9.2.

(FIGURE 9-9) **Thinking of peaceful scenes is one effective relaxation technique. Sit quietly and think of images you find restful.**

Check Up

Check Up

Have students read the Check Up silently and answer the questions to themselves. Then ask for a show of hands on each question. Tell students to ask themselves the same questions at various times during the day. Suggest that they use their observations to determine if there are certain times during the day when they are especially tense.

Background

Using Physical Exercise

Occasional exercise does little good; for general health benefits and stress management, exercise should be done daily. Warm-up exercises that stretch the body are very helpful. Good exercise activities include bicycling, swimming, aerobics, jogging, walking, racquetball, and tennis.

How Tense Are You?

As you begin to read this, *freeze*. Don't move a bit. Now notice how your body is positioned.

1. Can you drop your shoulders? If you can, your shoulder muscles were unnecessarily tense.

2. Can you relax your forehead more? If you can, you were tensing the muscles in your forehead for no useful purpose.

3. Can you relax the muscles in your arms more? If you can, you were unnecessarily tensing them.

4. Check the muscles in your abdomen and legs. Are they contracted more than necessary?

Unnecessary muscle contraction is called bracing. Most of us don't even notice that we are bracing because it has become such a natural response to stressful lives. As a result of bracing, many people develop tension headaches, back trouble, or shoulder pain. Some of the relaxation techniques in this section will help you stop bracing.

Laughing Laughing is one of the easiest and most natural relaxation techniques known. You don't have to be taught how to laugh. Many people find that when they are under a lot of stress, it helps to watch a funny movie or television program or read a humorous book. Some studies have shown that laughing may even strengthen the immune system, and a stronger immune system is better able to fight off infections.

Laughing only works as a relaxation tool when you really think something is funny. Laughing because you feel nervous or embarrassed won't help you reduce stress.

Yelling or Crying Sometimes you just have to go off somewhere private and yell or cry. After a good yell or cry, a person can feel much more relaxed and able to deal with a stressor.

(FIGURE 9-10) **You already know one of the best relaxation techniques available—laughing. Some studies have shown that laughing not only relaxes you but may also strengthen your immune system.**

(FIGURE 9-11) **The stress response is harmful to you only if you don't do something physical. When you feel stressed, do a vigorous exercise such as walking at a brisk pace.**

4 of the model by taking advantage of the body's readiness to do something physical.

Let's say you just had an argument with a friend and you are extremely angry. You can feel muscle tension in your shoulders, and your heart is beating rapidly. If you take a jog around the neighborhood, play basketball, or go for a swim, you use the tension in your muscles and your increased heart rate to do something physical. By exercising, you can use the stress response to your advantage instead of allowing it to hurt you.

Using Physical Exercise

If you don't stop stress from progressing, you could end up with a variety of physical responses, such as muscle tension, a racing heart, or high blood pressure. As you learned in Section 9.1, these changes are the result of the stress response, which prepares you to do something physical. The stress response is harmful to you only if you don't do something physical.

This is where exercise comes in. It sets up a stress intervention in front of Step

Review

1. Define the term stress intervention.

2. ■■ **LIFE SKILLS: Coping** *Give one example of a stressor, and explain how a person could use selective awareness to change his or her interpretation of that stressor.*

3. *Why is physical exercise a good way to relieve stress?*

4. ■■ **LIFE SKILLS: Coping** *Practice a relaxation technique at least once, and describe how you felt afterward.*

5. *Critical Thinking Regular practice of a relaxation technique helps many people feel more energetic. Offer an explanation of this fact.*

Review Answers

1. Stress intervention is any action that prevents a stressor from resulting in negative consequences.
2. Answers will vary. Accept any answer that shows an understanding and application of selective awareness.
3. Physical exercise enables the body to use the tension in the muscles, the increased heart rate, and some other physical changes that occur as part of the stress response in a positive, healthy way.
4. Answers will vary. Accept any answer that illustrates proper use of a relaxation technique.
5. Answers will vary. Relaxation techniques enable people to relax and become calm by taking their minds off problems as they focus their attention on a new activity. When a person feels calm or relaxed, he or she has more energy to devote to other activities rather than staying focused on the problem that caused the stress.

ASSESS

Section Review
Have students answer the Section Review questions.

Alternative Assessment
Which Roadblock?

Ask students to imagine being faced with these four stressors at once: (1) it's final-exam week; (2) you had to give up your summer job because you must baby-sit your cousin across town for the summer; (3) the route to baby-sit is through a dangerous neighborhood; and (4) you lost your watch, and although it was inexpensive, you needed it badly to keep you on schedule. Ask: **How would you intervene for each stressor?** *[1 and 2—selective awareness; relaxation, exercise; 3—elimination (find an alternate route, bicycle, or get a ride); 4—buy a new watch]*

Closure
Making It Work

Have students return to the list of stressful situations they compiled in the Closure feature of Section 9.1. Have them write beside each stressor an intervention they can use, and the specific thing they could do to make it work, such as how to eliminate the stressor, which specific positive thoughts to think, which relaxation method to use, or which exercise method to use.

SECTION 9.3

Life Skills Worksheet 9C

Assign the Getting Perspective Life Skills Worksheet.

Life Skills Worksheet 9D

Assign the Finding Help When Stress Is Overwhelming Life Skills Worksheet.

Section Review Worksheet 9.3

To reinforce the concepts presented in this section, assign Section Review Worksheet 9.3.

Section Quiz 9.3

Have students take Section Quiz 9.3.

Section 9.3

Managing Stress Is a Lifelong Process

Objectives

- *Explain how a support group helps a person deal with stress.*

- *Manage your time by setting goals and prioritizing.*
  LIFE SKILLS: Setting Goals

- *Know how to seek help if you or someone you know is overwhelmed by stress.*
  LIFE SKILLS: Using Community Resources

support group:

a group of people who trust each other and are able to talk to each other about their problems.

You learned in Section 9.2 how to deal with stressors as they come up on a daily basis. You can also protect yourself from stress by practicing stress-management techniques regularly throughout your lifetime.

Physical Health

Many of the negative consequences of stress can be prevented by taking the following steps to keep yourself physically well:

- Engage regularly in physical activity.
- Eat a balanced diet.
- Get enough rest and sleep.
- Do one of the relaxation techniques discussed on pages 202–204 every day.
- Do not use tobacco, alcohol, or other drugs.

A Support Group

One of the most effective ways to manage stress throughout your lifetime is to talk with other people about the things that bother you. You might be able to discuss your stressors with your family, your friends, or your teachers. Find a few people you can trust and call on them when you need to talk, and be available when they need to talk to someone. A group of people like this is called a **support group.** Sometimes just talking about a stressor with a member of your support group can reduce the stress you're under.

A Spiritual Life

Many people find that having a spiritual life—a sense of connection with something greater than oneself—helps them get through times of great stress. Some people believe in a supreme being who provides

(FIGURE 9-12) **Many people find the support group they need in religious communities such as churches and synagogues. A support group is one of the most effective ways to manage stress throughout your lifetime.**

Section 9.3 Lesson Plan

MOTIVATE

Journal 9E
Stressful Life Stages

This may be done as a warm-up activity. Write the following life stages on the chalkboard: infancy, childhood, adolescence, adulthood, and older adulthood. In their Journal, have students write two stressors they think are important during each stage. Tell them to write the life stage they believe is most stressful.

TEACH

Cooperative Learning
Devising a Health Program

Have students work in small groups, and have each group devise a physical health program. Ask them to plan a typical week, including exercise, meal patterns, sleep, and relaxation. Have the groups compare their plans.

Journal 9F
Support Groups

In their Journal, have students construct a personal support group. Have them write the names of individuals they trust to talk with about things that cause them stress.

Writing
Your Purpose in Life

Ask students to suppose their best friend has asked them two questions: "What do you believe about your purpose in life?" and "Does your belief help you deal with stress?" Have students write

*Life*SKILLS: Setting Goals

Managing Your Time by Setting Goals and Prioritizing . . . .

A stressor that almost everyone faces at one time or another is the feeling that you don't have enough time to do everything you need and want to do. The key to using time wisely is to set goals and prioritize them. The following steps will help you reduce the stress of "not having enough time."

1. List your goals for today.

2. Prioritize your goals. Beside each goal, write either an "A," a "B," or a "C." The goals you label "A" are the ones you absolutely must get done that day. The ones labeled "B" are those you would *like* to get done. The goals labeled "C" are not as important and may have to wait until later.

3. During your day, do what is necessary to reach your "A" goals first, then your "B" goals. If you have some time left, you can attend to your "C" goals.

This strategy can be adapted for shorter or longer periods of time than a day. You can develop goals for a single morning, for example, or for a week, a month, and even a year.

The following suggestions may also help you manage your time:

- Learn to say no. Do not take on tasks that you have no time to complete.

- Work on one task at a time. Don't go back and forth between tasks. The time it takes to constantly reorient yourself is time wasted.

- Ask for help from others when you are pressured for time.

*Life*SKILLS

Have students list their goals for tasks they want to complete today and prioritize them as described. Ask students to consider the following questions as they work on the list: Are there any activities or tasks I should say no to because I won't have enough time? Are there any goals that require me to get some help from others if I want to meet them? Who could I ask for help?

Reteaching Worksheet 9.3

Students who have difficulty with the material may complete Reteaching Worksheet 9.3.

---

a letter to their friend, answering the questions. Explain that this will help them understand themselves better. Assure them that no one will read their letters.

Class Discussion
Major Life Changes

Discuss the stressors of family violence, illness, loss of employment, and divorce. Have students weigh the merits of people with such problems seeking help from various sources, such as clergy, a therapist, a doctor, a hospital, the police, and hot lines. Explore the impact upon family and friends of their seeking help.

Reinforcement
Seeking Help

Remind students that if stress ever overwhelms them, they should get help and not try to handle it alone. Emphasize that dangerous stressors, such as suicidal thoughts, pregnancy, sexual abuse, physical beatings, and psychological abuse are too much for one person to deal with alone. Remind students that even though there is the risk of hurting other family members in talking about one's problems, it is always better to seek help.

Extension
Using Support Groups

Have students test their individual support groups by selecting the least sensitive problem from their Journal and actually talking to the person they indicated they could trust.

Review Answers

1. Talking with a trust-worthy, helpful person about a stressor can reduce the stress a person is feeling. Also, the support person might be able to suggest ways to better cope with the stressor.

2. Answers will vary depending on each individual student's goals.

3. You or the friend can talk with a trusted adult, or you or the friend can contact the police or the Department of Child Protective Services in your city or county.

4. Talk to an adult you can trust, or look in the phone book under "Suicide" and call the local suicide-prevention hot line.

5. Sample response: Tobacco is a stimulant; using tobacco can make a person feel even more stressed. Alcohol is a depressant; using alcohol can make the stress seem worse than it ordinarily would appear. Alcohol, along with other drugs, may make a person forget about a stressor for a very short time. Drugs do not, however, make the stressor go away, nor do they provide a long-term solution to dealing with the stressor.

comfort and guidance during hard times. And some people feel a strong connection with nature, which gives them a feeling of peace and a sense that they are part of a beautiful world. These are both ways of having a spiritual life. There are numerous other ways, perhaps as many ways as there are people.

Organized religions can help people deal with stress not only by offering spiritual guidance but also by helping people feel like they are part of a community. In this way, members of churches, synagogues, and other religious communities may find the support group they need to cope with the stressors in their life.

Some people would not call themselves "religious," but they know that they have a purpose—to help relieve the suffering of others, for example, or simply to act with honesty and integrity. Believing that one's life has purpose and meaning can help a person through very stressful times.

Getting Professional Help

At times a person can feel overwhelmed by stress. This can happen to anyone, even those who practice stress management. If you ever feel unable to cope with the stress in your life, you can get help from a professional. You might know a minister, priest, or rabbi you can turn to. Your school counselor is someone else who might be able to offer support.

You can also talk to a therapist if you feel overwhelmed by stress. Chapter 7 describes the different types of therapists and how to get in touch with them.

Many stressors cannot possibly be managed without the help of someone else. A person who is being physically, sexually, or emotionally abused should not be expected to deal with that stress all alone. If

you are being abused, or if anyone you know is being abused, you should talk with an adult you trust or call the police or the Department of Child Protective Services. You can even report abuse anonymously. Abuse is discussed in greater detail in Chapter 20.

Sometimes stress can be so overwhelming that ending one's life seems like the only way out. If you or someone you know is thinking of suicide, it is very important that you get help immediately. Talk to an adult you trust, or look in the phone book under "Suicide" and call your local suicide-prevention hotline. Chapter 11 of this book is devoted to discussing suicide prevention.

Review

1. How does a support group help a person deal with stress?

2. ▪▪ LIFE SKILLS: Setting Goals Set your goals for the next week and divide them into tasks you must get done, tasks you would like to get done, and tasks that can wait until later.

3. ▪▪ LIFE SKILLS: Using Community Resources If you or someone you know were being abused, what could you do to get help?

4. ▪▪ LIFE SKILLS: Using Community Resources If you or someone you know were thinking of suicide, what could you do to get help?

5. Critical Thinking How could the use of tobacco, alcohol, or other drugs contribute to stress?

ASSESS

Section Review

Have students answer the Section Review questions.

Alternative Assessment
Suggesting Ways to Cope

Have students write a paragraph suggesting ways a student in the following situation could cope with the stress she faces: Ellen has an after-school job

at a fast-food restaurant; she helps her mother care for her younger brothers, who are 7 and 3 years old; and she participates in sports that often have practices before school.

Closure
Testing the Relaxation Techniques

Ask students to choose one of the relaxation techniques described in the chapter and try it out the next time

they feel a stress response coming on. Have students report back to the class or write a paragraph on how successful the technique was for them.

Highlights

Summary . . . .

- A stressor is a new or potentially unpleasant situation.

- A stress response is a reaction of the body to a stressor. Stress responses include release of adrenalin, faster heart rate, faster breathing rate, higher blood pressure, greater muscle tension, and greater blood flow to the brain and legs.

- A stress response is helpful when a person is being physically threatened and needs to respond immediately.

- If not managed properly, stress can cause physical and mental disorders, or make such disorders worse.

- The stress model is a series of steps that describes how stress develops. If you know the way the stress model works, you can stop yourself from progressing from one step to the next.

- Using selective awareness, or thinking

positively, is one way to cope with a stressful situation.

- Changing your focus from your worries for a while can help you relax and reduce stress. Relaxation techniques include listening to music, reading a book, meditating, progressive relaxation, body scanning, and imagery.

- Physical exercise and relaxation techniques can relieve muscle tension caused by stress.

- One of the most effective ways to manage stress is to develop a support system, or a group of people you can talk to about your problems. Support systems usually include family members, friends, teachers, or clergy.

- When a person feels overwhelmed, he or she can get professional help from counselors, therapists, and clergy.

Vocabulary . . . .

stressor any new or potentially unpleasant situation.

stress response reaction of the body to a stressor.

stress the combination of a stressor and a stress response.

stress intervention any action that prevents a stressor from resulting in negative consequences.

selective awareness focusing on the aspects of a situation that help a person feel better ("thinking positively").

support group a group of people who trust each other and are able to talk to each other about their problems.

SUMMARY
Have students read the summary to reinforce the concepts they have learned in Chapter 9.

VOCABULARY
Have students review the definitions in the vocabulary section. Then ask them to describe how stress intervention, selective awareness, and support groups are related to stress reduction.

EXTENSION
Music can be stressful or relaxing, depending on its style and the listener's preference. Have students, working in pairs, experiment listening to two sequences of music, one they find stressful and one they find relaxing. They should then play the music for another pair of students and analyze any differences in the effect of the music on the other pair. Suggest that for relaxation purposes students may wish to try music they might not listen to ordinarily. Alternatively, students may wish to try this activity using different works of art instead of music.

Chapter Review

CHAPTER REVIEW

Concept Review

Sample responses:

1. People need enough stressors to make life interesting. Stress, however, can become bad for you when you can't control the stressors or relieve the stress. This type of stress can cause illness.

2. Your body releases adrenaline, which makes you breathe faster, your heart beat faster, your muscles tense, and your mouth feel dry.

3. Any event that involves a change in one's life situation, even a change that is positive, such as getting married, can be stressful.

4. Stress can make certain physical and mental disorders worse. Stress weakens the immune system and makes the body more susceptible to colds and flu. Because you can't concentrate very well when you are under stress, you can have an accident that may cause injuries.

5. tension headaches, backaches, TMJ syndrome, coronary heart disease, high blood pressure, chronic fatigue, depression

6. Eliminate some stressors, change your interpretation of a stressor (selective awareness), use relaxation techniques, and get physical exercise.

Concept Review

1. How can stress be both bad and good for you?

2. What changes can occur in your body during a stress response?

3. Can positive situations be stressful? Explain.

4. Explain how stress can make you ill and lead to injuries.

5. Describe at least four other consequences of stress.

6. What are three healthy ways to cope with stress?

7. At the end of a very stressful day, you find yourself unable to sleep. What can you do?

8. Explain why progressive relaxation is a good way to manage stress.

9. What can you do to maintain your physical health during times of stress?

10. What is a support system? How can it help you?

11. What can a person do if he or she feels totally overpowered by stressful situations and has tried all the usual coping techniques?

12. Stress often results from taking on too many tasks. Name three ways to protect yourself from this kind of stress.

Expressing Your View

1. Exam time is always a stressful time for you. While you are studying, you seem to know the material well; but during the exam, your anxiety level is so high that you can't remember anything. What can you do to cope better with the stress so that you can know the material on the next exam?

2. Name five jobs that you think are highly stressful. Name five jobs that you think are not stressful. Do you think everyone would classify these jobs as you did? Why, or why not?

3. Gary has been experiencing muscle tension and a rapid heartbeat. The problem seems to get worse every time he argues with his girlfriend. What can Gary do?

4. Laughter usually has positive results in coping with stress. Describe a situation in which humor might be inappropriate or have a negative effect.

7. Use one of the various relaxation techniques.

8. It helps relax tense muscles that are often caused by stress.

9. Reduce or eliminate stressors and use various methods that are effective in controlling stress.

10. A support system is a group of people you can trust and call upon if you need to talk. Sometimes just talking about a problem can reduce stress.

11. Get professional help.

12. Learn to say no, list your goals for the day, prioritize your goals, work on one task at a time, and ask others for help.

Expressing Your Views

Sample responses:

1. Try relaxation techniques before and during exams and talk with a counselor about how to take tests better.

Life Skills Check

1. Coping

Your friend seems very impatient, competitive, and even hostile with her friends lately. You think that she has overburdened herself with activities and responsibilities. Describe some relaxation techniques that might ease her stress.

2. Coping

You just found out that your family will be moving to another city. You know there will be many benefits for your family, but all you can think about are the changes you will have to make. You feel worried and scared. Make a list of five positive aspects of moving that might make you feel better.

Projects

1. Work with a group to make a list of stressors in the everyday lives of people in a certain age category (children, teenagers, adults, or elderly people). Then interview two people in the age category your group chose, to find out what their greatest stressors are. Compare the results to your first list and discuss the results.

2. Write a short essay focusing on findings that show a definite relationship between physical disorders and stress.

3. Find out if you are managing your time wisely by making a pie graph that shows how much time you spend on your daily activities. For example, you might spend 5 percent on chores, 30 percent in school, 15 percent with friends, 10 percent on extracurricular activities, 5 percent on homework, and 35 percent sleeping. Analyze your graph and decide whether managing your time better will reduce your stress.

Plan for Action

List one or two stressors in your life and devise a plan to lower your stress level using the suggestions in this chapter.

2. Student responses will vary. Accept any answer that is well thought out and shows an understanding of stressors and the stress response.

3. Try various methods in controlling stress, find out why he and his girlfriend argue, and try to resolve those problems. He must find ways to eliminate or reduce stressors.

4. Sometimes when people are nervous or embarrassed they try to cover it up by making a joke because they don't know what else to do. This would be inappropriate at a funeral, when someone is very sick, or when your parents are really mad about something.

Life Skills Check

1. Students may describe any of the relaxation techniques discussed in the chapter.

2. Accept any answer that lists five positive actions.

Projects

Have students plan and carry out the projects for managing stress.

Plan for Action

Before students choose their stressors and write their plan of action, review the stress reduction techniques. Students' plans should be practical and appropriate for the stressor. For example, if a student has a younger sibling who is annoying, a support group and relaxation techniques would be appropriate, but selective awareness would probably be less helpful.

ASSESSMENT OPTIONS

Chapter Test
Have students take the Chapter 9 Test.

Alternative Assessment
Have students do the Alternative Assessment activity for Chapter 9.

Test Generator
The Test Generator contains additional assessment items for this chapter.

SECTION	TITLE/OBJECTIVES	PERSONAL INVENTORY			LIFE SKILLS DEVELOPMENT			
		Personal Health Inventory	Journal	Check Up	Life Skills	Life Skills Worksheets	Media Message or Ethical Issues Worksheet	What Would You Do?
10.1 *pp. 213–218*	**DEATH AND DYING** • Describe the five stages terminally ill people generally pass through. • List three reasons why many people choose hospice care when they are terminally ill. • Describe the functions of a living will. ▪ Learn how to be of help to someone who is dying.	Ch. 10	10A 10B	p. 215		10A	Unit 3	
10.2 *pp. 219–222*	**THE GRIEVING PROCESS** ▪ Learn how to deal with your own grief. ▪ Learn how to give emotional support to someone who is grieving. • List three reasons for having funerals or memorial services.		10C		p. 221	10B 10C 10D		

KEY: ▪ Denotes Life Skill Objective

Text references denoted by page number.

Supplement references denoted by chapter or item numbers.

LINKING RESOURCES

INTERACTION		**OTHER RESOURCES**		**SECTION REVIEW AND ASSESSMENT**				
Making a Choice Cards	Parent Discussion Guide	Health Talk Audio Program	Teaching Transparencies and Directory	Section Review Worksheets	Section Quizzes	Reteaching Worksheets	Section Reviews	
10A	Ch. 10	Ch. 10	10A	10.1	10.1	10.1	p. 217	
10B				10.2	10.2	10.2	p. 222	

KEY FACTS

- Recognizing the significance and permanence of death is tied to maturity. Most people have a full awareness of death by adolescence.

- The Harvard Medical School established the following criteria to determine if a person is legally dead: unresponsiveness to painful stimuli, failure to breathe for over an hour, absence of muscular reflexes, and failure of the brain to generate electrical impulses (brain waves).

- Most terminally ill people pass through five stages in preparing for their death: denial, anger, bargaining, depression, and acceptance.

- A dying person needs to find support, maintain control over some part of his or her life, and die with dignity.

- Hospice programs for the terminally ill provide a homelike atmosphere in which the dying person and his or her family can prepare for death.

- Some people choose to sign a living will stating that they do not want their life prolonged artificially if they can never recover.

- Grief accompanies all loss, and people show their grief in different ways. People grieving over the loss of a loved one often go through stages similar to those of people coming to terms with their own imminent death.

CHAPTER REVIEW AND ASSESSMENT

TEXT

Chapter Review pp. 224–225

SUPPLEMENTS

Chapter Test 10

Alternative Assessment 10

Test Generator Chapter 10

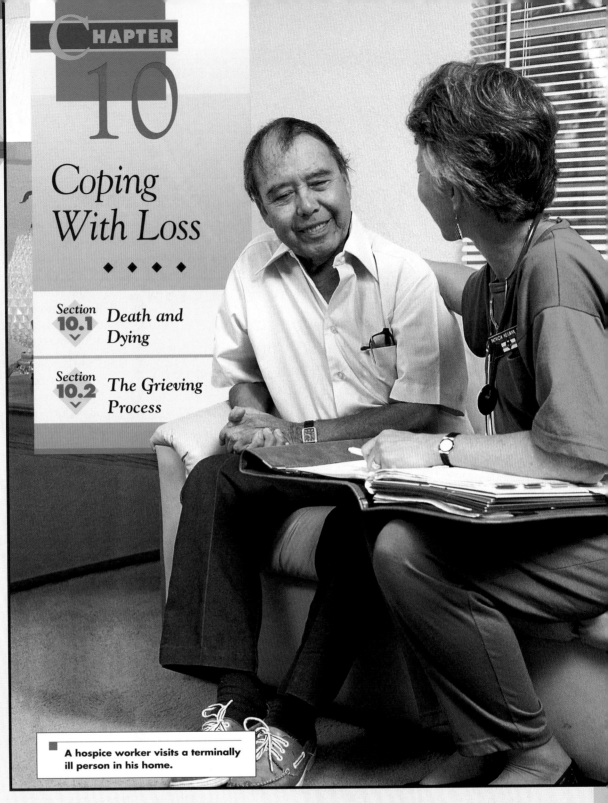

CHAPTER 10

Coping With Loss

◆ ◆ ◆ ◆

Section 10.1 Death and Dying

Section 10.2 The Grieving Process

A hospice worker visits a terminally ill person in his home.

MYTHS & MISCONCEPTIONS

- **You shouldn't talk to dying people about their impending death; it will make them feel worse.** Many people are very uncomfortable talking about death, so they avoid talking with terminally ill people about their illness. However, terminally ill people often want to discuss their feelings about death with someone, especially someone they are close to.

- **Young children do not understand death; therefore they do not go through a grief process.** Although young children do not yet understand the permanence of death, they do understand the loss of a loved one in their life and do go through a grief process.

- **A person who does not show strong emotion when a loved one dies is not grieving.** People show their grief in different ways. Some people, especially adolescents, repress their feelings of shock, depression, and denial to a level that they can manage.

Justin's brother, Chad, died last week. Chad had been in and out of the hospital for years with a serious illness; he died at home with his family close by. The funeral is over, and all the relatives have gone home. Now Justin has to go back to school. In a way this will be the hardest part, because he doesn't know how to act around his friends. What should he say? What will *they* say? He doesn't want to make anyone feel bad on his account. But he thinks it might help to talk with a friend about his brother.

Section
10.1 *Death and Dying*

O**bjectives**

- *Describe the five stages terminally ill people generally pass through.*

- *List three reasons why many people choose hospice care when they are terminally ill.*

- *Describe the functions of a living will.*

- *Learn how to be of help to someone who is dying.*
  LIFE SKILLS: Coping

If Justin were your friend, how would you help him? Would you feel embarrassed to say anything to him about his brother, afraid of saying the wrong thing? Most people would. Death is a topic that often makes us uncomfortable. But the more we know about it, the better we'll be able to help other people cope with death, and the better we'll be able to cope with our own losses.

Death is a natural part of life. Although we don't usually stop to think about it, death surrounds us all our lives. Even very young children are exposed to death—usually of pets or other animals. Children also learn about death through the media, especially from television. Those deaths seem remote and far away. By the time people become teenagers, however, most have known someone who has died. Often this is an older person, such as a grandparent, but sometimes it is a friend or brother or sister.

An understanding of death is greatly influenced by a person's age. For example, infants have no real concept of death. From age two to five, children recognize death but do not think it is permanent. They think that death is like sleep. From age five to nine, children come to view death as permanent, but not as something that could happen to them. Around age 10, children realize that death is inevitable and final. They know death happens but have trouble realizing it can happen to anyone at any time. Most people do not have a full awareness of death until adolescence.

Personal Health Inventory

Have students complete the Personal Health Inventory for this chapter.

English/Spanish CD Audio Program

Use the English/Spanish Health Talk audio program for students who need audio reinforcement of the concepts presented.

Parent Discussion Guide

Send home the Parent Letter for Chapter 10. As you progress through the chapter, send home the Parental Survey and The Extra Mile.

Section 10.1 Lesson Plan

MOTIVATE

Journal 10A
Loss Experience

This may be done as a warm-up activity. Encourage students to write in their Journal about some important loss they have experienced, such as a friend moving away, a parent leaving home due to divorce, or the death of a pet. Suggest that they describe their feelings about the loss and how those feelings have changed over time.

Class Discussion
Justin's Story

After students have read the story about Justin, ask: What would you say to Justin? Why? Encourage empathy for what Justin has gone through and what he must be feeling.

Background

Hospice

In medieval Europe, *hospice* meant "a refuge for weary travelers" and referred to the peace and refreshment provided by inns. Then religious orders began taking in the dying to provide nursing care and a final resting place for the end of their life, and the term shifted in meaning. The hospice concept as we know it originated with Dr. Cicely Saunders, who founded St. Christopher's Hospice in London in 1968.

Life Skills Worksheet 10A

Assign the Working Through the Stages of Grief Life Skills Worksheet.

When Does Death Occur?

According to the Harvard Medical School, all of the following criteria must be present for a person to be considered dead:

1. **Unreceptiveness and unresponsiveness.** *The patient is totally unresponsive to applied painful stimuli, such as poking with pins.*

2. **Unresponsiveness in breathing.** *For over an hour, the patient shows no spontaneous muscular contractions or breathing.*

3. **Lack of reflexes.** *The knee-jerk reflex is absent, or the pupil does not contract when light is pointed in the eye.*

4. **Flat EEG.** *For 20 minutes, the patient's brain does not generate an electrical impulse or brain wave.*

(FIGURE 10-1) **According to these criteria, a person who is kept functioning by life-support systems is alive until the machines are shut off.**

When Does Death Occur?

In the past, people considered death to occur when the lungs and heart ceased to function. Scientific and technological advances, though, have made it more difficult to determine when death occurs.

Today, people whose heart and lungs have stopped are sometimes revived by cardiopulmonary resuscitation (CPR) or by a machine. Life-support machines can sometimes keep people "alive" if they cannot breathe or if their heart will not beat on its own. Machines can feed people if they cannot eat, and they can clean the blood if the body's organs cannot do it. Even when

people are not emitting brain waves, they can still function artificially. When, then, is a person dead?

The Harvard Medical School has developed a definition of death that attempts to answer this question. According to this definition, the four criteria listed in Figure 10-1 must be met before an individual can be declared dead.

Stages in the Acceptance of Death

People who die suddenly do not have time to prepare for death. However, people who die from a terminal illness often have lots of time to think about death and to prepare for it.

Elisabeth Kubler-Ross, a noted physician, worked for years with patients dying from terminal illnesses. She identified five stages that most terminally ill patients go through when facing death. Understanding these stages can be valuable if you ever need to help a dying friend or relative.

Not all terminally ill people go through these stages in the same order. Some may skip a stage, revert to an earlier stage, or get stuck in one stage. People experience dying with the same individuality that they experience living.

Stage 1: Denial When people learn that they are going to die, their reaction is often to feel shock and denial. Denial acts as a buffer that gives people a chance to think about the news. People may think, "It can't be true, not me." Or they may prefer to believe that a cure will be found for their disease or that they will be the exception to the rule. At this point, it is helpful for patients to get a second opinion from a reputable physician in order to verify their condition. If you have a friend or relative in the denial stage, the best response is just to listen. Even if people who are dying talk

---

TEACH

 Journal 10B
Feelings About Death

Give students time to recall the way they thought about death when they were young. Then have them write in their Journal about how their thinking has changed as they have grown.

Class Discussion
Life Cycle Concepts

Have students think about and verbalize their own concepts of the life cycle. Have volunteers suggest a diagram that illustrates this concept. Sketch the diagram on the chalkboard, and then erase the portion representing death. Ask: **What happens to the concept of life cycle without death?** [*Encourage students to express in their own words the perspective that death is a natural occurrence and part of living.*]

Case Study
Life-Support Systems

In 1975, a drug overdose at a party left Karen Ann Quinlan in a vegetative, comatose state, attached to a respirator. After some months, it became evident that she would not emerge from the coma, and without the respirator would probably die. Although she had previously discussed with her family her wish to be allowed to die in such a circumstance, the courts at first would not permit the family's doctors to remove life

214 COPING WITH LOSS

about getting well soon, it is better not to contradict them. That could force them to accept their death before they are ready.

Stage 2: Anger When people realize they are really going to die, they are likely to think, "Why me?" and become angry. People may feel as if they are being treated unfairly. They may see someone who is mean and cruel but in perfect health and think, "Why should I have to die while this other person goes on enjoying life?"

In this situation, anger is often directed at medical staff, family, or friends. It is important to let them know they have a right to be angry. If the person gets angry at you, try to accept it without feeling hurt. Recognize that this is simply a stage that will pass. Providing an outlet for the anger can be helpful.

Stage 3: Bargaining Bargaining is a final attempt to avoid the inevitable. People who believe in God may promise to reform their life in exchange for a miraculous recovery.

Stage 4: Depression After passing through the first three stages, dying people often become depressed. Sometimes dying people have worries that it might be helpful for them to discuss—a friend or relative who is dying may ask you to adopt a pet or to visit periodically with his or her children or spouse.

Sometimes dying people are depressed because they feel they are losing everything, especially their friends and loved ones. What may be most helpful is just to be with them, often silently.

Stage 5: Acceptance Accepting your own death is hard to imagine, but most people who have a terminal illness eventually get to a point where they can do so. By this stage, people have usually taken care of all of their personal affairs, including wills,

funeral arrangements, and saying goodbye to special people in their life.

Death With Dignity

One of the most painful things about dying is that it can rob a person of his or her dignity. Recognizing this, the helping professions are exploring ways to allow dying people to have more control over what happens to them and to provide them with the support they need.

Check Up

How Do You Feel About Death?

On a separate sheet of paper, answer each of the following questions to determine how you feel about death. Use the following scale:

a = comfortable
b = somewhat comfortable
c = somewhat uncomfortable
d = uncomfortable

1. How comfortable are you talking about death and dying?

2. How comfortable would you feel if you had to visit and support someone you cared about who was terminally ill?

3. How comfortable would you feel if you had to provide support for a friend whose parent had died?

4. How comfortable would you feel about donating your kidneys for use upon your death?

5. How comfortable would you feel about signing a statement requesting that you not be kept alive if in a coma and on life-support mechanisms?

6. If you were legally responsible for someone being kept alive by life-support systems, and you knew the person would not want to remain in that state, how comfortable would you feel about ordering the withdrawal of the life-support equipment?

Check Up

Have students anonymously turn in their responses to the Check Up questions. Tally the results on the chalkboard and discuss reactions to the predominant feelings expressed. You might want to have them retake the Check Up at the end of the chapter to see if their attitudes have changed.

 Section Review Worksheet 10.1
To reinforce the concepts presented in this section, assign Section Review Worksheet 10.1.

Section Quiz 10.1
Have students take Section Quiz 10.1.

 Reteaching Worksheet 10.1
Students who have difficulty with the material may complete Reteaching Worksheet 10.1.

---

support. Some students may wish to research and report on the Quinlans' decade-long fight and what happened to Karen after life support was removed.

Debate the Issue
Life-Support Systems

Divide the class into two teams to debate whether life-support mechanisms should be used to prolong the life of a person who will never regain consciousness or will never be able to function normally again.

 ## Cooperative Learning
Kubler-Ross Model

Divide the class into five groups and assign to each group one stage of the Kubler-Ross model to explore. Encourage each group to create a list of statements that would illustrate things a dying person might say at that particular stage. Then have them write possible responses they might give to help the person through the stage.

Teaching Transparency 10A
Acceptance of Death or Loss

Use this transparency to help students understand how they could help a dying person as he or she goes through the stages in the acceptance of death.

Reinforcement
Ways to be Helpful

Help students list positive and practical things they could do for a friend or

Review Answers

1. Denial: When people are told that they will soon die, their reaction is usually one of disbelief. Anger: When people realize that they are really going to die, they are likely to become angry. Bargaining: People who believe in God may promise to reform their life in exchange for a miraculous recovery. Depression: When people realize that bargaining will not work, they may feel that their last hope has faded and they feel depressed. Acceptance: When people have accepted their condition and that death will soon come.

2. Students may answer that hospices provide a homelike atmosphere; they can provide a program of medical care and counseling for the patient, as well as counseling for the family; hospices sometimes provide care in the patient's own home; hospices freely provide medication for pain; visitation with the patient is unrestricted; hospice services also include legal counseling, spiritual support, home nursing care, and nutritional counseling.

will:

a legal document describing what should be done with a person's possessions after the person's death.

hospices:

places that offer housing, medical care, and counseling for terminally ill people and counseling for the family.

What Dying People Need Dying people need to be able to express their feelings, and they need a caring group of family and friends to listen.

Doctors used to be encouraged to withhold bad news from terminally ill patients because it was thought that the patients would be shocked, agitated, or depressed. But knowledge of an impending death can help improve communication and enhance relationships between the dying person and his or her friends and family. When asked, most people say they would want to be told if they had a terminal illness. Even if they are not told, most terminally ill patients know or suspect that they are going to die.

Just like the rest of us, dying people want some control over things that affect them. To have that control, they need honest answers to their questions. Dishonesty not only prevents them from managing their remaining time, but it also damages their trust in others, which is so vital when everything else seems to be falling away.

What kinds of things do people who are dying want to control? They want to decide who their doctors will be, which treatments they will accept, and who will visit them. In addition, they often wish to control their own funeral or memorial service. Decisions such as whether there will be a burial or cremation, who will officiate at the service, and what will be included in the service can be made in anticipation of death. Also, they want to control what will be done with their possessions. Dying people are often comforted by knowing their possessions will be in the right hands after they die. This is best handled through a **will,** which is a legal document describing what should be done after death. It also may contain directions for the care of surviving family members or even pets.

Hospices Many people would rather die at home than in a hospital. **Hospices**—programs that care for terminally ill people—help fill this need. Hospices provide a homelike atmosphere even though the patient is away from home. Although they do not have a hospital's extensive equipment, they can provide a program of medical care and support for the patient, as well as support for the family. Sometimes hospices can provide care in the patient's own home through medical specialists who visit the patient.

The hospice approach has several unique features. For example, medications are freely administered for pain, reflecting the philosophy that the patient's remaining time should be as comfortable as possible. Families visit freely without restrictions on hours or age, and volunteers visit and talk with dying patients.

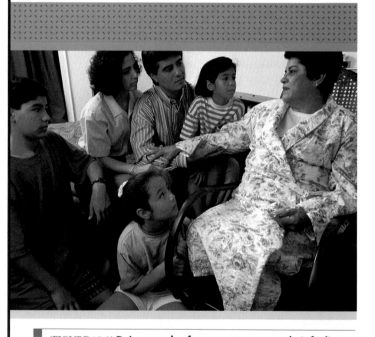

(FIGURE 10-2) **Dying people often want to express their feelings and need a warm group of family and friends to listen.**

• • • TEACH continued

relative who is terminally ill. Here is a start:

- Stay in touch—and remember that holding a hand or hugging the person are important.
- Take a favorite food in a disposable container (phone first).
- Take the children out for a few hours or offer to stay with the dying person so that the family can go out, to give everyone a break.

Class Discussion
Hospice Care

Have students suggest reasons a terminally ill person may prefer to go to a hospice rather than stay in a hospital or go home. If possible, have someone who works in a hospice come talk to the class. Students could prepare questions in advance to ask the speaker. If no speaker is available, have students investigate the availability of hospice care in their town.

Extension
Death and the Artist

Throughout the centuries, death and dying, and how they affect the meaning of life, have been the subject of numberous literary works. Interested students could research this topic and select favorite poems or passages to present to the class. Four famous works are "Hektor's Farewell to Andromache" in Homer's *Iliad*, A. E. Housman's poem "To an Athlete Dying Young," "Knoxville: Summer 1915" from James

When hospice care is provided in the patient's own home, families learn to participate in the patient's care. They may administer medications or perform other tasks.

Family members receive counseling to work through their grief and to be better prepared to interact with the dying person. Other hospice services include legal counseling, home nursing care, and support for the grieving family after the patient dies.

People who choose to die in their own homes often prefer hospice care. For example, George Jeffrey, a 78-year-old man, began to feel ill and had extensive tests that showed he had advanced cancer. Mr. Jeffrey was a retired commercial artist who lived with his daughter and son-in-law and his grandchildren. He loved to play golf, spend time with his family, and watch sports on TV.

Mr. Jeffrey and his family chose to receive hospice care in the home. Mr. Jeffrey stayed in the family home and continued to use his favorite easy chair. He continued to watch sports on TV and visited a great deal with his family.

The family was told what to expect throughout the dying process. Nurses from the hospice program made regular visits to Mr. Jeffrey and his family. As the time of death approached, the nurse gently explained to the family what was happening.

When the moment of death was very near, the family's greatest concern was for Mr. Jeffrey. They wanted him to know how much they loved him. They wanted him to know they would be fine and that he could let go and pass from this life.

He died with great courage and dignity. Most of all, he died in an atmosphere of great love.

Living Wills Many ethical decisions surround the topic of death. Should life be preserved at all costs—even if the person is in a coma or in excruciating pain? Or should death simply be allowed to take its course without intervention?

The **living will** is one way to deal with this complex issue. A living will is a simple statement people can sign that instructs their doctors not to use medical equipment just to keep them breathing and their hearts beating when they have no chance for meaningful recovery. It tells the medical staff to let nature take its course. This takes the burden off their families and lets the medical staff know their wishes. An example of a living will is shown in Figure 10-3. Living wills should not be confused with regular wills. Living wills are concerned with life-support mechanisms, while regular wills deal with the distribution of material goods and instructions for the care of others.

living will

a document expressing a person's wish to be allowed to die in case of terminal illness or incurable injury rather than be kept alive by artificial means.

Review

1. Describe the five stages terminally ill people generally pass through.

2. List three reasons why many people choose hospice care when they are terminally ill.

3. Describe the functions of a living will.

4. **LIFE SKILLS: Coping** You have a friend who is terminally ill and in the hospital. Your friend tells you the doctors are wrong and that he really isn't that sick. He wants to leave the hospital immediately and wants you to help him. What would you do?

5. **Critical Thinking** What types of patients might prefer hospital care to hospice care?

Answers to Questions 1 and 2 are on p. 216.

3. A living will is a statement that people can sign instructing their doctors not to use medical equipment just to keep them breathing and their hearts beating when they have no chance for meaningful recovery.

4. Answers will vary. Students may answer that they would listen to their friend and suggest that he talk to his doctor about being released and then seek a second opinion. They should not contradict the patient's belief that he does not have a terminal illness.

5. Sample response: Hospices do not have extensive medical equipment. Terminally-ill patients who desire the use of such equipment would prefer hospital care to hospice care.

Agee's autobiography, *A Death in the Family*, and Gabriel García Márquez's short story "Chronicle of a Death Foretold." Other students may wish to research musical compositions that were inspired by the death of a loved one, such as Eric Clapton's "Tears in Heaven."

ASSESS

Section Review

Have students answer the Section Review questions.

Alternative Assessment
Opinions on Hospice Care

Have students write a brief essay outlining their opinion about hospice care. They should explain what they think its value is, aspects they like or dislike, and needs they think hospice care does or does not meet.

Closure
Dealing With Grief

With the class, discuss various ways one could help a friend deal with the loss of a loved one.

Background

Living Will

Most people are not aware that a living will can be overridden by a family member. Once the patient is unable to respond, a loved one may have a change of heart and ask for resuscitation and/or life support. Medical staff then respond to the family member's wishes. For this reason, it is important for anyone making a living will to communicate his or her wishes in detail to family members.

Making a Choice 10A

Assign the Wills card. The card asks students to examine living wills and the emotions connected to inheritance.

Ethical Issues in Health Worksheet

Have students read this Unit 3 feature on pages 240–241. Then have them complete its companion worksheet.

Living Will Declaration

FIGURE 10-3

To My Family, Doctors, and All Those Concerned with My Care

I, _____, being of sound mind, make this statement as a directive to be followed if for any reason I become unable to participate in decisions regarding my medical care.

I direct life-sustaining procedures should be withheld if I have an illness, disease, or injury, or experience extreme mental deterioration, such that there is no reasonable expectation of recovering or regaining a meaningful life.

These life-sustaining procedures that may be withheld or withdrawn include, but are not limited to:

**Surgery   Antibiotics   Cardiac Resuscitation   Respiratory Support
Artificially Administered Feeding and Fluids**

I further direct that treatment be limited to comfort measures only, even if they shorten my life.

You may delete any provison above by drawing a line through it and adding your initials.

Other personal instructions:

These directions express my legal right to refuse treatment. Therefore, I expect my family, doctors, and all those concerned with my care to regard themselves as legally and morally bound to act in accord with my wishes, and in so doing to be free from any liability for having followed my directions.

Signed _____ Date _____

Witness _____ Witness _____

Proxy Designaton Clause

If you wish, you may use this section to designate someone to make treatment decisions for you if you are unable to do so. Your Living Will Declaration will be in effect even if you have a designated proxy.

I authorize the following person to implement my Living Will Declaration by accepting, refusing, and/or making decisons about my treatment and hospitalization:

Name _____

Address _____

If the person I have named above is unable to act on my behalf, I authorize the following person to do so:

Name _____

Address _____

I have discussed my wishes with these persons and trust their judgment on my behalf.

Signed _____ Date _____

Witness _____ Witness _____

Section 10.2 The Grieving Process

Objectives

- Learn how to deal with your own grief.
  - ◼◼ **LIFE SKILLS: Coping**

- Learn how to give emotional support to someone who is grieving.
  - ◼◼ **LIFE SKILLS: Communicating Effectively**

- List three reasons for having funerals or memorial services.

We experience grief when we suffer a great loss. People can grieve over losses other than death—the loss of a love relationship, for example, or even the loss of a treasured object. But grief is probably most intense when we lose someone through death.

The grief people feel when someone dies is influenced by several factors. For example, the feelings related to a sudden death are different from those resulting from death caused by a long illness. In one case, the death is an unexpected shock. In the other, you have time to prepare. Reactions to death also differ depending upon how close you were to the person who has died. However, regardless of who dies and how close you were to him or her, you will need to wrestle with the feeling of loss. Only the intensity of the loss will vary.

When people know a loved one is dying, they may go through the same stages of accepting death as the dying person. They may deny that death is imminent. They may become angry, sometimes at the patient, especially if they have been dependent on the dying person. They may spend a great deal of time praying and bargaining for the person to recover. They may get depressed. And, ultimately, they may come to accept the death and the need to survive in spite of it.

Dealing With Your Grief

Whether the death of someone close is anticipated or sudden, one thing is certain: expect the unexpected. No matter how much we plan and think about living without someone we love, we never really know how we will react to a death.

The loss of a parent through divorce is discussed in Chapter 19.

The loss of a love relationship is discussed in Chapter 17.

Ways to Deal with Your Grief

Speak to someone you can trust who will respect your feelings and keep your conversation confidential. This might be a close friend, teacher, coach, or school counselor. In some areas, there are support groups for the bereaved that your school counselor or a local hospital might know about.

It is important to get your feelings out. One way to do this would be to use phrases like: "I remember when ...." "What I remember most about ...."

Talking about the future will stress the permanence of death and help with adjustment. For example, you can say: "We're really going to miss ...." "What I will miss the most is ...."

Be honest with yourself and others when discussing your feelings about death.

(FIGURE 10-4)

Background
Coping With Grief

Grief is different for young people than it is for adults. Because they do not react in the same ways as adults, children's and teens' grief may not be recognized. The intense emotions of grieving are so painful and frightening that a child may approach and avoid them over a long period. Denial provides a numbness that allows grieving youngsters to bring overpowering emotions to a manageable level until they have regained the psychological strength to deal with them. For many grieving teens, the second year after the death is harder than the first year, in part because the numbness is past and a flood of painful emotions must be dealt with.

Life Skills Worksheet 10B
Assign the Support Groups for the Grieving Life Skills Worksheet.

Section 10.2 Lesson Plan

MOTIVATE

Journal 10C
Grieving

Ask students to recall a time when they went through a grieving process over the loss of a treasured item, a pet, or a relationship. Have them list in their Journal the stages of grief and explain how they felt and acted about their loss at each stage.

TEACH

Class Discussion
Grief Phases

Grief for someone dying or dead evolves in phases, in somewhat the same way the terminally ill experience stages in the progress of their illness. Have students talk about why the death of a loved one might cause feelings of denial, anger, and depression. (*The survivor is losing someone important, perhaps the emotional and economic center of his or her world.*)

Reinforcement
Grief Support Groups

Stress that releasing feelings of grief is an important part of the grieving process. Grief that is shared is less intensely suffered. Find out about grief support groups in your community and have students gather information to share with classmates.

 219

(FIGURE 10-5)

Life Skills Worksheet 10C

Assign the Writing a Condolence Letter Life Skills Worksheet.

Life Skills Worksheet 10D

Assign the Communicating With Those Who Are Grieving Life Skills Worksheet.

Making a Choice 10B

Assign the Dealing With Guilt card. The card asks students to examine strategies for dealing with guilt after a person's death.

Ways to Help a Grieving Person

If you have a classmate who has lost someone through death, it is important to express your sympathy as a show of support. You might say: "I was sorry to hear about your brother's death. He was a great guy." But unless you're a close friend, don't ask for details.

Try to put the person in touch with others who are grieving. For example, teenagers who have lost a parent through death can be of great help to another teenager whose parent has just died.

Reassure the person that guilt, sadness, despair, and similar feelings are normal.

Listen to, hold, and touch the grieving person. Let the person share the grief with you.

It is wise not to run away from feelings, because the hurt cannot be denied. It is best to let out the feelings, sharing them with people to whom you feel close. They can help by listening and by serving as a reminder that you are not alone.

During the grieving process, it may help to talk with a good friend about what you are experiencing. If you are a member of a church or synagogue, you may want to talk with your priest, minister, or rabbi. Organized support groups for people who have lost someone through death may also exist in your community. Another alternative is to talk to your school counselor or a therapist. Remember that seeking help is a sign of strength, not weakness. Figure 10-4 has some suggestions that can help you adjust to a death.

Helping Others Deal With Grief

If you know a person who is grieving, you can be of tremendous help. Try to imagine what would help if you were grieving.

What would feel good to you would probably also feel good to someone else.

Communicate your concern. Express friendship. Let the person know you're there if needed. You can show you care by being comforting. Avoid saying things like "Don't cry, you'll get over it." Crying is a healthful way to release feelings of grief. Offer to help the grieving person adjust. You might be able to help with schoolwork or household chores.

As you try to help, let the person set the speed of the recovery. Everyone handles this type of situation differently. Allow the person to decide how you can help. For example, don't insist on giving advice if the person doesn't want it. Respect the grieving person's wishes and take your lead from him or her. And remember that a grieving person often needs support not only right after a death, but also a week, a month, or a year later.

If you are helping someone who is grieving, you might find the suggestions in Figure 10-5 helpful.

• • • TEACH continued

Role-Playing
Communicating Effectively

Partners can review "Helping Others Deal With Grief" for appropriate responses to a grieving friend. Some pairs may wish to repeat their impromptu dialogue for the class. Allow time for students to respond to such performances, pointing out what they think is most helpful and why.

Class Discussion
Funerals and Memorial Services

Use the following questions to help students explore the nature and importance of funerals and memorial services to the bereaved. Ask: **When might a family have a memorial service instead of a funeral for a loved one who has died?** [*When the body has been lost or cremated, or when the service has to be held long after the death.*] **Some adults feel that children should not attend the funeral of a loved one, but should be**

shielded from their grief. What would you say in response to an attitude like this? [*The child misses a chance to realize that the death is real and final. The child is isolated from other family members at a vulnerable time and may feel terrified and abandoned. If the child feels that the dead person "went away" or "went to sleep" he or she may feel terrified that it will happen to another family member.*] Make the point to students, however, that no child should be forced to attend a funeral if he or she clearly does not want to go.

220 COPING WITH LOSS

Although negative emotions and re-adjustments accompany death, there are some positive outcomes. When families are close and communicate feelings openly, death can draw the survivors closer together and help them to grow from the experience.

Funerals and Memorial Services

When a person dies, the body is usually buried or cremated. When there is a burial, the body is placed in a casket and buried in a cemetery. In **cremation**, the body is reduced to ashes by intense heat. The ashes may be scattered or placed in an urn.

Within a few days of the death, there is almost always a funeral, which is a ceremony at which others pay respect to the person who has died. Usually the body is in a casket, which is sometimes open, sometimes closed. Often, a service is performed that includes a speech remembering the person who has died. This service may be held in a religious sanctuary or a funeral home.

cremation

the complete reduction of a body to ashes by intense heat.

*Life*SKILLS: Communicating Effectively

Helping a Grieving Friend . . .

With another student, role-play the following situation. Alternate roles, so that each of you has an opportunity to play both the grieving friend and the helping friend.

Situation

You are talking with your best friend, whose father just died. Your friend is really sad and needs to express his or her feelings. Using the guidelines in this chapter, talk with your friend and provide your support.

Here's one way you might start.

Friend: It doesn't seem real. I can't stop thinking Dad will come home after work, like he always did.

You: It's really tough, your dad dying. I know you miss him a lot.

SECTION 10.2

■■ ■ *Life*SKILLS

Pair students to complete the Life Skills activity. You may want to review the phases of grief with students and have them suggest statements a grieving person might make at any one of these junctures.

Section Review Worksheet 10.2
To reinforce the concepts presented in this section, assign Section Review Worksheet 10.2.

Section Quiz 10.2
Have students take Section Quiz 10.2.

Reteaching Worksheet 10.2
Students who have difficulty with the material may complete Reteaching Worksheet 10.2.

Extension
Hospice Programs

Hospice programs work with grieving family members as well as with the dying. Encourage some students to visit a hospice center to learn more about ways to help someone work through his or her grief. Sources of information include trained hospice volunteers, the hospice library, and the hospice staff.

Review Answers

1. Funerals and memorial services help people accept the finality of death and to adjust to their loss. These ceremonies are also a way for friends to show support to the grieving family. They also allow people to acknowledge the death spiritually.

2. Answers will vary but may include a good friend; family members; priest, minister, or rabbi; school counselor or therapist; teacher; coach; or an organized support group for people who have lost someone through death.

3. Students may answer that they would tell their friend that the grieving process takes a long time for many people to work through. Students may also relate their experiences with grief or the experiences of others.

4. Students may answer that just having someone there to listen to her would be of help. If this approach does not help Aunt Cindy work through the grief process, then she may need some professional help, such as a counselor, therapist, or support group.

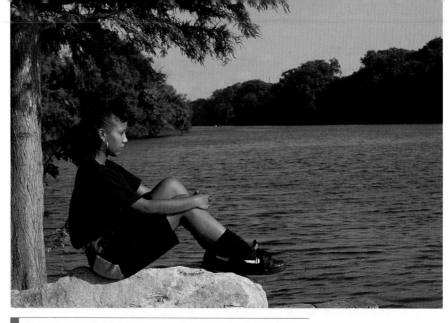

(FIGURE 10-6) **Grieving is a way to adjust to the idea that someone we love has died.**

When the body is to be buried, this indoor service is often followed by a short graveside service before burial.

Many times a memorial service is chosen instead of a funeral to pay respect to a person who has died. Memorial services differ from funerals in that the body is not present. Sometimes they take place after the body has been cremated or buried. Some memorial services are similar to funeral services, but others are more informal than traditional funerals.

Funerals and memorial services play an important role in helping people of our culture adjust to their loss and accept the finality of death. They can also assist people in observing the death spiritually.

In addition, these ceremonies provide a way for friends to show support to the grieving family. Seeing friends who knew and loved the person who has died can make the first few days of bereavement a little easier to bear.

Review

1. *Name three ways that funerals and memorial services help grieving people.*

2. **LIFE SKILLS: Coping** *If you were grieving over the death of a loved one, with whom could you talk?*

3. **LIFE SKILLS: Communicating Effectively** *Your friend tells you that she just can't get over the death of her mother, who died two months ago. What would you say to reassure her that her feelings are normal?*

4. **Critical Thinking** *Your Aunt Cindy's husband died a month ago. She stays home all the time, crying frequently. What do you think would help her most?*

ASSESS

Section Review

Have students answer the Section Review questions.

Alternative Assessment
Ways to Help

Have students make a collage or poster representing ways to help a grieving friend. They can attach a written paragraph explaining the circumstances under which each type of help is appropriate or explain their work orally to the class.

Closure
Grief Process

Ask students to write a short story or a series of diary entries that chronicle the grief process as a teenager might experience it.

Highlights

Summary

- Most people do not have a full awareness of death until adolescence.

- A person can be declared legally dead if the following criteria are met: unreceptiveness and unresponsiveness, unresponsiveness in breathing, lack of reflexes, and a flat EEG.

- Most terminally ill patients go through specific stages: denial, anger, bargaining, depression, and acceptance.

- A will is a legal document that states what to do with possessions and may contain directions for the care of surviving family members.

- A hospice provides medical care in a homelike environment for a person who is dying. Hospice care might also include counseling for the patient and his or her family.

- A living will allows a person to make the decision to die instead of being kept alive by machines.

- Grieving people may go through the same stages as dying people in accepting death. It may help a grieving person to talk with someone about how he or she is feeling.

- A good way to help a grieving friend is to express your concern and let him or her know that you want to help.

- Funerals help people accept the finality of death, allow friends to show support, and let people observe death spiritually.

Vocabulary

will a legal document describing what should be done with a person's possessions after the person's death.

hospices places that offer housing, medical care, and counseling for terminally ill people and counseling for the family.

living will a document expressing a person's wish to be allowed to die in case of terminal illness or incurable injury rather than be kept alive by artificial means.

cremation the complete reduction of a body to ashes by intense heat.

SUMMARY
Have students read the summary to reinforce the concepts they have learned in Chapter 10.

VOCABULARY
Have students use the four vocabulary terms and four other words or phrases from the chapter that were meaningful to them in a short essay that explains their attitudes toward dying and grief.

EXTENSION
Have students work in groups to create a video, filmstrip, play, or series of artworks that teaches others about the ordeal of the dying and the bereaved and shows ways to help them through these trying periods.

CHAPTER 10 ASSESSMENT

CHAPTER REVIEW

Concept Review

1. Death is a topic that makes many people uncomfortable, and they might be afraid that they will say the wrong thing.

2. Children aged 2 to 5 recognize death but do not think it is permanent. Children aged 5 to 9 see death as permanent, but not as something that could happen to them. At about age 10, children realize that death is inevitable, but have trouble realizing it can happen to anyone.

3. unreceptiveness and unresponsiveness, unresponsiveness in breathing, lack of reflexes, flat EEG

4. It can help you understand and help a dying person.

5. Answers may include any three of the following: a person wants to express his or her feelings, needs a caring group of family and friends to listen, and needs to feel that he or she some control over the things that affect him or her. In addition, most people want to be told the truth about their condition.

6. so they can manage their remaining time and prepare for their death

7. Hospices provide medical care for the terminally ill in a homelike atmosphere or in the home. They provide counseling for the patient and family;

CHAPTER 10

Chapter Review

Concept Review . . . .

1. Why might some people avoid a grieving person?

2. Describe a child's concept of death at various age levels.

3. List the four criteria for determining when death occurs.

4. Why is it helpful to know the five stages of accepting death identified by Elisabeth Kubler-Ross?

5. What are three needs of a dying person?

6. Why is it important to be honest with a dying person?

7. Describe some unique features of a hospice.

8. How is a regular will different from a living will?

9. How is the grief of a dying person similar to the grief of a survivor or other family member?

10. What factors influence the grief people feel?

11. What can you do during the grieving process to help adjust to a death? How can you help someone else deal with grief?

12. What is one positive outcome of death and grief?

13. How are burials different from cremations? How do funerals and memorial services differ?

Expressing Your Views . . . .

1. Your best friend just found out he has a terminal illness. He is convinced that a cure will be found soon and that he is not really going to die. It is hard for you to be around him because you are having trouble accepting the news too, but you want to help your friend if you can. How can you explain your friend's attitude? What would you do?

2. Your neighbor, who has two small children, is terminally ill. She has a full-time nurse at home so she doesn't need any kind of medical assistance. However, you want to help her in some way. What could you do?

3. Manuel has been grieving over his father's death for many months now. His friends don't understand his lingering depression. He is beginning to wonder if the grief he feels after all this time is normal and if it will ever go away. How could Manuel help himself?

administer medications to control pain; allow 24-hour family visitation; and provide legal counseling, spiritual support, and nursing care.

8. A living will makes clear what lifesaving measures a person will accept, while a regular will contains instructions for the distribution of material goods and the care of others after a person dies.

9. They both need to express their feelings, and both need a warm group of family and friends.

10. sudden death and closeness to the person

11. Sample response: I could talk to someone about how I am feeling, talk about the future, and be honest with myself about my feelings. To help someone else, I would let that person know that I care and that I'll be there if he or she needs me.

12. Death can draw the survivors closer and help them grow emotionally.

13. In a burial, the body is buried in a casket. In a cremation, the body is reduced to ashes by intense heat. The ashes may be scattered or placed in an urn. The deceased's remains are present at a funeral;

Life Skills Check . . . . . .

1. Coping
Beatrice is terribly depressed about her mother's death. She worries that her friends may get tired of hearing about it, but Beatrice does feel the need to share memories of her mother. What could you suggest to her?

2. Communicating Effectively
Your aunt is terminally ill and has been in and out of hospitals for almost a year. She always dreads her hospital stays because she misses her children and pets when she is away from home. What would you suggest to her as an alternative to hospital care? What would you say to explain how the alternative care would be different?

Projects . . . .

1. Burial customs vary from culture to culture. Choose another country or culture and research its customs and attitudes toward death. Write a brief essay summarizing your findings and comparing that society's customs with those of our society.

2. Find a newspaper or magazine article about a family that had to make the decision whether to keep a loved

one alive by life-support mechanisms, or an article about a situation where a family member carried out a patient's wishes through a living will. Bring the articles to class and discuss them in groups.

3. Invite a grief counselor or mental health professional to your class to lead a discussion about helping people deal with death.

Plan for Action . . . .

Friends and family can support a dying person and each other. List three things you can do in the future to help a dying friend.

in memorial services, the remains are not present.

Expressing Your Views
Sample responses:
1. He is going through the denial stage. The best thing to do is to be with him and listen, but not dispute what he is saying.
2. I would be there to listen, to run errands, to watch the children, to prepare meals, and to help with chores.
3. Manuel can talk with someone he trusts about his feelings.

Life Skills Check
Sample responses:
1. I would tell Beatrice that it is normal for her to want to talk to her mother. I would suggest that if she is uncomfortable talking to her friends, she could talk to the school counselor, an adult she feels close to, or to a religious leader.
2. I would suggest hospice care. This would allow her to be at home with the support of visiting nurses and her family.

Projects
Have students share the results of the projects on death with other students in the school.

Plan for Action
Have students think about what they would want done for them if they were dying. Then have students, using their own desires as a guide, write down three things that they could realistically do for someone with a terminal illness.

ASSESSMENT OPTIONS

 Chapter Test
Have students take the Chapter 10 Test.

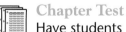 **Alternative Assessment**
Have students do the Alternative Assessment activity for Chapter 10.

 Test Generator
The Test Generator contains additional assessment items for this chapter.

11
Preventing Suicide

SECTION	TITLE/OBJECTIVES	PERSONAL INVENTORY			LIFE SKILLS DEVELOPMENT			
		Personal Health Inventory	Journal	Check Up	Life Skills	Life Skills Worksheets	Media Message or Ethical Issues Worksheet	What Would You Do?
11.1 *pp. 227–231*	**TEENAGE SUICIDE: A SERIOUS PROBLEM** • Define suicide. • Understand how serious the problem of suicide is among teenagers. • Name three possible reasons for the increase in teen suicides. • Name at least three myths and facts about suicide.	Ch. 11	11A					
11.2 *pp. 232–236*	**GIVING AND GETTING HELP** • List at least five warning signs of suicide. ▪ Learn strategies for dealing with someone who is suicidal. ▪ Learn how to use decision-making skills to help a friend in crisis. ▪ Know what to do if you feel suicidal.		11B 11C		p. 234	11A		p. 235

KEY: ▪ Denotes Life Skill Objective
Text references denoted by page number.
Supplement references denoted by chapter or item numbers.

LINKING RESOURCES

	INTERACTION	OTHER RESOURCES		SECTION REVIEW AND ASSESSMENT				
	Making a Choice Cards	Parent Discussion Guide	Health Talk Audio Program	Teaching Transparencies and Directory	Section Review Worksheets	Section Quizzes	Reteaching Worksheets	Section Reviews
	11A	Ch. 11	Ch. 11	11A 11B	11.1	11.1	11.1	p. 231
	11B				11.2	11.2	11.2	p. 236

KEY FACTS

- Suicide is the third leading cause of death for people aged 15 and 24.

- The suicide rate for teenagers has quadrupled in the last 40 years. The increase is attributed, in part, to the sense of isolation and the lack of family support that many of today's teenagers experience.

- Other suicide factors include a dysfunctional or abusive family, pressure to succeed, alcohol and drug use, and a romanticized view of suicide.

- Most suicidal people give warning signs that are a cry for help. People who talk about suicide should be taken seriously.

- People who are suicidal need professional help because they are too depressed or confused to see the alternatives to suicide.

- If a person kills himself or herself, no one is responsible but that person.

CHAPTER REVIEW AND ASSESSMENT

TEXT

Chapter Review pp. 238–239

SUPPLEMENTS

Chapter Test 11

Alternative Assessment 11

Test Generator Chapter 11

GETTING STARTED

Using the Chapter Photograph

Have students look at the chapter photo and the picture of Aaron on the facing page. Then have students suggest what Aaron might be thinking. Ask students how it might help Aaron to have someone outside of his family to talk about his problems with. Also, ask why Aaron's problems might need more help than a supportive friend could give.

Question Box

Have students write out any questions they have about suicide and suicide prevention and put them in the Question Box.

Sensitivity ALERT

Suicide is a difficult topic that can make both adults and students uncomfortable. Some students may be depressed or even suicidal, or they may have family members who are; their privacy must be respected. In addition, students need reassurance that all people go through some periods of depression in their lives. Suicidal people differ in the degree and number of symptoms, and in their ability to cope.

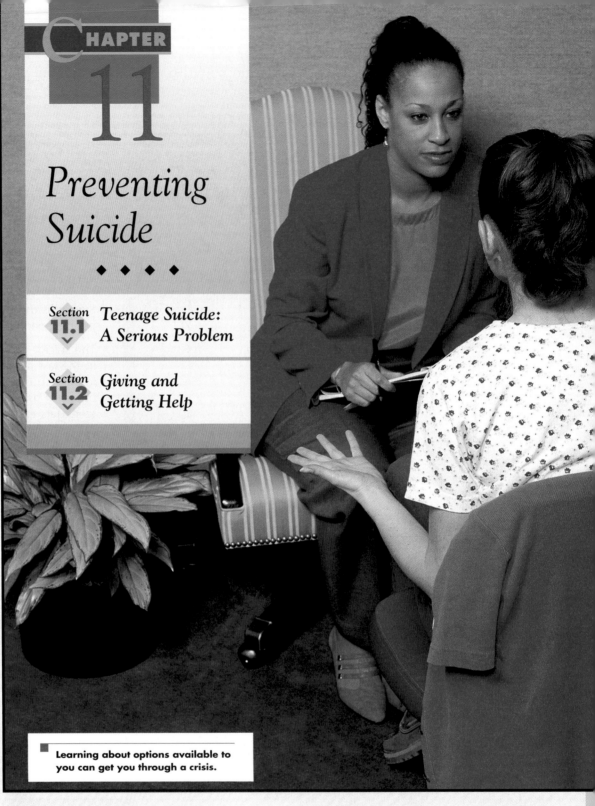

CHAPTER 11

Preventing Suicide

◆ ◆ ◆ ◆

Section 11.1 Teenage Suicide: A Serious Problem

Section 11.2 Giving and Getting Help

Learning about options available to you can get you through a crisis.

MYTHS & MISCONCEPTIONS

- **Suicidal people always appear depressed and lonely.** This is not always true; sometimes a suicidal person becomes overly active before attempting suicide.

- **If you dare a suicidal person to go ahead and commit suicide, he or she is not likely to do it.** Such a dare is a dangerous action and may only convince the suicidal person that no one really cares about him or her.

- **Once a person attempts suicide and fails, it is unlikely that he or she will try it again.** Often suicide victims make several suicide attempts before they succeed in taking their own life. It is important that a person who has attempted suicide receive professional help immediately.

A fter the divorce, things got really bad for Aaron. He lived with his mother, who was always on his case about something. Aaron knew that she was worried about money because his dad was having trouble paying the child-support payment and they could barely make ends meet.

Aaron was also having a hard time in school. He had flunked three tests in a row, and he knew that if he kept this up, he wouldn't get in to college. Even if he did get accepted, there probably wouldn't be enough money to pay for it. Aaron lay awake at night feeling desperate about his situation, and this made it even harder to concentrate at school.

Then the worst thing of all happened. Aaron's girlfriend, Ashley, who had stayed with him through all his troubles, told Aaron she didn't want to see him anymore. She had started going out with someone else. His whole life seemed so hopeless that he started to think about ending it all. He just wanted to go to sleep and never wake up.

Personal Health Inventory

Have students complete the Personal Health Inventory for this chapter.

English/Spanish CD Audio Program

Use the English/Spanish Health Talk audio program for students who need audio reinforcement of the concepts presented.

Parent Discussion Guide

Send home the Parent Letter for Chapter 11. As you progress through the chapter, send home the Parental Survey and The Extra Mile.

Section 11.1

Teenage Suicide: A Serious Problem

Objectives

- Define suicide.

- Understand how serious the problem of suicide is among teenagers.

- Name three possible reasons for the increase in teen suicides.

- Name at least three myths and facts about suicide.

Aaron reacted to the problems in his life by thinking about killing himself—committing **suicide.** He felt trapped. In his despair, he did not recognize that other options existed for him.

If you have ever been depressed like Aaron, you may have considered suicide. This is not unusual. Many people think about taking their own life when they feel extremely unhappy and hopeless. But if you have felt that suicide was the only way out of your troubles, you haven't learned about all the other options that exist.

In this chapter you will learn about the options available to you and your friends if life seems too painful to go on.

The Increase in Teen Suicides

Suicide is an increasingly serious problem among young people. The suicide rate among teenagers has quadrupled in the last 40 years. Suicide is the third leading cause

suicide:

the act of intentionally taking one's own life.

Section 11.1 Lesson Plan

MOTIVATE

Journal 11A
Aaron's Situation

This may be done as a warm-up activity. Ask students to write in their Journal a description of their feelings as they read about Aaron's situation. Suggest that they also describe how they would respond if he were their friend.

Writing
Aaron's Frame of Mind

Ask students to study the photograph of Aaron and write a descriptive paragraph or poem that reveals his frame of mind.

Background

Depression and Sunlight

Some cases of depression that occur in winter can be linked to the low levels of sunlight. Physicians call this condition season affective disorder (SAD) and define it as a temporary depression that occurs during the winter months. The reduced level of sunlight can cause changes in brain hormone levels that result in altered mood and metabolism. It is estimated that as many as 10 percent of those living in northern latitudes suffer from SAD. Researchers are experimenting with light therapy as a treatment for the disorder. In the meantime, some experts say that people prone to depression should try to get at least two hours of sunlight each day.

Making a Choice 11A

Assign the Group Discussion card. The card asks students to examine their feelings about statements concerning suicide.

of death among people between 15 and 24. A recent study showed that 27 percent of high school students have considered suicide at least once in their life. Of those who actually attempt suicide, 1 in 50 succeeds. Although the reasons for the increase are not clear, there are several factors that may contribute to teen suicide.

The rising divorce rate and breakup of families has created a situation in which many teenagers feel a sense of isolation and a lack of family support. Only a few decades ago, several generations of a family often lived in the same house. In this situation, young people usually had at least one close relative—a parent, a grandparent, an aunt, an uncle, or a cousin—that they felt they could relate to. Today teenagers live in smaller families, with fewer adults around to offer them the emotional support they need as a natural part of growing up.

Also, people today move from place to place more often than in earlier times. As a result of a parent's job loss or transfer to another city, children and teenagers often lose their old friends and must adjust to new schools. In times of trouble they may not be able to call on friends and relatives, who may be thousands of miles away.

Many teens live in troubled families, and feel that the love and care that they need is simply not there for them. Some teens may also experience physical, emotional, or sexual abuse.

Another factor may be the pressure to succeed in school and in future careers. Young people may feel like failures if they do not live up to their own or their parents' expectations.

The increased use of alcohol and other drugs among teens also contributes to suicides. Although mind-altering substances may provide a temporary escape from emotional pain, they make things worse in the long run. Using alcohol and drugs damages a person's ability to solve everyday prob-

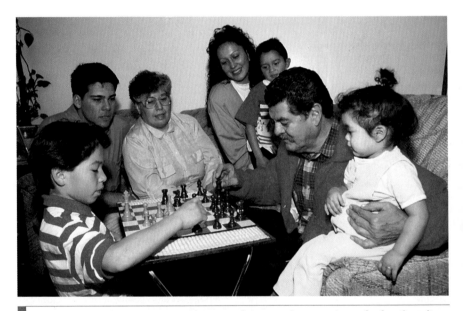

(FIGURE 11-1) **At one time, it was common for several generations of a family to live together. Teenagers in such families usually had at least one close relation to talk to.**

TEACH

Class Discussion
Celebrity Suicide

Some individuals identify to such an extent with the romanticized figure of a deceased celebrity who committed suicide that they also attempt suicide, sometimes successfully. As a class, discuss this phenomenon. Have students suggest reasons why this mythic status

granted by the media is so appealing to some individuals. Then discuss the fallacy of each reason. For example, some people may see suicide as the ultimate rejection of society. However, the reality is that the person who committed suicide was probably experiencing extreme pain and depression; it is more likely that he or she was seeking relief, not rejecting society. The person may have turned to alcohol or drug use instead of seeking effective

treatment for depression, making the problem worse.

Class Discussion
Do They Really Want to Die?

Ask: **In what sense is it true that a suicidal person doesn't want to die?** *[The suicidal person wants the pain or problem to end, not life. He or she, however, is too depressed and overwhelmed by feelings to see an end to the problem or options other than death.]*

(FIGURE 11-2) **Kurt Cobain, lead singer of the band Nirvana, committed suicide in 1994. Celebrities who commit suicide are sometimes glamorized by the media.**

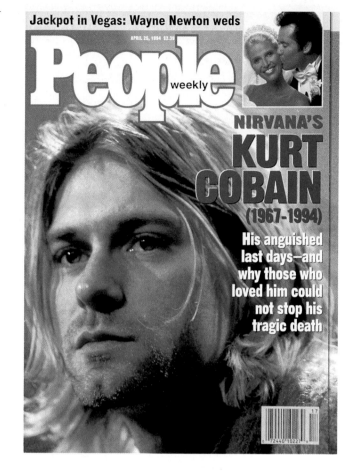

Jackpot in Vegas: Wayne Newton weds

People weekly

APRIL 25, 1994 $2.39

NIRVANA'S KURT COBAIN (1967-1994)

His anguished last days—and why those who loved him could not stop his tragic death

lems. And being drunk or high interferes with a person's judgment, and increases the chance that a person will act on a suicidal impulse.

Finally, the popular media have romanticized suicide to a certain extent. When famous people kill themselves, they are sometimes made to seem like mythic figures. Suicide, such a message may seem to say, is glamorous and romantic. But once a celebrity is dead, he or she is not around to enjoy the romantic image. Suicide is not a glamorous act; it brings only death.

Why Would Someone Want to Die?

The reasons why young people try to kill themselves are many and complicated. Most people don't really want to die—they just want to end the emotional pain that they are suffering.

How can things get that bad? Life as a teenager can seem extremely stressful, especially if a person has low self-esteem. If someone who is already under great stress experiences a crisis, it may make life seem unbearable.

A crisis to one person would not necessarily seem like a crisis to another. To Aaron, losing his girlfriend was the last straw—he felt it pushed him over the edge. His girlfriend provided the only emotional

support he had at that time. His father was gone, and his mother seemed preoccupied with earning enough money to pay the bills and keep a roof over their heads.

When a person is depressed, events that at other times would be tolerable might seem impossible to bear. Moving to another town, not making a team or club, or the death of a pet could trigger a crisis in an already depressed person. Even an event that would seem trivial to others—having a bicycle stolen, for example—could be the last unbearable thing for an extremely depressed person.

Background
Suicide Rates

Suicide rates vary according to sex and age. Men are three times more likely than women are to commit suicide. On the whole, the elderly are less likely than younger people are to commit suicide; however, the group with the highest suicide rate is white men over 85.

Although the teen suicide rate is relatively low, it is growing; from 1970 to 1994, it increased by 95 percent. The suicide rate for black males aged 15 to 24 is increasing rapidly. According to the Centers for Disease Control and Prevention, during the period of 1980 though 1993, this rate increased by 63 percent. Teens often commit suicide for reasons that are incomprehensible to adults. Researchers suggest that adults often do not appreciate the intensity of feeling that teenagers experience; thus they fail to recognize when a teenager feels that a situation is hopeless.

Teaching Transparency 11A
Myths and Facts About Suicide

Show the transparency of Figure 11-3 found on page 330. Explain that in the past, reluctance to talk about suicide has led to many wrong assumptions. Divide the class into pairs, assigning each pair one of the myths shown on the chart. Have them work out a brief

dialogue in which one speaker believes the myth and the other must convince him or her of the facts.

Extension
What About the Terminally Ill?

Have students investigate recent magazine and newspaper articles reflecting various viewpoints concerning the rights of the terminally ill. Have them summarize their findings for the rest of the class.

Section Review Worksheet 11.1

To reinforce the concepts presented in this section, assign Section Review Worksheet 11.1.

Section Quiz 11.1

Have students take Section Quiz 11.1.

Reteaching Worksheet 11.1

Students who have difficulty with the material may complete Reteaching Worksheet 11.1.

Myths and Facts About Suicide

Myth	Fact
Suicide usually occurs without warning.	While some suicides may be impulsive, usually the person has thought about suicide for a long time.
People who talk about killing themselves rarely commit suicide.	Most people who commit suicide have talked about it before.
If you ask a person if he or she is considering suicide, you will encourage that person to commit suicide.	You will not cause a suicide by asking if someone is thinking about it. People who are not suicidal will not be influenced by the question. People who are considering suicide will feel relieved that someone cares enough to ask and to listen to their problems.
All suicidal people want to die.	A suicide attempt is often a cry for help. The person may be asking for help to live.
When a suicidal person suddenly seems calm and serene, there is no longer any danger of suicide.	A suicidal person who suddenly acts calm and serene may have decided to commit suicide and therefore feels relief that a decision has been made.
If someone makes a suicidal comment while drunk or high, it isn't very serious.	People who are under the influence of alcohol or other drugs may be at a greater risk of acting on suicidal thoughts because their judgment is impaired and they may be more impulsive.
All people who commit suicide are mentally ill.	Many people who feel suicidal are not mentally ill. They may be in a period of intense emotional crisis.
Once a person is suicidal, he or she will always be suicidal.	Many people consider suicide for only a brief period in their lives. A person who attempts suicide and survives may never attempt it again if proper support and treatment is found.
The tendency toward suicide is inherited and passed from parent to child.	Suicide is a behavior and cannot be inherited. However, depression may have a genetic basis. Severely depressed people may harbor more thoughts of suicide than those who do not suffer from depression.

(FIGURE 11-3) **Because people avoid talking about suicide, many myths have arisen about the subject. Only by openly discussing suicide can people in trouble be recognized and helped.**

(FIGURE 11-4) **Suicide is a permanent response to what is usually a temporary problem.**

When people are in crisis situations, they may become confused and make poor decisions. They may develop "tunnel vision," which is the inability to see all the options available. Aaron thought killing himself was the only way to solve his problems. When someone feels that suicide is the only solution to the problems of living, he or she is said to have a **suicidal mindset.**

But other solutions to problems always exist, even in the worst of situations. If Aaron had committed suicide, it would have been a permanent solution to a temporary problem. Aaron didn't really want to *die*. He just wanted to end his pain and suffering. The key to preventing suicide is getting help from people who can offer alternatives to ending one's life.

Review

1. Define suicide.

2. Where does suicide rank among the causes of death of people aged 15 to 24?

3. Name three possible reasons for the increase in teen suicides.

4. Name three common myths about suicide and explain why each is not true.

5. **Critical Thinking** Describe some effects of alcohol and other drug use that might increase the possibility that a person would attempt suicide.

suicidal mindset:

the feeling that suicide is the only solution to the problems of living.

ASSESS

Section Review
Have students answer the Section Review questions.

Alternative Assessment
Alcohol and Drugs

Students can list several factors contributing to the suicide problem among young people and explain orally how alcohol and drug use increase the effects of these factors.

Closure
Teenage Suicide

Have students write a feature article on teenage suicide for a school newspaper, communicating facts about the seriousness of the problem, and dispelling common myths about suicide.

Section
11.2   *Giving and Getting Help*

According to The U.S. Department of Health and Human Services Task Force on Youth Suicide, suicide is the leading cause of death among lesbian and gay youth. In fact, 30 percent of all youth suicides committed each year in the United States fall within this group. Schools can protect these young people by having information about sexual identity problems readily available for those seeking it.

In addition to those indicators mentioned in the text, there are others that should be taken seriously. These include suicide notes, behavior that is very out-of-character (especially if it is self-destructive), drastic increase in use of alcohol and drugs, communication of a detailed plan for suicide, and talk about a means for killing oneself.

Section
11.2   *Giving and Getting Help*

Objectives

- *List at least five warning signs of suicide.*
- *Learn strategies for dealing with someone who is suicidal.*
  - ■ **LIFE SKILLS: Solving Problems**
- *Learn how to use decision-making skills to help a friend in crisis.*
  - ■ **LIFE SKILLS: Making Responsible Decisions**
- *Know what to do if you feel suicidal.*
  - ■ **LIFE SKILLS: Coping**

Because suicide is such a serious and scary issue, it's hard to know how to help someone who is considering it. Do the best you can to help them, but don't feel that the entire burden is on you. You shouldn't feel responsible if a friend commits suicide. If a person kills himself or herself, no one is responsible but that person.

The first step is to try to determine if a friend feels suicidal. Statistics show that 80 percent of the people who attempt suicide have given warning signals. Figure 11-7 on page 233 lists some possible warning signs of suicide.

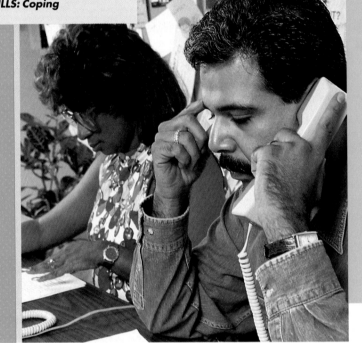

(FIGURE 11-5) **If you think a friend is suicidal, call a suicide hotline. The staff there will assist your efforts to find help.**

Intervention Strategies: What Should You Do?

Think back to Aaron at the beginning of this chapter. Assume that you are a friend of his and you've noticed that he has seemed really down lately. One night he says to you: "This may be the last time you will see me." Which of the following should you do?

1. Ask Aaron if he is thinking about committing suicide.
2. Avoid mentioning suicide but make an attempt to find out what is bothering Aaron.
3. Keep the talk light so as not to give Aaron any ideas about suicide.
4. Try to joke with Aaron about his problems and about suicide.

The first answer is the best one in this case. If Aaron isn't thinking about suicide, your mentioning it will not do any harm; you aren't going to make him suicidal by asking him if he is. But if Aaron is thinking about suicide, he urgently needs to discuss it. People who talk about suicide, or give any indication they are contemplating it, are often seeking help in the only way they know how.

Most suicidal people reach out to someone for help. In fact, many reach out repeatedly before they actually try to kill themselves.

If you have a friend who is suicidal, let your friend know you are listening and that you understand. Your friend may express feelings of being picked on, different, lonely, ugly, or stupid. Do not try to make your friend feel better by denying the feelings. Don't say, for example: "Oh, you're just imagining things. Snap out of it."

Be as understanding and patient as possible. To show you understand, you could say something like: "It must feel terrible to have all that pain and anguish."

(FIGURE 11-6) **If a friend seems depressed and possibly suicidal, let him or her know that you're there, and that you care.**

Possible Warning Signs of Suicide

Change in eating and sleeping habits

Withdrawal from friends, family, and regular activities

Violent actions, rebellious behavior, or running away

Use of alcohol or other drugs

Unusual neglect of personal appearance

Marked personality change

Persistent boredom, difficulty concentrating, or a decline in the quality of schoolwork

Frequent complaints about physical symptoms, such as stomachaches, headaches, or fatigue, which are often related to emotions

Giving away favorite possessions

Loss of interest in pleasurable activities

Not tolerating praise or rewards

(FIGURE 11-7) **Eighty percent of people who attempt suicide give warning signs that are a cry for help. If you recognize one or more of these signs in someone, talk with the person about your concerns. If their behavior continues, seek assistance from a professional.**

Background
Risk Factors for Suicide

There are many risk factors for suicide, but people who suffer from ongoing severe depression are most at risk. Often depression is related to a physical illness. It is estimated that physical illness is an important contributing factor in up to 50 percent of all suicides. Alcoholism is another risk factor. People with alcohol-abuse problems often begin drinking because they are depressed. The alcohol aggravates the depression and increases feelings of hopelessness in the abuser. As a result, the suicide rate for alcoholics is higher than that of the general public.

Cooperative Learning
Can You Help?

Many suicidal people can be helped if someone recognizes the problem and responds to it with appropriate actions. Divide the class into small groups, and have the groups make a list of ways that a student could suggest to another person that he or she is in danger and needs to seek professional help. Emphasize that while the support of friends is very helpful, a person who is suicidal needs professional help. Also, emphasize that if a person does commit suicide, the person's friends should not feel responsible.

Reinforcement
Showing Concern

Point out that it never hurts to show concern for someone who is struggling with depression or an emotional crisis, even if he or she is not suicidal.

• • • TEACH continues on p. 234

Life SKILLS

Have students do the Life Skills activity, brainstorming the names of adults who can be called on to help a suicidal friend. Bring phone books to class and have students locate phone numbers for suicide hot lines, crisis intervention lines, suicide counselors, counseling services, human services clinics, and so on.

 Life Skills Worksheet 11A

Assign the Peer Counseling Groups Life Skills Worksheet.

Making a Choice 11B

Assign the Helping a Friend in Trouble card. The card asks students to discuss and role-play situations in which they could help a suicidal friend.

After discovering that your friend is suicidal, get help. Contact an adult who you feel is caring and in a position to help. This person could be a parent or other relative, teacher, school counselor, school nurse, religious leader, or neighbor. Such a person may be able to help your friend, and may also offer advice on other places to go for help.

You could also call your local suicide hotline. Look in the phone book under ''Suicide'' or ''Crisis.'' The people staffing these phone lines will find help for you.

You can also call the 911 emergency number or the police department.

Your friend might make you promise not to tell anybody. It may seem like a difficult decision to make—keeping a promise you made to a friend, or going for help. But by confiding in you, your friend is asking for help. To help your friend, you *must* break the promise and notify a trusted adult of the danger that exists.

Remember, though, that you are not responsible for your friend's life. Only he or she can make the decision to live.

Life SKILLS: Solving Problems

Helping a Suicidal Friend . . . .

A friend tells you that he is failing school and feels humiliated because his father is a teacher and has high expectations of him. He says he feels stupid and knows he'll never amount to anything. If that's the way his life is going to be, he says, he might as well kill himself. You listen and let him know you care about him and that you understand how bad he must feel. You offer to help him find assistance.

On a separate sheet of paper, write down the names of as many adults as you can think of who could help your friend.

• • • TEACH continued

Class Discussion
Getting the Best Help

Refer students to Figure 11-8 and ask: **Which of these adults would be most helpful to someone who is considering suicide?** [Responses may vary, but ask students to express why they feel like they do.]

Journal 11C
Seeking Help

After discussing the importance of seeking help when your troubles are more than you can handle alone, have students write in their Journal a list of people they could turn to if they were facing what seemed like insurmountable problems. Then have them list two things they learned in the chapter that would make them more willing to seek help.

Extension
Another Perspective

Ask students to select an adult they trust and can talk to easily. Have each student talk with the person about difficult situations and stresses he or she faced in teenage years and find out the person's perspective on those problems today. How did he or she cope as a teenager?

If You Feel Suicidal

If you ever feel that life is too painful to continue, you must ask for help. The reason you need help is that you are too confused and desperate to see all the alternatives to suicide.

Contact one of the adults listed in Figure 11-8, or any other adult you trust. You might be surprised to find out how much other people care for you and how willing they are to help you.

You may need professional counseling with a psychologist or therapist. At the very least, talk to a therapist to see if counseling is necessary. Therapists can offer options you hadn't thought of before. They can also help you learn new skills so that you can succeed in basic goals like making friends, coping with stress, or getting along with your family. Most important, they may remind you that no matter how bad things may seem, there are things you can do to help yourself feel better.

■ (FIGURE 11-8) **Help is available for those in crisis. Talk to a trusted adult if you (or a friend) are thinking of suicide.**

What Would You Do **?**

Making Responsible Decisions

You Made a Promise

Julia is your best friend. She has been acting depressed lately because her boyfriend broke up with her. Julia came to you and told you that she is thinking about killing herself. But she made you promise you would not tell anyone.

After you talk with her, you begin to wonder if you should tell anyone about Julia's problem. But you *did* promise not to, and she *is* your best friend. What would you do?

Remember to use the decision-making steps:

1. State the Problem.
2. List the Options.
3. Imagine the Benefits and Consequences.
4. Consider Your Values.
5. Weigh the Options and Decide.
6. Act.
7. Evaluate the Results.

Some Adults Who Might Be Helpful in a Crisis

- Parent
- Grandparent, aunt, uncle, or other relative
- Teacher
- School counselor
- School nurse
- Therapist at a mental-health center
- Minister, priest, rabbi, or other religious leader
- Neighbor
- Person who staffs the local suicide hotline, the crisis hotline, or the 911 emergency number
- Person who answers the phone at the police department

 What Would You Do **?**

Review the steps in the decision-making process briefly. Point out that in this case a decision must be made quickly. Therefore, it is important to decide before the fact how you will handle such a situation if it arises.

Section Review Worksheet 11.2

To reinforce the concepts presented in this section, assign Section Review Worksheet 11.2.

Section Quiz 11.2

Have students take Section Quiz 11.2.

Reteaching Worksheet 11.2

Students who have difficulty with the material may complete Reteaching Worksheet 11.2.

Review Answers

1. Students may include any of the signs listed in Figure 11-7.

2. Ask the friend if he or she is contemplating suicide. If the friend says yes, even if you have promised not to tell anybody, immediately contact an adult who is in a position to help. If no one is available, call the local suicide hotline, 911, or the police department.

3. By confiding in the student, the friend is asking for help. To help the friend, the student must break the promise and notify a trusted adult of the situation.

4. You could ask for help from a trusted adult or call the local suicide prevention crisis line.

5. Answers will vary. Students may answer that a particular event, however trivial it may seem to someone else, may cause a person to feel suicidal if that person has been experiencing several stressful or depressing situations.

■ (FIGURE 11-9) **You might be surprised to find out how much other people care for you and how willing they are to help you.**

You need to be willing to take a risk—the risk of confronting and resolving your problems. If you are willing to talk openly and honestly about the things that are making you unhappy, you can create options for yourself that do not exist when you remain closed and depressed. Suicide is only one option out of thousands of options that life offers. If you choose it, then you won't have the chance to explore the others.

The teenage years are a difficult time for most people. Many adults who are now living happy lives once considered suicide or even attempted it when they were teenagers themselves.

Remember that with help, you can work through your pain. Don't try to solve a temporary problem with a permanent act like suicide. If you feel like hurting yourself, talk to a trusted adult now.

Review

1. *What are five signs that might indicate someone is suicidal?*

2. ■■ **LIFE SKILLS: Solving Problems** *Describe what you should do if your friend tells you he or she doesn't want to live.*

3. ■■ **LIFE SKILLS: Making Responsible Decisions** *Your friend made you promise that you would not tell anyone he was going to kill himself. Why should you break your promise?*

4. ■■ **LIFE SKILLS: Coping** *If you felt suicidal, how could you help yourself?*

5. *Critical Thinking* *Why do you think a particular situation will cause one person to feel suicidal, while another person in the same situation might not even be depressed?*

ASSESS

Section Review

Have students answer the Section Review questions.

Alternative Assessment

Ask students to write a letter to a counselor in which they express concern for a friend who exhibits some of the warning signs of suicide. Students may exchange letters and write a reply to the one they receive. Replies should show understanding of how to help a suicidal person.

Closure
Do's and Don'ts

Ask students to write a checklist of do's and don'ts for dealing with a person who may be suicidal. Suggest that they list four items in each column.

Highlights

Summary

- Suicide is one of the leading causes of death among people aged 15 to 24. The suicide rate among teenagers has quadrupled in the last 40 years.

- The following are possible reasons for the increase in teen suicides: (1) the rising divorce rate and breakup of families; (2) families moving from place to place more frequently; (3) absence of parental love and support in some families; (4) pressure to succeed in school and future careers; (5) increasing use of alcohol and drugs; and (6) glamorization of suicide by the media.

- Most people don't want to die but simply want to end the emotional pain they are suffering.

- Crises often seem more stressful if a person has low self-esteem. A crisis to one person may not be a crisis for someone else.

- Depression is a feeling that often accompanies suicide.

- When people are in crisis situations, they may become confused, make poor decisions, and be unable to see all the options available.

- Most people who attempt suicide display one or more warning signs. These signs or threats should always be taken seriously.

- Many adults who are now living happy lives once considered suicide or even attempted it when they were teenagers themselves.

- If you think a friend is thinking about suicide, get help as soon as possible. Contact a caring adult or call your local suicide hotline number.

- If you are in pain and are thinking about suicide, know that counseling is available from mental-health professionals such as psychologists.

- A person who is willing to talk openly and honestly about problems has options that do not exist for a person who remains closed and depressed.

Vocabulary

suicide the act of intentionally taking one's own life.

suicidal mindset the feeling that suicide is the only solution to the problems of living.

SUMMARY
Have students read the summary to reinforce the concepts they have learned in Chapter 11.

VOCABULARY
Using the vocabulary listed below and at least five other key words or phrases from the chapter, students might create a concept map that shows the relationships between these words and phrases and their relationship to the topic of teenage suicide. Suggest that students make their concept maps large enough to include illustrations that convey the concepts behind the words.

EXTENSION
Have students contact local mental health organizations or the National Mental Health Institute by phone or letter and request information on giving and receiving help for depression and suicidal tendencies. Encourage them to organize this information into a display for the classroom.

Chapter Review

CHAPTER REVIEW

Concept Review

1. Answers will vary. Possible reasons include the rising divorce rate and breakup of families, families moving from place to place more frequently, some families not providing love and care to children, pressure to succeed, increasing use of alcohol and drugs, and suicide being glamorized and romanticized by the media.

2. Most people don't want to die but simply want to end the emotional pain they are suffering.

3. The teen may feel he or she is the cause of the divorce. The teen may also feel isolated and sense a lack of family support.

4. The depression may lead to a crisis situation in which the person becomes confused, makes poor decisions, or cannot see options available. Without seeing options, the person may view the situation as hopeless and for this reason attempt suicide.

5. They may decide to attempt suicide.

6. Students may ask the friend if he or she is thinking of suicide. Students may let their friend know that they are listening and understand. Students can ask for help for their friend from parents, teachers, clergy, and school counselors.

Concept Review

1. Why is suicide a major problem among young people?

2. Is it true that all suicidal people want to die? Explain.

3. Explain why the breakup of families could contribute to the increase in teen suicides.

4. What makes the depression felt by a possible suicide victim different from the depression most people experience in everyday life?

5. What happens to people who are thinking of suicide when they find themselves in crisis situations?

6. How can you help if a friend is in a suicidal situation? Who are some adults who could help?

7. If a friend who is suicidal confides in you about his or her intentions and swears you to secrecy, should you keep your promise? Explain.

8. If you feel suicidal, how can it be helpful to take the risk of confronting and resolving your problems?

9. If you consider suicide once, will you always be suicidal? Explain.

Expressing Your Views

1. A good friend of yours has lost a lot of weight pretty quickly. Her grades have been dropping and she seems withdrawn. All of this has happened since her boyfriend broke up with her. You are concerned about her. What should you do?

2. Will's parents have recently divorced, and soon he will have to move to another town. He has been very depressed and has started seeing a psychologist. His friends don't know the whole story, but they say that Will is getting counseling because he's not strong enough to handle his problems on his own. What would you say to Will's friends?

3. Randall seems antisocial because he is always alone. Twice in the past week he has started strange conversations with you that ended with a suicide threat. When you told a friend what had happened, the friend said not to worry, that Randall threatens suicide all the time just to get attention. What do you think? Should you be concerned?

7. By confiding in you, your friend is asking for help. To help your friend, you must break the promise and notify a trusted adult.

8. Confronting and resolving personal problems may require professional help. A therapist can offer options you might not have thought of before. Following through with the professional help can help you see that no matter how bad things seem, there are things you can do to make yourself feel better.

9. No. Once you receive help and resolve the problem(s) you will not feel as depressed; you will feel more in control and happier; you will learn new skills in dealing with various problems. A situation may never arise again in which you feel so hopeless, helpless, and depressed.

Expressing Your Views
Sample responses:

1. Talk with her about what may be bothering her and let her know that I am

Life Skills Check . . . .

1. Coping

Let's say that during the past year you became terribly depressed. Your spirits were so low that at one point you were thinking about suicide. Instead, you got professional counseling, and now you feel as though you are recovering. As part of your therapy, your counselor has asked you to write down a list of the things that make you happy. What would you include on your list?

2. Solving Problems

Suppose a friend calls you to come over to her house right away. When you arrive, she appears very upset and begins to talk about suicide and death. No one is at home except the two of you. What should you do?

Projects . . . .

1. Work with a group to design a suicide-prevention pamphlet, using the information in your textbook. Include myths and facts about suicide, some warning signs of suicide, a list of adults to contact in a crisis, and the free hotline number. Distribute copies of the pamphlet throughout your school or publish it in the school newspaper.

2. Work with a partner to make up a problem situation and then role-play, providing support and receiving support. Devise a positive way to act out how to cope with the situation.

3. Using the library or the Internet to find newspaper and magazine articles, investigate a particular group of people that has a high suicide rate. Document your findings, and then brainstorm to make a list of actions that might help to lower that rate.

Plan for Action . . . .

Suicide is one of the leading causes of death among teenagers. Plan how you can prevent suicide in your life and in others' lives.

listening and I understand. Also, I would not attempt to make her feel better by denying any feelings she shares with me. If she is suicidal, I would get help.

2. I would tell them that they do not fully understand the situation and that Will is stronger than many people because he recognizes and admits feelings and is willing to risk con-fronting and re-solving his problems.

3. Randall may indeed be suicidal. I would be concerned and seek help for Randall by contacting a caring adult or calling the suicide hotline number.

Life Skills Check
Sample responses:

1. Answers will vary.

2. Be patient and understanding and let her know you are listening to what she is saying. Then get help as soon as possible by contacting a caring adult or calling the suicide hotline number, 911, or the police department.

Projects
Have students complete the projects on suicide.

Plan for Action
Ask the class to make a list of situations that might make a teenager think of suicide. Then have them come up with alternatives to suicide that will address each situation.

Pledge
Discuss the pledge for Chapter 11. A student's decision of whether to sign the pledge is personal and private.

ASSESSMENT OPTIONS

Chapter Test
Have students take the Chapter 11 Test.

Alternate Assessment
Have students do the Alternative Assessment activity for Chapter 11.

Test Generator
The Test Generator contains additional assessment items for this chapter.

ETHICAL ISSUES IN HEALTH

ISSUE: *Should terminally ill people have the right to determine how or when to die?*

Have students read the Ethical Issues in Health feature. Then divide the class into two teams, one for and the other against euthanasia. Have them debate whether a person who is terminally ill has the right to willfully end his or her own life.

Ethical Issues in Health

ISSUE: Should terminally ill people have the right to determine how or when to die?

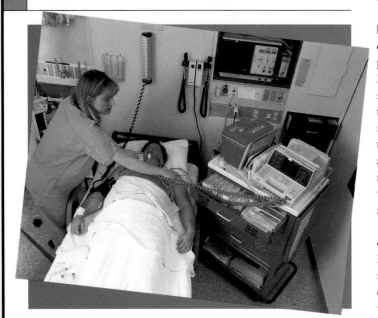

Death is the natural and inevitable end to life. Modern medical techniques, such as CPR and mechanical life support, have made it possible to avert death in situations where once a person certainly would have died. Modern technology is also capable of sustaining a person's life far beyond the point at which natural death would have occurred. Unfortunately, the technology to restore a healthy normal life to most of the people who survive with the aid of life-sustaining equipment does not exist. As a result, thousands of patients with no hope of recovery survive with mechanical support for weeks, months, and even years at great financial and emotional expense to their families and society.

Just as they did when they were healthy, people who are facing death need close relationships, honest communication, personal dignity, and control of their lives. Many people believe that the use of life-sustaining treatments, such as feeding through tubes and using equipment to maintain breathing and circulation, robs terminally ill patients of personal dignity and the right to control their lives. For this reason, many people believe that people with no hope of recovery should have the right to decide to die.

One way that people can retain control of their lives even when they are terminally ill is to establish a "living will." Recognized by most states, a living will is a legal document that allows people to specify what measures they want taken if they should have a serious disease or injury that will ultimately and inevitably result in death. Such a document allows a person to choose between receiving life-sustaining treatment or refusing all life-sustaining treatment so that death can occur naturally. A living will is executed only when the patient becomes permanently unconscious.

Some people want to be able to decide how and when to die, should they become terminally ill. Those who support the legal right to control the conditions of their own deaths make up the "right-to-die" movement. Sometimes terminally ill people request assistance from friends and family in

Issues in Health

what is often called "assisted suicide" or "assisted death." When a physician helps terminally ill patients die at their request, it is often referred to as "physician aid in dying."

An increasing number of people faced with death, particularly those in the latter stages of AIDS, are asking their friends and physicians to assist them by injecting them with painkillers in large enough doses to cause death. In 1989, the suicide rate among people with AIDS in the United States was six times higher than the rate for other adults. The suicide rate among people with other terminal illnesses is unknown.

The issue of assisted death gained national media attention when Dr. Jack Kevorkian of Michigan was tried for murder after he helped several people die with his controversial "suicide machine." Over the years, there have been several highly publicized court trials of people who caused the death of terminally ill family members suffering excruciating pain.

In the United States, a physician who purposefully causes the death of a terminally ill patient by injecting drugs or writing a prescription for drugs can be charged with murder, even if the doctor's actions were at the request of the patient. A person who is not a physician who helps end a life on request can also be charged with murder. However, very few people who have helped a terminally ill loved one die have been sent to jail. Dr. Kevorkian has been acquitted many times. Laws legalizing assisted death have been introduced in several states, but the idea is still very controversial. In the Netherlands, physicians who assist patients in ending their lives are not prosecuted.

People in the "right-to-die" movement defend assisted death. They argue that the practice is ethical because dying people have the right to have some control over both their lives and their deaths, especially the length of time it takes to die. Those who oppose assisted death say that even those who are dying do not have the right to ask others to participate in an act that is illegal and morally wrong.

Situation for Discussion

Martha is a 35-year-old woman who has cancer. The cancer began in an ovary and has spread to many parts of her body. More than one physician has confirmed that Martha is terminally ill. She suffers excruciating pain and has begun to slip in and out of consciousness. She has asked her doctor to help her die by prescribing a lethal dose of morphine.

a. If Martha's doctor prescribes this medication for her, could he be tried for murder? Research court cases of physicians who have assisted their patients in death. Has anyone been convicted for this action?

b. If Martha's doctor refuses to prescribe the morphine, what steps could she take to assure that she would not be put on machines that would prolong her life?

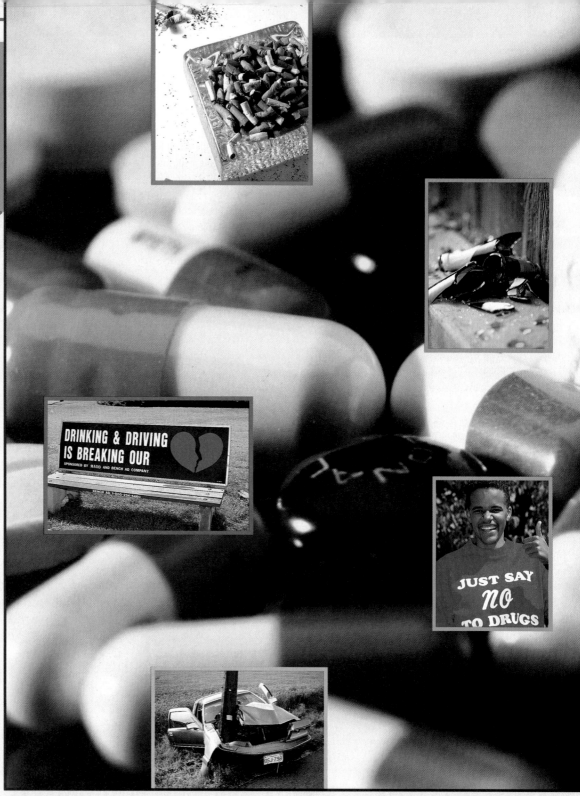

CHAPTER OVERVIEWS

CHAPTER 12

THE USE, MISUSE, AND ABUSE OF DRUGS

Students learn that although drugs can be useful in the prevention, treatment, or cure of many illnesses, drugs cannot solve *all* their problems. The chapter suggests drug-free pain treatments, names the seven categories of drugs, and explains the differences among drug use, drug misuse, and drug abuse. A thorough discussion of over-the-counter and prescription drugs follows. Students learn about the effects of drugs on the body, including drug interactions, side effects, and allergies.

CHAPTER 13

ALCOHOL: A DANGEROUS DRUG

The chapter begins with a discussion of the short- and long-term effects of alcohol. Students learn some reasons why people drink and some reasons *not* to drink. Myths and facts about alcohol are presented, as are strategies for coping with pressure to drink. The chapter also covers the three phases of alcoholism, its probable causes, and its most important risks. Treatment options for alcoholics are discussed.

CHAPTER 14

TOBACCO: HAZARDOUS AND ADDICTIVE

Students learn about the chemicals in tobacco and study the effects of the three most poisonous chemicals in tobacco smoke. The prevalent smoking-related diseases, plus the risks of passive smoking and using pipes, cigars, and smokeless tobacco are discussed. An explanation of why people may begin smoking and reasons *not* to smoke are given. The chapter ends with suggested strategies for quitting smoking.

CHAPTER 15

OTHER DRUGS OF ABUSE

The dangers of drug abuse and ways it can damage society are discussed, followed by a thorough presentation of the psychoactive drugs of abuse, and their dangers and effects. Students learn that people should not try to overcome drug dependency on their own and that there is no such thing as a fully recovered addict. Options for recovering addicts and alternatives for those who consider abusing drugs are suggested.

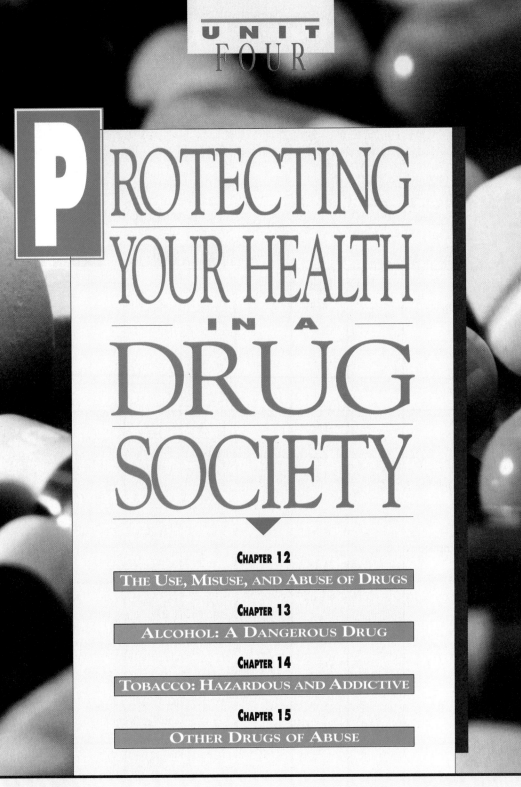

PROTECTING YOUR HEALTH IN A DRUG SOCIETY

CHAPTER 12
THE USE, MISUSE, AND ABUSE OF DRUGS

CHAPTER 13
ALCOHOL: A DANGEROUS DRUG

CHAPTER 14
TOBACCO: HAZARDOUS AND ADDICTIVE

CHAPTER 15
OTHER DRUGS OF ABUSE

This unit addresses the use of drugs—one of the most important health issues in our society. It provides students with the understanding of drug abuse they need to make responsible decisions. The reasons people use prescription drugs, over-the-counter drugs, alcohol, tobacco, and illegal drugs are explained and reasons *not* to use them given. The unit suggests drug-free alternatives for dealing with problems and offers suggestions for dealing with the pressure to use drugs. The chart below links the information and skills presented in this unit to the National Health Education Standards.

Unit 4	NATIONAL HEALTH EDUCATION STANDARDS*						
STANDARD	1	2	3	4	5	6	7
Chapter 12	•			•			
Chapter 13	•	•	•		•	•	•
Chapter 14	•		•		•		•
Chapter 15	•		•				

* For full text listing of each standard, see page 15T.

The Use, Misuse, and Abuse of Drugs

SECTION	TITLE/OBJECTIVES	Personal Health Inventory	Journal	Check Up	Life Skills	Life Skills Worksheets	Media Message or Ethical Issues Worksheet	What Would You Do?
		PERSONAL INVENTORY			LIFE SKILLS DEVELOPMENT			
12.1 *pp. 245–249*	**A DRUG-ORIENTED SOCIETY** • Name one problem with living in a drug-oriented society. • Name two ways to treat pain without using drugs. • Know the ways in which drug use, drug misuse, and drug abuse differ from each other.	Ch. 12	12A 12B					
12.2 *pp. 250–256*	**OVER-THE-COUNTER AND PRESCRIPTION DRUGS** • Describe three types of OTC medicines. • Know why prescription medications require a doctor's prescription. • Name three factors that may influence a medicine's effect. ▦ Know how to read the label on a prescription medicine.		12C 12D 12E 12F		p. 254	12A		

KEY: ▦ Denotes Life Skill Objective

Text references denoted by page number.

Supplement references denoted by chapter or item numbers.

LINKING RESOURCES

INTERACTION		OTHER RESOURCES		SECTION REVIEW AND ASSESSMENT			
Making a Choice Cards	Parent Discussion Guide	Health Talk Audio Program	Teaching Transparencies and Directory	Section Review Worksheets	Section Quizzes	Reteaching Worksheets	Section Reviews
	Ch. 12	Ch. 12	BSH1	12.1	12.1	12.1	p. 249
12A 12B			12A 12B	12.2	12.2	12.2	p. 256

For additional information about psychoactive drugs, see page 653 in the Body Systems Handbook.

KEY FACTS

- A drug is a substance that causes a physical, mental, or emotional change in a person.

- Taking legal drugs in their correct amounts is drug use. The improper use of any drug is drug misuse or drug abuse.

- Drug abuse occurs when a legal drug is used for a nonmedical reason or an illegal drug is used for any reason.

- Psychoactive drugs affect a person's mind, mood, or behavior.

- The most common types of over-the-counter drugs are analgesics, sedatives, and stimulants.

- The correct dosage of a drug is individual and varies according to a person's age, height, weight, and gender.

- Prescribed drugs may cause side effects or allergies, which should be reported to the prescribing doctor immediately.

CHAPTER REVIEW AND ASSESSMENT

TEXT
Chapter Review pp. 258–259

SUPPLEMENTS
Chapter Test 12

Alternative Assessment 12

Test Generator Chapter 12

The Use, Misuse, _and_ Abuse of Drugs

◆ ◆ ◆ ◆

| Section **12.1** | **A Drug-Oriented Society** |
| Section **12.2** | **Over-the-Counter and Prescription Drugs** |

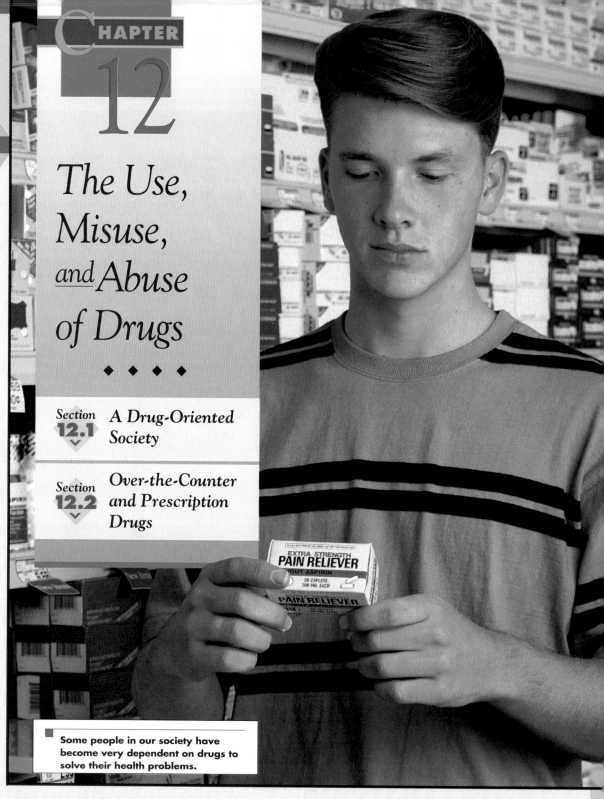

Some people in our society have become very dependent on drugs to solve their health problems.

GETTING STARTED

Using the Chapter Photograph

Ask students when they might take the over-the-counter (OTC) preparation shown in the photograph. Ask them if they know of any way to get rid of a headache without taking medication. Discuss with students whether people should rely heavily on nonprescription pain relievers and other OTC drugs. Tell students that the chapter will discuss the use, misuse, and abuse of drugs.

Question Box

Have students write out any questions they have about the use, misuse, and abuse of drugs and put them in the Question Box.

Sensitivity _ALERT_

The discussion of drug use may make some students uncomfortable. Some students may have someone close to them who abuses drugs or alcohol. Others may have someone close to them with a serious medical condition that requires heavy doses of prescription medicine. Be sure to avoid making any generalizations that may distress these students.

MYTHS & MISCONCEPTIONS

• **It's okay to take two different drugs at the same time as long as they are both prescribed by a physician.** It is okay if they are prescribed by the _same_ physician and if the physician knows you are taking them together. However, if they are prescribed by two different physicians who do not know what other drugs you may be taking, it is potentially very dangerous. Some drugs interact and can cause very serious side effects.

• **If you have the same symptom as someone else, it's okay to take a prescription drug that was prescribed for that person.** Similar symptoms do not always indicate the same condition, and it is not safe to take another person's prescription medicine. That drug was prescribed for the particular condition a doctor diagnosed for someone else and it may be completely inappropriate for you. In some cases, it could even make your condition worse.

Everything had gone wrong for Marisa today. The math test was a complete disaster. She had left her health assignment at home. Worst of all, she had a big fight with her best friend. By the time Marisa got home she was crying, and she had a terrible headache.

Without thinking about it, she went to her mother's medicine chest to find a pain reliever for her headache. As she swallowed the pills, Marisa looked at her puffy face in the bathroom mirror. She wished she could take a drug that would make her forget about her bad day.

Section 12.1

A Drug-Oriented Society

Objectives

- *Name one problem with living in a drug-oriented society.*
- *Name two ways to treat pain without using drugs.*
- *Know the ways in which drug use, drug misuse, and drug abuse differ from each other.*

We live in a drug-oriented society. The commercials we see on television make this clear. Have a headache? Take a painkiller. Is your stomach acting up? No problem—get some antacids. Feeling tired? Grab a cup of coffee. Want to relax? Have a beer. One reason our society has become so dependent on drugs is that we are constantly hearing about how great they are.

Every year, pharmaceutical companies spend about $25 billion on advertising. The alcohol industry spends an additional $18 billion to $20 billion. As a result, it is hard to find a magazine or a television program that doesn't feature at least one drug advertisement. In addition, many sports events are sponsored by beer manufacturers.

The message we receive from all the advertising is clear: If we take a drug, we'll feel better.

What is so bad about this message? After all, some drugs can save lives. Before the development of effective medicines, there was little relief for severe pain, and even minor infections could become deadly. Today, drugs can prevent, treat, or cure most illnesses. The problem is that many people think drugs can solve *all* their problems.

Healthier Options

Marisa's headache resulted from her stressful day at school. When she got home, she could have done some physical exercise that would have relaxed her, or she could have performed one of the relaxation exercises

Personal Health Inventory

Have students complete the Personal Health Inventory for this chapter.

English/Spanish CD Audio Program

Use the English/Spanish Health Talk audio program for students who need audio reinforcement of the concepts presented.

Parent Discussion Guide

Send home the Parent Letter for Chapter 12. As you progress through the chapter, send home the Parental Survey and The Extra Mile.

Section 12.1 Lesson Plan

MOTIVATE

Journal 12A
Headaches and Stress

This may be done as a warm-up activity. Ask students to write down in their Journal their reactions to Marisa's response to her day. Have them include how they would probably respond to the same kinds of problems.

Cooperative Learning
Marisa's Response

Have students form small groups to discuss why Marisa's first response was to take a pill to relieve her headache. Have them consider what influences people to take a pill or a capsule whenever they have the slightest pain. Point out that OTC drugs are sometimes necessary. Ask students to suggest some situations in which a pill or other medicine is appropriate. *(for an*

upset stomach, for a headache that persists after nondrug methods have failed, or for temporary allergy relief)

Background
Variable Drug Effects

Some substances act like drugs in some people yet have no effect whatsoever on other people. The flavor enhancer monosodium glutamate (MSG) is used in many foods. Most people have no problems after eating foods with MSG. However, others experience heart palpitations and nausea. Nutmeg, a common kitchen spice, causes distortions of time and space in some people; however, most people do not experience these effects.

drug:

a substance that causes a physical or emotional change in a person.

described in Chapter 9. Chances are, either of these would have made her head feel better.

Next time you have a headache or stomachache, ask yourself if the pain you are feeling has something to do with stress. If it does, see if physical exercise or a relaxation exercise makes you feel better, or just try talking to someone about your anxiety. You may find that the pain goes away without the use of a drug.

If you're feeling depressed or anxious about something, know that drinking alcohol or taking a drug will not solve your problem. The effects of these drugs last for a short period of time, and when they wear off, you might feel worse than you did before. Instead, you might try to find someone you can talk to. A parent, a friend, or a teacher may be able to offer some support.

What Is a Drug?

A **drug** is any substance that causes a physical or emotional change in a person. All drugs can be placed into one of the following seven categories: natural remedies, over-the-counter drugs, prescription drugs, tobacco products, alcohol, illegal drugs, and unrecognized drugs.

Cultural DIVERSITY

Medicines From the Rain Forest

People in so-called developing cultures are helping in the development of powerful new medicines. These cultures, which have existed for thousands of years in the tropical rain forests of the world, have already contributed a tremendous amount to the contents of our medicine cabinets. Tropical rain forests, shown in green on the map, are areas along the equator that have great amounts of rainfall and a huge number of different living things.

Quinine is an excellent example of a medicine that came to us from the rain forest. Made from the bark of the *Cinchona* tree in the Andean tropical forest of South America, quinine was long used as a medicine by the native people. Only later did people in more "advanced" societies discover that quinine cured malaria, an often fatal disease transmitted by mosquitoes.

Rain forest cultures introduced us to another important drug called curare. In the South American rain forest, native people extracted curare from woody vines and dipped their arrows into it to paralyze the animals they shot. In our society, curare serves not as a poison but as a muscle relaxant that is used during surgery.

Finally, nearly 70 percent of the plants known to be useful in the treatment of cancer come from rain forests. We know about most of these cancer-fighting plants from the native people who live where the plants grow.

TEACH

Class Discussion
A Pill for Every Problem

Discuss with students the emphasis in society on taking drugs for almost every possible ailment. Ask: **What do you think "a drug-oriented society" means?** *[a society in which taking a drug is the solution for every problem, including slight pains, stress, and just be-*ing tired]* **Why was Marisa wrong to think that problems can be solved by taking a pill?** *[Pills may just be an escape that keeps her from facing her real problem.]* **What are the dangers in taking a pill whenever you want to feel better?** *[A person who takes a pill for every problem does not develop strength and problem-solving techniques to face the bigger trials that may present themselves later on.]* **What are some actions you can take when you are upset by the way things are in your** life? *[Students may discuss ideas mentioned in the book, or they may add their own suggestions.]*

Role-Playing
Positive Alternatives to Drugs

Have students role-play a situation in which a teenager is upset after not making the team or after having an argument at home or with a friend. One student takes a pill to relieve the disappointment or stress. Another student uses a drug-free approach.

Natural Remedies Natural remedies contain substances that occur in nature and are used to treat or prevent ailments. You should always seek the advice of a trained practitioner before using natural remedies. Some of these substances can be dangerous if misused.

Over-the-Counter Drugs Over-the-counter (OTC) drugs can be legally bought without a doctor's prescription. Two examples of OTC preparations are aspirin and cough medicines.

Prescription Drugs Prescription drugs are drugs that require a doctor's prescription to buy. A **prescription** is a doctor's written order to a pharmacist that a patient be al- lowed to purchase a drug. A prescription includes the drug's name, directions for use, and amount of the drug to be used. Prescription drugs are usually more powerful than over-the-counter drugs.

Tobacco Products Tobacco products contain the drug nicotine. Examples of tobacco products are cigarettes, cigars, snuff, and chewing tobacco.

Alcohol Beer, wine, and distilled liquors all contain the drug alcohol, which is illegal for persons under the age of 21.

Illegal Drugs Illegal drugs are substances that cannot be legally sold, purchased,

prescription:

a doctor's written order for a specific medicine.

Sadly, the rain forests are rapidly disappearing, and along with them the native people who are most knowledgeable about these plants. If we protect the rain forest from destruction, we preserve not only the biological diversity but also the valuable *cultural* diversity of our world.

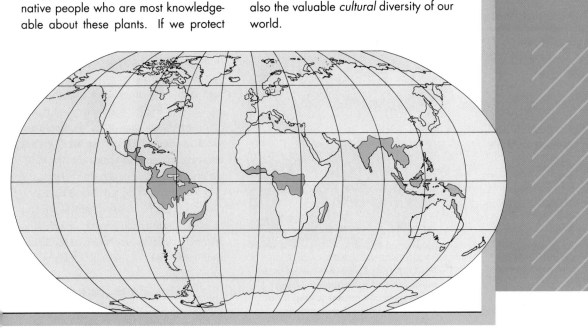

Reinforcement
Caution in Using Drugs

After students read about the seven categories of drugs, mention that all drugs, even those prescribed by a physician, should be used only according to the directions. Discuss why even OTC drugs have to be used with discretion.

• • • TEACH continues on p. 248

Section Review Worksheet 12.1

To reinforce the concepts presented in this section, assign Section Review Worksheet 12.1.

Section Quiz 12.1

Have students take Section Quiz 12.1.

Reteaching Worksheet 12.1

Students who have difficulty with the material may complete Reteaching Worksheet 12.1.

---

drug misuse:

improper use of a drug.

drug use:

taking a medicine properly and in its correct dosage.

drug abuse:

intentional improper use of a drug.

psychoactive effect:

an effect on a person's mood or behavior.

addiction:

a condition in which the body relies on a given drug to help it function.

---

or used. Powder cocaine, marijuana, crack cocaine, and heroin are all examples of illegal drugs.

Unrecognized Drugs Unrecognized drugs are found in products that are not usually classified as drugs. One example of an unrecognized drug is caffeine. Caffeine is an ingredient in coffee and colas.

Inhalants are another kind of unrecognized drug. Certain substances, when inhaled, cause a lightheaded feeling. Examples of inhalants are gasoline, spray paint, and correction fluid for paper. As you will learn in Chapter 15, inhalants are extremely dangerous.

Drug Use, Misuse, and Abuse

Taking drugs properly and in their correct amounts is called **drug use**. Let's say you wake up one morning with a sore throat and a high fever. You go to the doctor, who

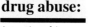
(FIGURE 12-1) **Some illnesses require medications for treatment. Using drugs correctly means taking them exactly as directed and in their proper doses.**

takes a throat culture and tells you that you have strep throat. The doctor gives you a prescription for antibiotics, which fight the bacteria that cause strep throat. When you take the antibiotics as the doctor directs, you are practicing proper drug use.

Drug misuse is the improper use of a drug. One way of misusing drugs is to take the wrong amount of a prescribed drug. If your doctor told you to take two tablets of a certain medicine each day, but you take *four,* you are misusing the drug. Taking too much of a medicine can lead to an overdose, which can be dangerous and even fatal.

Another way to misuse a drug is to stop taking it too soon. If the doctor told you to take two tablets a day until you finished the entire bottle, but you quit as soon as you felt better, you would be misusing the drug.

Taking medicine prescribed for someone else is another example of drug misuse. If you have a sore throat and take the medicine that is prescribed for your sister's sore throat, you are misusing a drug. Taking medicine prescribed for someone else can be very dangerous.

Drug abuse occurs when a person takes a legal drug for a nonmedical reason, or an illegal drug for any reason at all. A person who takes cough medicine to get high is abusing drugs, even though cough medicine is legal. A person who smokes marijuana is abusing drugs because marijuana is illegal. Other instances of drug abuse include smoking crack cocaine, sniffing powder cocaine, and taking heroin.

Many drugs that are abused have psychoactive effects. A **psychoactive effect** is an effect on a person's mood or behavior. Alcohol, caffeine, nicotine, tranquilizers, and heroin are all examples of psychoactive drugs.

The abuse of a drug can lead to **addiction.** When a person becomes addicted to a drug, it means that he or she has developed a

---

Role-Playing
Drug Use, Misuse, and Abuse

Have students make up skits that show examples of drug use, drug misuse, and drug abuse. The class should judge which category is being presented by the skit. Caution them to make a distinction between misuse and abuse so that both categories are not included in the same skit.

Journal 12B
Psychoactive Drugs

Have students write in their Journal their concerns about psychoactive drugs. Have them list their goals in life and tell how drug use could prevent them from reaching their goals.

Extension
What Do We Use?

Have students develop a survey to determine what types of OTC pain relievers are commonly used in their

high school. Stress that participation in the survey is on a voluntary basis. The survey could ask the name of the pain reliever (aspirin, ibuprofen, acetaminophen, etc.), whether it really provides relief, and if the recommended dosage instructions are followed. Have students analyze the data collected to see what, if any, conclusions can be drawn.

(FIGURE 12-2) **Abusing alcohol or other psychoactive drugs can be deadly.**

physical need for the drug and suffers withdrawal symptoms if unable to take the drug. Some common withdrawal symptoms are nausea, cramps, trembling, and nervousness. Drug abuse and addiction are discussed in more detail in Chapters 13, 14, and 15.

Psychoactive Drug Use and Risk Behaviors

One of the dangers of using psychoactive drugs is that they impair a person's ability to make good decisions. Someone who normally behaves responsibly might not be able to make the right decisions when under the influence of a psychoactive drug.

Joshua, for example, has decided to delay sexual intercourse until marriage. Usually he has little trouble sticking to his decision. But what if he gets drunk or high? Chances are, his decision will be harder to remember and harder to carry out. Not only would Joshua violate his own values if he had sexual intercourse, but he would also increase his risk of causing an unwanted pregnancy or getting a disease that is transmitted sexually. This can be especially

dangerous today, when the risk of getting AIDS can make the wrong decision a life-threatening one.

In addition, studies have shown that the use of psychoactive drugs is strongly associated with an increased risk of serious injury and violence. What this can mean is that you have a much greater chance of getting hurt in an accident or getting into a fight if you are drunk or high.

Review

1. What is one problem with living in a drug-oriented society?

2. What are two ways to treat pain without the use of drugs?

3. Define drug use, drug misuse, and drug abuse. How do they differ?

4. **Critical Thinking** Why might a person who has abused a drug be more likely to get AIDS than a person who has not?

ASSESS

Section Review

Have students answer the Section Review questions.

Alternative Assessment
Drug Use, Misuse, or Abuse?

Have students explain in their own words how drug use, misuse, and abuse are different. They could make a chart to display the differences.

Closure
Perspective on Drug Use

Have students explain the effects of drugs on the quality of life, both positive and negative.

Background
Food and Medications

Certain foods can make a medication act more slowly, more quickly, or not at all. For example, the calcium in milk, cheese, and yogurt can interfere with absorption of the antibiotic tetracycline. The information sheet that accompanies prescription medications usually covers any drug incompatibilities. Patients should read the sheet carefully and talk with the pharmacist if they have any questions.

stimulant:

a drug that speeds up body functioning.

medicine:

a substance used to treat an illness or ailment.

analgesic:

a medicine that relieves pain.

sedative:

a drug that slows down body functioning and causes sleepiness.

Section 12.2
Over-the-Counter and Prescription Drugs

Objectives

- Describe three types of OTC medicines.

- Know why prescription medications require a doctor's prescription.

- Name three factors that may influence a medicine's effect.

- Know how to read the label on a prescription medicine.
  LIFE SKILLS: Practicing Self-Care

Over-the-counter and prescription drugs are two kinds of **medicines**. Most medicines do at least one of four things: they battle bacteria and other organisms that cause disease; they protect the body from disease; they influence the circulatory system; or they affect the nervous system. For more information on the different types of medicines, see Figure 12-3.

Over-the-Counter (OTC) Drugs

OTC drugs are medicines that you can buy without a doctor's prescription. Three of the most common types of OTC drugs are analgesics, sedatives, and stimulants.

Analgesics are used to relieve pain. Three types of analgesics are aspirin, acetaminophen, and ibuprofen.

Sedatives are drugs that slow down body functioning and make you sleepy. OTC preparations that have sedatives in them include mild sleeping pills.

Stimulants are the opposite of sedatives; they make you more alert. The type of stimulant that is most commonly used in OTC medicines is caffeine. OTC preparations that contain caffeine include some headache remedies, cold remedies, and appetite suppressants.

Most people think that OTC preparations are completely safe. Unfortunately, no drug is free of risk. Aspirin can lead to stomach irritation and bleeding, and it also may be associated with a serious disease called Reye's syndrome. A number of people who have taken aspirin for chickenpox or flu have suffered this illness, which is why doctors now recommend that you use acetaminophen to treat any symptoms of these infections. Salicylates, the ingredients in aspirin that are believed to be linked to Reye's syndrome, are also contained in some other OTC medications. Teenagers suffering from flu and chickenpox should take special care to read all OTC labels carefully and to avoid all preparations that contain salicylates.

In addition, some OTC medicines can be misused or abused. Antihistamines can cause drowsiness and dizziness, which is why a person who has taken them should not try to drive. Over-the-counter appetite suppressants, which contain caffeine and a stimulant drug called phenylpropanolamine (PPA), can cause high blood pressure and increased heart rate.

One final warning about OTC preparations: Remember that sometimes pain is a helpful symptom of infection. By covering up a symptom with an OTC preparation instead of treating its cause, you may be making your infection worse than it already is.

Section 12.2 Lesson Plan

MOTIVATE

Journal 12C
Uses of Medications

This may be done as a warm-up activity. Encourage students to list in their Journal the OTC drugs and prescription drugs they are familiar with.

Tell them to write what each drug is used for.

TEACH

Teaching Transparency 12A
Drug Types and Effects

Use this transparency of Figure 12-3 to help students classify some common drugs according to the type of action they take in the body.

Class Discussion
Drug Types and Effects

Refer to the table in Figure 12-3 and ask: **How do vaccines differ from antisera?** [Vaccines cause the body to create antibodies before exposure. Antisera provide the body with antibodies to specific diseases after exposure. Antisera are stronger than vaccines.] **How do penicillin and tetracycline differ in their effects?** [Penicillin kills bacteria by preventing cell-wall formation;

Some Common Drug Types and Their Effects

Type of Drug	Type of Action	Effect	How Available
Vaccines	Protect body from disease	Cause body to set up agents to fight a specific disease before exposure	Doctor's office or clinic
Antisera	Protect body from disease	Provide the body with the antibodies that fight specific diseases after exposure	Doctor's office or clinic
Penicillin (antibiotic)	Battles organisms that cause disease	Kills bacteria by preventing cell wall formation	Prescription
Tetracycline (antibiotic)	Battles organisms that cause disease	Slows down growth and reproduction of bacteria	Prescription
Cardiac Glycoside (Digitalis)	Influence circulatory system	Increases force of heart contractions, corrects irregular heartbeat	Prescription
Diuretics	Influence circulatory system	Relieve body of excess water and salt	OTC or Prescription
Vasodilators	Influence circulatory system	Enlarge veins and arteries to increase flow of blood	Prescription
Antiarrhythmics	Influence circulatory system	Work to correct irregular heartbeat	Prescription
Hypertensives	Influence circulatory system	Work to reduce blood pressure	Prescription
Analgesics (aspirin, acetaminophen, ibuprofen)	Influence nervous system	Relieve pain	OTC or, in some cases, prescription
Stimulants	Influence nervous system	Prevent sleep, heighten awareness	OTC or, in some cases, prescription
Barbiturates	Influence nervous system	Relieve anxiety, insomnia, prevent certain types of seizures	Prescription
Tranquilizers	Influence nervous system	Relieve anxiety, insomnia; frequently milder than barbiturates	Prescription

(FIGURE 12-3) **Medicines can battle diseases and sometimes prevent them completely. Most OTC preparations, however, treat symptoms and do not fight infections.**

SECTION 12.2

Making a Choice 12A

Assign the Reasons for Use of Legal Drugs card. The card asks students to decide when over-the-counter (OTC) drug use is appropriate and to develop a set of guidelines for the use of OTC drugs.

tetracycline slows down growth and reproduction of bacteria.] **How do analgesics influence the nervous system?** *[They relieve pain, lower fever, and reduce swelling.]*

Cooperative Learning
Drug Action Symposium

Divide the class into four groups, according to the four types of actions caused by drugs, as shown in Figure 12-3. Each group will discuss and study the drugs that deliver one type of action shown on the chart: (1) protects body from disease, (2) battles organisms that cause disease, (3) influences the circulatory system, (4) influences the nervous system. Have each group work together to understand the action of each type of drug, its effects, and how it is available. Have them do this for each drug listed on the chart. Have groups report on their category.

• • • TEACH continues on p. 252

Background

Aspirin and Reye's Syndrome

Reye's syndrome is an acute and often fatal illness among children that usually develops after a viral illness. The first symptoms are fever, vomiting, and a headache, followed by disorientation and loss of consciousness. Swelling of the brain causes coma and convulsions, and fatty accumulations in the renal system can cause renal failure. Although recovery is possible, permanent brain damage can result. The cause-and-effect relationship between aspirin and Reye's syndrome is not well understood. However, the association is clear and the illness is very dangerous. Children and adolescents should never be given any product containing the analgesic aspirin to relieve symptoms of any viral illness, especially the "flu" or chickenpox.

Analgesics: Their Effects and Hazards

Analgesic	Effects	Potential Hazards
Aspirin	Relieves pain, reduces fever, reduces swelling	Causes stomach irritation and bleeding, associated with Reye's syndrome in children and adolescents, can cause overdose.
Acetaminophen	Relieves pain, reduces fever	Risk of overdose, may cause liver damage in high doses.
Ibuprofen	Relieves pain, reduces fever, reduces swelling	Can cause stomach irritation and bleeding.

(FIGURE 12-4) **Although analgesics are easily available, they are not without risk. If you must use these preparations, make sure that you take them according to their instructions and in their proper dose.**

Read the labels of all OTC preparations before you buy them. The labels should provide complete information about the correct amount to take and possible undesirable effects.

Prescription Drugs

Prescription drugs are usually more powerful than the medicines you can buy over the counter. For this reason, they cannot be purchased without a doctor's prescription.

A prescription always has a required **dose**—the correct amount of a drug to be taken at one time or at stated intervals. If you are using a prescribed medication, make sure you take the right dose each time. Be sure that you finish the entire prescription, even if the signs and symptoms of your disease have completely disappeared. It is particularly important that you continue

dose:

the exact amount of a drug.

taking antibiotics for an infection as long as the doctor instructs. Even though you may start to feel better after a few days, the bacteria that caused the infection may not be completely eliminated. If you stop taking the antibiotics too soon, the remaining bacteria can cause the infection to return.

Finally, prescription drugs can be abused. Some drugs that are prescribed, such as barbiturates and tranquilizers, have very strong psychoactive effects. They can also be addictive, which is why it is very important to take drugs like these only if they are prescribed for you.

It is extremely important that you follow the instructions on the label of any prescription medication. Remember that they are prescribed for a particular person with a particular condition. The only person who should be taking the medicine is the person whose name appears on the label. Even if you and your friend think you have the same

---

• • • TEACH continued

Journal 12D
Nonprescription Medications

Have students write in their Journal which of the following OTC medicines they may have taken at some time: an analgesic, a sedative, and a stimulant. Have them include the reason for taking each medication.

Class Discussion
Analgesics: Their Effects and Hazards

After students have looked at the table in Figure 12-4, ask: **Which analgesic would you use if aspirin irritates your stomach?** [*acetaminophen*] **Why should children and adolescents avoid using aspirin for chickenpox or flu?** [*Some children and adolescents who have taken aspirin for these diseases*

developed Reye's syndrome.] **What caution must be taken when using acetaminophen?** [*It may cause liver damage in high dosages.*]

Journal 12E
Taking Antibiotics

Have students write in their Journal the name of an antibiotic they have taken. Ask them to write down any special directions that they had to follow, such as taking the medication on illness, don't take his or her prescription medication. It could be that you don't have the same illness or that you are allergic to the medication offered to you.

Effects of Drugs on the Body

When a drug enters the body, it is absorbed into the bloodstream. Once there, the drug travels to the parts of the body it will affect.

One factor that influences the effect of a drug is the dose that has been taken. The amount of drug that is right for a person will vary according to that person's age, height, weight, and gender, among other factors. In general, the heavier a person is, the higher a dose he or she will require. All medicines have recommended doses.

In addition, the way a drug is administered, or taken, has a very important impact on its effect. Medicines are usually either swallowed or injected. Injected medicines go directly to the bloodstream, which is why they have faster effects than medicines that are swallowed.

SECTION 12.2

Making a Choice 12B

Assign the Using Legal Drugs Safely card. The card asks students to develop public service announcements that convey basic safety guidelines for the proper use of medications.

Guidelines for Appropriate Use of Medicines

Things You Should Remember About Use of Medicines

Don't mix medications without checking with a physician or pharmacist. When more than one drug is taken the results are often unpredictable.

Don't take a prescription medication unless it was prescribed for you. If you ever have an allergic reaction to a drug or food, make sure you tell a physician before using the same or another medication.

Don't use over-the-counter drugs for long periods of time. You may be delaying diagnosis of a serious problem.

Don't ever conclude that if a little bit of a drug makes you feel good, that more will make you feel better. Never take more of a medication than you are directed to.

Don't use a medicine prescribed for someone else, even if you seem to have the same problem.

Ask the pharmacist to tell you about the drug's purpose, its side effects, and its interaction with food and other drugs, as well as the dosage and length of time you should take the drug.

Keep all drugs away from children.

(FIGURE 12-5) **Keep in mind these basic safety rules for the proper use of medications. Medicines are anything but helpful when they are misused.**

an empty stomach or a certain number of hours before or after a meal. Have them explain why they think these precautions must be taken.

Class Discussion
Prescribed Medication

Ask: **Why do you think you need a prescription to purchase many of the drugs on the market?** *[Prescribed drugs are more potent than OTC drugs, and a physician needs to consider a patient's overall condition to determine whether a certain drug would have a harmful effect on him or her.]*

Case Study
Misuse of a Medication

A patient was regularly using decongestant nose drops for a sinus condition, every half-hour. He became addicted to the medication and began to suffer from terrifying hallucinations at night. When he stopped using the nasal decongestant, the hallucinations stopped. He did, however, have to be treated for withdrawal symptoms. Emphasize that although medications are helpful, they can also harm someone unless they are used responsibly.

• • • TEACH continues on p. 254

Life SKILLS

Have students review the Life Skills activity. Discuss what they can learn by reading a prescription label.

Life Skills Worksheet 12A

Assign the Comparing Medicine Prices Life Skills Worksheet.

When a medicine is taken orally—by mouth—it is often absorbed into the bloodstream through the stomach lining. This process can take a long time, especially if there is food in the stomach that can slow down the absorption process. The food can also protect the stomach lining from irritation, which is why doctors recommend that certain medicines should always be taken with a meal.

Drug Interactions Sometimes the effect of a medicine can be made either greater or smaller if there is already another drug in your system. This influence, called drug

*Life*SKILLS: Practicing Self-Care

How to Read a Prescription Label . . .

All prescription drugs should have clearly marked labels. If you have a medication prescribed for you, make sure you read the label carefully before beginning your treatment. The prescription number is often at the very top of the label, and your name should be underneath. If your name is not on the label, do not take the medicine. One of the most dangerous things you can do is take a prescription drug that has been prescribed for someone else.

Next to your name, your doctor's name should be listed, along with the date the prescription was filled. Underneath your name are directions explaining how often you should take the drug and how much you should take each time. This is followed by the drug's expiration date—the final date the drug can be safely used—and the name of the drug.

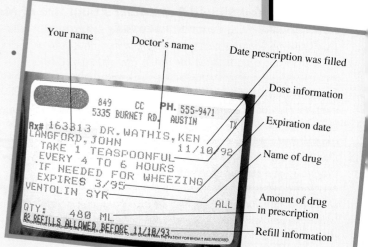

The bottom of the label should list the amount of the drug contained in the entire prescription dose, and should also provide instructions on how many times (if at all) the prescription can be refilled.

Not all labels will follow this exact order, but they all should contain this same information.

• • • TEACH continued

Debate the Issue
The Approval Process

Some OTC drugs were originally available only by prescription or in a reduced-strength form. Certain antibiotics that are available without a prescription outside the United States require a prescription here. Have student debate this question: Should the Food and Drug Administration approve more drugs in OTC form? Remind students that they must weigh the convenience against the risks.

Reinforcement
Drug Absorption

Ask: **Why do some prescriptions state that the patient should take a medication on an empty stomach?** *[If the medication enters the bloodstream through the stomach lining, food in the stomach can slow down the absorption process.]* **Why do injected medicines work faster?** *[Injected medicines go directly to the bloodstream.]*

Reinforcement
Drug Administration

Have students recall the ways drugs enter the body by drawing the outline of a body and labeling the places where drugs enter the body.

How drugs enter the body

1. Asthma medications that are inhaled directly affect the respiratory system.

2. Some medicines are placed under the tongue. These are absorbed into the bloodstream very quickly.

3. The medicines stored in transdermal patches are absorbed into the bloodstream through the skin.

4. Medicines that treat skin ailments such as cuts or burns can be applied topically, or directly onto the skin.

5. When medicines are swallowed, they are often absorbed into the bloodstream through the stomach.

6. Drugs can be injected either into a muscle or into a vein. Medicines that enter the body in this way have very strong effects, because they travel immediately to the bloodstream.

7. Some drugs that are swallowed enter the bloodstream through blood vessels that supply the intestine.

(FIGURE 12-6) **Drugs can enter the body in several different ways. Medicines that are absorbed into the bloodstream travel to the liver, where they are broken down into simple substances the body can use.**

Background
Dangerous Interactions
Emphasize that harmful reactions may occur when drugs interact. That is why it is important to let your doctor and your pharmacist know what medications you are taking and whether you drink or smoke. The combination of alcohol and some prescription *or* OTC medications, especially sedatives or painkillers, can easily be deadly.

 Section Review Worksheet 12.2
To reinforce the concepts presented in this section, assign Section Review Worksheet 12.2.

 Section Quiz 12.2
Have students take Section Quiz 12.2.

 Reteaching Worksheet 12.2
Students who have difficulty with the material may complete Reteaching Worksheet 12.2.

 Teaching Transparency 12B
Information on Drug Labels
Use this transparency to help students become more aware of the important information contained on the labels of prescription and OTC drugs.

Journal 12F
Drug Allergies
Ask students to write in their Journal whether they are allergic to any drug and the symptoms of the allergy.

Extension
Information from Pharmacists
Suggest that students visit a pharmacy to find out what kind of information a pharmacist gives with prescription drugs, beyond the literature provided by the pharmaceutical companies. As a class, make up a list of questions students would like to ask the pharmacist.

Deadly Combinations
Have students investigate the 1995 death of 17-year-old model Krissy Taylor. Although aspects of her death may remain a mystery, the combined effects of a prescription drug and an OTC medication are involved.

(FIGURE 12-7) Some prescription medications have suggestions or warnings concerning their use. Be sure to discuss these with your pharm-acist when you purchase a prescription drug.

side effect:

an effect that ac-companies the ex-pected effect of a drug.

drug allergy:

an unwanted effect that accompanies the desired effect of a drug.

interaction, is very difficult to predict. A drug interaction can be dangerous. For ex-ample, combining a prescribed barbiturate with alcohol has been known to cause coma or death.

Avoiding a harmful drug interaction is another good reason to read all label infor-mation on any OTC or prescription medica-tion you buy. If you have specific questions about how certain medicines interact, ask your doctor.

Side Effects and Allergies If you've ever taken a cold medicine that contains an antihistamine, you may have found that in addition to feeling your nasal passages clear, you felt a bit drowsy. The drowsiness you felt is called a **side effect**, because it is an effect that comes in addition to the drug's desired effect. Other common side effects of medicines include nausea, dizziness, and headaches.

A medicine can also have unpleasant effects when the person taking it has a **drug allergy**. Drug allergies occur when your body mistakes the medicine you have taken

for a disease-causing agent, and tries to re-ject it.

Symptoms of drug allergies include a rash, a runny nose, and a quickened heart and breathing rate. If you think you may be allergic to a medicine, make sure you talk with your doctor before you take that medi-cine again. Allergies get worse each time they occur. If their early effects are ig-nored, they can eventually be fatal.

Review

1. *Name three types of OTC medicines.*

2. *Name two reasons why prescription medicines require a doctor's prescription.*

3. *What are three factors that can influence the effect of a medicine?*

4. **LIFE SKILLS: Practicing Self-Care** *What are three important things to look for on a prescription label?*

5. *Critical Thinking* *Using your knowledge of drug effects and how they are influenced, explain why it can be dangerous to use a prescription drug that has been prescribed for someone else.*

Highlights

Summary

- We live in a drug-oriented society.

- Physical exercise or a relaxation exercise can often relieve pain without drugs.

- Drugs can be classified as natural remedies, over-the-counter drugs, prescription drugs, tobacco products, alcohol, illegal drugs, and unrecognized drugs.

- You can misuse a prescribed drug by taking the wrong dosage, by stopping it too soon, or by taking medicine prescribed for someone else.

- Drug abuse occurs when a person deliberately takes a legal drug for a nonmedical reason or an illegal drug for any reason.

- Psychoactive drugs such as alcohol, caffeine, nicotine, tranquilizers, and heroin impair a person's ability to make good decisions. Some of these drugs are associated with an increased risk of serious injury and violence.

- Three of the most common types of over-the-counter drugs are analgesics, sedatives, and stimulants. They should be taken according to the label directions.

- Drugs can sometimes cause side effects or allergies. Nausea, drowsiness, dizziness, and headaches are common side effects. Symptoms of drug allergies include a rash, a runny nose, and a quickened heart rate.

Vocabulary

drug a substance that causes a physical or emotional change in a person.

prescription a doctor's written order for a specific medicine.

drug use taking a medicine exactly as directed.

drug misuse unintentional improper use of a drug.

drug abuse intentional improper use of a drug.

psychoactive effect an effect on a person's mood or behavior.

addiction a condition in which the body relies on a given drug to function.

analgesic a medicine that relieves pain.

sedative a drug that slows down body functioning and causes sleepiness.

stimulant a drug that speeds up body functioning.

PH. 555-9471
849   CC   TX
5335 BURNET RD. AUSTIN
Rx# 163313 DR. WATHIS, KEN
                      11/10/92
LANGFORD, JOHN
   TAKE 1 TEASPOONFUL
   EVERY 4 TO 6 HOURS
   IF NEEDED FOR WHEEZING
   EXPIRES 3/95
VENTOLIN SYR
   QTY: 480 ML
   R2 REFILLS ALLOWED BEFORE 11/10/93

SUMMARY
Have students read the summary to reinforce the concepts they learned in Chapter 12.

VOCABULARY
Have students work in small groups to develop brief scenarios of a customer speaking to a pharmacist about a prescription. Students should include as many of the vocabulary words as possible in the dialogue.

EXTENSION
Have students examine magazines to find advertisements for OTC drugs. Ask them to make a chart that shows the different kinds of OTC drugs advertised and the ages of the people to whom the ads are directed. Tell students to tally their results and prepare a report on their findings.

CHAPTER REVIEW

Concept Review

Sample responses:

1. Drug use: taking prescription drugs according to the directions on the label. Drug misuse: because you missed a scheduled dose of a prescription drug, you take twice the amount this time to "catch up." Drug abuse: taking cocaine.

2. Some people may always turn to drugs to solve problems, even those that can be addressed in other ways.

3. Prescription drugs require a prescription; over-the-counter drugs do not. Prescription drugs are often more powerful and have more powerful psychoactive effects than OTC drugs do.

4. taking the wrong amount, not taking all the prescribed medication, taking medicine prescribed for someone else

5. Alcohol, caffeine, nicotine, tranquilizers, and heroin. The risk is addiction.

6. Addiction is when a person has developed a physical need for a drug. If a person suffers physical symptoms, such as nausea, cramps, trembling, or nervousness, when the drug is withdrawn, he or she is addicted to the drug.

7. Medications battle organisms that cause disease, they protect the body from disease, they

Concept Review . . . .

1. Give examples of drug use, drug misuse, and drug abuse.

2. Advertisements suggest that drugs make you feel better. How can this be a negative message?

3. Explain two differences between over-the-counter drugs and prescription drugs.

4. What are some ways you can misuse a drug?

5. What are some drugs that have psychoactive effects? What are the risks of abusing these drugs?

6. What does it mean when a person becomes addicted to a drug? How might a person know if he or she is physically dependent on a drug?

7. What are four things that medicines can do to your body?

8. What are some dangers of taking (a) aspirin? (b) appetite suppressants?

9. Why should a person who is taking antihistamines not drive a car?

10. Why is it important to finish a prescribed medication?

11. How are medicines usually administered? How does the method used influence the drug's effect?

12. What can happen if you take a drug when another drug is already in your system?

13. Define drug allergies and name two symptoms of them. What happens if they are ignored?

Expressing Your Views . . . .

1. Mario hurt his knee during hockey practice. That night he took some of his friend's prescription medicine for pain. Should Mario have taken this? Why or why not?

2. Your friend has had a fever and runny nose for several days. She has been taking ibuprofen along with an over-the-counter cold remedy to ease her suffering. How is

this risky behavior? What would you advise her to do?

3. It seems as if you have had a stuffy nose forever. You have been using a nasal spray for about a month. You realize it is not healthy to take drugs for a long time, but every time you stop using the spray, you can barely breathe through your nose. What do you think has happened?

influence the circulatory system, or they affect the nervous system.

8. Aspirin can lead to stomach irritation and bleeding and may be associated with Reye's syndrome. Appetite suppressants can cause high blood pressure and increased heart rate.

9. Antihistamines can cause drowsiness and dizziness.

10. If antibiotics are stopped too early, the bacteria may not be eliminated and the infection could return.

11. Most drugs are swallowed or injected. Injected medicines go directly into the bloodstream and therefore usually act more quickly than those that are swallowed.

12. You can have a drug interaction.

13. A drug allergy is an unwanted side effect that occurs when the body mistakes the medicine for a disease-causing agent and tries to reject it. Symptoms include a rash, a runny nose, and quickened heart and breathing rates. The result can be death.

Life Skills Check . . . . . .

1. Practicing Self-Care

You have had a sore throat and fever for several days. You haven't been eating well because it is painful to swallow. The doctor prescribed a medicine for strep throat, but shortly after you take the directed dosage your stomach starts to hurt. What could be the matter?

2. Practicing Self-Care

Your mother had been having trouble sleeping for a long time. Then her doctor prescribed a sleeping medication, or barbiturate, for her. She's been taking the medication for a week, and has been sleeping better. Last night when you went out to dinner with her, she had a glass of wine. Did she take a risk by drinking alcohol? Explain.

Projects . . . .

1. Select an advertisement for an over-the-counter drug. Analyze the claims and benefits and determine the accuracy of the ad. How does the ad try to sell the drug? Is the drug really needed? Rewrite the ad, giving suggestions for relieving the problem without use of the drug.

2. Invite a pharmacist to the classroom or visit a local pharmacy. Ask the pharmacist about over-the-counter drugs, prescription drugs, warnings, and directions for use.

3. Three common types of over-the-counter drugs are sedatives, analgesics, and stimulants. Go to the store and compare name brands, lists of ingredients, directions, and prices. Record your findings on a chart, and display it in the classroom.

Plan for Action . . . .

You have a choice regarding how much you rely on drugs to relieve symptoms of illness. Devise a plan to restrict your reliance on drugs.

Expressing Your Views

Sample responses:

1. No; taking medicine prescribed for someone else is a form of drug misuse and can be very dangerous.

2. She may be covering up her symptoms and making the infection worse. She should stop taking both medications and consult her doctor.

3. Using the OTC medication only covers up my symptoms. Since the underlying infection has not been treated, it may be getting worse.

Life Skills Check

1. You may be misusing the medicine. Read the prescription label to see if you should be taking the medicine with food. Call your doctor if the pain persists.

2. Yes. Never mix alcohol with any medications because of drug interaction.

Projects

Have students plan and carry out the projects on drugs.

Plan for Action

Have students write about their personal plans to avoid misusing and abusing drugs. They should use all they have learned in the chapter to come to decisions about their own behavior with regard to using drugs for medication, using them only when necessary, and always using them according to directions.

ASSESSMENT OPTIONS

Chapter Test
Have students take the Chapter 12 Test.

Alternative Assessment
Have students do the Alternative Assessment activity for Chapter 12.

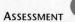

Test Generator
The Test Generator contains additional assessment items for this chapter.

CHAPTER 13

Alcohol: A Dangerous Drug

SECTION	TITLE/OBJECTIVES	PERSONAL INVENTORY			LIFE SKILLS DEVELOPMENT			
		Personal Health Inventory	Journal	Check Up	Life Skills	Life Skills Worksheets	Media Message or Ethical Issues Worksheet	What Would You Do?
13.1 pp. 261–266	**EFFECTS OF ALCOHOL ON THE BODY** • Discuss the effects of intoxication. • Name two diseases caused by long-term alcohol abuse.	Ch. 13	13A					
13.2 pp. 267–273	**TEENAGERS AND ALCOHOL** • Name two reasons why some people drink. • Name four reasons not to drink. • Discuss dangers of binge drinking. ∷ Name at least three ways you could refuse alcohol if a friend offers it to you. ∷ Use the decision-making steps to decide what to do if the person you are riding home with has been drinking.		13B 13C		p. 272	13A 13B		p. 271
13.3 pp. 274–277	**ALCOHOL ABUSE AND ALCOHOLISM** • Know the three phases of alcoholism. • Name the most important risks of alcohol abuse. • Know how alcohol can affect an unborn child. • Know the ways in which a family can be damaged by a family member's alcoholism.		13D			13C		
13.4 pp. 278–280	**HOPE FOR RECOVERY** • Discuss the treatment options for alcohol abuse. ∷ Learn how to get help if you or someone you know abuses alcohol.		13E			13D		

KEY: ∷ Denotes Life Skill Objective

Text references denoted by page number.

Supplement references denoted by chapter or item numbers.

LINKING RESOURCES

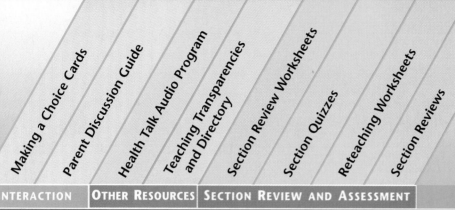

	Making a Choice Cards	Parent Discussion Guide	Health Talk Audio Program	Teaching Transparencies and Directory	Section Review Worksheets	Section Quizzes	Reteaching Worksheets	Section Reviews
INTERACTION		**OTHER RESOURCES**		**SECTION REVIEW AND ASSESSMENT**				
	Ch. 13	Ch. 13	13A	13.1	13.1	13.1	p. 266	
13A 13B			13B	13.2	13.2	13.2	p. 273	
			13C 13D	13.3	13.3	13.3	p. 277	
				13.4	13.4	13.4	p. 280	

KEY FACTS

- Anyone under the legal drinking age who drinks is violating the law, can be arrested and fined, and may acquire a criminal record.

- When alcohol is consumed, it quickly travels through the bloodstream to all cells in the body, including those in the brain.

- Blood alcohol level (BAL) is the percentage of alcohol in a person's blood; it is affected by weight, gender, drinking rate, and the amount of food in the stomach.

- The most serious short-term effects of alcohol abuse are poor judgment, reduced coordination, loss of control, and slowed reflexes. Long-term effects include liver damage, heart disease, brain damage, increased risk of certain cancers, and interpersonal problems.

- The cause of alcoholism is believed to be a combination of psychological, physical, and environmental factors.

- Alcoholism develops in three stages: abuse, dependence, addiction.

CHAPTER REVIEW AND ASSESSMENT

TEXT

Chapter Review pp. 282–283

SUPPLEMENTS

Chapter Test 13

Alternative Assessment 13

Test Generator Chapter 13

GETTING STARTED

Using the Chapter Photograph

Ask: **What is happening in this photograph?** *[The policeman is checking the driver's level of intoxication.]* **What might have happened if the driver were driving drunk and had not been stopped by the officer?** *[The driver could have been involved in or involved someone else in a serious accident.]* **What would you do if your friend, who was drunk, wanted to drive home from a party?** *[Try to talk the person out of driving; take the car keys.]*

Question Box

Have students write out any questions they have about alcohol and alcohol abuse and put them in the Question Box.

Sensitivity **ALERT**

Alcohol abuse is so prevalent that many of your students may have been touched by it in some way. Some students may have alcoholism in their family, may have known someone who was killed by a drunk driver, or may have an alcohol problem themselves. Such students may not want their situation known.

CHAPTER 13

Alcohol: A Dangerous Drug

◆ ◆ ◆ ◆

Section 13.1 Effects of Alcohol on the Body

Section 13.2 Teenagers and Alcohol

Section 13.3 Alcohol Abuse and Alcoholism

Section 13.4 Hope for Recovery

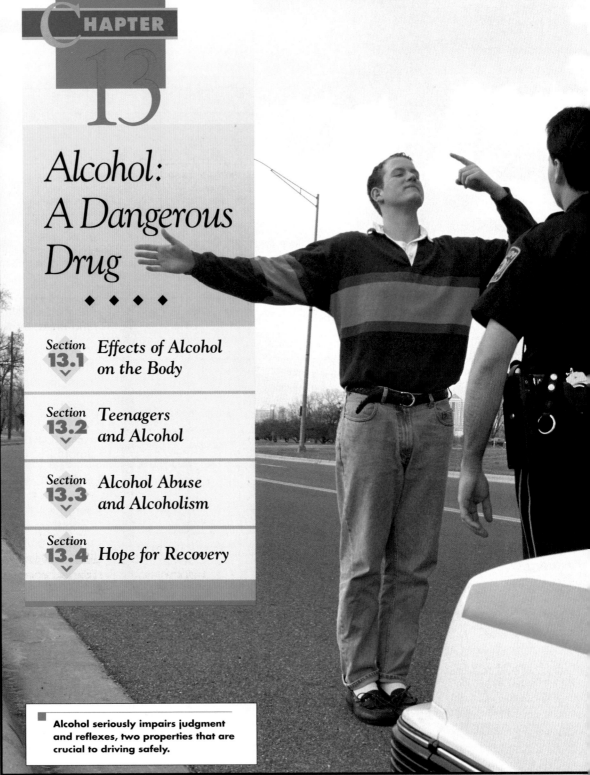

■ Alcohol seriously impairs judgment and reflexes, two properties that are crucial to driving safely.

MYTHS & MISCONCEPTIONS

- **Alcohol stimulates you and makes you livelier.** Just the opposite is true. Alcohol is a depressant that slows down the nervous system. The "loosening up" commonly associated with drinking is really a letting down of the inhibitions that usually govern a person's behavior. Frequently, people later regret alcohol-induced behavior.

- **I can drive just as well after drinking a few beers; in fact, I can drive better.** Alcohol frequently gives people a false feeling of confidence. Tests show that even low levels of alcohol in the blood cause a decrease in both perception and reaction time.

- **Alcoholic drinks such as brandy will help you stay warm when you are out in cold weather.** Actually, drinking alcohol cools the body. Alcohol causes blood vessels near the skin to dilate so that more blood flows through them. Although this may cause a sensation of warmth, body heat is actually lost through the skin.

Navorn was excited. School was out for the summer, and she had a great summer job lined up. Now she was celebrating at an end-of-school-year party, but it was getting late. Navorn saw Billy heading out the back door, and she was about to ask him for a ride home. Then she noticed that he seemed pretty drunk. So she asked a friend who hadn't been drinking for a ride.

The next day she heard the news. Billy had lost control of the car on his way home. It crashed into a ditch and hit several trees. Billy didn't make it. If Navorn had taken a ride with Billy, she might have been killed too.

Section
13.1
Effects of Alcohol on the Body

Personal Health Inventory

Have students complete the Personal Health Inventory for this chapter.

English/Spanish CD Audio Program

Use the English/Spanish Health Talk audio program for students who need audio reinforcement of the concepts presented.

Parent Discussion Guide

Send home the Parent Letter for Chapter 13. As you progress through the chapter, send home the Parental Survey and The Extra Mile.

Objectives

- *Discuss the effects of intoxication.*
- *Name two diseases caused by long-term alcohol abuse.*

Alcohol may be the most misunderstood drug. It is widely advertised and is often consumed at parties and restaurants. But alcohol is also a very dangerous drug that kills thousands of people every year and addicts millions more. It tears families apart and is involved in more than half the violent crimes committed in the United States. And, for Americans under 21, it is an illegal drug.

One reason alcohol is illegal for teenagers has to do with what happened to Billy. In 1994, over 6,000 people died in auto collisions in which teens were driving. Teenage drunken drivers were involved in almost 40 percent of these crashes. These numbers were even higher a few years ago, when some states allowed people as young as 18 to drink. Highway safety experts think the raised legal drinking age is responsible for saving many thousands of lives.

More and more people are deciding not to drink alcohol. They have made this decision not only because they worry about drunken driving, but also because they don't like what alcohol does to their body. Like any drug, alcohol changes the way your body functions. These changes are unhealthy and can be very dangerous.

When Alcohol Enters the Body

Your friend Leo loves beer. He says it's a better thirst quencher than any other beverage, which you find hard to believe. Now Leo is planning to go to Sandra's party, and you're worried that he will get into trouble.

The party is in full swing when Leo arrives. It doesn't take him long to find out where the beer is. From that moment on, Leo's evening is ruined.

Section 13.1 Lesson Plan

MOTIVATE

Journal 13A
Alcohol: Good or Bad?

This may be done as a warm-up activity. Have students write their responses to these questions in their Journal. What are some reasons why a person might start drinking? How do you think drinking alcohol might be bad for you?

Class Discussion
Alcohol at a Party

Have students discuss Navorn's decision not to ride with Billy because he was drunk. Ask: **What could she have done to stop him from driving?** [*persuaded him not to drive, found someone to take him home, sent him home in a taxi cab, had everyone physically block him from leaving, hidden his car keys, talked him into spending the night there, called his family*] Ask students if they or anyone they know has ever been in a similar situation. Have them describe the situation and the outcome.

Background
Alcohol Content

Alcoholic beverages vary widely in their alcohol content. Beers usually contain between 2 percent and 6 percent alcohol, but some specialty beers are stronger. Malt liquors are similar to beer but have a slightly higher alcohol content. Table wines have an alcohol content of about 10 percent to 15 percent. Fortified wines have alcohol contents of up to 24 percent. Distilled, or "hard," liquors generally have an alcohol content of 40 percent to 55 percent. The proof, or strength of an alcoholic beverage, is twice its alcohol content. For example, a whiskey that is 50 percent alcohol is 100 proof. The alcohol content of all distilled and most fermented beverages is shown on their label. There are two reasons why it is important for a consumer to know the alcohol content of a beverage: (1) the higher the proof, the faster a person will become intoxicated, and (2) alcohol contains calories—as proof increases, so does calorie content.

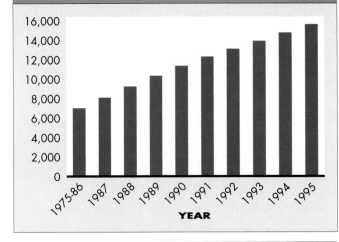

CUMULATIVE ESTIMATED LIVES SAVED BY MINIMUM DRINKING-AGE LAWS

(FIGURE 13-2) **Experts believe that minimum-drinking-age laws have saved more than 15,000 lives.**

blood alcohol level (BAL):

a way to measure the level of alcohol in a person's body.

intoxicated:

being affected by alcohol. Effects of intoxication can range from mild lightheadedness to severe and complete loss of judgment and reflexes.

Each gulp of beer Leo swallows makes its way first into his stomach and then into his small intestine. From his stomach and small intestine, the alcohol is absorbed into his bloodstream. It then travels to all Leo's cells and tissues, including his brain. Within *minutes*, Leo is feeling the effects of the beer.

Eventually the alcohol reaches Leo's liver, which breaks it down into carbon dioxide and water. The more Leo drinks, the harder his liver will have to work to help rid his body of alcohol. In fact, it will take Leo's liver more than an hour to break down the alcohol in each bottle of beer he drinks.

Blood Alcohol Level

One drink is enough to interfere with a person's judgment and reflexes. And the more a person drinks, the more alcohol interferes with judgment and reflexes.

The percentage of alcohol in a person's bloodstream is called the **blood alcohol level (BAL)**. A person's BAL can be influenced by gender, body weight, the amount of food in the stomach, and the rate of drinking.

One drink is enough to raise Leo's BAL to .025 or greater. According to new laws in most states, drivers under 21 are considered legally **intoxicated** at a BAL of .02, and adults are considered legally intoxicated at a BAL of .10. The lower limit for teenagers reflects intolerance for under-age drinking. Even this small amount is enough to impair Leo's judgment and vision. If he keeps drinking, Leo's BAL will keep getting higher.

Short-Term Effects of Alcohol

After a few beers, Leo starts feeling relaxed. He soon forgets about the rough day he had at school.

His face feels flushed and very warm because the alcohol has dilated, or widened, the blood vessels near his skin. He also has to urinate frequently, as his body tries to get rid of the alcohol in his system.

On his way to the bathroom, Leo knocks over an empty chair. He is too drunk to notice what he did, and when he

(FIGURE 13-3) **A 12-ounce bottle of beer, a 6-ounce glass of wine, and a 1.25-ounce glass of whiskey all have about the same alcohol content.**

TEACH

 Cooperative Learning
Questionnaire

Have students work in four groups to develop questions in four subject areas: drinking and teens, drinking in families, social attitudes toward drinking, and legal aspects of alcohol use. Have them combine their questions into a survey they can administer to a sample of other students in the school or complete themselves. Have students present their results in a written report or a set of pie graphs.

Teaching Transparency 13A
Alcohol in the Body

Use the transparency of Figure 13-4 to show how alcohol is distributed throughout the body. Have a volunteer trace and describe the pathway that alcohol takes to reach the brain and other organs. Ask students to explain how the body disposes of the alcohol.

Demonstration
Metabolizing Alcohol

Pose the following question and then demonstrate how you arrive at the answer using math. Ask: **How much alcohol is in a 1.5 oz serving of a liquor that is 40 percent alcohol?** *[Convert 40 percent to a decimal (0.4, the amount of the liquor that is pure alcohol). Then multiply 1.5 (ounces of liquor in one drink) times 0.4. The answer is 0.6 (ounce of alcohol in one drink).]* **If the liver breaks down**

Alcohol irritates the throat and esophagus on its way into the body.

Once in the bloodstream, alcohol travels throughout the body, including the heart and brain.

About 20% of the alcohol drunk is absorbed into the bloodstream through the stomach wall.

The alcohol remains in the bloodstream until it can be metabolized by the liver.

The alcohol that does not enter the bloodstream through the stomach wall gets there after it has passed into the small intestine.

(FIGURE 13-4) **The alcohol in one 12-ounce bottle of beer reaches the bloodstream very quickly. It then remains in the bloodstream until it is metabolized—a process that takes more than an hour for each bottle of beer.**

Background
Effects Differ by Sex

Generally, females become intoxicated more easily than males. The two major factors involved in intoxication are body weight and percentage of body fat. Body fluids dilute alcohol; as weight increases, so does the volume of body fluids. Fatty tissue contains less fluid than muscle tissue, and females have a higher fat-to-muscle ratio than males do. There are other factors to consider. In males, the stomach usually oxidizes alcohol more efficiently, so less alcohol passes into the bloodstream. Hormone levels also influence alcohol metabolism. A female's alcohol tolerance varies during her menstrual cycle. There is evidence that taking birth control pills reduces alcohol tolerance.

about 0.4 ounce of alcohol in 1 hour, how long will it take to rid the body of all the alcohol from the drink? *[Divide 0.6 ounce by 0.4 ounce per hour. The answer is 1.5 hours.]*

Debate the Issue
Legal Intoxication

Have students do research to find out why some states use a lower blood alcohol level for teens than they do for adults to establish legal intoxication. Then divide the class into two teams to debate this question: **Is justice** served by using a lower blood alcohol level to establish legal intoxication in teens?

• • • TEACH continues on p. 264

Background
Costs of Alcohol Use

In 1985, alcohol abuse in the United States cost society an estimated $70.3 billion. Several categories of costs are included in this estimate, including the medical costs incurred because of alcohol abuse and the loss of productivity in the workplace. The figure does not include the following costs, which are substantial: costs involving the criminal justice system, property loss from alcohol-related motor-vehicle accidents and fires, loss of productivity in the workplace by victims of alcohol-related crimes, and the cost of imprisonment due to alcohol-related crimes. As the population increases and inflation indexes rise, these costs to society will continue to rise.

Myths and Facts About Alcohol

Myth	Fact
You can't get as drunk from beer, wine, or wine coolers as you can from "hard" liquor like vodka and scotch.	A bottle of beer, a glass of wine, and a wine cooler all have around the same amount of alcohol as a shot of a distilled spirit like vodka or scotch. Therefore, they are just as intoxicating.
A person who looks and acts sober is sober.	Not everyone shows the effects of alcohol in the same way. Even people who seem completely sober are dangerous drivers if they have been drinking alcohol.
Alcohol can't be as dangerous as illicit drugs because it is easily available to people over the age of 21.	Even though alcohol is a legal drug for Americans over 21, when it is abused it is just as dangerous as many illicit drugs.

(FIGURE 13-5) **Myths about alcohol not only are untrue, but also can be dangerous to believe—particularly if a person is drinking and driving.**

hangover:

uncomfortable physical effects brought on by alcohol use. Symptoms of a hangover include headache, nausea, upset stomach, and dizziness.

returns from the bathroom he trips over it. Laughing loudly, he struggles to get up from the floor. Leo may find this funny, but his lack of coordination and inhibition has resulted from a serious event; the alcohol in his bloodstream has entered his brain, changing the way it functions.

Leo sees Roberto talking with a girl Leo used to date. The sight enrages him, and he grabs Roberto and shoves him against the wall. Roberto just shakes his head, rolls his eyes, and walks away.

Leo finds some more beer and sits in the kitchen, drinking by himself.

The next thing he knows, Leo is waking up on a kitchen floor—a kitchen floor he doesn't recognize. "Oh yeah," he realizes, "I guess I passed out in Sandra's kitchen." He has a dull headache, a sick

stomach, and he feels very dizzy. Leo has a **hangover.** "Just my luck," he says out loud.

Actually, Leo *was* pretty lucky. He could have seriously hurt Roberto or himself if Roberto hadn't ignored him. If Leo had tried to drive home, he could have easily had a wreck.

Leo's hangover lasts until late in the afternoon. (Nothing but time makes a hangover go away.) As a result, he plays poorly at basketball practice. "Okay, so I got drunk last night," Leo tells you when you ask him if he's all right. "What are you—my mother?"

Leo denies that the alcohol has had negative effects. He likes the relaxed feeling he gets while he is drinking. That means he'll probably drink again soon.

• • • TEACH continued

Class Discussion
Myths and Facts About Alcohol

Discuss the information shown in Figure 13-5. Ask: **We know that beer, wine, and hard liquors are all intoxicating. But beer and wine coolers often pose a greater hazard for teenagers than hard liquor. Why?** [They are cheaper, more widely available, and their lower alcohol content

misleads some into believing that a person can't get as drunk on them.]

 Teaching Transparency 13B
Blood Alcohol Level and Its Effects

Show the transparency of Figure 13-6. Point out that the BAL is for a 140-pound person, and ask: **If you weigh less than 140 pounds, would the same amount of alcohol affect you more, or less?** [More, because the same dose of alcohol would spread through a smaller quantity of blood, raising the

BAL.] **Which affects you more—a drink before dinner, or during a meal?** [A drink on an empty stomach affects you more, because the alcohol is very quickly absorbed by it. Eating food along with or before taking a drink spreads the absorption of alcohol over a longer time and causes a lower BAL.]

Debate the Issue
Setting the Legal Drinking Age

Divide the class into two teams and have the teams debate whether teenagers should be allowed to drink

Blood Alcohol Level and Its Effects

Number of Drinks in a 1-Hour Period (140-pound person)	Approximate Blood Alcohol Level	Effects on Body
1	.025	Feeling of relaxation, warmth, and well-being; slight impairment of judgment
2	.05	Inhibitions are lessened; judgment impaired, behavior can become impulsive or silly
3	.075	Reflexes and coordination impaired; speech and hearing slightly affected
4	.1	Legally drunk in most states; vision, hearing, judgment, reflexes, coordination impaired
6	.161	Intoxication; coordination seriously affected; vision blurred, speech and hearing severely impaired
8	.215	Intoxication extreme; no control over thoughts and perceptions; walking and even standing become difficult
12	.321	Intoxication severe and dangerous; nervous system may become affected, coma and death can result

(FIGURE 13-6) **This table shows the estimated blood alcohol level and its effects on a 140-pound person. A person's blood alcohol level will vary according to a number of factors, such as weight and gender.**

SECTION 13.1

Section Review Worksheet 13.1
To reinforce the concepts presented in this section, assign Section Review Worksheet 13.1.

Section Quiz 13.1
Have students take Section Quiz 13.1.

Reteaching Worksheet 13.1
Students who have difficulty with the material may complete Reteaching Worksheet 13.1.

at age 18. Remind students that both the pro and con teams should be able to refute one another's arguments with solid evidence.

Review Answers

1. A person who is intoxicated may become angry, behave impulsively and without inhibitions, and lose his or her reflexes. Coordination will become impaired, making the person clumsy. With increased levels of intoxication, the person can have difficulty walking and standing.

2. Answers will vary but may include hepatitis, cirrhosis, heart disease, and cancer.

3. Answers will vary. Students should point out the short-term effects and consequences of intoxication as well as some possible long-term consequences. Students may also suggest alternative ways to enjoy oneself at a party, other than drinking alcohol.

(FIGURE 13-7) **A normal liver (left), and a liver with cirrhosis (right). Cirrhosis is an incurable, untreatable disease caused by alcoholism.**

hepatitis:

an inflammation of the liver that can be caused by long-term alcohol abuse. Symptoms of hepatitis include high fever, weakness, and a yellowing of the skin.

cirrhosis:

a condition in which liver cells are replaced by useless scar tissue. Cirrhosis can be caused by long-term alcohol abuse.

Long-Term Effects

Over a period of time, the alcohol Leo drinks can seriously damage his body.

First, alcohol can harm his liver. As you now know, the liver works hard to break down the alcohol in his body into carbon dioxide and water. The liver does this job well, but pays a price each time. Studies show that even small doses of alcohol leave fat deposits on liver cells. The livers of alcoholics are often damaged beyond repair.

One liver disease that can result from alcohol abuse is **hepatitis** (hep-uh-TY-tis). Hepatitis is an inflammation or infection of the liver that can cause fever, a yellowing of the skin, weakness, and sometimes death. More information about hepatitis can be found in Chapter 21.

Another liver disease caused by alcohol abuse is **cirrhosis** (sur-OH-sis), which occurs when liver cells are permanently replaced with useless scar tissue. People with cirrhosis often suffer serious digestive problems, because their livers are no longer able to metabolize food properly. Research shows that people with cirrhosis who continue to drink have only about a 50 percent chance of living more than five years.

Alcohol abuse can have many negative effects on a person's health. It causes dam-age to the heart muscle and increases the risk of heart disease. Alcohol can also increase a woman's risk of developing breast cancer. It interrupts REM sleep, which is a necessary part of the sleep cycle. It can also lower a person's white blood cell count, reducing his or her ability to fight infection.

Alcohol kills brain cells. Unlike those in other parts of the body, the cells in the brain cannot be replaced. Loss of brain cells can lead to irreversible memory damage.

Finally, long-term alcohol abuse can also increase one's chances of suffering cancers of the liver, esophagus, pharynx, and larynx.

Review

1. *Explain how a person's behavior changes when he or she is intoxicated.*

2. *Name two diseases caused by long-term alcohol abuse.*

3. *Critical Thinking* *What could you say to Leo to persuade him to stop drinking?*

ASSESS

Section Review

Have students answer the Section Review questions.

Alternative Assessment
Lifelong Drinking Habits

Tell students about a person who started drinking a case of beer every weekend while still in high school. In college, the person progressed to drinking wine daily and hard liquor on weekends. As a young working person, it became a common practice to stop for a drink after work. Now the person is almost 40 and drinks half a bottle of wine or a beer or two each day. Have students describe what alcohol-related problems this person might face in the future.

Extension
Alcohol Laws

Have students contact your state's alcoholic beverage control agency to learn about the alcohol laws in your state. Ask students to prepare a report or poster summarizing their findings.

Closure
Feelings About Drinking and Driving

Have students assess their feelings about drinking. Then have them summarize orally their feelings about drinking and driving.

Section 13.2

Teenagers and Alcohol

If you watch a sporting event on television, or read a magazine, or drive a few miles on the highway, you are certain to see an advertisement for alcohol. Have a drink, the advertisements seem to say, and you can be like the people pictured—cool, glamorous, and sophisticated. Many people believe the ads so they drink to fit the image they see.

Some people think they have to drink to be relaxed, to be social. But as Leo experienced, drinking alcohol can make a person angry and aggressive. In this way, it can make a person *less* social.

Other people may drink to ease emotional pain. You saw how Leo forgot what was disturbing him after he had a few beers. Many teenagers who are having problems at home or at school may be looking for something to help them forget their worries. It's

completely understandable to feel this way. But alcohol tends to add to a person's problems, rather than solve them.

Some teenagers drink because it makes them feel independent. Others do so to rebel, or for excitement.

But whatever the reason, if you drink alcohol, you are putting your life on the line.

Drunken Driving

Alcohol severely damages judgment, reflexes, and vision. These effects happen to a person even if he or she doesn't *feel* drunk. In other words a person with a high blood alcohol level may not necessarily be slurring words, reeling, and staggering, but still is in no shape to be behind a wheel.

Blood Alcohol Level and Its Effects on Driving Ability

BAL	Decrease in Driving Ability
.04–.06	12%
.07–.09	23%
.10–.12	30%

(FIGURE 13-8) **A blood alcohol level of .04 or above can severely impair judgment, coordination, and vision, which are all important to safe driving.**

Background
Social Standards

Teaching students to say no to alcohol is complicated by our culture's double standard for drinking. Adults advocate sobriety, yet the media presents drinking as highly desirable. It may also seem paradoxical to teens that they are considered adult enough to drive, vote, marry, and serve in the armed forces, yet are not considered adults when it comes to alcohol. Thus, teaching students to say no to alcohol requires the support of society at large as well as parents, guardians, and teachers.

Life Skills Worksheet 13A

Assign the Hidden Persuasion Life Skills Worksheet.

A person doesn't have to be legally drunk in order to be dangerous on the highway. As little as one alcoholic beverage can cause enough impairment to cause a car crash. Figure 13-8 shows how different blood alcohol levels can affect a person's driving ability.

There are things you can do to minimize your risk of getting involved in a drunken-driving incident. First, don't drink. Of all reasons to turn down alcohol, this may well be the most important.

Second, don't accept a ride with anyone who has been drinking, even if he or she swears that you have nothing to worry about. Instead, call a sober person to pick you up. Maybe you can persuade the person you're with to come with you. You may want to show a parent or guardian a copy of the contract prepared by Students Against Driving Drunk (S.A.D.D.). This agreement guarantees that parents or guardians who are called for a ride home will pick up their teenagers—no questions asked. A copy of the contract is shown in Figure 13-10.

Binge Drinking

Remember that alcohol has very serious effects on the body. What you should also know is that alcohol is a poison. If a person drinks enough of it at one time, it can cause immediate death.

Although the amount of alcohol necessary to kill a person varies, a blood alcohol level of about .4 percent is usually enough to put a person in a coma and on the verge of death. For a 140-pound person, that's about 15 to 20 drinks in a one-hour period.

Binge drinking—drinking large amounts of alcohol quickly—can easily cause death by alcohol poisoning. Binge drinking is a very serious problem among teenagers and young adults who take part in drinking games.

Drunken Driving: Facts and Numbers

Among people up to age 34 in the United States, motor-vehicle accidents are the leading cause of death.

Approximately one-third of teenage deaths are the result of motor-vehicle accidents.

The risk of motor-vehicle accidents increases for young drivers who have even a very low concentration of blood alcohol in their systems.

Over 40,000 traffic deaths occur each year, and almost 41 percent of these deaths involve a driver who has been drinking alcohol.

Of the more than 40,000 traffic deaths each year, more than 5,200 involve a teenage driver. Of these deaths, almost 38 percent involve a teenage driver who had been drinking alcohol.

(FIGURE 13-9) **Studies show that drivers between the ages of 16 and 24 are three times as likely to die in a drunken-driving crash as older drivers.**

• • • TEACH continued

Class Discussion
Selling Beer

Have students recall beer ads they have seen and heard. On the chalkboard, write the heading MEDIA MESSAGES ABOUT BEER. Ask students to provide examples. (cool and refreshing, sports, sex, beautiful scenery, fun activities, social enjoyment, friendship, reward for a job well done)

Have students address the categories one by one to explain, first, how the connection with desirable rewards is made and, second, why the connection is false. For instance, beer is associated with sports by being sold in sports bars; drinking doesn't promote physical health, and real people who drink a lot don't look like the models in the ads.

Teaching Transparency 13C
Drunk Driving: Facts and Numbers

Use the transparency of Figure 13-9 to emphasize the relationship between fatal motor-vehicle accidents and drunk driving. Ask: **Considering that motor-vehicle accidents are the leading cause of death among teenagers, why should teenagers be concerned about drunk driving?** [Answers may include that about one-third

CONTRACT FOR LIFE

A FOUNDATION FOR TRUST & CARING

By agreeing to this contract, we recognize that SADD encourages all young people to adopt a **substance-free** life style. We view this contract as a means of opening the lines of communication about drinking, drug use and traffic safety to ensure the safety of all parties concerned. We understand that this contract does not serve as permission to drink, but rather, a promise to be safe.

Young Adult

I acknowledge that the legal drinking age is 21 and have discussed with you and realize both the legal and physical risks of substance use, as well as driving under the influence. I agree to contact you if I ever find myself in a position where anyone's substance use impairs the possibility of my arriving home safely. I further pledge to maintain safe driving practices at all times, including wearing my safety belt every trip and encouraging others to do the same.

_____
Signature

Parent or Guardian:

Upon discussing this contract with you, I agree to arrange for your safe transportation home, regardless of time or circumstances. I further vow to remain calm when dealing with your situation and discuss it with you at a time when we are *both* able to converse calmly about the matter.

I agree to seek safe, sober transportation home if I am ever in a situation where I have had too much to drink or a friend who is driving me has had too much to drink. Recognizing that safety belt usage is a vital defense against death and injury on the highway, I promise to wear my safety belt at all times and encourage others to do the same.

_____
Signature

_____
Date

Distributed by S.A.D.D. "Students Against Driving Drunk"

(FIGURE 13-10) S.A.D.D. published this contract between parents and teenagers for the sake of reducing the amount of drunken-driving incidents. This organization does not approve, however, of alcohol use among teenagers.

Making a Choice 13A

Assign the Alcohol-Free Activities card. The card asks students to brainstorm to make a list of fun activities that do not involve alcohol and a list of activities that require alertness and coordination that would be impaired by alcohol.

of all teenage deaths are the result of a car accident, 41 percent of fatal accidents involve drunk drivers, and 38 percent of teenagers who cause a fatal car crash are legally drunk.]

Class Discussion
Contract for Life

Give students a moment to read S.A.D.D.'s "Contract for Life" and then discuss what it says. Ask students to take a copy of the contract home and discuss signing it with their parents or guardian. Elicit a discussion of why someone may or may not want to sign the contract.

• • • TEACH continues on p. 270

Life Skills
Worksheet 13B
Assign the Resisting Pressure to Drink Life Skills Worksheet.

Blood Alcohol Level's Effect on Death Risk

BAL	Chance of Dying
.02–.04	1.5 times as likely
.05–.09	11 times as likely
.10–.14	48 times as likely
.15+	380 times as likely

(FIGURE 13-11) **Drinking alcohol in any amount can put a person's life in danger.**

Breaking the Law

People under 21 break a law every time they have any alcohol (except under special circumstances, such as religious purposes). Like all crimes, getting caught drinking alcohol under the age of 21 can lead to arrest, a fine, and even a criminal record. Many teenagers have decided that they'd rather not risk their futures by drinking alcohol now. In addition, driving while under the influence of alcohol is illegal for people of all ages. A person does not have to be in an accident in order to be caught driving drunk—the driver of any car exceeding the speed limit or noticeably weaving through traffic is subject to inspection and a possible blood alcohol level test.

Losing Control

One of the best reasons not to drink is that alcohol can make a person lose control. Drinking to the point of intoxication can remove inhibitions completely. As a result, drunk people may find themselves doing things they regret.

For example, Krystal and Claudio are the school's most popular couple. Wher-ever they go is *the* place to be. Whatever they do, everyone wants to do too. It's a secret, but one thing they *haven't* done is have sexual intercourse.

Claudio lives with his grandmother, who happens to be out of town for the weekend. He takes advantage of this opportunity, and throws the year's wildest party. By the end of the night, everyone is very drunk, including Claudio and Krystal. The house is severely damaged: the stereo is broken beyond repair, and part of the carpet has been badly burned.

Claudio doesn't know any of this yet, because Krystal has suddenly decided she's ready to have sex with him. The two of them have stumbled to his bedroom.

Hours later, Claudio wakes up, horrified and ashamed. He hadn't wanted it to be like that. How could he have been so stupid? He knows they both made a mistake and that it's too late to go back now. What if Krystal gets pregnant? What about sexually transmitted diseases? Claudio knows that if they hadn't been drunk, they wouldn't have lost control.

Teenagers who drink are more likely to engage in activities that conflict with their

---

• • • TEACH continued

Demonstration
Who Is Legally Drunk?

Prepare one index card for each student. Write LEGALLY DRUNK on 10 percent of the cards, and SOBER DRIVER on the remaining cards. Distribute the cards at random, face down, and ask the students to guess which cards say "legally drunk." This demonstrates that you can't tell which driver out of every 10 is drunk. Have students turn over their cards to discover which ones say "legally drunk." Explain that a driver should drive defensively and should not assume that all other drivers will act responsibly.

Debate the Issue
Prohibition

Divide the class into two teams to debate the pros and cons of passing a law prohibiting the use of alcohol. Suggest that before students begin the debate they find out about the positive and negative effects of Prohibition in the 1920s in the United States, which outlawed all alcoholic beverages containing more than 0.5 percent alcohol.

 Teaching Transparency 13D
Reasons Not to Drink

Use this transparency to summarize information on the risks of alcohol use.

personal and parental values. These actions can result in conflicts with family and friends, feelings of guilt, unwanted pregnancies, sexually transmitted diseases, and damage to public or personal property.

Standards Set by Parents or Guardians

Many teenagers decide not to drink because they want to abide by the standards set by their parents or guardians. Chances are that a lot of students in your class have decided not to drink for this reason.

An Alcohol-Free Life

People who choose not to drink do so because they like being sober. They find that being drunk interferes with a lot of activities they enjoy—like taking part in sports, or going to the movies, or socializing with friends, or reading. Being sober allows them to get the most out of the things that make them happy.

What Would You Do ?

Making Responsible Decisions

Should You Let Him Drive You Home?

You're at a party, and it's getting late. Your friend Cliff, who drove you to the party, says he's ready to drive you home. He tells you he hasn't been drinking, but you're pretty sure he's had at least two or three beers. What would you do?

Remember to use the decision-making steps:

1. State the Problem.
2. List the Options.
3. Imagine the Benefits and Consequences.
4. Consider Your Values.
5. Weigh the Options and Decide.
6. Act.
7. Evaluate the Results.

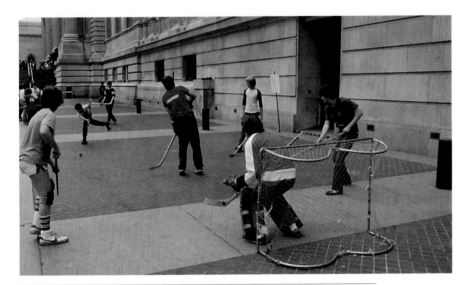

(FIGURE 13-12) **Life's healthiest and happiest activities never include drinking alcohol.**

What Would You Do ?

Have students read the description of the situation. Ask students how they would handle it. What would they say to Cliff, who does not appear drunk and may not acknowledge that he shouldn't drive? How would they find alternative transportation for themselves and for him? They should use the seven decision-making steps to help them make a reasonable choice.

 Section Review Worksheet 13.2

To reinforce the concepts presented in this section, assign Section Review Worksheet 13.2.

 Section Quiz 13.2

Have students take Section Quiz 13.2.

 Reteaching Worksheet 13.2

Students who have difficulty with the material may complete Reteaching Worksheet 13.2.

Cooperative Learning
Anti-drinking Advertisements

Have students form small groups to write anti-drinking ads that would appeal to teenagers. Tell them to be as creative as they wish and that the ads can be humorous.

Extension
Anti-drinking Organizations

If there is a chapter of S.A.D.D., M.A.D.D., or R.I.D. (Remove Intoxicated Drivers) in your school or community, have a representative meet with the class to explain their mission in stopping drunken driving.

Life SKILLS

Have students individually decide what to do in each situation. Then, with students sharing their decisions on a voluntary basis, discuss the different approaches to the situations presented.

Making a Choice 13B

Assign the Who Is Vulnerable? card. The card asks students to discuss traits and experiences that may predispose a young person to alcohol abuse. Students are also asked to suggest some better ways of handling those traits and experiences and to tell how a young person might be protected against alcohol abuse.

Saying No Thanks

You may find yourself in the position of having to turn down a drink at a party. There are a lot of ways to do this, but in general, the less you make of it, the easier it's going to be. If someone asks you if you want a drink, try just saying "no thanks." Remember that you don't owe anyone any explanations.

For many teenagers, saying no to alcohol is a matter of self-esteem. In general, the higher a person's sense of confidence and responsibility are, the better he or she may be at resisting pressure.

See the Life Skills activity below for some situations that test your ability to turn down alcohol.

Life SKILLS: Resisting Pressure

To Turn Down Alcohol . . . . .

It's never easy to decide not to do something a lot of other people are doing. Still, resisting pressure to drink alcohol is one of the healthiest decisions you can ever make. If you do have to turn down alcohol, it may help to have some idea of what you want to do or say. On a separate sheet of paper, write down what you would do, say, and feel in each situation.

1. You're at a party, and a friend is about to get herself a beer. She insists that you drink one.

2. You're with a group of friends who are passing around a bottle of liquor. The bottle comes to you, and you realize everyone is watching.

3. Four friends are sitting at a table playing a drinking game. They ask you to join them.

4. Your date buys some sodas at a drive-through restaurant, pulls out a bottle of liquor, and offers to mix some with your soda.

You don't have to make a big deal about the fact that you have chosen not to drink. But be firm about your decision. It is, after all, the right one for you.

Getting Involved

One of the most rewarding things you can do with your spare time is to volunteer for an anti-alcohol cause. This could mean planning an alcohol-free dance or other activities that bring people together without alcohol. You might want to think about organizing a discussion group for students in your school to talk about peer pressure or other things that tempt them to try alcohol.

In addition, look into joining your school or community chapter of S.A.D.D. or Remove Intoxicated Drivers (R.I.D.). Encourage your friends to volunteer with you. If you have trouble persuading them, remind them that drunken-driving crashes kill one teenager every three hours. Any organization that is working to bring that number down is worth the time and effort you put into it.

Review

1. *Name two reasons why some people drink.*

2. *What are two myths a lot of teenagers hear about alcohol?*

3. *What is the most dangerous consequence of binge drinking?*

4. **LIFE SKILLS: Resisting Pressure** *Name three ways you could refuse alcohol if a friend offers it to you.*

5. **LIFE SKILLS: Making Responsible Decisions** *Name two possible short-term negative consequences of accepting a ride with someone who has been drinking.*

6. **Critical Thinking** *Why are people who are intoxicated more likely to get into automobile crashes than people who are sober? Be specific.*

SECTION 13.2

Review Answers

1. Answers will vary but may include the following: to appear cool, glamorous, or sophisticated; to feel relaxed; to be sociable; to ease emotional pain; to feel independent; to rebel; for excitement.

2. Accept any thoughtful answer that reflects the fact that most advertisements imply that drinking will make you as cool, glamorous, and sophisticated as the people pictured seem to be.

3. Binge drinking can cause immediate death.

4. Answers will vary but should include a direct statement of refusal. For example, "No thanks" or "I don't want to break the law" or "I don't like the taste of alcohol."

5. Answers will vary but may include being involved in a drunken-driving accident and being injured.

6. Answers should reflect an understanding of the following facts: alcohol impairs coordination, vision, judgment, and reaction time, all of which decrease a person's ability to control a car.

ASSESS

Section Review

Have students answer the Section Review questions.

Alternative Assessment

Point out that many people drink heavily at parties, especially on holidays. Ask: **What are some of the dangers and results of this drinking?** *[Because of increased holiday traffic and drinking, the accident rate increases; in winter, bad road conditions may make driving even more dangerous; and regrettable behavior because of the influence of alcohol and hangovers can reduce the enjoyment of an occasion.]*

Closure
Using Common Sense

Have students suggest responses to friends who say the following:

• My mom drinks. Why shouldn't I drink?

• People say alcohol is just another drug, but it's not—it's legal.

Background
Alcohol Dependency

It was once believed that alcoholics were morally weak people who could stop drinking if they only tried harder, but that view has changed. Research shows that this is not the case. In the 1950s, the American Medical Association (AMA) recognized alcoholism as a disease of alcohol dependency that is characterized by compulsive drinking and withdrawal symptoms when the drinking stops. The term *alcohol dependency* is now the preferred medical term. The AMA identifies three factors that contribute to a person's development of the illness: personality, environment, and the addictive nature of the drug. According to the AMA, the factors that contribute to the development of alcohol dependence include heavy drinking over a long period of time; the availability and affordability of alcohol; social acceptance of alcohol consumption; stress, especially from loneliness or loss; insecure or immature personalities; and, in women, hormonal factors.

Section 13.3 Alcohol Abuse and Alcoholism

Objectives

- Know the three phases of alcoholism.
- Name the most important risks of alcohol abuse.
- Know how alcohol can affect an unborn child.
- Know the ways in which a family can be damaged by a family member's alcoholism.

alcoholism:

the state of being psychologically and physically addicted to alcohol.

(FIGURE 13-14)
Every teenager who drinks alcohol is an alcohol abuser.

Abuse

When a person who drinks alcohol cannot do so in moderation or at appropriate times, he or she is abusing alcohol. There are more people who abuse alcohol than you may realize. Every person who drives drunk, for example, is abusing alcohol. People who become violent or angry when they are drunk, or do things they wouldn't do when they are sober, are abusing alcohol.

Leo, Claudio, and Krystal are examples of teenagers who are abusing alcohol. In reality, all teenagers who drink alcohol are abusing it because they are doing something illegal.

People who abuse alcohol regularly can suffer in many ways. They often do poorly in school or at their jobs. And they are likely to engage in behaviors that risk the health and safety of themselves and others.

According to the American Medical Association, **alcoholism** is a disease just like cancer or heart disease. Most people who have this disease pass through three phases: abuse, dependence, and addiction.

Signs of Alcohol Abuse

Odor on the breath	Frequent absences
Intoxication	Unexplained bruises or accidents
Difficulty focusing, glazed eyes	Irritability
Uncharacteristically passive or aggressive behavior	Loss of memory (blackouts)
Decline in personal appearance or hygiene	Changes in peer-group associations and friendships
Decline in school or work performance	Damaged relationships with family members or close friends

Section 13.3 Lesson Plan

MOTIVATE

Class Discussion
Signs of Alcohol Abuse

Write the following on the chalkboard:

DRINKING → ABUSE → DEPENDENCE →ADDICTION

Explain that not all drinking leads to addiction, but when it does, this is the path it often follows. Ask: **What are signs of abuse?** *[drunken driving, poor schoolwork, behavioral changes]* Write student responses on the chalkboard under ABUSE. **What are signs of psychological dependence?** *[need alcohol to function, constant desire for it, no withdrawal symptoms if drinking stops]* **What are signs of addiction?** *[alcohol first priority, neglect everything else, withdrawal symptoms if drinking stops]*

Journal 13C
Alcohol and Behavior

Ask students to list in their Journal behaviors they associate with drunkeness. Ask them why Blood Alcohol Level is a better way of determining if someone is intoxicated than looking solely at his or her behavior.

Risk Factors for Alcoholism

Risk Factors You Cannot Control	Risk Factors You Can Control
Genes	Drinking before the age of 21
Environment	Associating with people who drink
	Bending to peer pressure
	Drinking beyond moderation
	Drinking at inappropriate times
	Drinking alone

(FIGURE 13-15) **Most risk factors for alcoholism can be avoided. For this reason, alcoholism is a preventable disease.**

Dependence

People in the dependence phase of alcoholism feel they need the drug to function properly. They have a very strong and constant desire for alcohol. At this point this desire is a psychological one only, which means that they are not yet physically addicted to alcohol. Even so, alcohol is beginning to dominate their lives.

Addiction

Eventually the dependence on alcohol becomes physical as well as psychological. Those who are physically dependent on alcohol suffer unpleasant withdrawal symptoms if they don't have a regular fix. Studies show that teenagers can become physically dependent, or addicted, much more quickly than adults. Teenagers who use alcohol can become addicted to it in as little as one to two years. It takes most adults about 5 to 20 years of alcohol abuse to become addicted.

Once a person becomes both psychologically and physically dependent on alcohol, he or she is an alcoholic.

Being addicted to alcohol means putting the drug before everything else. Alcoholics often neglect their job, their responsibilities, and even their family because their one focus—the one thing they think about—is getting more alcohol. Sometimes they will substitute alcohol for food, which can lead to serious health problems, such as malnutrition.

They may also be in a constant state of denial. People who are completely addicted to alcohol may resent any suggestion that they may have a drinking problem. They often claim that they can quit any time they want. In reality, such people usually need assistance in order to stop drinking.

Causes of Alcoholism It's not completely clear why some people can drink alcohol without becoming addicted, while others become alcoholics.

Background
Alcohol Poisoning
Alcohol is metabolized by the liver, but it takes about one hour for the liver to process 12 mL (10 g) of alcohol. This is the amount found in one glass of wine, a half pint of beer, or a shot of hard liquor, also called spirits. However, factors such as body weight, body chemistry, and the amount of food in the stomach influence how quickly alcohol is absorbed and metabolized. When more alcohol is consumed than the liver can process, the excess alcohol builds up in the body. Since alcohol is a toxin, a fatal quantity can accumulate. Some teenagers are under the impression that people pass out before they can drink enough to kill themselves. This is not true. Teens need to understand that death from alcohol poisoning can occur, even in a young, healthy person. Four hundred mL, the amount of alcohol found in a liter of hard liquor, is usually fatal. Teens need to be made aware that games such as drinking contests can lead to death.

TEACH

Debate the Issue
Who Is Responsible?

Explain that doctors and psychologists have argued for years whether alcoholics are people who drink too much and thus become addicted, or whether they are genetically predisposed to drinking. Then divide the class to debate the following topic: Alcoholics should not be held responsible for any crime they commit while under the influence of alcohol. Allow each side to state its case and make counterarguments.

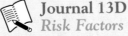

Journal 13D
Risk Factors

Go over the six risk factors that everyone can control (Figure 13-15). Reach a consensus on what each category means—for example, "drinking beyond moderation" might mean anything beyond one or two drinks; "drinking at inappropriate times" might mean drinking when one gets up in the morning. Then in their Journal, have students evaluate their risks according to their behavior. You may want to suggest that students use the following rating system: Never, Rarely, Sometimes, or Often.

Life Skills Worksheet 13C

Assign the Strategies for Raising Self-Esteem Life Skills Worksheet.

Section Review Worksheet 13.3

To reinforce the concepts presented in this section, assign Section Review Worksheet 13.3.

Section Quiz 13.3

Have students take Section Quiz 13.3.

Reteaching Worksheet 13.3

Students who have difficulty with the material may complete Reteaching Worksheet 13.3.

fetal alcohol syndrome (FAS):

a set of birth defects that can occur when a pregnant woman drinks alcohol. These defects include low birth weight, mental retardation, facial deformities, and behavioral problems.

Some evidence shows that children of alcoholics are more likely than others to become alcoholics as adults. And some evidence indicates that the likelihood of becoming an alcoholic may be inherited through genes.

But it is difficult to separate the possible effects of genetic traits from environmental factors. Children who grow up in alcoholic families are less likely than others to get their emotional needs met. So when they get older, they may use alcohol to numb their emotional pain.

Alcoholism probably results from a combination of psychological, environmental, and physical factors.

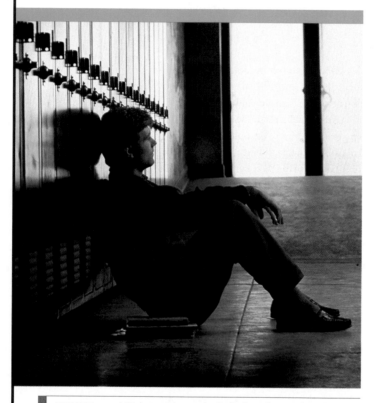

(FIGURE 13-16) **Living with an alcoholic family member can be confusing and lonely. But with proper treatment, the families of alcoholics can fully recover—regardless of whether the alcoholic they are living with does.**

Fetal Alcohol Syndrome

When a pregnant woman drinks alcohol, every bit of the drug in her system passes into the bloodstream of her unborn child. Babies who are exposed to alcohol in this way are at risk of suffering from a set of defects known as **fetal alcohol syndrome (FAS)**. These defects include low birth weight, mental retardation, facial deformities, and behavioral problems.

No one is exactly sure how much alcohol must reach the unborn child in order for FAS to occur, so many doctors advise women not to drink alcohol at all while they're pregnant. Women who are not addicted to alcohol have no trouble following this suggestion. Alcoholic women, however, may have difficulty staying away from alcohol for nine months.

Alcohol and the Family

Dennis's two sons love to be with him when he is sober. That's when he is warm and affectionate—that's when they know that he loves them. It's when he's drunk that everything becomes unpredictable. While drunk, he has beat them more times than they want to remember.

This behavior is not unusual—it is estimated that between 50 and 80 percent of all family violence involves alcohol.

But the damage alcoholism has caused Dennis's family goes beyond physical violence. The two sons don't talk about it, but they know that they must avoid their father when he is drunk. They also must make excuses for him when he is too intoxicated to go to work. They spend their time wondering what Dennis will be like at the end of the day. Will he have gone to work? Will he threaten them? Or will he be kind and loving, and make promises they know he won't keep? Dennis's addiction has taken over his entire family.

• • • TEACH continued

Reinforcement
Fetal Alcohol Syndrome

Refer students to Figure 13-17. Explain that this child has some facial deformity because her mother drank while she was pregnant. Ask: **What's the best way to prevent FAS?** [*Don't drink while pregnant.*] Explain that FAS children sometimes require special medical care costing many thousands of dollars. Discuss the following issues: Who do you think should pay for this special medical cost—the parents, a health-care plan, or the government? Would it be fair to levy a special tax on alcohol or the alcoholic beverage manufacturer? Why or why not? Stress that the entire FAS problem could be prevented by not drinking during pregnancy.

Cooperative Learning
Alcohol and the Family

Divide the class into groups of four or five students to discuss what Dennis' family should do to help him and themselves. Ask them to recommend specific steps for Dennis, such as going for counseling; specific steps for the family, such as taking him to court or leaving him. Then have the groups compare notes and reach a consensus on the best approach for Dennis and his family.

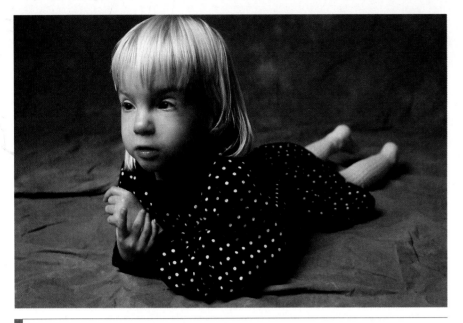

(FIGURE 13-17) **Fetal alcohol syndrome is a set of birth defects that can affect the babies of women who drink alcohol while pregnant.**

1. abuse, dependence, addiction

2. Answers will vary but may include drunk driving, violent behavior, breaking the law, doing poorly in school or on the job, engaging in risky behaviors, neglecting or abusing family and friends, and having health problems.

3. It may result in fetal alcohol syndrome, which includes defects such as low birth weight, mental retardation, facial deformities, and behavioral problems.

4. Answers will vary. Accept answers that indicate a variety of abusive behaviors by parents with this disease, such as physical abuse, mental abuse, and emotional abuse.

5. Answers will vary. Psychological factors might include desire to numb emotional pain and to feel relaxed; sociological factors might include to be one of the group, or to bend to peer pressure because everyone else is drinking.

Being controlled by a family member or a loved one's addiction is sometimes called being codependent. Teenagers who have an alcoholic parent often don't know what to expect when they come home from school. Some have learned that if they don't take responsibility for something, no one in the family will. They may find themselves doing responsible jobs at home, such as making sure the utility bill is paid, that teenagers from nonalcoholic families usually don't have to worry about. And even though they are doing so much for the family, these teenagers often feel as though they are somehow to blame for everything. They may think that they're constantly in the way.

The important thing for them to know is that their parent's drinking is *not* their fault, and that they can get help.

In the next section you'll learn about treatment for alcoholism and about the help available for family members of alcoholics.

Review

1. What are the three phases of alcoholism?

2. What are three dangers of alcohol abuse?

3. Explain how a pregnant woman's drinking can affect her unborn child.

4. How can a parent's alcoholism affect the children?

5. **Critical Thinking** What do you think are some psychological and sociological factors that can cause a person to become an alcoholic?

Extension
History of Alcohol

Have students use encyclopedias to discover the history of alcohol use in the United States from colonial times to the present, including the temperance movement and the era of Prohibition (1920–1933).

ASSESS

Section Review

Have students answer the Section Review questions.

Alternative Assessment
Drinking Behavior

Ask students to recall Leo, who liked to drink beer to forget about his rough day. Have them write a paragraph explaining which stage of alcohol use Leo is in and how they can tell.

Closure
Still a Problem

Discuss the following question: **Given all the problems with alcohol abuse and alcoholism, why do people in our society continue to drink?** *[Alcohol relaxes people, relieves physical and emotional discomfort, and makes people high; it is legal, unlike other drugs; it is widely available; it is heavily advertised; it is culturally sanctioned.]*

Section
13.4 Hope for Recovery

Background
Repeated Treatment
More than half of the alcoholics who undergo treatment are able to abstain from alcohol. But it is not unusual for an alcoholic to resume drinking, especially in response to a trauma such as the loss of a loved one or a job. Thus, alcoholics sometimes must go through withdrawal and treatment more than once.

Background
Alcoholics Anonymous
Alcoholics Anonymous (AA) was founded in Akron, Ohio, by two alcoholics, salesman Bill W. and surgeon Dr. Bob (AA does not use last names; hence the organization's name). A desire to stop drinking is the only prerequisite to becoming a member. No membership or attendance records are kept and no fee is charged—the meetings run on donations. AA is completely independent of government and religious and other organizations. AA has over 1 million members in the United States and over 2 million worldwide.

Section
13.4 Hope for Recovery

Objectives

- *Discuss the treatment options for alcohol abuse.*

- *Learn how to get help if you or someone you know abuses alcohol.*
  LIFE SKILLS: Using Community Resources

withdrawal: *the process of discontinuing a drug to which the body has become addicted.*

In order to quit drinking, an alcoholic must first admit that he or she is powerless over alcohol. Then the process of recovery can begin. Sometimes a person who is addicted to alcohol can reach this conclusion by himself or herself. Other times it may take intervention by friends and family to get an alcoholic to this point. But no matter how it happens, a person who has admitted this has completed the first step of the recovery process.

Withdrawal

When an alcoholic quits drinking, he or she goes through **withdrawal.** Withdrawal is the process of discontinuing a drug to which the body has become addicted. During withdrawal, a person may suffer extreme

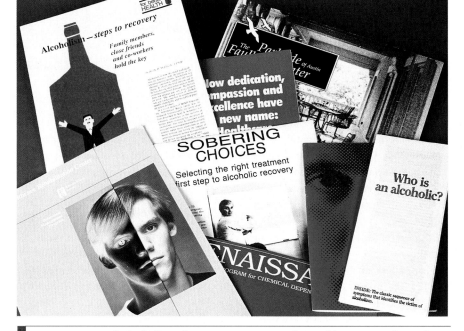

(FIGURE 13-18) **All alcoholics who want to overcome their addiction must first admit that their addiction to alcohol controls their life and that they need to get treatment.**

Section 13.4 Lesson Plan

MOTIVATE

Journal 13E
Attitudes Toward Drinking Now

This may be done as a warm-up activity. In their Journal, ask students to write about whether their attitude toward drinking has changed based on what they learned in this chapter. If it

278 ALCOHOL: A DANGEROUS DRUG

has changed, have students tell how it has changed. If it has not, have students tell what attitudes have been reinforced and why. Then have students tell what advice they would give about drinking to a younger sibling.

TEACH

Class Discussion
Getting Into Treatment

Write the following sequence on the chalkboard:

ADMIT → QUIT → WITHDRAWAL → RECOVERY

Have students explain how these steps are interrelated. Ask: **Why must alcoholics first admit that they are powerless over alcohol?** [Unless they admit they are powerless over alcohol, they can't be helped to get well.] **Does quitting drinking mean slowing down, or stopping entirely?** [stopping entirely] **Why should withdrawal be medically supervised?** [The seizures during withdrawal can be dangerous, and various prescription drugs are used nervousness, headaches, tremors, or seizures. Ordinarily these symptoms would go away once the alcoholic has some alcohol. But there is no such relief for a person who has decided to quit drinking. The withdrawal phase of recovery usually lasts no more than a few days. Those going through it, however, may want to be under constant medical supervision.

Inpatient and Outpatient Programs

Alcoholics who have gone through withdrawal are no longer physically addicted to alcohol. Now the harder part comes, because they have to stop being emotionally addicted as well. People who have at one time depended on alcohol to help them cope with problems may want a drink whenever times are hard. And because they are alcoholics, having just one drink is likely to make them physically and emotionally addicted once again. That's why patients in treatment programs are not allowed any alcohol at all.

Some recovering alcoholics decide to join hospital inpatient programs, which means that they live at the hospital while receiving treatment. Others choose to move home after completing withdrawal, and to participate in hospital outpatient programs. After going through withdrawal, patients in both programs receive counseling in order to understand why they became addicted to alcohol, and to help them cope with life without it. This may come in the form of individual sessions, or in group therapy, which gives the patient the opportunity to talk to other people going through the same thing. Many hospitals also offer therapy sessions and education classes for families of alcoholics, who are also in a recovery process—living with an alcoholic can be as damaging as being one.

Alcoholics Anonymous

There are many self-help programs for alcoholics. By far the most widely used of these is Alcoholics Anonymous (AA). Many hospital treatment programs require their patients to attend AA meetings. In addition, AA has helped a large number of alcoholics stop drinking without any other form of treatment.

The AA method for recovery involves 12 steps. The first and perhaps most important of these is for the alcoholic to recognize that he or she is powerless over alcohol.

Through regular meetings and shared experience, AA members bring themselves and each other closer to their goal of a life that is free of alcohol, and full of emotional, physical, and spiritual well-being. Such a goal, AA members know, can only be reached one day at a time. For this reason, many recovering alcoholics attend AA meetings every day, and learn to celebrate every day, week, month, and year they conquer without alcohol.

To find out about AA meetings in your area, look in the phone book under "Alcoholics Anonymous."

Al-Anon and Alateen

Having a parent, a sibling, or a spouse who is an alcoholic can make a person feel alone and lost. Al-Anon and Alateen were formed to bring people who are feeling this way together.

Al-Anon is designed to help family members talk about the problems of living with an alcoholic. Alateen was specifically designed to help teenagers cope with the same situation.

Meetings at Al-Anon and Alateen are very much like those of AA. People who feel like talking about their experiences can do so. Those who would rather just listen don't have to say anything. Knowing that

SECTION 13.4

Life Skills Worksheet 13D
Assign the Locating Resources for Breaking Addiction Life Skills Worksheet.

Section Review Worksheet 13.4
To reinforce the concepts presented in this section, assign Section Review Worksheet 13.4.

Section Quiz 13.4
Have students take Section Quiz 13.4.

---

to aid withdrawal.] **During recovery, why does the family, as well as the alcoholic, undergo counseling?** *[because living with an alcoholic can be psychologically and physically damaging]*

 Cooperative Learning
Finding Out About Available Services

Divide the class into five groups to research alcohol treatment, therapy, and support available in your area. Each group should prepare a report showing their contacts, addresses, and phone numbers, and present to the class a summary of the services.

Case Study
Classroom Visit

Contact the local AA chapter and ask for a member to visit the class to be interviewed for this case study. Ask students to prepare questions before the visit and review them with the class. Have each student write a summary of the interview.

Reinforcement
Abstinence

A recovering alcoholic's abstinence must be permanent. To reinforce this fact, ask: **How soon after recovery is it safe for an alcoholic to enjoy a small glass of wine?** *[Never. He or she must never drink again.]* **If a recovering alcoholic has a bad cold, should he or she use a cold remedy that contains alcohol?** *[No. He or she must never have any form of alcohol.]*

Review Answers

1. A person can join an in-patient program, an out-patient program, or a self-help program.

2. Look in the phone book under "Alcoholics Anonymous" for a number to call, or check the Internet for the Alcoholics Anonymous Web site.

3. Look in the phone book under "Alcoholics Anonymous" or "Alateen." Call and ask the person who answers the phone about meetings in your town. Also, check the Internet for the Al-Anon/Alateen Web site.

4. Students might answer that living with an alcoholic can be damaging because it can make other family members feel alone and lost. Often the other family members feel as though they are to blame for everything and that they are constantly in the way. Accept any well-supported answer.

(FIGURE 13-19) **Alcoholics Anonymous is the most widely used and the most successful of the self-help programs. It has helped many alcoholics stop drinking without hospital treatment.**

other people are going through the same thing can make some very difficult situations less painful.

One of the most important goals of groups like Al-Anon and Alateen is to help people realize that they can get help whether or not the alcoholic they are living with gets treatment. Even if the alcoholic keeps drinking, the family members can improve their own lives.

If you want to find out more about Al-Anon and Alateen, look in the phone book under Al-Anon or Alcoholics Anonymous. The person who answers the phone can provide you with meeting information. You may also check the Internet for the Alcoholics Anonymous Web site and the Al-Anon/Alateen Web site.

Review

1. *Describe three ways a person can begin recovery from alcoholism.*

2. **LIFE SKILLS: Using Community Resources** *How could you find out about meetings of Alcoholics Anonymous in your area?*

3. **LIFE SKILLS: Using Community Resources** *How could you find out about meetings of Alateen in your area?*

4. **Critical Thinking** *Do you agree with the statement: "Living with an alcoholic can be as damaging as being one?" Why or why not?*

• • • TEACH continued

Extension
Drug Therapy

Many recovering alcoholics take the drug disulfiram, which makes them quite sick if they drink. Have students research this drug to discover what it does, how it works, and why it is so helpful to a recovering alcoholic.

ASSESS

Section Review

Have students answer the Section Review questions.

Alternative Assessment
Going It Alone

An alcoholic has decided that he or she is stronger than alcohol and that he or she will begin an alcohol-free life without anyone's help. Have students write an explanation of why this method probably will fail.

Closure
Self-Esteem

Ask students to explain the relationship between low self-esteem and alcohol abuse. What is that relationship? Can low self-esteem be improved? Can damaged self-esteem be rebuilt?

Highlights

Summary

- One drink can impair a person's judgment, reflexes, and vision enough to cause an automobile accident.

- Drinking alcohol can cause hangovers, damage the liver and heart, kill brain cells, and increase a person's chances of getting cancers of the liver, esophagus, pharynx, and larynx.

- Minimize your risk of getting involved in a drunken-driving incident by not drinking, and by not accepting a ride with anyone who has been drinking.

- Alcohol can be deadly if a person drinks enough of it at one time.

- Teenagers who drink are much more likely to engage in activities that conflict with their personal and parental values.

- Alcoholics and the people who are close to them can be helped by groups and programs such as Alcoholics Anonymous, Al-Anon, and Alateen.

Vocabulary

blood alcohol level (BAL) a way to measure the level of alcohol in a person's body.

intoxicated being affected by alcohol. Effects of intoxication can range from mild lightheadedness to severe and complete loss of judgment and reflexes.

hangover uncomfortable physical effects brought on by alcohol use. Symptoms of a hangover include headache, nausea, upset stomach, and dizziness.

hepatitis (hep-uh-TY-tis) an inflammation of the liver that can be caused by long-term abuse. Symptoms of hepatitis include high fever, weakness, and a yellowing of the skin.

cirrhosis (sur-OH-sis) a condition in which liver cells are replaced by useless scar tissue. Cirrhosis can be caused by long-term alcohol abuse.

alcoholism the state of being psychologically and physically addicted to alcohol.

fetal alcohol syndrome (FAS) a set of birth defects that can occur when a pregnant woman drinks alcohol. These defects include low birth weight, mental retardation, facial deformities, and behavioral problems.

withdrawal the process of discontinuing the use of a drug to which the body has become addicted.

CHAPTER 13

Chapter Review

CHAPTER REVIEW

Concept Review

Sample responses:

1. Alcohol interferes with a person's judgment, reflexes, coordination, vision, speech, and hearing. A person may at first feel relaxed and uninhibited; he or she may be impulsive. With very high blood alcohol levels, a person could go into a coma and die.

2. Drinking alcohol lessens a person's inhibitions and judgment. This can lead to obnoxious behavior, such as laughing loudly and being rude. It can also cause a person to become angry and aggressive.

3. Drinking alcohol severely impairs a person's judgment, reflexes, and vision, making the person incapable of controlling a car or reacting quickly enough to avoid an accident; being arrested for drunk driving and being involved in an accident.

4. Students Against Driving Drunk; to reduce the number of drunk-driving incidents

5. In general, a person with high self-esteem also has a higher sense of confidence and responsibility, making it easier to say no to drinking.

6. The person may do poorly in school or at work and engage in risky behavior. Also, he or she has a strong desire for alcohol and may make up excuses to drink.

Concept Review . . . .

1. How does alcohol affect the mind and body?

2. What is one way that drinking alcohol can make an individual less social?

3. How does alcohol affect a person's driving? What are two consequences of driving drunk?

4. What is S.A.D.D.? What is the purpose of their "Contract for Life"?

5. How is saying "no" a matter of self-esteem?

6. What are some signs that a person has a drinking problem?

7. How is the dependence stage of alcoholism different from the addiction stage?

8. Why can some people drink alcohol without becoming addicted, while others become alcoholics?

9. What does being codependent mean?

10. What is the first step in recovering from alcoholism?

11. What help is available for a problem drinker?

Expressing Your Views . . . .

1. You're about to leave a party with a friend, but you realize that your friend has been drinking alcohol. What should you do?

2. People who drink at parties often try to get everyone else there to drink as well. Why do you think people who drink try to pressure others to drink?

3. Mothers Against Drunk Driving (M.A.D.D.) is an organization that promotes stricter penalties for people who drive drunk. Contact this organization to find out what your state's acceptable blood alcohol level is and what the local and state penalties are for drunken driving. Do you think these penalties are fair and adequate? Why or why not?

---

7. People in the dependence stage have a strong psychological desire for alcohol. In the addiction stage, the dependence on alcohol is both psychological and physical.

8. There is some evidence of a genetic predisposition to alcoholism.

9. In codependence, a person is controlled by a family member's or loved one's addiction to alcohol.

10. The alcoholic must first admit that he or she is powerless over alcohol.

11. Inpatient and outpatient programs, as well as self-help programs, such as

Alcoholics Anonymous, are available.

Expressing Your Views

1. Sample response: I would try to keep my friend from driving if we were using his or her car. If I were unable to do that, I would try to get a ride with someone who has not been drinking or call a family member to pick me up.

2. Sample response: Most people don't want to drink alone. They also think drinking is cool and that everyone should try it.

3. Answers will vary depending on state laws.

Life Skills Check . . . .

1. Using Community Resources
Charlie's mother is an alcoholic. Sometimes she's asleep on the living room couch when Charlie comes home from school. Other times she's awake, but impatient with Charlie and quick to get angry over small things. Charlie knows she needs help, and would also like to talk to someone about how his mother's drinking affects him. What can Charlie do to get help?

2. Resisting Pressure
Movies, television, and advertisements often seem to encourage audiences to drink by making alcohol consumption seem appealing and sophisticated. What are they not telling viewers about alcohol?

3. Communicating Effectively
You think your friend may have a drinking problem because she always smells like alcohol, and because she often seems drunk. What could you say to persuade her to contact a group that could help her with her problem?

Projects . . . .

1. Make a poster advertising Al-Anon and Alateen meetings. Display these posters throughout the school. Include suggestions and illustrations to help the problem drinker. You might also write to these organizations for any additional information to display.

2. Create a bulletin board to show alcohol's effect on various parts of the body such as the brain, kidneys, liver, stomach, and heart. Include illustrations and labels, along with diseases brought about by alcohol abuse.

Plan for Action . . . .

About half of all fatal driving accidents are related to alcohol use. Devise a plan to ensure that you will always drive sober.

Life Skills Check
Sample responses:
1. He can contact Al-Anon or Alateen.
2. Advertisements do not tell about the pain and suffering alcohol can cause. They show people drinking and enjoying themselves, and they do not show what can happen when people drink too much. Movies and television do show people who have had too much to drink, but seldom in a realistic manner.
3. I could tell her that I know something is wrong and there are people, including myself, who are willing to stand by her and help her. I would suggest she call Alcoholics Anonymous to find out where in the community help is available to her. I would also encourage her to attend a meeting and offer to go with her for support.

Projects
Have students plan and carry out the projects within the school.

Plan for Action
Ask students if they now have better ideas for resisting pressure to drink. Ask students to write out a plan of what they can do to ensure that they always drive sober.

Pledge
Discuss the pledge for Chapter 13. A student's decision of whether to sign the pledge is personal and private.

ASSESSMENT OPTIONS

Chapter Test
Have students take the Chapter 13 Test.

Alternative Assessment
Have students do the Alternative Assessment activity for Chapter 13.

Test Generator
The Test Generator contains additional assessment items for this chapter.

Tobacco: Hazardous and Addictive

SECTION	TITLE/OBJECTIVES	PERSONAL INVENTORY			LIFE SKILLS DEVELOPMENT			
		Personal Health Inventory	Journal	Check Up	Life Skills	Life Skills Worksheets	Media Message or Ethical Issues Worksheet	What Would You Do?
14.1 *pp. 285–291*	**THE EFFECTS OF TOBACCO ON THE BODY** • Name three major chemicals in tobacco. • Name two kinds of diseases smoking can cause. • Name one disease smokeless tobacco can cause. • Know the difference between mainstream and sidestream smoke. ▪▪ Demonstrate how to ask someone not to smoke in your presence.	Ch. 14	14A		p. 290	14A	Unit 4	
14.2 *pp. 292–294*	**A TOBACCO-FREE LIFE** • Know two reasons why people start using tobacco. • Know three reasons not to use tobacco. • Know two strategies you can use to quit smoking.		14B 14C			14B		

KEY: ▪▪ Denotes Life Skill Objective
Text references denoted by page number.
Supplement references denoted by chapter or item numbers.

LINKING RESOURCES

	Making a Choice Cards	Parent Discussion Guide	Health Talk Audio Program	Teaching Transparencies and Directory	Section Review Worksheets	Section Quizzes	Reteaching Worksheets	Section Reviews
	INTERACTION		**OTHER RESOURCES**		**SECTION REVIEW AND ASSESSMENT**			
	Ch. 14	Ch. 14	14A BSH8		14.1	14.1	14.1	p. 291
	14A 14B				14.2	14.2	14.2	p. 294

For additional information about the lungs and lung dysfunction, see pages 671–673 in the Body Systems Handbook.

KEY FACTS

- Smoking is the most avoidable cause of death in the United States; yet smoking-related illnesses cause 434,000 deaths each year.

- Tobacco contains 401 poisonous chemicals, including nicotine, tar, and carbon monoxide.

- Nicotine is an addictive, psychoactive drug. Many people find it difficult or impossible to break their addiction to nicotine.

- Lung cancer is the most common cause of death by cancer among both American men and women. It is estimated that 80 percent of all lung cancer is caused by cigarette smoking.

- Smoking-related illnesses include cardiovascular disease, many kinds of cancer, and respiratory diseases, such as chronic bronchitis and emphysema.

- Smokeless tobacco products can cause cancer of the mouth, throat, tongue, cheek, and gums.

- Nonsmokers who inhale the sidestream smoke of smokers are at an increased risk of developing respiratory infections, lung cancer, and heart disease.

CHAPTER REVIEW AND ASSESSMENT

TEXT

Chapter Review pp. 296–297

SUPPLEMENTS

Chapter Test 14

Alternative Assessment 14

Test Generator Chapter 14

GETTING STARTED

Using the Chapter Photograph

Ask students to read the cigarette warning labels. Ask why they think people continue to use tobacco despite the warnings. Have them review the similar government warning on alcoholic beverage containers and discuss why people continue to drink despite the warning.

Question Box

Have students write out any questions they have about smoking or other tobacco use and put them in the Question Box.

Sensitivity ALERT

Many students smoke or have relatives who smoke or who suffer from a smoking-related disease. This chapter's focus on the health risks associated with smoking may be interpreted by some as an implied criticism of the students or of their relatives. Help students recognize that the relationship between smoking and disease may not have been well established when their relatives started smoking. Also, point out that the addictive nature of nicotine makes it difficult for most people to stop smoking even if they want to.

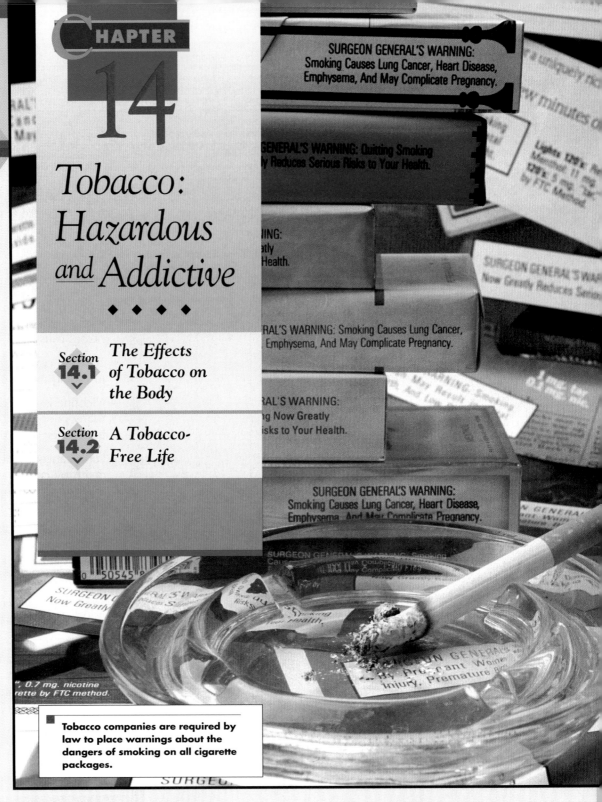

CHAPTER 14

Tobacco: Hazardous and Addictive

◆ ◆ ◆ ◆

Section 14.1 The Effects of Tobacco on the Body

Section 14.2 A Tobacco-Free Life

Tobacco companies are required by law to place warnings about the dangers of smoking on all cigarette packages.

MYTHS & MISCONCEPTIONS

• **Smoking makes you feel better.** Nicotine is a stimulant drug that provides a temporary lift. Smoking also calms some people. But to achieve these effects, a smoker must continually increase the dose, leading to addiction. In the long run, smoking makes people feel worse.

• **Low tar, low nicotine cigarettes are safe to smoke.** No cigarettes are safe. Also, smokers of low tar, low nicotine cigarettes tend to inhale more deeply and to smoke more cigarettes so that they receive a level of toxic substances similar to that received by those who smoke regular cigarettes.

• **Smokeless tobacco is safe.** No tobacco products are safe. Using smokeless tobacco products creates the same addiction to nicotine as smoking does. Smokeless tobacco can cause cancers, particularly oral cancer, and heart disease. Also, smokeless tobacco damages the teeth and gums.

Ethan has been smoking a pack of cigarettes every day for the past year. He didn't get hooked right away. In fact, the first few times he smoked, he got really sick. But soon he got used to it, and then he began to enjoy smoking. Now he finds it hard to get through each hour without smoking a cigarette. His girlfriend, Mara, hates his habit. She finds it really unattractive—his hair and clothes always reek of cigarette smoke. More important, she's worried about his health. He's always short of breath, and sometimes he coughs for minutes on end until his throat is raw. Mara knows he has to quit. The problem is, how can she persuade Ethan to give up cigarettes?

Section 14.1
The Effects of Tobacco on the Body

Objectives

- *Name three major chemicals in tobacco.*
- *Name two kinds of diseases smoking can cause.*
- *Name one disease smokeless tobacco can cause.*
- *Know the difference between mainstream and sidestream smoke.*
- *Demonstrate how to ask someone not to smoke in your presence.*
  ■ **LIFE SKILLS: Communicating Effectively**

Mara hopes that if she can teach Ethan enough about the risks of smoking, he'll find the courage and willpower to quit. She found some books and pamphlets on smoking and disease, and she is teaching Ethan some interesting facts. For example:

- Illnesses caused by smoking kill 434,000 Americans every year. That number is higher than the number of American military deaths during World War II.
- Cigarette smoking is considered the most avoidable cause of death in the United States.
- The death rate from heart disease is 70 percent higher for smokers than for non-smokers, and over 80 percent of lung cancer cases are caused by smoking.
- Tobacco smoke also creates a health hazard for all those around the smoker who rely on the same air supply. Each year an estimated 50,000 nonsmokers die from exposure to tobacco smoke released into the air by smokers.

The Chemicals of Tobacco

Tobacco contains more than 4,000 chemicals. More than 401 of these chemicals are poisonous. When Ethan smokes a cigarette,

SECTION 14.1

Personal Health Inventory
Have students complete the Personal Health Inventory for this chapter.

English/Spanish CD Audio Program
Use the English/Spanish Health Talk audio program for students who need audio reinforcement of the concepts presented.

Parent Discussion Guide
Send home the Parent Letter for Chapter 14. As you progress through the chapter, send home the Parental Survey and The Extra Mile.

Section 14.1 Lesson Plan

MOTIVATE

Journal 14A
Feelings About Smoking

This may be done as a warm-up activity. In their Journal, have students express their feelings about smoking. If they are smokers, ask them to tell how they feel when smoking and how smoking affects their body. If they don't smoke, have them tell how they feel about inhaling the smoke of others.

TEACH

Class Discussion
Does Ethan Have the Right to Smoke?

Have students name some problems Ethan's smoking might cause. These might include his health, the cost of his addiction, the risk of serious diseases, the hazard to Mara when she breathes his smoke, and her negative feelings. Does Ethan have the right to smoke, even when it affects someone

he loves? Does Mara have the right to convince him to stop smoking? Solicit ideas on how Mara might convince Ethan to give up smoking.

Cooperative Learning
Questioning Smokers

Form small groups. Have each group share observations about smokers: Do they know someone who smokes? When and how much do the people smoke? Are the smokers considerate of

Background

Tobacco: A New-World Crop

High-nicotine-content tobacco was first developed by the indigenous people of Mexico and Central America through the selective breeding of wild tobacco species. Its first use was probably in religious rituals. Columbus and other early explorers imported tobacco to Europe, where it became popular immediately. Soon, tobacco became a valuable crop, and it was an important factor in the English colonization of North America. Some tobacco was powdered for snuff, while leaf tobacco was processed primarily into pipe tobacco and later cigars. After 1915, improved methods in the production of cigarettes made them inexpensive, and cigarettes became extremely popular. By 1981, cigarette consumption in the United States had reached a high of 640 billion cigarettes annually. Since then, consumption has decreased steadily to an annual consumption of 485 billion cigarettes in 1994. Unfortunately, the teenage smoking rate has not decreased.

addictive:

causing a physical dependence; a person who is addicted to a drug requires that substance in order to function normally.

tar:

solid material in tobacco smoke that condenses into a thick liquid.

nicotine:

an addictive chemical found in tobacco.

psychoactive substance:

a substance that causes a change in a person's mood and behavior.

What's Really in Cigarettes?

Cigarette smoke is a collection of more than 4,000 chemicals.

Cigarette smoke contains cyanide, a deadly poison.

Fingernail polish remover, a poisonous gas, a preservative an insecticide, 401 poisons, and 43 known carcinogens (cancer-causing substances) are some of the ingredients in cigarette smoke.

Cigarette smoke contains methanol, a wood alcohol. Taken in sufficient amounts, methanol can cause blindness. It is also used as an additive in or substitute for gasoline.

Nicotine is a deadly poison. Taken in high doses, it can kill. One drop (70 milligrams) will kill an average person within a few minutes. Most cigarettes contain between .2 and 2.2 milligrams of nicotine. At one time, nicotine was used as an insecticide.

Cigarette smoke contains formaldehyde, a chemical used to preserve dissection specimen for biology.

(FIGURE 14-1) **It would be hard to find a list of ingredients that are more hazardous than those in tobacco.**

he inhales every one of those chemicals and every one of those poisons. Mara did some math and figured out that since Ethan is smoking one pack of cigarettes a day, he inhales these chemicals 70,000 times a year. Three of the most poisonous chemicals in tobacco smoke are tar, nicotine, and carbon monoxide.

Nicotine **Nicotine** is the psychoactive chemical in tobacco. A **psychoactive substance** causes a change in a person's mood and behavior. Nicotine is also the reason Ethan is hooked on smoking—it is a very **addictive** drug. A person who is addicted to a drug has trouble functioning without it. Because Ethan is addicted to nicotine, if he were to quit smoking, his body would go

through a physical withdrawal. The withdrawal symptoms of nicotine include irritability, headache, restlessness, and anxiety. These symptoms are unpleasant but temporary. Eventually Ethan's body would stop reacting in this way. Ethan is also psychologically dependent on nicotine. This means that he has a constant craving for it. A psychological addiction can be as difficult to overcome as a physical one.

Tar Tobacco smoke contains tiny pieces of solid matter called **tar.** When these tiny particles enter the lungs, they condense and form a sticky coating on the bronchial tubes. The bronchial tubes are lined with tiny hairs called cilia, which beat back and sweep away agents that cause disease. When the

• • • TEACH continued

nonsmokers nearby? Do they have any symptoms of smoking (cough, hoarse voice)? Does their smoking affect nearby nonsmokers in any way?

Game

Name Your Poison!

Have students write five questions on index cards about the three most poisonous chemicals in tobacco. For example: Which poison in tobacco is a

psychoactive substance? *(nicotine)* Which poison makes smokers short of breath? *(carbon monoxide)* Divide the class into two teams and give half the cards to each team. Have teams take turns asking each other the questions. Then have them trade cards and repeat.

Reinforcement

The More You Smoke, the Worse You Get

Emphasize that the effects of smoking are cumulative. The earlier you start,

the more years you smoke, the more cigarettes you smoke, the more you inhale, and the more of each cigarette you smoke—the worse the effects. Compare smoking to slow poisoning with cyanide: daily small doses accumulate until a person dies. Point out that people who abruptly stop smoking get much better and live longer.

cilia are damaged, they can't do their job. Ethan's cigarette habit puts a quart of tobacco tar into his lungs and cilia each year. If Ethan doesn't quit smoking soon, his cilia will be so damaged that they will not be able to protect him from getting a serious respiratory disease.

Carbon Monoxide As the cigarette burns, it releases an extremely dangerous gas called **carbon monoxide**. Carbon monoxide interferes with the blood's ability to carry oxygen. This is why Ethan is always so short of breath—he's not receiving as much oxygen as he should be.

The Effects of Nicotine

Every time Ethan takes a puff of a cigarette, the nicotine he inhales travels to his bloodstream and then to his brain. This entire process takes only seven seconds, so Ethan will start feeling the effects of the nicotine immediately. This means that Ethan's heart will beat more quickly, his blood pressure will increase, and he will begin to feel more alert and energetic. These effects last for only about 30 minutes, which is why Ethan usually craves another cigarette about half an hour after he has finished his last one.

carbon monoxide:

a poisonous gas released by burning tobacco.

Background
The Price of Smoking
Because cigarettes are relatively inexpensive to manufacture, the tobacco industry is one of the most profitable industries in the United States. However, the price society pays for smoking is high. In 1994, the medical costs of treating tobacco-related illnesses in the United States was $50 billion. These medical costs are paid by all of society, not just by smokers alone. This figure does not include the cost of lost productivity at work or school because of tobacco-related illnesses or the cost of damage from fires started by cigarettes.

(A) **Brain:** Smoking restricts oxygen flow and causes a narrowing of the blood vessels in the brain, which can lead to stroke.

(B) **Lungs:** Cigarette smoke introduces cancer-causing agents directly to the lung tissue. It also impairs the cilia's ability to clear these and other harmful foreign substances from the lungs, increasing the risk of lung cancer and emphysema.

(C) **Heart:** Nicotine increases heart rate and blood pressure, and constricts the blood vessels, which can lead to a heart attack.

(D) **Stomach:** Cigarette smoke can lead to ulcers.

(E) **Intestines:** Cigarette smoke can also cause ulcers in the small intestine.

(F) **Bladder:** Smoking can cause cancer of the bladder.

(FIGURE 14-2) **Cigarette smoke poses a danger to many major parts of the body.**

Teaching Transparency 14A
How Smoking Affects Your Body

Show the transparency of Figure 14-2. Point to each organ as you explain how smoking affects it. Ask students to define terms, such as cancer, cilia, and emphysema, as they arise.

Role-Playing
Would You Please Not Smoke Here?

Have students role-play the following situations. Before starting, assign specific roles, such as the smoker, the people who oppose smoking, the people who don't care if the smoker smokes, etc.

- In a group of friends, one person asks permission to smoke.
- In a group of strangers in a waiting room, one person asks the others for permission to smoke.
- In a group of friends, one lights up without asking.

- In a group of strangers in a waiting room, one person lights up without asking permission.
- In a restaurant, three people at a table light up in a nonsmoking section, refuse to douse their cigarettes, and claim that nonsmoking areas violate their civil rights.

After acting out each scenario, discuss how to handle each situation.

Evaluating Media Messages

Have students read this Unit 4 feature on pages 320–321. Then have them complete its companion worksheet.

(FIGURE 14-3) **A cancerous lung (left) and a healthy lung (right). The white areas on the otherwise blackened lung show the development of lung cancer.**

cancer:

a disease caused by cells that have lost normal growth controls and that invade and destroy healthy tissues.

Mara discovered why Ethan felt sick the first few times he smoked. When a person's body isn't used to nicotine, a condition called nicotine poisoning can result. Symptoms of nicotine poisoning include lightheadedness, rapid pulse, cold clammy skin, nausea, and sometimes vomiting and diarrhea. "I can't believe you kept smoking when it made you so sick," she told him.

Smoking and Disease

People who smoke put themselves in danger of developing a smoking-related disease. And mothers who smoke risk harming not only themselves but also their newborn and unborn children. For a list of these risks, see Figure 14-4. The risk of getting a smoking-related disease is highest among people who have smoked for a long time, who started smoking at a young age, and who smoke heavily. Mara figures that since Ethan started smoking as a teenager, he'll be at a very high risk of suffering a smoking-related disease if he doesn't quit soon.

Cancer Tobacco is a major cause of sev-

eral types of cancers. **Cancer** is a dangerous disease with formation and growth of malignant, or deadly, cells that attack and replace healthy cells. This can happen anywhere in the body. One major type of cancer caused by smoking is lung cancer. Lung cancer is the most common cause of cancer deaths among both American men and women and the second most common type of cancer among American men and women.

The bronchial tree, which is the hollow tubing that connects breathing passages from the mouth and nose to the lungs, produces a combination of saliva and mucus called sputum. Over a period of time the chemicals in cigarette smoke may cause changes in the cell genes of the sputum. These changes can lead to lung cancer.

There is no effective treatment for lung cancer. Every year, 120,000 Americans die from this disease. According to studies, cigarette smoking causes more than 80 percent of all cases of lung cancer in the United States.

Other cancers caused by smoking include cancers of the larynx, esophagus, bladder, kidney, and pancreas.

Debate the Issue
Should All Smoking Be Banned?

Pose these questions:

• Should people be allowed to smoke? If so, where? What about around babies or young children? around their pets? around elderly people? sick people? people with allergies? people with asthma?

• Is it fair to forbid adults to smoke?

After all, adults are not forbidden to drink alcohol.

Then divide the class into two teams to debate the question: Should all smoking be banned?

Class Discussion
Is Smokeless Tobacco Safer?

Write the following headings on the chalkboard: CIGARETTE, CIGAR, PIPE, and SMOKELESS. Ask students to name the diseases that are caused by each

form of tobacco, and write student responses on the chalkboard. *(cigarettes: lung cancer, chronic bronchitis, emphysema, atherosclerosis, heart attack, stroke; cigars: stomach cancer, cancer of the larynx; pipes: cancers of the tongue, lips, stomach, larynx; smokeless: cancers of the mouth, throat, tongue, cheeks, gums)* Point out that lung cancer and respiratory disease are not caused by smokeless tobacco because this tobacco is not burned and thus doesn't

Respiratory Diseases Ethan has a persistent cough because his smoking habit has caused mucus to accumulate in his respiratory tract. Over a period of time this condition can cause a respiratory disease such as chronic bronchitis or emphysema.

Chronic bronchitis is an inflammation of the bronchial tubes in the lungs and the production of excessive mucus. This results in a chronic cough and breathing difficulties. Smokers with chronic bronchitis often wake up in the morning coughing and spitting up mucus. Chronic bronchitis can eventually lead to emphysema.

Emphysema is a disease in which tiny air sacs in the lungs are ruptured, or torn. Under normal circumstances, these air sacs absorb oxygen coming into the body and help push carbon dioxide out of the body. When torn, they lose the ability to do this. This is why a person with emphysema is always short of breath. People with advanced emphysema constantly struggle for air. Sometimes they can't breathe without the help of a special oxygen tent.

Emphysema may last for years and is often fatal. Eighty percent of emphysema cases are related to smoking.

Cardiovascular Disease As you learned earlier in this section, nicotine increases heart rate and blood pressure, and carbon monoxide makes the circulatory system work very hard to deliver oxygen to the body's cells. Over a period of time, both of these chemicals put a great deal of strain on the body's blood vessels and cause cardiovascular disease, or disease of the heart and blood vessels. More than 120,000 smokers in the United States die every year from cardiovascular diseases.

Smoking can lead to atherosclerosis, which is the buildup of fat on the blood vessel walls. This can increase the chance that a blood vessel will become blocked or break

near the heart, resulting in a heart attack. Another type of cardiovascular disease, a stroke, can occur if a blood vessel breaks or becomes blocked near the brain.

Pipes, Cigars, and Smokeless Tobacco

"Maybe," Ethan said, "I could get my fix of nicotine from something else, like a cigar, a pipe, or even chewing tobacco." Mara and Ethan did some research and found that people tend to inhale the smoke from cigarettes more deeply than they do the smoke from cigars or pipes. For this reason, cigarettes are the most dangerous of

chronic bronchitis:

an inflammation of the bronchial tubes in the lungs and the production of excessive mucus.

emphysema:

a disease in which the tiny air sacs of the lungs lose their elasticity.

SECTION 14.1

Life Skills Worksheet 14A
Assign the Communicating With Smokers Life Skills Worksheet.

Reasons Mothers Shouldn't Smoke

There is a greater risk of miscarriage.

The baby might be born too early.

The baby might have a low birth weight or other serious health problems.

The baby might have a slow growth rate.

There is a greater risk of Sudden Infant Death Syndrome (SIDS).

There is a greater risk that the child will develop a respiratory illness.

The baby might receive nicotine from the mother's milk.

The baby could develop learning difficulties.

(FIGURE 14-4) **Pregnant women and mothers who smoke risk harming not only themselves but also their unborn and newborn children.**

---

produce tar and carbon monoxide. Ask: **Is smokeless tobacco safer to use than cigarettes?** [No. Smokeless tobacco doesn't cause lung cancer or respiratory disease, but it causes other cancers and heart disease.]

Reinforcement
Smoking and Pregnancy

Review Figure 14-4 with the students. Ask: **What are some ways that smoking during pregnancy can harm a**

fetus? [danger of miscarriage, premature birth, low birth weight] **What are some ways it might damage an infant or young child?** [increased risk of SIDS, increased incidence of respiratory and other serious illnesses, risk of nicotine addiction if a nursing mother smokes, increased incidence of learning disabilities]

• • • TEACH continues on p. 290

Life **SKILLS**

Have students consider the situation described in the text and then have them propose solutions.

 Section Review Worksheet 14.1

To reinforce the concepts presented in this section, assign Section Review Worksheet 14.1.

Section Quiz 14.1

Have students take Section Quiz 14.1.

 Reteaching Worksheet 14.1

Students who have difficulty with the material may complete Reteaching Worksheet 14.1.

---

chewing tobacco:

a form of smokeless tobacco that is placed between a person's cheek and gum.

the three. However, cigars and pipes have their own serious hazards. Pipe smokers have been known to suffer cancers of the tongue and lip, and certain types of cancers, such as cancer of the stomach and larynx, are more common among people who smoke cigars and pipes than among those who smoke cigarettes.

Smokeless Tobacco Smokeless tobacco comes in two forms. **Chewing tobacco** is placed between a person's cheek and gum. When this tobacco is chewed, it releases juices that contain nicotine and other chemicals. These juices mix with the saliva and are absorbed into the bloodstream.

The second kind of smokeless tobacco, snuff, is ground tobacco that is inhaled through the nose or placed between the cheek and gum. The nicotine and other chemicals are then absorbed into the bloodstream through the mucous membranes of

---

 *Life***SKILLS:** **Communicating Effectively**

A Cigarette With Dinner? . . . .

Studies show that people who are exposed to sidestream smoke are at risk of suffering the same diseases as smokers. For this reason, new laws have been passed to protect nonsmokers from the dangers of passive smoking. Federal buildings are now smoke-free, and many state, county, and city buildings are smoke-free. Some public places continue to allow smoking but provide designated nonsmoking areas.

Imagine that you and a friend have decided to sit in the nonsmoking section of a restaurant. During the meal, a person at the next table lights a cigarette. The smoke is ruining your meal. Role-play how you could use effective communication and solve the problem.

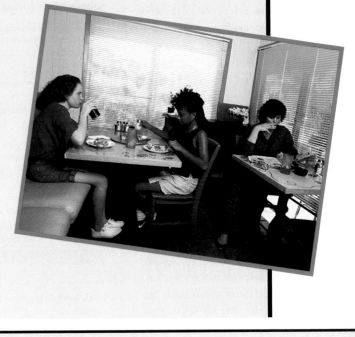

• • • TEACH continued

Writing
Mainstream Versus Sidestream Smoke

Reinforce the distinction between mainstream smoke and sidestream smoke. Then have students write answers to these questions as you read them: **Is it right for one person to light a cigarette and fill the air with sidestream smoke without asking** **others? Why or why not? What should the smoker do instead?** *[quit smoking or find a place to smoke]* **Is smoking a dangerous form of air pollution? Why?** *[Yes. Sidestream smoke promotes several diseases.]* Then discuss whether people should tolerate air pollution from a cigarette any more than they would tolerate air pollution from a garbage incinerator.

Extension
Ask the Experts

Have students use materials obtained from the American Cancer Society, American Lung Association, American Heart Association, and public health agencies to create an antismoking bulletin board. Encourage them to share the literature they obtained with friends who smoke.

the nose or mouth. Once in the bloodstream, the nicotine travels to the brain.

Both snuff and chewing tobacco can cause cancer of the mouth and throat, and chewing tobacco can also lead to cancer of the tongue, cheek, and gums.

The Risks of "Passive" Smoking

Mara saved her biggest weapon for last. If Ethan couldn't be persuaded to quit smoking to save his own health, maybe he would do so for hers. "It's dangerous for me to be around you when you smoke," Mara told him. "It could make me sick—it could even kill me."

Mara had learned that a burning cigarette releases two types of smoke:

- **Mainstream smoke** passes through the tobacco and filter when the smoker inhales.
- **Sidestream smoke** rises from the cigarette during the time the smoker is not inhaling.

Almost 75 percent of the smoke that comes from a burning cigarette is sidestream smoke. Sidestream smoke enters the environment and affects anybody who happens to be around. A person who inhales the sidestream smoke of a cigarette is a **passive smoker**. Sidestream smoke contains twice as much tar and nicotine, and three times as much carbon monoxide, as mainstream smoke. After 30 minutes in a smoke-filled room, a passive smoker has inhaled almost as much carbon monoxide as someone who has just smoked a cigarette.

Passive smokers are at an increased risk of suffering both lung cancer and heart disease. Sidestream smoke can also aggravate a person's allergies and cause respiratory infections. When Mara told Ethan these facts, he agreed to quit smoking.

(FIGURE 14-5) **Chewing tobacco can lead to serious facial deformities as well as certain types of cancer.**

Review

1. What are three major chemicals in tobacco?

2. What are two major types of diseases caused by smoking?

3. What is one disease caused by smokeless tobacco?

4. Define mainstream and sidestream smoke. How do they differ?

5. ■ **LIFE SKILLS: Communicating Effectively** What can you say if a person sitting next to you in a nonsmoking area lights a cigarette?

6. **Critical Thinking** If cigarettes did not contain tar, would they be safe to smoke?

mainstream smoke:

smoke that is inhaled directly into the mouth through a cigarette, pipe, or cigar.

sidestream smoke:

smoke that enters the environment from burning tobacco.

passive smoker:

A nonsmoker who is exposed to the sidestream smoke of a cigarette, cigar, or pipe.

Review Answers

1. tar, nicotine, carbon monoxide

2. Answers may include cancer, respiratory diseases, and cardiovascular disease.

3. cancer of the mouth and throat

4. Mainstream smoke passes through the tobacco and filter when the smoker inhales; sidestream smoke rises from the cigarette during the time the smoker is not inhaling. Two differences between mainstream and sidestream smoke are that mainstream smoke is filtered, whereas sidestream smoke is not; and mainstream smoke is inhaled by the smoker, whereas sidestream smoke is inhaled by the smoker and by all those around the smoker.

5. Students may answer that they could point out to the smoker that this is a nonsmoking section and that they would appreciate it if the person could refrain from smoking while sitting in this section.

6. No; tobacco contains more than 400 other chemicals that are harmful to one's health.

ASSESS

Section Review
Have students answer the Section Review questions.

Alternative Assessment
Why Is Tobacco Hazardous and Addictive?

Have students write a paragraph explaining why tobacco is both hazardous and addictive.

Closure
Setting an Example

Tell students to look ahead to a time when they may have children of their own. Ask: **What is the best way to teach your children not to use tobacco?** [Set a good example by not using it yourself.]

Section 14.2 A Tobacco-Free Life

Objectives
- Know two reasons why people start using tobacco.
- Know three reasons not to use tobacco.
- Know two strategies you can use to quit smoking.

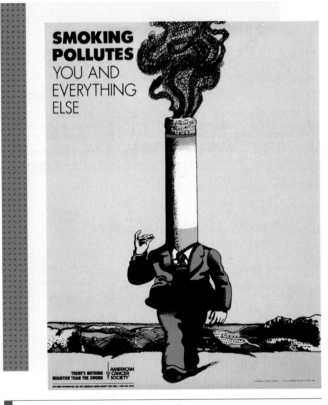

(FIGURE 14-6) **An advertisement from the American Cancer Society. Antismoking organizations are working to destroy the myth that smoking makes people glamorous and attractive.**

Every package of cigarettes and smokeless tobacco carries a warning from the Surgeon General on the dangers of tobacco use. These dangers are well known and well documented. Probably because these risks are so well understood, fewer people today use tobacco than ever before. But even so, more than 72 million Americans ignore these warnings and use tobacco products.

People use tobacco for different reasons. Peer influence and a parent's example may give someone the impression that it's O.K. to use tobacco. For example, Ethan's father has always smoked, and many of his friends smoke as well. If neither his dad nor his friends were smokers, Ethan might never have started smoking.

Another factor that may influence a person's decision to smoke is advertising. Models in cigarette and smokeless tobacco advertisements usually look glamorous and attractive. They can make tobacco use seem very appealing. Some organizations are working to destroy this idea by publishing posters showing the less attractive features of the habit.

Reasons Not to Use Tobacco

Just as peer pressure can tempt you to use tobacco, the influence of friends can help you make the decision *not* to use it. Many teenagers are aware of tobacco's dangers.

Having parents who don't use tobacco can also help a person make the same decision. Most parents realize how harmful tobacco is. They wouldn't want to see their sons or daughters jeopardize their lives by using a dangerous product.

Four Good Reasons to Avoid Tobacco

1. **It's dangerous:** Using tobacco causes cancer and can lead to high blood pressure, cardiovascular disease, and various lung disorders.

2. **It's expensive:** Smoking a pack of cigarettes a day costs more than $800 a year. Chewing a container of tobacco every two days costs about $600 a year.

3. **It leaves an unpleasant odor:** The smell of tobacco lingers on your breath, in your hair, and on your clothes.

4. **It's unattractive:** Tobacco can leave dark stains on your fingers and on your teeth. In addition, many teenagers find the sight of a person smoking or chewing tobacco unappealing.

(FIGURE 14-7)

As Figure 14-7 indicates, using tobacco is an expensive, smelly, and unattractive habit. But the most important reasons not to use tobacco products are that they can damage your health and shorten your life. As you learned earlier in this chapter, the diseases caused by smoking and chewing tobacco are serious and often fatal.

Quitting Smoking

If you avoid smoking altogether, you'll never have to worry about its health risks. But if you are a regular smoker, know that if you quit your habit for good, you can dramatically reduce your chances of getting a serious disease. If Ethan can stay away from cigarettes for five years, his chances of getting lung cancer will decrease by 50 percent. And in 15 years, his chances of suffering *any* smoking-related illness will be almost as low as a person who has never smoked. But even a few days after he stops smoking, Ethan will begin to feel less winded and healthier.

Some smokers are worried that they will gain weight if they stop smoking. In fact, most people don't gain weight. What they do gain is a sense of confidence about themselves. It's a great feeling to overcome a habit that once controlled you.

Even though it is difficult to quit, you can do it. Lots of people do. Here are some strategies that may help you:

Set a Quitting Date Select a date to quit before you actually do so. Choose a time when you can avoid being around other people who smoke and when you won't be stressed by other factors. Taking up a sport or a creative hobby can help distract you from smoking and relieve tension.

Decide Your Approach Different approaches work for different people. Many people prefer the "cold turkey" approach. They decide that, after the quitting date they have selected, they will never smoke again. Others prefer to gradually cut down the number of cigarettes they smoke, until they quit completely.

Prepare Your Environment If you decide to quit cold turkey, throw away all smoking materials and ashtrays in your

SECTION 14.2

Life Skills Worksheet 14B

Assign the Interviewing a Health-Care Professional Life Skills Worksheet.

Making a Choice 14A

Assign the Bulletin Boards About Smoking card. This card asks students to make bulletin boards dealing with reasons to quit smoking and alternatives to smoking.

Making a Choice 14B

Assign the Tobacco-Free-Life Skit card. This card asks students to write a skit that could be presented to younger students to convince them not to begin smoking or using smokeless tobacco.

Demonstration
Reasons to Avoid Tobacco

High up on the chalkboard, write in large letters: WE HAVE SPECIAL REASONS NOT TO USE TOBACCO! Then tell students:

- If you are an athlete or exercise regularly, please stand under the sign.
- If you play a brass or wind instrument in the band, please come up.
- If you, or anyone in your family, has allergies, asthma, problems breathing, chronic colds, or coughs, please come up.
- If anyone in your family has ever had a smoking-related illness, please come up.
- If you have a younger brother or sister, please come up.
- If you think that someday you may become a parent, please come up.
- If you want to live a full, healthy life and lower your risk of cancer, lung disease, or heart disease, please come up.

Join the group yourself, and close by pointing out that everyone has special reasons for not using tobacco.

Journal 14C
Confidential Tobacco Survey

Have students interview at least 10 tobacco users they know and ask them if they would like to stop and if so, why. Ask them to record the information in their Journal.

Section Review Worksheet 14.2

To reinforce the concepts presented in this section, assign Section Review Worksheet 14.2.

 Section Quiz 14.2

Have students take Section Quiz 14.2.

Reteaching Worksheet 14.2

Students who have difficulty with the material may complete Reteaching Worksheet 14.2.

Review Answers

1. Answers may include peer influence, parent's example, and advertising.

2. It damages one's health, it shortens one's life, and tobacco is an expensive, smelly, unattractive habit.

3. Set a quitting date, decide your approach, prepare your environment, get help if you need it, and find other ways to cope with stress.

4. Answers will vary but may include that it would be harder to quit because the person trying to quit would be around cigarettes all the time.

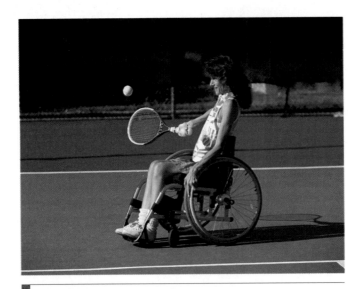

(FIGURE 14-8) **People who don't smoke are able to participate in and enjoy healthy, strenuous activity.**

house and car. If you decide to cut down, keep only one day's supply of cigarettes on hand at a time. If you have decided to smoke eight cigarettes the first day, for example, throw away the rest of the pack or have a friend keep it for you. That way, you won't be tempted to smoke more than you have allowed yourself.

Get Help if You Need It Make sure your family members and friends know that you are planning to quit smoking. You may need their encouragement. Avoid situations that trigger your desire to smoke; it may be helpful to enroll in a workshop or join a support group for people who are giving up smoking. Contact the American Lung Association or the American Cancer Society for information about cessation programs designed for teens.

Some people find that nicotine gum or nicotine patches (squares soaked in nicotine and placed on the skin) help them stop smoking without suffering nicotine withdrawal symptoms. Nicotine gum and patches are available without a prescription.

Find Other Ways to Cope With Stress
Most people who smoke want a cigarette most when they are under stress. There are healthier ways to handle anxiety. Getting regular exercise, for example, can be very relaxing. Try taking a long walk once a day. As your health and your wind improve, you'll be able to exercise for longer periods of time. In addition, the stress-management exercises described in Chapter 9 can help you cope with stress much more effectively than smoking.

After You Quit

Once you have stopped smoking for good, you'll start feeling better, both physically and psychologically. That feeling of being constantly short of breath will go away, and you'll even discover that the food you eat smells and tastes better. Although you may not have realized it, smoking dulls your senses of taste and smell.

In addition, you will enjoy the great sense of achievement that accomplishing a major goal can give you. By quitting smoking, you will have conquered a major addiction and taken a large step toward a long, healthy life.

· · · · ·

Review

1. *What are two reasons why people start using tobacco?*

2. *What are three good reasons not to use tobacco?*

3. *What are two things you can do to help yourself quit smoking?*

4. *Critical Thinking* *Why might it be harder for a person to quit if his or her friends and parents smoke?*

· · · TEACH continued

Extension
Do Quit-Smoking Devices Help?

Have students visit a pharmacy and ask the pharmacist questions about nicotine gum and skin patches. How effective are they? Why are they available only by prescription? What do they cost? Does the pharmacist know of a local quit-smoking program?

ASSESS

Section Review

Have students answer the Section Review questions.

Alternative Assessment
What Would You Tell a Child About Tobacco?

Ask students to think of a child who looks up to them, such as a little sister or brother or a neighbor's child. What advice would they give this child about using tobacco?

Closure
Why Do We Allow Tobacco Use at All?

Discuss these questions: Given all the negative aspects of tobacco, why do people continue to use it? Why do we allow the sale of tobacco?

CHAPTER 14

Highlights

Summary

- Tobacco smoke contains more than 4,000 chemicals; three of the most poisonous are tar, nicotine, and carbon monoxide.

- Nicotine, the psychoactive chemical in tobacco, leads to both psychological and physical dependence.

- Tar can damage the lining of the bronchial tubes, leaving a person vulnerable to several respiratory diseases.

- Carbon monoxide is a poisonous gas that interferes with the blood's ability to carry oxygen.

- Some diseases caused by smoking include cancer, chronic bronchitis, emphysema, and cardiovascular disease.

- Smoking pipes and cigars can lead to cancers of the lip, tongue, stomach, and larynx.

- Smokeless tobacco can cause cancers of the mouth, throat, tongue, cheek, and gum.

- Passive smokers are at an increased risk of suffering respiratory infections, lung cancer, and heart disease.

- Factors that may cause a person to start using tobacco include peer pressure and a parent's example. The same influences, however, can also help a person make the decision not to use tobacco.

- Once you decide to quit smoking, choose a plan and accept support from friends and family. Substituting other activities will help you cope with your day-to-day stresses.

Vocabulary

nicotine an addictive chemical found in tobacco.

tar solid material in tobacco smoke that condenses into a thick liquid.

carbon monoxide a poisonous gas released by burning tobacco.

chewing tobacco a form of smokeless tobacco that is placed between a person's cheek and gum.

mainstream smoke smoke that is inhaled directly into the mouth through a cigarette, pipe, or cigar.

sidestream smoke smoke that enters the environment from burning tobacco.

passive smoker a nonsmoker who is exposed to the sidestream smoke of a cigarette, cigar, or pipe.

CHAPTER 14
HIGHLIGHTS STRATEGIES

SUMMARY
Have students read the summary to reinforce the concepts they learned in Chapter 14.

VOCABULARY
Have students look at the vocabulary list and ask about any terms they do not understand.

EXTENSION
Have students investigate the smoking regulations in their town or city. Is smoking permitted in public buildings? Is smoking regulated in restaurants, theaters, and shopping centers? How long have any regulations been in effect?

Chapter Review

CHAPTER REVIEW

Concept Review

1. c	**5.** a
2. d	**6.** b
3. d	**7.** d
4. a	

Expressing Your Views

1. Sample response: Smoking is deadly. Smoking is addictive, and the more you smoke the more likely you are to become addicted to tobacco and the more likely you are to get colds, bronchitis, heart disease, lung cancer, and other cancers.

2. Sample response: I would approach management with the facts on passive smoking and ask if I could have a space to work in that was free of tobacco smoke.

3. Sample response: Athletes may chew tobacco because of their own peer group behavior or because they started to chew tobacco at an early age and are now addicted to it. Some athletes may feel pressure to perform and use the tobacco thinking it will relieve some of the stress. Since young children look up to athletes, these children may be influenced to try chewing tobacco simply because they want to be like their hero.

4. Answers will vary but may include the idea that more regulations should

be placed on the advertising of tobacco because of the influence advertising has on people to begin or to continue to use tobacco products.

Life Skills Check
Sample responses:

1. I would tell my aunt that cigarette smoke bothers me and ask her to ask her friend to refrain from smoking while in the car.

2. I would tell her that smoking is doing more harm than good. She should stop smoking and find healthy ways to deal with the stress. She could get regular exercise or try relaxation exercises. I would encourage her in her decision to stop smoking.

Concept Review . . . .

1. Which of the following causes the largest number of avoidable deaths in the U.S.?
   a. stress   c. cigarette smoking
   b. SIDS   d. drunken driving

2. Which of the following happens to most people the first few times they smoke?
   a. nausea   c. rapid pulse
   b. clammy skin   d. all of these

3. Which is a harmful effect of tobacco use?
   a. respiratory disease
   b. heart disease
   c. cancer
   d. all of these

4. Emphysema is
   a. a deadly respiratory disease.
   b. a cardiovascular disease.
   c. nicotine poisoning.
   d. a form of cancer.

5. Which of the following statements is true about smoking?
   a. Passive smoking carries health risks.
   b. Smokeless tobacco is a safe form of tobacco.
   c. Pipe or cigar smokers are not at risk for developing cancer.
   d. all of these

6. Which of the following statements about tobacco users is NOT true?
   a. Even a light smoking habit can leave a person winded.
   b. Tobacco users often have low blood pressure.
   c. Tobacco users become physically dependent.
   d. Smokers want a cigarette most when under stress.

7. Which of the following may influence people to use tobacco?
   a. peers   c. advertising
   b. parents   d. all of these

Expressing Your Views . . . .

1. Yesterday you caught your 13-year-old brother smoking a cigarette. What would you say to him to discourage him from smoking?

2. What would you do if you worked in an area where smoking was allowed? What are some ways to protect nonsmokers from environmental tobacco smoke?

3. You often see certain athletes using chewing tobacco. Why do you think they do this? Do you think the sight of them chewing tobacco will influence young people?

4. Do you think more or fewer regulations should be placed on the advertising of tobacco products? Explain.

Life Skills Check

1. Communicating Effectively

You are going on a long road trip with your aunt that the two of you have been planning for weeks. At the last minute she tells you that a friend of hers, who is a smoker, will be riding for at least half of the trip with the two of you. Cigarette smoke bothers you, especially when it's in a closed area like a car. What would you do?

2. Communicating Effectively

Your friend wants to quit smoking, but she says she's under tremendous stress at school, at her after-school job, and at home. She's afraid the anxiety will be overwhelming. What would you say to her?

SMOKING POLLUTES YOU AND EVERYTHING ELSE

THERE'S NOTHING MIGHTIER THAN THE SWORD | AMERICAN CANCER SOCIETY

Projects

1. Write to your local chapter of the American Lung Association, American Heart Association, or American Cancer Society for information on the effects of using tobacco and about ways to quit using it. Share this information with the class.

2. Find a magazine advertisement for tobacco and display it on one side of a poster board. Beside it, list the facts that the advertiser failed to mention about tobacco use. Display your poster in the classroom or around your school.

3. Research the current cost of a pack of cigarettes and figure out how much money a smoker would spend in a year if he or she smoked a pack a day. Then talk to smokers and ask them to list things they would buy, other than cigarettes, with this amount of money.

Plan for Action

Using tobacco is a very dangerous habit. Design a plan for becoming a nonsmoker or staying a nonsmoker.

Projects
Have students plan and carry out the projects for anti-smoking education.

Plan for Action
Ask students to form a plan to avoid starting to smoke or to quit smoking. For example, in either situation, a decision to not hang out with people who smoke would be a good start.

Personal Pledge
Discuss the pledge for Chapter 14. A student's decision of whether to sign the pledge is personal and private.

ASSESSMENT OPTIONS

Chapter Test
Have students take the Chapter 14 Test.

Alternative Assessment
Have students do the Alternative Assessment activity for Chapter 14.

Test Generator
The Test Generator contains additional assessment items for this chapter.

Other Drugs of Abuse

SECTION	TITLE/OBJECTIVES	Personal Health Inventory	Journal	Check Up	Life Skills	Life Skills Worksheets	Media Message or Ethical Issues Worksheet	What Would You Do?
		PERSONAL INVENTORY			LIFE SKILLS DEVELOPMENT			
15.1 *pp. 299–301*	**DRUG ABUSE AND ADDICTION** • Name two important dangers of drug abuse. • Name two ways in which drug abusers can damage society. ▪▪ Know how a person can become addicted to a drug.	Ch. 15	15A					
15.2 *pp. 302–312*	**THE EFFECTS OF DRUGS OF ABUSE** • Know the effects of one category of psychoactive drugs. • Name two dangers of crack cocaine. • Know how to avoid inhalant fumes. ▪▪ Discuss what you would say to a friend who is thinking of taking anabolic steroids.		15B 15C 15D		p. 311	15A		
15.3 *pp. 313–316*	**TREATMENT FOR DEPENDENCY** • Name two things everyone should know about treatment for drug dependency. • Know three options for recovering drug abusers. • Know a healthy alternative to abusing drugs.		15E 15F			15B		

KEY: ▪▪ Denotes Life Skill Objective
Text references denoted by page number.
Supplement references denoted by chapter or item numbers.

LINKING RESOURCES

Making a Choice Cards	Parent Discussion Guide	Health Talk Audio Program	Teaching Transparencies and Directory	Section Review Worksheets	Section Quizzes	Reteaching Worksheets	Section Reviews	
INTERACTION		**OTHER RESOURCES**		**SECTION REVIEW AND ASSESSMENT**				
15A	Ch. 15	Ch. 15		15.1	15.1	15.1	p. 301	
			15A BSH1	15.2	15.2	15.2	p. 312	
15B				15.3	15.3	15.3	p. 316	

For information on psychoactive drugs and the brain, see page 653 in the Body Systems Handbook.

KEY FACTS

- Although people who start using illicit drugs might think they can control their drug use, it almost always leads to physical or psychological addiction.

- Psychoactive drugs affect a person's mood and behavior, and their use plays a major role in family violence and other crimes.

- Five categories of psychoactive drugs are stimulants, marijuana and hashish, inhalants, narcotics, and sedative-hypnotics.

- Narcotics, such as morphine, cocaine, and heroin, are drugs derived from the opium poppy; they relieve pain but are highly addictive.

- Designer drugs are powerful psychoactive drugs created in a laboratory by slightly altering drugs that already exist; they are very dangerous.

- Drugs taken during pregnancy pass into the fetus's bloodstream, where they can cause deformities, retarded growth and mental development, and learning disabilities.

- Anabolic steroids are synthetic drugs similar to the male hormone testosterone. Their use has serious physical and psychological side effects, including liver damage and violent behavior.

- Drug dependency is extremely difficult to overcome and requires professional help.

CHAPTER REVIEW AND ASSESSMENT

TEXT

Chapter Review pp. 318–319

SUPPLEMENTS

Chapter Test 15

Alternative Assessment 15

Test Generator Chapter 15

GETTING STARTED

Using the Chapter Photograph

Ask students to look at the students in the photograph. Then ask them how being involved in something they really enjoy could be a good way of resisting peer pressure as well as the temptation to try drugs.

Question Box

Have students write out any questions they have about drugs and drug abuse and put them in the Question Box.

Sensitivity *ALERT*

The discussion of drugs and drug abuse may make students uncomfortable. Some students may have drug abuse problems or have family members or friends who do. Other students may be experiencing peer pressure to try drugs. Respect the students' privacy and present the information in a factual, nonjudgmental way.

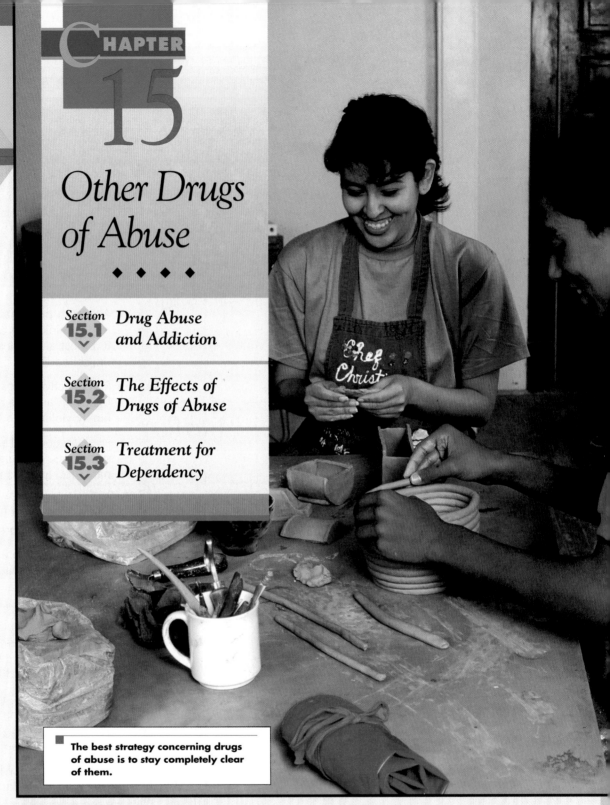

CHAPTER 15

Other Drugs of Abuse

◆ ◆ ◆ ◆

Section 15.1 Drug Abuse and Addiction

Section 15.2 The Effects of Drugs of Abuse

Section 15.3 Treatment for Dependency

The best strategy concerning drugs of abuse is to stay completely clear of them.

MYTHS & MISCONCEPTIONS

- **Trying drugs once or twice isn't harmful.** People have died the first time they tried crack. Some people are unable to try a drug just once or twice; after taking the drug once, they continue to take it, until they are addicted.

- **Cocaine causes no major health problems.** There are several health problems associated with cocaine. Some people are hypersensitive to cocaine and die if exposed to a small amount. Also, cocaine causes a sudden rise in blood pressure, which can cause a stroke. Cocaine also causes epileptic seizures in some people.

- **Marijuana is a safe drug.** Smoking marijuana may have a worse effect on the lungs than smoking tobacco does since its smoke is unfiltered. Marijuana impairs a person's ability to operate vehicles and mechanical equipment safely; doing so while under its influence is dangerous.

Max always looked forward to the weekends. Every Saturday night he would get together with the same four friends, and they would always find something fun to do. Sometimes they'd grab a hamburger and see a movie or go to someone's house and watch a ballgame. Then one night one of Max's friends wanted everyone to smoke marijuana. Max really didn't want to try it, but he did, and didn't like it. Now his friends are smoking pot more frequently and talking about getting some crack. This Saturday night they're supposed to get together and smoke it. This time Max knows he won't be joining his friends—but he doesn't know what to tell them.

Section
15.1
Drug Abuse and Addiction

Objectives

- *Name two important dangers of drug abuse.*
- *Name two ways in which drug abusers can damage society.*
- *Know how a person can become addicted to a drug.*
  LIFE SKILLS: Resisting Pressure

It turned out that Max's friend Troy felt the same way he did. Both of them had been concerned that their friends would think they were weird, and that they would end up being left out of the group.

You may feel uneasy about your decision to not use drugs. At first, a decision to stay away from friends who are abusing drugs can leave you feeling down. A longing for excitement, pleasure, and acceptance from friends can make it hard for teenagers to stay away from drugs. This is especially

true when it comes to **psychoactive drugs** of abuse. A psychoactive drug is a drug that affects a person's mood and behavior. Making the decision to abuse them can be deadly.

psychoactive drug:

a drug that affects a person's mood and behavior.

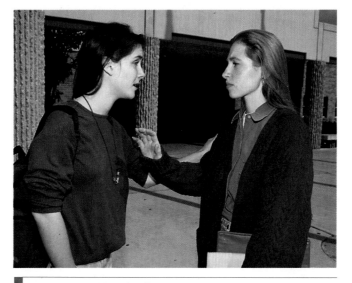

(FIGURE 15-1) **Knowing how to resist peer pressure is an important skill to have—especially when it comes to drug abuse.**

SECTION 15.1

Personal Health Inventory
Have students complete the Personal Health Inventory for this chapter.

English/Spanish CD Audio Program
Use the English/Spanish Health Talk audio program for students who need audio reinforcement of the concepts presented.

Parent Discussion Guide
Send home the Parent Letter for Chapter 15. As you progress through the chapter, send home the Parental Survey and The Extra Mile.

Section 15.1 Lesson Plan

MOTIVATE

Journal 15A
Pressure to Use Drugs

This may be done as a warm-up activity. Encourage students to record in their Journal their concerns about being pressured by friends to try drugs. They may also write their feelings about Max and his decision.

TEACH

Class Discussion
Dealing With Peer Pressure

To help students understand the problems caused by psychoactive drugs, ask: **Why are psychoactive drugs of abuse so dangerous to use?** [*These drugs affect your mood and behavior.*] To help students deal with peer pressure, ask the following questions: **How can peer pressure be a factor in taking a drug of abuse?** [*It's hard to turn down a friend's pressure on you to do*

something, even though you don't want to.] **What can you do to avoid falling into the drug trap?** [*Be aware of your own values and don't let anyone make you feel less worthwhile because you don't give in to their demands. You may need to find other friends.*]

Role-Playing
Not Caving In to Peer Pressure

Have students role-play a situation in which one friend is trying to convince

Background
Drug Testing

In general, employers may use random drug testing if there is reasonable suspicion of ongoing drug use. Employers often couple testing with education and rehabilitation programs. Even in jobs that do not directly affect public safety, testing is becoming more common. It may include pre-employment screening, random testing, or testing following a specific incident that has raised suspicion.

Making a Choice 15A

Assign the Pressure to Take Drugs card. The card asks students to discuss how a student who is new to a school can make friends and resist drug use.

Section Review Worksheet 15.1

To reinforce the concepts presented in this section, assign Section Review Worksheet 15.1.

Section Quiz 15.1

Have students take Section Quiz 15.1.

REMINDER

To *use* a drug means to take a medicine exactly as directed. To *misuse* a drug is to take a medication improperly. To *abuse* a drug is to take a legal drug for a nonmedical reason, or an illegal drug for any reason at all.

addicted:

the state of being physically dependent on a drug.

Max was glad that he had the self-esteem and the knowledge necessary to make the right choice. He also felt fortunate that he had Troy to talk to about his decision. It's important to have a high opinion of yourself in order to cope effectively with peer pressure. It's also important to know as much as you can about the risks you would face if you *didn't* make a good decision. Abusing drugs is highly dangerous for two reasons:

1. It can make a person lose control of the ability to make responsible decisions. Many who abuse drugs act irresponsibly, and sometimes violently.

2. It can cause a person to become **dependent**. A person who is dependent on a drug is controlled by a psychological or physical desire for it.

Drug Abuse

On Monday, Max and Troy found out that their friends had stolen a car after smoking

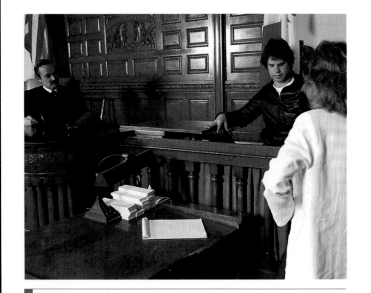

(FIGURE 15-2) **Drug abuse contributes to more than 35 percent of the crimes committed in the United States.**

---

crack on Saturday night. They had been caught by the police and were waiting to find out what would happen to them. Max and Troy think their friends would not have stolen the car if they hadn't been under the influence of crack.

People who abuse drugs place themselves, their families, and their society in danger. According to studies, more than 35 percent of all crimes in the United States are committed by people who are under the influence of illicit drugs. That number continues to grow, as drugs like crack have become widespread in many American cities and towns.

Drug abuse also plays a major role in many cases of child abuse and other instances of family violence. Finally, people who drive while under the influence of drugs are just as dangerous to society as those who drive drunk.

The Addiction Process

When a person is **addicted** to a drug, it means that his or her body has grown so used to the presence of the drug that it can't function without it. A lot of people think that drug addiction is something that could never happen to them. They believe that no matter how many times they take a certain drug, they will always have the power to stop when they want to. It's important to know that this isn't so. Addiction is a physical process. No matter how strong and invulnerable people may feel, the truth is that if they abuse addictive drugs, they will become physically dependent.

Just as you couldn't do without getting any sleep for a week, people who are addicted to drugs find it very difficult to function without the substance their bodies have come to demand.

Tolerance The body of a person who regularly uses or abuses a drug will eventually

---

• • • TEACH continued

the other that just trying crack once won't do any harm. The other person should use what he or she has learned so far about the effects of crack on the body. This person should make it clear that no matter how strong drug users think themselves to be, they can become physically dependent.

Class Discussion
How Drugs Affect the Body

After students learn about tolerance of a drug, ask: **What does forming a tolerance to a drug mean?** [*This means that higher and higher doses of the drug are needed to produce the same effect.*] **What are some physical withdrawal symptoms?** [*nausea, vomiting, sleeplessness, seizures*]

Extension
Is This Fair or Foul?

Some communities are trying to help police locate drug dealers. Neighborhood residents are encouraged to report the names of drug dealers and the locations where they operate to the police. Some people fear that the names of innocent people could be reported. Ask students to write their opinion of this practice.

form a resistance, or **tolerance**, to that substance. This means that higher and higher doses of the drug will be required in order to produce the same effects. If Max's friends were to abuse crack regularly, for example, they would soon discover the need to take more and more of the drug in order to get the same "high" they felt the first time they smoked it.

Crack cocaine is not the only type of drug whose use leads to tolerance. Many people who take prescription medications that relieve pain or anxiety also find that after a while they must increase the amount of drug they take in order to get the same relief that one or two pills used to give them. Tolerance is the first step in the addiction process.

Dependence Many psychoactive drugs will cause a person to become dependent. A drug dependency can be physical, psychological, or both. **Physical dependence**, or addiction, occurs when a person's body comes to expect the presence of a drug. If it doesn't receive the drug it expects, the body will go through a physical **withdrawal**. Common withdrawal symptoms include nausea, chills, depression, and sleeplessness. People who have developed a very high tolerance for a drug may suffer more serious and dangerous withdrawal symptoms, such as seizures. In general, the more addictive and powerful a drug is, the more serious its withdrawal symptoms will be.

A drug doesn't have to lead to tolerance and addiction in order to cause dependence. Many psychoactive drugs can lead to **psychological dependence**. People who are psychologically dependent on a drug are controlled by a constant craving for that substance. Some people with this type of dependency associate certain drugs with a feeling of happiness that they can't seem to find anywhere else.

(FIGURE 15-3) **Illegal drugs are not the only substances that can cause addiction. Some prescription medications can lead to tolerance and psychological and physical dependence.**

R eview

•••••

1. *What are two important dangers of drug abuse?*

2. *What are two ways in which drug abusers can damage society?*

3. *What are two major steps of the addiction process?*

4. **LIFE SKILLS: Resisting Pressure** *How would you have told Max's friends that you didn't want to smoke crack?*

5. *Critical Thinking* *Explain how a person who abuses a drug that is not physically addictive can still become dependent on that drug.*

physical dependence:

a condition in which the body becomes so used to the presence of a drug that it needs it in order to function.

withdrawal:

the body's reaction when it doesn't receive a drug it depends upon.

psychological dependence:

a constant desire to take a psychoactive drug.

Reteaching Worksheet 15.1
Students who have difficulty with the material may complete Reteaching Worksheet 15.1.

Review Answers

1. Answers may include irresponsibility, violence, and dependency.

2. Answers may include an increase in crime, child abuse, family violence, and accidents.

3. tolerance and dependence

4. Answers will vary. Students may answer that they would say they do not use drugs.

5. Psychoactive drugs can cause a psychological dependence in which the person associates a certain drug with a feeling of happiness that he or she cannot seem to find anywhere else.

ASSESS

Section Review

Have students answer the Section Review questions.

Alternative Assessment
Drugs Among Teenagers

Ask students at what age they think drug education should begin. Have them discuss how what they have learned about drugs will help them to avoid the pitfalls of drug abuse.

Closure
The Effects of Drugs

Discuss with students whether they think learning about the effects of drugs on the body will deter teenagers from taking drugs.

Background

Caffeine

Besides being present in coffee, caffeine is a drug that is present in many medications, such as tablets for cold symptoms and migraine headaches. All cola drinks, except those that are decaffeinated, also have caffeine. Even a slice of chocolate cake has a very small amount of this drug. Caffeine is a powerful stimulant of the central nervous system. In very high doses, caffeine stimulates the brain so much that it can cause convulsions and even death.

stimulant:

a drug that causes alertness and speeds up the activity of the body.

Section
15.2 *The Effects of Drugs of Abuse*

Objectives

- *Know the effects of one category of psychoactive drugs.*
- *Name two dangers of crack cocaine.*
- *Know how to avoid inhalant fumes.*
- *Discuss what you would say to a friend who is thinking of taking anabolic steroids.*
  LIFE SKILLS: Communicating Effectively

Psychoactive drugs of abuse fall into several categories according to the effects they have on the body. Of course, different drugs have different effects. A person who has taken cocaine will act very differently, for example, from a person who has taken marijuana. Still, it is important to know that every drug works by influencing a specific part of the body. This means that even if you have convinced yourself that a psychoactive drug you take will not affect you, it will. Once you have taken a psychoactive drug, you have limited control over the effects it has on you. For some information on the effects of specific psychoactive drugs, see Figure 15-9 on pages 308-309.

People who take drugs of abuse often lose control of themselves in certain situations and suffer impaired judgment. Things that require concentration, such as driving a car or making an important decision, can become difficult and often impossible when a person is under the influence of a psychoactive drug.

Stimulants

As you learned in Chapter 12, **stimulants** are drugs that cause alertness. Caffeine is the mildest of the stimulants, which is why it is legal to buy and to use. Other stimulants, such as cocaine and amphetamines, have much stronger effects and can be very dangerous.

Caffeine Caffeine is a naturally occurring stimulant. Aside from over-the-counter medications, caffeine can be found in some colas, in tea, and in coffee. A person who drinks a beverage containing caffeine will feel its effects within about 30 minutes. This is because caffeine is absorbed very quickly into the bloodstream through the gastrointestinal tract, and then travels to every part of the body, including the brain.

There is some evidence that caffeine stimulates the mind and body because it interferes with a chemical the brain produces called adenosine. Adenosine may normally influence certain effects in the brain that make a person weary and tired. Caffeine blocks adenosine from achieving these effects, which means that a person who has taken caffeine will be much more alert and much less tired than someone who has not. In high doses, caffeine can make a person irritable, nervous, and unable to sleep.

There is some evidence that caffeine can lead to tolerance and physical dependence. Regular coffee drinkers who give up their habit have been known to suffer such withdrawal symptoms as headache, irritability, drowsiness, and anxiety.

Cocaine and Crack Cocaine is a stimulant that is derived from the leaves of the

---

Section 15.2 Lesson Plan

MOTIVATE

Journal 15B
Risks of Drug Use

This may be done as a warm-up activity. Have students consider the short-term and the long-term risks of drug use. Then have them write in their Journal three reasons for not becoming involved in drug use.

TEACH

Class Discussion
Losing Control With Drugs

Ask: **What is one way in which drugs differ?** *[Different drugs affect specific parts of and have different effects on the body.]* **Why is driving a car when using psychoactive drugs so dangerous?** *[These drugs make you lose your ability to concentrate, which is necessary when driving a car.]* **Why wouldn't you trust someone taking psychoactive**

drugs with a responsible job? *[Someone taking drugs has a diminished ability to make sound decisions.]*

Class Discussion
Categories of Drugs of Abuse

Ask: **What are stimulants?** *[Stimulants are drugs that cause alertness.]* **How does caffeine work to stimulate the mind and body?** *[It interferes with a chemical the brain produces called adenosine. Ordinarily, adenosine makes a person feel tired. Caffeine blocks adenosine from doing this and the person feels*

Life Skills
Worksheet 15A
Assign the Marcy's Dilemma
Life Skills Worksheet.

(FIGURE 15-4) **Caffeine is a major ingredient in coffee, tea, chocolate, and certain soft drinks.**

coca plant. Cocaine is a very addictive and dangerous drug. It is sniffed, injected, or smoked (free-base and crack cocaine). Sniffing or snorting cocaine means inhaling the drug through the nose. When sniffed, the chemical enters the bloodstream through the membranes of the nasal passages and travels directly to the brain. Smoking or injecting cocaine allows higher doses to reach the brain faster than sniffing it does.

Cocaine use produces a sense of euphoria because it interferes with the reabsorption of dopamine, the chemical messenger in the brain that is associated with pleasure. The feeling of pleasure lasts 5 to 10 minutes when the cocaine is smoked and about 20 minutes when it is sniffed. Cocaine-related deaths are usually a result of cardiac arrest or seizures followed by respiratory arrest.

One important thing to know about this sense of pleasure is that it is often followed by irritability, anxiety, and exhaustion. These feelings will actually last longer than

the pleasurable emotions. Cocaine users find that in order to get the sense of pleasure back, they need to take the drug again.

There are many reasons why cocaine and crack are so dangerous. For one thing, they are extremely addictive. You read that a person who inhales cocaine wants to take more of the drug as soon as the effects wear off. This is true to an even greater extent for crack, since crack's effects are so strong and so immediate. Breaking an addiction to cocaine or crack is very difficult. A person going through cocaine withdrawal may experience an intense and constant craving for the drug and a severe loss of energy, as well as severe depression and anxiety.

In addition, crack and cocaine both cause severe psychological dependence. Many crack and cocaine abusers find that they are happy only when they are high. Ending a psychological dependence can be as difficult as breaking a physical one.

But even without their addictive qualities, crack and cocaine are highly dangerous

---

alert and less tired than he or she would without caffeine.] **What happens when people take high doses of caffeine?** [They become irritable, nervous, and cannot sleep.]

Role-Playing
Effects of High Doses of Caffeine

Have students role-play a situation in which one member has drunk several cups of coffee to keep awake in order to study for a test. The person with all the caffeine is excitable and cannot sleep. After not sleeping all night the

student is exhausted and unable to think when taking the test.

Journal 15C
Personal Risk

Have students write in their Journal their feelings about the personal risks of drug abuse.

Class Discussion
Facts on Crack

To help students understand and assimilate the information in Figure 15-5 on page 304, ask the following questions:

Why does crack use often trigger heart attacks? [Crack causes the blood vessels to constrict, making the heart overwork as it tries to move blood through the body.] **Why does crack cause strokes in some people who use it?** [The increased blood pressure caused by the drug may rupture blood vessels, which causes a stroke.] **Why is crack so addictive?** [It causes an intense stimulation of the reward center of the brain. This triggers an intense craving for more of the drug.]

Background

The Debate About Amphetamines

Amphetamines were first used to treat asthma, obesity, and to improve athletic performance. By 1947, the medical community became aware that amphetamines were being abused. Abusers began taking up to 30 tablets a day in order to lose weight. Soon these people experienced a mental and physical deterioration. The benefits of these drugs for weight loss are short term. They cause nervousness and excitation of the central nervous system. Since the drugs suppress hunger, the dieter never learns how to deal with hunger.

Facts on Crack

Crack is a form of cocaine that has been chemically altered so that it can be smoked. Because the process changes the cocaine into a chemical "base," crack belongs to a category of cocaine known as freebase.

Crack looks like small lumps or shavings of soap, but has the texture of porcelain. In some parts of the country crack is called "rock" or "readyrock."

The immediate effects of smoking crack are dilated pupils and a narrowing of blood vessels. Crack also causes increases in blood pressure, heart rate, breathing rate, and body temperature.

Crack can constrict the heart's blood vessels, making it work harder and faster to move blood through the body. In some people, this stress may trigger chest pain or heart attack, even for first-time users.

Crack can cause brain seizures, which are a disturbance of the brain's electrical signals. Some users have suffered strokes after using crack—the increase in blood pressure that the blood causes may rupture blood vessels.

Repeated use of crack without experiencing problems does not guarantee freedom from seizures in the future. The next dose—used in the same amount in the same way—can produce a fatal seizure.

Violent, erratic, or paranoid behavior can accompany the use of crack. Hallucinations are also common. Other psychological effects may include profound personality changes.

Crack is particularly alarming because it causes an intense stimulation of the reward center of the brain by allowing the brain chemical dopamine to remain active longer than normal. This causes changes in brain activity and triggers an intense craving for more of the drug, thus creating a powerful psychological dependence on the drug.

(FIGURE 15-5) **Smoking crack even once can be fatal.**

drugs. Cocaine constricts the body's blood vessels, making it harder for blood to circulate. This can put a strain on the heart, and it can even cause a heart attack. For this reason, trying crack or cocaine even once can be fatal.

Amphetamines In contrast to caffeine and cocaine, amphetamines—another type of stimulant—are not derived from natural substances. They are synthetic drugs, which means they are produced or manufactured in laboratories.

Amphetamine-type drugs are sometimes prescribed for neurological disorders and life-threatening obesity. Amphetamine use can result in tolerance, psychological dependence, and addiction. Withdrawal may cause depression.

Some amphetamines are illegally manufactured in secret labs. This process involves toxic and explosive chemicals that pose a health and safety threat to the surrounding community. Since there are no controls, the resulting drugs can have a wide range of concentrations and impurities.

One particularly dangerous form of amphetamine is called ice. Like crack, ice can be smoked. Remember that when a drug is smoked, it will reach the brain much more quickly than when it is taken orally or injected. Ice is very addictive. Its effects include dilated pupils, short attention span, and extreme talkativeness. Ice stays in the system for a very long time. Unlike those of crack, the effects of ice can be felt for several hours.

Hallucinogens

Hallucinogens such as LSD and PCP are very powerful psychoactive substances because they distort the senses. When the senses are affected in this way, it's not always easy to tell what's real from what is not. This is why people on hallucinogens

---

• • • TEACH continued

Cooperative Learning
Campaigning Against Crack

Have students work in cooperative groups to produce slogans that will point out the dangers of crack. Have them refer to Figure 15-5, "Facts on Crack," and the information in the text. Ask them to make posters that will display their slogans.

Debate the Issue
Should Amphetamines Be Used for Weight Control?

Hold a class debate on the topic: Should amphetamines be used for controlling the appetite? Have students do some research on the addictiveness of amphetamines, as well as on their effects on weight control.

Class Discussion
Hallucinogens

After the students have read about hallucinogens, ask: **What happens during a hallucination?** [During a hallucination a drug user begins to see and hear things that are not there.] **What causes some users of LSD to kill themselves?** [Sometimes an LSD experience is so frightening that the user becomes panicked, confused, and extremely anxious. In this drug-induced often forget where they are and may have difficulty keeping track of time. In some cases, hallucinogens have caused people to believe they have special powers. Hallucinogens include LSD, PCP, a designer drug called ecstasy, and some naturally occurring chemicals, such as mescaline, psilocybin, and psilocin.

LSD Lysergic acid diethylamide, or LSD, is made from a type of fungus that grows on rye and other grains. LSD is usually sold in the form of tablets or small paper squares with images on them. The effects of LSD are not always easy to predict. Sometimes the drug will stimulate the body like cocaine. Other times it acts as a **depressant,** which is a drug that slows down body functions such as heart rate and blood pressure.

A person who has taken LSD will begin to feel its effects within about 30 to 90 minutes. The user may see and hear things that are not there. This type of effect is known as a **hallucination.** At the same time, he or she may be experiencing huge emotional swings. People on LSD may be laughing hysterically one moment and violent the next.

Some LSD experiences are extremely frightening. Users can become panicked, confused, and extremely anxious. Some people have become so upset and scared while on the drug that they have killed themselves.

Sometimes a person who has had a bad LSD experience will suddenly start feeling the drug's effects again, long after the experience is over. This is called a **flashback.** People can experience flashbacks without warning, sometimes months after they have taken their last dose of LSD. Flashbacks can be as frightening and dangerous as the bad experiences that prompted them.

PCP Another dangerous hallucinogen is PCP. Also known as "angel dust," PCP is usually sprayed on tobacco or marijuana cigarettes and smoked. PCP has been known to cause severe mental disturbances that last from a few hours to a few weeks. People on PCP often act violently toward others or toward themselves.

Designer Drugs Some very powerful psychoactive drugs can be created by making slight changes in the chemistry of drugs that already exist. These are called **designer drugs.** One type of designer drug is MDMA, also called ecstasy.

Ecstasy is an illegal drug that is very close in its chemical makeup to amphetamines. Like amphetamines, it causes psychological and physical dependence. People who have used ecstasy say it makes them feel relaxed and happy. It can also cause confusion, depression, sleep problems, and severe anxiety. The physical effects of ecstasy include blurred vision, nausea, faintness, and chills and sweating. Ecstasy has been shown to cause brain damage in laboratory animals.

Peyote and Mushrooms The peyote cactus contains the drug mescaline, and certain species of mushrooms contain psilocybin and psilocin. These drugs can cause vomiting and cramping followed by hallucinations. Peyote cactus and mushrooms are traditionally used during religious ceremonies of native cultures in Mexico and the southwestern United States. However, concentrated extracts used by drug abusers can cause frightening experiences similar to those of LSD.

Marijuana and Hashish

Marijuana and hashish are organic drugs that come from the cannabis, or hemp, plant. It is not certain whether marijuana and hashish are physically addictive, but people have been known to become psychologically dependent on both drugs.

depressant: *a drug that slows body functioning.*

designer drugs: *synthetic drugs that are similar in chemistry to certain illegal drugs.*

hallucination: *imaginary sights and sounds, often induced by the use of a hallucinogen.*

flashback: *an unexpected return to an unpleasant LSD experience, often months after the original experience ended.*

hallucinogen: *a drug that distorts a person's senses.*

state, some people kill themselves.] **What is a flashback?** *[Long after the experience is over, an LSD user can suddenly start feeling the drug's effects again, with all the terrifying moments relived.]*

Reinforcement
Dangers of Heroin

Ask: **Why are heroin addicts at risk of contracting AIDS?** *[Heroin addicts usually inject heroin into their veins. Since they may share a needle with an HIV* infected person, they are at risk of introducing the HIV virus into their bloodstream.]* **What happens when abusers overdose on heroin?** *[Their breathing slows down so much that they lose consciousness, go into a coma, and often die.]*

• • • TEACH continues on p. 310

Background
Cannabis sativa

Until the twentieth century, hemp *(Cannabis sativa)* was a major cash crop in the United States, and its fibers were used to make many utilitarian items, such as rope, sails, and paper. Although hemp is still grown throughout the world, its use in the United States was outlawed because of its hallucinogenic properties. However, this form of hemp has a very low THC content, about 0.03 percent. Recently, there has been renewed interest in this low-THC hemp. Some environmentalists say that hemp yields much more pulp per acre than trees do and that using hemp, rather than paper pulp, would reduce deforestation.

Another form of hemp, which has been selectively bred to increase its THC content, is what is used to make marijuana. Marijuana is made from the dried leaves and flowering stalks of a form of hemp whose THC content is anywhere from 3 to 11 percent. Marijuana

• • • BACKGROUND continues on p. 307

inhalants:

chemicals that produce strong psychoactive effects when they are inhaled.

narcotic:

a drug with pain-relieving and psychoactive properties that is made from the opium poppy plant.

Marijuana and hashish may cause the user to suffer a loss of coordination and have difficulty concentrating. For these reasons, driving a car is very dangerous for people who are high on marijuana or hashish. These drugs can also cause a person to feel anxious or paranoid. Marijuana contains toxins that can damage the lungs, the reproductive system, and the immune system. Marijuana plants grown today yield a much higher concentration of THC than those produced in the 1960s; therefore, the effects are more damaging.

Inhalants

Inhalants are chemical vapors of solvents and gases that produce strong psychoactive effects. Inhalants include paint thinners, correction fluids, degreasers, glues, gasoline, medical anesthetic gases, aerosol propellants and associated solvents in spray paints and other aerosol products.

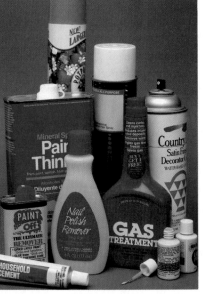

(FIGURE 15-6) **Many chemical products contain inhalant fumes.**

Inhalants enter the bloodstream and travel to the brain immediately after they are inhaled. A person abusing inhalants will experience an initial feeling of lightheadedness and giddiness. These effects are later replaced by dizziness, nausea, and headache. Repeated use can cause hearing loss, brain and nerve damage, bone marrow damage, and liver and kidney damage. Inhaling high concentrations of these deadly chemicals can cause suffocation and heart failure.

Many chemical products contain dangerous fumes. It's best to avoid these products completely, but if you have to use them, make sure you read the label and follow the instructions.

If you feel yourself getting lightheaded while using one of these products, go outside until the feeling goes away. Make sure that you close all containers after you have finished with them. Inhalants are very powerful drugs of abuse. You wouldn't want to leave yourself or anyone else exposed to their dangers.

Heroin and Other Narcotics

Narcotics, which are drugs that have been derived, or made, from the opium poppy plant, are something of a double-edged sword. Some narcotics serve useful medical purposes because they relieve pain so effectively. Morphine and codeine are two narcotic preparations used in hospitals for patients in severe pain.

On the other hand, narcotics are among the most physically addictive drugs of abuse. All narcotic medications should be taken only under the strict orders and observations of a doctor.

Not all narcotics have medical uses. One type of narcotic, heroin, is a very powerful, very addictive drug that is illegal to buy, sell, or use.

(FIGURE 15-7) **Heroin and other narcotics are all made from the opium poppy plant.**

Like all narcotics, heroin causes tolerance to the drug. People who are addicted to heroin have to keep increasing their doses in order to get the same effects. For this reason they run the constant risk of **overdose.** Large doses of heroin can severely depress the respiratory system. This can lead to a loss of consciousness, coma, or even death.

Heroin is most often bought and sold on the street, which means that it has some additional dangers. For one thing, drug dealers selling heroin often "cut," or mix, the drug with other substances. People who buy heroin never know if the drug they are taking is pure.

In addition, people who use heroin usually inject the drug into their veins. Heroin users who share dirty or contaminated needles run the risk of infecting themselves with hepatitis or AIDS. A growing number of needle-exchange programs are showing some success in reducing this risk.

overdose:

a serious, sometimes fatal, reaction to a large dose of a drug.

A person who has had an overdose needs medical attention immediately. What to do for a person who has had an overdose is discussed in Chapter 28 under **Poisoning.**

is known by several common names, including maryjane, Mary Jane, cannabis, grass, pot, weed, and hemp. Another drug, hashish, is made from the resin obtained from hemp. Hashish contains from five to eight times as much THC as marijuana does. Both marijuana and hashish are psychologically addictive, and their use is illegal in the United States, Canada, and many other countries.

In 1997, an article in *The New England Journal of Medicine* endorsed the use of marijuana for a limited number of medical conditions. Many are opposed to this endorsement. Continued research about marijuana's actions in the brain may resolve this conflict of opinion. Scientists have discovered a naturally occurring chemical in the brain, anandamine, that binds to the same receptor as THC does. Researchers are now trying to develop a synthetic analogue of marijuana that would mimic some of its actions in the brain but would not produce a high.

(FIGURE 15-8) **Intravenous drug users who share contaminated needles are at a high risk of contracting HIV.**

Characteristics of Some Drugs of Abuse

Drug	Health Hazards Associated With Abuse
Amphetamines and Methamphetamines	Drug dependence and addiction, elevated blood pressure, increased heart rate, sleep disturbance, fatigue, loss of appetite, stomach pains, abnormal heart rhythms, paranoia, picking at the skin, hallucinations, psychosis, mood swings
Barbiturates	Impaired judgment, loss of muscular control, respiratory depression, anxiety, insomnia, tremors delirium, convulsions, death
Benzodiazepines (minor tranquilizers)	Fatigue, drowsiness, headache, muscle weakness, depression, nausea, confusion, memory loss
Caffeine	Nervousness, irritability, elevated heart rate, sleep disturbance, insomnia
Cocaine, Crack	Brief feeling of euphoria, dysphoric crash, elevated heart rate, fatigue, depression, restlessness, irritability, anxiety, nasal damage, psychosis, death
Heroin	Short-lived euphoria, disorientation, drowsiness, slowed heart rate and breathing, decreased brain activity, depressed appetite, loss of muscle control, increased tolerance for pain, stupor, death
Inhalants	Hearing loss, limb spasms, central nervous sytem damage, bone marrow damage, liver and kidney damage, blood oxygen depletion, unconsciousness, death
LSD	Distorted perception, hallucinations, inability to make sensible judgments, anxiety, depression, flashbacks, increased heart rate and blood pressure
Marijuana (THC)	Bronchitis, emphysema, asthma, cancer, increased heart rate, impaired motor skills, increased appetite, cravings, paranoia, reduced short-term memory
MDMA (ecstasy)	Confusion, depression, sleep disturbance, drug craving, anxiety, paranoia, muscle tension, nausea, blurred vision, faintness, chills, sweating, increased heart rate
Mescaline, Psilocybin, Psilocin	Effects are similar to those of LSD; hallucinations, nausea, psychosis
PCP	Numbness, slurred speech, loss of motor control, anxiety, hallucinations, amnesia, mood disorders, paranoia, violent hostility, schizophrenia, false sense of strength

(FIGURE 15-9) **The effects of a particular drug can vary depending on the drug's concentration, the dose, the method of use, and the physical makeup of the user.**

Common Street Names	Methods of Use	Medical Uses
Speed, uppers, crystal meth, crank, ice	Pills, capsules, sniffing	Treatment for narcolepsy and mild depression, treatment for attention deficit disorder in children
Downers, barbs, gangster pills	Pills, capsules, injection	Sedation, induce sleep, prevent seizures
Downers, bennies, V, lib, blue angels	Pills, capsules	Sedation, induce sleep, relieve anxiety, prevent seizures
Joe, java	Beverages, chocolate, pills	Vasoconstrictor, mild stimulant
Snow white, base, caine, coke, line, rock	Sniffing, smoking, injection, ingestion	Was used as a local anesthetic in eye, nose, and throat surgery in the 1880s
Horse, smack, beast, brown	Injection, sniffing, smoking	Was used to treat pain in the late 1800s and early 1900s
Whippets, toncho, buzz bomb, whiteout	Inhalation	Some types used for medical anesthesia
Acid, A, blow, cid, blotters, microdots	Placed on the tongue and absorbed	Has been used to study mental illness
Pot, yerba, bud, chiba, weed, gangster, herb, blunt	Smoking, ingestion, pills	Antinauseant for patients undergoing chemotherapy, appetite stimulant for people with AIDS
Rolling, running, XTC, X, X-ing	Ingestion, sniffing	None
Mesc, cactus, tops, nubs, mushrooms, shrooms	Ingestion	None
Dust, rocket fuel, purple rain, super weed	Ingestion, smoking, injection	Was used as a veterinary anesthetic in the 1960s and 1970s

Background
Use of Tranquilizers

Tranquilizers are meant for those who have severe or incapacitating anxiety, panic, or tension. They are not designed to treat someone suffering from the ordinary tension of everyday life. The latter kind of tension is normal and can help motivate a person to attain worthwhile goals. Users of tranquilizers such as Valium develop withdrawal symptoms after taking large doses for a few days, moderate doses for a few months, or small doses for a few years. Combining alcohol with some tranquilizers can lead to death.

sedative-hypnotics:

drugs that depress the body systems and cause sleepiness.

Sedative-Hypnotics

Sedative-hypnotics are drugs that depress the body systems and cause sleepiness. Some common names for sedative-hypnotics are tranquilizers, sleeping pills, and sedatives.

The two major kinds of sedative-hypnotics are barbiturates and benzodiazepines. Barbiturates are sometimes prescribed for the prevention of seizures. They are also very addictive, abused drugs that are illegally bought and sold. Secobarbital and pentobarbital (sold under the brand names Seconal and Nembutal) are two common types of barbiturates.

Benzodiazepines (which are sometimes called minor tranquilizers) are prescription medications prescribed to relieve minor anxiety and insomnia. Some common benzodiazepines are diazepam (sold under the brand name of Valium), chlordiazepoxide (Librium), and chlorazepate (Tranxene).

Benzodiazepines and barbiturates are especially dangerous when used with alcohol or other drugs. A user's judgment may be severely impaired, resulting in uncharacteristic and dangerous behaviors.

Q. Can sniffing cocaine kill a person?

A. There have been several instances in which a person has died from sniffing cocaine.

♦♦♦

Q. Is marijuana as dangerous as alcohol?

A. Yes. Both alcohol and marijuana impair a person's judgment, lessen coordination, and diminish reflexes. A person who has had alcohol or marijuana should never try to drive. Both substances can also cause long-term damage to the body. Finally, both alcohol and marijuana are illegal substances for teenagers in the United States.

Drugs and Pregnancy Facts

Women who use marijuana when they are pregnant increase the risk that the baby will suffer low birth weight and delayed physiological development.

Women who use cocaine when they are pregnant are at increased risk of suffering hemorrhage (heavy bleeding), premature delivery, and miscarriage.

Heroin use during pregnancy increases the likelihood of stillbirth and infant death.

Babies born to women who are addicted to narcotics are often born with the same addiction.

(FIGURE 15-10) **Women who abuse drugs while they are pregnant endanger the lives and well-being of their unborn babies.**

Drugs and Pregnancy

Many drugs a woman takes when she is pregnant pass into the bloodstream of her unborn child. For this reason, women who are pregnant should always check with their doctor before using any medications. This is particularly true during the first several weeks of pregnancy, when the fetus is especially sensitive to any chemicals that may cause damage.

What if a drug abuser were to get pregnant? Drugs of abuse can pose very serious dangers to the growth and development of an unborn child. Babies born to women who abused drugs when they were pregnant have suffered such damage as facial and body deformities, retardation in growth and learning, brain damage, slowed reflexes, and severe learning disabilities. In addition, there is evidence that babies born to women who are addicted to drugs such as heroin and crack are born with the same addictions as their mothers.

*Life*SKILLS: Communicating Effectively

Should She Use Steroids? . . . .

Jessie hits the swimming pool every morning at 6:00. By the time most people wake up, she has been swimming for an hour. She is captain of the girls' varsity swim team, and she swims the anchor leg on the freestyle and medley relay teams.

Jessie's goal is to swim for a big university team one day. To do this, she needs to win a college scholarship for her swimming accomplishments. Unfortunately, Jessie feels that practice alone will not get her a college scholarship. She insists that her strength and speed will not hold up against larger female competitors. That is why she is thinking about using steroids. She says she knows some swimmers who have used them and have become more competitive.

You know that Jessie is serious and that you have to talk her out of using steroids. What are some good arguments you can use to convince Jessie to stay away from steroids?

SECTION 15.2

 Life SKILLS

Have students do the Life Skills exercise in the text, answering the question on paper.

 Section Review Worksheet 15.2

To reinforce the concepts presented in this section, assign Section Review Worksheet 15.2.

 Section Quiz 15.2

Have students take Section Quiz 15.2.

Reteaching Worksheet 15.2

Students who have difficulty with the material may complete Reteaching Worksheet 15.2.

• • • TEACH continued

steroids used by athletes are called anabolic steroids. Have students discuss why steroid use is dangerous to their health. Students may recall that athletes have been sent home from the Olympics and have been deprived of gold medals for using steroids.

 Journal 15D
Would You Take Steroids?

Encourage students to think about and write in their Journal their opinions about the use of steroids to improve athletic ability.

Cooperative Learning
Risks of Using Steroids

Have students work in cooperative groups to discuss the problem athletes face in taking or not taking steroids. Ask them If they knew steroids would help them win an important athletic contest, would they be tempted to take them? Have students list the opinions of the group and then share and debate these with the class.

Extension
Advice of the Athletic Director

Have students interview their athletic director or coach about the use of steroids to improve athletic ability. Have them share what they learned with the class.

Review Answers

1. Students should explain the effects of one of the following categories of drugs: stimulants, hallucinogens, marijuana and hashish, inhalants, heroin and other narcotics, sedative-hypnotics, or steroids. Explanations should include physical and behavioral effects and any health consequences that may result from the use of a drug in the category.

2. Answers may include addiction, violent behavior, increased risk of heart attack, and death.

3. Answers may include to read the label and follow the instructions; to use in a well-ventilated area; and to close all containers when finished.

4. Answers will vary. Students should include in their answers that steroids have dangerous side effects that far outnumber any benefits.

5. Yes. If a person does not follow the directions on the prescription label or those given by the doctor exactly, the person may misuse the drug and take too much of it or take the drug too often. This behavior can lead to addiction.

Effects of Steroid Use

Physical Changes	Rapid weight gain and muscle development Increased body hair Deepening of voice Acne Hair loss Breast enlargement (males) Elevated blood pressure Stomach upset Heart damage Liver damage Infertility and impotence Aching joints Enlarged prostate Swelling of extremities
Mental Changes	Increased aggression Hyperactivity and irritability Auditory hallucinations Paranoid delusions Manic episodes Depression and anxiety Panic disorders Suicidal thoughts

(FIGURE 15-11) **People who use steroids show certain physical and mental symptoms.**

anabolic steroid:

an artificially made, complex substance that can temporarily increase muscle size.

Anabolic Steroids

One of the most widespread problems in both professional and amateur sports is the use of **anabolic steroids** among athletes. Made to resemble the male hormone testosterone, anabolic steroids were originally developed and used to treat people suffering from certain types of anemia, as well as certain bone and joint disorders.

Because they can help a person gain weight and develop muscles, anabolic ste-

roids have become very popular drugs of abuse. Athletes have used them to help them run or swim faster, or to make them stronger. But the dangers of abusing anabolic steroids far outnumber what some people may think of as benefits.

For example, anabolic steroids can cause liver and heart damage, as well as very high blood pressure. Anabolic steroid abusers have been known to act aggressively and even violently. For more characteristics of anabolic steroid abuse, see Figure 15-11.

Athletes who use anabolic steroids may think they are at an advantage in competition. Anabolic steroids can be easily detected, however, and any athlete caught with anabolic steroids in his or her system is automatically disqualified from most competitions.

Review

1. Explain the effects of one category of psychoactive drugs.

2. Name two dangers of crack cocaine.

3. What is a good precaution to take if you have to use a product with inhalant fumes?

4. ■■ **LIFE SKILLS: Communicating Effectively** If your friend wanted to take anabolic steroids to get stronger, what would you say to him or her?

5. **Critical Thinking** Is it possible for a person using drugs for medical purposes to become addicted? Explain your answer.

ASSESS

Section Review

Have students answer the Section Review questions.

Alternative Assessment
A Drug-Free World

Ask students to speculate what it would be like if there were no drugs of abuse in the world.

Closure
What Stands Out Most

Ask students what made the most vivid impression on them as they learned about the effects of various drugs of abuse.

Section 15.3

Treatment for Dependency

Objectives

- *Name two things everyone should know about treatment for drug dependency.*
- *Know three options for recovering drug abusers.*
- *Know a healthy alternative to abusing drugs.*

Fighting a dependency to any drug is not easy. Most people who are addicted to drugs are psychologically dependent on them as well. The goal of all drug-treatment programs is to help a person battle not only the drug dependency itself but also the reasons why the drug abuse started in the first place. Fortunately, there are many options for people in this situation.

There are two things everyone who decides to seek treatment for a drug dependency should know. First, no one should try to overcome a drug dependency on his or her own. *Everyone* needs help when it comes to addiction or dependence. Another thing to realize about drug dependency is that there is no such thing as a *recovered* drug addict. Even if a person has not abused drugs for years, the chance that the person will relapse by abusing a drug again, and will become dependent again, is always there. Every recovering drug addict learns to take life without drugs one day at a time.

Methadone Maintenance Programs

People who are addicted to heroin have an especially difficult time overcoming their dependence. Their bodies have become so used to the presence of heroin that the withdrawal process can be very painful.

Some heroin addicts choose methadone maintenance to help them go through the withdrawal process. Like heroin, methadone is a narcotic. But its effects are not

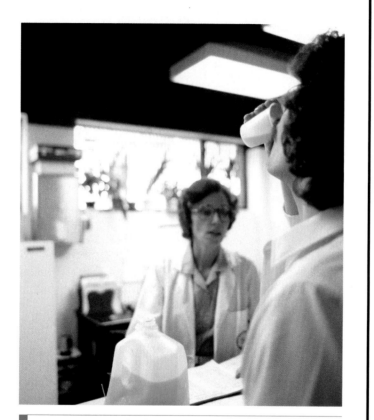

(FIGURE 15-12) **Methadone, a narcotic without the powerful effects of heroin, may help a person endure the painful process of heroin withdrawal.**

Background
Methadone Maintenance Programs

Methadone suppresses the symptoms of withdrawal from heroin for 24 to 32 hours. Like heroin, methadone is addictive, but unlike heroin, it is legal, does not produce euphoria, and can be taken orally. Oral treatment avoids the problem of dirty needles and the intravenous spread of HIV; however, many addicts continue to take heroin along with methadone. Because methadone's effects will not last more than 32 hours, some methadone clinics allow take-home doses for patients to use over the weekend. Unfortunately, some patients sell their weekend supply and use heroin in its place. These problems have caused methadone-maintenance programs to receive a lot of bad publicity. Due to the social stigma of drug addiction, most methadone-use cases that are considered success stories receive no publicity and go unnoticed by the general public.

Section 15.3 Lesson Plan

MOTIVATE

Journal 15E
On Seeking Help

This may be done as a warm-up activity. Have students write in their Journal what they would do if they were using drugs and wanted to stop. To whom would they turn for help? What would be their reasons for quitting drugs?

TEACH

Class Discussion
Fighting Dependency

Ask: **Why is it important for a person who has become addicted to a drug to find out why he or she became addicted in the first place?** *[If the person is not able to solve the problem that caused the addiction, the person may fall back into drug use again.]* **What are two things someone must remember when seeking treatment for de-**pendency on drugs? *[Everyone needs help when it comes to drug addiction; there is no such thing as a recovered drug addict.]* **Why does a person addicted to heroin have such a difficult time during treatment?** *[The withdrawal process is very painful because the body has become dependent upon the drug.]*

Background
Causes of Addiction
Researchers say that there does not seem to be an addiction-prone personality. However, people differ in their ability to withstand stress, which may be a factor in drug addiction. Rehabilitation must help addicts become aware of these differences and help them learn to manage their problems more effectively.

Life Skills Worksheet 15B
Assign the Where to Get Help Life Skills Worksheet.

Making a Choice 15B
Assign the A Family Disease? card. The card asks students to discuss the meaning of the term "family disease" when applied to drug addiction.

nearly as powerful or as appealing. People who go through methadone maintenance are able to provide their bodies with the narcotic they crave. The dosages of methadone are gradually decreased until the withdrawal process has been completed.

Withdrawing from a physical addiction is only the first step in the recovery process. The next hurdle all drug addicts must clear is the psychological dependency they have formed.

(FIGURE 15-13) **Group therapy sessions play an important role in all inpatient and outpatient drug-treatment programs.**

Inpatient and Outpatient Programs
Programs in hospitals and special treatment centers provide help for addicts going through withdrawal. Some recovering drug abusers need to live at the center while they receive treatment. Others will choose to stay at home and participate on an outpatient basis.

Although some programs provide methadone maintenance for recovering addicts, many treatment facilities help their patients go through withdrawal without the use of chemicals.

Inpatient and outpatient programs rely very heavily on education, one-on-one counseling, and group therapy to help recovering patients overcome their psychological dependencies. This is a very important part of the treatment process. In sessions, addicts talk to each other or to a counselor about the reasons why they started abusing drugs, and why they want to stop relying on them now.

Self-Help Programs
There are also programs available for drug abusers who want to quit without the help of professional counselors. Self-help programs like Narcotics Anonymous work in the same way as Alcoholics Anonymous. Participants follow a 12-step program and attend regular meetings, which are held at many times and locations. Members become part of a support system designed to help them change their lifestyle and overcome their addiction. Each person has a sponsor that he or she can call for support.

Options for Teenagers
Many teenagers who abuse drugs want to quit but aren't sure how to go about doing it. Most hospital and treatment-center programs have special divisions for teenagers with drug problems. Even so, some teenagers may find it intimidating to go to a stranger and admit that they have a problem with drugs.

For this reason, many schools now have student assistance programs available for students. Student assistance programs are set up to offer students information and sometimes to refer them to places that can help them overcome a drug dependency. Schools that don't provide student assistance programs usually have guidance counselors to perform the same functions. In addition, many towns and communities

Cooperative Learning
Helping a Friend on Drugs

Have students work in cooperative groups to discuss how they would handle the problem of a friend who needs help in dealing with drug dependency. Have them discuss whether they would tell a counselor or would go directly to the friend.

Class Discussion
Teenagers Trying to Quit Drugs

Ask: **Where can teenagers who are trying to quit drugs turn for assistance?** *[Schools have school assistance programs or guidance counselors to refer them to places that can help them overcome a drug dependency. The yellow pages in the phone book lists state and local councils on drug abuse.]* **When might you seek help from an intervention counselor?** *[If you have a friend who isn't seeking help for drug dependency, you might want help in learning*

how to confront the friend with his or her need for help.]

Role-Playing
Will a Drug Really Help?

Ask students to role-play a situation in which one member of a group is defending his or her experimentation with drugs to the other group members. For each defense the drug user presents, have group members suggest a drug-free way to handle the situation. For example, if the drug user says the drug helps him or her to relax, have state or local councils on drug abuse that can provide referral services for teenagers seeking treatment. State and local councils on drug abuse should be listed in your yellow pages.

A guidance counselor or student assistance program can also refer students to intervention counselors. If you know someone who is dependent on drugs and who isn't seeking the help he or she needs, you may want to think about using a formal group intervention strategy. Intervention means confronting a drug addict with his or her dependency and strongly encouraging him or her to seek treatment. If you decide that you want to use intervention, make sure you talk to an expert first.

If you have a drug abuse problem, there is nothing to be ashamed or embarrassed about. The important thing is to

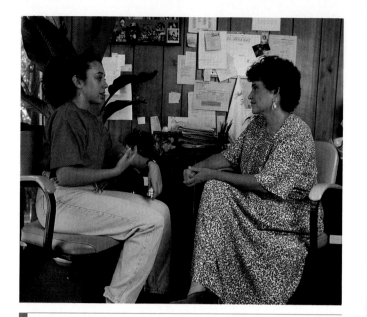

(FIGURE 15-15) **School guidance counselors can help teenagers with drug dependencies get proper treatment.**

(FIGURE 15-14) **Sometimes having a friend to talk to can make hard times less painful.**

SECTION 15.3

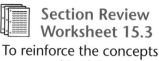 **Section Review Worksheet 15.3**
To reinforce the concepts presented in this section, assign Section Review Worksheet 15.3.

 Section Quiz 15.3
Have students take Section Quiz 15.3.

 Reteaching Worksheet 15.3
Students who have difficulty with the material may complete Reteaching Worksheet 15.3.

the group members might suggest a half hour of basketball followed by a shower or hot bath. The teacher could provide some help if the group members are unable to respond to a particular defense.

 Journal 15F
Options to Drugs

Have students write in their Journal the alternatives to taking drugs as a solution for everyday problems. Ask them which alternative they would choose and why.

Extension
Crisis Intervention

Have students visit a community clinic, family counseling center, or other agency that deals with people in crisis over drugs. Have them write questions ahead of time and prepare a brief report afterward about the kinds of problems drug users face and how they are being helped.

Review Answers

1. No one should try to overcome a drug dependency on his or her own; there is no such thing as a recovered drug addict.

2. methadone maintenance programs for heroin abusers, inpatient and outpatient programs, self-help programs

3. talking to someone you feel you can confide in about problems

4. A person who has abused drugs in the past most likely will have the tendency to abuse drugs again in certain circumstances. Therefore, a recovering drug abuser must learn to take life without drugs one day at a time.

(FIGURE 15-16) **Life's too short to be wasted on drugs.**

world around them. Why not take a drug, they may think, if it makes things seem easier for a while?

If you have felt this way, you're not alone. But taking drugs is the *worst* thing you can do. Drugs do not help people cope with problems. Their desired effects don't last forever, and when they end, things are usually worse. People who abuse drugs or alcohol often act impulsively and even dangerously. A person who is drunk or high, for instance, is more likely to commit suicide than a person who isn't.

There are people you can talk to about the things that are troubling you. If you don't think you can confide in a parent or close friend, you may want to speak to a coach, a teacher, or a religious leader. If they can't help you, they may be able to refer you to someone who can. The important thing to remember is that life can get better. Drugs may seem like a solution, but in the long run they don't solve problems—they only add to them.

admit you do have a problem and get help. One thing you *shouldn't* try to do is recover by yourself. No one can overcome a drug dependency alone—everyone needs help. Talk to someone in the student assistance program at your school, or call one of the programs listed in the Yellow Pages under "Drug Abuse and Addiction." Once you have admitted that you have a drug problem, you have taken a major step toward recovery.

Finally, if you have thought about abusing drugs, know that there are other options. Life can be very difficult. Many teenagers face struggles in their day-to-day lives—such as poverty, family problems, or depression—that can make it very hard to get through each day. Teenagers in these situations sometimes may feel a sense of hopelessness about themselves and the

Review

1. What are two things everyone should know about treatment for drug dependency?

2. Name three options for recovering drug abusers.

3. What's a healthier way to deal with problems than abusing drugs?

4. **Critical Thinking** Explain the reasoning behind the following statement: "There is no such thing as a recovered drug abuser."

ASSESS

Section Review

Have students answer the Section Review questions.

Alternative Assessment
Why Take the Risk?

Ask students to explain what makes drugs of abuse so attractive that people will take risks to obtain and use them. What kinds of personality traits and experiences make people most vulnerable to using drugs?

Closure
Letter of Advice

Ask students to write a brief letter to Josephine, a young woman who is thinking about taking drugs to help her face her problems. Tell them to make it clear that adding drugs to her problems will only make them worse.

Highlights

Summary

- One reason drug abuse is dangerous is that it can cause a person to act irresponsibly.

- Continued drug abuse can lead to psychological and physical dependence.

- Caffeine, cocaine and crack, and amphetamines are all examples of stimulants.

- Hallucinogens such as LSD and PCP are very dangerous psychoactive substances, because they distort the senses.

- Marijuana can impair a person's judgment and coordination.

- Many chemical products contain inhalant fumes that produce strong psychoactive effects when inhaled.

- Narcotics are highly addictive drugs. Some narcotics such as morphine and codeine have some medicinal value. The narcotic heroin, however, has no medical purpose and is illegal to buy, sell, and use.

- Steroid abuse can lead to very high blood pressure and can severely damage the heart and liver.

- No one should ever try to overcome a drug addiction alone.

- There is no such thing as a recovered drug abuser. Even if a person has not abused a drug in years, there is a chance that the person will abuse, and become dependent on, drugs again.

- Methadone maintenance programs, inpatient and outpatient programs, and self-help programs are three options for recovering drug abusers.

Vocabulary

psychoactive drug a drug that affects a person's mood and behavior.

stimulant a drug that causes alertness and speeds up the activity of the body.

hallucinogen a drug that distorts a person's senses.

narcotic a drug with pain-relieving and psychoactive properties that is made from the opium poppy plant.

sedative-hypnotics drugs that depress the body systems and cause sleepiness.

anabolic steroid an artificially made, complex substance that can temporarily increase muscle size.

Chapter Review

CHAPTER REVIEW

Concept Review

1. mood, behavior
2. physical
3. tolerance
4. physical; psychological
5. cocaine
6. illicit drugs
7. synthetic
8. hallucinogenic
9. flashback
10. marijuana, hashish
11. narcotic
12. liver, heart
13. recovered

Expressing Your Views

Sample responses:

1. Sharon is building up a tolerance to the medication. I would tell her to inform her doctor so that he or she can change the medication before she becomes addicted to it.

2. Barry could be addicted to amphetamines. I would encourage him to talk to someone in the student assistance program or to his counselor about the situation. I would support Barry in his decision to overcome his addiction and encourage him as he goes through a drug-abuse program.

Life Skills Check

Sample responses:

1. I would tell him not to use cocaine or crack under any circumstances. He does not have to explain to anyone why he doesn't want to try them. All he

Concept Review

1. A psychoactive drug is a drug that affects a person's _____ and _____.

2. Addiction is a _____ process.

3. _____ is the first step in the addiction process.

4. _____ dependence occurs when a person's body comes to expect the presence of a drug. _____ dependence is a strong desire to repeat the use of a drug for emotional reasons.

5. When _____ is inhaled, it enters the bloodstream, then travels to the brain.

6. Statistics show that 35 percent of all crimes in the United States are committed by people who are under the influence of _____ _____.

7. _____ drugs such as amphetamines are drugs produced or manufactured in laboratories.

8. People on _____ drugs often forget where they are, may have difficulty keeping track of time, and may believe they have special powers.

9. A _____ is an unexpected return to an unpleasant LSD experience, often months after the original experience ended.

10. _____ and _____ are two organic drugs that come from the cannabis, or hemp, plant.

11. Morphine, codeine, and heroin are examples of _____ drugs.

12. Steroids can cause _____ and _____ damage as well as high blood pressure.

13. There is no such thing as a _____ drug addict because even if a person has been off of drugs for years, that person could become dependent again.

Expressing Your Views

1. Your friend Sharon, who has been taking a prescription medication for several weeks, confides to you that she is having to take increasingly greater amounts of the drug in order to get the same pain relief she once got with the recommended dosage. Why is this happening to her? What would you tell her?

2. Your friend Barry takes amphetamines whenever he has to study for a test. "They keep me going," he's told you. But he's been absent from school a lot, and whenever you see him he's moody and anxious. What could be wrong with Barry? How can you help him get the treatment he needs?

has to do is say no. Cocaine and crack are addictive drugs; people on cocaine and crack often behave violently; cocaine and crack can be fatal, even the first time they are used.

2. I would tell my friends that I do not want to take PCP, and I would try to talk them out of taking it. I would tell them that taking PCP causes dangerous mental disturbances and often violent behavior and that I don't think this sounds like fun. I would try to convince them that because

we are out in the woods where no help is available, getting high on PCP seems especially dangerous.

Projects

Have students plan and carry out the projects on drugs and drug abuse.

Life Skills Check . . . .

1. Communicating Effectively

Your younger brother is planning to attend a party. You found out that several of the people there will be using cocaine and crack. What advice should you give him?

2. Resisting Pressure

While on a camping trip, two of your friends try to persuade you to try PCP. They assure you that the drug's effects will be gone by the time you return home the next day. You feel uneasy about using drugs, but you are also worried about what your friends will think if you refuse—saying no isn't easy. What should you do? What are some good reasons to say no?

Projects . . . .

1. Work with a partner to create a poster that describes information about different types of drugs. The following information could be included: street names, how the drug is taken, the physical and mental effects of the drug, and any other descriptive information. Display your poster in the classroom.

2. Work with a small group. Imagine that all of you in the group are parents. What kind of policies would you set to discourage your children

from abusing drugs? What could you do to encourage your children to follow healthy practices?

3. Certain athletes and other well-known personalities have had highly publicized bouts with drug abuse. Research the experience of one such celebrity. Why do you think this person may have turned to drugs? What other options do you think he or she may have had? Present the results of your research to the class.

Plan for Action . . . .

Life isn't easy for anyone, but people who abuse drugs when times are hard make things even worse for themselves. What are two things a person can do to cope with problems in a healthy way?

Plan for Action

Have small groups of students discuss positive things students could do to cope with life's problems. Then have each student write a coping-with-problems plan that identifies two actions he or she could take and how the plan could be implemented. For example, if a student's plan says that he or she would talk to someone about problems, the student should identify in advance who that person would be.

Pledge

Discuss the pledge for Chapter 15. A student's decision of whether to sign the pledge is personal and private.

ASSESSMENT OPTIONS

Chapter Test
Have students take the Chapter 15 Test.

Alternative Assessment
Have students do the Alternative Assessment activity for Chapter 15.

Test Generator
The Test Generator contains additional assessment items for this chapter.

Issues in Health

Evaluating Media Messages

How Bad Can It Be If Athletes Do It?

EVALUATING MEDIA MESSAGES

How Bad Can It Be If Athletes Do It?

Have students read the Evaluating Media Messages feature. Ask students how they would respond to Joel's habit of chewing tobacco. Would it offend them? Would they want to try it themselves? Can they think of another reason Joel may be so insistent? *(Tobacco is addictive and Joel may be habituated to it.)* What problems might Joel have in giving it up? *(overcoming addiction; giving up a habit he associates with people he admires or with people he sees a lot)*

Have interested students find out the number of young people who use smokeless tobacco. Have them choose a particular age range for their research. What percentage use smokeless tobacco? What percentage of young people in the same age range smoke cigarettes? Have students create pie graphs indicating the proportion of young people who have both habits.

Joel and Lucinda were walking home from school when Joel pulled out a pouch of chewing tobacco and put some in his mouth. Lucinda was horrified. ''What are you doing with that stuff, Joel?'' she cried.

''Oh, come on, Lucinda,'' Joel said. ''It's not like I'm smoking cigarettes—I mean I'm not bothering anyone, and it's not going to give me cancer.''

''You're wrong,'' Lucinda replied. ''My uncle used to do it, and he got cancer of the mouth.''

''So what?'' Joel replied. ''Your uncle's probably an old man who would've gotten cancer anyway.''

''No, actually he was in his twenties when he got sick.''

''Well, look at all the pro athletes who chew tobacco and dip snuff. Those guys are in great shape, so it must be okay.''

''Joel, my uncle played college baseball. He was in great shape too,'' Lucinda informed him.

Joel is one of a growing number of boys who use smokeless tobacco (chewing tobacco and snuff). While smoking has declined among teenagers in the United States, the use of smokeless tobacco has risen. In fact, the number of 17- to 19-year-old males using smokeless tobacco increased by a multiple of 8 during the 1980s. Researchers believe this increase resulted from the skillful marketing efforts directed at teens by tobacco companies.

Advertisers target teenagers because they are aware that teenagers can be very easy to influence. For instance, it is well known that many teens experience low self-esteem and a sense of being powerless. So advertisers portray people in tobacco ads as just the opposite—mature, self-confident, and independent. Such images make using tobacco very attractive to people who are looking for ways to appear more mature, to feel more confident, or to assert their individuality. Teens can fight back, but they must carefully evaluate the media messages in tobacco ads to combat their effect.

When evaluating a media message, it is helpful to refer to a simple model of communication. The SMCR model below breaks communication into four parts.

1. The *Source* of the communication creates a message that can be verbal, nonverbal, visual, or musical.
2. The *Message* is what the source wants to say.
3. The *Channel* is the means by which the message is transmitted. In mass media this could be television, magazines, newspapers, radio, etc.
4. The *Receiver* interprets the message on the basis of his or her individual experiences and values.

Issues in Health

Joel's comments to Lucinda indicate how he has been affected by media messages about smokeless tobacco. For example, one message that frequently appears in smokeless tobacco ads is that the product is good because it does not produce smoke, which bothers many people. Joel, the receiver, obviously agrees with the reasoning in this message; but Lucinda objects. "Sure, there's no smoke," she explains, "but when you use that stuff, you still do things that upset a lot of people—like spitting, drooling, and leaving smelly, wet tobacco in soft-drink cans." Joel may not have thought about how other people see these behaviors, because smokeless-tobacco ads don't mention them. Once he has considered Lucinda's remarks, he might evaluate messages about smokeless tobacco differently.

Joel's belief that chewing tobacco can't be very dangerous because athletes do it is an example of association, a very effective marketing tool. It is also an example of how powerful nonverbal communication can be. In using association, the source (an advertiser) makes a connection between something receivers like and the product the source wants to sell. If the channel is television or some other type of visual media, just the picture of a healthy athlete using smokeless tobacco can convey the false impression that the habit is not dangerous. Linking healthy athletes to unhealthy substances such as tobacco is actually a mixed message. When analyzed, mixed messages can be recognized as containing conflicting information.

Tobacco companies employ association not only by using athletes in their ads but also by giving free samples of smokeless tobacco to athletes—particularly major-league baseball players. The free

Media images make tobacco use attractive to people who want to feel more mature and confident.

samples are tremendously effective because millions of fans see their heroes using the products during televised games. To try to eliminate the association of athletes with smokeless tobacco, the National Cancer Institute and the National Institute for Dental Research have recently begun working with major-league baseball teams to help players quit using smokeless tobacco.

Critical Thinking

1. Find several tobacco or alcohol ads and analyze them using the SMCR Model.

2. Identify one product—tobacco, alcohol, antacid, cold medicine, pain reliever, diet pill—that you have bought or wanted to buy because of a media message. Evaluate the message by asking yourself the following questions:

- Who is the source?
- What is their message?
- How will they benefit if I do as they wish?
- How will I benefit if I do as they wish?
- What are my values?
- What is best for me?

3. What can you do to convince a friend who has started using smokeless tobacco to stop?

CHAPTER OVERVIEWS

CHAPTER 16

REPRODUCTION AND THE EARLY YEARS OF LIFE

This chapter describes the male and female reproductive systems and explains their functions in detail. Disorders of the reproductive systems are described, and proper care of the reproductive organs is discussed. Students learn about the development of human beings from fertilization of the egg through childhood.

CHAPTER 17

ADOLESCENCE: RELATIONSHIPS AND RESPONSIBILITIES

Students learn about the physical, emotional, and mental changes that occur during adolescence. To help them be more successful in interpersonal relations, the students also learn effective communication techniques. The chapter discusses sexuality and the possible consequences of sexual intimacy. Finally, students learn skills for responsible sexual behavior.

CHAPTER 18

ADULTHOOD, MARRIAGE, AND PARENTHOOD

This chapter covers the stages of adulthood, the process of aging, and the

needs of the elderly. It also explains the reasons why people get married, the ingredients that go into a successful marriage, and the difficulties teenagers may face in marrying early. It ends with a discussion of parental responsibilities.

CHAPTER 19

FAMILIES

Students learn the functions of a family, the different types of families, how families have changed, and some characteristics of a healthy family. Students also receive information on

coping with divorce and living in a dysfunctional family.

CHAPTER 20

PREVENTING ABUSE AND VIOLENCE

This chapter describes the forms of child, spouse, and elder abuse, and names sources of help for abusive families. It defines and discusses sexual assault, acquaintance rape, and sexual harassment. Students learn about risk factors related to homicides, the reasons why some teenagers join gangs, and some ways to avoid violence, including peer mediation.

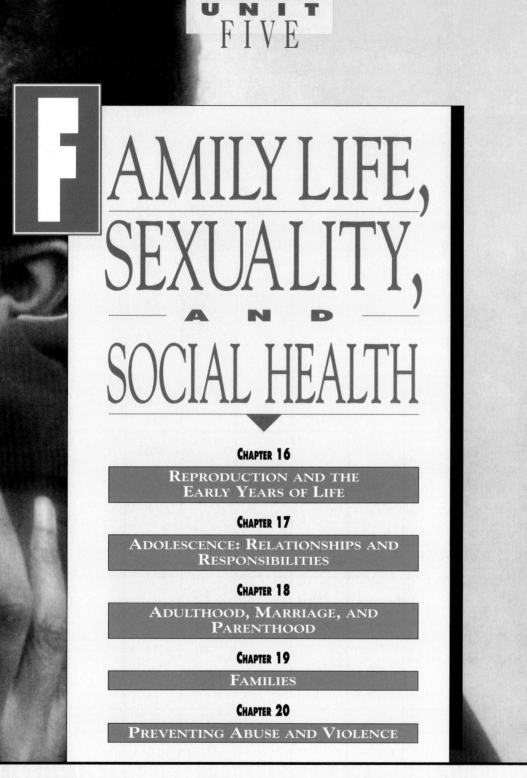

FAMILY LIFE, SEXUALITY, AND SOCIAL HEALTH

CHAPTER 16

REPRODUCTION AND THE EARLY YEARS OF LIFE

CHAPTER 17

ADOLESCENCE: RELATIONSHIPS AND RESPONSIBILITIES

CHAPTER 18

ADULTHOOD, MARRIAGE, AND PARENTHOOD

CHAPTER 19

FAMILIES

CHAPTER 20

PREVENTING ABUSE AND VIOLENCE

UNIT PREVIEW

The life stages of human beings from conception to old age are covered in this unit. The in-depth treatment of reproduction, adolescence, and sexuality provides students a sound basis for making responsible decisions about sexual behaviors. Students learn that the decisions they make at each stage of their life affect their short- and long-term wellness. The unit gives information to help students deal with family problems such as divorce and abuse. They also learn how to reduce their risks of being victims or perpetrators of sexual assault and other violent conflict. The chart below links the information and skills presented in this unit to the National Health Education Standards.

Unit 5	NATIONAL HEALTH EDUCATION STANDARDS*						
STANDARD	1	2	3	4	5	6	7
Chapter 16	•	•	•				
Chapter 17			•		•		
Chapter 18						•	
Chapter 19				•	•	•	
Chapter 20	•	•	•		•	•	

* For full text listing of each standard, see page 15T.

Reproduction and the Early Years of Life

SECTION	TITLE/OBJECTIVES	PERSONAL INVENTORY			LIFE SKILLS DEVELOPMENT			
		Personal Health Inventory	Journal	Check Up	Life Skills	Life Skills Worksheets	Media Message or Ethical Issues Worksheet	What Would You Do?
16.1 pp. 325–330	**THE MALE REPRODUCTIVE SYSTEM** • Name the major organs of the male reproductive system. • Explain the two functions of the testes. • Trace the path of the sperm from the testes to the outside of the body. • Describe how the sperm meets the egg and fertilizes it. ▪ Describe how to do a testicular self-examination.	Ch. 16	16A			16A		
16.2 pp. 331–338	**THE FEMALE REPRODUCTIVE SYSTEM** • Name the organs of the female reproductive system. • Trace the path of the egg from the ovary to the uterus. • Explain how the uterus changes during the menstrual cycle. ▪ Describe how to do a breast self-examination.		16B			16B		
16.3 pp. 339–348	**PREGNANCY, BIRTH, AND CHILDHOOD DEVELOPMENT** • List the substances that can pass from the mother to the placenta. • Describe the events that occur during birth. ▪ Use self-talk about childhood experiences to increase your self-esteem.		16C 16D		p. 347			

KEY: ▪ Denotes Life Skill Objective
Text references denoted by page number.
Supplement references denoted by chapter or item numbers.

LINKING RESOURCES

Making a Choice Cards	Parent Discussion Guide	Health Talk Audio Program	Teaching Transparencies and Directory	Section Review Worksheets	Section Quizzes	Reteaching Worksheets	Section Reviews
INTERACTION		OTHER RESOURCES	SECTION REVIEW AND ASSESSMENT				
			16A	16.1	16.1	16.1	p. 330
			16A	16.2	16.2	16.2	p. 338
16A 16B			16B 16C	16.3	16.3	16.3	p. 348

KEY FACTS

- The union of a sperm and an egg is called fertilization; it produces an embryo.

- The testes produce the hormone testosterone, which causes male sex characteristics to develop, and, in the sexually mature male, sperm.

- The ovaries produce female sex hormones and contain thousands of immature eggs. During ovulation each month, one of the eggs matures and is released.

- The female reproductive system provides a place for fertilization to occur. It also provides shelter and nourishment for the fetus until birth.

- Growth and development continue after birth through the stages of infancy, childhood, and adolescence.

- Monthly self-examinations, of the testes for males and of the breasts for females, are an important part of health care.

CHAPTER REVIEW AND ASSESSMENT

TEXT

Chapter Review pp. 350–351

SUPPLEMENTS

Chapter Test 16

Alternative Assessment 16

Test Generator Chapter 16

GETTING STARTED

Using the Chapter Photograph

Have students look at the chapter photograph and the photograph on the facing page. Ask them how they think having a baby changes a couple's lives. Discuss with students the ways teens could benefit by spending time with a very young niece, nephew, or cousin before becoming a parent.

Question Box

Have students write out any questions they have about the reproductive organs, conception, pregnancy, birth, and early childhood and put them in the Question Box.

Sensitivity ALERT

Many teenagers feel that their bodies should develop within a time frame and physical norms approved of by their peers. Stress that rate of maturation and individual development vary greatly among perfectly normal individuals. Also, many students may be uncomfortable discussing sexual intercourse, conception, pregnancy, childbirth, and parenting issues. Some of them may be dealing with the realities of these issues already.

CHAPTER 16

Reproduction and the Early Years of Life

◆ ◆ ◆ ◆

Section 16.1 The Male Reproductive System

Section 16.2 The Female Reproductive System

Section 16.3 Pregnancy, Birth, and Childhood Development

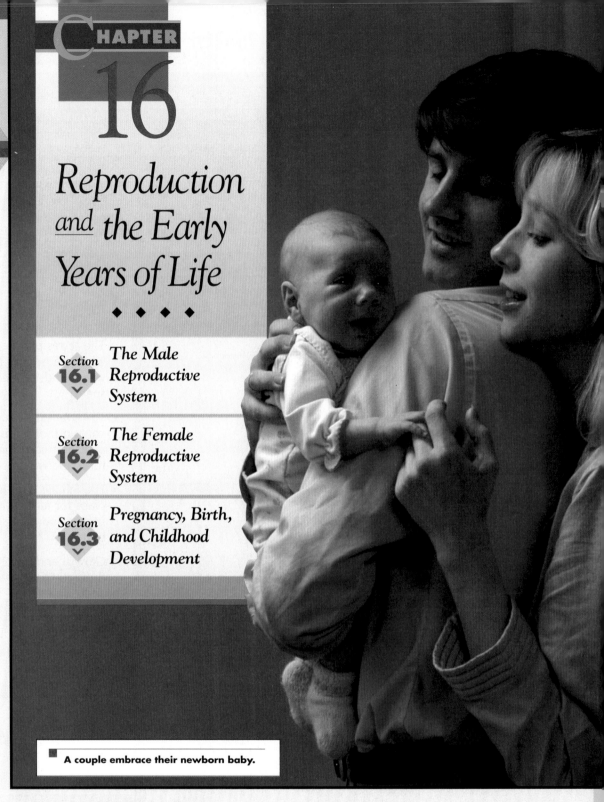

A couple embrace their newborn baby.

MYTHS & MISCONCEPTIONS

- **The more muscular a man is, the more virile he is.** There is no evidence to support this belief. It is not possible to predict a man's sperm count from his physical appearance. Fertility is not related to body shape or percentage of muscle mass.

- **Miscarriage may occur if a pregnant woman is very active or falls down.** Most aspects of daily life do not contribute to miscarriages. Factors that *do* increase the risk of miscarriage include fetal chromosomal abnormalities, maternal hormonal problems, an abnormally shaped uterus or cervix, smoking, and caffeine consumption.

- **Only sexually active women get vaginal infections.** Not all vaginal infections are caused by sexually transmitted organisms. For example, a yeast infection is an overgrowth of naturally occurring yeast cells that can be caused by many factors other than sexual activity.

Sabrena's older sister, Tonya, is pregnant. Tonya and her husband have been married for four years, and they have been looking forward to having a baby. Sabrena is extremely excited and can't wait to see her new niece or nephew. She has started thinking about what it would be like to have a baby. Sabrena isn't even sure she wants to have children. The idea of being responsible for a child's safety and well-being is pretty frightening. She's glad she doesn't have to make a decision about having children for a long time. Right now, she thinks, she will just enjoy her sister's baby.

Section
16.1
The Male Reproductive System

Objectives

- Name the major organs of the male reproductive system.
- Explain the two functions of the testes.
- Trace the path of the sperm from the testes to the outside of the body.
- Describe how the sperm meets the egg and fertilizes it.
- Describe how to do a testicular self-examination.
  LIFE SKILLS: Practicing Self-Care

Every person who has ever lived is the result of a process that began when a **sperm** cell from a male joined with an **egg** cell, or ovum, from a female. The male and female reproductive systems work together to bring the sperm and the egg together. This union of sperm and egg is called **fertilization.** Each sperm and each egg contains one-half of the instructions needed for the development of a new, unique human being.

The process of producing a new individual is called *reproduction.* In humans, the term reproduction means simply "having children."

One job of the male reproductive system is to produce sperm and transport them into the body of the female. Look at Figure 16-1, which shows the parts of the male reproductive system. The parts that you can see from the outside are the penis and the scrotum. The scrotum is the loose sac under the penis. Inside the scrotum are two testes, which produce the sperm. Connecting the testes and the penis are the two vas deferens, which are tubes through which the sperm travel. Along the way are glands that produce fluids that nourish and protect the sperm.

fertilization:
the union of a sperm and an egg.

sperm:
male reproductive cell; contains one-half of the instructions needed for the development of a new human being.

egg:
female reproductive cell, also called an ovum; contains one-half of the instructions needed for the development of a new human being.

Background
Vasectomy
Vasectomy is a male sterilization procedure in which the vas deferens (sperm ducts) are cut and tied so that sperm cannot pass through them and out of the body. The body reabsorbs the sperm, and unused sperm do not build up or cause any kind of problem. The surgery, which takes about half an hour, is done under local anesthesia in a doctor's office or out-patient clinic and involves making one or two small incisions in each scrotum. Normal function is restored within a day or two. Because some sperm may remain in the tubes above the places where they were cut, the man is not sterile immediately. A final sperm count is done approximately three months after the surgery to ensure that the sperm count is zero. Sexual function is in no way affected by a vasectomy.

 Personal Health Inventory
Have students complete the Personal Health Inventory for this chapter.

Section 16.1 Lesson Plan

MOTIVATE

Journal 16A
The Male Reproductive System

This may be done as a warm-up activity. Have students write in their Journal facts they know about the male reproductive system. Then have them list statements they have heard but do not know to be true. After they read the first section, have them refer to their journal to confirm the correctness of their facts and try to prove or disprove unproven statements.

Class Discussion
The Human Reproductive System

Discuss how the human reproductive system differs from other body systems. Point out that unlike other body systems, the reproductive system differs tremendously between the sexes.

Background

Orgasm and Ejaculation

Orgasm in males is followed almost immediately by the ejaculation of semen. This reflex action is controlled by the autonomic nervous system. It can, however, be influenced by impulses from higher brain centers that can delay or prevent ejaculation. The accessory glands—bulbourethral glands (Cowper's glands), seminal vesicles, and prostate gland—secrete fluids that protect and nourish the sperm and that help propel it from the body. The secretions of these glands make up the seminal fluid, the liquid portion of the semen. The bulbourethral glands may secrete a small amount of fluid just prior to ejaculation. Because this fluid contains some sperm, withdrawing the penis from the vagina just before ejaculation is not a reliable method of birth control.

testes:

male reproductive structures that make sperm and produce the male hormone testosterone.

The Testes

The **testes**, which are also called testicles, are two egg-shaped structures that hang inside the scrotum.

The testes have two functions. The first function of the testes is to make the sperm. The testes hang away from the body so that the temperature inside them is slightly cooler than the rest of the body. The temperature in the testes is very important to the sperm-making process. If the temperature is too high, the testes will make defective sperm that cannot fertilize an egg. The testes produce about 50,000 sperm every *minute*.

The second function of the testes is to produce the male sex hormone testosterone. Testosterone is necessary for the production of sperm and also for the development of male sex characteristics.

At puberty, the amount of testosterone in the male body increases, which causes boys' bodies to change. Coarse, curly hair called pubic hair begins to grow on the lower part of the abdomen around the penis. Similar coarse hair grows under the armpits. Teenage boys also begin to grow a beard on the lower part of the face. Some males begin to grow hair on the chest. The hormone testosterone is also responsible for the fact that males have bigger muscles, heavier bones, and deeper voices than women.

The Vas Deferens and the Urethra

The sperm must be able to travel to the outside of the body in order for reproduction to occur. Follow along the red line in Figure

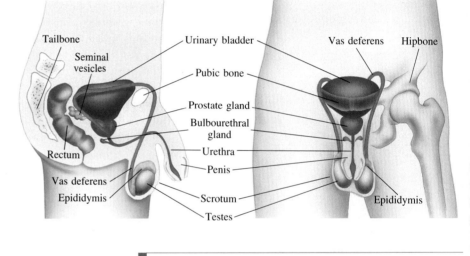

(FIGURE 16-1) **The function of the male reproductive system is to produce sperm that fertilize the egg of the female.**

TEACH

Teaching Transparency 16A
Male and Female Reproductive Systems

Show this transparency, which includes Figure 16-1. Have students describe the functions of various parts, tell how sperm are produced and protected, and trace the path sperm take out of the body.

Demonstration
Sperm and Egg Size

Tell students that an egg cell is about 0.005 inch in diameter, or about the size of a sharp pencil point. A sperm cell is so small—about 74 micrometers—that it cannot be seen without a microscope (1 micrometer = one-millionth of a meter). To help students visualize how small this is, have them look at the centimeter scale of a ruler and note the length of one

millimeter. Tell them that one millimeter equals 1000 micrometers. Ask students how many sperm could line up tail to tail along one millimeter. *(1000 divided by 74 is close to 13.5.)*

Demonstration
Sperm Mobility

To help students comprehend the difficulty of the sperm's journey to the egg, have them refer to a metric ruler. Explain that sperm swim at a rate of about 1 to 4 mm per minute. Have

16-2 to see the route the sperm take to leave the body.

After sperm are made in a testis, they travel to a structure called the epididymis, which is a tightly coiled mass of tubules located at the top of each testis. The sperm become fully mature while they are in the epididymis. After about two to ten days, the sperm leave the epididymis and travel through a tube called the vas deferens. Males have two of these tubes.

The vas deferens tubes lead to the urethra, which is the tube that runs through the center of the penis. The sperm leave the body through the urethra. The urethra is also the tube through which urine leaves the body during urination.

As the sperm travel through the vas deferens and the urethra, they pass by glands that add fluids to the sperm. These fluids nourish and protect the sperm, and enable the sperm to move on their own. The addition of these fluids to the sperm creates the fluid called semen.

The Penis

The **penis** is the body part that makes it possible for the sperm to reach the inside of the female's body. When the male becomes sexually excited, the arteries leading to his penis open wider, allowing more blood to flow into the penis. At the same time, some of the veins in the penis close or narrow so that less blood flows out.

The accumulated blood causes the penis to become larger, longer, and firmer and to point upward instead of hanging downward. When the penis is in this state, the male is said to have an erection. An erection makes it possible for the penis to be inserted in the female's vagina.

Ejaculation The process by which semen leaves the male's body is called ejaculation.

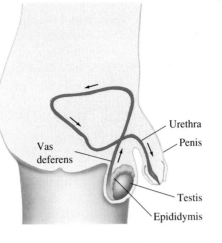

(FIGURE 16-2) **The red line shows the path of the sperm. Sperm originate in the testis, mature in the epididymis, travel through the vas deferens, and reach the outside of the body through the penis via the urethra.**

During ejaculation, muscles around the urethra and the base of the penis contract. The contraction moves the sperm out of the body. When the male ejaculates, he is said to have an orgasm.

Ejaculation can occur even while a male is sleeping. Especially in teenagers, the levels of testosterone may rise and fall unpredictably. These hormone fluctuations can cause an erection followed by ejaculation during sleep. Ejaculation during sleep is called a nocturnal emission or a "wet dream." Nocturnal emissions are very common in adolescent and adult males.

Pathway to Fertilization

During sexual intercourse, the sperm are deposited inside the female's vagina, a few inches away from the egg. But from a sperm's point of view, this is a long and difficult journey.

penis:

male reproductive structure that deposits sperm inside the female body.

Background
Sperm Mobility
At best, sperm move at about 4 millimeters per minute. Since they arrive in the fallopian tubes 30 to 60 minutes after ejaculation, there must be a second mechanism at work to help move them along. Evidence indicates that contractions of both the uterus and the fallopian tubes help transport the sperm.

students compute how far sperm would move in an hour and measure this distance on the ruler. (*The sperm would move 60 to 240 mm.*)

• • • TEACH continues on p. 328

Background
Testicular Cancer

In the United States, testicular cancer accounts for only 1 percent of all cancers in males; however, it is the most common abnormal growth in white males 15–34. (Whites are seven times more likely than blacks to develop testicular cancer.) Most deaths from testicular cancer occur among young adult men. When testicular cancer is detected and treated early, the prognosis is usually excellent. In both the United States and Europe, this cancer occurs two to four times more often than it did 50 years ago. There is mounting evidence that exposure to environmental contaminants, such as chemical fertilizers, phenols (used in solvents, resins, and weedkillers), chemical fumes, smoke, and estrogen-like substances, accounts for the increase in the occurence of testicular cancer.

Life Skills Worksheet 16A

Assign the Caring for the Male Body Life Skills Worksheet.

The sperm cell's structure enables it to make the trip. Each sperm has a tail that propels it forward. Also, sperm are streamlined and much smaller than most cells in the human body. Their streamlined shape and small size make it easier for them to swim quickly.

The semen in one ejaculation contains 40 million to 400 million sperm. Why are so many sperm released if only one will join with the egg?

First, the majority of the sperm will never make it to the egg. They will become trapped in mucus or die on the way to the egg.

Second, even though only one sperm can actually fuse with an egg, the presence of many sperm is necessary for this to happen. The egg is protected by a layer of many smaller cells. Sperm contain enzymes that break down this layer of cells. Only after *many* sperm have released their enzymes can *one* sperm make it to the inside of the egg. After one sperm has made it inside, a protective shield forms, which prevents others from fusing with the egg.

Circumcised or Uncircumcised?

Some males are circumcised, and some males are not. Circumcision is an operation in which a fold of skin called the foreskin is cut from around the tip of the penis in order to reduce irritation. Circumcision is usually done when a male is two to eight days old. Parents choose whether or not to have their male infants circumcised.

Figure 16-4 shows the difference between a male who has been circumcised and one who hasn't. Although they look different, circumcised and uncircumcised penises function in exactly the same way.

Males who have not been circumcised should pull the foreskin back when they wash. Cleaning under the foreskin prevents the buildup of a secretion that can cause irritation and odor.

(FIGURE 16-3) **(Top)** Sperm use their long tail to swim toward an egg. **(Left)** After one sperm has made it inside the egg, a protective shield prevents the other sperm from entering.

• • • TEACH continued

Reinforcement
Circumcision

Reassure students that circumcision is neither bad nor good, but simply a choice that some parents make and that can be culturally based. The presence or absence of the foreskin does not affect health or sexual performance.

Reinforcement
Care and Prevention

Stress the importance of cleaning and protecting the genitals. Males should wear a protector while participating in athletic events and strenuous exercise. Point out that fitted clothing is OK, but clothing that is too tight can cause pain in the groin.

Case Study
Testicular Cancer

In 1996, 25-year-old world-class cyclist Lance Armstrong was diagnosed with testicular cancer. Armstrong said that although he had annual physicals and blood tests, his testicles were never examined. By the time of his diagnosis, the cancer had spread to his lymph nodes, lungs, and brain. Ask students how a routine monthly testicular examination might have affected Armstrong's situation.

Circumcised ⎯⎯ Uncircumcised

Disorders of the Male Reproductive System

Even males who take good care of their reproductive system can have something go wrong. However, if a male knows as much as possible about male disorders, he will be prepared to seek the correct treatment.

Testicular Torsion Testicular torsion means "twisted testis." However, that's not exactly accurate. It is the spermatic cord, which suspends each testis in the scrotum and contains many blood vessels, that can become twisted during strenuous exercise or even during sleep. The condition is very rare, but it is an emergency situation, because testicular torsion can destroy the testes. Males who experience pain in the groin should seek treatment immediately.

Undescended Testes When some males are born, one or both of their testes remain inside the body rather than hanging loose in the scrotum. This condition is called undescended testes. If the testes do not descend into the scrotum by the age of two, medical treatment is necessary. Undescended testes are more likely than others to develop cancer. Because this condition interferes with the development of healthy sperm, infertility may result. Any male who thinks he may have this condition should seek medical treatment.

Inguinal Hernia Sometimes part of an intestine protrudes into the scrotum through a weakness in the abdominal wall. This condition is called an inguinal hernia. Inguinal hernias can be painful and usually require surgery to correct.

Infertility The condition of being unable to reproduce is called infertility. Both males and females can be infertile. Infertility in a male means that he has too few sperm or that his sperm are unable to fertilize an egg. Male infertility can be caused by a number of factors, including exposure to harmful drugs or X rays, the development of testicular mumps as an adult, or a genetic defect. Medical treatments are available for many kinds of male infertility.

Enlarged Prostate Gland As men get older, the prostate gland frequently gets larger and obstructs the outlet of the urinary bladder. The result is difficulty with urination. An enlarged prostate gland can be dangerous and uncomfortable.

Prostate Cancer Older men are also more likely to get cancer of the prostate gland, which requires surgical treatment. Prostate cancer is the most common cancer in American males, as well as the second most common cause of deaths due to cancer in American males.

Background
Prostrate Cancer

Prostate cancer, a disease that primarily affects men over 50, is the second most common cancer in men. In the 1980s, there was a steady rise in prostate cancer rates, but the rise may be due to increased screening. In the past, surgery was almost always recommended. Now, however, there is a great debate over the best treatment, since no treatment clearly reduces the death rate and some treatments greatly affect quality of life. Prostate cancer spreads slowly, but left untreated, it can cause death within 10 years.

 Section Review Worksheet 16.1

To reinforce the concepts presented in this section, assign Section Review Worksheet 16.1.

 Section Quiz 16.1

Have students take Section Quiz 16.1.

Extension
Male Infertility

In about 40 percent of the cases of infertility in couples, the male is thought to be infertile. Lifestyle and environmental factors, such as drug abuse and exposure to toxic agents, are sometimes the cause. Have students research these two factors and their impact on fertility.

Reteaching
Worksheet 16.1
Students who have difficulty with the material may complete Reteaching Worksheet 16.1.

Review Answers

1. testes
2. testes
3. passage of semen during ejaculation, passage of urine during urination
4. a tail that whips back and forth, its small size, its streamlined shape
5. Answers should include the steps described in Figure 16-5. Stand in front of a mirror and look for any swelling on the scrotum. Roll each testicle gently between the thumbs and fingers while feeling for any lumps, enlargements, tenderness, or change in texture. Report any abnormalities to a physician.
6. When the vas deferens are cut and tied off, mature sperm from the epididymis cannot travel to the urethra and to the outside of the body.

How to Do a Testicular Self-Examination

1. The best time to do the examination is after a warm bath or shower, when the scrotum is relaxed.

2. Stand in front of a mirror and look for any swelling of the scrotum.

3. Check for any lumps, enlargements, tenderness, or changes in texture by rolling each testicle gently between your thumb and fingers.

4. If you notice any abnormalities, report them to your doctor. In order to detect abnormalities as soon as possible, self-examinations should be performed monthly.

(FIGURE 16-5) **If testicular cancer is treated early, there is an excellent chance of recovery.**

Testicular Cancer Testicular cancer is cancer of the testes. It is the most common form of cancer in males between the ages of 15 and 35. The good news about testicular cancer is that if it is detected and treated early, there is an excellent chance of recovery. To make sure that this kind of cancer is detected early, males should do a monthly examination of their testes. See Figure 16-5 for instructions on how to perform a testicular self-examination.

Care of the Male Reproductive System

Males need to follow only a few simple steps to take care of their reproductive organs.

1. Wash the penis and scrotum daily, and check for any sores or bumps.
2. Don't wear extremely tight clothing. Tight clothing over the external reproductive organs can cause pain.
3. Do the testicular self-examination described in Figure 16-5 once a month to detect lumps or other abnormalities.

Review

1. Which male structure makes sperm?

2. Where is the male hormone testosterone produced?

3. What two functions does the male urethra serve?

4. What characteristics of sperm make it possible for them to swim quickly?

5. **LIFE SKILLS: Practicing Self-Care** Briefly describe how to do a testicular self-examination.

6. **Critical Thinking** A vasectomy is an operation in which the vas deferens are cut and tied off. Explain why a vasectomy is a very effective method of preventing pregnancy.

ASSESS

Section Review

Have students answer the Section Review questions.

Alternative Assessment
Male Reproductive System

Ask students to create an outline that documents the production of sperm, their journey, and the fertilization of an egg. The principal parts of the male reproductive system should be identified in the outline.

Closure
Paragraph Description

Have students describe the functions of the male reproductive system and explain how they are carried out.

Section 16.2
The Female Reproductive System

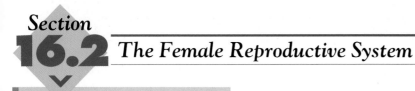

Objectives

- Name the organs of the female reproductive system.

- Trace the path of the egg from the ovary to the uterus.

- Explain how the uterus changes during the menstrual cycle.

- Describe how to do a breast self-examination.
  LIFE SKILLS: Practicing Self-Care

The job of the female reproductive system is to produce an egg and to provide a place where the egg and the sperm can join. After the egg and sperm join, the fertilized egg begins its development into a new individual. The female reproductive system provides the new individual with shelter and nourishment for the nine months before birth. And after birth, a woman's breasts are able to provide nourishment in the form of milk. Because of this, breasts are part of the female reproductive system.

The parts of the female reproductive system, except for the breasts, are shown in Figure 16-6.

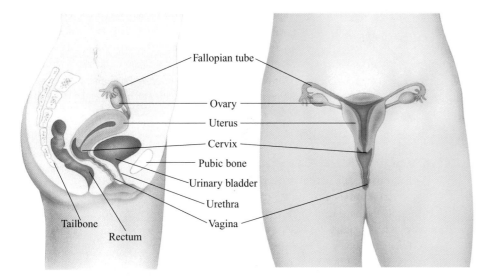

Fallopian tube
Ovary
Uterus
Cervix
Pubic bone
Urinary bladder
Urethra
Vagina
Tailbone
Rectum

(FIGURE 16-6) **The function of the female reproductive system is to produce an egg and provide a place for the egg to be fertilized and to develop.**

Background
Menstrual Cycle vs. Estrus Cycle
Humans are placental mammals. Although gestation times vary, the embryological development of all placental mammals is similar. The great apes—orangutans, chimpanzees, and gorillas—and some Old World monkeys go through a menstrual cycle just as humans do. However, most mammals go through an estrus cycle. During an estrus cycle, some blood may be discharged, but most of the uterine lining is absorbed into the female's body. Also, the female is sexually active only during estrus (also called heat).

Section 16.2 Lesson Plan

MOTIVATE

Journal 16B
The Female Reproductive System

This may be done as a warm-up activity. Have students use their Journal to state the facts they know about the female reproductive system and to list statements they have heard but do not know to be correct. As they read the section, students can verify their facts and unproven statements.

Class Discussion
Mammalian Reproduction

Discuss the ways in which human reproduction is similar to, and different from, reproduction in other mammals. Elicit questions and comments from the students about the female reproductive system.

Background
Hymen and Tampon Use

The hymen is a thin fold of mucous membrane that partly or almost completely covers the vaginal opening. Traditionally a ruptured hymen was considered a sign that a female had experienced sexual intercourse. This is not necessarily true. Hymens vary in thickness, and a thin hymen can be broken during vigorous physical activity, such as playing sports. The hymen may have an opening large enough to insert a tampon. However, some young women have difficulty inserting them, and in this situation, most doctors recommend the use of sanitary napkins. In addition, tampons (especially super-absorbent tampons) need to be changed frequently to prevent toxic shock syndrome. When insertion is difficult, some young women avoid it by leaving tampons in place too long, which puts them at risk of developing toxic shock syndrome.

ovaries:

female reproductive structures that produce eggs and female sex hormones.

ovulation:

the release of an egg from an ovary.

vagina:

female reproductive structure that receives the sperm.

cervix:

the base of the uterus, which bulges down into the vagina; has a small opening through which sperm can enter the uterus.

The Vulva

The parts of the female reproductive system that can be seen from the outside are collectively called the vulva.

The bone in the center of the lower part of the torso is called the pubic bone. Women have extra fat in front of the pubic bone that forms padding. The mound formed by the extra padding is called the mons pubis.

The other parts of the vulva are located between the upper part of the thighs. The two larger folds of skin are called the labia majora. At puberty, pubic hair begins to grow on the mons pubis and the labia majora. Inside the labia majora are two smaller folds of skin called the labia minora.

In between the two folds of the labia minora is the clitoris. Like the penis, the clitoris is the source of the greatest sexual excitement and has the capacity to become erect. It is covered by a hood of skin that is connected to the labia minora.

Below the clitoris is the opening of the urethra. Unlike the urethra of the male, the female's urethra does not have a role in reproduction. The only purpose of the female's urethra is to provide a way for urine to pass out of the body. Below the urethra is the opening of the vagina.

The Vagina and Cervix

The **vagina** is a muscular tube that receives the sperm. At the lower end of the vagina is the opening to the outside of the body. At the upper end is a part of the uterus called the **cervix**, which bulges down into the vagina. In the center of the cervix is a small opening through which sperm can enter the uterus.

During birth, the baby must pass through the cervix and the vagina. For this reason, the vagina is sometimes called the birth canal.

The Ovaries

Two **ovaries** are located in the lower part of the abdomen, one on each side of the uterus. Like the testes, the ovaries have two major functions. The first function of the ovaries is to produce the eggs. Ovaries usually produce only one mature egg at a time.

The second major function of the ovaries is to produce sex hormones. At puberty, these hormones cause a girl to develop breasts, wider hips, pubic and underarm hair, and a rounded body shape. After puberty and until a woman is in her 40's or 50's, these hormones control the monthly release of an egg and the menstrual cycle.

Before a female baby is born, her ovaries begin the development of several hundred thousand eggs. All of these eggs remain in the ovaries in a half-mature state until puberty. After the onset of puberty, hormones cause one of the eggs to complete the process of maturing about once a month. The release of an egg from an ovary is called **ovulation**. After ovulation, the egg is able to be fertilized by a sperm.

Follow the path of the egg as it travels to meet the sperm in Figure 16-7. The arrows show the path of the egg.

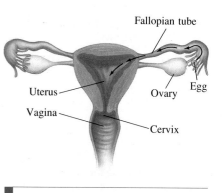

(FIGURE 16-7) **About once a month, an egg leaves a woman's ovary and travels through the fallopian tube to the uterus.**

TEACH

Teaching Transparency 16A
Male and Female Reproductive Systems

Show this transparency, which includes Figure 16-6. Have them point out specific parts of the female reproductive system and trace the path of the egg from the ovary to the uterus.

Class Discussion
Design of the Female Reproductive System

Discuss with students how the parts of the female reproductive system are well-designed to carry out their functions. For example, the vagina is muscular and able to stretch. The cervix remains small but it enlarges during labor to allow birth to occur. The uterus has thick walls, richly supplied with blood, and is also very stretchable. Be sure the students understand that the egg moves along the Fallopian tube to the uterus, whether or not it is fertilized. Ask: **Why is it advantageous for the egg to begin moving immediately rather than waiting for fertilization to occur?** *[Reasons include short life span of sperm, brief period of time during which the mature egg can be fertilized, and the need for the embryo to implant quickly in the uterus.]*

1. **Days 1–5** Menstruation begins. Since the lining of the uterus is not going to host a fertilized egg, the uterus sheds the lining, which then flows from the woman's body.

2. **Days 5–14** The uterine lining begins to thicken and continues to do so until ovulation occurs, which is around day 14.

3. **Days 15–28** The thickened uterine lining awaits a fertilized egg. If the egg is not fertilized, the lining begins to break down.

■ (FIGURE 16-8) **This diagram shows what happens inside the uterus if the egg is not fertilized. During the menstrual cycle, the uterine lining gets thicker and thicker. If the egg is not fertilized, the uterus sheds the lining, which then flows from the body during the menstrual period. However, if the egg is fertilized, the lining will be maintained, and the uterus will expand to many times its usual size.**

The Fallopian Tubes

When an egg has matured, fluid sweeps it from the ovary into one of the fallopian tubes. It is through a fallopian tube that an egg travels from an ovary to the uterus. A fallopian tube is also the place where fertilization occurs.

If the egg meets the sperm while in the upper third of the fallopian tube, it can be fertilized. If the egg is not fertilized within 12 to 24 hours after it is released from the ovary, the egg begins to break down. Once it begins to break down, it can no longer be fertilized. Whether it has been fertilized or not, the egg continues to travel toward the uterus. It reaches the uterus four or five days after it was released from the ovary. If the egg has not been fertilized, it will dissolve in the uterus. If it has been fertilized, it will implant in the wall of the uterus, where it will grow into an embryo.

The Uterus

The **uterus** is a hollow, muscular organ about the size of a fist. It is sometimes called the womb. The main job of the uterus is to provide a place for the baby to grow before birth. During pregnancy, the uterus is able to expand to many times its usual size.

The Menstrual Cycle

The uterus undergoes cyclical changes (approximately on a monthly basis), which prepare it to receive and nourish a fertilized egg. These changes in the uterus are called the menstrual cycle.

During the menstrual cycle, the inner lining of the uterus thickens, and many tiny blood vessels grow into this thickened lining. The changes in the uterine lining are caused by the female sex hormones. Once these changes have occurred, one of two

uterus:

the hollow muscular organ that provides a place for the baby to grow before birth; also called the womb.

Background
The Egg
In most women, only about 400 eggs actually mature over a lifetime. Each egg matures within a follicle, or a sac made of cells, which bursts open when the egg is ready for release. At this time, the follicle is about the size of a pea. The empty follicle is then known as the corpus luteum. The egg does not travel on its own. Rather, fringes and tiny hairs in the fallopian tube draw the egg in and sweep it along. The walls of the tube also contract to help move the egg.

Reinforcement
Menstrual Cycles

Reassure female students that there is a wide range of patterning that is considered normal for menstrual cycles. In addition, while the cycle is becoming established during puberty, it often varies a great deal. Also, outside factors such as illness or stress can delay the onset of a period.

Class Discussion
Multiple Births

Initiate a discussion of multiple births by asking students the following questions: **If a woman's ovaries contain many eggs and a man releases millions of sperm during an ejaculation, why is only one egg usually fertilized?** [Eggs mature in the ovaries at different times, and usually only one mature egg is released during each menstrual cycle.] **What might happen if two eggs were released from the ovaries at the same time?** [If both eggs were fertilized, fraternal twins would result. Since the twins resulted from two sperm and two eggs, they would be genetically different and would not look alike.] **What would happen if one egg were fertilized and later divided into two separate balls of cells?** [Identical twins would result.]

• • • TEACH continues on p. 336

Background
Monthly Cycles

The menstrual cycle, from the Latin word *menses,* meaning "month," is governed by the interaction of the following hormones: follicle-stimulating hormone (FSH), luteinizing hormone (LH), estrogen, and progesterone. This complex cycle can be summarized as follows: (1) The pituitary gland increases its production of FSH and LH. (2) FSH stimulates a follicle to mature, causing estrogen levels to rise. (3) LH triggers the follicle to rupture and release its egg. LH also causes the follicle to develop into a corpus luteum, which produces estrogen and progesterone. (4) The high estrogen and progesterone levels inhibit production of FSH and LH. (5) The estrogen and progesterone cause the uterus to prepare for the implantation of a fertilized egg. (6) If no egg is fertilized, the follicle degenerates and estrogen and progesterone levels drop. (7) In response to these low levels, the pituitary increases its production of FSH and LH, and the cycle is repeated.

things happens, depending on whether the egg has been fertilized by a sperm.

If the egg *has* been fertilized, hormones are released that tell the uterus to maintain its thickened lining. The female is pregnant.

Most of the time, though, the egg has not been fertilized, and the woman is not pregnant. The thickened uterine lining breaks down, and the female menstruates.

Except during pregnancy, most women release an egg approximately every month from puberty until about age 50. Even if a woman has many children, only a small percentage of her eggs will be fertilized and will result in pregnancy.

Menstrual Fluid If the egg has not been fertilized and the female is not pregnant, the blood vessels of the lining close up and then break. The cells of the lining come loose from the inside of the uterus. Blood from the broken blood vessels helps to wash these cells out of the uterus. This mixture of blood and cells is called menstrual fluid. The amount of menstrual fluid varies from female to female. Some females have a light menstrual flow—only about a tablespoon of menstrual fluid each cycle. Others have a heavy flow—eight or more tablespoons each cycle.

The Menstrual Period The menstrual fluid passes through the opening of the cervix and through the vagina to the outside of the body. The time during which the menstrual fluid flows out of the body is called the menstrual period. Most females have menstrual periods that last from three to seven days.

After the menstrual period is completed, the uterus begins to prepare a new thickened lining. This lining will be ready for the next egg that is released from the ovary and travels down the fallopian tube to the uterus.

The average menstrual cycle lasts about 28 days. This is the time from the first day of a menstrual period until the first day of the next menstrual period. However, the length of the menstrual cycle varies. One female might have a 25-day cycle, while her best friend has a 35-day cycle. Yet another female might have a cycle that is a different length each month. This is called an irregular cycle. Irregular cycles are especially common during the first few years after a female begins to menstruate. In addition, a female who usually has a regular cycle may occasionally have a period earlier or later than usual.

The age at which a female has her first menstrual period also varies from individual to individual. Most females begin to menstruate between the ages of 12 and 14. However, it is not unusual for a female to have her first period as young as age 9 or 10. Other females do not have a period until they are 17 or 18. Beginning menstruation at 10 or 13 or 18, having a regular 28-day cycle or one that's shorter or longer—all of these individual differences are perfectly normal.

Disorders of the Female Reproductive System

Menstrual Cramps Menstrual cramps are a very common problem, especially for teenagers. These are the cramps felt in the lower abdominal area that are caused by the contracting of the uterus as it works to expel its lining. Those who have cramps usually have them the first day or two of their menstrual periods, but sometimes the cramps last longer.

Warm baths and exercise can sometimes relieve cramps. However, medication is usually required for severe cramps. There are a variety of nonprescription pain medicines that are effective in relieving cramps. If an over-the-counter formula is not helpful, a doctor should be consulted. He or she may prescribe medication that alleviates menstrual cramps. Cramps usually decrease in severity as a female gets older unless there is an additional medical problem.

PMS (Premenstrual Syndrome) Some females experience a combination of problems before their menstrual periods called PMS (premenstrual syndrome). PMS seems to be most common in females in their thirties. The physical symptoms include swelling and tenderness of the breasts, a bloated feeling, constipation, headaches, and fatigue. The emotional signs of PMS are depression, crying, anxiety, and anger. A female with PMS may have all of these signs and symptoms, or she may have only a few. PMS usually occurs for one to three days before menstruation, but some females may have PMS for two weeks before each menstrual period.

Researchers do not yet know why some females have PMS and others do not. Nor do they know exactly what causes PMS, although hormonal fluctuations may be responsible.

Some women with PMS find that their symptoms are reduced if they restrict their intake of salt and sugar and completely avoid caffeine (in coffee, teas, colas, and chocolate) and nicotine (in tobacco). Regular physical exercise and relaxation exercises, such as those described in Chapter 9, are also reported to help some women. If a woman feels she has symptoms of PMS, she should seek medical treatment.

Vaginitis An infection in the vagina is called vaginitis. Most women will have vaginitis sometime during their lives. The signs and symptoms include itching or soreness of the vulva, an unpleasant odor, an increase in discharge from the vagina, and

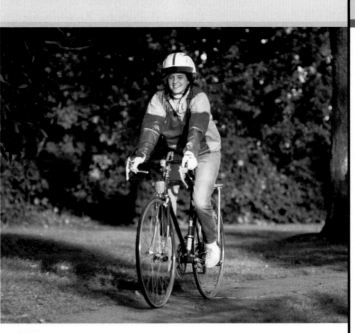

(FIGURE 16-9) **Getting plenty of exercise can help alleviate the pain and tension that sometimes accompany a woman's menstrual period.**

sometimes a burning sensation during urination. Vaginitis can be caused by a fungus, bacteria, or protozoa, and each kind of vaginitis requires a different kind of treatment. Douching for vaginitis is not recommended, because it may aggravate the infection. If a female has any of the symptoms of vaginitis, she should seek medical treatment to get the correct medication.

It is important to know that *most* fluids from the vagina are perfectly normal. If the fluid is clear or whitish and nonirritating, it is probably normal. Many factors besides an infection can create vaginal fluids— sexual excitement and hormonal changes are two examples. All women have these kinds of secretions. It is only when the fluid is irritating, has an offensive odor, or changes color that a woman should become concerned about infection.

SECTION 16.2

Life Skills Worksheet 16B
Assign the Caring for the Female Body Life Skills Worksheet.

Background
Disorders

Ovarian cysts often develop where a follicle has enlarged but has failed to break open and release an egg. The cyst may be fluid-filled or solid. Many are harmless and go away by themselves. Large ones can cause pain, abdominal swelling, or even abnormal menstruation. In these cases, surgery may be necessary.

Endometriosis is a disorder affecting some 10 million women in the United States. In the past, conventional surgery has been the only option to alleviate this condition. Now, thanks to laser laparoscopy, there is a quicker, safer option. A laparoscope (a thin, lighted telescope) is inserted through a small incision in the abdomen and used to view the reproductive organs and guide the laser. The laser is inserted through a second small incision and used to destroy unwanted tissues.

Pap test:

a medical procedure in which cells from the cervix are removed and tested for cancer.

Sexually transmitted diseases (STDs) can cause infertility. The relationship between STDs and infertility is discussed in Chapter 22.

Toxic Shock Syndrome Toxic shock syndrome, a rare but dangerous bacterial infection, is associated with the use of highly absorbent tampons. Tampons should be changed frequently (at least every 4–6 hours) to help prevent this infection.

The signs and symptoms of toxic shock syndrome are a high fever, nausea, diarrhea, dizziness, and a sunburn-like rash. The rash is often on the palms of the hands and the bottoms of the feet. A woman who has these signs and symptoms should remove the tampon and go to a hospital emergency room immediately because toxic shock syndrome can cause death.

Ovarian Cysts An ovarian cyst is a growth on the ovary. A woman with an ovarian cyst may experience pain or may have no signs or symptoms at all. Large cysts must be treated medically, but small cysts sometimes disappear without any treatment.

Cancers Cancer can occur in any part of the female reproductive system. The more sexual partners a female has, the greater her risk of developing cervical cancer is. Doctors recommend that all sexually active females, regardless of age, have a yearly pelvic examination to detect cancers early. The earlier the cancer is caught, the more successful the treatment will be. During the examination, the doctor will do what is called a **Pap test**, in which cells from the cervix are removed and tested for cancer. This test saves many lives every year.

Women should also get in the habit of checking their breasts for lumps and other abnormalities each month. Figure 16-10 describes how to do a breast self-examination. Most lumps are found this way and are not cancerous, but any lump should be checked out by a doctor to make sure.

Doctors recommend regular mammograms (an X ray of the breast) beginning when a woman is about 35 years old. If cancer of the breast is detected and treated early, there is an excellent chance of recovery. For this reason, regular breast self-examinations can be lifesaving.

Infertility Females, like males, can be infertile, or unable to have children. The most common cause of female infertility is failure to ovulate—to release an egg. Often, women who are underweight because of an eating disorder or excessive exercise do not ovulate. Another common cause of infertility is scar tissue in the fallopian tubes, which prevents the sperm from reaching the egg. The scar tissue may have been the result of an infection or previous surgery. Sexually transmitted diseases may result in infertility, as can endometriosis, a condition in which tissue from the endometrial lining of the uterus grows somewhere else in the abdomen. Many causes of infertility can be treated medically.

Care of the Female Reproductive System

The female reproductive system may seem more complicated than the male system, but it actually doesn't require much more care. Females should take the following simple steps to keep everything working smoothly:

1. Wash the external reproductive organs daily with a mild, nonirritating soap. Feel for any unusual bumps or sores.
2. Don't use "feminine hygiene" sprays. They can cause irritation. If daily washing doesn't keep you clean, you should seek the advice of a health care provider. An unpleasant odor may be a sign of an infection. Remember, though, that for vaginal secretions to have a scent is perfectly normal. As a female gets older, she gets better at telling the difference between the usual healthy scent and an odor that means infection.

---

3. Don't use douches unless they are medicinal douches recommended for you by your doctor. Like sprays, douches are usually unnecessary, and they can cause irritation.

4. During menstruation, change sanitary pads or tampons often—at least every 4–6 hours. In addition, do not use deodorant tampons, or tampons with greater absorbency than you need.

SECTION 16.2

 Section Review Worksheet 16.2
To reinforce the concepts presented in this section, assign Section Review Worksheet 16.2.

 Section Quiz 16.2
Have students take Section Quiz 16.2.

Reteaching Worksheet 16.2
Students who have difficulty with the material may complete Reteaching Worksheet 16.2.

How to Do a Breast Self-Examination

Do a breast self-exam once a month. Two or three days after your menstrual period ends is the best time because the breasts are less likely to be tender or swollen.

1. *Stand in front of a mirror and look carefully at your breasts. Look for anything unusual, such as a discharge from the nipples or a puckering, dimpling, or scaling of the skin.*

2. *Clasp your hands behind your head and press your hands forward. Do you notice any change in the shape of your breasts since the last time you did a breast self-exam?*

3. *Press your hands firmly on your hips and bow slightly forward. Pull your shoulders and elbows forward. Do you notice any change in the shape of your breasts since the last time you did a breast self-exam?*

4. *Raise your left arm. Use your fingers to examine your left breast. Beginning at the outer edge of your breast, press the flat part of your fingers in small circles, moving the circles slowly around the breast. Make sure to include the area between the breast and the armpit, as well as the armpit itself. Do you feel any unusual lumps under the skin? Repeat the step on your right breast with your right arm raised.*

5. *Gently squeeze each nipple, and look for any discharge.*

6. *Lie down and put a pillow or folded towel under your left shoulder. Raise your left arm. Examine your left breast the same way you did in Step 4. Repeat with your right breast.*

(FIGURE 16-10) **Breast self-examination should be done once a month to become familiar with the usual appearance and feel of your breasts. Most lumps are not cancerous, but any lump should be checked out by a doctor to make sure.**

Extension
Female Infertility

Blocked fallopian tubes and failure to ovulate are the two leading causes of female infertility. Have students research the underlying causes and the treatments for these two conditions.

Review Answers

1. ovary
2. fallopian tube
3. It breaks down and is shed.
4. Answers should include the steps described in Figure 16-10. Stand before a mirror and look at each breast for anything unusual. Repeat, clasping hands behind your head and pressing hands forward, and pressing hands on hips and bowing forward. Raise each arm in turn and use the fingers of the other hand to feel the breast and armpit for any lumps. Gently squeeze each nipple and look for any discharge. Lying down, repeat the examination of each breast.
5. When the fallopian tubes are cut and tied off, sperm cannot travel through the tubes to meet and fertilize an egg.

Highly absorbent tampons increase the risk of toxic shock syndrome, a rare but deadly disease. Deodorant tampons may cause irritation or infection.

5. Visit a health care provider once a year to make sure that your reproductive system is healthy. A gynecologist is a physician who specializes in caring for the female reproductive system. Young women should start getting yearly gynecological exams at the age of 18, or earlier if they are sexually active.

6. Perform a monthly breast self-examination to find lumps or other abnormalities. (See Figure 16-10.) The best time to do a self-examination is a few days after a menstrual period, when the breasts are less likely to be tender.

Q: I am almost 14 years old, and I still haven't started having menstrual periods. Could there be something wrong with me?

A: It is not abnormal for a girl to be 14 or 15 years old before she begins to menstruate. A girl who has reached the age of 16 and has not menstruated should probably see a doctor to make sure she doesn't have a medical problem.

◆◆◆

Q: Someone told me that a woman can't get pregnant the first time she has sexual intercourse. Is this true?

A: No. A woman is just as likely to get pregnant the first time as she is at any other time.

◆◆◆

Q: Can a woman get pregnant even if she doesn't have an orgasm during sexual intercourse?

A: Yes. Pregnancy can occur regardless of whether a woman has an orgasm.

◆◆◆

Q: Can a woman get pregnant if her partner ejaculates outside her body?

A: Yes. Sometimes fluid containing sperm is released before ejaculation. And when a man ejaculates when his penis is outside the vagina, there is still a chance that sperm can enter the vaginal passage and fertilize the egg, causing pregnancy.

Review

1. Which female structure produces the eggs?

2. In which structure do the egg and the sperm join?

3. What happens to the thickened uterine lining if fertilization does not occur?

4. ▪▪ **LIFE SKILLS: Practicing Self-Care** Briefly describe how to do a breast self-examination.

5. **Critical Thinking** A tubal ligation is an operation in which the fallopian tubes are cut and tied off. Explain why tubal ligation is a very effective method of preventing pregnancy.

ASSESS

Section Review

Have students answer the Section Review questions.

Alternative Assessment
Newspaper Health Column

Have students write an imaginary newspaper health column answering letters from teens with questions about the female reproductive system. Encourage them to use the information they learned in this section to answer the letters.

Closure
Female Life Cycle

Have volunteers use the chalkboard to summarize and illustrate what happens to an egg from the time a female is born until she conceives an offspring.

Section 16.3
Pregnancy, Birth, and Childhood Development

Objectives

- List the substances that can pass from the mother to the placenta.

- Describe the events that occur during birth.

- Use self-talk about childhood experiences to increase your self-esteem.

■■ LIFE SKILLS: Building Self-Esteem

For most parents, the birth of a child is both exciting and scary. Raising a child can bring parents a great deal of happiness and a sense that they are doing something truly worthwhile. When parents see a bit of themselves in the shape of their child's nose or in their child's way of laughing, they know that a part of themselves will live on after they are gone.

But having a child is also a tremendous responsibility. Parenthood means sacrifices and sleepless nights, losing freedom and gaining worries. The decision of whether to have children is important and shouldn't be taken lightly. This decision will be discussed in Chapter 18. In the rest of this chapter, you'll learn what happens after the sperm and the egg join.

■ (FIGURE 16-11) **Parenthood can be one of the most fulfilling experiences in life, but it is also a tremendous responsibility.**

SECTION 16.3

📇 Making a Choice 16A

Assign the Thoughts About Having Children card. The card asks students to examine their plans and feelings about having a family.

Section 16.3 Lesson Plan

MOTIVATE

Journal 16C
Feelings About Becoming Parents

This may be done as a warm-up activity. Refer students to the photograph shown in Figure 16-11. Ask: **How do you think the man and woman feel about becoming parents?** Have students write in their Journal what they think it would be like to become a parent.

Writing
Stages of Life So Far

Have students write a descriptive paragraph, poem, or short story about stages they feel they have passed through since birth. For each stage, they might describe the physical and psychological gains that were made.

Background
Ectopic Pregnancy

If a fertilized egg implants itself anywhere other than the uterus, an ectopic pregnancy results. Ninety-five percent of ectopic pregnancies occur in a fallopian tube. The number of ectopic pregnancies is rising. This rise is attributed to the increased incidence of pelvic inflammatory disease (PID). The tubule damage and scarring from PID inhibit the movement of the egg down the fallopian tube. This sometimes results in tubule implantation. As the embryo grows, the tube stretches and eventually ruptures, creating a life-threatening situation. Early detection can be difficult because the clinical symptoms of an ectopic pregnancy are very similar to those of spontaneous abortion. Several treatments are available, and the mortality rate for ectopic pregnancies has declined. However, if the tube is destroyed and the other tube has also been scarred by PID, fertility is greatly compromised and the risk of another ectopic pregnancy is high.

embryo:

a fertilized egg after it has attached itself to the wall of the uterus.

Implantation

Before fertilization, the sperm and the egg are two separate cells, which each contain *one-half* of the information needed for the development of a new person. After fertilization, there is only one cell, and it contains *all* of the information needed for the development of a new person.

After ejaculation, it usually takes the sperm between 15 minutes and an hour to reach the fallopian tube and fertilize the egg. The fertilized egg then travels toward the uterus. Figure 16-12 shows the path of the egg.

About 30 hours after fertilization, the egg divides into two cells. The two cells then divide into four cells, the four cells into eight cells, and so on. About four days after fertilization, the fertilized egg finally reaches the uterus.

As the fertilized egg comes to rest on the soft, thick lining of the uterus, it begins to burrow into the lining. It is now called an **embryo**. By the 10th day after fertilization, the embryo contains thousands of cells and is completely buried in the uterine wall. This process is called implantation.

From Mother to Baby

As the embryo implants itself in the wall of the uterus, it begins to use up all of the nutrients that were stored in the egg before fertilization. If the embryo is to survive, it must have a way to obtain everything it needs as it grows from the mother. The placenta is the structure that allows the embryo to get what it needs from the mother. The placenta is a disc-shaped organ that is attached to the inner wall of the uterus. It is connected to the embryo by a structure called the umbilical cord.

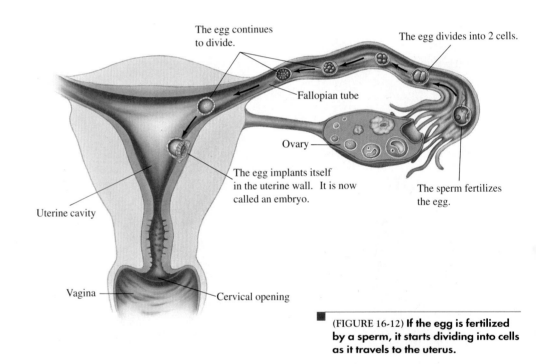

The egg continues to divide.

The egg divides into 2 cells.

Fallopian tube

Ovary

The egg implants itself in the uterine wall. It is now called an embryo.

The sperm fertilizes the egg.

Uterine cavity

Vagina

Cervical opening

(FIGURE 16-12) **If the egg is fertilized by a sperm, it starts dividing into cells as it travels to the uterus.**

TEACH

Teaching Transparency 16C
Fertilization

Show the transparency of Figure 16-12. Have students describe the changes the fertilized egg undergoes during this journey and explain what happens to it when it reaches the uterus.

Demonstration
Crossing the Placental Barrier

Divide an area of the chalkboard into two parts. One part will represent the mother's blood, the other the developing baby's blood. Draw a thick, shaded line between these two parts to represent the placenta. Provide students with a list of substances that are exchanged in the placenta. These include oxygen, carbon dioxide, nutrients, antibodies, and wastes. Ask students to draw arrows on the chalkboard, showing the movement of these substances between the mother and baby.

Reinforcement
Prenatal Care

Poor prenatal care is one major cause of the low birth weight and high mortality rate for infants born to teenage mothers. Have students suggest a list of do's and don'ts for a pregnant woman. Write these on the chalkboard

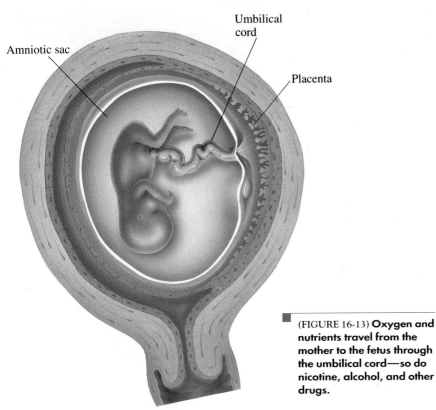

Amniotic sac

Umbilical cord

Placenta

(FIGURE 16-13) **Oxygen and nutrients travel from the mother to the fetus through the umbilical cord—so do nicotine, alcohol, and other drugs.**

Background
Calculating Date of Birth
The human period of gestation is 280 days, or about 9 months. To calculate the approximate date of a baby's birth, first determine when the pregnant woman's last period began. Then count back three months from the first day of this period. Add seven days plus one year.

The mother's blood does not flow into the baby. Instead, pools of blood are formed in the placenta that bathe the outside of the embryo's blood vessels.

Oxygen, antibodies, and nutrients from the mother's blood diffuse through the walls of the embryo's blood vessels in the placenta. These things then travel through the blood vessels in the umbilical cord to the baby.

Viruses and drugs can also pass from the mother's blood to the baby's blood. Some viruses and drugs can cause the baby to develop abnormally. For this reason, pregnant women should take good care of their health and avoid exposure to diseases. In addition, a pregnant woman should never take any drug without checking with her doctor first. This includes alcohol, nicotine, and nonprescription drugs, such as aspirin and cold remedies.

Changes During Pregnancy

Once implanted in the uterus, the embryo grows rapidly. A heart and brain begin to form. Eyes appear and the face takes shape. Small buds on the sides of the body become arms and legs. Internal organs like the lungs, stomach, and liver are developing. The embryo floats in a warm, fluid-filled pouch called the amniotic sac.

Eight weeks after fertilization occurs, the embryo is only 30 mm long (a little over 1 inch). However, all the major organ systems of its body are formed and growing. From the ninth week until birth, it is called a **fetus**.

fetus:

a developing individual from the ninth week of pregnancy until birth.

as students explain why each is important. *(The developing baby requires good food and plenty of fluid intake by the mother. Toxins and other harmful substances taken in by the mother can pass through the placenta and enter the blood of the embryo or fetus, where they can retard development or cause defects or congenital diseases. For these reasons, it is important that women who are pregnant eat well, drink plenty of healthful fluids, avoid alcohol, tobacco, and most drugs, and get the proper amount of exercise and rest.)*

Cooperative Learning
Stages of Development

Divide the class into small groups and assign each group a stage of embryo or fetal development to explore in depth. You might assign the stages shown in Figure 16-14 on page 342. Allow out-of-class or library time for students to locate information in books, magazines, and pamphlets. For each stage, have them tell what happens to the developing baby and how it can be affected by the mother's actions.

(FIGURE 16-14)

18 weeks

24 weeks

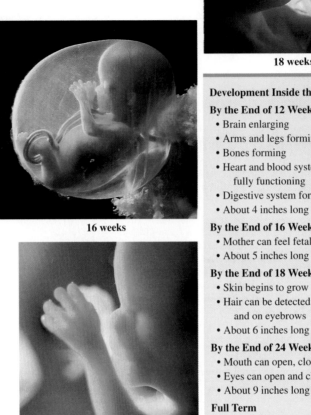

16 weeks

12 weeks

Development Inside the Uterus

By the End of 12 Weeks
• Brain enlarging
• Arms and legs forming
• Bones forming
• Heart and blood system fully functioning
• Digestive system forming
• About 4 inches long

By the End of 16 Weeks
• Mother can feel fetal movements
• About 5 inches long

By the End of 18 Weeks
• Skin begins to grow
• Hair can be detected on upper lip and on eyebrows
• About 6 inches long

By the End of 24 Weeks
• Mouth can open, close, and swallow
• Eyes can open and close
• About 9 inches long

Full Term
• Features, organs fully formed
• 18–22 inches long

full term

Pregnancy Tests

When a female misses a menstrual period, it is a sign that she *might* be pregnant. However, a number of other factors, like stress and illness, might also explain a missed period. A missed period is not a very reliable indicator of pregnancy.

An accurate pregnancy test detects a hormone called HCG (human chorionic gonadotropin). Three weeks after fertilization, a pregnant female will probably have enough HCG in her blood and urine for a positive test result. Doctors and health clinics can administer these tests.

Pregnancy "test kits" can be obtained at drug stores. These kits also test for the presence of HCG. However, they must be administered correctly to be accurate. If a negative result is obtained, the test should be done again. If the result is positive, the woman should visit a doctor or clinic to do another test to confirm the result.

• • • TEACH continued

Demonstration
Growth of the Fetus

Supply students with the following information on fetal size. Have students work in pairs to create three-dimensional models of a fetus at different developmental stages. Students will need rulers and modeling materials, such as clay or papier mâché. They may want to obtain reference books that show pictures or illustrations of fetal development. Each model should be accompanied by a written explanation including the following details about the fetus: length, weight, stage of development, and changes that occur at that stage.

Teaching Transparency 16D
Stages of Childbirth

Show the transparency of Figure 16-15. Have students explain the changes and events that are illustrated in each picture. The transparency may also prove useful for reference in answering questions students may have about childbirth, such as: What if the baby is not in the right position? How is a baby removed by Caesarean section?

End of	Size of Fetus
Month 1	.25 in. (0.6 cm)
Month 3	4 in. (10.2 cm); 1 oz. (28.3 g)
Month 5	12 in. (30.5 cm); 1 lb. (453.6 g)
Month 7	14–15 in. (35.6–38.1 cm); 2–2.5 lb. (907.2–1,134 g)
Month 9	18–20 in. (45.7–50.8 cm); 7–9 lb. (3,175.2–4,082.4 g)

Childbirth

The stages of the birth of a baby are shown in Figure 16-15. By the time the baby is ready to be born, it has usually moved so that its head is down against the cervix. The cervix is a ring of very strong muscles at the lower part of the uterus. These muscles are able to hold a developing fetus and surrounding fluids inside the uterus without relaxing until the baby is ready to be born.

Background
Baby's Head Shape
Several bones on the top of a baby's head (cranium) are not fused as they are in adults; they are soft and pliable. This allows them to shift during delivery so the head can pass through the birth canal. Often a baby's head appears somewhat misshapen at birth, but within a few days it returns to normal. (For more information about an infant's skull, see the Body Systems Handbook, p. 663.)

(2)

(3)

(4)

(1)

(5)

(FIGURE 16-15)

The birth of a child These drawings show various stages of childbirth. (1) A month or two before birth, the fetus drops to a lower position. (2) In the first stage of delivery (dilation), strong uterine contractions cause the cervix to dilate. (3) By the end of this stage, the cervix has completely dilated, the membranes surrounding the baby have ruptured, and the head has begun to extend into the birth canal. (4) During the second stage (expulsion), the head emerges fully and the shoulders rotate. (5) By the third stage (placental), the baby has been born. The uterus expels the placenta and the umbilical cord.

Debate the Issue
Pregnancy and Drugs

In some states, authorities think that women who abuse drugs during pregnancy should be prosecuted for child abuse. Debate this issue. Should the women be charged? What purpose will it serve if these women are convicted? Are there other ways to deter drug and alcohol abuse during pregnancy that do not involve criminal charges?

Extension
Memoirs

Have groups of students research a child's growth and developmental stages during the first 18 months of life. This research could be organized in several ways. Groups could be assigned specific time periods, for example, the first three months. Or they could be assigned to research specific behaviors, for example, changes in facial expressions, recognition of people and objects in the environment, movements, etc. Have each group make a presentation to the class that includes visuals.

Background
Postpartum Period

The first few weeks following childbirth are called the postpartum period. For the first two to three days, hormonal changes in the mother cause her breasts to secrete colostrum, a substance that contains proteins, antibodies, fat-soluble vitamins, and some minerals. Then other hormones cause milk production to begin. Between 10 percent and 15 percent of new mothers experience what is referred to as postpartum depression. Researchers now think this hormone-induced depression is caused by the relationships between the placenta, the hypothalamus of the brain, and the corticotropin-releasing hormone (CRH). During the last trimester of pregnancy, the placenta produces large amounts of CRH, so the hypothalamus reduces its production. After childbirth, the placenta is expelled, so CRH levels drop dramatically. It takes a while for the hypothalamus to increase its production again. In the meantime, some women become depressed because of low cortisol levels.

(FIGURE 16-16) **It is common for the father of the baby to take part in childbirth by providing comfort and encouragement to the woman in labor.**

Birth defects are discussed in Chapter 24.

Near the end of the pregnancy, muscles in the walls of the uterus begin to contract. Weak, irregular contractions may occur for several weeks before birth. When it is time for the baby to be born, the contractions become much stronger and last longer. They also start to come at regular intervals, closer and closer together. The final stage of pregnancy, when contractions are strong enough to push the baby out of the mother's body, is called labor. Labor usually takes between five and twenty hours.

Contractions press the baby's head against the cervix. They force the cervix to open wide enough for the baby to pass through. The baby then passes through the vagina and out into the world. Within a few seconds the baby takes its first breath. The baby no longer needs the placenta, so the umbilical cord is cut.

The placenta then separates from the wall of the uterus. Soon after the baby is born, the placenta and umbilical cord are pushed out of the uterus. The process of childbirth is then complete.

More and more hospitals are allowing fathers, friends of the mother, and even brothers and sisters of the newborn to be present at the birth. And some women choose to deliver their children at home with the help of a midwife—a person trained in childbirth—or a doctor. Some women receive pain-relieving medication during labor and delivery. In addition, many women take childbirth classes that help them and their birthing partner prepare for the process ahead.

Though most pregnancies and births go smoothly and normally, complications sometimes occur. Figure 16-17 on page 345 describes some complications of pregnancy and birth.

Complications of Pregnancy and Birth

Complication	Description
Ectopic pregnancy	The pregnancy tissue or embryo becomes implanted in the fallopian tube or somewhere else in the abdomen besides the uterus. The embryo may die and frequently must be removed by surgery.
Miscarriage (spontaneous abortion)	The pregnancy tissue or embryo is expelled from the uterus before it is sufficiently developed. Miscarriages may be caused by a genetic defect, illness in the mother, drugs the mother has taken, or other factors. Miscarriages usually occur during the first three months of pregnancy.
Toxemia	The pregnant woman has high blood pressure, swelling, and protein in the urine. Untreated toxemia can result in convulsions, coma, and the death of both mother and infant. It is most common among teenagers, older women, and women who already have health problems.
Rh incompatibility	A woman's blood produces an antibody that attacks a substance in the infant's blood cells. This may occur if the woman is Rh negative and the infant is Rh positive. The problem can be avoided by injections that prevent a woman's blood from making the Rh antibody.
Premature birth	A baby is born before it is fully developed. A baby is considered to be premature if it is born before the 37th week of pregnancy. Premature babies are placed in a newborn intensive-care unit, where the baby is protected while it continues to develop.
Cesarean section	If delivery through the birth canal is considered to be risky for any reason, an operation called a Cesarean section is performed. An incision is made through the abdomen and uterus, and the baby is taken from the mother's body.
Multiple births	Two or more infants are born together. Two infants are called twins, three are called triplets, and four are called quadruplets. The birth of five infants—quintuplets—is extremely rare.
Stillbirth	An infant that is born dead 22 weeks or more after conception.

(FIGURE 16-17) **Most pregnancies and births go smoothly and normally, but complications sometimes occur.**

Background
Cocaine Babies

The results of early research suggested that the children of mothers who used cocaine and crack cocaine suffered severe and perhaps permanent ailments. To date, there is a lack of definitive evidence to support these suggestions. However, cocaine use is not benign. Heavy cocaine users have a high rate of miscarriages, premature births, and low-birth-weight babies. Babies born to cocaine-addicted mothers often have a lengthy hospital stay, primarily because of their subnormal weight.

Section Review Worksheet 16.3

To reinforce the concepts presented in this section, assign Section Review Worksheet 16.3.

Section Quiz 16.3

Have students take Section Quiz 16.3.

Reteaching Worksheet 16.3

Students who have difficulty with the material may complete Reteaching Worksheet 16.3.

(FIGURE 16-18) **Babies who are born before they are fully developed are called premature babies. This premature infant weighed only 1 pound, 14 ounces at birth. Even babies this small respond to a parent's care.**

Infancy Through Childhood

Imagine what it was like living in the womb. You didn't have to eat or breathe, and you didn't have to adjust to different temperatures and different environments. Suddenly, all of that changed. After you were born, food had to be taken into the mouth, and air into the lungs. And you had to let it be known that you needed something (for example, you were cold and needed to be covered with a blanket).

After you were born, you continued to grow and develop. You grew taller and stronger throughout infancy and childhood, and you are probably *still* growing. In addition, you developed in other ways. About a month after you were born, you started to smile when you saw a human face. By six months, you could recognize the familiar people who cared for you, and you probably cried when a stranger tried to hold you. A few months later, you could sit up by yourself and play with simple toys.

(FIGURE 16-19) **You started to smile when you were about one month old.**

*Life*SKILLS: Practicing Self-Care

Using Self-Talk About Childhood Experiences . . . .

Your childhood experiences were probably the most important influences on your self-esteem. Some of the experiences made you feel great about yourself. Others, unfortunately, were painful and made you feel terrible. The following activity will help you understand *why* you feel the way you do about yourself, and it may help you increase your self-esteem.

1. Make a list of five childhood experiences that made you feel good about yourself.

2. Say positive things to yourself about each experience. If one of your positive experiences was winning an award for a piece of art you made, you could say, ''I'm proud that I can draw so well.''

3. For the following examples, try to think of something you could say to yourself that might help counteract negative feelings you would have if you were in that situation. For example, if it took Nick longer to read than it takes most kids, he could say to

himself, ''Well, at least I learned to read, which is something that a lot of people never learn to do.''

a. Felicia's parents got divorced last year, and now she spends the summers with her dad and the school year with her mom.

b. When Rudy was 10 years old, his parents had another child.

c. Kids at school made fun of Laura because she was the tallest kid in her class.

This kind of talking to yourself is called self-talk. Self-talk is a very effective way of making the most of positive experiences and minimizing the effect of negative ones.

Life SKILLS

Have students complete the Life Skills activity in the text, making the list and working through the suggested self-talk responses.

Making a Choice 16B

Assign the Childhood Memories card. The card asks students to recall some memories from early childhood and to identify one that made them feel good about themselves.

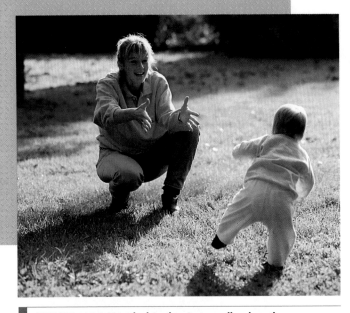

(FIGURE 16-20) **Most babies begin to walk when they are about one year old.**

When you were about one year old, you were determined to learn to walk. No one has to teach a baby how to pull itself up onto its own two feet and take its first steps. In fact, it would be difficult to stop a baby from learning to walk.

As a toddler, you were also learning how to talk. The sounds you had been hearing all your life began to have meaning, and you struggled to imitate them. You may have learned that "ba-ba" could cause an adult to give you a bottle of milk or that your mother was delighted when you waved and said "bye-bye."

During your childhood years, you learned how to be more independent. You learned to go to the cabinet for food when you were hungry, rather than sitting in your room and crying until you were fed. You were allowed to go to a friend's house by yourself. You learned how to cross the street safely. You went to school.

School occupied a major part of your day, and you learned a great deal there.

You learned a lot of facts, of course, but you also learned how to get along with people different from you and your family.

These years prepared you for adolescence. Your childhood experiences enabled you to make friends, prepared you to be able to study and learn well, and helped you to be confident that you can make effective decisions.

If you do the Life Skills activity on page 347, it may help you to understand how early experiences can affect your self-esteem.

You also grew *physically* in preparation for adolescence. Your height and weight increased quite a bit, and your coordination improved. These and other physical changes became even more dramatic as you approached puberty. In the next chapter, you'll learn about the changes that occur during adolescence.

Review

1. What substances pass through the placenta from the mother to the fetus?

2. Describe how the uterus and the cervix change during labor.

3. **LIFE SKILLS: Building Self-Esteem** Think of one aspect of yourself that you really like. Practice self-talk by stating a positive conclusion that you've made about yourself.

4. **Critical Thinking** AIDS is caused by a virus. Explain how this virus, HIV, may be transmitted from a pregnant woman to her developing child.

Highlights

Summary

- The union of sperm and egg is called fertilization.

- The testes, vas deferens, urethra, and penis are the major organs of the male reproductive system.

- The testes make sperm and produce the male hormone testosterone. The amount of testosterone increases at puberty, causing boys' bodies to change.

- Even though only one sperm can fuse with the egg, the presence of many sperm is necessary for this to happen.

- In the female, the vagina, the ovaries, the fallopian tubes, and the uterus make up the internal reproductive system.

- The ovaries produce eggs and sex hormones. After puberty, these hormones control the monthly release of an egg.

- The egg and sperm join in one of the fallopian tubes.

- The uterus provides a place for a baby to grow before birth.

- Monthly breast self-examinations and yearly visits to a gynecologist for a Pap test can help a women keep her reproductive system healthy.

- The fertilized egg implants itself on the wall of the uterus and gets oxygen and the nutrients it needs from its mother through the placenta and umbilical cord.

Vocabulary

sperm male reproductive cell; contains one-half of the instructions needed for the development of a new human being.

egg female reproductive cell, also called an ovum; contains one-half of the instructions needed for the development of a new human being.

fertilization the union of a sperm and an egg.

testes male reproductive structures that make sperm and produce the male hormone testosterone.

ovaries female reproductive structures that produce eggs and female sex hormones.

uterus the hollow muscular organ that provides a place for the baby to grow before birth; also called the womb.

embryo a fertilized egg after it has attached itself to the wall of the uterus.

fetus a developing individual from the ninth week of pregnancy until birth.

SUMMARY
Have students read the summary to reinforce the concepts they have learned in Chapter 16.

VOCABULARY
Have students play a game in which they guess vocabulary words by suggesting letters that fill in the blanks for a particular word. For example, embryo would start out as _ _ _ _ _ _, and letters would be filled in as students make correct suggestions. The student who guesses the word has the first chance to give the definition. Terms other than vocabulary words could also be included.

EXTENSION
Students who are interested could investigate child-raising customs from different cultures or periods of time. For example, today we think that infants need to be free to move, but many cultures still swaddle, or wrap, infants to restrict their movement.

Chapter Review

CHAPTER REVIEW

Concept Review

1. b	5. a
2. d	6. d
3. c	7. a
4. d	8. d

Expressing Your Views

Sample responses:

1. Responses will vary but should include abstaining from ingesting any substance that could be harmful to the fetus, such as alcohol, tobacco smoke, and illegal drugs. Also, answers should note that all drugs and medication should be used only with the physician's approval.

2. A large number of sperm are released to ensure that some will reach the egg. Many sperm die during their journey through the female reproductive tract. The head of the sperm contains an enzyme that breaks down the outer layer of the egg. Many sperm are needed to break down this layer so that one sperm can enter the egg.

Life Skills Check

1. Sample response: He should see his doctor immediately, as the swelling and soreness could be a sign of a serious problem.

2. Answers will vary depending upon the characteristic of their personalities students wish to change.

Concept Review

1. Sperm are made in the
   a. urethra.
   b. testes.
   c. penis.
   d. testosterone.

2. When a sperm joins with an egg, it is called
   a. ovulation.
   b. premenstrual syndrome.
   c. ejaculation.
   d. fertilization.

3. A disorder of the male reproductive system is
   a. circumcision.
   b. toxic shock syndrome.
   c. undescended testes.
   d. epididymis.

4. The female reproductive system includes
   a. the ovaries.
   b. the fallopian tubes.
   c. the uterus.
   d. all of these.

5. Egg cells and female sex hormones are produced in the
   a. ovaries.
   b. cervix.
   c. vagina.
   d. vulva.

6. When the uterus sheds its lining, it is called
   a. premenstrual syndrome.
   b. ovulation.
   c. vaginitis.
   d. menstruation.

7. Which of the following behaviors provides good screening for young women against breast cancer?
   a. monthly self-examinations
   b. loose-fitting clothing
   c. yearly mammograms
   d. body cleanliness

8. From the mother, the fetus can receive
   a. viruses.
   b. oxygen.
   c. nutrients.
   d. all of these.

Expressing Your Views

1. Keeping in mind that an embryo or fetus receives all of its nourishment from the mother through the placenta and the umbilical cord, list some practices you think a pregnant woman should avoid.

2. Millions of sperm are released in one ejaculation. Why do you think so many are released if only one is needed to fertilize an egg?

Life Skills Check

1. Practicing Self-Care

A friend has confided in you that he has been having soreness and swelling in his testes. He is hesitant to visit a doctor. What advice would you give him?

2. Building Self-Esteem

Most people have sides to their personality that they would like to change in order to feel better about themselves. Think of one aspect of your personality you think you would like to change. How could you change this trait or at least develop it to be more positive?

Projects

1. Go to the local library to look for information about the immunities passed from mother to baby in breast milk. Take notes on your findings, and present them to your teacher.

2. If you are male, find out if there are any risk factors for testicular cancer, and write a one-page report about your findings. If you are female, write a one-page report about behaviors or environmental factors that are associated with breast cancer.

Plan for Action

Males and females need to follow only a few basic steps to take care of their reproductive organs. Plan a daily, monthly, and yearly routine to ensure a healthy reproductive system and to prevent disorders from occurring.

Projects

Have students complete the projects on fetal immunity and breast or testicular cancer.

Plan for Action

Plans will vary. Be certain that students include monthly preventive checks in their plans.

ASSESSMENT OPTIONS

Chapter Test

Have students take the Chapter 16 Test.

Alternative Assessment

Have students do the Alternative Assessment activity for Chapter 16.

Test Generator

The Test Generator contains additional assessment items for this chapter.

CHAPTER 17
Adolescence: Relationships and Responsibilities

SECTION	TITLE/OBJECTIVES	PERSONAL INVENTORY			LIFE SKILLS DEVELOPMENT			
		Personal Health Inventory	Journal	Check Up	Life Skills	Life Skills Worksheets	Media Message or Ethical Issues Worksheet	What Would You Do?
17.1 pp. 353–356	**CHANGES DURING ADOLESCENCE** • Describe how puberty affects the male body. • Describe how puberty affects the female body. • Describe the nonphysical changes that occur during adolescence.	Ch. 17	17A 17B					
17.2 pp. 357–363	**COMMUNICATING EFFECTIVELY** :: Learn how to use "I" messages instead of "you" messages. :: Learn active-listening skills. :: Learn a method of verbally resisting pressure. :: Learn a method of resolving conflict.		17C		p. 358	17A		
17.3 pp. 364–369	**RELATIONSHIPS WITH PEERS** • Describe how to make and keep a friend. • Name three functions that dating serves. :: Name three actions you can take that will help you cope with a breakup.		17D					
17.4 pp. 370–376	**SEXUALITY AND RESPONSIBILITY** • Describe the difference between sexual and emotional intimacy. • Name three possible consequences of teenage pregnancy. • Describe the advantages of sexual abstinence. :: Consider how a pregnancy now would affect your life goals.		17E		p. 375			
17.5 pp. 377–380	**SKILLS FOR RESPONSIBLE SEXUAL BEHAVIOR** :: Learn how to resist internal pressure to become sexually intimate. :: Learn how to resist external pressure to become sexually intimate. :: Apply the decision-making model in this textbook to decisions about your own sexual behavior.		17F			17B		p. 379

KEY: :: Denotes Life Skill Objective

Text references denoted by page number.

Supplement references denoted by chapter or item numbers.

LINKING RESOURCES

	INTERACTION	OTHER RESOURCES		SECTION REVIEW AND ASSESSMENT			
Making a Choice Cards	*Parent Discussion Guide*	*Health Talk Audio Program*	*Teaching Transparencies and Directory*	*Section Review Worksheets*	*Section Quizzes*	*Reteaching Worksheets*	*Section Reviews*
	Ch. 17	Ch. 17	17A BSH10	17.1	17.1	17.1	p. 356
17A				17.2	17.2	17.2	p. 363
				17.3	17.3	17.3	p. 369
				17.4	17.4	17.4	p. 376
17B				17.5	17.5	17.5	p. 380

For additional information about hormones and the pituitary gland, see pages 677–678 in the Body Systems Handbook.

KEY FACTS

- Adolescence is a time of physical, emotional, mental, and social change.
- During puberty hormonal changes cause sexual maturity.
- The four levels of communication are: information giving, directing and arguing, exploring, and self-disclosing.
- Nonverbal communication includes eye contact, expressions, and body positions.
- There are several techniques you can learn to help you communicate more effectively.
- The strongest friendships are based on common interests and values.
- Sexuality is everything that makes one a sensual person.
- Teen sexual activity is risky and can lead to conflicts of values, damaged self-esteem, sexually transmitted diseases, and unplanned pregnancies.
- Exercising self-control and learning the difference between sexual and emotional intimacy can help teens resist the pressure to be sexually active.

CHAPTER REVIEW AND ASSESSMENT

TEXT

Chapter Review pp. 382–383

SUPPLEMENTS

Chapter Test 17

Alternative Assessment 17

Test Generator Chapter 17

GETTING STARTED

Using the Chapter Photograph

Ask students why they think the two girls in the photo are smiling. Who do they think is on the other end of the phone line—the girl's mother, a relative, her boyfriend, or someone else? Tell students that this chapter will focus on changes that occur during the teen years and on managing relationships with others.

 Question Box

Have students write out any questions they have about puberty, sexuality, and relationships and put them in the Question Box.

Sensitivity *ALERT*

Discussion of the physical and emotional changes of adolescence may embarrass some students because they are going through these changes themselves. Also, some may be involved in intimate relationships and may be sensitive about discussing such matters.

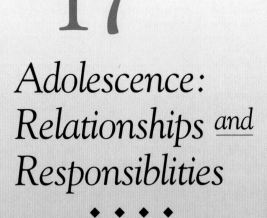

CHAPTER 17

Adolescence: Relationships and Responsiblities

◆ ◆ ◆ ◆

■ **Social interactions become very important during the adolescent years.**

MYTHS & MISCONCEPTIONS

- **Adolescence is a miserable time for adolescents and their families.** Adolescence is an emotional time, but not a miserable one; there are many exciting things about adolescence. Teens are discovering a great deal about themselves as individuals and are undergoing changes that will prepare them for adulthood.

- **There is no point in talking to teens because they never listen.** Teens may seem like they are not listening because they have already absorbed the values that the adults are trying to instill.

- **Teens who become pregnant are just careless.** While carelessness is one factor, another very important factor is peer pressure to become sexually active. That pressure, combined with positive media messages about sex and insufficient or inaccurate knowledge about birth control, results in many teen pregnancies. For some teens, becoming pregnant is intentional.

"**S**he'll never want to go out with me,"
Martin mutters as he shoves his books into his locker. Every time he gets up the nerve
to say hello to Caitlyn, he can't think of anything to say if she says
"Hi" back. He ends up just standing there feeling like a fool.
Martin's never really felt like this about anyone before—he's so
attracted to Caitlyn that he's almost afraid of her. Really he's afraid
that she wouldn't find him attractive. He figures, "Why would she
when I act so weird around her? If I did get up the courage to
ask her out, my heart would be beating so fast and my palms
would be so sweaty that she probably wouldn't want to
have anything to do with me anyway." Although many
people Martin's age go through the same thing, he is
convinced that he is the only one with these problems.

Section 17.1

Changes During Adolescence

Objectives

- *Describe how puberty affects the male body.*
- *Describe how puberty affects the female body.*
- *Describe the nonphysical changes that occur during adolescence.*

Martin doesn't realize it, but virtually everyone suffers similar discomforts during adolescence. If he could read Caitlyn's mind, he would probably find that she, too, has many of the same feelings.

Adolescence is a time of change—changing body, changing emotions, changing mental abilities, and changing social life. All these changes can cause feelings of awkwardness. It helps to know as much as possible about what is going on, and it also helps to realize that the changes are perfectly normal.

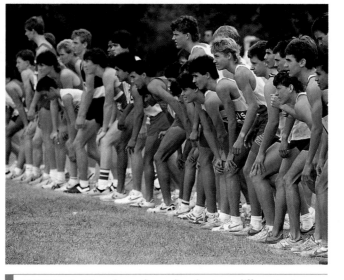

(FIGURE 17-1) **People go through puberty at different rates. Don't worry if you are maturing faster or slower than your friends.**

Section 17.1 Lesson Plan

MOTIVATE

Journal 17A
Being Shy

This may be done as a warm-up activity. Ask students to think about Martin's situation, and ask if they ever have felt shy or awkward with a person they like. Ask what Martin should do—remain silent and hope Caitlyn will talk to him, or work up his courage and ask her out? Then, in their Journal, have students describe a situation in which they felt shy or awkward and the steps they could have taken to overcome their shyness.

Personal Health Inventory
Have students complete the Personal Health Inventory for this chapter.

English/Spanish CD Audio Program
Use the English/Spanish Health Talk audio program for students who need audio reinforcement of the concepts presented.

Parent Discussion Guide
Send home the Parent Letter for Chapter 17. As you progress through the chapter, send home the Parental Survey and The Extra Mile.

Background

Developmental Differences

Adolescents develop at different rates, and it is important to make students aware that these differences are normal. Girls usually begin to mature before boys. Many boys do not reach their full height until after they graduate from high school. Among student in the same grade level, height differences of a foot or more are not unusual. This height increase requires so much of the body's energy that some adolescent boys appear quite thin because their body has not yet added muscle mass. Girls may have the opposite problem. As they mature and develop more body fat, many girls become overly concerned about staying thin. Emphasize to students that they should try not to compare their changing bodies with the "perfect" ones they see in the media.

Section Review Worksheet 17.1

To reinforce the concepts presented in this section, assign Section Review Worksheet 17.1.

puberty:

the period of physical development during which people become sexually mature and are able to produce children.

hormones:

chemical substances, produced by the endocrine glands, which serve as messengers within the body.

REMINDER

The endocrine glands are discussed in greater detail in the Body Systems Handbook on pages 677–679.

Physical Changes

The most dramatic changes during the adolescent years are the physical ones. You grow taller and larger, and enter the time of life called **puberty.** Puberty is the period of physical development during which people become able to produce children. Both males and females go through puberty. The age at which people begin puberty varies widely, from as young as 8 to as old as 16. It usually takes from two to four years for all of the changes of puberty to be completed.

Puberty is triggered by the release of specific **hormones.** Hormones are chemical substances, produced by the endocrine glands, which serve as messengers within the body.

The pituitary gland, located in the brain, releases hormones that send the message to other endocrine glands that it is time for them to begin releasing the hormones that cause puberty.

In males, the pituitary gland releases hormones that cause the testes to manufacture increased amounts of the hormone testosterone. Testosterone causes many of the changes of puberty. A male notices that his testes and penis begin to grow larger and that pubic hair appears around them. He gets taller and stronger. Later, hair grows

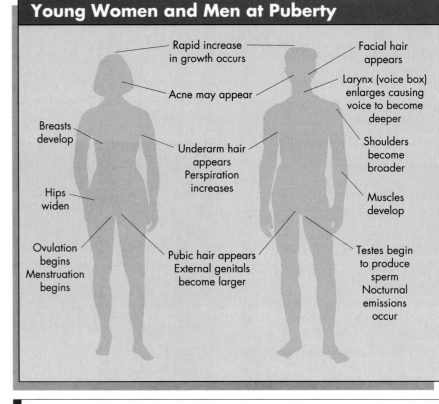

Young Women and Men at Puberty

- Rapid increase in growth occurs
- Acne may appear
- Breasts develop
- Underarm hair appears / Perspiration increases
- Hips widen
- Ovulation begins / Menstruation begins
- Pubic hair appears / External genitals become larger
- Facial hair appears
- Larynx (voice box) enlarges causing voice to become deeper
- Shoulders become broader
- Muscles develop
- Testes begin to produce sperm / Nocturnal emissions occur

(FIGURE 17-2) **Puberty is the time of life in which people become sexually mature and are able to produce children.**

TEACH

Teaching Transparency 17A
Young Women and Men at Puberty

Use this transparency of Figure 17-2 for the following activity: Divide the class into small groups. Tell each group to make a chart titled PUBERTY, with three headings: BOYS, GIRLS, and BOTH. Have them read the text and study the transparency, listing items in the proper columns on the chart and noting questions to discuss later. As a class, discuss the charts, and respond to any questions listed by the recorders.

Writing
Nonphysical Changes During Adolescence

Ask students to write a brief paragraph that (1) compares their emotions now with their emotions when they were 10 years old, (2) compares the kinds of problems their minds can solve now with those they could solve when they were 10, or (3) describes things they now can do independently that required an adult's help when they were 10. Ask volunteers to read examples and use these for class discussion on the nonphysical changes of adolescence.

Journal 17B
Concerns About Adolescence

Have students write in their Journal any concerns or questions they may under his arms and on his face. Testosterone also causes the larynx (voice box) to enlarge, resulting in the lower and deeper male voice. Before the voice stabilizes, however, it may break unpredictably for a while.

These types of changes may be welcome, but another aspect of puberty usually isn't. The increase in testosterone levels causes the oil glands to increase their production of oil. When these glands become clogged, acne can result.

An important part of male puberty is the beginning of sperm production by the testes, when boys start to experience **nocturnal emissions** ("wet dreams"). Nocturnal emissions are ejaculations of semen that occur during sleep. They are perfectly normal and no cause for alarm. Once sperm production has begun, a male is capable of causing pregnancy in a female.

In females, the pituitary gland releases hormones that cause the ovaries to produce the hormones estrogen and progesterone, the major female sex hormones. The female sex hormones cause female changes at puberty. The uterus, fallopian tubes, vagina, clitoris, and vulva grow in size. The breasts also start to grow, and pubic hair appears around the genitals. A female grows taller, and her hips widen.

During puberty, a female begins to ovulate and have menstrual periods. The first menstrual period usually occurs between the ages of 12 and 14, but it is not unusual for a girl to have her first period as young as 9 or as old as 17. Once a female has begun ovulation and menstruation, she is capable of becoming pregnant. As a result of hormonal changes during puberty, both males and females experience an increased sex drive and may find that they feel sexually aroused around some people.

Teenagers tend to develop at the same rate as their parents did. That does not

mean, however, that all teenagers develop at the same rate. If you are developing at a faster or slower rate than other people your age, don't worry. You are almost certainly developing normally. If you are concerned, speak to a health professional or other trusted adult.

Q: Is it possible for a girl to get pregnant before she has had her first menstrual period?

A: Actually it is possible, but only if she has had her first ovulation. Ovulation occurs two weeks before menstruation. A girl does not always feel ovulation and may not know when she is ovulating. So she could become pregnant if she has sexual intercourse after her first ovulation but before her first menstrual period.

◆◆◆

Q: Lately I've noticed that one of my testes is larger than the other. I've heard that testicular cancer is the most common kind of cancer for males my age, and I'm wondering if there's something wrong with me. Should I see a doctor?

A: Having one testicle that is larger than the other is very common, and it is usually nothing to worry about. However, hard lumps or an enlargement of the testes are things you should watch out for. It's always a good idea to perform the testicular self-examination on a regular basis and consult a doctor about anything that concerns you.

REMINDER
〰〰〰
Ovulation is the release of an egg from an ovary.

nocturnal emissions:

ejaculations of semen that occur during sleep.

Section Quiz 17.1
Have students take Section Quiz 17.1.

Reteaching Worksheet 17.1
Students who have difficulty with the material may complete Reteaching Worksheet 17.1.

Review Answers
1. The boy's body grows larger; increased oil production may cause acne; facial and underarm hair appears; larynx enlarges, which causes a deeper voice; shoulders become broader; muscles develop; penis and testes grow larger and pubic hair appears around them; sperm production begins; and nocturnal emissions occur.
2. The girl's body grows in size; increased oil production may cause acne; breasts develop; hips widen; the uterus, fallopian tubes, vagina, clitoris, and vulva grow in size; ovulation and menstruation begin; and pubic and underarm hair appears.

have about the changes they are undergoing as teenagers. Their concerns might include physical changes, emotional changes, or feelings toward others.

Extension
Identity Crisis

Have students use library sources to research the work of Erik Erikson, a psychoanalyst best known for his study of the adolescent identity crisis. Stu-

dents should prepare and present a report on Erikson's unusual adolescence and his contributions to the field of psychoanalysis.

Answers to Questions 1 and 2 are on p. 355.

3. Emotions may be more intense or a person may react to various familiar situations with different emotions; a person may recognize and better control his or her emotions; thinking becomes more logical and abstract; a person moves from being completely dependent on other people to being more independent; and there is an increasing awareness of the feelings of others and a desire for their approval.

4. People experiencing puberty may constantly wonder whether body changes taking place in them are normal. If an adolescent is developing faster or slower than others, he or she may feel self-conscious, awkward, and unattractive. These feelings can negatively affect a person's self-concept, and he or she may tend to withdraw.

(FIGURE 17-3) **Your mental abilities improve during adolescence, allowing you to think and reason in a logical, abstract manner.**

Other Changes

At the same time that your body is developing, your emotions, mental abilities, and social abilities are also changing.

As you mature, you experience emotions for different reasons, or perhaps you feel them more intensely. Things that didn't bother you when you were younger might cause you distress now. At the same time, you might be totally unaffected now by things that you used to feel strongly about.

With maturity, you can better recognize and control emotions. Controlling your emotions helps to keep them from having a negative effect on you. For example, when you feel angry, you should be able to control yourself so that you don't hurt yourself or someone else.

Emotional growth is influenced mainly by your environment, especially by the adults with whom you interact. Parents and other family members set examples, and you are likely to learn their ways of dealing with emotions. If they can control their

emotions, you probably will learn how to control yours too. If they cannot, you may have to work harder at this aspect of emotional growth.

During adolescence, you also grow mentally. You begin to think and reason in a different way. Your thinking becomes more logical and abstract. You are able to ask such questions as, ''Why is this correct?'' or ''Can this be done another way?''

You can deal with more complex problems. For example, you are able to consider the immense size of the sun and its constant chemical changes. As a child, you may have understood only that the sun provides light and heat.

Your improved mental abilities also allow you to make realistic plans because you can imagine the consequences of actions and think about alternatives. You can evaluate the results of decisions and learn from your successes and mistakes.

You also grow socially during adolescence. You move from being totally dependent on other people to being more independent. At the same time, you develop an increased awareness of the feelings of others, and you desire their approval.

Review

1. Describe how puberty affects the male body.

2. Describe how puberty affects the female body.

3. Describe the nonphysical changes that occur during adolescence.

4. *Critical Thinking* How might the changes of puberty affect a person emotionally?

ASSESS

Section Review
Have students answer the Section Review questions.

Alternative Assessment
What Would You Say?

Tell students to suppose a younger sister, brother, or friend is just entering puberty and is worried about the changes in his or her body. Ask how they would explain the changes to the younger child.

Closure
Which Change Is Most Difficult?

On the chalkboard, write the heading CHANGES DURING PUBERTY with these subheadings: PHYSICAL, EMOTIONAL, INTELLECTUAL, SOCIAL. Ask students which changes they think are most difficult to deal with and why.

Section 17.2

Communicating Effectively

Objectives

- *Learn how to use "I" messages instead of "you" messages.*
  - **LIFE SKILLS: Communicating Effectively**

- *Learn active-listening skills.*
  - **LIFE SKILLS: Communicating Effectively**

- *Learn a method of verbally resisting pressure.*
  - **LIFE SKILLS: Communicating Effectively**

- *Learn a method of resolving conflict.*
  - **LIFE SKILLS: Communicating Effectively**

As a teenager, you are beginning to learn how to communicate in a more adult way. If you learn effective communication techniques now, you'll be much more successful in your interpersonal relationships throughout your life.

Levels of Communication

There are four levels of communication, each of which is appropriate for different situations:

1. Information giving
2. Directing or arguing
3. Exploring
4. Self-disclosing

An example of Level 1 communication, information giving, is talking about the weather. Another example might be telling someone what you plan to wear to the football game on Friday night. Most casual conversations are conducted at Level 1, the least risky level of communication.

You might use level 2 communication, directing or arguing, when you tell a driver not to switch lanes because a car is there, or when you disagree with a statement another person has made.

Level 3 communication, exploring, is a safe way to find out how someone feels about something. For example, you might ask how your boyfriend or girlfriend feels about your relationship. Since you have not told the other person how you feel, you do not risk exposing your feelings. If the other person says your relationship is great, you can agree. If the person says he or she doesn't see much future together, you can also agree. Level 3 communication provides you with a safe way to explore another person's feelings, but it is not completely honest. The other person may never know how you really feel.

Level 4 communication, self-disclosing, is the deepest and the riskiest way of communicating. When you self-disclose, you reveal your feelings before you know how the other person feels. You might tell a friend, for example, that you really like her and want to spend more time with her. Her response might be positive or negative— she may tell you she feels the same way, or she may tell you that she doesn't share your feelings. Either way, you should have a good idea of where you stand, as a result of risking Level 4 communication. Self-disclosing can be a very honest and mature way of communicating.

Background
Communication Is Important

Leo Buscaglia, a well-known author of books on relationships, surveyed 1,000 adults to identify the most important qualities of relationships. The majority responded that the most essential ingredient of a relationship is communication, and the quality most destructive in relationships is a lack of communication.

Section 17.2 Lesson Plan

MOTIVATE

Game
Communication Warm-Up

Have students play the following game as a warm-up activity. Divide the class into two teams. Have each team write three statements for each of the four levels of communication. If necessary, provide these examples:

Level 1 (information giving)—The dance is tonight at eight.

Level 2 (directing)—You should ask Tina to the dance.

Level 3 (exploring)—Do you feel like going to the dance?

Level 4 (self-disclosing)—I don't feel much like going.

Have one team read their statements to the other team, which is to identify the level of each, and vice versa. Interrupt to discuss the interpretations as needed.

Life SKILLS

Have students complete the Life Skills feature, and then ask volunteers to read their "I" messages aloud. Extend the concept by practicing "I" messages in the context of talking with parents and teachers. On the chalkboard, write these "you" messages:

Parent: *You never remember to take out the trash.*

Parent: *Your music is awful. Turn that thing down.*

Teen: *You never let me go out with anyone!*

Teen: *You always buy my sister what she wants, but never me!*

Teen: *You teachers are always picking on me!*

Teacher: *Is giggling the only thing you people can do?*

Then, ask students to create "I" messages for each sentence and discuss their likely effect on the recipient.

"You" and "I" Messages

A "you" message is a blaming or shaming message, which is likely to put the other person on the defensive. Unfortunately, most people use "you" messages without thinking when they are upset. Jeremy, for instance, sent a "you" message to Angelique when she forgot to call him.

Jeremy: *You are so inconsiderate! How could you forget to call me when you promised? I'm not going to sit around waiting for you to call ever again!*

Angelique is likely to respond negatively to this "you" message. The conversation will probably go downhill without much chance of getting better.

Life SKILLS: Communicating Effectively

Sending "You" and "I" Messages . . .

Using "you" messages can lead to misunderstandings and arguments. We would get much better results if we translated our "you" messages into "I" messages. Practice this skill by thinking of "I" messages that could replace each of the following "you" messages:

"You" Messages

1. You jerk. You ruined another one of my tapes.

2. No, I'm not going to give you a ride because you always make me late.

3. You are so lazy. All you do is lie around watching T.V. while I clean the house.

4. How could you forget my birthday again? You are so thoughtless.

TEACH

Role-Playing
Mixed Messages

Have students act out the following scenarios, paying attention to body language. Ask them to indicate which situations have mixed messages:

1. Boy asks girl out; she says yes and really wants to go out.

2. Student asks two classmates to lend him or her lunch money. One does so willingly, the other unwillingly.

3. Student running for class secretary approaches several classmates for votes; some say they will, but they won't.

Cooperative Learning
Are You Actively Listening?

After reading the section on Active Listening on page 360, divide the class into groups of four. Have each group select a reader, two active listeners, and a monitor. Provide each group with letters to the editor or opinion columns from newspapers. In each group, the reader chooses an item and reads it aloud as the active listeners practice listening—identifying the main concepts, and providing feedback to the reader. The monitor listens and suggests improvements.

Class Discussion
Active Listening

Ask: **In what types of work is active listening especially important to**

(FIGURE 17-4) You send messages through your body language without even being aware of it. In the top drawing, the girl is very interested in what the other person is saying. In the bottom drawing, she is showing very little interest.

An ''I'' message, on the other hand, is much more likely to be successful because it doesn't put the other person on the defensive. The ''I'' message has three basic parts: the event, the results of the event, and feelings about the event.

Jeremy could have sent the following ''I'' message when Angelique forgot to call. Jeremy: *When you forgot to call me* (the event), *I wasted time waiting for you* (the result), *and I felt really angry with you* (feelings about the event).

Angelique is now likely to apologize to Jeremy, rather than snap at him defensively.

You can practice sending ''I'' messages by doing the Life Skills activity on page 358.

Nonverbal Communication

Words are important, but they are not the only messages we send. We also communicate through our behavior, through **nonverbal communication**. This kind of communication involves eye contact, facial expression, and body positions. Sometimes we communicate more with nonverbal communication than with verbal communication. If you are interested in something, you may lean forward in your chair and make direct eye contact. If you are bored, you may look around the room and lean back in your chair. You send messages about your feelings without even being aware of it.

If you pay attention to the nonverbal communication of your friends and family, you will have a better idea of how they are feeling. A friend, for example, may take his ring on and off when he is nervous. When you see him do this, you will know that he feels nervous.

nonverbal communication:

nonverbal behavior, such as eye contact, facial expression, and body position, that communicates information.

Background
Nonverbal Communication

Nonverbal communication occurs through facial expressions, eye contact, and body language. Kinesics is the study of the facial and body movements that accompany speech. Proxemics examines how different cultures use speaking distance, posture, and hand movements to silently communicate feelings and power. Generally, facial expressions communicate the same meanings worldwide, but eye contact and body language vary considerably among cultures. For example, in Arab culture, people may speak closely together and look intently into one another's eyes in a manner that would cause most Westerners discomfort.

Life Skills Worksheet 17A
Assign the Nonverbal Communication Life Skills Worksheet.

---

people? [counselors, teachers, doctors, psychologists, psychiatrists, clergy, attorneys, hotline operators, diplomats, talk-show hosts, salespeople] **In what family situations would active listening be especially helpful?** [during disagreements, when someone is hurt or upset, when someone is seeking advice]

 Journal 17C
Resisting Pressure Verbally

In their Journal, ask students to describe a situation in which a person might be under pressure to do something he or she does not want to do, such as accept an invitation to smoke or comply with a request to copy homework. Have them write down how the person could verbally resist the pressure using the five-step method.

Role-Playing
Practice Resisting and Reasserting

Have students role-play the Li/Kirsten dialogue (Resisting Pressure, pp. 360–362) to practice resisting verbally, resisting nonverbally, and reasserting resistance. Focus students' attention on the nonverbal resistance (looking straight in the eyes, standing firmly, and speaking confidently), which must accompany the verbal resistance to avoid sending a mixed message. Alternatively, have students devise another scenario to practice resistance techniques, such as saying no to alcohol, tobacco, or drugs.

••• TEACH continues on p. 362

Background

Active Listening

Active listening is used in many contexts. Marriage counselors, doctors, and nurses use active listening to find out what they need to know from patients. Company personnel specialists are trained in active listening to identify the concerns of dissatisfied employees. Clergy use this technique to help people talk out their problems. Community volunteers are trained in listening skills so that they can help social workers in agencies and crisis intervention.

mixed message:

a message that is sent when the verbal and nonverbal communications do not match.

active listening:

the process of hearing the words of the speaker and clarifying anything that is confusing.

A **mixed message** is sent when the verbal and nonverbal communications do not match. If Cynthia says she is interested in working with you on a project, but has a frown on her face and sits at the back of her chair with her arms crossed, she is sending a mixed message. When people receive mixed messages, they are more likely to believe the nonverbal communication than the spoken words.

Active Listening

Colleen was watching TV when her mom came home from work. Her mom asked Colleen about her day and continued talking to her. Colleen kept watching TV and didn't pay much attention, other than to grunt an occasional "ya" or "na." Finally her mom came into the room and asked Colleen if she had been listening. "Sure, Mom," Colleen answered.

Actually, Colleen was hearing the words her mother said, but she wasn't really listening to them. Consequently, her mother felt that Colleen didn't care about what she was saying.

You can improve your communication skills by practicing **active listening.** Active listening is the process of hearing the words of the speaker and clarifying anything that you find confusing. Here is how to practice active listening.

- Give the speaker your full attention. This means that you should not think about something else or about what you are going to say next.
- Try to identify the main concepts and ideas that are being communicated.
- Make eye contact with the speaker.
- Indicate you are listening by nodding your head or saying "um-hmm."
- Provide feedback to the speaker. Ask questions, or repeat in your own words

the speaker's comments to make sure you understand. For example, you might say, "If I understand you correctly, you are saying . . ."

- Wait until the speaker is finished before you start talking. Do not finish sentences for the speaker.

Resisting Pressure

The ability to resist pressure is extremely important to staying well. A person who cannot resist pressure to smoke cigarettes, for instance, or to take a ride with a person who is drinking, runs serious health risks. It is possible to resist pressure to do things that you don't want to do and still keep your friends.

Resisting Verbally Li's friend Kirsten got drunk last Saturday night and insisted that she drive Li home. Li knew she shouldn't ride with Kirsten, but she didn't know how to turn her down without looking stupid. Here is a five-step method of verbally resisting pressure that would have helped Li.

Step 1: Identify the problem.
Step 2: State your feelings about the problem.
Step 3: State what you would like to happen instead.
Step 4: Explain the results if the requested change is made.
Step 5: Explain the results if the requested change is not made.

Using this method, Li could have said to Kirsten:

When you want to drive me home after you've been drinking (identify the problem), *I'm afraid that we'll have a wreck* (state your feelings). *I'd like to drive you home or get someone else to take us home* (state what you would like to happen in-

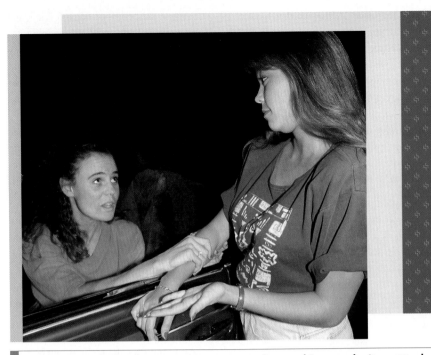

(FIGURE 17-5) **The best way to resist pressure to do something you don't want to do— like taking a ride with someone who has been drinking—is to state your feelings clearly and honestly.**

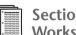

Section Review Worksheet 17.2

To reinforce the concepts presented in this section, assign Section Review Worksheet 17.2.

Section Quiz 17.2

Have students take Section Quiz 17.2.

Reteaching Worksheet 17.2

Students who have difficulty with the material may complete Reteaching Worksheet 17.2.

stead). *If you take my suggestion, I will feel good about going to other parties with you and I won't worry about you being hurt in a wreck—that's very important to me because I like you so much* (state results if change is made). *But if you insist on driving after you've been drinking, I won't ride with you and I'll think less of your judgment* (state results if change is not made).

In this way Li does not place herself in a dangerous situation, and she probably won't lose Kirsten's friendship either, because she let Kirsten know how much she cares about her.

Resisting Nonverbally If Li's nonverbal communication didn't reinforce what she said, Kirsten probably wouldn't take Li seriously. What if Li refused to look Kirsten in the eyes, shifted her weight back and forth, and laughed nervously as she spoke? Kirsten might feel that she could bully Li into doing what she wanted. To be effective in your resistance, you must look the other person directly in the eyes, stand straight and steady on both feet, and speak with confidence and sincerity.

Reasserting Your Resistance Sometimes people will continue to pressure you even after you've used the five-step method for resisting pressure. Then it's time to use other communication techniques. There are two that are particularly effective.

- The Broken Record—If the other person keeps pressuring, keep stating your resistance, like a broken record. Eventually, the other person may believe you are serious about resisting.

Making a Choice 17A

Assign the Using the RESPECT Method card. The card asks students to review the RESPECT method, to list situations in which it could be used to resolve conflicts, and to role-play the situations.

Review Answers

1. Answers will vary. Sample response: One "you" message might be, "You are so self-centered! You never listen to what I have to say." To change this message into an "I" message one might say, "When you don't pay attention to me while I'm talking to you (event), I feel that what I have to say is not important (the result), and my feelings get hurt (feelings about the event)."

2. Active listening requires that you give the speaker your full attention and not think about what you are going to say next.

- Separating Issues—Imagine that Kirsten said, "If you were really a good friend, you'd let me drive you home." Li can counter by separating the "good friend" issue from the "driving home" issue. Li could say, *I think I am a good friend because I spend a lot of time with you, especially when you need someone to talk to. But I don't want to put myself in a dangerous position by letting you drive me home after you've been drinking.*

If nothing works and you are truly in danger, you may have to resist physically. If someone were trying to pull you into a car against your will, for instance, physical resistance would be entirely appropriate.

Resolving Conflicts

Conflicts are a natural part of life. It would probably be impossible to go for a week without some sort of conflict arising with someone. But conflicts can usually be resolved if people show respect for each other. The following is an example of how not to resolve a conflict. Trina and Ronnie have been dating for a long time, but sometimes their tastes in friends are not the same.

Trina: *Let's go to Jenny's party tonight. I hear it's going to be great.*

Ronnie: *Are you kidding? Jenny's friends are boring. No way I'm going to that party!*

Trina: *Oh come on. How can you say Jenny's friends are boring? You're not the most exciting person in school, you know.*

Ronnie: *Who do you think you're talking to? I don't have to take that from anyone. Go out with yourself tonight. In fact, don't bother calling me again.*

Trina: *Don't worry about me calling you. No chance!*

When this conflict began, Trina and Ronnie wanted to spend the evening together. When it ended, not only did they not want to spend the evening together, but they had decided never to see each other again. The couple's predicament resulted from a lack of conflict-resolution skills.

Trina and Ronnie could have used the following RESPECT method for resolving conflicts, which requires that you show respect for the other person and for yourself.

1. **Recognize** that there is a difference of opinion.
2. **Eliminate** from your mind any thought of what you want for the time being. You'll get back to it later.
3. **Scan and listen** to what is being communicated by the other person in words and feelings.
4. **Paraphrase** what was communicated in words and state the feelings you believe the other person is experiencing.
5. **Express** what you want and describe your reasons for wanting it.
6. **Collect** several alternative solutions that meet both your needs.
7. **Try** the best of the alternative solutions.

Imagine that Trina had used the RESPECT method:

Trina: *Let's go to Jenny's party tonight. I hear it's going to be great.*

Ronnie: *Are you kidding? Jenny's friends are boring. No way I'm going to that party!*

Trina: (She recognizes there is a conflict and eliminates her own desires for the moment). *You sound as though you wouldn't be comfortable with Jenny's friends and wouldn't have a good time.* (Trina scans Ronnie's words and paraphrases them. She also paraphrases any feelings she thinks he might have, even those that were not expressed verbally.)

• • • TEACH continued

Role-Playing
Resolving Conflicts

On the chalkboard, write for reference:
- Recognize a difference of opinion.
- Eliminate your own thoughts for the time being.
- Scan other person's words.

- Paraphrase other person's words.
- Express what you want and why.
- Collect alternative solutions.
- Try the best one.

Divide the class into small groups. Ask students to think of a typical conflict between two people, and then act it out, applying the RESPECT method.

Conclude with a class discussion of the advantages of the RESPECT method.

Extension
Body Language in Other Cultures

Have students interview people from different cultures to find out about nonverbal communication in those cultures and whether it includes unfamiliar body language.

Ronnie: *That's right! All those people ever talk about are the honors and scholarships they're getting and the places that they travel to over summer vacation. I always feel out of place when they do that.*

Trina: *I know what you mean. Sometimes I feel out of place, too. But I like parties where I can dance and listen to music. I had a rough week, and I want to wind down tonight.* (Trina expresses what she wants and why she wants it.) *Let's see how many alternatives we can think of in which you feel comfortable and I can wind down.* (They collect several alternative solutions.)

Ronnie: *Well, maybe we could stay just a little while at the party.*

Trina: *Or we could go to the party but stay to ourselves. We really don't have to talk to anyone there, except to say hello. That way I can listen to music and you can be more comfortable there.*

Ronnie: *And I guess another possibility is for us to do what you want this time and for me to get my way next time we disagree.*

After generating several other alternatives, they try one. Using RESPECT, Trina and Ronnie both get what they need. If you respect the other person's needs, that person will be more likely to respect your needs.

Review

1. ■■ **LIFE SKILLS: Communicating Effectively** *Write a "you" message you might use and then translate it into an "I" message.*

2. ■■ **LIFE SKILLS: Communicating Effectively** *During a debate, each debater is thinking about his or her reply while listening to the other debater. Explain why this is not an example of active listening.*

3. ■■ **LIFE SKILLS: Communicating Effectively** *A friend is pressuring you to go to a party where you will see the person who broke up with you last week. You feel that you are not yet ready to socialize with this person. Using the five-step method of verbally resisting pressure, write down the words you would use in talking with your friend.*

4. ■■ **LIFE SKILLS: Communicating Effectively** *Daniel and his buddy Josh get together every Tuesday night to watch their favorite television show. Then the show is canceled. Daniel wants to continue getting together on Tuesday, but to play pool instead. Josh wants to switch to Monday nights and watch a different television show. Suggest several alternatives that could resolve their conflict.*

5. **Critical Thinking** *Name one situation in which Level 1 communication, information giving, would be inappropriate. Explain your answer.*

SECTION 17.2

Answers to Questions 1 and 2 are on p. 362.

3. Answers will vary. Sample response: I don't want to go to the party because the person I just broke up with will be there and I'm not ready for that. I would like to do something else with you instead of going to the party, but if you insist on going to the party, I will not go.

4. Answers will vary. Students might suggest that they alternate weeks—one week they can play pool on Tuesday and the next week they can watch a show on Monday. Accept any answers that show students' ability to recognize and resolve a conflict.

5. Answers will vary. Students may answer that level 1 communication would be inappropriate when trying to resolve a conflict. In conflict resolution, it is important to talk about what is causing the conflict. While some information may be necessary, feelings are the most important factor.

ASSESS

Section Review

Have students answer the Section Review questions.

Alternative Assessment
Identify the Communication Skill Needed

On the chalkboard, write the following statements:

1. That was rotten of you to make fun of me in front of my friends!

2. I made the team today!

3. If you like me, you'll go drinking with me.

4. If you make me stay, I'll never speak to you again.

Ask students to identify which communication skill is needed to reply in each case. ("I" message, active listening, resisting verbally, resolving conflicts with RESPECT) Assess further by having students think of responses to each.

Closure
Applying Your Skills

Ask students to describe to a partner a conflict they experienced recently. Have them tell whether any of the methods presented in this section were used to resolve the conflict. If none were used, which ones do they feel would have helped?

Background
Quiet, Shy, or Nonassertive?

The term *shy* is often used inaccurately to describe a person who is quiet, has difficulty talking to people, and is nonassertive. *Quiet* people simply don't talk a lot; this is not a social handicap. *Shy* people are anxious and usually at a loss for words, a definite handicap. *Non-assertive* people generally converse well enough but falter when they need to say "I want...," "I disagree...," or "No" because they can't assert themselves. Both shy and nonassertive people lack self-confidence and need encouragement and practice in dealing with others. About 40 percent of people consider themselves shy, including some famous people, such as TV personalities Barbara Walters and Jane Pauley.

Section
17.3 *Relationships With Peers*

Objectives

- *Describe how to make and keep a friend.*
- *Name three functions that dating serves.*
- *Name three actions you can take that will help you cope with a breakup.*
  LIFE SKILLS: Coping

relationship:

a connection between people.

A **relationship** is a connection between people. It can be long-lasting and strong, such as a relationship between a parent and child, or it can be shorter and fairly superficial, such as a relationship between a supervisor and a summer employee. It can involve romance, as a dating relationship does, or it can be linked to friendship.

Each of us has a variety of relationships, including those with peers. Because you spend so much time with your peers, it is crucial for you to understand the nature of peer relationships.

Friendships

A friend is someone you know and like. Most friendships are based on common interests and values. You may have different friends for the different things you like to do. Perhaps one friend is fun to play basketball with, and another is good to talk with on the telephone. If you were going on a class field trip, another friend might come to mind. As friendships grow, they provide opportunities for emotional closeness.

How to Make a Friend Some people are able to make friends easily. If you are shy, however, you may have difficulty making and keeping friends. Especially if you've just moved to a new town or started attending a new school, you may find yourself feeling lonely. It is possible that you have *no* friends. If you would like to make some new friends, you will have to take some positive risks.

First, look at the people around you and think about a person you would like as a friend. Try to find someone you think you would feel comfortable with, someone you wouldn't have to impress. Think about someone you would like to spend time with that you could trust. You may notice someone who seems to be alone a lot; that person may also be shy and would be happy to have a new friend. Don't try to fit in with people who don't show much interest in you, no matter how popular they are. It isn't much fun to be one of the "hangers-on" of an "in" group.

No matter how shy you are, you can find people who really like you and want to be your friend. After you've looked around, decide on one person you think would make a good friend for you.

Then approach the potential friend. Yes, this is a frightening prospect. What if the person looks at you like you're an idiot? What if the person just ignores you? These are definite possibilities, but you must risk rejection if you want to make friends. You can make it easier on yourself by first talking casually with the person about a class or other activity you share, or about something else that is happening in school. If that con-

Section 17.3 Lesson Plan

Journal 17D
Potential Friends

This may be done as a warm-up activity. In their Journal, have students list the names of three potential friends. Students should write about what they

have in common with these people and what they could do to develop a friendship with each of them.

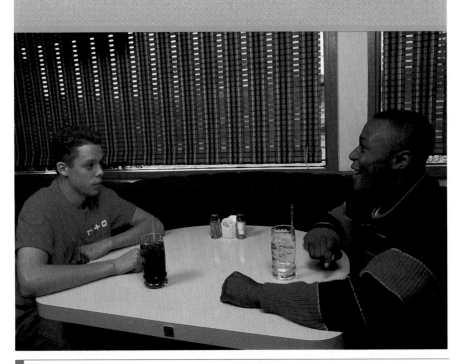

(FIGURE 17-6) **If you want to make new friends, you may have to take the first steps. After you've found someone you think would be a good friend, approach that person and start a conversation.**

versation goes fairly well, you can later invite your potential friend to do something with you—to go with a group of friends somewhere, for example, or to come over to your home to study.

If the person doesn't respond positively, don't take it too hard. Try not to think that you weren't "good enough." Everyone gets rejected sometimes. It is a fact of life that some people will like you and some people won't, no matter who you are. If you are rejected, just think to yourself, "It's their loss." If your first potential friend doesn't work out, try again with someone else, and keep trying until you find someone who responds positively. Eventually you'll find someone you like who also likes you.

How to Keep a Friend "You have to be a friend to have friends," goes an old saying. Different people require different qualities in friends, but there are some qualities that almost everyone values.

One of the most important qualities of a good friend is trustworthiness. It's very important that your friends know you won't tell other people personal things about them or any secrets that they have shared with you. It's also important that you don't criticize a friend to other people.

The way you talk with your friends is also critical to maintaining a friendship. Be honest, but temper your honesty with kindness. It would be better to tell someone that she looks best in blue, for example, instead of saying that she looks terrible in red.

TEACH

Class Discussion
How Can You Make Friends?

Ask students to tell how they make friends in various situations, such as moving to a new place, changing to a new school, joining a new organization, or going to a party where they know hardly anyone. Then, solicit suggestions for how shy or nonassertive people might go about meeting people and making new friends.

Class Discussion
Six Rules for Keeping Friends

On the chalkboard, write the heading SIX RULES FOR KEEPING FRIENDS and list them as follows:

1. Be trustworthy.
2. Be honest but kind.
3. Show empathy.
4. Say "I'm sorry" when necessary.
5. Be tolerant of differences.
6. Don't pressure.

Ask students to weigh their relationships with their friends using the six rules. Do they and their friends follow the rules? Then have them evaluate people they would like to have as friends using the six rules. Ask students if there are other rules they would add to the list.

Background
Teens Need Peer Groups

Pre-teen children primarily learn their rules from parents or other caregivers. But adolescence involves individual development and growing independence, so teens struggle to separate themselves from their parents. Because teens are going through this turbulent time together, they seek security with each other and form peer groups. These groups set their own values, standards, and define their own sense of "normal." Adolescents use each other to justify what they think, do, and like ("*Everyone* is doing it!"). To be a part of a group, one must conform, and anyone who does not is an outcast. Later in adolescence, each teen matures into a more individual self, and the importance of the peer group fades.

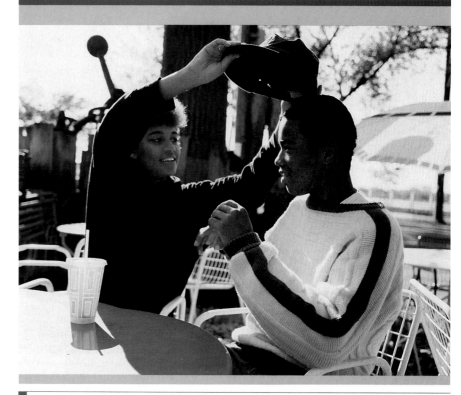

(FIGURE 17-7) **Besides just being fun, dating serves important functions in a person's social development.**

empathy:

the ability to understand how another person feels.

Show **empathy** when talking with your friends. Empathy is the ability to understand how another person feels; it involves putting yourself in your friend's place. For example, if your friend just found out that he didn't get a part in a school play, you could show empathy by saying: "I'm really sorry you didn't get that part. I know how rotten that feels." On the other hand, be sure to show your support when your friend succeeds, too.

If you have hurt someone's feelings, don't be afraid to say that you are sorry. The ability to admit that you are wrong demonstrates that you are mature, which is part of becoming an adult.

Try to be tolerant of any differences between you and a friend. The more toler-

ant you are of your friends, the more likely it is that they will be tolerant of you.

Finally, don't try to pressure someone else into doing something he or she feels uncomfortable doing. Just as you don't want to be pressured, others don't want to be pressured either.

Groups of Peers Peer groups provide you with a sense of belonging, support, and friendship. In a group of friends and acquaintances, you can learn how to present yourself to others and how to lead and follow others. You can talk about your values and what you believe is important. These experiences will allow you to compare your values and goals with others, as you decide what kind of adult you want to be.

 Cooperative Learning
Evaluating Relationships

On the chalkboard, draw the table shown, leaving a lot of vertical room.

IMPORTANCE OF QUALITIES
IN RELATIONSHIPS

Qualities	Friendship	Dating	Crush
[Fun to be with	3	2	1]

Ask students what they look for in people, and write their ideas in the Qualities column. (Add as needed: humor, intelligence, common interests, responsibility, maturity, trustworthiness, honesty, tolerance, no pressure.) Divide the class into three groups. Have each group complete a column in the table. Tell them to evaluate each quality for their column with the appropriate number from the following value scale: 0 = unimportant; 1 = not very important; 2 = pretty important; 3 = essential. Then, in a class discussion, have students compare their lists and evaluations.

• • • TEACH continues on p. 368

Your contact with peer groups probably started when you were a preschooler with a circle of friends. You learned about the give-and-take of relationships and began to practice social skills, such as learning how to compromise.

Sometime between the fourth and sixth grades, cliques start to form. Cliques are small groups of three to eight people who exclude others from the group. If you are in a clique, you probably don't mean to be deliberately exclusive. The result, though, is that many people are left out of your group.

Teenagers often belong to a crowd, which is a loosely knit group of peers. A crowd starts to form when cliques begin to interact with each other. A crowd helps its members become familiar with different types of people. If the crowd is diverse—that is, if it includes people of different genders, ethnicities, cultures, and religions—it is beneficial to be in a crowd. Toward the end of high school, crowds begin to break up, as dating becomes more important.

Dating and Romantic Relationships

Dating is a great way for teens to get to know each other. When young people start dating, it's often just a group of friends going out together. In a group, there is usually less awkwardness than in a one-on-one dating situation.

Though dating provides positive, enjoyable experiences for many people, not all people begin dating as teens. Some teenagers find that other activities provide a full life without dating.

Friends or Dates? It is common in elementary school for close friends to be of the same sex. In the teen years, however, close friendships often form with members of the other sex. Two people may not be inter-

ested in each other romantically, but they still enjoy being together. For example, a boy may find that he can relax with a certain girl because the relationship doesn't have the demands of a romantic relationship. Friendships like these are said to be "platonic" relationships.

Crushes Whether they are called crushes, infatuations, or puppy love, the short-lived romantic feelings many teenagers experience can be intense. Someone experiencing a crush may daydream about the other person and become fascinated with details of his or her life. The other person, however, may not even know about the crush.

> **❝***I wish I didn't have to be the one to ask people out on dates. What if she says no?***❞**
>
> **Martin**

Section Review Worksheet 17.3

To reinforce the concepts presented in this section, assign Section Review Worksheet 17.3.

Section Quiz 17.3

Have students take Section Quiz 17.3.

Reteaching Worksheet 17.3

Students who have difficulty with the material may complete Reteaching Worksheet 17.3.

Review Answers

1. To make friends, look at the people around you and think about who you would like as a friend. Decide on one person, approach the potential friend, and later suggest doing something together. To keep a friend, be trustworthy, be honest, show empathy, don't be afraid to say "I'm sorry," be tolerant of differences, and don't pressure anyone into doing something he or she doesn't want to do.

Such one-sided relationships are part of learning to love. Since the other person is not required to respond, a crush lets you explore romantic relationships in a safe way.

Beginning to Date It's normal to feel both excitement and fear about dating. And it's completely normal to be unsure about who to ask for a date. The qualities you look for in a friend are also good qualities to look for in a date.

In the past, it was almost always the boy who asked the girl out. But in recent years, it has become more common for girls to initiate dates.

As you begin to date, you learn how to talk and act with members of the other sex.

Suggestions for Successful Dating

Don't give up on yourself if you're rejected. It hurts if the person you like doesn't want to go out with you, but keep trying. You'll eventually find people you like who also appreciate you.

Have courage to date someone you like even if others don't agree with your taste.

Don't break a date unless you absolutely must. It is not acceptable to break a date just because something better came along.

Show up on time. If you must be late, call.

Don't expect every date to be wonderful.

Let your date know if you had a good time. Saying something like, "Thanks, you're fun to be with," is all it takes.

Don't accept bad treatment from your date. If your date is inconsiderate, don't go out with him or her again.

(FIGURE 17-8)

You might feel as though others are judging every move you make, but that's probably not true. In fact, they are probably more concerned about how they appear to you.

Besides just being fun, dating serves important functions in a person's social development. It provides an opportunity to learn skills such as being able to talk easily with others, cooperate with them, and be considerate of them. Through dating, you learn what characteristics you like in others and what kind of people you are compatible with. And knowing that you are attractive to someone else helps you gain confidence.

As a dating relationship develops, you can share your thoughts and feelings. You can have a companionship that doesn't necessarily lead to a long-term commitment.

As in other relationships, communication is crucial for success. Clearly communicating your feelings and expectations gives you a better chance for understanding each other. See Figure 17-8 for other ways to make your dates more successful.

Two people sometimes decide to date only each other. One advantage of "going steady" is the opportunity to get to know the other person very well. But there are also some disadvantages. Going out with only one person limits a person's opportunity to meet other people, and if the relationship ends, it might be difficult to begin dating other people.

Breaking Up When two people are going together, they usually don't think about the relationship ending. Yet in reality, most romantic relationships developed during adolescence end in a breakup. Even though breakups are so common, they can be very painful.

Usually the first stage of a breakup is shock and numbness. A person who has been rejected may find it difficult to believe the other person really wants to break up.

• • • TEACH continued

Class Discussion
Importance of Dating

Ask: **How is dating important to your social development?** [*learn how to talk and act with the other sex; learn skills such as talking easily with others, cooperating, and being considerate; discover with whom you are compatible; gain self-confidence*]

Demonstration
Breaking Up Is Hard To Do

During adolescence, romances and friendships often come to an end. Ask students why breaking up with someone or losing a friend can be so difficult. Then ask students which aspects of communication are important in a breakup situation. (*Responses will vary but should include stating the problem as you see it, using "I" messages that state how you feel, making eye contact,*

avoiding mixed messages, resisting pressure, and reasserting if necessary.) Have students suggest other things that will be important. (*For example, practice what you are going to say in front of a mirror, talk to the person in a physical situation where you can leave when you want to, and have a friend close by that you can talk to afterward.*) Students may wish to give some suggestions on things to avoid and what to do if someone ends a relationship with you. Stress the importance of communicating feelings, being sensitive to the

There is a tendency to deny the other person's words. It is easy to think the other person will want to get back together.

When the reality of a breakup is accepted, there may be anger. The other person's faults may be magnified. If the other person has started going with someone else, the anger may be directed at that person also, especially if the person was a friend.

A breakup can cause self-doubt, resulting in negative thoughts such as "If only I had been more fun" or "If only I were better looking." But it is better not to dwell on and give in to negatives. Instead, try to be very good to yourself.

If a relationship you were in has just ended, think of things you especially like to do and indulge yourself a little. Stay in contact with your friends. Remember that you are in the middle of a healing process and that the pain will end eventually. However, if you feel seriously depressed for more than a few weeks, seek help. Talk with a parent or guardian, or a school counselor, teacher, or coach.

Just remember that you will recover, that you will pick up your life and keep going. Although breaking up with someone is painful, it can also lead to personal growth. Your judgment about people becomes more reliable as you learn to evaluate people more realistically. Everything you have learned in this relationship will help you when you develop a deep and lasting relationship that doesn't break up. The suggestions in Figure 17-9 may help you cope with a breakup.

If you are the person who is ending the relationship, act with sensitivity and integrity. Tell the other person plainly that you want to break up. Don't just avoid the person and hope that the message is communicated. Be honest about your feelings, but don't say unnecessarily hurtful things.

Coping With a Breakup

Be very good to yourself. Do things you especially like to do, and stay involved with your friends.

When you start thinking or reminiscing about your ex-boyfriend or ex-girlfriend, command yourself to "Stop!"

Don't look at his or her photograph, reread old letters, or play "your song."

Ask trusted friends or family members if you may call them when you feel like calling your ex-boyfriend or ex-girlfriend.

If you are seriously depressed for more than a few days, seek help from a trusted adult.

Remember that you will recover from your loss.

Remember that you will find someone else.

(FIGURE 17-9)

Review

1. Describe how to make and keep a friend.

2. Name at least three functions that dating serves in a person's social development.

3. LIFE SKILLS: Coping Name at least three actions you can take that will help you cope with a breakup.

4. Critical Thinking Look at your answer to Question 2 of this Review. What activities other than dating could serve each function you listed?

Answer to Question 1 is on p. 368.

2. Answers may include: dating enables one to learn how to talk and act with a person of the opposite sex; it provides an opportunity to learn skills, such as being able to talk easily with others, cooperate with others, and be considerate of others; it enables one to learn what he or she likes in people; and it helps in gaining self-confidence.

3. Answers may include: be good to yourself and indulge yourself; try not to think about your ex-girlfriend or ex-boyfriend; don't look at photographs of your ex-girlfriend or ex-boyfriend; talk with trusted friends and family members; and remember you will recover from the loss and find someone else to be with.

4. Answers will vary but may include making and keeping friendships; becoming an active member of a club; and doing volunteer work.

---

other person's feelings, and seeking support from a friend or friends. Let students know that if they have been honest in a relationship and end it honestly, they have no reason to feel guilty.

Extension
Writing About Relationships

Have students write a poem that expresses their feelings about a friendship that is, or was, particularly important to them. Ask volunteers to read their poems aloud in class.

ASSESS

Section Review

Have students answer the Section Review questions.

Alternative Assessment
Helping a Friend

In any group of teens, someone right now is having difficulty with a friendship, a peer group, dating, or breaking up. Ask students to think about friends who are having problems with

relationships. Have students formulate a plan in which they can use their knowledge and skills in active listening, resisting pressure, and resolving conflicts to help their friends.

Closure
The Keys to Success and Failure

Ask students to summarize, while you write on the chalkboard, the keys to successful friendships and dating.

Section
17.4 Sexuality and Responsibility

Objectives

■ *Describe the difference between sexual and emotional intimacy.*

■ *Name three possible consequences of teenage pregnancy.*

■ *Describe the advantages of sexual abstinence.*

■ *Consider how a pregnancy now would affect your life goals.*
LIFE SKILLS: Setting Goals

heterosexuals:

people who are sexually attracted to those of the other sex.

homosexuals:

people who are sexually attracted to those of the same sex.

The adolescent years are a time of emerging sexuality. During this time a person's interest in sexual matters increases dramatically. This increased interest is a completely normal part of becoming an adult. Another important part of maturing is making responsible decisions about sexual behavior. The ability to use good judgment is crucial, not only to your current and future romantic relationships, but also to your health.

What Is Sexuality?

People often use the word "sexuality" as a synonym for "sexual activity." But sexuality is not just a physical act. It includes everything that makes someone a sexual person. Sexuality involves how we feel about our bodies, our desire for physical closeness with others, and all the thoughts and feelings we have about sexual intimacy. In fact, sexuality encompasses everything about being a male or female person. It isn't necessary to "have sex" to be a sexual person. In fact, people who abstain from sexual intimacy are just as sexual as those who don't. Everyone has sexuality, and everyone is a sexual being.

Most people are **heterosexuals**, people who are sexually attracted to those of the other sex. Some people are **homosexuals**, people who are sexually attracted to those of the same sex. Homosexual men are called gay men, and homosexual women are called gay women or lesbians. People who are attracted to members of both sexes are referred to as bisexual.

It is possible for adolescents to have sexual feelings for those of the same sex but be heterosexual as adults. Similarly, some people who are homosexual as adults have had sexual feelings for members of the other sex. It is the predominant sexual attraction—to those of the other sex or to those of the same sex—that determines whether a person is said to be heterosexual or homosexual in orientation.

No one knows for certain why some people are heterosexual and others are homosexual. Much of the evidence from recent studies indicates that homosexuality may result from a combination of biological and environmental factors.

Everyone—regardless of his or her sexual orientation—deserves to be treated with respect and dignity and without discrimination.

Influences on Sexuality As you grow up, your sexuality is influenced to a large extent by the people around you and the things you see, hear, and read. The earliest influences come from your family. If the people who raise you are comfortable showing affection through touch, you have a

---

Section 17.4 Lesson Plan

MOTIVATE

Writing
Feelings About Sexuality

Have students write a paragraph that expresses their concept of what sexuality is. In a discussion afterward, ask them to provide examples to illustrate the complexity of sexuality—which includes feelings, actions, and decisions.

TEACH

Class Discussion
Myths and Facts About Sexuality

Refer students to Figure 17-10, "Myths and Facts About Sexuality." Discuss the first myth in the table, asking their opinions on what *really* indicates that a couple is in love. Encourage discussion of each myth. Myth number four raises the opportunity to invite questions on homosexuality.

 Journal 17E
Setting Standards

In their Journal, have students write some standards for sexual and emotional intimacy that are important to them. Then, students should give their opinion of the way sex is depicted on TV and in the movies. Do they think most people their age agree with them about sexual behavior?

Myths and Facts About Sexual Intimacy

Myth	Fact
Becoming sexually intimate shows a couple is really in love.	Although sexual intimacy can be an expression of love, it doesn't prove that a couple is in love. Couples become sexually intimate for reasons other than being in love: curiosity, trying to hang on to a partner, proving to themselves that they are sexually normal, or because one partner wants to. It is possible for couples to express their love in ways that do not include sexual intimacy.
If a person has been sexually intimate once, there's no reason to say no to being sexually intimate again.	Many people are intimate once and decide there are many reasons not to do it again: fear of pregnancy or diseases, moral or religious beliefs, waiting for the right person, or wanting to wait until it can be a very satisfying experience.
One way to keep a boyfriend or girlfriend is to be sexually intimate.	Sexual intimacy doesn't guarantee a boyfriend or girlfriend will stay. Sometimes sex will keep a partner for a period of time because of a sense of duty or feelings of guilt. Sometimes a relationship will end after sexual intimacy because the challenge is gone or because a partner feels tied down and doesn't want to be.
If a male is a virgin when he graduates from high school, he's probably homosexual.	Many heterosexual males don't become sexually intimate until after high school because they believe they should wait for marriage. Others aren't ready for commitment, while still others don't want to jeopardize their plans for education and financial security.
The best way to get to know someone is to be sexually intimate with him or her.	Sexual intimacy is only one way of getting to know someone. There are many facets of a person's character one does not learn during sex. If sex replaces talking, spending time with mutual friends, and enjoying activities together, a couple may never truly get to know each other.

(FIGURE 17-10)

Debate the Issue
Censorship of TV and Movies

Divide the class into two teams and ask students to debate this question: Considering that preteens and younger teens are impressionable and prone to experimentation, should explicit and unrealistic sexual behavior be banned from TV and the movies? Close with a discussion attempting to reach a compromise on this issue.

• • • TEACH continues on p. 374

Background

Teen Pregnancy

After five years of no growth in the early 1980s, teenage pregnancy rates rose 9 percent from 1985 to 1990. In 1990, 6 percent of all young women aged 15–19 had babies. This is a 13 percent increase since 1980. For blacks and Hispanics, the rate was almost double this number. Why do so many teens become pregnant? The two main reasons are a failure to use effective contraception during sexual intercourse and the appeal that having a baby has for some girls. Emphasize to teens that if they choose to be sexually active, they need to know how to avoid conception. It is important to help young men and young women become aware of the realities of parenthood and of why they should postpone parenthood until they are more mature.

(FIGURE 17-11) **If the people who raise you are comfortable showing affection through touch, you are likely to feel comfortable with physical affection as well.**

sexual intimacy:

genital touching and sexual intercourse.

emotional intimacy:

sharing thoughts and feelings, caring for and respecting the other person, and gradually learning to trust one another.

pretty good chance of growing into a person who also shows physical affection easily. On the other hand, if your family is reserved and does not show affection readily, you may also be reluctant to show physical affection.

How your family talks about sexuality also can influence your attitudes about the subject. In some families, sexuality is openly discussed, and in others, there is an unspoken rule that it should not be discussed at all. Most families fall somewhere in between.

As you get older and enter adolescence, your peers become more important as sources of information about sexual matters. You hear what they think about sexuality and what they say they do. However, teenagers often misrepresent their sexual activities to impress others, so peer information may not be the most reliable.

An increasingly important influence on your sexuality is mass media—television, movies, magazines, and newspapers. Most of the information you get from the media is designed to sell you something. The more viewers a television show gets, the more it can charge for advertising time. And the more movie tickets are sold, the more money a movie makes. That's why the sex scenes in television shows and movies are usually so unrealistic: the more graphic the scenes are, the more money is made. Realistic sexual and emotional intimacy is rarely shown on the screen. What you see is what sells.

Sexual Intimacy Versus Emotional Intimacy Sexual intimacy and emotional intimacy are often confused. **Sexual intimacy** involves genital touching and intercourse. **Emotional intimacy** involves sharing thoughts and feelings, caring for and respecting the other person, and gradually learning to trust one another. It is entirely possible to have one kind of intimacy without the other.

"Casual sex" is an example of sexual intimacy without emotional intimacy. When people have casual sex, they are often using the other person for gratification without regard for the person's feelings. In this way they are treating the other person as an object rather than as a human being.

Sometimes a person who is lonely or uncomfortable around others will offer sexual intimacy in an effort to achieve emotional intimacy. This can be a painful experience and can be harmful to that person's emotional (and physical) health.

When people are sexually intimate, they allow themselves to be vulnerable, and for that reason it is very important to trust the other person a great deal. Trust is established over a period of time and requires commitment. When this type of lasting commitment exists between two emotionally mature, loving, and trusting people, sexual intimacy can be one of the best experiences in life.

Risks of Teenage Sexual Intimacy

Though sexual intimacy is a positive, pleasurable part of adult life, it can be harmful if it starts too soon. The risks of teenage sexual activity include conflicts with personal and parental values, sexually transmitted diseases, and unwanted pregnancy.

Conflicts With Personal and Parental Values Everyone must consider his or her own values—what he or she strongly believes—when making decisions about sexual behavior. Actions that conflict with one's own values can cause feelings of guilt and low self-esteem.

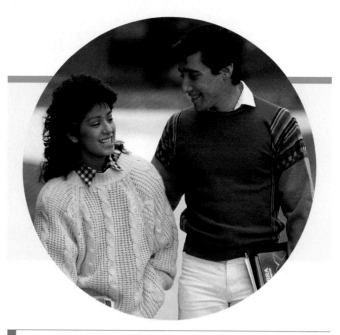

(FIGURE 17-12) **As people become emotionally intimate, they share their thoughts and feelings, care for and respect the other person, and gradually learn to trust one another.**

Teenage Pregnancy Facts

Each year, almost one million teenage females—11% of all females aged 15 to 19 and 20% of those who have sexual intercourse—become pregnant.

85% of teen pregnancies are unplanned, accounting for about one-quarter of all accidental pregnancies annually.

6 in 10 teen pregnancies occur among 18- to 19-year-olds.

Teen pregnancy rates are much higher in the United States than they are in many other developed countries—twice as high as in England and Wales or in Canada, and nine times as high as in the Netherlands or in Japan.

Among sexually experienced teens, about 8% of 14-year-olds, 18% of 15- to 17-year-olds and 22% of 18- to 19-year-olds become pregnant each year.

(FIGURE 17-13) **The United States has a higher teen pregnancy rate than does any other developed nation in the Western world. (Source: The Alan Guttmacher Institute)**

Background
Saying No
There is evidence that some teenage girls would like to say no to sexual intimacy but need help in learning how to send a clear and firm no message. Programs such as Marion Howard's "Postponing Sexual Involvement" at Grady Memorial Hospital in Atlanta are designed to teach this skill. They use role-playing techniques to reinforce assertiveness training so girls can say no effectively. While some analysts are not convinced of the validity of the results reported, others say that the girls who complete the programs have a lower pregnancy rate than those that don't.

Background

Cervical Cancer

Risk factors for cervical cancer in teenage girls include engaging in sexual activity early, contracting the human papilloma virus (genital warts), and having multiple sex partners. A sexually active teenage girl is putting herself in danger. While condoms may provide some degree of protection, abstinence reduces the risk to almost zero.

 Section Review Worksheet 17.4

To reinforce the concepts presented in this section, assign Section Review Worksheet 17.4.

Section Quiz 17.4

Have students take Section Quiz 17.4.

Reteaching Worksheet 17.4

Students who have difficulty with the material may complete Reteaching Worksheet 17.4.

STDs are fully discussed in Chapter 22.

HIV infection and AIDS are the subjects of Chapter 23.

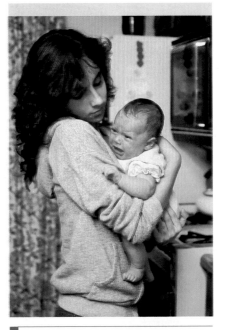

(FIGURE 17-14) **Caring for a child is a 24-hour-a-day responsibility. Teenage parents often find that they don't have time to do things they used to enjoy doing.**

Adolescents must also consider the values of their families. When you are part of a family, your decisions affect not just you, but other family members as well. If your parents believe, for example, that sexual intimacy before marriage is wrong, they would be disappointed and hurt if you became sexually active.

Sexually Transmitted Diseases A sexually active person risks contracting sexually transmitted diseases (STDs), including AIDS. Chapters 22 and 23 deal with STDs.

Teenage Pregnancy Adolescence is a time of coming of age—of emotional, social, and intellectual growth—and all this can be jeopardized by a pregnancy. A person may not be able to reach his or her goals in life because of a teenage pregnancy.

Many teenage pregnancies occur because teens tend to think: "It won't happen to me." But in fact, it does happen to about one million adolescent girls in the United States each year. This works out to 1 out of every 10 girls, the highest rate of teen pregnancy of any industrialized nation in the Western world.

A teenager who has become pregnant, or who has gotten someone pregnant, must face the consequences of his or her actions. Being a parent is hard for everyone, but it is especially difficult for teenagers, who are still developing the ability to make responsible decisions.

Because teenagers often delay making a decision about their pregnancies, they may not get adequate prenatal care. Partly as a result of less prenatal care, teenagers are more likely than older women to have health problems during a pregnancy. In fact, the risk of death due to complications is 60 percent higher for girls younger than 15 than for mothers who are older than 20. Many of these deaths are caused by a condition called toxemia, which is characterized by high blood pressure and fluid retention. Teenage mothers are also more likely to give birth to premature babies and to babies who weigh less than normal.

In addition to suffering health problems, teenage mothers experience educational, economic, and social disadvantages. They are less likely to finish high school, and once out of school, they are less likely to become employed. In addition, few teenage mothers marry the father of their children, and half of those who do are divorced within five years.

These dry facts, of course, do not begin to describe the emotional consequences to a teenager facing early parenthood. It can be very stressful to care for a helpless baby. The 24-hour-a-day responsibility, including middle-of-the-night feedings and diaper

---

••• TEACH continued

Class Discussion

Reasons to Avoid Pregnancy

Write two headings on the chalkboard: DISADVANTAGES OF TEEN PREGNANCY and ADVANTAGES OF TEEN PREGNANCY. Solicit entries for each heading and list them. Lead a discussion of the entries. Conclude with these questions:

- Which of you think your parents would be upset if you were involved in a pregnancy?
- Which of you would be upset if you were involved in a pregnancy?
- Which of you has plans for college or a job that would be disrupted by a pregnancy?
- Which of you has the money to pay for the birth of a baby and to care for it?

Class Discussion

Contraception

Ask: **What methods of contraception do you know about?** *[abstinence, withdrawal, rhythm method, condom, pill, foam, sponge, diaphragm, IUD, vasectomy, and tubal ligation]* Write them on the chalkboard. **Which method is 100 percent effective?** *[Abstinence— all other methods risk pregnancy, as well as STDs and side effects.]*

changing, exhausts the mother and takes its toll on her emotional resources.

When teenagers become parents, they usually find that they simply do not have enough time to do the things they previously enjoyed—going out with friends, for example, or dating or going to the movies. The constant care that a new baby requires can make something as simple as relaxing at home difficult for a new parent.

Teenage mothers are not the only ones who suffer the emotional consequences of premature parenthood. Teenage fathers may also experience major difficulties. They often feel guilty and depressed. They may find the sudden responsibility overwhelming. And like the mothers, teenage fathers are less likely to finish high school and are less successful financially than their peers who are not parents.

SECTION 17.4

Life **SKILLS**

Have students do this exercise independently. Then summarize their responses on the chalkboard under the headings: GOALS FOR NEXT YEAR, ONE-YEAR EFFECT, FIFTEEN-YEAR EFFECT.

Life **SKILLS:** Setting Goals

How Would a Pregnancy Affect Your Life Goals? . .

Take a few minutes to think about the consequences of becoming pregnant or having your girlfriend become pregnant. How would a pregnancy affect your goals?

1. List the personal, educational, or career plans that you have for the next year. What are some things that you are looking forward to?

2. Describe how the pregnancy would affect your goals for the next year.

3. Describe how the pregnancy would affect your goals for the next 5 years.

Review Answers

1. Sexual intimacy involves genital touching and intercourse, whereas emotional intimacy involves sharing thoughts and feelings, caring for and respecting another person, and learning to trust another person.

2. Answers will vary but may include you avoid conflicts with personal and parental values, you avoid sexually transmitted diseases, and you avoid an unwanted pregnancy.

Extension
What It's Really Like

Have someone who has counseled pregnant teens speak to the class. Ask the speaker to discuss the difficulties encountered by teenage parents that they did not anticipate. Allow some time for students to ask questions.

Answers to Questions 1 and 2 are on p. 375.

3. Answers will vary but should include the effect pregnancy would have on personal and educational plans. Students may also answer that they would not be free to do many activities with friends and that they could feel very stressed, guilty, and depressed.

4. Answers will vary. Sample response: Two people just meet, have sexual intercourse, and decide they love one another— all in one night. This is unrealistic. Love is a feeling that develops between two people over a period of time, as the two people get to know one another and have time to develop emotional intimacy. Sexual intimacy does not automatically lead to love.

Some Consequences of Teenage Pregnancy

Greater chance of suffering health problems during pregnancy

Greater chance of giving birth to premature babies

Difficult choice among pregnancy options

Stress of caring for an infant

Increased family conflict

Possible depression, guilt, and sense of isolation

Both mothers and fathers are less likely to finish high school

Both mothers and fathers are less successful financially

(FIGURE 17-15)

sexual abstinence:

delaying or refraining from sexual intimacy.

In addition, according to federal law the father must take financial responsibility for his child. This means that a male who fathers a child will be expected to pay for the support of that child for approximately 18 years. What if a male who fathers a child claims that he is not the father? In most states the mother can take legal steps to establish the paternity—who the father is—of her child without the father's permission. Once the paternity is established, the father is legally bound to support the child financially.

A teen pregnancy affects different people in different ways. The Life Skills activity on page 375 will help you get an idea of how a pregnancy would affect your life.

Although the consequences of teenage pregnancies are felt most deeply by the individuals directly involved, society as a whole also pays a cost. Teen pregnancies cost taxpayers an estimated $20 billion annually in public support.

Abstinence

A person who delays or refrains from sexual intimacy is practicing **sexual abstinence**. Being abstinent is a positive, responsible decision that allows you to avoid teenage pregnancy and sexually transmitted diseases.

Abstinence is the most responsible choice for a teenager because it allows you to delay sexual intimacy until you are in a stable, committed relationship, such as a marriage. Teenagers who practice sexual abstinence grow by acting responsibly and by learning to develop relationships that are not based on sexual intimacy. As adults, they may be better prepared to build strong, lasting relationships based on mutual trust and respect.

If you have already become sexually intimate, you can still choose to delay further intimacy and become abstinent until you know you are capable and ready to accept the consequences of sex.

Review

1. Describe the difference between sexual intimacy and emotional intimacy.

2. What are the advantages of delaying sexual intimacy until marriage?

3. ■■ **LIFE SKILLS: Setting Goals** How would a pregnancy now affect your life one year from now?

4. **Critical Thinking** Name one love scene in a movie, television program, or book that seems unrealistic to you, and explain why it is unrealistic.

ASSESS

Section Review

Have students answer the Section Review questions.

Alternative Assessment
Three Reasons to Abstain

Ask students to write the three most important reasons for abstaining from sexual intimacy until they are emotionally mature and in a stable, committed relationship.

Closure
What If?

Tell students to imagine that everyone stopped practicing abstinence, stopped using contraceptives, and focused upon sexual intimacy instead of emotional intimacy. What would happen to the pregnancy rate, disease rate, world population, and families? Ask students to imagine what would happen if everyone practiced abstinence.

Skills for Responsible Sexual Behavior

Objectives

■ *Learn how to resist internal pressure to become sexually intimate.*
  LIFE SKILLS: Resisting Pressure

■ *Learn how to resist external pressure to become sexually intimate.*
  LIFE SKILLS: Resisting Pressure

■ *Apply the decision-making model in this textbook to decisions about your own sexual behavior.*
  LIFE SKILLS: Making Responsible Decisions

Choosing to refrain from sexual intimacy is a sound, responsible decision. It doesn't help to decide to delay sexual intimacy, however, if you haven't developed the skills necessary to carry out your decision. In this section, you'll learn some valuable skills for responsible sexual behavior.

Resisting Internal Sexual Pressure

A person must first acknowledge sexual feelings before he or she can deal with them. The sex drive can be especially powerful during the teen years, when hormonal changes occur rather suddenly and an increased awareness of sexuality develops. The natural sex drive can make sexual inti-macy a very strong temptation, especially when you are in love.

The best way to deal with the internal pressure to be sexually intimate is to exercise self-control. You can also learn to express your romantic love for another person in ways other than sexual intimacy.

Other Ways to Show Love There are many ways to show love for another person while delaying sexual intimacy. Showing consideration for each other's feelings, doing special favors, hugging, kissing, and laughing together—all of these things show love.

A good way to think of ways to express love without sexual intimacy is to think of how you would want someone to show love to you. What could another person do that would make you feel cared for?

Practicing Self-Control We exercise power over our lives by practicing self-control. When you practice self-control, you make rules for yourself and act on them. It helps to think ahead about temptations and plan what you will do about them. For instance, you may feel that you are not ready for sexual intimacy. If you have given some thought to what your personal reasons for abstinence are, then it might be easier to remember to stick to your decision in a situation where you are tempted. In such a situation, you should ask your-self, What are the rules I have set for myself pertaining to sexual relationships?

Background
Everybody's Doing It!
Aside from peer-group opinion, where does the notion of "everybody's doing it" come from? Some experts point to TV and movies. One study counted 20,000 sex scenes in a typical year of TV watching. Typically, these scenes are romanti-cized and overblown— and birth control is sel-dom brought up.

Section 17.5 Lesson Plan

MOTIVATE

Cooperative Learning
Managing Internal Sexual Pressure

This may be done as a warm-up activity. Divide the class into four groups and appoint a recorder for each group. Have the groups brainstorm to make a list of ways to practice self-control in resisting internal sexual pressure. Then have them brainstorm to make a list of ways to show love besides sexual intimacy. Then ask the recorders to present their groups' ideas, and discuss their effectiveness.

Dealing With External Pressures

External pressures come from outside you. They include pressures from your boyfriend or girlfriend, your friends, or from media messages. Sometimes the external pressures can become internal pressures. If, for instance, you get the idea from television programs that virtually everyone your age is sexually active, you might begin to put pressure on yourself, telling yourself that something is wrong with you if you have not yet experienced sexual intimacy.

Old-fashioned stereotypes of male and female sexual behavior can contribute to the external pressures. Young men may feel that they are expected to be the sexual aggressor, to push for a greater degree of sexual intimacy, whether or not they really

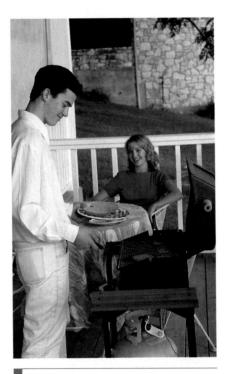

(FIGURE 17-16) **You can show your love for someone in nonsexual ways through gestures such as cooking a meal.**

want to. And a young woman may think that to please a boyfriend she must go further than she is emotionally ready to.

The most important thing to know is that you have a right to refuse sexual intimacy, anytime, for any reason. If you are not sure you are ready to be sexually intimate, you probably aren't. If someone tries to make you feel guilty or "no fun" because you don't want to do a certain thing with your body, that person probably doesn't respect you. Being pressured into sexual intimacy with someone who doesn't respect you is almost certainly going to be harmful to your self-respect, not to mention "no fun" for you.

Resisting Sexual Pressure Lisa and Jamal have been going out for about two months. They spend a lot of time together, talking and kissing, and things are starting to get serious. Lisa loves being with Jamal, and sometimes it's hard for her to keep from going further. Jamal, for his part, isn't even trying to restrain himself. He wants to have sexual intercourse, and the sooner the better. Though he hasn't tried to make Lisa feel bad about not going further, he has told her that he's extremely frustrated. Lately he's become insistent, making it more and more difficult for Lisa to resist.

Lisa genuinely cares for Jamal and wants to continue seeing him, but she doesn't feel ready for sexual intimacy. Deep down, it just doesn't feel like the right thing to do at this time in her life. Plus, she doesn't want to jeopardize her future by becoming pregnant or getting a sexually transmitted disease.

The resistance skills discussed in Section 17.2 could help Lisa avoid a degree of sexual intimacy she doesn't want, in a way that won't make Jamal feel that he has been attacked. The same conversation could work for a male who is being pressured by a female.

The five-step method of verbally resisting pressure is:

1. Identify the problem.
2. State your feelings about the problem.
3. State what you would like to happen instead.
4. Explain the results if the requested change is made.
5. Explain the results if the requested change is not made.

Here is how Lisa could express her feelings to Jamal:

The problem is that I don't want to go as far sexually as you do (identify the problem). *I like you a lot, and I want to keep going out with you. I'm also sexually attracted to you and love what we've been doing together, but I feel uncomfortable about going any further* (state your feelings). *I'd like you to respect my feelings about this and not pressure me* (state what you would like to happen instead). *If you do respect my feelings and back off, I'll keep seeing you, because I think you're great* (state results if change is made). *But if you keep pressuring me, I won't go out with you anymore* (state results if change is not made).

Lisa has stated how she feels and what she wants in a way that leaves no doubt about what she means. To be certain that Jamal gets a clear message, Lisa must reinforce her verbal statements with her nonverbal communication. She must look him straight in the eyes and speak confidently.

Sometimes we are in a situation in which we don't know what we want. If someone is putting on the pressure, we might do what he or she wants because we think we have to answer yes or no on the spot. But actually, we don't have to make a decision at that moment. We can say, "Let me think about it." Learning how to say this simple sentence can be a lifesaver.

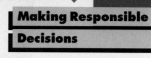

What if You've Already Become Sexually Active?

Making Responsible Decisions

Last night Sandra and Dylan had sexual intercourse for the first time. It seemed like the right thing to do—from stories Sandra had heard she thought that she and Dylan would become closer as a result. But Sandra doesn't feel any closer to him. In fact, now she feels really uncomfortable around Dylan. Things were fine before this happened, but now Sandra is thinking that she made a mistake.

By the end of the day, she's convinced that she doesn't want to continue the sexual intimacy. The problem is, Sandra and Dylan have plans to be together this weekend. She doesn't know whether to cancel the plans and risk ruining their relationship, or tell Dylan about her feelings. What should she do? What would you do?

Remember to use the decision-making steps:

1. State the Problem.
2. List the Options.
3. Imagine the Benefits and Consequences.
4. Consider Your Values.
5. Weigh the Options and Decide.
6. Act.
7. Evaluate the Results.

What if you've already become sexually intimate with someone and then you realize that it was a bad decision? You have the right to change your mind. Just because you've done something once doesn't mean you have to continue doing it. It is always your right to say no even if you've previously said yes.

Respecting Others Just as it is your right to resist pressure to do things with your body that don't feel right, it is also your

Have students apply the seven decision-making steps to determine whether to continue the sexual intimacy described in the situation. Stress the advantage of returning to abstinence.

Section Review Worksheet 17.5

To reinforce the concepts presented in this section, assign Section Review Worksheet 17.5.

Section Quiz 17.5

Have students take Section Quiz 17.5.

Reteaching Worksheet 17.5

Students who have difficulty with the material may complete Reteaching Worksheet 17.5.

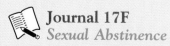
Journal 17F
Sexual Abstinence

In their Journal, have students write about how they feel about sexual abstinence at this point in their life. What would its advantages be? Also, have students consider with whom they could talk to help them make good decisions about sexual activity.

Reinforcement
Relationships Demand Respect

Refer students to the RESPECT method for solving conflicts in Section 17.2. Ask a volunteer to explain how this method could be used to resist sexual pressure. Tell students that in the best relationships, the couple balance their feelings of desire against their respect for one another.

Extension
Other Cultures

Have students research the dating customs and sexual mores of other cultures, particularly non-Western countries. Students can share their research by making oral presentations or by creating visual displays. If you have students from different ethnic backgrounds, have them report on dating customs

Review Answers

1. Exercise self-control and learn to express your romantic love for another person in ways other than sexual intimacy.

2. Identify the problem; state your feelings about the problem; state what you would like to happen instead; explain the results if the requested change is made; and explain the results if the requested change is not made.

3. Answers will vary but may include avoiding any activity that is high-risk for sexual intimacy, such as drinking and using drugs; avoiding being at home together when no one else is home; and becoming involved in group activities, such as going to movies and sport events.

4. Answers may include that external pressures from the media and from peers dictate that adolescents should be sexually active. Those who don't want to be sexually active may think that their feeling are out of step with society.

(FIGURE 17-18) **Participating in group activities is a healthy way to avoid the risk of unwanted sexual intimacy.**

obligation to respect the rights of others. People often don't realize when they are putting unfair pressure on others, especially in intimate situations.

If someone tells you that he or she doesn't want to do something sexually, back off. If the person appears reluctant but doesn't say anything, pay attention to the nonverbal signals. It's often difficult for people to admit that they feel uneasy about sexual intimacy. You might say something like, "You seem uncomfortable. Do you want to stop?"

High-Risk Situations Once you have chosen to delay sexual intimacy, avoiding situations that can make abstinence more difficult will help you stick to your decision.

The main things to avoid are drinking alcohol or using other drugs. These substances impair your judgment and self-control, making sexual activity more likely. Any party at which alcohol and other drugs are present is a high-risk situation.

Spending a lot of time alone with someone is also risky. Avoid being at home together when no one else is there, as well as parking in cars in isolated spots. Group ac-

tivities such as going to the movies and playing sports are best if you want to avoid sexual intimacy.

Review

1. **LIFE SKILLS: Coping** Describe how a person can deal with internal pressures to become sexually intimate.

2. **LIFE SKILLS: Resisting Pressure** Name the five steps of verbally resisting pressure.

3. **LIFE SKILLS: Making Responsible Decisions** If you made a decision to remain sexually abstinent, what steps would you take to ensure that you followed through on your decision?

4. **Critical Thinking** Why might it be difficult for a person to admit that he or she feels uneasy about sexual intimacy?

in their cultures. After reviewing all the information, have students discuss the differences they found and contrast them with American society. Are there any customs they prefer to ours? Why?

ASSESS

Section Review

Have students answer the Section Review questions.

Alternative Assessment
Avoiding Risky Situations

Point out that good intentions to keep in control of one's sexual behavior can fall apart in special situations. Ask students to name some of these situations and write them on the chalkboard. *(drinking, using drugs, parking, being home alone)* Discuss strategies for avoiding each situation.

Closure
Don't Create Sexual Pressure

This chapter has focused upon how to *resist* sexual pressure from others. Now, ask students to explain how they can avoid *creating* sexual pressure on someone else.

Highlights

Summary

- Adolescence, which is the gradual transition from childhood to adulthood, is a time marked by physical, emotional, mental, and social changes.

- Puberty is a period of physical development during which people become able to have children.

- Four types of communication are information giving, directing or arguing, exploring, and self-disclosing.

- Communication skills can be improved by using "I" instead of "You" messages, practicing active listening, and showing respect for the needs of others when conflicts arise.

- Most friendships are based on common interests and values. One of the most important qualities of a good friend is trustworthiness.

- Peer groups provide a person with a sense of support and friendship.

- The risks of teenage sexual activity include conflicts with personal and parental values, sexually transmitted diseases, and unplanned pregnancy.

- Pressures to be sexually intimate can be overcome by exercising self-control, learning to express romantic love in ways other than sexual intimacy, and avoiding high-risk situations.

Vocabulary

hormones chemical substances, produced by the endocrine glands, which serve as messengers within the body.

nonverbal communication nonverbal behavior, such as eye contact, facial expressions, and body position, that communicates information.

mixed message a message that is sent when the verbal and nonverbal communications do not match.

active listening the process of hearing the words of the speaker and clarifying anything that is confusing.

heterosexuals people who are sexually attracted to those of the other sex.

homosexuals people who are sexually attracted to those of the same sex.

sexual intimacy genital touching and sexual intercourse.

emotional intimacy sharing thoughts and feelings, caring for and respecting the other person, and gradually learning to trust one another.

sexual abstinence delaying or refraining from sexual intimacy.

SUMMARY
Have students read the summary to reinforce the concepts they learned in Chapter 17.

VOCABULARY
Review the vocabulary words with students for understanding. Be certain all are clear on the distinction between sexual intimacy and emotional intimacy.

EXTENSION
Adolescence is a time of developing the self and becoming independent. This self-exploration can result in conflicts and strained relationships with parents and other authority figures, such as teachers. Good communication is essential. Have students pick out one area of conflict they have in their life and assess how better communication could reduce the conflict.

CHAPTER 17 ASSESSMENT

CHAPTER REVIEW

Concept Review

1. c   4. c
2. a   5. d
3. b   6. a

Expressing Your Views

1. Answers will vary with individual opinions. Students most likely will answer emotional growth because emotions at this time may be more intense or the person may react to various familiar situations with different emotions than before. Adolescents may find that things will seem easier once they develop the ability to recognize and control emotions.

2. Answers will vary but may include: some people may be shy or they may have low self-esteem; they may not know how to communicate effectively; they may not be trustworthy; they may use "you" statements instead of "I" statements; they may not be active listeners; they may try to pressure friends into doing what they want to do instead of compromising and doing what their friends want to do; and they may not be tolerant of differences between themselves and their friends.

CHAPTER 17 Chapter Review

Concept Review

1. The period of physical development in which the body becomes able to produce children is called
   a. adulthood.   b. childhood.
   c. puberty.   d. adolescence.

2. Revealing your feelings before you know the feelings of another is the level of communication called
   a. self-disclosing.
   b. directing or arguing.
   c. information giving.
   d. exploring.

3. The process of hearing the words of the speaker and clarifying anything that is confusing is known as
   a. nonverbal communication.
   b. active listening.
   c. mixed messages.
   d. "you" and "I" messages.

4. The RESPECT method is used to
   a. resist pressure.   b. listen actively.
   c. resolve conflicts.   d. communicate nonverbally.

5. A friend is someone
   a. you feel comfortable with.
   b. who is trustworthy.
   c. who shows empathy.
   d. All of these.

6. Which of the following is not a high-risk situation if you have decided to delay sexual intimacy?
   a. group activities, such as movies and sports
   b. parties where alcohol is served
   c. using drugs on a date
   d. studying at home alone with your boyfriend or girlfriend

Expressing Your Views

1. In your opinion, what is the most difficult thing about adolescence? What would make it easier?

2. Some people find it hard to make and maintain friends. Why do you think this is true?

Life Skills Check

Sample responses:

1. I've discovered that several people know about the information I told you in confidence. I'm really angry and hurt. This changes how I view our friendship because I feel that my trust was violated and that I can no longer talk to you freely.

2. I could renew my acquaintance with my cousins. They will be a year older now, and maybe we will have more in common. I could bring my new CDs, and we could listen to them. Last year no one brought any sports equipment along, so I could bring my basketball; maybe we could shoot some hoops.

382 ADOLESCENCE: RELATIONSHIPS AND RESPONSIBILITIES

Life Skills Check . . . . . .

1. Communicating Effectively

Last week you told one of your friends something in confidence, and you just found out that your secret was shared with someone else. Using the method found on page 359, communicate an "I" message to let your friend know how you feel.

2. Coping

Your family is planning to attend the yearly family reunion. You can't imagine anything more boring than listening to the same old family stories. All you can think about is the upcoming school dance and whether your new friend will ask you out. You feel as if you must go to the reunion. What could you do to make your family day pleasant?

Projects . . . .

1. Select a biography or historical story about someone and note what you can about this person's teenage years. Look for events, circumstances, and behaviors that were different from the experiences of your adolescent years. Report your findings in writing.

2. Write *age 5*, *age 9*, and *age 14* across the top of a poster board. Under each age, list games and activities you enjoyed as well as any responsibilities you might have had

at that particular time in your life. Evaluate why the list changed from age to age and report this information to the class.

3. Choose three letters from an advice column dealing with teenage relationship problems. Without looking at the advice offered, write your own responses to the problems. Then compare your responses to the ones given in the paper. Bring the letters and both sets of responses to class for discussion.

Plan for Action . . . .

The period between childhood and adulthood is an intense time of change that can be very difficult. Create a plan to help you cope with this period of transition.

Projects

Have students complete the projects on adolescence.

Plan for Action

Students now need to apply the valuable skills they've learned in communicating and resisting pressure. Ask them to describe upcoming situations in which they will need these skills, such as a problem at home or in a relationship, or a special date. In each case, have the class formulate an action plan to handle the problem.

ASSESSMENT OPTIONS

Chapter Test
Have students take the Chapter 17 Test.

Alternate Assessment
Have students do the Alternative Assessment activity for Chapter 17.

Test Generator
The Test Generator contains additional assessment items for this chapter.

CHAPTER 18

Adulthood, Marriage, and Parenthood

SECTION	TITLE/OBJECTIVES	Personal Health Inventory	Journal	Check Up	Life Skills	Life Skills Worksheets	Media Message or Ethical Issues Worksheet	What Would You Do?
		PERSONAL INVENTORY			LIFE SKILLS DEVELOPMENT			
18.1 *pp. 385–392*	**ADULTHOOD** • Know the three stages of adulthood. • Define emotional maturity. • Name three concerns an elderly person might have. ▪▪ Identify the difficulty of coping with a grandparent who has Alzheimer's disease.	Ch. 18	18A		p. 388	18A 18B		
18.2 *pp. 393–398*	**MARRIAGE AND PARENTHOOD** • Name two reasons why people get married. • List three ingredients that can help a marriage be successful. • Name three difficulties teenagers who marry may face. • Name three responsibilities of parenthood.		18B	p. 397		18C		

KEY: ▪▪ Denotes Life Skill Objective

Text references denoted by page number.

Supplement references denoted by chapter or item numbers.

LINKING RESOURCES

	Making a Choice Cards	Parent Discussion Guide	Health Talk Audio Program	Teaching Transparencies and Directory	Section Review Worksheets	Section Quizzes	Reteaching Worksheets	Section Reviews
	INTERACTION		**OTHER RESOURCES**		**SECTION REVIEW AND ASSESSMENT**			
18A					18.1	18.1	18.1	p. 392
18B					18.2	18.2	18.2	p. 398

KEY FACTS

- The three stages of adulthood are young adulthood, middle adulthood, and late adulthood.

- People continue to change throughout all stages of adulthood.

- Developing emotional maturity is an important goal of young adulthood.

- Common concerns of the elderly include physical well-being and adjustment to physical change, filling leisure time, loneliness, age discrimination, and finding appropriate housing.

- A successful marriage requires emotional maturity; mutual love, respect, and trust; and the ability to compromise and communicate.

- The term *contraceptive* is commonly used for all methods of birth control. However, some methods, such as IUDs, are not technically contraceptives. Rather than preventing conception, they prevent the implantation of a fertilized egg.

- The demands of parenthood include putting the welfare of your children before everything else.

- Teenagers usually lack the necessary maturity and financial resources to meet the responsibilities of marriage and parenthood.

CHAPTER REVIEW AND ASSESSMENT

TEXT

Chapter Review pp. 400–401

SUPPLEMENTS

Chapter Test 18

Alternative Assessment 18

Test Generator Chapter 18

GETTING STARTED

Using the Chapter Photograph

Have students speculate about the decisions they think this couple made before deciding to get married. Ask students what qualities they think are needed to make a marriage work.

 Question Box

Have students write out any questions they have about adulthood, parenthood, or marriage and put them in the Question Box.

Sensitivity *ALERT*

Many of your students may be affected by divorce and the special concerns of caring for an older relative. Some students may be coping with parenthood. By creating a caring but direct approach to the topics of this chapter and fostering frank, open discussion, you may help these students feel at ease and willing to offer valuable insights.

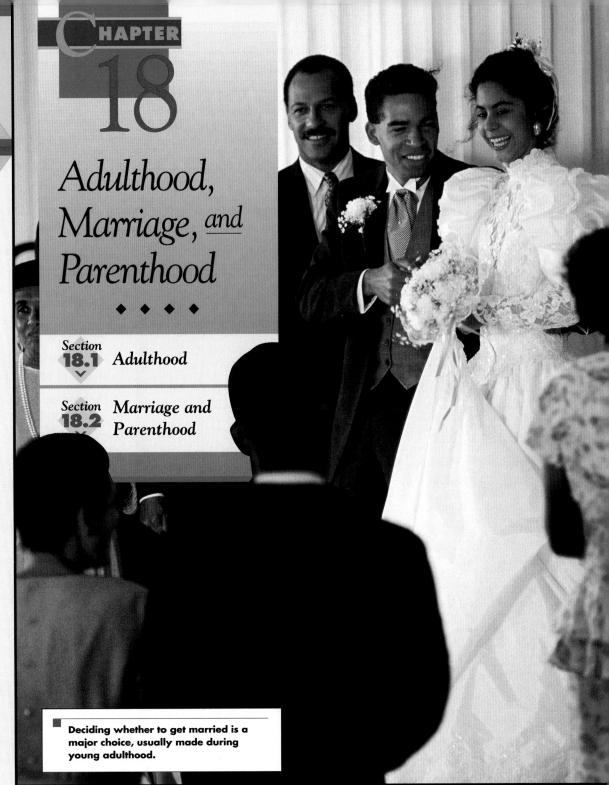

CHAPTER

18

Adulthood, Marriage, and Parenthood

◆ ◆ ◆ ◆

Section **18.1** Adulthood

Section **18.2** Marriage and Parenthood

■ **Deciding whether to get married is a major choice, usually made during young adulthood.**

MYTHS & MISCONCEPTIONS

• **Memory loss is inevitable with aging.** Researchers in the field of cognitive aging now believe that most types of memory loss are not normal and that memory loss is not inevitable. Although some types of memory decline with age, other types remain unchanged.

• **In old age, health problems are inevitable.** It is now known that many age-associated health problems are the result of years of eating a poor diet and

living a sedentary lifestyle; thus, they are largely avoidable. In addition, many medical conditions associated with old age respond well to medical treatment.

• **If a couple is really in love, their feelings won't ever change.** A couple's relationship evolves as they go through life together. Romantic love and physical attraction may be strongest in the beginning. As a couple's relationship matures, mutual respect, shared experiences, an appreciation of one another, and good companionship strengthen their bond.

Carmen had a pretty strange dream last night. She dreamed it was her wedding day but she hadn't bought a dress. She also hadn't chosen a place to live, a job she wanted to do, or even the person she was going to marry. When she awoke, Carmen laughed out loud. But she also had to admit that she was relieved she would not have to make those kinds of decisions for several more years. Being an adult, she thought to herself, can't be all that easy.

Section
18.1 *Adulthood*

Objectives

- *Know the three stages of adulthood.*
- *Define emotional maturity.*
- *Name three concerns an elderly person might have.*
- *Identify the difficulty of coping with a grandparent who has Alzheimer's disease.*
- **LIFE SKILLS: Coping**

It may seem as though you'll be young forever. The thought of being an adult might bring a mixture of excitement and anxiety. How will you know what choices to make? Will you want to get married, or remain single? What kind of parent will you be? As you leave your teenage years and enter your twenties, many of these questions will become clearer to you. Even so, every day of your adult life you will be faced with decisions—some obvious, others more difficult.

In that way, adulthood doesn't differ too much from adolescence. Decision making is never easy, but your adult years will offer you the opportunity to accomplish the goals that you are setting for yourself now, as well as the freedom to pursue your dreams.

The Stages of Adulthood

How will you know when you're an adult? Will you wake up one morning and just feel different? In the United States, a person is legally an adult when he or she turns 18. That doesn't mean, of course, that the person you are on your 18th birthday is the person you'll be for the rest of your life. In fact, you are likely to change just as much during your adulthood as you do during your teenage years. Adulthood is divided into three stages: young adulthood, middle adulthood, and older adulthood.

Young Adulthood Even though Americans are considered legal adults at the age of

Background
Aging Population
From 1900 to 1990, the number of Americans over age 65 grew 900 percent. From 1990 to 2030, the American population over 65 will increase another 75 percent. Persons over 85 are now the fastest-growing segment of the United States population.

Personal Health Inventory
Have students complete the Personal Health Inventory for this chapter.

Section 18.1 Lesson Plan

MOTIVATE

Class Discussion
As a warm-up activity, have students respond to these questions: When does a person become an adult? Is the meaning of adulthood different for a parent? a grandparent?

Making a Choice 18A

Assign the Emotional Maturity card. The card asks students to read about a conflict situation and come up with three ways to handle the conflict in a way that demonstrates emotional maturity.

young adulthood:

the period of adulthood between the ages of 20 and 40.

middle adulthood:

the period of adulthood between the ages of 41 and 65.

emotional maturity:

the capacity to act independently, responsibly, and unselfishly. Being emotionally mature requires having compassion, integrity, and self-esteem.

18, a person who is 18 is still technically a teenager. According to most guidelines, a person between the ages of 20 and 40 is in the stage of **young adulthood.** Young adulthood has its own series of decisions and challenges. Most people who marry, for example, do so during this stage of adulthood. You will most likely choose the career you want to pursue early in your adulthood as well. In addition, the friendships you form during your young adult years may be the longest lasting of your life.

Decisions such as these require a certain degree of maturity. There are two types of maturity. The first, physical maturity, is usually an automatic part of growing up. Being physically mature simply means being fully developed and fully grown. This happens to most people by the time they are in their early twenties. The second type of maturity, **emotional maturity,** is not as automatic. People who are emotionally mature have the capacity to form close relationships, yet act independently. They are able to make decisions that are responsible and unselfish. Being emotionally mature requires having the self-esteem to recognize your own strengths, even when times are hard.

No one can be emotionally mature all the time—everyone makes mistakes. But being equipped with a degree of emotional maturity will help you make better decisions throughout your life. For that reason, attaining emotional maturity should be a major goal during young adulthood.

Middle Adulthood The **middle adulthood** years, the period between the ages of 41 and 65, are, for some people, the most enjoyable time of adult life. Some of life's most difficult choices—about marriage, career, and parenthood, for example—have been made during the young adult years. Middle age can be a time to savor and appreciate the results of those choices.

 (FIGURE 18-1) **Finding the right job is one of the most important challenges young adults face.**

TEACH

Class Discussion
Kinds of Maturity

Write on the chalkboard "An adult is mature." Ask students what this statement means to them. To illustrate the aspects of maturity they discuss, provide the following model and add to it as students make suggestions.

An adult is mature physically when:
  sexually mature
  physiologically mature
An adult is socially mature when:
  responsible for self
  accepts responsibility for others
An adult is emotionally mature when:
  independent
  capable of sustained relationships

Ask: **How is maturity a lifelong process?** *[As people grow and develop, new relationships, situations, and challenges all affect their emotional development.]*

Cooperative Learning
Stages of Adulthood

Have students work in small groups to list experiences and characteristics they associate with the three phases of adulthood. Each group can clip or draw pictures and find quotes to create a collage, poster, or other visual impression of one of the phases.

386 ADULTHOOD, MARRIAGE, AND PARENTHOOD

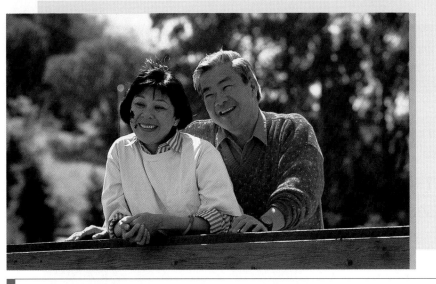

(FIGURE 18-2) **Middle adulthood is often a time to savor the romance of a good marriage and the satisfaction of a happy life.**

Middle adulthood does involve a series of physical and emotional changes. Hair may turn gray, some wrinkles may develop, and a few pounds will probably be gained. Most women stop menstruating during the middle adult years. Once a woman permanently ceases to menstruate, she can no longer bear children. Some women find this change, known as menopause, disheartening. Others welcome the end of their menstrual cycle. Middle-aged men and women who are unhappy in their career may begin to question whether the choices they made during young adulthood were the right ones. In addition, middle-aged adults often find themselves confronting the death of a spouse, a parent, or a close friend, a painful reminder that everyone's life ends at some point.

Parents in the middle-adult stage may also experience "empty-nest syndrome"—feelings of sadness when their children become adults and leave home. Although a change like that requires adjustment, some parents find that it returns romance to their relationship.

Older Adulthood Living to the age of 65 was once an almost miraculous accomplishment—a person born in the year 1900 had a life expectancy of only 47 years! Now, turning 65 simply marks the beginning of the **older-adulthood** stage. In fact, older adults are the fastest-growing segment of the population.

older adulthood:

the period of adulthood past the age of 65.

(FIGURE 18-3) **Older adults often find that they have more time for leisurely and healthy activities, such as exercise.**

Journal 18A
Growing Old

In their Journal, have students list and explain in detail their three largest concerns about growing old and aging.

Role-Playing
What About Grandparents?

Have small groups of students create a scenario for an extended family that wants to persuade a grandparent to make an important life change (give up driving, live with children, move to a retirement home). Have each group create a dialogue among family members; students can switch roles, so that each has a chance to consider the effects of the decision on child, parent, and grandparent.

Class Discussion
Debunking the Myths

Have students refer to Figure 18-4, Myths and Facts About Aging, on page 389 and point out the facts that most surprised them. Ask: **What might account for the increase in knowledge of the elderly?** [Life experience—most older people not only retain their mental ability, they continue to learn and grow and are frequently more creative and flexible in their approaches to problem solving than younger people.]

■■ *Life* SKILLS

Have students read the feature about a family member with Alzheimer's disease. Then have volunteers role-play scenes in which Nate talks to friends or family members about his grandfather. Discuss which responses seemed most helpful.

Background
Alzheimer's History and Facts

In 1906, Dr. Alois Alzheimer, a German neuropathologist, studied the brain tissue of a patient who had died after suffering loss of memory and reason. Under the microscope, he saw the two brain tissue abnormalities typical of Alzheimer's disease: tangled nerve fibers and plaque buildup around nerves.

Microscopic examination of brain tissue is still the only definitive method of diagnosing Alzheimer's disease. For patients with Alzheimer's symptoms, diagnosis comes only after thorough physical, psychological, and neurological examination. Over time, people with

● ● ● BACKGROUND continues
on p. 389

Life SKILLS: Coping

A Family Member With Alzheimer's Disease . . . .

At first Nate wasn't especially upset by his grandfather's forgetfulness. That just happens when people get old, he thought to himself. Then one night Nate's mother got a call from the police. Nate's grandfather had been found wandering around his neighborhood, lost. "How could Grandpa be lost in his own neighborhood?" Nate asked his mom, who was equally puzzled.

Nate's mom took his grandfather to a doctor. After doing some tests, the doctor asked Nate's family to come in for a meeting.

The news wasn't good. Nate's grandfather has Alzheimer's disease, an incurable illness that gradually destroys a person's memory. Eventually a person with Alzheimer's will not be able to remember how to do things that once came naturally—like reading and writing. The names of family members may be forgotten—many Alzheimer's sufferers don't recognize their own spouses or children.

In the several months since he was diagnosed, Nate's grandfather has gotten progressively worse. Sometimes he stares at Nate for long periods of time without speaking. Other times he'll yell at him for no reason.

The illness has been hard on Nate's mom, too. She spends time every day caring for her father. Sometimes he'll recognize and respond to her. Other times he won't. She has to help him get dressed—he no longer remembers how to do it himself. Soon she'll have to decide whether to put him in a nursing home, or hire 24-hour care for him.

Nate spends time every day thinking about his grandfather. He's also shared some memories of his grandfather with his friends from school. His friends know that Nate needs to talk about his grandfather, but they're not always sure what they should say to him. What would *you* say?

● ● ● TEACH continued

Extension
Contributions of the Elderly

The image of the elderly as sick, senile, and sedentary doesn't fit today. More and more people are remaining vital and productive into their 80s and 90s. Some students may enjoy researching and reporting on the late-life

contributions of the artists Grandma Moses, Pablo Picasso, and Georgia O'Keeffe; the playwright Arthur Miller; the physician and writer Benjamin Spock; the composer and conductor Nadia Boulanger; the architect Philip Johnson; the musicians Lionel Hampton and Vladimir Horowitz; the comedian George Burns; and others.

Young Adulthood: Making Decisions

Have students interview a young adult about job and family decisions and ways his or her perspectives have changed since adolescence.

Many people think of older adulthood as a time characterized by physical and mental deterioration. It's true that the older a person is, the more likely he or she is to get certain illnesses and conditions. Someone who is over 65 is much more likely to suffer from cancer, heart disease, or arthritis, for example, than a person who is 21. (These problems are discussed in greater detail in Chapter 24.) **Alzheimer's disease,** an incurable illness characterized by a gradual and permanent loss of memory, and **Parkinson's disease,** which causes a gradual loss of muscle function, are two other serious diseases that most commonly affect older adults.

However, many people remain happy and healthy well into their eighties and even nineties. For these individuals, older adulthood provides an opportunity to enjoy their family, relax, and reflect on their rich, fulfilling lives.

Aging

To a large extent, the choices you make now will affect your health as you grow older. For example, a person who exercises and eats regular, nutritious meals is much more likely to enjoy good health as an older adult than an inactive person who eats foods high in fat and cholesterol.

Common Concerns Physical well-being is an essential concern of aging, but it is not the only one. Jesse's grandparents, for example, had a happy life together for 40 years. But when Jesse's grandfather died last year, his grandmother was left alone. During the past year her health has gotten progressively worse. Jesse's parents are worried about her and have asked her to move in with them. But whenever they bring the subject up, Jesse's grandmother gets angry and defensive. "You don't trust me to take care of myself," she says.

Cancer, heart disease, and arthritis are discussed in greater detail in Chapter 24.

Alzheimer's disease:

an incurable illness characterized by a gradual and permanent loss of memory. Alzheimer's disease most commonly affects the elderly.

Parkinson's disease:

an incurable disease characterized by a gradual loss of control of muscle function. Parkinson's disease most commonly affects the elderly.

Alzheimer's disease experience a loss of memory and cognitive function. Physical deterioration also occurs, and death is usually caused by a secondary infection, often pneumonia. The cause of this progressive, degenerative disease is poorly understood. There appears to be a genetic aspect to early-onset Alzheimer's (before age 65), but it is an elusive one. None of the genetic studies have produced clear-cut links. Late-onset Alzheimer's (after age 65) is primarily a disease of older people, and it occurs in 20–30 percent of people 85 and older. In 1993, the drug yacrine was approved as a treatment for Alzheimer's symptoms, but it does not cure the disease. Researchers hope that by the mid-twenty-first century there will be drugs that will be able to cure Alzheimer's disease.

Myths and Facts About Aging

Myth	Fact
Most older people are sickly and unable to take care of themselves.	The majority of older people are fairly healthy and self-sufficient.
Intelligence declines with age.	People may become more knowledgeable as they age if they continue to exercise their mind.
Older people should stop exercising and get a lot of rest.	Exercise at any age strengthens heart and lung function. Older people can benefit as much from exercising as anyone else.
People's personalities change as they get older.	People's circumstances may change when they become older adults, but their personalities don't.

(FIGURE 18-4)

389

ADULTHOOD

**Life Skills
Worksheet 18B**
Assign the Caring for an
Older Person Life Skills
Worksheet.

One afternoon after school when Jesse stops by to say hello to his grandmother, she tells him that she's beginning to worry about finances. Her utility bills keep rising, and she's concerned that if she were to become very ill she wouldn't be able to afford good medical care.

"Why don't you move in with us?" Jesse asks her. "We'll take care of you." But his grandmother worries about that too. She doesn't want to burden her children. "You and your family have your own home and your own life," she tells Jesse. "You're not going to want to take care of a helpless old woman."

Jesse's grandmother's concerns are not at all unusual. As people get older, they must consider and cope with circumstances that younger people don't have to worry about. For example, most Americans stop working at some point during their sixties. This often results in financial strain, less contact with the outside world, and an abundance of free time.

Filling the sudden increase of time with fulfilling activities can be a challenge. Some people pursue options such as volunteer work, and some travel with enthusiasm. Others, though, find the sudden freedom overwhelming and depressing.

Cultural DIVERSITY

Growing Old in China

"I dread getting old," you hear people say. It seems that in our society, getting old often means losing much of what we value, such as independence and respect. But in other cultures, growing old has an entirely different meaning.

In many cultures, the older members of society are considered to be the most knowledgeable. They know how the weather affects crops, for example, or they know the habits of domesticated animals. They are the repositories of knowledge. To exclude

older people in these cultures would be akin to destroying libraries in our society.

Though many cultures have shown great respect for the old, ancient China was extreme in this characteristic. Respect for older people was one of the

Loneliness can also be a problem for elderly people. Jesse's grandmother is luckier than many older adults—even though she has lost a spouse, she has a loving family who wants her to move in with them. The death of a spouse can leave some elderly people completely alone and isolated.

Another problem older people sometimes face is age discrimination. Also called ageism, age discrimination occurs when a person is judged solely on the basis of his or her age. If, for example, a company chooses to hire a young person rather than an older person who is just as qualified for the job, that company is practicing age discrimination.

Like all prejudices, age discrimination results, at least in part, from ignorance. Judging a person on the basis of age is just as wrong as deciding not to like someone because of his or her race, religion, sexual orientation, or physical impairment.

Needs of the Elderly Jesse's grandmother used to love to cook. Recently, however, she has lost interest in preparing foods. She doesn't even enjoy eating any-

most important tenets of the Confucian system of ethics. The tradition of revering the elderly was so strong that, in large measure, it survived the communist revolution of the 1940s and the Cultural Revolution of the 1960s.

The respect that Chinese people owed their parents was called *xiao*. To show *xiao* meant to obey one's parents, to be extremely polite to them, and to care for them in their old age. It was thought that nothing could repay parents for the gift of life, but *xiao* was at least a meager attempt.

Older people were considered so special that only they could have birthday celebrations. A birthday was not considered to be noteworthy unless it was a 60th, 70th, 80th, 88th, or 100th birthday.

Even though the influence of old people is not quite as absolute in contemporary China as it was in the past, it is still understood that younger generations will care for their aging parents; very few elderly people live in nursing homes. In this way, the concept of *xiao*—a feeling of respect and obligation toward the aged—remains to tie the generations together.

SECTION 18.1

Section Review Worksheet 18.1
To reinforce the concepts presented in this section, assign Section Review Worksheet 18.1.

Section Quiz 18.1
Have students take Section Quiz 18.1.

Reteaching Worksheet 18.1
Students who have difficulty with the material may complete Reteaching Worksheet 18.1.

Review Answers

1. young adulthood, middle adulthood, older adulthood

2. Having the capacity to form close relationships yet act independently, responsibly, and unselfishly. Being emotionally mature requires having the self-esteem to appreciate your talents and to like yourself. Physical maturity happens to a person's body automatically.

3. Answers may include physical well-being; finances; loneliness; becoming a burden to his or her family; age discrimination; alternative housing; and nutrition.

4. Accept any response that shows students' understanding and empathy in dealing with a person who has a loved one with a debilitating disease that has no cure.

5. Students may answer that Jesse's grandmother still wants to remain independent; by responding the way she did, she may be trying to cover up the problems she is experiencing. Also, she may not want to burden her family with her problems.

Stress-management techniques are discussed in detail in Chapter 9.

more. Jesse's grandmother might be losing her sense of taste, which sometimes happens as a person gets older. She may need to eat specially prepared foods that are highly seasoned in order to enjoy meals again. Some organizations, such as Meals on Wheels, serve hot, specially prepared foods to people such as Jesse's grandmother, who are confined to their homes.

Another common need among elderly people is appropriate housing. Like Jesse's grandmother, most older adults prefer to live in their own homes for as long as they can. Modifications and adjustments can be made to make this possible. Special ramps, lighting, and wider doorways, for example, can make it possible for a person in a wheelchair to be mobile around the house.

If living at home becomes too difficult, though, a choice must be made. People who can afford to do so may choose to live in retirement communities, which offer special care and companionship.

Another option for people in this situation is to move in with family. Jesse's grandmother finally decided to do this. At first Jesse was surprised at how many adjustments had to be made. He could no longer listen to his radio late at night—it kept his grandmother awake. Sometimes he had to come straight home from school to care for her when no one else was around. But eventually Jesse grew to love living with his grandmother. She had great stories to tell, and she always had time to listen whenever something was troubling him.

Sometimes an elderly person will almost completely lose mental or physical functioning. When this happens, a nursing home may be the best option. A nursing home is a facility that offers special attention and long-term care for those who require it. Only a small percentage of elderly people in the United States live in nursing homes.

Tips for Healthy Aging The most important thing you can do now to stay healthy in the years to come is to practice good health habits. You learned earlier that getting regular exercise and eating a healthy diet decrease your risk of suffering certain diseases when you get older. Getting regular physical checkups, seeing a dentist regularly, and practicing good hygiene are some other things you can do to help yourself remain healthy during the years to come.

Avoiding tobacco, alcohol, and other drugs can also help you stay healthy throughout your life. Some people turn to these drugs to help them handle stress. When not managed properly, stress can cause physical disease, but there are better ways to manage stress than to use drugs. The techniques discussed in Chapter 9 can help you do this.

Review

1. Name the three stages of adulthood.

2. Define emotional maturity. How does it differ from physical maturity?

3. Describe three things an elderly person might be concerned about.

4. **LIFE SKILLS: Coping** What could you say to a friend who has just found out that his or her grandfather has Alzheimer's disease?

5. **Critical Thinking** Why do you think Jesse's grandmother reacted the way she did when Jesse's parents asked her to live with them? How do you think you would react?

ASSESS

Section Review

Have students answer the Section Review questions.

Alternative Assessment
Jesse's Point of View

Ask students to write a two-minute monologue in which Jesse speaks. It should reveal Jesse's understanding of his grandmother's situation and feelings, and his own mixed emotions about her living with his family.

Closure
Maturity versus Aging

Draw two large, overlapping circles on the chalkboard. Label one MATURITY and one AGING. Have students take turns coming to the board and writing a characteristic of aging or of maturity in the appropriate area. If a characteristic belongs to both, they should write it in the area of overlap.

Section 18.2 Marriage and Parenthood

Objectives

- Name two reasons why people get married.
- List three ingredients that can help a marriage be successful.
- Name three difficulties teenagers who marry may face.
- Name three responsibilities of parenthood.

Carmen, the girl discussed in the beginning of this chapter, has been seeing Danny for about two months. They really like being together—Carmen has feelings for Danny she's never had for anyone else. For that reason, she was kind of disturbed that Danny wasn't in her dream about getting married.

But the more she thought about it, the more she realized that it was pretty silly to think about marrying Danny—or anyone else, for that matter—at this time of her life. In fact, she wasn't all that sure she ever wanted to get married. As for having children—well, that can wait a while, too.

Why People Get Married

Carmen isn't certain how she feels about it yet, but when she gets older she may very well decide that she does want to get married. More than 90 percent of American adults have made that decision. There are several different reasons why people get married. The best reason for two people to get married is that they want to make a life-long commitment to be with the person they love and respect. Some people get married because they want to have children or because they seek the close companionship that marriage can provide. Others get married because they are seeking financial security. Still others marry because it is expected of them or because they are scared they will end up alone.

Successful Marriage

The most important ingredients two people can bring to a marriage are love and respect. Marriage often involves putting another person's needs before your own and making difficult sacrifices for the sake of your spouse's happiness. It takes a great deal of love and respect to do these things.

Other factors needed for a successful marriage are emotional maturity and the ability to compromise. The decisions you make when you are married affect both you *and* your spouse. What if a certain job you want involves moving across the country? What if you want to have children, but your spouse doesn't know if he or she wants them? A person who is not emotionally mature would probably have a difficult time making the kinds of compromises that are required to sustain the type of partnership that is necessary for a healthy and successful marriage.

One more ingredient that makes marriage successful is the ability to communicate effectively. Two people who are in a

Background
Marriage Statistics
The United States has the highest marriage rate of any industrialized country, but people marry at a later age. The average age for marriage in the United States is now almost 27 for men and 25 for women. Although demographers are cautious about predicting a trend, the divorce rate is somewhat lower now than it was in the late 1970s and early 1980s.

Section 18.2 Lesson Plan

MOTIVATE

Journal 18B
A Lasting Marriage

While love is important, sometimes it isn't enough to keep a marriage together. Have students list in their Journal the qualities that they think would help a marriage endure through both good and difficult times.

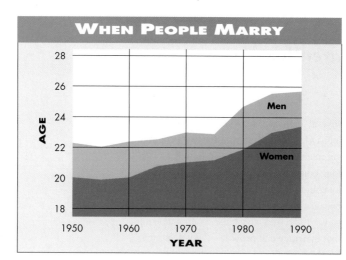

WHEN PEOPLE MARRY

(FIGURE 18-5) **Studies show that men and women are getting married at an older age than they once did.**

lifelong partnership must be able to tell each other how they are feeling and what they are thinking. As they do in all relationships, conflicts will inevitably arise in marriage. People who are in a good marriage are able to resolve these conflicts through communication and respect. Conflict-resolution skills are discussed in some detail in Chapter 17.

When two people are willing to make the commitment marriage requires, the result can be a rewarding, fulfilling relationship, well worth the work and compromise it requires.

Conflict-resolution skills are discussed in Chapter 17.

Reasons People Don't Get Married

Like all of life's choices, marriage is not for everyone and is not right for every partnership. Two people who enjoy being together but are not willing to make necessary compromises, for example, probably would not be happy married to each other.

People who have very busy jobs that require extensive travel or whose jobs require that they move often may also choose not to marry. It's not always easy to juggle a busy, demanding career with marriage, although it can be done.

Some people decide not to get married simply because they prefer to remain single. The decision to remain single is the right one for many people. Those who don't marry usually have more time for friends and career and are generally able to be completely independent and self-sufficient. Marriage, they may feel, would jeopardize these freedoms.

Teen Marriage

In addition to the challenges of every marriage, a marriage between teenagers has its own set of difficulties. It is almost impossible for teenagers who are still in school to support each other financially. In order to make ends meet, married teenagers often find that they must leave school to work full time.

Having enough money to live on becomes more important—and more difficult to accomplish—if the couple has a child to support. Married teenagers who are also parents will find it practically impossible to find the time and energy to do the things they once took for granted, such as going to the movies, eating out, or just being with friends.

The emotional responsibilities of marriage can also take their toll on teenagers. No one finds it easy to make the compromises and selfless decisions required for a successful marriage. But it can be especially difficult for teenagers, who are still developing emotionally and who are probably not ready to put another person's needs before their own.

TEACH

Class Discussion
Preparing for Marriage

Have students name and prioritize reasons why people get married. Let them discuss their points, then list the reasons on the board in order from most important to least important. Then ask: **What are you doing now that will prepare you for marriage?**

[Socializing and dating, taking on responsibilities at home, working and handling finances, making decisions; some may take classes or receive counseling just prior to marriage.] Then discuss the following questions with students: How do you think young men and women should prepare for marriage? What qualities would make a person "the perfect date"? How do they differ from the qualities you would list for "the ideal mate"?

Cooperative Learning
Marriage—Think Before You Leap

Have students meet in small groups to brainstorm a list of factors they think two people should consider before they marry. Provide the following list and have students phrase questions to be answered by the couple: values, goals and interests, communication, finances, sexuality, extended family, children, conflict resolution. You might have pairs of students role-play scenes

Divorce and Remarriage

Unfortunately, not all marriages are successful. When a marriage falters, some couples try living apart for awhile. Such an arrangement is called a separation. If one or both partners decide that the marriage is over, they will generally seek a divorce. A **divorce** is the legal end of a marriage.

A divorce can be very painful emotionally, not only for the two people going through it, but also for their sons and daughters. Sometimes, divorced people decide to marry again. Remarriage can also be difficult, particularly when there are children involved. Chapter 19 examines divorce and marriage in greater detail and offers some advice on ways to cope with the stress of divorce.

Parenthood

The decision to have children may be the most important one you will ever make. The commitment you make to a child is lifelong. Parenthood is rewarding and exciting, but it isn't easy. In fact, being a parent is a job that requires care and attention 24 hours each day, 7 days each week.

Family Planning If married couples don't want to start a family, they can prevent pregnancy by using contraceptives every time they have sexual intercourse. A **contraceptive** is a device or method that prevents the fertilization or implantation of a woman's egg. Some methods of contraception are more effective than others. Using a condom with spermicidal foam, for example, is a more effective method of con-

Chapter 19 discusses the effects of divorce and remarriage on teenagers.

divorce:

the legal end to a marriage.

contraceptive:

a device or method that prevents the fertilization or implantation of a woman's egg.

SECTION 18.2

 Making a Choice 18B

Assign the Parenthood: Doing It Right card. The card asks students to discuss with a partner three successful things their parents or guardians have done and three things they think are characteristics of good parents.

 Life Skills Worksheet 18C

Assign the Learning About Contraception Life Skills Worksheet.

(FIGURE 18-6) **Dating is an exciting and pleasurable activity for many teenagers. But teenagers who decide to get married must contend with some very difficult circumstances.**

in which couples work through the issues involved in these questions.

Class Discussion
When People Marry

Ask a volunteer to interpret the trend represented in Figure 18-5. Encourage students to give reasons why young adults might be waiting longer to marry. Ask students to think about themselves 10 years from now, as young adults. What will they be doing? Will they be married? How will they prepare for the future?

Debate the Issue
Teenage Marriages

Have student teams debate the topic: People should not marry as teenagers. You may wish to allow some out-of-class time for research and preparation of arguments. Debaters should be ready to present their arguments, give counterarguments, and take questions from the class.

Extension
More on Parenthood

Have volunteers recount their experiences baby-sitting or taking care of young relatives. Discuss the joys and trials of being with children, especially young children. Ask students why they think a person needs to be emotionally mature to be an effective parent. Suggest that students unfamiliar with young children visit a child-care facility

Background
Contraception

Point out to students that contraceptive methods, with the exception of condoms, do not provide protection against STDs, including AIDS. Students should not confuse protection against pregnancy with protection against disease. There is a renewed interest among contraceptive researchers in developing new "barrier" methods that can prevent both pregnancy and disease.

Also point out that the effective use of the rhythm method involves establishing the time of ovulation, which is tricky. Simply refraining from intercourse on certain days is not reliable.

In general, hormone implants are considered safe, but there are often side effects, such as irregular menstrual cycles, headaches, nausea, dizziness, acne, and weight gain. In addition, implant removal can be painful and may leave a scar. It is important for users to find out if the person who is removing the implant is fully trained to do so.

For information on fertilization and conception, see Chapter 16.

traception than simply using a condom. For definitions and reliability of different forms of contraception, see Figure 18-7.

Responsibilities of Being a Parent

Being a parent means caring for another human being completely. It means putting the welfare of your children before everything else. It means being able to support your children both financially and emotionally. It means feeding your children when you would rather be sleeping, laughing at their jokes when you've heard them thousands of times before, and letting them know you love them when they are convinced they are unlovable.

In other words, being emotionally mature is the most important key to being a

Actions and Effectiveness of Some Contraceptives

Method	Action	Effectiveness
Birth control pill	Temporarily stops a woman from ovulating and prevents the implantation of an ovum into the uterine lining; women take one pill every day.	97–99.9%
Condoms	Thin sheath that fits over penis and collects sperm.	88–98%
Diaphragm	Rubber cup that covers cervix and prevents sperm from reaching egg; most effective when used with spermicide.	72–94%
Spermicidal foams, creams, jellies, vaginal suppositories	Chemicals that are inserted inside the vagina to kill sperm and prevent sperm from entering the uterus; for greater effectiveness, should be used with a condom.	75–90%
IUD (intrauterine device)	A small device inserted by a health-care provider into the uterus, where it remains and prevents pregnancy for several years.	94–97%
Hormone implants	Six small capsules implanted in the skin of a woman's arm; releases a contraceptive hormone called progestin; effective for up to five years.	99.96%
Rhythm method	Requires that a couple determine when the woman is ovulating and abstain from sexual intercourse during that time.	80–86%

(FIGURE 18-7) **When used incorrectly, contraceptives offer no protection against pregnancy or sexually transmitted disease. Even when used correctly, no method of contraception is as effective as abstinence.**

• • • TEACH continued

to observe the children's interactions with each other and with care givers.

Check Up

Are You Ready to Be a Parent?

Answer the following questions to determine how ready you are to be a parent.

1. Could you handle a child and a job at the same time? Would you have time and energy for both?

2. Would you be willing to give up the freedom to do what you want to do, when you want to do it?

3. Would you be willing to decrease the time spent on your social life and spend more time at home?

4. Could you afford to support a child?

5. Would you want to raise a child where you now live? If not, can you afford to move? Are you willing to move?

6. Would a child fit into your career plans or educational plans for the future?

7. Are you willing to devote about 18 years of your life to the complete care of a child?

8. Do you understand how a child grows and develops or what children can be reasonably expected to understand?

9. Do you have the patience to cope with the noise and confusion that come with caring for a child?

10. Are you able to control your anger so that you won't take it out on a child?

11. Would you be able to discipline a child without being too strict?

12. Are you willing to take responsibility for a child's health and safety?

13. Would you be able to accept a child who developed values and ideas that are different from your own?

14. Would it matter to you whether the child you have is male or female?

15. Would you be as loving and accepting of an unhealthy child as you would be of a healthy child?

The more "Yes" answers you gave, the better parent you would probably be. Remember that becoming a parent is a serious responsibility. It is unfair—to you and to the child—to conceive a child without having considered your reasons for wanting to become a parent. Having a child doesn't make you "adult"; acting responsibly does.

Check Up

Have students answer the Check Up questions independently. Encourage them to discuss areas in which they feel least prepared for parenthood. What, in the next 10 years, might help them become more competent in these areas?

 Section Review Worksheet 18.2

To reinforce the concepts presented in this section, assign Section Review Worksheet 18.2.

 Section Quiz 18.2

Have students take Section Quiz 18.2.

 Reteaching Worksheet 18.2

Students who have difficulty with the material may complete Reteaching Worksheet 18.2.

Review Answers

1. Answers may include they want financial security, they want to have children, they seek close companionship, it is expected of them, they don't want to end up alone, and they want to make a lifelong commitment to be with a person they love and respect.

2. Answers may include love and respect, sacrifice, emotional maturity, and the ability to communicate effectively.

3. Answers may include meeting financial responsibilities, finding the time and energy to do the things they want to do, and being emotionally mature.

4. Answers may include putting the welfare of children before everything else, supporting your children financially and emotionally, meeting the physical and emotional needs of your children before your own, and discipline with compassion and love.

5. Answers will vary. Students may answer emotional maturity because this enables the parent to meet the needs of the child with love, unselfishness, and compassion.

(FIGURE 18-8) **Parenting requires time, patience, love, and a great deal of emotional maturity. But the rewards it offers are plentiful.**

Chapter 17 discusses the difficulties of teenage parenting.

successful parent. As you now know, emotional maturity is not a quality you can acquire overnight. It takes years of growth and experience to become a mature adult. This is one reason why teenage parents, who are still growing physically and emotionally, so often find their responsibilities overwhelming. The difficulties of being teenage parents are discussed in greater detail in Chapter 17.

Being financially secure also makes the job of parenting more manageable. Every state requires parents to support their children until the children reach age 18 (in some states it is 21). Clothing, feeding, and educating a child for 18 years is extraordinarily expensive.

It is also important for good parents to provide discipline. It is not easy to reprimand or punish a child for making mistakes. Some parents may remember making the same mistakes when *they* were younger. On the whole, discipline that is accompanied by compassion and love is the surest way to help a child understand what is right and what is wrong.

For all its difficulties and challenges, being a parent is one of life's most satisfying experiences. How good a parent do you think you'd be? Read the Check Up feature on page 397 to find out.

Review

1. What are two possible reasons why people get married?

2. Name three ingredients that can help a marriage be successful.

3. What are three difficulties teenagers who marry may face?

4. Name three responsibilities of parenthood.

5. **Critical Thinking** What do you think is the most important quality a parent can have? Explain your answer.

ASSESS

Section Review

Have students answer the Section Review questions.

Alternative Assessment

Successful Marriages

Have students work in small groups to prepare a visual or verbal summary of what they think goes into a successful marriage. Visual forms could include formulas, diagrams, and illustrations; verbal forms might be songs, dialogues, essays, or letters between spouses.

Closure

Life Decisions

Have each student submit a card with a summary of an important decision unique to a stage of adulthood. For example: Young Adulthood—couple decides when to start a family, or Middle Adulthood—a person decides whether to retrain for a new career or retire early. Divide the class into groups and have each group draw a card, make up characters for the situation it describes, and prepare to role-play the decision-making process.

Highlights

Summary

- Adulthood is divided into three stages: young adulthood, middle adulthood, and older adulthood.

- Decisions made during your adulthood require a certain degree of emotional maturity. For that reason, emotional maturity is a major goal to attain during young adulthood.

- Some middle-aged people may experience feelings of sadness when their children leave home, but middle adulthood also presents an opportunity to savor happy experiences.

- Common needs among elderly people include companionship, proper meals, and appropriate housing. As people grow older, they may elect to modify their own homes, move in with family, or live in retirement communities or nursing homes.

- The most important ingredients two people can bring to a marriage are love and respect.

- Marriage is particularly difficult for teens because they are still developing emotionally and may not be ready to put another person's needs before their own.

- Being emotionally and financially secure are important keys to being a successful parent. Good parents should also provide discipline accompanied by compassion and love.

Vocabulary

young adulthood the period of adulthood between the ages of 20 and 40.

middle adulthood the period of adulthood between the ages of 41 and 65.

older adulthood the period of adulthood past the age of 65.

emotional maturity the capacity to act independently, responsibly, and unselfishly. Being emotionally mature requires having compassion, integrity, and self-esteem.

Alzheimer's disease an incurable illness characterized by a gradual and permanent loss of memory. Alzheimer's disease most commonly affects the elderly.

Parkinson's disease an incurable disease characterized by a gradual loss of control of muscle function. Parkinson's disease most commonly affects the elderly.

contraceptive a device or method that prevents the fertilization or implantation of a woman's egg.

SUMMARY
Have students read the summary to reinforce the concepts they learned in Chapter 18.

VOCABULARY
Have students write a paragraph about adulthood and its events, using the vocabulary words correctly.

EXTENSION
Have students work in small groups to search the Yellow Pages and local community guides for agencies and services that help people make and carry out decisions about their lives at various stages of adulthood. These may include marriage counseling, family planning, and child care; financial planning, job retraining, vocational or professional education and career planning; single-parent, divorce, and surviving spouse support groups; and housing, food service, and medical assistance for the elderly. The class can organize the information into a community services directory.

CHAPTER
18

Chapter Review

CHAPTER REVIEW

Concept Review

1. young adulthood
2. emotional
3. middle adulthood
4. Alzheimer's disease, Parkinson's disease
5. age discrimination
6. nursing home
7. lifelong commitment, respect
8. communicate
9. divorce
10. compassion, love

Expressing Your Views

1. Answers will vary. Accept any answer that shows an understanding of the grandparents' needs and acknowledges that it is difficult, but often best, to give up independent living.

2. Sample response: Middle age can offer a time to benefit from the experiences you gained during young adulthood. It can be a time of peak professional ability. Married parents may find that it is a time to renew their romantic relationship. Middle age also involves physical changes such as gray hair, wrinkles, and menopause. Middle-aged adults may also have to confront death for the first time and may experience feelings of sadness when their children leave home.

3. Sample response: I would tell Jed that I feel it would be best if he waits

Concept Review . . . .

1. The period between the ages of 20 and 40 is known as _____ .

2. Age does not necessarily reflect _____ maturity.

3. Menopause occurs during _____ .

4. _____ and _____ are two incurable diseases that affect the elderly.

5. _____ occurs when a person is judged solely on the basis of his or her age.

6. A _____ may be recommended as housing for elderly people who lose almost complete mental and physical functioning.

7. Perhaps the best reason people get married is that they want to make a _____ to someone they love and _____ .

8. An important ingredient that makes a marriage successful is the ability to _____ effectively.

9. If one or both partners decide that the marriage has failed, a _____ will usually result.

10. Discipline that is combined with _____ and _____ is the best way to help a child understand what is right and what is wrong.

Expressing Your Views . . . .

1. Your grandparents are in their mid-seventies, and they are considering moving to a community of retired adults. It would provide a lot of opportunities for them, like tennis, book clubs, a new group of friends, and on-site health care, but it would mean they would have to give up their home. What do you think they should do?

2. What are some advantages of being middle-aged? What are some disadvantages?

3. Your friend Jed is planning to drop out of school and get married. He has asked you for your opinion of his decision. Explain how you would answer your friend.

4. Explain why you think compromise plays such an important role in the success of a marriage.

awhile before getting married and that he should finish school. It will be difficult to get a well-paying job without a completed education. Without a job that pays well, it will be hard to meet the financial obligations of marriage. Also, it is not easy for teenagers to make the compromises and selfless decisions that are required for a successful marriage. The possibility of having children often comes with marriage. Having children when you are not financially

or emotionally ready can be difficult on the parents and the marriage.

4. Sample response: Because marriage is a partnership, it is important to consider the needs and wants of the other person. The best way to meet your needs and those of your partner is through compromise. Marriage will not work if one partner is emotionally immature and always wants things his or her way.

Life Skills Check

1. Setting Goals

Think of two long-range goals you have for the next five years. Then list ways these goals would be affected by marriage and by parenthood. How can you help yourself stay on track and achieve your goals? Share your thoughts about the impact of marriage and parenthood on one's life with the class.

2. Coping

Your grandmother has just been placed in a nursing home. You know it is the best place for her because she is too sick to stay at home. You have always been close to your grandmother and you want to continue the close relationship; however, you feel uncomfortable visiting her in the nursing home. What should you do? How can you maintain a strong relationship with her?

Projects

1. Develop a questionnaire for adults. Interview three adults, one from each of the three age groups. Include the following questions: What are your goals now? How are they different from the goals you set during your teenage years? Share your results with the class.

2. Write a creative essay in which you describe yourself and your life at age 35 and at age 70. Include a discussion of your work, your family life, and your leisure time.

3. Work with a group to plan a budget for a newlywed couple. Include expenses such as rent, utilities, food, clothing, insurance, transportation, and entertainment. Consider who would be responsible for paying the bills and what would be done to cover emergency expenses.

Plan for Action

Marriage and parenthood are two of the most life-changing events that you can experience. Create a plan that you think would help you become better prepared for decisions regarding these actions.

Life Skills Check

1. Answers will vary. Accept all answers that state two goals and that clearly tell how the goals would be affected by marriage and parenthood.

2. Answers will vary but should include alternative ways to stay in contact with the grandmother, such as by telephone, through cards and letters, or by doing small errands or shopping. Some students may include innovative methods of communication, such as giving their grandmother a taped greeting she can play again and again.

Projects

Have students complete the projects on adulthood, marriage, and parenthood.

Plan for Action

Students' plans will vary. Suggest that students carefully consider their goals, the information and experiences they might need in order to make decisions affecting their goals, and who in the adult community is a possible source of information and guidance. Plans are extremely personal and should be shared only on a voluntary basis.

ASSESSMENT OPTIONS

Chapter Test
Have students take the Chapter 18 Test.

Alternative Assessment
Have students do the Alternative Assessment activity for Chapter 18.

Test Generator
The Test Generator contains additional assessment items for this chapter.

Section	Title/Objectives	Personal Health Inventory	Journal	Check Up	Life Skills	Life Skills Worksheets	Media Message or Ethical Issues Worksheet	What Would You Do?
		PERSONAL INVENTORY			LIFE SKILLS DEVELOPMENT			
19.1 *pp. 403–410*	**UNDERSTANDING FAMILY RELATIONSHIPS** • Name the three main functions of healthy families. • Explain how families have changed in recent years. • Name the characteristics of healthy families. ▪▪ Consider what your own family will be like when you are an adult.	Ch. 19	19A 19B		p. 409			
19.2 *pp. 411–414*	**COPING WITH FAMILY PROBLEMS** • Describe the common emotional reactions of a child to his or her parents' divorce. ▪▪ Name two actions a person can take to cope with parents' divorce. • Describe the effects on a child of growing up in a dysfunctional family. ▪▪ Name two actions that could help a teenager cope with living in a dysfunctional family. ▪▪ Apply the decision-making model to a family problem.		19C 19D				19A	p. 412

KEY: ▪▪ Denotes Life Skill Objective

Text references denoted by page number.

Supplement references denoted by chapter or item numbers.

LINKING RESOURCES

	Making a Choice Cards	Parent Discussion Guide	Health Talk Audio Program	Teaching Transparencies and Directory	Section Review Worksheets	Section Quizzes	Reteaching Worksheets	Section Reviews
	INTERACTION		OTHER RESOURCES		SECTION REVIEW AND ASSESSMENT			
	19A 19B			19A	19.1	19.1	19.1	p. 410
					19.2	19.2	19.2	p. 414

KEY FACTS

- Healthy families meet their members' basic physical needs, provide them with emotional support, and give structure to their lives.

- While the nuclear family is considered the traditional family type, there are many other types of families in today's society, including extended, couple, single-parent, and blended families, or any other non-traditional arrangement.

- Many forces, including the high divorce rate, the high cost of raising children, and the large number of working mothers, have helped change the American family structure.

- Within healthy families, members respect one another, communicate effectively, provide emotional support to one another, and adapt well to change.

- For some young people, the divorce of their parents or the remarriage of a parent creates a feeling of loss that can cause depression.

- Dysfunctional families do not meet the needs of their members, and children who grow up in a dysfunctional family often have low self-esteem.

CHAPTER REVIEW AND ASSESSMENT

TEXT

Chapter Review pp. 416–417

SUPPLEMENTS

Chapter Test 19

Alternative Assessment 19

Test Generator Chapter 19

GETTING STARTED

Using the Chapter Photograph

Ask students how the group in the picture fits their idea of family. How does it differ? Discuss the ways that our image of the ideal family is affected by how we feel about our own family.

Question Box

Have students write out any questions they have about families, family relationships, or coping with family problems and put them in the Question Box.

Sensitivity *ALERT*

Many students are anxious about some aspect of their family situation; they may be going through the pain of divorce or may come from a dysfunctional family. Try to alleviate this anxiety by assuring students that all families have troubles at one time or another. Point out that often people do not talk about their family troubles, so it is easy to get the idea that one's own family is the only one experiencing difficulties.

CHAPTER 19

Families

◆ ◆ ◆ ◆

Section 19.1 Understanding Family Relationships

Section 19.2 Coping With Family Problems

Families serve important functions.

MYTHS & MISCONCEPTIONS

- **It is best for a child to grow up in a nuclear family with both biological parents.** This is not always true. An intact nuclear family in which a member suffers from alcoholism, for example, may be much more harmful to a child than an alternative family structure. What a child needs is nurturing and a support system that can be relied on.

- **A healthy, normal family doesn't have problems.** All families must cope with problems. What is important is how a family deals with problems. Many people have difficulty acknowledging and addressing problems, so they deny that the problems exist. When members of a family function in this manner, problems that could be solved are not discussed. Health professionals often use the term *dysfunctional* to describe a family whose communication and problem-solving skills are not in good working order.

After Braylon's mother died he moved in with his grandparents. Since his father lived thousands of miles away, Braylon got to see him only a few times a year. It was a rough time—he loved his grandparents, but he also really missed his mother and father. His grandparents took good care of him though, and they were always ready to listen when he had something on his mind.

Things gradually started to settle down, and Braylon was able to concentrate on school again. Then his Uncle William moved back home, and Braylon had to share a bedroom with him! William was in his twenties—what right did he have to move back home and mess up Braylon's room with all his stuff? Braylon decided to talk to his grandfather about how he was feeling. Maybe his grandfather could help him cope with all of the changes.

Personal Health Inventory

Have students complete the Personal Health Inventory for this chapter.

Section 19.1

Understanding Family Relationships

Objectives

■ *Name the three main functions of healthy families.*

■ *Explain how families have changed in recent years.*

■ *Name the characteristics of healthy families.*

■ *Consider what your own family will be like when you are an adult.*
LIFE SKILLS: Setting Goals

Most of us grow up in some type of family. Your family may be the traditional kind, composed of a father, a mother, and one or more children. Or like Braylon's family, it may be less traditional.

Whatever kind of family you have, it probably means a lot to you. Healthy families provide us with love and support. They also teach us lessons about family relationships, which we use when we establish our own families. When people begin their own families, they tend to model them after the family relationships they experienced when they were children. If you grew up in a healthy family, this tendency to reproduce your childhood experience can have very positive effects.

Functions of Healthy Families

Although there is great diversity among families, all healthy families have similar functions. Whether a healthy family consists of just a parent and child, or if it also includes grandparents, a stepparent, and

---

Section 19.1 Lesson Plan

MOTIVATE

Cooperative Learning
Braylon's Situation

Have students form small groups and discuss Braylon's situation. Have them make suggestions for how he might cope with the changes. Have students imagine the conversations Braylon might have with Weldon, his grandfather, and his father.

Journal 19A
Family Relationships

Have students complete the statement, "An important relationship in my family is . . ." in their Journal. Then have students explain their choice.

Background
The Changing Family

The 1960s ideal of one parent who works, one parent who is a home-maker, and one or more children is a thing of the past. Today, economic conditions make it increasingly difficult—if not impossible—for one parent to stay home on a full-time basis. Family composition has also changed. Although divorce rates have decreased since a peak in 1981 and the number of two-parent households is on the rise, it is likely that one parent is a stepparent or an unrelated adult acting as a parent. At the same time, there has been a sharp increase in the number of households headed by single mothers. Forty-six percent of households headed by single mothers live below the poverty line, compared with 8 percent of households with two parents. The age of the parents also influences the family's financial status. Families with very young parents are much more likely to live near the poverty line than those with parents in their mid-twenties or older.

halfbrothers and sisters, it serves three basic functions.

First, families help provide basic physical needs such as food and shelter. When a family member is ill, the family provides the necessary care.

Second, families provide emotional support. The members of a supportive family know they can turn to each other when they have problems. Emotional bonding occurs in healthy families through shared experiences and close communication.

Third, families help provide structure for our lives. Your family helps you organize your activities and schedule your time.

You might want to stay up late at night, for example, but your parents or guardians probably require that you go to bed early so you will be rested the next day. A healthy family looks out for your best interests by providing structure.

Types of Families

The great variety of family types makes it difficult to define the word *family*. But regardless of who is included in the family structure, any family can be healthy and happy.

The traditional structure of a mother, father, and one or more children is known as

Cultural DIVERSITY

Extended Families of Hispanic Americans

Hispanic Americans are the second largest ethnic minority group in the United States. Immigrants and their descendants from Mexico, Cuba, Puerto Rico, Central and South America, and other Spanish-speaking areas make up this culturally diverse group. Despite their differences, Hispanic cultures share one important characteristic—the importance of family.

In Hispanic cultures, the word *familia* means not just the nuclear family but an extended network of parents, brothers and sisters, grandparents, aunts, uncles, cousins, and in-laws. Godparents, too, are considered to be members of the extended family. Through the

custom called *compadrazgo*, a *compadre* (godfather) or *comadre* (godmother) has real responsibility for the spiritual, emotional, and material welfare of the godchild.

TEACH

Class Discussion
Functions of Family Life

Have students name the three functions of any family. Discuss different ways families meet these needs. How do different family structures make it easier or more difficult to fulfill certain functions? For example, how does caring for a sick child in a single-parent

family differ from caring for a sick child in an extended family?

Reinforcement
Stages of Family Life

On the chalkboard, draw a model (such as the one that follows) for the stages of the family.

Ask students to explain how the model might differ for a couple family, adoptive family, extended family, foster family, single-parent family, or blended family. Add modifications

or create new models to represent each of these family types.

BEGINNING Establish household — PARENTING Raise children — EMPTY NEST Adjust as children leave — RETIREMENT leave work force — Children become independent a **nuclear family.** At one time, the father typically worked outside the home and the mother worked inside the home, taking care of the children and the household. Now, parenting roles are no longer so divided. This pattern is becoming less common as more women work outside the home and men take a more active role in parenting.

The nuclear family tends to go through the following four stages: beginning stage, parenting stage, empty-nest stage, and retirement stage.

The focus of the beginning stage is the establishment of the household by the new couple. They are adjusting to each other and are planning the things that will be important to them in their life together.

The parenting stage begins with the birth or adoption of the first child and lasts until the youngest child leaves home.

The empty-nest stage takes place when the children leave home, which used to be when the parents were middle-aged. It may now be later than middle age for parents who have children later in life or for parents whose children live at home for a while as adults. Some parents experience adjustment problems when their children leave home, especially if their children were the center of their activities. Others manage

nuclear family:

a family in which a mother, a father, and one or more children live together.

Background
Teenage Mothers
The United States has the highest teenage pregnancy rate among the world's industrialized nations. In 1995, 65 percent of all teenage mothers were unmarried. It is estimated that as many as 90 percent of unwed teenage mothers keep their babies, despite the extremely high risk of a lifetime of poverty. If the mother is able to continue school or to find employment, the primary parenting responsibility often passes to her mother, grandmother, or aunt, giving rise to a form of extended family known as skip-generation parenting.

A child who grows up in such a family therefore has the benefit of a great deal of social support.

Grandparents are highly respected members of traditional Hispanic families. As esteemed authority figures, they play a large role in the family decision-making process. The elders also make significant contributions to the family by helping with household tasks and child care.

A strong family system like this promotes good health by providing social support and an atmosphere of mutual respect.

Teaching Transparency 19A
Types of Families

Use this transparency to help students become aware of the makeup of modern families.

Debate the Issue
Moving Back Home

Have students debate the issue: Should young adults be allowed to live with their parents for as long as they want? After both sides are presented, list possible compromise arrangements on the board (grown child living at home must pay rent; parents and child must work out acceptable schedules and rules, and so on).

• • • TEACH continues on p. 406

(FIGURE 19-1) **Single-parent households are becoming increasingly common.**

couple family:

a family in which only a husband and a wife live together in the home.

single-parent family:

a family in which only one parent lives with the children in the home.

extended family:

an emotionally close family that includes relatives outside the central family unit.

perfectly well and, in fact, welcome the freedom to make decisions and to use their time without having to consider their children at home.

It is becoming more common for grown children to live at home with their parents. Many young adults cannot afford to live on their own, so they continue to live with their parents until they have the money to move. Others move out, find out they can't afford their own place or miss the emotional support of home, and move back in with their parents.

In the retirement stage, people adjust to changes associated with leaving the work force. They also deal with the changes that are part of aging.

An **extended family** includes relatives who are not part of the central family unit but who are emotionally close. They may be grandparents, grandchildren, aunts, uncles, or cousins. Years ago, it was very common for extended families to live together, but it is less common now.

A **couple family** has only the husband and wife living at home. Some couples never have children. They may choose not to have children, or they may be unable to reproduce or to adopt children. Others may have children who are living with someone else—a former spouse, a grandparent, or another relative.

A family in which only one parent lives with the children is called a **single-parent family.** The single parent may be divorced, never married, or widowed. Most single-parent families are headed by women, although many are headed by men. The single parent manages all aspects of the household alone, which can be extremely difficult if the parent also works outside the home. Juggling home and work responsibilities is not easy.

Sometimes divorced parents spend equal amounts of time with their children. In one arrangement, the children may spend one week with one parent and the next week with the other. Or the children may spend

---

Class Discussion

Changing Family Structures

Ask: **What is implied about the family in America by the many different types of structures?** *[The family unit is fluid, constantly changing, and often under great economic and emotional stress.]* Ask students to discuss some of the problems a blended family may face—such as children who spend

only part of the time in the family, and conflicts between children of different parents. Have they seen these problems on television programs? Have they seen these problems in life? Are the TV solutions realistic?

Reinforcement

Evolution of the Family

In recent history, most people grew up in families with several siblings.

Because of disease, not all children lived through childhood. Frequently there were grandparents or other relatives living in the household. Today, people in the United States tend to have small families. Have students explore their family history and record the number of children their parents, grandparents, and great grandparents had. If any students know about their great-great-grandparents, include that three or four days with one parent and then three or four days with the other parent. The important consideration for parents in this situation should be what is best for the child.

A **blended family** results when divorced or widowed parents remarry. The parents and their children from previous marriages combine to form the blended family. The parents may decide to have more children together. The parent who is not a child's biological father or mother is known as a stepparent. Some stepparents legally adopt their new spouse's children.

The members of a blended family face unique problems. They often must deal with changes in the family rules, for example, or they must work out arrangements in which unrelated children share a bedroom.

Some families don't fit any of the descriptions but are families nevertheless. A grandparent may take care of one or more grandchildren, for instance, or a child may live with a foster family. Sometimes people who aren't married or related choose to live together to support and care for one another. These people grow into a family, too.

How Families Have Changed

In recent years, families have changed a great deal. The typical family of the 1950s and 1960s was defined as a working father, a mother who stayed home, and two children. Today, only about 10 percent of families in the United States fit that description.

Years ago, women were expected to stay at home, care for their children, and tend to the household chores. But circumstances have changed. Today, most women with children work outside the home. Some women work primarily because of the

blended family:
a family that results when divorced or widowed parents remarry. The parents and their respective children from previous marriages live in the home together.

SECTION 19.1

Making a Choice 19A
Assign the Sharing Family Responsibilities card. The card asks students to assign household chores for an extended family in a logical manner that encourages appreciation among family members for each other.

Making a Choice 19B
Assign the Discovering How Families Have Changed card. The card asks students to identify the type of family they are a part of and to compare characteristics of today's families with those of the past.

(FIGURE 19-2) Blended families bring two households together.

information also. Graph these data and derive an average number of children per family for each of the generations represented.

• • • TEACH continues on p. 408

Section Review Worksheet 19.1

To reinforce the concepts presented in this section, assign Section Review Worksheet 19.1.

Section Quiz 19.1

Have students take Section Quiz 19.1.

Reteaching Worksheet 19.1

Students who have difficulty with the material may complete Reteaching Worksheet 19.1.

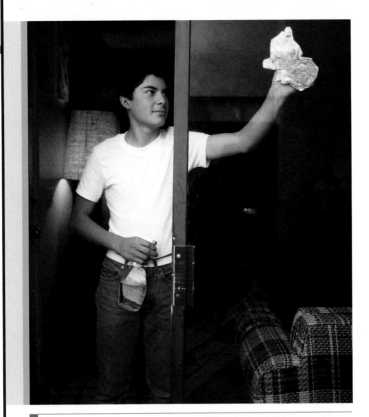

(FIGURE 19-3) **It is important for all family members to have responsibilities.**

satisfaction they receive from their accomplishments in the workplace. Others prefer not to work outside the home but must do so to support themselves and their family. Still other women prefer to stay at home and are able to do so. It is both challenging and rewarding to care for a family and a home. One of the benefits of recent changes in society is that many options are available to women, and each can be very satisfying.

Another major difference between today's families and those of the past is the number of single-parent families. Mostly as a result of the high divorce rate, single-parent families are much more common today than they were in earlier times. There are also many more blended families since most divorced people remarry.

Today's families are smaller in comparison with the families of the past. Before, having many children was beneficial if a family owned a farm or business; the children contributed to the material success of the family by working from an early age. Now, very few people in this country rely on their children for the family's economic survival. Even people who own a farm or business do not depend on their children as parents did years ago. These people usually hire other people to work in the business or on the farm and expect their children to help out only occasionally. Another reason for smaller families today is the high cost of raising children. It now costs a minimum of $100,000 to raise and educate one child through high school.

Characteristics of Healthy Families

Healthy families have certain characteristics in common. These include respect for family members, shared responsibilities, good communication, emotional support, and the ability to manage change.

Respect for Family Members Respect for family members is essential to a healthy family—this includes respect for privacy, property, and feelings. Respect means that you value what is important to another person. A brother might show respect for a sister, for example, by controlling an urge to read her diary. In this way he is respecting her privacy. A father might show respect for a teenage son by not telling him what he thinks of his friends. In this way he is respecting his son's feelings. If family members are not treated with respect, they might withdraw from the family.

Shared Responsibilities Responsibility helps us feel important and valuable. It is

---

• • • TEACH continued

Journal 19B
Respecting Others in Your Family

Have students write in their Journal ways they show respect for other members of their family. Then have them describe a way in which they want others in their family to show respect for them.

Demonstration
Healthy Families

Have students each write on an index card a line or two of dialogue that suggests poor family dynamics. *(I haven't time for that now; you'll do fine without my advice; you'll never learn to do that right.)* Shuffle the cards. Have each student draw one, read it aloud, and suggest a line of dialogue that would address the problem. *(For example, I would like to discuss that later, when we have time to talk.)*

Class Discussion
How Much Responsibility?

Ask the class to discuss the kinds of responsibilities they think are appropriate for a teenager. What happens when teens do not have enough responsibility? When they have too much?

Reinforcement
Communication Skills

Remind students of the communication skills they learned in Chapter 17. Have them practice effective family important that all family members have responsibilities, though they should be appropriate to each person's age and abilities. The responsibilities of a 4-year-old should be different from those of a 14-year-old, which should be different from those of a 40-year-old.

Good Communication Good communication is a vital ingredient of successful family relationships. People need to be able to express their feelings in an open and supportive environment. One of the most important communication skills is listening. Sometimes the best thing you can do for someone is simply to listen.

Effective communication can go a long way toward helping families work through their problems. Without it, the problems will probably get worse.

Communication skills are discussed in Chapter 17.

Life SKILLS

Have students answer questions 1–6 independently on a sheet of paper with their gender written at the top. Tally the yes and no answers for 1–4, separate responses of males and females, and place results on the chalkboard. What trends are shown? Discuss students' responses, including their responses to questions 5 and 6. Ask students what their ideas suggest about future changes in family structure.

Life SKILLS: Setting Goals

Your Future Family . . . . . .

What will your own family be like when you are an adult? You can start thinking about it now by answering the following questions.

1. Do you want to get married? If your answer is yes, when do you think you will be ready for marriage?

2. Will you work outside the home? Explain.

3. Will you want your spouse to work outside the home? Explain.

4. Do you want to have children? Explain.

5. If you want to have children, how many would you like?

6. Who will watch your children before they enter kindergarten? You? Your spouse? Another family member? A day-care center? Someone else?

communication by changing "you" messages (condemning) into "I" messages (revealing how you are affected by someone else's behavior). The following sentence can be a model for constructing "I" messages:

"When you *(state behavior),* I feel *(name the feeling).*" For example, "When you don't answer my questions, I feel unimportant and unloved."

Extension
Families Around the World

Have students research and report on the structure of families in the United States (for example, does family size vary in different regions of the country) and in other cultures. Have them devise a classification system that includes the different family structures found. Using the classification system, develop a method for presenting the results (histogram, pie chart, etc.).

Review Answers

1. meets basic physical needs, provides emotional support, provides structure

2. Extended families are less common now, more mothers work outside of the home, there is an increase in the number of single-parent families and blended families, and families are smaller in size.

3. respect for family members, shared responsibilities, good communication, emotional support, the ability to manage change

4. Answers will vary. Students' plans should reflect an understanding of the needs families meet for physical and emotional support and structure. They can practice good communication skills, lay the educational basis for a career, and make responsible decisions about sexual behavior.

5. Answers may include that women have been encouraged to pursue careers, that women need to work to support themselves and their families, and that many women are divorced. Society has changed so that many options are available to women.

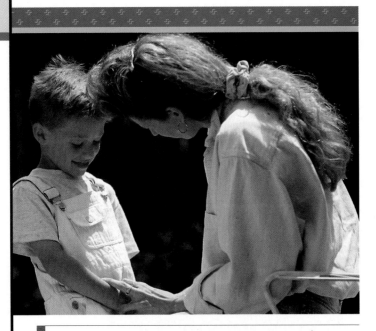

(FIGURE 19-4) **Good communication is an important characteristic of a healthy family.**

Emotional Support A healthy family provides emotional support to its members. For example, a teenager in a healthy family could turn to the family for support if he or she didn't make the track team or failed a test. A husband or wife can seek support from a spouse when going through a difficult time at work.

Ability to Manage Change Changes occur frequently in families. A healthy family can manage the variety of changes that occur during its members' lifetimes.

When family members are added to a household, the relationships between members may become more difficult, simply because it's a new situation. Living arrangements change when a baby is born, a grandparent moves in, a parent remarries, or grown children move back home after living on their own for a while. These changes aren't bad; they just mean the family has to

adjust to maintain good relationships. Space must be shared, new responsibilities must be assumed, and the family rules might have to be changed.

If a family member becomes disabled, the family must change to accommodate the disability. The physical structure of the apartment or house may have to be altered, and other family members may be called on to assist the disabled person, and to help him or her adapt to a new situation.

Disability and the addition of new family members are examples of dramatic changes that a family must adjust to. Most changes are less dramatic and occur over a longer period of time. As individual family members grow older, they develop new interests and begin to follow different life paths. Such changes are a completely normal part of life. Members of healthy families are usually able to accept and adapt to these new situations.

Review

1. Name the three main functions of healthy families.

2. Explain how families have changed in recent years.

3. Name the characteristics of healthy families.

4. **LIFE SKILLS: Setting Goals** Describe the kind of family you would like to have when you are an adult. What actions can you take now to help your plans succeed?

5. **Critical Thinking** What social changes have caused the shift in attitudes about women working outside the home?

ASSESS

Section Review

Have students answer the Section Review questions.

Alternative Assessment
Families in All Shapes and Sizes

Have students write a few sentences expounding on this thought: "The healthiness of a family has less to do with its size than with quality."

Closure
Family Problems and Solutions

Have each student write down a problem of an imaginary family and turn it in. Preview the problems, and place all appropriate ones in a container. Have a student pick a problem from the box and read it to the class. The other students should suggest ways that the problem could be addressed effectively. Repeat this process for the remaining problems.

Section
19.2 Coping With Family Problems

SECTION 19.2

Objectives

■ Describe the common emotional reactions of a child to parents' divorce.

■ Name two actions a person can take to cope with parents' divorce.
   ■ **LIFE SKILLS: Coping**

■ Describe the effects on a child who grows up in a dysfunctional family.

■ Name two actions that could help a teenager cope with living in a dysfunctional family.
   ■ **LIFE SKILLS: Coping**

■ Apply the decision-making model to a family problem.
   ■ **LIFE SKILLS: Making Responsible Decisions**

Although it would be wonderful if all families lived happily ever after, we know this is not the case. All families have problems. Some problems are temporary, and the family either copes with them or solves them. Other family problems are more serious and long lasting. As a teenager, you are not in a position to solve your family's problems, but you can find ways of coping with them.

If Your Parents Divorce

Each year, more than 1 million children experience the divorce of their parents. Although divorce is extremely common, it can be a shattering experience for all members of a family. When parents divorce, their children have to make major adjustments to cope with the changes that result.

Background
Codependency and Dysfunctional Families

When people support or condone the unacceptable behavior of a person who is dependent on them, their enabling actions are referred to as codependency. A codependent person becomes overly focused on the dependent person's problem behavior. In doing so, he or she often neglects his or her own needs and those of other family members. Codependent relationships are common in families with abuse problems.

(FIGURE 19-5) **If your parents divorce, you will have to make adjustments to cope with the changes that result.**

Section 19.2 Lesson Plan

MOTIVATE

Journal 19C
Troubled Families

No families are totally healthy all the time, and some families fail completely to meet the needs of their members. What do students consider to be abuse or neglect within a family? Have them write their thoughts in their Journal.

What Would You Do ?

Have students list options and decide what to do, and then form small groups to discuss the solutions.

Life Skills Worksheet 19A

Assign the How Can a Counselor Help a Family? Life Skills Worksheet.

Section Review Worksheet 19.2

To reinforce the concepts presented in this section, assign Section Review Worksheet 19.2.

Section Quiz 19.2

Have students take Section Quiz 19.2.

Emotional Reactions After parents divorce, children often see less of the parent who moved out. They may see that parent only on holidays or during the summer. In some extreme cases, they never see that parent again. This creates a tremendous sense

What Would You Do ?

Making Responsible Decisions

Should You Move Back Home?

Imagine that you graduated from college a year ago, and got a job as a copywriter at a small advertising company. You hope to work your way up the ladder there. In the meantime, you bought a used car and began sharing an apartment with two of your friends.

Then you discover that you never have enough money to make it from one paycheck to the next. You're constantly having to borrow money from your parents. Finally your father suggests that you just move back home until you make enough money to live on your own.

In a way, his idea is tempting; you have missed the refrigerator full of food and a washer and dryer in the house. But on the other hand, you have worked very hard to be self-sufficient, and you worry that others might think less of you for not "making it" in the real world. What would you do? What are your options?

Remember to use the decision-making steps:

1. State the Problem.
2. List the Options.
3. Imagine the Benefits and Consequences.
4. Consider Your Values.
5. Weigh the Options and Decide.
6. Act.
7. Evaluate the Results.

---

of loss for children who want to be close to the parent they no longer live with. It is natural to have strong emotional reactions—they are part of the grieving process.

At first, there may be anger at the parent who left; the child may feel betrayed and abandoned. There also may be anger at the parent who stays—a feeling that this parent has somehow caused the other parent to leave. It is common to take sides with one parent, but rarely does either parent deserve all the blame for a divorce. Because marriage is a very personal relationship, others outside the relationship cannot understand all the underlying reasons for the divorce.

Sometimes children feel very guilty after a divorce and blame themselves for their parents' decision. A person whose parents are divorcing may think, "If only I had been better, this would never have happened." But it's important to realize that getting married is a decision for adults, and therefore ending a marriage is also a decision for adults. Children are *not* responsible for their parents' divorces, although they may feel like they are.

Children of divorced parents may also experience anxiety about the future. Often there is anxiety about money or about whether the family will have to move. Again, these are matters for adults. Children are not responsible for their family's financial situation. They may, however, have to make some sacrifices to help make ends meet, especially during the initial adjustment period.

Another very common emotional reaction is depression. When parents divorce, the children may have problems sleeping and may find it harder to concentrate in school. They may have a poor appetite or feel generally listless and down. It is normal for children to experience a sense of sadness and loss when their parents divorce. If they are sad for more than a few weeks,

---

TEACH

Writing
Reacting to Divorce

Write the following questions on the board. Have students respond in writing to one of the questions as if it were a letter from a teen and they were an advice columnist.

1. Why can't my parents just get back together?

2. Did I cause my parents' divorce?
3. What if we can't pay the bills?
4. What if I have to move to a different home/neighborhood/school?
5. Can I still love both my parents? Should I?
6. When will this misery go away?

Ask volunteers to read their responses to the class.

Cooperative Learning
Stepsister, Stepbrother

Allow students to work in small groups to discuss conflicts that might arise be-

tween children in a blended family. How can they be resolved? Remind students what they have learned about active listening, problem solving, and conflict resolution.

Class Discussion
Defining Dysfunctional

Draw a horizontal line on the chalkboard and mark its midpoint. Label the left end of the line HEALTHY FAMILY RELATIONSHIPS—ALL NEEDS MET and the right end DYSFUNCTIONAL FAMILY RELATIONSHIPS—NO NEEDS MET. Explain that few families are 100 percent they should seek professional help. They could start by talking with a parent or a school counselor, who could refer them to a therapist or support group.

One good way to deal with your emotions is to communicate them to people you trust. In a situation like divorce, you might want to spend more time talking with your friends, especially those who have had a divorce in their family.

Another thing you could do is get involved in a new hobby or sport. Find something that absorbs your interest and takes your mind off problems that you cannot solve.

It's important to realize that attempting to escape from emotional pain by using alcohol or other drugs will not help, nor will expressing anger through violence or abuse. These behaviors create more serious problems and prolong the pain.

After children come to accept their parents' divorce, they will be able to look at the situation and evaluate it more objectively. A happy single-parent family suits some people better than an unhappy two-parent family.

Remarriage At some point, divorced parents may begin dating and eventually remarry. The remarriage of a parent can create new feelings of loss for the children. It might be the first time that a child has to abandon the dream that his or her family will someday get back together. The new stepparent may take away some of the attention a child was used to receiving from a parent. The stepparent may have children, and later there may be half-siblings, all of whom could threaten the child's sense of security in terms of how the parent spends his or her time and how money is distributed.

It takes some time to build a new family. If you are in this situation, be realistic,

and recognize that adjustments may be difficult. But also be aware that second marriages are often quite successful and that a happy, united family can emerge. Try to do your part to bring this about—be patient, and understand that all family adjustments take time to be successful—and you may find that, rather than losing a parent, you have gained valuable family members.

Dysfunctional Families

A family that fulfills the basic functions of a healthy family—to meet the basic physical needs of family members, to provide emotional support, and to provide structure—can be thought of as a functional family. A family that does not fulfill these basic functions is known as a **dysfunctional family.**

In some dysfunctional families, children may not be physically cared for. They may not be fed, clothed, or sheltered properly. In most dysfunctional families, however, the basic physical needs of children are met, but their emotional needs are not. Children might be neglected or abused. In some dysfunctional families children are rigidly controlled, while in others very little structure is provided.

Most dysfunctional families are a direct outgrowth of troubled parents. The parents may have an unhappy marriage, problems with alcohol or other drugs, or emotional problems. Usually, the parents grew up in troubled families. These parents don't intend to be inadequate parents; they are simply overwhelmed by their own problems and are therefore incapable of meeting their children's needs.

But regardless of parents' intentions, their behavior has a profound and lasting effect on children. Children who do not receive adequate parenting may develop low self-esteem, and grow up ashamed of their family and themselves. They often

dysfunctional family:

a family that does not fulfill the basic functions of a healthy family.

healthy or 100 percent dysfunctional. Review the attributes of a healthy family, and write them to the left of the midpoint. Ask the following questions, and list the responses to the right of the midpoint: **What are some problems that can cause families to become dysfunctional?** *[alcoholism, drug addiction, emotional or mental illness, abusive parents]* **In what ways does the problem show itself outwardly?** *[behaviors of children whose needs are not met; overt physical or emotional abuse of spouse or children; depression, anger, and low self-esteem of children]*

Journal 19D
When Things Are Bad . . .
Have students write in their Journal three positive actions a teenager in a dysfunctional family can take to meet his or her needs or to gain a better sense of personal worth.

Extension
Today's Family
Have students write articles, stories, poems, editorials, letters to the editor, etc. for an edition of a family magazine. Students may explore current

statistics on divorce and problems of dysfunctional families and may give advice to help solve these problems. Advertisements for family counseling or other related fields could be included. Students who are reluctant to write could design the cover or work on a layout for the magazine.

Answers to Questions 1–3 are on p. 413.

4. Answers will vary but may include: seek counseling for the family or just for himself or herself; get emotional support from other adults who are able and willing to give such support; and remember that he or she is a valuable and lovable person and that it is not a child's fault when a family is dysfunctional.

5. Answers will vary. Advantages may include getting emotional support and having physical needs met. Disadvantages may include still having to follow household rules and dealing with siblings.

6. Answers will vary. Students may answer that through counseling, the person may recognize the source and cause of the mistakes and how those mistakes affected his or her self-esteem, as well as how to avoid repeating the behaviors of the parents.

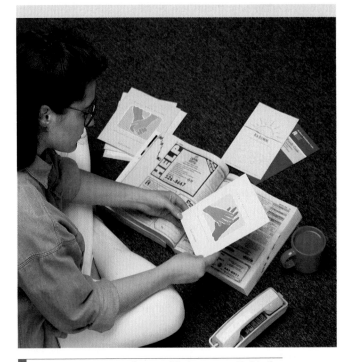

(FIGURE 19-6) **Many forms of help are available for troubled families.**

Emotional, physical, and sexual abuse are discussed in Chapter 20.

feel that they don't belong anywhere and that they are not ''good enough.'' As a result, they may be angry or depressed.

If Your Family Is Dysfunctional If you have grown up in such a family, know that help is available. Talk with an adult you trust about getting counseling. It would be most helpful if your entire family received counseling, but if that is not possible, don't hesitate to go by yourself.

It will also help to seek out adults who care about you and who will give you some of the emotional support you are missing. Do you have a relative—a grandparent, an aunt or uncle, or a brother or sister—that you can turn to for support? Perhaps there is a teacher, a religious leader, or another adult who would be willing to listen to you and help you.

While you do what you can to improve your situation, remember that you are a valuable person, even if your parents don't treat you that way. You are lovable, even if it sometimes seems that your parents don't love you. It isn't your fault that you are part of a troubled family.

When things seem especially bad, remind yourself that when you reach adulthood, you will have much more control over your life. You will be in a position to heal the old hurts and create the kind of life you want for yourself.

Review

1. Describe the common emotional reactions of a child to parents' divorce.

2. ■■ **LIFE SKILLS: Coping** Name two actions a person can take to cope with parents' divorce.

3. Describe the effects on a child of growing up in a dysfunctional family.

4. ■■ **LIFE SKILLS: Coping** Name two actions that could help a teenager cope with living in a dysfunctional family.

5. ■■ **LIFE SKILLS: Making Responsible Decisions** What are the advantages and disadvantages of continuing to live at home after high school graduation?

6. *Critical Thinking* How could a person who grew up in a troubled family avoid making the same mistakes with his or her own family?

ASSESS

Section Review
Have students answer the Section Review questions.

Alternative Assessment
Comparing Divorced and Dysfunctional Families

Have students decide which they think is less desirable: being part of a family split by divorce or belonging to a dysfunctional family. Ask them to write an explanation, including the way they see human needs being met in each circumstance.

Closure
Family Problems

Have students explain in their own words the differences between a family that copes with its problems and one that disintegrates or is dysfunctional. Have each student contribute his or her ideas to a class consensus.

 414 FAMILIES

Chapter

19

Highlights

HIGHLIGHTS
STRATEGIES

Summary

- Families help meet basic physical needs and provide emotional support and structure for our lives.

- There are a variety of family forms, including nuclear families, extended families, single-parent families, and blended families. Some families don't fit into any of these categories.

- In recent years the number of nuclear families has decreased, while the number of single-parent and blended families has increased.

- Healthy families have certain characteristics in common: respect for family members, shared responsibilities, good communication, emotional support, and the ability to manage change.

- A family that does not fulfill the basic functions of a healthy family is known as a dysfunctional family. In most dysfunctional families, physical needs are met, but emotional needs are not.

- Children who grow up without adequate parenting may have low self-esteem, be ashamed of their families and themselves, or be angry or depressed.

- Children of dysfunctional families can be helped through counseling or by seeking emotional support from other trusted adults.

Vocabulary

nuclear family a family in which a mother, a father, and one or more children live together.

extended family an emotionally close family that includes relatives outside the central family unit.

couple family a family in which only a husband and a wife live together in the home.

single-parent family a family in which only one parent lives with the children in the home.

blended family a family that results when divorced or widowed parents remarry. The parents and their respective children from previous marriages live in the home together.

dysfunctional family a family that does not fulfill the basic functions of a healthy family.

SUMMARY
Have students read the summary to reinforce the concepts they learned in Chapter 19.

VOCABULARY
For each vocabulary word, have each student write three words or phrases that could be associated with that vocabulary word. For example, for blended family, someone could write, "living with a stepbrother." Preview the words and phrases before distributing them to teams of students. Teams should take turns picking one of the words or phrases, reading it aloud, and stating which vocabulary word goes with it. Other teams can challenge their answer if they disagree.

EXTENSION
Arrange for a family-services counselor to speak to the class and answer questions. Have students prepare questions in advance about coping with divorce and other family problems.

HIGHLIGHTS STRATEGIES

Chapter Review

CHAPTER REVIEW

Concept Review

1. children
2. experiences, communication
3. empty-nest
4. extended family
5. single-parent; women
6. outside; smaller
7. respect
8. responsibilities
9. listening
10. disability, the addition of new family members or return of old ones
11. physical, emotional
12. unhappy marriage, alcohol or drug problems

Expressing Your Views

Sample responses:

1. As I get older, I assume more and greater responsibilities. Assuming these responsibilities now, under my parent's guidance, will help me become more capable and more efficient when dealing with these and similar responsibilities when I am on my own.

2. They can talk with other family members and help them share what they are feeling about the divorce. Teenagers can also help get younger siblings involved in activities so that they will not dwell on the divorce so much. Teenagers can help their friends who are experiencing a family breakup by giving emotional support, sharing how they

Concept Review . . . .

1. When people begin their own families, they tend to model them after the family relationships they experienced as _____.

2. Emotional bonding occurs in healthy families through shared _____ and close _____.

3. A nuclear family tends to go through stages. The _____ stage takes place when the children leave home.

4. Grandparents, uncles, aunts, and cousins make up an _____ _____.

5. A _____ family is a household in which only one parent lives with the children. Most of these families are headed by _____.

6. Today, most women with children work _____ the home. Also, today's families are _____ in size.

7. _____ for family members, which is essential to a healthy family, means that you value what is important to the other person.

8. It is important that all family members have _____, but they should be appropriate to each person's age and abilities.

9. One of the most important communication skills for a successful family is _____.

10. _____ and _____ are examples of changes that a family must adjust to.

11. In most dysfunctional families, the _____ needs of the children are met, but their _____ needs are not.

12. Most dysfunctional families are the result of _____, _____, or the emotional problems of the parents.

Expressing Your Views . . . .

1. How are your family responsibilities helping you prepare for independent life?

2. How can teenagers whose parents have divorced help other family members cope? How could they help friends experiencing a family breakup?

3. Many family problems are worked out through communication. Why do you think it is sometimes difficult for family members to communicate with each other?

4. What are some advantages of living within an extended family structure? What are some disadvantages?

felt when their parents divorced, or listening to how their friends are feeling and letting their friends know that they understand.

3. Some family members may not be emotionally mature or may not have developed good communication skills. Some family members may not have good listening skills. Some family members may find it difficult to express their feelings, especially if the family setting is not an open and supportive environment.

4. An advantage of an extended family is that there are more people to share in the household responsibilities. A disadvantage is that someone may have to give up a room or share a room with the person moving in.

Life Skills Check . . . . . .

1. Setting Goals

Sometimes just listening to someone is the most helpful thing you can do. How good are your listening skills? For a week, try to practice really listening to at least one person every day. Then evaluate your efforts. Set a goal to increase the amount of time you spend listening to people who are important to you.

2. Coping

Simira's mother is planning to remarry, and her mother's future husband has two small children. Simira and her mother have lived alone for almost all of Simira's life. Now Simira is afraid that she will never get to spend time with her mother, and she's worried that her new stepbrothers will complicate her life. What could you say to Simira to help her adjust to the change?

Projects . . . .

1. Working with a partner, research and compare the family structures of two different cultures. Give an oral report on your findings.

2. Work with a group to prepare a skit involving a family with two working parents, one teen, and one eight-year-old child; the family is trying to set up a schedule for household responsibilities and tasks. After pre-

senting your skit, evaluate how successful and fair the family was with the schedule.

3. Work with a group to create a bulletin-board display entitled "Healthy Families." Include family photographs, magazine pictures, or original art showing a variety of family types.

Plan for Action . . . .

A strong society depends on healthy family structures. Healthy families develop skills to work through problems. Devise a plan to help your family work out its problems and to help promote your family's health.

Life Skills Check

1. Evaluations and goals for listening skills will vary with each student.

2. Sample response: I might suggest that she talk with her mother about how she is feeling. Simira might also talk with her mother about what the new family rules and responsibilities will be as well as the living arrangements. I would assure Simira that, with compromise, all of the problems can be worked out to everyone's satisfaction.

Projects

Have students complete the projects on families.

Plan for Action

Have students work in small groups to create an imaginary case study of a dysfunctional family. After they have invented the family's difficulties, have students use what they have learned to make suggestions for the family's recovery. Suggest that students consider how they might apply any of the solutions they discussed to a situation in their own family that they wish to address.

ASSESSMENT OPTIONS

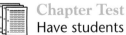 **Chapter Test**
Have students take the Chapter 19 Test.

 Alternative Assessment
Have students do the Alternative Assessment activity for Chapter 19.

 Test Generator
The Test Generator contains additional assessment items for this chapter.

SECTION	TITLE/OBJECTIVES	PERSONAL INVENTORY			LIFE SKILLS DEVELOPMENT			
		Personal Health Inventory	Journal	Check Up	Life Skills	Life Skills Worksheets	Media Message or Ethical Issues Worksheet	What Would You Do?
20.1 *pp. 419–423*	**ABUSIVE RELATIONSHIPS** • Name and define four different types of abuse. ▪▪ Use a decision-making model to decide what you would do if you suspected child abuse. ▪▪ Know at least two ways you could report an abusive situation.	Ch. 20				20A 20B		p. 422
20.2 *pp. 424–428*	**SEXUAL ASSAULT** • Define sexual assault. • Define acquaintance rape. • Discuss how young men can avoid committing acquaintance rape. ▪▪ Know what a victimized person should do to get help after a sexual assault. • Define sexual harassment.					20C		
20.3 *pp. 429–432*	**PREVENTING VIOLENT CONFLICT** • Name the three major risk factors associated with homicides. • Discuss the reasons why some teenagers join gangs. ▪▪ Know how to prevent your anger from turning into violence. ▪▪ Know how to resolve conflicts without violence. • Define peer mediation.		20A		p. 431	20D		

KEY: ▪▪ Denotes Life Skill Objective

Text references denoted by page number.

Supplement references denoted by chapter or item numbers.

LINKING RESOURCES

INTERACTION		OTHER RESOURCES		SECTION REVIEW AND ASSESSMENT			
Making a Choice Cards	Parent Discussion Guide	Health Talk Audio Program	Teaching Transparencies and Directory	Section Review Worksheets	Section Quizzes	Reteaching Worksheets	Section Reviews
20A	Ch. 20	Ch. 20		20.1	20.1	20.1	p. 423
			20A	20.2	20.2	20.2	p. 428
20B			20B	20.3	20.3	20.3	p. 432

KEY FACTS

- All forms of abuse—physical, sexual, child, spouse, elder, peer—are illegal.
- An abused child or adolescent is not responsible for the abuse.
- Abuse contributes to low self-esteem.
- More than 90 percent of all child abuse is inflicted by family members.
- Most child abusers were abused as children; counseling can help break this cycle.
- Sexual offenders cannot be identified by appearance, but there are behaviors known to be associated with sex offenders.
- Receiving education about how to prevent rape can reduce a person's risk of being raped.
- Major risk factors related to homicides are arguments turned violent, substance abuse, and possession of a gun.
- Anger is a natural emotion, but it needs to be managed and expressed in healthy ways.
- Training in non violent conflict resolution techniques can reduce violent conflicts.

CHAPTER REVIEW AND ASSESSMENT

TEXT

Chapter Review pp. 434–435

SUPPLEMENTS

Chapter Test 20

Alternative Assessment 20

Test Generator Chapter 20

GETTING STARTED

Using the Chapter Photograph

Ask students to describe what the children in the photograph are watching. Then ask students how common this kind of exposure is and what effect they think it has on American children.

Question Box

Have students write out any questions they have about abuse and violence and put them in the Question Box.

Sensitivity *ALERT*

This chapter deals with sensitive, difficult subjects. Teenagers may be embarrassed to discuss sexual abuse and assault; some students may be victims of rape or child abuse. Respect students' privacy, and do not encourage personal disclosure. Tell students that although the subject is hard to talk about and makes many people uncomfortable, it is too important a topic to ignore. Make it clear that jokes will not be tolerated.

CHAPTER

20

Preventing Abuse and Violence

◆ ◆ ◆ ◆

Section 20.1 Abusive Relationships

Section 20.2 Sexual Assault

Section 20.3 Preventing Violent Conflict

By the age of 18, the average person has seen approximately 250,000 violent acts on television.

MYTHS & MISCONCEPTIONS

- **No one should interfere with what goes on in a family.** The abuse of a spouse or a child is against the law. Law enforcement and family service agencies do have the right to intervene, and people do have the moral responsibility to report abuse.

- **An abused adult who stays with the abuser must like to be abused.** People, especially women, stay in such situations because of fear of retaliation if they leave,

because of financial dependence on and emotional attachment to the abuser, and because of their belief that the family should stay together.

- **Verbal abuse or neglect of children is not as serious as physical abuse or sexual abuse.** Although the legal penalties may not be as severe, withholding love, destroying a child's self-esteem, and neglecting a child's needs are serious forms of abuse.

Naomi and Carolyn are best friends, and they have always told each other everything. But Carolyn has a new boyfriend and is reluctant to tell Naomi about the time she spends with him. And instead of being happy about her new relationship, Carolyn is becoming quiet and withdrawn, and Naomi rarely sees her anymore. Although Carolyn insists that everything is fine, Naomi is beginning to think that something is very wrong.

A couple of weeks ago, Carolyn had a big bruise on her arm, but she had a very believable explanation when Naomi asked her about it. Last Sunday Naomi noticed that Carolyn had a swollen lip and some bruises on her leg. Naomi is beginning to think that Carolyn is being abused by her boyfriend. She has decided to confront her friend about her suspicions.

Section
20.1
Abusive Relationships

Personal Health Inventory
Have students complete the Personal Health Inventory for this chapter.

English/Spanish CD Audio Program
Use the English/Spanish Health Talk audio program for students who need audio reinforcement of the concepts presented.

Parent Discussion Guide
Send home the Parent Letter for Chapter 20. As you progress through the chapter, send home the Parental Survey and The Extra Mile.

Objectives

■ *Name and define four different types of abuse.*

■ *Use a decision-making model to decide what you would do if you suspected child abuse.*
   ■ **LIFE SKILLS: Making Responsible Decisions**

■ *Know at least two ways you could report an abusive situation.*
   ■ **LIFE SKILLS: Using Community Resources**

How would you react if you thought a friend was being abused? Would you intervene? What if someone was subjecting you to abusive behavior? These are some very difficult questions to answer.

This chapter is devoted to helping you understand the types of violent and abusive behaviors and their consequences. The behaviors take many forms: domestic abuse, sexual assault and harassment, homicides, and even terrorism. Through constant exposure to violent images on television and in the movies, we become numbed to the significance of violent or abusive behavior. Because these images don't shock us, we are more likely to accept them as a part of life. But think about these statistics:

Section 20.1 Lesson Plan

MOTIVATE

Class Discussion
What Is Abuse?

Ask students if there are kinds of abuse other than physical abuse. Then ask students to give examples of behavior that they consider abusive.

Case History
Unhealthy Relationships

It is not uncommon for high school girls to be abused by a steady boyfriend. Have the class, read Naomi and Carolyn's story. To help start a class discussion, ask: **Have you ever known of a similar situation? What should Naomi say to Carolyn? Can Naomi help her? What should Naomi do if Carolyn denies that there is a problem?** Discuss Naomi's options, and emphasize that it is not a breach of friendship if she turns to an adult to get help for Carolyn.

Background
Domestic Violence in America

Domestic violence cuts across age, race, religious, income, and class lines. About three million households in the United States experience one or more violent episodes a year. Spouse abuse and child abuse often go hand-in-hand. It is likely that over three million children witness family violence each year. Children who try to stop battering between their parents often end up injured. Even the unborn are affected: one in four abused women is pregnant, and many miscarry because of abuse. Violence between parents often escalates, and children are abused. However, simply witnessing such violence scars children emotionally. Finally, children learn that violence is acceptable and perpetuate the pattern as adults.

physical abuse:

bodily harm inflicted on another person.

sexual abuse:

sexual behavior between an adult or adolescent and a nonconsenting person.

neglect:

failure of a parent or legal guardian to provide for the basic needs of a person in his or her charge (child or adult).

- The United States ranks first among developed countries in deaths due to violent acts.
- The total number of deaths by firearms in the United States is higher than the totals of the next 17 countries combined.
- Homicide is the second leading cause of death among 15–24 year olds, and the murder rate among teens is increasing. On a typical day in the United States, 9 teenagers will be murdered, and 13 teens will commit murder.

All abuse—physical abuse, sexual abuse, emotional abuse, and neglect—is against the law, which means that the police or other authorities can intervene. They can arrest the offender or otherwise make sure that the abuse does not continue.

Physical Abuse **Physical abuse** occurs when a person inflicts bodily harm on another person. An abused child or adult may suffer scratches, bumps, bruises, broken bones, burns, or chipped teeth.

Though some cases of physical abuse are obvious, others are hard to detect. An abuser may be careful to hit a child, girlfriend, or wife in areas that are usually covered by clothing or may try to attribute the injury to an accident. It's likely that the abused adult or child may also try to conceal evidence of the mistreatment, which can make abuse even more difficult to detect.

Sexual Abuse **Sexual abuse** is sexual behavior between an adult or adolescent and a nonconsenting person. (A minor is legally unable to give consent.) Sometimes sexual abuse is called molestation. It usually involves the touching of private parts, but it can also include the watching or the photographing of sexual acts. It can involve force on the part of the abuser, but it is usually limited to threatening. Sexual abuse is most often inflicted upon girls between

the ages of 12 and 14 by a father, stepfather, other relative, or friend of the family.

Though young girls are the most common victims of sexual abuse, boys are also frequently sexually abused. It is difficult to estimate how many boys are sexually abused because they are less likely to tell anyone about the abuse.

It is rare for any child to report sexual abuse. As a result, it is very difficult to get an accurate estimate of the extent of sexual abuse. However, some experts estimate that as many as 40 million people in the United States have been sexually abused.

Programs have been developed in schools and other community settings to make sure that children and adolescents understand these important principles:

- Sexual abuse is against the law.
- Children and adolescents have the right to refuse any sexual contact and to run away and yell if they are being abused.
- It is illegal to have sex with a minor.
- In most states, you are required by law to report abuse if you suspect it.
- Children and adolescents should tell a trusted adult if they are being abused.
- Even if they did not seek help, children and adolescents should not blame themselves for what happened.

People who have experienced sexual abuse often have great difficulty forming close friendships and other intimate relationships. It is extremely important that people who have been sexually abused receive counseling so they can be assured that the abuse was not their fault.

Neglect Few people realize that **neglect** is a form of abuse. Neglect is the failure of a parent or guardian to provide for the basic needs of a person in his or her charge. Failure to feed a child or provide adequate supervision are examples of neglect.

TEACH

Class Discussion
The Roots of Child Abuse

Ask: **Why do some parents abuse their children?** [*It's a pattern they learned as children. They don't understand children or parenting. Usually, they lack the resources to work out their problems, so they take their frustrations out on children.*] **If child abuse is** **passed on from generation to generation, how can it be stopped?** [*Adults can learn new responses and skills so that they don't repeat their own parents' mistakes.*] **What do you think abused children can do to stop abuse?** [*Talk to a trusted adult, call 911, or keep talking until someone listens and takes action. Running away may stop the abuse, but it causes worse problems for the child.*]

 Cooperative Learning
Protecting Yourself

After students discuss the bulleted list of principles on page 420, have them work in small groups to develop a plan for educating children about protecting themselves from abuse. Plans should be frank and honest without inducing fear.

(FIGURE 20-1) **One of these people appears to be an abuser and the other a victim. In reality, however, most adults who abuse children were also the victims of child abuse.**

Emotional Abuse **Emotional abuse** is emotional mistreatment of another person. A parent may continually criticize a child or fail to show love and affection. Although the effects of emotional abuse aren't as visible as those of physical abuse, they can be just as devastating. One of the worst effects of emotional abuse is low self-esteem. Children or adolescents who are emotionally abused should report the abuse to a trusted adult or call 911 for help.

Child Abuse

The term **child abuse** refers to the mistreatment of children or adolescents. Child abuse can take the form of neglect or physical, emotional, or sexual abuse. Although some children are abused by people outside the family, more than 90 percent of child abuse is inflicted by family members.

Many abused children and adolescents run away from home. They hope that living on the streets will be better than living at home. But tragically, many runaways survive by prostitution and other behaviors that endanger their lives. They also run the risk of being victims of a violent crime.

There are many reasons why parents abuse children. Lack of money, unemployment, or alcohol or drug abuse can make a parent angry or frustrated. Some parents take out their frustration on their children.

Abusive parents may expect more mature behavior from a child than is reasonable. When the child isn't able to perform as the parent expects, the parent may become abusive.

People who were abused as children are most likely to abuse their own children. They may not even realize what they are doing. To them, excessive force or mental cruelty may seem like normal discipline. It's important to remember, however, that people who were abused as children can

emotional abuse:

emotional mistreatment of another person.

child abuse:

illegal treatment committed by an adult against a child that involves use of physical, sexual, or emotional force, cruelty, or neglect.

Life Skills Worksheet 20A
Assign the Making Positive Self-Statements Life Skills Worksheet.

Life Skills Worksheet 20B
Assign the Help for Abusive Families Life Skills Worksheet.

Class Discussion
It Isn't Only Physical

Ask: **Why are neglect and emotional mistreatment considered abusive?** *[Neglect means a child's most basic needs are not met, thereby endangering his or her life; failing to love a child and destructively criticizing a child can cause devastating psychological and emotional damage that lasts a lifetime.]* **What is an indicator that a child is neglected or emotionally abused?** *[low self-esteem]*

Class Discussion
Reporting Abuse

Many people who suspect or know about child abuse fail to report it, even though failure to do so is a crime. Ask students to list reasons why adults might fail to intercede. *(feel it's not their business, fear of retaliation)* Also have them give reasons why a child might not report abuse he or she had witnessed. *(fear that no one would listen, fear that things would get worse for*

the abused child) List these reasons on the chalkboard. For every reason listed, ask students to think of a reason why abuse should be reported.

Class Discussion
Linking Spouse and Child Abuse

In many families experiencing spouse abuse, child abuse is also occurring. Ask: **Why do you think spouse abuse and child abuse often occur together?** *[A dysfunctional adult who has*

...

What Would You Do ?

Have students write their responses; compare the responses to collect a range of options. Discuss the possible outcomes for each option.

Making a Choice 20A

Assign the Emergency Phone Numbers for Abuse card. The card asks students to compile a list of phone numbers of various types of agencies in their community that people can call for help in abusive situations.

Section Review Worksheet 20.1

To reinforce the concepts presented in this section, assign Section Review Worksheet 20.1.

Section Quiz 20.1

Have students take Section Quiz 20.1.

What Would You Do ?

Making Responsible Decisions

A Case of Child Abuse?

You have agreed to baby-sit for a family that you have never met before. They got your phone number from one of the other families that you baby-sit for.

When you get to the couple's house, you are told that their three-year-old son is asleep and shouldn't give you much trouble. But shortly after the couple leaves, the child starts screaming. You decide to pick him up and walk with him until he goes back to sleep. As you are lifting him out of bed you notice very large black-and-blue marks on both arms, and on looking further, you see huge welts on the child's back. You don't know what could have caused the injuries, but you are sure the boy is in a lot of pain.

You've just learned about child abuse in school. You think this child may have been beaten, but you aren't sure. What would you do? Use the decision-making steps found on page 25.

spouse abuse:

abuse of one's husband or wife.

elder abuse:

abuse of an elderly person.

prevent the cycle of abuse from continuing with their own children. They can stop the destructive patterns by learning appropriate parenting skills.

Spouse Abuse

Physical abuse of one's husband or wife is known as **spouse abuse** or spouse battering. When violence occurs between spouses, it is usually a woman who suffers injuries because of differences in strength. Approximately 20 percent of women in the United States are victims of spouse abuse at some point in their life, and about 2,000 women die each year as a result of abuse from their partner. Pregnant women are at the greatest risk. Between 3.9 percent and 8.3 percent of women in the United States are abused during a pregnancy.

A male abuser is usually a controlling person who becomes easily frustrated. Male abusers were often victims of abuse as children. In the majority of battering cases, the man had been drinking or using other drugs.

It may be difficult to understand why an abused woman would stay with her spouse. Experts think that many abused women have low self-esteem and believe they deserve the abuse. They may feel that abuse is normal in marriage, especially if they observed their own mothers being abused. Another reason abused women stay in the relationship is that they often don't have enough money to move out and live on their own. But the most common reason is that battered women are often more afraid to leave than to stay. In many cases the batterer has threatened to kill her or the children, to kidnap the children, or to harm himself if she leaves.

Some victims of this form of abuse do decide to leave their spouse. Many communities have established shelters for such people. The shelters provide a temporary home and help people find jobs or other means of financial support. In most communities, shelters for abused spouses are listed in the White Pages of the telephone book under "Battered Women."

Elder Abuse

Elder abuse is the abuse of an elderly person. As with other kinds of abuse, family members who abuse elders are often frustrated with their lives and take their frustrations out on someone else. When a case of elder abuse is reported, trained professionals will probably require that the family participate in some type of counseling. The elderly person may be placed in another living arrangement if the counseling does not end the abuse.

• • • TEACH continued

learned violence as a response to frustration or as a means of getting what he or she wants will likely strike an adult as well as a child.]

Debate the Issue
Media Messages

Have students debate the topic: American culture and role models are responsible for much of the abuse of women and children. You may want to initiate a discussion before the debate. Ask: **What messages do we often get from the media and society about what it takes to be a real man?** *[Real men are often portrayed as tough, strong, aggressive, financially successful, never-failing, and inexpressive.]* **In what ways do movies, television, books, and music appear to connect male sexuality with aggression and female sexuality with submission?** *[Much violence of men toward women is shown; some images even suggest that women deserve this or enjoy it. These* *messages present violence as the norm and appear to give social permission for force or violence.]*

Extension
Information on Advocates for Abuse Victims

Encourage students to visit local mental health clinics, family service agencies, or the police department to get pamphlets and brochures describing the advocacy groups in your area that help victims of abuse. Allow time for students to report their findings.

Peer Abuse

At the beginning of every school year, there are stories in the news about high school students or college students who have been injured or killed as a result of hazing. *Hazing* is defined as any physical or psychological abuse associated with initiation into a club or team. It includes whipping, beating, striking, branding, electronic shocking, sleep deprivation, excessive drinking, and the use of other drugs. Although most campuses have policies forbidding hazing, it is still a common practice because the nature of initiation involves secrecy. Hazing should be reported to the administration of the institution where it occurs. No club or organization is worth endangering your life.

Help for Victims of Abuse

No one deserves to be abused, whether the abuse is physical, emotional, sexual, or in the form of neglect. It is important to report abuse immediately. If you suspect abuse or are a victim of abuse, you can anonymously report the abuse to a trusted adult, the police, or the Department of Child Protective Services.

Families in which abuse and violence occur need professional help to break the cycle of abusive behavior. It is best if help is sought voluntarily, but it can be mandated by law.

Many victims feel responsible for the abuse. They believe that they are bad people who did something to deserve the abuse. Victims of abuse often need to undergo counseling to help them realize that they are not responsible for what has happened to them.

Counseling is available at many community health agencies for parents and children. The fees for counseling are usually based on ability to pay; if an individual has very little money, he or she will be charged very little or nothing for the counseling. Counseling with a private therapist will usually involve a set fee, but sometimes an agreement based on ability to pay can be arranged.

People who abuse children or fear they will do so can obtain help through Parents Anonymous, a national organization that helps parents cope without using violence. Many cities have local chapters of Parents Anonymous. Parents can call their local chapter of Parents Anonymous when they feel they are losing control. The people who answer the phones at the hotline number are trained to defuse the immediate situation and encourage parents to get on-going help.

Review

1. *Name and define four different types of abuse.*

2. **LIFE SKILLS: Making Responsible Decisions** *If you knew that a two-year-old child was frequently left alone for hours at a time, what would you do?*

3. **LIFE SKILLS: Using Community Resources** *To whom could you report a case of elder abuse?*

4. *Critical Thinking* *Why do you think sexually abused children often have trouble making friends?*

Reteaching Worksheet 20.1
Students who have difficulty with the material may complete Reteaching Worksheet 20.1.

Review Answers

1. physical abuse, sexual abuse, neglect, emotional abuse

2. Students might report the abuse to a trusted adult, the police, or the Department of Child Protective Services.

3. Students might talk with a trusted adult, call 911, or report the information to the police.

4. Answers will vary. Students may say that these children have low self-esteem and think that no one will like them or that the children may think they brought the abusive behavior on themselves because they are bad.

ASSESS

Section Review

Have students answer the Section Review questions.

Alternative Assessment
Why Abuse Is Hard to Stop

Have students write a brief essay explaining several reasons why abuse may be hard to detect and report, and why abusers and abused tend to perpetuate the problem rather than seek help.

Closure
Expressing Your Outrage

Have students create a poem, story, or artwork that expresses their feelings about any type of abuse.

Section
20.2 *Sexual Assault*

Background
Profile of the Rapist

Most rapists are males between 15 and 35 years of age, and they look and act normal. Rapists come from every social, economic, and religious group and may have any intelligence level. In most cases, the rapist has a sexual partner, so he is not sexually deprived. The rapist wants to control, overpower, and humiliate someone. He does not accept blame or see the harm in what he does; in fact, he blames the victim. He may be a loner or have few close friends. He may have been abused as a child. Without treatment, the rapist is likely to continue the pattern of sexual assault with others.

Objectives

- Define sexual assault.
- Define acquaintance rape.
- Discuss how young men can avoid committing acquaintance rape.
- Know what a victimized person should do to get help after a sexual assault.
  LIFE SKILLS: Using Community Resources
- Define sexual harassment.

sexual assault:

any sexual contact with a person without his or her consent.

Sexual assault is any sexual contact with a person without his or her consent. Sexual assault is a violent way to show dominance or anger. It includes the sexual abuse of children, forced sexual intercourse (rape), and sexual harassment. Approximately 75 percent of sexual assaults are committed by people known to the victim.

Each year, women are the victims of more than 5 million violent crimes, including approximately 500,000 rapes or other sexual assaults. Every 46 seconds a woman in this country is raped. It is difficult to know exactly how many assaults against women are committed—women victimized by people they know are not likely to report the crime because they are afraid of being victimized again—but approximately one out of every four women in the United States will be sexually assaulted.

Rapists do not discriminate on the basis of age, marital status, or physical appearance. Though most victims are female, males are also sexually assaulted, usually by heterosexual men.

Taking Precautions Against Sexual Assault

A person who is sexually assaulted is never responsible for what happened. It doesn't matter if the assaulted person left the doors or windows unlocked, wore ''provocative'' clothing, hitchhiked, or went out on a date with the assailant; the victim was not responsible for the assault.

A woman can *minimize* her chances of being assaulted, though, by taking the following precautions:

- Avoid walking alone in deserted areas.
- Have your keys ready for the car or the front door.
- Make sure that no one is in the rear seat of the car before getting in.
- Keep entrances and doorways to your house or apartment brightly lit.
- Use deadbolt locks on the doors of your house or apartment.
- Keep all windows and doors locked.

It is not possible to recognize a sex offender by their outward appearance. There are, however, some behaviors that are known to be associated with sex offenders. Be wary if someone does the following:

- acts as if he knows you better than he does
- stands too close to you and seems to enjoy your discomfort
- blocks your way
- grabs or pushes you

Section 20.2 Lesson Plan

MOTIVATE

Class Discussion
Sexual Assault

Write on the chalkboard, "A person who is sexually assaulted is not responsible for the assault." Elicit students' reactions to the statement. Then explore students' conceptions of sexual assault by asking questions such as the following: What is sexual assault? What is the typical rapist like? Why would anyone sexually assault another person? What is the typical victim like? How are victims of sexual assault hurt?

Myths and Facts About Rape

Myth	Fact
Only young, beautiful people are raped.	Rape victims include people of all ages and appearances.
People who hitchhike or wear sexy clothing are asking to be raped.	No one asks to be sexually assaulted; nor does any victim's behavior justify or excuse the crime.
Most rapes occur in dangerous places.	More than half of all rapes occur in the home. The next most common place is in an automobile.
Most rapes occur because the rapist is sexually starved.	Most rapes occur because the rapist has a desire to overpower and humiliate someone else.
Most rapes are committed by someone unknown to the victim.	Most rapes are committed by a person known to the victim.
It is common for a woman to falsely accuse a man of rape.	There are no more false reports of rape than of any other crime. Most victims do not even report the rape.
Men are never raped.	Men are raped, usually by heterosexual men. However, men are less likely to report a rape.

 (FIGURE 20-2)

The best protection is to act quickly when someone's behavior seems strange. It might require causing a scene in public, but that's better than being assaulted. Begin with a loud yell, which can intimidate the aggressor and give you confidence.

Physical resistance, including running and fighting, is entirely appropriate if you are in danger of being assaulted. It is also important to know, however, that a person who has been sexually assaulted and did not try to resist or run away has also acted ap-propriately. Anything a person does to stay alive during such an attack is absolutely acceptable and is nothing to be ashamed of.

Many people take self-defense classes to learn how to protect themselves. If you would like to do this, choose a class that deals specifically with self-defense in real-life situations, not martial arts such as judo and karate. Martial arts increase strength and build confidence, but they don't provide the kind of experience a person needs to de-fend against a sexual assault.

TEACH

Teaching Transparency 20A
Myths and Facts About Rape

Show the transparency of Figure 20-2, and have students point out facts about rape that surprised them and myths they previously believed were true. Then ask: **How do you think these myths became part of our culture? Do the media and advertisers affect your** view of acceptable sexual behavior? **What other factors influence your beliefs?** [Students' responses will vary according to their own experiences.]

Reinforcement
Precautions Against Sexual Assault

Emphasize the importance of taking precautions and responding actively to avoid putting yourself at risk of sexual assault. Review the precautions listed on page 424.

Class Discussion
Setting Limits

Write on the board, "Your date doesn't have ESP!" Around the statement, draw balloons with thoughts such as, "I wonder if it's okay to kiss him?" "Will she think I'm a wimp if I don't want to have sex?" "All I have to do is push a little, and she'll do it." "How do I get him to stop with just kissing?" Have students suggest other balloon

Background

When the Victim Is Male

Males are sexually assaulted, too. National statistics say one in seven young men is sexually assaulted (the number for young women is one in four). Most often, the attacker is an adult heterosexual male. This reinforces the notion that rape is about power and humiliation, not sexuality. Very few males report the assault, but these attacks are just as hurtful and criminal as sexual assaults on females.

Background

Date Rape

Point out that many studies show that alcohol consumption plays a major role in date rape. Under the influence of alcohol, both males and females make choices they might not make otherwise.

A Case of Acquaintance Rape

How Amy Described What Happened	*How Jim Described What Happened*
I first met Jim at a party. He was really good looking and he had a great smile. I wanted to meet him but I wasn't sure how. I didn't want to appear too forward. Then he came over and introduced himself. We talked and found we had a lot in common. I really liked him. When he asked me over to his place for a drink, I thought it would be O.K. He was such a good listener, and I wanted him to ask me out again. *When we got to his room, the only place to sit was on the bed. I didn't want him to get the wrong idea, but what else could I do? We talked for a while and then he made his move. He started by kissing. I really liked him, so the kissing was nice. But then he pushed me down on the bed. I was so startled. I tried to get up, and I told him to stop. He was so much bigger and stronger. I got scared and I started to cry. I froze and he raped me.* *It was terrible – he was so rough. When it was over he kept asking me what was wrong, like he didn't know. He had just forced himself on me, and he thought that was O.K. He drove me home and he said he wanted to see me again. I'm so afraid to see him. I never thought it would happen to me.*	*I first met her at a party. She looked really hot, wearing a sexy dress that showed off her great body. We started talking right away. I knew that she liked me by the way she kept smiling and touching my arm while she was speaking. She seemed pretty relaxed so I asked her back to my place for a drink. When she said yes, I knew that I was going to get lucky!* *When we got to my place, we sat on the bed kissing. At first, everything was great. Then, when I started to lay her down on the bed, she started twisting and saying she didn't want to. Most women don't like to appear too easy, so I knew she was just going through the motions. When she stopped struggling, I knew that she would have to throw in some tears before we did it.* *She was still very upset afterwards, and I just don't understand it! If she didn't want to have sex, why did she come back to the room with me? You could tell by the way she dressed and acted that she was no virgin, so why she had to put up such a struggle I don't know.*

(FIGURE 20-3) **These are two accounts of an acquaintance rape that occurred at a college. Notice that Jim has no idea he raped Amy. Whenever someone is forced to have sex, a rape has occurred.**

● ● ● TEACH continued

thoughts, and add them to the board. Ask students to come up with a set of "Daters' Communication Guidelines" that will clear up all this confusion. (*Possible responses might include thinking through your limits before the date; talking to your date about your feelings, limits, and expectations; and listening to your partner's limits and respecting them.*)

 Cooperative Learning
Miscommunication

Have students work in small groups to create a comic strip that illustrates one or more miscommunications during a date. Then have them prepare a second comic strip that shows good communication and an alternative outcome.

Role-Playing
Tell It Like It Is

Have students write descriptions of dating situations on index cards. (A couple is going with a large group to a party where liquor may be served and adult supervision may be lax; a couple is going on a hayride.) Each situation should present an opportunity for partners to communicate clearly what they want. Preview the cards for appropriate content. Have volunteers role-play each situation, focusing on skill building in these areas:

• Communicating limits
• Noticing power-play behavior
• Being assertive

Preventing Acquaintance Rape

Acquaintance rape, which is sometimes called ''date rape,'' occurs when a person is forced or coerced into sexual intercourse by an acquaintance or date. The force or coercion may be verbal pressure, threats, physical restraint, or physical violence. Any time a person's protests against engaging in sexual intercourse are ignored, a rape has occurred.

Acquaintance rape is partly the result of the way many men think they are supposed to behave with women. Some men assume they should always be aggressive and in control.

Some men see sexual intimacy as a competition between the man and the woman. As in playing sports, some young men might feel that they should ''win'' at any cost. Even the slang of sexual conquest is similar to that of sports: men speak of ''scoring'' with a woman. One young man described the situation this way: ''A man is supposed to view a date with a woman as a premeditated scheme for getting the most sex out of her. He's supposed to constantly pressure her to see how far he can get. She is his adversary, his opponent in a battle. . . .''

Most women, however, have not been socialized to think of sexual intimacy as a contest. Nor have they been encouraged to be assertive in resisting things they don't want to do. As a result, they may be unprepared to resist this type of aggression.

Read the two accounts of an acquaintance rape in Figure 20-3. The account on the left was given by a female college student who was raped. The one on the right is the account given by the male college student who committed the rape. Notice how differently each interprets the events.

As with any sexual assault, the burden of responsibility for preventing acquaint-ance rape lies with the offender, not the potential victim. It requires a fundamental change in the way many men view sexual encounters.

Males can avoid committing acquaintance rape by remembering that if someone says ''no'' at any point, they are obligated to accept ''no'' as the answer. If a woman voluntarily engages in some degree of sexual intimacy, it is not the same as agreeing to intercourse. One thing does not necessarily lead to another. No matter how quietly a woman objects, she still means ''no.''

It is important that young women communicate their limits clearly and assertively to the other person. It will help to review the discussion about resisting pressure on pages 378–379 in Chapter 17. As in any kind of sexual assault, running away or physically resisting is entirely appropriate.

After a Sexual Assault

After any sexual assault, a victimized person should contact the police as soon as possible. It is also helpful to call the local rape-crisis hotline, which can provide counseling and emotional support, as well as assistance with the judicial system. In addition, a medical examination will probably be necessary to collect legal evidence of the assault and to screen for possible sexually transmitted diseases and pregnancy. It is important that a victim of an assault get examined before washing or using the bathroom if at all possible. A worker from the rape-crisis center can accompany the person throughout this crisis and can provide assistance even if the person chooses not to report the crime to the police.

Unfortunately, most rapes are not reported because victims of a sexual assault often feel humiliated and ashamed. They may feel that reporting the crime might prolong their feelings of anguish and that it may be better to try to forget what happened and

acquaintance rape:

the forcing or coercion of a person into sexual intercourse by an acquaintance or date.

Life Skills Worksheet 20C

Assign the What Is Sexual Harrassment? Life Skills Worksheet.

Section Review Worksheet 20.2

To reinforce the concepts presented in this section, assign Section Review Worksheet 20.2.

Section Quiz 20.2

Have students take Section Quiz 20.2.

Reteaching Worksheet 20.2

Students who have difficulty with the material may complete Reteaching Worksheet 20.2.

Class Discussion
Help for Victims of Sexual Assault

Many victims of sexual assault choose not to report the crime. Discuss reasons why this occurs. *(Victims may assume wrongly that they are at fault, may want to avoid public shame or attention, may fear reprisal by the criminal, may want to put it out of their mind, may feel they won't be believed, and may fear punishment because they were breaking rules when it happened.)* Stress the positives of reporting:

- Victims need medical and counseling care.
- The criminal should not be able to hurt others.
- Victims can get protection and support.
- Police and other advocacy groups are trained to help the victim.
- Victims need to know if disease was transmitted.

Class Discussion
Sexual Harassment

Stress to the students that one inappropriate remark does not necessarily constitute harassment. People frequently disagree about what constitutes sexual harassment. Ask students to describe situations that they think involve sexual harassment. List each one on the board. Then elicit student opinions about each situation. Discuss why harassers seldom stop their behavior even

Review Answers

1. any sexual contact with a person without his or her consent

2. the forcing or coercion of a person into sexual intercourse by an acquaintance or date

3. Men have to change the way they view sexual encounters, and they must remember that if someone says no at any point, they are obligated to accept no as the answer to further sexual behavior.

4. unwanted, unwelcome, or offensive sexual behavior

5. Victims of sexual assault can contact the local rape-crisis hotline or call the police. They also may want ask a close friend to go with them if they decide to have a medical examination or go to the police station.

6. Just because Amy said yes to going to Jim's place, Jim assumed that Amy was also saying yes to sexual intercourse. When Amy told Jim to stop his sexual advances, Jim ignored her, feeling that Amy really wanted to have sex but didn't want to appear too easy.

(FIGURE 20-4) **Help for victims of sexual assault can be obtained by calling a local rape-crisis hotline.**

- staring at a person's body
- telling sexually-oriented jokes, stories, or remarks
- describing sexual acts or posting suggestive pictures or written material
- making unnecessary physical contact
- exerting pressure on someone for dates or sexual activity
- making unwelcome calls or writing unwelcome letters with sexual overtones
- making demands for sexual favors with implied threats related to benefits or opportunities

Any unsolicited conduct that fits these descriptions is sexual harassment. It is important that the victim communicates to the harasser that the conduct is unwelcome and must stop. Make sure you know the policies and procedures of your school or workplace so you know how to best handle a harassment situation.

get on with life. These feelings are completely understandable, but it is also important to know that rape is a serious crime. No matter whether the rape occurred between strangers, acquaintances, or even friends, the person who committed the rape is a criminal and deserves to be punished.

Sexual Harassment

sexual harassment:

unwanted, unwelcome, or offensive sexual behavior.

Sexual harassment is unwanted, unwelcome, or offensive sexual behaviors. Like rape, it has more to do with power than sex.

A male or female can be the victim or the perpetrator of sexual harassment. It most commonly occurs in school or the workplace. Each of the following are examples of sexual harassment:

- making demeaning remarks about a person's clothing, body, or activities

Review

1. Define sexual assault.

2. Define acquaintance rape.

3. Discuss how young men can avoid committing acquaintance rape.

4. Define sexual harassment.

5. ▣▣ **LIFE SKILLS: Using Community Resources** What can a victimized person do to get help after a sexual assault?

6. **Critical Thinking** Review the two accounts of a rape in Figure 20-3. What were the fallacies in Jim's thinking that led to his committing an acquaintance rape?

• • • TEACH continued

when asked. Ask students if they see any parallels between acquaintance rapists and sexual harassers?

Extension
What Happens After Sexual Assault?

Have students visit or phone local sexual assault, rape crisis, or mental health centers as well as the police department to find out about procedures

and victims' rights in each of the following areas: medical care, criminal justice procedures, prosecution, and emotional recovery.

ASSESS

Section Review

Have students answer the Section Review questions.

Alternative Assessment
Who Is the Villain?

Have students write an essay explaining and defending their point of view about who is responsible when an acquaintance rape occurs.

Closure
Ideas About Sexual Assault

Ask students to mention something they have learned about sexual assault that was entirely new to them or contradicted a previous belief.

Section 20.3
Preventing Violent Conflict

Objectives

- Name the three major risk factors associated with homicides.
- Discuss the reasons why some teenagers join gangs.
- Know how to prevent your anger from turning into violence.
  - ▪▪ LIFE SKILLS: Coping
- Know how to resolve conflicts without violence.
  - ▪▪ LIFE SKILLS: Solving Problems
- Define peer mediation.

It is estimated that by age 18, the average youth has watched 250,000 acts of violence and 40,000 attempted murders on television. These figures don't even include the violent acts depicted in movies, books, and magazines. Violence in the media often appears exciting and glamorous. Even grisly cult murders are presented in gory detail. It seems that violence has become so commonplace that we hardly react to it anymore. The lesson that many learn from all this is that if you have a problem, you solve it with violence.

What we know about violence in our society seems to indicate that too many people are attempting to solve their problems with violent acts. **Homicide**—a violent crime that results in the death of another person—is the second leading cause of death of all people aged 15 to 24.

One of the major risk factors related to homicide is the use of alcohol or other drugs. Substance abuse is a factor in almost half of all homicides in this country. Alcohol alone is involved in more than half of all violent crimes committed in the United States.

Another major risk factor is possession of a gun, since the most common weapon used to kill people is a firearm. A recent survey of high school students showed that approximately one out of 20 students had carried a gun at least once during the 30 days preceding the survey. Clearly, many deaths of young people could be prevented if people did not carry guns.

Arguments are also a major risk factor associated with homicide. As you can see in Figure 20-5, the most common event associated with a homicide is an argument. If

homicide:

a violent crime that results in the death of another person.

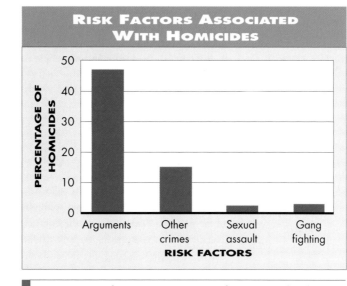

(FIGURE 20-5) **The event most commonly associated with a homicide is an argument.**

Background
Guns, Homicides, and the Law

FBI statistics reveal that the majority of homicides involving firearms result from arguments that become deadly because of easy access to a gun. In 1988, only about 7 percent of deaths caused by firearms were related to other actual or suspected illegal activities. The rest were homicides unrelated to any other felony, suicide, or accidental death. Experts disagree on how, or even if, gun-control laws would prevent these "arguments turned deadly." However, researchers agree on some of the following issues:

- Background checks on people who wish to purchase guns are necessary.
- Stricter regulations for acquiring a federal firearms dealer's license are needed.
- People who have been convicted of violent misdemeanors should be prohibited from buying or owning guns. Convicted felons cannot purchase guns. However, the present plea-bargain system often reduces felony charges to misdemeanor charges.

Section 20.3 Lesson Plan

MOTIVATE

Journal 20A
Feeling Your Anger Pulse

This may be done as a warm-up activity. Ask students to think about things that make them angry or upset. When have they been angry enough to hit someone? What did they do? Have them describe in their Journal an experience they had recently that required them to deal with their anger. Have students describe how they handled their anger.

TEACH

Class Discussion
Acceptance of Violence

Ask students to name TV shows, videos, and movies that depict violence; list these on the chalkboard. Have students describe their reaction to seeing violent acts on the screen. Discuss the effects of this constant exposure. (*Viewers become desensitized, cynical, and more accepting of violence; some may be persuaded to use violence*

themselves, either to get what they want or to resolve conflicts.)

 Cooperative Learning
Violence in Popular Culture

Divide the class into small groups and give each group a list of television programs and several super-hero comic books to analyze for violence. With the whole class, design an evaluation form. (It may include spaces for the program

Life Skills Worksheet 20D

Assign the Managing Anger Life Skills Worksheet.

Evaluating Media Messages

Have students read this Unit 5 feature on pages 436–437. Then have them complete its companion worksheet.

Making a Choice 20B

Assign the Resolving Conflict Without Violence card. The card asks students to describe a conflict that had a violent resolution, discuss possible nonviolent resolutions to the conflict, and role-play the different nonviolent solutions.

we can prevent violent arguments, especially when they occur between people who have been abusing drugs and who are carrying guns, many homicides can be avoided.

Managing Anger

Anger is a natural and even healthy emotion. Unfortunately, people often let this natural emotion change to violence. We all feel anger from time to time, and we will continue to do so throughout our life. But by learning to manage angry feelings and express them in healthy ways before they get out of control, we can help to prevent emotional and physical abuse.

Physical signals that you are getting angry are pretty easy to recognize: your heart starts to beat faster, your muscles automatically tense up, and you start to breathe more rapidly. Once you recognize what's happening, there are several things you can do.

Talking to someone about the way you are feeling is often the best way to work things out. But sometimes you need another kind of release, like running, walking, or punching a punching bag. When you are angry, it's very important that you do whatever it takes to keep from hurting people or damaging property.

Another technique for solving problems that lead to violence is peer mediation. This is a process for resolving disputes and conflicts in which a neutral person acts as a mediator for the process. This technique is often used in a school setting.

The mediators are students who help their classmates identify and find solutions to the problem that is causing the conflict. The purpose of peer mediation isn't to find out who is right or wrong, but rather to encourage students to learn how to get along with each other. The students who are in conflict are asked to tell their stories and ask

questions. The mediators help students identify ways to solve the conflict.

Situations involving name-calling, rumors, bumping into students in the hallways, and bullying are best dealt with through peer mediation. You'll find the steps of mediation in the Life Skills section on the facing page.

Resolving Conflicts Without Violence

The best way to deal with potentially violent conflicts is to avoid them. If someone seems to be picking a fight with you, walk away if you can.

If you cannot avoid the conflict, do what you can to keep the conflict from becoming violent. Take some deep breaths, stay calm, and do not raise your voice. Try to think of a way to compromise with the other person.

Gangs

Gang-related violence is increasing in this country, and more and more teenagers are becoming involved. Although many gang-related crimes are directed at enemy gang members, these crimes do not constitute the majority of gang incidents. Most of the time, people with no gang affiliation are the ones who are killed or assaulted.

Why do teenagers join gangs? Poverty and poor job prospects contribute to the proliferation of gangs. Gangs also provide a sense of family and a feeling of belonging that is lacking in many young people's lives. Michael, a former gang member who is serving time in prison, said that after his parents split up he didn't get the attention he needed. Then he joined a gang. "There I got a little attention—from the other gang members," Michael said. "I felt they loved me and they were a family."

• • • TEACH continued

or comic book's name, types of violence shown, frequency of violent episodes, and motivation for violence.) Then have each group review the evaluations. They should assign a numerical violence rating to each program or comic book. How violent are the programs and comics they reviewed? Are there any general differences between the two media?

Class Discussion
The Physical Effects of Anger

Remind students that anger is a normal emotion everyone experiences. Have students list things that make them angry. Ask them to describe physical changes they experience when angry. *(increased heart rate, faster breathing, muscle tension, flushed face, clenched fists, and so on)* Explain that anger creates physical reactions that require release.

Cooperative Learning
Dealing With Anger

Have students work in small groups to list situations that they feel are anger inducing and a number of different nonviolent responses to anger. *(Nonviolent responses include deep breathing, leaving the situation, exercising, hitting something soft, talking to a friend or teacher or counselor, finding the humor in the situation, or talking to the person you are angry at.)* Have each group take a situation from another group

But there are many clubs and organizations for teens that can also provide a feeling of belonging to a family without the goal of violence. Recreation centers generally sponsor youth groups, and many schools have athletic, academic, and social clubs for interested students. Check your phone book or your school guidance counselor's office for possible options.

The desire for status is another reason some people join gangs. Gang members may get "respect" from others. The media may also contribute to the appeal of gangs. A radio ad for a malt liquor, for example,

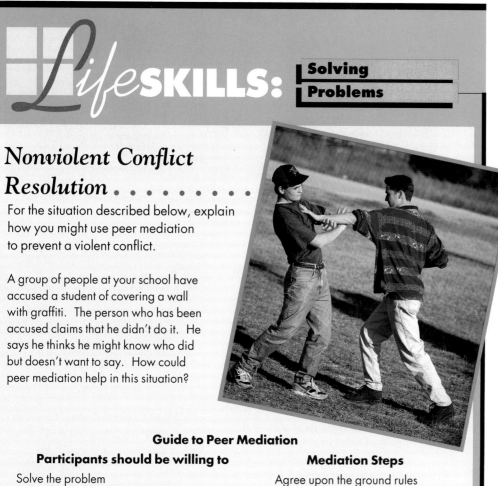

*Life*SKILLS: Solving Problems

Nonviolent Conflict Resolution . . . .

For the situation described below, explain how you might use peer mediation to prevent a violent conflict.

A group of people at your school have accused a student of covering a wall with graffiti. The person who has been accused claims that he didn't do it. He says he thinks he might know who did but doesn't want to say. How could peer mediation help in this situation?

Guide to Peer Mediation

Participants should be willing to

Solve the problem
Tell the truth
Listen without interrupting
Be respectful
Take responsibility for carrying out agreements
Keep the situation confidential

Mediation Steps

Agree upon the ground rules
Each student tells his or her story
Verify the stories
Discuss the stories
Generate solutions
Discuss solutions
Select a solution
Sign a contract

 Life **SKILLS**

Divide the class into small groups, and have each group use the peer-mediation technique to resolve one of the conflicts presented. Afterward, as a class, discuss students' reactions to and evaluation of this nonviolent conflict-resolution technique.

Section Review Worksheet 20.3
To reinforce the concepts presented in this section, assign Section Review Worksheet 20.3.

Section Quiz 20.3
Have students take Section Quiz 20.3.

Reteaching Worksheet 20.3
Students who have difficulty with the material may complete Reteaching Worksheet 20.3.

and decide how to respond, using their list of nonviolent responses. Students may wish to role-play their solutions. Discuss which responses worked best for each situation.

Reinforcement
Who Suffers Most From Gang Violence?

Remind students tht many of the victims of gang violence are innocent people who got in the line of fire. In over half of gang-related incidents, the people who are injured or killed are not gang members.

 Teaching Transparency 20B
People in Conflict

Use this transparency to discuss what the cartoon characters who are in conflict might be saying. Have students provide a possible dialogue for the people in the cartoon.

Extension
Nonviolent Conflict Resolution in History

Encourage students to research and report on famous figures—such as Mohandas K. Gandhi and Martin Luther King, Jr.—who have led by nonviolent example.

Review Answers

1. use of alcohol or drugs, possession of a gun, and arguments

2. poverty and poor job prospects, glorification by media, desire for status, sense of a family, a feeling of belonging

3. Peer mediation is a technique used to resolve disputes and conflicts nonviolently. A neutral person acts as a mediator for the process.

4. Answers will vary. Some students may answer that they would get out of the situation as soon as they began to feel angry and then channel that anger into some positive action, such as exercise. Students may also suggest that they try to resolve the differences that are causing the anger by compromising.

5. Answers will vary. Students may answer that they would ask for the jacket back and would resolve any conflicts using the peer-mediation technique.

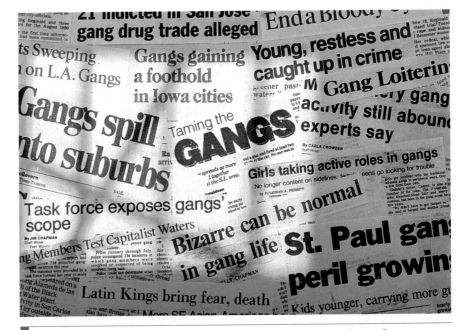

(FIGURE 20-6) In recent years, drive-by shootings and other incidents of gang violence have become more common on the streets of our cities.

refers to a gang tradition and compares the drink to a certain type of gun.

The status that members get from gangs is often short lived. Gang members are extremely vulnerable to homicide. A gang member who was locked up in a juvenile security camp in Los Angeles County described his life: "I've been stabbed four times, shot three times, and locked up and beaten up so many times that it's hard to keep count. The only thing left for me is to die, but I've been ready for that every day since I turned 13, and I'm 16 now."

There is hope for gang members; they can leave their gang and make a new life for themselves. After losing five friends in street warfare, Michael is learning to weld, and he hopes to get married and have kids when he gets out of prison. He said, "The guys in my neighborhood, I'll always love them. . . . But I don't want that life anymore."

Review

1. Name the three major risk factors associated with homicides.

2. Discuss the reasons why some teenagers join gangs.

3. Define peer mediation.

4. LIFE SKILLS: Coping If you felt yourself becoming extremely angry at a stranger, how could you prevent your anger from turning into violence?

5. LIFE SKILLS: Solving Problems If a fellow student stole your jacket, what could you do to resolve the conflict without using violence?

ASSESS

Section Review

Have students answer the Section Review questions.

Alternative Assessment
Reducing the Risk of Homicide

Have students make a collage featuring one factor that increases the risk of violent death. Each collage should also include a visual representation of how the violence might be prevented.

Closure
Joining a Gang

Ask students to consider what, if anything, could change in people's lives that might make them seriously consider joining a gang. (They may mention changes in family circumstances, encounters with gang members, or poor job prospects.)

Highlights

Summary

- Abuse can take the form of physical, emotional, and sexual abuse, as well as neglect.

- People who were abused as children are more likely to abuse others.

- Alcohol and other drug abuse is a factor in most cases of spouse abuse. When violence does occur between spouses, it is usually the woman who suffers injuries, because of differences in size and strength.

- Many abused women who stay in abusive marriages do so because they have low self-esteem.

- It is important to report abuse immediately. Families in which abuse and violence occur need professional help to break the cycle of abuse.

- Sexual assault is less a sexual act than a way to show dominance over or anger toward the victim. Most sexual assaults are committed by someone the victim knows.

- To avoid acquaintance rape, men should accept that when a woman says ''no'' she means ''no.'' It's also important for women to communicate their limits clearly and assertively.

- The best way to deal with potentially violent conflicts is to avoid them.

- Poverty, poor job prospects, the desire for status, and the need to belong are factors that cause youths to join gangs.

Vocabulary

physical abuse: bodily harm inflicted on another person.

sexual abuse: sexual behavior between an adult or adolescent and a non-consenting person.

neglect: failure of a parent or legal guardian to provide for the basic needs of a person in his or her charge (child or adult).

emotional abuse: emotional mistreatment of another person.

child abuse: illegal treatment committed by an adult against a child that involves use of physical, sexual, or emotional force, cruelty, or neglect.

sexual assault: any sexual contact with a person without his or her consent.

acquaintance rape: the forcing or coercion of a person into sexual intercourse by an acquaintance or date.

sexual harassment: unwanted, unwelcome, or offensive sexual behavior.

SUMMARY
Have students read the summary to reinforce the concepts they learned in Chapter 20.

VOCABULARY
Have students make a violence wheel, dividing a circle into sections. In each section, they place their own definition of one vocabulary word. Below the wheel, students can explain what all these forms of violence have in common.

EXTENSION
Encourage students to locate and read books and current articles on abuse, sexual assault, or violent crime in America. They can share what they learn from reading in a panel presentation.

Chapter Review

CHAPTER REVIEW

Concept Review

Sample responses:

1. A physical abuser may be careful to hit the abused person in areas that are covered by clothing or may attribute the injury to an accident. The abused person may try to conceal the evidence, especially if he or she thinks the abused will retaliate if the abuse is reported. The sexual abuse of children is rarely reported. The effects of emotional abuse are not visible.

2. Parents were abused as children; personal problems, such as lack of money, unemployment, and alcohol or drug abuse, can make parents angry and frustrated and cause them to take their feelings out on their children; and parents may not understand child development.

3. child abuse, spouse abuse, elder abuse

4. They have low self-esteem, they believe they deserve to be abused, and they may feel that they cannot make it on their own financially.

5. The man acts as if he knows you better than he does, stands too close to you and seems to enjoy your discomfort, blocks your way, or grabs or pushes you.

6. in order to collect legal evidence and to screen for sexually transmitted diseases and pregnancy

Concept Review

1. Why is it sometimes difficult to detect abuse?

2. What are three factors that might cause a parent to abuse a child?

3. Name three kinds of family violence.

4. Why do abused wives have trouble leaving their spouse?

5. List three behaviors that are known to be associated with sex offenders.

6. Why is a medical examination necessary after a sexual assault?

7. Which type of self-defense class is recommended for people wanting to learn how to protect themselves?

8. How prevalent is homicide in our society?

9. What signs does your body give you when you are getting angry?

10. How do gangs provide a sense of family?

Expressing Your Views

1. Do you think all forms of sexual assault should be reported? Explain.

2. Why do you think emotional abuse should not be ignored even though the effects aren't visible?

3. Your friend confides to you that her uncle has been sexually abusing her for over a year. She refuses to tell her parents because she thinks it was her own fault for being too friendly with her uncle. How could you help her?

4. Patty works late three nights a week and must walk across a large parking lot to her car. What precautions would you encourage her to take?

7. one that teaches a person how to protect and defend himself or herself in real-life situations

8. Very prevalent; homicide is the second leading cause of death for all people aged 15 to 24.

9. Your heart beats faster, you breathe more rapidly, and your muscles tense up.

10. They provide a sense of belonging by giving the attention and "love" that may be lacking in a family.

Expressing Your Views

Sample responses:

1. Yes. Sexual assault is against the law. When sexual assault is reported, the person committing the assault has a better chance of getting help to prevent him or her from doing the same thing again. Also, the victim can get the help he or she needs in dealing with the experience.

2. Emotional abuse can lead to low self-esteem. People with low self-esteem are not as successful in school and jobs, and are at a higher risk for self-destructive

Life Skills Check . . . . . .

1. Using Community Resources
Your cousin confided that she often feels as if she is losing control with her children and that she is afraid she might hurt them. What could you advise her to do?

2. Making Responsible Decisions
Katie's parents seem to criticize everything she does. They are hardly ever at home, and when they are, Katie never hears one kind or encouraging word from them. The situation has gotten so bad that she is thinking about running away. What alternatives does Katie have?

3. Coping
You like Ray a lot and enjoy some degree of sexual intimacy, but you do not want to have intercourse with him. The last time you were on a date, he assumed that because you enjoyed kissing him, you didn't want him to stop—you had to be really firm. The two of you are supposed to go out tonight. What should you do?

Projects . . . .

1. Most child-care centers are very reliable. However, child abuse does occasionally occur at these facilities. Interview a parent whose child attends a child-care center. How did the parent choose the center? What does the parent do to make sure no abuse is taking place? What would he or she do if child abuse were suspected? Share your findings with the class.

2. Work with a group to develop a puppet show to teach young children about child abuse and how to report it. Try to obtain permission to present the show to first- or second-graders in your school district.

Plan for Action . . . .

Crime is one of the major health problems facing Americans today. List 10 ways to reduce your risk of becoming a victim of violent crime.

behaviors, such as eating disorders and suicide.
3. I would tell her it isn't her fault and encourage her to talk with a trusted adult.
4. walk out with a friend or have the security guard escort her to her car, be alert to her surroundings, have her keys ready

Life Skills Check
Sample responses:
1. I would encourage her to seek help to find out why she is losing control. If she can talk about her problems, she probably won't feel so frustrated and will be less likely to take her frustrations out on her children.
2. Katie can talk to a trusted adult, such as a teacher, school counselor, or religious leader.
3. Before we leave on the date I should communicate my limits clearly and assertively to Ray. I would make it clear to him that I will leave and go home if he does not respect my request.

Projects
Have students complete the projects on abuse and violence.

Plan for Action
Students should consider their individual situation and should make a list of the ways they can protect themselves from crime.

Pledge
Discuss the pledge for Chapter 20. A student's decision of whether to sign the pledge is personal and private.

ASSESSMENT OPTIONS

 Chapter Test
Have students take the Chapter 20 Test.

 Alternative Assessment
Have students do the Alternative Assessment activity for Chapter 20.

 Test Generator
The Test Generator contains additional assessment items for this chapter.

Evaluating Media Messages

Violence and the Media

Issues in Health

EVALUATING MEDIA MESSAGES

Violence and the Media Have students read the Evaluating Media Messages feature. Ask them for their reactions. Do they think they are being influenced in any way when they see violence on TV or in a movie? Do they agree with the feature's contention that people who buy albums advocating violence or who watch violent movies or shows are "endorsing the destructive messages they contain"?

Hold a class debate on that question. Those who oppose the argument presented in the feature might suggest that violence experienced vicariously discharges emotions that might otherwise get out of control. Students might do research to find out whether such arguments are valid.

Andy couldn't believe it. Ten extra laps! What had he done this time? It didn't seem to matter; no matter what he did, the coach always managed to find something wrong. Kurt, on the other hand, could get away with anything. Andy didn't really blame Kurt—after all, they were good friends—but it did seem completely unfair. The more Andy thought about it, the angrier he got. By the time he started to step into the shower, he was ready to explode. At that moment, Kurt showed up and, with a grin, popped Andy with a towel. It took Andy only a split second to react. His arm shot up, and without thinking, he shoved Kurt against the wall.

Andy and Kurt were both stunned. Andy slowly lowered his hand, struggling to calm down. "I'm sorry, Kurt," Andy said. "I don't know what made me do that."

Andy is not the only teenager who has reacted violently to frustration and anger. Over the past several years, the incidence of violence has increased among young people to the point that homicide is now the second leading cause of death for people 15 to 24. Although aggressive and violent behavior can result from a number of factors, many psychologists and educators believe that mass media have had an enormous effect on the increase in these behaviors. From television programs to rock concerts, mass media too often depict people taking violent actions. It is possible, therefore, that Andy's behavior in the locker room could be linked to the amount of violence he has witnessed through mass-media channels.

One of the most powerful ways that mass media influence people is by providing role models. Like many living things, people learn much of their behavior by copying what they see. Someone whose behavior is copied is a role model. If the role model is an admired person, like a popular actor or athlete, association makes the role model an even more powerful factor in influencing behavior. Therefore, when a person (receiver) sees a role model coping with a problem by asking for help and

When people see acts of violence committed over and over again, they lose their natural horror of cruelty and gore.

talking about it calmly, he or she is likely to behave this way. And studies have shown that when people watch others using violence in movies or on television, their behavior tends to become more aggressive.

Another way media messages influence people is by attempting to teach attitudes and values. Unfortunately, too few of the situations used to teach values are based in reality. For instance, a Harvard University study found that many of today's cartoons represent the world as a very fearful place, where the criminals are so evil that the only way to deal with them is to destroy them completely. Even though the heros usually win, the world they live in and the solutions they use are not realistic. As a result, viewers cannot easily apply the values presented in these cartoons to real-life situations. In addition, the pain and humiliation that real victims of violence experience is generally missing from the media's treatment of violence. By not showing the negative consequences of violence, the source of a media message omits an important part of the values lesson—a reason for not using violence.

Seeing violence in the media also affects viewers in another, more subtle, way. When people are repeatedly exposed to stressful events, especially while in pleasant surroundings, the stress reaction is reduced. Consequently, when people see acts of violence over and over again, they lose their natural horror of cruelty and gore. Even news programs have this effect.

It is possible to reduce the amount of violence seen in mass media if you remember that receivers of media messages have power over the sources of those messages. Most media experts agree that violence is prevalent in the media because it attracts attention and sells products. But in a way,

people who buy albums that advocate violence or who watch violent movies and television programs are endorsing the destructive messages they contain.

As members of a major consumer group, teenagers have more power to affect the media than they realize. To help reduce the use of violence in the media and in society, think twice about spending money on something that uses violence as a marketing tool.

Critical Thinking

1. Think about how you usually react when someone makes you angry.

   - Have you always reacted this way?
   - Do people you admire behave this way? Who?
   - What kinds of things have influenced your behavior?

2. When you watch your favorite television programs tonight, take notes on how many times disagreements are handled with nonviolent solutions.

3. Analyze a movie or television program that contains violence by answering the following questions.

   - What is the source of the message to use violence?
   - What was the reason for making this movie or television program?
   - How do I benefit from the messages in this show?

4. Automobile accidents are the leading cause of death for teenagers. How do you think the scenes of car chases in movies and television programs might contribute to reckless driving and accidental deaths among teenagers?

5. Homicide is the second leading cause of death for people 15 to 24. How do you think media messages might affect violent behavior among teenagers?

UNIT 6
DISEASES AND DISORDERS

CHAPTER OVERVIEWS

CHAPTER 21

INFECTIOUS DISEASES

A general discussion of infectious diseases, including their causes, methods of transmission, and the body's defenses against them opens the chapter. This is followed by specific information about the symptoms, treatment, and prevention of the most common viral and bacterial diseases. Conditions and diseases caused by protists, animal parasites, and fungi are also described.

CHAPTER 22

SEXUALLY TRANSMITTED DISEASES

For each sexually transmitted disease (STD) described, students learn how it is spread, its symptoms, and the consequences of leaving it untreated. Ways of preventing STDs are discussed, particularly sexual abstinence. Students are also given information about where to go for help if they suspect infection.

CHAPTER 23

HIV INFECTION AND AIDS

This chapter describes the phases of HIV infection and emphasizes the difference between being HIV-positive and having AIDS. Students learn how HIV is transmitted and how they can protect themselves from infection. Sexual abstinence is emphasized as a means of prevention. HIV-related

concerns for teenagers, including risky behaviors and peer pressure, also are addressed. The chapter explores a number of social issues, such as the rapidly rising incidence of AIDS, reasons for anonymous testing, and discrimination against those who are HIV-positive.

CHAPTER 24

NONINFECTIOUS DISEASES AND DISORDERS

Hereditary, congenital, autoimmune, and degenerative diseases and ailments are described in this chapter. The difference between autoimmune diseases and AIDS is stressed. Students learn about lifestyle choices they can make to protect themselves from developing certain diseases in the future.

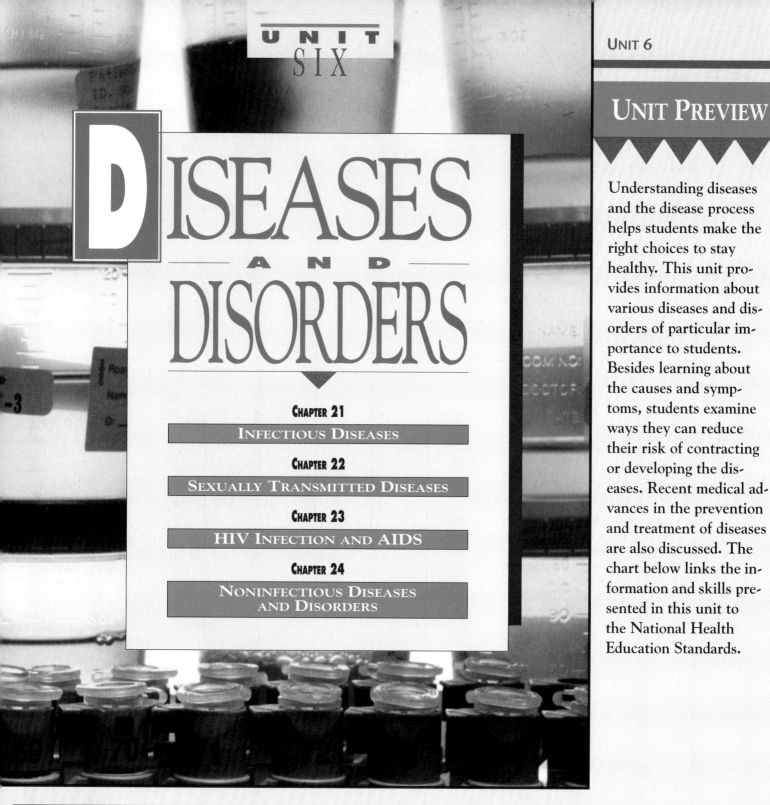

UNIT SIX

D ISEASES AND DISORDERS

CHAPTER 21
INFECTIOUS DISEASES

CHAPTER 22
SEXUALLY TRANSMITTED DISEASES

CHAPTER 23
HIV INFECTION AND AIDS

CHAPTER 24
NONINFECTIOUS DISEASES
AND DISORDERS

UNIT 6

UNIT PREVIEW

Understanding diseases and the disease process helps students make the right choices to stay healthy. This unit provides information about various diseases and disorders of particular importance to students. Besides learning about the causes and symptoms, students examine ways they can reduce their risk of contracting or developing the diseases. Recent medical advances in the prevention and treatment of diseases are also discussed. The chart below links the information and skills presented in this unit to the National Health Education Standards.

Unit 6	NATIONAL HEALTH EDUCATION STANDARDS*						
STANDARD	1	2	3	4	5	6	7
Chapter 21	•		•			•	•
Chapter 22	•	•	•		•	•	
Chapter 23	•	•	•		•		•
Chapter 24	•		•			•	•

* For full text listing of each standard, see page 15T.

PLANNING GUIDE

CHAPTER 21

Infectious Diseases

SECTION	TITLE/OBJECTIVES	PERSONAL INVENTORY			LIFE SKILLS DEVELOPMENT			
		Personal Health Inventory	Journal	Check Up	Life Skills	Life Skills Worksheets	Media Message or Ethical Issues Worksheet	What Would You Do?
21.1 *pp. 441–444*	**WHAT ARE INFECTIOUS DISEASES?** • Describe the causes of infectious diseases. • Identify the ways in which diseases are spread.	Ch. 21	21A 21B					
21.2 *pp. 445–451*	**FIGHTING DISEASE** • Distinguish between infection and disease. • Name the four ways the body resists infection. • Explain how an immunization can prevent disease.		21C					
21.3 *pp. 452–458*	**COMMON INFECTIOUS DISEASES** • List four common diseases caused by viruses. • Explain which kind of diseases antibiotics can cure, and which kind they can't. ▓ Know some ways to decrease your chances of getting an infectious disease.		21D		p. 456	21A		

KEY: ▓ Denotes Life Skill Objective
Text references denoted by page number.
Supplement references denoted by chapter or item numbers.

LINKING RESOURCES

Making a Choice Cards	Parent Discussion Guide	Health Talk Audio Program	Teaching Transparencies and Directory	Section Review Worksheets	Section Quizzes	Reteaching Worksheets	Section Reviews
INTERACTION		**OTHER RESOURCES**		**SECTION REVIEW AND ASSESSMENT**			
21A			21A	21.1	21.1	21.1	p. 444
			21B 21C BSH11	21.2	21.2	21.2	p. 451
21B				21.3	21.3	21.3	p. 458

KEY FACTS

- An infectious disease is a disease that can be passed from one living thing to another.
- A communicable disease is an infectious disease that is passed from one person to another.
- Infectious diseases are caused by agents called pathogens; bacteria, viruses, protists, fungi, and parasitic worms are pathogens.
- Pathogens can be passed to a person by another person; by an animal; by contact with contaminated objects, food, or water; or through the air.
- The body's defenses against pathogens include defensive barriers, such as the skin; chemical methods, such as the chemicals found in sweat; the inflammatory response; and the immune system.
- Immunity is protection against developing a certain disease; immunity may be innate, passive, or active.
- Bacterial diseases, such as strep throat or sinus infections, can be treated with antibiotics.
- Viral diseases, such as flu, chickenpox, or mononucleosis, do not respond to antibiotics.

CHAPTER REVIEW AND ASSESSMENT

TEXT

Chapter Review pp. 460–461

SUPPLEMENTS

Chapter Test 21

Alternative Assessment 21

Test Generator Chapter 21

For additional information on how the immune system combats disease organisms, see pages 680–681 in the Body Systems Handbook.

GETTING STARTED

Using the Chapter Photograph

Have students look at the chapter photograph, and then ask: **How could an infectious disease spread among this group of people without anyone realizing it?** *[primarily by coughing or sneezing, but also by sharing food or drinks and by touch]* **What two common diseases are spread in this manner?** *[colds and flu]*

 Question Box

Have students write out any questions they have about infectious diseases and put them in the Question Box. **Note:** STDs and AIDS are also infectious diseases, but they are covered in Chapters 22 and 23.

Sensitivity *ALERT*

Discussion of infectious diseases may make some students uncomfortable, particularly if they have visible signs of illness. Stress that with appropriate medical attention, most infectious diseases can be treated successfully. Some students may have questions they feel are too personal—or even too simple—to bring up before the class; encourage students to use the Question Box.

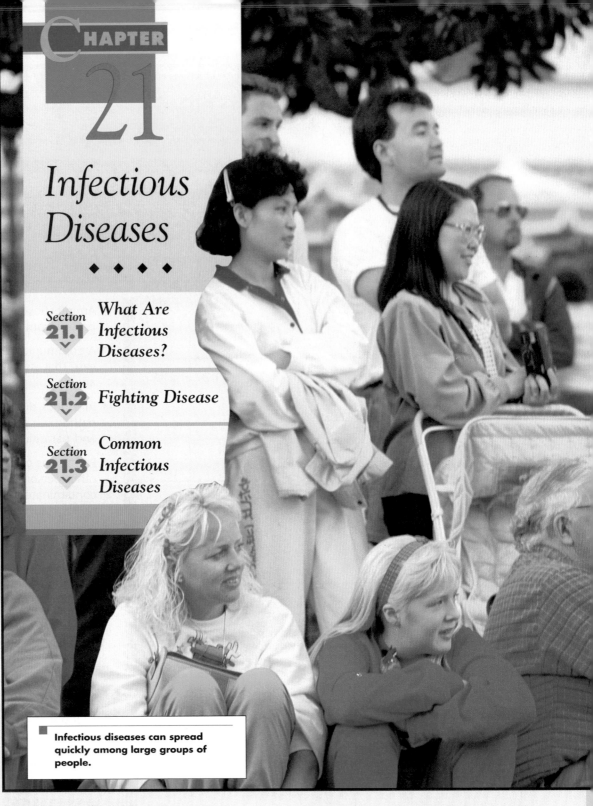

CHAPTER 21

Infectious Diseases

◆ ◆ ◆ ◆

Section 21.1 What Are Infectious Diseases?

Section 21.2 Fighting Disease

Section 21.3 Common Infectious Diseases

Infectious diseases can spread quickly among large groups of people.

MYTHS & MISCONCEPTIONS

- **Going outside during bad weather without a jacket or with wet hair will cause you to catch a cold.** Colds are caused by a virus, not by bad weather. However, research indicates that becoming chilled can weaken the immune system, leaving those who have become chilled more vulnerable to catching a cold.

- **I feel fine now, so I don't need to finish taking my prescription medicine.** To ensure that the medication kills all the pathogens responsible for an illness, it is necessary to take the entire amount exactly as directed.

- **Cold sores are unsightly but not dangerous.** Cold sores are caused by the herpes simplex virus type I. Because fluid from a cold sore can spread the virus to other areas of the body, a person with a cold sore must take precautions to prevent this spread.

The clock radio beside Tanita's bed suddenly blares out rock music, as it does every school morning at 6:30. But as she reaches out to turn down the volume, she realizes something is wrong. When she went to bed the night before, she thought she felt more tired than usual. She feels more than tired now. Her throat hurts and she feels feverish.

Tanita's best friend, Clarissa, has been out of school the past two days with the flu. Now it's Tanita's turn. She spends most of the day sleeping. When she's awake she drinks a little water and lies still, feeling queasy. Over the next several days, she gradually feels better. She's able to eat some soup and crackers, to watch TV, and to read a magazine.

Finally Tanita is well enough to go back to school. There's a history test to make up and she's way behind in her homework, not to mention the dance she missed last Friday. Being sick is no fun.

Section 21.1
What Are Infectious Diseases?

Objectives

- Describe the causes of infectious diseases.
- Identify the ways in which diseases are spread.

The disease that Tanita had is influenza, which is often called "flu" for short. If you have had influenza, you know that it makes you feel pretty miserable for a few days. But after resting and taking care of yourself, you soon feel like your old self again.

Influenza is an example of an **infectious disease**. An infectious disease is one that is caused by an agent that can pass from one organism to another. Influenza is also a contagious or **communicable disease**, an infectious disease that is passed from one person to another. Tanita feels sure that she "caught" the flu from Clarissa, and most likely she is right.

Not all diseases are infectious diseases. Illnesses like cancer and heart disease are not spread from one person to another. No one knows exactly why one person gets cancer or has a heart attack and another person does not. Researchers have found that certain factors—like smoking, a high-fat diet, and lack of physical activity—can increase your chances of getting these kinds of diseases. But you don't "catch" these diseases from another living thing.

communicable disease:

an infectious disease that is passed from one person to another.

infectious disease:

a disease caused by an agent that can pass from one living thing to another.

Background
Safe Sneezing
Covering the mouth during a sneeze reduces the spray but concentrates pathogens on the hand; from there they are easily transferred to another person by handshake or by handling food, doorknobs, and so on. Covering the mouth with a tissue during a sneeze and then promptly disposing of it is an effective way to reduce the spread of pathogens during a sneeze. Washing one's hands thoroughly with soap and warm water after throwing away the tissue will further reduce the spread of pathogens.

Personal Health Inventory
Have students complete the Personal Health Inventory for this chapter.

Section 21.1 Lesson Plan

MOTIVATE

Journal 21A
Diseases You Have Had
This may be done as a warm-up activity. In their Journal, ask students to list diseases they can remember having, what the symptoms were, and what was done to treat the disease.

Class Discussion
Infectious and Noninfectious
On the chalkboard, write the headings INFECTIOUS and NONINFECTIOUS. Discuss the distinction between these two types of disease, and write some key ideas and some sample diseases beneath the headings.

Background
Animals Spreading Disease

Animals that spread disease are called *vectors*, from a Latin word meaning "to carry." Listed below are some diseases, the type of pathogen that causes them, and their animal vectors.

- bubonic plague—bacteria; rats, fleas
- Lyme disease—bacteria; deer ticks
- rabbit fever (tularemia)—bacteria; rabbits, squirrels
- rabies—virus; dogs, cats, raccoons, bats, squirrels
- parrot fever (psittacosis)—viruslike organism; birds, especially parrots
- Rocky Mountain Spotted Fever—viruslike organism; wood tick
- ringworm—fungus; dogs, cats
- malaria—protist; mosquitoes
- liver fluke—parasitic worm; snails, sheep
- trichinosis—parasitic worm; pigs

pathogen:

any agent that causes disease.

microorganism:

a living thing that can be seen only with a microscope.

bacterium:

a type of microorganism that can cause disease.

What Causes Infectious Diseases?

Infectious diseases are caused by agents called **pathogens.** In the United States, the most common pathogens are bacteria and viruses. Bacteria and viruses are two different things, but they are sometimes grouped together and called germs.

Other pathogens include fungi, protists, and parasitic worms. Bacteria, protists, and many fungi are too small to be seen without a microscope. For this reason, they often are called **microorganisms.**

Some of the pathogens that can cause disease are shown in Figure 21-1.

Bacteria Bacteria are very simple living things. Each **bacterium** is a single cell, much smaller than the cells that make up your body. The vast majority of bacteria are harmless.

A few types of bacteria, however, are a real problem for people. They can spoil food or cause diseases. Common diseases caused by bacteria are strep throat, food poisoning, and urinary-tract infections.

A. Streptococcus Bacterium
Causes strep throat

B. Herpes Virus
Causes chickenpox, herpes, and shingles

C. Plasmodium (in red blood cell)
Causes malaria

D. Roundworm Parasite

(FIGURE 21-1) **Four causes of infectious diseases are bacteria, viruses, protists, and parasitic worms. Any agent that can cause an infectious illness is called a pathogen.**

TEACH

Teaching Transparency 21A
Four Agents of Infectious Disease

Show the transparency of Figure 21-1. Emphasize the tiny size of these microorganisms: one drop of saliva contains millions of bacteria and even more viruses. Viruses are so small that they can be seen only with an electron microscope. Some worms are large enough to be visible without a microscope.

Reinforcement
Word Origins

Write on the chalkboard:
pathos (suffer discomfort) + *genes* (to produce) = pathogen
Explain to students that knowing the etymology of a word will help them remember its meaning.

Journal 21B
Person to Person

Have students turn to their Journal and list all the person-to-person contacts they can remember having had yesterday. Tell them to include handshakes, contact sports, hugs, accidental bumps, or helping someone with their hair or clothing. Explain that no one will see their list; its purpose is to help them realize how many opportunities occur each day for them to exchange pathogens with someone else.

Viruses A **virus** is a microscopic disease-causing particle consisting of genetic material and a protein coat. Viruses cannot reproduce without first invading a living cell. Once inside a living cell, the virus's genetic material acts as a program that directs the cell to make more viruses. After the cell makes new viruses, it often dies and releases the viruses. These viruses spread to new cells, which also die.

Viruses are specialized to infect only certain types of cells. For example, some viruses attack only plant cells, while other viruses attack certain animal cells. If you have a dog, you know your pet needs to be immunized against certain diseases that affect only dogs. You also have your pet immunized against rabies, a viral disease that both humans and dogs can get.

Some common diseases caused by viruses include the common cold, the flu, cold sores, and measles.

How Are Infectious Diseases Spread?

You have seen that all infectious diseases are caused by pathogens that can be passed from one organism to another. In order for you to catch an infectious disease, a pathogen must first leave the body of a living thing and then enter your body. There are several ways that this can happen.

Through the Air Clarissa was sick with the flu because influenza viruses were invading cells in her respiratory system, mainly in her nose and throat. The viruses then moved from Clarissa to Tanita, and Tanita got sick.

How did the viruses get from Clarissa to Tanita? Influenza viruses usually travel through droplets in the air. When you sneeze, thousands of tiny drops of mucus and saliva are sprayed into the air, as shown

(FIGURE 21-2) **The viruses that cause influenza are spread through droplets in the air.**

in Figure 21-2. If your nose and throat are infected with viruses, some viruses are carried out into the air in the droplets. Someone nearby who breathes in the droplets can then become infected with the viruses.

Contact With Contaminated Objects A person who is sick may leave bacteria or viruses on objects like doorknobs, drinking glasses, toothbrushes, towels, or combs. Some agents of disease do not live for long outside of the human body, but other pathogens are tougher. These types of pathogens may be passed from one person to another when the second person opens the same door, shares a glass, or uses the sick person's toothbrush.

Person-to-Person Contact Sometimes the agents of disease are spread by direct person-to-person contact. For example, you can get some illnesses by shaking hands, kissing, or touching the ulcers or sores of a sick person. Some infectious diseases are spread by sexual contact. These diseases are discussed in more detail in Chapters 22 and 23.

virus:

a microscopic disease-causing particle consisting of genetic material and a protein coat.

Sexually Transmitted Diseases are discussed in Chapter 22. AIDS and HIV are discussed in Chapter 23.

SECTION 21.1

 Making a Choice 21A
Assign the What's Going Around? card. The card asks students to list all of the diseases that seem to be going around the school, to try to identify the pathogens that cause them, and to find out how the diseases are spread.

Section Review Worksheet 21.1
To reinforce the concepts presented in this section, assign Section Review Worksheet 21.1.

Section Quiz 21.1
Have students take Section Quiz 21.1

Reinforcement
Diseases and Their Pathogens

On the chalkboard, make a chart as shown. Allow room for about 10 diseases to be entered.

INFECTIOUS DISEASE	PATHOGEN	HOW SPREAD
Influenza	Virus	Through the air

Then have students name infectious diseases for you to enter, the pathogen that causes the disease, and how the disease is spread. (Influenza is shown as an example.)

Game
Disease Detective

Have students work in small groups. One person is It. He or she chooses a disease, a pathogen, and a method of transmittal (food poisoning, bacteria, potato salad). Other students question the person with the disease, who can only answer yes or no. Have you been on a picnic lately? Have you been camping? Did you boil the water? Do you feel queasy? Students must determine the disease, pathogen, and methods of transmittal.

Extension
Epidemics Around the World

Have students scan recent newspapers and magazines for articles on epidemics anywhere in the world. Have them photocopy the articles and post them on the bulletin board so classmates can read them. A geography and social studies link can be made by having students mark the locations of epidemics on a world map.

Review Answers

1. Bacteria—Streptococcus; virus—herpes; protist—plasmodium; parasitic worm— roundworm; accept any other examples discussed in class.

2. Answers may include through the air, person-to-person contact, contact with contaminated objects, animals, and food and water.

3. Answers will vary. Tanita would not have gotten the flu from Clarissa if she had stayed away from her friend the whole time Clarissa was ill. If Tanita attended any classes with Clarissa she may not have been able to avoid the flu, since it is spread through the air, person-to-person contact, and touching anything the infected person touched.

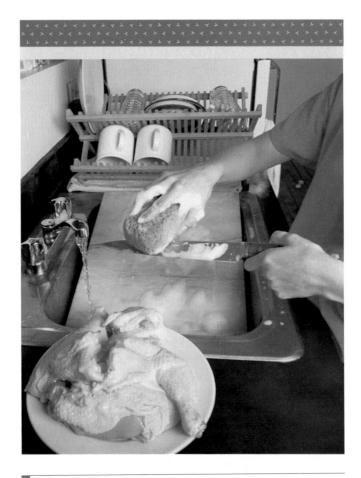

(FIGURE 21-3) **To help protect against food poisoning, always cook meat and eggs thoroughly and wash working surfaces, utensils, and hands with hot, soapy water after contact with meat.**

Animals That Spread Disease Some infectious diseases are spread by animals. Humans can get a fungus called ringworm from handling an infected dog or cat. It is possible for people to get rabies from the bite of an infected animal. A type of encephalitis, or inflammation of the brain, is spread by mosquitoes. Lyme disease, a serious bacterial infection, is carried by ticks. Hantaan virus, which causes a deadly hemorrhagic fever, can be transmitted through contact with feces from infected rodents.

Food and Water Eating contaminated food or drinking contaminated water can also spread disease. Diseases that affect the digestive system are often spread when feces from an infected person or animal contaminate food or water. This is why people who work with food are required by law to wash their hands thoroughly after every trip to the bathroom. For the same reason, fresh fruits and vegetables, particularly those that grow on the ground, should be washed thoroughly before they are eaten.

Large numbers of bacteria growing in food can cause food poisoning. Symptoms of food poisoning include nausea, vomiting, and abdominal pain. The best way to prevent this type of infection is to refrigerate food except while it is actually being prepared or served, keep hands and utensils clean while preparing foods, and cook food thoroughly to kill any bacteria present.

In the United States, drinking tap water is safe. But campers and hikers who drink water from streams must purify the water first, either by boiling or by using water purification tablets or special filtering systems, to protect themselves from disease.

Review

1. *Name four types of pathogens, and give an example of each.*

2. *What are three ways in which infectious diseases can be spread?*

3. *Critical Thinking* *Is there anything that Tanita could have done to avoid catching the flu from Clarissa?*

ASSESS

Section Review

Have students answer the Section Review questions.

Alternative Assessment
What's the Pathogen?

For each situation listed, ask what the disease could be, what the pathogen is, how it was communicated, and how it might be prevented.

(1) Anita ate some unrefrigerated potato salad and now has stomach cramps and diarrhea. *[food poisoning; bacterium; food; refrigerate the food]* **(2)** Jessie has a runny nose and sneezed several times during her last study session, and now her boyfriend has the same signs. *[cold; virus; through the air; avoid close contact and cover sneezes with a tissue]* **(3)** Several people in Consuela's class have been out sick and now Consuela has a fever and feels achy. *[flu; virus; person-to-person contact; avoid contact]*

Closure
Risks of Infection

Ask students to think about all the activities they are involved in today. Ask them which activities will most expose them to infectious diseases.

Section 21.2 *Fighting Disease*

Objectives

- *Distinguish between infection and disease.*
- *Name four ways the body resists infection.*
- *Explain how an immunization can prevent disease.*

Bacteria, viruses, and other agents of disease are everywhere around us. They are found in the air you breathe, on surfaces you touch, and even on your own skin. So why aren't you sick all the time?

Remember that in order for you to get sick, a pathogen must not only leave another organism, but also enter your body. Even if it enters your body, it cannot make you sick unless it survives, multiplies, and somehow causes damage to your system. Most of the time, pathogens are quickly destroyed or swept away before they have a chance to multiply in your body.

Infection and Disease

If pathogens do enter your system and begin to spread and reproduce, then you are infected. Being infected is not the same as having a disease, or actually being sick. Even after pathogens begin to multiply, your body can mount such a good defense against them that they can be destroyed or made harmless before they cause any actual damage. If this happens, you will probably never know that you have been infected. But if you are infected with certain disease-causing agents, you *can* pass them to someone else.

Disease If your defenses cannot stop the pathogen quickly enough, you may begin to feel sick. A disease is any harmful change in your body's normal activities. A pathogen can cause disease when it is able to multiply in your body and cause damage to your cells and tissues.

Signs and Symptoms The effects of a disease are called signs and symptoms. A sign of a disease is something another person can see or detect. Tanita had a fever,

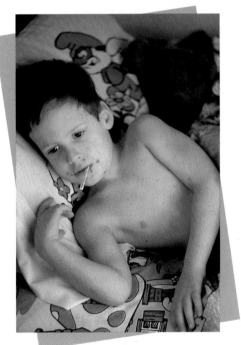

(FIGURE 21-4) **The effects of a disease are called signs and symptoms. One sign of the chickenpox is fluid-filled blisters.**

Background
Body Temperature

Oral body temperature averages 98.6°F (36.7°C) but can vary from person to person and with time of day, so readings a few tenths of a degree lower or higher can be normal for an individual. Fevers can be helpful. For example, when a virus attacks, the immune system signals the brain to raise body temperature to help fight the disease. This may cause a chill, compelling one to wrap up in a sweater or blanket, which insulates the body and helps drive up body temperature. Once a fever has done its job, body temperature returns to normal, sometimes accompanied by profuse sweating. Children often get a fever with a cold. This is less common with adults. Temperatures above 104°F can be dangerous, especially to the elderly and to those with heart problems. Fevers this high need prompt medical attention.

Section 21.2 Lesson Plan

MOTIVATE

Writing
Defective Immune Systems

This may be done as a warm-up activity. Tell students that on rare occasions a child is born with a genetic condition that results in a severely impaired or nonfunctional immune system. One famous case involved a boy named David who had a condition known as severe combined immunodeficiency (SCID). This condition occurs in about one out of every 100,000 newborns. David became known as the boy in a bubble because he had to spend his brief life (12 years) in an isolated environment. His "bubble" was actually a protective sterile room and a miniature space suit. Ask the students to write a few sentences explaining why David had to live in isolation. Explain that in this section they will learn about how our bodies fight disease.

Background
The Price of a Cold

In the United States, colds cost about $5 billion each year, which includes the cost of medical bills, symptom relievers, 60 million lost school days, and 50 million lost working days. The United States space program lost half a million dollars when a launch had to be postponed for a week because all three astronauts came down with colds!

mucous membranes:

the tissues that line the openings into your body; pathogens can enter the body through the mucous membranes, although many are trapped there.

---

which is a sign of influenza. Other diseases might have signs like sneezing, coughing, looking pale or flushed, or having skin eruptions like those shown in Figure 21-4.

A symptom is any feeling of pain or discomfort that you experience when you are sick. Tanita's sore throat, tiredness, and queasy stomach are all symptoms of influenza. Other symptoms of disease might include itching, tenderness, cramps, headache, or dizziness.

Defenses Against Infection

Your body has many ways of coping with disease-causing bacteria, viruses, and other pathogens.

Skin One of the functions of your skin is to protect the rest of your body from invasion by agents of disease. The outer part of your skin is very well designed for this job. The lower layers of this part of the skin are tightly joined so that it is difficult for anything to penetrate the skin and enter the tissues beneath it.

The upper layers of the skin are made of dead skin cells filled with a tough waterproof protein. Every day, millions of dead skin cells are shed from the surface of your skin and are replaced by new cells from the layers below. When you shower or bathe, you wash off even more skin cells. As the dead cells come off, they take any bacteria, viruses, or other pathogens that have settled on your skin with them.

Chemical Warfare on Germs Many of the chemical substances your body makes for its activities also act to destroy pathogens. For example, sweat and oils produced by your skin contain acids that can kill bacteria. Enzymes in tears and saliva also kill bacteria.

(FIGURE 21-5) **Every time you shower you remove dead skin cells from your body. Any agents of disease that have formed on these cells are washed away as well.**

Mucous Membranes The tissues lining the openings into your body, such as your mouth and nose, are different from the skin on the outside of your body. These tissues are called **mucous membranes** because cells in these tissues secrete a coating called mucus.

When you breathe through your nose, pathogens in the air are trapped in the sticky mucus that coats the passages of your respiratory system. The cells that line these passages have tiny projections on their surfaces called cilia, shown in Figure 21-6. In your nasal passages, the cilia sweep the mucus downward. In the tubes that lead to your lungs in the lower part of your respiratory system, the cilia sweep the mucus upward.

All of the mucus ends up in your throat and is swallowed, along with saliva from your mouth. This is a natural cleansing

---

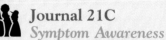

TEACH

Class Discussion
Signs and Symptoms

Often there are early signs of an illness coming on. If there is intervention at that time, a person may be able to avoid being so ill that they have to miss scheduled activities. Have students brainstorm to make a list of early signs or symptoms of illness. *(Signs and*

symptoms may include: painful swallowing; slight sore throat, nausea, fever, or chill; headache; fatigue; achiness; stuffiness; and tired eyes.)* Ask: **These symptoms may be early signs of what illnesses?** [throat infection, stomach virus or food poisoning, cold or flu, allergy, sinus condition] Ask: **What could you do at this point that might be helpful?** [Eat lightly, get extra sleep, and avoid close contact with others so you don't spread your illness.] Stress that sometimes a person becomes ill

despite efforts to avoid sickness but that it is possible to help the body fight off illnesses.

 Journal 21C
Symptom Awareness

In their Journal, ask students to record any symptoms they may have felt recently and any signs of illness they may have observed in family members and friends. Explain that the purpose of this exercise is to make them more aware and observant of signs and symptoms of diseases.

process that helps keep your respiratory passages free of microorganisms that might cause disease. Unless you have a disease that causes you to produce extra mucus, like a cold, you might not even be aware of it.

Stomach Acids Not all microorganisms enter your body through your respiratory system. A pathogen might get into your system through your mouth when you touch your fingers to your lips, breathe through your mouth, or bite your nails. Most microorganisms that enter your body in these ways are swallowed, and eventually they end up in your stomach.

Most of the microorganisms that reach the stomach are destroyed there. This is because your stomach contains acids that are 10 times stronger than the acid in pure lemon juice. The acids not only help digest your food, but they also help protect you from disease.

Helpful Microorganisms Remember that most microorganisms are harmless to humans. Many of these microorganisms,

(FIGURE 21-6) **The cells that line the passages of your respiratory system contain tiny projections called cilia, which help sweep disease-causing agents out of your body.**

especially bacteria, live on the skin and mucous membranes of every normal, healthy person. Within minutes after you were born, these microorganisms began to make themselves at home both on you and in you.

These microorganisms actually help protect you from pathogens. The harmless bacteria living in your mouth, for example, take up most of the space and use up most of the food available. When a pathogen is breathed in or eaten with a bite of food, it cannot multiply because there is simply no room for it.

Inflammation If you have ever had an infected cut, you may have noticed that it was swollen, red, painful, and warm to the touch. These are the signs of inflammation, which is caused by the body's defense reaction to the invasion by pathogens.

Your skin and mucous membranes are very effective at protecting the tissues underneath them from infection by pathogens. However, when you cut or burn yourself, pathogens are sometimes able to cross these protective barriers.

Fortunately, another set of defenses against pathogens is waiting in the tissues underneath the skin and mucous membranes. Any damage to these tissues results in the release of several different kinds of chemicals. The purpose of these chemicals is to act as signals for mobilizing the disease-fighting defenses.

First, small blood vessels expand to bring more blood to the injured area. Fluids from the blood and the white blood cells, called phagocytes, pour out of the blood and into the surrounding tissues. Then the phagocytes attack, eat, and destroy any microorganisms that they find in the vicinity. The extra blood and fluid cause the injured area to become swollen and warm and appear red or changed.

Background
Rabies
Rabies is an old disease, but it has recently become a problem in some eastern states. People are rarely bitten and infected, but when this does occur, rabies is fatal unless passive immunity is provided. The treatment for providing passive immunity is usually one injection of antirabies globulin followed by five injections of rabies vaccine. Dogs and cats can be vaccinated against rabies, and many cities have ordinances requiring vaccination. (For additional information about rabies, see page 641.)

Cooperative Learning
Defenses Against Infection

Divide the class into six groups and assign each group one of these defenses against infection: skin, chemical warfare, mucous membranes, stomach acid, helpful microorganisms, and inflammation. Allow each group a few minutes to discuss the text information on how their defense guards against invasion by microorganisms. Then, ask each group to explain to the class how their defense works when a pathogen tries to invade the body.

• • • TEACH continues on p. 448

Background
Polio Immunization

Polio immunization is extremely effective. In 1952, before the immunization was developed, there were 21,000 reported cases of polio in the United States. Between 1953 and 1955, polio vaccines were introduced, and by the 1980s, there were fewer than 10 cases reported annually. There are two types of vaccine, Sabin oral, which is a live but weakened virus, and Salk, which is an inactivated virus. Although both are effective, neither is perfect. An extremely small percentage of children vaccinated with the Sabin vaccine contract polio. Children recently vaccinated with the Salk vaccine can infect other people; therefore, unvaccinated adults should avoid contact with them. The CDC recommends that children receive two doses of the Salk vaccine as infants, and two doses of the Sabin vaccine before age six.

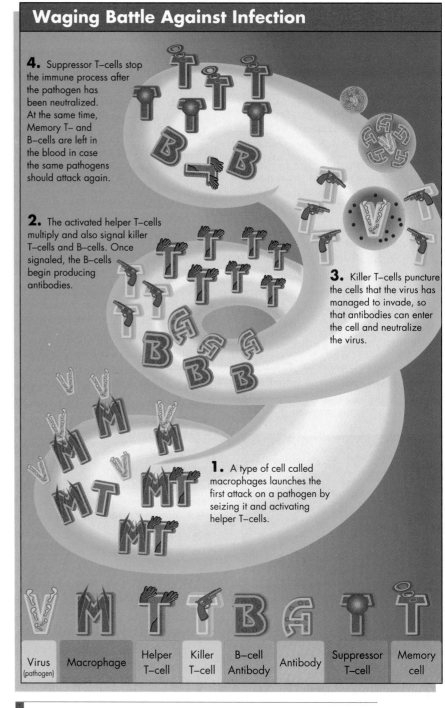

Waging Battle Against Infection

4. Suppressor T-cells stop the immune process after the pathogen has been neutralized. At the same time, Memory T- and B-cells are left in the blood in case the same pathogens should attack again.

2. The activated helper T-cells multiply and also signal killer T-cells and B-cells. Once signaled, the B-cells begin producing antibodies.

3. Killer T-cells puncture the cells that the virus has managed to invade, so that antibodies can enter the cell and neutralize the virus.

1. A type of cell called macrophages launches the first attack on a pathogen by seizing it and activating helper T-cells.

Virus (pathogen)	Macrophage	Helper T-cell	Killer T-cell	B-cell Antibody	Antibody	Suppressor T-cell	Memory cell

(FIGURE 21-7) **Your immune system launches an all-out war every time a pathogen invades your system.**

• • • TEACH continued

Class Discussion
Immune Cells

Ask everyone in the class who has keys to hold them up. Have students note how the keys are all different, each shaped to fit its own lock. Ask: **How are the keys similar to specialized immune cells?** *[Just as a key fits only the lock it is designed for, certain immune cells recognize only one type of invading molecule.]*

Reinforcement
Your Body's Watchdog

Compare the immune system to a watchdog. Explain that a watchdog always watches for intruders, and so does the body's immune system. When an intruder tries to get past the dog, it attacks (like killer T-cells), it barks to call for help (like helper T-cells), other dogs hear the noise and come running to help attack the intruder (like antibodies from B-cells), and the dog remembers the intruder if

it ever returns (like memory T-cells). Ask students to draw a cartoon strip showing the immune system as a watchdog.

 Teaching Transparency 21B
The Immune System

Use this transparency to help students visualize the role of the different types of cells that make up the immune system.

The Immune System All of the defenses that you have learned about so far will attack and destroy any and all possible agents of disease. In addition, your body has a complex system of fighting specific invaders. For example, if a measles virus gets past your other defenses, your body will launch an all-out war on measles viruses throughout your body.

The weapons your body is using to fight the measles virus work only on measles viruses. They have no effect on any other kind of pathogen. When the body mobilizes its defenses to fight one specific type of invader, the process that is activated is called the immune response. The cells and organs that fight the war against specific invaders are called the **immune system.**

Weapons of the Immune Response

Before a baby is born and during the first years of its life, the immune system produces millions of different kinds of immune cells. Each of these cells can attack a molecule of a certain shape. Such a molecule might be a protein in the outer coat of a virus or a poison molecule made by a bacterium. When an immune cell comes into contact with a molecule that is the right shape, biologists say that the immune cell ''recognizes'' that molecule.

There are millions of different kinds of these cells, and each kind recognizes a different shape of molecule. So no matter what kind of pathogen might invade your body, there are some immune cells ready to fight it. There are two main types of immune cells that are able to fight any pathogen that might come along.

T-Cells One type of immune cell is called **T-cells**. Certain T-cells mobilize to fight pathogens directly. These T-cells are called killer T-cells. When a pathogen invades your body, its molecules will be recognized by some of your killer T-cells. These cells will divide into many cells that then kill the invaders.

Another class of T-cells, called helper T-cells, get the immune response going by activating killer T-cells, phagocytes, and other immune cells. Helper T-cells are activated by macrophages, which are cells that form the first line of defense against a pathogen. Suppressor T-cells turn off the immune response after the pathogen has been defeated.

Antibodies The other main type of immune cell is called **B-cells.** Their job is to produce antibodies. **Antibodies** (AN tee bahd eez) are Y-shaped molecules that stick to and cover foreign molecules in the body. When a pathogen invades, the B-cells that recognize that pathogen divide rapidly and produce thousands of antibody molecules apiece. When a bacterium or virus is covered with antibodies, it has great difficulty attacking body cells.

Immunity

You may know that after you have had certain diseases, you can't catch them again. For example, after a person has had the mumps, that person doesn't have to worry about getting the mumps a second time.

You probably never had the mumps, however. Most people your age have been immunized against mumps and so never get this disease even once.

In other cases, it doesn't seem to count for anything if you've already had a disease. You may have had two colds this year alone, not to mention the one you had last year, and the one two years before that.

Why the difference? How can you be protected against some diseases entirely by an immunization, get other diseases only once, and get still others over and over?

B-cells:

cells in the immune system that produce antibodies against infection.

antibodies:

substances that stick to the surface of pathogens, slowing their action.

immune system:

the system that protects the body from disease.

T-cells:

cells that regulate the action of the immune system.

Background
Passive Immunity
The key difference between active immunity and passive immunity is the source of the antibodies. In active immunity, one's own body develops the antibodies in response to a pathogen, and "remembers" the invader. In passive immunity, a person is given antibodies from another person or animal, and the antibodies remain active in the body long enough to fight off the pathogen. Since the body did not generate these antibodies, it doesn't remember them, so the immunity is temporary. This is why the immunity an infant receives from its mother fades a few months after birth and why some vaccines are only temporary.

Teaching Transparency 21C
Waging Battle Against Infection

Use this transparency of Figure 21-7 to explain to students how the immune system defends the body against pathogens.

Extension
The Three Lines of Defense
The body's defenses against infection are usually categorized as the first, second, and third lines of defense. Have students do research to find out how these three lines of defense work. Have them explain how the inflammatory response differs from the immune response. Students could prepare an oral report or create a visual display to report their findings.

Computer Viruses
Computer viruses get their name because they spread in ways that can be compared with the way real viruses spread. Have students do research to discover the similarities and report their findings to the class.

Section Review Worksheet 21.2

To reinforce the concepts presented in this section, assign Section Review Worksheet 21.2.

Section Quiz 21.2

Have students take Section Quiz 21.2.

Review Answers

1. A person can be infected by a pathogen but have no signs or symptoms. The person has a disease when he or she develops signs and symptoms of illness.

2. Answers may include any four of the following ways: the skin protects the body from invasions of agents of disease; chemical substances, such as enzymes, kill pathogens; the mucous membranes trap microorganisms; strong acids in the stomach kill many microorganisms that are swallowed; helpful microorganisms living in the body use up available space and food resources; inflammation releases chemicals that kill invading microorganisms; and the immune system works to resist disease.

immunization:

injection of a small amount of a pathogen that will provide protection against an infectious disease.

Protection against developing a certain disease is called immunity. There are three basic types of immunity.

Innate Immunity You are immune to certain diseases just because you are who you are. First of all, you are a human being. You will never have to worry about diseases that affect only fish or rose bushes or horses. In addition, some people seem to inherit resistance to certain human diseases.

Active Immunity Once your body has launched an all-out war against a specific invader, it remains armed and ready to fight that same invader much more quickly and effectively if that same invader should ever show up again.

This happens because when the B- and T-cells that fight a specific invader multiply while they are fighting a pathogen, some of these cells are set aside as "memory cells." Any subsequent time that specific pathogen tries to invade your body, your immune system is ready for it. Memory cells multiply quickly and produce huge numbers of antibodies in a very short time. The invaders are defeated and destroyed so quickly that they don't have time to make you sick. You never even know that they were ever present in your body.

There are two ways that you can acquire active immunity. One way is by actually having the disease. For example, the cells of Tanita's respiratory system were attacked by an influenza virus. Some of her immune cells recognized the proteins on the outside of the viruses. Those T-cells and the B-cells then began to divide and fight the infection.

At the same time, Tanita's immune system set aside memory T- and B-cells that recognize this flu virus. If that exact same influenza virus ever attempts to invade Tanita's body again, her immune system will fight it off before she even knows it.

But people sometimes get the flu more than one time in their life. Why is that? Influenza viruses slowly change over time. After a while, a strain of flu may come along that is very different from the one Tanita is immune to. Her memory cells won't recognize this new flu virus, and she could get sick with the flu again.

Another way to acquire active immunity is through **immunization.** Sometimes called vaccination, immunization is a way of tricking your body into thinking that it has already had a disease. When you get an immunization, dead or weakened pathogens, or sometimes just parts of a pathogen, are injected into your body. These pathogens can't multiply and cause damage to your body, so they don't make you sick. However, your immune system recognizes them as foreign invaders and mobilizes the immune response to the pathogen.

You may be able to feel your immune system at work. For example, your immune system causes your temperature to go up when it is working hard. A slight to moderate fever is an immune response. When fever goes over a temperature of about 104°F, it may begin to do more harm than good. Some people get a little feverish and achy after an immunization—for example, after a diphtheria booster. This does not mean, however, that they got diphtheria from the immunization. It just means that they can feel their immune system going to work.

Just like actually having a disease, an immunization can leave memory cells behind. If you are effectively immunized against polio viruses, you cannot get polio. If polio viruses enter your body, your memory cells destroy them—and you don't even know that you have been infected.

Many serious pathogens do not change much over time. Having the disease or being immunized against it, like the person shown in Figure 21-8, will give many years of protection, although periodic boosters are sometimes needed. It is also possible to be immunized against diseases that do change, like influenza. However, every time a new strain of flu virus appears, a new vaccine must be developed to protect against it.

Why isn't there a vaccine for the common cold? The virus that causes the common cold changes even more rapidly than the influenza virus. There may be several different cold viruses being passed around at any one time, and they are changing all the time. Plus, the common cold is not a very serious disease. A vaccine for the common cold would be a waste of time and money. By the time it was ready, the strain going around would have changed so much that the vaccine would be useless. Research into new vaccines is much more useful if it is focused on preventing really serious diseases like hepatitis and AIDS.

Passive Immunity A third type of immunity to disease is called passive immunity. If you have passive immunity to a particular disease or infection, it means you have received antibodies from another person—or sometimes an animal—that have made you resistant to disease or infection.

Before you were born, some of your mother's antibodies passed from her to you. These antibodies gave you passive immunity that helped protect you from disease in the first few months of your life, until your immune system was mature enough to take care of your own body.

Antibodies are also injected into people who have been exposed to certain serious diseases. These antibodies may be extracted from the blood of humans or animals that have been exposed to the particular disease or venom. A person bitten by a dog with rabies is treated with injections of rabies antibodies. A person bitten by a poi-

(FIGURE 21-8) **Immunizations, such as this one for tetanus, trick the body into thinking it already has had a specific disease. When this happens, the body produces memory cells that will automatically destroy the pathogens that cause that illness.**

sonous snake is treated with snake venom antibodies.

Passive immunity lasts for only a short time. Eventually the antibodies break down and are removed from your bloodstream.

Review

1. *What's the difference between being infected and having a disease?*

2. *Name four ways that the body resists disease.*

3. *How does an immunization work to prevent disease?*

4. **Critical Thinking** *Is it always a good idea to take a medication that lowers fever? Why or why not?*

SECTION 21.2

Reteaching Worksheet 21.2
Students who have difficulty with the material may complete Reteaching Worksheet 21.2.

Answers to Questions 1 and 2 are on p. 450.

3. An immunization injects weakened pathogens or parts of pathogens into the body. The immune system then mobilizes the immune response to destroy these harmless pathogens. The immunization leaves memory cells behind. When an active form of the same pathogen invades the body, the memory cells multiply quickly to destroy the active pathogen.

4. No. A mild fever is an immune response. However, a temperature of 104°F or higher may begin to do more harm than good. Medical treatment may be needed for such a fever.

ASSESS

Section Review
Have students answer the Section Review questions.

Alternative Assessment
Microorganisms Everywhere

We are surrounded by microorganisms, and our bodies are constantly on guard against them. Have students write an explanation of why we become ill only occasionally, instead of almost constantly.

Closure
Living in Isolation

Encourage students to imagine they are living in an isolated room, shut off from people. There is a window for air, and someone supplies them with food, water, and clean clothing through a small door. Ask: **Would you be completely safe from infectious diseases? Why or why not?** [*You would not be safe because bacteria, viruses, protists, fungi, and parasites can travel in the air, water, food, and clothing.*]

Background
Meningitis

Meningitis is an inflammation of one of the three membranes (meningies) that cover the brain and spinal cord. It is usually caused by a bacteria and is often fatal. The high fever that accompanies meningitis can leave survivors with mild to severe brain damage. Because meningitis is so serious, the United States Public Health Service recommends immunization against it, especially for children less than one year old, who are most at risk. An outbreak in Canada in 1992 led to the largest immunization program in Canada since the polio epidemic of the 1950s.

Section 21.3 Common Infectious Diseases

Objectives

■ List four common diseases caused by viruses.

■ Explain which kind of diseases antibiotics can cure, and which kind they can't.

■ Know some ways to decrease your chances of getting an infectious disease.
■ **LIFE SKILLS: Practicing Self-Care**

(FIGURE 21-9) **Polio, a viral disease that reached epidemic proportions during the 1940s and 1950s, left thousands paralyzed and unable to breathe without the help of an iron lung.**

You know now that diseases are caused by bacteria, viruses, fungi, protists, and other parasites. It's not always easy to avoid some infectious diseases, particularly those that are easily spread. But in general, the more you know about preventing an individual illness, the better your chances are of avoiding it. When you are sick, it's always a good rule of thumb to see your doctor. Keep in mind that even diseases that are not serious can have complications.

Viral Diseases

Some of the most common infectious diseases in the United States are caused by viruses. These include the common cold, influenza, cold sores, warts, mononucleosis, chickenpox, and AIDS.

Preventing Viral Disease A number of viral diseases that were common when your parents and grandparents were young are now quite rare in the United States. In the 1940s and early 1950s, a polio epidemic left many children paralyzed. Some polio victims were unable to breathe on their own, like the child shown in Figure 21-9. Until the 1960s, almost everyone got measles, mumps, and rubella (sometimes called German measles) when they were children.

Today, almost all children are immunized against these diseases, which are now rarely seen. One exception is measles. Recently there have been several outbreaks of measles among high school- and college-aged young adults. Because of this, many people in this age group have had to get extra booster immunizations. In contrast,

Section 21.3 Lesson Plan

MOTIVATE

Journal 21D
Personal Experience With Disease

This may be done as a warm-up activity. On the chalkboard, write the heading DISEASES and list the following: cold, flu, chickenpox, measles, mononucleosis, hepatitis, strep throat, sinus infection, mumps, tonsillitis, and ear infection. For each disease, ask students if they or anyone in their family has had the disease. Record the number of cases beside each disease on the chalkboard. This will provide a reference for today's discussions. In their Journal, have students describe a personal experience involving one of these diseases. Suggest that students describe any signs and symptoms they, a family member, or a friend experienced.

TEACH

Cooperative Learning
Folk Medicine

Have students form small groups to discuss and prepare a list of folk "cures" for the cold. Have the groups present their list. Make sure students understand that although such cures may relieve symptoms, there is no scientific evidence that they halt the reproduction of viruses in the respiratory tract. Point out that herbs, potions, and poultices used among many the immunization campaign against small-pox, a disease that killed thousands of people several centuries ago, was so successful that smallpox has been eliminated.

The most deadly viral disease in the United States today is AIDS. So far, there is no vaccine to prevent AIDS, but researchers in many laboratories are working hard to develop one.

Curing Viral Diseases   Most of the time when you recover from a viral disease, it is because your immune system has destroyed the viruses in your body or made them harmless.

Antibiotic (an tee by AHT ik) drugs like penicillin and tetracycline work by preventing the growth and cell division of living bacterial cells. Eventually the bacteria die. Viruses, however, cannot be killed by antibiotics.

What follows is a list of the most common viral infections. For symptoms, vaccine information, and treatment suggestions for each type of infection, see Figure 21-11.

The Common Cold   The common cold should really be called the common colds. That is because more than 200 different viruses can cause the cold. A cold may make you feel really miserable, but it usually lasts only two or three days.

Each year, Americans spend more than $500 million on cold remedies. None of these remedies can actually cure a cold, but they can make you feel better while you are waiting to get well. Some over-the-counter drugs can help clear a stuffy nose or ease aching muscles.

Although there is no way to cure the common cold, there are some things you can do to reduce your chances of getting one. For one thing, try to avoid people who are sick with a cold. Colds are very contagious, especially through person-to-person contact. Washing your hands often will reduce

(FIGURE 21-10) **There is no immunization against the common cold. Fortunately, most colds last for only a few days.**

antibiotics:
drugs that kill or limit the growth of bacteria.

your risk of being infected with a cold virus.

If you do get a cold, rest, eat nutritious foods, and drink plenty of water. Studies show that a diet rich in vitamin C can lessen the severity of your symptoms.

Influenza   Like the common cold, influenza is caused by a viral infection of the respiratory tract. The flu usually lasts longer than an ordinary cold. A cold usually lasts only two to three days, while it may take 7 to 10 days to feel like your old self again after having the flu.

Most people who are basically healthy recover from the flu without any serious problems. However, influenza may have serious complications and can be life threatening for the elderly and people with respiratory problems. These people may choose to be immunized against influenza.

Background
Widespread Diseases
When an infectious disease affects many people, it is called an *epidemic*. If epidemics occur simultaneously at multiple locations in the world, they form a *pandemic*. Infectious diseases that occur continually in a particular region—such as malaria in parts of Africa—are called *endemic*.

Life Skills Worksheet 21A
Assign the Evaluating Advertisements Life Skills Worksheet.

Making a Choice 21B
Assign the Common Infectious Diseases card. The card asks students to find out more about common infectious diseases discussed in the chapter and to present the information to the class.

---

groups of people throughout the world may bring symptomatic relief and comfort. In some cultures, a folk healer is an esteemed and trusted person in the community.

Class Discussion
Colds and Flu

Ask the following questions and have students answer and discuss them. **Why is it so difficult to develop vaccines against the many common cold viruses and the various flu strains?** *[because there are so many viruses involved]* **Are the symptom-relieving drugs of value even though there are no cures for the flu and colds?** *[Yes, they may make you feel better.]* **What is proper treatment for these diseases, and when is it necessary to get medical help?** *[Rest and drink fluids. You should see a doctor if your symptoms become severe.]*

Debate the Issue
Immunization

Remind students that vaccines are not 100 percent safe. But, if too many

people in the population decide against being vaccinated against a disease, the incidence of that disease will increase and it may become a public-health problem again. Because of this, schools commonly require students to be vaccinated for certain diseases. Have students debate this question: Should individuals have the right to refuse vaccinations that carry a very small risk of causing some harm but keep the population as a whole

Background
Measles

Healthy, well-nourished children seldom suffer complications from measles and usually recover completely. However, children who are in poor health or who are undernourished can suffer permanent effects from this disease. There is evidence that people with measles are more vulnerable to other infections. The risk of developing complications from measles increases with the age of the infected individual. Complications include lung infection, hearing loss, pneumonia, and brain damage.

The measles vaccine was introduced in 1963 and was so effective that by the 1980s health officials believed that the disease was under control. The vaccination schedule was changed from two doses to one, which did not ensure immunity. As a result, the number of reported measles cases began to rise. In the 1990s, several college campuses in the United States experienced a record number of cases. It is now recommended that physicians follow a two-dose immunization schedule.

Common Viral Diseases

Disease	Signs and Symptoms	Treatment
Common Cold	Sneezing, stuffy nose, sore throat, aches, fever, fatigue	Rest, fluids
Influenza	Chills, fever, sore throat, muscle aches, fatigue, cough, weakness	Rest, fluids
Chickenpox	Blisters, rash, fever, muscle soreness	Rest, fluids
Mononucleosis	Swollen lymph nodes, fatigue, fever, sore throat, enlarged liver and spleen	Rest, fluids, balanced diet
Hepatitis	Fever, weakness, loss of appetite, nausea, jaundice (yellowing of skin)	Gamma globulin, interferon, rest
Measles	Rash, high fever, sore throat, conjunctivitis, swollen lymph nodes	Gamma globulin, fluids, rest

(FIGURE 21-11) **The best way to treat most viral diseases is to get plenty of rest and to drink lots of fluids.**

If you do get the flu, check with your doctor if your symptoms become severe—for example, if you experience difficulty breathing or have a high fever.

Chickenpox Chickenpox is caused by one of the herpes viruses. It is usually a mild disease and treatment is limited to relieving the itching and fever. Aspirin should not be used because of the possible link to Reye's syndrome, a rare but serious disease that affects the brain and the liver.

Chickenpox can be dangerous for children who suffer from other diseases. It can also be serious for people who are infected as adults. A vaccine is now available, but the duration of the immunity provided is uncertain. People who get chickenpox won't get it again, but they might have a flare up of the virus later in life. This condition is called shingles.

Measles One of the most serious viral diseases is measles. Without proper care, measles can lead to complications such as encephalitis and meningitis (an infection of the brain and spinal cord).

Like influenza, measles can spread through droplets in the air that can enter the body through the eyes, nose, and throat.

Mononucleosis Mononucleosis, often called mono for short, is caused by the Epstein-Barr virus, or EBV. This virus is usually spread by contact with the saliva of an infected person. Children are usually exposed to EBV at an early age and have

---

• • • TEACH continued

healthier? Have students research the subject before they prepare their arguments.

Reinforcement
Reduce Your Chance of Infection

Stress that mononucleosis, colds, flu, and other diseases are spread by sharing drinks, sharing food, sharing personal items, and personal contact. Have students think about anything they have done today, or may do later today, that might expose them to an infectious disease. Then, remind them to avoid such contacts when possible.

Game
Defenders

Divide the class into two teams to play "Defenders." Write this list of diseases on the chalkboard: cold, flu, chickenpox, measles, mono, hepatitis, polio, diphtheria, tetanus, whooping cough, strep throat, TB, sinus infection, trichinosis, mumps, and rabies.

Start with a student on one team, and give the student the first disease on the list to defend himself or herself against. Students on the team must take turns naming a defense, such as "I'm vaccinated!," "I already had it!," "I don't share food and drinks with my friends," and "I'll take an antibiotic." Give the team one point for each correct answer. If an answer is incorrect or if the student cannot think of a defense, it is the other team's turn. That symptoms so mild that the illness is mistaken for a brief cold or flu. These children develop immunity and can continue to transmit the virus through out their life.

Mononucleosis seldom lasts for more than three or four months. If symptoms last more than six months, the illness might more appropriately be described as chronic fatigue syndrome, or CFS.

Hepatitis Hepatitis is a viral disease that can cause serious damage to the liver. There are three main types of hepatitis—Type A, Type B, and Type C hepatitis. These three diseases are caused by three different viruses. Type A hepatitis is usually spread by food contaminated with feces. The most effective way to prevent hepatitis A is to wash your hands frequently when you prepare or serve food.

Hepatitis B is more serious than hepatitis A. It is usually spread through infected blood, semen, or saliva. Therefore, it can be spread through intravenous drug use,

sexual contact, or tattoo needles and ear-piercing equipment that are not sterile. Hepatitis C is most often spread through blood transfusions. It is also very serious. Studies show, though, that hepatitis C can be treated with an antiviral agent called interferon.

A vaccine for Type B hepatitis has recently been developed. In addition, people exposed to hepatitis are often treated with an injection of gamma globulin, which is the part of the blood that contains antibodies. Therefore, gamma globulin injections can provide some temporary passive immunity for hepatitis.

Common Bacterial Diseases

Immunization can prevent some bacterial diseases, such as tetanus. In addition, antibiotics are very effective against bacterial diseases. If left untreated, however, bacterial diseases can be serious. That's why it's

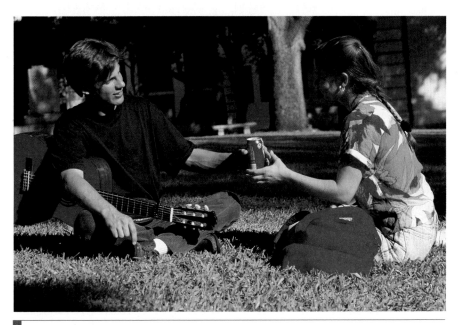

(FIGURE 21-12) **Mononucleosis is spread through contact with the saliva of an infected person.**

SECTION 21.3

Background
Tuberculosis
About 10 to 15 million Americans carry tuberculosis all the time, but their immune systems keep them from becoming ill. However, people who have impaired immune systems and those who are malnourished are vulnerable to the TB bacterium. Although antibiotics can usually control tuberculosis, treatment programs are not always successful. An estimated 20 percent of tuberculosis patients who start an antibiotic treatment program do not complete it. When this happens, the bacteria most resistant to the antibiotic survive. The person remains infected and goes on to infect others with a more virulent strain of tuberculosis. These new strains are resistant to many of the standard antibiotics that were effective against tuberculosis in the past. By 1993, multi-drug resistant strains of tuberculosis were reported in more than 36 states. Continued research to develop new treatments and better public-education programs are necessary to combat this disease.

team can continue defending the disease or can start with the next disease on the list. Repeat the procedure until all the diseases have been defended against. The team with the most points wins.

To make the game more lively, you could use a harmless object such as a styrofoam ball or sponge as the "pathogen" for a disease. Toss the object to any student to start the game. Once that student has answered, he or she should toss the pathogen to someone on either team. The game continues as described above except that students cannot be certain when they will "catch" the pathogen.

Role-Playing
What Do I Have?

Divide the class into groups of three or four and have them role-play a situation in which a member shows disease signs and complains of symptoms from the text ("I have a skin rash, fever, and muscle soreness."). Other group members try to identify the disease (chickenpox) and inform the person of the necessary treatment (rest, fluids, seek a doctor). Have students take turns with different diseases.

Extension
Diseases Arriving With the Europeans

Many scholars believe that more Native Americans died from diseases introduced by Europeans than from warfare with them. Have students research this topic and report on it to the class.

Life SKILLS

Have students write an evaluation of their personal self-care as it relates to steps 1–6. Point out that this will help make them aware of things they can do to protect themselves against infectious diseases.

Life SKILLS: Practicing Self-Care

Tips on Preventing Infectious Diseases . .

To decrease your chances of getting an infectious disease and increase your chances of staying healthy, you can do the following things:

1. Try to avoid close contact with other people who might be sick. When you must be exposed to people who are sick, wash your hands often. Do not share personal items like hairbrushes and toothbrushes. Avoid sharing food or drinks with other people.

2. Reduce the amount of refined sweeteners in your diet. Follow the nutrition principles described in Chapter 4. A balanced diet is a key factor in strengthening your immune system.

3. High stress levels can decrease the efficiency of your immune system. Practice the effective stress management skills discussed in Chapter 9. Make time for rest, and participate in relaxing activities that you enjoy.

4. Drink 8–10 cups of water a day—more if you are very active or live in a hot climate. Water is vital for your immune system.

5. Make sure you are up-to-date on your immunizations.

6. Get regular checkups by doctors and dentists.

7. Design and maintain an appropriate exercise program as outlined in Chapter 3.

a good idea to see a doctor if you think you have a bacterial disease.

Strep Throat

A sore throat caused by the *Streptococcus pyrogenes* bacterium is not a very serious disease in itself, but it can have serious complications. These complications include permanent heart and kidney damage. Unlike sore throats caused by the cold or flu viruses, strep throat can be easily cured by taking antibiotics.

Any severe sore throat, or a sore throat that lasts more than two days, should be checked by a doctor. A simple test that takes only a few minutes in a doctor's office can show if your sore throat is caused by a *Streptococcus* bacterium. If so, you will need to take antibiotics to avoid serious complications.

Tuberculosis

The bacteria that cause tuberculosis, or TB, attack the lungs and cause fluid to build up there. Not surprisingly, people with tuberculosis suffer severe coughing spells. Other symptoms of TB include high fever, weakness, and loss of appetite.

Tuberculosis is another disease spread through droplets in the air. Fortunately, it is not easy to become infected, even if you inhale these droplets. Unless you are in close contact for a prolonged period of time with a person who has TB, chances are you won't catch the disease. In recent years tuberculosis cases have increased dramatically, partly because people with AIDS are very vulnerable to it. Other factors that have contributed to the increase of tuberculosis include malnutrition and alcohol and

SECTION 21.3

Section Review Worksheet 21.3

To reinforce the concepts presented in this section, assign Section Review Worksheet 21.3.

Section Quiz 21.3

Have students take Section Quiz 21.3.

Reteaching Worksheet 21.3

Students who have difficulty with the material may complete Reteaching Worksheet 21.3.

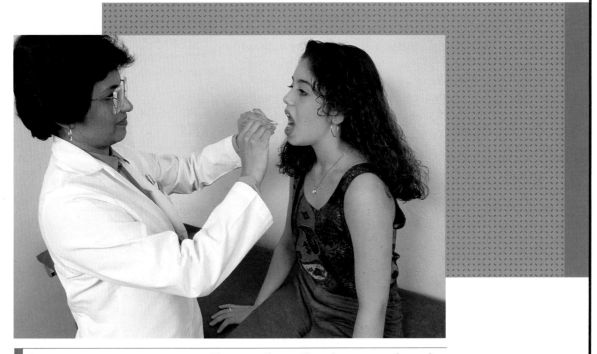

(FIGURE 21-13) **A teenager gets tested for strep throat. If you have a sore throat that lasts for more than two or three days, see your doctor. Strep is easily cured with antibiotics, but it can have serious consequences if left untreated.**

Review Answers

1. Answers will vary but may include chickenpox, common cold, influenza, measles, mononucleosis, and hepatitis.

2. bacterial; viral

3. Answers will vary but may include getting immunizations, reducing person-to-person contact, not sharing items like soft-drink cans or bottles, washing hands before preparing or serving food, not sharing tattoo needles or body-piercing equipment, and taking good care of your body.

4. Polio and AIDS are both caused by viruses. Polio is now preventable through immunization. There is no immunization for the virus that causes AIDS.

(FIGURE 21-14) **Malaria, which strikes 200 million people every year, is spread from person to person by mosquitoes.**

drug abuse. Tuberculosis can be effectively treated with antibiotics, although some strains of the disease have proven to be resistant to treatment.

Sinus Infections A cold, flu, or allergy that leads to heavy mucus production can lead to a bacterial infection in your sinuses. The most common signs and symptoms of a sinus infection are thick, greenish mucus, headaches, and sinus pain. A doctor can determine if you have a bacterial infection that needs to be treated with an antibiotic.

Other Diseases

Remember that there are diseases caused by pathogens other than bacteria and viruses. Fungi, protists, and animal parasites may also be agents of disease.

Three common conditions caused by fungi are athlete's foot, jock itch, and ringworm. These are discussed in Chapter 6.

Diseases caused by protists (which are complex, one-celled organisms) are not widespread in the United States, although they are common in other parts of the world. The most widespread and serious of these diseases is malaria. Each year, as many as 200 million people suffer from malaria, and one to two million people die from it.

Malaria is caused by a protist that is carried from one person to another by mosquitoes.

Diseases can also be caused by animal parasites. Animals like hookworms, flukes, pinworms, and tapeworms can live inside the human body and cause disease. One kind of parasitic roundworm causes a disease called trichinosis. This roundworm can be found in the muscle tissue of pigs. For this reason, pork must always be cooked thoroughly before it is eaten.

Review

1. What are four common diseases that are caused by viruses?

2. What kind of diseases can antibiotics cure? What kind can't they cure?

3. ■■ LIFE SKILLS: Practicing Self-Care Name four ways you can lower your chances of getting an infectious disease.

4. *Critical Thinking* What do polio and AIDS have in common? How are they different?

ASSESS

Section Review

Have students answer the Section Review questions.

Alternative Assessment
When Do Antibiotics Work?

Ask students to imagine that several students and teachers have become sick with fever and sore throat and are feeling weak. All are treated with antibiotics. Soon half of them improve, but the other half remain sick with the same signs and symptoms. Ask: **How could this happen? Is it one disease or two? What could the diseases be?** *[The half made well by the antibiotics had a bacterial infection, possibly strep throat. The other half have a viral infection, possibly the flu.]*

Closure
Protecting Yourself

Although it is not always possible to prevent common illnesses, often they can be avoided if preventive measures are taken. Have individual students brainstorm to make a list of behaviors that could help avoid infection. For example, they could wash their hands before meals, especially if they are around someone with a cold. As a class, use the lists to create a class list. Post one copy of the list in a conspicuous place in the classroom and another copy in the school cafeteria.

Highlights

Summary

- Infectious diseases are diseases that pass from one organism to another. Communicable, or contagious, diseases are infectious diseases that pass from one person to another.

- In the United States, the most common infectious diseases are caused by bacteria and viruses. Other disease-causing pathogens are fungi, protists, and parasitic worms.

- A sign of a disease is something another person can observe, such as a fever, cough, sneeze, or rash. A symptom of a disease is any feeling of pain or discomfort a person experiences with a disease.

- Some of the body's defenses against disease are skin, mucous membranes, stomach acids, and body chemicals.

- The immune system is a complex system of organs and cells that fight specific agents of disease.

- A person can acquire active immunity to a disease by having the disease or by getting immunized, or vaccinated, against it.

- The common cold, influenza, hepatitis, mononucleosis, chickenpox, and AIDS are diseases caused by viruses.

- Strep throat, tuberculosis, and sinus infections are common bacterial diseases.

Vocabulary

infectious disease a disease that is caused by an agent that is passed from one living thing to another.

communicable disease an infectious disease that is passed from one person to another.

pathogen any agent that causes disease.

bacterium a type of microorganism that can cause disease.

virus a microscopic disease-causing particle consisting of genetic material and a protein coat.

immune system the system that protects the body from disease.

immunization injection of a small amount of a pathogen that will provide protection against an infectious disease.

antibodies substances that stick to the surface of pathogens, slowing their action.

antibiotics drugs that kill or limit the growth of bacteria.

SUMMARY
Have students read the summary to reinforce the concepts they have learned in Chapter 21.

VOCABULARY
Discuss the definitions of *infectious disease, pathogen, virus, bacterium, immune system,* and *immunization* and briefly review the relationships among them.

EXTENSION
Rejection is a major problem with organ transplants because the immune system responds to the transplanted organ as it would to a pathogen and attacks it. Have students research this topic and present a report to the class.

Chapter Review

CHAPTER REVIEW

Concept Review

1. bacteria

2. Answers can include any two of the following: ringworm, mosquito-borne encephalitis, malaria, trichinosis, or any other disease borne by an animal vector that was discussed in class.

3. food poisoning

4. skin

5. inflammation, the body's defense system reacting to an invading pathogen (accept either answer)

6. immune system

7. innate, active, passive

8. immunization

9. viruses

10. antibiotic

11. malaria

Expressing Your Views

Sample responses:

1. Yes. There may be a problem with food and water contamination. Also, people living in these countries might not have received vaccinations against many preventable infectious diseases and therefore could infect others.

2. No. Buddy could have something like strep throat and could be contagious. The lozenges may give him some relief, but they won't cure his sore throat. If his sore throat is severe or if it lasts for more than a few days, he should have it checked out by his doctor.

3. Throw it away. Food that should have been refrigerated may now be contaminated with so much bacteria that it could cause food poisoning if eaten.

Life Skills Check

Sample responses:

1. I would tell my friend about my concerns so she wouldn't think I was selfish. I would tell her that I will share if she has a cup, but that I don't want to drink out of the same soda can.

2. I would ask my parents if the immunizations I received as an infant are sufficient. If they didn't know, we could talk to my doctor or to the school nurse about what to do.

Concept Review

1. Food poisoning and urinary tract infections are diseases caused by _____.

2. _____ and _____ are two diseases that affect humans but are spread by animals.

3. Refrigerating, cooking foods thoroughly, and washing hands and utensils help prevent _____ _____.

4. The _____ acts as a barrier to protect the rest of your body from pathogens.

5. If an infected cut is swollen, red, painful, and warm to the touch, it is a sign of _____.

6. The _____ _____ produces special kinds of cells that attack pathogens.

7. The three basic types of immunity are _____, _____, and _____.

8. Sometimes called a vaccination, _____ is a way of artificially acquiring immunity.

9. Measles and influenza are diseases caused by _____.

10. Bacterial infections can be cured with _____ drugs.

11. _____ is the most serious and widespread disease caused by a protist.

Expressing Your Views

1. Dion and Sam are planning to visit a foreign country that has poor living conditions. Do you think they will be at an increased risk of getting a disease? Why or why not?

2. Buddy is home with a sore throat. He says he can't afford to miss any more work, so he plans to stock up on throat lozenges and go back to work. Do you think that is a wise thing for Buddy to do? Why or why not?

3. Last night you had a party and had a lot of leftover food. You were too tired to put all the food away so you left most of it out all night on the counter. What should you do with the leftover food now? Explain.

CHAPTER 21 ASSESSMENT

Life Skills Check

1. Practicing Self-Care

You are drinking a soda when a close friend comes over and asks you to share. You would really like to share but are concerned about spreading germs. What should you do?

2. Practicing Self-Care

You were immunized against measles and mumps when you were an infant. You thought the immunizations were good for life, but you just read that there is an outbreak of measles at the local college. What should you do?

Projects

1. Choose a common infectious disease and create a poster containing information about it. Show the causes, symptoms, method of transmission, long-term effects, and treatments of the disease. Display your poster at a suitable place in your school.

2. Contact your doctor or school nurse and ask for a copy of your immunization record. The record should have vaccinations you have received during your life and the date when each was given. Make a list of diseases you have been vaccinated against, and record the date when your next booster shots, if any, are due.

3. Work with a partner to collect information about natural remedies and preventive measures for common illnesses. Use library references or call a naturopathic doctor for information about alternatives to over-the-counter drugs. Find out how the substances are taken and how they affect the body. Write a report that includes the benefits and the possible side effects of the alternative medicines.

Plan for Action

There are several strategies a person can take to control the spread of infectious diseases. What are some things you can do to help keep infectious diseases from spreading?

Projects

Have students plan and carry out the projects on infectious diseases, immunizations, and natural remedies.

Plan for Action

As a class, review the strategies for preventing the control of infections, and then have students make a plan for their life using any strategies that are applicable.

ASSESSMENT OPTIONS

Chapter Test
Have students take the Chapter 21 Test.

Alternative Assessment
Have students do the Alternative Assessment activity for Chapter 21.

Test Generator
The Test Generator contains additional assessment items for this chapter.

PLANNING GUIDE

CHAPTER 22

Sexually Transmitted Diseases

SECTION	TITLE/OBJECTIVES	PERSONAL INVENTORY			LIFE SKILLS DEVELOPMENT			
		Personal Health Inventory	Journal	Check Up	Life Skills	Life Skills Worksheets	Media Message or Ethical Issues Worksheet	What Would You Do?
22.1 *pp. 463–474*	**WHAT ARE SEXUALLY TRANSMITTED DISEASES?** • Define the term sexually transmitted disease. • Know the names of four common sexually transmitted diseases. • Know how sexually transmitted diseases are spread from one person to another. • Know the signs and symptoms of sexually transmitted diseases.	Ch. 22	22A 22B 22C 22D	p. 464		22A		
22.2 *pp. 475–480*	**PREVENTING SEXUALLY TRANSMITTED DISEASES** • Know what you can do to decrease your chances of getting an STD. ▪▪ Name 10 ways you can show love for someone without sexual intimacy. ▪▪ Know where to go for testing and treatment for STDs.		22E 22F 22G	p. 476				

KEY: ▪▪ Denotes Life Skill Objective

Text references denoted by page number.

Supplement references denoted by chapter or item numbers.

LINKING RESOURCES

	Making a Choice Cards	Parent Discussion Guide	Health Talk Audio Program	Teaching Transparencies and Directory	Section Review Worksheets	Section Quizzes	Reteaching Worksheets	Section Reviews
	INTERACTION		**OTHER RESOURCES**		**SECTION REVIEW AND ASSESSMENT**			
	Ch. 22	Ch. 22	22A	22.1	22.1	22.1	p. 474	
22A 22B			22B	22.2	22.2	22.2	p. 480	

KEY FACTS

- A sexually transmitted disease (STD) is passed from one person to another during sexual contact.

- Pelvic inflammatory disease (PID) is an inflammation of the uterus and fallopian tubes. Unless PID is diagnosed and treated early, it can cause infertility.

- The most common STDs are AIDS, gonorrhea, chlamydia, genital herpes, and syphilis; AIDS is the most dangerous STD.

- Other STDs are nongonoccal urethritis, genital warts (which may be the fastest growing STD in the United States), vaginal infections not caused by yeast, Hepatitis B, and parasitic infections, such as pubic lice and scabies.

- Some diseases, such as Hepatitis B, can be spread both sexually and nonsexually.

- Some sexually transmitted diseases, such as genital herpes, can be transmitted from mother to infant during childbirth.

- Sexual abstinence is the most effective way of preventing STDs.

- People who think they have an STD should seek treatment immediately and should abstain from sexual activity until their doctor says it is okay. If an STD is diagnosed, they should notify any recent sex partners.

CHAPTER REVIEW AND ASSESSMENT

TEXT

Chapter Review pp. 482–483

SUPPLEMENTS

Chapter Test 22

Alternative Assessment 22

Test Generator Chapter 22

GETTING STARTED

Using the Chapter Photograph

Have students look at the photograph showing educational literature about STDs. Ask them if they know what kind of information is usually found in such literature. Ask students why it is important to be educated about sexually transmitted diseases. Ask students what surprised them most about what Vanessa's mother said about the effects of sexually transmitted diseases.

Question Box

Have students write out any questions they have about STDs and put them in the Question Box.

Sensitivity **ALERT**

The discussion of STDs may make students uncomfortable. For some, discussing diseases caused by sexual activity may be embarrassing. For others, it may be a difficult topic because they are concerned that their behavior may have put them at risk. Prepare the class to be respectful of others' privacy and sensitive to others' feelings.

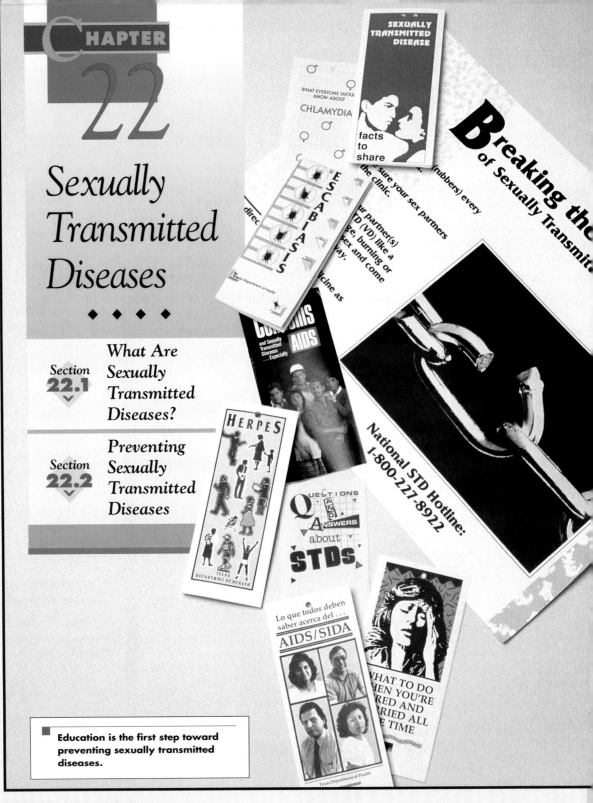

CHAPTER 22

Sexually Transmitted Diseases

◆ ◆ ◆ ◆

Section 22.1 What Are Sexually Transmitted Diseases?

Section 22.2 Preventing Sexually Transmitted Diseases

Education is the first step toward preventing sexually transmitted diseases.

MYTHS & MISCONCEPTIONS

- **Nice people don't contract or transmit STDs.** Anyone can contract or transmit an STD.

- **A person who has had sex only once couldn't have an STD.** It takes only one sexual encounter with an infected person to get an STD.

- **Using condoms provides complete protection against STDs.** While the use of condoms decreases the risk of contracting

an STD, it does not provide complete protection.

- **The only way a person can get an STD is through sexual contact.** STDs are transmitted through sexual contact. However, certain diseases that are frequently transmitted sexually, such as herpes and hepatitis B, can also be transmitted by nonsexual means.

Vanessa and her best friend, Han, agree that sometimes it seems like everybody takes it for granted that all teenagers are sexually active. In movies and on TV sitcoms the teenage characters joke about birth-control pills and losing their virginity. The songs on the radio are pretty explicit. It all adds up to a lot of pressure to have sex. At the same time, worrying about diseases that you could get makes sex seem pretty scary.

One evening Han was having supper with Vanessa and Vanessa's mother at their apartment. Han was surprised when Vanessa asked her mother about these diseases. Vanessa's mom is a nurse, so she was able to tell the girls a lot of what they wanted to know. Vanessa's mom said that AIDS is the most deadly disease you can get through sexual activity, but that there are others that are also dangerous. Some of them can cause infertility, the inability to have children. Vanessa didn't intend to get pregnant any time soon, but she had always assumed that some day she would have children. Finding out that a disease might make it impossible to have children made her realize that these diseases are serious.

Personal Health Inventory
Have students complete the Personal Health Inventory for this chapter.

English/Spanish CD Audio Program
Use the English/Spanish Health Talk audio program for students who need audio reinforcement of the concepts presented.

Parent Discussion Guide
Send home the Parent Letter for Chapter 22. As you progress through the chapter, send home the Parental Survey and The Extra Mile.

Section 22.1
What Are Sexually Transmitted Diseases?

Objectives

- Define the term sexually transmitted disease.

- Know the names of four common sexually transmitted diseases.

- Know how sexually transmitted diseases are spread from one person to another.

- Know the signs and symptoms of sexually transmitted diseases.

Each year, about 2.5 million teenagers are infected with sexually transmitted diseases. A **sexually transmitted disease**, or **STD** for short, is a disease that is passed from one person to another during sexual contact. These diseases used to be called venereal diseases (VD). Some of these diseases are merely uncomfortable, while others can be quite serious.

The most dangerous STD is AIDS. It cannot be cured and is eventually fatal. Because AIDS is such a serious threat, the next chapter will be devoted entirely to AIDS and the virus that causes it. This chapter will tell you about other diseases that are spread by sexual activity.

sexually transmitted disease (STD):

a disease that is passed from one person to another during sexual contact.

HIV infection and AIDS are discussed in Chapter 23.

Section 22.1 Lesson Plan

MOTIVATE

Journal 22A
Talking About STDs

This may be done as a warm-up activity. Encourage students to write down in their Journal the names of any STDs they have heard about. Have them write why it was easy for Vanessa and Han to talk to Vanessa's mother.

TEACH

Class Discussion
Staying Informed

Discuss the meaning of the term *sexually transmitted diseases*. Mention that these diseases are sometimes called venereal diseases. Tell students that, even though this is an uncomfortable topic, it is important for them to receive all the information they need to avoid these diseases. Ask: **Would you prefer to**

discuss this topic in small groups? With members of your own sex only? Are there topics you do not feel comfortable talking about? Before discussing the students' responses, stress that there are no right or wrong answers to these questions. Encourage students to continue to use the Question Box if they have any questions they wish to ask anonymously.

Check Up

Have students anony-mously turn in their an-swers to the Check Up questions. Tally the results on the chalkboard. Iden-tify the number of re-sponses to each question. Discuss the correct an-swers to questions often missed. You might want to have students retake the Check Up at the end of the chapter and com-pare the class results with those obtained earlier.

Check Up

How Much Do You Already Know About STDs?

1. Can someone have an STD and not know it?
2. Are STDs common among sexually active teenagers?
3. Do birth-control pills prevent STDs?
4. Can STDs be prevented by washing carefully after sex?
5. Can the use of latex condoms greatly reduce the risk of getting an STD?
6. Can a person get an STD from oral sex?
7. Is it easy to tell if someone has an STD?

1. yes 2. yes 3. no 4. no 5. yes 6. yes 7. no

gonorrhea:

an STD caused by bacteria that can infect the mucous membranes of the penis, vagina, throat, or rectum.

REMINDER

Antibiotics are drugs that kill or limit the growth of bacteria.

Gonorrhea

One of the most common STDs is **gonorrhea** (gahn-uh-REE-uh). Gonorrhea is an infection caused by a bacterium. The gonorrhea bacterium attacks mucous membranes. It can infect the mucous membranes of the penis, vagina, throat, or the rectum.

About one million cases of gonorrhea are reported each year. Because many cases are not reported, however, the actual number is probably closer to three million cases each year.

What Are the Signs and Symptoms of Gonorrhea? As you learned in Chapter 21, a sign of a disease is something another person can see or detect. A symptom of a disease is any feeling of pain or discomfort you may experience. As many as 80 percent of women who have gonorrhea have no signs and symptoms or have signs and symptoms that are so mild that they aren't noticed. Because of this, most women with gonorrhea do not even realize that they have the disease.

One sign of gonorrhea in females is ir-ritation of the vagina that is accompanied by a discharge. Since a female may have a vaginal discharge for other reasons, this is not a sure sign of gonorrhea. Females with gonorrhea may also have pain in the lower abdomen. But since this pain is usually mild, it is a symptom that is often ignored.

Unlike women who have gonorrhea, men infected with gonorrhea usually have signs and symptoms. One sign of gonor-rhea is a heavy yellow discharge of pus from the penis. Symptoms of gonorrhea include frequent, painful urination, tenderness in the groin or testicles, and swelling of the lymph nodes in the groin. These signs and symp-toms usually appear about 2 to 10 days after infection. Sometimes the signs and symp-toms go away, but that doesn't mean that the infection is gone.

One reason why gonorrhea is such a common disease is that a large number of people who are infected do not have signs or symptoms. These people may not realize that they have gonorrhea, but they can still pass the bacteria to their sex partners.

How Can a Person Become Infected with Gonorrhea? Gonorrhea is spread by sexual contact or from mother to infant at delivery. The gonorrhea bacteria can be passed from one person to another only by moving directly from one warm, moist body surface to another. It is not true that gonor-rhea can be caught from dirty toilet seats, cups, or towels. This is because these bac-teria must have the right combination of temperature, humidity, atmosphere, and nutrients to grow. A gonorrhea bacterium on a toilet seat would live for only a few seconds, because it dies when it is exposed to the air.

What Happens if Gonorrhea Is Not Treated? Gonorrhea can be completely cured by the appropriate antibiotics.

• • • TEACH continued

Class Discussion
Myths and Facts

Discuss the information found In Figure 22-1. Ask students to cover the fact column as you present each myth for discussion. Ask them to comment on each myth and provide a response that they believe is true. Have them check their responses with the fact col-umn. One myth not on the list is that

sexual activity in itself causes STDs. Students should be aware that sexual activity does not cause STDs. Sex pro-vides the method of transmission, and sex organs provide a moist, warm lo-cation for the microbes to flourish.

Journal 22B
Surprising Myths

Have students write in their Journal the myth and fact about STDs that sur-prised them most.

Game
Myths and Facts About STDs

Have students play a short game using the information in Figure 22-1. A member of one team makes a state-ment from the table without mention-ing whether the statement is from the myth or fact column. A player from the other team must identify the state-ment as a myth or a fact. Have stu-dents tally correct answers.

Myths and Facts About STDs

Myth	Fact
Birth-control pills prevent STDs.	Birth-control pills provide no protection against STDs.
Washing the genitals after sex prevents STDs.	Washing is not an effective way to prevent STDs.
It is best to see if an STD goes away on its own before going to a doctor.	STDs do not go away on their own. Even if the symptoms go away, it does not mean the STD is cured.
The medicine prescribed for one kind of STD will cure any STD.	Each STD requires different treatment. A doctor must be consulted for proper treatment.
As soon as a person feels better, he or she can stop taking the medicine prescribed for an STD.	All of the medicine prescribed by the doctor must be taken, even if a person starts feeling better before the medicine is all gone.
If one sex partner is treated for an STD, it isn't necessary for the other partner to be treated.	Both sex partners must be treated so they will not continue to reinfect each other.
It is easy to tell when a person has an STD.	Some people show no signs of illness even though they have an STD.

(FIGURE 22-1) **A national survey, *The National Adolescent Student Health Survey*, showed that many teenagers have misconceptions about STDs that could endanger their health.**

However, untreated gonorrhea in females may spread to the reproductive organs inside the pelvic cavity. Infection of the uterus and fallopian tubes is called **pelvic inflammatory disease (PID).** PID can be caused by several different kinds of microorganisms, including the bacterium that causes gonorrhea. The signs and symptoms of PID may include painful sexual intercourse, uterine bleeding, vaginal discharge, abdominal pain, and fever. PID can be a very serious disease. It must be treated with powerful antibiotics and may even require hospitalization. PID can cause scarring of the fallopian tubes, resulting in infertility.

A woman with untreated gonorrhea can also pass the gonorrhea bacterium to her baby at birth. This can cause blindness in the infant. To reduce this risk, it is standard procedure to treat the eyes of babies with medicated eyedrops immediately after birth.

pelvic inflammatory disease (PID):

an infection of the uterus and fallopian tubes often caused by STDs; if untreated, may result in infertility.

Writing
Dangers of Infertility

Have students write an article for the school newspaper stressing the dangers of infertility caused by STDs such as gonorrhea and chlamydia.

Journal 22C
If You Had an STD

Have students write in their Journal how they think they would feel if they found out they had an STD.

• • • TEACH continues on p. 466

Background
STDs in History

STDs are not a modern affliction. Many famous people in history have suffered from STDs: Henry VIII of England, Napoleon Bonaparte, Franz Schubert, Adolf Hitler, and Al Capone, to mention a few. The search for a cure has an equally long history. Not until the advent of antibiotics was there an effective way to cure some of these diseases.

📑 **Life Skills Worksheet 22A**

Assign the Preventing the Spread of STDs Life Skills Worksheet.

(FIGURE 22-2) **The photograph on the left shows normal tissue from a woman's fallopian tube. The photograph on the right shows the effects of pelvic inflammatory disease (PID). Some sexually transmitted diseases can cause PID and result in infertility.**

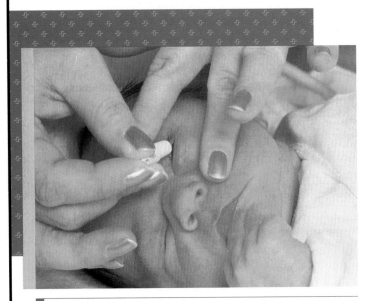

(FIGURE 22-3) **A newborn baby's eyes are treated with medicated eyedrops. This is standard procedure to prevent possible STD infections that could cause blindness.**

chlamydia:

the most common STD in the United States; caused by bacteria.

A male who has been infected with gonorrhea may suffer serious complications in a short period of time, sometimes in just two to three weeks. Infection can spread quickly throughout the male reproductive system and cause pain, fever, and urinary problems. Eventually, the man may become infertile as a result of scarring of the reproductive organs.

Chlamydia

Chlamydia (klam-ID-ee-uh) is the most common STD in the United States. There are from 3 to 10 million new cases each year. Chlamydia is caused by a small bacterium. It is not a new disease, although it has become more common in recent years.

What Are the Signs and Symptoms of Chlamydia? Like gonorrhea, chlamydia does not cause signs and symptoms in the majority of women who are infected. Also, about one-fourth of infected men do not get signs and symptoms. In people who get them, the signs and symptoms of chlamydia will usually appear one to three weeks after exposure.

In males, the signs and symptoms of chlamydia infection include painful and difficult urination and a white or yellow watery discharge from the penis. In females, signs and symptoms may include painful urination, vaginal discharge, pain in the lower abdomen, and bleeding between menstrual periods.

• • • TEACH *continued*

Class Discussion

Fears and Treatment for Herpes

Ask: **What do people fear most about both herpes simplex type I and type II?** *[There is no cure for either of these viruses. Once infected, you are infected for the rest of your life.]* **If there is no cure for herpes, why are people treated for it?** *[Treatment reduces* the pain and often causes the symptoms to go away sooner.]* Mention to students that many people who have cold sores on their lips have herpes simplex type I. Remind them that the virus can be reactivated by various conditions such as irritation, stress, hormonal changes, or eating certain foods.

 Teaching Transparency 22A
Sexually Transmitted Diseases

Show the transparency of Figure 22-5 on pages 468–469. Ask students to group the diseases, based on similarities and differences in the causes, methods of spreading, symptoms, and cures of the disease. For example, they may group all those caused by bacteria together and all those caused by viruses together.

How Can a Person Become Infected With Chlamydia? Chlamydia is transmitted from one person to another through sexual contact. One reason chlamydia is such a common STD is that it is often spread by people who don't know that they have the disease.

What Happens if Chlamydia Is Not Treated? In women, the bacterium that causes chlamydia is another microorganism that can cause PID. Like PID caused by gonorrhea, PID caused by chlamydia can damage a woman's reproductive system, making her infertile. In men, an untreated chlamydia infection can also result in infertility.

Women with chlamydia are more likely to have problems during pregnancy, and babies born to women with chlamydia may get eye infections or pneumonia. Because of this, pregnant women should be screened for chlamydia even if they have no signs and symptoms.

Genital Herpes

Infection with the herpes simplex virus in the genital region is called **genital herpes** (HUR-peez). Two types of the herpes simplex virus exist—type I and type II. Usually, type I is found above the waist, appearing as a cold sore or fever blister on the mouth. Type II is usually found below the waist. There are more than 40 million Americans with genital herpes. About 500,000 more become infected each year.

What Are the Signs and Symptoms of Genital Herpes? Only about 25 percent of people infected with genital herpes have signs and symptoms. The other 75 percent still have the disease and can give it to someone else.

If there are signs and symptoms, they usually take from 2 to 10 days to develop. In females, painful blisters may appear on the cervix, vagina, or vulva. In males, blisters and ulcers may appear on the penis. Pain may also be experienced when urinating. In both sexes, redness and blisters may appear at any site of contact.

In addition, some people experience itching, tingling, or burning sensations just before the sores appear. Other symptoms of herpes may include a sluggish feeling, fever, and flulike symptoms.

There is no cure for herpes. Once you are infected with the virus that causes herpes, you are infected for the rest of your life. If you do not have signs and symptoms, or when they go away, the herpes-causing virus stays inactive in the nerves. The virus may be reactivated by anything that stresses the immune system.

genital herpes:

an STD caused by a virus that often causes painful blisters or ulcers; cannot be cured.

(FIGURE 22-4) **Painful blisters like these are the result of genital herpes. However, most people infected with genital herpes have no symptoms.**

Background
Genital Herpes
Genital herpes is usually caused by herpes simplex type II, but a genital infection with herpes simplex type I is possible. The initial outbreak of herpes is frequently the most severe, but for some people it is so mild that they do not realize they have been infected. Some people never experience another outbreak, while others have painful outbreaks lasting roughly 10 to 21 days several times a year. Many people have very mild recurrences and thus are unaware that they are contagious. These unpredictable, mild recurrences often result in the spread of disease. The incidence of herpes infection has risen almost 300 percent in the last 30 years. It is estimated that as many as 20 million people in the United States are infected with herpes simplex type II. Transmission almost always occurs through direct contact. Because nonsexual transmission is possible, although not typical, contact with any active herpes lesion should be avoided. This includes cold sores on the lips or nose.

Game
What Do You Know About STDs?

Prepare two sets of cards or have students prepare them. Each card of the first set will bear one of the following terms: Cause, Method of Spreading, Symptoms, Treatment. Each card of the second set will have one of the following: gonorrhea, chlamydia, genital herpes, syphilis, nongonococcal urethritis, genital warts, vaginitis, hepatitis B, pubic lice, scabies. (You will probably want to include only those cards in the second set that have STDs covered thus far. The other cards will be added when all the diseases have been discussed.) Each player will select a card from each pile and must provide the information requested by the card of the first set about the disease mentioned on the card in the second set.

• • • TEACH continues on p. 472

STDs and Infertility

Females are more susceptible to STD infection and less likely to show early symptoms than males are. Thus, by the time an STD is diagnosed in a female and the treatment is begun, permanent damage to her reproductive system may already have occurred. One of the greatest risks is the development of pelvic inflammatory disease (PID), a leading cause of infertility. A female who has had PID has an increased risk for a spontaneous miscarriage or an ectopic (tubular) pregnancy, which is a life-threatening condition. In males, STDs can cause infertility when immune cells attack sperm cells as well as the invading bacteria.

Sexually Transmitted Diseases

STD	What Causes It?	How Is It Spread?
Gonorrhea	Neisseria gonorrhoese bacterium	Sexual contact; mother to infant at birth
Chlamydia	Chlamydia trachomatis	Sexual contact; mother to infant at birth
Genital herpes	Herpes simplex virus	Sexual contact; contact between sores and mucous membranes or break in skin; mother to infant at birth
Syphilis	Treponema pallidum bacterium	Sexual contact; contact between chancre or rash and mucous membranes or break in skin; mother to infant before birth
Nongonococcal urethritis (NGU)	Several causes, such as chlamydia, ureaplasma, mycoplasma, trichomonas, herpes	Most often spread by sexual contact, but some microorganisms can be spread by other means
Genital warts	Virus	Sexual contact
Vaginitis	Several causes, such as candida, gardnerella, herpes, trichomonas, mycoplasma	Often spread by sexual contact, but some microorganisms can be spread by other means
Hepatitis B	Hepatitis B virus	Sexual contact; sharing needles; sharing items like razors, toothbrushes, eating utensils; mother to infant at birth
Pubic lice	Insect	Sexual contact
Scabies	Mite	Sexual contact

(FIGURE 22-5) A sexually transmitted disease (STD) is a disease that is passed from one person to another during sexual contact. AIDS is another STD, and is discussed in Chapter 23.

What Are the Signs and Symptoms?	How Is It Treated?
Females: *often no signs or symptoms; vaginal irritation and discharge; pain in lower abdomen* **Males:** *frequent, painful urination; heavy yellow discharge of pus from penis; tenderness in groin or testicles; swollen lymph nodes on groin*	Antibiotic
Females: *usually no signs or symptoms; painful urination; vaginal discharge; pain in lower abdomen; bleeding between menstrual periods* **Males:** *often no signs or symptoms; painful, difficult urination; white or yellow discharge from penis*	Antibiotic
Females: *usually no signs or symptoms; painful blisters on cervix, vagina, vulva, thighs, or buttocks; sluggish feeling; fever; flulike symptoms; lymph node enlargement* **Males:** *usually no signs or symptoms; blisters on penis, thighs, or buttocks; painful urination; sluggish feeling; fever; flulike symptoms; lymph node enlargement*	No cure but acyclovir can ease symptoms
First sign: *small, red bumps at the point of infection, which becomes an open sore oozing fluid (called a chancre)* **Later signs and symptoms:** *a rash; a dull, depressed feeling; fever, joint pain; hair loss; large moist sores around the sex organs or mouth* **Final stage:** *Blindness; brain damage; paralysis; can cause death*	Antibiotic
Painful urination; discharge	Antibiotics or other drugs depending on cause
Warts in the genital or anal area	No cure; trichloracetic acid; podophyllin; laser; liquid nitrogen; surgery
Itching or pain in vaginal area; vaginal discharge that is yellowish or has an unpleasant odor	Antibiotics or other drugs depending on cause
Flulike symptoms; dark urine; yellowing of skin	No cure; interferon and gamma globulin can ease symptoms; vaccine available
Intense itching and possible rash in genital area; occasional swelling of lymph nodes in the groin	Medicated lotions and shampoos
Intense itching in genital area, under the breast, in the armpits, between the fingers, or elsewhere	Medicated lotions and shampoos

Background
Treating Bacterial STDs
Bacterial resistance to antibiotics is a serious problem that is getting worse. Both gonorrhea and syphilis were once easily cured with penicillin. Because of new, resistant strains, however, this is no longer true; often more than one antibiotic has to be used. Researchers would like to develop a vaccine for gonorrhea and syphilis. Vaccines work by causing the production of antibodies in the bloodstream. Unfortunately, the gonorrhea bacteria does not appear in the bloodstream until well after primary infection; by the time it is present, the disease has been in the body for a long time and has already caused considerable damage. A syphilis vaccine presents a different—but equally difficult—problem. The syphilis bacterium can survive only inside a warm, living body. (Rabbits are often used in research.) Researchers say it will be difficult to develop a vaccine against syphilis until a means of culturing it in a test tube is developed.

Background

History of Syphilis

Some historians have tried to trace the terrible outbreak of syphilis in Europe in 1493 to Christopher Columbus's sailors returning from the New World. Supposedly, some bones of pre-Columbian natives resemble syphilitic bones. However, it has not been established that syphilis originated in the New World. The ruins of Pompeii, A.D. 79, contain some writing about a disease that could have been syphilis. If that is the case, the disease was present in Europe long before Columbus's journey occurred.

syphilis:

an STD caused by bacteria, that can spread through the bloodstream to any organ of the body.

How Can a Person Become Infected With Genital Herpes?

Herpes is almost always transmitted by sexual contact. However, any direct contact with a herpes sore can cause infection with herpes. The tiny blisters that form during a herpes outbreak are filled with a clear fluid that contains the virus. When blisters appear, the disease is in its most infectious state. That is the time when genital herpes can most easily be transmitted to another person. The open lesions will eventually crust over as the healing begins.

This does not mean that you cannot get herpes if you do not see herpes blisters on your partner's genitals. For one thing, although herpes is most contagious when blisters are present, it can also be transmitted when there are no blisters—for example, right before an outbreak of blisters. Also, blisters may be present but not seen. For example, if the infection were on a female's cervix, it would not be seen. Still, it could infect her sex partner.

What Happens if Genital Herpes Is Not Treated?

Some people who have genital herpes will never experience signs and symptoms. Some may have signs and symptoms when they are first infected and never have them again. Still others may have herpes signs and symptoms that come and go. The signs and symptoms may appear once every few years or as often as every few weeks.

Although there is no cure, there is a drug that can be helpful to people with herpes. For people whose signs and symptoms return again and again, the drug acyclovir is used. Although acyclovir does not cure herpes, it can reduce the pain of the signs and symptoms and cause them to go away sooner than they would have without treatment. Acyclovir is available in capsules or as a cream.

The most important serious effects of genital herpes are the long-term problems. First, living with an incurable condition that can flare up at any moment can cause much stress and worry. Second, if a pregnant woman has an outbreak of herpes during childbirth, a Caesarean section may be necessary to prevent the baby from being born infected. Herpes infections in newborn babies are very serious. Fifty percent of newborns infected with herpes die, and half of the surviving babies will have severe brain or eye damage.

Syphilis

Syphilis (SIF-uh-lis) is caused by a bacterium. Syphilis is a very serious disease because it can spread through the bloodstream to any organ of the body. More than 120,000 new cases of syphilis are reported each year.

What Are the Signs and Symptoms of Syphilis?

The first sign of syphilis is a painless sore called a chancre (SHANG-ker). The chancre starts out as a small red bump that later becomes an open sore that oozes fluid filled with syphilis bacteria. The chancre forms at the part of the body where the infection occurred.

A chancre on the penis or on the lips of the vagina is most likely to be noticed. However, the chancre may also form on the cervix, inside the vagina, in the mouth, in the throat, or in the rectum. Since the chancre is small and painless, it is usually not noticed if it forms in these areas. A chancre on the lips may be mistaken for a cold sore. While the chancre is present, the infected person has primary syphilis.

It usually takes about three weeks for the chancre to appear after infection, although it may appear as soon as 10 days after infection. In some people it may not appear for as long as three months. Before

(FIGURE 22-6) The first sign of syphilis is a painless sore called a chancre [left]. A later sign of the disease is a rash, which sometimes appears on the soles of the feet [right].

the chancre forms, a blood test for syphilis may be negative even though the bacterium is present in the body and the disease is progressing.

The chancre disappears with or without treatment within one to five weeks. However, disappearance of the chancre does not mean the disease is cured. It is just progressing to the next stage.

The next stage of the disease is called secondary syphilis. The signs and symptoms of secondary syphilis appear about two to six months after exposure. The most common sign of secondary syphilis is a rash that appears on the body. Sometimes the rash appears on the palms of the hands and the soles of the feet. The rash does not itch, and it goes away without treatment after a few weeks, although it may come back and go away again several times.

A person with secondary syphilis may also have a dull depressed feeling, fever, sore throat, joint pain, or hair loss. Large, moist sores sometimes develop around the sex organs or in the mouth. Like the chancre that is characteristic of primary syphilis, the signs and symptoms of secondary syphilis disappear without treatment. Syphilis then enters the latent stage.

Latent syphilis has no signs and symptoms. This stage may last for a few years or for an entire lifetime. However, latent syphilis may progress to tertiary syphilis. Tertiary syphilis is the stage of the disease in which the syphilis bacteria cause severe damage to parts of the body such as the skin, blood vessels, heart, bones, spinal cord, and brain. Tertiary syphilis can cause blindness, brain damage, paralysis, and, in some cases, even death.

How Can a Person Become Infected With Syphilis?

The bacterium that causes syphilis is very frail and cannot survive drying or chilling. It dies within a few seconds after exposure to air. Therefore, as with gonorrhea, you cannot get syphilis from toilet seats or dirty towels. Syphilis is usually transmitted during sexual contact. The bacterium is passed from the chancre or rash of

The Spread of STDs

STD	Approximate New Cases Each Year
Gonorrhea	1–3 million
Chlamydia	3–10 million
Genital herpes	500,000
Syphilis	120,000
Genital warts	1 million

(FIGURE 22-7) **Sexually transmitted diseases are spreading at an alarming rate. One reason for the rapid spread is that many people do not have signs and symptoms of disease and unknowingly infect others.**

genital warts:

an STD caused by the human papilloma virus, or HPV; causes warts in the genital and anal areas and has been linked to cervical cancer and penile cancer.

an infected person to the mucous membrane of the vagina, penis, mouth, or rectum of the other person. It is also possible for syphilis to be transmitted from a chancre or rash to an open wound or sore. An infected woman can also pass syphilis to her unborn child during pregnancy.

What Happens if Syphilis Is Not Treated? Syphilis can be cured at any stage by using the right antibiotics. Treatment for the disease is easiest during the first year of infection.

After a year, syphilis can still be successfully treated, but the medication must be taken for a longer period of time.

If syphilis progresses to the final tertiary stage, treatment can stop the progression of the disease but cannot reverse the damage that has already occurred. As you already read, tertiary syphilis can cause blindness, paralysis, and even death.

Other STDs

The most common STDs are the ones already discussed. However, there are other STDs as well.

Nongonococcal Urethritis (NGU) Any infection of the urethra—the tube that carries urine from the bladder to the outside of the body—that is not caused by gonorrhea is called nongonococcal urethritis. Several different organisms cause NGU, but most cases are caused by chlamydia. The proper antibiotic must be prescribed to cure NGU.

Genital Warts **Genital warts** may be the fastest growing STD in the United States. There are more than one million new cases each year. Warts may appear in the genital and anal areas.

Genital warts are caused by the human papilloma virus (HPV). HPV is not curable, but its symptoms may be treated with drugs, lasers, liquid nitrogen, or surgery. HPV is associated with penile and cervical cancers, so people who have been infected should be screened for cancer regularly.

Vaginitis Vaginitis is any inflammation of the vagina. Signs and symptoms may include itching or pain in the vaginal area or any unusual vaginal discharge. It is normal for the vagina to secrete a small amount of clear liquid. It is also normal for the amount and thickness of the secretion to vary somewhat during the monthly cycle. However, if the discharge is yellowish, if it has an unpleasant odor, or if there is much more than usual, it is a sign of vaginitis.

Vaginitis can be caused by the gonorrhea or chlamydia bacteria, as well as by other microorganisms. Trichomoniasis (also called "trick") is caused by a one-celled organism that burrows under the mucus in the vagina. It is often transmitted through sexual intercourse. It can also be contracted by exposure to moist objects

---

• • • TEACH continued

Class Discussion
Treatment Is Important

Discuss syphilis as a potentially life-threatening disease. Ask: **Why is it important to seek treatment for syphilis even if the chancre disappears?** *[When the chancre disappears, the disease has not been cured; instead the second stage is just beginning.]*

Journal 22D
On STDs and Friends

Have students write in their Journal how they would feel if they found out that a friend had an STD. Tell them to write whether it would change their feelings for this friend. Also have them write how they personally would want to be treated if they contracted an STD.

Extension
Old and New STDs

Students may want to know if people had problems with STDs in the past and what, if any, treatments were available. Have them do library or Internet research to find out which STDs are old diseases and which ones are relatively new diseases. Have students report their findings in the style of a television or magazine investigative-journalism report.

containing the organism. For example, this could happen if you used someone else's wet towel or bathing suit.

Vaginitis can also be caused by a fungus called candida. This kind of infection, candidiasis, is commonly known as a yeast infection. A yeast infection is not necessarily sexually transmitted. Any imbalance in the normal environment inside the vagina can give candida a chance to grow and to cause problems.

Hepatitis Hepatitis (hep-uh-TY-tis) is an inflammation of the liver that can be caused by several different viruses. The type of hepatitis that is called hepatitis A is not usually transmitted sexually, but it can be passed from one person to another by oral-anal contact.

The hepatitis B virus, on the other hand, is easily transmitted through sexual contact. It may be present in the body fluids—saliva, urine, blood, semen, and vaginal secretions—of an infected person.

But sexual contact is not the only way hepatitis B is spread. Practices such as sharing toothbrushes, razors, or needles with an infected person can also transmit the disease.

Hepatitis B is a serious disease. It can cause damage to the liver and result in serious health problems. Early signs and symptoms may be similar to those of the flu and may also include dark urine and yellowing of the skin and the whites of the eyes. If you are exposed to hepatitis B, it is important for you to seek treatment right away.

A vaccine is now available that prevents hepatitis B. If you are concerned about this type of hepatitis, talk to a doctor or another health professional about receiving the vaccine.

Parasitic Infections Pubic lice ("crabs") and scabies can be spread by either casual or sexual contact. Pubic lice are small insects that live in the pubic hair and attach their eggs to hair shafts. Pubic lice grip the pubic

(FIGURE 22-8) **One of the early signs of hepatitis B is yellowing of the skin and the whites of the eyes.**

Review Answers

1. a disease that is passed from one person to another during sexual contact

2. The most common STDs are gonorrhea, chlamydia, genital herpes, and syphilis.

3. sexual contact; mother to infant during birth

4. In both males and females there may be no symptoms or there may be painful blisters on the sex organs. Some people experience an itching, tingling, or burning sensation just before the herpes sores appear. Other symptoms include a sluggish feeling, fever, and flulike symptoms.

5. Yes. A person with an STD but no symptoms may unknowingly infect another person. Also, some people may not recognize or may ignore the symptoms of an STD and fail to get treatment.

(FIGURE 22-9) **Pubic lice [left] live in the pubic hair, causing irritation and itching. Scabies is caused by a tiny mite that burrows under the skin.**

hair and feed on tiny blood vessels of the skin. The lice irritate the skin and cause itching and occasional swelling of the glands in the groin.

Scabies (SCAY-beez) is caused by a tiny mite that can barely be seen. The mite burrows under the skin and causes intense itching and the formation of pus. In addition to the genital area, scabies may appear under the breasts, in the armpits, between the fingers, and elsewhere.

Special medicated shampoo is used to treat pubic lice, and medicated lotion is used to treat scabies. However, pubic lice and scabies can be found in clothes and bed linen. Therefore, all clothing and bed linen must be washed in hot water and either dried in a hot clothes dryer or dried in bright sunshine in order to eliminate these parasites.

Review

1. What is a sexually transmitted disease?

2. Name four common sexually transmitted diseases.

3. Name two ways that chlamydia can be transmitted.

4. What are the signs and symptoms of genital herpes?

5. **Critical Thinking** Is it possible for someone to transmit an STD to another person without realizing it? Explain.

ASSESS

Section Review

Have students answer the Section Review questions.

Alternative Assessment
The Spread of STDs

Ask students to summarize in a paragraph what the STDs discussed in this section have in common. Have them discuss why these diseases are easily spread by sexual contact.

Closure
Remaining Questions

Ask students to list for themselves three questions they still have about STDs. Use the Question Box or initiate open discussion to encourage students to express these questions and get answers. Follow up on any questions to which you don't know the answer.

Section
22.2
Preventing Sexually Transmitted Diseases

Objectives

- *Know what you can do to decrease your chances of getting an STD.*
- *Name 10 ways you can show love for someone without sexual intimacy.*
  - **LIFE SKILLS: Communicating Effectively**
- *Know where to go for testing and treatment for STDs.*
  - **LIFE SKILLS: Using Community Resources**

Vanessa said that she thought these diseases must be pretty rare. After all, she had heard a lot of people talking about sex, but she had never known anyone personally who had gotten one of these diseases. But her mother pointed out that most people who get an STD are embarrassed about it. They aren't likely to go around telling everybody that they have one of these diseases.

Han said that she thought the people who got STDs were probably very promiscuous, with many sex partners. Vanessa's mom said that it's true that the more sex partners you have, the more likely you are to get one of these diseases. However, you can get an STD by having sexual contact just once, if your partner is infected.

Staying Healthy

STDs can be prevented by making responsible decisions. You can stay healthy by refusing to take part in behaviors that put you at risk for STDs.

Delaying Sexual Intimacy Many of these diseases are transmitted only by sexual contact or mainly by sexual contact. If you are not sexually active, you will probably never have to worry about getting gonorrhea, syphilis, or chlamydia.

Although it is theoretically possible to get genital herpes, trichomoniasis, pubic lice, or scabies in other ways besides sexual contact, it is very unlikely. You can reduce your risk of these diseases to practically zero if you avoid sexual contact and also practice good hygiene. That means not sharing towels, clothing, or bed linen with anyone else unless those items have been thoroughly washed. In addition, you must avoid direct contact with any open sores another person might have.

(FIGURE 22-10) **If two people abstain from sexual activity until marriage and remain faithful to each other, they will be protected from STDs.**

Background
Speaking Frankly

In the United States, approximately 12 million new cases of sexually transmitted diseases occur annually. The Centers for Disease Control and Prevention estimates that two-thirds of these cases occur in people under the age of 25. People 15 to 19 are at the greatest risk of contracting STDs. Having multiple partners or unprotected intercourse makes the risk even greater. It is estimated that 56 million people are infected with a viral, non-AIDS STD, such as genital herpes or human papilloma virus. Considering these figures, it is obvious that talking frankly with a sex partner about STDs is absolutely necessary. In addition, it is unwise to assume that a casual sex partner will be honest about his or her sexual history. Also, because STDs are not always symptomatic in their early stages, a person who insists that he or she is disease-free may unknowingly pass on a serious infection.

Section 22.2 Lesson Plan

MOTIVATE

Journal 22E
Prevention of STDs

This may be done as a warm-up activity. Ask students to write in their Journal ways to prevent sexually transmitted diseases.

Class Discussion
The Spread of STDs

Discuss Vanessa's idea that STDs must be rare. You may want to remind students of the data shown on page 472 in Figure 22-7, "The Spread of STDs." Ask: **Which of those diseases in the figure can be cured?** *[gonorrhea, chlamydia, syphilis]* Ask students what they think of Han's conclusion

that only promiscuous people contract STDs. Discuss the possibility of contracting an STD if you have just one sex partner.

*Life*SKILLS

Ask students if they think the couple in the photograph love each other. Ask them how they can tell. Have them suggest other ways to show love nonsexually.

Making a Choice 22A

Assign the Public Health Campaign card. The card asks students to design a public-information campaign to publicize the causes and treatments of sexually transmitted diseases.

Making a Choice 22B

Assign the Designing a Game card. The card asks students to design a game that teaches practices that will help prevent the spread of sexually transmitted diseases.

As you already learned, delaying or abstaining from sexual intimacy is called sexual abstinence. If you decide to practice abstinence until you are older, that doesn't mean that you will not have sexual feelings for someone in the meantime. There are many safe ways to express sexual affection for someone. Talking, hugging, and holding hands, for example, are the safest possible expressions of feelings.

In spite of the messages you may be getting from music, movies, TV, or even your friends, the truth is that many teenagers are not sexually active. Teenagers choose to delay sexual intimacy for a variety of reasons. For some teens it is a matter of avoiding sexually transmitted diseases and pregnancy. For others, the primary reason for delaying intimacy involves personal goals and values. People are generally happier when they live up to their values and accomplish their goals.

Remember, if two people abstain from sexual activity until marriage and remain faithful to each other, they will be protected from STDs.

*Life*SKILLS: **Communicating Effectively**

Showing Love Nonsexually . . . .

The teenage years are a time of strong sexual feelings. Even though you know that choosing abstinence is the best way to avoid STDs, you may want to show your affection for someone by becoming sexually intimate.

When you are in love and really care for someone, it's natural to want to show it. But sexual intercourse is not the only way to show affection. For example, one of the nicest things you can do for a person is to listen to what he or she has to say with genuine interest. This shows that you take the person seriously and that his or her thoughts and feelings are important to you.

On a separate sheet of paper, write down at least 10 other ways besides sex that you can show you love your girlfriend or boyfriend.

TEACH

Class Discussion
Sexual Abstinence

Discuss the zero risk of STDs if a person practices sexual abstinence. Ask students to name other advantages of sexual abstinence. Have them discuss whether they think it is possible to convince someone who thinks differently to change his or her ideas.

Class Discussion
Avoiding STDs

With student participation, build the following concept map on the chalkboard. Provide the title AVOIDING STDs and the two ways: Staying in Control and Reducing Risks. Ask students to state two ways to stay in control. Fill these in on the map. Ask for two ways to reduce the risks. Fill these in on the map. As students provide

suggestions, ask them questions about each suggestion and fill in their responses on the map. "Using a condom" is provided here as an example.

AVOIDING STDs

Staying in Control Using alcohol and other drugs can be harmful to your health in more ways than their direct effects on your body. Drinking or doing drugs can also increase your risk of getting an STD. How? Drugs and alcohol interfere with your judgment and decision-making abilities. With drugs or alcohol clouding your thinking, it is much easier to convince yourself that it's okay "just this once."

Besides avoiding drugs and alcohol, it can also help to avoid situations where you might be pressured to participate in sexual activity. For example, group dating with friends who share your values can make it easier to avoid temptation. Also, getting involved in sports, after-school clubs, hobbies, or volunteer work can reduce your need to alleviate boredom or find satisfaction through sex.

Reducing the Risk of STDs There are some sexual practices that—although they are not completely safe—can reduce the risk of getting an STD during sexual contact. For example, the **latex condom,** a covering for the penis, helps protect both partners from sexually transmitted diseases and helps prevent pregnancy. For a condom to be effective though, it must be used properly. The condom must be put on before any physical contact and must be worn until contact has ended. When putting the condom on, the reservoir tip at the top of the condom must be pinched as the condom is unrolled to the base of the penis. To prevent the condom from slipping off inside the vagina, the penis must be withdrawn while still erect while the condom is held snugly to the base of the penis. High temperatures weaken latex, so condoms should never be stored in a car or in a wallet carried in a hip pocket. Also, condoms weaken over time, so remember to check the expiration date printed on the package. Using a spermicide

can give added protection against STDs and pregnancy. Although water-based lubricants do not protect against STDs or pregnancy, they do reduce the risk of condom breakage. Caution: Any oily substance can weaken the latex and cause the condom to break.

Breaking the Cycle of Infection Sexually transmitted diseases have become epidemic in the United States. One reason why so many people have them is that STDs are spread from one sex partner to another in a seemingly endless chain by people who don't know that they have a disease, who do not get proper treatment for the disease, or who don't inform their partners.

As Figure 22-11 shows, if an infected person passes an STD to two sex partners and those people pass it to two partners, and so on, the disease can spread from one person to many people in a relatively short time.

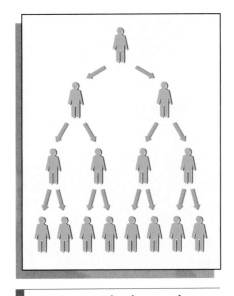

(FIGURE 22-11) **This diagram shows how rapidly an STD can spread if each infected person passes it to two sex partners.**

latex condom:

a covering for the penis that, when used correctly, helps protect both partners from sexually transmitted diseases and helps prevent pregnancy.

Teaching Transparency 22B
The Chain of Infection

Show the transparency of Figure 22-11, which demonstrates the spread of an STD if each infected person has two sex partners. Ask students to discuss the responsibility a person with an STD has to both himself or herself and to his or her sex partners.

• • • TEACH continues on p. 478

Background
The Law and STDs

If a case of reportable STD is made known to public officials, they are required by law to contact all recent sex partners of the infected person. If the sex partners will not seek treatment voluntarily, police action may force the person to have a medical examination and to start treatment if necessary. Some states now have laws that authorize the treatment of minors for STDs without requiring parental consent.

If you think you might have an STD, it is very important that you break this chain of infection. If you do not act responsibly to stop the disease, there could be serious consequences to your own health. You could also be responsible for the infection of many other people.

If You Think You Might Have an STD

If you have any reason to think you have been exposed to one of these diseases, you must find out for sure if you have it even if you do not have signs or symptoms. Only a doctor or a health professional at a clinic can diagnose STDs.

Where to Go for Help You have several choices about where to go for proper diagnosis and treatment. You can go to your family doctor or to another private doctor. Remember, doctors have a professional duty to keep information regarding their patients confidential.

If you don't have a private doctor, or if you cannot afford to pay for private treatment, there are public health clinics that offer free or low-cost treatment. To find the number for a public clinic, look in the local government section of the Blue Pages under "Health and Human Services." Other clinics that offer testing services are listed in the Yellow Pages under "Clinic—Medical."

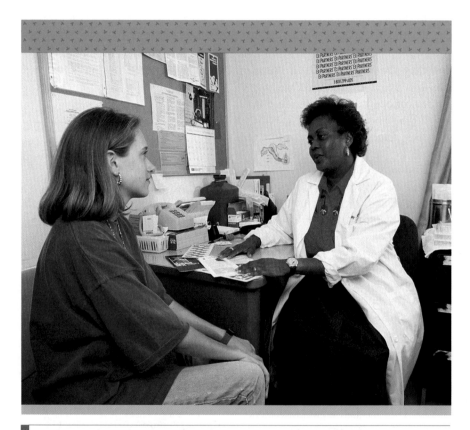

(FIGURE 22-12) **Public health clinics will keep your name, your diagnosis, your treatment, and any other information about you completely confidential.**

• • • TEACH continued

Reinforcement
Seeking Help

It is normal that someone may not want to acknowledge that he or she has an STD. But it would be irresponsible to knowingly expose someone else to the disease. Ask students what the consequences of not seeking help would be to themselves and to any sex partners.

Debate the Issue
Revealing Names

Tell students that a person who has been diagnosed as having an STD may be asked for the names of sex partners. Hold a class debate on whether this is an invasion of privacy. Tell them to consider this both as a matter of law and as a matter of moral responsibility.

Journal 22F
Sexual Abstinence

Ask students if their feelings about sexual abstinence have changed in any way since they have learned about STDs. In their Journal, have students explain their answer.

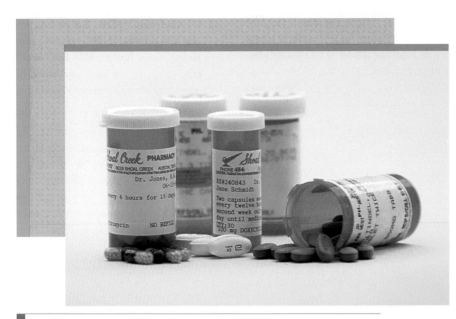

(FIGURE 22-13) **People with STDs should take all the medicine they are prescribed and follow the doctor's orders exactly.**

You can also call the National STD Hotline number, which is listed with Directory Assistance, to find out where in your area you can go for STD testing and treatment. The people staffing the hotline can answer any questions you have about STDs.

It is the law in most states that anyone can be treated for a communicable disease. This means that anyone who seeks treatment for a sexually transmitted disease can receive it.

Don't worry about the health workers in the clinics being shocked or upset that you might have an STD. Remember, dealing with STDs is just part of their daily routine. Their goal is to stop the spread of these diseases. Public health workers are more likely to be upset by people who do not get treatment and who continue to spread the disease. Public health clinics will keep your name, your diagnosis, your treatment, and any information you give them completely confidential.

If you are diagnosed with certain STDs, workers at the clinic may ask for the names of your sex partners. They do this so that they can inform your partners of possible exposure to the disease. For many people, telling their partners is the hardest part of dealing with an STD. If a person with an STD wishes, a health clinic worker will contact the sex partners but not reveal the name of the person with the STD.

Treatment for STDs Different STDs require different treatments, so a visit to a health professional is necessary to receive the correct treatment.

Many people think they have to take their medicine only until they feel better. This is not true! Once a person feels better and is not so worried, it may take some effort to keep taking the medicine until it is gone. However, it is very important to do so. People with STDs should take all the medicine they are prescribed and follow the doctor's instructions exactly.

Section 22.2 sidebar

Section Review Worksheet 22.2
To reinforce the concepts presented in this section, assign Section Review Worksheet 22.2.

Section Quiz 22.2
Have students take Section Quiz 22.2.

Reteaching Worksheet 22.2
Students who have difficulty with the material may complete Reteaching Worksheet 22.2.

Review Answers
1. Answers will vary but may include the following: do not become sexually active; do not share unclean towels, linens, or clothing; avoid direct contact with open sores on other people; stay in control by not using alcohol or drugs; limit dating to group dating; become involved in activities that interest you, such as sports or a hobby; and, if you do become sexually active, use a latex condom correctly each time you have sex.

Reinforcement
See a Doctor

Remind students that, since many of the symptoms of an STD do not show up immediately, it is important to see a doctor if they think they have been exposed to an STD or if they find out that a sex partner was having sexual intercourse with someone else.

Class Discussion
STD Treatment

Ask: **Why is it necessary that a patient take all the medicine prescribed in order to cure the STD?** *[Physicians prescribe a certain amount of antibiotics to be taken. A smaller amount may not kill all the harmful bacteria. It may kill only the weaker ones, leaving the stronger ones to develop a resistance to the antibiotic.]* **Why it is necessary for both partners to be treated at** the same time for certain STDs? *[If only one of the sex partners is treated and if the couple continues their sexual relationship, the untreated partner will reinfect the treated partner.]*

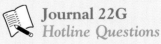

Journal 22G
Hotline Questions

Have students write in their Journal any questions they might want to ask on the National STD Hotline.

479

Answer to Question 1 is on p. 479.

2. Answers will vary but may include hugging, holding hands, doing something nice for the person, listening to the person, respecting the opinions and feelings of the person, and talking.

3. The friend could go to his family doctor or to another private doctor. If he wanted to go to a public clinic, he could locate one by looking in the local government section of the Blue Pages under "Health and Human Services." Other clinics that offer testing are listed in the Yellow Pages under "Clinic—Medical."

4. Sample response: If a person does not take all the antibiotic prescribed for a bacterial STD, he or she won't be cured of the disease.

REMINDER

〜〜〜〜

Bacteria can develop immunity to any antibiotic that is not taken as directed.

Medicine must not be shared with anyone else. For one thing, it might be the wrong medicine to cure someone else's disease. And if two people are taking medicine prescribed for one person, there may not be enough medicine to completely cure both people.

Though they shouldn't share the same medicine, sex partners should be treated at the same time for certain STDs. A person with an STD should ask a health professional if his or her partner should also be treated. If both sex partners are not treated at the same time, they can continue to reinfect each other.

Q. A friend told me that the best way to avoid STDs is to take a shower right after having sex. He said that if you can't take a shower right away, you should at least wash off the best you can. Is this true?

A. No. Washing after sexual contact will not prevent STDs. If you have unprotected sexual contact with an infected partner, disease-causing microorganisms can cross mucous membranes and enter your body before you can wash them off.

◆◆◆

Q. Is it true that taking birth-control pills can prevent STDs?

A. No, definitely not. Birth-control pills prevent pregnancy but do nothing to prevent STDs.

◆◆◆

Q. My boyfriend told me that he has had sex with previous girlfriends. He says he has never had an STD, but I'm still concerned. If we have sex, could he give me a disease without knowing it?

A. Not everyone who gets an STD has signs or symptoms of the disease. If a previous girlfriend had an STD but failed to inform your boyfriend, you are at risk. People are often secretive about STDs, so getting tested is the best way for a sexually active person to find out if he or she is infected. You and your boyfriend can be tested for STDs even if you have no symptoms. A health professional will probably advise you and your boyfriend to be tested now, and then again after a waiting period.

Review

∙ ∙ ∙ ∙ ∙

1. *Name four actions you can take that will eliminate or reduce your risk of getting an STD.*

2. ▪▪ **LIFE SKILLS: Communicating Effectively** *Name 10 ways you can show love for someone without becoming sexually intimate.*

3. ▪▪ **LIFE SKILLS: Using Community Resources** *If a friend told you that he thought he might have an STD but didn't know where to go to find out for sure, how could you help him?*

4. *Critical Thinking What do you think will happen if a patient being treated for a bacterial STD does not take all of the antibiotic?*

Extension
STDs and Teens

Encourage students to do library research about the prevention of STDs among teenagers.

ASSESS

Section Review

Have students answer the Section Review questions.

Alternative Assessment
Stopping the Spread

Have students explain in a paragraph how STDs are spread and how they can be contained.

Closure
Letter to a Friend

Have students write a letter to a friend who has told them that he or she has an STD but can't bring himself or herself to get treatment or to tell any sex partners of the infection. The letter should try to convince the friend why someone infected with an STD is obliged to receive treatment and to report his or her sex partners.

CHAPTER 22

Highlights

Summary

- The most dangerous STD (sexually transmitted disease) is AIDS. It cannot be cured and is eventually fatal.

- Some other serious STDs include gonorrhea, chlamydia, genital herpes, syphilis, and HPV.

- Gonorrhea is an infection caused by a bacterium. Many people with gonorrhea do not have symptoms but can pass the bacteria to their sex partners.

- Genital herpes is caused by a virus; there is no known cure. Fifty percent of newborns infected with herpes die, and half of the surviving babies will have severe brain or eye damage.

- Syphilis is caused by a bacterium and progresses in stages. It can be cured

at any stage with the right antibiotic, but if it progresses to the final stage, the damage that has occurred cannot be reversed.

- Other common STDs include genital warts, hepatitis, and pubic lice.

- When used properly, a condom and spermicide can reduce the risk of getting an STD. Safe lubricants for a condom are "water-soluble" ones.

- Confidential diagnosis and treatment for STDs can be obtained from a private doctor or a public health clinic.

- Sexual partners should be treated at the same time for STDs, but they shouldn't share the same medicine.

Vocabulary

sexually transmitted disease (STD) a disease that is passed from one person to another during sexual contact.

gonorrhea an STD caused by bacteria that can infect the mucous membranes of the penis, vagina, throat, or rectum.

pelvic inflammatory disease (PID) an infection of the uterus and fallopian tubes often caused by STDs; if untreated, may result in infertility.

chlamydia the most common STD in the United States; caused by bacteria.

genital herpes an STD caused by a virus that often causes painful blisters or ulcers; cannot be cured.

syphilis an STD caused by bacteria that can spread through the bloodstream to any organ of the body.

genital warts an STD caused by the human papilloma virus, or HPV; causes warts in the genital and anal areas and has been linked to cervical cancer and penile cancer.

CHAPTER 22 HIGHLIGHTS STRATEGIES

SUMMARY

Have students read the summary to reinforce the concepts they learned in Chapter 22.

VOCABULARY

Have students write questions that use the vocabulary words. Have them work in pairs, asking questions of their partner and answering their partner's questions.

EXTENSION

Have students write an article for a teen magazine discussing what they think every teenager should know about STDs. Tell them to keep the article upbeat but serious.

CHAPTER 22 ASSESSMENT

CHAPTER REVIEW

Concept Review

1. b	5. d
2. d	6. c
3. a	7. c
4. d	8. b

Expressing Your Views

Sample responses:

1. I would tell her that genital herpes can also be transmitted when there are no blisters, for example, right before an outbreak of blisters. Therefore, condoms should be used all the time.

2. Sexual intercourse needs to take place only once with an infected person in order for the other partner to become infected. I would tell him that his partners need to be told so that they can seek treatment. Also, both partners need to be treated to prevent passing the disease back and forth and to other people.

3. People do not use protection, such as condoms, during sexual intercourse; people do not recognize symptoms and/or are reluctant to seek treatment; and people do not inform their sexual partners that they have been exposed to an STD.

Concept Review

1. An incurable STD is
   a. gonorrhea.
   b. herpes.
   c. syphilis.
   d. chlamydia.

2. An STD that can cause sterility and pelvic inflammatory disease is
   a. syphilis.
   b. genital warts.
   c. vaginitis.
   d. chlamydia.

3. How are some sexually transmitted diseases commonly spread?
   a. from mother to infant
   b. by closed-mouth kissing
   c. by using dirty toilet seats
   d. all of these

4. An STD associated with cancer is
   a. vaginitis.
   b. NGU.
   c. scabies.
   d. genital warts.

5. Hepatitis B can be spread by
   a. sharing toothbrushes.
   b. sexual contact.
   c. sharing needles.
   d. all of these.

6. Special medicated shampoos or medicated lotions are used to treat
   a. genital warts.
   b. PID.
   c. parasitic infections.
   d. genital herpes.

7. Which of the following behaviors provides the best protection against STDs?
   a. using a condom
   b. using a condom with spermicide
   c. practicing abstinence
   d. getting tested for STDs

8. To find out if you have an STD, you should
   a. talk to a counselor.
   b. visit a doctor or clinic.
   c. talk to your sex partner.
   d. get an over-the-counter drug from the pharmacist.

Expressing Your Views

1. Your friend has confided to you that she has genital herpes. Her boyfriend does not use a condom during sexual intercourse. She says she will not infect her boyfriend as long as she doesn't have an outbreak of blisters. How would you respond to this statement?

2. You have a friend who has been diagnosed as having a sexually transmitted disease. He has received treatment but is too embarrassed to tell his sex partners about his problem. He keeps telling himself that he didn't have sexual intercourse with them often enough for them to be infected. Why is it important for him to inform his partners?

3. Why do you think sexually transmitted diseases continue to spread?

Life Skills Check

1. Students' scripts will differ. Accept all scripts that include correct information about the diagnosis and treatment of STDs and that treat the subject seriously.

2. Sample response: Visit your doctor or a clinic to have the sore properly diagnosed.

Life Skills Check . . . . . .

1. Communicating Effectively

Write a script for a play to be acted out by members of your class in which one character informs his or her sex partner that they are most likely both infected with an STD. Include conversations the two characters might have with friends and relatives about the situation. End the play with the couple deciding on a course of action to resolve their problem.

2. Communicating Effectively

You have noticed a small, painless, leaky sore in your mouth. Ordinarily you would dismiss it as a cold sore. But lately you have been behaving in a way that would put you at risk for a sexually transmitted disease, and you wonder if that is what it could be. How could you find out for sure in a confidential manner?

Projects . . . .

1. Use telephone books and library research to compile a list of telephone numbers and addresses of local agencies that could provide information, counseling, and testing for sexually transmitted diseases. Display the lists in the classroom and around the school.

2. Work with a group to create a bulletin board describing the STDs covered in this chapter. Include symptoms, dangers, and treatments of each disease.

3. Design a cartoon illustrating a way for people to cope with a risky situation or peer pressure.

Plan for Action . . . .

STDs are a major health concern because of their increase among teens and young adults. Make a plan to protect yourself and to help control the spread of these diseases.

Projects
Have students plan and carry out the projects on STDs.

Plan for Action
Have students create a list of negative responses they can give to someone pressuring them to have sexual intercourse and a list of ways to reduce their risk of contracting an STD if they do have intercourse.

Personal Pledge
Discuss the pledge for Chapter 22. A student's decision of whether to sign the pledge is personal and private.

ASSESSMENT OPTIONS

 Chapter Test
Have students take the Chapter 22 Test.

 Alternative Assessment
Have students do the Alternative Assessment activity for Chapter 22.

 Test Generator
The Test Generator contains additional assessment items for this chapter.

CHAPTER 23

HIV Infection and AIDS

SECTION	TITLE/OBJECTIVES	PERSONAL INVENTORY			LIFE SKILLS DEVELOPMENT			
		Personal Health Inventory	Journal	Check Up	Life Skills	Life Skills Worksheets	Media Message or Ethical Issues Worksheet	What Would You Do?
23.1 *pp. 485–491*	**WHAT IS HIV INFECTION?** • Define AIDS. • Describe how HIV works in the body. • Describe the three phases of HIV infection. ■ Find out where to get an HIV-antibody test.	Ch. 23	23A 23B	p. 487		23A		
23.2 *pp. 492–497*	**TRANSMISSION OF HIV** • Name the four body fluids that may contain enough HIV to infect another person. • List the four behaviors that put you at risk for HIV infection. • Name at least five behaviors that don't put you at risk for HIV infection. ■ Find out where you can get answers to any questions about HIV that are not covered in this chapter.		23C 23D		p. 495			
23.3 *pp. 498–501*	**HOW TO PROTECT YOURSELF FROM HIV** • Discuss abstinence as the most effective way to prevent the sexual transmission of HIV infection. ■ Practice resisting pressure to be sexually intimate. ■ Explain how to reduce your risk of HIV infection if you are sexually active.		23E		p. 499	23B		
23.4 *pp. 502–504*	**HIV INFECTION AND SOCIETY** • Describe the medical treatments available for HIV infection. • Name at least two actions you can take to help people with HIV infection.		23F			23C	Unit 6	

KEY: ■ Denotes Life Skill Objective
Text references denoted by page number.
Supplement references denoted by chapter or item numbers.

LINKING RESOURCES

| INTERACTION | OTHER RESOURCES | | SECTION REVIEW AND ASSESSMENT | | | | |
Making a Choice Cards	Parent Discussion Guide	Health Talk Audio Program	Teaching Transparencies and Directory	Section Review Worksheets	Section Quizzes	Reteaching Worksheets	Section Reviews
	Ch. 23	Ch. 23	23A 23B 23C	23.1	23.1	23.1	p. 491
			23D	23.2	23.2	23.2	p. 497
23A 23B				23.3	23.3	23.3	p. 501
				23.4	23.4	23.4	p. 504

KEY FACTS

- AIDS is a sexually transmitted disease caused by the human immunodeficiency virus (HIV), which attacks and weakens the body's immune system.

- AIDS is the sixth leading cause of death among people 15 to 24.

- Although there are some promising treatments, there is no cure for or vaccine against AIDS.

- The transmission of AIDS can be prevented; abstinence or a monogamous relationship with someone who is not infected are the best ways to avoid HIV infection.

- Many HIV-positive people look perfectly healthy, but they can still transmit the disease.

- The three phases of HIV infection are (1) infection with no sign of illness, (2) infection with some signs and symptoms of illness, and (3) full-blown AIDS.

- The following body fluids contain enough HIV to infect another person: blood, semen, vaginal secretions, and breast milk.

- Behaviors that put a person at high risk for contracting AIDS are sharing equipment for injecting drugs, tattooing, or body piercing and having any kind of unprotected sexual intercourse with a person whose HIV status is positive or unknown.

CHAPTER REVIEW AND ASSESSMENT

TEXT

Chapter Review pp. 506–507

SUPPLEMENTS

Chapter Test 23

Alternative Assessment 23

Test Generator Chapter 23

GETTING STARTED

Using the Chapter Photograph

Ask students how the person in the picture is taking action against AIDS. Discuss how this action might increase public awareness of the disease and why increased awareness is important.

Question Box

Have students write out any questions they have about HIV and AIDS and put them in the Question Box.

Sensitivity _ALERT_

To explain the transmission of HIV, it is necessary to discuss sexual activities explicitly. This may make some students uncomfortable. In addition, some students may have a friend or relative who is HIV-positive or who has AIDS. This chapter provides an opportunity to clear up the myth that homosexuals are responsible for the AIDS epidemic. Prepare the class to be receptive to new information and respectful of the feelings and situations of other students.

HIV Infection _and_ AIDS

◆ ◆ ◆ ◆

Section 23.1 ▽
What Is HIV Infection?

Section 23.2 ▽
Transmission of HIV

Section 23.3 ▽
How to Protect Yourself From HIV

Section 23.4 ▽
HIV Infection and Society

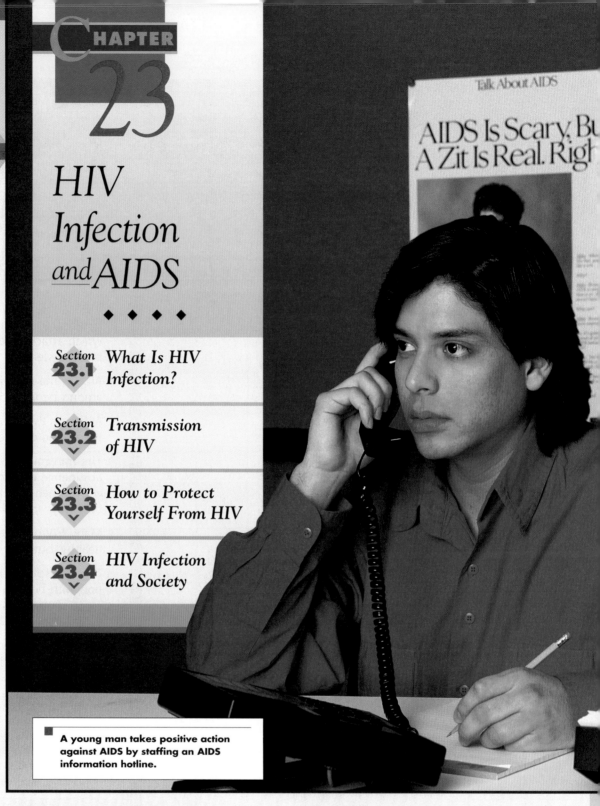

A young man takes positive action against AIDS by staffing an AIDS information hotline.

MYTHS & MISCONCEPTIONS

- **It is possible to get AIDS from casual contact.** There are no documented cases of a person becoming infected with HIV through casual contact with an HIV-positive person. Behaviors such as touching, breathing the same air, and sharing utensils do not transmit AIDS.

- **HIV-positive people look very sick.** People in the final stages of AIDS look very ill. However, many people who are HIV-positive show no signs of illness for many years.

- **It is dangerous to donate blood.** Sterile needles are used to draw blood, so donating blood is completely safe.

- **You can avoid infection with HIV by using a condom during intercourse.** Condoms can leak, break, or come off. Also, only latex condoms protect against HIV transmission, and they must be used from the beginning to the end of a sexual encounter.

Michael and Bryan had been friends since the fourth grade. So Michael noticed immediately that something was really bothering Bryan; he was quiet and looked sad. But Bryan wouldn't talk about what was wrong.

Finally, Michael lost his patience and told Bryan he needed to know what was bothering him. Bryan said he'd think about it, which kept Michael wondering what the problem could be. A couple of days later, Bryan told Michael that his older brother Aaron had tested positive for HIV. Michael felt like he had just been punched in the stomach. He had no idea what to say. "Does that mean Aaron has AIDS?" he blurted out, and then he wanted to kick himself for asking that question. But Bryan didn't seem surprised. He told Michael that so far Aaron didn't seem sick. Then Bryan said that he trusted Michael not to tell their other friends.

Michael was in a daze for the rest of the day. Was Bryan's brother going to die? How did he get infected? Was there any possibility that Bryan could be infected by the AIDS virus? Michael decided he needed to find out more about AIDS.

Personal Health Inventory

Have students complete the Personal Health Inventory for this chapter.

English/Spanish CD Audio Program

Use the English/Spanish Health Talk audio program for students who need audio reinforcement of the concepts presented.

Section 23.1 — What Is HIV Infection?

Objectives

- *Define AIDS.*
- *Describe how HIV works in the body.*
- *Describe the three phases of HIV infection.*
- *Find out where to get an HIV-antibody test.*
  LIFE SKILLS: Using Community Resources

Michael sat down at a computer to search for information about HIV infection and AIDS. In this chapter, you'll learn what Michael learned as he read the information he found.

The most important thing to know about HIV infection is that it is preventable. You can keep from getting it by learning about how it is spread and then avoiding behaviors that might allow you to be infected. In other words, you can choose responsible behaviors to protect yourself. And you can relax about behaviors that don't put you at risk.

Section 23.1 Lesson Plan

MOTIVATE

Journal 23A
Concerns About AIDS

This may be done as a warm-up activity. Encourage students to record their concerns about AIDS in their Journal.

Cooperative Learning
Michael's Response

Have students form small groups to discuss Michael's reaction to the news that his friend has AIDS. How do they think they would have reacted?

TEACH

Class Discussion
AIDS Can Be Prevented

Write on the chalkboard, "AIDS is a preventable disease." Ask: **What does this mean?** *[By avoiding behaviors that lead to infection, a person can prevent getting AIDS.]* **What are some other diseases that are influenced by a person's actions?** *[in some cases, lung cancer, heart disease, diabetes]* **What are some diseases that a person cannot prevent?** *[hereditary diseases, including hemophilia, sickle cell anemia, and muscular dystrophy]* **If a person gets a preventable disease, is that person responsible? Why or why not?** *[It would depend on how well informed the person was about the risks and whether he or she had an opportunity to prevent the disease.]*

Background
Origins of AIDS

Several sensational theories concerning the origin of acquired immunodeficiency syndrome (AIDS) have been reported in the media, most of which have no basis in fact. As of 1996, the general belief among most AIDS researchers was that AIDS developed in western Africa, where certain monkeys carry the simian immunodeficiency virus (SIV). SIV appears to be harmless to the monkeys. It is, however, closely related to human immunodeficiency virus 1 (HIV-1), which in turn is closely related to HIV-2, the virus that causes AIDS. Humans may have been infected with SIV through the bite of a monkey or by eating infected monkey meat. The theory is that SIV mutated into HIV, but just how this happened is not yet known. The earliest confirmed case of AIDS, diagnosed from stored blood and tissue samples, is that of a British sailor who died in 1959.

AIDS:

a disease, caused by a virus, that cripples a person's immune system; AIDS is classified as a sexually transmitted disease, but it can also be spread in other ways, such as through sharing infected equipment for injecting drugs, tattooing, or ear piercing. AIDS is the last phase of HIV infection.

REMINDER

A virus is a microscopic agent that can cause disease.

HIV:

(human immunodeficiency virus) the virus that causes AIDS; also called the "AIDS virus."

(FIGURE 23-1) **The virus that causes AIDS is called HIV (human immunodeficiency virus).**

AIDS, the last phase of HIV infection, is considered to be a sexually transmitted disease because it is most often spread through sexual contact. The name **AIDS** stands for Acquired Immune Deficiency Syndrome. When you break the name of the disease down into its parts, the name makes sense.

Acquired means that a person gets AIDS during his or her lifetime, rather than inheriting it from parents (although a pregnant woman with HIV infection can pass the virus on to her baby).

Immune Deficiency means that the body's immune system, the system that defends the body against infection and disease, is no longer able to do its job. In other words, the immune system becomes deficient.

Syndrome refers to the many diseases and conditions that result from having AIDS.

AIDS is caused by a kind of virus called **HIV** (human immunodeficiency virus). HIV is often referred to as the "AIDS virus." You can see a diagram of one of these viruses in Figure 23-1.

HIV actually attacks the body's immune system, making it difficult for the immune system to defend the body against infection. What this means is that infections that normally wouldn't be very dangerous can kill a person with AIDS.

There is still no cure for HIV infection. Once the virus is able to enter a person's body, there is no way to remove it. There is currently no form of vaccination that can keep you from getting infected with HIV. That's why it's important to read this chapter carefully and take precautions to protect yourself from HIV infection.

The Spread of HIV Infection

The first cases of AIDS were diagnosed in the United States in 1981. Since that time, the number of people with AIDS has grown tremendously, as you can see in Figure 23-2. At the end of 1981, there were 379 cases of AIDS in the United States. Ten years later, the number had increased to more than 200,000. By the end of 1995, the number of cases was well over 500,000 and 62 percent had already died.

There are probably many more people that are infected but don't know it yet because they show no symptoms of the disease. The World Health Organization estimates that 18 million adults and 1.5 million children have been infected with HIV.

Many of the people who first had AIDS in the United States were homosexual men. As a result, some people thought that only homosexuals could get AIDS. That is now known to be a myth. Anyone who engages in risky behaviors can get HIV, whether that person is homosexual or heterosexual. Heterosexual contact is becoming an increasingly common method of

---

 Teaching Transparency 23A
HIV

Show the transparency of Figure 23-1 which shows an illustration of HIV. Tell students that HIV is a retrovirus. A retrovirus contains RNA as its genetic material. As with all viruses, HIV contains genetic material, but it cannot reproduce itself unless it infects another living cell. Then point out that the blue, knoblike structures on the outer surface of the virus in the illustration represent the proteins that allow HIV to bind to specific receptor proteins on the T4 blood cells' surface.

Class Discussion
AIDS on the Increase

Have students look at Figure 23-2, which shows how the number of cases of AIDS is increasing each year. Discuss why the number of cases is rising even though it is now known how AIDS can be prevented. *(Some people*

are uneducated about the way HIV is transmitted and some people think that it can't happen to them, so they engage in risky behaviors.)

Reinforcement
About the Epidemic

Tell students that the AIDS epidemic in the United States first took hold in the homosexual community. This led to early speculation that the disease might be related to homosexuality and transmission. In fact, in some parts of the world, heterosexuals make up the largest group of people with AIDS.

Something that is particularly disturbing about the spread of HIV is the large number of people in their twenties who have it. Since it often takes years from the time of infection until a person actually gets sick, this means that many people were in their teens when they were originally infected with HIV. Among people 15 to 24 years of age, AIDS is now the sixth leading cause of death.

How HIV Works

Among people aged 25–44, AIDS is now the leading cause of death in men and the third leading cause of death in women. If you know the way in which HIV works in the body, you'll understand why certain behaviors increase your chances of being infected with the virus.

Check Up

How Much Do You Already Know About HIV Infection?

1. Can you get HIV by drinking from a glass that someone with HIV has once used?

2. Can you get HIV by holding hands with a person with HIV?

3. Can you get HIV by having sexual intercourse with a person with HIV?

4. If a restaurant cook with HIV sneezes on your food, could you get HIV?

5. Can a woman with HIV infect her baby during delivery?

6. Can you get HIV by donating blood?

7. Can you tell by looking at someone whether he or she has been infected with HIV?

8. Is there a blood test that shows whether a person has been infected with HIV?

1. no 2. no 3. yes 4. no 5. yes 6. no 7. no 8. yes

Note: Any time the blood of an infected person can enter another person's bloodstream through an open cut, sore, or other wound, the potential for infection exists.

Check Up

Have students anonymously turn in their answers to the Check Up questions. Tally the results on the chalkboard. Identify the number of correct responses to each question. Discuss the correct answers to questions often missed. You might want to have students retake the Check Up at the end of the chapter and compare the class results obtained earlier.

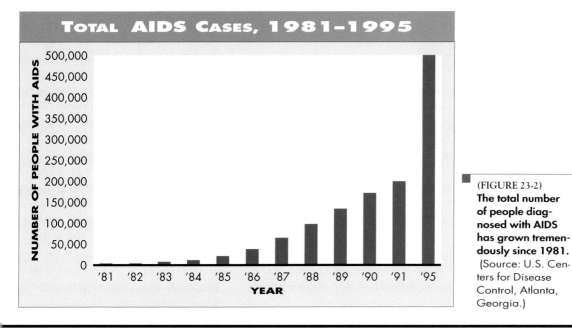

TOTAL AIDS CASES, 1981–1995

(FIGURE 23-2)
The total number of people diagnosed with AIDS has grown tremendously since 1981. (Source: U.S. Centers for Disease Control, Atlanta, Georgia.)

would be confined to that group. That turned out not to be the case. The disease began among heterosexuals in other countries and is spreading among them in the United States as well. At the same time, it has slowed down among homosexuals, who not only have lobbied for funds to support research and care but also have become highly organized to prevent the spread of AIDS and attend to those who already have the disease.

• • • TEACH continues on p. 488

Life Skills
Worksheet 23A
Assign the Local HIV Test-
ing Life Skills Worksheet.

AIDS AMONG YOUTH

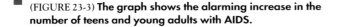

(13 to 19 years) (20 to 24 years)

(FIGURE 23-3) **The graph shows the alarming increase in the number of teens and young adults with AIDS.**

First, HIV must get into a person's bloodstream. The virus can enter the bloodstream directly through shared needles or syringes, or the virus can be transmitted through some form of sexual intercourse with an infected person.

In the body, HIV targets a special kind of blood cell—white blood cells called T4 cells. T4 cells are an extremely important part of a person's immune system because they are the cells that coordinate the body's defense against infection. The attack on T4 cells is what makes HIV so dangerous—it targets the cells that are most important in fighting off infection.

The virus enters the T4 cells and slowly destroys them. The virus forces the T4 cell to make thousands of copies of HIV. The T4 cells become tiny factories, making nothing but HIV—a process that eventually kills the immune system cells.

HIV-antibody test:

a test used to determine whether a person has been infected with HIV.

The newly made viruses then go on to target and attack other T4 cells. As more and more cells are destroyed, the person's immune system gets weaker and weaker. Without a working immune system, a person's body is defenseless against other viruses, bacteria, fungi, and cancer cells. These other infections and cancers are what kill a person with AIDS, not HIV itself.

There are two main points to remember about how HIV works. First, the virus has to get into a person's bloodstream before it can cause infection. What this means to you is that you have to avoid doing things that might let HIV into your bloodstream.

Second, HIV can be in a person's body for years before any signs or symptoms of illness appear. Sometimes more than 10 years can pass before an infected person has any outward signs of the disease. That means you can't tell by looking at someone whether he or she has been infected with HIV. Someone who carries the virus but is not sick can still infect others.

HIV-Antibody Tests

A person can find out if he or she is infected with HIV by going to a health clinic, hospital, or doctor's office and asking for an **HIV-antibody test.** The HIV-antibody test checks a person's blood for antibodies to HIV. Antibodies are substances the body makes to fight infectious agents.

Many clinics offer what is called "anonymous" testing, which means that no one at the clinic or lab that analyzes the test knows the name of the person being tested. Instead the person being tested is assigned a number. Testing is usually free at public-health clinics.

HIV test kits are now available at pharmacies. An individual can perform the test at home and mail the materials to a special

• • • TEACH continued

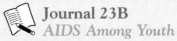

Teaching Transparency 23B
AIDS Among Youth

Have students study the transparency of the graph shown in Figure 23-3. As a class, interpret the information shown. To help the students in their interpretation, ask: **What is the pattern shown for young adults from 1983 to 1995?** *[The number of AIDS cases has risen sharply since 1985.]* **What is the pattern shown for**

teens? *[The number of cases has risen each year but not as dramatically.]* **What might account for the difference in these two patterns?** *[The young adults became infected with HIV as teens but did not develop AIDS until early adulthood.]* **Does this pattern mean that teens are less at risk for AIDS than are young adults?** *[No, it simply reflects the fact that AIDS usually does not develop until a number of years after the initial infection with HIV.]*

Journal 23B
AIDS Among Youth

In their Journal, have students write the thoughts that occur to them while looking at the graph shown in Figure 23-3. Have students consider what they know about the spread of AIDS, and then have them offer explanations for the increasing number of AIDS cases in their age group.

lab for analysis. The test materials are labeled by number, so the people in the lab do not know the identity of the person taking the test. The test results are made available when the person calls the lab and provides the identification number. A positive test result should be followed up immediately by a visit to a doctor for confirmation of the results because there may be other reasons why the results could show up positive.

Myths and Facts About HIV Infection

Myth	Fact
HIV and AIDS are the same thing.	HIV (human immunodeficiency virus) is the name of the virus that causes AIDS. AIDS is the last phase of HIV infection.
People who are infected with HIV look very sick.	Although people with advanced AIDS may look very sick, many people with HIV look perfectly healthy. You can't tell by looking at people whether they have the virus. Even HIV-positive people who look healthy can infect others.
A person who is young and healthy cannot be infected with HIV.	Anyone can be infected with HIV. Unfortunately, many teenagers see themselves as "immune" to misfortunes such as HIV infection.
Birth control pills can prevent the transmission of HIV.	Birth control pills have no effect whatsoever on the spread of HIV.
A person who uses a new latex condom each time he or she has intercourse runs no risk of getting HIV.	Although latex condoms provide good protection, they are not 100 percent effective in preventing HIV transmission. Condoms sometimes tear or are used incorrectly.
Sharing needles to inject insulin, antibiotics, or steroids is not risky for HIV transmission.	Sharing needles for any purpose is risky, even if the injected drugs are legal.
It is possible to get HIV by donating your blood.	Donating your blood does not put you at risk for HIV. Blood-donation centers use a new, sterile needle with each donor.
If a mosquito bit someone with HIV and then bit you, you could get HIV.	There have been no cases of HIV transmission by an insect or any other animal.
It is possible to get HIV by eating food that a person with HIV has handled.	There have been no cases of HIV transmission through food or beverages.

(FIGURE 23-4)

Reinforcement
How HIV Strikes

Reassure students that HIV cannot affect a person unless it enters his or her body. It must reach the bloodstream to have an effect. Stress the fact that symptoms of HIV infection do not show up immediately. A person who appears healthy may be infected with HIV and can pass the disease to others.

Reinforcement
Myths and Consequences

After students review Figure 23-4, ask them to explain what the consequences of believing these myths would be. Ask if they believe that these misconceptions contribute to the spread of HIV.

Class Discussion
Anonymous Testing

Ask students for possible reasons why many clinics offer anonymous testing for HIV. List the reasons on the chalkboard. Then lead a discussion about the need for anonymous testing. Who should have access to the results of an HIV-antibody test?

Class Discussion
HIV Testing

Ask: **Why might a person infected with HIV get a negative result from an HIV-antibody test?** *[It can take up to 6 months after infection for antibodies*

Section Review Worksheet 23.1

To reinforce the concepts presented in this section, assign Section Review Worksheet 23.1.

Section Quiz 23.1

Have students take Section Quiz 23.1.

Reteaching Worksheet 23.1

Students who have difficulty with the material may complete Reteaching Worksheet 23.1.

HIV-positive:

the condition of being infected with HIV.

The HIV antibody test has one major drawback. It takes a while for an infected person's body to make enough antibodies to show up on the test—usually from 6 to 12 weeks, but sometimes up to 6 months. If a person gets tested immediately after possibly being infected, the test results will be negative. So even when the test results are negative, there is still some chance that a person could be carrying HIV.

There are two very compelling reasons to be tested if you think you might be infected with the virus. First, it may be possible to slow the progress of the disease with early treatment. Early treatment can prolong life if an individual starts medication before he or she gets sick. The second reason is that if you know you are infected, you can take precautions not to infect others.

Phases of HIV Infection

There isn't a timetable for the progression of HIV infection, but people tend to go through the following three phases.

Phase 1: Infection With No Signs or Symptoms of Illness Some people—infants, people who already have chronic diseases, and older people, for example—show signs and symptoms of infection very quickly. Others can be infected with HIV for years, sometimes 10 years or longer, without any noticeable illness. They seem perfectly healthy and wouldn't even know they were infected if they hadn't tested positive on the HIV-antibody test.

People who have been infected with HIV are said to be **HIV-positive.** It's important to remember that people can be HIV-positive and not have AIDS. People who are HIV-positive will probably get sick eventually; however, researchers might find a way to prevent the disease from progressing. The main thing to remember now is that people who are infected with HIV but don't show any signs or symptoms of illness can still transmit the virus to other people.

Phase 2: Infection With Signs and Symptoms of Illness During the second phase of HIV infection, a person's immune system will begin to fail. A person in this phase may have one or more of the following signs and symptoms:

- swollen lymph glands in the neck and armpits
- extreme tiredness
- fever
- diarrhea
- severe weight loss
- excessive sweating during the night
- white patches on the inside of the mouth

You might be thinking to yourself, "I've had some of those signs. Does that mean I might be infected with HIV?" Remember that these signs and symptoms can also be caused by other infections, such as a cold or the flu. If you have these signs and symptoms, it doesn't necessarily mean that you're infected with HIV. One difference between the signs and symptoms of an HIV infection and a cold or flu is that the signs and symptoms of HIV infection tend to last a lot longer. If you have any of the signs or symptoms for more than two weeks, it's a good idea to see a doctor just to be on the safe side.

In addition to these infections, females can develop problems of the reproductive system. Often the first symptom of a weakened immune system in women is a series of severe vaginal infections.

Phase 3: AIDS According to the Centers for Disease Control and Prevention, there are two ways in which an HIV-infected person is considered to have AIDS. As it is clinically defined, a person has AIDS when

---

• • • TEACH continued

to form.] Stress the importance of retesting if a person has engaged in any high-risk behaviors during the six months prior to the test.

Have students give reasons why at-risk individuals should be tested. *(In addition to getting treatment to delay the onset of disease and to preventing the infection of others, students may mention putting worries to rest and being motivated to stop risk behaviors.)*

Role-Playing
HIV With No Symptoms?

Have students role-play a situation in which one member of a couple is trying to convince the other that he or she is not infected with HIV because he or she has no symptoms. The other person should use facts about the virus to counteract the arguments. In a variation, the first person says he or she has had an antibody test and the other asks questions to determine whether the results would be reliable.

Teaching Transparency 23C
The HIV Iceberg

Use this transparency to complement the three phases of HIV infection described in the text. Ask: **Why are the three phases of HIV infection compared to an iceberg?** *[The visible portion of an iceberg, its tip, is only a small portion of the entire iceberg, which may be enormous. Actual cases of AIDS (Phase 3) are small in number when compared with the number of cases of what is called AIDS-related complex*

the level of T4 cells in his or her blood is fewer than 200 cells per microliter, which is less than 14 percent of the white blood cells in the blood. This level indicates that a person's immune system has been severely damaged.

The second factor that doctors look for in diagnosing AIDS is the development of serious conditions that result from long-term damage to the immune system. Among these serious conditions are opportunistic infections. They are called opportunistic infections because they take the "opportunity" created by a weakened immune system to attack a person's body.

One of the most common opportunistic infections affecting people with AIDS is a kind of pneumonia called *Pneumocystis carinii pneumonia,* which causes difficulty in breathing, chest pain, and coughing. Another common opportunistic infection is *Kaposi's sarcoma,* which is a rare form of cancer that causes purple patches or bumps on the skin and on the internal organs. It is very unusual for someone who does not have AIDS to get Pneumocystis carinii pneumonia or Kaposi's sarcoma because a normally functioning immune system can successfully defend against these infections. Pulmonary tuberculosis is another opportunistic infection. This type of tuberculosis and a low T4 count are used to diagnose AIDS. HIV-infected women are more likely than other women to get cervical cancer.

People with HIV who have a large number of functioning T4 cells often appear healthy. They are energetic for long periods of time and can work or go to school. Those with fewer T4 cells are more likely to become ill and develop opportunistic infections and cancers.

There is still no cure for AIDS, but researchers continue to develop new treatments that can help people with AIDS lead longer, healthier lives.

(FIGURE 23-5) **People with AIDS are more susceptible to infections and cancers than people who have fully functioning immune systems.**

Review

1. *Define AIDS.*

2. *Define HIV.*

3. *Can a person infected with HIV who shows no outward signs of illness infect another person? Explain your answer.*

4. ▓ **LIFE SKILLS: Using Community Resources** *Make a list of the resources in your community that you can consult to find out more about AIDS.*

5. *Critical Thinking Is it possible for a person who was infected with HIV at the age of 14 to have no outward signs of illness at the age of 19? Explain your answer.*

Review Answers
1. Answers may vary but should include the following information: AIDS is a viral disease caused by HIV and is the last phase of HIV infection. AIDS is diagnosed when an HIV-positive person either has a T4 cell level that is less than 200 cells per microliter, which is less than 14 percent of the white blood cells in the blood, or has developed serious infections (opportunistic infections) due to long-term damage to the immune system.
2. HIV (human immunodeficiency virus) is a virus that attacks the body's immune system, leaving it unable to defend the body against infection.
3. Yes. Outward signs do not have to be present. Anyone who is HIV-positive can pass the infection on if his or her blood or body fluids come in contact with an uninfected person's blood.
4. Available resources will vary depending on the community in which the student lives.
5. Yes. It can take 10 years, and sometimes longer, for symptoms to show.

(Phase 2) and the number of HIV-positive people who show no sign of infection (Phase 1).]

Extension
The Research Frontier

Interested students may find recent articles describing promising medical research, medicines, and techniques for fighting HIV and AIDS. Have them report to the class on their findings.

ASSESS
Section Review

Have students answer the Section Review questions.

Alternative Assessment
Phase 1 HIV Infection

Have students explain what the delay between HIV infection and the appearance of symptoms means for individuals and for society.

Closure
HIV and AIDS

Have students write a paragraph that explains the difference between being infected with HIV and having AIDS.

Section
23.2

Background
Other Bodily Fluids

HIV has been found in small amounts in tears, saliva, and urine. However, the amounts present in these fluids are considered insufficient to infect someone, and there are no documented cases of HIV having been transmitted by them.

Section 23.2 *Transmission of HIV*

Objectives

■ *Name the four body fluids that may contain enough HIV to infect another person.*

■ *List the four behaviors that put you at risk for HIV infection.*

■ *Name at least five behaviors that don't put you at risk for HIV infection.*

■ *Find out where you can get answers to any questions about HIV that are not covered in this chapter.*

LIFE SKILLS: Using Community Resources

Fortunately, HIV is not transmitted like the viruses that cause the common cold or flu. Cold and flu viruses are transmitted easily by contact between two people. If you shake hands with a person who has a cold or flu, for example, and then you touch your mouth, you are very likely to catch the virus from that person. HIV is much harder to catch because it is not transmitted through the air. By far, the most common way that HIV is transmitted from one person to another is through body fluids. Only some of these fluids contain enough of the virus to infect someone else. The following body fluids can contain enough HIV to infect another person:

- blood
- semen
- vaginal secretions
- breast milk

(FIGURE 23-6) **You can't get AIDS from being around a person in an ordinary, everyday kind of way.**

Section 23.2 Lesson Plan

MOTIVATE

Journal 23C
How a Person Gets AIDS

This may be done as a warm-up activity. Have students complete this sentence in their Journal: "A person can get AIDS by . . ."

Transmission of HIV

Risky Behaviors	Safe Behaviors ("Casual Contact")
• Sharing equipment for injecting drugs, tattooing, or piercing	• Working at the same place or going to the same school
• Anal intercourse with an infected person	• Living in the same home
• Vaginal intercourse with an infected person	• Shaking hands, holding hands, or hugging
• Oral intercourse with an infected person	• Sharing a toilet or using a public toilet
• Having multiple sex partners	• Using the same locker room
• Exercising poor judgment regarding sexual activity as a result of using alcohol or other drugs	• Using the same telephone
	• Using the same water fountain
	• Swimming in the same pool
	• Being breathed on, coughed on, or sneezed on
	...and any other ordinary, everyday kind of contact

(FIGURE 23-7) **Risky behaviors involve the exchange of blood, semen, or vaginal secretions.   Safe behaviors don't involve those body fluids.**

Remember that HIV must enter a person's bloodstream for infection to occur. It must go from the blood, semen, vaginal secretions, or breast milk of an infected person into the bloodstream of another person. But how does HIV get into the bloodstream?

First, HIV can be transmitted directly from an infected person's blood into another person's bloodstream when needles and syringes used to inject drugs are shared.

Second, HIV can enter the bloodstream through the **mucous membranes** of the body. Mucous membranes are moist, pink tissues that line the openings to the body—the mouth, the vagina, the anus, the rectum, and the opening at the tip of the penis. If there are sores or tiny breaks in the mucous membranes, there is a simple pathway for HIV to enter the bloodstream. But even if a person has no breaks in the mucous membranes, documented cases show that HIV can still enter the body through the mucous membranes during sexual intercourse.

mucous membranes:

moist, pink tissues of the body; includes membranes of the mouth, vagina, anus, rectum, and the opening at the tip of the penis.

TEACH

Class Discussion
Transmission of HIV

Ask: **What are the four body fluids that may contain enough HIV to infect another person?** *[blood, semen, vaginal secretions, breast milk]* **Why are other body fluids, such as tears and saliva, not considered to be infectious even though they may contain HIV?** *[The concentration of HIV is not high enough to infect someone, and there may not be a means to transmit*

the fluid into another person's bloodstream.]* Be alert for misconceptions students have about the way HIV is spread. They may think it is spread in urine, tears, saliva, by sneezing, by sharing a toilet, by kissing, and so on.

Reinforcement
Two Ways Into the Bloodstream

Emphasize to students that HIV has two ways to get into the bloodstream: directly (through shared needles, breaks in the skin, or contaminated blood products) or indirectly (through

mucous membranes). HIV can pass through these membranes even if they are not torn.

 Teaching Transparency 23D
Transmission of HIV

Show the transparency of Figure 23-7. Have students think of other risky behaviors that might be added to the left half of the chart; discuss their suggestions. Ask for additional safe behaviors for the right half.

Actions That Put You At Risk

People used to talk about HIV risk groups—groups of people who are more likely than others to get HIV. Now we know that anyone who takes part in certain risky behaviors is at risk of contracting HIV.

Sometimes it is hard to talk about risky behaviors because it involves discussing intimate sexual matters and illegal activities. But knowing about HIV transmission is a life-or-death matter, so it is necessary for you to be aware of any actions that put you at risk of contracting the disease.

There are four behaviors that put you at risk of HIV infection. By choosing to avoid these behaviors, you can protect yourself from infection.

> *I was really scared about AIDS until I took this health class. I'd heard all kinds of wild stories about how you could get it.*
>
> Mei

Sharing Equipment for Injecting Drugs, Tatooing, or Body Piercing

Any sharing of needles or other equipment for injecting drugs, tatooing, or body piercing is very risky behavior. When people use the same needle to inject drugs, blood from the first person can go directly into the second person's body. If the blood on the needle contains HIV, the virus is injected along with the drugs. It does not matter what kind of drug is injected—cocaine, heroin, or steroids. Even injecting vitamins, insulin, or antibiotics can expose a person to HIV if the needles or syringes are shared.

Body piercing has become increasingly popular among teens. Body piercing increases a person's chance of contracting many infections. It is an extremely risky behavior if unsterilized needles are used for piercing. A safer option is to go to a licensed practitioner who performs body piercing using sterilized equipment.

Sexual Intercourse With an Infected Person

Vaginal intercourse is one kind of sexual intercourse. It is the most common kind of intercourse between a man and a woman. During vaginal intercourse, a man puts his penis into a woman's vagina.

HIV can be transmitted during vaginal intercourse. If the man is infected with HIV, the virus in his semen can be transmitted into the woman's bloodstream through the mucous membranes in her vagina.

If the woman is infected with HIV, the virus can be transmitted from the fluids in her vagina to her partner through the mucous membranes around the opening at the tip of his penis.

Although either partner can transmit the virus to the other, women are at a greater risk than men because the mucous membranes of the vagina have a much larger surface area, resulting in more exposure to the virus. Also, because semen may remain in

---

··· TEACH continued

Cooperative Learning
The Path of Transmission

Ask: **What are the two main risk activities for contracting HIV?** *[sharing equipment for injecting drugs, tattooing, and body piercing; any sexual activity with an infected person that involves the exchange of body fluids]* Have students form groups to analyze the path of transmission for each activity. Then have them make a list of questions

that have not been answered by any discussion thus far. List these questions on the board. Answer any questions you can. For questions that cannot be answered immediately, have the groups do research to find out the answer and report their findings to the class. Students might ask questions such as the following: Can HIV live in dried blood? Why isn't the concentration of HIV in saliva high enough to be infectious? Can a woman become pregnant at the same time she contracts the disease? Can you have sex

with an HIV-positive person and not be infected? How can you be certain that a shop uses disinfected needles for tattooing or body piercing?

Journal 23D
Considering Risk Activities

Have students review the four main factors for HIV infection and their journal entries for how a person can get AIDS. Then have them write in their Journal their feelings about discussing the risk factors for AIDS. Are they uncomfortable discussing any of them?

a woman's vagina for some time after intercourse, the likelihood of infection is increased. More women are infected with HIV from vaginal intercourse than men.

During oral intercourse, also called oral sex, the virus can be passed to either partner through tiny cuts or through the mucous membranes of the mouth or genitals.

During anal intercourse, it is possible for either partner to transmit the virus to the other. HIV can pass through the mucous membranes of the anus, the rectum, or the opening in the penis.

Other Methods of Transmission

Although transmission of the virus through body fluids is most common, there are other ways people have contracted AIDS that have nothing to do with risky behaviors. Nearly all children who are HIV positive contracted the virus from their mothers while still in the womb or during the birth process. Any woman who has had sex with someone at risk for HIV or who has a history of intravenous drug use should be tested for HIV before thinking about becoming pregnant.

Life SKILLS

Have students gather the information requested in steps 1–5 in the text. Each student should do this exercise independently in order to benefit from the experience. Give each student an index card on which to record and retain the information gathered.

Life SKILLS: Using Community Resources

Getting HIV Information . . . .

You may have questions about HIV infection that haven't been answered in this chapter. Don't worry; you can get answers to your questions. You may be comfortable talking to a parent or teacher, or you may prefer to call someone who doesn't know you. After you do the following exercise, you'll be able to get the information you need.

1. Look in the phone book under "AIDS" and write down the name of every organization you see.

2. Write down the phone number of the local AIDS hotline.

3. Find the CDC Web site for HIV infection and AIDS. Make a list of some of the information that is available.

4. Where could you call to talk to someone about whether you are at risk of being infected with HIV?

5. Write down the name and phone number of a place where you can get an HIV-antibody test. (You may have to call one of the phone numbers you've already looked up to get this information.)

Do they agree with Dr. C. Everett Koop, the former surgeon general, that it is necessary to discuss these risk behaviors?

Reinforcement
Other Methods of Transmission

Draw a simple diagram on the chalkboard, with three lines extending from a central circle labeled "Other Methods of Transmission." Ask students to name methods of transmitting HIV other than the main risk behaviors, and write them on the spokes leading

to the center. *(to a child in the womb or during the birth process, to a health-care worker during an accidental needle prick, through a transfusion with contaminated blood)* Remind students that although these are not common sources of infection, they are important to know about.

Class Discussion
Thoughts on HIV Transmission

Ask questions like the following to extend students' thinking about other methods of transmission: Is it a good

idea for an HIV-positive woman to become pregnant? If a woman who is HIV-positive bears a child who is not infected, should she breast-feed the baby? What kinds of precautions should be taken with hypodermic needles? Is it reasonable to be afraid of going to the dentist because of the possibility of AIDS infection? Is it reasonable to be afraid of receiving a blood transfusion?

Background
HIV and Pregnancy

Pregnant women who are HIV-positive have a 25 to 30 percent chance of giving birth to a baby who is HIV-positive. In 1994, the FDA approved the drug AZT for use in preventing the transmission of HIV from mother to fetus. Studies show that a dose of AZT daily during pregnancy and an infusion of intravenous AZT during labor and delivery reduces the chances of transmission by two-thirds, to just over 8 percent. The newborn infants in this study were also given oral AZT for six weeks after birth. Long-term follow-up studies on these infants are underway. Any pregnant woman who has engaged in at-risk behavior should be tested immediately to protect the health of her unborn child. If she is HIV-positive, she should discuss the possibility of treatment with her doctor.

 Section Review Worksheet 23.2

To reinforce the concepts presented in this section, assign Section Review Worksheet 23.3.

Some health-care workers have contracted the virus while working with infected patients. If a worker has cuts or other breaks in the skin which come in contact with infected blood, they can be infected. Cases have been reported in which health care workers have been stuck accidentally with needles used to draw blood from an infected patient. Health-care workers now use "universal precautions" which are a set of guidelines for handling all patients to reduce the risk of a worker's exposure to the virus. These precautions apply to dental workers as well.

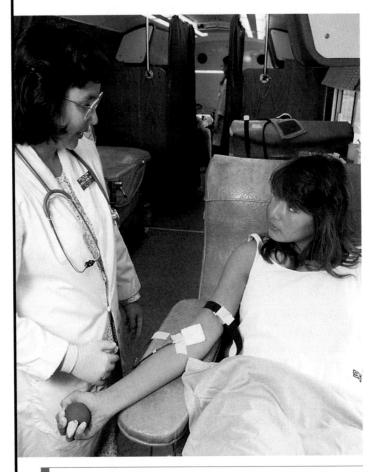

(FIGURE 23-8) **All blood that is donated in the United States is tested for HIV, and all blood that is infected is discarded.**

Before 1985, people contracted the virus while receiving blood transfusions or other blood components that were contaminated with HIV. People with hemophilia (a blood-clotting disorder) were particularly at risk. Because their blood does not clot, people with hemophilia may often need transfusions. The blood components in those transfusions often came from many different donors. Because the risk of transmission in blood was not known at the time, many people who received life-saving transfusions in hospitals later found out that they had contracted the virus. There are also reported cases of HIV transmission resulting from organ transplants and artificial inseminations from infected donors.

Since 1985, all blood donated in the United States is tested for HIV, and any HIV-infected blood is discarded. If you know in advance that you will need to replace lost blood, for example, after major surgery, you can donate your own blood for a later transfusion. All donated tissue is now tested for the virus before it is made available for transplant. Unfortunately, you should be aware that there are reported cases of HIV transmission where tissue samples were HIV negative at the time of donation or transplant.

You can see that transmission of the virus occurs in very specific ways. The list of all the ways you can't get HIV is much longer than the list of ways that you can get HIV. You can't get HIV by having what is called "casual contact" with someone who tests HIV positive. In other words, you can't get HIV by being around an infected person in ordinary day-to-day contact. There has not been a single case of transmission of the virus through casual contact with an infected person. Even family members and friends who live with people with AIDS and help care for them have not been infected with HIV through casual contact.

• • • TEACH continued

Debate the Issue
The Right to Know?

Debate this issue: Does a person have a right to know if his or her health-care provider is HIV-positive? Have students do some research, and then allow presentations, counterarguments, and questions from the audience. Remind students that in a debate, sometimes you are not arguing the side you believe in but rather trying to put forth the best possible arguments for an assigned position.

Class Discussion
Jobs and HIV

Ask students their opinions about mandatory testing of health-care workers for HIV. Should HIV-positive workers continue in their jobs?

Extension
Health-Care Precautions

Suggest that students visit a dental or medical office to find out what precautions its personnel take against transmission of HIV.

Q and A ✕✕✕✕✕✕✕

Q: Is it possible to get HIV from kissing?

A: You can't get HIV from a "simple" kiss, the kind in which people just put their lips together. If you could, a lot of people would already have been infected this way. There have been no reported cases of this happening. But it is theoretically possible for the virus to be transmitted through "French" kissing—deep, open-mouth kissing—since HIV has been found in the saliva of infected people. HIV researchers think it usually takes many viruses to cause infection, however, and saliva contains very few viruses. And here again, there have been no reported cases of HIV being transmitted in this way.

◆◆◆

Q: Isn't it true that you can get AIDS if you donate your blood?

A: No, absolutely not. This is something that many people are confused about. Blood-donation centers use a new, sterile needle with each donor. Don't let a myth like this keep you from donating blood to those who need it.

◆◆◆

Q: I've heard people say that you could get HIV if a mosquito bites a person with HIV and then bites you. Is that true?

A: No. If mosquitoes could transmit HIV, there would already be many cases of that happening by now. In fact, there

are no reported cases of HIV being transmitted by any kind of insect or other animal.

◆◆◆

Q: What should I do if I think I might be infected with HIV?

A: Talk to someone you trust about getting an HIV-antibody test—a parent, teacher, coach, school nurse, counselor, doctor, or someone at a health clinic. You can also call an AIDS hotline number to find out where you can go for HIV testing and counseling.

◆◆◆

Review • • • • •

1. *Name four body fluids that can contain enough HIV to infect another person.*

2. *Name the four behaviors that put you at risk for HIV infection.*

3. *Name at least five behaviors that don't put you at risk for HIV infection.*

4. ▪▪ **LIFE SKILLS: Using Community Resources** *Name two people you could talk to about whether a certain behavior could put you at risk for getting HIV.*

5. *Critical Thinking Could you get infected with HIV by wiping away the tears of a baby with HIV? Explain your answer.*

SECTION 23.2

📄 **Section Quiz 23.2**
Have students take Section Quiz 23.2.

📄 **Reteaching Worksheet 23.2**
Students who have difficulty with the material may complete Reteaching Worksheet 23.2.

Review Answers
1. blood, semen, vaginal secretions, breast milk
2. sharing equipment for injecting drugs, for tattooing, or for body piercing; vaginal, oral, or anal intercourse with an infected person
3. Students should list five of the safe behaviors listed in the table shown in Figure 23-7 or any others mentioned in class.
4. You could talk with someone you trust who is knowledgeable about AIDS, or you could call a local AIDS hotline.
5. It is extremely unlikely. Tears can contain HIV, but wiping tears does not allow for direct contact between the virus and the bloodstream or the mucous membranes.

ASSESS

Section Review
Have students answer the Section Review questions.

Alternative Assessment
The Nature of HIV and Infection

Have students write a brief narrative about how a person can and cannot contract AIDS.

Closure
Risk of Infection

Ask students to speculate about how a person who has never injected drugs and has only one sexual partner might become infected with HIV.

Making a Choice 23A

Assign the Couple's Discussion card. The card asks students to examine the issues of how to talk about protection against HIV infection and how a couple can express affection without having sexual intercourse.

Making a Choice 23B

Assign the Advertising card. The card asks students to discuss the issue of advertising contraceptives on television.

Section 23.3 *How to Protect Yourself From HIV*

Skills for delaying sexual intimacy are discussed in Chapter 17.

Objectives

- *Discuss abstinence as the most effective way to prevent the sexual transmission of HIV infection.*

- *Practice resisting pressure to be sexually intimate.*
  LIFE SKILLS: Resisting Pressure

- *Explain how to reduce your risk of HIV infection if you are sexually active.*
  LIFE SKILLS: Solving Problems

In this section you'll learn exactly how to reduce your risk of becoming infected with HIV. Protecting yourself requires knowledge about HIV and the skills to put your knowledge to use.

Abstinence

The only way to be 100 percent safe from getting HIV sexually is to avoid the three kinds of sexual intercourse that were discussed in Section 23.2. When a person decides against taking part in sexual intercourse, that person is said to be choosing abstinence.

Being abstinent doesn't mean that a person has no sexual feelings. Everyone has sexual feelings—they are a perfectly natural and pleasurable part of being human. It's just that people who choose abstinence decide not to act on their sexual feelings in ways that could endanger them. There are many ways to show affection for

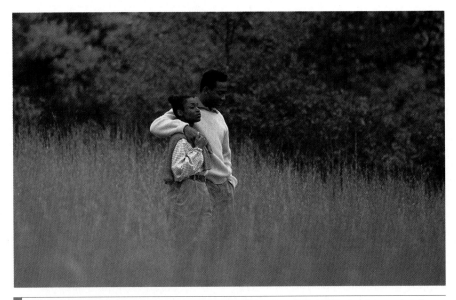

(FIGURE 23-9) **People who are sexually abstinent can show affection for each other in ways that don't put them at risk for getting HIV.**

Section 23.3 Lesson Plan

MOTIVATE

Journal 23E
On Delaying Sexual Intercourse

This may be done as a warm-up activity. In their Journal, have students write down the pros and cons of sexual abstinence at this point in their life. Are there more reasons not to have sex than to have sex? Have students include the benefits and consequences as they see them.

other people that don't put you at risk of getting HIV. The Life Skills activity below will prepare you to resist the pressure to do things you really don't want to do or take risks you really don't want to take.

One final note about abstinence: You will have a harder time sticking to your decision to remain abstinent if you drink or use other drugs. Any resolutions can be ignored or forgotten when a person is drunk or high.

Monogamy

The only sexual intercourse that is completely safe from HIV infection is sexual intercourse between two disease-free adults

SECTION 23.3

Life SKILLS

Have students do the Life Skills exercise in this section, answering the five questions on paper. After they have done the exercise, have students share their responses. Discuss which ones students think would be most effective and which ones they think would be least effective and why.

Life SKILLS: Resisting Pressure

Saying No . . . .

One of the ways to keep from doing things that put you at risk for HIV is to become resistant to pressure. See if you can think of a resistant response to each of the statements below.

1. "We'll just play around some. We can stop whenever you want."

2. "If you really loved me, you would make love to me."

3. "You must not have any sexual feelings at all."

4. "But I hate using condoms. It takes all the fun out of it."

5. "I'll pierce your ears and then you can pierce mine."

Although it helps to think of responses to certain statements, remember that you aren't required to have a reason. If you don't want to explain, all you have to say is "I don't want to." You don't have to debate what to do with your own body.

TEACH

Class Discussion
Social Pressures

Most HIV is transmitted sexually; abstaining from sex is the surest way to avoid this transmission. Ask students to comment on social pressures for or against delaying sexual activity. If there is peer pressure to have sex, is there a good way to cope with it? Stress the value of anticipating and avoiding

situations in which there is pressure to have sex, and remind students that no one has the right to force them to have sex. They can refuse verbally or simply leave the situation.

Reinforcement
Understanding the Dangers of Serial Monogamy

Many teens are serially monogamous. Have students differentiate clearly between lifelong monogamy and serial

monogamy. Stress that serial monogamy is *not* an effective preventive strategy. Ask: **Can you believe that a partner is telling the truth about their previous sexual encounters?** *[not necessarily]*

Reinforcement
Drugs and Alcohol and Judgment

Aside from the direct danger of infection from injecting drugs, there is

Life Skills
Worksheet 23B

Assign the Magazine
Advertisements Life Skills
Worksheet.

Section Review
Worksheet 23.3

To reinforce the concepts
presented in this section,
assign Section Review
Worksheet 23.3.

Section
Quiz 23.3

Have students take
Section Quiz 23.3.

Reteaching
Worksheet 23.3

Students who have diffi-
culty with the material
may complete Reteaching
Worksheet 23.3.

monogamy:
*when two people
have intercourse
with only each other
for their entire
lives.*

who practice safe behaviors and who are emotionally mature enough to be faithful to each other for their entire life. When two adults have sexual relations with each other over a lifetime, they are said to be practicing **monogamy.**

What if someone says that he or she has never had any form of sexual intercourse before. Can you assume that this person does not have HIV? The answer is a definite no. Unfortunately, people do not always tell the truth when it comes to sexual matters. For example, studies show that people have lied to their sexual partners about past encounters in order to have sexual intercourse.

All too often, a person has intercourse out of fear of losing a boyfriend or a girl-friend. It is difficult to resist this kind of pressure, especially when it comes from someone you love. However, if your partner truly loves you, that love would not be used to pressure you to do something that you don't feel ready for. A young woman named Amy Dolph has some advice to share about this problem. She says you should not allow another person, even someone you love, to determine when you will die. "Do you want to put your life in that other person's hands?" she asks. "Is that boy or girl worth dying for? I doubt it." Amy contracted HIV during high school from a boyfriend.

The risk of HIV infection is something that extends well beyond your teen years. During your adult life, you will be exposed to many of the same risks you may now encounter. Remember that when you become an adult, the risks are still there. During adulthood, the following two steps should

(FIGURE 23-10) **Group activities such as team sports can help teenagers form close relationships without the risk of sexual intimacy.**

● ● ● TEACH continued

another danger. Remind students that drugs and alcohol impair body functions and cloud judgment. Research shows that when people are using drugs and alcohol they are much more likely to engage in risky sexual practices.

Cooperative Learning
Protection From HIV

Have the class prepare a bulletin board describing the ways people can protect themselves from HIV. They might divide the bulletin board in half—one half showing decisions they personally can make to protect themselves, and the other half showing steps society can take.

Extension
HIV in Your Community

Have students create a newsletter called AIDS Update. The newsletter could include investigative stories, answers to frequently asked questions, editorials, the latest statistics concerning teens, AIDS-education articles, and news briefs on the latest medical discoveries about HIV.

be taken to reduce your lifelong risk of HIV infection:

1. **Practice Monogamy** The fewer sex partners a person has, the less likely he or she is to have intercourse with someone who is HIV-positive. But remember that it takes only one HIV-infected partner to infect a person with the virus.

2. **Use Latex Condoms During Intercourse** Sex partners must use latex condoms to reduce their risk of HIV infection. Condoms are not 100 percent effective in preventing the spread of HIV, but when used properly they can make sexual intercourse less risky. To be effective in protecting against HIV, a condom must be made of latex (a kind of rubber). No other material provides the same degree of protection in preventing the spread of the virus from one partner to the other. If a condom is made of latex, it will say it on the package.

It is important to remember that a condom must be used the whole time—from start to finish—during intercourse. Condoms can not be reused. A new condom must be used each time a person has intercourse. If the outside surface of a condom touches the tip of the penis, semen can be deposited there. This condom should be discarded because it no longer provides protection against HIV or pregnancy.

Don't Inject Drugs

If you haven't used injected drugs, don't start. If you do use them, seek treatment to help you quit. See Chapter 15 for information about drug-treatment programs.

Sharing needles to inject drugs is one of the major causes of HIV transmission. Even when all equipment is cleaned with bleach-and-water solution before and after each use, the possibility for infection still exists.

What If You've Already Engaged in Risky Behavior?

What if you haven't followed these guidelines? Should you just forget about it because it's already too late? No, absolutely not. You haven't necessarily been infected, even if you know you've engaged in risky behavior with an HIV-infected person.

If you think there is a chance you've been infected, get an HIV-antibody test immediately. Protect yourself, and protect other people.

Review

1. *What is the best way to prevent the transmission of HIV through intercourse?*

2. **LIFE SKILLS: Resisting Pressure** *If your friend wanted the two of you to give each other tattoos, what would you do or say to protect yourself against the possibility of HIV infection?*

3. **LIFE SKILLS: Solving Problems** *If you have decided to have intercourse, how could you reduce your risk of becoming infected with HIV?*

4. **Critical Thinking** *Explain the reasoning behind this statement about the transmission of HIV: "When you have intercourse with someone, you're also having intercourse with everyone that person has ever had intercourse with."*

Review Answers
1. Practicing abstinence and participating in sexual activity only within a lifelong monogamous relationship with an uninfected person are the two best means of avoiding the transmission of HIV through intercourse.
2. Sample response: I would tell my friend why I feel uncomfortable about us giving each other tattoos and why I will only get a tattoo at a place where I know that the equipment is correctly sterilized.
3. Sample response: I could practice monogamy with a person who is not infected and use latex condoms every time I have intercourse.
4. Because HIV is transmitted sexually, every previous partner of a person may have given him or her the virus. You can become infected, too.

ASSESS

Section Review
Have students answer the Section Review questions.

Alternative Assessment
Advice About HIV

Have students write a letter to a younger teen that explains how to avoid HIV. The letter should include all types of risky behavior and should give advice on what to do if a person thinks he or she may be infected.

Closure
Feelings About Sexual Abstinence

Ask students if the information in this section has altered their attitude about sexual abstinence in any way. Tell them that being even more strongly convinced that abstinence is best for teens can be considered a change. Then have students summarize why condoms do not provide complete protection against HIV infection and why a person has to be cautious about all situations in which needles are shared, even legal ones.

Section 23.4
HIV Infection and Society

Objectives

- *Describe medical treatments available for HIV infection.*

- *Name at least two actions you can take to help people with HIV infection.*

HIV doesn't just affect individuals. It affects society. Millions of dollars are being spent searching for new treatments for HIV infection, even as discrimination against people with HIV continues.

(FIGURE 23-11) **AIDS activists have pressured government agencies to increase spending on HIV research and on programs to help those with the disease. Elizabeth Glaser worked tirelessly for this cause until her death from AIDS in December 1994. She contracted the disease from a transfusion during the birth of her last child.**

But a society is made up of individuals. Each individual can do his or her part to eliminate the disease and care for the people affected by it.

Medical Advances

Recent medical advances have made it possible to ease the symptoms of HIV infection and perhaps delay the onset of illness. Researchers discovered that combinations of drugs such as AZT (zidovudine), ddI (dideoxyinosine), and nevirapine show promise in postponing symptoms in people who have tested HIV-positive but are not yet sick. AZT, ddI and other similar drugs slow down the rate at which the virus reproduces inside the body. Combinations of drugs are generally used because the virus has the ability to adapt and change rapidly in response to a single drug.

Because of the development of drugs and other treatments, HIV infection is now considered to be a chronic condition that can be managed for many years. Researchers continue to search for a cure for HIV infection. They also hope to develop a vaccine to prevent infection in the first place. But because the virus can change quickly, developing a vaccine is very difficult; it may take many years before the attempts are successful. In the meantime, your first line of defense against HIV is you.

Section 23.4 Lesson Plan

MOTIVATE

Journal 23F
A Roommate With HIV

Pose the following situation to students, and have them write their response in their Journal: You are attending a convention or athletic event away from home. As soon as you meet your assigned roommate, he or she tells you, "I am infected with HIV." How would you feel about the revelation? Would it change your expectations about the person? about sharing a room? Would it matter to you how the person contracted HIV? Have students explain their answer.

TEACH

Writing
Questions About AIDS

Students may have questions that they would like to ask an AIDS patient.

Have each student make a list of questions. The list might include questions such as the following: Do you know how you got AIDS? What kind of help do you need? Are you sad often? Are your family and friends supportive? As a class, share the questions and make a list of the top five or ten questions. Contact a local AIDS organization, and ask if it is possible to have someone answer the questions either by letter or through a class visit.

(FIGURE 23-12) Dawn Marcel was infected with HIV when she was a senior in high school. She is now a speaker for an AIDS-education program in San Francisco. "I've been on AZT for three years," Dawn said. "I take it for one month, then go off it for one month because it destroys my liver. I don't look sick. I'm chubby, or I think I'm chubby. People don't imagine that I could be sick, but you can't tell by looking at someone."

Life Skills Worksheet 23C

Assign the Teenagers and Sex Life Skills Worksheet.

Ethical Issues in Health Worksheet

Have students read this Unit 6 feature on pages 534–535. Then have them complete its companion worksheet.

Section Review Worksheet 23.4

To reinforce the concepts presented in this section, assign Section Review Worksheet 23.4.

Section Quiz 23.4

Have students take Section Quiz 23.4.

Reteaching Worksheet 23.4

Students who have difficulty with the material may complete Reteaching Worksheet 23.4.

Teens and Risk

Teens have special needs when it comes to HIV prevention. It is normal for teens to experiment and be eager to try new things. Much of this experimentation is a healthy part of the maturation process. But studies show that teens often engage in activities that put them at great risk. When it comes to HIV, teens who have intercourse or experiment with injected drugs are risking their lives and the lives of their friends. A study done in 1995 indicates that 53.1 percent of high school students have engaged in sexual intercourse. Among sexually active high school students, 45.6 percent had not used a condom the last time they had intercourse. Fortunately, the study shows much smaller numbers of students are injecting drugs. But it should be obvious that teens are ignoring tremendous risks by engaging in these activities.

In Chapter 17, you learned that part of growing up means accepting responsibility for your actions. Plan now to protect yourself as well as those you care about by taking what you have learned in this chapter seriously. If you have placed yourself at risk from intercourse or drugs, get tested. Resolve to change your life to ensure that you will be able to keep on living.

Living With HIV Infection

People often avoid and isolate people who have HIV infection. When the people in Ryan White's town found out he had AIDS, for example, they made life rough for him. "Lots of kids in school flattened themselves against walls when I walked by," Ryan said. "When I went to restaurants, people would get up and leave. Even in church, no one would shake my hand."

Michael's friend Bryan was afraid that he would lose his friends if people found out that his brother had HIV. Bryan knew only too well that some people think they can

Review Answers

1. A combination of AZT (zidovudine), ddI (dideoxyinosine), and nevirapine shows great promise in postponing symptoms in people who are HIV-positive.

2. Teens often engage in activities, such as unprotected sexual intercourse, that put them at great risk.

3. Because the virus that causes AIDS can change quickly, developing a vaccine is very difficult.

4. Sample response: HIV-positive people fear discrimination and the loss of their job.

5. Sample response: I could help them with things like shopping or housecleaning. I could be friendly and not act like I don't want to be around them.

(FIGURE 23-13) **Earvin "Magic" Johnson, former Los Angeles Lakers basketball star, discovered in 1991 that he was HIV-positive.**

(FIGURE 23-14) **You can help people with HIV infection by doing volunteer work for AIDS organizations. These teens are working at an AIDS education center in Massachusetts.**

become infected with HIV just by being around someone who is HIV positive. Even though this is not true, people with HIV infection may face discrimination at work, at school, and in their personal relationships. They are forced to face this discrimination at the same time that they are fighting a deadly disease.

Taking Positive Action Against HIV

You have already learned what you can do to protect yourself against HIV infection. But what else can you do to stop the spread of this disease?

You can educate others. If someone says something that is not true about HIV, you can give him or her the correct information. You can be a tremendous help to people with HIV infection by helping others overcome their prejudices based on misinformation.

You can treat people with HIV infection as you would treat any person who has a life-threatening illness—or anyone else, for that matter—with respect, compassion, and acceptance.

Review

1. Describe medical treatments that may delay the onset of HIV symptoms.

2. Why are teens at greater risk for HIV infection than adults?

3. Why has it been difficult to develop a vaccine for AIDS?

4. **Critical Thinking** Why do many people with HIV infection choose not to tell their fellow students or co-workers about their HIV test results?

5. **Critical Thinking** What are some ways you could help people with AIDS?

• • • TEACH continued

work is available that would be suitable for teens. Encourage students to discuss with their family the possibility of doing volunteer work.

ASSESS

Section Review

Have students answer the Section Review questions.

Alternative Assessment

Have students write a public service announcement they think will persuade teenagers to treat people with HIV as they would want to be treated if they contracted HIV.

Closure

Ask students to explain why teens have special needs when it comes to HIV prevention.

CHAPTER
23

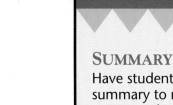

Summary

- AIDS is a sexually transmitted disease that is caused by a virus.

- The virus that causes AIDS is called HIV (human immunodeficiency virus).

- AIDS is the last phase of HIV infection.

- Even though an HIV-infected person appears healthy, he or she can still transmit the virus to another person.

- The four behaviors that put a person at risk for getting HIV are: 1) sharing equipment for injecting drugs, tattoo-ing, or ear piercing with an infected person; 2) having anal intercourse with an infected person; 3) having oral intercourse with an infected person; and 4) having vaginal inter-course with an infected person.

- The behaviors that are most effective in preventing HIV infection are absti-nence from sexual intercourse and abstaining from drugs.

- Properly using latex condoms reduces the risk of sexual transmission of HIV.

- People with HIV infection must strug-gle with discrimination at the same time they are fighting a deadly dis-ease. They do not want to be thought of as passive "victims."

Vocabulary

AIDS a disease, caused by a virus, that harms a person's immune system; AIDS is classified as a sexually transmitted dis-ease, but it can also be spread in other ways, such as through sharing infected equipment for injecting drugs, tattoing, or ear piercing. AIDS is the last phase of HIV infection.

HIV (human immunodeficiency virus) the virus that causes AIDS; also called the "AIDS virus."

mucous membranes moist, pink tis-sues of the body; HIV can enter the body through the mucous membranes of the mouth, vagina, anus, and rectum, and the opening at the tip of the penis.

monogamy when two people have sex with only each other for their entire lives.

latex condom a covering for the penis that helps protect both partners from sexually transmitted diseases and also helps to prevent pregnancy.

SUMMARY
Have students read the summary to reinforce the concepts they learned in Chapter 23.

VOCABULARY
Have students write a paragraph about AIDS that uses the vocabulary words correctly.

EXTENSION
Have students make AIDS awareness posters to be displayed in the school. The posters could con-cern myths about AIDS, steps that can be taken to prevent HIV infection, or volunteer opportunities for students to help peo-ple with AIDS.

Chapter Review

CHAPTER REVIEW

Concept Review

1. b	**4.** d
2. a	**5.** a
3. a	**6.** c

Expressing Your Views

Sample responses:

1. It is extremely risky to use a needle that has not been sterilized. If my friend uses an unsterilized needle to pierce my ears and that needle was used to pierce the ears of an HIV-positive person, I could become infected with HIV.

2. Discourage your friend from having sexual intercourse because of the risk of HIV infection, among other reasons. Practicing safer sex does not eliminate the risk of HIV infection. A person who is under the influence of drugs is less likely to practice safe sex.

3. Some people are prejudiced against people who are HIV-positive because they do not fully understand how HIV can be transmitted. They may believe that they could become infected by touching or working near the infected person.

Life Skills Check

Sample responses:

1. She could look in the phone book under AIDS and call an organization that deals with AIDS. She could search the Internet

Concept Review . . . .

1. When a person has HIV infection, it means that he or she
 a. has AIDS.
 b. can infect other people with HIV.
 c. has Kaposi's sarcoma.
 d. has used injected drugs.

2. A person can find out if he or she has been infected with HIV by
 a. getting an HIV-antibody test.
 b. calling the AIDS hotline.
 c. asking all previous sexual partners if they are HIV-positive.
 d. talking with a school counselor.

3. Which of the following behaviors can put a person at risk for HIV infection?
 a. sharing needles to inject steroids with an HIV-infected person
 b. shaking hands with an HIV-infected person
 c. sharing an elevator with an HIV infected person
 d. all of the above

4. Which of the following types of sexual intercourse with an HIV-infected person is risky for HIV infection?
 a. vaginal intercourse
 b. oral intercourse
 c. anal intercourse
 d. all of the above

5. Which of the following behaviors provides the best protection against HIV infection?
 a. practicing abstinence from sexual intercourse
 b. using condoms
 c. showering every day
 d. practicing French kissing

6. Which of the following actions would help people with HIV infection?
 a. raising money for agencies that help people with HIV infection
 b. treating people with HIV infection no differently from anyone else who had a life-threatening illness
 c. both of the above

Expressing Your Views . . . .

1. You are planning to get your ears pierced. One of your friends offers to pierce your ears for free. What problems could develop in accepting your friend's offer?

2. At a party your best friend gets drunk and confides to you that he or

she is going to "do it" tonight. What do you think you should do?

3. Why do you think some people are prejudiced against people who have HIV infection?

for information about HIV and AIDS.

2. I would tell her that condoms can help prevent HIV infection, but they are not 100 percent effective. Abstinence and sexual activity with only one, uninfected partner are the most effective ways to prevent HIV infection.

Life Skills Check . . . . . .

1. Using Community Resources
Debra needs to find out if something that she is doing puts her at risk for HIV infection. She feels that she cannot talk to her parents or any of her teachers or counselors. In fact, she feels that she cannot talk to anyone who knows about this. How might Debra get the information she needs?

2. Resisting Pressure
You are being pressured by your boyfriend or girlfriend to have sexual intercourse. In talking about this situation with a friend, she tells you that you have nothing to worry about if you use a condom. How would you respond to this statement?

Projects . . . .

1. Design a survey to find out how much other students in your school know about HIV infection. Think of five questions to ask in your survey, and work in a group of 3-4 students to collect responses from the whole student body. Tabulate your results and present your data and conclusions to your class.

2. Work with a group of students to come up with a plan to inform the students in your school about HIV prevention. Present your group plan to the principal.

3. Have a health fair at your school in which a variety of health topics are introduced, including HIV infection.

Plan for Action . . . .

HIV infection is a communicable disease that can be prevented. Devise a plan to protect yourself from getting infected with HIV.

Projects
Have students plan and carry out the projects for HIV infection and AIDS.

Plan for Action
Before students devise their plans, hold a class discussion to brainstorm suggestions that could help teenagers
- resist peer pressure to engage in risk behaviors
- avoid situations in which risk behaviors are likely
- promote healthy sexuality without promoting pre-marital sex

ASSESSMENT OPTIONS

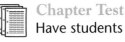
Chapter Test
Have students take the Chapter 23 Test.

Alternative Assessment
Have students do the Alternative Assessment activity for Chapter 23.

Test Generator
The Test Generator contains additional assessment items for this chapter.

CHAPTER

24

Noninfectious Diseases and Disorders

SECTION	TITLE/OBJECTIVES	Personal Health Inventory	Journal	Check Up	Life Skills	Life Skills Worksheets	Media Message or Ethical Issues Worksheet	What Would You Do?
		PERSONAL INVENTORY			LIFE SKILLS DEVELOPMENT			
24.1 *pp. 509–517*	**HEREDITARY AND CONGENITAL DISEASES** • Define noninfectious disease. • Distinguish between hereditary and congenital diseases. • List three factors that may cause congenital disease.	Ch. 24	24A					
24.2 *pp. 518–520*	**AUTOIMMUNE DISEASES** • List three common autoimmune diseases. • Explain the difference between autoimmune disease and AIDS.		24B					
24.3 *pp. 521–530*	**DEGENERATIVE DISEASES** • Describe what happens to arteries during the development of atherosclerosis. • Explain the relationship between atherosclerosis and high blood pressure. • List three kinds of cancer to which tobacco use contributes. ▪▪ Name four things you can do to reduce your risk of cardiovascular disease. ▪▪ Name two things you can do to reduce your risk of getting cancer.		24C 24D		p. 528	24A 24B 24C 24D		

KEY: ▪▪ Denotes Life Skill Objective

Text references denoted by page number.

Supplement references denoted by chapter or item numbers.

LINKING RESOURCES

Making a Choice Cards	Parent Discussion Guide	Health Talk Audio Program	Teaching Transparencies and Directory	Section Review Worksheets	Section Quizzes	Reteaching Worksheets	Section Reviews
INTERACTION		**OTHER RESOURCES**		**SECTION REVIEW AND ASSESSMENT**			
			24A	24.1	24.1	24.1	p. 517
				24.2	24.2	24.2	p. 520
24A 24B			24B 24C BSH6 BSH7	24.3	24.3	24.3	p. 530

For information about the heart and the circulatory system, see pages 668–670 in the Body Systems Handbook.

KEY FACTS

- Noninfectious diseases are diseases that are not passed from one organism to another.
- Hereditary diseases are diseases that are caused by defective genes inherited from one or both parents.
- Congenital diseases are diseases that are present at birth but are not hereditary. Some, such as fetal alcohol syndrome, are completely avoidable.
- Autoimmune diseases occur when a person's immune system attacks and damages an organ in his or her own body.
- Degenerative diseases result from gradual damage to an organ over time.
- Cardiovascular diseases, such as heart attack, stroke, atherosclerosis, and high blood pressure, result from progressive damage to the heart and blood vessels.
- Eating a healthful diet, exercising regularly, avoiding tobacco, and limiting alcohol consumption can greatly reduce the risk of developing cardiovascular disease or cancer.

CHAPTER REVIEW AND ASSESSMENT

TEXT

Chapter Review pp. 532–533

SUPPLEMENTS

Chapter Test 24

Alternative Assessment 24

Test Generator Chapter 24

Noninfectious Diseases and Disorders

◆ ◆ ◆ ◆

Section 24.1 Hereditary and Congenital Diseases

Section 24.2 Autoimmune Diseases

Section 24.3 Degenerative Diseases

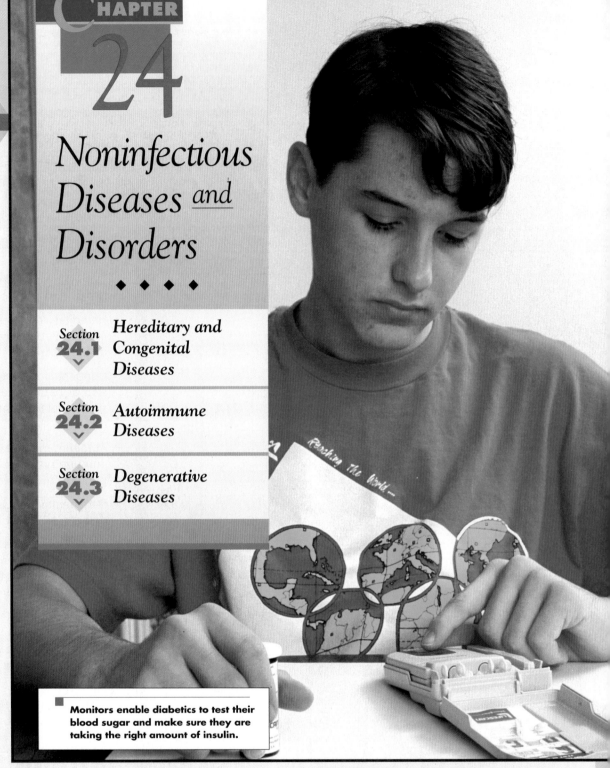

Monitors enable diabetics to test their blood sugar and make sure they are taking the right amount of insulin.

GETTING STARTED

Using the Chapter Photograph

Ask students how the person in the picture is dealing with his illness. Discuss how mainstreaming can help both the student with a health problem and the others in the class.

Question Box

Have students write out any questions they have about noninfectious diseases and disorders and put them in the Question Box.

Sensitivity *ALERT*

Discussion of diseases may make students uncomfortable. Some students or someone close to them may have one of the noninfectious diseases. They might be interested in finding out more about the disease, or they might be embarrassed and want to avoid the subject. Prepare the class to be respectful of privacy and receptive and sensitive to other people's feelings.

Carrier

MYTHS & MISCONCEPTIONS

- **For a child to inherit a disease like cystic fibrosis, one of the parents must have the disease.** A parent can be a carrier (a person who has one gene for a hereditary disease) and not have the disease. If both parents are carriers, it is possible for the child to inherit one defective gene from each parent and develop the disease even though neither parent has cystic fibrosis.

- **If there is heart disease in your family, there's nothing you can do to prevent developing it.** To a great extent, heart disease can be avoided by eating a balanced diet that is low in fat and by getting plenty of exercise.

- **You should avoid being around people with cancer so you won't catch it from them.** Cancer is not caused by an infectious agent; it cannot be passed from one person to another.

Shawn's pretty lucky; he had ear infections and a case of the chickenpox when he was very young, but during the last few years the only disease he's had to worry about has been an occasional cold. Some of the people he knows, and even some people in his own family, have had much more serious illnesses. His mother has high blood pressure. His cousin has sickle cell anemia. And two years ago, his grandfather died of lung cancer. Shawn has some questions about these diseases.

For example, is there any need to worry about being around people who have these diseases? Are any of them contagious? Could he inherit high blood pressure from his mother, or lung cancer from his grandfather? Is there anything he can do to avoid getting these diseases?

Personal Health Inventory

Have students complete the Personal Health Inventory for this chapter.

Section 24.1 — Hereditary and Congenital Diseases

Objectives

- Define noninfectious disease.
- Distinguish between hereditary and congenital diseases.
- List three factors that may cause congenital disease.

High blood pressure, sickle cell anemia, and cancer are all examples of **noninfectious diseases.** A disease is a condition that prevents your body from functioning normally. When a disease is noninfectious, it means that you can't catch it from viruses or microorganisms that pass from another person or other organism. A cold is an infectious disease. You can ''catch'' a cold from your best friend, when viruses pass from your friend's body to yours from casual contact. You can't catch sickle cell anemia or cancer because these diseases are not spread by viruses or microorganisms.

There are many different noninfectious diseases. Some people are born with a disease such as sickle cell anemia or cystic fibrosis and are affected by the disease throughout their life. Other noninfectious diseases, like cancer and heart disease, usually show up later in life. When you say that a person was ''born with'' a certain disease, you are referring to either a hereditary or a congenital disease.

Hereditary Diseases

A **hereditary disease** is a disease caused by defective genetic information passed from one or both parents to a child. In order to understand how this happens, it is important

REMINDER

A microorganism is a living thing that can be seen only under a microscope.

noninfectious disease:

a disease that a person cannot catch from another person or any other organism.

hereditary disease:

a disease caused by defective genes inherited by a child from one or both parents.

Infectious Disease D. Florence

Section 24.1 Lesson Plan

MOTIVATE

Journal 24A
Concern About Diseases

This may be done as a warm-up activity. Have students record in their Journal their reactions to Shawn's concerns about the diseases of those around him. Have students predict what their reactions would be in a similar situation. Then have students suggest resources Shawn could use to answer his questions.

Cooperative Learning
Infectious Versus Noninfectious Diseases

Have students form small groups to discuss the difference between infectious and noninfectious diseases. Have them list ways to avoid getting both kinds of diseases.

TEACH

Class Discussion
Inheriting a Disease

Ask: **How can a disease be inherited?** *[If a gene inherited from one parent has incorrect information, it can cause a hereditary disease.]* **What is a gene?** *[A gene is a short segment of the DNA molecule that serves as a code for a particular bit of genetic information. It provides a person with a characteristic he or she*

509

Background

Adaptive Value of the Sickle Cell Gene

People who carry one gene for the sickle cell trait are less susceptible to malaria, a mosquito-borne disease found in many areas of the world. The gene is relatively rare. It occurs most frequently in people whose genetic origins are from western Africa, the Middle East, or the Mediterranean—all areas with a history of a high incidence of malaria. The value of a single gene in protecting against malaria seems to outweigh any disadvantage the disease presents.

chromosomes:

cell structures that carry hereditary information.

gene:

a short segment of a DNA molecule that serves as a code for a particular bit of hereditary information.

to know something about heredity. Many of your characteristics, such as the way you look and certain talents you have, were passed on to you from your parents. This kind of information is carried from your parents to you in the form of tiny structures within the body's cells known as **chromosomes**. Chromosomes contain the hereditary material deoxyribonucleic acid, better known as DNA.

Each chromosome is made up of thousands of genes. A **gene**, which serves as a code for a particular bit of inherited information, is a short segment of the DNA in a chromosome. The genes that you inherited from your parents determined many of your characteristics; for example, whether you have blue, green, or brown eyes. Tens of thousands of genes determine the inherited characteristics of an individual. Genes don't always carry correct information,

however. If one single gene does have incorrect information, it can cause a hereditary disease.

Sickle Cell Anemia One hereditary disease that occurs when genes carry incorrect instructions is sickle cell anemia, the illness Shawn's cousin Nelson has. The genes that carry incorrect information in Nelson's body affect the construction of a protein called hemoglobin. This protein, which is found inside the body's red blood cells, carries oxygen from the lungs to the other tissues in the body.

Because the hemoglobin inside Nelson's red blood cells isn't constructed correctly, the hemoglobin forms long, stiff chains. This causes the red blood cells—normally smooth, round disks—to sickle, or become spiky, such as those that are shown in Figure 24-2.

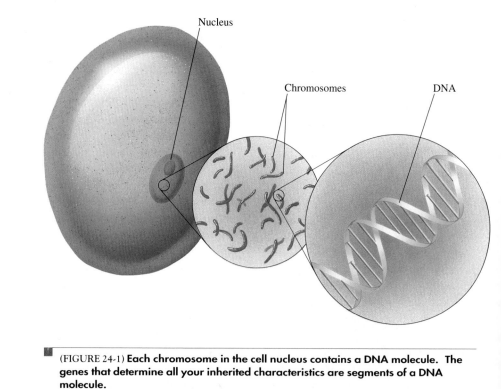

Nucleus

Chromosomes

DNA

(FIGURE 24-1) **Each chromosome in the cell nucleus contains a DNA molecule. The genes that determine all your inherited characteristics are segments of a DNA molecule.**

• • • TEACH continued

receives from a parent.] **What is sickle cell anemia?** *[Sickle cell anemia is a hereditary disease that causes the hemoglobin in the red blood cells to be sickle shaped rather than disk shaped. This causes the red blood cells to become stuck inside the smallest blood vessels. This in turn causes intense pain and damage to the vital organs.]* **From which parent does a child inherit sickle cell anemia?** *[For a child to*

inherit sickle cell anemia, he or she has to inherit a gene for the disease from each parent.]

Teaching Transparency 24A
Cell Nucleus, Chromosomes, and DNA

Show the transparency of Figure 24-1. Point out to students that each chromosome contains thousands of DNA sequences. Some of these sequences are genes, most of which occupy a specific place on a chromosome. Some DNA sequences appear to have no

funtion and are sometimes referred to as junk DNA. Some scientists think that this is a misnomer and that in the future the purpose of these sequences will be discovered.

Reinforcement
Genes Specific to Geographic Locations

Remind students that 1 in 10 African Americans carries one gene for sickle cell anemia and that 1 in 20 white Americans carries one gene for cystic fibrosis. People of eastern European

(FIGURE 24-2) **The red blood cells of a person who has sickle cell anemia (left) become long, spiky, and sickled. Note how different they look from normal red blood cells (right).**

Anything that reduces oxygen in Nelson's body, such as stress, respiratory disease, or strenuous exercise, can cause a sickle cell crisis. During the crisis, a high percentage of red blood cells sickle. Spiky, sickled red blood cells rupture easily and tend to stick inside the smallest blood vessels, the tiny capillaries. Intense pain and damage to vital organs may result.

For a person to have sickle cell anemia, he or she must inherit two copies of the sickle cell gene, one from each parent. People who have inherited only one sickle cell gene from one parent are usually quite healthy. Almost 10 percent of African-American people carry the gene for sickle cell anemia.

Cystic Fibrosis The most common serious inherited disease among white Americans is cystic fibrosis. Cystic fibrosis is a

hereditary disease that results in the secretion of very thick mucus in the lungs and digestive tract.

Unlike normal mucus, which is regularly cleared from the lungs, the thick mucus produced by people with cystic fibrosis builds up and blocks small air passages inside the lungs. This makes breathing difficult and increases the likelihood of lung infections. Mucus in the digestive tract interferes with the action of digestive enzymes. Because of this, people with cystic fibrosis have difficulty getting adequate nourishment from food.

The symptoms of cystic fibrosis can be treated with physical therapy and drugs that loosen mucus in the lungs. These drugs may be delivered to the lungs by using a vaporizer, like the one shown in Figure 24-3. Unfortunately, this treatment provides only temporary relief. Cystic fibrosis is a very serious, and eventually fatal, disease.

Background
Cystic Fibrosis

Cystic fibrosis is most common among people of European background, who have an occurrence rate of about 1 out of 1,600. Like sickle cell disease, cystic fibrosis occurs only when a person inherits two genes for the disease. There is evidence that people with one gene (carriers) have a greater resistance to tuberculosis than non-carriers do. From the 1700s to the early 1900s, tuberculosis epidemics were common in Europe. Some experts believe that a cystic fibrosis carrier would have been more likely to survive tuberculosis than a non-carrier.

---

ancestry are more likely to have a gene for Tay-Sachs disease. At one time, these genes may have had a useful function.

Reinforcement
Cystic Fibrosis

Remind students that in cystic fibrosis an unusually thick and sticky mucus interferes with the normal functioning of the lungs and the digestive system. It also blocks sweat glands, making people with the disease unusually sensitive to heat. The recent discovery of the

gene locus for the disease may lead to the development of a gene transfer therapy that could cure the disease.

Class Discussion
Coping With Diabetes

After reading the section on Type II diabetes on page 512, discuss with students its symptoms and the lifestyle changes that a person who is diagnosed with the disease must make. **Ask: What lifestyle changes do people diagnosed with diabetes have to make?** [Those with Type II diabetes have

to adhere to a strict, balanced diet and exercise. People with Type I diabetes must take daily injections of insulin.]

Case Study
Allergies

After reading the section on allergies on page 513, have students put together a case study of a person with allergies. They should describe the difficulties the person has in pinpointing the substances causing the allergies.

• • • TEACH continues on p. 514

Background

Human Genome Project

In 1990, the Human Genome Project was launched. The goal of this effort is to map all the genes in the human body. (It is estimated that there are about 100,000 genes and that the project will take 20 years.) This knowledge will have a profound effect on how genetic diseases are treated. Researchers already are working on ways to cure inherited diseases for which the defective gene is known. Animal experiments have shown that it is possible to implant genetically engineered cells into a mammal's body. This is a first step toward finding effective treatments. Many medical scientists predict that this project will make gene transfer therapy an important medical treatment in the twenty-first century.

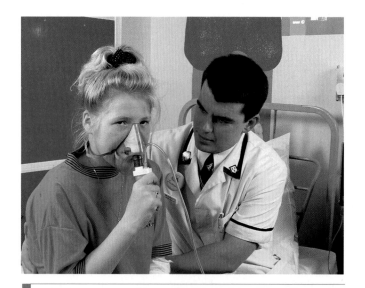

(FIGURE 24-3) **Cystic fibrosis causes mucus to build up and block air passages in the lungs. Vaporizers that deliver special medications to clear these air passages can help people with this disease breathe more easily.**

Like sickle cell anemia, cystic fibrosis strikes only those who have inherited two cystic fibrosis genes—one from each parent. About one in twenty white Americans carries one gene for cystic fibrosis.

Tay-Sachs Disease Tay-Sachs disease is a condition caused by a defective gene that causes fat to accumulate in the brain, destroying normal brain tissue. Although babies born with Tay-Sachs seem normal at first, by the time they are a few months old, symptoms begin to appear. These symptoms include seizures, mental retardation, and blindness. Death generally occurs by the age of three or four.

The gene that causes Tay-Sachs disease is most common in families of eastern European origin.

Muscular Dystrophy Muscular dystrophy refers to several genetic diseases that cause muscles to weaken and degenerate. One of the more common forms, Duchenne muscular dystrophy, affects only boys.

Children with this form of muscular dystrophy develop normally at first, but between the ages of two and ten, they become clumsy and uncoordinated as their muscles begin to weaken. As the disease progresses, they have difficulty standing and they fall frequently. By their teens, people with muscular dystrophy must use a wheelchair. The disease is fatal when it progresses to the point that the muscles that control breathing fail. This usually occurs when patients reach their early twenties.

There is currently no cure for muscular dystrophy. However, the gene that is responsible for Duchenne muscular dystrophy has been identified. Researchers hope that better understanding the functioning of the gene will lead to an effective treatment for this disease.

Type II Diabetes Diabetes is a disease that results when a hormone called insulin is lacking in, or is not used properly by, the body. Hormones are chemicals produced in the body to regulate body functions. Insulin helps blood sugar enter the body's cells. Blood sugar is the body's major source of energy, even for people who don't eat many sweets. Starchy foods like potatoes contain sugars that are broken down and used for energy. But when insulin is lacking or cannot be used properly, as is the case in people with diabetes, the body's cells are unable to use the sugar that is in the blood.

When sugar cannot enter a person's cells to provide energy, the cells begin to use fats and proteins for energy. Breaking down large amounts of fats and proteins produces dangerous levels of toxic waste products. For this reason, diabetes that is not treated is often fatal.

The most common form of diabetes, called Type II diabetes, usually appears in middle age. People with Type II diabetes do produce insulin; however, their bodies cannot use it properly. There is evidence that Type II diabetes is hereditary. Studies have shown that if one identical twin has Type II diabetes, there is a 100-percent chance that the other twin will have the disease. Other factors that may contribute to the onset of Type II diabetes include age and obesity. Type II diabetes can sometimes be controlled by a strict, healthy diet (most Type II diabetics are obese) and exercise. Drug therapy such as insulin is often needed as well.

Type I diabetes is a more serious form of the disease that usually begins during childhood. Only about 10 percent of diabetics have Type I diabetes. Unlike Type II diabetes, Type I diabetes does not appear to be an inherited illness. People with Type I diabetes must take daily injections of insulin to replace this substance, which is missing from their body. You'll learn more about Type I diabetes in the next section.

Allergies Allergies affect about one of every seven people in the United States—more than 35 million Americans. An allergy is the overreaction of a person's immune system to a common substance—such as dust, pollen, certain foods, mold spores, or animals—that has no effect on nonallergic people. A person can inherit a tendency to have allergies.

Allergic reactions take many forms. When an inhaled substance triggers an allergic attack, the person may experience a stuffy nose, red itchy eyes, and sinus pain. Allergies to foods or certain drugs sometimes cause hives, itchy welts, or bumps to develop on the skin.

Although allergies are generally not life-threatening, they do make life miserable. If you have an allergy, the best way to treat it is to avoid the thing that you're allergic to. For example, if you are allergic to cat dander and saliva, as many people are, you'd be wise to choose another kind of pet.

(FIGURE 24-4) **(Left)** A person who is allergic to a substance that is inhaled may experience red eyes, a stuffy nose, and sinus pain. **(Right)** An allergy to a food or drug can cause hives or welts to develop on the skin.

SECTION 24.1

Background
Diet and Type II Diabetes
Although diabetes was rare among Native Americans before the 1940s, they now have a higher incidence of Type II diabetes than any other ethnic group in the United States. By the 1970s, 50 percent of the Pima people in southern Arizona over the age of 35 were diagnosed with Type II diabetes. While it is now known that the Pima people have a genetic predisposition to Type II diabetes, researchers are also investigating the role of diet in the development of this disease. The Phoenix Indian Hospital did studies comparing a modern American diet that is high in fats and sugars with a turn-of-the-century Pima diet, which contains higher-than-average levels of a starch called amylose. Many desert foods are high in amylose; these foods slow down carbohydrate digestion and lower insulin and blood sugar levels after meals. Preliminary studies suggest that Pima people who return to their tribe's traditional diet experience a reduction of blood-sugar levels.

(FIGURE 24-5) **Specially prescribed inhalers can prevent asthma attacks or lessen their severity.**

these types of allergic reactions are not really serious. However, about 15 million people suffer from asthma, which is a very serious disease that is often a form of allergic reaction.

Take a deep breath. The air you just inhaled travels through a series of air passages that branch into smaller and smaller tubes inside your lungs. These tubes are encircled by small muscles that adjust the width of the tubes.

Changing the diameter of the tubes is one of the ways in which your body adapts to allow you to take in more air when you are exercising, and less air when you are sitting quietly.

During an asthmatic attack, these muscles overreact, causing the air passages to become constricted. Taking in enough air becomes very difficult. To make matters worse, the linings of the air passages may swell and become filled with mucus. Sometimes the small tubes collapse and make it even more difficult to exhale than it is to inhale.

An asthmatic attack can be life-threatening. More than 6,000 people a year die from asthma, and the number is increasing. Fortunately, there are effective treatments for asthma. Most deaths from asthma occur because the person had not been diagnosed or was not getting proper treatment.

Once they understand that asthma must never be taken lightly, asthmatics can usually lead normal, healthy lives, provided they faithfully follow the treatment prescribed by a doctor. Drugs breathed into the lungs from an inhaler, like the one shown in Figure 24-5, can often prevent asthmatic attacks or reduce their severity.

Such treatments have made it much safer for people with asthma to participate in athletic activities. In fact, not only is exercise beneficial for most people with

If you're allergic to house dust, on the other hand, you will suffer much less if you live in a house that has wood or tile floors rather than carpeting.

Sometimes it is simply impossible to avoid the substance causing the allergic reaction. In that case, medicines called antihistamines can help relieve the allergic symptoms. Histamine is the substance released by the immune system that causes the unpleasant effects of an allergy. Antihistamines work by interfering with the action of histamine. Some allergies can also be treated by a series of injections that reduce the sensitivity of the allergic person to a particular substance.

Asthma Even though hay fever or hives can make a person very uncomfortable,

---

asthma, but many people with this condition excel at sports.

A person with asthma who does perform strenuous exercise, however, must follow certain precautions. For some people, this may mean avoiding exercise in cold, dry air or when air pollution levels are high. To prevent attacks, most asthmatics must take medication before engaging in strenuous exercise.

Down's Syndrome: An Inherited Disorder

One in every 800 to 1,000 babies born each year in the United States has a disorder called Down's syndrome. Down's syndrome is caused by the presence of an extra chromosome in body cells.

Normally, cells in the human body contain 46 chromosomes. The exceptions are sperm and egg cells, which each contain 23 chromosomes. When the sperm and egg unite at fertilization, the fertilized egg has the normal complete set of 46 chromosomes. Sometimes, however, a sperm or egg with 24 chromosomes is produced. Sperm with extra chromosomes are usually so abnormal that they are unable to fertilize an egg. For this reason, it is unlikely that sperm with extra chromosomes will contribute to the formation of an abnormal embryo. However, an egg with an extra chromosome can be fertilized.

An extra chromosome always causes serious problems in the development of an embryo. In most cases, the deformities caused by the extra chromosome are so severe that the embryo dies before birth. Survival is possible, however, if the extra chromosome is one of the smaller ones. Down's syndrome results when there is an extra copy of chromosome 21, one of the smallest chromosomes.

Background
Down's Syndrome
People with Down's syndrome have an extra copy of chromosome 21. In most cases, this extra copy comes from the egg cell. The overall incidence of Down's syndrome is about 1 in every 1,000 live births. As a woman gets older, the risk of giving birth to a child with Down's syndrome increases. For mothers over 45, the risk is as high as 1 in 16. For this reason, pregnant women over 35 often have a procedure called amniocentesis performed to detect the condition. In this procedure, a small amount of the amniotic fluid surrounding the fetus is extracted. Fetal cells present in the fluid are used to prepare a fetal karyotype (set of chromosomes), which will reveal the presence of an extra chromosome.

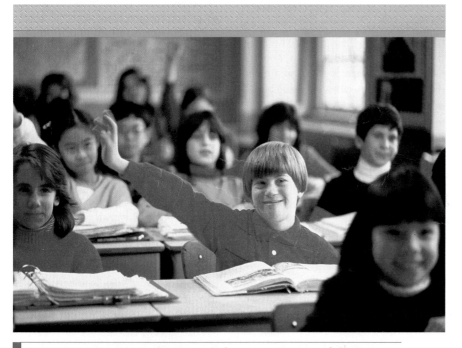

(FIGURE 24-6) **Down's syndrome results from an extra copy of chromosome 21 in body cells.**

Class Discussion
Inherited Tendency

As a class, discuss the difference between diseases that are clearly caused by inheriting defective genes and those thought to have a genetic basis. Ask: **Of the diseases we have discussed so far, which are caused by an identifiable defective gene that is inherited?** [*sickle cell anemia, cystic fibrosis, Tay-Sachs, muscular dystrophy*]

Which diseases may have a hereditary basis? [*Type II diabetes, allergies, possibly asthma*]

• • • TEACH continues on p. 516

Section Review Worksheet 24.1

To reinforce the concepts presented in this section, assign Section Review Worksheet 24.1.

Section Quiz 24.1

Have students take Section Quiz 24.1.

Reteaching Worksheet 24.1

Students who have difficulty with the material may complete Reteaching Worksheet 24.1.

Review Answers

1. A noninfectious disease is one that a person cannot catch from another person, animal, or other organism. An infectious disease is one that a person can catch in any of these ways.

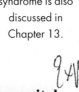

Fetal alcohol syndrome is also discussed in Chapter 13.

congenital disease:

a disease that is present from birth, but is not inherited.

All people born with Down's syndrome show some degree of mental retardation. The severity of the impairment varies from person to person. Other effects of Down's syndrome include defects in the thyroid gland and heart. Heart defects are fairly common, and they are often fatal during infancy. People with Down's syndrome can live a long and healthy life if the effects of the syndrome are not severe.

Genetic Screening Sophisticated genetic testing and prenatal screening can help couples with family histories of hereditary disorders. A couple planning to have a child can find out if they are at risk for passing defective genes to their unborn child. Tests can determine the presence of genes that may carry Tay-Sachs disease, cystic fibrosis, or sickle cell anemia. Parents can then be made aware of the likelihood of passing on a disease based on its inheritance pattern.

Pregnant women who are at risk of having a child with a hereditary disorder can undergo specific tests that can detect some genetic defects in the fetus. For example, women over the age of 35 are at a higher risk than younger women for giving birth to a child with Down's syndrome. Many doctors recommend that pregnant women over the age of 35 undergo a test called amniocentesis. This test is given at the end of the woman's first timester of pregnancy. Amniocentesis can detect the presence of Down's syndrome, as well as other chromosomal defects.

Congenital Diseases

A **congenital disease** is a disease that is present from birth but is not inherited. In other words, a congenital disease is not caused by an abnormal gene present in the egg or sperm at the time of fertilization, but by an accident or incident that occurs during fetal development or birth. For example, if a woman contracts rubella (German measles) during pregnancy, her baby may be born with cataracts or heart defects. Besides exposure to certain diseases, exposure to certain drugs or to environmental dangers such as radiation or pollution, during pregnancy can cause a congenital disease. It is therefore very important for a pregnant woman to carefully read the labeling of any medication she may consider taking during her pregnancy.

Fetal Alcohol Syndrome One drug that can cause a serious congenital disease is alcohol. A woman who drinks heavily during pregnancy risks having a baby with fetal alcohol syndrome. The effects of this congenital disease include low birth weight, mental retardation, facial deformities, and heart defects.

Many doctors believe that drinking smaller amounts of alcohol during pregnancy causes a mild form of fetal alcohol syndrome that may result in mental retardation with less obvious physical deformities. For this reason, pregnant women are generally advised to refrain from drinking alcohol during pregnancy.

Cerebral Palsy Cerebral palsy is caused by damage to the brain. This damage results in a form of paralysis that makes it impossible for a person to control his or her muscles. The muscles may be limp and unresponsive or may contract randomly and uncontrollably. Random contraction of the muscles is known as spastic paralysis.

People with cerebral palsy sometimes find it difficult to walk or talk because of the difficulty of controlling their muscles. Although some people with cerebral palsy are mentally retarded, many are of completely normal intelligence and are as capable of achievement as those born without the disease.

• • • TEACH continued

Class Discussion
Congenital Versus Hereditary Disease

Ask: **How does a congenital disease differ from a hereditary disease?** *[A congenital disease is caused by an incident that occurred during pregnancy or at birth, whereas a hereditary disease is caused by an abnormal gene.]* **What is an example of an incident occurring during pregnancy that could cause a** disease in the child? *[If a woman has German measles during pregnancy, her child may be born with cataracts or heart defects. Exposure to drugs, radiation, or pollutants in the environment could also cause congenital diseases.]*

Class Discussion
Cerebral Palsy

Ask: **What causes cerebral palsy?** *[brain damage resulting from lack of oxygen during birth as well as exposure during pregnancy to radiation, certain drugs, and some diseases]* **What are** the symptoms of cerebral palsy? *[A person with severe cerebral palsy cannot control his or her muscles, causing difficulty with walking and talking. Some people with cerebral palsy are retarded, but others have normal intelligence.]*

Class Discussion
Epilepsy

Ask: **If it is normal to have electrical impulses in the brain, what is epilepsy?** *[Epilepsy is abnormal electrical activity in the brain.]* **How do grand mal and petit mal seizures differ?**

The brain damage that causes cerebral palsy can result from several factors. Lack of oxygen during birth is one possible cause. Exposure during pregnancy to radiation, certain drugs, or some diseases can also be a factor.

Epilepsy Epilepsy is a disease in which electrical activity in the brain becomes abnormal for short periods. Epilepsy is not mental retardation. People with this disorder have the same mental abilities as people who are not epileptic.

Epilepsy takes different forms, depending on which type of abnormal brain activity occurs. The periods of abnormal brain activity are called epileptic seizures.

The most serious form of epilepsy is grand mal epilepsy. During a grand mal seizure, the person loses consciousness, and may fall to the floor and thrash about. The movements can be so forceful that people have been known to injure themselves by hitting objects such as desks or other furniture.

A grand mal seizure is often very frightening to witness. If someone around you should have a grand mal seizure, the best thing you can do to help the person is to move furniture out of the way to reduce the risk of injury. Do not try to touch or move the person while he or she is having a seizure. Grand mal seizures usually last only a few minutes. After the seizure, the person will probably sleep for a short time.

Grand mal seizures are also frightening for the person who experiences them. The person may feel disoriented and confused after a seizure. Many epileptics are embarrassed by their seizures or feel guilty because of the disruption and worry they have caused. It is very important that people who witness a seizure be understanding and supportive.

Fortunately, medication helps most people with grand mal epilepsy avoid having seizures. Once the proper drug therapy is prescribed, an epileptic may go for many years, or for the rest of his or her life, without a seizure.

There are two other forms of epilepsy. Petit mal epilepsy causes a person to simply ''go blank'' for a minute or two. Convulsions do not occur. This form of epilepsy usually occurs during childhood and disappears by adolescence. Psychomotor epilepsy causes seizures in which the person does not fall or have convulsions but may repeat simple movements over and over. Epilepsy may be a hereditary or congenital disease, or it may be caused by a head injury or a tumor later in life.

People with epilepsy, or with any type of congenital or hereditary disease, should be treated the same way as anyone else: with compassion and respect.

Review

1. *What is a noninfectious disease? How does it differ from an infectious disease?*

2. *Define hereditary disease and congenital disease. How do they differ?*

3. *List three factors that can cause a congenital disease.*

4. ***Critical Thinking*** *Should a person born with fetal alcohol syndrome be able to sue his or her mother for damages if it can be proven that the mother used alcohol during pregnancy, knowing of its risks? Why or why not?*

Answer to Question 1 is on p. 516.

SECTION 24.1

2. A hereditary disease is caused by a defective gene or genes passed from one or both parents to a child. A congenital disease is present from birth but is not hereditary. A hereditary disease involves a defective gene that was present in the egg or the sperm, or both, at the time of fertilization. A congenital disease is caused by an accident or incident that happened during the pregnancy or birth.

3. Answers may include radiation, pollution, drugs, diseases, or lack of oxygen during birth.

4. Answers will vary. Students may say yes because the mother knew she was potentially damaging the child and because anyone who inflicted such damage on another person could be prosecuted in other circumstances. Others may say that even if she knew the consequences, the mother may have been unable to refrain from drinking or that a lawsuit for such a reason within a family is inappropriate.

[In grand mal seizures, a person loses consciousness and thrashes about. Petit mal seizures simply cause a person to blank out for a minute or two; there are no convulsions involved.]

Extension
Research Organizations

Have students investigate organizations that sponsor research on specific noninfectious diseases, such as muscular dystrophy. Encourage students to find out how they can help the organization of their choice.

ASSESS

Section Review

Have students answer the Section Review questions.

Alternative Assessment
What's the Difference

Have students explain in their own words the difference between a hereditary disease and congenital disease. Then have them give an example of each and explain its cause, symptoms, and any treatment that is available.

Closure
Congenital Diseases

Have students write a one-page paper on one of the congenital diseases discussed in the chapter or in class. The paper should discuss the cause of the disease, its symptoms, and any treatment that is available.

Section
24.2 *Autoimmune Diseases*

Background
Type I Diabetes

Young people with Type I (insulin-dependent) diabetes must be more careful than other teens to develop a wholesome lifestyle. They must exercise to keep their weight and body composition within the healthy range and to keep their body using insulin efficiently. And they must eat well-selected foods. Eating too much sugar or eating irregularly can throw off the carefully regulated insulin levels. Too much insulin in the body causes blood-sugar levels to drop below normal. This condition is called hypoglycemia. Too much insulin in diabetics can cause them to become so hypoglycemic that they have an insulin reaction, sometimes called insulin shock. This is a life-threatening condition. It can be handled by eating a sugar-rich food immediately; for that reason, diabetics often carry candy with them. The young person with Type I diabetes has to take responsibility for eating well, exercising, and following a healthful lifestyle.

Section
24.2 *Autoimmune Diseases*

Objectives

- *List three common autoimmune diseases.*
- *Explain the difference between autoimmune disease and AIDS.*

Your immune system consists of an amazing set of specialized cells that destroy potentially dangerous viruses, microorganisms, and poisons that enter your body. Cells of the immune system constantly patrol your blood and tissues, checking out every cell and substance they meet. When an immune system cell recognizes a cell or molecule, it leaves it alone. But an immune system cell will attack and destroy anything that it does not recognize.

You could not survive without this patrol system. However, in some people, the immune system mistakes a cell type or a certain kind of body tissue for a foreign invader and attacks it. When a person's immune system attacks and damages an organ of his or her own body, the person has an **autoimmune disease.**

What Causes Autoimmune Disease?

There seem to be several factors that trigger the immune attack. Some tissues in the body are not normally patrolled by, or exposed to, the immune system. An example is the thyroid gland. If an injury or infection brings immune cells into contact with thyroid cells, the immune system behaves as if this "new" tissue is foreign.

autoimmune disease:

a disease in which a person's own immune system attacks and damages an organ of his or her own body.

Sometimes a virus or bacterium contains molecules that are very similar to molecules found in the human body. If a person is infected by one of these viruses or bacteria, the immune system fights the infection in the normal way. However, after the infection is over, the immune system then goes on to attack the similar molecules in the body. For example, molecules on heart valves are similar to molecules found in the streptococcus bacterium that causes strep throat. After a strep throat infection, the immune system may attack the heart valves and damage them. This autoimmune disease is called rheumatic fever.

Even though autoimmune diseases are disorders of the immune system, it is important not to confuse them with HIV infection or AIDS. Infection with HIV leads to the gradual destruction of the immune system until it is unable to defend the body against invaders. With autoimmune disease, the immune system is strong and effective against foreign invaders, but it also attacks some part of the "self."

The most important distinction between AIDS and autoimmune diseases is that AIDS is a communicable disease. That is, it is passed from one person to another. Autoimmune diseases are noncommunicable diseases. You do not have to worry about "catching" them from someone else.

Multiple Sclerosis Multiple sclerosis (MS) is classified here as an autoimmune disease because it is often the result of an immune system attack on the fatty coverings of nerves. The resulting nerve damage affects different parts of the nervous system

---

in each patient. Early symptoms include vision disturbances, stiffness and fatigue in limbs, dizziness, and emotional disturbances. Complete paralysis, numbness, double vision, speech problems, general weakness, difficulty in swallowing, and other problems may occur in the advanced stages.

The exact trigger for the autoimmune attack is unknown. The disease usually shows up in early adulthood. One characteristic of multiple sclerosis is the cycle of temporary recovery from symptoms followed by periods when the disease gets worse. There is no cure for the disease, and the periods during which the symptoms are less severe make it very difficult to judge the value of any particular treatment.

Type I Diabetes You have already learned how important it is for the body's cells to be able to use sugars for energy, and that in order to use the sugars, the body must have insulin. Insulin is a hormone that is made by the pancreas.

Type I diabetes, which is sometimes called juvenile diabetes, is believed to be caused by an autoimmune attack on the insulin-producing cells of the pancreas. Once their insulin-producing cells are destroyed, people with Type I diabetes must receive insulin every day. There is no "insulin pill" that works, because the insulin would be destroyed by acids and enzymes in the digestive tract. The insulin must be delivered directly to the bloodstream, either by injections ("shots") or by an insulin pump. Diabetics must carefully monitor the level of sugars in their blood to make sure that they are taking the right amount of insulin. Some diabetics use a device like the one shown at the beginning of this chapter.

Some symptoms of diabetes are excessive thirst, excessive hunger, excessive urination, unexplained weight loss, slow healing of cuts and bruises, low energy, intense

(FIGURE 24-7) **People with Type I diabetes must take insulin every day.**

itching, vision changes, and pain in the extremities. If these symptoms appear, a doctor can perform a urine or blood test to determine whether the person has diabetes.

When a diabetic does not get enough insulin, a diabetic coma may occur. A person about to enter a diabetic coma may develop a fever, appear quite ill, complain of thirst, and vomit. A diabetic who receives too much insulin may suffer from insulin shock. Weakness, moist pale skin, and tremors or convulsions are all symptoms of insulin shock. Sugar (orange juice, soft drinks, granulated sugar on the tongue) may be given if the person is conscious.

Although diabetes is a serious disease, treatment is very effective. Diabetics who monitor and control their intake of insulin carefully, maintain a healthy, specially designed diet, get regular exercise, and avoid tobacco can lead healthy lives.

SECTION 24.2

Background
Hypoglycemia
Hypoglycemia, the condition of having too little glucose or sugar in the blood, most commonly occurs among diabetics who take insulin. If the dosage of insulin is too large, low blood sugar results. Symptoms can include hunger, headache, nervousness, sweating, and accelerated heartbeat. In extreme cases, convulsions, unconsciousness, and even death can result. A balanced diet of foods containing proteins and carbohydrates is recommended for the management of hypoglycemia.

damages any organ of his or her own body.] **Why is AIDS not an autoimmune disease?** *[AIDS is an infection that leads to the gradual destruction of the immune system. AIDS does not cause a person's immune system to attack his or her own body. Also, an autoimmune disease cannot be contracted from someone else.]*

 Cooperative Learning
Symptoms of Some Autoimmune Diseases

Have students work together in groups to produce a chart of autoimmune diseases, showing the symptoms of each and its effect on the body.

 Journal 24B
What Is an Autoimmune Disease?

Have students choose one of the autoimmune diseases discussed in this section and write in their Journal how they think their daily life would change if they suffered from it.

Extension
Research on Autoimmune Diseases

Have students obtain brochures from a local chapter of the Multiple Sclerosis Society, the National Diabetes Information Clearinghouse, and the Rheumatic Diseases Research Foundation. Ask them to display the brochures with posters soliciting support for research on these three diseases.

Section Review Worksheet 24.2

To reinforce the concepts presented in this section, assign Section Review Worksheet 24.2.

Section Quiz 24.2

Have students take Section Quiz 24.2.

Reteaching Worksheet 24.2

Students who have difficulty with the material may complete Reteaching Worksheet 24.2.

Review Answers

1. Answers may include rheumatic fever, multiple sclerosis, Type I diabetes, rheumatoid arthritis, Hashimoto's thyroiditis, and Graves' disease.

2. AIDS is a communicable disease; an autoimmune disease is not communicable.

3. Too much insulin can cause insulin shock. Not enough can cause a diabetic coma.

(FIGURE 24-8) **Former First Lady Barbara Bush suffers from Graves' Disease, a disorder that causes irregular heartbeat and a protruding of the eyeballs.**

Rheumatoid Arthritis Rheumatoid arthritis occurs when the immune system attacks the membranes that line the spaces between joints. Eventually, the joints may be destroyed and the bones may even fuse together. Unlike osteoarthritis, which is very common in older people, rheumatoid arthritis usually shows up at a younger age. It is more common in women and often first appears between the ages of 30 and 40.

Rheumatoid arthritis may also cause other problems, like anemia and heart disease. It is treated with anti-inflammatory drugs and gentle exercise.

Hashimoto's Thyroiditis and Graves' Disease Hashimoto's thyroiditis and Graves' disease are both caused by an immune attack on the thyroid gland, but oddly, they have opposite effects. In the case of Hashimoto's thyroiditis, the immune system destroys tissues of the thyroid gland and not enough thyroid hormone is produced. People with this disease must take thyroid hormone pills every day to replace the missing hormone.

In Graves' disease, the immune system attacks the thyroid, and the thyroid gland is tricked into making too *much* thyroid hormone. The usual treatment for this disease is to remove the thyroid or destroy it with radioactive iodine. Then the person takes thyroid pills to restore and maintain a normal level of the hormone.

Review

1. Name three common autoimmune diseases.

2. What is an important distinction between AIDS and autoimmune diseases?

3. *Critical Thinking* Why is it so important for a person to monitor the amount of insulin he or she takes?

ASSESS

Section Review

Have students answer the Section Review questions.

Alternative Assessment
Autoimmune Diseases

Have students explain what an autoimmune disease is and how such a disease differs from AIDS. Then have students choose one autoimmune disease and tell how it affects the body and what its symptoms are.

Closure
Graves' Disease in the White House

Have students consider the diagnoses of physicians that former President Bush, his wife Barbara, and their dog suffer from Graves' Disease. Ask them to write whether the disease could have spread from one to the others? *(Graves' disease is a noninfectious disease, so it could not have spread.)*

Section 24.3 Degenerative Diseases

Objectives

- Describe what happens to arteries during the development of atherosclerosis.

- Explain the relationship between atherosclerosis and high blood pressure.

- List three kinds of cancer to which tobacco use contributes.

- Name four things you can do to reduce your risk of cardiovascular disease.
  LIFE SKILLS: Practicing Self-Care

- Name two things you can do to reduce your risk of getting cancer.
  LIFE SKILLS: Practicing Self-Care

Degenerative diseases are diseases that result from gradual damage to organs over time, and that are more likely to occur as a person gets older. In this section, you will learn about three degenerative diseases: osteoarthritis, cardiovascular disease (disease of the heart and blood vessels), and cancer.

Osteoarthritis

Osteoarthritis is very different from rheumatoid arthritis, the autoimmune disease. Osteoarthritis seems to be caused by wear and tear on joints over time. Osteoarthritis is very common among the elderly, although the age at which it appears varies from person to person. Some people begin to feel its effects in middle age or even earlier, while other people in their seventies or eighties are free of it. Some researchers think that the age at which osteoarthritis appears is determined by your genes, but that everyone who lives long enough would eventually get it.

Osteoarthritis is usually treated with aspirin or ibuprofen. Gentle exercise, which is often prescribed by a doctor or therapist, can slow the progression of the disease, relieve stiffness and pain, and prolong freedom of movement.

Cardiovascular Disease

Progressive damage to the heart and blood vessels is called **cardiovascular disease.** Damage to blood vessels usually occurs slowly, over many years. It may even begin in childhood. In the early years of the disease, it causes no pain or other symptoms, which means that some people in their teens and early twenties are suffering from cardiovascular disease and don't know it.

Although the early stages of cardiovascular disease don't have symptoms, the effects of the illness can be deadly. Heart disease is the leading cause of death in the United States. Stroke, which is also caused by cardiovascular disease, is the nation's third leading killer.

Atherosclerosis **Atherosclerosis**, the most common cause of cardiovascular disease, is a narrowing of the arteries caused by a buildup of fatty material. Arteries are blood vessels that carry blood away from the heart. Atherosclerosis begins with a small injury to the inner wall of an artery.

cardiovascular disease:

progressive damage to the heart and blood vessels.

degenerative diseases:

diseases that result from gradual damage to organs over time.

Background
Causes of Osteoarthritis
Rheumatologists now believe that there is no single cause for osteoarthritis (OA); it probably results from a combination of genetic factors and the process of aging. Obesity is the primary risk factor. Severe or repeated joint injury may cause degeneration to occur in younger adults. Other causes include infection and anatomical abnormality in a joint. Exercise does not appear to cause OA. In fact, a suitable exercise program strengthens bones. However, once a person develops OA in weight-bearing joints such as the knees or hips, exercise may become difficult or impossible.

Section 24.3 Lesson Plan

MOTIVATE

Journal 24C
Degenerative Diseases

This may be done as a warm-up activity. Have students write in their Journal what they would like to know about the degenerative diseases—osteoarthritis, cardiovascular diseases, and cancer—and why. Ask them to write whether they ever worry about having one of these diseases someday.

TEACH

Class Discussion
Osteoarthritis

Ask: **What seems to cause osteoarthritis?** [wear and tear on the joints over time] **At what age do people develop osteoarthritis?** [It can begin in middle age or even earlier, but is more common in older people.] **Why does the age at which it develops vary?** [Researchers believe genes determine the age at which it begins.]

Demonstration
Change in Blood Flow

Use a rubber tube to demonstrate how blood flows through a normal artery. Pour water into one end of the tube and call attention to the diameter of the water flow from the other end. Insert a plastic tube that fits snugly into the far end of the rubber tube. When you pour water into the other end of the rubber tube, ask students what they notice about the water flowing

Background
Avoiding High Blood Pressure

Excessive consumption of salt is one cause of high blood pressure. Americans consume from two to six times the recommended daily allowance of sodium, which is 2400 mg. Since salt is the main source of sodium for most people, the daily allowance of salt is ½ to 1½ teaspoons of salt. Abstaining from salty foods and not adding salt to food at the table are two ways to lower your blood pressure. Other factors that contribute to high blood pressure are excess body weight, lack of exercise, and excess alcohol consumption.

what is it

Causes

Explain

This triggers the cells lining the artery to multiply and take in certain substances circulating in the bloodstream. One of these substances is cholesterol.

Cholesterol is found only in animal cells. A certain amount of cholesterol is essential for your body to function normally. Cholesterol makes up part of your cell membranes and provides the raw material for certain essential hormones. Your body can make all the cholesterol it needs. Even strict vegetarians who do not eat eggs, meat, or cheese do not show any cholesterol deficiency. If your diet includes cholesterol, your body will make less and use some of the cholesterol in your food to supply its needs. However, the average American eats far more cholesterol than the body is able to use.

A diet high is saturated fats can also increase a person's cholesterol to an unhealthy level. When this occurs, more fatty deposits or plaque are deposited on the inside the artery walls. There is more information on fats, plaque, and cholesterol in Chapter 4.

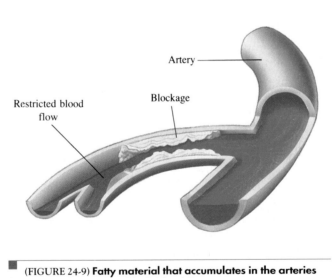

(FIGURE 24-9) **Fatty material that accumulates in the arteries can interfere with or block blood flow.**

The regions in arteries where plaque is deposited tend to thicken over time, narrowing the opening through which blood flows, as shown in Figure 24-9. Eventually, the arteries stiffen because of the accumulation of calcium, which restricts blood flow even further. When the disease becomes this severe, it is called **arteriosclerosis,** which means "hardening of the arteries."

People who have high cholesterol levels can develop atherosclerosis at an early age. In addition to eating foods high in cholesterol and fat, high levels of cholesterol in the blood can be increased by smoking, lack of exercise, or heredity—or in most cases, by several of these factors combined.

High Blood Pressure Another major cause of cardiovascular disease is high blood pressure. As you now know, your blood circulates from your heart to the rest of your body through tubular blood vessels called arteries. Your blood travels through your arteries in much the same way that water travels through a garden hose. Just like water in a garden hose, the blood in your arteries is under pressure. Imagine that you turn the water faucet connected to your garden hose on and off repeatedly. The pressure rises when water rushes out of the faucet and then falls when you turn the water off.

A person with a strong, healthy heart and flexible, healthy arteries should have a blood pressure reading of about 120/80 or less. A blood pressure measurement greater than 140/90 is considered high. These numbers represent the highest and lowest pressure inside your arteries.

While your heart contracts, squeezing blood into your arteries, the pressure inside your arteries is at its highest. This pressure is your systolic blood pressure, which is what the first number represents. When the heart muscle relaxes, the pressure in your arteries falls. The lowest pressure—the

---

Class Discussion
Heart Attack and Stroke

If possible, show the class an illustration of the exterior of the heart that clearly details the coronary arteries. Ask: **What causes a heart attack?** *[If the coronary arteries are narrowed by atherosclerosis, a spasm in the muscle layer of the artery or a tiny blood clot can block the coronary artery. When part of the heart muscle receives no oxygen, it begins to die in a few minutes.]* **Why do some people survive a heart attack?**

[When the damaged region is not too large and the person receives medical treatment quickly, a heart-attack victim may survive, but the damaged tissue will be replaced by scar tissue.] **How are a stroke and a heart attack similar, and how are they different?** *[Both a stroke and a heart attack involve loss of the blood supply to a vital organ. A stroke occurs when a part of the brain is deprived of its blood supply, and a heart attack happens when a part of the heart does not receive blood.]*

(FIGURE 24-10) **A heart attack does permanent damage to the heart by replacing healthy muscle (left) with scar tissue (right).**

Making a Choice 24A

Assign the Smoking card. The card asks students to summarize their knowledge about the health consequences of smoking cigarettes.

Making a Choice 24B

Assign the Avoiding Arterial Damage card. The card asks students to analyze foods in terms of their relation to heart disease.

pressure of the blood in between contractions of the heart—is the second number. This is called your diastolic blood pressure.

High blood pressure can damage the inner walls of arteries and accelerate the process of atherosclerosis. As fat is deposited and arteries narrow, the heart must pump harder in order to push blood through the body. Blood pressure rises even higher, causing even more damage to blood vessel walls.

Heart Attack The heart is the hardest working muscle in your body. It contracts continually throughout your life, never resting, not even when you sleep. A plentiful, oxygen-rich supply of blood is essential to the health of your heart.

Since the heart is filled with blood, you might think that the blood inside the heart supplies the heart muscle with all of the oxygen and nutrients that it needs. However, this is not the case. In fact, the inner lining of the heart actually acts as a barrier to the transfer of oxygen and nutrients.

When blood leaves the heart, it is pumped out through the largest artery in the body, the aorta. However, before blood is carried to any other part of the body, some of the blood detours into small blood vessels leading off from the aorta, where it connects to the heart.

These vessels on the outside of the heart are the coronary arteries. They have one of the most important jobs in the entire blood vessel system—that is, to supply blood to the heart muscle itself.

If the coronary arteries have been narrowed by atherosclerosis, a spasm in the muscle layer of the artery—or a tiny blood

The circulatory system is discussed in greater detail in the Body Systems Handbook.

The symptoms of a heart attack are discussed in Chapter 28.

Game

Cardiovascular Concentration

Ask students to work in pairs to make cards, each with the name of one of the cardiovascular diseases mentioned in this section. Have these pairs of students also make cards with the definitions of the disorders. Have students play concentration by matching the name with the definition.

• • • TEACH continues on p. 524

Background
Diet and Cancer Prevention

Many foods contain nutrients that help reduce one's chances of getting cancer. Cabbage-type vegetables, such as broccoli, cauliflower, kale, and brussels sprouts, protect against cancers of the colon, rectum, stomach, and lungs. High-fiber foods, such as bran cereals, whole wheat bread, rice, popcorn, and potatoes protect against cancer of the colon. Foods with vitamin A, such as carrots, peaches, squash, and broccoli protect against cancer of the esophagus, larynx, and lungs. Foods with vitamin C, such as grapefruit, oranges, strawberries, and tomatoes guard against cancer of the esophagus and stomach.

The symptoms of stroke are discussed in Chapter 28.

cancer:

a disease caused by cells that have lost normal growth controls and that invade and destroy other tissues.

clot—can block the coronary artery. Part of the heart muscle receives no oxygen and begins to die within a few minutes. When this happens, a heart attack has occurred. If the damaged region of the heart is not too large, and the person receives medical treatment quickly, there is a good chance that the heart attack victim will survive. After recovery, however, the damaged heart muscle will be replaced by scar tissue.

Stroke Like the heart, the brain needs blood and the nutrients it carries in order to survive. When a region of the brain is cut off from its blood supply, a **stroke** occurs. Some strokes result when blood traveling through blood vessels damaged by cardiovascular disease can't reach the brain. A

(FIGURE 24-11) **Cancer results when cells that have undergone a rapid and uncontrolled growth invade other cells and body tissue.**

stroke can be caused by a blood clot, by a broken blood vessel if it swells and puts pressure on the brain, or when the artery that supplies blood to the brain is severely narrowed by atherosclerosis.

Nearly 150,000 people die each year of stroke. If you think someone you're with is having a stroke, call a doctor immediately and describe the symptoms. If a physician is unavailable, call an ambulance or take the person to the hospital immediately.

Cancer

Your body makes millions of new cells every day. Normally, this is a controlled process in which cells divide to provide replacement cells for the ones that are worn out. Sometimes, though, cells divide and multiply in an uncontrolled way.

Cancer is a disease caused by cells that have lost normal growth controls. These irregular cells accumulate rapidly. They can invade, compress, and destroy the surrounding healthy tissue. These cells may form a solid mass called a tumor. A benign tumor does not invade the surrounding tissues. Most tumors are benign and may be safely ignored, whereas others will need to be removed through surgery. When a tumor spreads to the surrounding tissues it eventually damages vital organs. A malignant tumor consists of cells that can spread the cancer.

Cells in almost any part of the body can become cancerous. When a cancer arises, it usually grows for a while in the part of the body where it began—sometimes for years. Eventually, however, some of the cancer cells may metastasize, or move to other parts of the body. The cancer cells often travel through the blood or lymph fluid and give rise to new malignant tumors.

• • • TEACH continued

Class Discussion
Learning About Cancer

Discuss with students what cancer is and what it does to the body. Ask: **Why is cancer a noninfectious disease?** *[Cancer is not caused by an infectious organism, and it cannot be passed on to someone else.]* **What is the difference between a benign tumor**

and a malignant tumor? *[A benign tumor is harmless and can often be ignored. A malignant tumor invades and destroys tissues of the body.]*

Cooperative Learning
Treatment for Cancer

Have students form groups to research and report on cancer treatments. They should find out about surgery, radiation, chemotherapy, and alternative therapies, such as visualization and

meditation. For what kinds of cancer are they each used? For what stages of a cancer's development? Are they sometimes used together, or in sequence?

• • • TEACH continues on p. 526

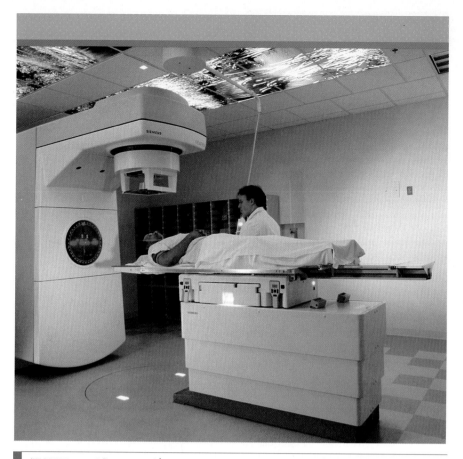

(FIGURE 24-12) **Persons with cancer sometimes require radiation therapy.**

Life Skills
Worksheet 24A
Assign the Giving Good
Health-Care Advice Life
Skills Worksheet.

Life Skills
Worksheet 24B
Assign the Knowing
When to See a Doctor Life
Skills Worksheet.

Cancer Treatments At one time, the vast majority of cancers were incurable. Today, many cancers can be controlled, and often cured. Even so, cancer remains a very serious disease. It is the second leading cause of death in the United States.

The first step in treating cancer is usually to surgically remove the cancerous growth. Surgery is most effective in the early stages of cancer. A small cancer that has not spread to other parts of the body can be completely removed in this way. Some skin cancer surgery is performed with lasers, which can cut through the cancerous tissue without causing damage to the surrounding tissue.

Some cancer patients receive radiation treatments or chemotherapy, either alone or in addition to surgery. The purpose of radiation therapy is to kill any cancer cells near the original tumor that were not removed by surgery. The goal of chemotherapy, which is treatment with special anti-cancer drugs, is to destroy cancer cells that have traveled to other parts of the body.

When cancer is not diagnosed until after it has grown and spread into vital organs such as the lungs, the pancreas, or the brain, surgery is often useless. Radiation or chemotherapy may be used to treat advanced cases of cancer. In these cases, a cure is very unlikely. However, treatment

Life Skills Worksheet 24C

Assign the National and Local Organizations Life Skills Worksheet.

Life Skills Worksheet 24D

Assign the Making Healthful Lifestyle Decisions Life Skills Worksheet.

Seven Warning Signals for Cancer

Change in bowel or bladder habits.

A sore that does not heal.

Unusual bleeding or discharge.

Thickening or lump in breast or elsewhere.

Indigestion or difficulty in swallowing.

Obvious change in wart or mole.

Nagging cough or hoarseness.

(FIGURE 24-13) **Having one or more of the above signs and signals does not mean that you have cancer. But to be on the safe side, see a doctor.**

Complete information on breast and testicular self-examinations is provided in Chapter 16.

sometimes reduces the size of tumors, reduces pain, and prolongs life.

Early Detection of Cancer It is important that everyone know the early warning signs of cancer. Remember, cancer caught early is very often completely curable. You can begin protecting yourself by learning the seven warning signals for cancer that have been developed by the American Cancer Society, listed in Figure 24-13. If you have one of these warning signals, see your doctor immediately.

Some cancers do not have symptoms that you can feel or see in their early stages, yet they can be detected by certain diagnostic tests. This is one reason why regular checkups are so important. Regular self-examination of breasts or testicles is the most effective way to detect cancer in these regions at an early stage. See Chapter 16 for more information regarding these important self-exams.

Preventing Cardiovascular Disease and Cancer

It's not always easy to determine the exact reason why a particular person gets cardiovascular disease or cancer. There is evidence that a person can inherit a tendency to suffer a certain degenerative disease from his or her parents, and it is also known that older people are more likely to get degenerative diseases than are younger people.

Risk Factors for Degenerative Disease

Factors You Can't Control	Factors You Can Control
Gender	Poor Dietary Habits
Heredity	High Blood Pressure
Age	Lack of Exercise
	Smoking
	Drinking Alcohol

(FIGURE 24-14) **Most of the risk factors for degenerative disease are within your control.**

••• TEACH continued

Journal 24D
Plan for Monthly Self-Examination

Have students outline in their Journal a plan for a monthly self-examination, and ask them to give several reasons for implementing such a plan.

Class Discussion
Risk Factors and Cardiovascular Disease

Discuss the factors that can't be controlled in contracting a degenerative disease. Ask: **How can heredity place one person more at risk than another to contract a cardiovascular disease?** *[If several members of a person's family have cardiovascular problems, that person may have inherited a tendency toward these problems.]*

What could you do to reduce the risk of your contracting one of the cardiovascular diseases? *[You could avoid the factors that you can control, such as poor dietary habits, high blood pressure, lack of exercise, smoking, and drinking alcohol.]*

Role-Playing
Preventing Cancer

Have students role-play a situation where a teen is trying to convince his or her father or mother to quit smoking.

(FIGURE 24-15) **Some studies have shown that certain foods contain nutrients that may reduce a person's chances of suffering cancer.**

Age and heredity are two disease-causing factors a person can't do anything about. But there are things you *can* do to decrease your chances of getting certain diseases. The decisions you make concerning the care of your body—starting now—can have a very strong influence on your health as you grow older.

By making healthy choices, you may be able to avoid getting a certain degenerative disease. Even if you don't avoid the disease entirely, you may be able to postpone the age at which a disease shows up, or reduce its severity.

Cardiovascular Disease It may not seem especially important to think about preventing cardiovascular disease while you're still a teenager. But in fact, the choices you make now about diet, exercise, tobacco, and alcohol are already affecting your heart and blood vessels. For some measures you can take to reduce your risk of

getting cardiovascular disease, read the Life Skills feature on pages 528–29.

Preventing Cancer In order for cells to become cancerous, a series of changes must occur in cells in a particular sequence. These changes cause the cells to lose their normal growth controls. Scientists have discovered several factors that cause some of these changes in cells. Regular exposure to these factors increases your risk that some of the cells in your body will undergo the unlucky combination of changes that results in cancer.

High doses of radiation and certain very toxic chemicals are known to cause cancer. Fortunately, you are unlikely to be exposed to these factors. However, many people are concerned that low doses of less toxic chemicals common in the environment may also be causing cancer in some people. Research continues to explore the relationship between environmental factors and cancer.

Have them mention the five kinds of cancer caused by cigarette smoking and any ideas they have learned about reducing the risk of cancer.

Debate the Issue
Avoiding the Risk Factors

Hold a class debate on the topic: People should not deprive themselves of so many things they want to do all their life, just to add a few years to their life at the end. Divide the class into two teams, one pro and one con.

Each team should prepare for the debate by listing arguments the other side is likely to make and composing their counterarguments.

Class Discussion
Seven Warning Signals for Cancer

Discuss the chart shown in Figure 24-13. Emphasize that early detection may mean the difference between life and death. At an early stage, cancer does not move to other parts of

the body. It can more easily be controlled at this stage. Have students read the information about breast self-examination and testicular self-examination. Ask them to outline the steps appropriate to them.

 Cooperative Learning
Environmental Cancer Risks

Have students work together to chart the risks of cancer that may be present

Life SKILLS

Have students read the Life Skills feature in the text. Ask them whether they feel the steps suggested are practical. Are there any that would be difficult for them to take? If so, ask them to explain why. Are some easy, requiring only a minimal adjustment? What are the rewards of following these steps?

Life SKILLS: Practicing Self-Care

Reducing Your Risk of Cardiovascular Disease . . . . .

Here are some steps you can take—starting now—to reduce your chances of getting cardiovascular disease.

1. *Don't smoke.* Smoking cigarettes or using any other form of tobacco increases your risk of heart attack and stroke more than any other factor that you can control. Smokers are two to six times more likely to have a heart attack than are nonsmokers. Smokers who have heart attacks are more likely to die from them. The best thing that you can do to maintain good health is to never start smoking. If you have started, quit. For some suggestions on ways to stop smoking, see Chapter 14.

2. *Have your blood pressure checked regularly.* Most people with high blood pressure can bring their blood pressure down to normal levels and greatly reduce their risk of heart attack and stroke. Many people return to normal blood pressure readings

simply by quitting smoking, not drinking alcohol, maintaining a normal weight, and getting regular exercise. Some people also need to take medication to lower their blood pressure.

• • • TEACH continued

in the environment and plan how to counteract them. Suggest they make a simple chart with four categories down the left side (radiation, toxic chemicals, tobacco, sun) and two wide columns across the top (times you may be exposed to these dangers, ways to minimize exposure). When each group has finished, combine all the ideas on a single chart on the chalkboard.

 Teaching Transparency 24C
Factors That Increase the Risk of Heart Disease and Cancer

Use this transparency to reinforce the connections between diet, exercise, smoking, and other habits and the development of heart disease or cancer.

Extension
Spreading the News

Have students develop two fliers: one for the prevention of cardiovascular disease and one for the prevention of cancer. Fliers should stress things that students can do now. Students may wish to include graphics or charts. Fliers could be passed out at a school assembly or during lunch period.

3. *If you are diabetic, be sure you follow medical advice to control it.* Diabetics develop more severe atherosclerosis earlier in life. If you have diabetes, be sure that you see a doctor regularly, and follow his or her instructions regarding insulin shots and general self-care. In addition, a healthy lifestyle is even more important for you than for nondiabetics.

4. *Eat healthy foods.* Eating a healthy variety of foods in moderate amounts reduces your risk of obesity, which in turn reduces your risk of suffering cardiovascular disease. You should make a special effort to avoid foods that are high in fat. Chapter 4 offers specific information on choosing a nutritious diet.

5. *Exercise regularly.* Regular aerobic activity can strengthen the heart and has been shown to increase the internal diameter of arteries, allowing more blood to pass through. Exercise can also lower blood cholesterol. If you don't exercise, not only will you lose these protective effects, but you will find it much more difficult to maintain normal weight.

6. *Learn how to manage stress.* Everyone suffers from stress now and then. But having a continuous amount of high stress can contribute to heart disease. Learning how to manage the stress in your life can make you not only happier, but healthier too. Some specific approaches for stress management are discussed in detail in Chapter 9.

7. *Schedule regular medical checkups.* An examination by a health professional can let you know if you are developing risk factors such as high blood pressure, diabetes, or high blood cholesterol levels. You can then treat these conditions before they cause serious damage to your heart and blood vessels.

Section Review Worksheet 24.3

To reinforce the concepts presented in this section, assign Section Review Worksheet 24.3.

Section Quiz 24.3

Have students take Section Quiz 24.3.

Reteaching Worksheet 24.3

Students who have difficulty with the material may complete Reteaching Worksheet 24.3.

Review Answers

1. The arteries become narrow because of a buildup of fatty material called plaque. Eventually the arteries narrow and stiffen, restricting blood flow.

2. Atherosclerosis causes the blood flow through the arteries to be restricted, increasing blood pressure. High blood pressure can damage the inner walls of the arteries and accelerate the process, causing the blood pressure to become even higher.

3. Answers may include cancer of the lung, bladder, kidney, liver, esophagus, larynx, pharynx, or pancreas.

4. Answers may include don't smoke; have your blood pressure checked regularly; eat healthful foods; exercise regularly; manage stress; control your diabetes if you are a diabetic; and get regular medical checkups.

5. Answers may include don't smoke or use tobacco products; avoid exposure to radiation, toxic chemicals, and pollutants; avoid overexposure to the sun; and use a sunscreen with a high sun-protection factor number.

6. Answers should reflect an understanding of the following information. What you do now can affect you later in life. Cardiovascular disease can begin in childhood. The accumulative effects of years of smoking greatly increase your chance of developing cancer and cardiovascular disease later in life.

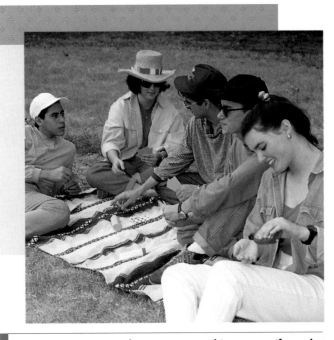

(FIGURE 24-16) **Too much sun can cause skin cancer. If you do spend time in the sun, be sure to cover up as much as possible and to use proper protection.**

There are several proven measures you can take to decrease your risk of getting cancer. First, don't use tobacco. Smoking cigarettes is the number-one cause of lung cancer in this country. Chewing tobacco and snuff can cause cancers of the bladder, pancreas, and kidney. Long-term tobacco use is associated with a higher risk of liver, esophagus, larynx, and pharynx cancers. By avoiding tobacco, you can significantly lessen your chances of getting any of these diseases.

It is also important to follow a healthy diet and exercise plan. Eating low-fat foods and getting plenty of exercise can help you maintain a healthy body weight and reduce your chances of getting many diseases—including cancer. In addition, some evidence indicates that certain nutrients are anticarcinogens, which are substances that can prevent cancer.

Another thing you can do to help protect yourself from cancer is to avoid overexposure to the sun. Ultraviolet rays from the sun are known to cause skin cancer.

Some forms of skin cancer are easily treated and rarely fatal. However, one form of skin cancer that is on the rise, melanoma, can be incurable unless detected early. A single case of sunburn in childhood serious enough to cause blisters can dramatically increase the risk of melanoma.

If you do spend time in the sun, be sure to use a sunscreen with a high sun protection factor number. For more information on selecting a proper sunscreen, see Chapter 6.

Review

1. *Explain the ways in which the arteries are affected by atherosclerosis.*

2. *Describe the relationship between atherosclerosis and high blood pressure.*

3. **LIFE SKILLS: Practicing Self-Care** *List three kinds of cancer that tobacco use can cause.*

4. **LIFE SKILLS: Practicing Self-Care** *Name four things you can do to reduce your risk of cardiovascular disease.*

5. *Name two things you can do to reduce your risk of getting cancer.*

6. **Critical Thinking** *A friend of yours who smokes cigarettes and eats a diet high in fats tells you it's stupid to worry about cardiovascular disease while you're still a teenager. What could you say in response?*

ASSESS

Section Review

Have students answer the Section Review questions.

Alternative Assessment
Avoidable—or Not?

Have students decide how they feel about this statement: Degenerative diseases are largely avoidable. Students should support or deny the validity of this statement by using examples from the book; they should also include a definition of degenerative disease.

Closure
Choosing to Live Longer

Ask students to suggest steps they could take to avoid one of the degenerative diseases later in life.

Highlights

Summary

- Diseases that are not transmitted from one organism to another are called noninfectious diseases. Hereditary, congenital, autoimmune, and degenerative diseases are all types of noninfectious diseases.

- Hereditary and congenital diseases are diseases people are "born with."

- Genes are responsible for transmitting hereditary characteristics. Some hereditary conditions are sickle cell anemia, cystic fibrosis, Tay-Sachs disease, Down's syndrome, muscular dystrophy, Type II diabetes, allergies, and asthma.

- Exposure during pregnancy to some drugs, environmental factors, and certain diseases can cause congenital diseases. Some congenital diseases are fetal alcohol syndrome, cerebral palsy, and epilepsy.

- Autoimmune diseases are disorders of the immune system. The most important distinction between AIDS and autoimmune diseases is that AIDS is an infectious disease, and autoimmune diseases are not.

- Three types of degenerative disease are osteoarthritis, cardiovascular disease, and cancer.

- Many types of cancer and heart disease can be prevented by avoiding certain environmental and lifestyle risks. Early detection and treatment can cure some types of cancer and control cardiovascular disease.

Vocabulary

noninfectious disease a disease that a person cannot catch from another person, animal, or other organism.

hereditary disease a disease caused by defective genes inherited by a child from one or both parents.

congenital disease a disease that is present from birth but is not inherited.

autoimmune disease a disease in which a person's own immune system attacks and damages an organ of his or her own body.

degenerative diseases diseases that cause gradual damage to organs over time.

cardiovascular disease progressive damage to the heart and blood vessels.

cancer a disease caused by cells that have lost normal growth controls and invade and destroy other tissues.

CHAPTER REVIEW

Concept Review

1. noninfectious
2. chromosomes, genes (accept either)
3. cystic fibrosis
4. Down's syndrome
5. autoimmune
6. atherosclerosis
7. noncancerous
8. melanoma
9. diet, exercise

Expressing Your Views

Sample responses:

1. He might be experiencing a heart attack. I should call 911 for emergency help.

2. Yes. I would move furniture out of the way to reduce the risk of injury to Wendy. I would also not try to touch or move her while she is having a seizure. I would be understanding and supportive.

3. I would suggest that he eat a low-cholesterol diet and begin an exercise program. If he smokes, I would suggest that he quit.

4. Some people may want to know if they have inherited a fatal disease so they can make plans for things they might like to do while they are still healthy.

Life Skills Check

Sample responses:

1. I would use a sunscreen with a high SPF number.

Concept Review . . . .

1. High blood pressure, sickle cell anemia, and cancer are all examples of _____ diseases.

2. The characteristics that were passed from your parents to you are carried on tiny structures within the body's cells known as _____ .

3. _____ is a hereditary disease that results in breathing and digestive difficulties caused by the secretion of thick mucus in the lungs and digestive tract.

4. _____ is caused by the presence of an extra chromosome in the body cells.

5. When a person's immune system attacks and damages an organ of his or her own body, the person has an _____ disease.

6. The most common cause of cardiovascular disease is _____, a narrowing of the arteries caused by a buildup of fatty materials.

7. A _____ tumor is called a benign tumor.

8. _____ is one form of skin cancer that is on the rise and can be fatal unless detected early.

9. The choices you are making now concerning _____, _____, alcohol, and tobacco are already affecting your heart and blood vessels.

Expressing Your Views . . . .

1. Your uncle, who has just returned from jogging, says he has an uncomfortable feeling of pressure in the middle of his chest and then becomes short of breath and dizzy. What might he be experiencing, and what should he do?

2. Your new friend, Wendy, has just told you that she suffers from epilepsy. Would you ask her any questions about her disease? What would you do if she had a seizure when you were alone with her?

3. Your father just found out that his cholesterol level is dangerously high. What things would you suggest he do to bring his cholesterol level down?

4. Do you think most people would want to know if they had possibly inherited a fatal disease? Explain.

2. No. I would follow my doctor's advice on how to control my asthma when I participate in athletic activities. The advice is usually to avoid activities in cold, dry air or when air pollution levels are high and to premedicate to prevent an attack during the activity or exercise.

3. I might be experiencing an allergic reaction. I might see an allergist for testing to find out what I am allergic to. Then I would try to find that source in the house and eliminate or minimize it. I might also need to take medication, called antihistamines, if I can not avoid the substance causing the allergic reaction.

Life Skills Check

1. **Practicing Self-Care**
On a hot summer day, you and your friends plan to go to the beach. You are sure you will spend all day there and you are worried about sunburn. What could you do to protect yourself?

2. **Practicing Self-Care**
You have recently been diagnosed as having asthma. Does this mean you can no longer participate in athletic activities? What can you do to minimize your attacks?

3. **Practicing Self-Care**
Since your family moved to a new house, you have had a stuffy nose, itchy eyes, and frequent sneezing. What might you be experiencing? What could you do to relieve your misery?

Projects

1. Research the cause and nature of a given noninfectious disease. Then prepare an oral report that describes the disease, its prevention, and its treatment, and that identifies any behaviors that could minimize the risk of getting the disease.

2. Work with a group to write public service announcements that inform the public of ways to prevent cancer. Deliver your announcements to the class.

3. Work with a group to create a bulletin board that illustrates ways to lower your chances of developing cardiovascular disease.

4. Several cultures around the world have low rates of heart disease. Work with a partner to research the diet of one of these cultures. Prepare a meal that is representative of the foods they eat.

Plan for Action

Early habits and attitudes play an important role in the prevention of cardiovascular disease and cancer. Create a plan to reduce your chances of getting one of these diseases.

Projects
Have students plan and carry out the projects for noninfectious diseases.

Plan for Action
Have students work in cooperative groups to plan how they can avoid developing a degenerative disease. Ask them to draw up strategies to improve their lifestyle with regard to diet, exercise, and avoiding carcinogens. In addition, have students write a personal plan.

ASSESSMENT OPTIONS

Chapter Test
Have students take the Chapter 24 Test.

Alternative Assessment
Have students do the Alternative Assessment for Chapter 24.

Test Generator
The Test Generator contains additional assessment items for this chapter.

Issues in Health

Ethical Issues in Health

ETHICAL ISSUES IN HEALTH

ISSUE: *Should clean needles be distributed to intravenous drug users in order to slow the spread of AIDS?*

Have students read the Ethical Issues in Health feature. Ask them which side of the controversy they are on. If the class divides over the issue of needle-exchange programs, hold a debate. Allow students to do library research to support their arguments. If the class agrees—either pro or con—have them do research to counteract the arguments that might be raised against their positions. Finally, discuss how a needle-exchange program could possibly help prevent HIV infection in infants.

▶ **ISSUE:** Should clean needles be distributed to intravenous drug users in order to slow the spread of AIDS?

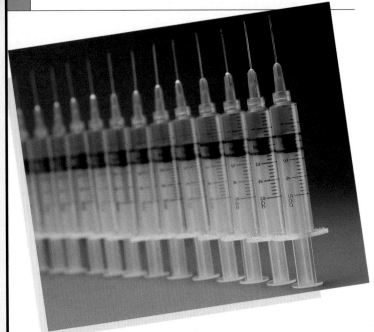

Intravenous drug use has become a major factor in the spread of AIDS because of a very dangerous practice—sharing needles. According to the Centers for Disease Control and Prevention, 23 percent of AIDS cases reported in the United States in 1992 resulted from intravenous drug users sharing needles contaminated with HIV.

Public-health authorities have proposed a method to slow the spread of HIV infection by intravenous drug users. The method involves distributing clean needles and supplies such as bottles of bleach and water for cleaning needles and syringes.

These items are included in a "survival kit." The popular name for such an effort is "needle exchange program." Reactions to this method have sparked national and international debate.

Those who oppose needle exchange programs argue that the programs will increase intravenous drug use and encourage youngsters to use drugs. Some opponents also argue that intravenous drug users will not take advantage of programs to protect their health. They believe that by using drugs, users show a lack of concern for themselves.

Advocates of needle exchange programs contend that most persons addicted to drugs are concerned about AIDS and will take steps to prevent HIV infection, if they are assisted in doing so. Supporters also argue that making clean needles available will not increase the use of drugs but will improve the relationship between public-health workers and people addicted to drugs. This improved relationship, they believe, will increase the likelihood that people with addictions will get into treatment programs.

During a two-year experiment in New Haven, Connecticut, researchers at Yale University collected information about the effects of a needle exchange program. Their data showed that the program had several positive effects. First, the needles returned for exchange were in circulation for a shorter length of time than needles in circulation before the program began. This indicates that fewer people used each of the needles. Second, the percentage of needles infected with HIV dropped by one-third. Third, referrals to drug treatment centers increased.

The Yale study showed that in New Haven, drug use did not increase when a needle exchange program was begun, as many had feared. In fact, it may have decreased somewhat. In addition, the chief of police in New Haven reported a 20-percent decrease in the area's crime rate. He speculated that the reason for the drop may have been an improved relationship between public-health workers and the drug-using community. Since the average participant in the program was 35 years old and had been shooting drugs for an average of seven years, the Yale study also suggests that the New Haven program did not encourage more adolescents to use drugs.

Currently, there are many legal barriers to conducting needle exchange programs. In some states, it is just as illegal to carry needles and syringes as it is to use or possess drugs. Public-health workers who distribute "survival kits" in these states often risk being arrested.

State and federal lawmakers who support needle exchange programs have begun to address the legal barriers. On the local level, several city governments have authorized needle exchange programs despite unanswered legal questions. These cities have obtained police cooperation to prevent the arrest of health workers and needle recipients.

One group that could benefit from needle exchange programs is children. Seventy percent of all AIDS cases among children are linked to intravenous drug use by a parent. These children were infected with HIV before birth. One mayor who had opposed a needle exchange program in his city changed his mind and became an advocate after seeing HIV-infected newborns in a hospital.

Situation for Discussion

Ben is a 28-year-old married man who has used intravenous drugs for more than 10 years. He frequents a "shooting gallery" where needles are shared. Ben is aware of the danger of HIV infection and the possibility of infecting his wife and future children, but his wife is unaware of his addiction and wants to start a family. Ben wants to get treatment for his addiction but worries that he will be fired if he uses the insurance his employer provides. He has heard about a needle exchange program near the shooting gallery but fears he will be arrested for carrying needles if he participates.

a. What course of action is open to Ben? What keeps him from getting help? What are some positive and negative aspects of participating in the needle exchange program?

b. If you were a public official, would you support or oppose a needle exchange program? What data would you gather to support your position? What steps would you take to start or stop such a program?

CHAPTER OVERVIEWS

CHAPTER 25

ENVIRONMENTAL AND PUBLIC HEALTH

Students learn that a healthy environment is important to personal and public health. The chapter defines *ecosystem* and discusses interactions within an ecosystem. It describes the elements of a healthy environment and explains how overpopulation and pollution threaten the health of the environment. The major types of pollution, their causes, and their health effects are discussed. Students learn the benefits of conservation, recycling, and reuse in fighting pollution and explore specific ways they can help. The chapter defines public health and describes public health activities. The public health concerns of developed and developing countries are compared. The chapter ends with a description of the functions of local, state, national, and international public and private health organizations.

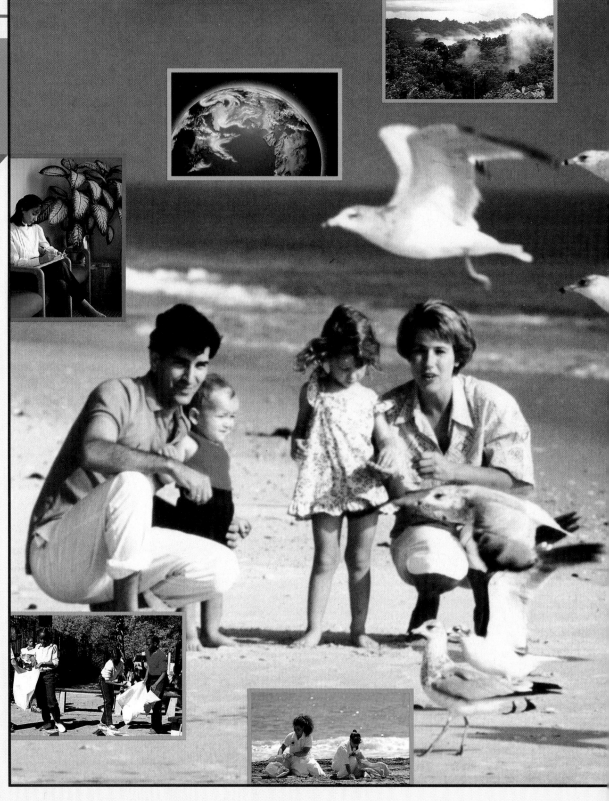

CHAPTER 26

BEING A WISE CONSUMER

The chapter describes the process of selecting a doctor and explains the Patient's Bill of Rights. Students learn why health care costs in the United States are rising. They learn about the advantages and disadvantages of traditional health insurance policies, HMOs,

and PPOs. They learn how to find and use free health services and how to protect themselves against quackery.

UNIT SEVEN

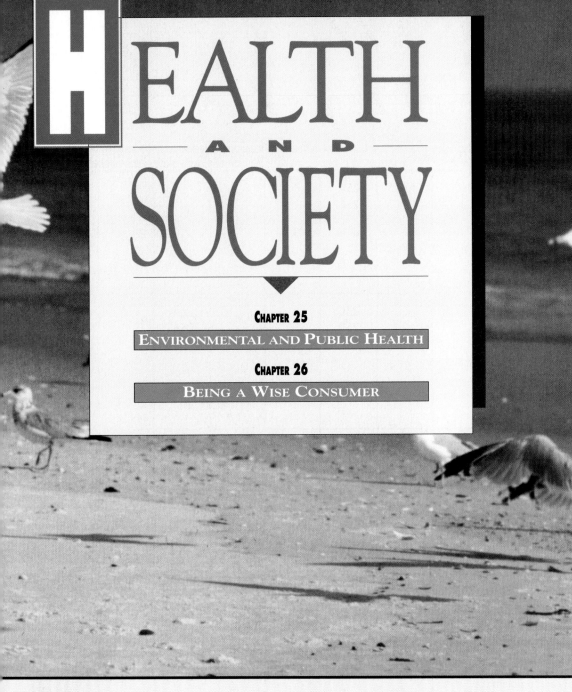

HEALTH AND SOCIETY

CHAPTER 25

ENVIRONMENTAL AND PUBLIC HEALTH

CHAPTER 26

BEING A WISE CONSUMER

UNIT PREVIEW

This unit provides information that helps students understand how a healthy environment is essential to personal and public health. This in turn helps them make responsible decisions about environmental issues. Students learn the roles of various agencies and organizations in maintaining public health. To prepare them to be informed consumers of health care, the unit describes how to select and communicate with a doctor. It explains the rights of patients as well as some of the plans that are available to pay for health care costs. The chart below links the information and skills presented in this unit to the National Health Education Standards.

Unit 7	NATIONAL HEALTH EDUCATION STANDARDS*						
STANDARD	1	2	3	4	5	6	7
Chapter 25	•	•	•	•		•	•
Chapter 26	•	•	•		•		

* For full text listing of each standard, see page 15T.

CHAPTER 25

Environmental and Public Health

SECTION	TITLE/OBJECTIVES	PERSONAL INVENTORY			LIFE SKILLS DEVELOPMENT			
		Personal Health Inventory	Journal	Check Up	Life Skills	Life Skills Worksheets	Media Message or Ethical Issues Worksheet	What Would You Do?
25.1 pp. 539–544	**THE ENVIRONMENT AND HEALTH** • Identify the characteristics of an ecosystem. • Describe the components of a healthy environment. • Identify the consequences of overpopulation and pollution.	Ch. 25	25A 25B					
25.2 pp. 545–552	**ENVIRONMENTAL POLLUTION** • Identify the main cause of environmental pollution. • Describe the environmental consequences of air pollution. • Identify health problems caused by various types of pollution.		25C 25D			25A 25B		
25.3 pp. 553–556	**WHAT CAN YOU DO?** • Describe the benefits of responsible waste management, recycling, and conservation. • List specific ways each individual can help reduce pollution. ▪▪ Make a recycling and reuse plan for your household.		25E 25F			25C		p. 558
25.4 pp. 557–566	**PUBLIC HEALTH** • Define public health. • Describe four public-health activities. • Compare the public-health concerns of developed and developing countries. ▪▪ Discover what the major public-health issues are in your community and find out where to get help for a public-health problem.		25G 25H		p. 565	25D		

KEY: ▪▪ Denotes Life Skill Objective

Text references denoted by page number.

Supplement references denoted by chapter or item numbers.

LINKING RESOURCES

Making a Choice Cards	Parent Discussion Guide	Health Talk Audio Program	Teaching Transparencies and Directory	Section Review Worksheets	Section Quizzes	Reteaching Worksheets	Section Reviews
INTERACTION		**OTHER RESOURCES**	**SECTION REVIEW AND ASSESSMENT**				
			25A	25.1	25.1	25.1	p. 544
			25B 25C BSH3	25.2	25.2	25.2	p. 552
25A 25B				25.3	25.3	25.3	p. 556
				25.4	25.4	25.4	p. 566

For additional information on hearing and hearing loss, see page 660 in the Body Systems Handbook.

KEY FACTS

- Living things and their physical surroundings (environment) make up ecosystems, all parts of which are interdependent.

- The environment provides certain materials and conditions that are essential for healthy existence, including water, air, food, and shelter.

- Overpopulation and pollution are two factors that disturb the balance of an ecosystem.

- Human activities are the primary cause of environmental pollution.

- Air, water, land and noise pollution have a negative impact on health.

- Conservation, the wise use of natural resources, and recycling help protect and preserve the environment.

- Individuals can help preserve the local environment by reducing their personal pollution and supporting conservation organizations.

- Local public-health agencies are concerned with the health of all people in a community.

- Public-health agencies provide services at local, state, national, and international levels.

CHAPTER REVIEW AND ASSESSMENT

TEXT
Chapter Review pp. 568–569

SUPPLEMENTS
Chapter Test 25

Alternative Assessment 25

Test Generator Chapter 25

GETTING STARTED

Using the Chapter Photograph

Ask students what they find appealing about the chapter photograph. Elicit from students the relationship between a clean, healthy environment and an individual's feeling of personal well-being.

Question Box

Have students write out any questions they have about the relationship between the environment and their health and put them in the Question Box.

Sensitivity *ALERT*

Some students may live in areas where, due to various types of pollution, the environmental quality is poorer than that of other areas. Students should not be made to feel that their surroundings reflect their personal worth or that a better environment means a better individual. Nor should they be made to feel responsible for all of our environmental problems. The use of public-health facilities, as opposed to private ones, is a sensitive issue for some students. Emphasize that agencies concerned with public health set health standards that affect the entire community.

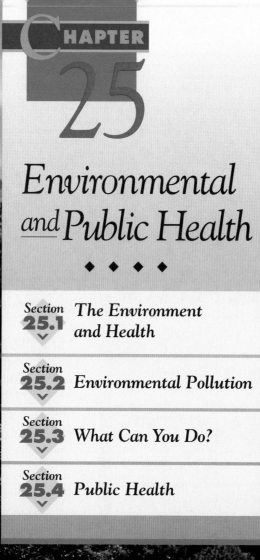

CHAPTER 25

Environmental *and* Public Health

◆ ◆ ◆ ◆

Section 25.1 The Environment and Health

Section 25.2 Environmental Pollution

Section 25.3 What Can You Do?

Section 25.4 Public Health

For many people, enjoying the outdoors is part of a healthy lifestyle. But even if you don't enjoy outdoor activities, a healthy environment is essential to your health and to the health of all people.

MYTHS & MISCONCEPTIONS

- **The world is so huge that there is nothing I can do to change it—for better or for worse.** The actions of every individual count. It is only through the collective action of individuals that the changes that are needed to preserve the environment can take place.

- **Low levels of pollutants in the atmosphere are safe.** The presence of even minute quantities of toxic materials can have devastating effects on ecosystems. For some toxins, no safe level of exposure is safe.

- **Except for AIDS, infectious diseases are not a serious problem in the United States.** Infectious diseases, such as pneumonia, kill many people, particularly the young and the elderly. Drug-resistant strains of many bacteria are a growing threat to public health.

The trouble started when Teresa's sister wound up in the hospital with pains in her abdomen. Before long, several other people in the neighborhood began to have the same symptoms. People were upset because the doctors at the local clinic hadn't been able to figure out what was making everyone sick. Eventually, officials from the health department were called in to help solve the mystery.

Within a few weeks, health officials announced that Teresa's sister and her neighbors were suffering from gasoline poisoning. Small amounts of gasoline in the neighborhood's drinking water had caused liver and nerve damage. In other words, the environment in the neighborhood was unhealthy. To inform as many people as possible of the danger, a neighborhood meeting was arranged. Teresa decided to go to find out what was going on.

Section
25.1 *The Environment and Health*

Objectives

- Identify the characteristics of an ecosystem.
- Describe the components of a healthy environment.
- Identify the consequences of overpopulation and pollution.

At the meeting, several environmental and health specialists spoke to people from Teresa's neighborhood. As she listened to the speakers, Teresa began to get a better idea of how all living things are related to their environment. Teresa learned that a healthy environment promotes good health, and that when the environment is damaged, the health effects can be enormous.

Discussing the environment in health class may seem strange, but a healthy environment is an important element in both personal and public health. Every year thousands of people—like the people in Teresa's neighborhood—find out how important the environment is to their health. In this chapter, you will discover how the environment is important to your health.

Ecosystems

Every living thing is part of an **ecosystem**, which consists of many groups of living things and their physical surroundings (environment). For example, a lake and all the organisms (living things) that live in it make up an ecosystem. All the living things on Earth and the places where they live make up a worldwide ecosystem. From the smallest to the largest, all ecosystems have several things in common.

ecosystem:

a system made of living things and their physical surroundings.

Background
The Gaia Hypothesis
The idea that Earth itself is a living being is found among the mythologies of ancient peoples. In 1979, a scientist named James Lovelock proposed the Gaia hypothesis, named in honor of the ancient Greek mother goddess, *Gaia*. This hypothesis suggests that Earth itself is a giant organism. It envisions all of Earth's creatures and physical components as part of that organism. The complex interactions between organisms and between organisms and physical systems, such as the ocean and atmosphere, maintain conditions suitable for life. Thus, according to the Gaia hypothesis, Earth actively maintains its homeostasis. Although discounted by many scientists, Lovelock's hypothesis has generated considerable discussion and debate.

Personal Health Inventory
Have students complete the Personal Health Inventory for this chapter.

Section 25.1 Lesson Plan

MOTIVATE

Journal 25A
Your Environment

This may be done as a warm-up activity. Ask students to record in their Journal some things about their environment that affect their health in positive ways. Then ask them to record some things that affect their health in negative ways. Suggest that they re- view their lists as they read the chapter and modify the lists if necessary.

TEACH

Class Discussion
Teresa's Environment

Discuss with students how they might react to the situation in Teresa's neighborhood if they lived there. Ask them to consider whether they would become involved and in what ways. Have them identify questions they might ask at a neighborhood meeting and the kind of action they would want the community to take.

Demonstration
Ecosystems

Display a small ecosystem, such as an aquarium or a terrarium, to the class. (You may be able to borrow such an ecosystem from the biology department.) Have students identify the living things in the ecosystem. Have

Interactions One characteristic of an ecosystem is that its living and nonliving parts interact with one another. Some living things feed on others. Living things also take the water and nutrients they need from the environment and then return the materials that are needed by other living things. For example, you inhale oxygen and exhale carbon dioxide. Plants take in carbon dioxide and give off oxygen. In other words, each living thing provides something that other living things need.

Nonliving materials interact as well. For example, oxygen reacts chemically with certain elements to form new compounds. The rusting of iron represents this type of reaction. Another example of interaction between nonliving parts of the environment is the effect that carbon dioxide has in the atmosphere. Carbon dioxide helps maintain the temperature of our surroundings by trapping heat from the sun inside our atmosphere.

Interdependency Consider what could happen if most of the Earth's plants died. For one thing, there would be less oxygen and more carbon dioxide. Both you and the environment would be affected. Your body would have to adjust to having less oxygen. The extra carbon dioxide might make the climate warmer—imagine summertime temperatures 10 to 20 degrees warmer than they are now. This could happen if certain human activities (such as releasing large amounts of carbon dioxide by burning oil and gas and clearing away large areas of the world's forests) are not reduced.

You can see that whatever happens to one part of an ecosystem affects other parts. In other words, the parts of an ecosystem are interdependent. The water, air, land, and climate, plus the kinds of organisms and the size of their communities, are all important to the health of an ecosystem. If one part of an ecosystem is damaged, the environment in the ecosystem could become unhealthy.

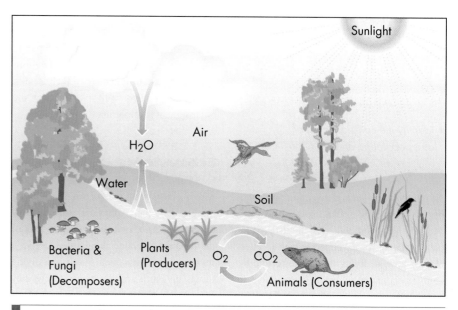

(FIGURE 25-1) **The parts of an ecosystem interact and are independent. Here you can see how living and nonliving elements of an ecosystem affect each other.**

• • • TEACH continued

them identify the nonliving parts, or physical factors, in the ecosystem. If you cannot display a small ecosystem, try to take students outdoors to observe a local ecosystem and have them identify the living and nonliving parts.

Class Discussion
People and the Environment

Emphasize the interaction between people and the environment. Ask:

What are some things the environment supplies that are necessary for life? *[Air, water, food, and shelter are examples.]* Point out that animals depend on plants for oxygen. Plants are also a source of food, both directly and indirectly. Ask students to explain how eating meat is, indirectly, dependent on a supply of plant life. Finally, remind students that animals exhale carbon dioxide, which plants need to make food.

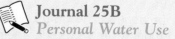 **Teaching Transparency 25A**
Parts of an Ecosystem

Show the transparency of Figure 25-1. Have students distinguish the ecosystem's living and nonliving parts.

Journal 25B
Personal Water Use

Have students record in their Journal the ways in which they use water each day. Then have them decide if they are wasting water in any of these uses.

(FIGURE 25-2) **In addition to the many everyday activities for which we use water, each of us uses about 40 gallons of water per day just for personal washing and toilet flushing.**

Change and Homeostasis Fortunately, living things are able to adjust to changes in their environment. When it's cold, for instance, you shiver and get goose bumps. This is an automatic change your body makes to warm you up. Organisms rely on such changes to maintain a balance inside their bodies. Maintaining this balance is called **homeostasis**.

Ecosystems also change constantly. For example, the temperature changes from day to night and from season to season. Materials such as water and air, as well as the living things, constantly come and go. In healthy ecosystems, there is a balance between the materials that are entering and leaving. The internal balance that exists in an ecosystem also represents a type of homeostasis.

Elements of a Healthy Environment

Even though living things can adjust to many of the changes in their surroundings, there are limits to this ability. The environment provides certain materials and conditions that are essential for the healthy existence of living things. Among these essentials are water, air, and adequate food and living space.

Water Water is one substance that is vital to all living things. It is home to many organisms (living things). But more important, all of the body processes that sustain life require water. In fact, most of an organism's body is water. For instance, water makes up as much as 65 to 70 percent of your body as a whole, and 80 percent

homeostasis:

the tendency of any living thing to maintain a balance in its inner systems.

Students can also record ways to reduce their water usage.

• • • TEACH continues on p. 542

Background

Population Growth

Population growth is often expressed in terms of doubling time, that is, the time required for a population to double in size. Earth's population in 1600 was approximately 500 million. It was not until about 1850, 250 years later, that the population had doubled, reaching 1 billion. If the birth rate is constant as population increases, the time it takes for the population to double decreases. Thus, about 50 years later in the first part of the twentieth century, Earth's population reached 2 billion. By 1960, the population reached about 3 billion. In 1995, the world's population was estimated as 5.76 billion. Even though the overall birth rate is declining, Earth's projected population for 2030 is 8.5 billion.

food chain:

a sequence of organisms that begins with a food producer and continues with one or more organisms, each of which eats the one before it.

of your brain. Human activities require a great deal of water as well. In addition to the water we must drink daily to maintain good health, we also use water for personal and household cleanliness, food preparation, and recreation. Agriculture and industry use huge amounts of water to grow food, process food and raw materials, and manufacture other necessities.

Unfortunately, less water is available for our use than most people realize. Almost 97 percent of Earth's vast water supply is salt water. Most of the remaining 3 percent is frozen in the polar icecaps and glaciers. This means that only about 0.5 percent of the Earth's water supply is fresh water that is suitable for use by humans and the other organisms that require fresh water.

Air Air is another substance that is vital to all living things. Without it, you could survive for only a few minutes. Oxygen is the most important gas you get from air. It allows you to obtain energy from your food. Other gases, such as carbon dioxide and ozone, are also important to you. In addition to trapping the sun's heat, carbon dioxide is used by plants to make the food on

which all animals depend. The ozone layer of the atmosphere protects living things from the damaging ultraviolet rays in sunlight.

Other Essentials Nutrients (food and minerals) are another requirement for living that comes from the environment. All living things are part of a **food chain**. In a food chain, an organism, such as a frog, eats another organism, such as a dragonfly. The frog may then be eaten by a fish, and the fish may be eaten by a human. As you can see in Figure 25-3, all food chains begin with a life form, such as a plant, that makes its own food out of nonliving materials from the environment.

If something affects one of the life forms in a food chain, the others are usually affected as well. For example, if all of the frogs disappeared, there would be more dragonflies. And because the fish would have less food, there would be fewer fish, which would mean there would also be less food for the humans.

Living things also require a certain amount of room in which to live. The amount of space needed by a particular type

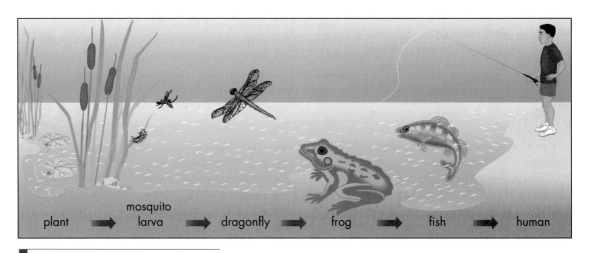

plant ➡ mosquito larva ➡ dragonfly ➡ frog ➡ fish ➡ human

(FIGURE 25-3) **A typical food chain.**

• • • TEACH continued

Demonstration
A Food Chain

Divide the class into groups of three or four. In each group, students should assume the identity of an organism that could be part of a food chain. Students must adhere to the following rules: one person in each group must be a plant; at least one person in each group must be a plant-eater; at least

one person in each group must be a meat-eater (grass, cow, person). Have each group demonstrate how the organisms might form a food chain. Check to determine if students' food chains are valid, that is, determine if their particular food chain could actually exist in nature. You may wish to provide students with food chains rather than have them create their own. To extend the activity, allow groups to exchange members to construct different food chains.

Debate the Issue
Overpopulation

Select two teams of students to debate the question: Should national governments limit family size in their countries? Give students time to research factors involved in the issue, including the relationship between birth rate and population growth, and attitudes toward an individual's right to privacy. Allow each team to present its arguments. Then allow other members of the class to question team members about their stand on the question.

of organism depends on many things, such as the type of shelter it needs and the amount of light, water, air, and food it requires for living. These factors help determine how many individuals of a certain kind can be supported by the environment of a particular area.

Upsetting the Balance

If you have ever had food poisoning from eating contaminated food or become dehydrated from perspiring too much, you know how bad you can feel when your homeostasis is disrupted. Your health suffers when your internal balance is upset. Likewise, the health of the environment is threatened when the homeostasis of an ecosystem is disturbed. **Overpopulation** and pollution are two factors that disturb the healthy balance in an ecosystem.

Overpopulation If you had been born in 1900, you could have expected to live about 47 years. Babies born in the United States in the 1990s are expected to live about 76 years. Better health care and cleaner living conditions are primary reasons for this dramatic increase in *life expectancy* (the average length of time a person is expected to live). However, as life expectancy has increased, the number of people living on Earth has also increased.

The world's population is currently growing at a rate of about 255,000 people per day, or 93 million people per year. At this rate, the world's population will double in about 60 years. Such a rapidly growing population places a burden on natural resources. When the population of a region becomes too large to be supported by the available resources, overpopulation has occurred.

The effects of increasing population are serious. At its worst, overpopulation results in poverty and starvation when food production cannot keep up with population

(FIGURE 25-4) **Overpopulation has resulted in a shortage of food in Dhaka, Bangladesh. These conditions have made it necessary for the people there to wait in long lines just to get a small ration of milk for their children.**

growth. In addition, there are severe shortages of usable land and other natural resources. Currently, Earth's **nonrenewable resources** such as petroleum and mineral ores such as coal are being used at an alarming rate. Even **renewable resources** such as timber and seafood are being consumed at a much faster rate than they are currently being replaced.

overpopulation:

the point at which the population of an area is so large that it can no longer be supported by the available resources.

nonrenewable resources:

natural resources such as coal and oil that cannot be replaced once they are used.

renewable resources:

natural resources such as trees that can be replaced continually.

 Section Review Worksheet 25.1
To reinforce the concepts presented in this section, assign Section Review Worksheet 25.1.

Section Quiz 25.1
Have students take Section Quiz 25.1.

Reteaching Worksheet 25.1
Students who have difficulty with the material may complete Reteaching Worksheet 25.1.

Extension
Looking at the Problems

Have students check newspapers and weekly newsmagazines for stories about human hardships that are in some way connected to problems in the environment. Such stories might range from local environmental problems, similar to the problem in Teresa's neighborhood, to more extensive tragedies, such as famine. Have students bring the stories to class. Select stories to discuss and emphasize the relationship between environmental degradation and human hardship.

Review Answers

1. Some characteristics of an ecosystem are: it is made up of living and nonliving parts that interact; its parts are interdependent—if there is a change in one part, there will be a change in other parts; ecosystems change constantly but maintain an internal balance.

2. water, air, food, adequate living space

3. Overpopulation can lead to poverty, starvation, and shortages of usable land and natural resources. Pollution can lead to the extinction of life forms, climate changes, and shortages of food and clean water.

4. Answers will vary. Sample response: Yes. Humans should make sure that the environment remains balanced and healthy. They can do so by not polluting the environment and by using natural resources wisely.

Consequences of Pollution and Removal of Resources

Extinction of life forms, such as the passenger pigeon.

Destruction of ecosystems, such as the tropical rain forests of Central and South America.

Climate changes, such as global warming due to the greenhouse effect.

Shortages of food and clean water, which lead to famine and disease.

(FIGURE 25-5) **Since the parts of the environment are interrelated, any one of these events could trigger the others.**

Pollution The balance in an ecosystem is also disturbed when one or more of its parts is damaged by pollution. Pollution occurs when substances that are harmful to living things contaminate the air, water, or soil. Such substances include poisonous chemicals, garbage, and radioactive wastes. Even excess amounts of otherwise beneficial materials such as carbon dioxide can also be considered as pollutants (substances that cause pollution). It is difficult to predict how pollution will ultimately affect Earth and its inhabitants, but it has already greatly affected human and environmental health. In Figure 25-5, you will find some of the many possible consequences of pollution.

(FIGURE 25-6) **When properly managed, forests like this one can be renewable resources. What are some of the other natural resources that can be renewed?**

Review

1. List the characteristics of an ecosystem.

2. What do living things need from their environment for a healthy existence?

3. How do overpopulation and pollution affect an ecosystem?

4. **Critical Thinking** Do you think that humans are a part of the natural ecosystems on Earth? If so, what responsibility, if any, do you think humans should take for the other parts of ecosystems?

Section Review
Have students answer the Section Review questions.

Alternative Assessment
Parts of an Ecosystem

Have students give an example of an ecosystem. Then have them name some living and nonliving things in that ecosystem. Finally, have students identify one or more ways in which the homeostasis of that ecosystem might be upset.

Closure
Overpopulated Ecosystems

Have students explain how overpopulation in a natural ecosystem, such as a pond or a forest, places a burden on the resources of that ecosystem. *(The rapid reproduction of algae in a pond is an example. Decomposing algae cause an oxygen shortage in the water; the algae on the surface block sunlight from reaching lower levels, killing plants that depend on photosynthesis and animals that depend on those plants.)*

Section
25.2

Environmental Pollution

Objectives

- Identify the main cause of environmental pollution.
- Describe the environmental consequences of air pollution.
- Identify health problems caused by various types of pollution.

The situation in Teresa's neighborhood is just one example of how pollution can damage the environment and affect human health. You have probably heard or read about many other incidents that are similar, or even more serious. In this section, you will learn about several forms of environmental pollution and discover how they may affect your health.

Although Teresa had learned a lot at the neighborhood meeting, she was still upset. "Did you hear?" Teresa asked her boyfriend, Jaime. "The health department found out there's gasoline in our drinking water! That's what made my sister and our neighbors sick. They say the gasoline's coming from some gasoline storage tanks in our neighborhood."

"I heard," Jaime said. "My dad works for a company that owns some of those tanks. That's all he talked about last

Background
Magnifying Pollutants

Dumping even small amounts of pollutants into bodies of water can result in serious damage to the environment. Organisms that live in the water may take in the pollutants, concentrating them in their tissues. The pollutants are further concentrated as they are passed along the food chain. Thus, an animal, such as an eagle, that consumes fish, may be affected by pollutants that were initially absorbed by aquatic plants. The increasing concentration of pollutants through the food chain is called biomagnification.

(FIGURE 25-7) **Sources of water pollution. Public drinking water comes from two main sources: surface waters (precipitation that collects in rivers, lakes, and reservoirs) and ground water (precipitation that seeps into the ground). The quality of drinking water varies, depending on its source and its exposure to pollutants.**

Section 25.2 Lesson Plan

MOTIVATE

Journal 25C
Pollution Around You

This may be done as a warm-up activity. Encourage students to record in their Journal examples of pollution in their environment. Suggest that they look for pollution both in their neighborhoods and around the school. Have them identify the sources of the pollution, if possible.

Role-Playing
Community Concerns

Have two or three students play the roles of officials from a company that owns gasoline tanks in Teresa's neighborhood. Have other students play the roles of community representatives. The company officials should try to convince the community representatives that the tanks should be repaired but not removed. Allow the community representatives to respond as they believe they should.

TEACH

Teaching Transparency 25B
Sources of Water Pollution

Use the transparency of Figure 25-7 to discuss the issue of water pollution. Have students identify the sources in the diagram and then indicate if any of these sources could affect the drinking water in their communities.

Background
Acid Rain

Acid rain (rain with a pH of less than 5.6) is a harmful outcome of certain kinds of air pollution. It damages soil and surface waters, destroys forests and agricultural crops, and endangers human health. The main causes of acid rain are the sulfur dioxide and nitrogen oxides given off by coal-burning power plants and motor vehicles. These gases interact with sunlight and water vapor in the air, forming acid compounds. When ordinary precipitation (rain or snow) passes through air containing acid compounds, it picks them up and falls to the ground as acid rain, snow, or sleet.

Genetics and the Environment: How Do They Relate?

Like height or eye and hair color, physical disorders can be inherited. Some people have a genetic predisposition for certain illnesses or diseases. This means that a person is predisposed (inclined) to develop a certain physical condition because he or she has inherited genes related to that condition. Whether a person will actually develop symptoms of a disease or illness he or she has a predisposition for depends on many factors.

Environmental pollution is a good example of something that triggers physical illness. It not only aggravates asthma and allergies but also increases the risk of activating certain diseases for which people may have a genetic predisposition. Leukemia and breast cancer are two examples of such diseases.

You can see again that environmental factors play important roles in our health. If you are aware of your surroundings and of how they affect you, you can use this information to your best health advantage.

■ (FIGURE 25-8)

night. According to him, those tanks can't be leaking gasoline, because they have some kind of pollution controls. But, come to think of it, I always smell gasoline when I drive by the tank farm.''

"Me too," Teresa agreed. "Well, I think we should demand that all the tanks be removed from our neighborhood! Those companies don't have the right to make everybody in our neighborhood sick by polluting the water!''

Water Pollution

Our increasing need for water, combined with the pollution of our water supply, is moving us steadily toward a health disaster. Part of our limited supply of fresh water is already too polluted for human use. As a result, many communities, like Teresa's,

have health problems due to polluted drinking water. Entire populations of some countries suffer from life-threatening health problems caused by severe shortages of clean, fresh water. Imagine what life would be like if you did not have enough water for drinking, bathing, cooking, or washing clothes.

Industry, agriculture, and our everyday activities create a vast amount of waste water that contains many dangerous chemicals and disease-causing organisms. Although cholera and typhoid (two diseases spread by polluted water) have been virtually eliminated in the United States, chemicals such as lead, gasoline, oil, fertilizers, and disinfectant byproducts impose many health risks. These and other hazardous chemicals increase the risk of cancer and birth defects, as well as nerve, stomach, kidney, and liver disorders.

Air Pollution

The quality of our air and the critical balance of gases in our atmosphere are also threatened by pollution. Air pollution is caused by the release of toxic gases and particles into the atmosphere by automobiles, factories, power-generating plants, and burning trash. These pollutants can be carried long distances by the wind or can rise into the upper levels of the atmosphere, where they can cause major worldwide problems.

Many health problems are linked to air pollution. The Environmental Protection Agency (EPA) blames air pollution for at least 2,000 new cases of cancer each year. There is also evidence that polluted air is a factor in birth defects and many other health problems. Young children, the elderly, and people who suffer from allergies or respiratory diseases such as asthma, bronchitis, and emphysema are especially at risk.

• • • TEACH continued

Class Discussion
Your Drinking Water

Determine if students know where their household water comes from—a reservoir or other surface water, such as a river, or underground water obtained from wells. Tell them that water from reservoirs and rivers is treated to remove bacteria and is tested periodically for toxic materials. If some students obtain water from underground

sources, ask them how the water is tested to ensure that it is free of contaminants. If the community has experienced problems with its water supply, discuss this situation with the class.

 Cooperative Learning
How's the Air?

Have students form groups to discuss the air quality in their area. Students should note whether smog or atmospheric haze is common. Ask them to

check local newspapers to see if air quality data are given. Have each group suggest what they think is the most important factor contributing to air pollution in the area.

Teaching Transparency 25C
Friend in the Sky, Foe on the Ground

Use this transparency to help students understand how ozone can be both helpful and harmful.

Destruction of the Ozone Layer

Ozone is an unstable form of oxygen. In the lower atmosphere, ozone is an undesirable gas that contributes to air pollution and is often a major component of smog. But the ozone found in the region of the upper atmosphere called the ozone layer is vital to living things.

The ozone layer completely surrounds the planet and protects living things from the ultraviolet (UV) light rays of the sun. UV light is dangerous to living things because it damages cells. In the early 1970s, scientists discovered a hole in the ozone layer over Antarctica. In the early 1990s, another hole was detected over the Northern Hemisphere. These holes in the ozone layer allow more of the damaging UV light to reach the Earth's surface.

Chemicals called chlorofluorocarbons (CFCs) have been linked to the destruction of the ozone layer. Sunlight causes these chemicals to break down. When they do, chlorine that is released from CFCs breaks down ozone molecules. Aerosol sprays (such as hairspray and deodorant) and chemicals used for cooling in air-conditioning systems and refrigerators are the main sources of ozone-damaging CFCs. However, coolants containing CFCs are slowly being phased out, and the ultimate goal is to have a total ban on CFCs by the year 2000. In addition, new regulations have been passed regarding the disposal of ozone-depleting chemicals.

Increased exposure to UV rays has been linked to an increase in several health problems, including skin cancer. Each year over 500,000 new cases of skin cancer are diagnosed.

Global Warming and the Greenhouse Effect

A greenhouse is a great place to be when it's cold outside, but not such a great place to be in the summer when it's hot.

Precautions you can take to avoid overexposure to the sun are discussed in Chapter 6.

Background
Ozone: Increase and Decrease

The thinning of the ozone layer in the stratosphere, caused by CFCs, leads to an increase in ultraviolet radiation reaching the earth's surface. According to one EPA study, a decrease of 1 percent in stratospheric ozone could lead to a 5 percent rise in skin cancer in the United States. Increased UV radiation also damages plants and animals, including the microscopic plankton that form the base of the food chains in the sea.

Additionally, human activities—such as driving gas-powered vehicles, manufacturing, and power production—indirectly add ozone to the lower atmosphere, where it is neither needed nor wanted. Ozone in the lower atmosphere is a pollutant that damages plants and causes respiratory problems in humans. Thus, our activities are destroying ozone where we need it and adding it where it is harmful.

Sun's Energy Warms the Earth

Gases Trap Heat and Radiate it Back to Earth

Gases Given Off by Industry and Vehicles

Earth Radiates Heat Back into Atmosphere

(FIGURE 25-9) **The greenhouse effect causes warming of the atmosphere. Many scientists predict that as the concentration of greenhouse gases in the atmosphere increases, global warming (an overall rise in the Earth's temperature) will result.**

Debate the Issue
Black-Market CFCs

As of 1996, CFCs can no longer be manufactured in the United States, and the sale of aerosols containing them is illegal. However, since many refrigeration systems and older air conditioning systems still rely on CFCs as a coolant, a large, international black-market trade in CFCs has developed. This bootlegged supply is much cheaper than the dwindling supply of legal CFCs. Have students debate the issue: How severe should penalties be for using illegal CFCs? What could the government do to stop this illegal trade?

Demonstration
Global Warming in a Car

On a sunny day, heat trapped within a car that has the windows closed can raise the inside air temperature considerably. Even on a cool day, the effect is noticeable. Demonstrate this effect by having students measure the temperature inside and outside the car, using thermometers. Have students report any difference in warmth between the inside air and the outside air. Use the car as an analogy to help students understand how such a greenhouse effect could lead to global warming.

Life Skills Worksheet 25A
Assign the Avoiding Tobacco Smoke Life Skills Worksheet.

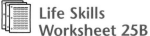

Life Skills Worksheet 25B
Assign the Protection from Noise Pollution Life Skills Worksheet.

Some Indoor Air Pollutants

Formaldehyde *chemical used in making furniture, foam insulation, and pressed wood—can cause dizziness, headaches, nausea, and burning eyes and lungs.*

Asbestos *fibrous mineral once used in insulation—linked to lung cancer and other respiratory diseases.*

Radon *radioactive gas that occurs naturally in certain kinds of rocks—linked to lung cancer.*

Carbon monoxide *invisible, odorless gas that escapes from faulty furnaces—causes drowsiness and death.*

(FIGURE 25-10) **Your home, school, or workplace could contain one or more of these indoor air pollutants. Your local health department can help you find out how to determine if any of these pollutants are present in your home.**

greenhouse effect:

the trapping of heat from the sun by certain gases in the atmosphere called greenhouse gases.

The glass or plastic that covers a greenhouse traps heat from the sun's rays, warming the inside. The **greenhouse effect** is the name given to this warming. The term is also used to describe the warming effect of certain gases in the atmosphere that trap heat from the sun's rays. These gases, called greenhouse gases, include carbon dioxide, water vapor, methane, ozone, nitrous oxide, and CFCs. In the right amounts, the greenhouse gases keep Earth's surface warm enough for life.

Today, certain agricultural, industrial, and consumer practices are increasing the amount of greenhouse gases—such as carbon dioxide—in the atmosphere. At the same time, vast numbers of trees, which consume carbon dioxide, are cut down each year. Water pollution also threatens to kill algae and small water plants that take up carbon dioxide and give off oxygen. The overall effect of these changes may be a gradual increase in the temperature of the planet—**global warming**.

global warming:

long-term increase in temperature that is related to air pollution and the greenhouse effect.

Already, global warming has resulted in a rising sea level and the erosion of many coastal areas. Experts believe that by the year 2100, increasing temperatures could melt many glaciers and raise the sea level another two to seven feet. A seven-foot rise of sea level would flood 50 to 80 percent of our coastal wetlands (bays and swamps) and cause extensive destruction of coastal property, wildlife, and beaches.

Indoor Air Pollution Most of us are exposed daily to air pollution in our homes, schools, and workplaces. In tightly sealed buildings, air pollutants may be more concentrated than they are outdoors. In general, air pollution tends to aggravate health problems such as asthma, bronchitis, heart disease, and emphysema. Certain pollutants can cause cancer and other serious illnesses.

Tobacco smoke is a common indoor air polluter. You learned in Chapter 14 that if you smoke or live with a smoker you are more likely to develop cancer, cardiovascular disease, or respiratory diseases than someone who is not exposed to smoke on a regular basis. Figure 25-10 lists some other indoor pollutants and their effects. Notice how dangerous a carbon monoxide leak can be—it's important to have carbon monoxide detectors installed in your home.

Land Pollution
Overpopulation and modern technology are creating another pollution problem. Land pollution is the spoiling of the land so that it is unfit to be inhabited by living things. As the population grows, more land area will be required to house the human race. This land will become unfit for other purposes, such as growing food and supporting wildlife. But an even greater land-pollution problem is the accumulation of wastes that are produced and discarded by humans.

• • • TEACH continued
Class Discussion
A Warmer Future
Point out that global warming not only means a rise in sea level but a wide range of other consequences as well. For example, dramatic changes in climate, including patterns of rainfall and average annual temperatures, would likely occur in most regions. Ask students to consider how such changes might affect agricultural pro-duction, recreational activities, fuel consumption, and other human activities.

Debate the Issue
Diapers: Cloth or Disposable?
Have students find out about the differences between disposable and cloth diapers, in terms of their environmental impact. They should look at the amount and kinds of material used in manufacture, the energy consumed in manufacture, the energy used in washing, the landfill space used in disposal, and so on. Have them debate the question: Which is better, cloth or disposable? Then discuss whether there is a clear preference between the two kinds of diapers in terms of the environmental impact.

Journal 25D
My Garbage

Have students refer to Figure 25-11 to identify the types of garbage that humans produce. Then ask them to record in their Journal the types of

Solid Wastes Solid wastes include all of the materials that humans discard. In the United States, agriculture, manufacturing, mining, health care, and just everyday living produce more than 150 million tons of solid wastes each year. Each one of us generates about four pounds of trash per day. Figure 25-11 shows the type of materials that the average American throws away.

The most common way of dealing with solid wastes has been to dump them "as far away as possible" so that they could be forgotten. But open dumps (where wastes are left on the ground) are breeding grounds for odors and disease-carrying insects and rodents. Today, the amount of solid wastes has grown so much that finding a safe place to put them is a serious problem.

Most solid wastes are now placed in sanitary landfills, where they can take years to decompose (break down). At these sites, the wastes are covered with a layer of soil to prevent the spread of disease. However, materials often escape from landfills and pollute the air and water. Some wastes are burned in incinerators (industrial plants where solid wastes are burned). Unfortunately, burning waste can pollute the air.

Sanitary landfills and incinerators are healthier than open dumps. However, all of these methods take up land that could be used for other purposes, and none are completely safe for human and environmental health. This is why it is so important for us to focus our efforts on reducing the amount of trash we generate.

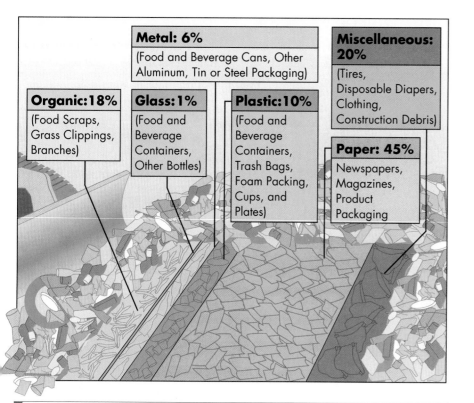

Metal: 6%
(Food and Beverage Cans, Other Aluminum, Tin or Steel Packaging)

Miscellaneous: 20%
(Tires, Disposable Diapers, Clothing, Construction Debris)

Organic: 18%
(Food Scraps, Grass Clippings, Branches)

Glass: 1%
(Food and Beverage Containers, Other Bottles)

Plastic: 10%
(Food and Beverage Containers, Trash Bags, Foam Packing, Cups, and Plates)

Paper: 45%
Newspapers, Magazines, Product Packaging

■ **(FIGURE 25-11) Do you know what's in your trash? Some of these figures may surprise you.**

SECTION 25.2

Background
Household Hazardous Waste (HHW)
Households are exempt from the stringent regulations that govern the disposal of industrial hazardous wastes. For this reason, it is important that consumers are able to identify what products found in the home could pose disposal problems. The product's label is sometimes a good source for information concerning its potential environmental hazards. HHWs include paint, some household cleaners and polishes, flashlight batteries and other small batteries, pesticides, motor oil, antifreeze, and lead-acid vehicle batteries. These products can pollute ground water, soil, and even air. HHWs frequently accumulate under the sink or in the garage because people don't know what to do with them. Because they need special handling, more and more communities are developing collection programs for HHWs. Although HHWs make up a small portion of household waste, it is extremely important to dispose of them properly.

garbage they throw away each day for a week. Have them classify the materials based on the categories shown in Figure 25-11. Then ask them to outline steps they could take to help reduce the problem of garbage disposal.

Reinforcement
The Problem of Solid Wastes

Have students distinguish the three categories of wastes that can pollute the environment.

- Solid wastes—garbage, or refuse, that is disposed of in open dumps or in sanitary landfills

- Hazardous wastes—toxic materials that can cause serious health problems for all living things

- Nuclear wastes—hazardous wastes that are radioactive and that cause health problems even in small doses

Ask students to discuss how these wastes must be disposed of so they do not pollute the environment and endanger health.

 Cooperative Learning
Hazardous Chemicals in Common Use

Many common chemicals used in homes and schools are classified as hazardous. When sold they are accompanied by a Material Safety Data Sheet (MSDS). Obtain copies of the MSDSs for chemicals used in your school. (Schools are required to have MSDSs on file; check with the chemistry departments or the director of the

Background
Nuclear Wastes

How and where to permanently store the nuclear wastes that have accumulated over the last 50 years remains an unsolved problem. The radiation released by these wastes remains dangerous for hundreds, and in some cases thousands, of years. Today there are only temporary nuclear-waste storage facilities. Although these facilities are not considered dangerous, there is mounting political pressure to find a long-term solution. Opponents of plans for permanent sites argue that their safety has not been established. So far, no one wants these wastes stored in "their backyard."

Section Review Worksheet 25.2

To reinforce the concepts presented in this section, assign Section Review Worksheet 25.2.

Section Quiz 25.2

Have students take Section Quiz 25.2.

---

hazardous wastes:

wastes that are dangerous to the health of living things or that are harmful to the environment.

Hazardous Wastes Certain types of wastes are classified as **hazardous wastes** because they may cause injury, illness, or death. Heavy metals, such as lead and mercury, and many chemical wastes, such as paint, paint removers, automobile fluids, pesticides, herbicides, and even batteries, are all examples of hazardous wastes. These substances are toxic (poisonous) to living things and are responsible for a lot of human health problems, including many birth defects and cases of cancer. Even plastic bags and balloons are considered hazardous wastes. When swallowed by wildlife, they can block the digestive system, causing starvation or disease.

Nuclear wastes are another type of hazardous waste. These highly dangerous radioactive materials result from nuclear-weapons research and production, nuclear-power generation, and medical treatments. It takes 10,000 years for some dangerous radioactive elements to decay into safe substances. Exposure to a large dose of radiation from nuclear wastes can be deadly. Even small amounts of radiation have been shown to cause bone marrow damage, skeletal abnormalities, and cataracts, as well as leukemia and other types of cancer.

Noise Pollution

The average amount of sound in our environment doubles every 10 years. Each day, you are exposed to many sources of noise pollution, including cars, trucks, heavy equipment, and jet aircraft. Sounds from radios, televisions, stereos, and loud concerts are also major noise pollutants.

Loud or constant noise can not only damage your hearing, but also cause stress, fatigue, irritability, anger, and anxiety. Prolonged exposure to loud sounds can even rupture your eardrum and may cause permanent hearing loss. Figure 25-13 shows some sources of noise pollution, their volume, and the type of damage they may cause.

(FIGURE 25-12) **Live rock concerts often produce sound levels that can cause some people pain and may even result in hearing loss.**

---

physical plant.) Have students form small groups, and give each one a different MSDS. Have the group review its sheet to identify the hazardous chemicals, the kinds of hazards they present, and the recommendations for handling and disposing of the chemicals. Have each group report its findings to the class. Ask students if they were surprised about any of the substances classified as hazardous.

Class Discussion
Noise Around Me

Have students identify sources of noise in and around their homes. The stereo, vacuum cleaner, and lawn mower are some examples. Suggest they discuss with family members ways of reducing noise around the home or ways of reducing exposure to noise.

Extension
Your Community's Garbage

Have a speaker from the local sanitation department speak to the class about the ways in which the community's solid wastes are disposed of. Also have the speaker discuss any plans for changing the way that solid wastes will be disposed of in the future.

LOUDNESS OF COMMON SOUNDS

THE DECIBEL SCALE. The decibel (dB) is the unit of sound loudness. It is based on the faintest sound people can hear. The decibel scale is exponential, which means that an increase of 10 dB produces a sound that is ten times louder. Therefore, an increase from 20 dB to 40 dB does not double the loudness of sound—it increases it 100 times. The graph below compares the loudness of some common sounds.

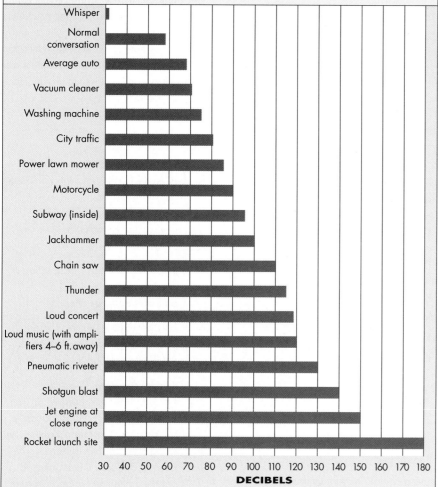

(FIGURE 25-13) The slightest sound that the human ear can detect has a loudness of 0 decibels (dB). Sounds in the 40–60 dB range are considered comfortable. Constant exposure to sounds above 70 dB (10 million times louder than the slightest sound) can be annoying and may begin to damage your hearing. Serious damage to hearing occurs with exposure to sounds of 120 dB. Sounds of 140 dB or more can cause pain, and at 180 dB, immediate and irreversible hearing loss occurs.

Check Up

Have students complete the Check Up, using Figure 25-13 as a guide to the decibel levels of noises in the environment. After completing the Check Up, have students record their conclusions concerning personal hearing loss. Students should also record any action they think they should take to protect their hearing.

Answers to Questions 1 and 2 are on p. 551.

3. Answers will vary but may include the following, plus any other threats to health discussed in class. Solid wastes can escape from landfills and cause air and water pollution. Wastes burned in incinerators can cause air pollution. Hazardous wastes contain toxic substances.

4. Answers will vary depending on the individual opinions of students.

Check Up

Are You Protecting Your Hearing?

There are several ways that noise can increase your anxiety level or permanently damage your hearing:

- prolonged exposure to sounds above 70 dB (increased anxiety level),

- 8 hours of exposure to 90 dB or more (hearing damage),

- short-term exposure to 120 dB or more (serious hearing damage),

- or exposure to 150 dB or more for any length of time (eardrums may rupture). Damage may occur with or without apparent symptoms.

Use Figure 25-13, Loudness of Common Sounds, as a guide, and evaluate your potential for hearing loss by responding "yes" or "no" to the following questions. Write your answers on a separate sheet of paper.

1. Do you attend loud concerts?

2. Do you frequently go to places that play loud music?

3. Do you listen to your stereo, videogames, or T.V. with the volume turned very high?

4. Do you use earphones when you listen to music?

5. Do you live or work around sources of loud noises, such as construction, airports, or major industry?

6. Do you sit up front when you go to:
   movies?
   concerts?
   other places that play loud music?

7. Do you hunt with a rifle or a shotgun or practice using firearms at a shooting range?

8. Have you ever been exposed to extremely loud noises (above 120 dB)?

If you responded yes to any of the questions above or if you frequently have trouble hearing certain sounds, you may have suffered some hearing loss. You should seriously consider changing your behavior so you do not further damage your hearing.

Some teenagers have already damaged their hearing. Studies indicate that many college freshmen suffer some degree of hearing loss. Much of this damage occurs during the middle school and high school years, in spite of the fact that hearing can easily be protected. Turning down the volume of radios and televisions and using protective earplugs when operating machinery and firing guns are ways that you can protect your hearing. To determine whether your hearing is damaged, complete the "Check Up: Are You Protecting Your Hearing?" to the left.

Review

1. What is the main cause of environmental pollution?

2. How does air pollution cause the greenhouse effect? destruction of the ozone layer? What are the potential dangers of each?

3. List five ways in which solid and hazardous wastes are harmful to the health of living things.

4. **Critical Thinking** Recently, smoking has been banned or restricted in most public places—schools, transportation systems, the workplace, and restaurants. This poses a difficult ethical question. Smokers often feel unfairly treated and resentful when they are not allowed to smoke. Nonsmokers usually find the smell of cigarette smoke very unpleasant. It is also hazardous to their health. How do you think this problem could be handled?

ASSESS

Section Review

Have students answer the Section Review questions.

Alternative Assessment
Pollution and Health

Have students make up charts that show health risks associated with each type of pollution. The chart should have the heads WATER POLLUTION, AIR POLLUTION, LAND POLLUTION, and NOISE POLLUTION. Students can then fill in the charts.

Closure
Pollution Around Me

Have students give examples of pollution they have observed, experienced, or caused. In each case, have the student classify the pollution as water pollution, air pollution, land pollution, or noise pollution.

Section
25.3 *What Can You Do?*

Objectives

- *Describe the benefits of responsible waste management, recycling, and conservation.*
- *List specific ways each individual can help reduce pollution.*
- *Make a recycling and reuse plan for your household.*
  LIFE SKILLS: Setting Goals

After what they had learned about the effects of environmental pollution on health, both Teresa and Jaime wanted to know what

they could do to protect their health. By collecting brochures and reading books and articles on the subject, they found that there are many ways to protect environmental and personal health.

Protecting Natural Resources and the Environment

As you learned in Section 25.1, the environment provides the materials that living things need for survival. This includes the many materials that people use for manufacturing the growing number of products and appliances they depend on. Currently, many natural resources are being used at an

(FIGURE 25-14) **Strip mining is one way that natural resources such as copper and coal are gathered. Frequently, these methods are very harmful to the environment.**

Background
Alternative Energy Sources—Wind

In past centuries, wind was a source of mechanical energy. Windmills were used to pump water and to grind grain into flour. As electric motors came into use, windmills became rare. Now, windmills are making a comeback—to generate electricity. Large windmill "farms" are efficient generators of electricity. Windmills have certain advantages—the wind is free and windmills produce no pollutants. Of course, wind does not blow steadily and some areas experience more wind than others. However, some experts think that wind-generated electricity could supply most electrical needs in many parts of the United States, particularly in the Midwest.

 Life Skills Worksheet 25C
Assign the Caring for the Environment Life Skills Worksheet.

Section 25.3 Lesson Plan

MOTIVATE

 Journal 25E
Environmental Awareness

This may be done as a warm-up activity. Have students record in their Journal the things they are currently doing to help preserve and protect the environment. Point out that they will learn more ways of protecting the environment as they read this section.

TEACH

Cooperative Learning
Resources From the Environment

Have students meet in small groups to brainstorm ways in which they are dependent on resources from the environment. Suggest that they consider materials that they use every day, materials needed for a comfortable home, materials needed for transportation, and materials that help them remain

healthy. Each group should compile a list of resources from the environment that supply these needs.

Writing
Conservation Ads

Have students compose advertisements or slogans that commend the benefits of conservation. Students might want to include artwork with their advertisements and construct posters. They could display their posters in the school or community.

Background

Radon

Another important indoor pollutant is *radon,* a naturally occurring radioactive gas found in many types of rocks and soils. Outdoors, it is relatively harmless. Indoors, however, radon can build to unhealthy levels, especially in basements. High levels of radon can damage lung tissue and eventually cause lung cancer. The EPA recommends that all homes be tested for radon. Test kits are available at most hardware stores. In most homes, the radon level is safe. However, if the radon level is found to be above a safe level, a ventilation system should be installed and any cracks in the building's foundation should be sealed.

Making a Choice 25A

Assign the Producing Less Waste card. The card asks students to examine ways to reduce their use of disposable products.

alarming rate, while the manner in which they are used pollutes the environment. If we don't reverse this trend, we will be left with an environment that can no longer support life as we know it. Fortunately, there are healthier and more responsible alternatives to the activities that are endangering the health of our environment.

conservation: *the wise use and protection of natural resources.*

Conservation **Conservation** is the protection and wise use of natural resources. By taking fewer natural materials from the environment, particularly those that are nonrenewable, we can help ensure that these resources will continue to be available in the future. One example of a pressing need for conservation efforts is in the way we produce energy. Much of our electricity is generated by burning coal and oil. Gasoline is burned to power most motor vehicles.

 (FIGURE 25-15) **Many products that are sold in aerosol cans are available in pump sprays, which do not contain CFCs or damage the ozone layer.**

However, burning fuels such as coal, oil, and gasoline is very harmful to the environment. In addition, supplies of these fuels are limited. Using less electricity and driving less helps to extend the supplies of burnable fuels and slow down the rate of pollution. It also helps each of us save money.

Conservation also means protecting the environment from pollutants by using products that are less toxic (safer). Safer alternatives to many toxic products are available. For example, pump sprays do not contain CFCs and do not damage the ozone layer. Low-phosphate and no-phosphate laundry detergents are less polluting to the water than high-phosphate detergents. Safer alternatives to burning fuels for energy include solar power, wind power, and water power. These energy sources are also renewable.

Recycling and Reusing Many of the materials that we discard can be reused. Ways of reusing materials include:

- recycling—the reusing of materials either directly or indirectly by making them into another product (For example, glass bottles can be used again or ground up and remelted to make a new item.)
- composting—the converting of organic matter into fertilizer by allowing it to be broken down by the action of bacteria
- pulverizing and compacting—the pounding of solid wastes into bricks that can be used in constructing landfills, roads, or other structures

About 80 percent of the solid waste produced is reusable. The advantages of reusing these materials include reducing the volume of solid waste and slowing down the rate at which resources are removed from the environment. Unfortunately, it costs more in many instances to recycle items than to produce them from scratch. As a result, less than 10 percent of reusable solid wastes is actually being recycled, but researchers are actively striving to develop low-cost methods of recycling. Most cities and towns now have centers that will accept recyclable items. Since some recycling centers pay for the materials, this is a good way to clean up the environment and raise money for a good cause.

Reducing Personal Pollution

There is much that each individual can do to limit the amount of pollution that enters the environment. Teresa and Jaime decided to list easy ways that they could begin to make their environment cleaner and safer. The following are some of the things they listed as personal goals.

Preserving the Air To help keep the air as clean as possible, we will:

- Walk, bicycle, use public transportation, or carpool whenever possible.
- Purchase safer alternatives to products sold in aerosol cans.
- Choose not to smoke or spend time with those who do.
- Keep the car well tuned, and have the exhaust system checked frequently.
- Avoid purchasing products that contain formaldehyde or CFCs.
- Use less electricity.
- Plant trees by participating in a community program.

Preserving the Water To conserve water and help keep it cleaner, we will:

- Use only biodegradable, low-phosphate detergents.
- Fix leaky faucets and toilets quickly.
- Put displacement devices in all toilet tanks. (See Figure 25-17 to find out how to make a displacement device out of common household products.)

(FIGURE 25-16) **Community recycling centers accept a variety of recyclable materials. These materials must be separated according to their type. It's a good idea to do this ahead of time if you plan to recycle.**

- Take shorter showers, use less water in the tub for baths, and replace shower heads with water-conserving models.
- Fertilize and water lawns sparingly.
- Avoid using pesticides, and use the least-toxic products available when they are necessary.
- Dispose of all hazardous household chemicals safely. (Contact the local EPA office or city sanitation department for instructions and disposal sites in your community.)

Reducing Solid and Hazardous Waste To help reduce pollution and preserve non-renewable resources, we will:

- Recycle and reuse whenever possible.
- Reduce household trash by purchasing reusable items and products with minimal packaging.

SECTION 25.3

 Making a Choice 25B
Assign the Assessing Threats to Health card. The card asks students to consider environmental threats to health in their local community.

Section Review Worksheet 25.3
To reinforce the concepts presented in this section, assign Section Review Worksheet 25.3.

Section Quiz 25.3
Have students take Section Quiz 25.3.

 Reteaching Worksheet 25.3
Students who have difficulty with the material may complete Reteaching Worksheet 25.3.

other members of the class evaluate the effectiveness of the arguments.

Class Discussion
Local Issues

Have students check the local newspaper for several days to find out about environmental issues that concern the local community. Engage the class in a discussion of those issues. Students should decide how the issues affect them, what they think should be done, and what actions, if any, they want to take.

Extension
Time to Recycle

Have students find out if their community has a recycling program. If so, have students report on the types of materials recycled and how the community handles such materials. If recycling is voluntary, have students organize a campaign to increase participation among community residents. Students can help distribute information about what to recycle and how. If no recycling program exists,

have students organize a campaign to start a recycling program in the community. Students can write letters to local officials and put up posters in the school and around the community urging that the local government start a recycling program.

1. Recycling reduces the volume of solid waste and slows the rate at which resources are removed from the environment. Conservation helps ensure we will have natural resources in the future and helps protect the environment from pollutants.

2. Water pollution: Answers may include to fertilize and water lawns sparingly, to avoid using pesticides, and to dispose of all household chemicals safely. Air pollution: Answers may include to walk, cycle, or carpool whenever possible, to use less electricity, and to not smoke. Land pollution: Answers may include to recycle and reuse, to start a compost pile, and to purchase environmentally safe cleaning products.

3. Students might use the Yellow Pages, their city government, or the local library to find the locations of recycling centers. Students' plans will vary depending on the type of materials students plan to recycle and reuse.

4. Students might use symbols that convey the dangers of hazardous and nuclear wastes.

(FIGURE 25-17) **You can reduce the amount of water used in flushing the toilet by placing a displacement device into the tank. A plastic milk or juice bottle filled with water and a few rocks to weight it down is ideal for this purpose. Your city water board should be able to give you more information on how to conserve water.**

- Start a compost pile for biodegradable garbage.
- Limit the use of chemical fertilizers and pesticides.
- Purchase environmentally safe cleaning products.

Other Ways to Make a Difference

In addition to adopting personal behaviors that reduce pollution, there are many ways people can work together to promote a cleaner, safer environment. Some of the ways you could help are listed here.

- Join or support the efforts of environmental groups such as the Sierra Club, Friends of the Earth, the Wilderness Society, and the Nature Conservancy.
- Call problems to the attention of those who can help, such as conservation groups, newspapers, and city hall.
- Help attorneys prosecute violators by identifying sites of pollution and providing evidence such as photos.
- Participate in the law-making process by voting and by writing or talking to elected officials about your concerns.
- Encourage the school to obtain and use programs that build environmental awareness: Project WILD, Project Learning Tree, and the National Wildlife Federation CLASS PROJECT.

Review

1. *What are the benefits of recycling and conservation?*

2. *List three ways individuals can help reduce each of the following: water pollution, air pollution, and land pollution.*

3. **LIFE SKILLS: Setting Goals** *Find out where the recycling centers are in your community and what materials they accept. Then outline a recycling and reuse plan for your household and plan to carry it out.*

4. **Critical Thinking** *How would you label hazardous and nuclear wastes so that someone living 10,000 years in the future would be able to understand their danger even though they may not speak your language?*

ASSESS

Section Review

Have students answer the Section Review questions.

Alternative Assessment
For My Own Good

Have students write a brief paragraph showing the connection between helping protect the environment and protecting their own health.

Closure
Protecting the Environment

Have each student suggest three things that he or she thinks are most important in protecting the environment. List these on the chalkboard as they are suggested. Keep a tally of the number of students mentioning each one. Then reorder or number the steps in the order of importance to the class.

Life Skills Check . . . .

1. Communicating Effectively
Write a letter to one of your local legislative representatives describing an environmental concern and what you would like him or her to do about it.

2. Setting Goals
Someday you will move into a place of your own. Suppose you were to design your house or apartment. What are some things you would put in your plans that would be energy efficient and foster environmental protection? Include plans for landscaping, materials for building the house, and plumbing fixtures.

3. Using Community Resources
You would like to provide public-health support by doing volunteer work. You don't really want to work with a government agency. Who else might need your help? What could you do for them?

Projects . . . .

1. Write a brief report about your community's trash disposal system. Does your community have a sanitary landfill? If not, how does your community dispose of trash? Is the system environmentally safe? If your community has a landfill, does the landfill prevent environmental pollution? How? If possible, include pictures with your report.

2. By reading the newspaper or watching the local news, monitor the "pollution index" of your area for a week. Then find out what the pollution index was six months ago. (You can do this by looking up old newspapers in the library.) Compare the numbers. What do they mean? How could they affect your health? Report your findings to your class.

Plan for Action . . . .

The responsibility for your community's environment ultimately rests with the individuals of the community. Devise a plan to adapt your behaviors in order to promote a healthy environment in your community.

---

as contaminate fish and other food sources.
2. Answers will vary. Accept any thoughtful response.
3. Answers will vary. Accept any thoughtful response.

Life Skills Check

1. Letters will vary according to students' concerns.
2. Answers may include skylights, solar panels, computer-controlled thermostats, and water-conserving faucet heads.
3. Answers will include a variety of volunteer agencies that deal with problems such as AIDS, drug abuse, homelessness, and teen pregnancies.

Projects
Have students complete the projects on environmental and public health.

Plan for Action
Have the class vote on a single environmental or health issue that they would like to support or promote as a group. Have students brainstorm a list of actions they can take to help achieve their goal.

Personal Pledge
Discuss the pledge for Chapter 25. A student's decision of whether to sign the pledge is personal and private.

ASSESSMENT OPTIONS

Chapter Test
Have students take the Chapter 25 Test.

Alternative Assessment
Have students do the Alternative Assessment activity for Chapter 25.

Test Generator
The Test Generator contains additional assessment items for this chapter.

CHAPTER 26

Being a Wise Consumer

SECTION	TITLE/OBJECTIVES	Personal Health Inventory	Journal	Check Up	Life Skills	Life Skills Worksheets	Media Message or Ethical Issues Worksheet	What Would You Do?
		PERSONAL INVENTORY			LIFE SKILLS DEVELOPMENT			
26.1 *pp. 571–573*	**WHAT YOU CAN EXPECT IN HEALTH CARE** ▦ Develop a plan to select a physician. ▦ Learn how to communicate with medical personnel. • Understand your rights as a patient.	Ch. 26	26A 26B			26A		
26.2 *pp. 574–580*	**FINANCING YOUR MEDICAL COSTS** • Understand why health-care costs in the United States are rising. ▦ Know the advantages and disadvantages of traditional private health-care insurance and HMOs. ▦ Learn how to locate free health care in your community. ▦ Learn how to recognize quackery.		26C 26D		p. 577	26B 26C	Unit 5	

KEY: ▦ Denotes Life Skill Objective

Text references denoted by page number.

Supplement references denoted by chapter or item numbers.

LINKING RESOURCES

	INTERACTION		OTHER RESOURCES		SECTION REVIEW AND ASSESSMENT			
Making a Choice Cards	Parent Discussion Guide	Health Talk Audio Program	Teaching Transparencies and Directory	Section Review Worksheets	Section Quizzes	Reteaching Worksheets	Section Reviews
26A			26A	26.1	26.1	26.1	p. 573
26B				26.2	26.2	26.2	p. 580

KEY FACTS

- Having a primary-care physician is critically important to maintaining good health.

- To evaluate a person's health accurately, a doctor must do a physical examination and take a complete medical history. It is important that the patient gives the doctor complete and accurate information.

- A patient has the right to obtain a second opinion from another doctor.

- Hospitals should give all patients a copy of the Patient's Bill of Rights.

- Health-care options include traditional health insurance, HMOs, PPOs, and free or low-cost health care funded by the government.

- Quackery, the promotion of worthless or unproven medical services or products, can be dangerous when it delays accurate diagnosis and appropriate treatment of a disease.

CHAPTER REVIEW AND ASSESSMENT

TEXT

Chapter Review pp. 582–583

SUPPLEMENTS

Chapter Test 26

Alternative Assessment 26

Test Generator Chapter 26

Being a Wise Consumer

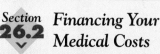

◆ ◆ ◆ ◆

Section 26.1 *What You Can Expect in Health Care*

Section 26.2 *Financing Your Medical Costs*

GETTING STARTED
• • • • • • • • • • • •

Using the Chapter Photograph

Ask: **How is the young man in the picture taking responsibility for maintaining his health?** *[by visiting a doctor]* Ask how they think the young man went about choosing the doctor and how he or his family might be paying for the visit.

 Question Box

Have students write out any questions they have about choosing a doctor and paying for medical services and put them in the Question Box.

Sensitivity **ALERT**

Many people have no health insurance, family doctor, or dentist and have difficulty paying for health care. Don't assume that everyone has or can afford regular health care. One student's level of health care may be unavailable to another. Be sensitive to these varying economic levels in your class. Also, a student undergoing treatment for a personal problem, such as a psychological disorder, may be uncomfortable discussing medical services, so be alert to discomfort levels in students.

■ **The right doctor is critically important to maintaining good health.**

MYTHS & MISCONCEPTIONS

• **Health-care advertising must be true because there are government agencies that monitor it.** Several government agencies try to identify fraudulent services and products. However, no thorough controls over health-care advertising exist. View all advertising that promises quick or unusual results with suspicion.

• **Since the doctor knows best, there is no need to question recommended treatments.** It is important to ask your doctor questions about any aspect of your medication or treatment that you do not understand.

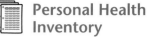

Cam sat in the middle of the living room looking at all the boxes that surrounded her. Books were strewn across the floor, and her cat was having a great time running through the maze. Cam could hear her parents in the next room hanging pictures. It seemed they had been here longer than just two days.

All of a sudden, Cam began to wheeze from all the dust in the room. ''Oh, no,'' she thought. ''I hope I don't get an asthma attack *now*. Not when we just moved to this town. We don't even have a doctor yet.''

Personal Health Inventory

Have students complete the Personal Health Inventory for this chapter.

Life Skills Worksheet 26A

Assign the Finding a Primary-Care Physician Life Skills Worksheet.

Making a Choice 26A

Assign the Doctor-Patient Interactions card. The card asks students to role-play an interview between a doctor and prospective patient and between a doctor and first-time patient.

Section 26.1
What You Can Expect in Health Care

Objectives

- *Develop a plan to select a physician.*
  - **LIFE SKILLS: Being a Wise Consumer**

- *Learn how to communicate with medical personnel.*
  - **LIFE SKILLS: Communicating Effectively**

- *Understand your rights as a patient.*

Like Cam and her family, practically everyone needs a **primary care physician** (family medicine physician). Although the right doctor is critically important to maintaining good health, many people don't know how to find a good doctor. People often seem unconcerned with how they choose their physician. In fact, some studies indicate that the average American spends more time selecting a mechanic than in selecting a doctor. In this chapter, you'll learn how to select a doctor and how to communicate with doctors. You'll find out what your rights are in dealing with them. And you'll learn about some of the plans that are available to pay for the costs of health care.

primary care physician:

a family physician, a pediatrician, or a general internal medicine physician.

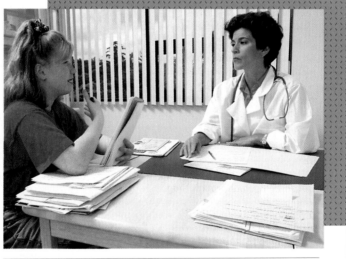

(FIGURE 26-1) **It is important that you feel free to be direct and assertive with your doctor and to ask any questions that concern you.**

Section 26.1 Lesson Plan

MOTIVATE

Journal 26A
Thinking About Health Care

Ask students to list in their Journal the images that come to mind when they hear the term *health care*. Also, have them describe any feelings that are attached to those images.

TEACH

Class Discussion
Why You Need a Doctor

On the chalkboard, write, "Why You Need a Doctor." Write the reasons as students volunteer them. *(to maintain good health; for physicals and immunizations; for care if there is illness or an emergency)* Have students discuss the role of the primary-care physician, or where they go when they need medical attention. Ask: **If you don't have a family** doctor, or if you can't get your doctor during an emergency, where can you go for medical help?** *[a public hospital emergency department]*

Teaching Transparency 26A
Patient's Bill of Rights

Use this transparency of Figure 26-2 to review a patient's rights. Discuss how rights and responsibilites are related. For example, if a patient does not understand what a health professional

Section Review Worksheet 26.1

To reinforce the concepts presented in this section, assign Section Review Worksheet 26.1.

Section Quiz 26.1

Have students take Section Quiz 26.1.

Reteaching Worksheet 26.1

Students who have difficulty with the material may complete Reteaching Worksheet 26.1.

The Selection Process

As an adult, you will need to decide who your doctor will be. You may decide to keep the same physician you have always had. If you decide to change doctors, it's best to go ahead and make the change while you are healthy.

There are several ways to go about finding a new doctor. One way is to ask your relatives and friends about their physicians. Another method is to locate a medical school that is affiliated with a nearby hospital. Then, call the school, and ask for a list of its staff physicians. The county medical society can also provide you with a list of physicians.

After making your choice, call the doctor's office to find out if he or she is accepted by your medical plan and to make sure new patients are welcome. Check on hours and fees as well.

During your first appointment, your doctor will record your reason for coming in, your specific signs and symptoms (temperature, blood pressure, heart rate, type of pain, etc.), medication you are taking, and your diet and exercise habits. Information about previous illnesses, surgery, treatment, allergies, and reactions to medications will also be needed to establish your medical history. During the examination, you can help by pointing out pains, lumps, growths, or previous injuries that cause pain or concern. Keep in mind that your doctor is trying to learn and record as much about you as possible to aid diagnosis and treatment.

It is important for you to feel comfortable enough with your doctor that you are able to be direct and assertive, and to ask questions. You might ask, How long will it take to heal? Will the medicine produce any side effects? Should I take the medicine with food or on an empty stomach? When should I come back? Can I exercise and go to soccer practice? You should expect answers to all of your questions, no matter how trivial they may seem. Some people like to write down their questions and bring the list with them. You may also want to write down any special instructions the doctor gives you during the office visit. Do not allow the doctor to rush you or brush you off to get to the next patient. Avoid making a final decision about a new doctor until after a few visits. If you are hurried, treated like a child, cannot get direct answers, sense questionable business prac-

(FIGURE 26-2)

Patient's Bill of Rights

As a patient, you have the right to:

considerate and respectful care.

obtain complete information concerning your diagnosis, treatment, and prognosis in language you can understand.

information (risks, benefits, alternative treatments) you need in order to give informed consent before treatment.

refuse treatment, once you are aware of the facts, to the extent permitted by law.

privacy (refusal to be examined in front of people not involved in your case) and confidentiality of records.

a reasonable response when you ask for help.

information about any possible conflicts of interest (hospital ownership of labs, professional relationships among doctors who are treating you).

be told if the hospital plans to make your treatment part of a research project or experiment.

an itemized explanation of your hospital bill.

know what hospital rules apply to your conduct as a patient.

expect good follow-up care.

• • • TEACH continued

tells them, it is the responsibility of the patient to say so.

Journal 26B
A Patient's Bill of Rights

Ask students to recall the last time they had medical or dental treatment. Then, in their Journal, have them evaluate their experience based on the Patient's Bill of Rights.

Role-Playing
Visiting the Doctor

Have students role-play a visit to a doctor. The patient has the following symptoms: sore throat, slight fever, and fatigue. Assign these roles: receptionist (greets patient, asks patient for insurance card, accepts payment or gives insurance papers), nurse or physician's assistant (obtains brief statement of symptoms, takes temperature and blood pressure), doctor (examines, asks questions, rec-

ommends treatment, and prescribes medicines), and patient. Discuss the roles before beginning. Emphasize the importance of good communication between patient and doctor. Remind the patient to ask questions if anything is unclear. For each role-play, evaluate how well the patient and doctor communicated.

Reinforcement
Caring for Yourself

Emphasize that each student is responsible for his or her own health care. Point out that students also should

(FIGURE 26-3) **You and your family may have to consult a team of doctors if someone close to you has a major illness and requires long-term medical care.**

tices, or do not feel comfortable, then change doctors.

Remember that you have a right to get the opinion of another doctor at any time. This can be especially important when surgery or another major procedure has been recommended. The recommendation of the second doctor is called a "second opinion."

Patient's Bill of Rights

The basic rights of human beings include freedom of expression, the right to make one's own decisions and to act upon them, and the right to maintain one's personal dignity. These rights should be preserved for you when you are a patient. If you are hospitalized for any reason, you should receive your copy of the Patient's Bill of Rights, shown in Figure 26-2. Although it is not a legal document, it does set forth standards that hospitals are expected to follow. Becoming aware of your rights as a patient is your first step toward getting quality health care. It is your own personal responsibility to look out for yourself, insisting on good

care and freely expressing your needs and concerns.

Review

1. **LIFE SKILLS: Being a Wise Consumer** List three ways to select a physician.

2. **LIFE SKILLS: Communicating Effectively** This is your third visit to your doctor about the headaches you have been having. Your doctor hasn't told you what is causing the headaches or whether they will go away. Write down four questions you can ask your doctor to get clear information on your condition.

3. **Critical Thinking** Why should a hospital tell you if it plans to make your treatment part of an experiment it is conducting?

SECTION 26.1

Review Answers
1. Ask relatives and friends about their physicians, locate a medical school in your area and call its affiliated hospital for a list of its staff, or contact your county medical society.
2. Answers will vary but may include: What do you think is causing the headaches? Can I expect the headaches to go away? What tests might be done to find the cause of the headaches? What can I do to prevent the headaches? What can I do to treat the headaches once they start?
3. Answers will vary but should reflect the following: You have a right to know whether the treatment received is experimental or approved, and if the treatment is experimental, you have a right to know the risks involved and how your medical information will be used.

apply the Patient's Bill of Rights any time they see a doctor or dentist. They should always communicate clearly with medical people, be assertive, ask questions, and feel free to find a second opinion or another doctor.

Extension
Choosing a Health-Care Provider

Ask the school nurse or other health-care professional to visit the class to talk about finding physicians, hospitals, clinics, pharmacies, and health insurance, and to answer students' questions concerning health care.

ASSESS

Section Review

Have students answer the Section Review questions.

Alternative Assessment
A Dangerous Mistake

Suppose you don't tell a doctor all of your symptoms or don't ask all of your important questions. Why could this be a dangerous mistake?

Closure
Health Care Is Your Responsibility

Ask students to think about what they will do after high school, such as go to college, get a job, or start a family. Discuss whose responsibility it will be to find a family doctor.

Background
History
In Colonial America, medical care was rare and doctors were few. Most people received only home remedies as treatment for disease. Hospitals began to appear in the 1700s. Modern health-care innovations include health insurance, HMOs, and Medicare for the elderly and Medicaid for the poor. Today, many people think our massive health-care system needs overhauling, but people can't agree on how to change it.

Background
Wasteful Spending
Studies estimate that $130 billion is spent on unnecessary surgery, tests, and hospitalization days, and that $70 billion is wasted through administrative inefficiency. Various studies indicate that many Caesarean births, hysterectomies, back surgeries, and MRI scans (Magnetic Resonance Imaging, which displays computer-generated images of the body) are unnecessary.

defensive medicine:

use of numerous and sometimes unnecessary diagnostic tests to avoid a lawsuit.

premium:

payment a person makes to an insurance company in exchange for coverage.

Section 26.2 *Financing Your Medical Costs*

Objectives

- *Understand why health-care costs in the United States are rising.*

- *Know the advantages and disadvantages of traditional private health-care insurance and HMOs.*
  - **LIFE SKILLS: Being a Wise Consumer**

- *Learn how to locate free health care in your community.*
  - **LIFE SKILLS: Using Community Resources**

- *Learn how to recognize quackery.*
  - **LIFE SKILLS: Being a Wise Consumer**

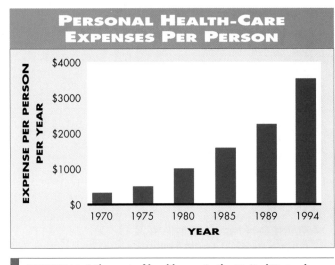

PERSONAL HEALTH-CARE EXPENSES PER PERSON

(FIGURE 26-4) **The cost of health care in the United States has been rising rapidly, making it difficult for many people to obtain health care. (Source: U.S. Bureau of the Census.)**

We are spending more and more each year for personal health care as physician costs, dental costs, and hospital-care costs rise rapidly. You can see this trend in Figure 26-4. High tech equipment, organ transplants, the AIDS epidemic, malpractice insurance, and **defensive medicine** (use of numerous and sometimes unnecessary diagnostic tests to avoid a lawsuit) are some of the causes, and they will continue to increase costs in the future. Unless something is done to reduce these costs, the number of Americans unable to afford medical or dental care will continue to grow.

The U.S. government and businesses are exploring ways to make medical care affordable for everyone by examining proposals for socialized medicine (health care paid from tax dollars), shared-cost programs, and managed care.

Your Family Health Insurance Plan
A good health insurance plan is an absolute necessity in the United States today. Employees of major industries, the government, and other companies often pay a fee, called a **premium**, for their insurance coverage. For an additional fee, they may add family members. Unfortunately, many small businesses and other employers have no such plans, and their employees cannot afford the high health insurance premiums of individual policies. High medical costs have also forced many companies to reduce their benefits and to increase premiums, especially for employees with unhealthy lifestyle behaviors such as smoking. The monthly insurance premium is taking a big-

Section 26.2 Lesson Plan

MOTIVATE

Demonstration
What Do We Spend on Health Care?

Have students review the health-cost figures in Figure 26-4. Then have students multiply the 1994 health-care cost per person, $3,500.00, times the United States population for that year,

an estimated 261 million people, to find out approximately how much we spent on health care that year. *(about $913.5 billion)* Elicit student responses to this figure.

(FIGURE 26-5)

SECTION 26.2

Check Your Insurance Coverage

Can you choose any physician, or is there a limited list of providers?

Is there a deductible? That is, do you have to pay anything before the insurance company begins paying?

What deductible amount is suited to your family income and predicted health needs?

Is disability or lost-income protection provided? Is there a lump-sum payment to dependents in case of death?

Is full coverage provided for hospital, medical, and surgical costs? Can you go outside the plan and still be covered?

Is major medical insurance available for serious illness and accidents?

Are expenses for care during pregnancy and delivery covered?

Is this a "commercial policy" (one that can be canceled if the holder becomes a bad risk after the claim for a current illness is paid)?

Is a group policy available? These are less expensive.

Is coverage provided for mental and emotional disorders?

Is coverage provided for dental care?

Are dependents covered?

Do any restrictive clauses eliminate coverage of pre-existing conditions or require a waiting period before such conditions are covered?

What happens if I am covered by a group policy at work and I get fired or resign? Could I keep my insurance, or would the policy be canceled?

Background
What Health Insurance Covers
Coverage usually includes hospital expense (shared room, meals, tests, medications, nursing, operating room), surgical expense (doctor's fee), outpatient expense (nonsurgical), and major medical (cost from a serious illness or accident, office visits, therapy, medications). Some policies include dental, vision, and disability income.

Ethical Issues in Health
Have students read this Unit 7 feature on pages 584–585. Then have them complete its companion worksheet.

Life Skills Worksheet 26B
Assign the Free or Low-Cost Health Services Life Skills Worksheet.

ger and bigger portion of the employee's take-home pay. In addition, health insurance pays only part of the bill. For those who are stricken with a serious illness, family savings are often quickly drained.

Traditional Policies Traditional private health insurance policies have advantages and drawbacks. One big advantage is that the insurance company will pay for treatment by any doctor or hospital the insured person chooses. This can be very important if a person has had the same physician for a long time and does not want to change.

One drawback is that the insured person must pay for any doctor visits or medical expenses up front, and then fill out a claim form in order to be reimbursed.

Another disadvantage is that the insured person must pay a yearly **deductible,**

deductible:

the amount of medical costs an insured person must pay before the insurance company begins paying.

TEACH

Debate the Issue
Can We Cut Health-Care Costs?

Have students select one of the reasons for rising health-care costs, formulate a question, and debate the pros and cons. Some sample questions to debate are: Should limitations be placed on organ transplants? Should caps be placed on malpractice awards to encourage doctors to stop practicing defensive medicine?

Demonstration
Teacher's Health Insurance

As an example, explain to students your school district's health-care plan for teachers. Describe where the money comes from, the types of coverage provided, any additional fees for family coverage, deductibles, any premium you must pay, and so on. Show the arithmetic for a specific claim on the chalkboard to illustrate how the system works.

Journal 26C
Your Family's Health Insurance

Have students ask the adults at home questions about how their family health-care costs are met. Then, in their Journal, have students explain their family's arrangement.

Making a Choice 26B

Assign the Choosing a Health Insurance Plan card. The card asks students to make up a list of questions to help them decide whether to enroll in a traditional health insurance plan, a PPO, or an HMO.

HMOs (health maintenance organizations):

organizations that offer subscribers complete medical care in return for a fixed monthly fee.

PPOs (preferred provider organizations):

organizations that offer subscribers discounted medical care when they use preselected health-care providers.

(FIGURE 26-6)

or set fee, before the insurance company begins paying for any of the costs. And routine checkups at a doctor's office are usually not reimbursed—only office visits for illness or injury. Insurance companies reimburse only a percentage of office visit costs, usually 80 percent. The remaining amount is paid by the insured person. Insurance companies also pay only a percentage of hospital costs, usually 80 percent as well.

Before purchasing a traditional health insurance policy, it would be helpful to find out the answers to the questions in Figure 26-5. You might also find it helpful to call your state insurance department for assistance. A representative can analyze any policy, explain its terms, and provide information on how to get reimbursed for claims.

HMOs and PPOs A more recent type of health-care plan is an **HMO (Health Maintenance Organization),** a group of health-care providers who offer complete medical care in return for a fixed monthly fee. In addition, some HMOs charge a small fee for office visits and prescriptions.

HMOs have several advantages. First, patients do not have to submit claim forms for reimbursement. Another advantage is that HMOs practice preventative medicine. Because HMOs receive almost the same amount of money from members no matter how many times members use their services, it is financially advantageous for HMOs to have healthy members. Therefore, HMOs emphasize checkups, immunizations, and other ways of staying healthy.

A big drawback of HMOs is that you can't freely see any doctor of your choice. If you see a specialist outside an HMO without the consent of the HMO, you must pay for the services yourself.

There is another type of health-care plan that combines features of both traditional policies and HMOs—**Preferred Provider Organizations (PPOs).** As a

Traditional Insurance Policies Versus HMOs

Traditional Insurance Policies	HMOs
Focus is on treatment	Focus is on prevention
Regular checkups usually not covered; only a percentage (usually 80 percent) of hospital costs and office visits reimbursed; reimbursement doesn't begin until costs exceed the deductible	Most health-care costs paid, except for a small fee (copayment) charged by some HMOs for office visits or prescriptions
Can see any primary care physician you choose	Must use one of the HMO's participating primary care physicians
Can see any specialist you choose	Must have the HMO's consent to see a specialist, or the HMO will not pay costs

• • • TEACH continued

Case Study
Traditional Health Insurance

Present the following information to students: Anna has a traditional health insurance plan at work with $500 deductible, 80 percent payment, and no dental or eye coverage. Last year she had hospital bills ($1,100), doctor bills ($300), prescriptions for drugs ($100), dental care ($75), and new glasses ($125). Ask: **How much did Anna pay? How much did her insurance pay?** [Anna's paid $200 for dental and eye care. Her insurance covers the $1,500 for hospital, doctor, and prescriptions, but she had to pay the first $500 (the deductible). That left $1,000, of which the insurance company paid 80 percent or $800; Anna paid the remaining $200. Altogether, the insurance company paid $800, and Anna paid $900.]

Class Discussion
How Can Everyone Be Covered?

Have students discuss the idea of universal basic health-care coverage. Ask how they think it could be paid for considering the enormous costs involved. Consider this scenario: the breadwinner of a moderate-income family recently lost his or her job. Although the family could keep their insurance policy, they would have to pay the entire $220 monthly premium.

member of a PPO, you may either select your health-care provider from a pre-approved group, the ''preferred providers,'' or you may choose to be in the care of someone outside of the group. However, the insurance company has arranged to have services performed by a preferred provider at a discounted rate. What this ultimately means is that although you can go to any doctor you want, it will cost you less money if you choose to go to a doctor that your PPO has selected.

*Life*SKILLS: Being a Wise Consumer

Traditional Policy or HMO?

Someday you will need to select a health insurance policy of your own. Get some practice now by evaluating the following situation.

At your new job, your take-home pay is $1,100 a month. You're married and have a small child. Your spouse does not have health insurance at work, but you can get either a traditional policy or join an HMO where you work.

The traditional policy would cost you $71 per month. It would cost you $22 per month to add your spouse and child. The traditional policy has a $250-a-year deductible for you, or $500 for you and your dependents (spouse and child), and it pays 80 percent of hospital costs.

You would pay $56 per month for the HMO. It would cost $22 per month to add your spouse and child. In addition, each time you or a member of your family visited the doctor or bought a prescription medicine, you would pay a $5 copayment. There would be no copayment required of you if you or a member of your family entered the hospital.

Everyone in your family is enjoying good health right now. Your child will need a checkup at least once a year. You are happy with the pediatrician who cares for your child. You and your spouse, however, have not yet chosen a primary care physician.

Which family members would you insure? Would you choose the HMO or the traditional policy? Why?

Life SKILLS

Have students consider the facts presented in the text and decide on their own whether the traditional health insurance policy or the HMO is more advantageous in this case.

The family could not do this and continue to meet their basic living expenses. Because they were all in good health, they took a chance and dropped the insurance policy. Suddenly a family member needs a $15,000 operation. Should the family receive help in paying for this surgery? Should they be allowed to pay at a reduced rate? Should the government help? Stress that this is not an unusual situation in society today.

• • • TEACH continues on p. 578

Background

Health Care for the Poor and Uninsured

People who are poor or lack insurance have difficulty getting health care. Medicaid patients sometimes are refused service by doctors and hospitals because Medicaid pays too little to cover the total cost. Private hospitals make money from well-insured patients, often leaving public and non-profit hospitals to serve the poor and uninsured, limiting the care they can provide.

Life Skills Worksheet 26C

Assign the Responding to People Selling Products Life Skills Worksheet.

How to Find and Use Free Health Services

Most states and communities have some form of free or reduced-cost health care. Medicaid, which is funded by every employed person in the United States, provides federal aid to the blind, disabled, low-income families with dependent children, and those who live at or below the federally designated poverty level. Medicare provides federal aid for the elderly.

Community health resources are also available to the public. State health departments and county or city health units exist to help residents with specific health problems. Immunization centers for disease control, special clinics for sexually transmitted diseases, and maternal and child health services are generally available. Some places charge small fees for their services.

"Free clinics" have also been established in most cities to treat or counsel people for unplanned pregnancies, sexually transmitted diseases, and drug abuse. Many of these clinics also treat other types of ailments for those people who are unable to afford medical care.

Cultural DIVERSITY

Native Americans and Health Care

The United States health-care system is enormous. It includes a large number and variety of hospitals, health-care centers, doctors, nurses, and other health professionals. Some people find that the options available within this system meet their health needs quite effectively. Others, however, have customs and beliefs that lead them to seek different sources of treatment, called "alternative" health-care systems. Native American cultures are examples of cultures that provide alternative health systems for their people.

According to the philosophy of these cultures, all elements of the world—inanimate objects as well as living things—have life, spirit, power, and specific roles to play. Each element is related to the others, and each affects the entire universe. When there is harmony among these elements, a state of well-being results. But an imbalance among the elements can cause illness.

When such an imbalance occurs, a Native American may seek the help of a traditional healer. Healers are trained men and women who perform ceremonies to right the imbalance and in so doing heal the illness. Such healing ceremonies may include prayers, rituals, special medicines, and the use of visual symbols.

Though the practices of Native American healers may seem quite differ-

---

However, funding for these clinics is usually low, so they must restrict the medical services they offer to a small number of patients and limit the services provided. Check the yellow pages for a list of health-care clinics that are in your area, or call your state, county, or city health department.

Quackery

Quackery—the promotion of medical services or products that are worthless or unproven—can endanger your health.

Worthless so-called miracle remedies for weight loss, arthritis, cancer, epilepsy, and other serious disorders flood the market and confuse the public. Fake treatments and worthless medication may delay accurate diagnosis and appropriate treatment until the problem is very serious.

And even when worthless treatments don't actually endanger your health, such as creams that are advertised as breast enlargers, they waste your money.

It is often very difficult to know which health products and services to purchase for special problems and which ones to avoid. Television, radio, magazine, and mail advertising is designed to get you to buy vari-

quackery:

the promotion of medical services or products that are worthless or unproven.

ent from those of medical doctors, there are similarities. Like medical doctors, Native American healers must undergo years of special training. They must learn the right ceremonies and rituals to perform for the different types of imbalance. Also like medical doctors, Native American healers sometimes specialize in certain kinds of health problems. The healers may refer a patient to another healer or to a medical doctor if an illness is not within their area of expertise.

The alternative health-care systems of Native Americans are perhaps the best known, but they are by no means

the only ones. Some African-Americans, Asian-Americans, Hispanic-Americans, and people who live in the Appalachian Mountains also practice alternative health care.

Section Review Worksheet 26.2
To reinforce the concepts presented in this section, assign Section Review Worksheet 26.2.

Section Quiz 26.2
Have students take Section Quiz 26.2.

Reteaching Worksheet 26.2
Students who have difficulty with the material may complete Reteaching Worksheet 26.2.

Review Answers

1. Answers may include high-tech equipment, organ transplants, the AIDS epidemic, malpractice insurance, and defensive medicine.

2. Answers will vary. Students might say that they would choose a traditional insurance policy so that they could continue to see the same doctor, otherwise they would have to change to a doctor who participates in the HMO. A PPO may not be attractive if the person's doctor is not on the list.

Class Discussion
Spotting Quackery

Obtain a supermarket tabloid and have the class study and discuss the ads for quack products, using the guidelines in Figure 26-7 on the following page. Likely candidates include weight-control products; intelligence enhancers; cures for migraines; breast enlargers; baldness cures; sex enhancers; and 900-line health advisers. For 900 numbers, have students calculate the charge for a 10-minute call.

Extension
Another Viewpoint

Ask a representative from a hospital or HMO or someone from your city's Department of Health and Human Services to visit the class, discuss the problem of providing affordable health care for everyone, and answer students' questions.

Answers to Questions 1 and 2 are on p. 579.

3. Answers may include the blind, disabled, families with dependent children, and those who live at or below the poverty level.

4. Answers may include your physician, a reference resource such as The Medicine Show or Consumer Reports, National Health Council, World Health Organization, Food and Drug Administration, Department of Health and Human Services, American Heart Association, and American Lung Association.

5. Answers may include those who are unemployed, those who cannot afford high health-care costs or individual insurance policy premiums and whose employers don't provide health-care plans, those who work part-time jobs, and those who are poor, elderly, or disabled.

ous products. Each media message does its best to convince you that its product is the absolute best way to eliminate a particular health concern.

Quackery is not always practiced by dishonest people. Some people who sell worthless products or services truly believe in what they are selling.

Your best protection is to analyze carefully every product or treatment method you are considering. You may have to contact your physician or a reputable agency or nonprofit organization for advice. One good resource for information on drugs and cosmetics is a book called *The Medicine Show,* an unbiased report on numerous products by the editors of *Consumer Reports* magazine. Other sources of health-related consumer information are the National Health Council, the World Health Organization, the Food and Drug Administration, the Department of Health and Human Services, and various nonprofit associations, such as the American Heart Association and the American Lung Association. Any time you are in doubt, check the product out before you purchase it. Figure 26-7 gives you some tips to help identify a quack or an unsound product.

Are You Dealing with a Quack?

If you encounter the following, you may be dealing with a quack:

The promise or guarantee of a quick cure

The use of a "secret remedy" or an unorthodox treatment

The use of advertising to gain patients

Testimonials by patients who have been cured

Claims that a product will cure a wide variety of ailments

Claims that sound too good to be true

Request for a large payment in advance

Claims by the manufacturers or sponsors of the product that the medical profession is persecuting them

(FIGURE 26-7) **Spectacular claims are often a sign that you're dealing with a quack.**

Review

1. List three reasons why health-care costs are rising in the United States.

2. ■■ **LIFE SKILLS: Being a Wise Consumer** You have a chronic condition for which you've been seeing the same doctor for years. You have a great deal of confidence in your doctor and don't want to change. Would you choose a traditional insurance policy, an HMO, or a PPO? Explain why.

3. ■■ **LIFE SKILLS: Using Community Resources** List three groups of people who can receive health care through Medicaid.

4. ■■ **LIFE SKILLS: Being a Wise Consumer** You are considering buying a health product that guarantees a quick cure for your condition. Name two groups you could consult to determine whether you are dealing with a quack.

5. **Critical Thinking** Which people in the United States are least likely to have access to good health care?

ASSESS

Section Review

Have students answer the Section Review questions.

Alternative Assessment

Health-Care Systems Improvements

Have students write a paragraph on improvements they would like to see made in the health-care system.

Closure

Being a Wise Consumer

Ask: **What things can you do to get the best health care at the lowest cost?** *[The many possibilities include avoiding unnecessary treatment; getting a second opinion; comparison-shopping for doctors, hospitals, dentists, eye care, pharmacies, therapists, and health-care plans; using free clinics if you qualify to do so; being alert to quackery; and never spending money for suspicious services or products.]*

Highlights

Summary

- When choosing a doctor, ask friends and relatives about their physicians, or obtain a list of the staff physicians at a nearby hospital.

- It is important to feel comfortable and to be able to communicate well with your doctor. You should ask any questions that concern you and insist that the doctor explain special instructions clearly.

- As a patient, you have the right to get another doctor's opinion at any time.

- An advantage of a traditional private health insurance policy is that the insured person can choose any doctor. Disadvantages are that the insured person must pay a yearly deductible and usually must pay medical fees before being reimbursed. Also, tradi-

tional health insurance does not reimburse the cost of preventative practices.

- Two advantages of HMOs are that their practitioners stress preventative medicine and patients do not have to submit claim forms for reimbursement. One drawback of HMOs is that patients can't always see a doctor of their choice.

- PPOs combine aspects of traditional policies and HMOs, and discount the services of preselected doctors.

- Many community health resources are available to the public. Some services are free, while others require small fees.

Vocabulary

primary care physician a family physician, a pediatrician, or a general internal medicine physician.

defensive medicine the use of numerous and sometimes unnecessary diagnostic tests to avoid a lawsuit.

premium the payment a person makes to an insurance company in exchange for coverage.

deductible the amount of medical costs an insured person must pay before the insurance company begins paying.

HMOs (health maintenance organizations) organizations that offer subscribers complete medical care in return for a fixed monthly fee.

PPOs (preferred provider organizations) organizations that offer subscribers discounted medical care when they use preselected health-care providers.

quackery the promotion of medical services or products that are worthless or unproven.

CHAPTER REVIEW

Concept Review

Sample responses:

1. reason for visit; specific signs and symptoms; medication taken; exercise habits; information about previous illnesses, surgery, allergies, and reactions to medications

2. The doctor will record your specific signs and symptoms, such as temperature, blood pressure, heart rate, and weight.

3. the recommendation of a second doctor; when surgery or any other major procedure is recommended by the first doctor

4. When a person is hospitalized for any reason. It sets forth standards that hospitals are expected to follow.

5. Health-care costs are rising because of high-tech equipment, organ transplants, the AIDS epidemic, malpractice insurance, and defensive medicine. Health-care costs in the future are likely to be higher still.

6. socialized medicine, managed care, shared-cost programs

7. high medical costs

8. An advantage of a traditional private health insurance policy is that the insured person can choose any doctor. Disadvantages of traditional policies are that the insured person must pay a yearly deductible and also

Concept Review

1. What types of information make up a medical history?

2. What is included in a routine physical examination?

3. What is a "second opinion"? When might a patient need one?

4. When would an individual receive a copy of the Patient's Bill of Rights? What does it do?

5. Are health-care costs rising or falling? Why? What is the outlook for health-care costs in the future?

6. What are two approaches being considered by the U.S. government and businesses to make medical care affordable for everyone?

7. Why have many companies had to reduce the health insurance benefits they provide for employees?

8. Name one advantage and one disadvantage of traditional private health insurance policies.

9. Who can you contact to help you choose a traditional health insurance policy? How can they help you?

10. What is an HMO? Describe its service.

11. Name three types of health services that are available through state health departments and county or city health units.

12. What kind of treatment or counseling do "free clinics" provide? Who do they treat?

13. Name four instances in which a health consumer should suspect quackery.

Expressing Your Views

1. You need to select a primary care physician. What professional and personal characteristics of a doctor are important to you? What would you do if, after you found a doctor, you were not satisfied with him or her?

2. Your primary care physician has recommended that you have surgery. You are wondering if you should see another doctor for a second opinion. What advantages are there to getting an opinion from another doctor?

3. Why do you think some people continue to buy worthless products?

must pay medical fees before being reimbursed. Traditional health insurance does not reimburse the cost of routine checkups.

9. The state insurance department. They will help a person analyze any policy, explain its terms, and provide information on how to get reimbursed for claims.

10. HMOs, or health maintenance organizations, offer subscribers complete medical care and preventive medicine in return for a fixed monthly fee. HMOs offer services such as special testing with high-tech machinery.

11. medicaid, immunization centers, clinics for STDs, maternal and child health services

12. Treatment and counseling for undesired pregnancies, sexually transmitted diseases, and drug abuse. They treat people who cannot afford medical care.

13. Students should list four of the instances listed in Figure 26-7.

Life Skills Check . . . .

1. Communicating Effectively
You have your first appointment with your new primary care physician concerning a recent health problem. What information should you take to the doctor with you? What are three questions you could prepare to ask the doctor?

2. Being a Wise Consumer
Your family has been offered a fantastic deal on a traditional health insurance policy. What questions should you ask the insurance agent before purchasing the policy? Where else could you check to be sure the company is sound and that the policy is a good one for your family?

Projects . . . .

1. Some countries have a national health insurance program. Many people think we should have such a program in the United States. Work with a group to research the national health insurance program of another country and compare that program with the health services available in our country. Organize a class debate on whether our federal government should institute national health insurance.

2. Work with a partner to create a short skit about quackery. The skit can be humorous or outrageous. One partner should pretend to be a quack using some of the common practices listed in Figure 26-7. The other partner should pretend to be a consumer. Lead the audience to see the possible negative consequences of being misled by quackery.

Plan for Action . . . .

A health-care system cannot be expected to care for your health if you are not willing to do your part in caring for yourself. Make a plan to find a doctor if you do not have one and list three local health-care facilities you could use if necessary.

Expressing Your Views

1. Answers concerning personal characteristics will vary. Students should find another doctor if they are not satisfied with their current one.

2. Sample response: Surgery may not be necessary. You would be saved the cost, time, and pain of surgery.

3. Sample response: They are hoping for a fast or easy cure to their medical problems.

Life Skills Check

1. The results of any tests you had and the names of any medication you are taking or have taken for the health problem. How long will my condition take to heal? Should I take medicine with food? Can I go back to school? Can I exercise?

2. What is the deductible? Is full coverage provided for hospital, medical, and surgical costs? What is the monthly premium? State insurance department.

Projects

Have students plan and carry out the projects for health care.

Plan for Action

Ask students why a preexisting partnership with a physician or health maintenance organization is a better health-care option than relying on intervention only when there is a health crisis. Have students develop a plan for locating a primary-care physician and a dentist. Provide reference materials that students can use to locate free or low-cost health services.

ASSESSMENT OPTIONS

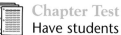
Chapter Test
Have students take the Chapter 26 Test.

Alternative Assessment
Have students do the Alternative Assessment activity for Chapter 26.

Test Generator
The Test Generator contains additional assessment items for this chapter.

Issues in
Health

Ethical Issues in Health

ETHICAL ISSUES IN HEALTH

ISSUE: *Should family leave be an employment benefit in the same way as sick leave?*

Have students read the Ethical Issues in Health feature. Ask students to speculate—or report— about how families without family leave handle the needs described in the article. Sometimes parents use their own sick days to care for children, sometimes parents or other caretakers work part time, or sometimes people lose their jobs or have to quit. In what way are the needs of a family the responsibility of the society as a whole? Have each student write a paragraph, story, or poem about a family crisis that would be affected by family leave.

▶ **ISSUE:** Should family leave be an employment benefit in the same way as sick leave?

There are times in everyone's life when the attention of family is required. When you were a baby, for instance, you needed constant care. Chances are that a parent or guardian remained at home for a period of time to provide that care for you. Even after you started school, someone probably stayed home to take care of you when you were sick. You may also remember a time that a family member helped out when a serious injury, illness, or death occurred in your family. Such physical and emotional care is an important function of families.

For many families, caring for each other is also a financial necessity. Today's soaring medical costs make hospital care unaffordable for many people, especially when they require continuous care for a long period of time. For example, someone who has been seriously hurt in an accident may require 24-hour care for weeks, months, or even years. People who have

Parkinson's or Alzheimer's disease also require constant care. Since the number of older persons in our society is rapidly increasing, family members will be called on more and more in the future to care for older adults suffering from cancer, heart disease, arthritis, loss of memory, or muscle disease. Unfortunately, people with full-time jobs often find it impossible to work and still provide regular care for a family member in need.

Employers can make such situations easier to manage by allowing employees to take a leave of absence from their jobs—as they would if they were sick—to take care of family members. This type of leave is usually called family leave. Some companies continue paying an employee's salary and insurance premiums while he or she is on family leave. Others simply provide assurance that the same job, or a similar one, will be available when the employee is able to return to work. Child-care leave is a specific type of family leave that many companies provide for women who have just had babies. In some companies, child-care leave is available to new fathers as well.

Many people believe family and child-care leave should automatically be part of the benefits and rights for all employees. These advocates contend that government and the business community have a responsibility to help families cope with the consequences of birth, death, illness, and disability. They stress that home care is better and much less expensive than the care given in a hospital, day-care center, or nursing home. Since health-care costs are often paid for by the insurance plans provided by employers or by tax dollars (as with Medicare and Medicaid), some experts predict that family leave would reduce the overall cost of health care.

In one of the first acts of his administration, President Clinton signed into law the Family and Medical Leave Act. This legislation requires all businesses with more than 50 employees to provide up to 12 weeks of unpaid family leave to all employees who have worked at the company at least one year and who work at least 25 hours per week. Employers must also offer the same job or a comparable job to employees returning from leave and must pay employees' health insurance costs while they are on leave. Several states have laws that require smaller companies to provide family-leave benefits as well.

Opponents of family-leave laws argue that a company should be responsible only for providing its employees fair salaries and reasonable benefits. They argue that a company should not have to take responsibility for the well-being of an employee's entire family. They predict that if employers are required to provide family-leave benefits, some private businesses could be driven out of existence as a result.

Those who oppose family-leave laws also predict that such policies would increase taxes, as well as the price of products and services. Taxes would increase because the large number of government employees would receive family-leave benefits. Prices of products and services would increase because the cost of temporarily replacing an employee is high. In order to survive, many companies will have to add this cost to the prices customers pay.

Situation for Discussion

In the Garcia family, both parents work at a small company in order to support their four children, who range in age from 8 to 16. Mrs. Garcia's 78-year-old father, Mr. Peña, lives alone in an apartment near the family's home. Several months ago, Mr. Peña was diagnosed with bone cancer. Although he has been able to care for himself until now, he is about to undergo a series of chemotherapy treatments that will make it necessary for him to have constant care for at least a couple of months.

a. How can the Garcia family manage this situation? What choices do they have?

b. If Mr. Garcia or Mrs. Garcia could take family leave, should the company hold a job until he or she returns, or hire a person who is equally qualified for the job? Should the com-

pany pay full salary during the leave? What would the company have to do to continue normal operations during the leave?

c. Should the government reimburse a company for the cost of family leave?

UNIT 8

SAFETY AND EMERGENCY CARE

CHAPTER OVERVIEWS

CHAPTER 27

SAFETY AND RISK REDUCTION

This chapter examines ways in which personal behaviors can be modified to reduce accidents. Students learn to recognize the factors that contribute to motor vehicle and bicycle accidents. They also learn behaviors that reduce their risks of being injured in such accidents. The most common accidents around the home and how to avoid them are discussed. Students learn how to reduce their risk of injury in the workplace and in the event of disasters. A discussion of safety in sports, swimming and diving, and camping, hiking, and hunting ends the chapter.

CHAPTER 28

FIRST AID AND CPR

Students learn that first aid often makes the difference between life and death when an accident or other emergency occurs. The chapter describes the first steps that should be taken during an emergency. The ABC procedure for assessing and treating medical priorities is explained. The CPR procedure is described, and students are encouraged to attend a training class in CPR. First aid for injuries, choking, and heart attack is covered thoroughly. The Heimlich maneuver is described, and students are

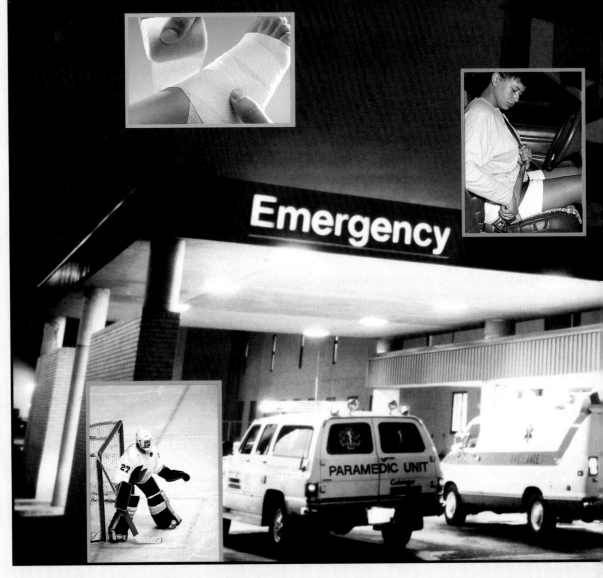

encouraged to learn how to perform it. Students also learn how to deal with emergencies caused by extreme heat and cold, bites, stings, and poisoning. The chapter also describes steps to take in treating hyperventilation, nosebleeds, electric shock, burns and scalds, and other conditions.

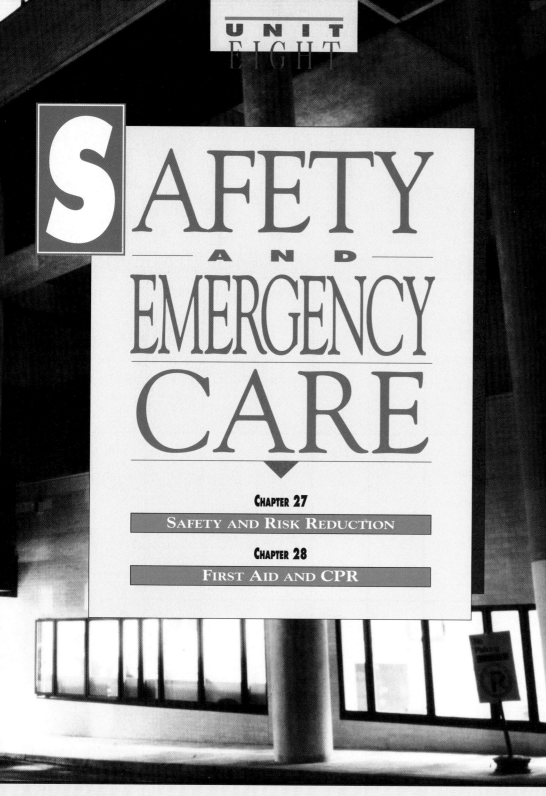

SAFETY AND EMERGENCY CARE

CHAPTER 27

SAFETY AND RISK REDUCTION

CHAPTER 28

FIRST AID AND CPR

Accidents are the leading cause of death for people between the ages of 15 and 24. In this unit, students learn that carelessness and taking unnecessary risks are factors in most accidents. Students' safety awareness—knowledge about risks and how to reduce them—is raised by thorough coverage of vehicle safety; home, workplace, and community safety; and recreational safety. Students' readiness to deal with accidents and other emergencies is enhanced through the unit's presentation of first aid procedures. The chart below links the information and skills presented in this unit to the National Health Education Standards.

Unit 8	NATIONAL HEALTH EDUCATION STANDARDS*						
STANDARD	1	2	3	4	5	6	7
Chapter 27	•		•			•	•
Chapter 28	•	•	•		•	•	•

* For full text listing of each standard, see page 15T.

CHAPTER 27

Safety and Risk Reduction

SECTION	TITLE/OBJECTIVES	PERSONAL INVENTORY			LIFE SKILLS DEVELOPMENT			
		Personal Health Inventory	Journal	Check Up	Life Skills	Life Skills Worksheets	Media Message or Ethical Issues Worksheet	What Would You Do?
27.1 *pp. 589–592*	**ACCIDENTS AND RISKS** • Recognize that accidents are the leading cause of death for people between the ages of 15 and 24. • Recognize that risky or careless behaviors are factors in most accidents. ▪ Identify ways in which your personal behavior can be modified to reduce your risk of accidents.	Ch. 27	27A		p. 591			
27.2 *pp. 593–597*	**VEHICLE SAFETY** • Recognize factors that contribute to motor-vehicle accidents. • Identify behaviors that reduce the risk of being injured in a motor-vehicle accident. • List some ways to maintain a bicycle for safety. • Identify behaviors that reduce the risk of being injured in a bicycle accident.		27B					
27.3 *pp. 598–606*	**SAFETY AT HOME AND AT WORK** • Recognize the relationship between accidents that frequently occur in the home and personal behavior. • Identify potential accident hazards in the home and in the community. ▪ Recommend steps to reduce the potential for accidents in the home and in the community. • Identify ways to maintain safety in the workplace.		27C			27A		p. 605
27.4 *pp. 607–610*	**RECREATIONAL SAFETY** • Recognize potential hazards in recreational activities. ▪ Identify ways to reduce the risk of accidents in recreational activities.		27D 27E				Unit 8	

KEY: ▪ Denotes Life Skill Objective

Text references denoted by page number.

Supplement references denoted by chapter or item numbers.

LINKING RESOURCES

	Making a Choice Cards	Parent Discussion Guide	Health Talk Audio Program	Teaching Transparencies and Directory	Section Review Worksheets	Section Quizzes	Reteaching Worksheets	Section Reviews
	INTERACTION		**OTHER RESOURCES**		**SECTION REVIEW AND ASSESSMENT**			
27A					27.1	27.1	27.1	p. 592
					27.2	27.2	27.2	p. 597
					27.3	27.3	27.3	p. 606
27B					27.4	27.4	27.4	p. 610

KEY FACTS

- Accidents are the leading cause of death among people 15 to 24 years old; three-fourths of these deaths are from motor-vehicle accidents.

- Engaging in risky behavior and carelessness are factors in most accidents; changing these behaviors can reduce accidents.

- Drugs and alcohol, speeding, and reckless driving are the cause of most motor-vehicle accidents.

- Falls are the second greatest cause of accidental deaths; most fatal falls occur in the home.

- Fires are the third most common cause of accidental death in the home.

- Careless behavior and ignoring basic safety rules cause most home accidents.

- Plans should be drawn up beforehand to determine what to do in case of a natural disaster.

- Although some accidents cannot be avoided, following basic safety guidelines can help prevent assaults, job-related accidents, and recreational accidents and injuries.

CHAPTER REVIEW AND ASSESSMENT

TEXT

Chapter Review pp. 612–613

SUPPLEMENTS

Chapter Test 27

Alternative Assessment 27

Test Generator Chapter 27

GETTING STARTED

Using the Chapter Photograph

Have students look at the chapter photograph and ask: **What safety precautions is the climber taking?** *[wearing a helmet, using climbing ropes attached to a harness, wearing special soft-soled climbing shoes, carrying appropriate gear on his belt]* **What other precautions might the climber have taken?** *[received instruction in rock-climbing techniques and safety, become physically conditioned for climbing, told someone where he was going and when he should be back, checked the weather forecast]*

 Question Box

Have students write out any questions they have about safety and risk reduction and put them in the Question Box.

Sensitivity *ALERT*

Students who have been injured in a serious accident or who have a close friend or relative who has been injured may feel self-conscious. If they were responsible for the accident, it may upset them to read that caution might have prevented the accident.

CHAPTER 27

Safety and Risk Reduction

◆ ◆ ◆

Section 27.1 Accidents and Risks

Section 27.2 Vehicle Safety

Section 27.3 Safety at Home and at Work

Section 27.4 Recreational Safety

Physical activity is an important part of good health, and some activities are more dangerous than others. Rock climbers follow certain procedures and use the proper safety equipment to reduce their risk of injury and have fun at the same time.

MYTHS & MISCONCEPTIONS

- **People are usually not responsible for accidents that happen to them.** In many cases, people are at least partly responsible for the accidents that happen to them either because they have taken a risk or because they are not attentive to what they are doing.

- **I'm a good driver, so I don't have to worry about accidents.** Unless you practice defensive driving, you aren't really a good driver. Defensive driving involves expecting other drivers to do the unexpected, such as changing lanes or turning unexpectedly, and being prepared to deal with the situation quickly and safely.

- **When you are at home, you are safe from accidents.** Most accidents occur in or just outside of the home; fires, falls, and poisonings are most likely to occur at home.

Sarah hung up the telephone and turned toward her mother. "That was Jan, Mom. Her little brother, Billy, just got back from the emergency room. He flipped off his bike today and broke his wrist. The lace of his sneaker jammed the bike chain and he was thrown over the handlebars."

"Poor Billy, he won't have much of a summer vacation this year," said Sarah's mother.

"It could've been a lot worse," said Sarah. "He hit his head on the curb, but his bicycle helmet cushioned the blow. The doctor told his mother that if he hadn't been wearing a helmet, Billy's injuries would've been more serious."

Sarah thought of her younger sister, Lynette. "Mom, I think it's time we bought a bike helmet for Lynette."

"And what about you, Sarah? Can you be sure that you'll never take a fall from your bike?"

Section 27.1 Accidents and Risks

bjectives

- *Recognize that accidents are the leading cause of death for people between the ages of 15 and 24.*
- *Recognize that risky or careless behaviors are factors in most accidents.*
- *Identify ways in which your personal behavior can be modified to reduce your risk of accidents.*

■■ **LIFE SKILLS: Practicing Self-Care**

Billy's broken wrist was the result of an **accident.** In this chapter, you will learn that even though they are unexpected, many accidents can be prevented.

Accidental Deaths

Accidents are the number-one cause of death in the United States among people aged 15 to 24. Among people of all ages, accidents are the fourth leading cause of death. Figure 27-1 on the next page breaks down the number of deaths that occur each year because of specific types of accidents. Notice that motor-vehicle accidents are responsible for the greatest number of accidental deaths—approximately the same amount as all the others combined.

Different age groups tend to have different types of accidents. Among 15- to 24-year-olds, for example, most fatal accidents involve motor vehicles or alcohol, or both. Very young children and elderly people are more likely to be injured or killed in falls. Children under five account for many cases of accidental poisoning.

accident:

any unexpected event that causes damage, injury, or death.

Section 27.1 Lesson Plan

MOTIVATE

 Journal 27A
Critiquing One's Own Safety Awareness

This may be done as a warm-up activity. Encourage students to rate themselves on a scale of one to ten as to whether they make an effort to practice safety and avoid risks. Have them explain in their Journal the rating they gave themselves and the ways they could improve their safety-related behavior.

Cooperative Learning
Accidents as News

Have students form small groups to read newspapers for stories about accidents. Have them draw up a list of the accidents they find. Have them note how each of these accidents might have been avoided.

Background
Lowering Risks
A safe life is not necessarily a dull, inactive one. Remote regions of the world —such as deserts, mountains, and the polar regions—have been explored by successful risk takers who knew how to anticipate and prepare for emergencies. Mountain climbers condition themselves slowly to the higher altitudes so as to avoid sickness and disorientation; explorers in the cold regions carefully store food and supplies at intervals along their way to supply their return trip. Anyone planning to engage in a risky activity should first master the related safety rules. It's important to be aware of one's own physical capabilities, reactions, and emotional state before beginning.

Personal Health Inventory
Have students complete the Personal Health Inventory for this chapter.

Making a Choice 27A

Assign the Accident Survey card. The card asks students to list accidents in which they or members of their group have been involved and discuss possible ways each accident could have been prevented.

Section Review Worksheet 27.1

To reinforce the concepts presented in this section, assign Section Review Worksheet 27.1.

Section Quiz 27.1

Have students take Section Quiz 27.1.

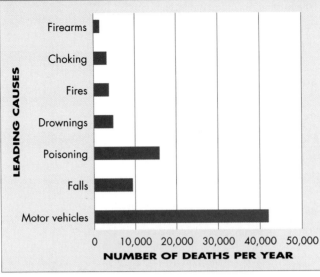

(FIGURE 27-1) Accidents are currently the fourth leading cause of death in the United States. For young adults 15 to 24, they are the leading cause of death.

risk:

an action that is potentially dangerous; the chance of injury.

safety awareness:

knowledge about risks and how to reduce them.

Risks and Carelessness

Sometimes a person has no control over the things that lead to an accident. For example, when an earthquake causes bricks to fall from a building, someone may be injured. Such events, however, make up a minority of accidents.

Most accidents result from the actions, or inactions, of people. Have you noticed that certain people seem to have more accidents than others? You've probably also heard or used phrases such as "He is an accident waiting to happen" and "She's accident prone" many times. Such phrases suggest that the person may be at least partly responsible for many of the accidents that happen to him or her. A person's behavior may greatly affect his or her chances of being involved in an accident. Understanding why accidents occur can help you avoid most accidents.

Taking Risks One type of behavior that increases the likelihood of having an accident is taking risks. A **risk** is an action that involves danger of some kind. Many everyday activities involve risk. Every time you cross a busy street, for example, you are taking a risk. But your chances of being injured are fairly low if you pay attention and obey traffic signals.

Many people, however, take unnecessary risks. Dodging traffic to cross the street in the middle of the block is far more likely to lead to an accident than crossing at the corner. Drinking alcohol and taking drugs increase the risk of accidents because these substances impair a person's ability to make good judgments, alter his or her perceptions, and impede normal physical skills.

The high number of accidents among teenagers is related to the fact that they take more risks than older people. You can minimize risk by making responsible decisions.

Being Careless Putting dishes away, as the boy in Figure 27-2 is doing, is not, by nature, dangerous. But notice that by not paying attention to his task, the boy has managed to push a bowl off the shelf—and possibly onto his head! His behavior is not risky—it is careless. Carelessness is a lack of concern about the possible effects of one's actions, or not paying attention while performing a task. As with taking unnecessary risks, carelessness can lead to accidents that could have been avoided.

Safety and Behavior

Avoiding unnecessary risks and being attentive are important to your safety. **Safety awareness** is knowing about risks and how to reduce them. Assuming that they don't wish to be injured, why do so many people lack safety awareness? There are several answers to this question.

TEACH

Class Discussion
Statistics on Accidental Deaths

Before students look at Figure 27-1, have them write down what they think are the three most frequent causes of accidental death in the United States. Tally their choices on the chalkboard. Have them compare their class list with the table. Ask them why they think motor vehicles cause the most

deaths. Discuss why they think the insurance for drivers between the ages of 15 and 24 is so high.

Role-Playing
Who's Responsible?

Have students role-play a situation in which several teens are urging another to do something dangerous. Examples might include climbing a water tower, climbing under a suspension bridge, jumping into a river from a rock, anything that involves risk. The lone person should assess the situation and decide

whether to resist the pressure or to go along. After the role-play, have class members give additional reasons why the activity would be dangerous and other ways the person could have resisted the pressure to become involved.

Class Discussion
Necessary Versus Unnecessary Risks

Write on the chalkboard these headings: NECESSARY RISKS and UNNECESSARY RISKS. Have students suggest some necessary risks they take often,

Life SKILLS: Practicing Self-Care

Analyze Your Safety Awareness . . . .

The teens in this photo are demonstrating their safety awareness by buckling their seat belts. You can protect yourself from many accidental injuries by being safety-conscious and practicing behaviors that promote safety as well.

To analyze your safety awareness and behavior, answer the following questions on a separate sheet of paper. Thousands of 10th-graders answered similar questions when they took the *National Adolescent Student Health Survey*, a project developed by health educators and funded by agencies of the U.S. Department of Health and Human Services. Later in this chapter, you will discover how your behavior and safety awareness compare to that of these 10th-graders.

1. How many times in the past month did you ride with a driver who had used alcohol or drugs?

0 times	7–10 times
1–3 times	11–20 times
4–6 times	Over 20 times

2. Did you wear a seat belt the last time you rode in an automobile?

Yes No Don't remember

3. How often do you wear a helmet when riding a bicycle?

Never	Usually
Rarely	Always
Sometimes	

4. How often do you warm up before exercising?

Never	Usually
Rarely	Always
Sometimes	

5. How often do you swim alone or in a restricted or unsupervised area?

Never Sometimes

Once you have identified behaviors that place you at risk of being injured in an accident, work on modifying these risky behaviors to protect yourself.

Life SKILLS

Have students review their daily activities and analyze them for risky behavior. Ask them to identify any risky behaviors they engage in that could affect other people. Give each student an index card on which to record and retain the results of their review and analysis.

Reteaching Worksheet 27.1

Students who have difficulty with the material may complete Reteach Worksheet 27.1.

such as crossing the street or riding a bike. List these on the chalkboard. Have students discuss whether the risks mentioned are truly necessary or simply a more convenient or easier way of completing a task. Ask students to suggest unnecessary risks that they might be tempted to take, such as crossing the street in the middle of the block or riding a bike without a helmet. List these on the board and have students discuss why these risks should be avoided.

Debate the Issue
Car Phones

Today, many people are talking on cellular telephones while driving. Often these calls divert the driver's attention away from the road. The use of car phones is completely unrestricted. Debate this issue: Should the use of car phones be limited in any way? If so, what should the limitations be? Have students research the issue before taking a position.

Extension
Interviews on Risk Taking and Accidents

Encourage students to interview family members, neighbors, or adult friends about risks they took as teens or young adults. Do the adults now regret the risks they took? Do they now see ways that they could have avoided the risky behavior and still have had a satisfying social life? Have students share their findings.

Review Answers

1. motor-vehicle accidents

2. Risks and carelessness. A risk is an action that involves danger of some kind. Carelessness is inattentive behavior while one is performing a task.

3. The behaviors students choose to eliminate or modify will vary.

4. Yes. However, infants and toddlers do not yet understand that their behavior is risky. This is why they need constant supervision by someone who is aware of the risks. Student examples will vary but may included the following: Infants and toddlers can put small objects into their mouths and choke. They can chew on electrical cords and reach for hot items on a stove. They can also easily fall from high objects such as a chair, bed, or the top of the stairs.

(FIGURE 27-2) **Not paying attention to what you are doing is a factor in many accidents.**

Ignorance and lack of caution can lead to dangerous situations. For example, Rob is on the school swimming team. While out with friends, he decided to swim across a small river to show his ability. Rob assumed the current was not very strong. However, he was swept downstream and had to be rescued by people fishing from a small boat. Rob did not know the strength of the current. He exercised poor judgment and was not cautious. Among young people, such lack of caution can stem from the feeling that "it can't happen to me."

The use of alcohol and other drugs increases risky behavior and carelessness as well. A person is far more likely to attempt a foolish—even dangerous—act if he or she is under the influence of alcohol or other drugs.

A person's emotional state can also contribute to risky behavior. For example, someone who is angry is likely to act on impulse and with little or no regard for what

might happen. Such a person may drive over the speed limit, putting himself or herself and others at risk. Someone suffering from depression may also be indifferent to personal safety and may act in a way that could lead to an accident.

Peer pressure can influence individuals to take unnecessary risks. For example, Meda was with a group of friends when they found a fallen tree that made a bridge over a deep gorge. Her friends took turns walking on the tree to cross the gorge. Meda could see the tree wasn't steady, but her friends dared her to cross and she did. Everyone, at some point, has been dared to do something dangerous. Taking a dare, even though the results could be fatal, becomes a test of one's courage, but it is neither mature nor responsible behavior.

Personal responsibility is the key to avoiding accidents. To discover whether your behavior demonstrates safety awareness, complete the Life Skills activity on page 591.

Review

1. What is the leading cause of death among young people 15 to 24?

2. Name and describe the two factors that contribute to avoidable accidents.

3. ■■ **LIFE SKILLS: Practicing Self-Care** This week, eliminate or modify at least one behavior that contributes to your likelihood of having an accident.

4. **Critical Thinking** Can infants and toddlers engage in risky behaviors that lead to accidents? Support your answer with examples.

ASSESS

Section Review

Have students answer the Section Review questions.

Alternative Assessment
Learning to Be Cautious

Have students write a fable about a foolish person who ignores prudent advice and takes an unnecessary risk. The story should include a moral.

Closure
Proper Procedures When in a Motor Vehicle

Have students suggest factors that contribute to motor-vehicle accidents. *(emotions, inexperience, inattention, showing off)* List them on the chalkboard. For each one, have another student suggest an accident it could cause. What are ways of handling these factors so that they do not cause an accident?

Section 27.2 *Vehicle Safety*

Objectives

- *Recognize factors that contribute to motor-vehicle accidents.*

- *Identify behaviors that reduce the risk of being injured in a motor-vehicle accident.*

- *List some ways to maintain a bicycle for safety.*

- *Identify behaviors that reduce the risk of being injured in a bicycle accident.*

Riding in or on any vehicle involves risk. And because of their size, weight, and the speed at which they travel, motor vehicles have great potential for doing damage. Now look again at Figure 27-1 and recall that motor-vehicle accidents account for more deaths than any other kind of accident. For these reasons alone, vehicle safety should be a priority for you.

As a teenager, you may already have a license and be driving. You probably also ride with friends. Unfortunately, drivers under the age of 24 have more accidents than drivers in other age groups. There are also more deaths from motor-vehicle accidents among 15- to 24-year-olds than in any other age group. In fact, three-fourths of all accidental deaths in this age group are related to motor vehicles. Half of these deaths also involve alcohol. By learning to avoid certain risky behaviors, you could avoid having an accident that could result in injury or death.

Behavior and Auto Accidents

As with accidents in general, motor-vehicle accidents are usually linked to human behavior. The automobile in Figure 27-3 was demolished in an accident, and the driver and passengers were injured. Quite possibly, the driver's behavior was at fault.

Using alcohol or other drugs is a behavior that is a factor in many motor-vehicle accidents. In Chapters 13 and 15, you studied some of the effects of these substances: reaction time is slowed, judgment is impaired, and general awareness is lowered. Thus, a person driving under the influence of alcohol or other drugs is not in full control of a vehicle that can be a deadly weapon.

The effects of alcohol and other drugs on the body are discussed in Chapters 13 and 15.

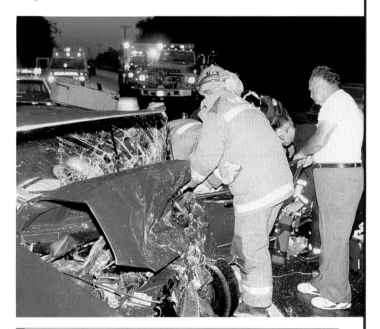

(FIGURE 27-3) **Alcohol is a factor in at least half of all automobile accidents.**

Background
Effect of Drugs and Alcohol on Driving

In 1982, alcohol-related traffic fatalities constituted 57.3 percent of all traffic fatalities; by 1993, that number had dropped to 43.5 percent. Safety experts attribute this decline to increased public concern over the problem of drunken driving and to tougher laws against drunken drivers. At one time, every state considered a driver legally intoxicated if his or her blood alcohol concentration (BAC) was .10 percent (100 milligrams per deciliter) or greater. By 1995, 11 states had lowered the limit to .08 percent. Unfortunately, the statistics for teenagers have not changed significantly. In 1993, 16.2 percent of the drivers 16–20 who were involved in a fatal accident were intoxicated.

Drugs also impair a person's ability to operate a vehicle safely. In the 1980s, the railroad industry began mandatory drug testing. Since then, the industry has experienced a dramatic reduction in the number of on-the-job injuries.

Section 27.2 Lesson Plan

MOTIVATE

Journal 27B
Reducing Risks in Motor Vehicles

This may be done as a warm-up activity. Encourage students to record in their Journal any risky behavior they or someone they know engages in when in a motor vehicle, such as clowning around or racing other cars.

Have them describe the outcome of the behavior. Then have students consider the risk involved and tell if the outcome could have been more serious.

TEACH

Reinforcement
Behavior and Auto Accidents

Ask students why they think teens are more prone to motor-vehicle accidents than any other group. Have them suggest unnecessary risks that some teens take when driving a motor-vehicle. Ask them to suggest ways to avoid accidents in motor vehicles. If they do not mention being careful and paying attention to what they are doing, bring this up for discussion. If practicing defensive driving is not mentioned, bring it up for discussion. Lead students to the conclusion that thinking about what might result from their actions is good common sense.

Background
Rescuing Accident Victims
Technology has helped in rescuing accident victims trapped inside a car or pinned underneath wreckage. Air bags have been developed that are less than 2.5 cm wide, making it possible to insert them into tight places where a person is trapped. Air is then pumped into the bag, forcing apart whatever is trapping the victim. Air bags have the power to move objects weighing over 50,000 kg.

Other behaviors that increase the risk of having an accident are speeding and reckless driving. Mark is a high school senior who enjoys driving his own car. But in three months he has received three speeding tickets. His response is, "What's the big deal? I like to drive fast." This attitude is dangerous to Mark and to others.

For several reasons, speeding increases the risk of accidents and injuries. One reason is a driver's reaction time (the time between deciding to apply the brakes and applying them). Although reaction time is usually less than one second, a car moves some distance in that second. And a car traveling at 45 mph goes much farther in that time than a car traveling at 25 mph. Furthermore, a car traveling at a faster speed has a longer braking distance and takes more time to stop. Finally, the faster a car is traveling upon impact, the more likely it is that people will be seriously injured. So speeding increases both the likelihood that an accident will occur and the risk of serious injury or death.

Reckless driving is careless behavior. Being distracted from driving for just a moment—tuning the radio, talking to a passenger, reading signs or a road map, or trying to get a wasp out the window—can get you into trouble. Even more serious are deliberate actions, such as not obeying traffic rules and signs, trying to turn or pass with too little time, or running a light.

Reducing Auto Injuries
Avoiding automobile accidents is the best way to reduce your risk of injury. The first step is never drink and drive or ride in a car with a driver who is under the influence of alcohol or other drugs. If you know someone is under such influence, try to keep him or her from driving.

Obeying traffic laws, including posted speed limits, will also reduce your risk of being involved in an auto accident. If you know someone who disregards safe driving practices, is careless, or takes chances behind the wheel, don't ride with that person.

10th Graders Who Rode With Drivers Who Had Used Alcohol or Other Drugs

Number of Times	Male	Female	Total
0 times	57.0%	54.0%	55.6%
1-3 times	23.4%	30.8%	27.0%
4-6 times	7.6%	7.1%	7.4%
7-10 times	4.5%	4.5%	4.5%
11-20 times	3.1%	1.8%	2.5%
over 20 times	4.4%	1.8%	3.2%

(FIGURE 27-4) This is how the 10th-graders who participated in the *National Adolescent Student Health Survey* responded to the question: "How many times in the past month did you ride with a driver who had used alcohol or other drugs?"

• • • TEACH continued
Class Discussion
Braking Time
Ask: **How does the speed at which you are driving affect your braking time?** [The faster you are going, the longer it takes to stop.] **What other factor might affect your braking time?** [the condition of the road—whether it is wet, icy, or dry; the condition of the brakes—good, fair, or poor] **How should these conditions affect your driving?** [Under unfavorable conditions, you should always drive more slowly and more cautiously.]

Role-Playing
Responsible Driving
Have students role-play situations in which someone who has been drinking or using drugs wants to drive a car. The others should provide alternatives, such as offering to drive the car.

 Cooperative Learning
Reducing Injuries From Motor-Vehicle Accidents
Have students work in groups to produce a bulletin board to convince teens to drive carefully and avoid unnecessary risks. They should include messages about not speeding, avoiding drugs and alcohol, driving defensively, obeying all traffic laws, using seat belts, and wearing helmets and goggles when on motorcycles.

Seatbelt Use Among 10th Graders

Wore Seat Belts	Female	Male	Total
Yes	39.9%	40.3%	40.1%
No	58.3%	57.6%	57.9%
Don't Remember	1.8%	2.1%	1.9%

(FIGURE 27-5) This is how the 10th-graders who participated in the *National Adolescent Student Health Survey* responded to the question: "Did you use a seat belt the last time you rode in a vehicle?"

When you drive, practice **defensive driving** to avoid accidents. Defensive driving involves expecting other drivers to drive recklessly, like changing lanes suddenly or turning from the wrong lane. You will be better able to handle such situations if you assume they might happen.

Wearing a seat belt is the best way to reduce your risk of being injured or killed in a car accident. Forty-six percent of people killed in auto accidents were not wearing seat belts.

Safety and Other Motor Vehicles

Motorcycles, minibikes, snowmobiles, and all-terrain vehicles (ATVs) are other types of motor vehicles. They are fun to ride, but they can also be dangerous. In accidents involving these vehicles, the risk of serious head injury is very high. Approximately 60 percent of 10th-graders surveyed reported having recently ridden on a motorcycle or minibike, but less than 30 percent reported that they always wore a helmet.

To protect yourself from injury, take the following safety measures when riding on one of these vehicles. Always wear a helmet to reduce your risk of suffering a serious head injury. Wear goggles to protect your eyes, especially if the vehicle has no windshield. Sturdy, close-fitting clothing can also help prevent an injury in the event of an accident. Obey all traffic laws as you would when driving a car. Don't use alcohol or drugs or ride with someone who has.

Bicycle Safety

As with any vehicle, there are hazards involved in bicycle riding. And once again, risky behavior and carelessness—the human factors—contribute to many bicycle accidents.

When Billy's shoelace got caught in his bicycle chain, it resulted in an accident. Clothing catching in the chain or wheels is a leading cause of bicycle accidents. The sudden jamming of the chain or wheel can cause the rider to be thrown from the bike. When riding a bicycle, make sure your laces are tucked into your shoes or tied so that they hang toward the outer side of your shoes. It is also best to wear clothing that is closefitting.

Losing control of a bicycle can also result in an accident. Hitting a hole or turning suddenly to avoid a person walking can cause a rider to lose control. As with motor

defensive driving: *driving as though you expect other drivers to drive recklessly.*

Class Discussion
Causes of Bicycle Accidents

Discuss with students the causes of bicycle accidents. List the causes on the chalkboard as they mention them. Have them state a way to avoid accidents from each cause.

Role-Playing
Good Advice

Have students role-play a parent and adolescent in conflict over the use of a bicycle helmet. One student should play a young person who is reluctant to wear the helmet and gives his or her reasons; another student should play the parent or guardian who explains why the helmet is important.

Extension
Safety in the Community

Have students visit a bicycle shop to inquire about safety devices on bicycles. Encourage them to contact a cycling club to find out how safety rules are promoted by the club.

Section Review Worksheet 27.2

To reinforce the concepts presented in this section, assign Section Review Worksheet 27.2.

Section Quiz 27.2

Have students take Section Quiz 27.2.

Reteaching Worksheet 27.2

Students who have difficulty with the material may complete Reteaching Worksheet 27.2.

Review Answers

1. Answers may include driving under the influence of drugs or alcohol, speeding, and reckless driving.

2. Answers may include the following: do not speed, do not drive recklessly, do not drive while under the influence of drugs or alcohol, do not ride with a driver who is under the influence of drugs or alcohol or who drives recklessly, obey traffic laws, drive defensively, and always wear a seat belt.

Hand Signals for Bicycle Riders

Left turn   Right turn   Stop or slow

(FIGURE 27-6) **By warning the traffic behind you that you intend to change direction or speed, you can help to protect yourself from being injured in an accident while riding a bicycle.**

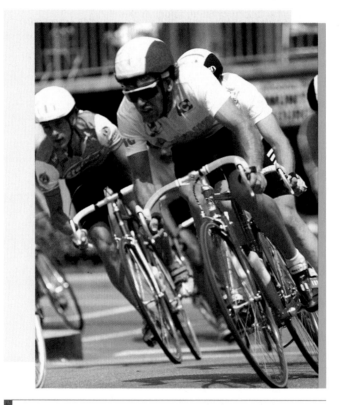

(FIGURE 27-7) **Serious cyclists wear specialized equipment to reduce their risk of having an accident or being seriously injured in an accident.**

vehicles, maintain control by not speeding and ride defensively.

Bicyclists must generally obey the same traffic laws as other vehicles. A bicycle, for example, should be ridden in the direction that traffic flows. Hand signals, as shown in Figure 27-6, should be used to signal a change in direction or speed. If you ride at night, your bicycle should be equipped with lights and reflectors.

Sometimes bicycle accidents are caused by mechanical problems with the bicycle. Maintaining the bicycle in a safe condition is important. Keep the fenders, spokes, pedals, and handlebars undamaged and tightly attached. Adjust the saddle height and handlebars for comfortable fit. Keep the chain lubricated, and be sure it is in good condition. The bell or horn, lights, and reflectors should be working perfectly. Keep the tires filled with air, and check them for wear, leaks, or embedded pebbles and nails.

The cyclists in Figure 27-7 are skilled riders—they race bicycles. Notice that they are wearing helmets. But as Figure 27-8 indicates, 10th-grade bicycle riders

Bicycle Helmet Use Among 10th Graders

Helmet Is Used	Female	Male	Total
Never	94.3%	89.2%	91.6%
Rarely	2.9%	5.2%	4.1%
Sometimes	1.4%	3.4%	2.5%
Usually	0.7%	1.7%	1.3%
Always	0.7%	0.4%	0.6%

(FIGURE 27-8) **This is how the 10th-graders who participated in the *National Adolescent Student Health Survey* answered the question: "How often do you wear a bicycle helmet when riding a bicycle?"**

almost never wear helmets. Head injuries account for the majority of fatal injuries in bicycle accidents. Deciding to wear a helmet will reduce your risk of being seriously injured or killed in a bicycle accident.

Pedestrian Safety

People riding in motor vehicles are not the only victims of motor-vehicle accidents. People are often struck and killed by motor vehicles while crossing the street. Some accidents occur when young children run from between parked cars into the street. In other accidents, people are hit by a vehicle when they cross a busy street carelessly. Don't assume that a car will stop for you or that it will turn if its turn signal is on. Frequently, impairment from alcohol or other drugs is a factor in these accidents.

Only about one-third of 10th-graders questioned said that they always or usually cross busy streets at the corner. At busy intersections, pedestrian walk signs may be provided, and there is usually at least a painted crosswalk. Once again, the behavior you choose affects the probability that you will be involved in an accident.

Review

1. Describe two factors that contribute to motor-vehicle accidents.

2. What are some ways that a person can reduce his or her chances of being injured in a motor-vehicle accident?

3. List some ways to maintain a bicycle for safety.

4. What are some ways that a person can reduce his or her chances of being injured in an accident while riding a bicycle?

5. *Critical Thinking* Some drugs, such as stimulants, increase awareness and may cause a person to react more quickly. Why, then, would a person who is under the influence of such a drug still be a hazard when driving a motor vehicle?

Answers to Questions 1 and 2 are on p. 596.

3. Keep the fenders, spokes, pedals, and handlebars undamaged and tightly attached. Adjust the saddle height and handlebars for comfortable fit. Keep the chain lubricated and in good condition. The bell or horn, lights, and reflectors should be working well. Keep the tires filled with air and check them for defects.

4. Answers may include the following: wear close-fitting pants; do not wear scarves, long coats, or other items that can get caught in the spokes or chain; don't ride over objects or holes; don't speed; ride defensively; ride with traffic; use hand signals; ride with lights and reflectors at night; keep the bicycle in a safe condition; and always wear a helmet.

5. That person may respond too quickly or too much. An overreaction can be as dangerous as a sluggish response in driving.

ASSESS

Section Review

Have students answer the Section Review questions.

Alternative Assessment
Appeal for Safer Roads

Ask students to write an article for the school newspaper on vehicle safety, especially as it relates to teens.

Closure
Personal Vehicle Safety

Have students write a brief paragraph in which they evaluate their own compliance with the rules of safety when driving or riding in vehicles.

Section 27.3 Safety at Home and at Work

Objectives

■ *Recognize the relationship between accidents that frequently occur in the home and personal behavior.*

■ *Identify potential accident hazards in the home and in the community.*

■ *Recommend steps to reduce the potential for accidents in the home and in the community.*
   ■ **LIFE SKILLS: Problem Solving**

■ *Identify ways to maintain safety in the workplace.*

People spend much of their time at home. Most adults and some teenagers also spend part of their day at the place where they work. Unfortunately, accidents are common in both places. This section contains tips that will help you reduce your risk of accidental injury at home and at work.

Safety Around the Home

Look again at Figure 27-1. Many of the types of accidents listed are likely to occur at home. Most falls, which are the cause of the second greatest number of accidental deaths, do not occur outdoors while hiking or climbing but in the home. Accidents involving fires and poisons are also most likely to occur at home. So making sure that your home is a safe place to be is extremely important.

Falls About 50 percent of fatal accidents that occur in the home are due to falls. The chances of dying in a fall increase with age. In fact, for people over 65, falls make up from one-third to one-half of all accidental deaths! Young children are also more likely to be injured or killed in falls, often as a result of climbing onto or off of furniture and other items.

Many falls occur on staircases. Surprisingly, however, falls on level surfaces are more numerous and cause more fatalities. Examine the photos in Figure 27-9 for hazards that could lead to falls. Notice the objects on the floor at the top of the staircase. Anyone could stumble over one of these objects and fall down the stairs. The curled rug is another hazard that could lead to a fall. Finally, that highly polished floor may look very nice, but it could easily cause someone to slip and fall. Check your home for such hazards when you go home today.

The following are some measures that can be taken to help reduce the risk of falls:

• If you have staircases, the handrails should be sturdy and the steps should have nonslip treads or flat carpeting.

• Floors should be kept free of clutter—toys, electrical cords, or books—that could cause someone to trip.

• Frayed rugs and broken floor tiles should be repaired.

• The bottom of the bathtub should have a nonskid texture. If elderly people live in the house, there should be handrails on the walls beside the bathtub as well.

• Floor mats in the bathroom should also be nonskid to prevent slipping when stepping into and out of the tub or shower.

(FIGURE 27-9) **Any of these situations could cause someone to fall and be injured.**

Some falls occur just outside the home. Icy sidewalks and steps are very hazardous. Broken sections of pavement, exposed tree roots, and objects left on the ground should be fixed, covered, or cleared away.

Fires Fires are the third most common cause of accidental death in the home. Careless smoking, often in connection with alcohol use, is a leading cause of home fires. Other causes include faulty electrical wiring and faulty heating units, cooking accidents, children playing with matches, and improper use of fireplaces.

Carelessness, whether while cooking, smoking, or using electricity, contributes to many household fires. Use the following list to check your home for fire hazards:

- Do not overload electrical outlets.
- If you have fuses, use only fuses of the specified amperage. If you have circuit breakers, keep them in good working order.
- Have the heating system inspected regularly by a professional.
- If you have a fireplace, use a protective metal screen and have the chimney cleaned regularly.
- Keep the kitchen stove free of grease.

SECTION 27.3

Background
Fire Extinguishers

Home fire extinguishers can be effective in putting out small, contained fires. However, the fire department recommends that people first call 911 to report the fire and then use the fire extinguisher. Many people mistakenly believe that they can put out a fire when they cannot. The delay in calling the fire department allows the fire to get out of control. The fire department also cautions people to consider their personal safety before that of their possessions; unless the fire is very small, they should leave the house rather than try to extinguish the fire.

Life Skills Worksheet 27A

Assign the Looking at Fire Extinguishers Life Skills Worksheet.

---

help? *[The smoke detector would alert the dozer to the fire. The fire extinguisher could put out the fire.]* Then tell students that kitchen fires are very common. Ask: **Why do many fires start in the kitchen?** *[The burners get too hot and the food or cooking oil catches fire.]*

Role-Playing
Rules to Be Observed During a Fire

Have students role-play a situation in which a family discovers that a fire has broken out in the house. They should illustrate the appropriate behaviors outlined in the text. Ask students to evaluate the behaviors demonstrated in the skits and point out any adjustments that should be made.

 ### Cooperative Learning
Preventing Fires at Home

Have students write a one-paragraph summary of information they would convey to a youngster about fire prevention in the home. (The summaries should be clear and complete, and they should include signs of danger that a younger child could perceive.)

Background
Smoke Detectors

Smoke detectors are help-ful, but only if they work. The National Smoke Detector Project estimates that there are 16 million smoke detectors that do not work in homes in the United States. This num-ber is greater than the number of homes with no smoke detector at all. The most common reason smoke detectors do not work is that their "test button" is tested incor-rectly or is not opera-tional. Using the test button is not the best way to test a smoke de-tector. To determine if a smoke detector is opera-tional, use an aerosol smoke-detector product, available in most hard-ware stores. The product should be sprayed toward the smoke detector from a distance of about three feet. If the smoke detec-tor goes off, it is in good working order.

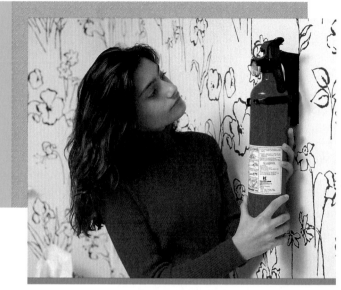

(FIGURE 27-10) Smoke and carbon-monoxide detec-tors should be checked at regular intervals to be sure they are working properly. Place fire extinguishers where they will be visible and easily accessible in case of an emergency.

electrocution:

death resulting from the flow of electrical current through the body.

All homes should have smoke detec-tors and fire extinguishers. But in a recent study, about 20 percent of students ques-tioned reported not having smoke detectors in their homes. Smoke detectors should be located on every floor and should be tested regularly to make sure they are working. It's a good idea to make a chart showing the dates smoke detectors have been checked. Fire extinguishers should be placed in kitchens, basements, and storage areas to deal with small fires.

Finally, you should have a plan for escape in case of fire. The plan should be practiced, and all family members should take part in fire drills. If a fire does break out in your home, observe the following safety precautions:

- If possible, alert the other members of your household, and leave by one of the exits established in your escape plan.
- If there is smoke, cover your nose and mouth with a wet cloth, drop to the floor, and crawl toward the prearranged exit.
- If a closed door is warm to the touch, do not open it. There could be fire on the other side of the door.
- Close doors behind you, if possible.
- Once outside, call the fire department from the nearest phone.
- If your hair or clothing catches on fire, stop, drop, and roll to extinguish the flames. Do not run.

Electrical Safety Faulty electrical wiring and improper use of fuses can result in fires. Electricity also presents an additional dan-ger. **Electrocution** is death resulting from the passage of electric current through the body. About 1,000 people are accidentally electrocuted each year.

Many electrical accidents involve ap-pliances that are not installed or used prop-erly. Any electrical appliance that is not working properly should be unplugged right away. It should be repaired by a qualified

---

• • • TEACH continued

Demonstration
Fuses and Circuit Breakers

Explain that the purpose of a fuse or circuit breaker is to prevent fires caused by overloaded circuits. If a cir-cuit containing a fuse becomes too hot, the metal band in the fuse melts, breaking the circuit. Caution students that fuse boxes must be used correctly to provide protection against an elec-trical fire. If some other metal with too

high a melting point is used instead of a fuse, the metal will not melt before the wires get overheated and the cir-cuit will not be broken in time to pre-vent a fire. A circuit breaker also provides protection against overheated wires. In most home circuit breakers, a temperature-sensitive device similar to a thermostat causes a switch to break the circuit if the wires become over-heated. To reset the circuit, the circuit-breaker switch is turned back on. Many appliances contain a type of cir-

cuit breaker called a ground fault cir-cuit interrupter (GFCI). A GFCI helps prevent electrical shocks from faulty appliances by automatically shutting off the electricity to the appliance. If possible, bring in a newer model hair dryer that contains a GFCI.

Class Discussion
Accidents Caused by Electricity

Ask: **When might a person be in danger of electrocution in or near the home?** [After a severe storm, an technician, or it should be replaced. Never attempt to fix an appliance that is plugged into an outlet!

Careless use of electrical appliances around water is very dangerous. Because water is a good conductor of electricity, someone who is wet or has wet hands can become a pathway for electric current. Avoid using hair dryers and other appliances in the bathroom. Never place a radio or other electrical device near a tub or sink. Bathroom outlets should have built-in circuit breakers.

A worn electrical cord is both a fire hazard and an electrocution hazard. Inspect the electrical cords in your home. Tell a parent or guardian about any defective wiring that you find.

Electricity is especially dangerous to young children. They should not be allowed to play with electrical cords or appliances nor permitted to plug in or unplug

(FIGURE 27-11) **This outlet has a built-in ground fault protector to break the circuit automatically in case an electrical appliance comes in contact with water.**

such appliances. Outlet caps should be placed over electrical outlets to keep young children from sticking objects into the holes.

Poisoning Most cases of accidental poisoning involve children under five. These children may swallow medicines, cleaning chemicals, pesticides, or other poisons. Improper storage of poisonous substances or failure to put them away after use are the most common ways that poisons get into the hands of youngsters.

To make your home safer for children, all medicines should be placed in cabinets that are out of a child's reach. Cleaning fluids and other poisonous materials should not be stored under sinks or in closets where children can reach them. A locked cabinet is the best storage location. Since basements are often collection places for a variety of dangerous chemicals, they should be inspected carefully and childproofed.

Older children and adults can also be victims of accidental poisoning. Storing liquids in plastic soda bottles is a very dangerous practice that can lead to someone accidentally drinking a poisonous material. Always store materials in their original containers, and make sure they are clearly marked.

Sometimes people are accidentally poisoned when handling pesticides and weedkillers. Before using any of these chemicals, read the label carefully and follow the instructions given. When using such products, you should wear gloves. If you spray pesticides indoors, the windows should be open, and it is a good idea to go outside afterward. If you need to spray outdoors, do not do so on a windy day.

Accidental poisoning can also result from taking medicine that was prescribed for someone else. Since your present health condition can affect how you react to a drug, you should take only medicines that were

SECTION 27.3

Background
Electrical Accidents
If a person comes into contact with a "hot" wire, the current can flow through parts of the body. If the circuit is completed through the hand, a shock or a burn would result. But if the circuit is completed through the body from one hand to the other or from hand to foot, the person may lose muscle control and not be able to let go. Large amounts of current can cause breathing difficulties and uncontrolled contractions of the heart.

To rescue a person who has had an electrical accident and is still in contact with the source of the electricity, the rescuer should first disconnect the equipment, touching only the plug. Then the rescuer should pull the victim away from the contact with a long, dry pole, a rope, or cloth. The rescuer must have dry hands and be standing on a dry surface.

electrical wire may fall to the ground. Anyone touching the wire could be electrocuted. Using an appliance when standing in water can do the same. Touching a worn wire of a plugged-in appliance can also cause electrocution.] **How can young children be protected from the dangers of electricity?** [By not letting them play with electrical wires or plugs; by placing outlet caps over electrical outlets so they cannot stick objects into the holes.]

Reinforcement
Accidental Poisonings at Home
Discuss ways in which young children become victims of accidental poisoning. Ask where medicine should be stored if there is a young child in the house. Also discuss the danger of chemicals, such as cleaning fluids and pesticides, and the proper places where they should be stored. Discuss ways in which other family members may also be poisoned accidentally when poisonous substances are not properly labeled or stored.

Cooperative Learning
Unsafe Materials in the Home
Have students work in groups to prepare posters that show how dangerous household products should be stored, labeled, and kept from the hands of young children. Some posters should point out that older members of the family are also in danger from mislabeled bottles.

Background
Preparing for an Emergency

After a major earthquake or other disaster, electricity, water, and gas may be out of service. Emergency aid may not reach victims for several days. Homes, offices, and cars should be equipped with the following items: fire extinguisher, first aid kit, wrench for turning off gas and water valves, flashlight and extra batteries, water and disinfectant, radio and extra batteries, dry or canned food that does not require cooking, blankets, clothing, and shoes for walking through the debris. Everyone in an at-risk area should have these items located in a place where they can easily be reached.

Carbon Monoxide: A Deadly Poison

Each year in this country, as many as 1,500 people die from accidental exposure to carbon monoxide (CO), an odorless, colorless, tasteless gas, and 2,300 people use it to commit suicide. Carbon monoxide poisoning is generally the result of defective heating and cooking systems, the burning of certain fuels and solid waste products, or cigarette smoke. The following steps will reduce your risk of CO poisoning:

Never leave a car running in the garage, especially if the garage door is closed or if the garage is attached to your house.

Put carbon monoxide detectors in your home.

Make sure fuel-powered equipment is working correctly and is properly ventilated.

Keep your car windows rolled up when you are in heavy traffic, especially if you are in enclosed space, such as a tunnel.

(FIGURE 27-12) **Carbon monoxide causes more deaths in the United States than any other environmental poison. You can take a few easy measures to protect your family. (Source: Wayne State University School of Medicine.)**

prescribed for you. Combining drugs is another risky behavior. It can result in a drug interaction that is dangerous to your health. Such a situation is also a case of accidental poisoning.

Everyone should inspect his or her home for poison hazards and take steps to poisonproof it. One step that is a must is to have the telephone number of the nearest Poison Control Center next to your phone. By calling that number, you can get instructions for helping someone who has been poisoned.

Safety in a Disaster

An event that seriously affects the lives and health of the people living in one or more communities is called a **disaster.** Many disasters, such as storms and earthquakes, are acts of nature. People have no control over such events. However, it is possible to reduce your risk of injury from these events.

Thunderstorms Thunderstorms are powerful but short-lived events that are most common in spring and summer. Although

disaster:

an event that affects the lives and health of people in one or more communities.

most thunderstorms would not be considered disasters, strong winds that sometimes accompany thunderstorms can blow objects around and cause widespread damage as well as injuries.

The most dangerous aspect of any thunderstorm is the lightning. Lightning is a gigantic discharge of electricity. It often strikes the tallest object in the area. However, the electricity can move from an object to your body if you are nearby. More people are killed each year by lightning than by any other weather-related event.

To reduce your risk of being injured during a thunderstorm, observe the following precautions:

- If you are outdoors, try to find shelter in a building or car.
- If you are on or in water, such as a lake or swimming pool, leave the water immediately. High winds, waves, and lightning are dangerous to boaters and swimmers.
- Never stand under a tall, isolated tree or other tall object.
- If you are in an open area, discard anything that might attract lightning, such as a large metal belt buckle, metal-frame backpack, or golf club. Crouch down to avoid being the tallest object in the area.
- If you are indoors, close the windows and stay away from them. Do not use the telephone, computer, or other electrical appliances. If lightning strikes a nearby electrical transmission line, the electricity can be transferred to you.

Tornadoes Like thunderstorms, tornadoes are most common in the spring and summer. Although they are fairly brief, the winds in tornadoes can be as high as 300 mph. Thus, tornadoes are able to destroy homes and send objects, including cars, flying through the air. The following are some safety tips to follow if a tornado is sighted or a warning is issued in your area:

• • • TEACH continued

Reinforcement
Natural Disasters

Discuss with students the kinds of natural disasters that strike from time to time. Certain disasters are more likely to threaten one part of the country than another. For example, the West Coast has concerns about earthquakes, the Atlantic and Gulf Coasts about hurricanes, the Midwest about tornadoes. Many parts of the country have severe

thunderstorms. Any low-lying region near a river may be flooded. Ask students how injuries can occur during each of these disasters.

 Cooperative Learning
Preparing for a Disaster

Have students work in cooperative groups to draw up plans of action for when a severe thunderstorm occurs in their area. Their plans should include meetings with family members to review the proper procedures to protect themselves and their property when a

watch has been put into effect or in case the disaster occurs without warning.

Class Discussion
Hurricanes and Tornadoes

Ask: **What are some dangers during a hurricane?** [*People can be struck by flying objects, including broken glass, bricks, boards, and debris. Vehicles and mobile homes can be overturned.*] **What precautions should be taken during a tornado?** [*If you are outdoors, try to go indoors. Go to the lowest part of the*

- Try to get indoors, then go to the lowest part of the building. Basements and interior bathrooms, closets, and hallways on the ground floor will provide the most protection.
- Stay away from windows and doors. Windows may be shattered by the winds. Doors can be ripped from their hinges and thrown about.
- If you are in a vehicle or mobile home as a tornado approaches, get out of it and go to a safer place. A tornado can overturn most vehicles and mobile homes. If you cannot get indoors, lie in a ditch or the lowest place you can find.

Hurricanes Hurricanes are strong tropical storms that occur most often in late summer and fall. Hurricane winds range from 75 to more than 150 mph, and the rain from a hurricane is usually very heavy. Hurricanes are very large storms that may travel great distances. Fortunately, there is usually some time to prepare for a hurricane. Observe the following precautions if a hurricane is forecast for your area:

- If you live along the coast, be prepared to leave if local officials advise it. The huge ocean waves and flooding produced by a hurricane do great damage to coastal areas and are a major cause of injuries and deaths from these storms.
- Have a supply of canned food, drinking water, flashlights, fresh batteries, candles, and first-aid materials in your home.
- If possible, board up windows or tape the inside of each pane. Place indoors all objects that might be blown away if left outside, such as lawn chairs or bicycles.
- Remain indoors until authorities advise that the storm is over. Once outside, avoid downed electrical wires and flooded areas.

(FIGURE 27-13) **Severe thunderstorms, like the one shown here, can produce dangerous lightning, damaging winds, hail, heavy rain, flash flooding, and even tornadoes. If you live in a part of the country that is prone to these types of storms, learn to recognize the signs of an approaching storm, and know what to do to protect yourself from storm-related injuries.**

building, such as a basement or cellar. Stay away from windows or doors. Get out of a car or mobile home. If you cannot go indoors, lie in a ditch or on the lowest ground you can find.]

 Cooperative Learning
Possibility of a Disaster in Your Area

Have students research newspapers and magazines to find information on the kinds of disasters that have struck your part of the country in the past. Some students may have experienced these disasters. Encourage them to share their experiences with the class. Ask students to discuss how they will respond to similar problems in the future.

• • • TEACH continues on p. 604

Section Review Worksheet 27.3

To reinforce the concepts presented in this section, assign Section Review Worksheet 27.3.

Section Quiz 27.3

Have students take Section Quiz 27.3.

Reteaching Worksheet 27.3

Students who have difficulty with the material may complete Reteaching Worksheet 27.3.

(FIGURE 27-14) **This building collapsed during an earthquake in San Francisco, CA. In earthquake-prone areas, building codes now specify earthquake-resistant designs.**

Earthquakes An earthquake is a sudden movement of Earth's crust. Earthquakes are brief, lasting only a minute or two. However, one earthquake can mean others will occur over the next few days. Powerful earthquakes and their aftershocks can cause great damage and loss of life. In North America, most serious earthquakes occur near the West Coast. Safety during an earthquake is often a matter of thinking quickly. The following are suggestions that could save your life:

assault:

a personal attack in which you are threatened or harmed.

Ways to avoid being a victim of violence are discussed in Chapter 20.

- If you are outdoors, get away from buildings and other tall objects. Material falling from them could injure or kill you.
- If you are in a car, pull over but remain in the car.
- If you are indoors, stand in a doorway between rooms or get under a heavy table. Stay away from windows, doors with glass panes, and objects that might shake loose from walls.

Other Disasters Although many disasters are caused by nature, some, such as gas explosions and forest fires, often result from the activities of people. During any disaster, follow the instructions of the emergency workers in charge. It is a good idea to listen to the emergency information on a local radio station so that you know what to do.

Assaults

A personal attack in which you are threatened or harmed is called an **assault.** Many assaults occur in connection with robberies, but some assaults, such as sexual assaults, are often committed by people known to the victim. Therefore, to reduce your risk of being assaulted, take precautions and be alert when you are alone with someone you are acquainted with as well as when interacting with strangers. Consider the following safety precautions:

• • • TEACH continued

Class Discussion
Avoiding Assault

Discuss the list of safety precautions in the text. Have students suggest other precautions for avoiding assault. If no suggestions are made, tell students that it is appropriate for them to go into a store and ask to call the police if they feel threatened on the street. In some cities, store owners participating in safe-haven programs display a window sticker so people will know that they can seek help there.

 Cooperative Learning
Resisting Attack— Is It Wise?

Have small groups of students discuss when it is best to resist attack and when it is best not to resist. Then, as a class, draw up a list of conditions, if any, under which they agree that resistance is advisable.

Class Discussion
Occupational Safety

Ask students what they think are the most dangerous occupations. Then have them look at Figure 27-15 on page 606, which shows the death rates among workers in various industries. Ask: **Why do you think you hear more about accidents that occur in manufacturing plants than in farming?** *[More people are usually involved in a single manufacturing accident, but many more farm accidents*

- When at home, keep doors locked both day and night. Never unlock the door for a stranger. If a service person comes to the door, have the person show identification at a window.
- Never let a stranger know that you are home alone, even if the stranger is on the telephone. If you receive a threatening or obscene phone call, hang up and then call the police.
- Do not walk outside alone, particularly at night. Even when you are with friends, avoid deserted areas, alleys, and poorly lighted parks.
- When in a car, keep the doors locked. At night, keep the windows partially rolled up. If a stranger approaches your car, drive away.

If you are attacked, let good judgment determine your actions. Escape if you can. If your attacker has a weapon, do not try to resist unless you think that your life is in immediate danger. Afterward, report the attack to the police.

Occupational Safety

Many people are injured or killed each year in job-related accidents. According to a study by the National Safety Council, personal behavior—such as being careless and disregarding safety requirements—is a factor in 82 percent of these accidents. Close to 20 percent of work-related accidents are caused wholly by such behavior. Faulty machinery and unsafe working conditions also contribute to many injuries and deaths.

As a student, you are preparing for your future occupation. Some occupations, such as mining and the manufacturing of chemicals and explosives, are obviously risky. But as the graph in Figure 27-15 indicates, agriculture, construction, and transportation can also be considered risky occupations.

What Would You Do ?

Making Responsible Decisions

Your On-the-Job Safety Is Threatened

Suppose that you work for a company that uses hazardous materials in its everyday operation. You like the job and the people you are working with. Then one day, one of your co-workers shows you a copy of the *Material Safety and Data Sheet* for a chemical that you use frequently, saying that you should read it carefully.

Material Safety and Data Sheets are government publications that contain information about the hazards of chemicals and the types of protective clothing and equipment that are needed for handling them safely. After reading the data sheet, you realize that you have not been provided with the proper protective equipment. What would you do?

Remember to use the decision-making steps:

1. State the Problem.
2. List the Options.
3. Imagine the Benefits and Consequences.
4. Consider Your Values.
5. Weigh the Options and Decide.
6. Act.
7. Evaluate the Results.

What Would You Do ?

Have students do the exercise, using the decision-making model to decide what to do as a worker who has to handle hazardous chemicals but who has not been provided with the proper protective equipment.

may occur every day.] Discuss the kinds of accidents that occur in the mining industry.

Extension
Safety in the Workplace

Have students interview the managers of local manufacturing plants or businesses to find out how they handle occupational safety.

Review Answers

1. Answers will vary but may include being careless while cooking or by not repairing frayed rugs or broken tiles. Accept any accurate examples.

2. Answers will vary but may include using slippery bath mats or overloading electrical outlets.

3. Plans for fire safety will vary with each student and home. Fire safety plans should enable fires to be detected as early as possible, and escape routes should be as direct an exit from the house as possible.

4. Occupational Safety and Health Administration (OSHA); OSHA helps protect workers by setting safety standards such as requirements for storing large amounts of chemicals, types of safety equipment workers must wear, and allowable amounts of exposure to dangerous materials such as poisonous vapors and radiation.

5. Answers will vary according to occupation. Accept any answer that demonstrates the ability to recognize potential hazards and ways to eliminate or reduce those hazards.

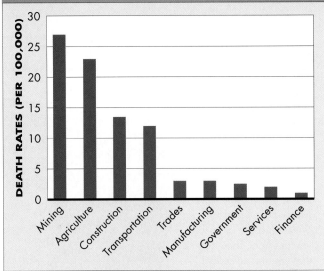

DEATH RATES AMONG WORKERS IN VARIOUS INDUSTRIES

(FIGURE 27-15) **This data supplied by the Bureau of Labor Statistics indicates the most hazardous occupations. Remember that both you and your employer are responsible for your safety.**

The Occupational Safety and Health Administration (OSHA) is a federal agency that sets safety standards in the workplace. State and local governments may also set standards for safety in various occupations. Fire safety, requirements for storing large amounts of chemicals, and the types of safety equipment that workers must wear are examples of factors the government regulates. In industries that expose workers to dangerous materials such as poisonous vapors and radiation, the government sets limits on how much exposure a worker is permitted to have.

Work-related illnesses and injuries affect close to two million Americans each year. Many workers once employed in the asbestos industry developed serious lung diseases as a result of contact with asbestos. Illnesses caused by contact with irritating or toxic materials continue to affect the health of many workers each year. To practice protecting yourself at work, complete the "What Would You Do?" activity on page 605.

Although the accident rate in the workplace has, in general, been declining, such accidents are still an important factor in the total number of accidental injuries and deaths. The same principles that apply to accidents in general also apply in the workplace. Both employers and employees are responsible for ensuring safe working conditions and preventing accidents.

Review

1. Cite some examples of how careless behavior can contribute to accidents in the home.

2. What unsafe conditions can you identify in your home that might lead to accidental falls? to electrical accidents?

3. **LIFE SKILLS: Problem Solving** Review the fire safety of your home. Then develop a plan to improve it. Discuss your plan with a parent or guardian. With his or her assistance, put your plan into action.

4. What federal agency oversees the safety of workers? List three ways this agency helps protect workers from injury on the job.

5. **Critical Thinking** Choose one of the occupations shown on the graph in Figure 27-15. What potential hazards associated with that occupation might be regulated by government agencies to help ensure the safety of the workers?

ASSESS

Section Review

Have students answer the Section Review questions.

Alternative Assessment

Government Help During Disasters

Ask students to speculate about what it would be like if the government did not help restore an area to normal after a disaster strikes.

Closure

Student Responsibility to Safety at School

Ask students to suggest ways students sometimes endanger themselves and others when at school (for instance, by goofing off on stairways or by leaving articles in places where others may trip over them).

Section 27.4 Recreational Safety

Objectives

- *Recognize potential hazards in recreational activities.*
- *Identify ways to reduce the risk of accidents in recreational activities.*
  LIFE SKILLS: Problem Solving

Activities such as swimming, hiking, and playing baseball provide fun and exercise, and can reduce stress. Recreation also involves risk, but there are things you can do to reduce the risk of accidents and injury.

Sports and Safety

The student in Figure 27-16 is on a high school track team. But right now he is not running; he is warming up. Figure 27-17

gives information about warm-up practices among 10th-graders who exercise or play sports outside of school.

Warming up stretches ligaments and tendons—tissues that connect bones and hold muscles to bones, respectively.

(FIGURE 27-16)
Warming up protects against sports injuries.

Background
Warming Up the Joint Fluid

Warming up before sports activities helps prevent injury during playing time. Warming up causes an increase in the amount of synovial fluid that lubricates the joints. Without a sufficient amount of synovial fluid, the bones that meet at the joints are stressed and are more easily injured.

Warm-up Practices of 10th Graders

Warm Up Before Exercises	Female	Male	Total
Never	9.8%	14.9%	12.5%
Rarely	11.1%	14.1%	12.7%
Sometimes	20.7%	18.1%	19.3%
Usually	22.7%	20.7%	21.6%
Always	35.7%	32.1%	33.8%

(FIGURE 27-17) **This is how the 10th-graders who participated in the *National Adolescent Student Health Survey* answered the question: "How often do you warm up before exercising?"**

Section 27.4 Lesson Plan

MOTIVATE

Journal 27D
Sports and Safety

This may be done as a warm-up activity. Ask students to name a sport or form of exercise that they participate in. Then, in their Journal, have then tell what safety guidelines a person should follow when participating in that activity.

Cooperative Learning
Warm-up Activities

Have students form groups. Have them discuss the importance of warm-ups, then tally how many in the group always warm up before exercising, usually warm up, sometimes do, rarely do, and never do. Copy the categories on the chalkboard and find the class profile by combining the totals for each category for all the groups. Compare the results with the national averages.

Background
Accidental Drownings

Many people who drown are accomplished swimmers. They may swim out too far, then become too tired to return to shore. Strong currents may carry them into deep water. Sometimes cramped muscles cause a swimmer to lose the ability to continue swimming. Some swimmers take unnecessary risks, others swim while under the influence of alcohol. Swimming is usually safe for those who follow the rules and are aware of the risks.

 Making a Choice 27B

Assign the Planning for Safety card. The card asks students to analyze safety hazards of their activities and to plan how to avoid potential accidents.

 Ethical Issues in Health

Have students read this Unit 8 feature on pages 650–651. Then have them complete its companion worksheet.

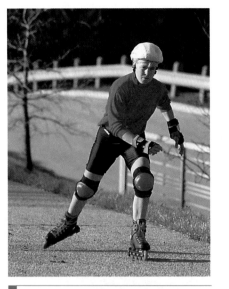

(FIGURE 27-18) **In-line skaters wear helmets, kneepads, and other protective gear to reduce their risk of injury.**

The importance of warming up properly is discussed in greater detail in Chapter 3.

Warming up also slowly increases the flow of blood, and thus oxygen, to muscles. Beginning physical activity without first warming up can result in pulled ligaments and muscles and in muscle strains. Such injuries are common among people who participate in sports.

Water Safety Among 10th Graders

Behavior	Never Do	Sometimes Do
Swim alone	62.0%	38.0%
Swim in restricted/ unsupervised area	70.7%	29.3%

(FIGURE 27-19) **This is how the 10th-graders who participated in the *National Adolescent Student Health Survey* answered the question: "How often do you swim alone or in restricted or unsupervised areas?"**

The most serious injuries in sports often occur because of the misuse—or lack of use—of protective equipment, such as helmets and mouthguards. As with riding bicycles and motorcycles, playing sports often requires the use of safety equipment. Batting helmets are required in Major League Baseball. No player in the National Football League would head onto the field without his helmet and his mouthpiece. Professional athletes reduce their risk of injury by using such equipment. Unfortunately, amateurs don't always take the same precautions.

In-line skating, which has become very popular, is a sport that causes many broken bones and other injuries. Notice the types of protective equipment being worn by the skater in Figure 27-18. If you participate in this activity or a similar activity, such as roller-skating or skateboarding, be sure you are protected against accidental injury—wear protective equipment.

Water Safety

As you might suspect, the recreational activity that results in the greatest number of accidental deaths is swimming. Figure 27-1 shows that drowning is the fourth leading cause of accidental death. This is partly because a great number of people head for the water on hot summer days.

Swimming and Diving Many drownings occur in home swimming pools. Because of carelessness, young children are frequently the victims. Children should never be left unattended in or near a pool. Many communities require pools to be fenced so that youngsters cannot wander into them.

Older children and adults, including those who can swim, are also victims of drowning. In many cases, risky behavior contributes to an accidental drowning.

TEACH

Class Discussion
Proper Equipment for Sports and Exercise

Ask students to name the sports and other forms of exercise they participate in. Write them on the chalkboard. Then ask what kinds of equipment are needed to make these activities safe, and write these next to the activity.

Have students mention accidents they know of that occur during these activities, and the effect of proper equipment on reducing injuries.

 Journal 27E
Water Safety

Discuss the table shown in Figure 27-19. Ask students to write in their Journal about whether they are familiar with basic water-safety rules. If they are familiar with them, have them list the ones they always follow and the ones they don't follow.

Class Discussion
Boating Safety

Ask students to discuss some unsafe boating practices. Discuss the consequences of these risky behaviors.

• • • TEACH continues on p. 610

Swimming alone and swimming in an unprotected area are two such behaviors. Figure 27-19 shows that approximately one-third of 10th-graders surveyed engage in such risky behavior at least some of the time. To reduce the risk of drowning, you should always swim with a friend and swim where there are lifeguards.

Learning how to swim will reduce your risk of drowning. But if you are in trouble in deep water and no immediate help is available, a technique called **drown proofing** can help keep you afloat. The steps in drown proofing are as follows:

- First, take a deep breath and relax, allowing your face to enter the water. Let your legs hang down in the water and your arms float forward.
- Next, slowly exhale underwater. Then move your arms downward as you kick with your feet to raise your head above the surface.
- Take a breath and begin again.

Diving into water requires caution. Learn to dive from someone who knows how. Diving into an unknown area or into water of unknown depth is a very risky behavior. Hitting bottom can cause serious head, neck, and spinal injuries. Paralysis or death often results from such accidents.

Boating Safety Some drownings occur as a result of boating accidents. The girls in Figure 27-20 are reducing their risk of drowning by wearing life jackets. All boaters, regardless of their swimming ability, should wear a life jacket *at all times*.

Boating accidents usually result from carelessness or risky behavior. As with a car, speeding in a boat can result in loss of control. Alcohol is another factor in many boating accidents. Ignoring warning buoys and other markers and weaving unnecessarily can also result in accidents. Sudden

drown proofing:

a technique to stay afloat that can be used even by those who cannot swim.

SECTION 27.4

Section Review Worksheet 27.4
To reinforce the concepts presented in this section, assign Section Review Worksheet 27.4.

Section Quiz 27.4
Have students take Section Quiz 27.4.

Reteaching Worksheet 27.4
Students who have difficulty with the material may complete Reteaching Worksheet 27.4.

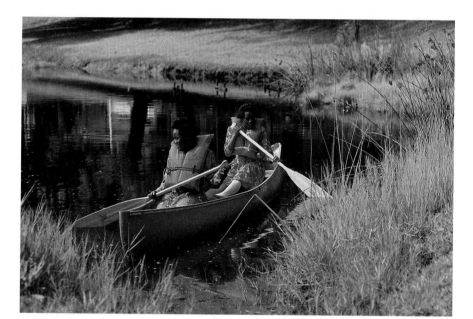

(FIGURE 27-20) **As these girls are demonstrating, every person in a boat should have his or her own life jacket.**

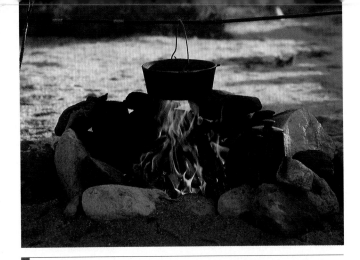

(FIGURE 27-21) **This is one safe way to manage a campfire. Campfires should not be left unattended and should be extinguished completely before the last person leaves the area.**

storms and overloading a small boat with people and equipment can result in capsizing, or turning the boat over. If you use a boat, learn how to handle it. Also learn the rules of boating safety.

Wilderness Safety

Hiking, camping, and hunting are outdoor activities enjoyed by millions of people. Although some people are injured by animals such as bears and snakes, such incidents are rare. Hazards such as getting lost, losing control of a fire, and being injured with firearms are far more common.

Hiking in the woods involves thinking ahead. For example, when Gary and Lien planned to hike for a day, they bought a trail map of the area, studied it, then let their parents know where they were going and when they expected to return. As they hiked, Gary and Lien followed the marked trail. They did not try to cut across the forest to reach their destination. Carrying a map and staying on the trail helped Gary and Lien avoid getting lost. Letting people know where they were going hiking was

another good precaution to take in case something went wrong.

Careless handling of campfires and other fires results in many forest fires each year. Damage runs into the millions of dollars, and loss of life can result. Like the campfire in Figure 27-21, a campfire should be built only in a fire ring of metal or stone, or in a stone fireplace. Using inflammable liquids to start a fire or get it burning better is a risky behavior that can result in injuries. A fire of any kind must never be left unattended. If the fire danger in the area is high, it is unlikely that campfires will be permitted.

Hunting accidents often result from carelessness. If you hunt, wear bright red or orange clothing so that you are visible to other hunters. When preparing to shoot, be sure that your target is the intended animal. If you are not certain about what you are shooting at, don't shoot. Firearms should always be stored and transported unloaded. But when you are handling a firearm, always assume that it is loaded until you have checked it!

Review

1. *In what ways do careless and risky behaviors contribute to accidental drowning?*

2. *LIFE SKILLS: Problem Solving Discuss some ways to reduce injuries resulting from participation in sports.*

3. *Critical Thinking Review your recreational activities for potential hazards. Identify actions that you can take to reduce the risk of accidents.*

Highlights

Summary

- To reduce the risk of accident or injury in a motor vehicle, wear seat belts, obey traffic laws, drive defensively, and never drive after using alcohol or other drugs or ride with a driver who is under the influence of alcohol or other drugs.

- To reduce the risk of accident or injury on a bicycle or motorcycle, wear a helmet and proper clothing, avoid speeding, ride defensively, obey traffic laws, and keep bikes in good working order.

- To prevent injury from fire, install fire extinguishers and smoke detectors; properly maintain heaters, stoves, fireplaces, and electrical wiring; and have a home evacuation plan.

- To reduce the risk of accidental poisoning, keep medicines and other poisonous substances out of the reach of chil-

dren, store them in properly marked original containers, and follow the directions for their proper use.

- To reduce the risk of carbon monoxide poisoning, install CO detectors in your home and make sure fuel-powered equipment and cars are working and are properly ventilated.

- To reduce the risk of being assaulted, keep doors locked, avoid strangers and deserted areas when alone, and when in a car, keep the doors locked.

- To reduce the risk of accidental injury or death when engaging in outdoor activities, use the proper safety equipment and follow the safety rules for each activity, tell someone where you are going and when you will be back, and never go alone.

Vocabulary

accident any unexpected event that causes damage, injury, or death.

risk an action that is potentially dangerous; the chance of injury.

safety awareness knowledge about risks and how to reduce them.

defensive driving driving as though you expect other drivers to drive recklessly.

electrocution death resulting from the flow of electrical current through the body.

disaster an event that affects the lives and health of people in one or more communities.

assault a personal attack in which you are threatened or harmed.

drown proofing a technique to stay afloat that can be used even by those who cannot swim.

SUMMARY

Have students read the summary to reinforce the concepts they learned in Chapter 27.

VOCABULARY

Have students write several safety rules in which they use all the vocabulary words correctly.

EXTENSION

Have students make posters that raise community awareness to the need for safer practices in sports activities. Have students ask that their posters be displayed in the public library, banks, and health clubs.

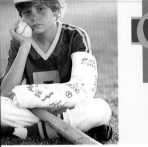

Chapter Review

CHAPTER REVIEW

Concept Review

1. safety awareness
2. motor vehicle
3. is under the influence of alcohol or drugs
4. driving defensively
5. helmet
6. falls
7. smoke detectors, fire extinguishers
8. water
9. children under five
10. lightning, strong winds
11. mining, agriculture
12. swimming
13. life jacket
14. unloaded

Expressing Your Views

1. Sample response: Teenagers often take more risks than other people would because they typically feel that an accident "can't happen to me." Some teenagers may feel that wearing a seat belt or a bicycle helmet doesn't look "cool." Also, some teenagers may not wear safety devices because their friends don't.

2. Answers will vary with individual opinions. Accept any opinion that is well supported.

3. Sample response: Lock all medicines in a cabinet that is out of reach, lock all cleaning materials in a cabinet, put away all small items that the child might put in his or her mouth and possibly

Concept Review

1. Knowledge about risks and how to avoid them is called _____ .

2. _____ accidents account for more deaths than any other kind of accident.

3. You can reduce your risk of being involved in a motor-vehicle accident by not riding with a person who _____ .

4. _____ involves expecting other drivers to do the unexpected.

5. Wearing a _____ when riding a bicycle or motorcycle can reduce your chances of suffering a serious injury.

6. For people over 65, _____ cause from one-third to one-half of all accidental deaths.

7. Two types of devices that reduce the risk of injury from a fire are _____ and _____ .

8. Electrical appliances should never be used around _____ .

9. _____ have the highest risk of being poisoned by improperly stored medicines and poisons.

10. _____ and _____ are the most dangerous aspects of a thunderstorm.

11. The two most risky occupational fields are _____ and _____ .

12. The recreational activity that results in the greatest number of accidental deaths is _____ .

13. All boaters should wear a _____ .

14. For safety, firearms should be stored and transported _____ .

Expressing Your Views

1. Why do you think so many teenagers fail to use safety equipment such as seat belts and bicycle helmets, as indicated by the tables in Figures 27-5 and 27-8?

2. Many states have laws that require passengers in cars to wear seat belts and motorcyclists to wear helmets. Do you think people should be required by law to wear such equipment? Why or why not?

3. If your one-year-old cousin were coming to your house for a visit, what changes would you make in your home to assure his safety?

swallow or choke on, put out of reach all items that are breakable or have sharp edges, put electrical outlet safety plugs in all outlets that are not in use, and close and lock doors that lead to stairs or put up a child safety gate in front of stairs.

Life Skills Check

Sample responses:

1. If I did not drive to work I would have someone pick me up directly in front of the restaurant or I would get a ride home with another employee who I knew well and could trust. If I did drive to work I would park as close to work as possible, in a well-lighted area, and lock all doors when I left the car. I would have my car keys in my hand as I walked to my car. I would make sure no one was in the back seat before I got into the car. If there were strangers near my car, I would go back into the restaurant and find someone to escort me to my car, or call the police.

2. I would not go with my friend. Swimming and diving at night is not safe, especially in an area not open to swimmers and

Life Skills Check

1. Practicing Self-Care
You just got a late-night job at a restaurant downtown, about eight blocks from your house. What safety precautions could you take to make sure you get home safely each night?

2. Making Responsible Decisions
Your friend tries to talk you into going swimming and diving with him in a water-filled quarry late one night. You try to persuade your friend to do something less dangerous, but he won't listen. What should you do?

3. Problem Solving
Tornadoes, hurricanes, and earthquakes are natural disasters. What could you do at home and at school to prepare for each of these disasters?

Projects

1. Divide a sheet of poster board into four parts. Create a "What Is Wrong?" picture in each part, showing an important safety rule being violated. Present these to the class and have volunteers guess what is wrong in each picture.

2. Working with a group, contact your local police department, hospital, or EMS squad to find out the numbers and types of accidents that are most common in your community. Ask if

any prevention programs are being used to reduce these problems. Present your findings to the class along with your suggestions for ways to limit these accidents.

3. Develop a fire-escape plan for your home. On a floor plan of your home, diagram the escape routes for every member of your household, and make a list of the directions to share with your family.

Plan for Action

The home is a place where people spend much of their time, and unfortunately, it is a place where accidents are common. Create a plan to help reduce the risk of accidents in your home.

without lifeguards. I would continue trying to convince my friend to do something else.

3. I could make a disaster plan for each of the natural disasters. One plan would tell what I would do if I were at home; the other plan would tell what I would do if I were at school. I would practice my plan so that it would be familiar to me, if and when I should need to put it into action.

Projects
Have students plan and carry out the projects for safety and risk reduction.

Plan for Action
Suggest that students talk with their family before developing their plan. They may want to take a tour of their home with their family to identify any areas where accidents could occur.

ASSESSMENT OPTIONS

Chapter Test
Have students take the Chapter 27 Test.

Alternative Assessment
Have students do the Alternative Assessment activity for Chapter 27.

Test Generator
The Test Generator contains additional assessment items for this chapter.

CHAPTER

28

First Aid and CPR

SECTION	TITLE/OBJECTIVES	PERSONAL INVENTORY			LIFE SKILLS DEVELOPMENT			
		Personal Health Inventory	Journal	Check Up	Life Skills	Life Skills Worksheets	Media Message or Ethical Issues Worksheet	What Would You Do?
28.1 *pp. 615–623*	**EMERGENCY PRIORITIES** • Name the first steps that should be taken during an emergency. ▪ Describe the procedure for rescue breathing. ▪ Describe the procedures for stopping or controlling bleeding. • Describe the signs of shock and its treatment. ▪ List two facilities that might offer CPR training.	Ch. 28	28A 28B		p. 617			
28.2 *pp. 624–628*	**INJURIES** • Differentiate among five types of wounds and their treatments. • Describe the first-aid steps for a fracture. • Describe the first-aid procedures for suspected injuries of the head and spine.		28C 28D					
28.3 *pp. 629–633*	**CHOKING, HEART ATTACK, AND OTHER EMERGENCIES** • Describe the first aid for a heart-attack victim. • Explain what to do if you find a person unconscious from an unknown cause. ▪ Know how and when to perform the Heimlich maneuver.		28E			28A		p. 633
28.4 *pp. 634–646*	**COMMON EMERGENCIES** • Contrast two health emergencies caused by heat, and compare their treatments. ▪ Know how to identify and protect your body from cold-related health emergencies. • Describe three types of burns and their treatment. • List the steps to be taken when poison is swallowed.		28F 28G		p. 637	28B 28C 28D		

KEY: ▪ Denotes Life Skill Objective
Text references denoted by page number.
Supplement references denoted by chapter or item numbers.

LINKING RESOURCES

								KEY FACTS
Making a Choice Cards	Parent Discussion Guide	Health Talk Audio Program	Teaching Transparencies and Directory	Section Review Worksheets	Section Quizzes	Reteaching Worksheets	Section Reviews	
INTERACTION		**OTHER RESOURCES**		**SECTION REVIEW AND ASSESSMENT**				
			28A	28.1	28.1	28.1	p. 623	
			28B	28.2	28.2	28.2	p. 628	
28A 28B				28.3	28.3	28.3	p. 633	
				28.4	28.4	28.4	p. 646	

KEY FACTS

- First aid is immediate emergency care given to a sick or injured person until professional help is available. This chapter is designed to familiarize students with first-aid procedures, but it does not take the place of professional instruction in first aid.

- Cardiopulmonary resuscitation (CPR) can revive people whose breathing and heartbeat have stopped; it should be performed only by someone trained in the procedure.

- The Heimlich maneuver is the recommended method for dislodging an object from the throat of a person who is choking.

- A person should not risk his or her life in order to rescue or to provide first aid to another person.

- Shock, a condition in which the body's vital processes are severely depressed, is life threatening and can occur in accident victims that appear uninjured. Knowing simple procedures used to treat shock can save lives.

- Familiarity with emergency procedures will help a person remain calm when dealing with an accident or sudden illness. Remaining calm prevents panic and can save lives.

CHAPTER REVIEW AND ASSESSMENT

TEXT
Chapter Review pp. 648–649

SUPPLEMENTS
Chapter Test 28

Alternative Assessment 28

Test Generator Chapter 28

CHAPTER 28

First Aid and CPR

◆ ◆ ◆ ◆

Section **28.1** Emergency Priorities

Section **28.2** Injuries

Section **28.3** Choking, Heart Attack, and Other Emergencies

Section **28.4** Common Emergencies

People who are not physicians but are trained to give emergency medical care often help save lives. With training in First Aid and CPR, you may someday be able to save a life as well.

MYTHS & MISCONCEPTIONS

- **In a life-threatening emergency, the safest action is to wait for medical help to arrive.** Medical help may not arrive in time to save a person's life, and first aid administered by an informed person can mean the difference between life and death.

- **In a life-threatening emergency, a person should always try to rescue a person who is in danger.** A person should attempt to rescue another person only if doing so does not endanger his or her life as well.

- **Frostbite should be treated by rubbing snow on the affected area.** Frostbite is the freezing of tissues. Treatment involves warming the tissues.

- **A person who swallows poison must be made to vomit.** Many poisons are caustic and should be diluted with fluids rather than evacuated by vomiting.

The late afternoon sun hung low in the sky as Sonya walked home, her jacket collar pulled up against the chill autumn air. She heard the swish of leaves behind her, and Masahiko streaked past her on his bicycle.

While Sonya watched in horror, a driver pulled out of a parking place directly in front of Masahiko. Unable to brake in time, Masahiko crashed into the side of the car and flew off his bike. His head slammed into the curb.

Looking around for help, Sonya saw no one. She was on her own. What should she do first? How could she tell whether Masahiko was injured seriously? How should she treat his injuries?

Section 28.1

Emergency Priorities

Objectives

- Name the first steps that should be taken during an emergency.
- Describe the procedure for rescue breathing.
  ■■ **LIFE SKILLS: Intervention Strategies**
- Describe the procedures for stopping or controlling bleeding.
  ■■ **LIFE SKILLS: Intervention Strategies**
- Describe the signs of shock and its treatment.
- List two facilities that might offer CPR training.
  ■■ **LIFE SKILLS: Using Community Resources**

You never know when an emergency may occur, or in what form. You could be needed to help the victims of a hurricane, earthquake, car collision, or sporting accident. A classmate could be wounded in metal shop, or a person near you at a concert could collapse from a drug overdose.

In this chapter you will learn how to respond in an emergency when lives could depend on what you do next. You will learn what to do first and about treatment priorities. After studying the chapter, you will know how to treat many medical emergencies. To find out how to get specialized training, complete the Life Skills activity on page 617.

First Aid: The Difference Between Life and Death

First aid is the immediate care given until professional medical personnel arrive at the

first aid:

emergency care given to an ill or injured person before medical attention is available.

SECTION 28.1

Background
First Aid
Standard first-aid techniques were introduced by the St. John's Ambulance Association in 1877 in London. In 1882, the State Charities Association in New York became the first American group to offer training in first aid. Other groups, including the American National Red Cross, became interested in first aid and began teaching courses. In 1907, Clara Barton was instrumental in setting up the International First Aid Committee, an organization of groups from many countries committed to instruction in first aid.

Personal Health Inventory
Have students complete the Personal Health Inventory for this chapter.

Section 28.1 Lesson Plan

MOTIVATE

 Journal 28A
Emergencies

This may be done as a warm-up activity. Encourage students to record in their Journal descriptions of an emergency situation they have witnessed or heard about. Have them note what they or others did to help the victim.

scene of an accident or sudden illness. Sonya knew that appropriate first aid could mean the difference between life and death or between recovery and permanent injury. If Masahiko was seriously injured, Sonya had only seconds to act. Prompt medical attention was essential.

Sonya made an effort to compose herself, then ran to Masahiko. He wasn't moving. The car's driver, a man of about 50, seemed unhurt but was almost hysterical. He was beating his fists on the steering wheel and crying, "What have I done?" Grabbing the man by the arm, Sonya asked him to calm down, find a telephone, dial 911, report the emergency, and then come back to tell her when the ambulance and paramedics would arrive.

Sonya then turned to Masahiko, tapped him on the shoulder, and asked in a loud voice, "Masahiko, are you all right?"

Masahiko still did not move, but he groaned and muttered "No."

Steps To Take in a Medical Emergency

1. Survey the scene.

2. Rescue the person if necessary to prevent further injury.

3. Send for help.

4. Treat life-threatening conditions.

5. Go for help yourself if nobody has done so.

6. Identify other injuries, and provide first aid.

7. Remain with the victim until medical help arrives. Monitor breathing and heart rate, and prevent further injury.

(FIGURE 28-1) **Follow these steps if you are the first person to arrive at the scene of a medical emergency. Do not risk your safety to rescue or give first aid to someone else.**

First Steps in a Medical Emergency

If you are the first person to arrive on the scene of a medical emergency, there are certain steps you should take. Figure 28-1 summarizes these steps. Do not, however, risk your own safety in order to rescue or provide first aid to another person.

Survey the Scene First, evaluate the situation and the area for possible danger to you or to the victim. Determine what happened and how many people are injured. Look for and call out for bystanders who can help you.

Rescue If you can do so safely, your next step is to rescue anyone whose life is endangered. For example, a victim in deep water or a burning car will need to be moved to a safer place before you can even begin to check for injuries. Otherwise, *never* move an injured person until medical help arrives. Moving someone who has a head, neck, or spine injury could cause further serious, or fatal, injury. Instead, do what you can to protect the person from further injury.

Because of the nature of Masahiko's accident, Sonya knew that he could have suffered a head or neck injury. Until she knew the full extent of Masahiko's injuries, moving him would risk making his injuries worse. Luckily, a motorist stopped to help. Sonya asked her to park her car crosswise in the street, providing a barrier to protect Masahiko from oncoming traffic. This was Sonya's rescue step.

Send for Medical Help If others are available, send them for medical help. If not, shout "Help!" Do not leave the injured person, even to go for help, until you have checked for and treated life-threatening conditions. People who call for help in an emergency should use the procedure given at the top of page 619.

TEACH

Class Discussion
What Actions Were Needed?

Have students discuss why someone in an emergency situation might fail to take appropriate action. Point out that, in an emergency, someone with knowledge about how to proceed is better prepared to deal with the situation than someone who has never

thought about what he or she might do. How do students judge Sonya's actions as described in the text?

Case Study
When to Rescue

Rescue is the second step to be taken in an emergency—if it can be done safely. Read a news story to the class about a rescue that involved serious risk to the rescuer. Pose the question, "Do people who risk their lives to save others violate recommended steps for dealing with an emergency?"

Reinforcement
Dealing With an Emergency

Review with students Figure 28-1, which outlines the steps that a person should take in dealing with an emergency. Have students describe Sonya's action for each step.

• • • TEACH continues on p. 618

*Life*SKILLS: Using Community Resources

First Aid and CPR Training . .

You never know when you may be called upon to give emergency care to help save a life, prevent further injury, or simply lessen discomfort. People in certain professions are required to study emergency care. For example, boat captains, flight attendants, police officers, and firefighters all need to be certified in first aid and cardiopulmonary resuscitation (CPR). Knowledge of emergency care can also be extremely important for anyone who spends time in the wilderness. On a hunting or backpacking trip, for instance, people may be miles from the nearest vehicle or medical facility. First aid may be the only care an injured person receives for hours, days, or even weeks.

First-Aid Training If you have not already taken a first-aid course, you may wish to do so. The course will give you hands-on experience that will help you remember the techniques described in this book. First-aid courses are given by the American Red Cross, local community colleges, and hospitals.

CPR Training Someday you may be able to save a life if you are trained in CPR. A local chapter of the American Red Cross or the American Heart Association will be able to tell you where training is available.

1. To find out where you can receive training in first aid or CPR, call a hospital, college, or organization such as the American Red Cross or the American Heart Association.

2. Find out when the courses are given.

3. Ask if there is a charge for the course.

• Caution: If you haven't had CPR training, *do not* attempt to administer CPR. If done improperly, CPR can cause further injury or even death.

SECTION 28.1

■■ *Life* SKILLS

Have students read the Life Skills feature. Then have them investigate where they can obtain first-aid training and training in CPR. Encourage students to consider enrolling in such courses with friends.

Rescue Breathing:

1. Open the airway by tipping the head back and lifting the chin.

2. Check for breathing by placing your cheek next to the person's nose and then listening and feeling for breath.

3. If the victim is not breathing, pinch the nose closed with one hand while keeping the airway open by holding the chin up with the other hand.

4. Tightly seal your mouth over the victim's mouth and blow air into the victim's lungs, or hold the mouth closed and blow into the nose.

5. After two breaths, check for a pulse and signs of breathing.

6. Continue to give one slow breath every 5 seconds until medical help arrives, you are too exhausted to continue, or the victim begins to breathe.

For young children and babies:
1. Blow into the mouth and nose at the same time.
2. Give one breath every 3 seconds.
3. Use smaller puffs of breath because the lungs are smaller.

(FIGURE 28-2) **Procedure for opening the airway and giving rescue breathing. Note the differences in the procedure for young children and babies.**

• • • TEACH continued
Demonstration
Rescue Breathing

Bring in a doll to use in demonstrating how to perform rescue breathing. Ask for a volunteer to act as a rescuer who must save a young child who has stopped breathing. Allow the student to refer to Figure 28-2 as he or she administers rescue breathing. Have the class critique the procedure.

618 FIRST AID AND CPR

Teaching Transparency 28A
Rescue Breathing

Use this transparency of Figure 28-2 to discuss the procedure for opening the airway and giving rescue breathing.

Demonstration
Finding the Carotid Artery

Show students how to locate their carotid artery. They can refer to Figure 28-3 for assistance. Have selected students find the artery on each other, demonstrating the proper technique for the class.

Role-Playing
Getting Help

Present an accident scenario to the class. Then have a student role-play a person calling 911 to report the accident. Have another student role-play the 911 operator. Using the guidelines on page 619 as a prompt, have the first student give information to the operator. The operator should ask for any information the person omits. As a class, review the 911 call and

When calling for help:

- Speak slowly and clearly.
- Tell exactly where the victim is, including town, address, description of the location, and any landmarks.
- Describe the accident, number of people injured, and nature of the injuries.
- Ask what you should do while waiting for medical help to arrive, and listen carefully to the instructions.
- Let the other person hang up first, to be sure they have no more questions or advice for you.

Initial Assessment Priorities

When giving first aid, treat life-threatening conditions first by following the procedure described below.

Determine Whether the Victim Is Conscious Tap the person on the shoulder, and ask loudly, ''Are you all right?'' Even though Masahiko answered ''No,'' his answer told Sonya that he was conscious.

Check ABCs If the person is unconscious, call 911, then check the ABCs: *A*irway, *B*reathing, and *C*irculation of blood. Check in this order, because a person whose airway is closed will stop breathing, and when breathing stops, the heart will soon stop circulating blood. Sonya checked all ABCs at once by asking if Masahiko was all right. Anyone who can talk, however poorly, has an open airway, can breathe, and has a beating heart.

Airway To open the airway, turn the person gently onto his or her back after checking for head, neck, and spinal injuries. If the person has these injuries, *do not move him or her until the head and neck have been stabilized.* With one hand under the chin and one on the forehead, lift the chin and tip the head back. See Figure 28-2.

Breathing Check for breathing by putting your cheek next to the person's nose and mouth and listening and feeling for breath. Also watch the chest to see if it is rising and falling. If the victim is not breathing, start rescue breathing at once, using the procedure shown in Figure 28-2. If the person's airway is open, your breath should easily enter his or her lungs and the chest will rise. The person should exhale automatically when you remove your mouth. If your breath will not enter the victim's lungs, repeat the procedure for opening the airway. If it still doesn't work, follow the procedures on page 629 for an unconscious choking victim.

Circulation of Blood Look for a pulse to determine whether the heart is working. The easiest pulse to find is usually at the carotid artery in the neck. You can find it in the groove on either side of the windpipe, beside the Adam's apple. See Figure 28-3.

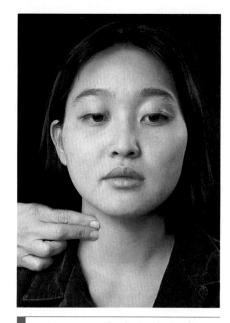

(FIGURE 28-3) **Check circulation by feeling for a pulse at the carotid artery on the side of the neck.**

make helpful suggestions if necessary. Repeat the procedure several times using different scenarios.

• • • TEACH continues on p. 622

CPR for Adults:

1. Lay the person on his or her back.

2. Open the airway as previously described, and give two slow breaths.

3. Place the heel of your hand nearest the victim's head on the victim's breastbone, starting two finger-widths up from the bottom of the breastbone. Then place your other hand on top of your first hand.

4. With your arms straight, put your weight on your hands and press down on the sternum, and then release the pressure so the chest can expand. Give compressions at a rate of 80–100 thrusts per minute. After 15 compressions, give two rescue breaths. After 4 sets of 15 compressions and two breaths, stop and check for a pulse. If the victim has a pulse, stop giving compressions. If not, repeat this step.

CPR for Young Children and Babies:
Follow the same basic procedure as above, with the following exceptions.
1. An infant should be held, with one hand supporting the head.
2. Use two or three fingers instead of your hands.
3. Depress the sternum only 1/2 to 1 inch.
4. Give compressions at a rate of 2 per second, about as fast as you can do it.
5. After 5 compressions, give one slow breath.

(FIGURE 28-4) **Procedure for performing CPR. Note the differences for young children and babies.**

CPR Procedures Do not attempt **cardio-pulmonary resuscitation (CPR)** *with the instructions from this or any other book unless you've had CPR training. Instead, study these directions for an understanding of CPR, or use them for review if you are trained.*

If you cannot find the victim's pulse and you are trained in the procedure, you may be able to save his or her life with CPR. Figure 28-4 describes CPR. When administered improperly, CPR can cause further injury.

CPR is hard work. It's all right not to start CPR if you don't feel up to it or aren't sure you know how. If you do start CPR, be prepared to keep on without pause until you are relieved by another trained CPR provider or you are simply too exhausted to continue. If, after CPR, the victim's heart starts beating on its own, check for breathing and continue rescue breathing if needed.

CPR is given *only* when a person is not breathing and has no pulse (heartbeat). If CPR is successful in reviving the person, he or she will most likely require additional medical treatment to remain alive. For this reason, you should always call 911 for emergency medical assistance, or send someone to call for you, before beginning CPR.

Control Bleeding If an injured person's breathing and circulation are adequate, the next priority is to stop severe bleeding that is life threatening. Use direct pressure, as described in Figure 28-5.

If you do not have sterile gauze, you will have to make do with whatever clean materials you have. Sanitary napkins make ideal dressings, and sometimes they are available when other materials are not. They are sold in restroom vending machines, and female bystanders may be carrying them in their purses.

cardiopulmonary resuscitation (CPR):

a lifesaving procedure designed to revive a person who is not breathing and has no heartbeat.

Procedure to Stop Bleeding

1. *Wash your hands with soap and water. Cover your hands with something that blood will not soak through.*

2. *If possible, cover the wound with a sterile dressing, such as gauze.*

3. *If possible, raise the bleeding wound above the heart.*

4. *Use your palm to apply pressure directly over the dressing on the bleeding wound. Keep applying pressure for at least 10–12 minutes to give blood clots time to form.*

5. *If bleeding starts again, resume pressure until it stops.*

6. *Wrap a pressure bandage tightly over the dressing. If blood soaks through, place another dressing on top.*

7. *Monitor ABCs.*

(FIGURE 28-5) **Follow these steps to stop or control severe bleeding. If it is not stopped, the victim might bleed to death before medical help arrives. Take steps to avoid direct contact with someone else's blood.**

SECTION 28.1

Section Review Worksheet 28.1
To reinforce the concepts presented in this section, assign Section Review Worksheet 28.1.

Section Quiz 28.1
Have students take Section Quiz 28.1.

Reteaching Worksheet 28.1
Students who have difficulty with the material may complete Reteaching Worksheet 28.1.

Background
Shock

Shock, which is severe circulatory distress, should not be confused with electric shock, which is the passage of an electric current through the body. During shock, the blood supply to the extremities, including the skeletal muscles and skin, is reduced. Heart action is weak, and breathing is shallow. The victim may feel lightheaded and weak. Shock may occur immediately after an injury, or it may develop several hours later. When treating victims, the rescuers must always be alert for signs of shock. Left untreated, shock can be fatal.

Review Answers

1. Survey the scene, rescue the person if necessary to prevent further injury, and send for medical help.

2. Answers should agree with information shown in Figure 28-2.

3. Answers should agree with information given in Figure 28-5. Students should also mention applying pressure to a pressure point if direct pressure does not stop the bleeding.

(FIGURE 28-6) **The body's pressure points are the locations of main arteries and veins. To stop bleeding, apply pressure with your fingers or the heel of your hand to the pressure point *nearest* the bleeding wound that is *between* the heart and the wound. Except for the head, this point would be just above the wound.**

If direct pressure and elevation do not stop bleeding on the head or a limb, apply pressure to the main artery supplying blood to the affected part. The places on the body where these arteries are located are called pressure points. Figure 28-6 shows the body's pressure points.

Try to avoid direct contact with someone else's blood, because it can carry an organism or a virus that causes a very serious disease such as hepatitis or AIDS. If your first-aid kit has rubber gloves, wear them. Otherwise, put something between your hand and the wound. You can, for example, place the victim's hand between yours and the wound. After providing first aid to a bleeding victim, wash your hands immediately. Meanwhile, do not eat or drink, and keep your hands away from your eyes, nose, and mouth.

Treat Poisoning As soon as the victim's ABCs are in order and bleeding is stopped, you must treat poisoning if it has occurred. (You'll learn how to treat poisoning later in the chapter.)

Assess Other Injuries The next step in handling an emergency is to look carefully for other injuries. If the person is conscious, ask him or her what hurts. Very gently, inspect the person's body for anything that looks broken or not quite right.

Look for Signs of Shock You must watch for signs of shock when helping an injured person or a victim of a serious accident. Shock is a condition in which the body's vital processes are severely depressed—circulation and breathing slow way down. If the shock process is not stopped, the person will die. Shock can result from major injuries, loss of blood, burns, poisoning, electric shock, allergic reactions, and sudden temperature changes. Even when the victim of a serious accident appears uninjured, he or she can have hidden injuries that could cause shock. Shock can kill a person even when the injury that triggered it is not life threatening.

The signs of shock include rapid, shallow breathing; rapid heartbeat; a weak pulse; pale, clammy skin; blue color around lips and fingernails; nausea; apathy; agitation; and weakness. Any time you start to see signs of shock, call immediately for an ambulance equipped with oxygen.

Role-Playing
Treating Shock

Have a student role-play an accident victim who is going into shock. Have another student play the role of a person who is administering first aid. Have this person demonstrate the proper procedure for preventing and treating shock. Have the class critique the effort. Repeat the role-playing with two more students.

Debate the Issue
Being a Good Samaritan

Select two small teams of students to debate whether it is okay to refuse to give first aid to an injured person because of the risk of being sued for incompetent treatment. Point out that although most states have laws protecting individuals who try to help victims, laws vary and final interpretation may be in the hands of a judge or jury. After the debate, poll the class about their attitudes on the proposition.

Journal 28B
Reviewing First Aid

Have students read over their Journal entries describing emergencies they witnessed. Have them compare how the emergencies were handled with the emergency procedures discussed in this section. Ask them to write in their Journal whether, in view of the knowledge they now have about handling emergencies, they would act differently if the accident happened today.

Treatment for Shock To treat shock, keep the victim calm, lying face up with feet elevated 10 to 12 in. This helps supply more blood to the brain. Victims who are unconscious or who may vomit should have their head turned to the side so they will not choke on their vomit. Do not elevate the feet if you suspect a head injury.

A shock victim's normal body temperature needs to be maintained. In some cases, you may need to cool an overheated shock victim, but usually you need to keep the victim warm. Cover or wrap the victim just enough to maintain body temperature.

Sonya treated Masahiko for shock immediately after checking his ABCs and determining that he was not bleeding severely. She knew that treatment is much more likely to be successful, and to save a life, if it is begun *before* signs of shock have started to appear. This means that any time you are treating an injury that might cause shock, you should begin treating for shock right away.

Because it was a chilly afternoon and getting colder, Sonya sent the motorist who had stopped to help to get blankets from a nearby home. She covered Masahiko with them and watched him closely. Knowing that a shock victim's breathing or heartbeat can fail, Sonya was ready to provide rescue breathing and, because she was trained, start CPR if necessary.

Attitude

It is important to approach an emergency situation with a calm and reassuring attitude. If you are upset or panicky, the victim will sense it and possibly become more panicked. That's why Sonya took control of herself after Masahiko's accident. Try to reassure injured persons that you will help them and that they will be all right. Since fear can bring on shock, calm reassurance

can help save a victim's life. The power of fear is so great that people have died after being bitten by nonpoisonous snakes!

Good Samaritan Laws

Most states have a Good Samaritan law that will protect you from legal liability if you help someone in an emergency. As long as you do your best, use common sense, and are careful not to cause additional harm to the injured person, the law should shield you from any legal problems. However, do not attempt procedures in which you have had no training.

Review

1. *What are the first three steps that should be taken in an emergency?*

2. **LIFE SKILLS: Intervention Strategies** *Explain how to provide rescue breathing.*

3. **LIFE SKILLS: Intervention Strategies** *How would you stop severe bleeding?*

4. *When and how would you treat a person for shock?*

5. **LIFE SKILLS: Using Community Resources** *Find out where you can get CPR and first-aid training in your community. Write or call two of these places and obtain a schedule of their classes.*

6. **Critical Thinking** *You are the first to arrive on the scene of an auto accident where there are two victims. What should you do?*

SECTION 28.1

Answers to Questions 1–3 are on p. 622.

4. When the person has suffered major injuries or shows one of the following signs of shock: rapid, shallow breathing; rapid heart beat; a weak pulse; pale, clammy skin; blue color around lips and fingernails; nausea; apathy; agitation; and weakness. Treatment involves maintaining the victim's normal body temperature, keeping the victim calm, and having the victim lie face up with feet elevated. Unconscious victims should have their head turned to the side.

5. A local chapter of the American Red Cross or the American Heart Association will be able to tell students where CPR training is available. First-aid courses are given by the American Red Cross, local community colleges, and hospitals.

6. Answers will vary but students should indicate the need to call 911 immediately. Students who are trained in first aid should check each victim's ABCs, treating the most severely injured victim first. Students with no first-aid training could check each victim for signs of shock and treat if necessary.

Extension
Obtaining Expert Advice

Have students write a class letter to a paramedic team that works in your area, describing the accident used as an example at the beginning of this section (Masahiko's bicycle accident). Have students describe what Sonya did and ask the paramedics whether she acted correctly and what else, if anything, she should have done.

ASSESS

Section Review

Have students answer the Section Review questions.

Alternative Assessment
Responsible Action

Tell students to imagine that they have witnessed an accident in which a person has fallen down a flight of stairs and is not moving. Have students write down the steps that they would

take if they were the first or only person on the scene.

Closure
The Danger of Shock

Have students describe shock and how to treat it. Then have them explain why an accident victim must always be checked for signs of shock. Ask each student, in turn, to suggest an incident in which a victim might go into shock.

SECTION 28.2

Background
Tourniquets

A tourniquet is a constricting device that should be used only as a last resort to control severe bleeding. A tourniquet is applied only when a large artery in a limb is severed and cannot be closed or when a section of a limb has been partially or totally severed.

A tourniquet is made by wrapping a length of cloth twice around the limb, just above the wound. The cloth is then tied once, and a stick, piece of metal, or other sturdy, elongated object is centered on the tied cloth. The cloth is then knotted over the stick and the stick is twisted in a circle until the bleeding stops. Once applied, a tourniquet should be released only by a doctor.

Section 28.2 Injuries

Objectives

- Differentiate among five types of wounds and their treatment.
- Describe the first-aid steps for a fracture.
- Describe the first-aid procedures for suspected injuries of the head and spine.

Injuries that may require first aid occur frequently in daily life. For instance, during athletic events, outdoor activities, or even common activities in the home, you or someone nearby may require first aid for an injury. The following are the recommended first-aid treatments for some common types of injuries.

Wounds

Wounds are among the most common injuries. Figure 28-7 shows the different kinds of wounds and their treatment.

Infections With any type of wound, there is danger that an infection will later develop as invading bacteria begin to multiply. Signs of infection include fever, pus, pain, swelling, and redness. Immunization helps prevent tetanus, which is a very serious, life-threatening infection. Anyone with a serious wound should have a tetanus shot if they are not up-to-date with their immunizations. Anyone who has not had a tetanus shot for more than 10 years should get one whether they have a wound or not.

Scalp Wounds The head has a large supply of blood, and much of it runs near the surface. Consequently, a relatively minor wound of the scalp or face can cause profuse bleeding that must be stopped by applying pressure.

Embedded Foreign Body When a foreign body, such as a piece of glass or even a knife, is embedded in a body part, it should be left in place. If you attempt to take it out, you could easily do more damage than good. Bandage the wound with the foreign body held in place, and get medical help for the victim.

Avoid Contact With Blood Remember that blood and some other body fluids can carry organisms and viruses that cause serious diseases. It is extremely important to avoid all contact with blood or other body fluids when you are treating another person's bleeding wounds.

Blisters

Pressure or friction may cause blisters. Treat blisters as follows:

- Protect an unbroken blister and avoid further pressure or friction.
- Wash a broken blister with soap and water and cover it with a sterile dressing.
- If a blister is likely to break,
  1. wash the area with soap and water,
  2. *do not* attempt to pierce and drain the blister,
  3. cover the blister with a bandage or sterile dressing,
  4. watch for signs of infection, and seek medical attention as needed.

Laceration
In a laceration the skin is torn. Lacerations usually bleed freely, and risk of infection is small if the wound is kept clean. First-aid steps:
1. Stop severe bleeding.
2. Make sure the cut is clean.
3. Cover with a clean sterile dressing.
4. Take victims with serious wounds to a doctor. Even if you doubt that seeing a doctor is necessary, go anyway. It's best not to take chances.

Incision
An incision is a clean cut, as made by a knife or a sharp piece of glass. Incisions usually bleed freely, and risk of infection is small if the wound is kept clean. First-aid steps:
1. Stop severe bleeding.
2. Make sure the cut is clean.
3. Cover with a clean sterile dressing.
4. Take victims with serious wounds to a doctor. Even if you doubt that seeing a doctor is necessary, go anyway. It's best not to take chances.

Abrasion
Skin is scraped away or worn away in an abrasion. A skinned knee from falling off a bicycle is a typical abrasion. Many abrasions do not bleed very freely and will need to be washed clean to avoid infection. First-aid steps:
1. Rinse carefully under running water.
2. If dirt or other matter is stuck in the abrasion, try to remove larger pieces by wiping very gently with a clean, damp cloth or tissue. Small bits can be left in place, if necessary, and will work their way out as the wound heals.
3. Cover with a bandage.

Puncture
A puncture wound is a hole through the skin and into deeper tissue. Stepping on a nail causes a puncture wound. Puncture wounds are difficult to clean, because they are deep and narrow. They seldom bleed much, and risk of infection is greater than with other kinds of wounds. First-aid steps:
1. Encourage the wound to bleed, to help clean it.
2. Wash the area around the wound to help prevent infection.
3. Because tetanus germs can thrive in a puncture wound, any victim of such a wound should be up-to-date on tetanus shots or make arrangements for a booster immediately.

Avulsion
In an avulsion, skin or another part of the body is torn off, or nearly torn off and attached by a flap of skin. First-aid steps:
1. Use direct pressure on the wound to stop the bleeding.
2. If a flap of skin is cut off or hanging loose, gently lay it back in place before bandaging the wound.
3. If a body part has been removed, send it to the hospital with the victim. If possible, wrap the body part in sterile gauze, place it in a plastic bag, and put the bag on ice, but don't delay getting the victim to a hospital.
4. Treat for shock.

(FIGURE 28-7) **Types of wounds and their treatment.**

Background
Tetanus
In any type of wound, including an open fracture, the danger of infection exists. Tetanus is a serious infection caused by the bacterium *Clostridium tetani.* The bacteria thrive under conditions of low oxygen, which helps explain why puncture wounds are candidates for infection with this microbe. The bacteria release a toxin that affects the nervous system, eventually causing paralysis. Death occurs when the respiratory muscles cease to function. Vaccines that give immunity are available, but periodic booster injections are required to ensure immunity. If untreated, the fatality rate exceeds 50 percent.

risky behavior and carelessness contribute to many accidents.

• • • TEACH continues on p. 626

Background

Concussion

Any head injury that results in unconsciousness, and even injuries that do not result in such, may include concussion. *Concussion* can be defined as a brain bruise. It results in a temporary state of confusion or in unconsciousness that can be fleeting, or it may last for hours or even days. A concussion is produced by the slamming of the brain tissue into the bones that form the skull. Any type of blow to the head can toss the head rapidly, causing the brain tissue to be compressed against the skull. Concussions can involve damage to the blood vessels and the nerve tissue in the brain. Because a concussion can cause permanent brain damage or death, medical treatment is required. (For more information about concussions, see the Body Systems Handbook, p. 661.)

fracture:

a broken bone.

First Aid for Fractures

1. *Avoid moving fracture victims unless you need to move them out of danger or transport them to a medical facility. If medical help is on the way, keep the injured person still.*

2. *Treat fracture victims for shock.*

3. *Build a splint to hold the broken bone in whatever position you find it. Trying to straighten out a fractured bone could cause further damage.*

4. *Place the splint so it immobilizes both the broken bone and the joints immediately above and below the fracture.*

5. *Provide padding between the splint and the skin. For example, for a broken forearm, you can splint the break so the wrist is supported as well as the bone, and then support the forearm in a sling so the elbow doesn't move.*

6. *Don't make the splint too tight. Fractures often cause swelling. Check to make sure the victim has a pulse on the side of the splint away from the heart; that tells you that the splint is not too tight.*

(FIGURE 28-8) **A splint prevents further injury by immobilizing a bone. Splints can be made from pieces of wood; from rolled-up magazines, newspapers, or pillows; or from pieces of stiff cardboard.**

Fractures

A broken bone is called a **fracture**. Fractures can be either open or closed. With a closed fracture, also called a simple fracture, the skin is unbroken. If the skin is broken at the site of the fracture, it is called an open fracture, or a compound fracture. Open fractures are more serious because germs and contamination that cause infection can reach the bone, making the fracture more difficult to treat.

Sometimes a fracture is obvious, because the bone is exposed or a limb is lying at a strange angle that would be possible only with a broken bone. Sometimes the victim cannot move toes or fingers without pain. You may even hear a snap as the bone breaks. Swelling, discoloration, or loss of movement are often present with fractures.

A fracture must be immobilized so that the bone can't move and further injure the victim. To immobilize a bone, use a splint as described in Figure 28-8. A splint is a rigid strip of wood, metal, or some other material that will not easily bend. Other parts of the body can also be used as a splint. For example, a broken leg may be bound to the other leg to immobilize the broken bone. If the fracture is open, cover the wound with a clean dressing before applying a splint. You may need to stop bleeding as well.

You won't always know whether an injury is a fracture or something else. Sometimes all you know is that the victim is in pain. To administer first aid, you need not be certain that the injury is a fracture. If you suspect a fracture, treat it as such and splint it.

• • • TEACH continued

Role-Playing

Treating a Fracture

Obtain some wooden splints, gauze padding, adhesive tape, and a towel (to use as a sling). Select a student to play the role of a person who has suffered a closed fracture of the lower arm. Have two or three other students play the roles of passersby who must administer first aid. Have them place a splint on the injured person, securing it loosely with tape. Then have them place the arm in a sling. Allow other members of the class to inspect the splint to see how effective it is. Repeat the exercise with other students.

Demonstration

Pupils of the Eye

If possible, obtain a number of penlights. Have students form pairs. Distribute penlights to as many pairs as possible. Darken the classroom and have students wait five minutes. Then have one member of each pair use the penlight to examine the eyes of the other member. Have them note how the pupil of each eye responds as the penlight is shone on the eye. Then have the remaining pairs of students do the demonstration.

Reinforcement

Injuries and Shock

Have students review the procedures for treating wounds, fractures, dislocations, and injuries to the neck and spine. Have them note that in all cases, it may be necessary to treat the victim

Dislocations

In a **dislocation**, the end of a bone comes out of its joint. The dislocated joint will be swollen and deformed, and the person will feel severe pain. Dislocations should be splinted in the same way as fractures. For a dislocated shoulder, splint the upper arm with the elbow supported in a sling and the upper arm strapped to the side of the chest. This gives the dislocated joint the greatest possible support. Treat the victim for shock.

Neck and Spine

An accident victim who complains of pain in the neck or back may have a fractured neck or spine. Moving someone with a broken spinal column could paralyze or kill the person. If the slightest chance of a broken neck or back exists, do not move the person. Treat for shock, send for medical help, and stay until help arrives. Place your hands or a rolled-up blanket or coat on either side of the person's head to keep it from moving.

Head Injury

Any bump on the head that causes a victim to lose consciousness, even if only for a second or two, is potentially serious. Blood vessels sometimes break inside the skull, and then pressure may build and squeeze the brain. This can happen quickly or take place slowly over hours or days. Nausea, slurred speech, slowed breathing, convulsions, and loss of memory can be signs of a head injury, as can blood or body fluid leaking from the ears or nose.

You can sometimes find clues to internal head injuries by examining the pupils of the victim's eyes. Pupils are normally the same size on both sides, or nearly so, and they react to light, becoming smaller in bright light and bigger in dim light. If one pupil is significantly bigger than the other, or if the pupils do not react to light and dark, assume the individual has a serious head injury. You can check for reaction to light by shining a flashlight into one eye then the other, or by shading first one eye then the other from a strong light.

When you suspect a head injury, do the following:

- Treat for shock, but *do not* elevate the victim's feet.
- Stay with the victim, watching carefully for signs of deterioration.
- Monitor breathing. Be ready to give rescue breathing if needed, or CPR if you are trained. If you do so, however, do not tilt the head back. Keeping the head and neck still, pull the jaw forward. Use this procedure also when you suspect an injury to the neck or spine.

dislocation:

an injury in which the end of a bone comes out of its joint.

SECTION 28.2

Section Review Worksheet 28.2
To reinforce the concepts presented in this section, assign Section Review Worksheet 28.2.

Section Quiz 28.2
Have students take Section Quiz 28.2.

Reteaching Worksheet 28.2
Students who have difficulty with the material may complete Reteaching Worksheet 28.2.

(FIGURE 28-9) **Examine the eyes if you suspect a head injury. If the pupils are not the same size or do not react to light, it may indicate a serious head injury.**

for shock. Elicit from students that shock is a possible consequence of any serious injury. A person giving first aid must always be alert for signs of shock and must always be ready to treat it.

Class Discussion
Head Injuries

Discuss whether head injuries tend to be more serious than injuries to other parts of the body. Have students consider why protective headgear is required or recommended in so many diverse activities (baseball, football, bicycle riding, motorcycle riding). In addition, ask students to consider non-fatal consequences of head injuries as opposed to nonfatal consequences of other types of injuries.

Demonstration
Treating a Sprain

Obtain an elastic bandage. Demonstrate for students the proper method for wrapping a sprained ankle or wrist with the bandage. Allow students to examine the secured bandage. If possible, have students practice placing the bandage on their own wrists.

 Journal 28D
My Injury—Evaluated

Have students review their description of an injury they experienced and its treatment. In their Journal, have students evaluate the treatment they received in light of what they have learned about proper treatment of injuries. Have them include any thoughts on how the treatment could have been improved.

Review Answers

1. laceration—torn skin; incision—clean cut; abrasion—skin scraped or worn away; puncture—hole through the skin and into deeper tissue; avulsion—skin or other part of the body torn off or nearly torn off

2. Answers should include basic information about making a splint, described in Figure 28-8, and the following: avoid moving the fracture victim and treat for shock.

3. Do not move the victim because this could paralyze or kill the person.

4. A puncture wound, because it is harder to clean and thus the risk of infection is greater. Also, at the time of treatment for a puncture wound, the victim can receive a tetanus shot or a booster, because tetanus germs can thrive in a puncture wound.

(FIGURE 28-10) **A splint can be used to immobilize a limb that has suffered a sprain or a strain, as well as to immobilize a fracture.**

sprain:

a torn or stretched ligament.

strain:

a stretched or torn muscle or tendon.

Sprains and Strains

When a ligament is torn or stretched, the resulting injury is called a **sprain**. In a **strain**, the muscle itself is torn or stretched. Sharply twisting a joint, for example, may cause a sprain, while strains often occur when a person is lifting a heavy weight.

RICE—First Aid for Sprains and Strains

Rest: Do not use the injured part.

Ice: Use ice packs to prevent swelling.

Compression: Wrap the injured part in an elastic bandage.

Elevation: Elevate the injured part above the level of the heart.

(FIGURE 28-11) **Remember the steps for treating a sprain or a strain as RICE—Rest, Ice, Compression, Elevation.**

With either a sprain or a strain, the victim will experience pain and swelling.

It can be difficult to tell a sprain or strain from a fracture. If you think the injury might be a fracture, you should treat it as a fracture instead of as a sprain. Leave off the elastic bandage and apply a splint instead. It never does any harm to treat a sprain or a strain as a fracture. Otherwise, use the procedure shown in Figure 28-11.

Internal Injuries

Following any accident, a victim may have injuries inside the body that you can't easily detect. Internal bleeding is especially dangerous. Pain in the chest or abdomen is cause for concern. When an accident victim seems to deteriorate without obvious reason, suspect internal injuries. The victim may turn pale, or the person's breathing and pulse may be unusually rapid. If you suspect internal injuries, treat for shock and get the victim to a doctor right away.

Review

1. List and describe five types of wounds.

2. What steps should be taken for a fracture until the victim can see a doctor?

3. What is the most important thing to remember when giving first aid to a victim with a possible neck or spine injury?

4. **Critical Thinking** Assuming both wounds were minor, would it be more important to have a doctor examine a puncture wound or an incision? Explain.

Extension
Paramedics

Have a member of a local emergency squad speak to the class about how to treat wounds. Ask the person to demonstrate the proper techniques for treating wounds, using students as simulated victims. In many communities, emergency squads are composed of trained volunteers. Some students may be interested in finding out how to become members of such squads.

ASSESS

Section Review
Have students answer the Section Review questions.

Alternative Assessment
Wounds and Their Treatment

Have students make posters that include drawings of the five major types of wounds and a description indicating how each type of wound should be

treated. Display the posters in the class and throughout the school.

Closure
First Aid for Injuries

Have students mention signs that indicate an injury to the neck or spine, then signs that indicate an injury to the head. List them on the chalkboard. Have the students compare the first-aid treatment for each type of injury.

Section 28.3
Choking, Heart Attack, and Other Emergencies

Objectives

- *Describe the first aid for a heart-attack victim.*
- *Explain what to do if you find a person unconscious from an unknown cause.*
- *Know how and when to perform the Heimlich maneuver.*
    - **LIFE SKILLS: Intervention Strategies**

The most serious emergencies are those in which the victims would die or suffer permanent damage without intervention. For example, a classmate sitting next to you in the cafeteria could start choking. It is also possible that an individual could collapse in your presence from a heart attack or a stroke. Knowing what to do and acting quickly could save a life. The information in this section will help prepare you to give aid, should a life-threatening emergency occur.

Choking

A person chokes when something, such as a piece of food, gets stuck in his or her airway and prevents breathing. To save a choking person's life, you must act immediately. You don't have time even for a telephone call. Brain cells die when they are deprived of oxygen for even a few minutes. Unless the obstruction is removed immediately, a choking victim will die or suffer permanent brain damage.

Signs of Choking A choking victim will usually grab his or her neck. The victim may be breathing very shallowly, or not at all, and he or she may be trying to cough but be unable to do so. If you think someone is choking, do the following:

- Ask the person if he or she is choking and needs help. Because people need air to talk, a person who can talk is not choking.
- If the choking person is able to cough at all, encourage him or her to continue coughing as hard as possible.
- If other people are nearby, send someone to call for medical help.
- If the victim is unable or barely able to cough, take immediate action to dislodge the object blocking the airway.

The Heimlich Maneuver You can often dislodge an object from a person's airway by using the **Heimlich maneuver,** which is a series of sharp thrusts to the abdomen. These thrusts compress the lungs, forcing the air out. The air, in turn, sometimes pushes the obstruction out of the airway. The procedure to use when performing the Heimlich maneuver for a conscious person is shown in Figure 28-12.

If a person becomes unconscious, lay the person on his or her back. Using your finger, dislodge any obstruction from the person's throat. Alternate a rescue breath with 8 to 10 abdominal thrusts and a finger sweep until the obstruction is dislodged or help arrives. Don't give up hope. As the victim's body becomes starved for oxygen, the muscles in the throat will start to relax. You may suddenly be successful even after you have started to think it is too late.

Heimlich maneuver:

a series of sharp thrusts to the abdomen, used to dislodge an object from a choking person's airway.

Section 28.3 Lesson Plan

MOTIVATE

Class Discussion
What Would You Do?

Ask the class how many of them would know exactly what to do if they were in the presence of someone who was choking. Volunteer students can give brief descriptions of how they would react. Tell students that choking causes more than 3,000 deaths a year in the United States. Most people choke on food, but others, especially small children, choke on small objects, such as parts from toys or stuffed animals.

TEACH

Role-Playing
The Heimlich Maneuver

Select a student to play the role of a choking victim and a second student to play the role of a passerby who performs the Heimlich maneuver to dislodge the object caught in the victim's throat. The rescuer can refer to Figure 28-12 when applying the Heimlich maneuver. **Caution:** Students should NOT apply pressure against the abdomen. Have several teams of students practice the maneuver.

Background
Stroke

A stroke generally affects one side of the brain. In cases where paralysis of the limbs occurs, it generally affects one side of the body. Since the left side of the brain controls the muscles on the right side of the body, a stroke on the left side of the brain paralyzes the right side of the body, and vice versa. A person who shows paralysis on the right side of the body is more likely to suffer losses in the ability to speak, read, or understand speech. In most people, these functions are controlled by the left side of the brain.

Life Skills Worksheet 28A

Assign the Responding to an Emergency Life Skills Worksheet.

The Heimlich Maneuver

1. Have the choking person stand up, positioning yourself behind him or her.

2. Reach around the victim with both hands, placing one fist with its thumb side against the abdomen, a little above the navel and below the rib cage. Grasp the fist in your other hand.

3. Make a sharp, hard thrust with your fist into the abdomen and up toward the rib cage. Continue making hard, vigorous thrusts until you dislodge the obstruction, or until the victim collapses and becomes unconscious.

(FIGURE 28-12) **The Heimlich maneuver. This lifesaving first-aid measure can dislodge an object that is causing someone to choke.**

If a baby is choking, lay the baby face down on your lap with its head slightly lowered. With one hand supporting the baby's head, slap the baby's back forcefully five times. Then turn the baby on its back and give five *chest* thrusts to its breast bone, using only two fingers instead of your fist. Alternate back blows with chest thrusts until the baby's airway is clear. If the baby becomes unconscious, stop after each set of chest thrusts to check the airway and attempt to give two slow breaths.

If *you* are choking, you can perform the Heimlich maneuver on yourself. To do this, lean over the back of a chair, fence, or similar object, and thrust your abdomen into the object, hard, as shown in Figure 28-13.

• • • TEACH continued

Journal 28E
Choking

This may be done as a warm-up activity. In their Journal, have students write how they think they would react if they saw someone choking. Then have them tell how being trained in using the Heimlich maneuver would change the way they would handle a choking person. Students should tell why it is important for people to be trained in emergency first aid.

Reinforcement
Remember Your ABCs

Have students recall from Section 28.1 the initial steps in treating a person who is unconscious. Check the ABCs:

- Airway—Place the victim on his or her back and gently lift the chin and tip the head back.
- Breathing—Place your cheek next to the victim's nose and mouth and listen and feel for breathing; watch the chest to see if it rises and falls. Start rescue breathing if necessary.
- Circulation—Determine whether the person's heart is beating by trying to find a pulse. Administer CPR if needed and only if you are trained to do so.

• • • TEACH continues on p. 632

(FIGURE 28-13) **If you begin to choke on an object while you are alone, you can use the Heimlich maneuver on yourself. One technique for doing so is being demonstrated here.**

In a choking emergency, you need to act immediately. Therefore, you may wish to practice the Heimlich maneuver in advance with a friend. However, you should fake the thrusts. You can cause damage by thrusting too hard when it is not needed.

Heart Attack

During a heart attack, part of the heart is not receiving enough blood, and the heart is not pumping well. The signs and symptoms of a heart attack include:

- sudden pain in the chest under the breastbone, possibly radiating into the arms, shoulders, side of the neck, or jaw
- weakness, nausea, or sickness
- rapid, weak, or irregular pulse
- pale or blue skin
- perspiration, anxiety, or fear

To treat a heart attack, follow the steps in Figure 28-14. **Cardiac arrest** may follow a heart attack, meaning that the heart will stop working altogether. In case of cardiac arrest, perform CPR if you are trained.

cardiac arrest:

condition in which the heart stops working.

Steps in Treating a Heart Attack

1. Sit or lay the victim down, propping up the head.

2. Help administer any heart medication the person may have, unless the person is unconscious.

3. Immediately send for an ambulance equipped with oxygen, and contact the victim's own doctor if possible.

4. Stand by in case rescue breathing becomes necessary.

5. In case of cardiac arrest, perform CPR if you have been trained.

6. Treat for shock.

(FIGURE 28-14) **In the event a person suffers a heart attack, you could save his or her life by acting quickly and following these steps.**

Background
Aspirin and Heart Attacks
In a recent study of male subjects, researchers found that those who took one aspirin tablet every other day had fewer heart attacks than those who took a placebo. This is due to aspirin's effect on the formation of blood clots: it reduces the accumulation of platelets, and consequently, the formation of a blood clot when bleeding takes place. Because heart attack results from the blockage of a coronary artery by a blood clot, aspirin's action to reduce clotting is beneficial. But some people should not routinely take aspirin—for them it could be harmful. These include people who have had a stroke resulting from a cerebral hemorrhage and those who have high blood pressure, a history of stroke in the family, a bleeding disorder, ulcers, or impaired liver or kidney functions.

Unconsciousness

If a person becomes unconscious and you don't know why, check ABCs and send for help immediately. Check for medical alert identification that could tell you about any special medical condition. The information

(FIGURE 28-15) **A medical alert identification tag warns of conditions such as diabetes, heart conditions, allergies, or even contact lenses.**

might appear on a bracelet, necklace, or anklet such as those shown in Figure 28-15. Some people carry medical alert information on a card, so check the victim's pockets and wallet.

While waiting for help to arrive, treat the individual for shock and stand by in case rescue breathing is needed. If the person vomits, turn his or her head sharply to the side to prevent choking. Use your finger, covered with a cloth if possible, to wipe out the mouth.

Convulsions

Convulsions may result from epilepsy, poisoning, high fever, or other conditions. During convulsions, every muscle suddenly becomes rigid, then the body starts jerking violently. The victim may also lose control of bowels and bladder. Convulsions can be frightening and upsetting to an observer. It is important to keep yourself calm while attempting to give aid.

Individuals who are convulsing should be prevented from causing themselves injury—for example, from rolling off a

---

Treatment for Stroke

1. Send for an ambulance equipped with oxygen, immediately.

2. Keep the stroke victim quiet and lying on the side in case of vomiting. If the victim vomits, make sure the head is turned sharply to the side, to reduce the chance of choking.

3. Treat for shock by keeping the victim warm, but do not raise the legs.

4. Be ready to give rescue breathing if necessary or CPR if you have been trained.

(FIGURE 28-16) **Some of the symptoms of a stroke are similar to other, less life-threatening conditions. If there is any doubt in your mind, follow these first-aid steps for treating a stroke.**

---

sidewalk into traffic. Loosen tight clothing, and remove any objects from the immediate area. Otherwise, there is nothing you can do except wait for the convulsions to stop.

Do not try to put anything into a person's mouth while he or she is convulsing or if he or she is unconscious. If the victim is unconscious, turn his or her head to the side. Observe the victim's breathing, in case you need to provide rescue breathing. The convulsions will go away in a minute or two. If the victim has medicine for convulsions, you may help administer it *after* the convulsions have stopped and *only* if the person is conscious. Victims who are unconscious after convulsions should be laid on their sides. Send for medical help, or take the individual to a doctor.

Stroke

In a **stroke**, also called a cerebral vascular accident, blood supply to part of the brain is obstructed because a blood vessel in the brain has burst or become plugged with a clot. Stroke victims may show some or all of the following signs and symptoms:

- dizziness or loss of consciousness
- difficulty in breathing or talking
- mental confusion or slurred speech
- partial paralysis on one side of the body
- mouth pulled sideways
- pupils of unequal size
- bright red face
- bulging neck veins

Figure 28-16 lists the treatment for stroke.

Something Wrong— Cause Unknown

If a person appears to be ill or in pain but you can't tell what the problem is, treat for shock and send for help. Watch the person in case rescue breathing becomes necessary.

Review

1. *Explain what to do for someone who is having a heart attack.*

2. *What is the first-aid procedure for a victim who is unconscious from an unknown cause?*

3. **LIFE SKILLS: Intervention Strategies** *Describe the steps and purpose of the Heimlich maneuver.*

4. *Critical Thinking* *Is it always possible to determine whether a victim is suffering from shock or a stroke? Explain.*

stroke:
the rupture or blockage of an artery in the brain, leading to oxygen deprivation and damage to brain cells.

What Would You Do ?

Have students read the What Would You Do? feature. Have a volunteer state the procedure that he or she would follow. Then have the class evaluate the person's procedure, based on what they have read in Section 28.3.

Review Answers

1. Answers should include the steps shown in Figure 28-14.

2. Send for help, check ABCs, check for medical alert identification, and treat for shock; stand by in case rescue breathing becomes necessary.

3. Answers should agree with Figures 28-12 and 28-13. The purpose of the Heimlich maneuver is to dislodge whatever is obstructing the person's airway.

4. No. Some stroke symptoms are similar to those for shock and other head injuries.

ASSESS

Section Review

Have students answer the Section Review questions.

Alternative Assessment
Emergency Situations

Organize students into three groups. Assign each group one of the following emergency situations: heart-attack, unconsciousness from an unknown cause, or choking. Have each group develop a presentation on how to deal with the emergency assigned to their group. Presentations can be oral, visual, or a combination of both. If a video camera is available, students may wish to do a video presentation.

Closure
Heart Attack and Stroke

As an oral review, ask students to compare the signs of a heart attack with the signs of a stroke. Have them include the emergency steps for treating both conditions.

Section
28.4 Common Emergencies

Objectives

• • • • •

- Contrast two health emergencies caused by heat, and compare their treatments.

- Know how to identify and protect your body from cold-related health emergencies.
  ■■ **LIFE SKILLS: Practicing Self-Care**

- Describe three types of burns and their treatment.

- List the steps to be taken when poison is swallowed.

This section covers emergencies you could encounter—indoors or outdoors—at school, home, work, or sporting events.

Heat-Related Emergencies

Overexertion in too much heat can lead to emergencies that require first aid.

Heat Exhaustion With heat exhaustion, a person collapses from heat, exertion, and loss of water and salt through perspiration. The victim starts to go into shock, and the body's cooling mechanisms may begin working too hard, actually over-cooling.

(FIGURE 28-17) **Vigorous exercise or hard work, especially during warm months, can result in heat exhaustion or heatstroke due to overheating and the loss of body fluids and salts. Knowing the difference between these two common conditions could help you save a friend's life.**

Section 28.4 Lesson Plan

MOTIVATE

Journal 28F
Common Emergencies

This may be done as a warm-up activity. Ask students to record in their Journal three examples of common emergencies that are likely to occur inside the home and three examples of emergencies that are likely to

occur outdoors. Tell the students to note which, if any, of these emergencies they have experienced and how the emergencies were handled.

TEACH

Class Discussion
Heat Exhaustion and Heatstroke

Stress to the class that heat exhaustion and heatstroke are two very different emergencies. Ask: **How can you tell whether a person is suffering from**

heat exhaustion or whether he or she is suffering from heatstroke? *[In heat exhaustion the skin is cool and moist; in heatstroke the skin is hot and dry.]* **What cooling mechanism is working in heat exhaustion but has failed in heatstroke?** *[perspiring]* Point out that heat exhaustion is related to the loss of water and salts by the body; heatstroke is related to a failure of the body's cooling mechanisms. Ask: **Which of these conditions presents a critical emergency?** *[heatstroke]*

The person's skin will feel clammy (cool and moist). Other signs and symptoms include weakness, dizziness, headache, nausea, rapid and shallow breathing, and dilated pupils.

A victim of heat exhaustion should lie down in the shade and cool off. If the victim is conscious and not nauseated, replace body fluids by giving the victim plenty of drinking water. Suggest that the victim avoid heat and strenuous exercise for a few days, even when feeling better.

Heatstroke (Sunstroke) After working or exercising strenuously in a hot environment, a person can suffer from heatstroke. The skin becomes red and very hot and dry. With heat exhaustion, the body is still trying to cool off by perspiring freely. With heatstroke, the hot, dry skin tells you the body's mechanism for cooling itself is not working anymore. It has been overwhelmed by too much heat and exercise. The internal body temperature becomes very high—106° F or even higher. Heatstroke is life threatening. If the following steps are not taken to cool the body, the victim will die.

- Call EMS
- Move the victim out of the heat.
- Put the victim in cool (not cold) water, or apply wet cloths all over the body.
- If conscious, the person should drink water in small quantities.
- Take the victim to a hospital emergency room as quickly as possible.

Heat Cramps A cramp is a sudden, very painful knot in a muscle, often a leg muscle. Heat cramps are caused by exercising in conditions where too much body salt and water are being lost through perspiration. Generally, a cramp will go away if you stretch out the affected muscle. You can also give drinking water to a person with heat cramps to replace body fluids.

Treatment for Frostbite

1. Cover the affected area, and provide extra blankets or clothing. Take the victim indoors if possible.

2. Gently thaw the frozen part by soaking in warm—not hot—water, wrapping in warm blankets, or treating with a warm object. Any water or object that feels hot on your own hand is too hot for thawing frostbite.

3. Stop applying heat as soon as the skin is flushed.

4. Avoid damaging tissue. Do not rub the affected area, since this may cause gangrene.

5. Keep the victim away from hot fires or stoves.

6. Do not allow the blisters to break.

(FIGURE 28-18) **Frostbite may occur during exposure to extreme cold. If you must give first aid for frostbite, follow these steps, but wait until you are sure the frozen parts will remain thawed.**

Cold-Related Emergencies

Overexposure to cold or the loss of too much body heat can also lead to emergencies that require first aid.

Frostbite With frostbite, ice crystals form in the fluids of soft tissues of the body. Typically, whitish or yellowish spots appear on the nose, fingers, toes, ears, or cheeks. Blisters may develop later. To treat frostbite, follow the steps in Figure 28-18.

Frostbitten tissue has been injured and may take time to heal. Have the person gently exercise any affected parts except the feet. It is better not to thaw frostbitten tissue until you can keep the tissue thawed. Frostbitten tissue can be severely damaged if it thaws out and refreezes before it has a chance to heal. In most cases, a frostbite victim should consult a doctor.

Role-Playing
Treating Frostbite

Select one student to play the role of a hiker who has frostbite of the fingers of both hands. Select a second student to play the role of a person living in a nearby cabin who comes across the victim of frostbite on the hiking trail. Have this student demonstrate the proper procedure for treating frostbite. (Provide a pan of warm water, a blanket, and some towels for the student to use.) The student can refer to Figure 28-18 as he or she treats the victim of frostbite. Allow other teams of students to role-play the incident.

Reinforcement
Heatstroke and Hypothermia

It may be useful to compare the conditions of heatstroke and hypothermia and the recommended treatments, since these emergencies are almost mirror images of each other. You might make a comparison chart on the chalkboard, like the one at right.

	Heatstroke	**Hypothermia**
Body Temp.	Too high	Too low
Temp. Regulation	Sweating stops	Shivering stops
Treatment	Cool the body	Warm the body
Risk to Life	Critical	Critical

• • • TEACH continues on p. 638

**Life Skills
Worksheet 28B**
Assign the First-Aid Supplies Life Skills Worksheet.

hypothermia:

below-normal body temperature.

Hypothermia The prefix "hypo" means low, or under. **Hypothermia,** therefore, is a condition in which a person's body temperature is too low. This condition results not just from being exposed to cold but also from losing heat from the body faster than the body can rewarm itself.

As the body loses heat and its internal temperature begins to drop, the body takes steps to protect itself. First, some of the blood flow to the extremities (arms, legs, and head) is cut off. Shivering begins, to rewarm the body, and may become violent.

Eventually, the heart rate and breathing rate slow, the victim loses muscle strength and coordination, and other signs and symptoms such as slurred speech, fatigue, confusion, hallucinations, and irrational behavior may appear. Finally, the victim stops shivering. This means that the victim's body has lost the ability to rewarm itself.

Like heatstroke, hypothermia is a life-threatening condition. The treatment for hypothermia is described in Figure 28-19. To find out how to avoid hypothermia, complete the Life Skills activity on page 637.

Treatment for Hypothermia

If the victim is shivering:	**1.** A shivering person will recover if you eliminate further loss of heat. Move the victim to a warm place, wrapping him or her in coats, blankets, or sleeping bags to help the body rewarm itself.
	2. Give warm drinks to rewarm the body from the inside, if the person can hold the glass alone. Never give alcoholic drinks to a cold person. Alcohol may make people feel warmer, but it actually increases heat loss.
If the victim has stopped shivering:	**1.** A person who has ceased shivering will die unless you rewarm his or her body. Get the person to a hospital if you can do it quickly.
	2. Warm the central part of the body first, without warming the extremities. Soak the person in a warm—not hot—bath with arms and legs hanging out, or use warm objects such as water bottles or electric heating pads next to the trunk.
	3. Giving warm drinks will help, if the person is conscious and sufficiently coordinated to hold the glass alone. A person without enough coordination to hold a glass is in danger of choking or breathing liquid into the lungs.

(FIGURE 28-19) **Follow these steps if you must give first aid for hypothermia.**

Life SKILLS: Practicing Self-Care

Life SKILLS

Have students read the Life Skills feature. Then tell them to answer the questions. When students have finished, discuss the answers in class.

Preventing Hypothermia . . . .

Preventing hypothermia is much easier than treating this life-threatening condition. Remember, it is easier to stay warm than it is to rewarm your body after it has lost heat.

As you get cold, 50 percent of your body's heat loss can be through your head and neck. This is because a large portion of the blood in your body flows through your head and neck, much of it near the surface. Air currents carry away heat as it radiates from your blood.

Water is a better conductor of heat than air is, and if it is cooler than your body temperature, it will conduct heat from your body faster than air. This is why you may feel cold in water that is 70°F , when air at 70°F is comfortable. Even though the water is not very cold, you can develop hypothermia if you stay in it for too long. Solids conduct heat even faster than liquids do, so you can also lose body heat quickly by lying or sitting on something cold.

Answer the following questions to see if you know how to prevent hypothermia.

1. If you are wearing a warm jacket and start to feel cold, what items of clothing might you add to prevent heat loss?

2. Why do you suppose people wore nightcaps before houses were heated efficiently?

3. Assume you are in water at 70°F, and the air temperature is 70°F. If you start shivering or feeling chilled, what should you do? Why?

4. Why should you put down a blanket before laying an injured person on the ground?

(FIGURE 28-20) **Any snake with a triangular head is dangerous. The coral snake, for which the harmless king snake is often mistaken, is the only poisonous snake in North America that does not have a triangular head. You can distinguish the coral snake from the king snake by remembering this rhyme: red on yellow kill a fellow, red on black, venom lack. Notice the difference between the toothmarks of a nonpoisonous snake, such as the king snake, and those of a poisonous snake, such as the pit vipers and the coral snake.**

• • • TEACH continued

Cooperative Learning
Poisonous Snakes

Obtain several copies of field guides that discuss reptiles. (*A Field Guide to the Reptiles and Amphibians of Eastern/Western North America* is an excellent choice.) Then have students meet in small groups, with each group having access to a field guide. Have the groups use the plates and the maps in the field guide to identify the poisonous snakes found in their area of the country. Have students study the pictures of the poisonous snakes in their area so that they can easily identify these snakes on sight.

Demonstration
A Constricting Band

Explain the usefulness of a constricting band in treating a poisonous snake bite. Then cut a piece of cloth about 1 inch wide and about 8 inches long. Have a student assist you in demonstrating where and how to tie a constricting band on your arm. Refer to Figure 28-21 for instructions. **Caution:** Do NOT allow a student to place a constricting band on another student.

• • • TEACH continues on p. 640

Drowning

Drowning may occur in deep water some distance from shore, in a swimming pool a few feet from the side, or even in a bathtub. In a drowning emergency, *do not* attempt to swim to the victim unless you have received the proper training in water-safety and life-saving techniques. Instead, toss a flotation device or rescue line to the victim and then call for help.

Once retrieved, potential drowning victims who have stopped breathing must be given rescue breathing immediately and continually until they begin to breathe. If the victim was in deep water, you should begin rescue breathing as soon as the victim reaches shallow water. If it is necessary, provide CPR if you are trained to do so. Send for medical help immediately.

Snakebite

Only four of the hundreds of kinds of snakes in the United States are poisonous. They are pictured in Figure 28-20. The coral snake, which is related to the deadly cobra, is rarely seen. The others belong to a family of snakes called pit vipers, which includes rattlesnakes, copperheads, and water moccasins (also called cottonmouths). All pit vipers have a triangular-shaped head and two large fangs in the upper jaw.

A pit viper's bite usually leaves two prominent holes where the fangs went in. The poison is in the fangs, so if you are ever bitten by a pit viper that doesn't leave fang marks, don't worry. Even with a bite that does leave fang marks, a victim may not have been poisoned.

Snakebites are rarely fatal, but they often cause permanent damage that can sometimes make it necessary to amputate a limb. Therefore, a poisonous snakebite should be treated as a serious emergency. Take the following steps to treat a snakebite:

Procedure for Applying a Constricting Band

1. Tie the band 2 to 4 inches above any swelling from the bite, but not around a joint. The ideal band would be 1 to $1\frac{1}{2}$ inches wide, but a shoelace would serve if nothing else is available.

2. Check snugness. The band should be snug enough to dimple the skin all the way around, but still loose enough for you to slide a finger under it.

3. Check for a pulse below the band. If there is none, loosen the band until there is.

(FIGURE 28-21) **CAUTION: The purpose of a constricting band is to slow circulation just under the skin, where most poison travels, NOT to cut off circulation altogether.**

- Wash the wound with soap and water to reduce the chance of infection.
- To slow the spread of poison through the body, keep the person quiet and calm, preferably lying down.
- If the bite is on an arm or leg, keep the affected part below the level of the heart and follow the steps in Figure 28-21 to help slow the spread of poison.
- Monitor ABCs and watch for shock.
- Do not apply tourniquet, attempt to remove venom, or apply ice.

A snakebite victim needs medical treatment within four hours. Whenever possible, the victim should be carried to the doctor, rather than being allowed to walk. Fear and panic can aggravate snakebite symptoms, so you should try to be soothing and reassuring. If you are bitten when you are alone and you must walk for help, you should apply a constricting band and then walk at a slow pace, resting frequently, in order to keep your blood circulating as slowly as possible.

Background
Poisonous Snakes

Although there are only four types of poisonous snakes in the United States, there are several varieties of each type. For example, there are three varieties of cottonmouths (Eastern, Western, and Florida), all confined to the southeastern section of the country.

A number of different species of rattlesnake occur in the United States. The timber rattlesnake is the only one that lives in the Northeast. The canebrake rattlesnake, eastern diamondback, and several varieties of pygmy rattlesnakes are found in the Southeast. Several types of massasauga rattlesnakes and the prairie rattlesnake are found in the middle of the country. And in the western United States live the western diamondback, mojave rattlesnake, black-tailed rattlesnake, and several other types. Thus, it might be useful for students to become familiar with the rattlesnakes found in their section of the country.

Life Skills
Worksheet 28C

Assign the Emergency
Medical Help Life Skills
Worksheet.

Life Skills
Worksheet 28D

Assign the Taking Appro-
priate Action Life Skills
Worksheet.

Stings

If you have been stung by a bee, hornet, wasp, or scorpion, you know it can cause intense pain, burning, and itching at the sting site. First aid for insect and scorpion stings includes the following steps:

- Examine the sting site carefully. If part of the stinger is still embedded in the wound, *do not* try to pull it out. It may have the poison sac still attached, and by grasping it, you can squeeze more poison

(FIGURE 28-22) **The brown recluse (above) and the black widow (right). Both black widow and brown recluse spider bites require medical treatment. On rare occasions, they can be fatal.**

into the wound. Instead, scrape it out with a fingernail, broken stick, or the edge of a credit card.

- Use a paste of baking soda, a towel soaked in ammonia, or ice to help reduce the pain and swelling.
- Observe the victim for a while. A small percentage of people are allergic to bee stings and can experience a severe, life-threatening reaction. Victims who are in obvious distress, feeling nauseated, dizzy, faint, or who are having trouble breathing should be treated for shock and be examined by a doctor right away.
- Stand by to perform rescue breathing, if necessary, or CPR if you are trained to give it.

Spider Bites

Of the thousands of species of spiders in the United States, only two are poisonous—the black widow and the brown recluse. The black widow's bite is painful and will make a victim extremely ill, but it is rarely fatal except to the seriously ill, the very young, or the very old. Only the female black widow is poisonous. The brown recluse spider's

Journal 28G
Insect Stings

Have students record in their Journal incidents in which they have suffered insect stings. Have the students describe their reactions. Encourage students who feel that they may have experienced an allergic reaction to a sting to discuss this fact with their parents or guardians.

Role-Playing
Treating Hyperventilation

Have one student play the role of a person who is hyperventilating. Have a second student play the role of a friend who is trying to reassure the victim and to treat the hyperventilation. Allow other students to role-play the situation. Have the class critique the treatment given in both roles.

bite can form a bad sore in a few hours, but it is not likely to be fatal.

If you must give first aid for a spider bite, follow the steps below.

- Wash the bite with soap and water to reduce the chance of infection.
- Use a paste of baking soda and water, a towel soaked in ammonia, or ice to reduce the pain and swelling.
- Treat for shock and be prepared to give rescue breathing if necessary.
- Seek medical attention immediately.

Human and Animal Bites

The mouths of humans and other mammals are full of bacteria, so their bites carry danger of serious infection. To prevent infection, human and other animal bites should be washed with soap and water, then rinsed thoroughly under running water. Dress a bite as you would any other wound. For severe or infected bites, the victim should see a doctor. Because bites can cause tetanus, bite victims should receive tetanus shots if they are not up to date on immunizations.

The most serious risk from animal bites is rabies. This viral infection of the nervous system is always fatal without preventive treatment. After a bite, observe the animal for unusual behavior or signs of illness. Rabid animals may drool or be unusually calm or excited. If you can do it safely, confine the animal so that it can be examined by a veterinarian or health department official. *Do not* get near the animal in order to capture it, and *do not* handle it. Only a professional should do so. Rabies can always be prevented if treatment is started soon enough. However, the series of treatments is long and painful. Victims can avoid suffering through it if a doctor can be sure that the animal did not have rabies.

Hyperventilation

Hyperventilation is rapid breathing that may be accompanied by chest pains, tingling of the fingertips and around the mouth, dizziness, or fainting. Emotional distress or poor circulation to the brain can precipitate it. Hyperventilation lowers the level of carbon dioxide in the blood. The following treatment is designed to raise the blood level of carbon dioxide to normal.

- Try to calm the victim. Have the person sit and lower his or her head.
- Have the person breathe into a paper bag or cupped hands. Breathing exhaled air helps restore the normal level of carbon dioxide in the blood.
- Seek medical attention if the symptoms persist.

(FIGURE 28-23) **Your breath contains more carbon dioxide than the surrounding air. By breathing into a paper sack for a few minutes, you can raise the level of carbon dioxide in your blood and get rid of the symptoms of hyperventilation.**

Background
Rabies

Rabies, a form of viral encephalitis transmitted in the saliva of infected animals, has been known and feared for centuries. In domestic animals, the disease is found most frequently in cats, dogs, and cattle, but the availability of vaccines has kept the incidence of disease low. Among wild animals, rabies is found most frequently in raccoons, skunks, and bats. In the United States, bats account for the majority of human exposures, even though some people with bat rabies do not recall having contact with a bat. This suggests that even indirect contact with infected saliva can cause transmission via the mucous membranes. For this reason, people should avoid contact with stray domestic animals which may not be vaccinated, and with wild animals, especially those known to carry rabies. Early symptoms of rabies infection can be mistaken for other illnesses. If treatment is delayed until symptoms are present, death will occur. (For information on the treatment of rabies, see p. 447.)

Making a Choice 28A

Assign the Precaution and Preparation card. The card asks students to discuss health emergencies that might arise in several different situations.

Making a Choice 28B

Assign the Putting Yourself on the Line card. The card asks students to assess the risks of giving first aid in various circumstances.

Nosebleeds

A nosebleed is spontaneous bleeding from a nostril that usually results from drying and cracking of the membranes lining the inside of the nose. Most nosebleeds will stop on their own fairly easily. If the bleeding does not stop soon on its own, use the following procedure.

- Use latex gloves if it is necessary to come in contact with the victim's blood.
- Have the victim sit upright, lean slightly forward, and firmly pinch both nostrils closed for 10 to 15 minutes.
- Apply cold cloths firmly against the bleeding nostril.

- If the bleeding continues, try putting a plug of rolled-up gauze into the bleeding nostril. Do not use cotton for this purpose, because it could be hard to remove later.
- If the bleeding continues and nothing seems to help, take the victim to a doctor. Something else might be wrong.

Electric Shock

Electric shock occurs when an electric current passes through a person's body. The current may cause cardiac arrest (the heart stops beating) and respiratory failure (the person stops breathing). In case of electric shock, follow the steps in Figure 28-24.

Steps to Take in Case of Electric Shock

1. *Do not touch an electric shock victim who is still touching a live wire or other source of electricity.*

2. *Turn off the current if you can do so quickly and safely. Otherwise, use an object made of a substance that does not conduct electricity (such as wood or plastic) to pull any wires away from the victim. Do not use metal! Stand on insulating material such as paper, wood, or rubber. Be sure your hands and the materials you use are dry.*

3. *Check the victim's ABCs—airway, breathing, and circulation (heartbeat).*

4. *If the airway is open and the victim isn't breathing, begin rescue breathing at once. If there is no pulse, begin CPR as well, if you are trained. If the victim doesn't regain consciousness right away, do not give up hope. Victims who have been struck by lightning, or who have suffered other serious electrical shock, may need rescue breathing for an hour or more before they begin breathing on their own again.*

5. *Send for medical help.*

6. *Treat the victim for shock.*

(FIGURE 28-24) **In addition to these lifesaving measures, an electric shock victim may also need treatment for burns.**

• • • TEACH continued

Demonstration
Treating a Nosebleed

Many people instinctively tilt the head back when treating a nosebleed. Review with students the proper position for stopping a nosebleed. To reinforce the proper technique, demonstrate the position that a person being treated for nosebleed should assume.

Cooperative Learning
Antidotes for Poisoning

Have students ask their parents or guardian if there are any substances in their home that have a poisonous warning label. If so, have the student copy the names of the substances and any instructions on what to do if the poison is ingested. Allow students to meet in small groups to exchange information. Each group can prepare a brief list of the poisons that they discussed and the recommended treatment for each. However, point out to

students that it is essential to call 911 or contact a poison control center before treating a person for poisoning. The first-aid instructions on labels may not be correct.

Class Discussion
The Dangers of Carbon Monoxide Poisoning

Have students describe conditions under which there is likely to be a danger of carbon monoxide poisoning. *(running a car in a closed garage; using an oil space heater in a poorly insulated*

Poisoning

Poisons can cause intense pain, permanent injury, impaired health, and even death. The steps you take immediately after a poisoning can save a life and prevent permanent injury.

A victim of poisoning needs medical attention immediately. Until medical help is available, monitor the victim's pulse and breathing. Be ready to give rescue breathing, or if you are trained, CPR.

Poisoning by Ingestion If victims are conscious and able to talk, you can usually ask what they drank or ate. Sometimes eyewitness accounts can be useful. If a person is unconscious or unable to talk, you should suspect poison if you detect the symptoms in Figure 28-25. For the benefit of the medical personnel who will assist, save the container or label of the suspected poison. If the person vomits, save a sample of the material for examination.

If you must give first aid to a person who drank or ate a poison, do not give anything by mouth or try to induce vomiting until you have determined what the poison is and checked with the nearest poison control center for instructions. They may tell you to dilute the poison by having the victim drink a glass of water or milk immediately. Often they will tell you to induce vomiting. Syrup containing *ipecac* is often recommended for this purpose. However, some poisons that can be swallowed contain strong acids or alkalis that damage tissue on contact. Because they cause as much damage coming up as going down, you will be told not to induce vomiting in those cases.

You can reach the poison control center in an emergency by dialing 911, or O for operator, and asking to be connected. Find out the number of the nearest poison control center in advance and keep it posted by your telephone.

Signs and Symptoms of Poisoning

Presence of a poisonous substance or its container

Sudden, unexplained illness or pain, especially in the abdomen

Nausea or vomiting

Burns near the lips or mouth

Odor of chemicals or fuel on the breath

Changes in the pupils (dilation or constriction)

(FIGURE 28-25) **These symptoms may indicate poisoning. Your first step should be to call 911 or contact the nearest poison control center.**

Drug Overdose Drugs are a common cause of poisoning. Even nonprescription drugs can be poisonous if taken in large doses or in bad combinations. Outdated drugs may be poisonous as well. Follow the same steps for a drug overdose as for poisoning by ingestion. In addition, try to keep the person awake and calm.

Poisoning by Inhalation Many substances can be poisonous if they are inhaled, including a number of chemicals, fuels, and gases. Carbon monoxide is a frequent cause of inhalation poisoning. Produced by incompletely burned fuels, carbon monoxide accumulates in poorly ventilated areas where fuels are being burned or where fuel-burning engines are running. Because it is odorless, it can overcome victims before they are even aware of the danger.

If you attempt to rescue a victim of inhalation poisoning, *exercise extreme caution*. Take several deep breaths before entering a closed space where someone has collapsed, and hold your breath while you

room; using any charcoal-burning cooking device indoors) Stress that carbon monoxide is odorless and invisible. A person who is being poisoned by carbon monoxide may not realize what is happening. Point out that today many people install carbon monoxide detectors in their homes. Discuss why such a detector could be a life-saving investment.

• • • TEACH continues on p. 644

Section Review Worksheet 28.4

To reinforce the concepts presented in this section, assign Section Review Worksheet 28.4.

Section Quiz 28.4

Have students take Section Quiz 28.4.

Reteaching Worksheet 28.4

Students who have difficulty with the material may complete Reteaching Worksheet 28.4.

(FIGURE 28-26) **Defective or improperly maintained space heaters and automobile exhaust systems are common sources of poisonous fumes, such as carbon monoxide. Sudden or unexplained drowsiness is a symptom of inhalation poisoning by carbon monoxide.**

immediately move the victim to fresh air. If the person is not breathing, perform rescue breathing. Send for an ambulance equipped with oxygen, and treat for shock.

Contact Poisoning Several types of poisonous substances can burn the skin or be absorbed through it on contact. Treatment for contact poisoning is the same as that for chemical burns: remove clothing and flush the area thoroughly with water for at least five minutes. If the poison is a pesticide, send for an ambulance. Chapter 6 tells you how to treat for contact with poisonous plants such as poison ivy.

Muscle Cramps

A cramp is a sudden knotting of a muscle, usually in the foot, leg, or abdomen. Cramps can be very painful, and they may last anywhere from a few minutes to a few hours. You can help the cramp go away sooner by massaging or stretching the muscle. If a muscle cramps when you are swimming, tread water while you massage the muscle. Call for help if you need it.

Burns and Scalds

Skin can be burned by fire, sun, hot liquids, heated objects, chemicals, and electricity. Burns are classified by the depth and degree of tissue damage. Figure 28-27 describes the classes of burns and their treatment.

Chemical burns can also be first-, second-, or third-degree, depending on how many layers of skin have been damaged. Take the following steps to treat chemical burns:

- Remove any clothing that covers the affected area or has the chemical on it.
- Hold the burned part under running water for as long as 10 to 15 minutes to wash away all traces of the chemical. If burns are extensive, you may use a hose or shower.
- Once the burn is free of the chemical, you may be able to treat it as you would any other burns. Call a poison control center or doctor to be sure of proper treatment.

If the chemical is in the victim's eye, the eye must be washed out under running water for a full 15 minutes. Hold the person's head under a water fountain or faucet so that the flow of water is away from the nose and toward the ear. Bandage *both* eyes with a soft material to rest the injured eye. If the good eye can see, it will move and the injured eye will move too. Take the victim to a doctor as soon as possible.

• • • TEACH continued

Demonstration
Safety in the Science Lab

Burns from chemicals and from heat can occur in the science lab. Well-equipped science labs have an eye-wash station and may even have a fire shower. If the science lab in your school has either or both of these facilities, have a science teacher demonstrate their uses for the class.

Reinforcement
Care of the Eyes

Caution students that in attempting to remove a foreign body from their eye or from someone else's eye, their hands must be clean, and any item, such as a cloth, used to remove the object must also be clean. Use Figure 28-28 on page 646 to review with students methods for inspecting both the lower and upper eye-lid for the presence of a foreign body.

Class Discussion
I Feel Faint

Have students recall incidents in which they felt faint, including factors that contributed to the feeling of faintness, how they felt, and what they did about it. Then have them explain what they would do now if they felt faint.

Extension
Water Safety

Interested students might wish to research water safety or lifesaving

1st-Degree Burns

A first-degree burn affects only the epidermis, the top layer of skin. The skin turns red and may hurt but does not blister. Sunburn is the most common first-degree burn. Even without treatment, a first-degree burn will heal in a few days.

▶ **Treatment**

Cold water and ice can help lower the skin temperature, stop the burning, and relieve the pain. So can pain-relieving preparations you can buy in the drugstore.

1st-Degree Burns

2nd-Degree Burns

2nd-Degree Burns

A second-degree burn forms blisters and affects both layers of skin— the epidermis and dermis. Unless they affect more than 15 percent of the body, second-degree burns are not serious.

▶ **Treatment**

1. Place the burned area into cool water right away. Cooling it will stop further burning and help relieve the pain.
2. Cover the burn with a clean dressing to prevent infection.
3. Do not pop blisters. The intact skin protects the burned part from infection. Blisters heal on their own in a few days.

3rd-Degree Burns

In a third-degree burn, the dermis and epidermis are destroyed. The tissue underneath is injured and may be partly destroyed as well. Third-degree burns are easily infected. They are typically whitish in color, though they may be charred brown or black. The burns may not hurt at all at first, if the nerve endings have been destroyed.

▶ **Treatment**

1. Rinse the burned area with cool water only. Very cold water can bring on or intensify shock.
2. Do not apply ointments or creams.
3. Do not remove pieces of clothing stuck to the burns.
4. Cover the burns lightly with sterile dressings or clean cloth.
5. Keep burned limbs elevated, above the heart if possible.
6. Unless victims are unconscious or vomiting, have them drink water to replace fluids lost through the burn.
7. Treat for shock.
8. Monitor breathing.
9. Send for medical help immediately, or take the victim to a hospital or doctor. Third-degree burns will not heal on their own.

3rd-Degree Burns

(FIGURE 28-27) **First-, second-, and third-degree burns are easily distinguished. Note that the treatment is different for each of these three types of burns.**

techniques for dealing with emergencies in water. They might contact the local office of the American Red Cross or use library references for this information. Suggest that students make a poster that summarizes their findings.

Rabies in Wild Animals

Have students contact the offices of state parks and forests to request information on the extent of rabies in wild mammals in the state. Such offices should be able to supply information on which animals are likely to be infected, on signs of infection, and to whom suspect animals should be reported. Have students report their findings to the class.

Answer to Question 1 is on p. 645.

2. Answers should reflect an understanding that it is easier to prevent hypothermia than to treat it. Answers may include that the student should warm up before leaving the house again and that he or she should wear clothing appropriate for the weather, such as a warm jacket, hat, and gloves.

3. Answers should agree with Figure 28-27.

4. Answers will vary but should include the following steps. Ask the victim what he or she swallowed if possible; call the poison control center, give them all the information you have and follow their instructions; monitor the victim's pulse and breathing; and, if necessary, administer rescue breathing or CPR.

5. The deep, whitish colored burn is more serious because it is a third-degree burn. Third-degree burns need medical attention, as they will not heal on their own.

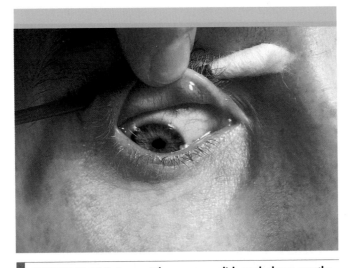

(FIGURE 28-28) **To inspect the upper eyelid, push down gently on the lid with a small stick, such as a matchstick or cotton swab, placed across the lid. Grasping the eyelashes, pull the eyelid upward against the stick and have the person look down while you inspect the lid.**

Foreign Body in the Eye

To remove a foreign body from the eye, first have the victim try blinking several times. Often, blinking and tears will wash the foreign body away. Pulling on the eyelashes of the upper lid may help as well. Gently pulling the upper lid down over the lower lid can permit tears and the lower eyelashes to dislodge the object.

If blinking and tearing don't work, move the person to good light so you can see the eye clearly. To inspect the inside of the lower lid, pull the lid down by pressing on the eyelashes. Use the procedure shown in Figure 28-28 to inspect the inside of the upper lid. If the object is on the inner surface of an eyelid, gently remove it with the corner of a moist, clean cloth or tissue twisted to a point.

If you find an object of any sort embedded in the surface of the eyeball, gently bandage both eyes to restrict their movement. Then take the victim to a doctor.

Fainting

Temporary loss of consciousness is called fainting. Usually, the cause is a shortage of blood flow to the brain. Sometimes a person will be pale and dizzy before fainting. Usually, the victim regains consciousness in a few minutes.

If a person faints near you, keep the person lying down. Elevate his or her feet to increase circulation to the brain. If *you* feel faint, lie down with your head lowered and your feet elevated to increase the blood flow to your brain. If this is not possible, sit down or kneel and bend over so that your head is lower than your heart.

Review

1. *Contrast the treatments for heat exhaustion and heatstroke. Which condition is more serious?*

2. **LIFE SKILLS: Practicing Self-Care** *The temperature is below freezing. You have come in after getting the newspaper and are shivering. You must now walk to school. How can you prevent hypothermia?*

3. *Explain how the treatments for second- and third-degree burns differ.*

4. *What steps would you take if you discovered someone who had swallowed poison?*

5. *Critical Thinking A burn victim has two burns. One is blistered and painful, and the other is deep and whitish colored but does not hurt. Which is the more serious burn? Explain.*

ASSESS

Section Review

Have students complete the Section Review questions.

Alternative Assessment
Dealing With an Emergency

From the emergency situations discussed in this section, have students select one that they think they might encounter. Have each student write a brief paragraph discussing how he or she would deal with the emergency.

Closure
Emergencies Differ

Make two columns on the chalkboard. At the top of one column write VERY SERIOUS; write LESS SERIOUS at the top of the other. Have students classify the emergencies discussed in this section into these categories.

Highlights

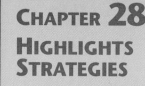
Summary

- Appropriate first aid can mean the difference between life and death or between recovery and permanent injury.

- The steps to take in an emergency are: survey the scene; rescue the victim; send for medical help; treat the life-threatening conditions; identify injuries and provide first aid; remain with the victim, monitoring breathing and pulse until medical help arrives.

- Check the airway, breathing, and circulation (ABCs) of unconscious persons, in that order, before beginning first aid.

- CPR can revive people whose breathing and heartbeat have stopped. It should be attempted only by trained individuals.

- To stop bleeding, apply direct pressure and elevate the wound above the heart.

- All victims of serious injury or illness should be treated for shock. Shock can kill a person even when the injury that triggered it is not life-threatening.

- People with fractures or neck and spinal injuries should not be moved except to be rescued from immediate danger.

- Being calm and reassuring while giving first aid helps prevent panic, which can kill someone even if an injury or illness is not life-threatening.

- Call 911 or the nearest poison control center for advice before giving first aid for poisoning.

Vocabulary

first aid emergency care given to an ill or injured person before medical attention is available.

cardiopulmonary resuscitation (CPR) a lifesaving procedure designed to revive a person who is not breathing and has no heartbeat.

fracture a broken bone.

dislocation an injury in which the end of a bone comes out of its joint.

sprain a torn or stretched ligament.

strain a stretched or torn muscle or tendon.

Heimlich maneuver a series of sharp thrusts to the abdomen, used to dislodge an object from a choking person's airway.

cardiac arrest condition in which the heart stops working.

stroke the rupture or blockage of an artery in the brain, leading to oxygen deprivation and damage to brain cells.

hypothermia below-normal body temperature.

Chapter Review

CHAPTER REVIEW

Concept Review

1. Tell exactly where the victim is, describe the accident and the injuries, ask what you should do while waiting for medical help, and let the other person hang up first.

2. Check airway, breathing, and circulation of blood.

3. Keep the victim calm, lying face up with feet elevated if you do not suspect a head injury. Victims who are unconscious or may vomit should have their heads turned to the side. Keep the victim warm. Untreated shock can lead to death.

4. Behave calmly. Having the victim further upset might cause shock.

5. pus, pain, redness; infection

6. Loss of consciousness, nausea, slurred speech, slowed breathing, convulsions, loss of memory, and blood or body fluid leaking from the ears or nose. A clue is whether pupils react to light normally or are dilated.

7. sudden pain in the chest and possibly radiating to the arms, shoulders, side of the neck, or jaw; weakness, nausea, or sickness; rapid, weak, or irregular pulse; pale skin; perspiration, anxiety, or fear

8. Loosen clothing; remove large objects from the immediate area; if the victim is unconscious,

Concept Review

1. What information should you remember to give when making an emergency telephone call?

2. What are the ABCs of emergency treatment?

3. What is the first-aid treatment for shock and why is this treatment so important?

4. It is important to approach an emergency with the right attitude. How should you behave and why?

5. What are some danger signs to watch for around a wound? What do these signs indicate?

6. What are some symptoms of a head injury? What clues should you look for if you suspect a head injury?

7. What are four symptoms of a heart attack?

8. What is the first-aid treatment for a victim of convulsions?

9. What parts of the body most often suffer from frostbite? What is the most important thing to remember when giving first aid for frostbite?

10. What are the four poisonous snakes in the United States? How soon after being bitten does a snakebite victim need medical treatment?

11. How should the stinger of an insect be removed from its victim? Why? What is the main danger from an insect sting?

12. Why should a person who has swallowed a strong acid be advised not to vomit?

13. Describe the appearance of a first-degree burn.

Expressing Your Views

1. You have started baby-sitting to make some extra money. You are afraid an emergency might arise while the children are in your care. Which first-aid procedures would be important for a baby sitter to know?

2. Do you think the good samaritan laws are fair? Why or why not?

3. Suppose you were bitten by a strange dog while walking near your home. What would you do?

4. You and your friends are planning a camping trip. What do you think should be included in a first-aid kit?

turn his or her head to the side; watch the victim's breathing; if the victim has medicine for convulsions, help administer it; and send for medical help or take the victim to the doctor after the convulsion.

9. Fingers, toes, nose, ears, cheeks. It is better not to thaw frostbitten tissue until you can keep the tissue thawed.

10. coral snake, rattlesnake, copperhead, water moccasin; within four hours

11. Scrape the stinger out with a fingernail, broken stick, or the edge of a credit card. If

you try to pull the stinger out and the poison sac is still attached, you could squeeze more poison into the wound. Allergic reaction is the main danger.

12. The acid can do as much damage coming up as it did going down.

13. The skin turns red and hurts but does not blister.

Expressing Your Views

1. rescue breathing; emergency choking aid; treatment for burns, cuts, and poisoning

Life Skills Check . . . .

1. Intervention Strategies
Rescue breathing is a technique that can save lives in a number of different kinds of medical emergencies. If a family member or friend were to stop breathing, what steps would you take to give rescue breathing?

2. Practicing Self-Care
If you suffer from diabetes or epilepsy, what can you do to ensure that others are aware of your condition?

3. Practicing Self-Care
Suppose you want to be an ambulance driver. Knowing that you will have to treat bleeding victims, what steps should you take to protect yourself from a serious disease such as hepatitis or AIDS?

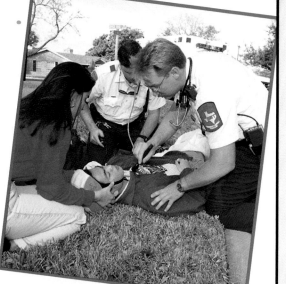

Projects . . . .

1. Inventory the first-aid supplies at home, and make suggestions to a parent or guardian about what items are needed. You might also put together a first-aid kit for your car.

2. Working with a group, present a short skit in which a group member experiences one of the emergencies discussed in the chapter. Others in the group should portray people arriving at the scene—police officers, medics, friends, and family members.

Without performing the actual techniques, show the audience correct emergency first-aid procedures.

3. Interview an EMT, paramedic, or emergency-room nurse. Ask about the type of training required and the personal qualities they feel are necessary for the job. Also ask the person to relate a particularly rewarding experience he or she has had on the job. Share what you learn with the class.

Plan for Action . . . .

First aid and CPR are very important lifesaving skills. Make a list of your activities, and identify the ways you could save lives during an emergency by knowing and using first aid or CPR.

2. Most students will answer yes, as the laws enable a person to administer first aid without worrying about a lawsuit.

3. Wash the bite and call the doctor for further instructions. Notify the police and try to find out whether the dog has had rabies shots.

4. sterile bandages, antibiotic ointment, elastic bandage, cotton swabs, tweezers, splints, baking soda, ice packs

Life Skills Check

1. Students should respond with the steps given in Figure 28-2.

2. Wear a medical ID bracelet or necklace identifying the condition.

3. Put on rubber gloves before treating the wounds. If rubber gloves are not available, cover the wound with sterile gauze and then place the victim's hand on top of the material and your hand on top of the victim's hand. Afterward, wash your hands.

Projects

Have students plan and carry out the projects for first aid and CPR.

Plan for Action

Have students quiz each other orally in a round-robin fashion. The first student poses an emergency situation, the second describes what first-aid measures should be taken in that situation and then poses a situation for the next student.

ASSESSMENT OPTIONS

Chapter Test
Have students take the Chapter 28 Test.

Alternative Assessment
Have students do the Alternative Assessment activity for Chapter 28.

Test Generator
The Test Generator contains additional assessment items for this chapter.

Ethical Issues in Health

ETHICAL ISSUES IN HEALTH

ISSUE: *Should gun-control laws be passed to reduce the number of violent deaths from gunshot wounds?*

Have students read the Ethical Issues in Health feature. Ask them to suggest reasons for and against the enactment of gun-control laws. List these in two columns on the chalkboard. Is it difficult to separate arguments and feelings when it comes to gun control? Can students suggest compromises that might be reached in gun-control legislation (for instance, limiting access to certain kinds of guns)?

▶ **ISSUE:** Should gun-control laws be passed to reduce the number of violent deaths from gunshot wounds?

Guns have become a factor that seriously affects teenage health and safety. In a recent survey at an inner-city high school, more than half the students interviewed said they knew someone who had brought a gun to school, and most said they knew someone who had been shot. Sadly, this is not a surprising statistic. Accidents, homicides, and suicides are the leading causes of death among American teenagers. Many of the accidents and a majority of the homicides and suicides of teens involve guns. Statistics from the National Center for Health show that guns were used in more than 70 percent of teenage homicides and in more than 60 percent of the suicides by teenage males. As a result, gunshot wounds are the second leading cause of death among 15- to 19-year-olds in the United States.

To try to stop students and other people from bringing guns to school, schools across the nation are beginning to use metal detectors. In the same way that these devices are used in airports, metal detectors can be installed in a school's doorways so that all students must pass through one of the devices before entering the school. Hand-held metal detectors can also be used to search individuals suspected of carrying a gun or knife. Nearly half of the students surveyed in one inner-city school agreed that metal detectors should be installed in schools to prevent the entry of guns and other weapons. Many school board members and administrators also believe that as long as guns continue to be a serious problem in schools, metal detectors will be necessary to protect students and school employees.

One reason why guns play such a major role in the deaths of American teenagers may be the large number of guns that are available. Studies show that half of all homes in the United States have firearms (rifles, shotguns, and handguns). It is estimated that 70 million Americans own about 200 million firearms, many of them handguns. Although many people feel that having guns in their homes provides safety, those most likely to be injured by gunshots are the family members of people who have guns. Other high-risk groups include male teens, those who abuse alcohol, and people who frequently get into physical fights to settle arguments.

In an attempt to reduce the impact of guns on the health of all Americans, several laws have been proposed that would control the sale of firearms (handguns, rifles, and shotguns). Some of these laws would require people to obtain a license to own guns. Others would require a waiting period for the purchase of a gun.

Advocates of gun-control laws point out that most people are shot and killed as the result of arguments and fights with family members. They argue that requiring a waiting period before the purchase of a gun would reduce the number of homicides and suicides, because an enraged or depressed person would not have immediate access to a gun. They also argue that licensing would help reduce gunshot injuries, because people with criminal records or histories of mental illness would be denied licenses to own and carry guns.

Those who oppose gun control point out that by itself, a gun cannot kill or injure people—it must be fired by someone. Since most people who own guns use them responsibly, opponents of gun control believe that only those who use guns unlawfully should be punished. Opponents of gun-control laws are also concerned that such laws will not be obeyed by criminals, leaving law-abiding citizens defenseless. The National Rifle Association (NRA) is the most powerful group in the United States that opposes gun-control laws. Citing the United States Constitution, the NRA's philosophy is that all citizens have the right to own and use guns for self-defense, hunting, and recreational purposes.

Situation for Discussion

Mark and George attend the same high school. Last Saturday night, Mark saw George and Wendy dancing and kissing at a friend's party. Mark had been dating Wendy, but they had recently split up. As the party broke up, a loud confrontation between Mark and George began on the front lawn. Several blows were exchanged, but the fight was stopped by other party-goers. As George was leaving, Mark yelled, "I'll see you later, George! You're a dead man!"

a. What is the potential outcome of this situation?

b. Could a gun-control law prevent an injury or homicide in this case? Explain.

c. What other ways are there to protect George, Mark, their families and friends, and other students at their school from injury or death?

d. How could the disagreement be settled without physical harm to either person?

The Nervous System and Its Organs

▶ Your nervous system regulates and coordinates your body activities in response to
▶ changes in the internal and external environment. The changes, called stimuli, initiate
▶ impulses in millions of **sensory receptors** spread throughout your body. The most familiar
▶ are the **sense organs:** the eyes, ears, nose, skin, and tongue. In addition to these organs,
▶ there are other sensory receptors within the body and close to the surface of the skin.

Brain

Spinal cord

Spinal nerves

CENTRAL NERVOUS SYSTEM ◆

The **brain** and **spinal cord** make up the central nervous system. The brain is the organ responsible for thought, memory, consciousness, creativity, and emotion. It also receives sensory impulses, controls and coordinates muscular movements, and regulates vital body processes. The spinal cord is the pathway for sensory and motor nerve impulses traveling to and from the brain. It also processes some information without the aid of the brain, as demonstrated by reflexes such as the withdrawal reflex.

Cerebrospinal fluid fills the open spaces in the brain and surrounds the spinal cord. This fluid acts as a shock absorber, protecting the brain and spinal cord from damage. It transports metabolic wastes out of the central nervous system. Nutrients, hormones, and other vital substances are transported throughout the central nervous system by the cerebrospinal fluid.

PERIPHERAL NERVOUS SYSTEM ◆

The 31 pairs of **spinal nerves** as well as all the other nerves and nerve cells outside of the central nervous system make up the peripheral nervous system. This system carries nerve impulses to and from the body's sensory cells and the central nervous system. The central nervous system analyzes the information it receives from the peripheral nervous system and responds to it. The motor neurons of the peripheral nervous system carry out the instructions received from the central nervous system.

Dendrites

Neuron

Cell body

Axon

NERVOUS TISSUE

The tissue of the nervous system is composed of two basic types of cells, neurons and glia (glial cells). A **neuron** consists of a **cell body; dendrites,** branched structures that conduct impulses to the cell body; and an **axon,** a long fiber that transmits impulses away from the cell body. There are three types of neurons. **Sensory neurons** send signals from the sense organs to the spinal cord and the brain. **Motor neurons** send signals from the brain and the spinal cord to the body's muscles. **Association neurons** link sensory neurons to motor neurons. **Glial cells** help support and nourish neurons and account for approximately one-half of the volume of the nervous tissue. There are four types of glial cells, each with a different function.

◆ NEUROTRANSMITTERS

Neurons are separated from each other and from other body cells by a tiny gap called a **synapse.** When a nerve impulse reaches a synapse, the axon releases a chemical called a **neurotransmitter.** The neurotransmitter transfers the impulse across the synapse to the target cell. Then, the synapse is cleared so that another impulse can cross. Over 60 different chemicals have been identified either as neurotransmitters or as substances that modify the activity of neurotransmitters.

Axon

Target cell

Synapse

Neurotransmitter molecules

Neurotransmitters and Drugs

The use of **psychoactive drugs** alters the transmission of nerve impulses. For example, caffeine stimulates the nervous system by facilitating synaptic transmission. Cocaine, amphetamines, and some antidepressant drugs cause substances to remain in the synapse longer. The result is prolonged stimulation of the nervous system. Some psychoactive drugs are addictive. The body adjusts to the changes these drugs cause. If the drug is withdrawn, the body will be unable to function as it had previously. The addicted drug user will then experience withdrawal symptoms.

Body Systems Handbook

653

BRAIN

The brain contains about 1 trillion cells, and it consists of three basic parts: the cerebrum, the cerebellum, and the brain stem. The **cerebrum,** which is the largest part of the brain, initiates all the body's voluntary actions. The **cerebellum** controls balance and muscle movement. The **brain stem,** which connects the cerebrum to the spinal cord, has nerve centers that regulate swallowing, the digestive process, circulation and respiration.

CEREBRAL HEMISPHERES

The cerebrum is made up of a right hemisphere and a left hemisphere, each divided into four lobes. Each hemisphere controls the actions of the opposite side of the body. In most people, the left hemisphere is dominant. In general, the left hemisphere is responsible for speech, writing, and reading. It also plays a major role in verbal, analytical, and computational skills. The right hemisphere is more involved with nonverbal functions, such as emotion, intuition, awareness and interpretation of space, and creativity. The cerebrum's hemispheres are connected by a structure called the corpus callosum, and there is constant communication between the two sides.

Blood-Brain Barrier

Some substances taken into the body can interfere with the proper functioning of the brain. Fortunately, a structure called the **blood-brain barrier** prevents most harmful substances from passing from the capillaries of the brain into the cerebrospinal fluid. The cells lining the brain's blood vessels are tightly joined together and play the primary role in forming the blood-brain barrier. In addition, projections from one type of glial cell cover the outside of the brain's blood vessels, making passage into the brain even more difficult. A special carrier system allows water, oxygen, carbon-dioxide, glucose, and nutrients to pass through the blood-brain barrier.

BRAIN INJURY

Accidents and illnesses can damage or destroy brain cells. When permanent damage is done to enough cells, disability results. The degree and type of disability depend on how many brain cells are injured and on where the damage occurs. Severe trauma to the head as well as repeated minor trauma to the head, such as that incurred by boxers, can cause permanent brain damage.

◆ SPINAL CORD

The **spinal cord** is a cable of nerve tissue that extends from the base of the brain to just below the level of the ribs. In adults, it is about the thickness of the little finger. The spinal cord is surrounded by the spinal column (backbone), which protects it. Thirty-one pairs of spinal nerves connect the spinal cord with the rest of the body. The spinal nerves are composed of both sensory neurons and motor neurons. These neurons transfer millions of messages between the body and the brain.

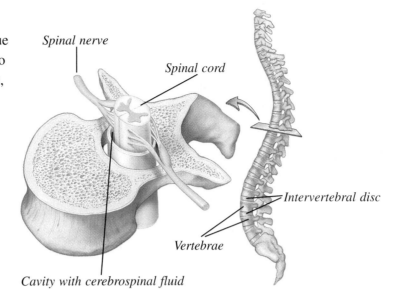

Spinal nerve

Spinal cord

Intervertebral disc

Vertebrae

Cavity with cerebrospinal fluid

SPINAL-CORD INJURIES

Spinal-cord injuries are relatively common. About 45 percent of all spinal-cord injuries are incurred in motor-vehicle accidents. Injuries to the spinal cord can alter or prevent communication between the brain and the body. If the injury is serious enough paralysis can occur. In general, the higher up on the spinal cord the injury is, the more severe the damage will be. Damage to the spinal cord in the neck can result in paralysis from the neck down, while injures lower on the spinal cord may produce paralysis only in the legs.

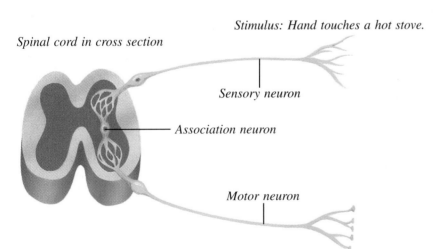

Spinal cord in cross section

Stimulus: Hand touches a hot stove.

Sensory neuron

Association neuron

Motor neuron

Reflex: Muscle moves hand away from stove.

REFLEXES ◆

Reflexes are involuntary responses to stimuli and are not controlled by the brain. Reflex movements take only a split second to occur. For example, when a person touches a hot stove, a nerve impulse travels through a sensory neuron in the person's hand to the spinal cord. There, it is transferred first to an association neuron and then to a motor neuron traveling quickly back to the hand. In a split second, the withdrawal reflex pulls the hand away from the stove. If this message had to go through the brain, the response time would be longer increasing the possibility of injury.

Sensory Receptors and Sense Organs

Your senses are the window through which you view the world around you. They allow you to interpret changes in your internal and external environment. One day you may feel well; the next day you may have a headache. Your senses are what provides this information to the brain, which in turn, interprets it. Not everyone interprets information in the same way. That's why some people love hot chili peppers, while others prefer more subtle flavorings.

INTERNAL SENSORY RECEPTORS

Sense receptors located deep within the body enable a person to feel internal pain, hunger, thirst, tiredness, and nausea. Other receptors located in skeletal muscles, tendons, and the connective tissue surrounding joints are sensitive to changes in stretch and tension. They continuously relay information about body position, equilibrium, and movement to the central nervous system, and together they make up what is called the **kinesthetic** sense. Many internal sensations are not recognized at a conscious level. For example, some sensors monitor blood pressure; the information they send to the brain is not processed by the cerebrum, so an individual is not aware of this sensation.

SENSATION AND THE SKIN

Touch is the sensation produced by pressure on the surface of the body and is sometimes called the **tactile** sense. Pressure receptors are located all over the skin. On sensitive parts of the body, such as the tongue, lips, and finger pads, their concentration is very high. Touch messages are transmitted by bundles of **sensory nerve fibers** that come through the **subcutaneous layer** to the **dermis,** or inner layer of skin. The bundles split into fibers, some of which reach into the **epidermis,** or outer layer of the skin. These **nerve endings** in the epidermis are sensitive to pressure. Other sensory nerve fibers end in specialized receptors in the dermis, which sense temperature or pain.

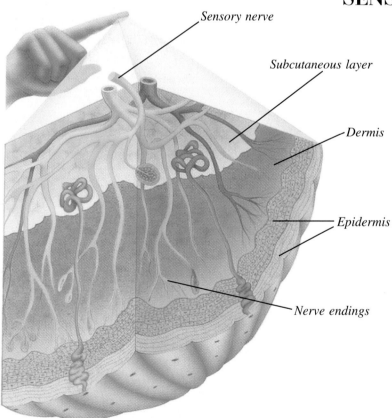

Sensory nerve

Subcutaneous layer

Dermis

Epidermis

Nerve endings

▶ Smell and Taste

▶
▶ Your sense of taste and your sense of smell are both stimulated by chemicals. Their
▶ main purposes are to help you detect harmful substances and to stimulate your
▶ appetite and digestion. Even though taste and smell messages travel separately to
▶ different regions of the brain, they create a combined feeling of either pleasure
▶ or displeasure when you are eating. For example, think of how the aroma of a
▶ delicious meal can make your mouth water.

SMELL ◆

Olfactory (smell) receptors are located in a dime-sized area in the roof of the nasal passages. They are able to sense minute amounts of chemicals in the air. These receptors are actually specialized neurons whose dendrites are modified into hairlike projections called cilia. Their axons transmit nerve impulses through an opening in the skull directly to the olfactory bulb in the forebrain. When a person has a stopped-up nose, little air passes over the olfactory receptor cells, resulting in a diminished sense of smell. Compared to some other mammals, humans have a poor sense of smell. For example, humans have anywhere from 5 million to 20 million olfactory receptors, while dogs have 40 million or more.

Olfactory nerve

Olfactory bulb

Receptor cells with cilia

Nasal passage

◆ TASTE

The tongue is covered with small, rough bumps called papillae. Each papilla is covered with **taste buds**, clusters of taste sensors. Taste receptors sense chemicals—classified as sweet, sour, salty, or bitter—in foods and beverages. When chewed-up food mixed with saliva washes across the papillae, the chemicals in the food stimulate the taste receptors. The receptors transmit nerve impulses to the brain through the gustatory nerve, and the brain interprets the taste. Babies have about 10,000 taste buds, but this number decreases as a person gets older. There are other reasons why the ability to taste can diminish. For example, there is good evidence that long-term cigarette smoking damages taste receptors, adding to the loss that normally comes with age.

Pore

Hair

Taste buds

Nerve fiber

▶ Vision

Human beings have excellent eyesight. In fact, only birds can see better than humans can, although squids and octopuses can see just as well. Your vision is a response to light falling on the retina of the eye. Light rays enter your eye through the pupil and are focused onto the retina, which is actually an extension of your brain. Nerve fibers of the retina join to form the optic nerve, which transmits nerve impulses to the occipital lobe of your brain. Your brain then interprets these impulses as an image, and you "see" it.

◆ EYE

The outer surface of the eye is covered by the **cornea,** a transparent membrane that protects the eye but allows light to enter. Behind the cornea is the **iris,** a thin, colored, circular membrane. In the center of the iris is an opening called the **pupil.** Muscles in the iris control the amount of light that is let in by altering the diameter of the pupil. The pupil dilates, or enlarges, to let more light in and contracts to let in less light. Behind the pupil is the **lens,** a thick, curved structure that focuses the light rays so that they will fall on the **retina,** the thin lining on the back of the eye. Notice that the image on the retina is inverted.

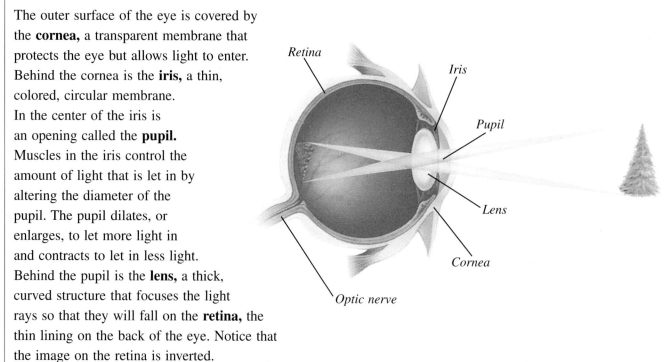

◆ RECEPTOR CELLS

There are approximately 1 billion receptor cells in the retina. **Rods** are cells that are extremely sensitive to light; however, they cannot detect color, and they produce poorly defined images. **Cones** are cells that detect color and produce sharp images. At the center of the retina is a concentration of about 3 million cone cells. People usually move their eyes so that the light rays from an object they want to see fall on this area. There are no cones or rods at the point where the optic nerve enters the retina. Light that falls on this area does not stimulate any sight receptors, resulting in a "blind spot" in the field of vision.

EYE DISORDERS

Some people are nearsighted or farsighted; others have an astigmatism. Why is this? For an image to appear clear, the lens must focus light rays directly onto the retina. The lens does this by using tiny muscles and ligaments to adjust its thickness. If the shape of the eyeball is too elongated or too short, the lens will be unable to change sufficiently to focus the image properly. In nearsighted people, the focal point is in front of the retina, resulting in poor distance vision. In farsighted people, the focal point is behind the retina, resulting in poor close vision. Astigmatism is caused by an irregularly shaped cornea. This causes the light rays to be focused erratically and to mostly miss the retina. Corrective lenses adjust the light ray's focal point so that it is on the retina.

Color blindness, a condition that is almost always genetic in origin, is the inability to distinguish colors. It is caused by an abnormality of one or more of the three types of light-sensitive pigments in the cone cells. The inability to distinguish red light from green light is the most common type of color blindness. About 10 percent of all males have some degree of color blindness while less than 1 percent of females are affected. Total color blindness is extremely rare.

When a person has cataracts, the lens of the eye is no longer transparent. Light cannot pass through the lens easily, so vision is diminished. Although aging is the most common cause of cataracts, they can also result from a reaction to a drug, from radiation including solar exposure, and from disease. In the past, people with cataracts became blind; however, today the condition can be corrected surgically. The faulty lens is removed and replaced with an artificial one. Glasses or contact lenses are then prescribed to adjust the vision.

Some diseases cause scarring of the cornea. When this occurs, blindness may result because light cannot pass through the damaged cornea. This condition can be corrected by a corneal transplant. The central portion of the scarred cornea is removed and replaced with a cornea from an organ donor.

Brain

Optic nerves split

Optic nerves

THE BRAIN FORMS AN IMAGE ◆

When the eyes view an image, each eye sees the image from a slightly different angle. About one-third of the visual fields overlap, but the other two-thirds differ. This overlap produces **binocular vision,** which enables people to perceive depth. Also, the optic nerves do not connect to only one hemisphere. About one-half of each optic nerve crosses over into the opposite side of the brain; because of this, each hemisphere receives visual information from both eyes. The brain combines all the information it receives to produce one image.

Hearing and Equilibrium

When you think of your ears, you may only consider your external ear, the part that sticks out on each side of your head. But you also have a middle ear and an inner ear, the portions responsible for sensing sound.

HEARING

The **external ear** funnels sounds through the **ear canal** to the **eardrum.** On the other side of the eardrum is an air-filled cavity called the **middle ear.** This part of the ear opens to the back of the throat through a tube called the eustachian tube. As sound waves apply pressure to the eardrum, the eardrum vibrates. Three bones located in the middle ear—the **hammer,** the **anvil,** and the **stirrup**— transfer this vibration to a fluid-filled chamber, the **cochlea.** Inside are tiny hair cells that serve as sound receptors. They respond to the vibrations and send impulses to the brain, which interprets the vibrations as sound.

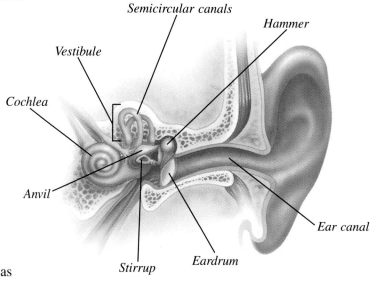

Semicircular canals

Hammer

Vestibule

Cochlea

Anvil

Stirrup

Eardrum

Ear canal

Equilibrium

The two other portions of the inner ear, the **semicircular canals** and the **vestibule,** are involved with the sense of equilibrium. The semicircular canals detect movement of the head. The vestibule contains sensory cells that respond to changes in head position with respect to gravity. It is the inner ear that contains the sense cells, which enable you to hear, and that produces your sense of equilibrium, or balance and stability in space.

HEARING LOSS

Certain conditions, diseases, and types of trauma can result in hearing loss. For example, a buildup of wax in the ear or an ear infection can create a barrier to sound waves entering the ear, preventing vibration of the ear drum and the inner-ear bones. Repeated inner-ear infections can result in scarring of the eardrum and damage to the bones of the inner ear. If this occurred, sound waves would not be conducted as well and hearing would be diminished. This type of hearing loss is referred to as conductive deafness.

Repeated exposure to excessively loud sounds will destroy the tiny hair cells in the cochlea, resulting in hearing loss. Once destroyed, these hair cells can never be replaced. Rock concerts and exposure to other loud noises, such as power saws, cause this type of hearing loss. Wearing ear plugs protects the ears from this type of damage. There is now evidence that prolonged exposure to even moderately loud sounds, such as head phones, has a cumulative effect and can cause hearing loss classified as nerve deafness.

Q and A

Q: I've heard that exercise leads to a "runner's high." What is that?

A: The body produces neurotransmitters that travel to other parts of the body and affect them in various ways. Endorphins are one type of neurotransmitter. One endorphin, enkephalin, is produced by the brain and spinal cord in response to stress. Enkephalin binds to the same receptors in the brain as the narcotic morphine does. Enkephalin secretion results in lessened pain and a sense of well-being. Another endorphin, betaedorphin, is produced by the pituitary gland. These two endorphins are secreted during exercise and are responsible for what is called a "runner's high."

Q: What is a concussion?

A: When the head receives a violent blow—such as from a fall—the brain is jarred. The force of the brain hitting the skull interferes with normal brain function and is called a concussion. If the force is mild, loss of consciousness may occur but will usually last only a few seconds. However, if the force is intense, loss of consciousness may be prolonged and damage may be extensive. It is common for a person to experience confusion or even amnesia following a concussion. Although the damage may not be obvious from the outside, concussions can be very dangerous.

Q: Where does earwax come from?

A: Sebaceous glands and ceruminous glands, specialized sweat glands, located in the ear canal produce this waxlike secretion. Earwax, called cerumen, protects the ear from infection and traps debris or small insects that enter the ear. It also helps prevent the ear drum from drying out. Usually the wax moves outward, moving anything it trapped along with it.

Q: Why can certain smells trigger emotions or vivid memories?

A: Scientists are not completely certain; they do know that the olfactory system is so sensitive that as few as four molecules of a substance can stimulate an olfactory receptor, even though there may be no conscious recognition of a smell. They also know that the olfactory nerve fibers link directly to areas of the brain where memories and emotions are held. The perfume industry is aware of these connections and makes full use of it when developing new scents.

Q: Is it safe to wear contact lenses overnight?

A: Wearing contact lenses, even soft lenses, overnight prevents the cornea from receiving adequate oxygen, and low-oxygen conditions increase the growth of some bacteria. People who wear their lenses overnight increase their risk for bacterial infection 10 to 15 times. Since bacterial infection of the eye can cause permanent damage to a person's vision, it is not worth the risk.

Q: Where do tears come from, and what is their purpose?

A: Tears are produced by a gland found above and to the outside of each eyeball. Each gland produces a watery secretion that mixes with a slightly oily secretion from accessory glands. The tear glands have between 10 and 12 ducts, and every time the eyes blink, tears are spread across the surface of the eye. Tears protect the eyes by lubricating them and washing away debris. Also, they contain an enzyme that helps prevent eye infection. Tears drain into two ducts in the inner corners of the eye. These ducts drain into the back of the nose.

The Skeletal System

Your skeletal system supports and protects the soft tissues and vital organs of your body. Your heart and lungs are shielded by your ribs, your spinal cord is protected by your vertebrae, and your brain is protected by your skull. Without rigid bones and flexible joints, you would not be able to stand, sit, bend, walk, or run. By themselves, bones cannot move. Your skeletal system moves because muscles attached to your bones contract or relax in response to messages sent from the nervous system. Some of the skeletal bones are held together by strong fibers called **ligaments.**

HUNDREDS OF BONES

The skeleton contains about 206 bones, depending on how they are counted. The pelvis, for instance, can be counted as a single bone or as six bones fused together. Children have 33 vertebrae in their spine, but in adults the bottom five become fused to form the sacrum. There are 24 ribs in 12 pairs, and there are 56 phalanxes (finger and toe bones). The hard shell of the skull consists of 28 bones and provides protection for the brain and the delicate sense organs.

The bones of the body vary greatly in size. The thigh bone, or femur, is the largest single bone in the body.

Stirrup   Anvil   Hammer

The smallest bones—the stirrup, the anvil, and the hammer— are found in the ear and are less than one-half inch long.

Skull
Clavicle (collar bone)
Scapula (shoulder blade)
Rib cage
Sternum (breast bone)
Humerus
Radius
Ulna
Carpus
Ilium
Sacrum
Coccyx (tailbone)
Metacarpal
Ischium
Pubis
Phalanges
Femur
Patella
Tibia
Fibula
Tarsus
Metatarsal
Phalanges

VIEW OF A BONE

They may seem hard and lifeless, but bones are made of living tissue. The outer membrane of the bone, called the **periosteum,** contains many nerves, as well as blood vessels that transport food and oxygen to the bone's many cells. Inside the periosteum is the **bony layer,** which contains more blood vessels, bone cells (osteoblasts), and nerves. At the center of some bones is the **marrow,** which makes blood cells and stores fat.

Periosteum

Marrow

Bony layer

Blood vessels

BONE GROWTH

The long bones of the body, such as the femur, continue to grow until a person is about 20 years old. In the end of long bones is a band of cartilage called the **epiphysis,** or growth plate. Here, cartilage forms that will later be replaced by bone. As a young person matures, this cartilage formation slows down and finally stops. The growth plate becomes completely hardened, and growth in the length of the bone is no longer possible.

At birth, the bones of an infant's skull are incompletely developed and are separated by areas of soft tissue called **fontanels,** or soft spots. Fontanels allow for movement of the skull bones as the baby passes through the birth canal. There are no growth plates in these bones. The skull bones simply grow until they meet, closing up the soft spots. Some fontanels close up as early as two months after birth, but the one at the top of the head does not close up until about one year after birth.

There are several factors that can interfere with bone growth. If the epiphysis is injured, growth in the bone may stop. Deficiencies in the diet—especially of the vitamins A, C, and D—can interfere with bone growth. Steroid use by young people can cause premature closure of the epiphysis.

CARTILAGE

Cartilage is a tough connective tissue found in various regions of the body. In the skeletal system, cartilage connects the ribs to the sternum, helps form the movable joints, and is found between the bones of the pelvis. The tip of the nose and the outer ears are made of cartilage, as are the **intervertebral disks.** These disks, which are shown on page 655, serve as cushions that prevent the vertebrae from rubbing and scraping against each other. Sometimes a disk becomes compressed and presses against a spinal nerve, which can be very painful. As people age, a disk's outer layer may develop cracks. If the inside of the disk protrudes through a crack, a condition called a herniated disk results. Disk damage can also result from misuse of the spine, such as the repeated improper lifting of heavy objects.

◆ PELVIS

Although the bones of males and females are essentially alike except for size, the pelvis is an exception. To accommodate pregnancy and childbirth, the female's pelvis has a slightly different shape than that of the male. It is usually wider so there is enough room for a developing fetus. The opening at the bottom of the pelvis is larger so that a baby's head can pass through during childbirth. The female pelvic bones are usually lighter and have less muscle attachment. This lighter structure causes females to be more susceptible to pelvic fractures than males.

JOINTS ◆

Joints are the locations where bones come together. There are three basic types of joints. **Immovable joints** provide little or no movement. For example, the bones that make up the skull's cranium are joined by immovable joints called **sutures. Slightly movable joints** allow limited movement. This type of joint is found between the vertebrae of the spine.

The names of the **freely movable joints** suggest the kind of motion each allows—hinge, pivot, ball-and-socket, and gliding. **Hinge joints,** found in the knees and elbows, allow back-and-forth movement—like a hinge in a door. **Pivot joints,** such as those in the neck, allow either back-and-forth movement or up-and-down movement. The shoulder and hip joints are **ball-and-socket joints,** which allow the greatest range of movement. **Gliding joints,** found in the wrist and ankles, allow for flexibility.

*Shoulder
(ball-and-socket joint)*

*Neck
(pivot joint)*

*Knee
(hinge joint)*

*Wrist
(gliding joint)*

Q and A

Q: What is scoliosis? Do many teenagers have it?

A: Scoliosis, a sideways curve in the spine, is fairly common among young people. While most people have a small degree of curvature of the spine, it is usually not severe enough to require medical treatment. With scoliosis, the curvature is more pronounced and can result in pain and lack of mobility. Surgery may be required to straighten the vertebrae, but early detection eliminates the need in most cases. Other symptoms of scoliosis include unlevel shoulders or hips, a hump on the back, or a prominent shoulder blade.

Q: What does it mean when someone says an athlete has been "scoped"?

A: The severity of a joint injury can be assessed by inserting a thin, tubular instrument called an arthroscope through the skin and into the joint. In many cases, another tube that contains other instruments can be used to repair the damage. This procedure is called an arthroscopy, commonly called "scoping."

The Muscular System

Your muscular system enables your body to move. Each muscle consists of muscle cells that can contract or relax. Because muscle cells are usually long and slender, they are called fibers. Skeletal muscles move your bones and help protect your inner organs. Smooth muscles deep within your body help move food, air, and body fluids. Cardiac muscle is a special type of muscle found only in your heart. Your body has more than 600 muscles, which make up about 30 percent of the female body and about 40 percent of the male body.

◆ SKELETAL MUSCLES

Muscles attached to bones are called skeletal muscles. They are also called "voluntary" muscles because a person can choose whether to move them. In addition to muscle fibers, skeletal muscles contain connective tissue, nerves, and blood vessels. Each muscle is surrounded by a fibrous membrane. At one end of the muscle, the fibers of this membrane connect with a tough band of elastic tissue called a **tendon.** Tendons connect most skeletal muscles to bones.

Frontalis

Trapezius

Deltoid

Pectoralis major

Biceps brachii

Abdominal muscles

Sartorius

Rectus femoris

Tibialis anterior

Trapezius

Deltoid

Triceps brachii

Latissimus dorsi

Gluteus maximus

Biceps femoris

Gastrocnemius

SMOOTH AND CARDIAC MUSCLES ◆

Smooth muscles are found in internal organs, such as the stomach, intestines, urinary bladder, uterus, and blood vessels. Unlike skeletal muscles, which can be contracted voluntarily, smooth muscles are involuntary. Smooth muscles are responsible for the contractions of the esophagus and the intestines called **peristalsis.** Smooth muscles are also responsible for the contractions of labor during childbirth.

Cardiac muscle fibers are strong like skeletal muscles, but the heart is an involuntary muscle. The contraction and relaxation of cardiac muscle fibers pumps blood through the body automatically and rhythmically.

*The Achilles'
tendon joins
the calf muscles
to the heel
bone; it can be
felt by touching
the back of the
ankle while
wiggling the
foot.*

Achilles tendon

◆ MUSCLE ACTION

Muscle fibers respond to nerve impulses by contracting. When enough nerve impulses are received, the entire muscle contracts and pulls any attached tissue along with it, resulting in movement of that tissue. Skeletal muscles often work in pairs to bend and straighten joints. The biceps and triceps muscles move the arms at the elbow. In the illustration, notice how the biceps is attached to two different bones. Contracting the biceps muscle pulls upward on one of the bones of the lower arm, causing the arm to bend. When the biceps relaxes and the triceps contracts, the arm is pulled in the opposite direction.

*Biceps
contracts*

Triceps relaxes

*Biceps
relaxes*

Triceps contracts

*Even the simplest body move-
ments involve the coordination
of many muscles. For example,
it takes 13 muscles to smile and
34 muscles to frown.*

COMMON MUSCLE PROBLEMS

Considering that muscles are used every time you move, it is not surprising that muscle injuries are common. Although regular exercise preceded by a proper warm-up reduces the risk of muscle injury, it can still occur—especially when a person ignores his or her limitations. Charley horses and pulled hamstrings are common jogging-related injuries. A **charley horse** is a painful contusion, or bruising, of the muscle and is frequently accompanied by a tear in muscle fibers. A **pulled hamstring** is an overextension or strain of one of the muscles in the back of the thigh. Inflammation of the flexor muscles of the front portion of the lower leg causes another common condition, known as **shin splints.** A **muscular cramp** is a prolonged and painful involuntary muscular contraction. A **spasm** is a brief, involuntary contraction. The exact cause of muscle cramps and spasms is unknown. Experts suggest that they may result from several causes: insufficient oxygen, calcium, or magnesium; fatigue; or various drugs. **Tendinitis** is the inflammation of the connective tissue surrounding a tendon.

Q _and_ A ◆◆◆◆◆◆◆◆◆

Q: Why does muscular fatigue develop?

A: The causes of muscular fatigue are not well understood. One explanation is that when muscles contract they produce lactic acid. Lactic acid creates an environment in which muscles are not able to respond to stimulation. However, new research indicates that there are other contributing factors, such as depletion of stored energy and muscle glycogen, inadequate blood flow to the muscles, and low oxygen levels. Well-conditioned athletes experience less muscle fatigue. It is known that they accumulate less lactic acid in their muscles and that conditioning actually increases the capillary density of the skeletal muscles, increasing blood flow.

Q: Why does weight training make a person look muscular?

A: Muscles develop differently depending on the type of exercise they receive. For example, when a muscle is contracted moderately but repeatedly, as in swimming, it develops new capillaries and some increased strength. When a muscle is contracted in short, forceful actions, as in weightlifting, the muscle fibers increase in diameter and the entire muscle enlarges more than in repeated, moderate activity. This form of exercise increases the strength of the muscle, but a weight lifter will not have the endurance of a swimmer.

Q: What does it mean if a person has TMJ?

A: Stress or a poor bite (malocclusion of the teeth) can cause some people to clench their jaw, especially in their sleep. Contracting the jaw muscles in this way causes pressure on the temporomandibular joint located in the jaw just below the ear. This can result in headaches, earaches, or pain in the jaw, neck, or shoulder. This condition is called temporomandibular joint syndrome, or TMJ. Stress management and dental splints are often prescribed for sufferers of TMJ.

The Circulatory System

Your circulatory system includes the cardiovascular system and the lymphatic system. The cardiovascular system, which consists of the heart (cardio-), blood, and blood vessels (-vascular), transports oxygen, nutrients, antibodies, and infection-fighting cells to each cell in your body. It also helps rid the body of wastes. In addition to blood, your body has another fluid, lymph, that circulates throughout it. The lymphatic system is a drainage subsystem for the larger circulatory system and is active in fighting disease.

◆ BLOOD

Blood consists of various specialized cells and a fluid called **plasma.** The yellowish plasma contains water, nutrients, wastes, and other materials. The cells found in blood include **red blood cells,** which carry oxygen; **white blood cells,** which protect the body against disease; and **platelets,** which initiate the process of blood clotting.

Platelets

Red blood cells

White blood cells

Heart

Arteries

Veins

◆ BLOOD VESSELS

The blood vessels of the circulatory system form a continuous system. There are three types of blood vessels. **Arteries** are the thick-walled vessels that carry blood from the heart to all parts of the body. **Veins,** which have thinner walls, carry blood back to the heart from all parts of the body. Veins also contain tiny valves that prevent blood from flowing downward from the pull of gravity. **Capillaries,** which are the smallest of the blood vessels, link the arteries to the veins. Because of their small diameter, blood cells must pass through capillaries in single file. No cell in the body is more than a few cells away from a capillary.

Artery

Vein

The wall of a capillary is only one cell thick, which allows oxygen and nutrients to leave the bloodstream easily and be taken up by the body's cells.

HEART

The heart is the circulatory system's pump. Actually, the heart is two pumps placed side-by-side. The right side of the heart pumps blood to the lungs, and the left side pumps blood to the rest of the body. The atria receive blood and pump it into the ventricles. The ventricles push the blood out of the heart. The ventricles' job requires a greater force, so the ventricles are larger and more muscular. Valves in the heart allow blood to move through it in one direction only.

Blood enters the **right atrium** of the heart and is pumped into the **right ventricle.** When the right ventricle contracts, blood is pumped through the **pulmonary arteries** to the lungs, where the blood gives off carbon dioxide and picks up oxygen.

Oxygen-rich blood returns to the heart through the **pulmonary veins** and enters the **left atrium.** It is then pumped to the **left ventricle.** The left ventricle contracts, pumping blood into the **aorta** and out to various parts of the body.

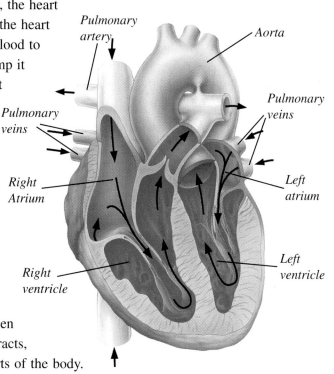

Pulmonary artery

Aorta

Pulmonary veins

Pulmonary veins

Right Atrium

Left atrium

Right ventricle

Left ventricle

CARDIAC OUTPUT

During exercise, the muscles and the body organs need more oxygen and nutrients. The heart accommodates this need in two ways. First, it pumps blood out faster, increasing the **heart rate.** Second, the heart increases its **stroke volume,** the amount of blood pumped out of the heart with each heartbeat. The amount of blood pumped with each beat multiplied by the number of beats per minute is called **cardiac output.** As a person exercises regularly and becomes more conditioned, the heart begins to work more efficiently and stroke volume increases. In very well-conditioned athletes, the heart itself enlarges in response to the increased demand. This type of enlargement is not harmful and disappears rapidly if the exercise level diminishes.

HEART ARRHYTHMIA

The heart beats in a regular rhythm as the walls of the atria and ventricles alternately contract and relax. This is called the **cardiac cycle.** If the cardiac cycle is disrupted and the heart gets out of rhythm, a condition called **arrhythmia** results. Arrhythmia can lead to serious consequences, including death. When a person begins to exercise, the heart adjusts to the greater demand for oxygen by increasing its rate. If the person exercising has a heart problem or is in a weakened condition, there is a chance that as the heart rate increases, the heart will get out of rhythm. When the heart's atria get out of synch, a person can survive because blood is still able to move through the heart. However, if the ventricles are affected, sudden death may occur because blood does not get pumped to the vital organs. To help avoid exercise-related heart-rhythm problems, always warm up first so the heart can adjust slowly. There are other causes for arrhythmia. For example, the drug cocaine can cause arrhythmia by disabling the nerves that regulate the contractions of the heart.

THE ROLE OF THE LYMPHATIC SYSTEM

The cells of the body are bathed in a clear watery fluid called **lymph.** This fluid helps move materials between the capillaries and the body's cells. Lymph is formed from water, proteins, and other nutrients that move out of the blood into the spaces between the body's cells. This fluid must be returned to the circulatory system. A system of **lymphatic vessels** similar to the veins and capillaries collect the fluid and return it to the circulatory system. The lymph capillaries parallel the blood capillary system and are connected to larger lymph vessels that eventually connect to one of two ducts. These two ducts, the thoracic and the right lymphatic, open into two veins just above the heart.

The lymphatic system is also a part of the body's immune system. In addition to the lymph fluid and vessels, this system includes the lymph glands, the thymus gland, the spleen, and the tonsils. For information about the role of the lymphatic system in fighting disease, refer to the section in this handbook on the immune system.

Q: What does the doctor actually listen for with a stethoscope?

A: A stethoscope amplifies heart sounds so they can easily be heard. Heart sounds are produced by the contracting and relaxing of the heart and the opening and closing of its valves. These heart sounds can provide information about the health of the heart. One thing the doctor listens for is a heart murmur. A murmur is a sound that occurs when the heart's valves do not function properly. For example, a valve may not close completely, thereby allowing blood to leak back into the chamber it just left. Often heart murmurs are not serious. However, when they do create a problem, open heart surgery can be performed to repair or replace a damaged valve.

Q: What's a pacemaker?

A: Two small groups of cells in the wall of the heart set the pace for cardiac contraction. They are the heart's natural pacemaker. Sometimes disease causes these cells to become slow in their initiation of the contraction. If medication does not help, doctors can insert an electronic, artificial pacemaker near the heart. This pacemaker is battery-operated, and wires from it send a small electric impulse to the heart at regular intervals. Over 50,000 people in the United States have either external or internal pacemakers.

Q: Why have some young athletes died suddenly from heart failure?

A: Young athletes who have healthy hearts and who do not abuse drugs seldom die of heart failure. However, athletes with underlying, undiagnosed heart conditions are at risk. The most common cause of sudden death from heart disease is hypertrophic cardiomyopathy (HCM). HCM is a genetic disease that causes an abnormal thickening of the left ventricle. This condition can kill with no prior symptoms of disease, and it accounts for roughly half of the heart-related fatalities in young athletes. In some other cases of sudden death, the suspected cause is the use of an illegal drug, which can cause a fatal heart arrhythmia.

The Respiratory System

Every breath you take provides your body's cells with essential oxygen. As they perform their various tasks, the cells produce the waste product carbon dioxide. Your respiratory system provides a way to remove carbon dioxide from your body and to obtain oxygen from the atmosphere. The respiratory system includes the pharynx, the larynx, the trachea, the bronchi, and the lungs.

◆ RESPIRATORY TRACT

Normally, air enters the body through the **nostrils.** Hairs in the nose help filter out dust and other small particles. The cells of the nasal cavity warm and moisten the air before it enters the lungs. Some cells lining the **nasal cavity** secrete mucus, which also traps debris. If a person breathes through his or her mouth, the air passes through the **oral cavity.** The nasal and oral cavities meet at the throat, or **pharynx.** Air from the nose or mouth passes through the pharynx to the voice box, or **larynx,** where the vocal cords are located. The larynx is attached to the windpipe, or **trachea.** This long passageway leads to the **lungs.** In the illustration, notice that the pharynx leads to both the esophagus (food passageway) and the trachea. When a person swallows, the **epiglottis** covers the opening to the trachea, preventing foods or liquids from entering the lungs.

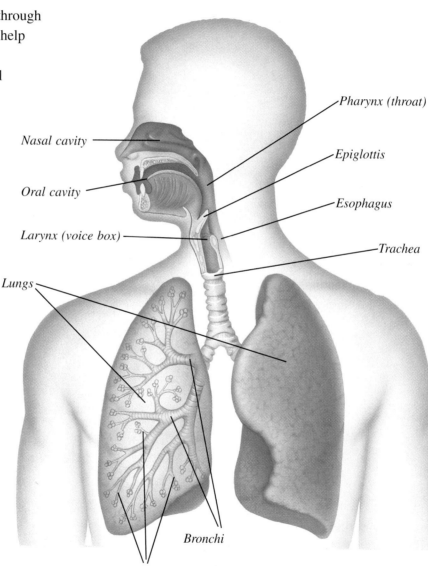

Pharynx (throat)

Nasal cavity

Epiglottis

Oral cavity

Esophagus

Larynx (voice box)

Trachea

Lungs

Bronchi

Bronchioles

LUNGS ◆

The lungs are located in the chest cavity. Below the lungs is a sheet of muscle tissue, the **diaphragm,** which separates the chest cavity from the abdominal cavity. Two tubes known as **bronchi** connect the trachea to the **lungs.** The bronchi are subdivided many times, forming smaller and smaller passages, the smallest of which are known as **bronchioles.** At the end of each bronchiole is a cluster of tiny air sacs called **alveoli.** Each lung contains about 150 million alveoli, each of which is surrounded by **capillaries.** Oxygen passes from the alveoli into these capillaries for delivery to the body's cells. Simultaneously, carbon dioxide in the bloodstream moves from the capillaries into the alveoli, where it is exhaled from the lungs. This simultaneous exchange of gases is called **respiration.**

Bronchiole

Capillaries

Alveoli

Oxygen

Carbon dioxide

◆ BREATHING

Air moves into and out of the lungs with every breath. Why is this? The movement of the diaphragm and rib muscles changes the size of the chest cavity. When a person **inhales,** the diaphragm contracts and moves downward and the rib muscles expand the chest cavity upwards and outwards. This causes the chest cavity to enlarge. Air rushes into the lungs, and the alveoli expand as they fill with air. When a person **exhales,** the diaphragm relaxes and moves upward and the rib muscles relax. The chest cavity becomes smaller, and air is pushed out of the lungs. This process is automatic and is regulated by the respiratory control center in the brain stem.

Inhalation

Exhalation

Diaphragm contracts

Diaphragm relaxes

LUNG DYSFUNCTION

Efficient breathing depends on two factors: an adequate amount of oxygen must reach the alveoli, and there must be adequate surface area available for gas exchange in the alveoli. There are numerous reasons why the first condition might not be met. If the diaphragm and rib muscles do not function correctly, air will not flow into the lungs. An inhaled object or an abnormal growth can block the air passage. (Chapter 28 describes how the Heimlich maneuver is used to remove objects from the air passages.) In a disease such as asthma, the air passages can become constricted, restricting the flow of air to the lungs. Many conditions that block air passages can be treated successfully.

Anything that impairs the function of the alveoli reduces the total surface area available for gas exchange. For example, if the alveoli are filled with fluid, as with pneumonia, or covered with the debris found in cigarette smoke, respiration is diminished. The disease emphysema causes the alveoli to be less elastic. Because they are unable to expand sufficiently, less oxygen fills the alveoli and gas exchange is diminished. If the alveoli are punctured, as sometimes happens with a broken rib, they lose air pressure and collapse. The alveoli can also be damaged by noxious fumes. For example, the dangerous practice of inhaling chemical substances for nonmedical reasons damages the alveoli as well as the brain. Diseases that cause oxygen deficiency are extremely debilitating. Abstaining from smoking is the most important thing a person can do to prevent respiratory problems. Keep in mind that there is no way to replace damaged or destroyed alveoli.

Q and A

Q: Why do people yawn?

A: Even when people breathe normally, not all of the alveoli are filled with oxygen. That means that some blood may pass through the lungs without getting enough oxygen. It is thought that this low blood-oxygen concentration triggers the yawn reflex. Yawning causes a person to take a deep breath, which makes more oxygen available to the alveoli and increases the blood-oxygen concentration.

Q: What's wrong when a person has laryngitis?

A: Sometimes an infection or an irritation from inhaling noxious vapors can cause the cells lining the larynx to become inflamed. When this occurs, the vocal cords may not vibrate as easily as usual and the voice may sound hoarse. This condition is known as laryngitis. Laryngitis is usually mild and goes away by itself. However, if the tissue becomes so swollen that it obstructs the airway, a tracheotomy may have to be performed. In this procedure, a hole is made in the trachea below the larynx, allowing air to reach the lungs.

Q: What is diaphragmatic breathing?

A: Usually when people breathe, they do not fully utilize the lower third of their lungs. In diaphragmatic breathing, the diaphragm is lowered, allowing air to fill the abdominal area, which appears to blow up like a balloon. Diaphragmatic breathing is a very effective way to relax. To practice diaphragmatic breathing, place your hands on your abdomen and breathe in, trying to fill your abdomen with air. If done correctly, the abdomen should raise and lower as air goes in and out of the lungs.

The Digestive System

The digestive system allows your body to take in and process food to nourish its cells. Digestion begins in the mouth and continues in the stomach and the small intestine. Other digestive organs, such as the pancreas, liver, and gallbladder, contribute to the process of digestion.

◆ MOUTH

Digestion begins in the mouth with three pairs of **salivary glands.** The smell, and even the thought, of food causes these glands to increase their production of saliva. **Saliva** contains enzymes that break down starches and other complex carbohydrates in food. As a person chews, food is broken into small pieces and mixed with the saliva, which moistens it, making it easier to swallow. Once the food is chewed sufficiently, swallowing forces it into the esophagus.

◆ ESOPHAGUS AND STOMACH

After food is swallowed, it passes through a muscular tube called the **esophagus** and enters the **stomach.** Glands in the stomach lining secrete a variety of enzymes and other chemical compounds. These secretions aid in digesting the food and are collectively called **gastric juices.** Most of the protein and carbohydrates in food are broken down in the stomach. The churning action of the stomach muscles furthers the digestion process by mixing the food and enzymes. After about four hours, the food has become a liquid called **chyme.** The chyme then passes into the small intestine.

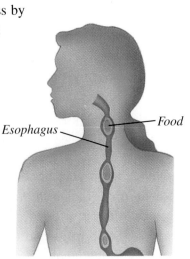

A wavelike motion called peristalsis pushes food through the esophagus and into the stomach.

◆ SMALL INTESTINE

Digestion is completed in the **small intestine.** Enzymes secreted by the liver and pancreas enter the portion of the small intestine close to the stomach. The digestion of carbohydrates and proteins continues, and the digestion of fats occurs. The remainder of the small intestine has the critical function of absorbing the digested food.

The walls of the small intestine are covered with tiny projections called **villi.** Each villus contains capillaries and lymph vessels and is covered with hairlike projections called **microvilli.** Nutrients move from the small intestine into the capillaries, where they are transported to the cells of the body. The presence of the villi and microvilli increases the total surface area available for nutrient absorption. In fact, for the average person, the total surface area available for nutrient absorption is larger than a tennis court! The middle section of the small intestine contains the greatest concentration of villi, and most absorption takes place there.

Villi

Microvilli

Capillaries

◆ PANCREAS, LIVER, AND GALLBLADDER

The small intestine produces only a few digestive enzymes. Others are supplied by the pancreas and the liver. These organs communicate with each other through hormonal messages that coordinate their enzyme secretions. The **pancreas** secretes enzymes that are active in the digestion of carbohydrates, proteins, and fats. The **liver** secretes a greenish fluid called **bile.** Bile enables large molecules of fat to be broken down. The **gallbladder,** a small, muscular, green sac attached to the liver, stores excess bile until it is needed. The pancreas and the liver have other functions as well. The liver is vital in regulating metabolism. Toxins, such as drugs and alcohol, are broken down by the liver. It also filters damaged red blood cells, debris, and pathogens from the bloodstream. The pancreas produces insulin, which is vital in regulating blood-sugar levels.

LARGE INTESTINE ◆

Undigested food moves into the **large intestine,** or colon, where water is absorbed from the waste and returned to the bloodstream. No food absorption takes place here. Peristalsis moves the solid waste, called feces, through the colon to the **rectum.** Here, it is stored briefly and then eliminated from the body through an opening called the **anus.**

DISORDERS OF THE DIGESTIVE SYSTEM

The two most common disorders of the digestive system, constipation and diarrhea, are discussed in Chapter 5, page 118. Another common problem is a **gastric ulcer,** an open sore that develops in the stomach. If the sore creates damage to blood vessels in the stomach wall, a **bleeding ulcer** can develop. Left untreated, bleeding ulcers can cause death. It is now known that most, but not all, ulcers are caused by the bacteria *H. pylori* and can be treated successfully with antibiotics.

The gallbladder removes water from bile and stores it in a concentrated form. Sometimes bile becomes too concentrated, and hard concentrations of minerals and salts, called **gall-stones**, form. If the gallstones are large enough to block the flow of bile out of the gallbladder, they cause a great deal of pain and must be removed surgically. Smaller gallstones can be removed or destroyed by less invasive techniques. One technique involves using directed sound waves to shatter the gallstones.

Q *and* A ◆◆◆◆◆◆◆◆

Q: How long does it take food to pass through the digestive system?

A: Some foods take longer to digest than others. Studies have been conducted in which people volunteered to eat small beads with a meal. About 70 percent of the beads appeared in the feces within 72 hours. However, it took a full week to recover all of the beads.

Q: Is the appendix a part of the digestive system?

A: The vermiform (worm-shaped) appendix is located off the large intestine close to where it meets the small intestine. This rounded saclike structure is about 3.5 inches long. The appendix serves no function in digestion, and its purpose is unknown. The appendix can become inflamed, and if it ruptures, it is a life-threatening situation. However, an inflamed appendix is not caused by contaminated food.

Q: What causes a person to vomit?

A: One way the digestive system responds to irritations is by eliminating the irritant. The vomiting reflex is an efficient method of eliminating the contents of the upper digestive system. First, a person salivates heavily and feels nauseated. Then the muscle separating the stomach and small intestine relaxes, and strong peristaltic waves travel upward. Regurgitation of the contents of the stomach and upper small intestine results. This reflex is controlled by the vomiting center in the medulla of the brain and can also be stimulated by strong emotional experiences.

Q: What causes indigestion?

A: Indigestion is a broad term that covers a variety of conditions. Most causes are not serious and are related to food. Some people have difficulty digesting highly-seasoned foods or carbonated beverages. Other people experience indigestion if they eat too fast or too much. Your emotional and physical state greatly influence your ability to digest food. Emotions can cause the stomach muscles to contract forcefully, causing it to churn. It is not a good idea to eat when you are overly tired or upset.

The Endocrine System

Your endocrine system is composed of specialized tissues called **endocrine glands.** Unlike other glands, your endocrine glands do not have ducts (tubes) that deliver their secretions to a particular point. Instead, they secrete chemical substances called hormones directly into the bloodstream. The main endocrine glands are the thyroid, the pituitary, the adrenals, the endocrine cells in the pancreas, and the reproductive organs. Hormones are also produced by the hypothalamus of the brain, the pineal gland, the parathyroid glands, the thymus, and the walls of the stomach and the intestine.

HORMONES AND THE CENTRAL NERVOUS SYSTEM

Hormones act as chemical messengers and regulate many body functions. Each hormone carries a particular message to specific cells of the body. The central nervous system regulates the secretion of these hormones. In fact, the central nervous system and the endocrine system are so closely linked that they are sometimes called the **neuroendocrine system.**

Coordinating centers in the **hypothalamus** of the brain regulate the activities of these two systems. The hypothalamus is sometimes called the master switch of the endocrine system because most endocrine glands are either directly or indirectly under its control. The hypothalamus constantly monitors the internal state of the body and sends out messages that keep body functions stable. Sometimes the messages are in the form of nerve impulses; at other times, they are hormonal. Nerve impulses produce rapid changes, while the release of hormones causes slower but longer-lasting effects.

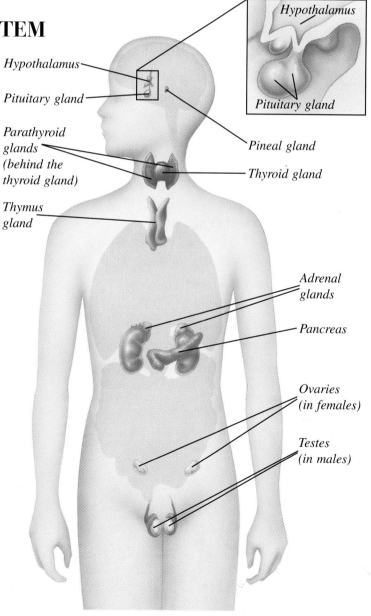

Hypothalamus

Pituitary gland

Parathyroid glands (behind the thyroid gland)

Thymus gland

Hypothalamus

Pituitary gland

Pineal gland

Thyroid gland

Adrenal glands

Pancreas

Ovaries (in females)

Testes (in males)

677

PITUITARY GLAND

The pea-sized **pituitary gland** lies at the base of the brain and is connected to the hypothalamus by a slender stalk. Hormones produced by the hypothalamus move through the pituitary gland. In response to these hormones, the pituitary gland produces at least six hormones of its own. These hormones regulate growth and direct the reproductive organs, the adrenal glands, and the thyroid gland. In women, pituitary hormones stimulate uterine contractions during childbirthand the release of breast milk during nursing. Because the pituitary gland controls so many different functions—and even controls other glands—it is often called the master gland.

THYROID GLAND

The butterfly-shaped **thyroid gland** is located at the base of the front of the neck. It secretes hormones that play a crucial role in determining the speed at which the body transforms food into energy (metabolic rate) and the speed at which the body uses that energy. One thyroid hormone is responsible for normal growth of the brain, bones, and muscles during childhood. The thyroid gland also helps maintain a normal heart rate, has a roll in maintaining the body's calcium level, and affects reproductive functions.

Thyroid gland

ADRENAL GLANDS AND "FIGHT OR FLIGHT"

There is an **adrenal gland** located on top of each kidney. These glands produce dozens of different hormones. The adrenal's inner layer secretes hormones that cause a "fight-or-flight" response to stressful situations. The outer layer secretes hormones that help regulate the body's metabolism and its salt-and-water balance.

When the brain senses danger, the hypothalamus stimulates the release of adrenal hormones. These hormones stimulate other body responses.

Brain perceives danger; stimulates adrenal gland

Breathing rate increases

Heart rate accelerates; blood pressure increases

Liver releases extra blood sugar

Hair stands on end

OTHER ENDOCRINE GLANDS

Several other endocrine glands aid in maintaining normal body functions. The **pancreas** secretes two hormones that help regulate how much glucose is in the bloodstream. The **pineal gland** is thought to control the body's internal time clock. The **parathyroid glands** control the calcium level in the blood. The reproductive organs—**testes** in males and **ovaries** in females—produce hormones that regulate the development of sex characteristics and initiate the production of reproductive cells. The **thymus** plays an important role in immune response and is discussed in the section on the immune system.

HORMONE DISORDERS

Many hormonal disorders are well recognized and are fairly easily treated. Others can be difficult to diagnose, and their treatment may cause side effects that will also need treatment. Some disorders are characterized by the under-production of a particular hormone. For example, if a child's pituitary gland produces inadequate amounts of growth hormone, the growth that precedes puberty will not occur, and the child will remain short. (Not everyone who is short has this condition; many people just inherit a short stature.) Supplying the missing hormone can correct the condition. A number of hormone deficiencies can be treated by simply supplying the missing hormone.

Q _and_ A ◆◆◆◆◆◆◆◆◆◆

Q: Is it safe to take hormones?

A: The use of hormones to replace a missing hormone is called hormone replacement therapy. When prescribed by a physician to treat a specific condition and when used exactly as directed, hormone replacement therapy is usually safe. For example, the hormone insulin is commonly used to treat diabetes. When closely monitored, this has proved safe and effective. The safety of some types of hormone replacement therapy is not well established. For example, after menopause a woman's estrogen level drops dramatically. Often, hormone replacement therapy is used to replace the missing estrogen. Research indicates that this will help prevent osteoporosis and reduce a woman's risk of developing heart disease. However, the effects of long-term estrogen use are unknown, and some studies indicate that it may increase the risk of developing breast cancer.

Estrogen belongs to a group of hormones called steroid hormones. These hormones are secreted by the cortex of the adrenal glands, the ovaries, the placenta, and the testes. Steroid hormones have the ability to pass into the nucleus of a cell, where they can trigger changes in the chromosomes. There are legitimate medical uses for these hormones; however, the abuse of steroid hormones is quite dangerous. Anabolic steroids are powerful synthetic chemicals that resemble one of the hormones produced in the testes. They increase muscle size, but because they can alter the chromosomes, they have serious and potentially deadly side effects.

The Immune System

You constantly come in contact with bacteria and viruses that have the potential to make you ill, but your body's defense system manages to control these organisms. Chapter 21 of your textbook discusses this defense system. When the body's nonspecific defenses are unable to overcome an invading organism, your immune system goes to work. Rather than being an organ system, your immune system is a functional system; it works by using components of the lymphatic and circulatory systems.

WHITE BLOOD CELLS

The white blood cells, or **leukocytes,** defend the body against infection. They begin their lives as immature cells in the bone marrow. As they mature, leukocytes become specialized for specific functions. The leukocytes that are important in the immune response are the **macrophages** and several types of **lymphocytes.** As shown in the photograph, the macrophages can surround and digest bacteria and other invaders. Some can move from the bloodstream through the fluid that surrounds the body cells to reach the site of an infection. The lymphocytes are involved in the production of antibodies, in recognizing and destroying specific types of cells, and in remembering a specific pathogen in case it is encountered again.

—*Macrophage*

—*Bacteria*

THYMUS GLAND

Some of the immature lymphocytes leave the bone marrow and go to the **thymus gland.** There they undergo a change and become one of the different types of **T-cells** (for thymus) of immune system. This change takes place just before birth and during the first months of life. The thymus also functions as an endocrine gland. Its hormone, thymosin, is important to the maturation of T-cells and is thought to influence them after they leave the thyroid. At about 12 years of age, the thymus begins to shrink. In adults, the thymus is very small, and its function is not clearly understood.

Tonsils

Thymus

Right lymphatic duct

Lymphatic vessels

Lymph nodes

Thoracic

Spleen

LYMPH NODES AND GLANDS

Once the macrophages and the lymphocytes mature, they circulate in the bloodstream until they reach one of the secondary lymphatic organs, such as the lymph nodes, the spleen, or the tonsils. The lymphatic vessels and the **lymph nodes** are described in the section on the circulatory system. As lymph circulates through these nodes, macrophages along the walls engulf any pathogens, damaged cells, or cell debris present in the lymph fluid. Large lymph nodes are called **lymph glands** and are located in the armpits, in the groin, and at the base of the neck. The "swollen" glands that accompany some infections are actually enlarged lymph glands.

STRESS AND THE IMMUNE SYSTEM

Researchers now know that the central nervous system can communicate chemically with the immune system and that the immune system produces chemicals that can reply to the nervous system. A new field of medicine called **psychoneuroimmunology** investigates what influence these two systems have on each other. One area of particular interest is the effect that stress has on the immune system and on subsequent illnesses or diseases. Researchers have found that stressful events can actually suppress the immune system, causing the person under stress to be more susceptible to illness. As knowledge about the relationship between the central nervous system and the immune system increases, new ways of preventing and treating disease will emerge.

SPLEEN AND TONSILS

The **spleen** performs the same function for the blood that the lymph nodes do for the lymph. Here, white blood cells rid the blood of foreign matter. The spleen contains more lymphatic tissue than any other part of the body. The **tonsils** are large lymph nodes found in the walls of the pharynx. At birth, the tonsils are quite small. They increase in size until about age six or seven, when they begin to shrink. The lymph nodes in the tonsils are not always able to disable invading organisms, and the tonsils frequently become infected. At one time it was standard practice to remove the tonsils if repeated infections occurred. Now they are viewed as a line of defense against invading bacteria, and if possible, they are left in place.

Q and A

Q: What is pus?

A: Pus is a mixture of white blood cells, dead pathogens, debris from broken-down body cells, and blood plasma. It is a sign that the body's defense system is at work. When pus collects in an infected region of the body, an abscess occurs. No abscess, no matter how small, should ever be squeezed. This can cause bacteria to enter to bloodstream and spread to another part of the body.

Q: What are antihistamines?

A: During an allergic response, the body produces histamines. Histamines cause an inflammatory reaction and increase mucus production. They are responsible for the teary eyes, the runny nose, and the itchy throat that are associated with allergies. Certain medications—appropriately called antihistamines—block the histamines' effects and alleviate allergy symptoms.

The Excretory System

Your excretory system removes the waste products of metabolism from your body. It also removes excess water and minerals. Your kidneys are the main organ of excretion, but your respiratory and digestive systems also play a role. In addition, a small amount of waste products are excreted by the sweat glands.

◆ KIDNEYS AND URINARY TRACT

In addition to its role in digestion, the liver converts the toxic waste products of metabolism into less toxic ones: urea and uric acid. These and other toxic substances in the bloodstream must be removed. The renal arteries carry blood containing toxic substances to the kidneys. The **kidneys** remove urea and uric acid from the bloodstream and turn them into a liquid called **urine.** Peristaltic contractions move urine from the kidneys through the **ureters** to the **bladder.** Urine collects in the bladder until it leaves the body through the **urethra.**

In addition to forming urine, the kidneys maintain the body's internal chemical balance by first removing water and minerals from the bloodstream and then reabsorbing the amount of water and minerals needed by the body. The clean blood with its adjusted chemical composition then leaves the kidneys through the renal veins. The kidneys are amazingly efficient; one healthy kidney can easily meet the body's needs.

Another waste product, perspiration, is excreted by the skin. Perspiring is also the body's way of keeping itself cool.

Kidney

Ureter

Bladder

Urethra

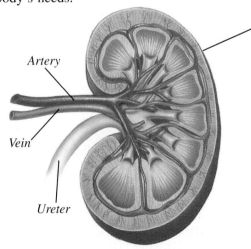

Artery

Vein

Ureter

URINE FORMATION

Each kidney contains a little over 1 million blood-filtering units called **nephrons.**
Nephrons consist of a tiny tube, or tubule, with a cup-shaped structure at one end, and
they produce urine in a two-phase process. First, **filtration** occurs. Blood coming from the
renal artery flows into the capillary network in the cup. Pressure forces water and small
molecules, such as urea, out of the capillaries and into the long tubule connected to the
cup. Second, **reabsorption** takes place. About 99 percent of the water and some of the
other substances that were filtered out of the blood move into capillaries that surround the
tubule. The fluid that remains in the tubule is urine. The tubules join to form larger tubes,
which connect with the ureter where it joins the kidney. **Urine** is a concentrated mixture of
water, urea, and various mineral salts. Complex mechanisms regulate urine formation, and
the contents of the urine can vary depending on the state of the body. This is why an
analysis of the urine, called a urinalysis, is so useful in diagnosing some diseases.

DISORDERS OF THE URINARY SYSTEM

Urinary-tract infections are fairly common, especially in females. This is because the female's
urethra is much shorter than that of the male. This allows bacteria easier access to the bladder and ureters. It is important to treat urinary-tract infections early. Once an infection is
well established, it can travel up the urinary tract to the kidneys and cause a kidney infection. Acute or repeated kidney infections can cause permanent damage to the nephrons.

Kidney stones are more common in males than in females. They consist of
hardened calcium salts, uric acid, and other by-products that collect inside the
kidneys. Approximately 60 percent of kidney stones pass through the urethra
and leave the body. If a stone becomes lodged in the ureter, it must be removed.
Surgical removal was once the only option, but less invasive methods are now
available. For example, fiber-optic laser surgery is used to break the stones into
pieces that are small enough to pass through the urethra.

If the kidneys do not function properly, **hemodialysis** equipment can be used to filter waste
products from the blood. As shown in the photograph on the right, blood is pumped from an
artery in the wrist to the machine, where it is cleansed; it is then pumped back to the body.
There are undesirable side effects to dialysis, and for many people, a kidney transplant is a
better long-term solution.

Q: How do people control when they urinate?

A: Two circular muscles at the base of the bladder control the flow of urine from the body.
Adults have voluntary control of the outermost
muscle, but young children do not. The bladder can hold up to 600 mL of urine, a little
over half a liter. Stretch receptors in the wall
of the bladder sense how full it is, and when
it contains about 200 mL, a person usually
feels the need to urinate. When the volume
approaches 300 mL, the need to urinate
becomes urgent.

Medical and Dental Careers

Many health-care workers provide direct care to help improve a person's health. These highly trained professionals diagnose limitations, illnesses, and injuries; provide necessary treatment; and operate highly specialized medical equipment.

◆ PHYSICIAN

Physicians examine, diagnose, and treat medical conditions. Many physicians treat patients for a variety of illnesses and conditions. Such physicians are called general practitioners, or family doctors. Many other physicians specialize in treating certain types of conditions. For example, cardiologists diagnose and treat people with heart ailments, obstetricians care for pregnant women and deliver babies, and orthopedists specialize in treating disorders of the bones, joints, tendons, and muscles.

To become a physician, a person usually completes a four-year college program in science. Four years of medical school follow. After graduating from medical school, physicians must complete an internship and, if he or she has chosen a specialty, a residency at a hospital, during which he or she receives another three to four years of intense training in both general medicine and the specialty.

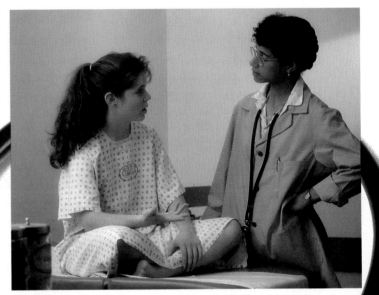

A general practitioner, or family practice physician, performs physical exams and diagnoses and treats a variety of common ailments.

X-RAY TECHNOLOGIST

X-ray technologists operate X-ray equipment. They are often called on to prepare and administer special formulas that make certain body parts more visible on the X ray. If, for example, an X ray is to be taken of the stomach, the technologist gives the patient a drink that highlights the contents of the patient's stomach. An X-ray technologist may also operate medical imaging equipment, such as a CAT scan or an MRI.

A person who wants to become an X-ray technologist can receive training in college or at a hospital or technical school.

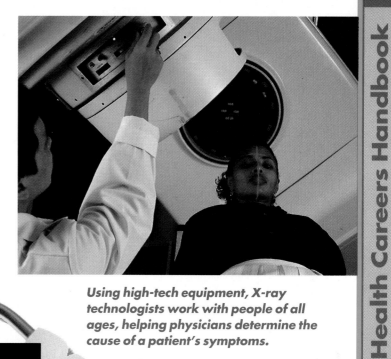

Using high-tech equipment, X-ray technologists work with people of all ages, helping physicians determine the cause of a patient's symptoms.

PHYSICAL THERAPIST

A **physical therapist** helps people with physical disabilities regain the strength to function as independently as possible. People who have amputations, broken bones, nerve or spinal injuries, severe back pain, or diseases such as cerebral palsy or multiple sclerosis can be helped by physical therapy. Therapists use ice packs, hot baths, electrodes, deep massage, exercise, and traction in their treatments.

Physical therapists work in nursing homes, hospitals, and rehabilitation centers. They must have patience, good coordination and physical strength, and good communication skills. Training programs and certification requirements vary from state to state.

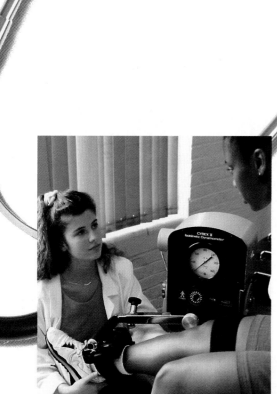

A physical therapist uses massage, exercises, and many other treatments to improve the strength of a person with a physical disability.

Emergency medical technicians, or EMTs, must react quickly to administer medical care in emergency situations.

◆ EMERGENCY MEDICAL TECHNICIAN

An **emergency medical technician** (EMT) provides quick medical attention in emergency situations, such as automobile accidents. EMTs are trained to assess the seriousness of an injury or illness and to provide care for victims of heart attacks, near drownings, motor-vehicle accidents, accidental poisoning, and serious wounds. EMTs treat victims at the scene of the accident and often transport them to hospitals for additional medical care.

An emergency medical technician must be at least 18 years old, hold a high-school diploma, and have a valid driver's license. After completing an extensive training program, those certified as EMTs find jobs at hospitals, police or fire departments, or with private companies. With advanced training, a person can earn an EMT paramedic rating, which enables him or her to perform more advanced medical procedures.

◆ NURSE

A **nurse** works to care for those in need of medical attention. Depending on their level of training and their specialty, nurses perform a variety of duties, such as performing physical exams, observing and assessing patient symptoms, administering medication and treatments, and helping patients with proper nutrition, personal hygiene, and general health care.

Registered nurses (RNs) are licensed to practice by a state board. States have different education requirements that may include a diploma, an associate degree, or a bachelor's degree from an accredited college or university. With additional specialized training, an RN may become a nurse practitioner (NP). Licensed practical nurses (LPNs) usually complete a two-year college program or a technical-school program. In addition to many hours of clinical experience during their schooling, nurses must pass a state-board examination before they can be hired.

This surgical nurse has received special training to allow her to assist physicians in performing surgery.

A dentist treats patients for diseases of the teeth and gums and repairs mechanical damage to the teeth to improve their appearance or function.

DENTAL LABORATORY TECHNICIAN

A **dental laboratory technician** makes retainers, dentures, braces, bridges, and crowns according to a dentist's exact specifications. He or she must have excellent manual dexterity, because precision and accuracy are crucial to the perfect fit of dental devices.

Most dental laboratory technicians acquire their skills in commercial laboratories. On-the-job training also is provided by hospitals and federal agencies. Schooling without the actual hands-on training takes about two years. Training with no formal schooling can last as long as five years.

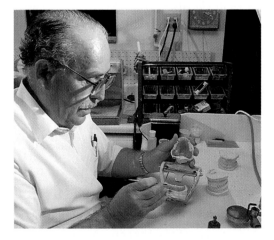

The procedures followed by a dental laboratory technician require manual dexterity and artistic ability.

DENTIST

A **dentist** examines and treats patients for diseases and conditions of the teeth and gums. A general dentist checks teeth for abscesses, fills decayed teeth, determines whether orthodontic devices are needed, and instructs his or her patients on home dental care. He or she also does the preliminary work for fitting a patient with dentures, crowns, or bridges. As with physicians, there are many dental specialties as well.

After successfully completing college and four years of dental school, every aspiring dentist must pass many practical and written examinations as well as a state board exam. Specialists must complete two to three years of additional study and pass exams in their field of specialization.

Careers in Health-Care Administration

Hospitals and other health-care facilities must employ administrators to coordinate the activities of all employees—medical and nonmedical—so that patients receive the best possible care. Health-care administrators range from housekeepers to computer specialists to hospital directors.

MEDICAL RECORDS TECHNICIAN

A **medical records technician** is responsible for what happens to the information recorded by the nurse and doctor on your medical record or chart. They collect the information, classify it, use it to compute statistics, and finally transcribe the data into hospital files.

A medical records technician often holds an associate's degree in this field. However, a person who has earned a bachelor's degree in biology needs only to finish a one-year program for certification. Those who hold bachelor's degrees in medical records administration often supervise medical records technicians.

A medical records technician must organize information about many patients and monitor its accuracy and completeness.

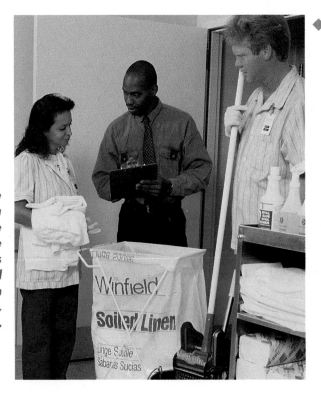

An executive housekeeper in a hospital must see to it that the facility is always clean and sanitary, and in some cases, sterile.

EXECUTIVE HOUSEKEEPER

An **executive housekeeper** trains and manages a hospital's housekeeping staff, which can include custodians, kitchen workers, and laundry attendants. He or she is responsible for assuring that the proper precautions are taken to maintain the sanitary or even sterile environment required in certain areas of a hospital.

A hospital's executive housekeeper must be certified by the National Executive Housekeepers' Association. In addition to several college-level courses, he or she must complete a vocational or technical training program and possibly a management training program.

MEDICAL CLAIMS EXAMINER

A **medical claims examiner** evaluates the charges listed on an insurance claim form to determine whether they are proper and covered by the patient's insurance policy. If the examiner suspects errors have been made, he or she helps work out any problems before making payment to either party. Medical claims examiners work for insurance companies.

Most medical claims examiners hold a college degree. In addition, everyone entering this field should possess a general understanding of medical terms and procedures in order to evaluate each claim properly.

A medical claims examiner spends a great deal of time on the telephone, evaluating the validity of insurance claims and determining whether certain procedures are covered by a policy.

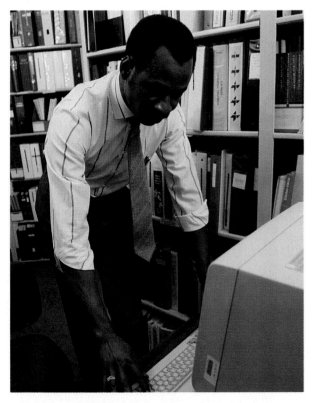

A systems analyst for a health care facility must help meet the changing computer needs of the facility.

SYSTEMS ANALYST

A **systems analyst** evaluates how information should be processed by a computer system. In a health-care institution, he or she is responsible for determining what type of computer system is needed by the facility. The analyst also chooses the printers, terminals, and software that will best meet the facility's current and future needs.

The educational background of a health-care systems analyst can range from a two-year degree with work-related experience to a master's degree in business or computer science. A general knowledge of health-care facilities and the functions they perform is quite useful in this field.

Community Service Careers in Health

Many people assist in the field of health care by providing a multitude of services and products to hospital personnel and patients, and to the general public. Some service careers require extensive training, while others can be started after a few courses beyond high school or with on-the-job training.

◆ PHARMACIST

A **pharmacist** dispenses drugs according to strict specifications provided by physicians and dentists. He or she also discusses possible side effects and drug interactions and advises customers on the proper usage of many nonprescription medications. Most pharmacists work in pharmacies or hospitals.

To become a pharmacist, a person must graduate from a five-year pharmacy program at an accredited college or university. Successful completion of an internship under the direct supervision of a registered pharmacist is also required. Finally, a pharmacy student must pass a state examination to become a registered pharmacist.

A pharmacist fills prescriptions and advises customers about the use of prescription and nonprescription drugs.

One of the tasks of an environmental health inspector is to check the temperatures of certain foods to ensure that they are safe to eat.

◆ ENVIRONMENTAL HEALTH INSPECTOR

An **environmental health inspector** works for a local, state, or federal government agency, monitoring facilities such as restaurants, dairies, and food-processing plants. Inspectors routinely test the air and the food and water used in these establishments for harmful pathogens and pollutants to determine whether the facilities are complying with government regulations regarding hygiene.

Environmental health inspectors generally have earned a four-year college degree. Some agencies also require several years of job-related experience.

COUNSELOR

A **counselor** works with individuals and families who are having difficulties in their social, economic, and personal lives. He or she helps people overcome the problems associated with drug and alcohol dependency, illness, and relationship, marriage, and family issues. A counselor begins by talking to his or her clients about their problems; he or she then assesses the situation and makes recommendations for how the problems could be resolved. The counselor also refers clients to other professionals and organizations if more-specialized help is needed.

Most counselors have at least a bachelor's degree in psychology or social work, but a master's degree in one of these fields is usually necessary for employment. In most parts of the country, a state examination is required to obtain a license.

This counselor is telling a young woman how long it will be until her HIV antibody test results are available. She will also answer questions about AIDS and HIV infection.

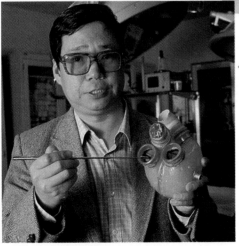

Dr. Kevin Cheng has helped save many lives by designing an artificial heart, which he is demonstrating here.

BIOMEDICAL ENGINEER

A **biomedical engineer** designs new medical equipment and does research to improve existing devices. Biomedical engineers are often assisted by biomedical equipment technicians, who install and service complicated pieces of machinery, such as lasers, electrocardiographs (EKGs), and electroencephalographs (EEGs).

A biomedical engineer usually works for a research facility such as a university, a health-care company, or a large hospital. He or she must have at least a bachelor's degree in engineering with specialization in biomedical training. Research positions require a master's degree or even a doctorate of philosophy in biomedical engineering.

areers in Health Education

Education is part of any health-care worker's job. However, there are many types of health-care professionals who specialize in educating people about how to improve their overall physical and mental health.

◆ HEALTH TEACHER

A **health teacher** conducts courses on health in public or private schools. He or she helps students understand the material by starting class discussions, delivering lectures on health topics, and giving exams. Often, a health teacher discusses health concerns with individual students who feel uncomfortable talking about their concerns in class.

A health teacher should hold at least a bachelor's degree in health education. A strong background in human anatomy and physiology, biology, psychology, sociology, or other health-related topics is also quite useful. Teaching at the college level usually requires a graduate degree.

A health teacher gives lectures and answers questions about health-related topics.

◆ SCHOOL PSYCHOLOGIST

A **school psychologist** works closely with students, teachers, and parents to help students overcome social and emotional problems and neurological disorders that might interfere with learning. He or she often administers tests to assess mental health but spends most of his or her time talking to students and listening to what they have to say about their situations. School psychologists also advise a school's administrative body and suggest how policies might be changed to enhance learning.

Nearly all psychologists have at least a master's degree in psychology. Some hold doctorate degrees in psychology, which usually require eight years of schooling at a college or university. Most psychologists obtain clinical experience during their formal education by assisting and observing other psychologists interacting with patients.

A school psychologist assists students with various problems that might interfere with their ability to learn.

◆ SPECIAL-EDUCATION INSTRUCTOR

A **special-education instructor** uses knowledge of sign language and Braille to help people who are deaf or hard of hearing and people who are visually impaired develop better communication skills. Such instructors work in clinics, rehabilitation centers, and schools.

A special-education instructor must complete a bachelor's degree in special education. A master's degree with specialization in either the visually or hearing impaired is usually necessary as well. Some clinical work with visually- and hearing-impaired people is required before graduating with either degree.

A special-education instructor often works with his or her students on a one-to-one basis. Here the instructor is teaching her student how to say "bear" in sign language.

◆ REGISTERED DIETICIAN

A **dietician** manages the food-service program in restaurants and cafeterias, hospitals, nursing homes, health-care clinics, private companies, and the military. He or she works closely with the kitchen staff to make sure that nutritious meals are served. Some dieticians are self-employed and work with individuals to help them improve their eating habits or control certain illnesses through proper nutrition.

A registered dietician must have a bachelor's degree in dietetics and must become certified with the American Dietetic Association.

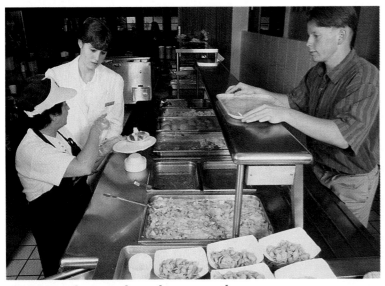

Dieticians plan meals and manage the food-service program of many health-care facilities.

GlossaryIndex

*Page numbers in **boldface** type indicate the introduction of vocabulary terms.*

Body weight *(cont.)*
    weight-loss strategies, 55, 110–112
    weight management concepts,
    105–106
Bone density, 41
Bracing, 204
Brain tumor, 163
Brain waves *electrical patterns produced by the brain that fluctuate greatly during the sleep cycle,* **60,** 61
Bread, cereal, rice, and pasta group, 84–86
Breakup of relationship, 368–369
Breast, 331
    development at puberty, 355
    self-examination of, 336–338
Breast cancer, 266, 336, 546
Breathing, assessment of injured person, 618–619
Bronchitis, 289, 546, 548
Brown recluse spider, 640–641
Brushing of teeth, 139–140
Bulbourethral gland, 326
Bulimia *an eating disorder based on a cycle of bingeing and purging food,* 104, **115,** 116, 163, 166
    with anorexia, 116
Burns, 644–645
B vitamins, 96

C

Caffeine, 62, 248, 250, 302–303, 308–309, 335
Calcium, 78–79, 83, 87, 96
Calculus *hardened plaque,* **138**
Calf stretch, 58
Calorie *a unit of measurement for energy; 1 nutrition calorie = 1 kilocalorie,* **70**
    calculating caloric needs, 109
    number burned in aerobic exercise, 56
Camping, 610
Cancer *a disease caused by cells that have lost normal growth controls and that invade and destroy healthy tissues,* 13, 22–23, 41, 69, 108, 266, **288,** 509, **524,** 525–526, 530, 546, 550
    bladder, 287–288, 530
    breast, 266, 336, 546
    cervical, 336, 472, 491
    colon, 71

    diet and, 530
    esophageal, 266, 288
    kidney, 288, 530
    laryngeal, 266, 288, 290, 530
    liver, 266, 530
    lung, 23, 287–288, 291, 530
    oral, 291
    prevention of, 526–527, 530
    prostate, 329
    skin, 131, 530, 547
    testicular, 330
    tongue, 290–291
    treatment of, 525–526
Carbohydrate(s) *class of nutrients containing starches, simple sugars, glycogen, and dietary fiber,* **70,** 71
    complex, 71
    dietary, 82–83, 91
    reading labeling about, 90
Carbon dioxide, 540, 542, 544, 548, 641
Carbon monoxide *a poisonous gas released by burning tobacco,* **287,** 291, 548, 602, 643–644
Carcinogen, 286
Cardiac arrest *condition in which the heart stops working,* **631**
Cardiac glycoside, 251
Cardiopulmonary resuscitation (CPR) *a lifesaving procedure designed to revive a person who is not breathing and has no heartbeat,* 214, 240, **621**
    procedure for, 620–621
    training in, 617–618
Cardiorespiratory endurance, 10
Cardiovascular disease *progressive damage to the heart and blood vessels,* 13, 22–23, 69, 73, 78, 108, 196, 266, 285, 289, 291, **521,** 522–524, 548, 559
    diet and, 529
    physical activity and, 529
    prevention of, 526–529
    smoking and, 289, 528
    stress and, 529
Careers
    community service in health, 674–675
    health-care administration, 672–673
    health education, 676–677
    medical and dental, 668–671
Centers for Disease Control and Prevention, 563

Cereal crops, 84–86
Cerebral palsy, 516–517
Cervical cancer, 336, 472, 491
Cervix *the base of the uterus, which bulges down into the vagina; has a small opening through which sperm can enter the uterus,* **332,** 343–344
Cesarean section, 345
Chancre, 470–472
Cheilosis, 77
Chewing tobacco *a form of smokeless tobacco that is placed between a person's cheek and gum,* **290,** 291, 320–321
Chickenpox, 250, 442, 445, 452, 454
Child abuse *illegal treatment committed by an adult against a minor that involves use of physical, sexual, or emotional force, cruelty, or neglect,* 29, 156, 178, 420, **421**
Childbirth, 343–345
Child development, 346–348
China, older adults in, 390–391
Chinese foods, 93
"Chinese restaurant syndrome," 120
Chlamydia *the most common STD in the United States; caused by bacteria,* **466,** 467–469, 472, 475
Chloride, 118
Chlorine, 78
Chlorofluorocarbons, 547–548, 554
Choking, 629–631
Cholesterol *fatlike substance that is part of all animal cells and is needed for the production of some hormones and fat digestion; can block the arteries and cause heart disease,* **73,** 83, 87, 108, 196, 522
Chromium, 78–79
Chromosomes *cell structures that carry hereditary information,* **510,** 515–516
Chronic bronchitis *an inflammation of the bronchial tubes in the lungs and the production of excessive mucus,* **289**
Chronic fatigue, 196
Chronic fatigue syndrome, 455
Chronic obstructive pulmonary disease, 13, 22–23
Cigarette smoking. *See* Smoking; Tobacco
Cigar smoking, 289–291
Cilia, 446–447

Depression, 40, 42, 62, 68, 115,
156–157, 166–167, 172, 246, 369,
412, 592
stress and, 157, 196
suicide and, 227, 229–230
in terminally ill person, 215
Dermatitis, 77
Dermatologist, 128
Dermis *the second layer of skin;*
contains the most important
structures of the skin, **127**
Designer drugs *synthetic drugs that are*
similar in chemistry to certain illegal
drugs, **305**
Diabetes, 13, 22, 41, 69, 108, 508–509,
529
type I, 513, 519
type II, 512–513
Diabetic coma, 519
Diaphragm, as contraceptive, 396
Diarrhea *loose bowel movements that*
occur when food moves too quickly
through the digestive system, **118**
Diastolic blood pressure, 523
Diet, 91, 111–112. *See also* Food
selection; Nutrition
cancer and, 530
vegetarian, 96–97
Dietary fiber *a subclass of complex*
carbohydrates with a high ratio of
plant material that is not absorbed
by the body, **71,** 83, 90
Dietary Guidelines for Americans, 82
Digestive disorders, 118–120
Digestive system, 674–676
Disaster *an event that affects the lives*
and health of people in one or more
communities, **602,** 603–604
Disease, 445
infectious. *See* Infectious disease
noninfectious, 509–530
signs and symptoms of, 445–446
Dislocation *an injury in which the end*
of a bone comes out of its joint, **627**
Displacement, as defense mechanism,
160
Dissociative disorder *a condition in*
which someone's personality changes
to the point that the person believes
he or she is someone else, **165,**
166–167
Diuretic, 116, 251

Diving safety, 608–609
Divorce *the legal end to a marriage,*
395, 406–407, 411–413
emotional impact on children,
412–413
DNA, 510
Dose *the exact amount of a drug,* **252,**
253
Douching, 337
Down's syndrome, 515–516
Drinking water, 444, 545–546
Drowning, 608–610, 639
Drown proofing *a technique to stay*
afloat that can be used even by those
who cannot swim, **609**
Drug *a substance that causes a physical*
or emotional change in a person,
246
absorption of, 254–255
accidental poisoning with, 601–602
dose of, 252–253
effects on the body, 253–256
healthier options, 245–246
illegal, 247–248, 261
over-the-counter. *See* Over-the-
counter drugs
passage from mother's blood to
fetus, 341
prescription. *See* Prescription drugs
psychoactive, 249, 299–316
from rain forest plants, 246–247
side effects and allergies, 256
unrecognized, 248
Drug abuse *intentional improper use of*
a drug, 228, **248,** 252, 299–316. *See*
also Intravenous drug use
depression and, 157
first aid in drug overdose, 643
HIV transmission from, 501
needle exchange programs, 534–535
during pregnancy, 310–311
sexual activity and, 477
vehicle accidents and, 593–594
violent behavior and, 429
Drug addiction, 299–301. *See also*
Addiction
Drug allergy *an unwanted effect that*
accompanies the desired effect of a
drug, **256**
Drug dependence, 300–301
treatment for, 313–316
Drug interactions, 254–256, 602

Drug misuse *improper use of a drug,*
248
Drug-oriented society, 245–249
Drug tolerance, 300–301
Drug-treatment programs, 313–316
Drug use *taking a medicine properly*
and in its correct dosage, **248**
during pregnancy, 341
Drunken driving, 261, 267–268, 271,
593–594
Dying, 213–218
needs of terminally ill person, 216
suicide and terminal illness, 240–241
Dysfunctional family *a family that does*
not fulfill the basic functions of a
healthy family, **413,** 414

E

Ear-piercing equipment, 455, 494
Earthquake, 604
Eastern Indian foods, 93
Eating disorders *compulsive eating*
behaviors caused by emotional
problems or an obsession with body
weight, 104–105, 113–117, 163, 166,
336
Ecosystem *a system made up of living*
things and their physical
surroundings, **539,** 540–541, 544
Ecstasy, 305, 308–309
Ectopic pregnancy, 345
Egg *female reproductive cell, also called*
an ovum; contains one-half of the
instructions needed for the
development of a new human being,
325, 332
Ejaculation, 327–328
Elder abuse *abuse of an elderly person,*
422
Electric shock, steps to help in
emergency, 642
Electrocution *death resulting from the*
flow of electrical current through the
body, **600**
Electrolysis, as hair removal, 135
Electrolyte balance, 78, 116, 118
Embryo *a fertilized egg after it has*
attached itself to the wall of the
uterus, **340,** 341
Emergency. *See also* Accident; Injury
choking, heart attack, and others,

viral, 452–455

Infertility, 329, 336, 463, 465–467

Influenza, 13, 196, 441, 443, 446, 450–454, 558

Inhalants *chemicals that produce strong psychoactive effects when they are inhaled,* 248, **306,** 308–309

Inhalation poisoning, 643–644

Injury. *See also* Accident; Safety
  avoiding injuries during exercise, 50–52, 58
  exercise-related injuries, 52
  unintentional, 22
  work-related, 605–606

Insomnia *temporary or continuing loss of sleep,* **61,** 62

Insulin, 512–513, 519

Insurance. *See* Health insurance

Interferon, 455

Intoxicated *being affected by alcohol; effects of intoxication can range from mild lightheadedness to severe and complete loss of judgment and reflexes,* **262**

Intrauterine device (IUD), 396

Intravenous drug use, 307, 455, 493–494, 501, 534–535

Iodine, 78–79

Iron, 78–79, 83, 96

IUD. *See* Intrauterine device

J

Jealousy, 157

Jock itch, 129, 458

Journal writing, 12–13

Juvenile diabetes. *See* Diabetes, type I

K

Kaposi's sarcoma, 491

Killer T-cells, 448–449

"Kosher" items, 92

L

Labor, 343–344

Laceration, 625

Lactose intolerance, 119

Landfill, 549

Land pollution, 548–550

Latex condom *a covering for the penis that helps protect both partners from sexually transmitted diseases and also helps prevent pregnancy,* 395–396, **477,** 501

LDL (low-density lipoproteins) *compounds that carry cholesterol to cells for cell processes,* **73**

Lean mass *total body weight minus the weight due to fat,* 106, **107**

Lifestyle, 11
  underlying causes of death, 13

Life-support machines, 214, 240

Lipids, 72

Living will *a document expressing a person's wish to be allowed to die in case of terminal illness or incurable injury rather than be kept alive by artificial means,* **217,** 218, 240

Love, 152
  in marriage, 393
  nonsexual ways of expressing, 377–378, 476, 498–499

Low-density lipoproteins. *See* LDL

LSD, 304–305, 308–309

Lung cancer, 23, 287–288, 291, 530

M

Magnesium, 78–79, 83

Mainstream smoke *smoke that is inhaled directly into the mouth through a cigarette, pipe, or cigar,* **291**

Makeup, 128

Malaria, 442, 458

Male reproductive system, 325–330
  care of, 330
  disorders of, 329–330

Mammogram, 336

Marijuana, 248, 299, 305–306, 308–309

Marriage, 393–394

Maslow's hierarchy of needs, 162

Maturity, 386

Measles, 443, 452, 454, 559

Meat, poultry, fish, dry beans, eggs, and nuts group, 87–88

Media messages
  about body image, 178–179
  about body weight, 146–147
  definition of, 34–35
  drug advertisements, 245
  influence on your sexuality, 372

romanticism of suicide, 229
  SMCR model to evaluate, 320–321
  about tobacco, 292, 320–321
  about violence, 429, 436–437

Medicaid, 579

Medical alert identification, 632

Medical checkup, 529

Medical costs, 574–580

Medicare, 579

Medicine *a substance used to treat an illness or ailment,* **250,** 251
  guidelines for appropriate use of, 253

Melanin, 125, 127, 133

Memorial service, 216, 221–222

Memory loss, 266, 388

Menopause, 387

Menstrual cramps, 334–335

Menstrual cycle, 333–334

Mental disorders, 163–167
  stress and, 195–196
  suicide and, 230
  treatment for, 168–172

Mental health *the ability to recognize reality and cope with the demands of daily life,* 6, **8,** 151–159
  assessment of your health, 153
  exercise and, 42
  strategies to promote, 159–162

Mercury, 120

Mescaline, 308–309

Metabolism, body weight and, 105–112

Metal detector, 650

Metastasis, 524

Methadone maintenance programs, 313–314

Methamphetamine, 308–309

Methane, 548

Mexican foods, 92–93

Microorganism *a tiny living thing that can be seen only with a microscope,* **442**
  helpful, 447

Middle adulthood *the period of adulthood between the ages of 41 and 65,* **386,** 387

Middle Eastern foods, 93

Midwife, 344

Milk, yogurt, and cheese group, 87

Minerals *inorganic substances that are generally absorbed to form structural components of the body,*

sleepiness, **310**

Seizure. *See* Convulsion

Selective awareness *focusing on the aspects of a situation that help a person feel better (thinking positively),* **200,** 201

Selenium, 78–79

Self-concept *the current mental image you have of yourself,* **161,** 192

Self-defense class, 425

Self-disclosure *telling another person meaningful information about yourself,* **185,** 357

Self-esteem *feeling good about yourself and your abilities; pride in and acceptance of yourself; sense of personal worth,* **9,** 159, 162–163, **177,** 272

    assessment of, 180–181

    body image and media messages and, 178–179

    building of, 158, 182–186

    childhood experiences and, 347

    eating disorders and, 115–117

    emotional abuse and, 421

    importance of, 177–181

Self-examination

    of breasts, 336–338

    of testes, 330

Self-help program, 314

Self-ideal *your mental image of what you'd like to be,* **161**

Self-image, 163

Self-talk, 154–155

    about childhood experiences, 347

    positive, 183

Semen, 327

Seminal vesicles, 326

Sense organs, 652, 656

Sensory receptors, 652, 656

Sex hormones

    female, 332–333

    male, 326

Sexual abstinence *delaying or refraining from sexual intimacy,* **376,** 475–476, 498–499

Sexual abuse *sexual behavior between an adult and a child or adolescent,* 208, **420,** 421

Sexual assault *any sexual contact with a person without his or her consent,* **424,** 425–428, 604. *See also* Rape;

Sexual harassment

    help for victim of, 427–428

    precautions against, 424–425

Sexual harassment *unwanted, unwelcome, or offensive sexual behavior,* 424, **428**

Sexual intimacy *genital touching and sexual intercourse,* **372,** 373, 427

    contraception, 395–396

    dealing with external pressure, 378–380

    drug and alcohol abuse and, 477

    high-risk situations, 380

    with HIV-infected person, 494–495

    myths and facts about, 371

    resisting sexual pressure, 377

    risks for teens, 373–376

    saying "No" to, 499

    unwanted, 378–380

Sexuality, 370–373

Sexually transmitted disease (STD) *a disease that is passed from one person to another during sexual contact,* 11, 336, 374, 455, **463,** 464–475

    breaking cycle of infection, 477–478

    finding help for, 478–480

    myths and facts about, 465

    prevention of, 462, 475–480

    reducing the risk of, 477

    testing your knowledge of, 464

    treatment for, 479–480

Sexually transmitted disease (STD) hotline, 479

Shampoo, 134

Shaving, 135

Shingles, 442, 454

Shock

    signs of, 622

    treatment for, 623

Shoulder pain, 204

Sickle cell anemia, 509–511, 516

Side effect *an effect that accompanies the expected effect of a drug,* **256**

Sidestream smoke *smoke that enters the environment from burning tobacco,* 290, **291**

Simple sugars, 70–71

Single-parent family *a family in which only one parent lives with the children in the home,* **406,** 408

Sinus infection, 458

Skeletal system, 662–664

Skin

    care of, 125–132

    defenses against infectious disease, 446

    functions of, 126

    problems with, 127–131

    structure of, 127

    sun exposure and, 131–132, 530

Skin cancer, 131, 530, 547

Sleep, 60–62

    exercise and, 42, 61–62

    tips for sound sleeping, 61–62

Sleeping pills, 62, 250, 310

Smallpox, 453, 559

Smoke detector, 600

Smoke-free environment, 290

Smokeless tobacco, 289–291, 320–321

Smoking, 7, 23, 62, 284, 530. *See also* Tobacco

    cardiovascular disease and, 528

    disease and, 287–289

    fire dangers from, 599

    indoor air pollution, 548

    during pregnancy, 289

    quitting, 285–286, 293–294

    risks of passive smoking, 291

    tobacco-free life, 292–294

Snacks, 67, 95

Snakebite, 639

    application of constricting band, 639

    snake identification, 638

Social health *interactions with people to build satisfying relationships,* **8**

Social justice, 26, 165

Social support *deriving positive feelings from sharing life situations with others,* 9, **10**

Social worker, 169

Sodium, 78–79, 83, 118

Solid waste, 549, 555–556

Somatoform disorder *an emotional condition in which there are physical symptoms but no identifiable disease or injury; the physical symptoms are caused by psychological factors,* 166, **167**

Sperm *male reproductive cell; contains one-half of the instructions needed for the development of a new human being,* **325,** 326

    pathway to fertilization, 327–328

Acknowledgments

For permission to reprint copyrighted material, grateful acknowledgment is made to the following sources:

Allyn & Bacon: From "Stretching exercises for flexibility" from *Exploring Health: Expanding the Boundaries of Wellness* by Jerrold S. Greenberg and George B. Dintiman. Copyright © 1992 by Prentice-Hall, Inc. All rights reserved. From "Why Do Men Rape Women?" from *Sex on Your Terms* by Elizabeth Powell. Copyright © 1991 by Elizabeth Powell.

American College Health Association: From "A Case of Acquaintance Rape" from a brochure by the American College Health Association. Copyright © 1997 by American College Health Association.

Joseph Bauer: From "Letters to You from Teenagers in Jail" by Joseph Bauer from *Seventeen,* August 1991. Copyright © 1991 by Joseph Bauer.

Mercel Dekker, Inc.: Adapted from "Anabolic steroids, a review of the clinical toxicology and diagnostic screening" from *Clinical Toxicology,* vol. 28, no. 3, 1990, pp. 287-310. Copyright © 1990 by Marcel Dekker, Inc.

Amy Dolph: Quote by Amy Dolph from "Teenagers and Aids" by Barbara Kantrowitz from *Newsweek,* August 3, 1992. Copyright © 1992 by Amy Dolph.

Elsevier Science Inc., 655 Avenue of the Americas, New York, NY 10010-5107: Table "Ranking of Stressors by High School Students" from "What's Bad About Stress?" from *Journal of Psychosomatic Research,* vol. 16, 1972. Copyright © 1972 by Pergamon Press.

ETR Associates, Santa Cruz, CA: Excerpted and adapted from "Sexuality Myth Activity Answer Sheet" (Retitled: "Myths and Facts About Sexual Intimacy") from *Entering Adulthood: Coping with Sexual Pressures* by Nancy Abbey and Elizabeth Raptis Picco. Copyright © 1989 by Network Publications, a division of ETR Associates. All Rights Reserved. For information about this and other related materials, call 1-800-321-4407.

The Alan Guttmacher Institute: Adapted from graph "Teenage Pregnancy in the United States" (Retitled: "Adolescent Pregnancy Rates of Western Nations") by James Trussell from *Family Planning Perspectives,* vol. 20, no. 6, November/ December 1988. Copyright © 1988 by The Alan Guttmacher Institute.

Prentice Hall, a division of Simon & Schuster Inc.: Adapted from graph "Factors Associated with the Occurrence of Homicide" from *Violence Prevention: Curriculum for Adolescents* by Deborah Prothrow-Stith. Copyright © 1987 by Deborah Prothrow-Stith. Published by Education Development Center, Inc.

Scholastic Inc.: From "Who Am I not to Fight?" by Lauren Tarshis from *Scholastic Update.* Copyright © 1991 by Scholastic Inc.

Sports Illustrated: From "Senseless: 'You See a Red Rag, Shoot'" by Rick Telander from *Sports Illustrated,* vol. 72, no. 20, May 14, 1990. Copyright © 1990 by Time Inc. All rights reserved.

Texas Commission on Alcohol and Drug Abuse: From Alcohol . . . Is a Drug, from Crack . . . Shattered Dreams!" by Texas Commission on Alcohol and Drug Abuse.

Weekly Reader Corporation: Adapted from graph "Teens Know, Ignore Risks" from *Current Science®,* vol. 78, no. 2, September 18, 1992. Copyright © 1992 by Weekly Reader Corporation.

PHOTO CREDITS

Abbreviations used: (bkgd) background, (t) top, (c) center, (b) bottom, (l) left, (r) right.

710